Reading is not enough, Now ***Listen, Learn & Practice***
Every Chapter

i. Golden Points

Get **500+** Chapter-wise One Liners in **PODCAST form** (audio) for quick revision of chapters

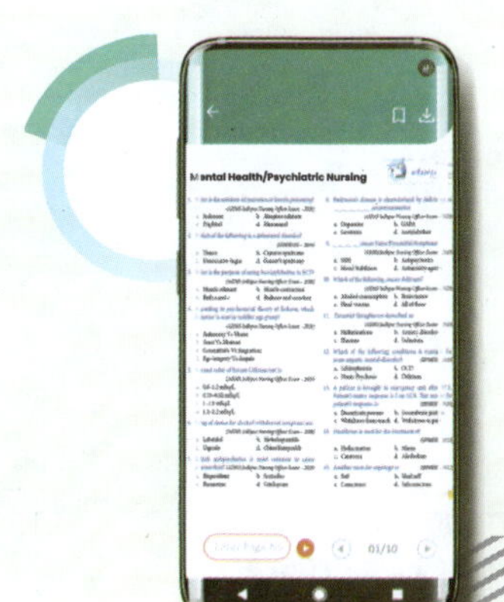

ii. Solved Exercises

Subjective and Objective exercises of the book have been given with their solution (in PDF) to evaluate and assess the complete chapter knowledge

- **50+** Long Answer Questions
- **50+** Short Answer Questions
- **50+** Multiple Choice Questions

iii. MCQs

200+ Chapter-wise Multiple Choice Questions in Practice and Review mode to provide in-depth concept clarity

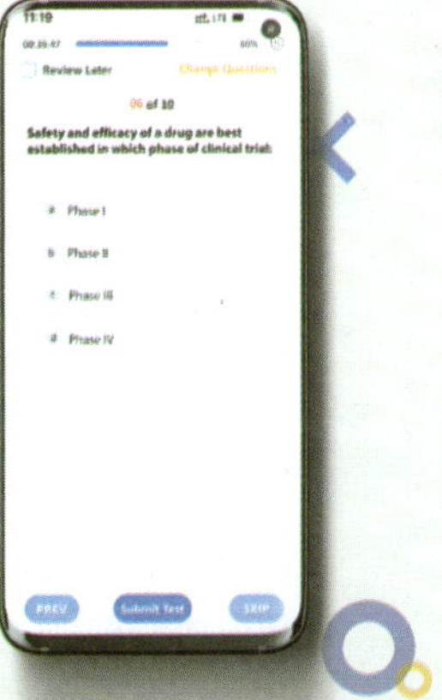

Mapping of the most important topics from the Book at one place with one click search

Get 50+ Important topics of the book at one click

Chapter 1: Introduction to Psychiatric Nursing

- Indicators of Mental Health
- Scope of Psychiatric Nursing
- Functions of Psychiatric Nurse in Various Settings

Chapter 2: Principles and Concepts of Mental Health Nursing

- Psychoanalytic Theory
- Steps in Neurotransmission

Chapter 3: Assessment of Mental Health Status

- Mental Status Examination
- Mini Mental Status Examination or Folstein Test

Chapter 4: Therapeutic Communication and Nurse-Patient Relationship

- Johari Window of Interpersonal Relationship

Chapter 5: Treatment Modalities and Therapies used in Mental Disorders

- Psychotherapy
- Key Concepts of Milieu Therapy
- Nurses Responsibility in Milieu Therapy

Chapter 6: Nursing Management of Patients with Schizophrenia and Other Psychotic Disorders

- Positive and Negative Symptoms of Schizophrenia
- Types of Schizophrenia

Chapter 7: Nursing Management of Patients with Mood Disorders

- Bipolar Disorder
- Stages of Mania
- Etiology of Mood Disorders
- Treatment of Bipolar Disorder
- Nursing Management
- Types of Depression

Chapter 9: Nursing Management of Patients with Substance use Disorders

- Treatment of Alcohol Withdrawal
- Alcohol Withdrawal Syndromes
- Nursing Diagnosis and Interventions for Patient with Substance Abuse
- Prevention of Substance use Disorder

Chapter 10: Nursing Management of Patients with Sexual, Personality and Eating Disorders

- Personality Disorders
- DSM-5 Diagnostic Criteria for Eating Disorders
- Treatment of Anorexia Nervosa

and Many more...

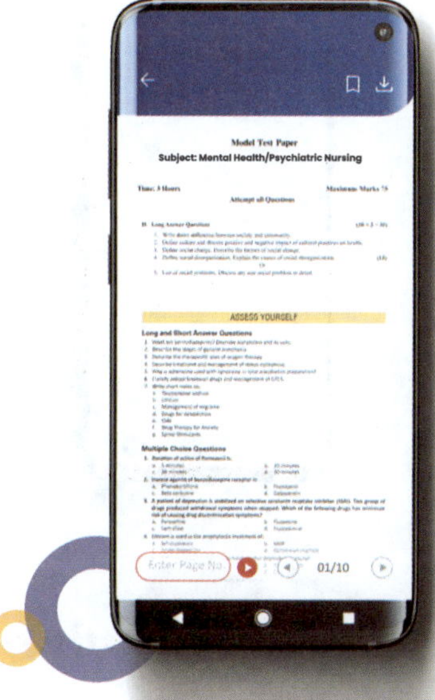

Solved Papers

Get Qs Bank covering the complete subject in the form of subjective exercises and extra exercises with their solutions

- **150+** Long Essay Questions
- **150+** Short Essay Questions
- **500+** Multiple Choice Questions

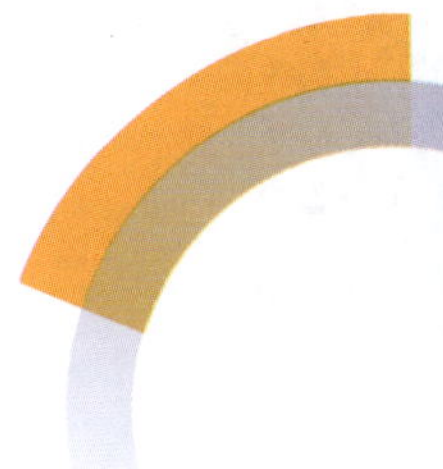

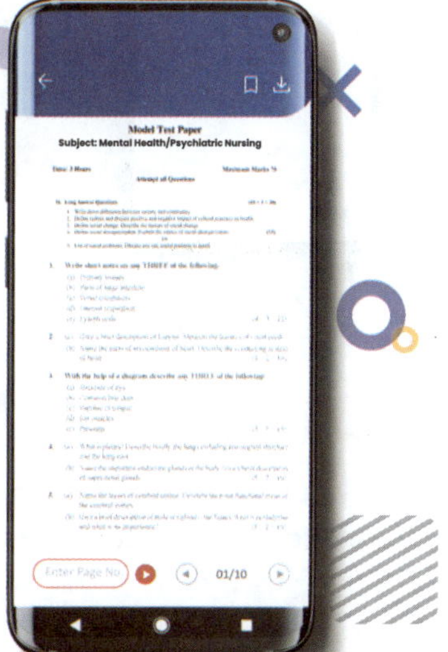

Unsolved Papers

Explore the pool of **20+** unsolved previous year exam papers of top Universities, like Delhi University, RUHS, KUHS, CCS University, MGR University and many more (Year/Semester-wise in PDF Format)

CBS Phygital Books >
Textbook of Mental Health/ Psychiatric Nursing PHYGITAL

Scan the QR Code to Download the App

Assess Yourself

Every Step Counts

It's time to do self-assessment. Are you ready for the competition!

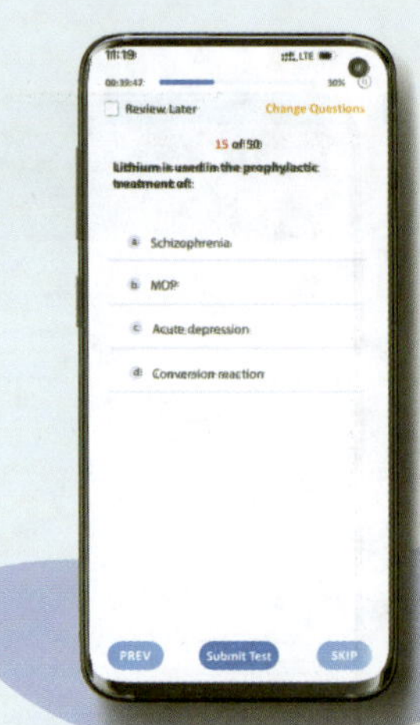

i. Mini Test *(Topic-wise)*

6 Tests covering **300** Questions with rationale (in Practice/Review mode) of the respective subject covering all important topics

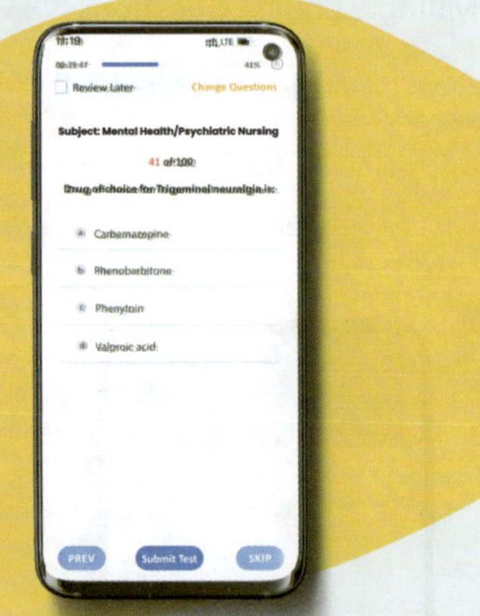

ii. Semester/Year-wise Test *(All Subjects)*

2 Tests covering **200+** MCQs based on important topics of respective year

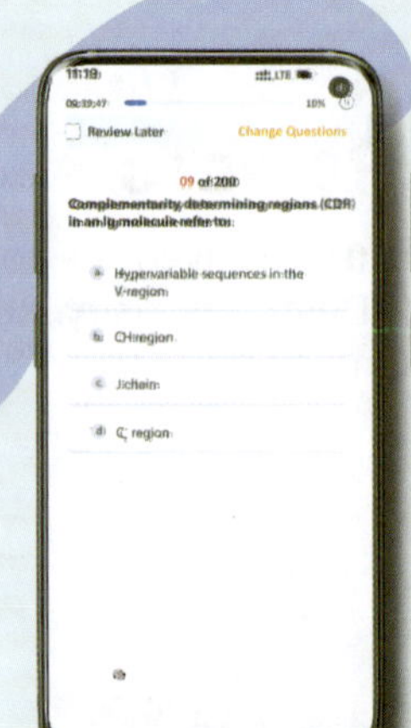

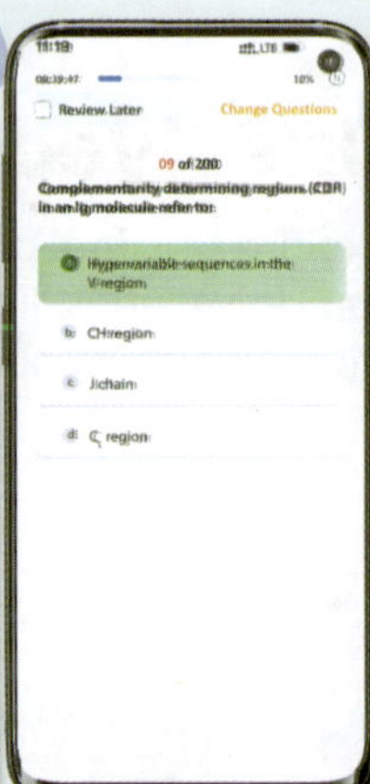

iii. Mega Grand Test *(All subjects)*

2 Grand Tests covering **400** MCQs with futuristic approach covering all subjects from all the years

Scan the QR Code to Download the App

Download the App

Nursing Next Live

The Next Level of Nursing Education

CBS Phygital Books >

Textbook of Mental Health/ Psychiatric Nursing PHYGITAL

High Yield Topics

Revise on the Go

Get 50+ Topic-wise Selective Images & Tables with their descriptions for LMR and Quick reference, based on the topics of University examination

List of High Yield Topics

and Many more...

Dil Mange More Content

Don't settle for less, go beyond with Recent Updates, E-books & much more...

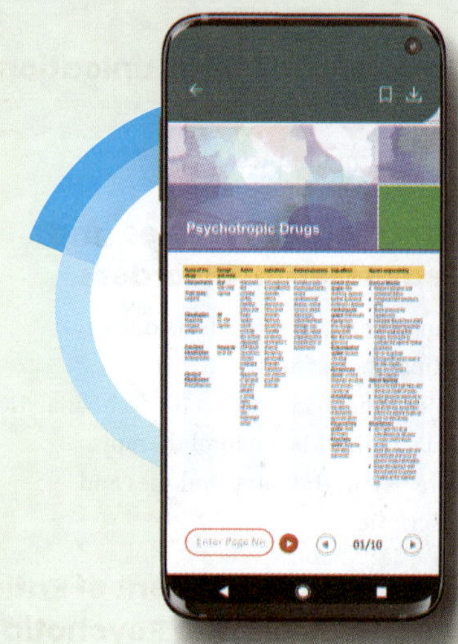

i. Recent Update

Regular updates related to **Recent advancement** and **Book Errata**

ii. E-book

Get PDFs of important chapters/sections **(Annexures/ Appendices)** of book

(This feature is for Institutions and pro-users)

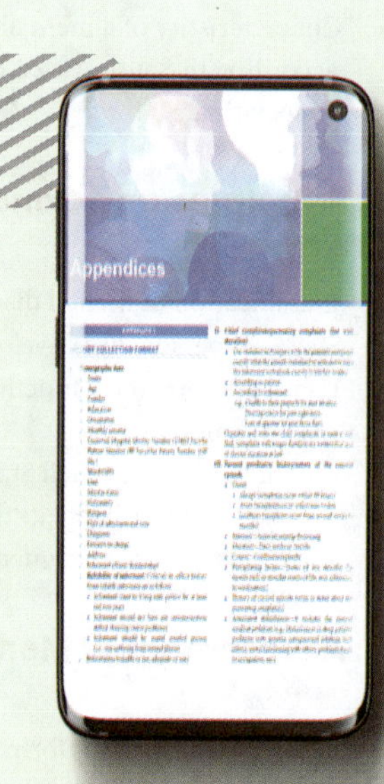

Scan the QR Code to Download the App

CBS Phygital Books >
Textbook of Mental Health/ Psychiatric Nursing PHYGITAL

Nursing Knowledge Tree
An Initiative by CBS Nursing Division

Textbook of
Mental Health/ Psychiatric Nursing
for BSc Nursing Students

As per the Revised INC Syllabus (2021–22) for BSc Nursing

Second Edition

P Prakash PhD (N), MBA (HM)
Assistant Professor
College of Nursing
Prince Sattam Bin Abdulaziz University
Al-Kharj, Kingdom of Saudi Arabia (KSA)

CBS Publishers & Distributors Pvt Ltd
• New Delhi • Bengaluru • Chennai • Kochi • Kolkata • Lucknow • Mumbai
• Hyderabad • Jharkhand • Nagpur • Patna • Pune • Uttarakhand

Textbook of
Mental Health/ Psychiatric Nursing
for BSc Nursing Students
As per the Revised INC Syllabus (2021–22) for BSc Nursing

ISBN: 978-93-94525-18-4

Second Edition: 2024

First Edition: 2020

Published by **Satish Kumar Jain** and produced by **Varun Jain** for

CBS Publishers & Distributors Pvt Ltd

4819/XI Prahlad Street, 24 Ansari Road, Daryaganj, New Delhi 110 002, India.
Ph: +91-11-23289259, 23266861, 23266867 Website: www.cbspd.com Fax: 011-23243014
e-mail: delhi@cbspd.com; cbspubs@airtelmail.in.

Corporate Office: 204 FIE, Industrial Area, Patparganj, Delhi 110 092
Ph: +91-11-4934 4934 Fax: 4934 4935
e-mail: feedback@cbspd.com; bhupesharora@cbspd.com

Branches

- **Bengaluru:** Seema House 2975, 17th Cross, K.R. Road, Banasankari 2nd Stage, Bengaluru-560 070, Karnataka
  Ph: +91-80-26771678/79 Fax: +91-80-26771680 e-mail: bangalore@cbspd.com
- **Chennai:** 7, Subbaraya Street, Shenoy Nagar, Chennai-600 030, Tamil Nadu
  Ph: +91-44-26680620, 26681266 Fax: +91-44-42032115 e-mail: chennai@cbspd.com
- **Kochi:** 68/1534, 35, 36-Power House Road, Opp. KSEB, Cochin-682018, Kochi, Kerala
  Ph: +91-484-4059061-65 Fax: +91-484-4059065 e-mail: kochi@cbspd.com
- **Kolkata:** Hind Ceramics Compound, 1st Floor, 147, Nilganj Road, Belghoria, Kolkata-700056, West Bengal
  Ph: +033-2563-3055/56 e-mail: kolkata@cbspd.com
- **Lucknow:** Basement, Khushnuma Complex, 7-Meerabai Marg (Behind Jawahar Bhawan), Lucknow-226001, Uttar Pradesh
  Ph: +0522-4000032 e-mail: tiwari.lucknow@cbspd.com
- **Mumbai:** PWD Shed, Gala No. 25/26, Ramchandra Bhatt Marg, Next to J.J. Hospital Gate No. 2, Opp. Union Bank of India, Noor Baug, Mumbai-400009, Maharashtra
  Ph: +91-22-66661880/89 Fax: +91-22-24902342 e-mail: mumbai@cbspd.com

Representatives

- **Hyderabad** +91-9885175004
- **Jharkhand** +91-9811541605
- **Nagpur** +91-9421945513
- **Patna** +91-9334159340
- **Pune** +91-9623451994
- **Uttarakhand** +91-9716462459

Printed at: Goyal Offset Works Pvt. Ltd.

Dedicated to

My Friends, Family
and
Nursing Students

About the Author

P Prakash *PhD (N), MBA (HM)* is presently working as an Assistant Professor in Department of Nursing at Prince Sattam Bin Abdulaziz University, Kingdom of Saudi Arabia (KSA), and Adjunct Teaching Faculty cum Post-Doctorate Research Fellow in Nursing at Lincoln University College, Malaysia.

He has 11 years of experience in Nursing as a Teaching faculty, ward in-charge (Psychiatric Unit), and Nursing Officer (Liver Transplantation Unit). He is a recognized research guide cum international examiner for scholars pursuing a doctorate program in Nursing. He has been awarded a Doctorate in Nursing at Meenakshi Academy of Education & Research (MAHER), Chennai. He completed Master's degrees in Psychiatric Nursing from Sri Ramakrishna Institute of Paramedical Sciences (SRIPMS), Coimbatore and in Hospital Administration from Alagappa University, Karaikudi. Besides, he also completed a diploma in Operation Theatre Techniques and yoga from Annamalai University & Madurai Kamaraj University respectively.

The author received the prestigious Florence Nightingale Award for Best Nurse in Philanthropy in 2016 by Doctors United Charitable Trust (DUCT). He has also been awarded a merit certificate in his post-graduation for obtaining second place in General Proficiency. He received a gold medal from 'His Excellency of Governorship, Surjit Singh Barnala,' for securing State level First rank in the conversational English program conducted at the State Bank Officers Association, Chennai. He was awarded twice for best poster presentation in national seminars. He was also awarded gold certificate in the Yogathon Challenge Competition for the completion of 108 rounds of Surya Namaskar on World Health Day April 7, 2012.

Dr P Prakash is a Certified Master trainer for the Promotion of Mental Health Services in collaboration with the World Health Organization (WHO) & Ministry of Health/Family Welfare, Govt. of India. He is an American Heart Association Certified Advance Cardiac Life Support (ACLS) Provider. He is an assessor of the Health Sector Skills Council. He worked as a Medical Investigator at Ayu Health, Chennai. He is a content developer for 'The CBS Nursing Next Mobile application.' He is a Life Member of the International Palliative Care Family Career Research Center, University of Melbourne in Australia, the American Travel Health Nurses Association, the Indian Red Cross Society, the Trained Nurses Association of India & Senior Member of the Asian Researchers Society.

The author is Editor-in-Chief, Editorial Board Member, and Reviewer of various Indexed International journals. He has authored *Textbook of Applied Sociology and Psychology* published by CBS Publishers. Besides, he has published books titled *Pocket Clinical Guide* for Nurses and *Health/Nursing Informatics* published by reputed medical book publishers.

Last but not least, he has presented topics as a resource person at the international conferences and has published research articles in Scopus-indexed journals, organized workshops, and has presented scientific papers at national and international levels.

Contributors and Reviewers

CONTRIBUTORS

E Elamathi

(Psychiatric Nursing) Masters at MMC, Chennai

Assistant Professor
Department of Psychiatric Nursing
Hindu Mission College of Nursing
Chennai, Tamil Nadu

Hyrune Zohara

MSc (Mental Health Nursing)

Assistant Professor
Department of Psychiatric Nursing
Ithaya Jyothi College of Nursing
Tirunelveli, Tamil Nadu

Joseph Jeganathan

(Psychiatric Nursing) Masters at NIMHANS and PhD at INC Consortium

Assistant Professor
Department of Psychiatric Nursing
University of Bahrain

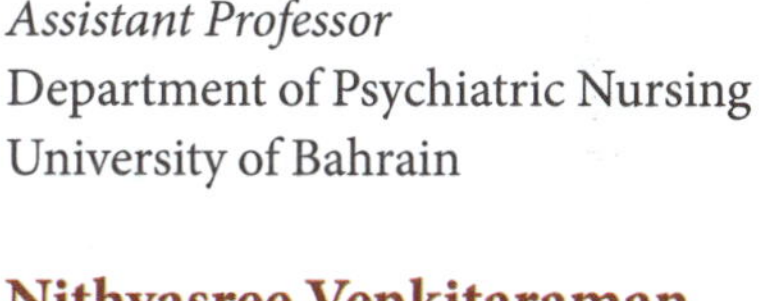

Nithyasree Venkitaraman

(Neuro Psychology)

Mental Health Professional
Birmingham Women's and Children's
NHS Foundation Trust, UK

Parthasarathy V

MD (Psychiatry), Gold Medal Achiever, Post Graduation at JIPMER

Associate Professor
Department of Psychiatry
Pondicherry Institute of Medical Sciences (PIMS)
Puducherry

Pastin Pushpa Rani P

Post-Graduation at CMC Vellore and PhD at INC Consortium

Associate Professor
College of Nursing
CMC Vellore Chittoor Campus
Andhra Pradesh

Sampoornam V

(Psychiatric Nursing), PhD (N), MSc (C&P)
MSc (Psy), SEFM, GRN, OWCN, ATHNA, IFNA

Professor cum Principal
Bhavani College of Nursing
Varadhanallur, Bhavani
Erode, Tamil Nadu

The names of the contributors are arranged in an alphabetical order.

REVIEWERS

Aldrin Vas
PhD (N), MSc Nursing (Psychiatric Nursing)
Professor cum Principal
Tejasvini Nursing Institute
Mangaluru, Karnataka

Jesudian K Nath
MSc (Mental Health Nursing)
Professor
United Institute of Nursing and Paramedical Sciences
Prayagraj, Uttar Pradesh

Anitha
MSc (Mental Health Nursing)
Associate Professor
Sri Vijay Vidyalaya College of Nursing and Research
Bagur, Krishnagiri, Tamil Nadu

Kirandeep Dhaliwal
PhD (N), MSc (Mental Health Nursing)
Principal
MM Institute of Management
Maharishi Markandeshwar (DU)
Mullana, Ambala, Haryana

Barnali Mukherjee
MSc (Psychiatric Nursing)
Professor
Government College of Nursing
Burdwan Medical College and Hospital
Purba Bardhaman, West Bengal

Lida Antony
PhD (N), MSc (N)
Vice Principal
Dr Moopen's Nursing College
Meppadi, Wayanad, Kerala

Baskar
PhD (N), MSc (Mental Health Nursing)
Professor
Department of Mental Health Nursing
PSG College of Nursing
Coimbatore, Tamil Nadu

Manisha Gupta
PhD (N), MA (Sociology), RM, RN
Dean and Principal
Rabindranath Tagore University Institute of Nursing
Bhopal, Madhya Pradesh

Gomathi M
PhD (N) Scholar
MSc (Mental Health Nursing)
JIPMER, Puducherry

Moushumi Purkayastha Mukherjee
(Psychiatrist) MBBS, DPM (NIMHANS), DNB (GMCH, Chandigarh)
Professor
Department of Psychiatry
JIPMER, Puducherry

The names of the reviewers are arranged in an alphabetical order.

Narendra Kumar Sharma
MSc (Mental Health Nursing)
Principal
Chitrini Nursing College
Prantij, Gujarat

Neetu Bhatnagar
MSc (Applied Psychology and Psychiatric Nursing)
Diploma in Nursing Administration
Principal
Bee Enn Nursing Institute
Chak Bhalwal
Jammu and Kashmir

Nuziba Begum
MSc (Mental Health Nursing)
Professor
Department of Mental Health Nursing
Sri Ramakrishna Institute of
Paramedical Sciences (SRIPMS)—
College of Nursing
Coimbatore, Tamil Nadu

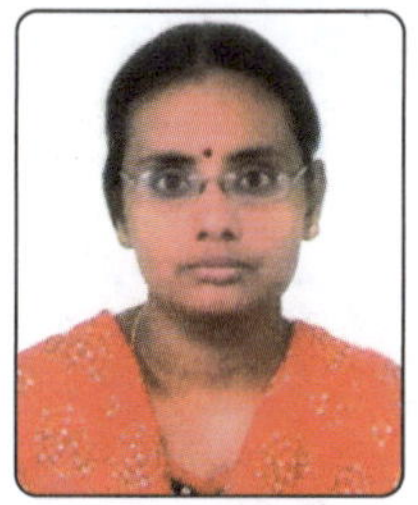

P Jamunarani
MSc (Mental Health Nursing)
Professor
Department of Mental Health Nursing
KMCH College of Nursing
Coimbatore, Tamil Nadu

R Sridevi
PhD (N), MSc (N)
Professor cum Principal
EGS Pillay College of Nursing
Nagapattinam, Tamil Nadu

Ruba A
PhD (N), MSc (N)
Professor cum Principal
Mariamman Nursing College
Tiruchirappalli, Tamil Nadu

Sadhya Ghai
PhD (Psychiatric Nursing)
Consultant/Senior Advisor
JHPIEGO, Lucknow, Uttar Pradesh
Former Principal
PGININE, Chandigarh

Sangeetha P
MSc (Mental Health Nursing)
Professor and Head
Department of Psychiatric Nursing
Adhiparasakthi College of Nursing
Melmaruvathur, Chennai, Tamil Nadu

Sathish Rajamani
MSc (Psychiatric Nursing)
Professor
DRIEMS School and College of Nursing
Cuttack, Odisha

Sibin K Dummini
BSc (N)
Principal
Jeevandeep School of Nursing
UP State Medical Faculty
Lucknow, Uttar Pradesh

The names of the reviewers are arranged in an alphabetical order.

Smitha P M
MSc (Mental Health Nursing)
Professor/HOD
Department of Mental Health Nursing
Narayana College of Nursing
Vellore, Andhra Pradesh

Varun Toshniwal
PhD (N)
Professor cum Head
College of Nursing
IIMT University
Meerut, Uttar Pradesh

Sonia Nanda
MSc Nursing (Psychiatric Nursing)
Associate Professor
Rajiv Gandhi College of Nursing
Chak Bhalwal
Jammu and Kashmir

Vinodh Selvan Vincent
MSc (Mental Health Nursing)
Assistant Professor
Department of Psychiatric Nursing
College of Nursing
Pondicherry Institute of Medical Sciences
Puducherry

V Nirosha
MSc (N)
Professor
Vivekanandha College of Nursing
Elayampalayam, Tamil Nadu

Preface to the Second Edition

Numerous books on psychiatry are available in the market but most of them are not appropriate and suitable from the students' point of view. This book has been written to equip the nurses with easy understanding of subject, as I intended that each aspect of the psychiatry should be imbibed by the students.

For this, I have tried to present the text in lucid language. This second edition of "Textbook of Mental Health/Psychiatric Nursing" has been written based on Revised Syllabus of Indian Nursing Council. This book is equipped with the recent updates such as ICD-11 criteria, DSM-5 criteria, Mental Healthcare Act (2017), POCSO Act (2012), Trends in Psychiatric Nursing, etc. Each chapter is organized by following a uniform pattern as Chapter Outline, Learning Objectives, Key Terms, Description, Summary, Probable Questions and MCQs with Answers.

'Assess Yourself' at the end of every chapter includes the possible Essay Type Questions, Short Notes and Multiple-Choice Questions (with answers) to help the students to revise the chapter easily. This book has been prepared with the selected key points that are included in every chapter to ensure that student excels in university exams.

A number of illustrations and photographs are presented in all chapters which will help students enhance their presentation skill in the university exams. All-important concepts have been explained with appropriate examples. "Glossary" at the end of book will help the students to memorize important terms in Psychiatric Nursing in one go.

"Appendices" including Formats for Mental Health Assessment, Psychiatric History Collection and the Checklists will guide the students to understand the formats followed in practice along with implementation of core concepts of Psychiatry. "Learn the Differences" which are included in the annexure will help the students explore the differences between the important terminologies used in Psychiatric Nursing.

Moreover, case scenarios of all the vital Psychiatric nursing topics have been covered with appropriate answers for the same. In addition to that, viva voce questions with answers are included in the textbook.

OSCE, Abbreviations, Psychotropic Drugs and Syndromes in Psychiatry have been included in the textbook to give a concise view of important topics.

I am confident that this book will provide adequate information to the teachers as well as students for understanding the basic concepts of Psychiatric Nursing. Suggestions from the teachers and students are always welcome for the improvement of the content of this textbook.

P Prakash
email: prakash.lalitha88@gmail.com

Preface to the First Edition

Numerous books on psychiatry are available in the market but most of them are not relevant from the students' point of view. This book has been written to equip the nurses with easy understanding of subject, as I intended that each aspect of the psychiatry should be imbibed by the students.

I have tried to present the text in lucid language. "Textbook of Mental Health/Psychiatric Nursing" has been written on the basis of Revised Syllabus of Indian Nursing Council. This book is equipped with the recent updates such as DSM-5 criteria, Mental Healthcare Act (2017), Trends in Psychiatric Nursing, etc. Each and every chapter is organized by following a uniform pattern as Chapter Outline, Learning Objectives, Key Terms, Description, Summary, Probable Questions and MCQs with Answers.

'Assess Yourself' at the end of every chapter includes the possible Essay Type Questions, Short Notes and Multiple Choice Questions (with answers) to help the students to revise the chapter easily. This book has been prepared with the selected key points that are included in each and every chapter to ensure that student excels in university exams.

A number of illustrations and photographs are presented in all chapters which will help students to enhance their presentation skill in the university exams. All important concepts have been explained with appropriate examples. "Glossary" at the end of book will help the students to memorize important terms in Psychiatric Nursing in one go.

"Appendices" including Formats for Mental Health Assessment, Psychiatric History Collection and the Checklists will guide the students to understand the formats followed in practice along with implementation of core concepts of Psychiatry. "Learn the Differences" which are included in the annexure will help the students to explore the differences between the important terminologies used in Psychiatric Nursing.

Abbreviations, Psychotropic Drugs and Syndromes in Psychiatry have been included in the textbook to give a glimpse of important topics.

I am pretty sure that this book will provide valuable information to the teachers as well as students for understanding the basic concepts of Psychiatric Nursing. Suggestions from the teachers and students are always welcome for the improvement of the content of this textbook.

P Prakash
email: prakash.lalitha88@gmail.com

Acknowledgments

First of all, I would like to thank the Almighty God for helping me at every step and for bestowing wisdom and patience to achieve this grand success. My heartfelt thanks go to my parents Mr Palanivelu and Mrs Lalitha. I convey sincere thanks to my wife Mrs Dhivya and my daughter Taeju, who kept patience and supported me. I express thanks to my sister Mrs Anitha, who always encouraged me.

I am thankful to Dr Parthasarthy, Associate Professor at Pondicherry Institute of Medical Sciences, for his excellent guidance. I am so thankful to all the reviewers, editors, and content designers for their remarkable contributions.

My special thanks is due to **Mr Satish Kumar Jain** (Chairman) and **Mr Varun Jain** (Managing Director), M/s CBS Publishers and Distributors Pvt Ltd for their wholehearted support in publication of this book. I have no words to describe the role, efforts, inputs and initiatives undertaken by **Mr Bhupesh Aarora** [Sr. Vice President – Publishing & Marketing (Health Sciences Division)] for helping and motivating us.

Last but not least, I sincerely thank the entire CBS team for bringing out the book with utmost care and attractive presentation. I would like to thank Ms Nitasha Arora (Publishing Head and Content Strategist – Medical and Nursing), Ms Daljeet Kaur (Assistant Publishing Manager) and Dr Anju Dhir (Product Manager cum Commissioning Editor – Medical) for their editorial support. I would also extend my thanks to Mr Shivendu Bhushan Pandey (Sr. Manager and Team Lead), Mr Ashutosh Pathak (Sr. Proofreader cum Team Coordinator) and all the production team members for devoting laborious hours in designing and typesetting the book.

CBS Nursing Knowledge Tree

Extends its Tribute to

Florence Nightingale

For glorifying the role of women as nurses,
For holding the title of "The Lady with the Lamp,"
For working tirelessly for humanity—
Florence Nightingale will always be
remembered for her
selfless and memorable services to the
human race.

Florence Nightingale
(May 1820 – August 1910)

From Publisher's Desk

Dear Reader,

Nursing Education has a rich history, often characterized by traditional teaching techniques that have evolved over time. Primarily, teaching took place within classroom settings. Lectures, textbooks, and clinical rotations were the core teaching tools; and students majorly relied on textbooks by local or foreign publishers for quality education. However, today, technology has completely transformed the field of nursing education, making it an integral part of the curriculum. It has evolved to include a range of technological tools that enhance the learning experience and better prepare students for clinical practice.

As publishers, we've been contributing to the field of Medical Science, Nursing and Allied Sciences and earned the trust of many. By supporting **Indian authors**, coupled with **nursing webinars and conferences**, we have paved an easier path for aspiring nurses, empowering them to excel in national and state level exams. With this, we're not only enhancing the quality of patient care but also enabling future nurses to adapt to new challenges and innovations in the rapidly evolving world of healthcare. Following the ideology of **Bringing learning to people instead of people going for learning**, so far, we've been doing our part by

- Developing quality content by qualified and well-versed authors
- Building a strong community of faculty and students
- Introducing a smart approach with Digital/Hybrid Books, and
- Offering simulation Nursing Procedures, etc.

Innovative teaching methodologies, such as modern-age Phygital Books, have sparked the interest of the Next-Gen students in pursuing advanced education. The enhancement of educational standards through **Omnipresent Knowledge Sharing Platforms** has further facilitated learning, bridging a gap between doctors and nurses.

At Nursing Next Live, a sister concern of CBS Publishers & Distributors, we have long recognized the immense potential within the nursing field. Our journey in innovating nursing education has allowed us to make substantial and meaningful contributions. With the vision of strengthening learning at every stage, we have introduced several plans that cater to the specific needs of the students, including but not limited to **Plan UG** for undergraduates, **Plan MSc** for post graduation aspirants, **Plan FDP** for upskilling faculties, **SDL** for integrated learning and **Plan NP** for bridging the gap between theoretical & practical learning. Additionally, we have successfully completed seven series of our **Target High** Book in a very short period, setting a milestone in the education industry. We have been able to achieve all this just with the sole vision of laying the foundation of diversified knowledge for all. With the rise of a new generation of educated, tech-savvy individuals, we anticipate even more remarkable advancements in the coming years.

We take immense pride in our achievements and eagerly look forward to the future, brimming with new opportunities for innovation, growth and collaborations with experienced minds such as yourself who can contribute to our mission as Authors, Reviewers and/or Faculties. Together, let's foster a generation of nurses who are confident, competent, and prepared to succeed in a technology-driven healthcare system.

Mr. Bhupesh Aarora
(Sr. Vice President- Publishing & Marketing)
bhupeshaarora@cbspd.com| +91 95553 53330

Special Features of the Book

Learning Objectives in the beginning of every Chapter help readers understand the purpose of the chapter.

LEARNING OBJECTIVES

After studying this chapter, the student will be able to understand the basic concepts of psychiatric nursing.

CHAPTER OUTLINE

- Perspectives of Mental Health and Mental Health Nursing
- Mental Health Team or Multidisciplinary Team
- Nature/Philosophy of Psychiatric Nursing

Chapter Outline gives a glimpse of the content covered in the chapter.

Key Terms are added in each chapter to help understand difficult scientific terms in easy language.

KEY TERMS

Mental health nursing, Mental health, Mental health policy, Mental health team, Normal behavior, Abnormal behavior, Evolution of mental health services, Functions of psychiatric nurse.

Table 3.14: Drug levels in blood

Name of the drug	Blood therapeutic value
Lithium	0.6–1.8 mEq/L
Carbamazepine	6–12 mg/mL
Sodium valproate	50–100 mg/mL

Numerous **Tables** have been used in the chapters to facilitate learning in a quick way.

The book is well illustrated with relevant colorful **Figures**, etc.

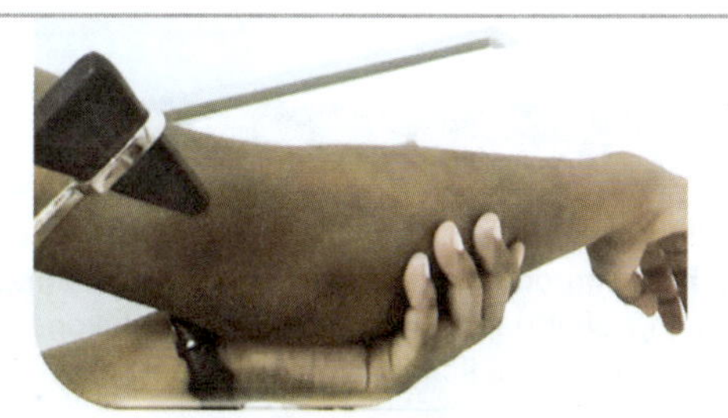

Figure 3.7: Assessment of triceps reflex

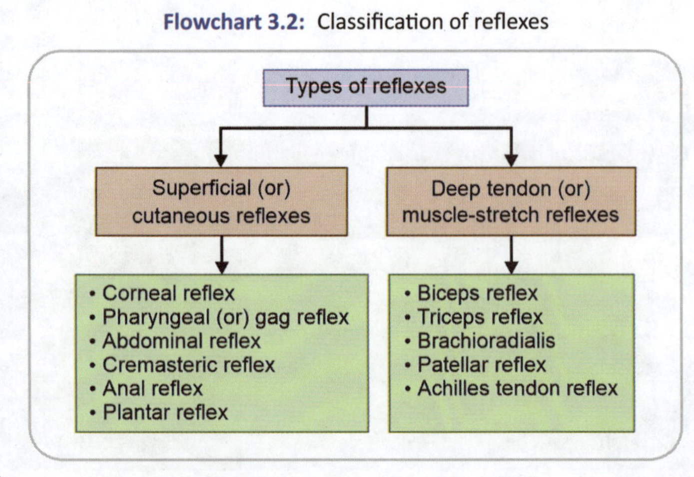

Flowchart 3.2: Classification of reflexes

Flow Diagrams are used in-between the text to enhance students' learning experience in one go.

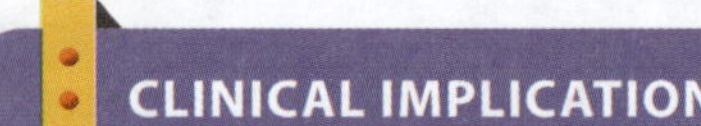

CLINICAL IMPLICATION

Frontal Lobe Syndrome

Damage to the dorsolateral (upper and outer) areas of the frontal lobes may cause symptoms such as lack of drive and spontaneity. Damage to the anterior aspects of frontal lobes might lead the changes in mood or affect, which in turn exhibits the impulsive and inappropriate behavior in patients.

Evolving conceptual details for application in clinical situations are depicted in **Clinical Implication** boxes.

NURSING IMPLICATION

Implications for Nursing Practice

- Understanding the psychosexual stages of childhood provides a framework for understanding behaviors observed in adult patients.
- Effective parenting can be promoted by teaching parents about the child's needs during each psychosexual stage.

Clinical correlations from nursing point of view have been covered under **Nursing Implication** or **Nursing Responsibility** boxes.

NOTE

Light therapy used for skin conditions might emit ultraviolet rays that should not be used for other conditions because it might harm the eyesight.

Extra knowledge related to the respective topic is covered under the **Note** boxes.

DO YOU KNOW

Some Indian celebrities who spoke boldly that they were suffering from mood disorders were Manisha Koirala, Yo Yo Honey Singh, Shahrukh Khan, Deepika Padukone, Anushka Sharma, Varun Dhawan, Randeep Hooda and Ileana D'Cruz.

Do You Know boxes give an overview of important facts and terms of the concerned topic.

Numerous **Mnemonics** have been added in whole book to help the students remember complex topics in easy way.

Mnemonic

Mnemonic to remember lithium side effects are "LITHUM"

L : Leukocytosis
I : Insipidus (Nephrogenic diabetes insipidus)
T : Tremors (or) thirst (or) taste as metallic (or) teratogenic (Teratogenics–Ebstein anomaly)
H : Hypothyroidism
U : Urinary (Polyuria)
M : Miscellaneous

EXTRA EDGE

Types of Schizophrenia

Paranoid Schizophrenia

It is most common type of schizophrenia. Onset is late and has good prognosis. Personality is said to be preserved, i.e., client is able to perform activities of daily living (ADLs) and has good social interaction. Hallucination, delusion and thought disorders are peculiarly seen. Examples of hallucinatory themes are commenting, arguing, threatening, body sensations/movements. Examples of thought disorders are irrelevant, incoherent and neologisms in speech.

Extra Edge boxes provide highly useful additional information to enhance the knowledge of the students.

Important takeaway points of respective chapters have been highlighted under **Summary** boxes.

SUMMARY

- Antipsychotics are medications to treat psychotic disorder and psychosis related to other psychiatric and medical disorders.
- The other names of antipsychotics are D_2 receptor blockers, major tranquilizers, neuroleptic agents, ataractics and anti-schizophrenic drugs.

ASSESS YOURSELF

Long Answer Questions

1. Explain the scope of psychiatric nursing practice.

Short Answer Questions

1. Name the members of a mental health care team.

Short Notes

Write short notes on:

1. Functions of psychiatric nurse

Multiple Choice Questions

1. Misperception of taste is ________ hallucination.

a. Auditory
b. Visual
c. Functional
d. Gustatory

At the end of chapters, **Assess Yourself** section is given which contains frequently asked questions in exams and multiple choice questions to help students attain mastery over the subject.

Case Study demonstrates example(s) of specific clinical scenarios covered in separate section from clinical and applied aspects.

CASE 2 PATIENT WITH DEPRESSIVE DISORDER

Mr K, 63-year-old male, unmarried, he is a carpenter, completed Higher Secondary Certificate (HSC). Mr K has a pervasive low mood, poor appetite, decreased sleep, fearfulness, lack of interest in activities, decreased self-care and social withdrawal.

Giving extra edge to book from the practical point of view **OSCE** station and **Viva Voce** covered in a separation section.

Objective Structured Clinical Evaluation (OSCE)

STATION 1–ANXIOUS PERSONALITY DISORDER

Instructions to the Examinee

Ms X aged 28 years came with complaint of avoiding social gathering and family functions. Her mind is preoccupied with being criticized or rejected and she also shows extreme anxiety, nervousness and low self-esteem.

Participant number: ________ **Date:** ________

Viva Voce

1. **Define mental illness.**
   Mental illness is a maladjustment in living which produces disharmony in life.

Important terms with their one-line definition covered under **Glossary**.

Glossary

Acute depression: It's a sudden abrupt onset of depression.

Apraxia: Inability to perform learned motor activities.

Biceps reflex: Flexion of forearm occurs when arm is gently flexed at elbow, tap the biceps brachii tendon.

Coprophilia: Sexual pleasure with feces.

Syllabus

Mental Health Nursing-I

Placement: V Semester **Theory:** 3 Credits (60 Hours)

Unit	Time (Hrs)	Learning Outcomes	Content	Teaching/Learning Activities	Assessment Methods
I	6 (T)	• Describe the historical development and current trends in mental health nursing • Discuss the scope of mental health nursing • Describe the concept of normal and abnormal behavior	**Introduction** • Perspectives of mental health and mental health nursing, evolution of mental health services, treatments and nursing practices • Mental health team • Nature and scope of mental health nursing • Role and functions of mental health nurse in various settings and factors affecting the level of nursing practice • Concepts of normal and abnormal behavior	• Lecture discussion	• Essay • Short answer
II	10 (T)	• Define the various terms used in mental health nursing • Explain the classification of mental disorders • Explain the psychodynamics of maladaptive behavior • Discuss the etiological factors and psychopathology of mental disorders • Explain the principles and standards of mental health nursing • Describe the conceptual models of mental health nursing	**Principles and Concepts of Mental Health Nursing** • Definition: Mental health nursing and terminology used • Classification of mental disorders: ICD-11, DSM-5, Geropsychiatry manual classification • Review of personality development, defense mechanisms • Etiology biopsychosocial factors • Psychopathology of mental disorders: Review of structure and function of brain, limbic system and abnormal neurotransmission • Principles of mental health nursing • Ethics and responsibilities • Practice standards for psychiatric mental health nursing (INC practice standards) • Conceptual models and the role of nurse: ▪ Existential model ▪ Psychoanalytical models ▪ Behavioral model ▪ Interpersonal model • Preventive psychiatry and rehabilitation	• Lecture cum discussion • Explain using charts • Review of personality development	• Essay • Short answer

Contd...

Unit	Time (Hrs)	Learning Outcomes	Content	Teaching/Learning Activities	Assessment Methods
III	6 (T)	Describe nature, purpose and process of assessment of mental health status	**Mental Health Assessment** • History taking • Mental status examination • Mini mental status examination • Neurological examination • Investigations: Related blood chemistry, EEG, CT and MRI • Psychological tests	• Lecture cum discussion • Demonstration • Practice session • Clinical practice	• Essay • Short answer • Assessment of mental health status
IV	6 (T)	• Identify therapeutic communication and techniques • Describe therapeutic relationship • Describe therapeutic impasses and its interventions	**Therapeutic Communication and Nurse-Patient Relationship** • Therapeutic communication: Types, techniques, characteristics and barriers • Therapeutic nurse-patient relationship • Interpersonal relationship • Elements of nurse-patient contract, • Review of technique of IPR—Johari window • Therapeutic impasse and its management	• Lecture cum discussion • Demonstration • Role play • Process recording • Simulation (video)	• Essay • Short answer • OSCE
V	10 (T)	Explain treatment modalities and therapies used in mental disorders and role of the nurse	**Treatment Modalities and Therapies used in Mental Disorders** • **Physical therapies:** Psychopharmacology • Electroconvulsive therapy • **Psychological therapies:** Psychotherapy, behavior therapy, CBT • **Psychosocial:** Group therapy, family therapy, therapeutic community, recreational therapy, art therapy (dance, music, etc.), occupational therapy • **Alternative and complementary:** Yoga, meditation, relaxation • **Consideration for special populations**	• Lecture cum discussion • Demonstration • Group work • Practice session • Clinical practice	• Essay • Short answer • Objective type
VI	8 (T)	Describe the etiology, psychodynamics/ pathology, clinical manifestations, diagnostic criteria and management of patients with schizophrenia, and other psychotic disorders	**Nursing Management of Patient with Schizophrenia, and Other Psychotic Disorders** • Prevalence and incidence • Classification • Etiology, psychodynamics, clinical manifestation, diagnostic criteria/formulations **Nursing Process** • Nursing assessment: History, physical and mental assessment • Treatment modalities and nursing management of patients with schizophrenia and other psychotic disorders • Geriatric considerations and considerations for special populations • Follow-up and home care and rehabilitation	• Lecture and discussion • Case discussion • Case presentation • Clinical practice	• Essay • Short answer • Assessment of patient management problems
VII	6 (T)	Describe the etiology, psychodynamics, clinical manifestations, diagnostic criteria and management of patients with mood disorders	**Nursing Management of Patient with Mood Disorders** • Prevalence and incidence • Mood disorders: Bipolar affective disorder, mania depression and dysthymia, etc. • Etiology, psychodynamics, clinical manifestation, diagnosis • Nursing assessment history, physical and mental assessment	• Lecture and discussion • Case discussion • Case presentation • Clinical practice	• Essay • Short answer • Assessment of patient management problems

Contd...

Unit	Time (Hrs)	Learning Outcomes	Content	Teaching/Learning Activities	Assessment Methods
			• Treatment modalities and nursing management of patients with mood disorders • Geriatric considerations/considerations for special populations • Follow-up and home care and rehabilitation		
VIII	8 (T)	Describe the etiology, psychodynamics, clinical manifestations, diagnostic criteria and management of patients with neurotic, stress related and somatization disorders	**Nursing Management of Patient with Neurotic, Stress Related and Somatization Disorders** • Prevalence and incidence • Classifications • Anxiety disorders—OCD, PTSD, Somatoform disorders, phobias, Dissociative and conversion disorders • Etiology, psychodynamics, clinical manifestation, diagnostic criteria/formulations • Nursing assessment: History, physical and mental assessment • Treatment modalities and nursing management of patients with neurotic and stress related disorders • Geriatric considerations/considerations for special populations • Follow-up and home care and rehabilitation	• Lecture and discussion • Case discussion • Case presentation • Clinical practice	• Essay • Short answer • Assessment of patient management problems

Mental Health Nursing-II

Placement: VI Semester

Theory: 1 Credit (40 hours)

Unit	Time (Hrs)	Learning Outcomes	Content	Teaching/Learning Activities	Assessment Methods
I	6 (T)	Describe the etiology, psychodynamics, clinical manifestations, diagnostic criteria and management of patients with substance use disorders	**Nursing Management of Patients with Substance Use Disorders** • Prevalence and incidence • Commonly used psychotropic substance: Classifications, forms, routes, action, intoxication and withdrawal • Psychodynamics/etiology of substance use disorder (Terminologies: Substance use, abuse, tolerance, dependence, withdrawal) • Diagnostic criteria/formulations • Nursing assessment: History (substance history), Physical, mental assessment and drug and drug assay • Treatment (detoxification, antabuse and narcotic antagonist therapy and harm reduction, brief interventions, MET, refusal skills, maintenance therapy) and nursing management of patients with substance use disorders • Special considerations for vulnerable population • Follow-up and home care and rehabilitation	• Lecture cum discussion • Case discussion • Case presentation • Clinical practice	• Essay • Short answer • Assessment of patient management problems

Contd...

Unit	Time (Hrs)	Learning Outcomes	Content	Teaching/Learning Activities	Assessment Methods
II	6 (T)	Describe the etiology, psychodynamics, clinical manifestations, diagnostic criteria and management of patients with personality, and sexual disorders	**Nursing Management of Patient with Personality and Sexual Disorders** • Prevalence and incidence • Classification of disorders • Etiology, psychopathology, characteristics, diagnosis • Nursing assessment: History, physical and mental health assessment • Treatment modalities and nursing management of patients with personality, and sexual disorders • Geriatric considerations • Follow-up and home care and rehabilitation	• Lecture cum discussion • Case discussion • Case presentation • Clinical practice	• Essay • Short answer • Assessment of patient management problems
III	8 (T)	Describe the etiology, psychopathology, clinical manifestations, diagnostic criteria and management of childhood and adolescent disorders including mental deficiency	**Nursing Management of Behavioral and Emotional Disorders Occurring during Childhood and Adolescence** (Intellectual disability, autism, attention deficit, hyperactive disorder, eating disorders, learning disorder) • Prevalence and incidence • Classifications • Etiology, psychodynamics, characteristics, diagnostic criteria/formulations • Nursing assessment: History, physical, mental status examination and IQ assessment • Treatment modalities and nursing management of childhood disorders including intellectual disability • Follow-up and home care and rehabilitation	• Lecture cum discussion • Case discussion • Case presentation • Clinical practice	• Essay • Short answer • Assessment of patient management problems
IV	5 (T)	Describe the etiology, psychopathology, clinical manifestations, diagnostic criteria and management of organic brain disorders	**Nursing Management of Organic Brain Disorders (Delirium, Dementia, Amnestic Disorders)** • Prevalence and incidence • Classification • Etiology, psychopathology, clinical features, diagnosis and differential diagnosis • Nursing assessment: History, physical, mental and neurological assessment • Treatment modalities and nursing management of organic brain disorders • Follow-up and home care and rehabilitation	• Lecture cum discussion • Case discussion • Case presentation • Clinical practice	• Essay • Short answer • Assessment of patient management problems
V	6 (T)	Identify psychiatric emergencies and carry out crisis intervention	**Psychiatric Emergencies and Crisis Intervention** • Types of psychiatric emergencies (attempted suicide, violence/aggression, stupor, delirium tremens and other psychiatric emergencies) and their managements • Maladaptive behavior of individual and groups, stress, crisis and disaster(s) • Types of crisis • Crisis intervention: Principles, techniques and process ▪ Stress reduction interventions as per stress adaptation model ▪ Coping enhancement ▪ Techniques of counseling	• Lecture cum discussion • Case discussion • Case presentation • Clinical practice	• Short answer • Objective type

Contd...

Unit	Time (Hrs)	Learning Outcomes	Content	Teaching/Learning Activities	Assessment Methods
VI	4 (T)	Explain legal aspects applied in mental health settings and role of the nurse	**Legal Issues in Mental Health Nursing** • Overview of Indian Lunacy Act and The Mental Health Act, 1987 • (Protection of Children from Sexual Offence) POCSO Act • Mental Health Care Act (MHCA) 2017 • Rights of mentally ill clients • Forensic psychiatry and nursing • Acts related to narcotic and psychotropic substances and illegal drug trafficking • Admission and discharge procedures as per MHCA 2017 • Role and responsibilities of nurses in implementing MHCA 2017	• Lecture cum discussion • Case discussion	• Short answer • Objective type
VII	5 (T)	• Describe the model of preventive psychiatry • Describe community mental health services and role of the nurse	**Community Mental Health Nursing** • Development of Community Mental Health Services: • National Mental Health Policy viz. National Health Policy • National Mental Health Program • Institutionalization versus deinstitutionalization • Model of preventive psychiatry • Mental health services available at the primary, secondary, tertiary levels including rehabilitation and nurses' responsibilities • Mental health agencies: Government and Voluntary, National and International • Mental health nursing issues for special populations: Children, adolescence, women elderly, victims of violence and abuse, handicapped, HIV/AIDS, etc.	• Lecture cum discussion • Clinical/field practice • Field visits to mental health service agencies	• Short answer • Objective type • Assessment of the field visit reports

Contents

Abbreviations

A

AA: Alcoholic Anonymous

AAMR: American Association on Mental Retardation

AN: Anorexia Nervosa

ABPN: American Board of Psychiatry and Neurology

ACT: Acceptance and Commitment Therapy

ACTH: Adrenocorticotropic Hormone

AD: Alzheimer's Disease (or) Adjustment Disorder

AIMS: Abnormal Involuntary Movement Scale

ADD: Attention Deficit Disorder

ADHD: Attention Deficit Hyperactive Disorder

APA: American Psychiatric Association

ARDSI: Alzheimer's & Related Disorders Society of India

ASPD: Antisocial Personality Disorder

ASD: Autism Spectrum Disorder

ATS: Amphetamine-Type Stimulant

AvPD: Avoidant Personality Disorder

B

BAI: Beck Anxiety Inventory

BDI: Beck Depression Inventory

BDRS: Bipolar Depression Rating Scale

BED: Binge Eating Disorder

BDD: Body Dysmorphic Disorder

BEHAVE: AD Behavioral Pathology in Alzheimer's Disease

BHS: Beck Hopelessness Scale

BMI: Body Mass Index

BPRS: Brief Psychiatric Rating Scale

BPSD: Behavioral and Psychological Symptoms of Dementia

C

CATIE-AD: Clinical Antipsychotic Trials of Intervention Effectiveness for Alzheimer's Disease

CA: Chronological Age

CAM: Complementary and Alternative Medicine

CAMQ: Common Mental Disorder Questionnaire

CAPU: Child and Adolescent Psychiatric Unit

CAT: Cognitive Analytic Therapy

CBCL: Child Behaviour Checklist

CBT: Cognitive Behaviour Therapy

CD: Conduct Disorder

CGI: Clinical Global Impressions

CGI-C: Clinical Global Impression of Change

CID: Critical Incident Debriefing

CIT: Crisis Intervention Team

CIMH: Center for International Mental Health

CLF: Community Living Facility

CMAI: Cohen-Mansfield Agitation Inventory

CMHN: Community Mental Health Nurse

CNS: Central Nervous System

CPRP: Community Psychiatric Rehabilitation Program

CRH: Corticotropin Releasing Hormone

CROMP: Centre for Rehabilitation of Mental Patients

CRSD: Circadian Rhythm Sleep Disorders

CT: Computed Tomography

CVA: Cerebrovascular Accident

D

DBS: Deep Brain Stimulation

DID: Dissociative Identity Disorder

DiG: DiGeorge Syndrome
DLB: Dementia with Lewy body
DBT: Dialectical Behaviour Therapy
DISC: Diagnostic Interview Schedule for Children
DMHP: District Mental Health Program
DMHT: District Mental Health Team
DOES: Disorder of Excessive Somnolence
DPN: Diploma in Psychiatric Nursing
DSH: Deliberate Self Harm
DSM-IV: Diagnostic and Statistical Manual of Mental Disorders, 4th Edition
DSM-5: Diagnostic and Statistical Manual of Mental Disorders, 5th Edition
DT: Delirium Tremens
DXM: Dextromethorphan
DZP: Diazepam

E

ED: Emotional Disturbances
EBP: Evidence-Based Practice
ECT: Electroconvulsive Therapy
ECG: Electrocardiogram
EDNS: Eating Disorder Not otherwise Specified
EEG: Electroencephalogram
EMG: Electromyogram
EIT: Early Intervention Team
EMPS: Emergency Mobile Psychiatric Services
EOMI: Episodes of Mental Illness
EPDS: Edinburgh Postnatal Depression Scale
EPQ: Eysenck Personality Questionnaire
EPS: Extrapyramidal Symptoms
EQ: Emotional Quotient
ERP: Exposure and Response Prevention
EUPD: Emotionally Unstable Personality Disorder

F

FAS: Fetal Alcohol Syndrome
FAA: Food Addicts Anonymous
FAP: Functional Analytic Psychotherapy
FAST: Functional Assessment staging
FGA: First-Generation Antipsychotic
FTD: Formal Thought Disorder (or) Frontotemporal Dementia

G

GA: Gamblers Anonymous
GABA: Gamma Amino Butyric Acid
GAD: Generalized Anxiety Disorder scale
GAF: Global Assessment of Functioning scale
GAI: Geriatric Anxiety Inventory
GAS: General Adaptation Syndrome
GBL: Gamma-Butyrolactone
GGT: Gamma Glutamyl Transpeptidase
GHB: Gamma Hydroxybutyric acid
GHQ-12: General Health Questionnaire, 12 item version
GRADE: Grading of Recommendations Assessment, Development and Evaluation
GTS: Gilles de Tourette's Syndrome
GIP: Global Initiative in Psychiatry

H

HADS: Hospital Anxiety and Depression Scale
HDRS: Hamilton Depression Rating Scale
HGH: Human Growth Hormone
HT: Healing Touch
HIV: Human Immunodeficiency Virus

I

IDEA: Individuals with Disabilities Education Act
IDS: Inventory of Depression Symptomatology
ITP: Inferior Thalamic Peduncle
ICD-10: International Classification of Diseases, 10th Revision
IEC: Information Education Communication
IED: Intermittent Explosive Disorder
IOP: Intensive Outpatient Program
IPT: Interpersonal Therapy
ILA: Indian Lunacy Act
IQ: Intelligent Quotient
IR: Immediate Release
IRF: Inpatient Rehabilitation Facility
IRR: Incidence Rate Ratio
ISMH: Indian System of Medicine & Homeopathy
ISMO: International Society for Mental Health Online
ISPN: Indian Society of Psychiatric Nurses
ITAQ: Insight and Treatment Attitude Questionnaire
ITT: Intention to Treat

L

LAAM: Levacetylmethadol

LSD: Lysergic Acid Diethylamide

M

MA: Mental Age

MADRS: Montgomery-Asberg Depression Rating Scale

MAOIs: Monoamine Oxidase Inhibitors

MARIs: Mono Amine Reuptake Inhibitors

MBCT: Mindfulness Based Cognitive Therapy

MBSR: Mindfulness Based Stress Reduction

MDAD: Mixed Depressive Anxiety Disorder

MDD: Major Depressive Disorder

MDE: Major Depressive Episode

MDMA: Methylene Dioxy Phenethylamine

MDP: Manic Depressive Psychosis

MFT: Marriage and Family Therapist

MHA: Mental Health Act

MI: Motivational Interviewing

MMD: Major Mental Disorder

MMSE: Mini-Mental State Examination

MPA: Medico Pastoral Association

MR: Mental Retardation

MRI: Magnetic Resonance Imaging

MSIR: Morphine Sulphate IR

MSW: Master of Social Work

MHCOP: Mental Health Care of Older People

MH Hx: Mental Health History

MHW: Mental Health Worker

N

NA: Narcotics Anonymous

NANDA: North American Nursing Diagnosis Association

NAMI: National Alliances for the Mentally Ill

NCCAM: National Centre for Complementary and Alternative Medicine

NCMH: National Council for Mental Health

NE: Norepinephrine

NES: Night Eating Syndrome

NIA: National Institute on Aging

NIMH: National Institute of Mental Health

NIMHANS: National Institute of Mental Health and Neurosciences

NCMH: National Council for Mental Health (or) National Center for Mental Health

NINCDS/ADRDA: National Institute of Neurological and Communicative Diseases and Stroke/Alzheimer's Disease and Related Disorders Association

NMS: Neuroleptic Malignant Syndrome

NMHP: National Mental Health Programme

NPI: Neuropsychiatric Inventory

NPI-NH or NPI/NH: Neuropsychiatric Inventory—Nursing Home

NPI-Q: Neuropsychiatric Inventory Questionnaire

NREM: Non-Rapid Eye Movement

NQF: National Quality Forum

O

OCD: Obsessive-Compulsive Disorder

ODD: Oppositional Defiant Disorder

ODDRS: Oppositional Defiant Disorder Rating Scale

OPQ: Occupational Personality Questionnaire

P

PCP: Phencyclidine

PD: Parkinson Disease

PBD: Pediatric Bipolar Disorder

PCIT: Parent Child Interaction Therapy

PCLN: Psychiatric Consultation Liaison Nurse

PDD: Pervasive Developmental Disorder

PDD: Persistent Depressive Disorder

PE: Prolonged Exposure Therapy

PET: Positron Emission Tomography

PESU: Psychiatric Emergency Service Unit

PHP: Partial Hospitalization Program

PLMD: Periodic Limb Movement Disorder

PPD: Paranoid Personality Disorder

PPP: Postpartum Psychosis

PRS: Psychiatric Rehabilitation Services

PTSD: Post-Traumatic Stress Disorder

PSSD: Post SSRI Sexual Dysfunction (or) Post SSRI Sexual Disorder

PSW: Psychiatric Social Worker

PANSS-EC: Positive and Negative Symptom Scale—Excitement Component

Q

QTc: Corrected QT interval

R

RAS: Reticular Activating System
REM: Rapid Eye Movement
REBT: Rational Emotive Behavior Therapy
RLS: Restless Leg Syndrome
RTC: Residential Treatment Center

S

SAD: Seasonal Affective Disorder (or) Separation Anxiety Disorder (or) Social Anxiety Disorder
SDMI: Severe Disabling Mental Illness
SCC: Subcallosal Cingulate Cortex
SDD: Specific Developmental Disorders
STN: Subthalamic Nucleus
SAS: Simpson-Angus Scale
SFRS: Schneider's First Rank Symptoms of Schizophrenia
SGA: Second-Generation Antipsychotic
SIB: Severe Impairment Battery
SMD: Standardized Mean Difference
SSRI: Selective Serotonin Reuptake Inhibitors
SNRI: Selective Serotonin and Norepinephrine Reuptake Inhibitor
SPD: Schizoid Personality Disorder
SUD: Substance Use Disorder
SZA: Schizoaffective Disorder

T

TAT: Thematic Appreciation Test
TBI: Traumatic Brain Injury
TCA: Tricyclic Antidepressant
TCL: Training in Community Living
TD: Tardive Dyskinesia
THC: Tetrahydrocannabinol
THP: Trihexyphenidyl
TLE: Temporal Lobe Epilepsy
TMD: Transitory Mood Disorder
TMS: Transcranial Magnetic Stimulation
TRADA: Total Response to Alcohol and Drug Abuse
TRD: Treatment-Resistant Depression
TRH: Thyrotropin Releasing Hormone
TS: Tourette Syndrome
TT: Therapeutic Touch
TIA: Transient Ischemic Attack

V

VCA/S: Ventral Capsule and Ventral Striatum
VNS: Vagus Nerve Stimulation
VTA: Ventral Tegmental Area
VH: Visual Hallucinations
VTE: Venous Thromboembolism

W

WAIS: Wechsler Adult Intelligence Scale
WFMH: World Federation for Mental Health
WISC: Wechsler Intelligence Scale for Children
WIAT: Wechsler Individual Achievement Test
WHO: World Health Organization
WRAT: Wide Range Achievement Test

X

XR: Extended Release

Y

YBOCS: Yale-Brown Obsessive-Compulsive Scale
YGTSS: Yale Global Tic Severity Scale.

Introduction to Psychiatric Nursing

CHAPTER 1

LEARNING OBJECTIVE

After studying this chapter, the student will be able to understand the basic concepts of psychiatric nursing.

CHAPTER OUTLINE

- Perspectives of Mental Health and Mental Health Nursing
- Mental Health Team or Multidisciplinary Team
- Nature/Philosophy of Psychiatric Nursing
- Scope of Psychiatric Nursing
- Current Trends and Issues in Care of Mentally Ill Patients
- Functions of Psychiatric Nurse in Various Settings
- Factors Affecting the Level of Practice of Psychiatric Nurse
- Concepts of Normal and Abnormal Behavior

KEY TERMS

Mental health nursing, Mental health, Mental health policy, Mental health team, Normal behavior, Abnormal behavior, Evolution of mental health services, Functions of psychiatric nurse.

PERSPECTIVES OF MENTAL HEALTH AND MENTAL HEALTH NURSING

Definitions of Mental Health

The adjustment of human beings to the world and to each other with the maximum of effectiveness and happiness.

—***Karl Menninger, 1893***

A dynamic state in which feelings and behavior are age appropriate and congruent with the local and cultural norms.

—***Robinson, 1983***

Mental health is simultaneous success at working, loving and creating with the capacity for mature and flexible resolution of conflicts between instincts, conscience, other important people and reality.

—***American Psychiatric Association, 1980***

The capacity of an individual to form harmonious relationships with others and to participate in or contribute constructively to changes in social environment.

—***World Health Organization (WHO), 1950***

Mental health is defined as, 'state of well-being in which every person realizes one's own potential, is able to cope with the normal stresses of life, able to work productively or fruitfully, and is able to make a valuable contribution to the community.

—***World Health Organization (WHO), 2014***

Aspects of Mental Health

- **Individual aspect:** Free from internal conflict, self-confident, feels adequate.
- **Social aspect:** Establishes a satisfactory relationship between himself and his environment.

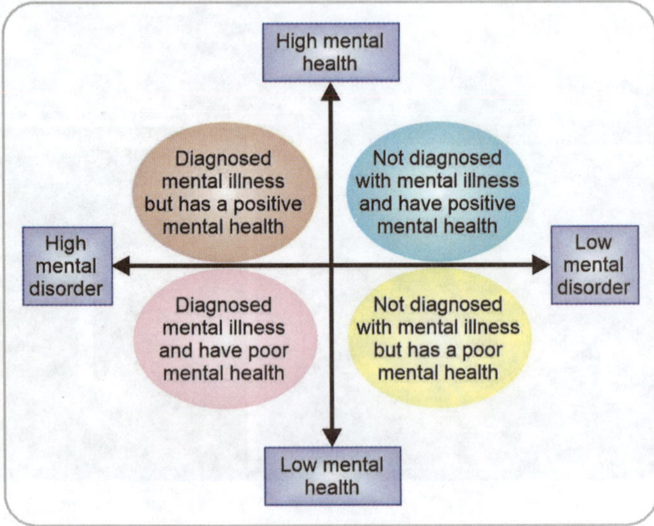

Figure 1.1: Mental health continuum

Mental Health Continuum

Continuum of mental health ranges from low mental health to high mental health and high mental disorder to low mental disorder. Component present between the high mental health and high mental disorder is diagnosed with mental illness but has a positive mental health. Component present between the high mental health and low mental disorder is not diagnosed with mental illness and has a positive mental health. Component present between the low mental health and low mental disorder is not diagnosed with mental illness but has a poor mental health. Component present between the low mental health and high mental disorder is diagnosed mental illness and has poor mental health (Fig. 1.1).

Ten Facts on Mental Health by World Health Organization (WHO)

1. Approximately 20% of adolescents and children have psychiatric illness.
2. Psychiatric illness and substance use disorders are the chief cause of disability worldwide.
3. Around eight lakh people commit suicide every year.
4. War and disasters have a huge impact on psychosocial well-being and mental health.
5. Psychiatric illness is an important risk factor for other diseases.
6. Stigma and discrimination will prevent the people from seeking mental health treatment.
7. Violation of human rights in regard to mental and psychosocial disability was reported routinely in most of the countries.
8. There is an inequality in the distribution of skilled human resources in mental health.
9. There are five key barriers to increase the availability of mental health services such as absence of mental health from public health agenda with its implications for funding, organization of mental health services, absence of integration within primary care, lack of human resources for mental health and lack of public mental health leadership.
10. Financial resources to enhance the mental health services are relatively small.

Indicators of Mental Health

Marie Jahoda (1958) has identified six indicators of mental health:

1. **A positive attitude toward self:**
   - An objective view of self.
   - Knowledge and acceptance of strengths and limitations.
   - A strong sense of personal identity.
   - Feel of security within the environment.
2. **Growth, development and the ability for self-actualization**
   - Successful achievement of tasks associated with each level of development.
3. **Integration**
   - Ability to adaptively respond to the environment.
   - Development in regard with the philosophy of life.
4. **Autonomy**
   - Ability to perform in an independent self-directed manner.
5. **Perception of reality**
   - Perception of the environment without distortion.
   - Capacity for empathy and social sensitivity—a respect and concern for the wants and needs of others.
6. **Environmental mastery**
   - Ability to achieve a satisfactory role within the group/ society or environment.

United Nations adopted the Sustainable Development Goals (SDGs) with two mental health indicators that are listed here:

1. **Promotion of mental health:** By the year 2030, one-third of mortality of noncommunicable diseases should be reduced through prevention/treatment measures and mental health/well-being should be promoted.
2. **Harmful use of alcohol:** Prevention and treatment measures of substance abuse including the harmful use of alcohol and narcotic drug abuse.

Flowchart 1.1: Components of mental health according to 'Keyes'

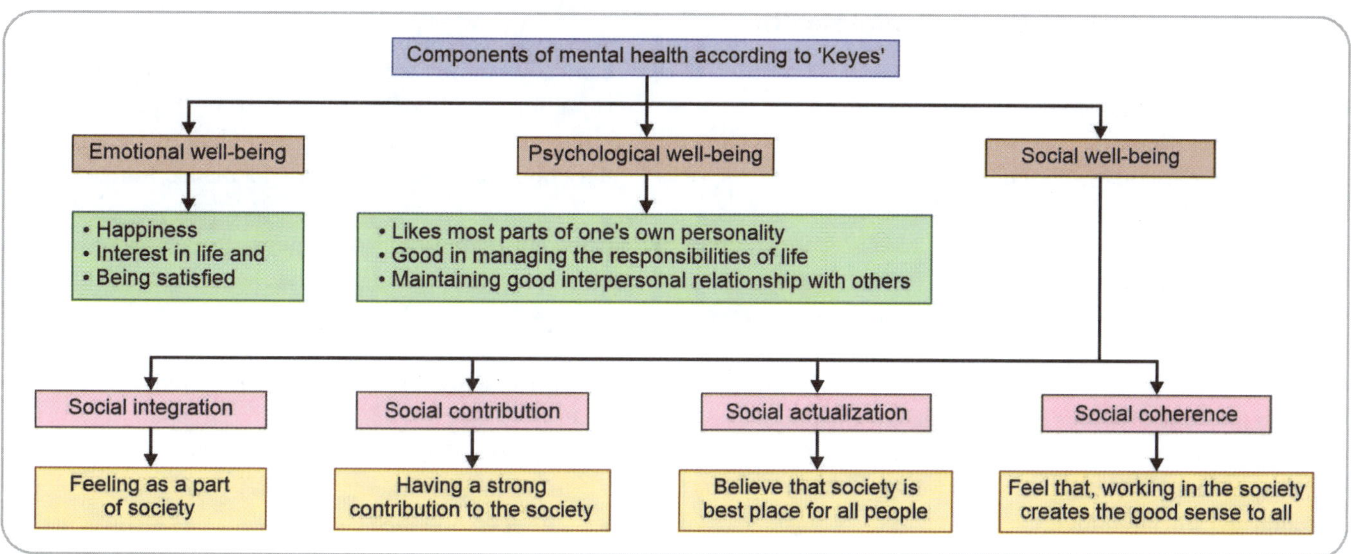

Principles of Mental Health

There are two basic principles of mental health:

1. **Self-knowledge:** Individual must be aware of himself, his strengths and weaknesses.
2. **Harmonious social relationship:** Individual must be able to establish and maintain a harmonious relationship.

Components of Mental Health

Components of mental health include:

- Ability to accept self
- The capacity to feel right toward others
- The ability to fulfil life's tasks

According to Keyes, components of mental health were classified as emotional well-being, psychological well-being and social well-being (Flowchart 1.1). Emotional well-being includes having interest in life, being satisfied and stay happy with life. Psychological well-being includes, the satisfaction with the most parts of one's own personality, well in managing the responsibilities of life and maintaining good interpersonal relationship with others. The social well-being includes the social integration, social contribution, social actualization and social coherence. Social integration means, 'individual feels that he/she is a part of a society.' Social contribution means, 'individual feels that he/she is having a strong contribution to the society.' Social actualization means, 'individual believes that society is the best place for all people.' Social coherence means 'individual feels that, working in the society makes a good sense to all.'

Criteria for Mental Health

- Adequate contact with reality
- Control of thoughts and imagination
- Efficiency in work and play
- Social acceptance
- Positive self-concept
- A healthy emotional life

Characteristics of a Mentally Healthy Person

- Has an ability to make adjustments.
- Has a sense of personal worth, feels worthwhile and important.
- Solves his problems largely by his own effort and makes his own decisions.
- Has a sense of personal security and feels secure in a group.
- Shows understanding of others' problems and motives.
- Has a sense of responsibility.
- Can give and accept love.
- Lives in a world of reality rather than fantasy.
- Shows emotional maturity in his behavior and develops capacity to tolerate frustration and disappointments in his daily life.
- Has developed a philosophy of life that gives meaning and purpose to his daily activities.
- Has a variety of interests and generally lives a well-balanced life of work, rest and recreation.

Characteristics of a Mentally Healthy Person According to National Mental Health Association (2004)

- Feels good about oneself.
- Individual will not be overwhelmed by emotions, such as anger, fear, jealousy, love, guilt, anxiety, etc.
- Has a satisfying personal relationship with others.
- Feels comfortable with others.
- Can laugh with others.
- Has self-respect and for others even with the presence of differences.
- Is able to accept life's disappointments.
- Can meet the demands of life and handle the problems.
- Takes own decisions.
- Shapes the environment whenever possible and gets adjusted when required.

Characteristics of a Mentally Healthy Person According to South Africa Federation Association (2014)

A mentally healthy person feels good about himself/herself; feels comfortable with others and is able to meet the demands of life as shown in Figure 1.2.

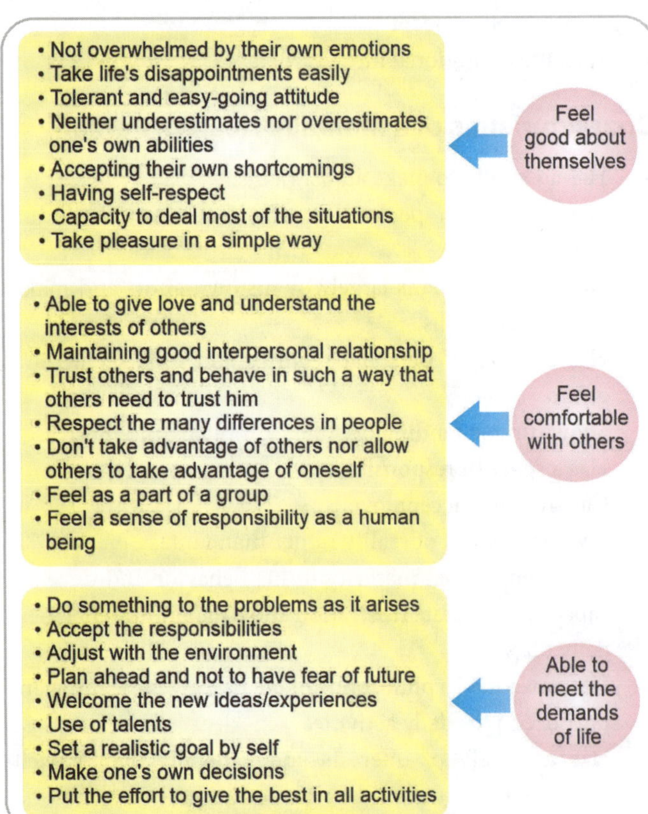

Figure 1.2: Characteristics of a mentally healthy person according to South Africa Federation Association

Definitions of Mental Disorder

- A mental disorder is a syndrome characterized by clinically significant disturbance in an individual's cognition, emotional regulation, or behavior that reflects a dysfunction in the psychological, biological, or development processes underlying mental functioning.
  —DSM-5
- Clinically significant conditions are characterized by alterations in thinking, mood (emotions) or behavior are associated with personal distress and/or impaired functioning. *—WHO, 2001*
- In general, an individual may be considered to be mentally ill, if:
  - The person's behavior is causing distress and suffering to self and/or others.
  - The person's behavior is causing disturbance in his day-to-day activities, job and interpersonal relationships.

Features of Mental Illness

- **Disturbances in bodily functions:** Disturbed sleep, increased or decreased food intake, disturbances in bowel and bladder functions and changes in libido.
- **Disturbances in mental functions:** Behavioral disturbances, abnormal speech pattern, abnormal thoughts, disturbed perception, impaired attention and concentration, memory disturbances, poor judgment and sometimes disturbed consciousness.
- **Changes in individuals and their social activities:** Neglected physical care, poor social sense and strange behavior with family members, friends, colleagues and others.
- **Somatic complaints:** Aches and pains in different parts of the body, fatigue, weakness, involuntary movements, etc.

Evolution of Mental Health Services/Psychiatry

Developments in the field of psychiatry are discussed here in a nutshell:

- **Soul friends:** In the history of psychiatry, Christian Europe created models of care for the mentally ill which include, partnering of the insane with "Soul friends" who will help to reconnect with themselves and society. In many ways, these soul friends could be seen as forerunners of the modern psychiatric nurse.
- **Exorcism:** Exorcism is the religious practice of evicting demons or other spiritual entities from a person or an area which they are believed to have possessed either by commanding the spirit, or by making a hole on the skull

of the affected person or torturing the spirit by beating and chaining the affected person.

- **The Witches' Hammer:** This was a book published in 1487.
  - It was written by Dominican monks Jacob Sprenger and Heinrich Kramer.
  - This book rationalized mental illness in terms of magical explanation.
- **Era of moral treatment:** During this period, there was a revolution in the model of care for the mentally ill persons. Many humanitarians strived to bring in a least restrictive way of caring. Few of them are as follows:
  - In 1974, Philippe Pinel treated inmates in the French institutions with humanity.
  - In England, William Tuke focused on "moral treatment" in a humane milieu called York Retreat.
  - In America, Benjamin Rush focused on humanitarianism and moral treatment at the Pennsylvania Hospital.
- **Decade of the brain:**
  - The 1990s has been called the "Decade of the Brain." The advent of numerous imaging techniques opened up a new world of understanding the neurophysiology and neuroanatomy of the brain.
  - This knowledge leads to a revolution in the understanding of mental health, providing evidences that most serious mental disorders should be viewed as "diseases of the brain."
  - Thus, there has been a major shift in the way of treating people suffering from mental diseases, mainly through psychopharmacology.

Development or Evolution of Mental Health Nursing

Psychiatric nursing is a specialized area of nursing practice employing theories of human behavior. It is used in the diagnosis and treatment of human response to actual and potential mental health problems. Evolution of psychiatric nursing takes place along with the developments of psychiatry. A record of these historic events helps us to get a vivid picture of the development of psychiatric nursing.

Phase 1: The Emergence of Psychiatric/Mental Health Nursing (1773–1881)

- Special institutions for individuals with psychiatric disorders were built.
- Benjamin Rush wrote the first American textbook on psychiatry.
- Attendants were hired to socialize with patients.
- Philippe Pinel classified clients according to their observable behaviors.
- Schools of nursing were established in Boston and Philadelphia by 1872.
- The first American graduate nurse, Ms Linda Richards, graduated from the 'New England Hospital for Women and Children' in 1873.
- Dorothea Lynde Dix devoted time to improve the conditions of mentally ill persons.

Phase 2: Development of the Work Role of Psychiatric Nurses (1882–1914)

- Training schools for nurses in the psychiatric setting were established at McLean Hospital in Belmont, Massachusetts and at Buffalo State Hospital in New York in 1882.
- It was a two-year program, focusing mainly on the custodial care of the patients.
- Trained nurses were employed in State mental hospitals (1890).
- National Society for Mental Hygiene was founded in 1909.
- John Hopkins University started a School of Nursing and the fully developed curriculum for Psychiatric Nursing was implemented in 1913.

Phase 3: Development of Undergraduate Psychiatric Nursing Education (1915–1935)

- Student nurses received clinical experience in state mental hospitals.
- Textbooks focusing on psychiatric nursing practice were written.
- Educational objectives for undergraduate were discussed at National League for nursing conventions.
- Harriet Bailey wrote the first psychiatric nursing textbook 'Nursing Mental Diseases'.
- Insulin Shock Therapy, ECT and Prefrontal lobotomy were introduced in the psychiatric clinical setting.
- The National Committee for Mental Hygiene was established.

Phase 4: Development of Graduate Psychiatric Nursing Education (1936–1945)

- Clinical experiences in psychiatric hospitals were standardized by 1937.
- Approximately, half of all nursing schools provided psychiatric nursing courses; however, participation in psychiatric courses did not become a requirement for nursing licensure until 1955.
- The National League of Nursing education has framed curriculum guidelines for psychiatric nursing graduate education. By 1943, three universities were sponsored with the existing graduate program.

Phase 5: Development of Consultation and Research in Psychiatric Nursing Practice (1946–1990)

- The Mental Health Act provides funding to graduate nursing programs in order to prepare psychiatric clinical nurses.
- Yearly grants were given to the National League for nursing to evaluate psychiatric programs.
- Psychiatric nursing was added as a subject in the nursing curriculum in many schools of nursing in western countries.
- In 1950, National League for Nursing started the training of student nurses in psychiatric units, which was found essential.
- In 1950, psychiatric nurses were able to define their role as a scientific observer, a creator of therapeutic environment, a socializing agent and a psychotherapeutic agent.
- In 1952, Hildegard Peplau developed 'Theory related to Interpersonal relations in Psychiatric Nursing'.
- In 1953, Maxwell Jones wrote a book on 'Therapeutic Community'. He mentioned the therapeutic aspect of the Nurses' role in his book.
- In 1960, first Doctoral Program in Psychiatric Nursing was started in Boston.
- In 1960, the name 'Psychiatric Nursing' was changed to 'Psychiatric Mental Health Nursing'.
- In 1963, 'The Journal of Psychiatric Nursing and Mental Health Services' was published.
- In 1970, the name 'Psychiatric Mental Health Nursing' was again changed to 'Psychosocial Nursing'.
- In 1985, Standards of Psychiatric Mental Health and Clinical Nursing Practice were published by American Nurses Association.
- In 1990, integration of neurosciences into holistic biopsychosocial practice of Psychiatric Nursing took place.

Development of Psychiatric Nursing in India is shown in Table 1.1.

Table 1.1: Development of Psychiatric Nursing in India

Year	Milestone development of psychiatric nursing in India
1954	Nur Manzil Mental Health Center, Lucknow introduced 4–6 weeks' orientation course in psychiatry for the employed nurses
1956	Health Survey Committee recommended a 1 year post certificate course in Psychiatric Nursing. The duration of this course was reduced to 11 months by 1974 –77
1962	Mysore Government started a 9 months' course in Psychiatric Nursing for male nurses in lieu of Midwifery. In 1976, the course duration was reduced to 6 months.
1965	Indian Nursing Council incorporated Psychiatric Nursing as a compulsory subject in BSc Nursing.
1966	Psychiatric Nursing was added as a compulsory subject in Diploma in General Nursing and Midwifery.
1975	Psychiatric Nursing was offered as an elective subject in MSc Nursing at RAK College of Nursing, New Delhi.
1988	Psychiatric Nursing was offered as a specialization in MSc Nursing.

MENTAL HEALTH TEAM OR MULTIDISCIPLINARY TEAM

Mental health care is a product of collaborative care rendered by a team of mental health care professionals. They form a multidisciplinary team named mental health team. They meet within 48 hours of admission to determine a comprehensive treatment plan, set goals of therapy and assign responsibilities to provide intervention. All members will sign the treatment plan and meet weekly to update the plan as needed.

Mental health team members:

- Psychiatrist
- Psychiatric nurse
- Clinical psychologist
- Psychiatric social worker
- Occupational therapist
- Counselor
- Pharmacist

Qualifications and functions of mental health team members have been listed in Table 1.2.

Psychiatric Paraprofessionals or Technical Staff

- **Psychiatric nursing aid:**
  - Provides care under supervision by assisting the client in meeting daily living activities.
  - Aids in maintaining therapeutic environment.
- **Electroconvulsive therapy (ECT) technician:**
  - Prepares the ECT room, ECT machine and other articles required for the procedure.
  - Assists the psychiatrist in administering ECT.
  - Gives ECT under the supervision of psychiatrist or anesthetist.
- **Dietician:** Plans and distributes therapeutic diet to the clients according to the physician's order.
- **Clergymen/Chaplain**
  - They visit patients once or twice a week based on client's faith.
  - Identifies and attends the spiritual needs of the clients and family members.
  - Provides comfort and spiritual support through counseling.

Table 1.2: **Qualification and functions of mental health team members**

Mental health team members	Qualification	Functions
Psychiatrist	MBBS with diploma or a postgraduation in psychiatry	• Admission of patients into mental health care setting • Formulating diagnosis and prescribing pharmacological treatment • Administering physical and psychological methods of treatment • Leading the mental health team and coordinating institutional services, treatment and rehabilitation of mentally ill patients • Discharging the patient from hospital and extending services in the community setting
Psychiatric nurse	Diploma/Basic BSc (N), Post Basic BSc (N), MSc (N) or PhD (specialization in psychiatric nursing)	• Formulating the nursing care plans • Administering and monitoring medications ordered by psychiatrist • Organizing and assisting the various therapies • Providing Psychoeducation to the patient and patient's family members. • Maintaining the patient's records • Creating awareness program in the community in order to promote mental health.
Clinical psychologist	Postgraduate degree or Doctoral degree in clinical psychology	• Performing psychological assessment and contributing to formulation of diagnosis • Providing psychological therapies to the patients and families
Psychiatric social worker	Postgraduate degree or Doctoral degree in social work (specialized in psychiatric field)	• Performing family case work by applying skills in interview techniques and group dynamics • Providing social assistance to clients with mental illness • Helping the family members to understand the nature of treatment • Working for reintegration of patients into community • Emphasizing interventions in social environment where the patient lives
Occupational therapist	Bachelor of occupational therapy (BOT) or postgraduate in occupational therapy (MOT)	• Conducting recreational, occupational and activity programs • Assisting the patients to gain pre-vocational, vocational and home making skills • Helping the patients to gain or retain employment
Counselor	MSc (Psychology)/ MSc counseling and Psychotherapy	• Providing supportive counseling • Assisting in psychological therapy • Assisting in psychoeducational and recreational activities
Pharmacist	D Pharm/B Pharm/M Pharm (Diploma to masters in pharmacy)	• Dispensing the psychotropic agents as per prescription

- **Speech therapist:** The qualification of speech therapist is Bachelor in Audiology and Speech Language Pathology (BASLP). Speech therapist will treat the patients with speech related problems.

NATURE/PHILOSOPHY OF PSYCHIATRIC NURSING

Hildegard Peplau is known as the mother of psychiatric nursing. She identified that the heart of psychiatric nursing is the role of a nurse as a counselor or psychotherapist. Therapeutic nurse patient relationship is a core part of this.

The practice of mental health nursing is based on certain philosophical beliefs:

- The individual has intrinsic worth, dignity and respect.
- The goal of all individuals is growth, health, autonomy and self-actualization.
- Every individual has the potential to change.
- Each person functions as a holistic being who acts on, interacts with, and reacts to the environment as a whole person.
- All people have common, basic needs such as physical requirements, safety, love, belonging, esteem and self-actualization.
- Behavior of the individual is meaningful.
- Individuals vary in their coping capacities.
- All people have rights to utilize the equal opportunity for adequate health care.
- Each individual has a right to participate in decision-making regarding his/her health.
- The goal of nursing care is to promote wellness.
- An interpersonal relationship can produce change and growth.

SCOPE OF PSYCHIATRIC NURSING

The psychiatric nurse provides holistic care to the client with emphasis on the psychological component which is a core value of essential nursing care. The scope of psychiatric nursing practice can be discussed at three levels:

1. Basic Roles

As a basic nurse, his/her functions and responsibilities can be categorized into:

- **Patient care**
  - Assess the patient's needs and give individualized nursing care according to their needs.
  - Develop care plans to meet long-term goals.
  - Assist the multidisciplinary team members in diagnostic and therapeutic measures.
  - Provide therapeutic environment.
  - Assist in personal hygiene and provide facilities for those who can take care of themselves.
  - Assist patients in meeting nutritional needs and give feed to those who are unable to feed themselves.
  - Carry out mental status examination.
  - Set limits with the unacceptable patient's behavior.
  - Provide activities to channelize the patient's energy with constructive work to improve their self-esteem.
- **Education and supervision**
  - Make use of opportunities to give group or individual health education.
  - Teach nursing students about Psychiatric Nursing care and assist them to take care of the mentally ill patients.
  - Supervise the work of subordinates.
  - Change the misconceptions of mental illness by conducting health teaching program.
- **Ward management**
  - Write the daily report of acutely ill patients.
  - Periodically evaluate the chronic patient's progress and record it.
  - Assess the cleanliness of ward and take steps to improve it.
  - Give a brief report about patient's behavior changes while hand over the patient to another staff nurse, this will help to maintain the consistency in nursing care.
  - Accompany the multidisciplinary team for clinical rounds and give report based on her observation.
- **Interpersonal relationship and communication**
  - Establish and maintain cordial relationship with patients, their families and team members.
  - Coordinate the nursing services with psychosocial therapies.
  - Communicate the patient's behavior to the concerned personnel. (For example, intimating the abscond of patient to police).
  - Share the knowledge about the community resources with patients and their families for future rehabilitation.
- **Role in other therapies:** The nurse plays an interdependent role in various therapies such as pharmacological, psychological, social and physical therapies. The nurse has a key role in milieu therapy and therapeutic community.

2. Expanded Roles

Expanded role of psychiatric nurse means enlargement of nursing responsibilities within the boundaries of psychiatric nursing. The expanded roles in psychiatric nursing are as follows:

- **Registered psychiatric nurse:** Provides psychiatric mental health nursing care to individuals, families and groups to enable them to function at an optimal level of psychological wellness through more effective adaptive behaviors and increased resilience to stress.
- **Nurse practitioner:**
  - Utilizes psychological processes and phases in rendering psychological reassurance and counseling services to the client.
  - Assists the clients in meeting his/her total needs especially emotional needs and delivers holistic care.
- **Clinical Nurse Specialist (CNS):**
  - Psychiatric clinical nurse specialist holds a master's degree in psychiatric mental health nursing.
  - CNS is an advanced practice nurse who is usually a primary health care provider, functions autonomously, often work in a semi-isolated situation.
  - Has medication prescription privileges, manages the overall care of people with emotional and psychiatric problems.
  - Usually has a consultative arrangement with a psychiatrist.
- **Nurse clinician:**
  - Identifies the emotional and behavioral problems of the clients.
  - Provides comprehensive care, emotional support.
  - Makes the client to learn coping strategies and helps them to understand and adapt to the situations.
- **Nurse counselor:** Provides counseling services to both family and to the client whenever the need arises.

- **Nurse researcher:**
  - Undertakes research projects and contributes to the evidence of psychiatric nursing.
  - Modifies the existing practice based on the current evidence.
  - Communicates the research findings through publications or paper presentations.
- **Nurse case manager:** Nurse case managers act as advocates for patients and their families by coordinating care and linking the patient with the physician, other members of the health care team, resources and the payers.

3. Extended Roles

It is the responsibility assumed by the psychiatric nurse beyond traditional functioning of the psychiatric nurse and it requires additional professional preparation or educational qualification.

- **Community Mental Health Nurse:**
  - Community mental health is the application of knowledge of psychiatric nursing in preventing mental illness and promoting and maintaining mental health of the people.
  - It includes early diagnosis, appropriate referrals, care and rehabilitation of mentally ill people.
- **Psychiatric Home Care Nurse:**
  - Provides holistic mental health care at the doorstep of the people.
  - Provides comprehensive care including physical assessment, mental status assessment, direct nursing care, behavioral management, crisis intervention, psychoeducation, in-home detoxification, medication management, case management and consultation with the colleagues.
- **Forensic Psychiatric Nurse:**
  - Forensic psychiatric nurse works with the individuals who have mental health needs of those who have entered the legal system.
  - Nurses in this role perform physical and psychiatric assessment and develop plans of care for the patients.
- **Psychiatric Consultation—Liaison Nurse:**
  - It is an advanced practice where nurses practice psychiatric and mental health nursing in a medical setting/non-psychiatric setting.
  - They provide consultation and education to patients, families and health care team and the community.
  - They provide assessment, recommendations and supportive therapy to patients who are anxious, depressed or experiencing other psychological problems or emotional distress.
- **Geropsychiatric nurse:** Nurses provide care to aged people who have been affected by emotional and behavioral disorders such as dementia, chronic schizophrenia, delirium, etc.
- **Parish nurse:**
  - Parish nursing is a program that promotes health and wellness of body, mind and spirit.
  - The parish nurse is a pastorally called, spiritually mature, licensed registered nurse with a desire to serve the members and friends of his or her congregation.

CURRENT TRENDS AND ISSUES IN CARE OF MENTALLY ILL PATIENTS

A psychiatric nurse faces various challenges because of changes in the inpatient care approach. Some of these changes that affect the role are as follows:

- **Trends in health care**
  - Increased mental health problems
  - Provision for quality and comprehensive services
  - Multidisciplinary team approach
  - Providing continuity of care
  - Care is provided in alternative settings
- **Economic issues**
  - Industrialization
  - Urbanization
  - Raised standard of living
- **Changes in illness orientation:** Shift from illness to prevention (modification of style), specific to holistic, quantity of care to quality of care.
- **Changes in care delivery:** Care delivery is shifted from institutional services to community services, genetic services to counseling services, nurse-patient relationship to nurse-patient partnership.
- **Information technology**
  - Telenursing
  - Telemedicine
  - Mass media
  - Electronic systems
  - Nursing informatics
- **Consumer empowerment**
  - Create awareness to the health team members in community for early detection and treatment of mental illness as well as proper utilization of available psychiatric hospitals.

- Patients are health care consumers demanding quality health care services at affordable cost with less restrictive and more humane rates.
- **Deinstitutionalization:** Bringing mental health patients out of the hospital and shifting the nursing care at community level.
- **Physician shortage and gaps in service:** Physician shortage can provide the opportunity for new roles (e.g., Nurse practitioner). In respect to gaps in services, nurses always meet the needs of people for whom services are not available (e.g., home visiting nurse).
- **Demographic changes:**
  - Increasing number of the elderly group.
  - Type of family—increased number of nuclear families.
- **Change in needs of the patient:**
  - Wanting a more holistic orientation in health care.
  - Culturally specific and sensitive nursing care.
  - Preventive health in the place of promotive health.

Issues and Challenges in Psychiatric Nursing

- Misconceptions about the mental illness—stigma and discrimination.
- Misconceptions in mental health nursing profession.
- Deinstitutionalization of mental illness care (Closure of psychiatric hospitals).
- Limited access to psychiatric nurse.
- Reduction in hospital stay for patients with mental disorders.
- Decline in psychotherapy and more use of psychopharmacology.
- Lack of health insurance for mentally ill.
- Government initiatives to render financial help to mentally ill.
- Rapid shift toward mental health hospitals from community based mental health services.
- Issues related to the safety and security for the mentally ill patients in ward.
- Lack of protocols/policies to take care of the patients with psychiatric illness.
- Lack of trained psychiatric nurse in the hospitals.
- Resources are limited.
- Uncertainty of the role specified.

Priorities of the Helsinki Declaration (1964–2013)

- Create the awareness in regard with significance of mental health.
- Tackle the stigma, inequality and discrimination collectively.
- Support the individuals and family members with mental health problems by providing treatment.
- Promote, prevent, treat and give rehabilitation to mentally ill.
- Emphasize the need of competent workforce in all settings.

FUNCTIONS OF PSYCHIATRIC NURSE IN VARIOUS SETTINGS

- **Psychiatric inpatient ward**
  - Enhancing environmental safety.
  - Performing comprehensive psychosocial assessment.
  - Meeting the biological and emotional needs of the patients.
  - Administering the psychotropic agents as per order.
  - Assisting the psychiatrist in somatic therapies.
  - Organizing and assisting in psychological therapies.
  - Observing and documenting the peculiar change in behavior of mentally ill patient.
  - Providing psychoeducation to the patients and family members.
  - Coordinating the mental health team.
  - Planning discharge, community referral and follow-up of patients.
  - Ward administration.
- **Psychiatric outpatient department**
  - Performing clinical assessment.
  - Assisting in psychometric assessment.
  - Assisting in psychological therapies.
  - Counseling the patients and family members.
  - Drug compliance counseling.
  - Conducting group therapy.
  - Providing psychoeducation to the patients and family members.
- **ECT room nurse**
  - Educating the family members on ECT.
  - Preparing the patients for ECT.
  - Providing nursing care during ECT.
  - Providing nursing care after ECT.
  - Reassuring the patients and reducing their anxiety.
- **Psychotherapy unit**
  - Advanced practice psychiatric nurses can practice individual or group psychotherapy.
  - Establishing a therapeutic relationship with the patient.
  - Facilitating ventilation of patient's feelings.
  - Helping the patients in gaining insight about the problem.
  - Helping the patients in learning new skills.
  - Reinforcing desirable behaviors.
  - Providing consistent emotional assistance.

- **Day care centers**
  - Performing clinical assessment.
  - Accurately observing and documenting the patient's behaviors.
  - Medication management.
  - Social skills training.
  - Counseling the patients and family members.
  - Providing psychoeducation.
  - Assisting in occupational or recreational therapy.
  - Providing vocational assistance.
- **Family therapy units**
  - Assess the conflicts existing among the family members.
  - Facilitation of family's use of positive coping strategies.
  - Encouraging positive family communication.
  - Promoting adaptive family functioning.
  - Delivering psychoeducation.
- **Child and adolescent psychiatry units**
  - Psychosocial need assessment
  - Developmental assessment
  - Assessment of child's strengths and abilities
  - Providing a safe environment to the child
  - Interdisciplinary care approach
  - Self-care training to the child
  - Provide genetic counseling if necessary
  - Deliver psychoeducation
  - Provide emotional support to the child.
- **Home setting**
  - Performing routine psychosocial assessment
  - Performing physical assessment
  - Supervising regularity of medications
  - Providing Psychoeducation on drug compliance, diet and rehabilitation
  - Providing family counseling
  - Performing necessary basic investigations and nursing procedures.
- **Community mental health center**
  - Screening and identification of patients in the community.
  - Referring the identified cases to appropriate centers of care.
  - Making home visits and providing direct care to the patients in the community.
  - Follow-up care with special emphasis on drug compliance, patient prognosis, management of side effects and improvement done in patient's functional ability.
  - Conducting mental health awareness programs.
  - Training paraprofessionals, community leaders, school teachers and other care giving professionals in the community.
  - Locating and managing resources in the community.
  - Direct services, like care of families at risk for violence, abuse and dysfunction, care of homeless mentally ill patients.
- **Hospice care centers**
  - Provide the cancer patients with pain relief through psychological measures.
  - Facilitate the normal grieving process.
  - Provide supportive psychotherapy to patients and their families.
- **Emergency department**
  - Crisis intervention during natural disasters, accidents, unexpected illnesses causing increased anxiety, stress or immobilization.
  - Helping the mother in labor and support them to cope up with the stress during labor.
  - Providing support to bereaved parents in the event of fetal demise, abortion, birth of an infant with congenital anomalies.
- **Medical inpatient wards:** Psychosocial intervention for chronic illnesses with major psychological effects. For example, Alzheimer's disease, HIV/AIDS, diabetes mellitus, Parkinson's disease, multiple sclerosis, hemophilia, colon cancer, amputation, etc.
- **Industrial medical centers**
  - Implementing or participating in industrial substance abuse programs for employees.
  - Providing crisis intervention during accidents (or) in the acute onset of a physical or mental illness.
  - Teaching stress management techniques.
- **Forensic psychiatry units**
  - Forensic psychiatric nurses assist patients with self-care, administration of medications and monitor the effectiveness of the treatment.
  - Promote coping skills.
  - Advanced nurses are able to diagnose and treat individuals with psychiatric disorders.
  - Provide psychotherapy
  - Forensic evaluation for legal sanity
  - Assessment of risk for violence
  - Parole/probation considerations
  - Assessment of racial/cultural factors during crime
  - Sexual predator screening and assessment
  - Submitting formal written reports to court
  - Reviewing police reports
  - On scene consultation to law enforcement.

FACTORS AFFECTING THE LEVEL OF PRACTICE OF PSYCHIATRIC NURSE

Role of the psychiatric nurses and their activities include a wide variation in levels of performance. Individual nurses have primary responsibility and accountability for their own practice. Four major factors play a part in the roles engaged in by each nurse. These are as follows:

1. **Laws:** Laws are the primary factor affecting the level of nursing practice. Each state has its own nursing practice act, which regulates entry into the profession and defines the legal limits of nursing practice that must be adhered to by all nurses. Nurse practice acts also address aspects of advanced practice, including prescriptive authority. Nurses must be familiar with the nursing practice act of their state and define and limit their practice accordingly.
2. **Qualifications:** A nurse's qualifications include education, work experience, and certification. Two levels of psychiatric- mental health clinical nursing practice, basic and advanced have been identified. Basic level nurses work as staff nurse, case manager, nurse manager and other nursing roles in psychiatric setting. The advanced practice psychiatric nurse focuses on clinical practice which applies knowledge, skills and experience autonomously to complex mental health problems.
3. **Practice setting:** The role of a nurse in any psychiatric mental health setting depends on the following:
   - Philosophy, mission, values, and goals of the treatment setting.
   - Definitions of mental health and mental illness that prevail in the setting.
   - Needs of the consumers of the mental health services.
   - Number of clinical staff available and the services they are able to provide.
   - Organizational structure and reporting relationships in the setting.
   - Consensus reached by the mental health care providers about their roles and responsibilities.
   - Resources and revenues available to offset the cost of care needed and provided.
   - Presence of strong nursing leadership and mentorship.

   A supportive environment for psychiatric nurses is characterized by:
   - Open and honest communication among staff.
   - Interdisciplinary respect.
   - Recognition of nurses' contributions.
   - Nursing involvement in decision making.
   - Delegation of nonessential nursing tasks.
   - Opportunities to expand into new roles and responsibilities.
   - Encouragement from professional activities and organizations.
4. **Personal initiative:** The personal competence and initiative of the psychiatric nurse will influence the roles and activities of the nurse. This is a very important factor. Psychiatric nurse can use one strategy to enhance the personal growth and competence by joining and participating with support groups.

CONCEPTS OF NORMAL AND ABNORMAL BEHAVIOR

Defining the concepts of normal and abnormal behavior is found to be difficult. Abnormality is the deviation from the norms or standards or rules and regulations. When the abnormal behavior persists for longer duration, it is termed maladaptive behavior (Fig. 1.3). Several models have been put forward in order to explain the concept of normal and abnormal behavior. Some of these are as follows:

- **Medical model:** Mental health refers to a state that is free from undue pain, discomfort and disability. Medical model describes mental illness as a result of organic pathology. According to this model, abnormality is characterized by the disturbances in thought, emotions and behavior due to the organic pathology.
- **Statistical model:** Statistically normal mental health falls within two standard deviations (SDs) of the normal distribution curve. Therefore, mental illness falls outside two SDs of the normal distribution curve.
- **Utopian model:** Utopian model states that individual's ability is based on the normal mental health. Mental illness might interfere with the ability to function at optimum level.

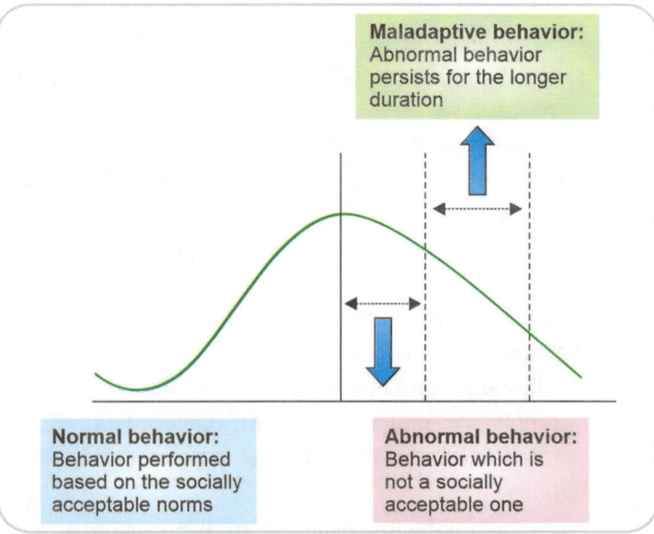

Figure 1.3: Concepts of normal and abnormal behavior

- **Subjective model:** According to this model, normality is viewed as an absence of distress, disability, or help-seeking behavior resulting thereof. When there is a subjective distress in the emotional domain, he/she is said to be abnormal.
- **Social model:** Normality is defined in context with social norms prescribed by the culture. A normal person is expected to behave in a socially 'acceptable' way. When there is a deviation from the social norms, it is considered an abnormal behavior.
- **Process model:** Normal behavior is the result of interacting system. Normality is a dynamic and changing process, rather than a static process. This model focuses on the need for developmental changes in the attainment of mature adult functioning.
- **Behavioral model:** Behavior that is adaptive and socially acceptable is considered normal. Abnormal behavior is a set of faulty behaviors acquired through learning.
- **Continuum model:** According to this model, normality and mental disorder are as falling at the two ends of a continuum, rather than being disparate entities. According to this model, level of severity (scores above the 'cut-off') that determines whether a particular individual constitutes a symptom of a disorder or falls on the healthy side of the continuum.

Some of the following traits are more commonly found in 'normal' individuals:

- Reality orientation.
- Self-awareness and self-knowledge.
- Self-esteem and self-acceptance.
- Ability to exercise voluntary control over their behavior.
- Ability to form affectionate relationships.
- Pursuance of productive and goal-directed activities.

The personal world of an individual is abnormal, when it:

- Is universally abnormal.
- Separates the individual from others emotionally.
- Does not provide the person with a sense of spiritual and material security.

SUMMARY

- **Mental health is defined as** 'state of well-being in which every person realizes one's own potential, is able to cope with the normal stressors of life, able to work productively or fruitfully, and is able to make a valuable contribution to the community. (WHO, 2014)
- **Continuum of mental health** ranges from low mental health to high mental health and high mental disorder to low mental disorder.
- Marie Jahoda (1958) has identified six indicators of mental health that are positive attitude toward self, growth/development and the ability for self-actualization, integration, autonomy, perception of reality and environmental mastery.
- **United Nations adopted the Sustainable Development Goals (SDGs)** with two mental health indicators that are suicide mortality and harmful use of alcohol.
- There are **two basic principles of mental health** that are self-knowledge and harmonious social relationship.
- According to Keyes, **components of mental health** were classified as emotional well-being, psychological well-being and social well-being. Emotional well-being includes interest in life, being satisfied and happy. The psychological well-being includes that most parts of one's own personality is liked by self, well in managing the responsibilities of life and maintaining good interpersonal relationship with others. The social well-being includes the social integration, social contribution, social actualization and social coherence.
- **Characteristics of a mentally healthy person** by South Africa Federation Association (2014) are feeling good about themselves; feel comfortable with others and able to meet the demands of life. National Mental Health Association (2004) also suggested the characteristics of mentally healthy person.
- **Mental illness** is defined as, 'A clinically significant behavioral or psychological syndrome or pattern that occurs in an individual which is associated with present distress or disability or with a significant increased risk of suffering' (DSM-IV).
- **Evolution of mental health services/psychiatry** discussed in the topics: Soul friends, Exorcism, Witches' Hammer, Era of Moral Treatment and Decade of the Brain.
- **Development and evolution of mental health nursing** is classified into the following phases:
  - **Phase 1:** The Emergence of Psychiatric Mental Health Nursing (1773–1881)
  - **Phase 2:** Development of the Work Role of Psychiatric nurses (1882–1914)
  - **Phase 3:** Development of Undergraduate Psychiatric Nursing Education (1915–1935)
  - **Phase 4:** Development of Graduate Psychiatric Nursing Education (1936–1945)
  - **Phase 5:** Development of Consultation and Research in Psychiatric Nursing Practice (1946–1990)
- **Mental** health team members include Psychiatrist, Psychiatric Nurse, Clinical Psychologist, Psychiatric Social Worker, Occupational Therapist, Counselor and Pharmacist. Psychiatric Paraprofessionals or Technical Staff such as Psychiatric Nursing aid, ECT technician, Dietician, Clergy men/Chaplain and Speech Therapist.
- The **scope of psychiatric nursing practice** can be discussed at three levels such as basic role, expanded roles and extended roles. Basic roles are patient care, education, supervision, ward management, interpersonal relationship, communication and role in other therapies. Expanded roles are registered psychiatric nurse, nurse practitioner, clinical nurse specialist, nurse clinician, nurse researcher, nurse counselor and case manager. Extended roles are community mental health nurse, psychiatric home care nurse, forensic psychiatric nurse, psychiatric consultation—liaison nurse, geropsychiatric nurse and parish nurse.

Contd...

- **Trends in mental health** are increased mental health problems, provision for quality and comprehensive services, multidisciplinary team approach, providing continuity of care and care has to be provided in alternative settings.
- **Issues in mental health** are discussed in the headings: Economic issues, changes in illness orientation, changes in care delivery, information technology, consumer empowerment, deinstitutionalization, physician shortage and gaps in service, demographic changes and change in needs of the patient.
- **Functions of psychiatric nurse in various settings** were discussed in the headings: Psychiatric inpatient ward, psychiatric outpatient department, ECT room nurse, psychotherapy unit, day care centers, family therapy units, child and adolescents' psychiatry units, home setting, community mental health center, hospice care centers, emergency department, medical inpatient wards, industrial medical centers and forensic psychiatry units.
- **Factors affecting the level of practice** discussed as four major factors such as laws, qualifications, practice setting and personal initiative.
- Abnormality is the deviation from the norm or standard or rules and regulations. When the abnormal behavior persists for longer duration, it is termed maladaptive behavior. Several models have explained the **concept of normal and abnormal behavior** that are medical model, statistical model, utopian model, subjective model, social model, process model, behavioral model and continuum model.

ASSESS YOURSELF

Long Answer Questions

1. Explain the scope of psychiatric nursing practice.
2. Describe the characteristics of a mentally healthy person.

Short Answer Questions

1. What are the three levels of the scope of psychiatric nursing practice?
2. Name the members of a mental health care team.

Short Notes

Write short notes on:

1. Functions of psychiatric nurse
2. Mental health team
3. Concept of normal and abnormal behavior
4. Evolution of mental health nursing
5. Components of mental health
6. Continuum of mental health

Multiple Choice Questions

1. **Development of the work role of Psychiatric nurses happened in ________.**
   a. 1773–1881 b. 1882–1914
   c. 1915–1935 d. 1936–1945
2. **Mental illness interferes with the ability for optimal functioning explained in ______ model.**
   a. Subjective b. Utopian
   c. Social d. Process
3. **Normal mental health falls within two Standard Deviations (SDs) of the normal distribution curve explained in ______ model.**
   a. Subjective b. Utopian
   c. Continuum d. Statistical
4. **National Society for Mental Hygiene was founded in:**
   a. 1908 b. 1909
   c. 2002 d. 2005
5. **Which of the following is emotional well-being component of mental health according to 'Keyes'?**
   a. Social integration b. Social coherence
   c. Social contribution d. Being satisfied
6. **_________ is called 'decade of brain'.**
   a. 1980s b. 1990s
   c. 2000s d. 2010s
7. **Who wrote the first American Textbook of Psychiatry?**
   a. Philippe Pinel b. Dorothea Lynde Dix
   c. Sigmund Freud d. Benjamin Rush
8. **In which year, Indian Nursing Council incorporated Psychiatric Nursing as compulsory subject in BSc Nursing?**
   a. 1954 b. 1962
   c. 1965 d. 1975
9. **Who work for the reintegration of patients into community?**
   a. Psychiatrist
   b. Psychiatric nurse
   c. Psychiatric social worker
   d. Occupational therapist
10. **Who conducts the recreational and activity programs to the patient?**
    a. Psychiatrist
    b. Psychiatric nurse
    c. Psychiatric social worker
    d. Occupational therapist

ANSWER KEY				
1. b	**2.** a	**3.** d	**4.** c	**5.** d
6. b	**7.** d	**8.** b	**9.** b	**10.** d

Principles and Concepts of Mental Health Nursing

CHAPTER 2

LEARNING OBJECTIVE

After studying this chapter, the student will be able to understand the basic concepts and principles of mental health nursing to take care of the mentally ill patients.

CHAPTER OUTLINE

- Definitions
- Terminology
- Classification of Mental Disorders
- Review of Personality Development
- Perspectives in Personality Theory
- Theories of Personality Development
- Defense Mechanisms
- Biopsychosocial Etiology of Mental Illness
- Psychopathology of Mental Disorders: Review of Structure of Brain, Functions of Brain, Limbic System and Abnormal Neurotransmission
- Principles of Psychiatric Nursing
- Standards of Psychiatric Nursing
- Conceptual Models in Psychiatric Nursing

KEY TERMS

Mental health nursing, Psychiatric nurse, Personality, Psychoanalytic theory, Psychosocial theory, Social learning theory, Personality traits, Defense mechanism, Cerebral hemisphere, Limbic system, Cerebellum, Brain stem, Pineal gland, Frontal lobe syndrome, Basal ganglia, Amygdala, Thalamus, Cingulate gyrus, Hippocampus, Medulla oblongata, Pons, Mid brain, Autonomic nervous system, Neurons, Neurotransmitters, Action potential, Neuroplasticity, Existential model, Psychoanalytical model, Behavioral model, Interpersonal model.

DEFINITIONS

Mental Health Nursing

Mental health nursing is defined as a branch of nursing which deals with the study of measures in order to:

- Prevent mental illnesses
- Promote mental health
- Restore the patient with mental illnesses.

Mental health nursing is focused on prevention, treatment and nursing care of individuals who suffer from mental illness and its effects. Despite continuing improvements in health care and living conditions in many countries of the world, extended life expectancy as well as improved economic growth have brought an increase in the number of individuals who suffer from mental illness.

—***World Health Organization (WHO, 1998)***

Psychiatric Nurse

Psychiatric nurse is an expert in performing mental status assessment, crisis intervention, administering psychotropics, therapies and patient assistance. Psychiatric nurses work with patients to help them in order to manage their psychiatric illness and live productive and fulfilling lives.

—American Psychiatric Nurses Association (APNA)

TERMINOLOGY

Terminology Related to States of Mind

- **Mood:** The pervasive feeling tone which is sustained or lasts for some length of time and colors the total experience of the person.
- **Affect:** The outward bodily expression of emotions that range from joy to sorrow or anger.
- **Insight:** The ability to perceive oneself realistically and to understand oneself and the motives behind one's behavior.
- **Judgment:** The ability to make logical decisions.

Terminology Related to Mental Disorders

- **Alzheimer's disease:** A neurodegenerative disease that is characterized by progressive, irreversible and lethal structural damage to the brain that results from the presence of β-amyloid proteins and that leads to a loss of cognitive functions with the symptoms of progressive dementia.
- **Anorexia nervosa:** An eating disorder in which one is preoccupied with food or eating behavior which suppresses the desire to take food. It can be achieved by compromising nutritional intake and not necessarily by a loss of appetite.
- **Amnestic disorders:** Impairment of memory that occurs without delirium and dementia.
- **Autism:** A pervasive developmental disorder that is characterized by marked impairment of social and cognitive abilities.
- **Body dysmorphic disorder:** A somatization disorder in which one becomes obsessed with an imagined defect in one's body or body parts.
- **Bulimia nervosa (Earlier known as "bulimarexia"):** An obsession with thinness, dieting and a compulsive cycle of bingeing and purging.
- **Conversion disorder:** A disorder in which one perceives deficits that affect sensory or motor functions that are unrelated to a medical condition.
- **Delirium:** A disturbance of consciousness and a change in cognition that develops over a short period of time that tends to fluctuate during the course of day. It is characterized by disorientation to time or place, reduced ability to focus, sustain or shift attention, incoherent speech and continual aimless physical activity.
- **Dementia:** A global impairment of intellectual (cognitive) functions (e.g., thinking, remembering, reasoning) that is usually progressive and of sufficient severity to interfere with a person's social and occupational functioning.
- **Depression:** A mood disorder that is characterized by persistent and pervasive sadness or low mood, changes in appetite, sleep, weight, activity, libido and energy that may or may not be accompanied by suicidal thoughts.
- **Dissociative amnesia:** The inability to recall important personal information that is generally of a traumatic or stressful nature.
- **Dissociative fugue:** A sudden or unexpected travel away from one's home or work place with an inability to recall the past.
- **Dysthymia:** Chronic low-level depression that lasts for more than two years and that may lead to more severe depression, if left untreated.
- **Factitious disorder:** The intentional way of producing the symptoms of illness so that one can assume a sick role.
- **Hypochondriasis:** Individual may have a fear or belief that one has a serious illness despite medical reassurance.
- **Hypomania:** A mood of elation with higher-than-usual activity, but not as expansive as full mania.
- **Phobias:** A group of disorders that are primarily characterized by the avoidance of a specific situation or escaping, if the situation is unexpectedly encountered.
- **Psychosis:** A form of serious mental illness in which the patient is unable to recognize reality, displays bizarre behavior and is unable to deal with life's demands.

Terminology Related to Thinking

- **Autistic thinking:** Disturbances in thought that result from the intrusion of a private fantasy world that is internally stimulated. This type of thinking results in abnormal responses to people and events in the real world.
- **Cognition:** The process of being aware, thinking, knowing and reasoning.
- **Critical thinking:** An intellectual and disciplined process of actively and skillfully conceptualizing, applying, analyzing, synthesizing and evaluating information through observation, experience, reasoning and communication as a guide for belief or action.
- **Intuition:** Knowing or sensing without the use of rational processes such as reasoning.

Terminology Related to Substance Abuse

- **Abstinence:** A voluntary act of refraining from behavior or from the use of a substance (e.g., alcohol, drugs, food and gambling, spending, sex) that has caused problems in the psychosocial, physical, cognitive/perceptual or spiritual/belief dimensions of an individual's life.
- **Blackout:** The loss of memory about the events that occur after the onset of the causative agent or condition (e.g., memory loss after the ingestion of alcohol or drugs).
- **Alcoholic blackout:** An episode of forgetting all or part of what occurred during or after the intake of alcohol.
- **Codependence:** A relationship in which the actions of a family member or a close friend or a colleague of an alcohol or drug dependent person tend to perpetuate the person's dependence and thereby retard the process of recovery.
- **Gateway drugs:** Substances that have been implicated as forerunners to polysubstance use or drug dependence (e.g., tobacco, alcohol, marijuana).
- **Detoxification:** It is the physiological or medicinal removal of toxic substances from a living organism. It is recommended for patients with substance use disorders. This treatment assists an individual in getting rid of the physical effects of substances.
- **Intoxication:** The physiologic state of being poisoned by a drug or other toxic substance.

Terminology Related to Crisis, Loss and Grief

- **Bereavement:** The objective state of grieving that occurs after loss, especially of a loved one.
- **Grief:** The dynamic natural response to loss.
- **Anticipatory grief:** Grief that is experienced before the death or loss occurs (e.g., when loved one has a terminal illness).
- **Complicated grief:** Grief that is expressed with a significantly greater or lesser intensity over a longer or shorter period of time than is culturally expected. This may manifest as serious physical or emotional disabilities.
- **Crisis:** An event that threatens one's well-being (e.g., death of a family member in an earthquake) and that exceeds the person's ability to cope with the threat.
- **Crisis intervention:** Therapeutic techniques for helping individuals who are experiencing a crisis.
- **Distress:** A subjective response to internal or external stimuli that are threatening or perceived as threatening to the self.
- **Eustress:** A nonspecific stress response associated with desirable events such as marriage, the birth of a child, or a job promotion.
- **Cope:** The ability to adapt with the situation and promote well-being by using a variety of tools, including adaptive or maladaptive maneuvers. Internal coping involves changes in thinking and use of psychic defense; external coping occurs through the actions.
- **General adaptation syndrome (GAS):** This process was given by Hans Selye which shows the physiological changes of our body responses during stress in three stages. The GAS occurs in three stages, i.e., alarm, adaptation and exhaustion.
- **Loss:** The process of losing or being deprived of someone or something that is characterized by a series of overlapping stages that includes the psychological and behavioral manifestation.
- **Maladaptation:** A response that may result in unfavorable circumstances, situations or conditions for an individual who is unable or unwilling to meet the standards that are accepted by the medical or social community.
- **Mourning:** The social and psychological expression of grief.

Terminology Related to Mental Health Nursing

- **Countertransference:** It is the redirection of a psychotherapist's (Nurses) dependent feelings toward the patient.
- **Forensic nursing:** A branch of nursing that focuses on the clinical observation and treatment of individuals who are victims of crimes or who have mental health problems or who are charged with or convicted of crimes.
- **Clinical pathway:** A standardized format that is used to provide and monitor patient care and progress by way of case management and interdisciplinary health care delivery system. It is also known as a critical pathway, care path or care map.
- **Empathy:** Projecting sensitivity and an understanding of other's feelings.
- **Johari window:** A model of communication that helps the nurse to look at self-awareness through interpersonal learning styles.
- **Process recording:** A written account of an interaction between a nurse and a patient that helps the nurse to examine the relationship.
- **Transference:** The feelings or responses that a patient has toward the nurse that are associated with someone who is significant in the patient's life.

Terminology Related to Psychiatric Symptomatology

- **Ambivalence:** Simultaneously holding two different attitudes, emotions, thoughts, or feelings about a person, object or situation.

- **Anhedonia:** The loss of interest and inability to experience pleasure in activities that were previously enjoyed by an individual. This state is seen in depressive disorder.
- **Aggression:** Acting out behaviors that can lead to harm or injury to the self and others.
- **Agnosia:** The loss of comprehension of auditory, visual or other sensations although the senses are intact.
- **Agraphia:** The loss of ability to write.
- **Akathisia:** A syndrome that is caused by dopamine-blocking drugs and is characterized by both motor restlessness and a subjective feeling of inner restlessness.
- **Alexia:** Inability to read caused by a lesion or dysfunction of the central nervous system.
- **Alexithymia:** A condition that causes individuals to have difficulty in identifying and describing their emotions. Individuals with eating disorders often have a restricted emotional life and thus, exhibit this condition.
- **Apathy:** Indifference, disinterest or dull attitude. This manifests as a negative symptom of schizophrenia.
- **Aphasia:** The inability to speak or write (expressive aphasia) or the inability to comprehend what is being said or written; it may progress to babbling or mutism (receptive aphasia).
- **Apraxia:** The loss of abilities to carry out purposeful or complex movements and to use objects properly.
- **Avolition:** A lack of motivation or will. It is noted in patients with schizophrenia or other mental illnesses.
- **Battering:** Physical or sexual abuse of a person by intimate partner or by someone with whom he/she has been intimate.
- **Blunted affect:** The restricted expression of emotions.
- **Cataplexy:** A sudden loss of muscle tone and voluntary muscle movement.
- **Circumstantiality:** A type of speech that is characterized by unnecessary details and indirectness before the point or intent is reached. It may be noted in patients with schizophrenia or other mental illnesses.
- **Compulsion:** An unremitting and repetitive impulse to perform a behavior or a mental act. The object of the compulsion is to prevent or reduce anxiety or distress. Compulsive acts often occur to reduce the distress that accompanies an obsession.
- **Confabulation:** The fabricating of stories to fill in memory gaps. It may be an attempt to preserve self-esteem, and not to be mistaken for lying. It is often seen in patients with Alzheimer's disease or other types of dementia.
- **Double bind communication:** A situation in which contradictory messages are given to one person by another; and a response or a choice between two opposing alternatives is demanded.
- **Dysarthria:** Difficulty with articulating words. It is more commonly found in patients with vascular dementia, stroke and major head injuries.
- **Dyspareunia:** Painful sexual intercourse that does not result from a general medical condition.
- **Delusion:** A false, unshakable belief which is not amenable to reasoning, and is not in keeping with the patient's sociocultural and educational background.
- **Shared delusion:** A phenomenon in which a person takes on the delusion of another person and often manifests similar characteristics of delusion. It is also known as '*Folie a deux*'.
- **Depersonalization:** Feelings of unreality or personal dissociation. Individuals who are experiencing depersonalization have difficulty in distinguishing themselves from others.
- **Derealization:** An alteration in the perception of external world so that the feeling of the reality of external world is (as if) temporarily changed or lost.
- **Disorientation:** A loss of familiarity with place, time, person and situation.
- **Echolalia:** The involuntary repetition of words spoken by another person.
- **Echopraxia:** The spontaneous imitation of movements made by another person.
- **Encopresis:** The repeated passage of feces in inappropriate places whether involuntary or intentional (most commonly seen in children).
- **Enuresis:** The repeated voiding of urine into the bed or clothing, whether involuntary or intentional.
- **Euphoria:** Mild elevation of mood in which an individual experiences a sense of well-being and happiness, not keeping with ongoing events. This state is seen in hypomania.
- **Euthymia:** Normal range of mood with absence of depressed or elevated mood.
- **Ecstasy:** Very severe elevation of mood in which an individual experiences an intense sense of rapture or blissfulness.
- **Flat affect:** The lack of outward expression of emotions.
- **Flight of ideas:** The shifting from one idea to another without completing the previous idea or an abrupt change of topics expressed in a rapid flow of speech.
- **Grandiosity:** A characteristic that is noted in patients with mania in which they experience a sense of inflated self-esteem or exaggerated confidence. It is also known as self-aggrandizement.
- **Hallucination:** A perceptual disturbance of one or more of the five senses in the absence of external stimuli.

- **Hyper-religiosity:** A preoccupation or obsession with religion, God or another deity.
- **Hypervigilance:** An excessive watchfulness and scanning of the environment that is generally manifested in patients who are experiencing delusions or hallucinations and that may preclude acts of aggression or violence.
- **Inappropriate affect:** An affect that is not congruent with the emotion being felt (e.g., laughing when sad).
- **Ideas of reference:** Incorrect interpretations of external incidents and events that have a particular or special meaning specific to the person.
- **Labile affect:** A disorder where the patient has excessive display of emotion, or expresses emotions that are not congruent with the situation. Labile affect is also called pseudobulbar affect or emotional incontinence.
- **Looseness of association:** A thought disturbance in which the speaker rapidly shifts his/her expression of ideas from one subject to another in an unrelated and fragmented manner. This is most commonly noted in patients with schizophrenia.
- **Negative symptoms:** Symptoms that include flat affect, poverty of speech, poor grooming, withdrawal and avolition that are seen in patients with schizophrenia.
- **Neologisms:** Invented words to which meanings are attached; coining of new words for which patients have personal meaning.
- **Nihilism:** The belief that existence is senseless and useless. Patients with schizophrenia may experience nihilistic delusions in which they believe the world is nonexistent.
- **Obsessions:** Persistent ideas, thoughts, impulses or images that involve death, sexual matters, religion, or any themes which lead to the person's efforts to resist them. It may result in marked anxiety or distress.
- **Panic:** A circumscribed period of extreme anxiety. During panic, one's perceptions are distorted; and the ability to integrate and separate environmental stimuli is impaired.
- **Perseveration:** The excessive and persistent repetition of the same ideas in response to different questions.
- **Positive symptoms:** Symptoms that include hallucinations, delusions, increased speech production with loose associations, bizarre behavior. These are often seen in patients with schizophrenia.
- **Poverty of thought:** A psychopathologic thought disturbance seen in patients with schizophrenia. Patient's inability to think logically and sequentially is reflected in the poverty of content of his or her speech, which is vague, repetitious and disconnected.
- **Pressured speech:** Rapid speech with an urgent quality. It is often noted in patients with mania.
- **Psychomotor agitation:** Agitated motor activities such as restlessness, pacing and irritability.
- **Psychomotor retardation:** The slowing of physiologic processes that result in slow movement, speech and reaction time. It is often noted in patients with depression.
- **Residual symptoms:** Minor disturbances that may remain after an episode of schizophrenia but do not include delusions, hallucinations, incoherence or gross disorganization.
- **Secondary gain:** Any benefit that results from illness, such as personal attention, sympathy from others, or escape from unwanted responsibilities.
- **Somatization:** The conversion of mental state or experiences into bodily symptoms that are associated with anxiety.
- **Sundowner's syndrome:** The confusion and irritation that are commonly seen in patients with dementia at the end of the day, as a result of tiredness and inability to mentally process any more information as they struggled whole day long to understand the environmental clues.
- **Tangentiality:** Responding in a manner that is irrelevant to the topic.
- **Thought blocking:** An abrupt interruption in the flow of thoughts or ideas that results from a disturbance in the speed of association.

Terminology Related to Treatment Modalities

- **Cognitive behavioral therapy:** Therapy that is focused on changing irrational or self-defeating thoughts and behaviors into realistic ones.
- **Deinstitutionalization:** The discharge of a patient from the psychiatric institution or hospital into the community.
- **Milieu therapy:** A type of therapy that recreates a community atmosphere in an inpatient treatment setting to facilitate interaction among patient peers to identify and solve issues that occur when relating to others.

Terminology Related to Drug Side Effects

- **Acute dystonia:** Abnormal muscle tonicity and spasm of the face, head, neck and back. It is a side effect of some antipsychotic medications.
- **Extrapyramidal syndrome (EPS):** The collective term that is used to describe the troubling motor side effects of dopamine blocking medications. It includes acute dystonia, akathisia, Parkinsonism and tardive dyskinesia.
- **Hypertensive crisis:** Any severe elevation of blood pressure that is a medical emergency. It may occur as a result of food or drug admixtures with some psychotropic medications.

- **Neuroleptic malignant syndrome (NMS):** A rare but potentially lethal toxic reaction to dopamine-blocking drugs that presents with a constellation of symptoms including fever, autonomic instability, increased muscular rigidity and altered mental status.
- **Serotonin syndrome:** An adverse drug reaction that results in excessive production of serotonin in the brain. It may be life-threatening.

CLASSIFICATION OF MENTAL DISORDERS

Classification of mental disorders has been illustrated in Flowchart 2.1.

ICD-11 Classification of Mental Disorders

1.2.4.1 Coding Scheme

- The coding scheme always has a letter in the second position to differentiate from the codes of ICD-10.
- In ICD-11, the first character of the code always relates to the chapter number. It may be a number or a letter. The code range of a single chapter always has the same character in the first position.
- In order to describe a causal relationship between conditions in a code title, the preferred term is 'due to'.
- In order to indicate the concurrence of two conditions in a code title, the preferred term is 'associated with'.

The codes of ICD-11 are alphanumeric and cover the range from 1A00.00 to ZZ9Z.ZZ. Codes starting with 'X' indicate an extension code (see Extension codes). The inclusion of a forced number at the 3rd character position prevents spelling 'undesirable' words. The letters 'O' and 'I' are omitted to prevent confusion with the numbers '0' and '1'. Chapters are indicated by the first character. For example, 1A00 is a code in Chapter 1, and BA00 is a code in Chapter 11.

1.2.4.2 Extension codes

ICD-11 allows for adding specific detail to coded entities by using the following mechanisms:

- The extension codes comprise groups of codes, e.g., anatomy, agent, histopathology and other aspects that may be used to add detail to a stem code. Extension codes are not to be used alone but must be added to a stem code. Not all extension codes can be used with every stem code.
- 'Code also' instructions provide additional etiological information which is mandatory to code in conjunction with certain categories, because that additional information is relevant for primary tabulation. The 'code also' instruction marks the categories that must be used in conjunction with the indicated condition. In some instances, they may be a reason for treatment in their own right, where etiology is unknown.
- ICD-11 has an explicit way of marking codes that are post coordinated to describe one condition, called cluster coding. This is a notable new feature in ICD-11 that creates an ability to link core diagnostic concepts (i.e., stem code concepts) when desired, and/or to add clinical concepts captured in extension codes to primary stem code concepts. Either way, it should be emphasized that the clustering ability inherent to ICD-11 is one of the significant changes relative to ICD-10.

Flowchart 2.1: Classification of mental disorders

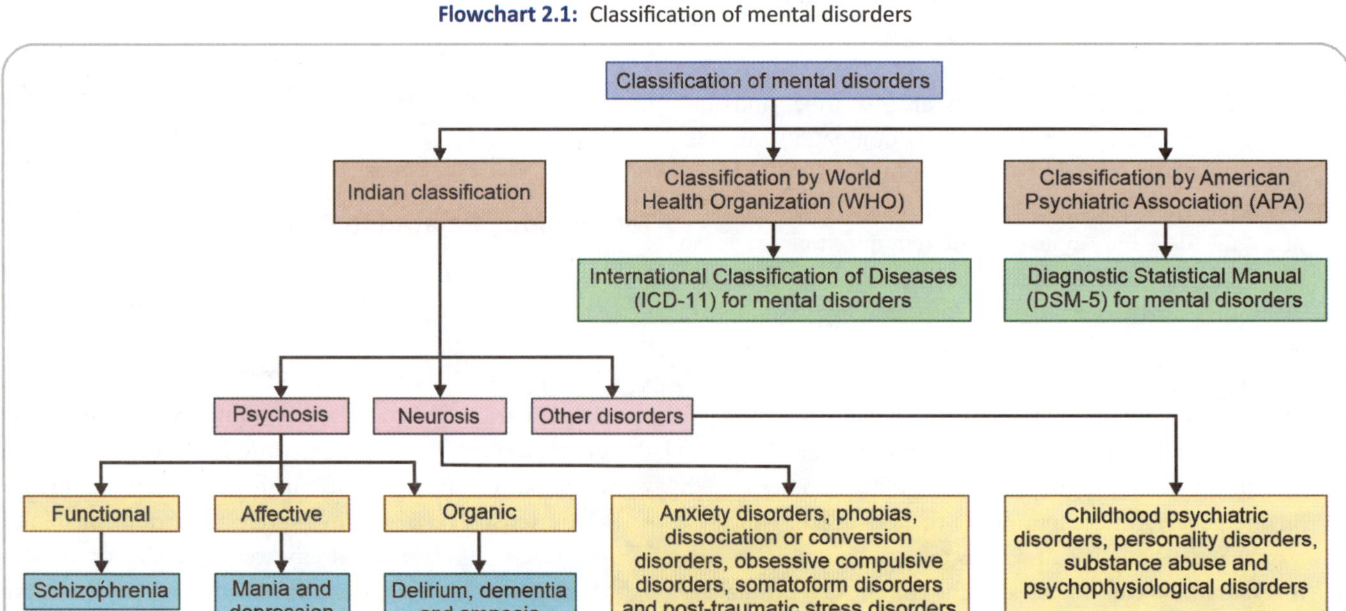

DSM-5 Classification of Mental Disorders

Diagnostic Statistical Manual (DSM) Classification of Mental Disorders has been given by American Psychiatric Association (APA). DSM-I was released in 1952 and various revisions have been done. DSM-5 was released in 2013 which replaced the previous version of DSM-IV. This is the standard classification used by mental health professionals in the United States. DSM-5 diagnostic chapters are as follows:

- Schizophrenia spectrum and other psychotic disorders
- Bipolar and related disorders
- Depressive disorders
- Anxiety disorders
- Obsessive-compulsive and related disorders
- Trauma and stressor-related disorders
- Dissociative disorders
- Somatic symptom and related disorders
- Feeding and eating disorders
- Elimination disorders
- Sleep-wake disorders
- Sexual dysfunctions
- Gender dysphoria
- Disruptive, impulsive and conduct disorders
- Substance-related and addictive disorders
- Neurocognitive disorders
- Personality disorders
- Paraphilic disorders
- Other mental disorders

ICD-11 and DSM-5 Classification of Mental Disorders

Table 2.1 shows ICD-11 and DSM-5 classification of mental disorders.

Table 2.1: ICD-11 and DSM-5 classification of mental disorders

ICD-11	DSM-5	Classification of mental disorders
Neurodevelopmental disorders		
Intellectual disability (intellectual developmental disorder)		
6A00.0	—	Mild intellectual disability
6A00.1	—	Moderate intellectual disability
6A00.2	—	Severe intellectual disability
6A00.3	—	Profound intellectual disability
6A00.4		Provisional intellectual disability
—	315	Global developmental delay
6A00.Z	319	Unspecified intellectual disability (intellectual developmental disorder)
Communication disorders		
6A01	315.39	Language disorder
6A01.0	315.39	Speech sound disorder
—	315.35	Childhood-onset fluency disorder (stuttering)
—	307.0	Adult-onset fluency disorder
6A01.22	315.39	Social (pragmatic) communication disorder
6A01.Z	307.9	Unspecified communication disorder
Autism spectrum disorder		
6A02	299.00	Autism spectrum disorder
—	293.89	Autism spectrum disorder with catatonia
Attention-deficit/hyperactivity disorder		
6A05.0	314.00	Predominantly inattentive presentation
6A05.1	314.01	Predominantly hyperactive/impulsive presentation
6A05.2	314.01	Combined presentation
6A05.Y	314.01	Other specified attention-deficit/hyperactivity disorder
6A05.Z	314.01	Unspecified attention-deficit/hyperactivity disorder

Contd...

ICD-11	DSM-5	Classification of mental disorders
Specific learning disorder		
6A03.0	315.00	With impairment in reading
6A03.1	315.2	With impairment in written expression
6A03.2	315.1	With impairment in mathematics
Motor disorders		
—	315.4	Developmental coordination disorder
6A06	307.3	Stereotypic movement disorder
Tic disorders		
8A05.00	307.23	Tourette's disorder
—	307.22	Persistent (chronic) motor or vocal tic disorder
—	307.21	Provisional tic disorder
—	307.20	Other specified tic disorder
—	307.19	Unspecified tic disorder
Other neurodevelopmental disorders		
6A0Y	315.8	Other specified neurodevelopmental disorder
6A0Z	315.9	Unspecified neurodevelopmental disorder
Schizophrenia spectrum and other psychotic disorders		
6A20	295.90	Schizophrenia
6A21	—	Schizoaffective disorder
6A22	301.22	Schizotypal (personality) disorder
6A23	—	Acute and transient psychotic disorder
6A24	297.1	Delusional disorder
—	298.8	Brief psychotic disorder
—	295.40	Schizophreniform disorder
—	295.70	Schizoaffective disorder (bipolar type)
—	295.70	Schizoaffective disorder (depressive type)
—	293.81	Psychotic disorder due to another medical condition (with delusions)
—	293.82	Psychotic disorder due to another medical condition (with hallucinations)
6A40	293.89	Catatonia associated with another mental disorder (catatonia specifier)
—	293.89	Catatonic disorder due to another medical condition
6A41	—	Catatonia induced by psychoactive substances, including medications
6A4Z	293.89	Unspecified catatonia
—	298.8	Other specified schizophrenia spectrum and other psychotic disorder
—	298.9	Unspecified schizophrenia spectrum and other psychotic disorder
Bipolar and related disorders		
Bipolar I disorder		
—	296.41	Current or most recent episode manic (mild)
—	296.42	Current or most recent episode manic (moderate)
—	296.43	Current or most recent episode manic (severe)
6A60.5	296.44	Current or most recent episode manic (with psychotic features)
6A60.B	296.45	Current or most recent episode manic (in partial remission)
6A60.F	296.46	Current or most recent episode manic (in full remission)
6A60.E	296.40	Current or most recent episode manic (unspecified)

Contd...

ICD-11	DSM-5	Classification of mental disorders
Bipolar II disorder		
6A61	296.89	Bipolar II disorder
6A62	301.13	Cyclothymic disorder
6A6Y	296.89	Other specified bipolar and related disorder
6A6Z	296.80	Unspecified bipolar and related disorder
Depressive disorders		
—	296.99	Disruptive mood dysregulation disorder
6A70.0	296.21	Single episode depression (mild)
—	296.22	Single episode depression (moderate)
6A71.1	—	Single episode depression (moderate without psychotic features)
6A71.2	—	Single episode depression (moderate with psychotic features)
6A71.3	—	Single episode depression (severe without psychotic features)
6A71.4	—	Single episode depression (severe with psychotic features)
—	296.23	Single episode depression (severe)
—	296.24	Single episode depression (with psychotic features)
6A70.6	296.25	Single episode depression (in partial remission)
6A70.7	296.26	Single episode depression (in full remission)
6A70.Z	296.20	Single episode depression (unspecified)
6A71.0	296.31	Recurrent episode depression (mild)
—	296.32	Recurrent episode depression (moderate)
6A71.1	—	Recurrent episode depression (moderate without psychotic features)
6A71.2	—	Recurrent episode depression (moderate with psychotic features)
—	296.33	Recurrent episode depression (severe)
6A71.3	—	Recurrent episode depression (severe without psychotic features)
6A71.4	—	Recurrent episode depression (severe with psychotic features)
—	296.34	Recurrent episode depression (with psychotic features)
6A71.6	296.35	Recurrent episode depression (in partial remission)
6A71.7	296.36	Recurrent episode depression (in full remission)
6A71.Y	296.30	Recurrent episode depression (unspecified)
6A7Z	300.4	Persistent depressive disorder (dysthymia)
—	625.4	Premenstrual dysphoric disorder
—	293.83	Depressive disorder due to another medical condition
Anxiety disorders		
6B00	300.02	Generalized anxiety disorder
6B01	300.01	Panic disorder
6B02	300.22	Agoraphobia
6B03	300.29	Specific phobia
6B04	300.23	Social anxiety disorder (social phobia)
6B05	309.21	Separation anxiety disorder
6B06	312.23	Selective mutism
—	293.84	Anxiety disorder due to another medical condition
6B0Y	300.09	Other specified anxiety disorder
6B0Z	300.00	Unspecified anxiety disorder

Contd...

ICD-11	DSM-5	Classification of mental disorders
Obsessive-compulsive and its related disorder		
6B20	300.3	Obsessive-compulsive disorder
—	300.7	Body dysmorphic disorder
6B24	300.3	Hoarding disorder
6B25.0	312.39	Trichotillomania (hair-pulling disorder)
6B25.1	698.4	Excoriation (skin-picking) disorder
—	294.8	Obsessive-compulsive and related disorder due to another medical condition
—	300.3	Other specified obsessive-compulsive and related disorder
6B20.Z	300.3	Unspecified obsessive-compulsive and related disorder
Trauma- and stressor-related disorders		
6B44	313.89	Reactive attachment disorder
6B45	313.89	Disinhibited social engagement disorder
6B40	309.81	Post-traumatic stress disorder
—	308.3	Acute stress disorder
6B43	—	Adjustment disorders
—	309.0	Adjustment disorders (with depressed mood)
—	309.24	Adjustment disorders (with anxiety)
—	309.28	Adjustment disorders (with mixed anxiety and depressed mood)
—	309.3	Adjustment disorders (with disturbance of conduct)
—	309.4	Adjustment disorders (with mixed disturbance of emotions and conduct)
—	309.9	Adjustment disorders (unspecified)
6B4Y	309.89	Other specified trauma- and stressor-related disorder
6B4Z	309.9	Unspecified trauma- and stressor-related disorder
Dissociative disorders		
6B60	—	Dissociative neurological symptom disorder
6B61	300.12	Dissociative amnesia
—	300.13	Dissociative amnesia (with dissociative fugue)
6B62	—	Trance disorder
6B63	—	Possession trance disorder
6B64	300.14	Dissociative identity disorder
6B65	—	Partial dissociative identity disorder
6B66	300.6	Depersonalization-derealization disorder
6B6Y	300.15	Other specified dissociative disorder
6B6Z	300.15	Unspecified dissociative disorder
Somatic symptom and related disorders		
—	300.82	Somatic symptom disorder
—	300.7	Illness anxiety disorder
—	300.11	Conversion disorder (functional neurological symptom disorder)
—	316	Psychological factors affecting other medical conditions
—	300.19	Factitious disorder
—	300.89	Other specified somatic symptom and related disorder
—	300.82	Unspecified somatic symptom and related disorder

Contd...

ICD-11	DSM-5	Classification of mental disorders
Feeding and eating disorders		
6B80	307.1	Anorexia nervosa
6B80.10	—	Restricting type
6B80.11	—	Binge eating/purging type
6B81	307.51	Bulimia nervosa
6B82	307.51	Binge eating disorder
6B83	307.59	Avoidant/Restrictive food intake disorder
6B84	307.52	Pica
6B85	307.53	Rumination disorder
6B8Y	307.59	Other specified feeding or eating disorder
6B8Z	307.50	Unspecified feeding or eating disorder
Elimination disorders		
6C00	307.6	Enuresis
6C01	307.7	Encopresis
—	788.39	Other specified elimination disorder (with urinary symptoms)
—	787.60	Other specified elimination disorder (with fecal symptoms)
6C00.Z	788.30	Unspecified elimination disorder (with urinary symptoms)
6C01.Z	787.60	Unspecified elimination disorder (with fecal symptoms)
Sexual dysfunctions		
HA00	302.71	Hypoactive sexual desire disorder
HA01.0	302.72	Female sexual interest/arousal disorder
HA01.1	302.72	Erectile disorder
HA02	302.73	Female orgasmic disorder
HA03.0	302.75	Premature (early) ejaculation
HA03.1	302.74	Delayed ejaculation
—	302.76	Genito-pelvic pain/penetration disorder
HA03.Y	302.79	Other specified sexual dysfunction
Gender dysphoria		
—	302.6	Gender dysphoria in children
—	302.85	Gender dysphoria in adolescents and adults
—	302.6	Other specified gender dysphoria
—	302.6	Unspecified gender dysphoria
Disruptive, impulse-control and conduct disorders		
6C90	313.81	Oppositional defiant disorder
6C73	312.34	Intermittent explosive disorder
6C91.0	312.81	Conduct disorder (childhood-onset type)
6C91.1	312.82	Conduct disorder (adolescent-onset type)
6C91.Z	312.83	Conduct disorder (unspecified onset)
—	301.7	Antisocial personality disorder
6C70	312.33	Pyromania
6C71	312.32	Kleptomania
6C7Y	312.89	Other specified disruptive, impulse-control, and conduct disorder
6C7Z	312.9	Unspecified disruptive, impulse-control, and conduct disorder

Contd...

ICD-11	DSM-5	Classification of mental disorders
Personality disorders		
6D10	—	Personality disorders
6D10.0	—	Personality disorders, mild
6D10.1	—	Personality disorders, moderate
6D10.2	—	Personality disorders, severe
6D10.Z	—	Personality disorders, unspecified severity
6D11	—	Predominant personality traits
6D11.0	—	Negative affectivity in personality disorder
6D11.1	—	Detachment in personality disorder
6D11.2	—	Dissociality in personality disorder
6D11.3	—	Disinhibition in personality disorder
6D11.4	—	Anankastic personality disorder
6D11.5	—	Borderline pattern personality disorder
Cluster A personality disorders		
—	301.0	Paranoid personality disorder
—	301.20	Schizoid personality disorder
—	301.22	Schizotypal personality disorder
Cluster B personality disorders		
—	301.7	Antisocial personality disorder
—	301.83	Borderline personality disorder
—	301.50	Histrionic personality disorder
—	301.81	Narcissistic personality disorder
Cluster C personality disorders		
—	301.4	Obsessive-compulsive personality disorder
—	301.82	Avoidant personality disorder
—	301.6	Dependent personality disorder
Other personality disorders		
	310.1	Personality change due to another medical condition
	301.89	Other specified personality disorder
Medication-induced movement disorders and other adverse effects of medication		
—	332.1	Neuroleptic-induced parkinsonism
—	333.92	Neuroleptic malignant syndrome
—	333.72	Medication-induced acute dystonia
—	333.99	Medication-induced acute akathisia
—	333.85	Tardive dyskinesia
—	333.72	Tardive dystonia
—	333.99	Tardive akathisia
—	333.1	Medication-induced postural tremor
—	333.99	Other medication-induced movement disorder
Gender dysphoria (DSM-5) and gender incongruence (ICD-11)		
HA60	302.85	Gender dysphoria in adolescents and adults
HA61	302.6	Gender dysphoria in children

Contd...

ICD-11	DSM-5	Classification of mental disorders
HA8Y	302.6	Other specified gender dysphoria
HA6Z	302.6	Unspecified gender dysphoria
Paraphilic disorders		
6D30	302.4	Exhibitionistic disorder
6D31	302.82	Voyeuristic disorder
6D32	302.2	Pedophilic disorder
6D33	302.84	Sexual sadism disorder
6D34	302.89	Frotteuristic disorder
—	302.83	Sexual masochism disorder
F65.0	302.81	Fetishistic disorder
—	302.3	Transvestic disorder
6D35 and 6D36	302.89	Other specified paraphilic disorder
6D3Z	302.9	Unspecified paraphilic disorder

ICD-11 Classification of Amnestic Disorder

6D72 Amnestic Disorder

- 6D72.0 Amnestic disorder due to diseases classified elsewhere.
- 6D72.1 Amnestic disorder due to psychoactive substances including medications.
- 6D72.10 Amnestic disorder due to use of alcohol.
- 6D72.11 Amnestic disorder due to use of sedatives, hypnotics or anxiolytics.
- 6D72.12 Amnestic disorder due to other specified psychoactive substances including medications.
- 6D72.13 Amnestic disorder due to use of volatile inhalants.
- 6D72.2 Amnestic disorder due to unknown or unspecified etiological factors.
- 6D72.Y Other specified amnestic disorder.
- 6D72.Z Amnestic disorder, unspecified.

ICD-11 Classification of Dementia

6D80 Dementia

- 6D80 Dementia due to Alzheimer's disease.
  - 6D80.0 Dementia due to Alzheimer's disease with early onset.
  - 6D80.1 Dementia due to Alzheimer's disease with late onset.
  - 6D80.2 Alzheimer's disease dementia, mixed type, with cerebrovascular disease.
  - 6D80.3 Alzheimer's disease dementia, mixed type, with other nonvascular etiologies.
  - 6D80.Z Dementia due to Alzheimer's disease, onset unknown or unspecified.
- 6D81 Vascular dementia.
- 6D82 Dementia due to Lewy body disease.
- 6D83 Frontotemporal dementia.
- 6D84 Dementia due to psychoactive substances including medications.
  - 6D84.0 Dementia due to use of alcohol.
  - 6D84.1 Dementia due to use of sedatives, hypnotics or anxiolytics.
  - 6D84.2 Dementia due to use of volatile inhalants.
  - 6D84.Y Dementia due to other specified psychoactive substances.
- 6D85 Dementia due to diseases classified elsewhere.
  - 6D85.0 Dementia due to Parkinson's disease.
  - 6D85.1 Dementia due to Huntington's disease.
  - 6D85.2 Dementia due to exposure to heavy metals and other toxins.
  - 6D85.3 Dementia due to human immunodeficiency virus.
  - 6D85.4 Dementia due to multiple sclerosis.
  - 6D85.5 Dementia due to prion disease.
  - 6D85.6 Dementia due to normal pressure hydrocephalus.
  - 6D85.7 Dementia due to injury to the head.
  - 6D85.8 Dementia due to pellagra.
  - 6D85.9 Dementia due to Down syndrome.
  - 6D85.Y Dementia due to other specified diseases classified elsewhere.
- 6D86 Behavioral or psychological disturbances in dementia.
  - 6D86.0 Psychotic symptoms in dementia.
  - 6D86.1 Mood symptoms in dementia.
  - 6D86.2 Anxiety symptoms in dementia.

- 6D86.3 Apathy in dementia.
- 6D86.4 Agitation or aggression in dementia.
- 6D86.5 Disinhibition in dementia.
- 6D86.6 Wandering in dementia.
- 6D86.Y Other specified behavioral or psychological disturbances in dementia.
- 6D86.Z Behavioral or psychological disturbances in dementia, unspecified.

- 6D8Z Dementia, unknown or unspecified cause.
- 6E0Y Other specified neurocognitive disorders.
- 6E0Z Neurocognitive disorders, unspecified.

ICD-11 Classification of Substance Use Disorders

- 6C40 Disorders due to use of alcohol.
- 6C41 Disorders due to use of cannabis.
- 6C42 Disorders due to use of synthetic cannabinoids.
- 6C43 Disorders due to use of opioids.
- 6C44 Disorders due to use of sedatives, hypnotics or anxiolytics.
- 6C46 Disorders due to use of stimulants including amphetamines, methamphetamine or methcathinone.
- 6C47 Disorders due to use of synthetic cathinones.
- 6C48 Disorders due to use of caffeine.
- 6C49 Disorders due to use of hallucinogens.
- 6C4A Disorders due to use of nicotine.
- 6C4B Disorders due to use of volatile inhalants.
- 6C4C Disorders due to use of MDMA or related drugs, including MDA.
- 6C4D Disorders due to use of dissociative drugs including ketamine and phencyclidine [PCP].
- 6C4E Disorders due to use of other specified psychoactive substances, including medications.
- 6C4F Disorders due to use of multiple specified psychoactive substances, including medications.
- 6C4G Disorders due to use of unknown or unspecified psychoactive substances.
- 6C4H Disorders due to use of non-psychoactive substances.
- 6C4Y Other specified disorders due to substance use.
- 6C4Z Disorders due to substance use, unspecified.

Table 2.2 shows DSM-5 classification of delirium.

Table 2.2: DSM-5 classification of delirium

Delirium	
292.81	Medication-induced delirium
293.0	Delirium due to another medical condition (or) Delirium due to multiple etiologies
780.09	Other specified delirium (or) unspecified delirium

Table 2.3 shows DSM-5 classification of major and mild neurocognitive disorders (dementia).

Table 2.3: DSM-5 classification of major and mild neurocognitive disorders (dementia)

Major and mild neurocognitive disorders	
294.11	Probable major neurocognitive disorder due to Alzheimer's disease with behavioral disturbance
294.10	Probable major neurocognitive disorder due to Alzheimer's disease without behavioral disturbance
331.9	Possible major neurocognitive disorder due to Alzheimer's disease
331.83	Mild neurocognitive disorder due to Alzheimer's disease
294.11	Major or mild frontotemporal neurocognitive disorder with behavioral disturbance
294.10	Major or mild frontotemporal neurocognitive disorder without behavioral disturbance
331.9	Possible major neurocognitive disorder due to frontotemporal lobar degeneration
331.83	Mild neurocognitive disorder due to frontotemporal lobar degeneration
294.11	Major or mild neurocognitive disorder with Lewy Bodies with behavioral disturbance
294.10	Major or mild neurocognitive disorder with Lewy Bodies without behavioral disturbance
331.9	Possible major neurocognitive disorder with Lewy Bodies
331.83	Mild neurocognitive disorder with Lewy Bodies
290.40	Probable major vascular neurocognitive disorder with behavioral disturbance
290.40	Probable major vascular neurocognitive disorder without behavioral disturbance
331.9	Possible major vascular neurocognitive disorder
331.83	Mild vascular neurocognitive disorder
294.11	Major neurocognitive disorder due to traumatic brain injury with behavioral disturbance
294.10	Major neurocognitive disorder due to traumatic brain injury without behavioral disturbance
331.83	Mild neurocognitive disorder due to traumatic brain injury
294.11	Major neurocognitive disorder due to hiv infection with behavioral disturbance
294.10	Major neurocognitive disorder due to hiv infection without behavioral disturbance
331.83	Mild neurocognitive disorder due to hiv infection
294.11	Major neurocognitive disorder due to prion disease with behavioral disturbance
294.10	Major neurocognitive disorder due to prion disease without behavioral disturbance

Contd...

Major and mild neurocognitive disorders	
331.83	Major neurocognitive disorder due to prion disease
294.11	Major neurocognitive disorder probably due to Parkinson's disease with behavioral disturbance
294.10	Major neurocognitive disorder probably due to Parkinson's disease without behavioral disturbance
331.9	Major neurocognitive disorder probably due to Parkinson's disease
331.83	Mild neurocognitive disorder probably due to Parkinson's disease
294.11	Major neurocognitive disorder due to Huntington's disease with behavioral disturbance
294.10	Major neurocognitive disorder due to Huntington's disease without behavioral disturbance
331.83	Mild neurocognitive disorder due to Huntington's disease
294.11	Major neurocognitive disorder due to another medical condition with behavioral disturbance
294.10	Major neurocognitive disorder due to another medical condition without behavioral disturbance
331.83	Mild neurocognitive disorder due to another medical condition
294.11	Major neurocognitive disorder due to multiple etiologies with behavioral disturbance
294.10	Major neurocognitive disorder due to multiple etiologies without behavioral disturbance
331.83	Mild neurocognitive disorder due to multiple etiologies

Table 2.4 shows DSM-5 classification of substance use disorders.

Table 2.4: DSM-5 classification of substance use disorders

Alcohol	
305.00	Alcohol use disorder (mild)
303.90	Alcohol use disorder (moderate or severe)
303.00	Alcohol intoxication
291.81	Alcohol withdrawal
291.9	Unspecified alcohol-related disorder
Caffeine	
305.90	Caffeine intoxication
292.0	Caffeine withdrawal
292.9	Unspecified caffeine-related disorder
Cannabis	
305.20	Cannabis use disorder (mild)
304.30	Cannabis use disorder (moderate or severe)
Inhalants	
292.89	Inhalant intoxication
292.9	Unspecified inhalant-related disorder
Opioids	
305.50	Opioid use disorder (mild)
304.00	Opioid use disorder (moderate or severe)
292.89	Opioid intoxication
292.0	Opioid withdrawal
292.9	Unspecified opioid-related disorder
Sedative, hypnotic or anxiolytic-related disorders	
305.40	Sedative, hypnotic or anxiolytic use disorder (mild)
304.10	Sedative, hypnotic or anxiolytic use disorder (moderate or severe)
292.89	Sedative, hypnotic or anxiolytic intoxication
292.0	Sedative, hypnotic or anxiolytic withdrawal
292.9	Unspecified sedative-, hypnotic- or anxiolytic-related disorder
Stimulant-related disorders	
305.70	Stimulant use disorder, mild amphetamine-type substance use (or) use of unspecified substances
305.60	Stimulant use disorder, mild cocaine substance use
304.40	Stimulant use disorder, moderate or severe amphetamine-type substance use (or) use of unspecified substances
304.20	Stimulant use disorder, moderate cocaine substance use
292.89	Stimulant intoxication
292.0	Stimulant withdrawal
Tobacco	
305.1	Tobacco use disorder, mild
305.1	Tobacco use disorder, moderate
305.1	Tobacco use disorder, severe
292.0	Tobacco withdrawal
292.9	Unspecified tobacco-related disorder
Miscellaneous	
305.90	Other (or unknown) substance use disorder, mild
304.90	Other (or unknown) substance use disorder, moderate
304.90	Other (or unknown) substance use disorder, severe
292.89	Other (or unknown) substance intoxication
292.0	Other (or unknown) substance withdrawal
292.9	Unspecified other (or unknown) substance-related disorder

Contd...

REVIEW OF PERSONALITY DEVELOPMENT

The term 'personality' has been derived from the word '*persona*' which means the mask that the Roman and Greek actors used to wear in dramas, which indicated to the audience whether they played the good or bad characters. Thus, the mask distinguished one actor from the other actor.

Personality

- Personality is defined as a characteristic set of behaviors, cognitions and emotional patterns that evolve from biological and environmental factors.
- Personality is a characteristic way of thinking, feeling and behaving oneself.
- Personality embraces moods, attitudes and opinions that are most clearly expressed in interactions with other people.
- It includes behavioral characteristics, both inherent and acquired, that distinguish one person from another, can be observed in people's relations to the environment or the social group.

Related Terms

- **Temperament:** It refers to those aspects of an individual's personality that are often regarded as innate rather than learned. It is a natural disposition. There are three major temperament types—*Easy, difficult and slow to warm up.*
- **Character:** It is the sum total of the acquired dispositions of an individual. It is a mental structure which is organized, lasting and enduring. It influences the conduct and social behavior all the time.

PERSPECTIVES IN PERSONALITY THEORY

There are several ways in which the characteristic behavior of human beings can be explained. The personality is still difficult to measure precisely and scientifically. Hence, there is no single explanation of personality that all can agree on. There are four main perspectives in personality theory (Fig. 2.1).

Psychoanalytic perspective	Behaviorist perspective
Humanistic perspective	Trait perspective

Figure 2.1: Perspectives in personality theory

1. **Psychoanalytic perspective:** It focuses on the role of unconscious mind in the development of personality.
2. **Behaviorist perspective:** The approach focuses on the effect of behavior on the environment.
3. **Humanistic perspective:** This arises as a reaction against the psychoanalytic and behaviorist perspectives and focuses on the role of each person's conscious life experiences or the choices in personality development.
4. **Trait perspective:** The psychoanalytic, behavioristic and humanistic perspectives all seek to explain the process that causes personality to form into its unique characteristics, whereas trait theorists are more concerned with the end result, 'the characteristics'.

THEORIES OF PERSONALITY DEVELOPMENT

Psychoanalytic Theory

Sigmund Freud's psychoanalytical theory of personality has been based primarily on his concept of unconscious nature of personality. This theory assumes that man is motivated more by unseen forces than by conscious and rational thoughts. He emphasized that the major force which motivates a human being is his unconscious framework. This framework includes three conflicting psychoanalytic concepts, namely the id, the ego and the superego (Table 2.5).

1. Id is the foundation of the unconscious behavior and is the source of psychic energy and seeks immediate satisfaction of biological or instinctual needs.
2. Ego is the conscious and logical part because it is concerned about the realities of external environment. The ego of a person keeps the id in check whenever it demands immediate pleasure.
3. Superego is a higher-level force to restrain the id and it is described as the conscience of a person. Superego represents the norms of an individual, his family, society and is an ethical constraint on the behavior.

Freud believed that personality develops through a series of childhood stages in which the pleasure-seeking energies of the id become focused on certain erogenous areas, an area of the body that is particularly sensitive to stimulation. Each stage of development is marked by conflicts that can help in growth or self-development, depending upon how they are resolved. If these psychosexual stages are completed successfully, they result in the development of a healthy personality. Early experiences play a major role in personality development and continue to influence behavior later in life.

Table 2.5: Principles and level of consciousness involved in structure of mind

Structure of mind	Description	Behavior	Principle	Level of consciousness highly involved
Id	Needs or wishes or pleasure	Animalistic	Pleasure	Unconscious mind
Ego	Think about right and wrong; Gains control over the behavior	Humanistic	Reality	Conscious mind
Superego	Moral concepts or ideals	Spiritualistic	Morality	Unconscious and conscious mind

Neo-Freudian Approaches

Alfred Adler, one of Freud's earlier associates, agreed that early childhood experiences are important to development but believed that much of our personality is determined by our efforts to overcome **feelings of inferiority**. He said that birth order can influence the development of personality. The schema that depicts the differences in personality is given in Table 2.6.

Table 2.6: Schematic representation showing differences in personality based on the birth order (Neo-Freudian approaches)

The eldest child	Set goals to get back the attention of parents and others, which was lost after the birth of younger sibling
Middle children	Either very social or very competitive
The youngest child	More secure, but generally pampered and dependent

Jung's Theory

Carl Jung explained that the **collective unconscious** contains more than the repressed thoughts and feelings (personal unconscious state). Collective unconscious contains memories which are shared by all mankind stored in the form of archetypes. The aim of healthy personality is to achieve a kind of wholeness in which all parts of personality are fully developed and harmoniously interpreted.

Erikson's Theory of Psychosocial Development

Erik H Erikson proposed that personality develops in a predetermined order. In his theory, he explained how the process of socialization affects a child's sense of self. According to him, personality is unfolded through eight different stages, each with two possible outcomes. Each stage involves accomplishment of specific developmental task that may lead to acquisition of certain virtues or psychosocial strength. Failure to accomplish these tasks may result in development of maladaptive behavior (Table 2.7).

Bandura's Social Learning Theory

Albert Bandura emphasized the role of social learning in personality. He said that human beings can think and regulate their own behavior. There is a continuous mutual interaction between the person (P), his behavior (B) and the external environment (E) (Fig. 2.2).

Process of Social Learning

- We learn to observe the behavior of others and we later reproduce it when required.
- We also create new and original behaviors.
- Human beings can think and regulate their behavior through self-observation.
- People are more likely to engage in certain behaviors when they believe they are capable of implementing those behaviors successfully (self-efficacy).

Rogers Theory of Personality

Carl Rogers viewed personality structure in terms of 'self-concept'. He referred to self-concept as "the organized, consistent set of perceptions and beliefs about oneself." Self-concept is influenced by the actual life experiences of an individual and his/her interpretation of those experiences. Self-concept and life experiences may or may not be congruent with each other which in turn determine the kind of personality developed within an individual. Being genuine, showing acceptance and empathy are the conditions required for growth-promoting climate of a child (Table 2.8).

Congruence between self-concept and life experiences may result in self-actualization. Such individuals are well adjusted, well-balanced and interesting to know.

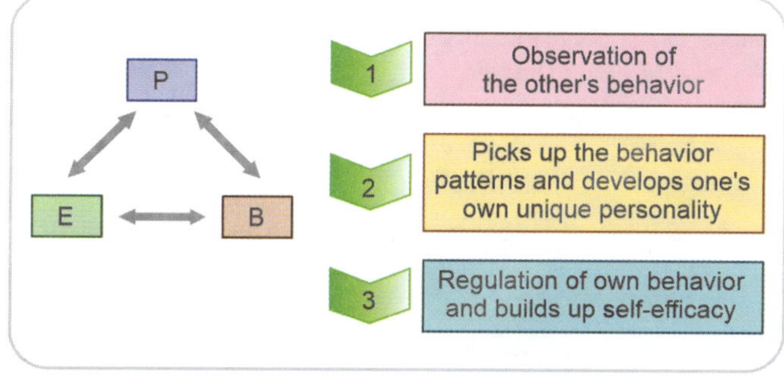

Figure 2.2: Bandura's social learning model and development of personality

Table 2.7: Stages of personality development

Stage	Psychosocial crisis	Virtues	Developmental tasks	Success in tasks	Failure in tasks
Infancy (0–1 year)	**Basic trust vs mistrust**	Hope	• Learn to develop trust based on their interaction with their caregivers • Feels secure when receives consistent care from caregivers • Lack or inconsistent care giving process may result in mistrust and a sense of fear in the child.	Feel secure	Suspiciousness
Early Childhood (1–3 years)	**Autonomy vs shame and doubt**	Will	• Learn to be independent • Want to make their own choices • Learn motor skills • Develop a sense of autonomy when they are allowed to function independently • Doubt themselves or feel shameful when they are denied to be independent	Feel independent	Low self-esteem
Middle childhood (3– 6 years)	**Initiative vs guilt**	Purpose	• Develop a sense of initiative and feel secure in their ability to lead others and make decisions • Develop a sense of guilt when they are criticized or controlled or fail to develop initiative	Self-content	Being a passive personality
Late childhood (6–12 years)	**Industry vs inferiority**	Competence	• Develop a sense of pride in their accomplishments and gain • self-confidence • Develop a feeling of inferiority when they are confronted with failures or negative feedbacks	Self-confident	Inferiority complex
Adolescence (12–18 years)	**Identity vs role confusion**	Fidelity	• Look at the future in terms of career and relationships • Begin to form new identity based on exploration of possibilities and observation of adult roles • If development of self-identity is hindered, it results in confusion about themselves and their role	Clear with role performance	Improper personal relations
Young adulthood (18–25 years)	**Intimacy vs isolation**	Love	• Develop a sense of intimacy from a mutually satisfying marital relationship • Failure to develop close relationships may lead to isolation, loneliness and even depression	Intimate personal relations	Immature behavior and lack of personal relations
Middle adulthood (25-45 years)	**Generativity vs stagnation**	Care	• Accomplishing family commitments, work place demands and sociocultural duties lead to a sense of generativity • Failure in fulfilling these tasks can result in stagnation. • Feelings of stagnation can lead to a feeling of being unproductive	Being a part in welfare of others	No concern for others
Old age (45 years to death)	**Ego integrity vs Despair**	Wisdom	• Develop sense of ego integrity when recalling the life's accomplishments • If one sees life as unproductive, it may bring feelings of despair	Feeling satisfied	Hopelessness

Table 2.8: Differences between congruence and incongruence

Congruence	Incongruence
• Self-concept and actual life experiences may be consistent with each other • Accepts and learns from the life experiences • Becomes an individual who is able to function at full extent.	• Disparity between one's self-concept and actual life experiences • Distortion or denial of experiences • Impaired psychological well-being

Rogers also identified the following five characteristics of a fully functioning or self-actualizing person:

1. Open to experience
2. Existential living
3. Trust feeling
4. Creativity
5. Fulfilled life

Trait Approach

The following **Big Five** are the most widely accepted personality traits: (Mnemonic **OCEAN**)

1. **O – Openness**
2. **C – Conscientiousness**
3. **E – Extraversion**
4. **A – Agreeableness**
5. **N – Neuroticism**

The **Big Five** are the ingredients that make up each individual's personality. Each individual has all these traits but in varying degrees.

1. O – Openness

Openness refers to "openness to experience". People who are high in openness will enjoy adventure. They are curious and appreciate the art, imagination and novelty. People with low openness prefer to stick to their habits and avoid new experiences. Changing personality is usually considered a tough process, but openness is a personality trait which is subjected to change in adulthood.

2. C – Conscientiousness

People who are conscientious are organized and have a strong sense of duty. They are dependable, disciplined and achievement-focused. People with low conscientiousness are more spontaneous or freewheeling and they may tend toward carelessness. Conscientiousness is a helpful trait as it has been linked to achievement in school and on the job.

3. E – Extraversion

Extroverts are chatty, sociable and draw energy from crowds. They tend to be assertive and cheerful in their social interactions. Introverts, on the other hand, prefer to spend most of their time lonely, perhaps because their brains process social interaction differently.

4. A – Agreeableness

Agreeableness measures the extent of a person's warmth and kindness. If the individual is mostly agreeable, he is more likely to be trustful, helpful and compassionate. Disagreeable people are cold, suspicious of others and they are less likely to cooperate.

5. N – Neuroticism

People high in neuroticism worry frequently and easily slip into anxiety and depression. If all is going well, neurotic people tend to find things to worry about. In contrast, people who are low in neuroticism tend to be emotionally stable and even-keeled.

DEFENSE MECHANISMS

Definitions

- A defense mechanism is an unconscious psychological mechanism that reduces anxiety arising from unacceptable or potentially harmful stimuli.
- Defense mechanism is defined as, 'unconscious processes which defend the individual and protect from the anxiety'.

  —***Sigmund Freud***

Psychoanalytic Basis of Defense Mechanism

In psychoanalytic theory, defense mechanisms are psychological strategies brought into the performance by the unconscious mind **to manipulate, deny or distort reality** in order to defend against feelings of anxiety and unacceptable impulses and to maintain one's self-schema or other schemas.

Defense Mechanism in Relation with Origin

Table 2.9 shows defense mechanisms used in various age groups.

Table 2.9: Defense mechanisms used in various age groups

Period	Age group	Defense mechanisms
Oral	0–2 years	• Fixation • Compensation • Denial • Displacement
Habit training	1–3 years	• Conversion • Identification • Sublimation • Reaction formation • Introjection • Transference
Late childhood	3–6 years	• Repression • Rationalization • Regression
Latency period	6–12 years	• Projection

Normal and Pathological Use

Healthy persons normally use different defenses throughout life. An ego defense mechanism becomes pathological, when the persistent use leads to maladaptive behavior which affects the physical or mental health.

Key Aspects

Defense mechanism is a false coping mechanism which is said to be **unconscious** and not to be confused with usual coping strategies. **Repression** is considered a base for all defense mechanisms. The purposes of defense mechanism are as follows:

- To protect the self, mind and ego from anxiety.
- To help in situations where coping mechanism fails.

Views of Psychologists about Defense Mechanism

- **Robert Plutchik (1979)** viewed the defenses as derivatives of basic emotions.
  As per his theory:
  - Reaction formation is related to joy and manic features.
  - Denial is related to acceptance and histrionic features.
  - Repression is related to fear and passivity.
  - Regression is related to surprise and borderline traits.
  - Compensation is related to sadness and depression.
  - Projection is related to disgust and paranoia.
  - Displacement is related to anger and hostility.
  - Intellectualization is related to anticipation.
- **Otto F Kernberg (1967)** developed a theory of borderline personality. The ***borderline defenses*** are projection, denial, splitting, devaluation and projective identification.
- **Anna Freud (1936)**, daughter of Sigmund Freud, enumerated 10 defense mechanisms such as regression, repression, isolation, reaction formation, projection, undoing, introjection, turning against one's own person, sublimation and displacement.

Vaillant's Categorization of Defense Mechanisms

George Eman Vaillant (Fig. 2.3), a psychiatrist, described four-level classification of defense mechanisms (Fig. 2.4).

Figure 2.3: George Eman Vaillant

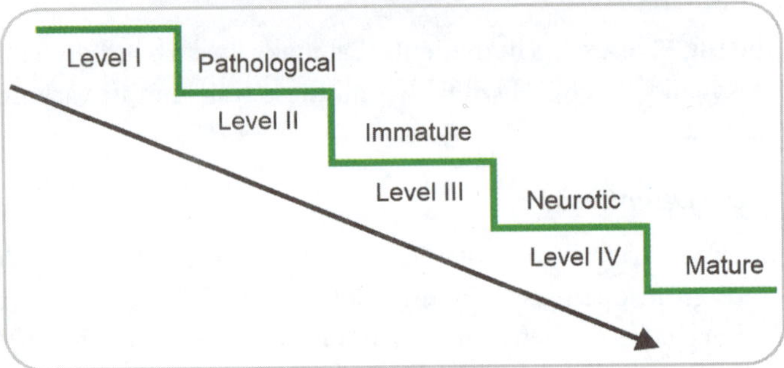

Figure 2.4: Vaillant's levels of defense mechanism

1. Pathological Defenses

- Pathological defenses are severely pathological when used predominantly.
- These defenses, in conjunction, allow an individual to effectively experience and eliminate the need to cope with reality.
- Pathological users of these mechanisms may appear "irrational" or "insane" to others.

Table 2.10 describes the pathological defenses with examples.

2. Immature Defenses

- Immature mechanisms are often present in adults.
- Excessive use of such defenses is considered socially undesirable because they are immature, difficult to deal with and out of touch with reality.
- This decreases the distress and anxiety produced by the threatening people or by an uncomfortable reality.
- These mechanisms lead to problems in a person's ability to cope effectively.
- These defenses are often seen in major depression and personality disorders.

Table 2.11 describes the immature defenses with examples.

3. Neurotic Defenses

- Neurotic defenses are quite common in adults.
- These defenses have short-term advantages in coping. But they can cause long-term problems in relationships and work when used as one's primary style of coping.

Table 2.12 describes the neurotic defenses with examples.

4. Mature Defenses

- Mature defenses are found among emotionally healthy adults.
- These are considered mature defenses, even though many have their origins in an immature stage of development.
- They have been adapted in order to optimize success in human relationships.
- These defenses help to integrate conflicting emotions and thoughts.

Table 2.10: Description of pathological defenses with examples

Level 1 pathological defenses	Description	Examples
Conversion	The intrapsychic conflicts are exhibited outside as physical symptoms such as deafness, blindness, seizures, paralysis or numbness.	Student might get conversion fits, when the teacher punishes him.
Denial	Refusing to accept the external reality since it is extremely threatening.	Patient will not accept that he has been diagnosed with Human Immunodeficiency Virus (HIV) or Acquired Immunodeficiency Syndrome (AIDS) when the western blot test reveals the positive result.
Superiority complex	Having a greater feel of superiority with extraordinary talents and feel special with arrogant behavior which increases difficulties in work or relationship with others.	Mother may feel that "I am the only person with special talents and so the child has to obey my words" without giving any importance to the feelings of the child, which will enhance hatred in the child.
Inferiority complex	Individual will feel that he/she is having a lack of self-worth and not meeting up to the level of standards when compared to others.	Student who fails in a subject feels that, 'I am not capable to study and I am inferior to others'.

Table 2.11: Description of immature defenses with examples

Level 2 immature defenses	Description	Examples
Acting out	Direct the expression of an unconscious wish or impulse into action without the conscious awareness of emotion which drives into the expressive behavior.	Father beats his son because he feels so angry about the behavior of his son that he is not behaving as per the father's expectations.
Fantasy	Using fantasy in order to resolve inner conflicts.	An individual has a lot of issues in a job, takes his casual leave and thinks of his promotion or salary when he/she is employed in other organization.
Wishful thinking	Take decisions which are pleasing to imagine instead of giving importance to the reality.	Decision to enjoy in a park even when there is an important work in the office.
Idealization	Perceive the other individual with more positive qualities more than the actual potential.	Father perceives his daughter as too good even after her daughter's professor tells many complaints about her poor academic performance.
Passive aggression	Aggression expressed toward others either indirectly or passively	Teacher failed the student in the exam because the student did not join the tuition classes.
Projection	Conscious or unconscious way of blaming others for one's own mistake.	Student replies that I failed in the exam because the evaluator did not evaluate my answer script properly.
Somatization	Transformation of negative feeling toward oneself in terms of pain, illness and anxiety.	Boy saying that he was having severe pain in leg because he was emotionally upset.

Table 2.12: Description of neurotic defenses with examples

Level 3 neurotic defenses	Description	Examples
Displacement	Unconscious manner of letting the feelings toward the less threatening object	In a family, father scolds the mother for her mistake. Mother shows the anger to the child and in turn child beats the doll.
Dissociation	Modifying one's own identity in order to prevent psychological distress.	Adult forgets everything about his childhood sexual abuse.
Hypochondriasis	An excess preoccupation or concern about health	Even with insignificant symptoms, individual worries about his illness.
Intellectualization	Focus on the intellectual aspects so that one can prevent the anxiety-provoking emotions.	Person shows no emotional expression in a quarrel.

Contd...

Level 3 neurotic defenses	Description	Examples
Isolation	Separation of the feelings from ideas.	Be lonely when you dislike an individual.
Rationalization	Try to make excuses to convince self that he/she is not wrong.	A student came late to college, reasons out that he came late because his bike tyre got punctured.
Reaction formation	Converting the unconscious wishes or ideas or impulses which are perceived as dangerous or unacceptable by their opposites.	A jealous girl who hates her elder sister might show high level of respect and affection toward her.
Regression	Temporary state of the ego put into the earlier stage of development instead of handling the unacceptable impulses as an adult.	Adult cries like a child to get the things done from his parents.
Repression	Unconscious way of suppressing the negative feelings which is a threat	Forgetting the birthday of loved one after the fight.
Undoing	An individual tries to 'undo' destructive or unhealthy thoughts in reverse of the unacceptable.	Giving a gift to an individual with a dislike feeling toward him.
Withdrawal	Withdraw oneself from interactions or stimuli or events due to the threat of painful thoughts and feelings.	Student taking leave often because he feels that his teacher will scold him badly in front of other students.
Upward and downward social comparisons	Will compare oneself with other person to be low and find oneself comfortable with one's performance.	A student compares oneself with other student who secures less marks than him.

Table 2.13 describes mature defenses with examples.

Table 2.13: Description of mature defenses with examples

Level 4 mature defenses	Description	Examples
Patience	Being silent under difficult circumstances such as provocation, delay, criticism, quarrel, etc.	At the time of quarrel with his friend, Raja is being silent.
Acceptance	Person accepts the reality of a situation.	Driver accepts that the road traffic accident happened due to his carelessness.
Mindfulness	Orientation of one's experiences in present moment.	Mother making her daughter aware that the mistake has been committed.
Humility	Humility is intelligent self-respect given to oneself.	Raj gives importance and respect to one's own ideas or thoughts
Courage	Psychological willingness and ability to confirm the pain, danger, fear, conflicts, obstacles, despair, etc.	Boxer has physical courage to fight. A counselor has mental courage to give solutions to the problem.
Gratitude	Feeling of thankfulness or appreciation toward the person.	Patient says thanks to the nurse at the time of discharge for efficient care.
Altruism	Constructive social service to others which gives personal satisfaction.	Ram is helping the orphan children, which gives personal satisfaction to Ram.
Forgiveness	Being merciful and forgiving the mistake of others.	Mother forgives the mistake of children.
Anticipation	Plan in a realistic way for future discomfort.	A person who knows that he is going to lose his job, psychologically prepares for that incidence.
Emotional self-sufficiency	Not being emotionally dependent on the approval or disapproval of others.	Wife is not happy with an encouragement from her husband.
Humor	Channeling of unacceptable impulses or thoughts into a light-hearted story or joke.	Turns out the serious situation in a joyful way by cracking jokes.
Emotional self-regulation	Individual who modifies the intensity and duration of expressing the emotions.	A person who gets angry will move away from that particular place to divert oneself.

Contd...

Level 4 mature defenses	Description	Examples
Thought suppression	The conscious way of pushing out the negative thoughts or feelings.	A student writing the exam keeps on thinking about the quarrels with his friend. He puts off this incident from his mind so that he can write his exam well.
Sublimation	It refers to transformation of socially unacceptable impulses or thoughts into socially acceptable actions or behavior, resulting in a long-term conversion of the initial impulse.	A person who is getting aggressive thoughts will engage oneself in the sports actively.
Identification	Unconscious modeling of one's self toward another person's character and behavior.	Girl wants to become nurse because she got impressed with the care rendered by a nurse in the hospital.

BIOPSYCHOSOCIAL ETIOLOGY OF MENTAL ILLNESS

The causes of mental disorders vary from one another. Mental illnesses are caused by a combination of biological, psychological, environmental and social factors.

Biological Factors

- **Genetic factors:** Individuals having family history of mental illness are at a higher risk of developing psychiatric disorders. Mental illness occurs from the interaction of multiple genes and other factors such as stress, abuse or a traumatic event which can influence or trigger an illness in a person who is having inherited susceptibility. Chromosome 1 and 7 defects lead to substance abuse disorders. Chromosome 1, 9, 11, 13q defects might lead to panic disorder. Chromosome 14q defect might lead to specific phobia/social phobia/panic disorder. Chromosome 3q defect might lead to agoraphobia. Chromosome 16q defect might lead to social/simple phobia. Down's syndrome, Fragile X syndrome and Prader-Willi syndrome might contribute to mental retardation in children. Abnormality in chromosome 12 and 15 is seen in depression. The deletion of 30–40 genes in middle of chromosome 22 (DiGeorge Syndrome) might lead to schizophrenia.
- **Biochemical factors:** Abnormal functioning of nerve cell circuits or pathways that connect particular brain regions may lead to mental illness. The increased or decreased levels of neurotransmitters and their associated psychiatric disorders are listed in Table 2.14.
- **Structural damage to brain:** Defects or injuries to certain areas of the brain are linked to some mental illnesses. For example, organic psychosis may occur in people who meet with an accident and sustain brain injury. Rapid blood flow and metabolic activity seen in frontal lobe, cingulum and basal ganglia are seen in patients with obsessive compulsive disorder. Anatomical abnormalities of prefrontal cortex, basal ganglia and cerebellum are seen in patients with schizophrenia. Decreased metabolism of caudate nucleus is seen in eating disorders. Dysfunction in prefrontal cortex, frontal/temporoparietal cortex, fusiform cortex, subcortical region, basal ganglion, thalamus and lingual gyri (particularly with nondominant part of brain) is seen in organic brain disorders.
- **Infections:** Certain infections may cause brain damage and therefore, they develop mental illnesses or worsen the symptoms of mental illnesses. For example, a condition known as Pediatric Autoimmune Neuropsychiatric Disorders associated with Streptococcal Infections (PANDAS) leads to the development of obsessive-compulsive disorder and other mental illnesses in children.
- **Maternal factors:** Exposure to environmental stressors, inflammatory conditions, toxins, alcohol or drugs during prenatal period can lead to mental illness.
- **Prenatal damage:** Evidence suggests that a disruption of early fetal brain development or trauma at the time of birth or hypoxia at birth may be associated with the development of mental illnesses.
- **Hormonal factors:** Some endocrine disorders are closely associated with the development of mental illnesses. For example, depression in hypothyroidism. Imbalance in the growth hormone, prolactin, thyroid releasing hormone and oxytocin might lead to schizophrenia. Cortisol increases in stress-related disorders due to the stimulation of Hypothalamic-Pituitary-Adrenal (HPA) axis. Pineal gland secretes melatonin, which decreases in depressive disorders. Overactivity of HPA axis is seen in anxiety disorders.
- **Other factors:** Poor nutrition and exposure to toxins such as lead may play a role in the development of mental illnesses.

Table 2.14: Imbalanced levels of neurotransmitters and their association with psychiatric disorders

Psychiatric disorder	Neurotransmitters	
	Increased	Decreased
Schizophrenia	Dopamine, epinephrine and norepinephrine	Gamma-Amino Butyric Acid (GABA)
Mania	Dopamine, epinephrine and norepinephrine	–
Depression	Acetylcholine	Epinephrine, norepinephrine and histamine
Parkinson's disease	–	Dopamine
Anxiety disorder	Serotonin	Gamma-Amino Butyric Acid (GABA), epinephrine and norepinephrine
Aggression, suicide and impulsivity	–	Serotonin
Huntington's disease	Somatostatin	–
Alzheimer's disease	–	Somatostatin
Eating disorder and sleep disorder	Gamma-amino butyric acid (GABA)	–

Psychological Factors

Psychological factors that may contribute to mental illnesses include:

- Severe psychological trauma suffered during childhood period, such as emotional, physical or sexual abuse
- Death of a parent
- Neglect
- Poor coping ability

Environmental Factors

Certain stressors can trigger an illness in a person who is susceptible to mental illness. These stressors include:

- Divorce
- A dysfunctional family life
- Feelings of inadequacy, low self-esteem, anxiety, anger and loneliness
- Changing jobs or schools frequently
- Social or cultural expectations

Social Factors

- Adverse housing conditions
- War
- Experience of social discrimination and stigma
- Social deprivation

PSYCHOPATHOLOGY OF MENTAL DISORDERS: REVIEW OF STRUCTURE OF BRAIN, FUNCTIONS OF BRAIN, LIMBIC SYSTEM AND ABNORMAL NEUROTRANSMISSION

Mental disorders cannot be traced to specific physiological or psychological problems. These are complex syndromes consisting of biopsychosocial symptoms that cluster together. All human behaviors result from actions that originate in the brain and its interconnection of neural networks. Complex circuit of the brain interacts with the external environment, memories and experiences. Through the spinal column and peripheral nerves, along with the endocrine and immune systems, the brain constantly receives or processes information. Therefore, it is important for the nurse to understand basic nervous system and its functioning.

Central Nervous System

The central nervous system (CNS) is composed of the brain, the spinal cord and associated nerves that control voluntary acts.

Brain

Structurally, the brain is divided into:

Cerebrum

Cerebral hemispheres: Cerebrum is divided into right and left hemispheres. All lobes and structures are found in these halves except pineal gland.

- The pineal body is an endocrine gland which is located between the hemispheres.
- The corpus callosum is a pathway connecting the two hemispheres and coordinating their function.
- The left hemisphere controls the right side of the body. It is the center for logical reasoning and analytical functions such as reading, writing and mathematical tasks.
- The right hemisphere controls the left side of the body. It is the center for creative thinking, intuition and artistic abilities.

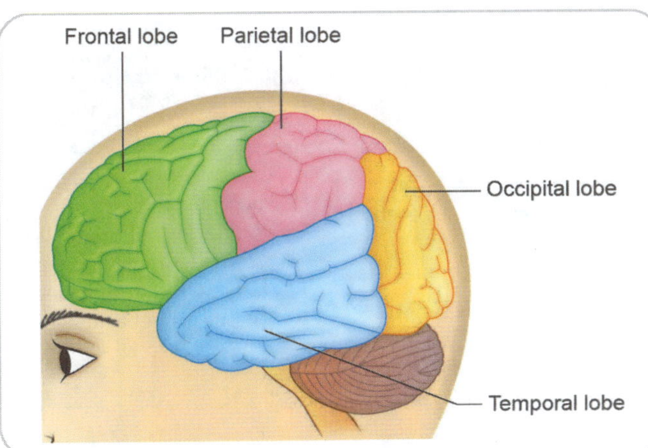

Figure 2.5: Lobes of brain

Lobes: *Each cerebral hemisphere is divided into four lobes (Fig. 2.5):*

1. Frontal lobe
2. Parietal lobe
3. Temporal lobe
4. Occipital lobe

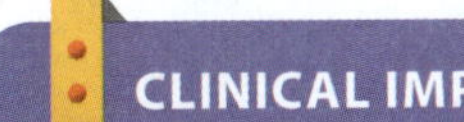

CLINICAL IMPLICATION

Frontal Lobe Syndrome

Damage to the dorsolateral (upper and outer) areas of the frontal lobes may cause symptoms such as lack of drive and spontaneity. Damage to the anterior aspects of frontal lobes might lead the changes in mood or affect, which in turn exhibits the impulsive and inappropriate behavior in patients.

Some functions of the lobes are distinct; others are integrated (Table 2.15).

Cerebellum

- Cerebellum is located below the cerebrum and is the center for coordination of movements and postural adjustments.
- It receives and integrates information from all areas of the body such as muscles, joints, organs and other components of the CNS.

CLINICAL IMPLICATION

Inhibited transmission of dopamine, a neurotransmitter, in this area is associated with the lack of smooth, coordinated movements in diseases such as Parkinson's and dementia.

Brain Stem

- Brain stem includes the midbrain, pons and medulla oblongata and the nuclei for cranial nerves III-XII (Table 2.16).

Extrapyramidal Motor System

It is a bundle of nerve fibers connecting the thalamus to the basal ganglia and cerebral cortex. Muscle tone, common reflexes and automatic voluntary motor functioning (e.g., walking) are controlled by this nerve tract.

Table 2.15: Lobes of brain, their functions and impact of abnormalities

Lobes	Functions	Associated abnormalities
Frontal lobes	Control the organization of thought, body movement, memories, emotions and moral behavior	Abnormalities in the frontal lobes are associated with schizophrenia, attention deficit hyperactivity disorder and dementia
Parietal lobes	• Parietal lobe plays an important role in integrating sensory information from various parts of the body, knowledge of numbers and the manipulation of objects • It is also involved in processing information related to the sense of touch • Portions of the parietal lobe are involved with visuospatial processing	• Lesions in the parietal lobe of the dominant hemisphere are associated with dyslexia, a group of disorders that involve difficulty in learning to read or interpret words, letters and other symbols. • Cognitive processes regulated by parietal lobe, such as perception, attention, memory, planning, motor control, mental calculation, language, self-awareness and emotion regulation, are impaired in schizophrenia • These cognitive functions may be impaired in schizophrenia due to the decreased volume of parietal lobe.
Temporal lobes	Center for smell, hearing, memory and emotional expression	Research results have shown that temporal lobe epilepsy is highly associated with psychiatric disorders such as anxiety disorder and depression
Occipital lobes	Assist in coordinating language generation and visual interpretation perception in-depth.	• There is evidence in the reduction of the overall occipital lobe volume in schizophrenic patients • Functional abnormalities, such as decreased activation of occipital lobe areas during episodic memory encoding, episodic memory recovery and emotion processing tasks, are found to be associated with schizophrenia

Table 2.16: Brain stem structures, location, functions and psychiatric implications

Brain stem structures	Location/description	Functions	Clinical implications
Medulla oblongata	Located at the top of the spinal cord	Contains vital centers to regulate respiration and cardiovascular functions	• The **locus coeruleus,** a small group of norepinephrine- • producing neurons in the brain stem, is associated with stress, anxiety and impulsive behavior
Pons	Above the medulla and in front of the cerebrum	• Bridges the gap between medulla and cerebrum both structurally and functionally • Serves as a primary motor pathway	
Midbrain	• Connects the pons and cerebellum with cerebrum (2 cm in length) • Includes most of the reticular activating system and the extrapyramidal system	• Reticular activating system influences motor activity, sleep, consciousness and awareness • The extrapyramidal system relays information about movement and coordination from the brain to the spinal nerves	

Extrapyramidal syndrome (EPS) is a group of side effects caused by the dopamine blockade effect of typical antipsychotic drugs. As the extrapyramidal tract is severely affected, it may produce involuntary motor movements.

Pineal Body

Pineal body is located above and medial to the thalamus. It contains secretory cells that emit the neurohormone melatonin and other substances. These hormones are thought to have a number of regulatory functions within the endocrine system. Information received from light-dark sources controls the release of melatonin, which has been associated with sleep and emotional disorders. A modulation of immune function has been postulated for melatonin from the pineal gland.

Limbic System

The limbic system is essential to understand many hypotheses related to psychiatric disorders and emotional behavior in general. It is a complex set of structures found on the central lower part of the cerebrum. It comprises inner sections of the temporal lobes and the bottom of the frontal lobe. It is called a "system" because it comprises several small structures that work in a highly organized way.

Basic emotions, needs, drives and instincts are modulated in the limbic system. Hate, love, anger, aggression and caring are basic emotions that originate within the limbic system. It combines higher mental functions and primitive emotions into a single system. It is often referred to as the 'emotional nervous system' or the 'emotional brain'. It is not only responsible for our emotional lives but also for our higher mental functions, such as learning and formation of memories.

Components of limbic system: Components of the limbic system are: (**Mnemonic - BATCH**)

- **B – Basal Ganglia**
- **A – Amygdala**
- **T – Thalamus and Hypothalamus**
- **C – Cingulate gyrus**
- **H – Hippocampus**

- **B-Basal ganglia:** The basal ganglia are a group of nuclei lying deep in the subcortical white matter of the frontal lobes that organize motor behavior. The **caudate, putamen** and **globus pallidus** are major components/parts of the basal ganglia (Fig. 2.6). The basal ganglia serve as a gating mechanism for physical movements, inhibiting potential movements until they are fully appropriate to the context.
  The basal ganglia are also involved in:
  - Rule-based habit learning (e.g., initiating, stopping, monitoring, temporal sequencing and maintaining appropriate movement).

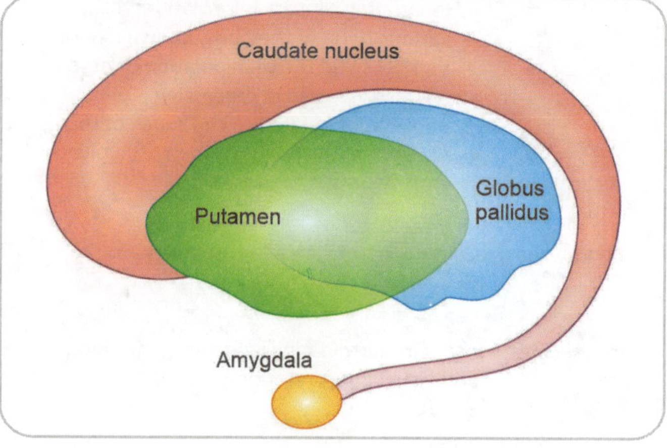

Figure 2.6: Parts of basal ganglia

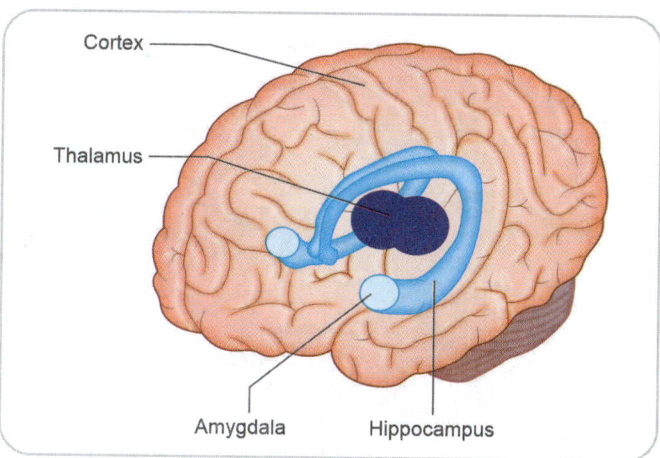

Figure 2.7: Placement of amygdala, thalamus and hippocampus in limbic system

- Inhibiting undesired movements and permitting desired ones.
- Choosing from potential actions.
- Motor planning.
- Sequencing
- Predictive control
- Working memory
- Attention

- **A-Amygdala:** The amygdala, also known as the emotional center of the brain, is a small almond-shaped structure, located in each of the left and right temporal lobes. It is involved in evaluating the emotional valence of situations (e.g., happy, sad, scary). It helps the brain to recognize potential threats and helps to prepare the body for fight-or-flight reactions by increasing the heart rate and respiration rate. The amygdala is also responsible for learning on the basis of reward or punishment. Since it is very close to the hippocampus (Fig. 2.7), the amygdala is involved in the modulation of memory consolidation, particularly the emotionally-laden memories.
- **T-Thalamus and hypothalamus:** Both the thalamus and hypothalamus are associated with changes in emotional reactivity. The hypothalamus is a small part of the brain located just below the thalamus on both sides of the third ventricle. Lesions of the hypothalamus interfere with several unconscious functions (such as respiration and metabolism) and some motivated behaviors like sexuality, combativeness and hunger. The lateral parts of the hypothalamus seem to be involved with pleasure and rage. The medial part is linked to aversion, displeasure and a tendency for uncontrollable and loud laughter.
- **C-Cingulate gyrus:** The cingulate gyrus is located in the medial side of the brain next to the corpus callosum. Its frontal part links smell and sight with pleasant memories of previous emotions. This region also participates in our emotional reaction to pain and in the regulation of aggressive behavior.
- **H-Hippocampus:** The hippocampus is found deep in the temporal lobe and is shaped like a sea horse. It consists of two horns curving back from the amygdala. It plays an essential role in the formation of new memories about past experiences. It is also responsible for general declarative memory (memories that can be explicitly verbalized, such as memory of facts and episodic memory).

CLINICAL IMPLICATION

Disturbances in the limbic system have been implicated in a variety of mental illnesses such as:

- Memory loss that accompanies dementia.
- Poorly controlled emotions and impulses seen with psychotic or manic disorder.

Damage to the hippocampus usually results in the difficulties of forming new memories (*anterograde amnesia*) and access to memories formed before the brain damage (*retrograde amnesia*).

Autonomic Nervous System

Autonomic nervous system (ANS) is a subdivision of the peripheral nervous system (PNS) and is closely associated with the spinal cord but not lying entirely within its column. This system contains efferent nerves (nerves moving away from the Central Nervous System) or motor system neurons which affect target tissues such as cardiac muscle, smooth muscle and the glands. It also contains afferent nerves which are sensory and conduct information from these organs back to the central nervous system.

Autonomic nervous system is further divided into the sympathetic and parasympathetic nervous systems. These systems are involved in the emergency "Fight-or-Flight" response as well as the peripheral actions of many medications.

Neurons and Nerve Impulses

Neurons or nerve cells are the fundamental units of the brain and nervous system (Fig. 2.8). These cells are responsible for receiving sensory input from the external world, and for sending motor commands to our muscles. They transform the electric signals from a neuron to other neuron.

- Each neuron has **a cell body or soma** which holds the nucleus, containing most of the cell's genetic information. The soma also includes other organelles such as ribosomes and endoplasmic reticulum which carry out

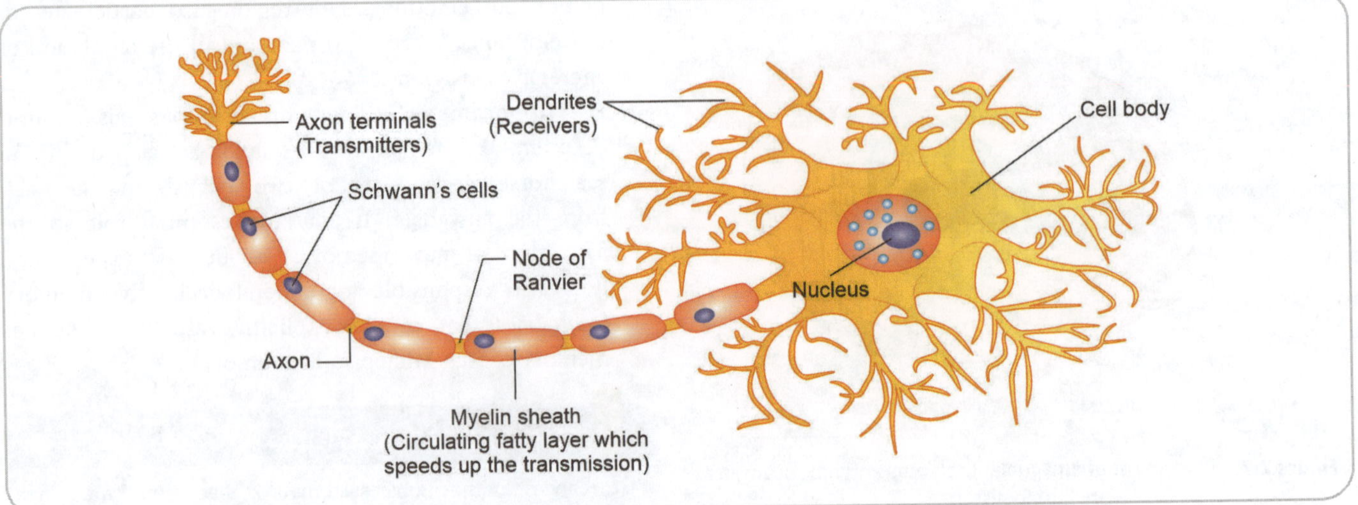

Figure 2.8: Parts of a neuron

protein synthesis, the Golgi apparatus which contains enzymes to modify the proteins for specific functions, vesicles which transport and store proteins or lysosomes that are responsible for degradation of these proteins. Mitochondria containing enzymes (cell's engine) are located throughout the neurons which provide the basis for secreting numerous chemicals by which the neurons communicate.

- Neurons have a structure called **axon** that varies in length and conducts impulses away from the soma and has numerous **dendrites** that receive signals from other neurons. Axons may branch as they terminate and have multiple contacts with other neurons.
- The cell's membrane is a double layer of phospholipid molecules with embedded proteins. Some of these proteins provide water-filled channels through which inorganic ions may pass. Each of the common ions such as sodium, potassium, calcium and chloride, has their own specific molecular channel. These channels are voltage gated and thus, opening or closing in response to the change in the electrical potential across the membrane takes place.

Action Potential

Nerve signals are prompted to fire by a variety of chemical or physical stimuli when the stimulation of action potential starts and electrical communication of the nerves takes place. Table 2.17 differentiates the events that occur during rest and with action potential of neurons.

> **Neuroplasticity**
> - Neuroplasticity is a continuous process of modulation in neuron structure and function due to the response of changing environment.
> - It contributes to understanding that how the brain function may be restored over time after brain damage.

Neurotransmission (Synaptic Transmission)

Neurotransmission is the fundamental process that transfers information between neurons. It is essential for the process of communication between two neurons. It occurs at specialized regions between neurons called the synapse. The synapse is a highly specialized contact between a presynaptic and a postsynaptic neuronal cell.

Table 2.17: Differences between events that occur during rest and with action potential of neurons

Neurons at rest	Neurons with action potential
Membrane is polarized	Membrane is depolarized
Outside of the cell is positively charged	Outside the cell is negatively charged
270-mV charge is present inside the cell	Inside the cell is positively charged
Passive diffusion of potassium across the membrane	Voltage-gated sodium channels open
Sodium pump uses energy to move sodium from inside the cell against a concentration gradient	Sodium moves into the cell and this action potential begins

It is the process by which signaling molecules (neurotransmitters) has been released by axon terminal of the neuron (presynaptic neuron) will bind and activates the receptors of the dendrites in the another neuron.

Factors Determining Neurotransmission

- Availability of neurotransmitter.
- Release of neurotransmitter by exocytosis.
  (Exocytosis is a form of active transport and bulk transport in which a cell transports molecules, such as neurotransmitters or proteins, out of the cell by secreting them through an energy-dependent process).
- Binding of the postsynaptic receptor by the neurotransmitter.
- Functional response of the postsynaptic cell.
- Subsequent removal or deactivation of the neurotransmitter.

Steps in Neurotransmission

The following are the steps of neurotransmission (Fig. 2.9):

Step 1: Neurotransmitter Synthesis

There are two types of neurotransmitters:

1. Large neuropeptides.
2. Smaller amines/amino acids.

Large peptides are synthesized in the cell body of the neuron and are transported to the synaptic terminal through the axon. The smaller amines/amino acids can be synthesized at the presynaptic terminal itself.

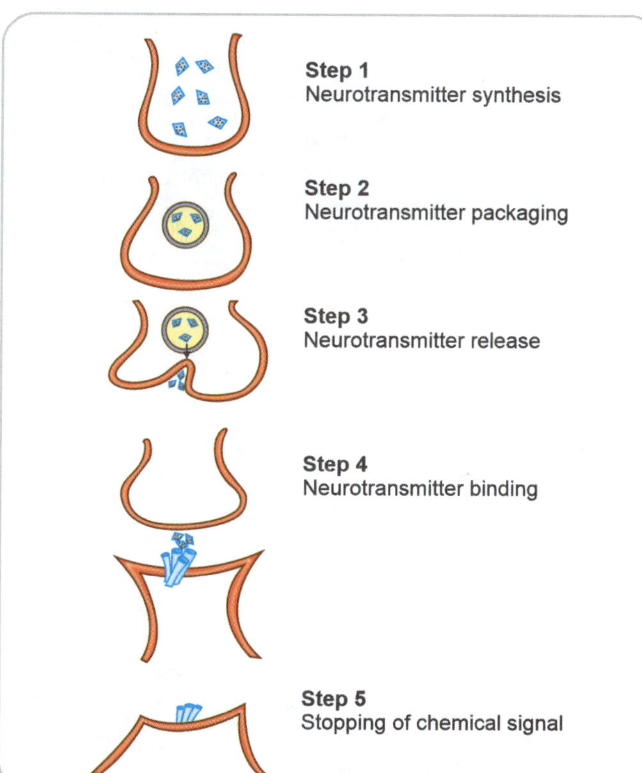

Figure 2.9: Steps in neurotransmission process

Step 2: Neurotransmitter Packaging

This is the process by which the synthesized neurotransmitters are packaged into "small groups" or "vesicles" that are ready for transmission across the synaptic cleft.

Step 3: Neurotransmitter Release

- Paced neurotransmitters are released in the synaptic cleft when they receive an order from Ca^{2+} ions.
- When the electrical signal reaches the presynaptic terminal, it opens some voltage gated Ca^{2+} channels in the membrane.
- Once these channels are open, calcium ions from the surrounding extracellular environment rush into the presynaptic terminal.
- As the calcium ions encounter the vesicles, the membrane of the vesicles fuses with the membrane of the presynaptic terminal at the synaptic cleft.
- As the vesicles fuse with the membrane, the neurotransmitters are "expelled" into the synaptic cleft.

Step 4: Neurotransmitter Binding

- The neurotransmitters diffuse through the synaptic cleft, until they reach the postsynaptic neuron.
- The membrane of the postsynaptic neuron contains a few channels (receptors) which control neurotransmitters in synapse to bind with the postsynaptic neuron.

Step 5: Stopping of Chemical Signal

- Once the chemical signal has been translated into an electrical signal, the postsynaptic receptors need to be cleared very quickly for two purposes.
  - To receive new neurotransmitters from new signals.
  - To prevent the traffic of neurotransmitters.
- **Fate of neurotransmitters after the clearance of postsynaptic receptors**
  - Recycled back to the presynaptic terminal.
  - Degraded.
  - Absorbed by postsynaptic terminal.

Classification of neurotransmitters is given in Flowchart 2.2. Neurotransmitters and their functions have been described in Table 2.18.

PRINCIPLES OF PSYCHIATRIC NURSING

Principles of psychiatric nursing are formulated based on the concept that every individual has an intrinsic worth or dignity, potential and capabilities. Principles form the guidelines which will help the client to meet his/her emotional needs and also bring the desirable changes in his/her behavior. The following are the principles of psychiatric nursing:

- Accept the client exactly as he or she is:
  - Acceptance conveys the feeling of being loved and cared for.

Flowchart 2.2: Classification of neurotransmitters

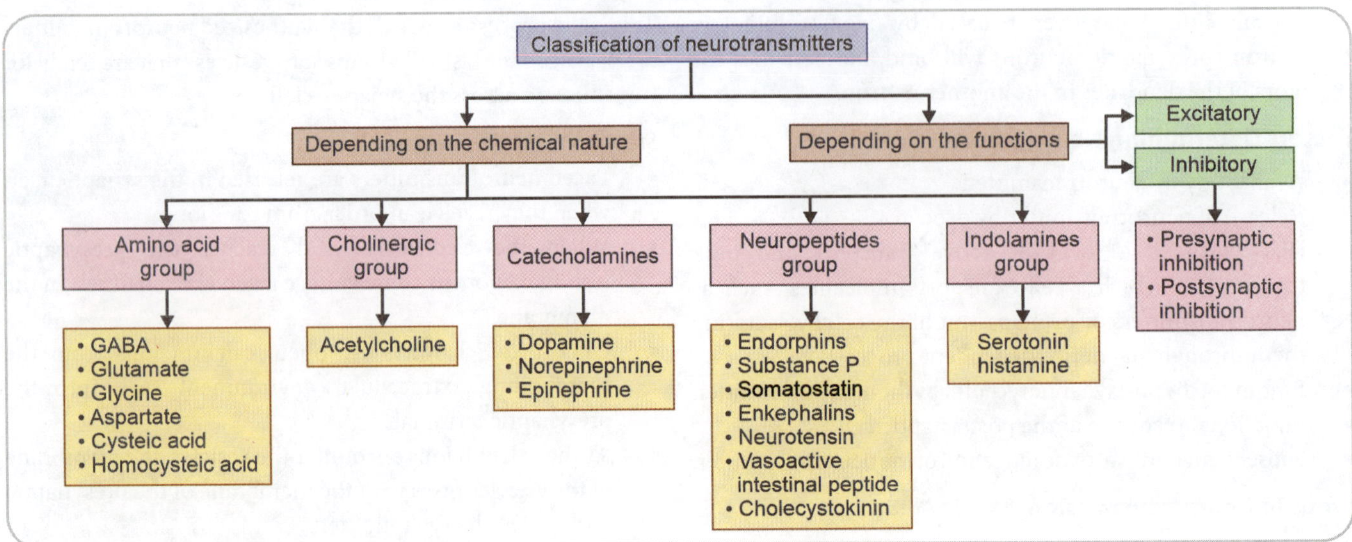

Abbreviation: GABA, gamma aminobutyric acid

Table 2.18: Neurotransmitters and their functions

Neurotransmitter	Function	Clinical implications (or) abnormal neurotransmission
Biogenic amines: Catecholamines		
Dopamine	Involved in pleasurable feelings and complex motor activities	• Increased—Schizophrenia and mania • Decreased—Depression and Parkinson's disease
Norepinephrine	Regulates awareness of environment, attention, learning, memory and arousal	• Increased—Schizophrenia and mania • Decreased—Anxiety, depression and sleep disorders
Epinephrine	Contributes to the "fight-or-flight" response	
Biogenic amines: Indolamines		
Serotonin	Contributes to temperature regulation	• Increased—Anxiety disorders (fearfulness, avoidance) • Decreased—Depression, aggression, suicidal ideations and impulsivity
Histamine	Involved in allergic responses, gastric acid secretion, arousal, suppression of eating, control of pituitary hormone secretion and cognitive function	• Weight gain associated with psychotropic meditations • Decreased level—Depression
Biogenic amines: Cholinergics		
Acetylcholine	Mediates cognitive functioning directly or by modulating another neurotransmitter indirectly; contributes to sleep-wake cycles	• Increased—Depression • Decreased—Alzheimer's disease
Neuropeptides group		
Neuropeptides: Endorphins and enkephalins, somatostatin, neurotensin, vasoactive intestinal peptide, cholecystokinin and substance P	Play a secondary messenger role and contribute to modulating the pain response	Somatostatin increases in Huntington's disease and decreases in Alzheimer's disease. Deficit of endorphins leads to increased pain perception by the body
Amino acids		
Excitatory: Aspartic acid, glutamic acid, cysteic acid and homocysteic acid	Sparse information available; high levels can be toxic	Disturbances in excitatory amino acids might cause schizophrenia, delirium or dementia
Inhibitory: Gamma-amino butyric acid (GABA)	Slows down body activity	• Decreased—Schizophrenia, some forms of epilepsy and anxiety disorders • Increased—Sleep and eating disorders

Flowchart 2.3: Punitive methods to be avoided

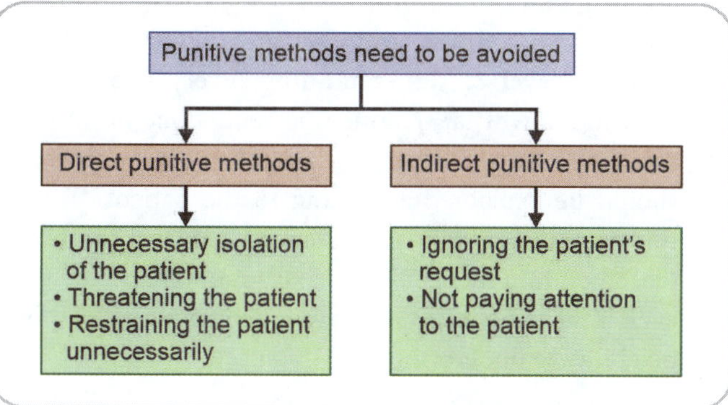

- Acceptance conveys to the client that he/she is respected as an individual.
- Being accepted by nurses will lower the anxiety among clients.
- Nurses should not judge clients by their appearance, behaviors or socioeconomic background.

  Acceptance is expressed in the following ways:
  - **Being nonjudgmental and nonpunitive:** The client's behavior should not be judged as right or wrong. Client should not be punished for his/her undesirable behavior. All direct and indirect methods of punishment must be avoided (Flowchart 2.3).
  - **Being sincerely interested in the patient:** This can be demonstrated by:
    - Observing the patient's behavior pattern
    - Involving the patient in decision-making process
    - Identifying his/her likes and dislikes
    - Being honest with him/her
    - Sparing time to listen to the patient's words
    - Handling sensitive issues judiciously
  - **Recognizing and reflecting the feelings which patient may express:** The nurse should not only focus on the content of conversation but also recognize and reflect the feelings associated with the patient's communication.
  - **Talking with a purpose:** The nurse must use the therapeutic communication techniques when she interacts with the patient. Nurse must be conscientious not to use nontherapeutic communication techniques.
  - **Listening:** Listening is an active process. The nurse should spend reasonable time to listen what the patient is saying. Nurse has to be a sympathetic listener. He/she needs to show genuine interest in conversation. Listening conveys acceptance to the patient.
  - **Permitting patient to express strongly-held feelings:** Emotionally painful and suppressed emotions are bound to the psychopathology. The purpose of therapeutic alliance is to facilitate the discharge of these emotions. The nurse must encourage and accept the expression of patient's strong negative feelings in a more comfortable way.
  - Bottled up emotions might damage the personality of the individual. Therefore, sharing sadness will reduce it to half.

- **Use self-understanding as a therapeutic tool:** A psychiatric nurse should have a realistic self-concept and should be able to recognize one's own feelings, attitudes and responses. If the nurse is able to understand one's own strengths or limitations, then only the nurse can understand the patient's strengths, limitations, needs and problems.
- **Use consistent behavior to contribute to the patient's security:** Consistency in nurses' approach is necessary to develop a trusting relationship between the nurse and patient. Nurses' consistency must reflect in their attitude, ward routines or by defining limitations in the patient's behavior.
- **Give reassurance in an acceptable and subtle manner:** Nurse has to provide psychological support to the patient. The right and appropriate psychological support is termed 'reassurance'. Nurse should not give a false hope to the patient or caregivers. The manner of providing false hope is termed 'false assurance'.

  Example: Patient who has been recently diagnosed with HIV/AIDS and depressive disorder has to be reassured that taking antiretroviral drugs will help in enhancing the life span to a great extent. He/she should not be given false assurance that antiretroviral drugs will completely cure HIV/AIDS.
- **Change the client's behavior by emotional experience rather than rational interpretation:** Major focus in psychiatry is on feelings and not on the intellectual aspect. Advising or rationalizing with patients is not effective in changing behavior. Role play, sociodrama and transactional analysis are few ways of creating emotional experience in a patient about one's own behavior.

  Example: The behavior of a patient with alcohol dependence syndrome can be modified with psychodrama because it might touch the patient emotionally and exhibit the behavior change, instead providing the health teaching by saying that it is waste of time, because patient knows all the complications of alcoholism before the health teaching itself.
- **Avoid unnecessary increase in patient's anxiety:** Anxiety is a feeling of apprehension. It is also a threat to biological integrity or self-system (ego) of the person.

Psychiatric patients already have some amount of anxiety due to their illness, disapproval and seclusion from the family. Psychiatric nurses must not further increase anxiety of the patients by:

- Exhibiting one's own anxiety
- Showing attention to the patient's deficits
- Contradicting his psychotic thoughts
- Demanding the patients to complete difficult tasks
- Making the patient face repeated failures
- Passing sharp comments and showing indifference

- **Use objective observation to understand patient's behavior:** Objectivity is an ability to evaluate exactly what the patient wants to say and not mix up one's own feelings, opinion or judgment. To be objective, the nurse should indulge in introspection and make sure that her own emotional needs do not take precedence over patient's needs. The nurse may lack objectivity in the following situations:
  - Nurse is criticizing the patient
  - Defending or justifying himself/herself
  - Demanding that the patient should treat him/her in certain ways
  - Judging the patient's behavior right or wrong
- **Maintain a realistic nurse-patient relationship:** Realistic nurse-patient relationship is a planned, goal-oriented relationship which is based on patient's needs. It focuses upon the personal and emotional needs of the patients and not on nurse's needs. It is an interpersonal process aimed at bringing adaptation, integration and emotional maturity in patient. To maintain such professional relationship, the nurse should be able to empathize and understand the feelings of the patient.
- **Avoid physical and verbal forces as much as possible:** Any kind of force applied on the patient results in psychological trauma. Under some circumstances, it may be inevitable. But it must be used judiciously. If a nurse is an expert in predicting patient's behavior, she can mostly prevent an onset of undesirable behavior. Restraining should never be used as measure of reducing nurses' duty.
  Example: Mr Raj, a psychiatric patient, who has been scolded by the nurse is an example of verbal force. Nurse beats Mr Raj and restrains him is an example of physical force. Both should not be done as per the principles of psychiatric nursing.
- **Focus nursing care on the patient as a person rather than controlling symptoms:** Two patients having similar symptoms may be expressing two different needs. Analysis and study of symptoms are necessary to reveal their meaning and significance to the patient. Nursing care should focus on the patient as a person and not on the symptoms.
- **Explain procedures and routines according to the patient's level of understanding:** Every patient has a right to know what treatment is being done for him and the reason for performing the treatment. Every procedure should be explained according to the patient's level of understanding. This may depend on the limitations placed on him by his illness. Explanation has to be given even if the patients do not have touch with reality or have no ability to understand.
- **Many procedures are modified but basic principles remain unchanged:** In the field of psychiatric nursing, many methods are adapted according to individual needs of the patients, but the underlying scientific principles remain the same. Basic nursing principles are as follows:
  - Safety
  - Comfort
  - Privacy
  - Therapeutic effectiveness
  - Economy in the utilization of resources to be followed in all procedures

STANDARDS OF PSYCHIATRIC NURSING

In 1973, the American Nurses Association (ANA) issued standards to improve the quality of care provided by psychiatric and mental health nurses. These standards were revised in 1994, which are now applicable to generalists and specialists working in any setting, where the psychiatric and mental health nursing is being practiced. These are discussed under the following three are as follows:

1. Standards of Care
2. Standards of Professional Performance
3. Indian Nursing Council Standards in Mental Health Nursing

Standards of Care

Standards of care pertain to professional nursing activities that are demonstrated by the nurse through the nursing process. These include:

- **Standard I: Assessment**—The mental health nurse collects the patient's health data.
- **Standard II: Diagnosis**—The mental health nurse analyzes the assessment data for determining the diagnosis.
- **Standard III: Outcome identification**—The mental health nurse identifies the expected outcomes which are specific to every patient.

- **Standard IV: Planning**—The mental health nurse develops a plan of care that prescribes interventions.
- **Standard V: Implementation**—The psychiatric and mental health nurse implements the interventions identified in the plan of care.
  - **Standard Va: Counseling**—The mental health nurse uses counseling interventions to assist patients in improving or regaining their previous coping abilities, fostering mental health, preventing mental illnesses and disabilities.
  - **Standard Vb: Milieu therapy**—The mental health nurse provides, structures, maintains a therapeutic environment in collaboration with the patient and other health care providers.
  - **Standard Vc: Self-care activities**—The mental health nurse structures interventions around the patient's activities of daily living to foster self-care, mental and physical well-being.
  - **Standard Vd: Psychobiological interventions**—The mental health nurse uses knowledge of psychobiological interventions, applies clinical skills to restore the patient's health and prevents further disability.
  - **Standard Ve: Health teaching**—The mental health nurse, through health teaching, assists patients in achieving satisfying, productive and healthy patterns of living.
  - **Standard Vf: Case management**—The mental health nurse provides case management to coordinate comprehensive health services and ensure continuity of care.
  - **Standard Vg: Health promotion and health maintenance**—The mental health nurse employs strategies and interventions to promote and maintain mental health and prevent mental illnesses.
  - **Standard Vh: Psychotherapy**—The mental health nurse uses individual, group and family psychotherapy, child psychotherapy and other therapeutic treatments to assist patients in fostering mental health, preventing mental illnesses or disabilities, improving or regaining previous health status and functional abilities.
  - **Standard Vi: Prescription of pharmacological agents**—The mental health nurse uses prescription of pharmacologic agents in accordance with the State Nursing Practice Act to treat symptoms of psychiatric illnesses and improve functional health status.
  - **Standard Vj: Consultation**—The mental health nurse provides consultation to health care providers and others to influence the plan of care for patients and to enhance the abilities of others to provide psychiatric and mental health care and effect change in systems.
- **Standard VI: Evaluation**—The mental health nurse evaluates the patient's progress in attaining expected outcomes.

Standards of Professional Performance

Standards of professional performance describe a competent level of behavior in a professional role. These include:

- **Standard I: Quality of care**—The mental health nurse systematically evaluates the quality of care and effectiveness of mental health practice.
- **Standard II: Performance appraisal**—The mental health nurse evaluates his/her own practice in relation to professional practice standards, its relevant statutes and regulations.
- **Standard III: Education**—The mental health nurse acquires and maintains current knowledge in nursing practice.
- **Standard IV: Collegiality**—The mental health nurse contributes to the professional development of peers, colleagues and others.
- **Standard V: Ethics**—The mental health nurse's decisions and actions on behalf of patients are determined in an ethical manner.
- **Standard VI: Collaboration**—The mental health nurse collaborates with the patient, his/her significant others and health care providers in providing care.
- **Standard VII: Research**—The mental health nurse contributes to nursing and mental health through the use of research.
- **Standard VIII: Resource utilization**—The mental health nurse considers factors related to safety, effectiveness, cost in planning and delivering patient care.

Indian Nursing Council Standards in Mental Health Nursing

- The Practice Standards for Psychiatric Mental Health Nursing were launched in 2019.
- Standards were launched in order to create the scope in terms of nursing practice, nursing education, nursing administration, evidence-based practice or research and other standards of professional performance.
- Standards include:
  - 14 major standards
  - 18 substandards
  - 143 measurement criteria
- Description of Indian Nursing Council Standards and Sub-standards in Mental Health Nursing with their measurement criteria is shown in Table 2.19.

Table 2.19: Indian Nursing Council Standards in mental health nursing, its description, sub-standards and measurement criteria

Indian Nursing Council Standards in mental health nursing	Description and Sub-standards	Measurement criteria
Standards of Practice		
Standard 1: Assessment	Mental health nurse has to perform comprehensive assessment for the health care consumers to take appropriate health care decisions	• Level of knowledge the mental health nurse possesses about the etiology, symptoms, diagnostic criteria of mental illnesses and substance dependence • Skills to maintain rapport in order to obtain the data from patient and family members • Systematic and accuracy in performing history collection, physical examination and mental status examination
Standard 2: Nursing diagnosis	Mental health nurse has to frame the appropriate nursing diagnosis	• Skills to frame the nursing diagnosis on the basis of subjective and objective data • Skill to interpret the various diagnostic tests • Modify the diagnosis on the basis of ongoing assessment
Standard 3: Expected outcomes of care	Mental health nurse has to identify the realistic goals with the existing situation	• Skills to explore realistic goals within the stipulated time frame • Involve the health care consumers and their family members while setting the goal • Modify the goal on the basis of ongoing assessment, if required
Standard 4: Planning	Mental health nurse has to plan the nursing care as per the framed goals	• Develop the individualized care plan with the health care consumers and their family members • Coordinate the plan with other health team members • Ensure the plan is in congruence with the organizational policies • Ensure the continuity of care and follow-up while planning out the interventions • Review and modify the plan, if required
Standard 5: Implementation (mental health nurse needs to implement the planned nursing care for the health care consumers)	Standard 5a: Nursing care delivery to health care consumers	• Provide holistic care • Manage the emergencies effectively • Implement the plan well with the use of current evidence-based practices • Coordinate with other health team members to implement effectively • Consider the developmental stages (children/old age) in implementation • Utilize all the available resources well • Document the interventions clearly and timely
	Standard 5b: Assistance in the delivery of biological therapies	• Administer the psychotropic agents on the basis of therapeutic response and alert the adverse effects timely to take necessary action for the same • Have competent assistance in electroconvulsive therapy before, during and after delivering it • Have competent assistance in transcranial magnetic stimulation and stereotactic techniques for intractable psychiatric disorders • Document the implemented biological therapies
	Standard 5c: Psychotherapeutic interventions	• Organizes and coordinates various psychotherapeutic interventions such as cognitive behavior therapy, family therapy, recreation therapy, social skills training, vocational training, etc. • Active involvement with the family members to implement psychotherapeutic interventions effectively • Clearly document the delivered psychotherapeutic interventions and their therapeutic response
	Standard 5d: Safe and therapeutic environment	• Orient the health care consumers about the structured schedule of the hospital • Orient the family members of health care consumers with regard to their rights and responsibilities • Skills to follow the patient safety protocols • Document if any untoward events happens and along with the steps taken to minimize the same

Contd...

Indian Nursing Council Standards in mental health nursing	Description and Sub-standards	Measurement criteria
	Standard 5e: Health education	• Health teaching with regard to the promotion of mental health, prevention of mental illnesses and rehabilitation of patients with mental illnesses • Skills to use appropriate audio-visual aids • Provide the information, education and communication (IEC) material to the health care consumers • Document the health education provided
	Standard 5f: Community mental health nursing services, including reintegration of health care consumers into the community	• Assessment of community with the use of key informant reports, community surveys and qualitative techniques • Provide psychotherapeutic interventions and psychoeducation to the individuals and family • Provide effective rehabilitation measures in home setting • Perform regular follow-up as per the organizational policy • Participation in the community mental health outreach programs • Early identification of risk factors of mental illnesses • Utilize the locally available community resources • Create public awareness to alleviate stigma of mental illness • Document the services rendered in community
Standard 6: Evaluation	Mental health nurse evaluates the extent to which the goal has been achieved	• Conduct systematic and ongoing clinical evaluation • Modify the nursing diagnosis and goal on the basis of ongoing assessment • Document the results of evaluation
Standards of Education		
Standard 7: Academic excellence (mental health nurse needs to equip oneself with the required knowledge and skills to render quality nursing care to the health care consumers)	Standard 7a: Personal academic development	• Actively participate in the staff development programs such as conferences, workshops, seminars, etc. • Actively participate in the interprofessional educational activities • Strive for higher qualification for the progress of career development • Have commitment with lifelong learning
	Standard 7b: Capacity Building	• Mentor the subordinates effectively • Encourage the subordinates for higher education • Organize the in-service education programs
Standards of Administration		
Standard 8: Administrative efficiency	Standard 8a: Personal vision, commitment, technical expertise	• Have clear vision on goals and implement the same • Demonstrate scientific and technical expertise on the basis of current trends
	Standard 8b: Team building	• Promote a healthy work environment with mutual trust and respect • Be loyal and maintain integrity as team leader • Have effective interprofessional collaboration to promote high quality care
	Standard 8c: Quality assurance	• Ensure the delivery of high-quality care to the patients • Conduct and participate in the quality assurance programs • Use the resources such as technology, education and research to provide high-quality care • Effectively work with interprofessional team members to ensure quality • Document the quality care rendered timely
	Standard 8d: Continuing nursing education	• Actively participate in the staff development programs such as conferences, workshops, seminars, etc. • Support the career advancement of subordinates
	Standard 8e: Leadership	• Be resourceful, courageous while dealing with problematic situations • Find innovative solutions to the problems • Implement the right health care policy to promote mental health • Perform key roles in administrative teams • Revise the institutional policies or protocols to ensure quality

Contd...

Indian Nursing Council Standards in mental health nursing	Description and Sub-standards	Measurement criteria
	Standard 8f: Performance appraisal	• Actively participate in the performance appraisal of subordinates • Support the subordinates to enhance their work performance • Take decision with regard to the promotions, incentives, training, disciplinary measures of the subordinates
	Standard 8g: Organizational and professional advancement	• Actively participate in the national and international professional organizations • Support the superiors to promote the welfare of health care consumers
Standards of evidence-based practice and research		
Standard 9: Responsible and ethical conduct of research and integration into practice	Standard 9a: Research ethics	• Gather accurate research data to disseminate the research findings • Report unethical research practices to the appropriate authorities
	Standard 9b: Integration of research into practice	• Actively participate in research activities • Develop knowledge with regard to the current and best research evidence • Make the work environment full of motivation to support the implementation of best evidences into practice • Disseminate the research findings through publication in indexed journals and through scientific presentation in conferences
	Standard 9c: Teaching scientific rigor to young nurse investigators	• Teach the subordinates about the importance of doing the research • Guide the subordinates to perform the research activity
Other standards of professional performance		
Standard 10: Self-care and Self-awareness	Mental health nurse has to know about oneself and care about self	• Having strong insight about the strengths and weaknesses • Use self-evaluation and peer evaluation to improve work performance
Standard 11: Ethics	Mental health nurse has to follow right ethical practices in nursing care	• Adhere to the professional code of conduct • Protect the rights of health care consumers • Maintain the confidentiality of the patient information • Report the unethical practices timely
Standard 12: Communication	Mental health nurse has to communicate effectively to the health care consumers, their family and the health team members	• Use active listening skills • Build rapport with the health care consumers, their family and the health team members • Convey right information to the health care consumers in both oral and written form to ensure the clarity in message.
Standard 13: Culturally sensitive care	Mental health nurse has to render nursing care by considering the cultural values of health care consumers	• Understand the cultural background of health care consumers • Be empathetic to health care consumers from diverse cultures • Provide culturally sensitive care effectively
Standard 14: Legally safe practice	Mental health nurse has to render nursing care as per the legal system	• Good knowledge with regard to mental health policies and legislation • Utilize the knowledge well to protect the rights of health care consumers • Has to perform all tasks within the scope of practice • Keep records complete, clear and up to date

A. Standards of Practice

- Standard 1: Assessment
- Standard 2: Nursing diagnosis
- Standard 3: Expected outcomes of care
- Standard 4: Planning
- Standard 5: Implementation
  - Standard 5a: Nursing care delivery to health care consumers
  - Standard 5b: Assistance in the delivery of biological therapies
  - Standard 5c: Psychotherapeutic interventions
  - Standard 5d: Safe and therapeutic environment
  - Standard 5e: Health education
  - Standard 5f: Community mental health nursing services, including reintegration of health care consumers into the community
- Standard 6: Evaluation

B. Standards of Education

- Standard 7: Academic excellence
  - Standard 7a: Personal academic development
  - Standard 7b: Capacity building

C. Standards of Administration

- Standard 8: Administrative efficiency
  - Standard 8a: Personal vision, commitment, technical expertise
  - Standard 8b: Team building
  - Standard 8c: Quality assurance
  - Standard 8d: Continuing nursing education
  - Standard 8e: Leadership
  - Standard 8f: Performance appraisal
  - Standard 8g: Organizational and professional advancement

D. Standards of Evidence-Based Practice and Research

- Standard 9: Responsible and ethical conduct of research and integration into practice
  - Standard 9a: Research ethics
  - Standard 9b: Integration of research into practice
  - Standard 9c: Teaching scientific rigor to young nurse investigators

E. Other Standards of Professional Performance

- Standard 10: Self-care and self-awareness
- Standard 11: Ethics
- Standard 12: Communication
- Standard 13: Culturally sensitive care
- Standard 14: Legally safe practice

CONCEPTUAL MODELS IN PSYCHIATRIC NURSING

Theories and models in the field of psychiatry are used by mental health professionals to determine the basis of behaviors and to plan necessary initiations. Many psychosocial theories have been developed based on theorists' personal experiences. Therefore, it is appropriate to refer to these as models rather than theories.

A model is a conceptual system that describes and explains the relationship between the cause (factors contributing to illness or etiology) and effect (occurrence of illness). In this way, a conceptual model serves as a tool to guide and shape human behavior. When models are applied to real nursing events, they serve to guide the understanding and behavior of nurses.

Existential Model/Theory

Existential theory is a branch of philosophy that deals with what it identified as existential questions. These are questions about the meaning of life such as "why do human exists?", "how do human exists?", "what do I value?", "who am I?" and "how can I contribute to my world?".

Assumptions of Existential Model

Existential psychology assumes that human beings strive to live a meaningful life. The following are the specific assumptions (Fig. 2.10) based on which the theory is conceptualized:

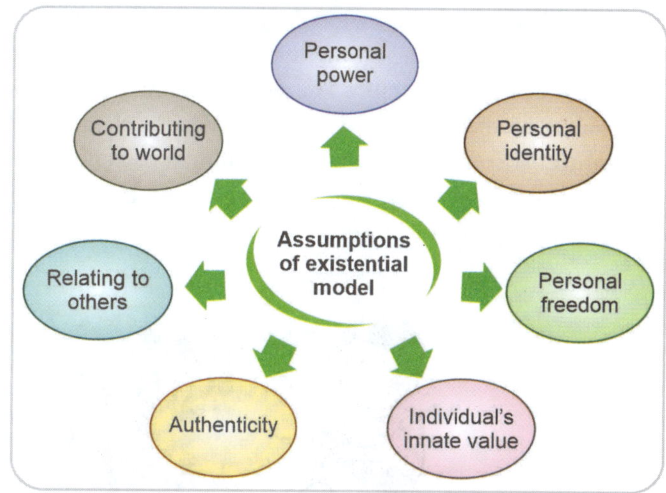

Figure 2.10: Assumptions of existential model

- **Personal power:** Existential theory believes in the power of individuals to choose their actions.
- **Personal identity:** When an individual knows what he/she is as a human, he/she can understand in a better way what is right and wrong for him/her. Through introspection and talking with others, he can consider what unique things make him/her an individual.
- **Personal freedom:** Existential theory believes in the personal freedom of individuals to make their own choices. It also recognizes the difficulty of making important life choices.
- **Individuals' innate value:** Existential model believes in individual's abilities to choose or make choices which are found crucial to live a meaningful life.
- **Authenticity:** Being authentic helps an individual to live in meaningful ways.
- **Relating to others:** Relating to others is an essential part of a human life.
- **Contributing to world:** One way of exploring the meaning of one's life is by contributing to the society.

Basic Dimensions of Human Existence

There are four basic dimensions of human existence: physical, social, psychological and spiritual (Fig. 2.11). These are interwoven and provide a complex four-dimensional force field for people's existence. Individuals are stretched between a positive pole of what they aspire on each dimension and a negative pole of what they fear.

- **On the physical dimension:** Individuals relate to their environment and the natural world around them. This includes their attitude toward the body, to the concrete surroundings they find themselves in, to the climate or weather, to objects or material possessions, to the bodies of other people, their own bodily needs, to health or illness and their mortality. The struggle on this dimension is between the search for domination over the elements of nature. There is a need to accept the limitations of natural boundaries by recognizing the limitations in order to deliver a significant release of tension.
- **On the social dimension:** Individuals relate to others as they interact with the public around them. This dimension includes their response to the culture as well as to the class and race they belong to. The struggle is between acceptance versus rejection and belonging versus isolation.
- **On the psychological dimension:** Individuals relate to themselves to create a personal world. This dimension includes views about their character, their past experience and their future possibilities. Contradictions are often experienced regarding personal strengths and weaknesses. Activity and passivity are important polarities in this dimension.
- **On the spiritual dimension:** Individuals relate to the ideal world, an ideology and a philosophical outlook. They find meaning by putting all the pieces of the puzzle together for themselves. The contradictions are often between purpose and absurdity, hope and despair.

Existential Therapy

Existential psychotherapy is a form of psychotherapy that contains elements of philosophies, phenomenology and existentialism.

- Within existential therapy, clinicians work with their clients to help them accept responsibility for their lives.
- Existential therapy deals with people with a restricted existence, i.e., they have a limited awareness of themselves and the nature of their problems. They often see few options available to them and feel helpless or trapped.
- The goal of existential therapy is to understand the subjective world of clients and help them come to new understanding and new options.
- This therapy can be applied to a variety of settings such as individual therapy, group therapy, family or couples therapy and community outreach areas.
- The client is the central focus of the therapy and is given respect, freedom of choice and responsibility for his/her actions.

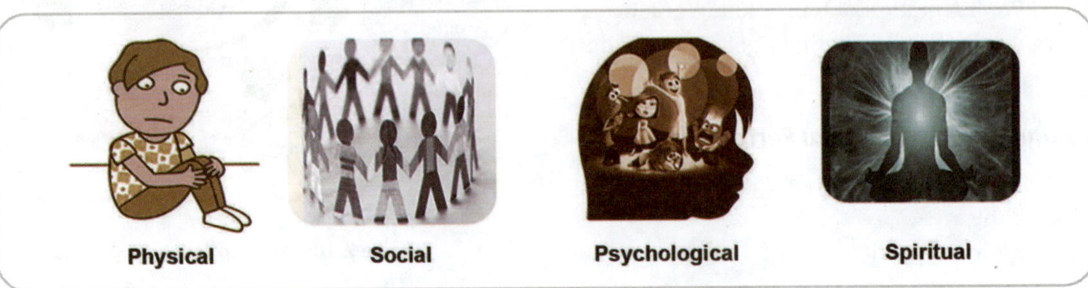

Figure 2.11: Basic dimensions of human existence

- The limitation of this therapy is lack of a defined and systematic approach.

Other Therapies based on Existential Theory

- **Rational-emotive therapy (Albert Ellis):** It is an active directive, cognitive-oriented therapy. Confrontation is used to assume responsibility for the patient's behavior. The patient is encouraged to accept himself/herself as he/she is, not because of what he/she does. He/she is taught to take risks and to try out new behavior. Action is emphasized for both the patient and the therapist.
- **Logo therapy (Viktor E Frankl):** It is a future-oriented therapy. The patient is confronted with and oriented toward the meaning of life. This search for meaning (logos) is viewed as a primary life force. This includes meaning in the spiritual sense. Without a sense of meaning, life becomes an "existential vacuum".

The aim of logo therapy is to promote awareness regarding one's own responsibility. In essence, the patient is guided to take control of his/her own life and to determine the meaning for him/her.

- **Reality therapy (William Glasser):** Central themes are the need for identity reached by sense of being loved, feeling worthwhile and behaving responsibly. The patient is helped to recognize his/her life goals and the way he/she keeps himself/herself motivated toward accomplishing his/her goals. The process includes making the individual aware of the alternatives available. Another focus of therapy is development of the capacity for caring, through the warm acceptance of the therapist. The patient is directed to talk about any topic but must focus on behavior rather than feelings.
- **Gestalt therapy (Frederic S. Pearls):** The patient is encouraged to identity feelings by enhancing self-awareness. There is focus on body sensations as they reflect feelings. The increased awareness makes the patient more sensitive to other aspects of his/her existence. Self-awareness is expected to lead to self-acceptance. The patient is assisted in dealing with unfinished business by becoming aware of the totality of his/her responses. More assertion is focused on the "how" and "what" behavior rather than "why".
- **Psychosynthesis (Roberto Assagioli):** Focus on the self. "Self" is considered "an inner center of awareness and peace".

  Three developmental stages are described:

  1. The pre-personal in which an individual asks, "Do I exist?"
  2. The personal, "I exist, who am I?"
  3. The transpersonal, "I know who I am. What is the meaning of my life?"

  The therapist helps the persons to use techniques such as guided imagery and meditation for obtaining self-awareness and control over the course of his/her life.
- **Encounter group therapy (William C Schultz, Carl Rogers):** Encounter group therapy focuses on the establishment of intimate interactions in a group setting. Therapy is oriented to 'here and now' principle. The patient is expected to assume responsibility for his/her own behavior. Feeling is stressed; intellectualization is discouraged. Group exercises are frequently used. Group members are encouraged to share their thoughts and feelings honestly.

Psychoanalytic Model (Psychodynamic Theories or Concepts)

Psychoanalytic Model or Psychodynamic theories explain the development of mental or emotional processes and their effects on behavior or relationships. Sigmund Freud (1856–1939) is known as the father of psychoanalytic theory. His theory states that deviations in human behavior result from unsuccessful task accomplishment during earlier developmental stages. His model is useful in the development of therapeutic relationships, techniques and interventions.

Basic Tenets of Psychoanalytic Model

- Structure of personality or mind
- Topography of mind
- Psychosexual development
- Object relations and identification
- Behavioral motivation

Structure of Personality or Mind

The personality consists of three structures: Id, ego and superego.

- **Id**
  - The id is present at birth and is not oriented to reality.
  - The id is formed by unconscious desires, primitive instincts and unstructured drives including sexual and aggressive tendencies that arise from the body.
  - Since the id always seeks immediate reduction from tension, it operates on the pleasure principle.
- **Ego**
  - The ego begins to develop at three years of age.
  - The ego develops because the id must negotiate with external reality to meet its needs.

- The ego consists of certain mental mechanisms such as perception, memory and motor control as well as specific defense mechanisms.
- The capacity to form mutually satisfying relationship is a fundamental function of the ego, which is not present at birth but it is formed throughout the child's development.

- **Superego**
    - The superego begins to develop at age of three and it is an outgrowth of the ego.
    - It projects the conscience, one's inner sense of right and wrong.
    - It is associated with ethics, standards and self-criticism.

Topography of Mind

In this model, human mind is conceptualized in terms of conscious mental processes and unconscious mental processes. Conscious mental process refers to the awareness of events, thoughts and feelings with the ability to recall them. Unconscious mental processes include thoughts and feelings that are outside awareness and are not remembered (Fig. 2.12).

- **The conscious level mind is a part of the ego**
    - The conscious mind is much smaller than the unconscious mind.
    - The conscious mind is reality based.
    - Any mental information readily available to an individual is located in the conscious mind.
- **The subconscious level mind is a part of the ego**
    - The subconscious acts as a filtering device between the external environment and the ego.
    - Information stored in the subconscious can be called into conscious awareness.
- **The unconscious level mind is a part of the superego**
    - Comparatively, the unconscious mind is much larger than the conscious mind.
    - The unconscious mind is not reality based.
    - Information stored in the unconscious mind affects behavior and this information is unavailable to the conscious mind.

Figure 2.12: Iceberg metaphor of mind

Psychosexual Development

When development occurs, a child must master the specific psychosexual conflicts to become a healthy and functioning adult. The names of the stages reflect the body, and are mostly associated with the child's source of gratification.

- **Oral stage occurs between birth and age of 18 months**
    - The child's needs are satisfied by oral gratification: feeding, exploring objects by placing them in the mouth or exploring by using the lips.
    - If needs are met, the child gains a feeling of trust and well-being.
    - If needs are not met by the desired level of satisfaction, the child becomes an adult who is afraid and becomes ill easily.
- **Anal stage occurs between the age of 18 months and 3 years**
    - The child develops an awareness of fullness in the rectum.
    - The child takes pleasure in retaining or eliminating feces.
    - If this stage is negotiated effectively, the child becomes an adult who can delay gratification to attain future goals.
    - If this stage is inadequately negotiated, the child becomes an adult who is either excessively rigid and conservative or messy and destructive.
- **Phallic (Oedipal) stage occurs between the age of 3 and 6 years**
    - The child takes pleasure in exploring and manipulating genitalia.
    - The child is attracted to the opposite-sex parent but realizes that he/she cannot sexually relate with his parent: the dilemma is resolved by identifying with the same-sex parent.
    - During this stage, the superego develops and the conscience is formed.
    - If needs are adequately met during this stage, the child develops a sex-appropriate identity.
    - If needs are inadequately met during this stage, the child becomes an adult whose sexual identity is confused and who has problems relating to authority figures.
- **Latency stage occurs between the age of 6 and 12 years**
    - The child has learned to express inner drives and urges in socially acceptable ways: sexual tension is sublimated into age-appropriate activities.

   - If this stage is successfully negotiated, the child becomes an adult who can deal with various life situations.
   - If this stage is not successfully negotiated, the child becomes an adult who has difficulty in developing social skills and who feels inferior to others.
- **Genital stage occurs between the age of 13 and 20 years**
   - Corresponding with genital maturation is a reawakening of the sex drive.
   - The child expands energy establishing psychological independence from parents and family.
   - If this stage is completed successfully, an adult emerges whose personality structure is integrated, allowing the development of love and work relationships.
   - Unsuccessful completion of this stage results in an adult whose ability to establish intimacy and a strong personal identity is greatly compromised.

Object Relations and Identification

'Object relations' is a concept introduced by Sigmund Freud that refers to the psychological attachment to another person or object. He believed that the choice of a sexual partner in adulthood and the nature of that relationship depends on the quality of the child's object relationships during the early formative years.

The child's first love object is the mother, who is the source of nourishment and the provider of pleasure. Gradually, as the child separates from the mother, the nature of this initial attachment influences future relationships. The child incorporates her mother as a love object, identifies with her and grows up to become like mother.

Behavioral Motivation

Behavior which is motivated by anxiety acts as the cornerstone of psychopathology.

NURSING IMPLICATION

Implications for Nursing Practice

- Understanding the psychosexual stages of childhood provides a framework for understanding behaviors observed in adult patients.
- Effective parenting can be promoted by teaching parents about the child's needs during each psychosexual stage.
- Successfully identifying manifestations of anxiety provides clues for planning nursing care.
- Defense mechanisms protect a patient from overwhelming anxiety; the nurse should not deliberately interfere with them.
- All behavior is meaningful, often representing the unconscious needs and wishes of patients who do not always know why they behave as they do.

- Anxiety arises when unresolved conflicts are stimulated.
- Severe anxiety may produce behavioral regression to an early developmental level.

Behavior is always meaningful and often unconsciously motivated.

Behavioral Model (Behavioral Psychology or Behaviorism)

Behavioral model is a theory of learning based upon the idea that all behaviors are acquired through conditioning. John B Watson, BF Skinner and Ivan Pavlov advocated this concept and it dominated the field of psychology during the early half of the twentieth century. Behavioral techniques are still widely used in therapeutic settings to help clients learn new skills and behaviors.

Under Behavioral model, several types of learning exist with the contributions of behaviorists. The most basic form is associative learning, i.e., making a new association between the events in the environment. There are two forms of associative learning: **classical conditioning** and **operant conditioning**.

1. **Classical conditioning by Ivan Pavlov:** It is a reflexive or automatic type of learning in which a stimulus acquires the capacity to evoke a response that was originally evoked by another stimulus.
2. **Operant conditioning by BF Skinner:** It is based on the fundamental idea that behaviors which are reinforced will tend to continue, while behaviors which are punished will eventually end.

Concept of Behaviorism by John Watson: Watson studied how a certain stimulus provokes organisms to make responses. He believed psychology was only an objective observation of behavior.

Basic Assumptions of Behavior Theory

- All human behavior is a response to a stimulus or stimuli from the environment.
- Human beings can control or determine the behavior of others.
- The human personality is a mere pattern of stimulus-response chains or habits.
- Both adaptive and maladaptive behavior are learned or strengthened through reinforcement.
- Maladaptive behavior can be unlearned and replaced by adaptive behavior if the person receives exposure to specific stimuli or reinforcements for the desired adaptive behavior.

Basic Premises

- There is no such thing as a defect in the personality structure.

- Behavior that is rewarded will persist, whether the behavior is good or bad.
- Diagnostic labels are irrelevant; the focus of treatment is the behavior that requires change.

Therapeutic Approaches

- **Assertive training:** It seeks to alleviate anxiety when the patient's anxiety is arising from interpersonal relationships. Assertiveness implies the ability to stand up for one's own rights while not infringing on the rights of others. It is differentiated from aggressive behavior which violates others' rights. In assertiveness training, the patient identifies his/her usual mode of behavior. This increases self-esteem and sense of self-control.
- **Token economy system:** It is a positive reinforcement program. Usage of this system is to encourage socially acceptable behavior. The person is rewarded with a token when the desirable behavior occurs. He/she is penalized by removal of tokens when undesirable behavior takes place. When enough tokens are accumulated, they may be spent for snacks, to watch a movie or whatever is meaningful to the patient. This pleasurable experience reinforces the future repetition for the desired behavior.
- **Systematic desensitization:** In this therapy, the client will attain a state of complete relaxation and is then exposed to the stimulus that elicits the anxiety response. There are three steps in this procedure:
  1. Relaxation training
  2. Constructing a hierarchy of anxiety provoking stimuli
  3. Desensitization of the stimuli
- **Aversion therapy:** It is a form of behavior modification approach in which an aversive (causing a strong feeling of dislike or disgust) stimulus is paired with an undesirable behavior in order to decrease or eliminate that behavior.
- **Flooding:** Involves patients to a phobic object or situation in a nongraded manner with no attempt to reduce anxiety. Here, the person is exposed to a phobic stimulus but escape is made impossible. Prolonged contact with the phobic stimulus with therapist's guidance and encouragement might decrease the level of anxiety.

Interpersonal Model

Interpersonal theories emphasize the importance of human relationship; instincts and drives are less important. ***Harry S Sullivan*** is the originator of interpersonal theory. He viewed interpersonal relations as the basis of human development and behavior. Sullivan believed that the health or sickness of one's personality is determined by the characteristic pattern of interpersonal relations.

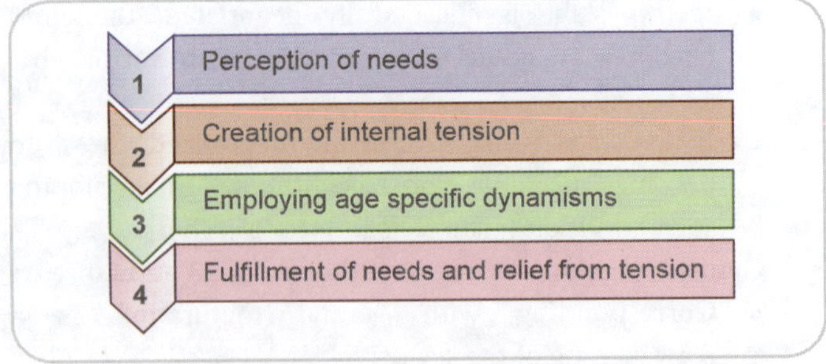

Figure 2.13: Schema representing the process of need fulfillment according to interpersonal model

Theoretical Foundations by Sullivan

Sullivan believed that all human behavior is directed toward the fulfillment of two needs: **Need for satisfaction and the need for security.** Need for satisfaction is derived from the person's biological needs for air, food, sex, shelter and so on. Need for security by a person is derived from emotional needs of feeling such as interpersonal intimacy, status and self-esteem.

An individual employs a variety of methods to meet these needs, thereby reducing tension. The first step in the process of need fulfillment is perception of needs. The second step is the creation of internal tension after the needs have been perceived. The third step in the process of need fulfillment is employing the age-specific dynamisms. Final step is the fulfillment of needs and release of tension (Fig. 2.13).

Response to Anxiety

Anxiety is a central theme in the interpersonal theory. Anxiety is a response to feelings of disapproval from a significant adult. The feelings of disapproval may or may not be based on reality.

When a child experiences anxiety, he defends against anxiety by using any of the security operations mentioned in Table 2.20.

Table 2.20: Security operations used to defend against anxiety

Apathy	Apathy is the complete absence of emotional expression. So, the emotional expression will not been associated with the anxiety producing situation.
Somnolent detachment	A primitive defense in which an individual falls asleep when confronted by a highly threatening, anxiety producing experience
Selective inattention	Anxiety producing aspects of a situation are not allowed into awareness, enabling the individual to maintain a sense of stability
Preoccupation	Consuming interest in a person, thought or event to the exclusion of the anxiety-producing reality

Self-concept

Self-concept is an idea which is self-constructed from the beliefs one holds about oneself and the responses of others. The development of self-concept begins in infancy and is closely related to the quality of the infant's feeding experiences. Sullivan described three types of self-concept: Good me, Bad me and Not me.

Good me: If infants frequently experience satisfaction and security from the mothering they receive during the feeding process, they begin to see themselves as worthwhile individuals; they start to develop "Good me" concept.

Bad me: If the infants' needs for satisfaction and security are not met, it will result in anxiety and infants believe that they are not worthwhile. This leads to the development of "Bad me" concept.

Not me: If infants are severely deprived or when the majority of the interpersonal relationships are brought with great threats to their existence, infants defend themselves by dissociating the anxiety-generating experiences. Since they cannot develop a sense of self from reflected appraisals, infants develop a "Not me" concept, which leads to severe emotional problems.

Application to Nursing

- It helps to interact successfully with others.
- It helps to assist clients to achieve interpersonal security and a sense of well-being.
- It is used to help the clients to achieve a higher degree of independence and interpersonal functioning.

EXTRA EDGE

ICD-10 Classification of Mental Disorders

ICD-10 is 10th revision of the International Statistical Classification of Diseases and Related Health Problems (ICD), a medical classification list by the World Health Organization (WHO). It contains codes for diseases, signs or symptoms, abnormal findings, complaints, social circumstances, and external causes of injuries or diseases. Work on ICD-10 began in 1983, was endorsed by the Forty-third World Health Assembly in 1990, and was first used by member states in 1994.

The fifth chapter of ICD-10 contains the *International Classification of Mental and Behavioral Disorders*. It has two separate publications. The ***clinical descriptions and diagnostic guidelines ("Blue Book")*** are for clinical and general educational use. The ***diagnostic criteria for research ("Green Book")*** are intended for research purposes and to be used in conjunction with the guidelines within it. The following are the contents of fifth chapter:

F00–F09: Organic, including symptomatic, mental disorders

- F00 Dementia in Alzheimer's disease
- F01 Vascular dementia
- F02 Dementia in other diseases classified elsewhere
- F03 Unspecified dementia
- F04 Organic amnesic syndrome, not induced by alcohol and other psychoactive substances
- F05 Delirium, not induced by alcohol and other psychoactive substances
- F06 Other mental disorders due to brain damage or dysfunction and physical disease
- F07 Personality and behavioral disorders due to brain disease, damage or dysfunction
- F09 Unspecified organic or symptomatic mental disorder

F10–F19: Mental and behavioral disorders due to psychoactive substance use

- F10 Use of alcohol
- F11 Use of opioids
- F12 Use of cannabinoids
- F13 Use of sedatives and hypnotics
- F14 Use of cocaine
- F15 Use of stimulants including caffeine
- F16 Use of hallucinogens
- F17 Use of tobacco
- F18 Use of volatile solvents
- F19 Multiple drug use and use of other psychoactive substances
- All the conditions coded from F10–19 have the following subtypes:
  - F 1x.0 Acute intoxication
  - F 1x.1 Harmful use
  - F 1x.2 Dependence syndrome
  - F 1x.3 Withdrawal state
  - F 1x.4 Withdrawal state with delirium
  - F 1x.5 Psychotic disorder
  - F 1x.6 Amnestic syndrome
  - F 1x.7 Residual and late-onset psychotic disorder
  - F 1x.8 Other mental and behavioral disorder
  - F 1x.9 Unspecified mental and behavioral disorder

F20–F29: Schizophrenia, schizotypal and delusional disorders

- F20 Schizophrenia
  - F20.0 Paranoid schizophrenia
  - F20.1 Hebephrenic schizophrenia (Disorganized schizophrenia)
  - F20.2 Catatonic schizophrenia
  - F20.3 Undifferentiated schizophrenia
  - F20.4 Post-schizophrenic depression
  - F20.5 Residual schizophrenia
  - F20.6 Simple schizophrenia
  - F20.8 Other schizophrenia
    - Cenesthopathic schizophrenia
    - Schizophreniform disorder not otherwise specified (NOS)
    - Schizophreniform psychosis NOS
  - F20.9 Schizophrenia, unspecified
- F21 Schizotypal disorder
- F22 Persistent delusional disorders
- F23 Acute and transient psychotic disorders
- F24 Induced delusional disorder

Contd...

- F25 Schizoaffective disorders
- F28 Other nonorganic psychotic disorders
- F29 Unspecified nonorganic psychosis

F30–F39: Mood (affective) disorders
- F30 Manic episode
- F31 Bipolar affective disorder
- F32 Depressive episode
- F33 Recurrent depressive disorder
- F34 Persistent mood (affective) disorders
  - F34.0 Cyclothymia
  - F34.1 Dysthymia
  - F34.8 Other persistent mood (affective) disorders
  - F34.9 Persistent mood (affective) disorder, unspecified
- F38 Other mood (affective) disorders
- F39 Unspecified mood (affective) disorder

F40–F48: Neurotic, stress-related and somatoform disorders
- F40 Phobic anxiety disorders
  - F40.0 Agoraphobia
  - F40.1 Social phobias
    - Anthropophobia
    - Social neurosis
  - F40.2 Specific (isolated) phobias
    - Acrophobia
    - Animal phobias
    - Claustrophobia
    - Simple phobia
  - F40.8 Other phobic anxiety disorders
  - F40.9 Phobic anxiety disorder, unspecified
- F41 Other anxiety disorders
  - F41.0 Panic disorder (episodic paroxysmal anxiety)
  - F41.1 Generalized anxiety disorder
- F42 Obsessive-compulsive disorder
- F43 Reaction to severe stress, and adjustment disorders
  - F43.0 Acute stress reaction
  - F43.1 Post-traumatic stress disorder
  - F43.2 Adjustment disorder
- F44 Dissociative (conversion) disorders
- F45 Somatoform disorders
- F48 Other neurotic disorders

F50–F59: Behavioral syndromes associated with physiological disturbances and physical factors
- F50 Eating disorders
  - F50.0 Anorexia nervosa
  - F50.1 Atypical anorexia nervosa
  - F50.2 Bulimia nervosa
  - F50.3 Atypical bulimia nervosa
  - F50.4 Overeating associated with other psychological disturbances
  - F50.5 Vomiting associated with other psychological disturbances
  - F50.8 Other eating disorders
  - F50.9 Eating disorder, unspecified
- F51 Nonorganic sleep disorders
  - F51.0 Nonorganic insomnia
  - F51.1 Nonorganic hypersomnia
  - F51.2 Nonorganic disorder of the sleep-wake schedule
  - F51.3 Sleep walking (somnambulism)
  - F51.4 Sleep terrors (night terrors)
  - F51.5 Nightmares
- F52 Sexual dysfunction, not caused by organic disorder or disease
  - F52.0 Lack or loss of sexual desire
  - F52.1 Sexual aversion and lack of sexual enjoyment
  - F52.2 Failure of genital response
  - F52.3 Orgasmic dysfunction
  - F52.4 Premature ejaculation
  - F52.5 Nonorganic vaginismus
  - F52.6 Nonorganic dyspareunia
  - F52.7 Excessive sexual drive
  - F52.8 Other sexual dysfunction, not caused by organic disorder or disease
  - F52.9 Unspecified sexual dysfunction, not caused by organic disorder or disease
- F53 Mental and behavioral disorders associated with the puerperium, not elsewhere classified
- F54 Psychological and behavioral factors associated with disorders or diseases classified elsewhere
- F55 Abuse of non-dependence producing substances
- F59 Unspecified behavioral syndromes associated with physiological disturbances and physical factors

F60–F69: Disorders of adult personality and behavior
- F60 Specific personality disorders
  - F60.0 Paranoid personality disorder
  - F60.1 Schizoid personality disorder
  - F60.2 Dissocial personality disorder
  - F60.3 Emotionally unstable personality disorder
  - F60.4 Histrionic personality disorder
  - F60.5 Anankastic personality disorder
  - F60.6 Anxious (avoidant) personality disorder
  - F60.7 Dependent personality disorder
  - F60.8 Other specific personality disorders
    - Eccentric personality disorder
    - Haltlose personality disorder
    - Immature personality disorder
    - Narcissistic personality disorder
    - Passive-aggressive personality disorder
    - Psychoneurotic personality disorder
  - F60.9 Personality disorder not otherwise specified/ Personality disorder unspecified
- F61 Mixed and other personality disorders
- F62 Enduring personality changes, not attributable to brain damage and disease
- F63 Habit and impulse disorders
  - F63.0 Pathological gambling
  - F63.1 Pathological fire-setting (pyromania)
  - F63.2 Pathological stealing (kleptomania)
  - F63.3 Trichotillomania
  - F63.8 Other habit and impulse disorders
    - Intermittent explosive disorder
- F64 Gender identity disorders
  - F64.0 Transsexualism
  - F64.1 Dual-role transvestism
  - F64.2 Gender identity disorder of childhood
- F65 Disorders of sexual preference
  - F65.0 Sexual fetishism
  - F65.1 Fetishistic transvestism
  - F65.2 Exhibitionism

Contd...

- F65.3 Voyeurism
- F65.4 Pedophilia
- F65.5 Sadomasochism
- F65.6 Multiple disorders of sexual preference
- F65.8 Other disorders of sexual preference
  - Frotteurism
  - Necrophilia
  - Zoophilia
- F66 Psychological and behavioral disorders associated with sexual development and orientation (Specifically states that "sexual orientation by itself is not to be considered a disorder")
  - F66.0 Sexual maturation disorder
  - F66.1 Ego-dystonic sexual orientation
  - F66.2 Sexual relationship disorder
  - F66.8 Other psychosexual development disorders
  - F66.9 Psychosexual development disorder, unspecified
- F68 Other disorders of adult personality and behavior
  - F68.0 Elaboration of physical symptoms for psychological reasons
  - F68.1 Intentional production or feigning of symptoms or disabilities, either physical or psychological (factitious disorder)
    - Munchausen syndrome
  - F68.8 Other specified disorders of adult personality and behavior
- F69 Unspecified disorder of adult personality and behavior

F70–F79: Mental retardation

- F70 Mild mental retardation
- F71 Moderate mental retardation
- F72 Severe mental retardation
- F73 Profound mental retardation
- F78 Other mental retardation
- F79 Unspecified mental retardation

F80–F89: Disorders of psychological development

- F80 Specific developmental disorders of speech and language
  - F80.0 Specific speech articulation disorder
  - F80.1 Expressive language disorder
  - F80.2 Receptive language disorder
  - F80.3 Acquired aphasia with epilepsy (Landau-Kleffner)
  - F80.8 Other developmental disorders of speech and language
    - Lisping
  - F80.9 Developmental disorder of speech and language, unspecified
- F81 Specific developmental disorders of scholastic skills
  - F81.0 Specific reading disorder
    - Developmental dyslexia
  - F81.1 Specific spelling disorder
  - F81.2 Specific disorder of arithmetical skills
    - Developmental acalculia
    - Gerstmann syndrome
  - F81.3 Mixed disorder of scholastic skills
  - F81.8 Other developmental disorders of scholastic skills
  - F81.9 Developmental disorder of scholastic skills, unspecified
- F82 Specific developmental disorder of motor function
  - Developmental coordination disorder
- F83 Mixed specific developmental disorders
- F84 Pervasive developmental disorders
  - F84.0 Childhood autism
  - F84.1 Atypical autism
  - F84.2 Rett's syndrome
  - F84.3 Other childhood disintegrative disorder
  - F84.4 Overactive disorder associated with mental retardation and stereotyped movements
  - F84.5 Asperger's syndrome
- F88 Other disorders of psychological development
- F89 Unspecified disorder of psychological development

F90–F98: Behavioral and emotional disorders with onset usually occurring in childhood and adolescence

- F90 Hyperkinetic disorders
  - F90.0 Disturbance of activity and attention
    - Attention-deficit hyperactivity disorder
    - Attention deficit syndrome with hyperactivity
  - F90.1 Hyperkinetic conduct disorder
  - F90.8 Other hyperkinetic disorders
  - F90.9 Hyperkinetic disorder, unspecified
- F91 Conduct disorders
  - F91.0 Conduct disorder confined to the family context
  - F91.1 Unsocialized conduct disorder
  - F91.2 Socialized conduct disorder
  - F91.3 Oppositional defiant disorder
  - F91.8 Other conduct disorders
  - F91.9 Conduct disorder, unspecified
- F92 Mixed disorders of conduct and emotions
- F93 Emotional disorders with onset specific to childhood
  - F93.0 Separation anxiety disorder of childhood
  - F93.1 Phobic anxiety disorder of childhood
  - F93.2 Social anxiety disorder of childhood
  - F93.3 Sibling rivalry disorder
  - F93.8 Other childhood emotional disorders
    - Identity disorder
    - Overanxious disorder
  - F93.9 Childhood emotional disorder, unspecified
- F94 Disorders of social functioning with onset specific to childhood and adolescence
  - F94.0 Elective mutism
  - F94.1 Reactive attachment disorder of childhood
  - F94.2 Disinhibited attachment disorder of childhood
  - F94.8 Other childhood disorders of social functioning
  - F94.9 Childhood disorder of social functioning, unspecified
- F95 Tic disorders
- F98 Other behavioral and emotional disorders with onset usually occurring in childhood and adolescence
  - F98.0 Nonorganic enuresis
  - F98.1 Nonorganic encopresis
  - F98.2 Feeding disorder of infancy and childhood
  - F98.3 Pica of infancy and childhood
  - F98.4 Stereotyped movement disorders
  - F98.5 Stuttering (stammering)
  - F98.6 Cluttering
  - F98.8 Other specified behavioral and emotional disorders with onset usually occurring in childhood or adolescence
  - F98.9 Unspecified behavioral and emotional disorders with onset usually occurring in childhood or adolescence

F99: Unspecified mental disorder

F99.0 Mental disorder, not otherwise specified

EXTRA EDGE

DSM IV-TR

The need for a classification of mental disorders has been clear throughout the history of medicine. Various systems for categorizing mental disorders have differed with respect to whether their principal objective was used in clinical areas, research, or in administrative settings.

Diagnostic and Statistical Manual of Mental Disorders, 4th Edition, Text Revision, also known as *DSM-IV-TR,* is a manual published by the American Psychiatric Association (APA) in 1994 that includes all currently recognized mental disorders.

Components of DSM-IV-TR

- Instructions on how to use the manual
- DSM-IV classification system
- Multi axial system
- Diagnostic criteria

Salient Features of DSM-IV

- It provide the framework for classifying the disorders and defining the diagnostic criteria for the list of disorders, in which some disorders are first diagnosed in infancy, childhood or adolescence.
- Adult diagnosis can be used for children who are considered for a specific diagnosis.
- Criteria for mental retardation are more compatible with the definitions as per the American Association of Mental Retardation.
- Categories of organic mental disorders fall under delirium, dementia and amnestic and other cognitive disorders.
- This section of schizophrenia and other psychotic disorders brings together these sections of DSM-III-R that were all characterized by having psychotic symptoms as their main features.
- The mood disorder criteria have been polished (e.g., in order to qualify as mania, symptoms have to be present for at least a week).
- The section of anxiety disorders starts by noting that panic attacks can be a feature of a variety of anxiety disorders.
- Acute stress disorder has been added to cover acute reactions to stress.
- The diagnostic classes of dissociative disorder and sleep disorders are more compatible with the ICD-10.
- The diagnostic classes of somatoform disorders and personality disorders have been clarified. There is a special effort to avoid gender bias in the section on personality disorders.
- In the multiaxial system, Axis IV codes psychosocial and environmental problems rather than a rating scale for severity of stressors.

Multiaxial System of DSM-IV-TR

- **Axis I** provides information about clinical disorders. Any mental health conditions, other than personality disorders or mental retardation, would have been included here. Disorders which would have fallen under this axis include:
    - Disorders usually diagnosed in infancy, childhood or adolescence
    - Delirium, dementia, amnesia and other cognitive disorders
    - Mental disorders due to a general medical condition
    - Substance-related disorders
    - Schizophrenia and other psychotic disorders
    - Mood disorders
    - Anxiety disorders
    - Somatoform disorders
    - Factitious disorders
    - Dissociative disorders
    - Sexual and gender identity disorders
    - Eating disorders
    - Sleep disorders
    - Impulse-control disorders not classified elsewhere
    - Adjustment disorders
    - Other conditions that may be a focus of clinical attention.
- **Axis II** provides information about personality disorders and mental retardation. Disorders which would have fallen under this axis include:
    - Paranoid personality disorder
    - Schizoid personality disorder
    - Schizotypal personality disorder
    - Antisocial personality disorder
    - Borderline personality disorder
    - Histrionic personality disorder
    - Narcissistic personality disorder
    - Avoidant personality disorder
    - Dependent personality disorder
    - Obsessive-compulsive personality disorder
    - Personality disorder not specified otherwise
    - Mental retardation
- **Axis III** provides information about any medical conditions that were present which might impact the patient's mental disorder or its management.
- **Axis IV** is used to describe psychosocial and environmental factors affecting a person. Factors which might have been included here are as follows:
    - Problems with a primary support group
    - Problems related to the social environment
    - Educational problems
    - Occupational problems
    - Housing problems
    - Economic problems
    - Problems with access to health care services
    - Problems related to interaction with the legal system/crime
    - Other psychosocial and environmental problems.
- **Axis V** is a rating scale called the Global Assessment of Functioning (GAF); the GAF goes from 0 to 100 and provides a way to summarize in a single number that denotes the overall functioning of an individual. A general outline of this scale would be as follows:
    - 100: No symptoms.
    - 90: Minimal symptoms with good functioning.
    - 80: Transient symptoms that are expected reactions to psychosocial stressors.
    - 70: Mild symptoms or some difficulty in social, occupational or school functioning.
    - 60: Moderate symptoms or moderate difficulty in social, occupational or school functioning.

Contd...

- 50: Serious symptoms or any serious impairment in social, occupational or school functioning.
- 40: Some impairment in reality testing or communication or major impairment in several areas such as work or school, family relations, judgment, thinking or mood.
- 30: Behavior is considerably influenced by delusions or hallucinations or serious impairment in communication or judgment or inability to function in almost all areas.
- 20: Some danger of hurting self or others or occasionally fails to maintain minimal personal hygiene or gross impairment in communication.
- 10: Persistent danger of severely hurting self or others or persistent inability to maintain minimal personal hygiene or serious suicidal act with clear expectation of death.

DSM-IV-TR Classification System

Disorders usually first diagnosed in infancy, childhood or adolescence.

Mental Retardation

- 317 Mild mental retardation
- 318.0 Moderate mental retardation
- 318.1 Severe mental retardation
- 318.2 Profound mental retardation
- 319 Mental retardation; severity unspecified

Learning Disorders

- 315.00 Reading disorder
- 315.1 Mathematics disorder
- 315.2 Disorder of written expression
- 315.9 Learning disorder not otherwise specified

Motor Skills Disorders

315.4 Developmental coordination disorder

Communication Disorders

- 315.31 Expressive language disorder
- 315.32 Mixed receptive-expressive language disorder
- 315.39 Phonological disorder
- 307.0 Stuttering
- 307.9 Communication disorder not otherwise specified

Pervasive Developmental Disorders

- 299.00 Autistic disorder
- 299.80 Rett's disorder
- 299.10 Childhood disintegrative disorder
- 299.80 Asperger's disorder
- 299.80 Pervasive developmental disorder not otherwise specified

Attention-deficit and Disruptive Behavior Disorders

- Attention-deficit hyperactivity disorder
  - 314.01 Combined subtype
  - 314.01 Predominantly hyperactive-impulsive subtype
  - 314.00 Predominantly inattentive subtype
  - 314.9 Attention-deficit hyperactivity disorder not otherwise specified

Conduct Disorder

- 312.81 Childhood onset
- 312.82 Adolescent onset
- 312.89 Unspecified onset
- 313.81 Oppositional defiant disorder
- 312.9 Disruptive behavior disorder not otherwise specified

Feeding and Eating Disorders of Infancy or Early Childhood

- 307.52 Pica
- 307.53 Rumination disorder
- 307.59 Feeding disorder of infancy or early childhood

Tic Disorders

- 307.23 Tourette's disorder
- 307.22 Chronic motor or vocal tic disorder
- 307.21 Transient tic disorder
- 307.20 Tic disorder not otherwise specified

Elimination Disorders

- 307.6 Enuresis (not due to a general medical condition)
- 307.7 Encopresis, without constipation and overflow incontinence
- 787.6 Encopresis, with constipation and overflow incontinence

Other Disorders of Infancy, Childhood or Adolescence

- 309.21 Separation anxiety disorder
- 313.23 Selective mutism
- 313.89 Reactive attachment disorder of infancy or early childhood
- 307.3 Stereotypic movement disorder
- 313.9 Disorder of infancy, childhood or adolescence not otherwise specified

Delirium, Dementia, and Amnestic and Other Cognitive Disorders

Delirium

- 293.0 Delirium due to... [indicate the general medical condition]
- 780.09 Delirium not otherwise specified

Dementia

- Dementia of the Alzheimer's type, with early onset
  - 294.10 Without behavioral disturbance
  - 294.11 With behavioral disturbance
- Dementia of the Alzheimer's type, with late onset
- Vascular dementia
- Dementia due to HIV disease
- Dementia due to head trauma
- Dementia due to Parkinson's disease
- Dementia due to Huntington's disease
- Dementia due to Pick's disease
- Dementia due to Creutzfeldt -Jacob disease
- Dementia due to... [indicate other general medical condition]
- 294.8 Dementia not otherwise specified

Amnestic Disorders

- 294.0 Amnestic disorder due to... [indicate the general medical condition]
- 294.8 Amnestic disorder not otherwise specified

Other Cognitive Disorders

- 294.9 Cognitive disorder not otherwise specified

Mental Disorders due to a General Medical Condition Not Elsewhere Classified

- 293.89 Catatonic disorder due to... [indicate the general medical condition]
- 310.1 Personality change due to... [indicate the general medical condition]
  - (Subtypes: Labile, disinhibited, aggressive, apathetic, paranoid, other, combined, unspecified)

Contd...

- 293.9 Mental disorder not otherwise specified due to... [indicate the general medical condition]

Substance-related Disorders

Alcohol-related Disorders
- 305.00 Abuse
- 303.90 Dependence
- 291.89 Induced anxiety disorder
- 291.89 Induced mood disorder
- 291.1 Induced persisting amnestic disorder
- 291.2 Induced persisting dementia
- 291.5 Induced psychotic disorder, with delusions
- 291.3 Induced psychotic disorder, with hallucinations
- 291.89 Induced sexual dysfunction
- 291.89 Induced sleep disorder
- 303.00 Intoxication
- 291.0 Intoxication delirium
- 291.9 Related disorder not otherwise specified
- 291.81 Withdrawal
- 291.0 Withdrawal delirium

Amphetamine (or amphetamine-like) Related Disorders
- 305.70 Abuse
- 304.40 Dependence
- 292.89 Induced anxiety disorder
- 292.84 Induced mood disorder
- 292.11 Induced psychotic disorder, with delusions
- 292.12 Induced psychotic disorder, with hallucinations
- 292.89 Induced sexual dysfunction
- 292.89 Induced sleep disorder
- 292.89 Intoxication
- 292.81 Intoxication delirium
- 292.9 Related disorder not otherwise specified
- 292.0 Withdrawal

Caffeine-related Disorders
- 292.89 Induced anxiety disorder
- 292.89 Induced sleep disorder
- 305.90 Intoxication
- 292.9 Related disorder not otherwise specified

Cannabis-related Disorders
- 305.20 Abuse
- 304.30 Dependence
- 292.89 Induced anxiety disorder
- 292.11 Induced psychotic disorder, with delusions
- 292.12 Induced psychotic disorder, with hallucinations
- 292.89 Intoxication
- 292.81 Intoxication delirium
- 292.9 Related disorder not otherwise specified

Cocaine-related Disorders
- 305.60 Abuse
- 304.20 Dependence
- 292.89 Induced anxiety disorder
- 292.84 Induced mood disorder
- 292.11 Induced psychotic disorder, with delusions
- 292.12 Induced psychotic disorder, with hallucinations
- 292.89 Induced sexual dysfunction
- 292.89 Induced sleep disorder
- 292.89 Intoxication
- 292.81 Intoxication delirium
- 292.9 Related disorder not otherwise specified
- 292.0 Withdrawal

Hallucinogen-related Disorders
- 305.30 Abuse
- 304.50 Dependence
- 292.89 Induced anxiety disorder
- 292.84 Induced mood disorder
- 292.11 Induced psychotic disorder, with delusions
- 292.12 Induced psychotic disorder, with hallucinations
- 292.89 Intoxication
- 292.81 Intoxication delirium
- 292.89 Persisting perception disorder
- 292.9 Related disorder not otherwise specified

Inhalant-related Disorders
- 305.90 Abuse
- 304.60 Dependence
- 292.89 Induced anxiety disorder
- 292.84 Induced mood disorder
- 292.82 Induced persisting dementia
- 292.11 Induced psychotic disorder, with delusions
- 292.12 Induced psychotic disorder, with hallucinations
- 292.89 Intoxication
- 292.81 Intoxication delirium
- 292.9 Related disorder not otherwise specified

Nicotine-related Disorders
- 305.1 Dependence
- 292.9 Related disorder Not Otherwise Specified
- 292.0 Withdrawal

Opioid-related Disorders
- 305.50 Abuse
- 304.00 Dependence
- 292.84 Induced mood disorder
- 292.11 Induced psychotic disorder, with delusions
- 292.12 Induced psychotic disorder, with hallucinations
- 292.89 Induced sexual dysfunction
- 292.89 Induced sleep disorder
- 292.89 Intoxication
- 292.81 Intoxication delirium
- 292.9 Related disorder Not Otherwise Specified
- 292.0 Withdrawal

Phencyclidine (or Phencyclidine-like) Related Disorders
- 305.90 Abuse
- 304.60 Dependence
- 292.89 Induced anxiety disorder
- 292.84 Induced mood disorder
- 292.11 Induced psychotic disorder, with delusions
- 292.12 Induced psychotic disorder, with hallucinations
- 292.89 Intoxication
- 292.81 Intoxication delirium
- 292.9 Related disorder not otherwise specified

Sedative, Hypnotic or Anxiolytic Related Disorders
- 305.40 Abuse
- 304.10 Dependence
- 292.89 Induced anxiety disorder
- 292.84 Induced mood disorder
- 292.83 Induced persisting amnestic disorder
- 292.82 Induced persisting dementia

Contd...

- 292.11 Induced psychotic disorder, with delusions
- 292.12 Induced psychotic disorder, with hallucinations
- 292.89 Induced sexual dysfunction
- 292.89 Induced sleep disorder
- 292.89 Intoxication
- 292.81 Intoxication delirium
- 292.9 Related disorder not otherwise specified
- 292.0 Withdrawal
- 292.81 Withdrawal delirium

Polysubstance-related Disorder

- 304.80 Polysubstance dependence

Other (or unknown) Substance-related Disorder

- 305.90 Abuse
- 304.90 Dependence
- 292.89 Induced anxiety disorder
- 292.81 Induced delirium
- 292.84 Induced mood disorder
- 292.83 Induced persisting amnestic disorder
- 292.82 Induced persisting dementia
- 292.11 Induced psychotic disorder, with delusions
- 292.12 Induced psychotic disorder, with hallucinations
- 292.89 Induced sexual dysfunction
- 292.89 Induced sleep disorder
- 292.89 Intoxication
- 292.9 Related disorder not otherwise specified
- 292.0 Withdrawal
- 293.0 Delirium due to general medical condition

Schizophrenia and Other Psychotic Disorders

- Schizophrenia
  - 295.20 Catatonic type
  - 295.10 Disorganized type
  - 295.30 Paranoid type
  - 295.60 Residual type
  - 295.90 Undifferentiated type
- 295.40 Schizophreniform disorder
- 295.70 Schizoaffective disorder
- 297.1 Delusional disorder
  - Erotomanic subtype
  - Grandiose subtype
  - Jealous subtype
  - Persecutory subtype
  - Somatic subtype
  - Mixed type
- 298.8 Brief psychotic disorder
- 297.3 Shared psychotic disorder
- Psychotic disorder due to... [indicate the general medical condition]
  - 293.81 With delusions
  - 293.82 With hallucinations
- 298.9 Psychotic disorder not otherwise specified

Mood Disorders

- 293.83 Mood disorder due to...[indicate the general medical condition]
- 296.90 mood disorder not otherwise specified

Depressive Disorders

- 300.4 Dysthymic disorder
- Major depressive disorder
  - Major depressive disorder, recurrent
    - 296.36 In full remission
    - 296.35 In partial remission
    - 296.31 Mild
    - 296.32 Moderate
    - 296.33 Severe without psychotic features
    - 296.34 Severe with psychotic features
    - 296.30 Unspecified
  - Major depressive disorder, single episode
    - 296.26 In full remission
    - 296.25 In partial remission
    - 296.21 Mild
    - 296.22 Moderate
    - 296.23 Severe without psychotic features
    - 296.24 Severe with psychotic features
    - 296.20 Unspecified
- 311 Depressive disorders not otherwise specified

Bipolar Disorders

- 296.80 Bipolar disorder not otherwise specified
- Bipolar I disorder, most recent episode depressed
  - 296.56 In full remission
  - 296.55 In partial remission
  - 296.51 Mild
  - 296.52 Moderate
  - 296.53 Severe without psychotic features
  - 296.54 Severe with psychotic features
  - 296.50 Unspecified
- 296.40 Bipolar I disorder, most recent episode hypomanic
- Bipolar I disorder, most recent episode manic
  - 296.46 In full remission
  - 296.45 In partial remission
  - 296.41 Mild
  - 296.42 Moderate
  - 296.43 Severe without psychotic features
  - 296.44 Severe with psychotic features
  - 296.40 Unspecified
- Bipolar I disorder, most recent episode mixed
  - 296.66 In full remission
  - 296.65 In partial remission
  - 296.61 Mild
  - 296.62 Moderate
  - 296.63 Severe without psychotic features
  - 296.64 Severe with psychotic features
  - 296.60 Unspecified
- 296.7 Bipolar I disorder, most recent episode unspecified
- Bipolar I disorder, single manic episode
  - 296.06 In full remission
  - 296.05 In partial remission
  - 296.01 Mild
  - 296.02 Moderate
  - 296.03 Severe without psychotic features
  - 296.04 Severe with psychotic features
  - 296.00 Unspecified
- 296.89 Bipolar II disorder
- 301.13 Cyclothymic disorder
- 293.83 Mood disorder due to... [indicate the general medical condition]
- 296.90 Mood disorder not otherwise specified

Contd...

Anxiety Disorders
- 300.02 Generalized anxiety disorder
- Panic disorder
  - 300.21 With agoraphobia
  - 300.01 Without agoraphobia
- 300.22 Agoraphobia without history of panic disorder
- 300.29 Specific phobia
- 300.23 Social phobia
- 300.3 Obsessive-compulsive disorder
- 309.81 Post-traumatic stress disorder
- 308.3 Acute stress disorder

Somatoform Disorders
- 300.81 Somatization disorder
- 300.82 Undifferentiated somatoform disorder
- 300.11 Conversion disorder
- Pain disorder
  - 307.89 Associated with both psychological factors and a general medical condition
  - 307.80 Associated with psychological factors
- 300.7 Hypochondriasis
- 300.7 Body dysmorphic disorder
- 300.82 Somatoform disorder not otherwise specified

Factitious Disorders
- 300.19 With combined psychological and physical signs and symptoms
- 300.19 With predominantly physical signs and symptoms
- 300.16 With predominantly psychological signs and symptoms
- 300.19 Factitious disorder not otherwise specified

Dissociative Disorders
- 300.6 Depersonalization disorder
- 300.12 Dissociative amnesia
- 300.14 Dissociative identity disorder
- 300.15 Dissociative disorder not otherwise specified

Sexual and Gender Identity Disorders

Sexual Dysfunctions
- 625.8 Female hypoactive sexual desire disorder due to... [indicate the general medical condition]
- 608.89 Male hypoactive sexual desire disorder due to... [indicate the general medical condition]
- 302.71 Hypoactive sexual desire disorder
- 302.79 Sexual aversion disorder
- 302.72 Female sexual arousal disorder
- 302.72 Male erectile disorder
- 607.84 Male erectile disorder due to... [indicate the general medical condition]
- 302.73 Female orgasmic disorder
- 302.74 Male orgasmic disorder
- 302.75 Premature ejaculation
- 302.76 Dyspareunia (not due to a general medical condition)
- 625.0 Female dyspareunia due to... [indicate the general medical condition]
- 608.89 Male dyspareunia due to... [indicate the general medical condition]
- 306.51 Vaginismus (not due to a general medical condition)
- 625.8 Other female sexual dysfunction due to... [indicate the general medical condition]
- 608.89 Other male sexual dysfunction due to... [indicate the general medical condition]
- 302.70 Sexual dysfunction not otherwise specified

Paraphilias
- 302.4 Exhibitionism
- 302.81 Fetishism
- 302.89 Frotteurism
- 302.2 Pedophilia
- 302.83 Sexual masochism
- 302.84 Sexual sadism
- 302.3 Transvestic fetishism
- 302.82 Voyeurism
- 302.9 Paraphilia not otherwise specified

Gender Identity Disorders
- Gender identity disorder
  - 302.85 In adolescents or adults
  - 302.6 In children
  - 302.6 Gender identity disorder not otherwise specified
- 302.9 Sexual disorder not otherwise specified

Eating Disorders
- 307.1 Anorexia nervosa
- 307.51 Bulimia nervosa
- 307.50 Eating disorder not otherwise specified (EDNOS)

Sleep Disorders

Primary Sleep Disorders
- 307.44 Primary hypersomnia
- 307.42 Primary insomnia
- 347 Narcolepsy
- 780.59 Breathing-related sleep disorder
- 307.45 Circadian rhythm sleep disorder
- 307.47 Dyssomnia not otherwise specified
- 327.03 Insomnia related to mood disorder (ICD 9)

Parasomnias
- 307.47 Nightmare disorder
- 307.46 Sleep terror disorder
- 307.46 Sleepwalking disorder
- 307.47 Parasomnia not otherwise specified

Other Sleep Disorders
- Sleep disorder
  - Sleep disorder due to... [indicate the general medical condition]
  - 780.54 Hypersomnia type
  - 780.52 Insomnia type
  - 780.59 Mixed type
  - 780.59 Parasomnia type
- 307.42 Insomnia related to... [indicate the Axis I or Axis II disorder]
- 307.44 Hypersomnia related to... [indicate the Axis I or Axis II disorder]

Impulse-Control Disorders Not Elsewhere Classified
- 312.34 Intermittent explosive disorder
- 312.32 Kleptomania
- 312.31 Pathological gambling
- 312.33 Pyromania
- 312.39 Trichotillomania
- 312.30 Impulse-control disorder not otherwise specified

Contd...

Adjustment Disorders
- 309.9 Unspecified
- 309.24 With anxiety
- 309.0 With depressed mood
- 309.3 With disturbance of conduct
- 309.28 With mixed anxiety and depressed mood
- 309.4 With mixed disturbance of emotions and conduct

Personality Disorders (AXIS II)

Cluster A (odd or eccentric)
- 301.0 Paranoid personality disorder
- 301.20 Schizoid personality disorder
- 301.22 Schizotypal personality disorder

Cluster B (dramatic, emotional or erratic)
- 301.7 Antisocial personality disorder
- 301.83 Borderline personality disorder
- 301.50 Histrionic personality disorder
- 301.81 Narcissistic personality disorder

Cluster C (anxious or fearful)
- 301.82 Avoidant personality disorder
- 301.6 Dependent personality disorder
- 301.4 Obsessive-compulsive personality disorder

NOS

301.9 Personality disorder not otherwise specified

Additional Codes
- V62.3 Academic problem
- V62.4 Acculturation problem
- 995.2 Adverse effects of medication not otherwise specified
- 780.9 Age-related cognitive decline
- Antisocial behavior
  - V71.01 Adult antisocial behavior
  - V71.02 Child or adolescent antisocial behavior
- V62.82 Bereavement
- V62.89 Borderline intellectual functioning
- 313.82 Identity problem
- Medication-induced
- Movement disorder
  - 333.90 Movement disorder not otherwise specified
  - 333.1 Postural tremor
- Neglect of child
  - V61.21 Neglect of child
  - 995.5 Neglect of child (if focus of attention is on victim)
- Neuroleptic-induced
  - 333.99 Acute akathisia
  - 333.7 Acute dystonia
  - 332.1 Parkinsonism
  - 333.82 Tardive dyskinesia
  - 333.92 Neuroleptic malignant syndrome
- V71.09 No diagnosis on Axis II
- V71.09 No diagnosis or condition on Axis I
- V15.81 Noncompliance with treatment
- V62.2 Occupational problem
- V61.20 Parent-child relational problem
- V61.10 Partner relational problem
- V62.89 Phase of life problem
- Physical abuse
  - V61.1 Physical abuse of adult
  - 995.81 Physical abuse of adult (if focus of attention is on victim)
  - V61.21 Physical abuse of child
  - 995.5 Physical abuse of child (if focus of attention is on victim)
- 316 Psychological factors affecting medical condition
- Relational problem
  - V62.81 Relational problem not otherwise specified
  - V61.9 Relational problem related to a mental disorder or general medical condition
- V62.89 Religious or spiritual problem
- V61.1 Sexual abuse of adult
- 995.83 Sexual abuse of adult (if focus of attention is on victim)
- V61.21 Sexual abuse of child
- 995.53 Sexual abuse of child (if focus of attention is on victim)
- V61.8 Sibling relational problem
- 300.9 Unspecified mental disorder (non-psychotic)
- 799.9 Diagnosis deferred on Axis II
- 799.9 Diagnosis or condition deferred on Axis I
- V65.2 Malingering

SUMMARY

- Mental health nursing is defined as a branch of nursing which deals with the study of measures in order to prevent mental illnesses, promote mental health and restore the patient with mental illnesses.
- **International Classification of Diseases (ICD)** has been given by World Health Organization (WHO). The codes of ICD-11 are alphanumeric and cover the range from 1A00.00 to ZZ9Z.ZZ. Codes starting with 'X' indicate an extension code (see Extension codes). The inclusion of a forced number at the 3rd character position prevents spelling 'undesirable' words. The letters 'O' and 'I' are omitted to prevent confusion with the numbers '0' and '1'. Chapters are indicated by the first character. For example, 1A00 is a code in Chapter 1, and BA00 is a code in Chapter 11.
- **Diagnostic Statistical Manual (DSM) Classification of Mental Disorders** has been given by American Psychiatric Association (APA). DSM-5 diagnostic chapters are as follows:
  - Schizophrenia spectrum and other psychotic disorders
  - Bipolar and related disorders
  - Depressive disorders
  - Anxiety disorders
  - Obsessive-compulsive and related disorders
  - Trauma and stressor-related disorders

Contd...

- Dissociative disorders
- Somatic symptom and related disorders
- Feeding and eating disorders
- Elimination disorders
- Sleep-wake disorders
- Sexual dysfunctions
- Gender dysphoria
- Disruptive, impulsive and conduct disorders
- Substance-related and addictive disorders
- Neurocognitive disorders
- Personality disorders
- Paraphilic disorders
- Other mental disorders

- Personality is defined as a set of behaviors, cognitions and emotional patterns that evolve from biological and environmental factors.
- Perspectives in personality theory are psychoanalytic perspective, behaviorist perspective, humanistic perspective and trait perspective.
- Theories of personality development include psychoanalytic theory, Neo-Freudian approaches, Jung theory, Erikson's theory of psychosocial development, Bandura's social learning theory, Rogers theory of personality and trait approach.
- Defense mechanism is defined as 'unconscious processes which defend the individual and protect from the anxiety'.
- George Eman Vaillant, a psychiatrist, described four-level classification of defense mechanisms as pathological, immature, neurotic and mature type.
- Pathological defense mechanisms are conversion, denial, superiority complex and inferiority complex.
- Immature defense mechanisms are acting out, fantasy, wishful thinking, idealization, passive aggression, projection and somatization.
- Neurotic defense mechanisms are displacement, dissociation, hypochondriasis, intellectualization, rationalization, reaction formation, regression, repression, undoing, withdrawal, upward and downward social comparison.
- Mature defense mechanisms are patience, acceptance, mindfulness, humility, courage, gratitude, altruism, forgiveness, anticipation, emotional self-regulation, humor, emotional self-sufficiency, thought suppression, sublimation and identification.
- Biopsychosocial etiology of mental illness includes biological factors (genetic factors, biochemical factors, structural damage to brain, infections, maternal factors, prenatal damage, hormonal factors and other factors), psychological factors, environmental factors and social factors.
- Structurally, the brain is divided into cerebrum, cerebellum, brain stem and limbic system.
- Neuron is the structural and functional unit of brain. Neurotransmission is the fundamental process that transfers information between neurons. Neurotransmitters are classified based on the chemical structure (amino acid group, cholinergic group, catecholamines, neuropeptides group, indolamines group) and they depend on the functions (excitatory and inhibitory).
- Principles of psychiatric nursing include:
  - Accept the client exactly as he/she is
  - Use self-understanding as a therapeutic tool
  - Use of consistent behavior might contribute to the client's security
  - Give reassurance in an acceptable and subtle manner
  - Change the client's behavior by emotional experience rather than rational interpretation
  - Avoid unnecessary increase in client's anxiety
  - Use objective observation to understand client's behavior
  - Maintain a realistic nurse-client relationship
  - Avoid physical and verbal forces as much as possible
  - Focus nursing care on the patient as a person rather than controlling symptoms
  - Give all explanations of procedures and routines according to the client's level of understanding
  - Many procedures are modified but basic principles remain unchanged.
- Standards of care include:
  - Standard I: Assessment
  - Standard II: Diagnosis
  - Standard III: Outcome identification
  - Standard IV: Planning
  - Standard V: Implementation
    - Standard Va: Counseling
    - Standard Vb: Milieu therapy
    - Standard Vc: Self-care activities
    - Standard Vd: Psychobiological interventions
    - Standard Ve: Health teaching
    - Standard Vf: Case management
    - Standard Vg: Health promotion and health maintenance

Contd...

  - Standard Vh: Psychotherapy
  - Standard Vi: Prescription of pharmacological agents
  - Standard Vj: Consultation
- Standard VI: Evaluation

- Standards of professional performance include:
  - Standard I: Quality of care
  - Standard II: Performance appraisal
  - Standard III: Education
  - Standard IV: Collegiality
  - Standard V: Ethics
  - Standard VI: Collaboration
  - Standard VII: Research
  - Standard VIII: Resource utilization
- Conceptual models in psychiatric nursing include existential model, psychoanalytical model, behavioral model and interpersonal model.

- **Indian Nursing Council Standards in Mental Health Nursing**

  A. Standards of Practice
  - Standard 1: Assessment
  - Standard 2: Nursing diagnosis
  - Standard 3: Expected outcomes of care
  - Standard 4: Planning
  - Standard 5: Implementation
    - Standard 5a: Nursing care delivery to health care consumers
    - Standard 5b: Assistance in the delivery of biological therapies
    - Standard 5c: Psychotherapeutic interventions
    - Standard 5d: Safe and therapeutic environment
    - Standard 5e: Health education
    - Standard 5f: Community mental health nursing services, including reintegration of health care consumers into the community
  - Standard 6: Evaluation

  B. Standards of Education
  - Standard 7: Academic excellence
  - Standard 7a: Personal academic development
  - Standard 7b: Capacity building

  C. Standards of Administration
  - Standard 8: Administrative efficiency
    - Standard 8a: Personal vision, commitment, technical expertise
    - Standard 8b: Team building
    - Standard 8c: Quality assurance
    - Standard 8d: Continuing nursing education
    - Standard 8e: Leadership
    - Standard 8f: Performance appraisal
    - Standard 8g: Organizational and professional advancement

  D. Standards of Evidence-Based Practice and Research
  - Standard 9: Responsible and ethical conduct of research and integration into practice
    - Standard 9a: Research ethics
    - Standard 9b: Integration of research into practice
    - Standard 9c: Teaching scientific rigor to young nurse investigators

  E. Other Standards of Professional Performance
  - Standard 10: Self-care and self-awareness
  - Standard 11: Ethics
  - Standard 12: Communication
  - Standard 13: Culturally sensitive care
  - Standard 14: Legally safe practice

ASSESS YOURSELF

Long Answer Questions

1. Define mental health nursing/psychiatric nursing. Explain the principles of psychiatric nursing with appropriate examples.
2. Elaborate various defense mechanisms with examples.
3. Elaborate the classification of mental disorders.
4. Describe the theories of personality development.
5. Explain the psychopathology of mental disorders.

Short Answer Questions

1. What is collective unconscious?
2. Define Freud's psychoanalytical theory of personality.
3. Which standards are included in standards of professional performance?
4. Define self-concept.

Short Notes

Write short notes on:

1. Standards of psychiatric nursing
2. Conceptual models in psychiatric nursing
3. Neurotransmitters
4. Etiology of mental disorders

Multiple Choice Questions

1. **ICD-11 Code for Autism Spectrum disorder is:**
   a. 6A02 b. 6A70
   c. 6A30 d. 6A52
2. **Level of dopamine in Schizophrenia is:**
   a. Increased b. Decreased
   c. Normal range d. Not specific
3. **__________ is the structural and functional part of the brain.**
   a. Neuron b. Cell
   c. Tissue d. Myocytes
4. **Carl Rogers views the personality in terms of ______.**
   a. Self-esteem b. Self-concept
   c. Self-confidence d. Self-control
5. **The outward bodily expression of emotions that range from joy to sorrow or anger is termed:**
   a. Mood b. Affect
   c. Anhedonia d. Depression
6. **In Erikson's theory of psychosocial development, stage of old age is:**
   a. Initiative versus guilt
   b. Industry versus inferiority
   c. Generativity versus stagnation
   d. Ego Integrity versus despair
7. **________ denotes pleasure principle in psychoanalytic theory.**
   a. Id b. Ego
   c. Superego d. Superior ego
8. **The conscious way of pushing out the negative thoughts or feelings is:**
   a. Repression b. Suppression
   c. Regression d. Rationalization
9. **__________ is considered the emotional brain.**
   a. Cerebrum b. Cerebellum
   c. Brain stem d. Limbic system
10. **___________ is the originator of interpersonal relational theory.**
    a. Harry S Sullivan
    b. Albert Ellis
    c. Sigmund Freud
    d. Hippocrates

Answer Key

1. a	2. a	3. a	4. b	5. b
6. d	7. a	8. b	9. d	10. a

Assessment of Mental Health Status

CHAPTER 3

LEARNING OBJECTIVE

After studying this chapter, the student will be able to gain knowledge regarding assessment in psychiatric nursing to render the quality nursing care for mentally ill patients.

CHAPTER OUTLINE

- Psychiatric History Collection
- Mental Status Examination
- Neurological Assessment
- Mini Mental Status Examination or Folstein Test
- Investigations in Psychiatry
- Psychological Tests

KEY TERMS

History collection, Mental status examination, Mini-mental status examination, Psychological test, Insight, Form of thought, perseveration, Flight of ideas, Clang association, Mood, Affect, Premorbid personality, Pedigree, Omega sign, Otto veraguth folds, Nasolabial folds, Delusion, Hallucination, Illusion, Circumstantiality, Tangentiality, Neologism, Fear, Anxiety, Mutism, Panic attack, Thought block, Thought retardation, Thought broadcasting, Amnesia, Paramnesia, Retrograde amnesia, Anterograde amnesia, Confabulation, Déjà Vu, Jamais Vu, Abstract thinking, Glasgow coma scale, Cranial nerve assessment, Reflexes, Romberg test, Tandem walking test, Stereognosis, Baragnosis, Calorie test, Graphesthesia, Toxicology screening, Drug levels, Electrophysiological test, Brain imaging test, Neuro-endocrine test, Neuropsychological test, Personality test, Occupational test, Intelligence test, Aptitude test, Interest test, Individual/Group tests, Paper-pencil/Performance test, Speed/Power tests, Computer-assisted tests.

PSYCHIATRIC HISTORY COLLECTION

Introduction

History means inquiry or the knowledge acquired by investigations. Its roots lie in the past and are supported by available written documents. In nursing, history means the story of a patient which might be collected from patient, caregivers/family members/informant (who meet the criteria of reliability). Collateral history collection means collecting history from friends, police and strangers who might know the information about the patient. Collecting history is a vital part for a nurse to have strong knowledge about patient.

Table 3.1 shows differences between general history collection and psychiatric history collection.

Purposes

- To know about the patient.
- To use it as a pathway to perform right health assessment.
- To provide the baseline data about patient.
- To understand the past treatment and outcomes.
- To identify the causative factors for each issue.
- To compare the patient's condition/symptoms before the onset of illness.

Table 3.1: Differences between general history collection and psychiatric history collection

Aspects	General history collection	Psychiatric history collection
Information collected	Maximum from patient	**For psychosis:** Maximum history collected from informant in case of psychosis (so, reliability of informant has to be checked before collecting history). **For neurosis:** Maximum history collected from patient.
Present and past psychiatric history	Included only if, there is psychiatric problem to patient or to family members	A vital component of history collection.
Family history	Two-generation chart can be drawn	Three-generation chart to identify the root cause/genetic influences.
Behavior problems in personal history	Addressed only if, it is present	Act as vital source for problem identification.
Premorbid personality	Not necessary	It is essential to identify the differences in patient before and after the onset of illness. For example, patient himself an anxious person from childhood might be diagnosed as anxious personality disorder; not to be diagnosed as generalized anxiety disorder.

History Collection Format

I. Demographic data

- Name
- Age
- Gender
- Education
- Occupation
- Monthly income
- Universal Hospital Identity Number (UHID No.)/In Patient Number (I.P.No.)/Out Patient Number (O.P.No.)
- Ward/OPD
- Unit
- Marital status
- Nationality
- Religion
- Date and time of admission
- Diagnosis
- Doctors in-charge
- Address
- Informant (Name/Relationship)
- Reliability of Informant

Criteria to collect history from reliable informant are as follows:
- Informant should have a close relationship with patient and he/she should be living together with the patient from last 2 years.
- Informant should not have any communication deficit (hearing/vision problems).
- Informant should be a sound minded person (i.e., not suffering from any mental illness).
- Information provided by the informant should be reliable and adequate.

II. Chief complaints/presenting complaints (list with duration):

- Use verbatim technique (write the patient's complaint exactly in the same words as verbalized by the patient or informant). Organize and write the chief complaints in such a way that, 'complaints with longer duration should be written first and shorter duration at the last'.

  Example: Unable to sleep properly for past 10 days, Hearing male voices for past 8 days, Loss of appetite for past 3 days

III. Present psychiatric history/nature of the current episode

- **Onset**
  - Abrupt (symptoms occur within 48 hours)
  - Acute (symptoms occur within 2 weeks)
  - Insidious (symptoms occur from several weeks to months)
- **Intensity:** Same/increasing/decreasing
- **Duration:** Days, weeks or months
- **Course:** Continuous/episodic
- **Precipitating factors:** Yes/no (if yes, describe the factors such as stressful events of life, nonadherence to medications, etc.)
- **History of current episode** (write in detail about the presenting complaints)
- **Associated disturbances:** Includes present medical problems (e.g., disturbances in sleep pattern, problems with appetite, interpersonal relations with others, social functioning with others, problems faced in occupation, etc.)

IV. Past psychiatric history

- Number of episodes with onset, duration of each episode, intensity and course
- Complete or incomplete remission of symptoms
- Treatment details and its side effects, extrapyramidal effects, if any
- Prognosis of the previous treatment/hospitalizations
- Previous suicidal attempts, if any
- Description of any precipitating factor, if present.

V. Medical history, surgical history, obstetrical history (if the patient is female)

VI. Family history

- **Family genogram:** Draw three-generation chart which should include grandparents. Include the particular generation which has specific psychiatric family history. Table 3.2 shows some symbols of genogram.
- **Types of family:** Joint/Nuclear/Extended
- **Consanguinity:** Present/Absent

VII. Personal history

- **Birth history**
  - **Prenatal history:** Fetus having exposure to radiation, maternal infections and other maternal complications.
  - **Natal history:** Type of delivery (normal/cesarean/vacuum/forceps), newborn cried at birth, neonatal infections and other complications.
  - **Milestones:** Normal or delayed
- **Behavior during childhood**
  - Excessive temper tantrum
  - Feeding habits or pica
  - Habit disorders
- **Illness during childhood**
  - Seizures
  - Neurotic disorders
  - Central nervous system infections
  - Malnutrition
- **Schooling/educational history**
  - Age of joining school
  - Academic performance in the school
  - Relationship with peer group
  - Relationship with teachers
  - Learning disability and attention deficit in childhood
  - Reason for discontinuation from education
- **Play history**
  - Involvement in play activities
  - Preferred type of play
  - Preferred play materials

Table 3.2: Genogram symbols

Pedigree/family tree/genogram
Male
Female
Pregnancy
Relationship
Female died
Male patient
Female patient
Consanguineous marriage
Divorce
Consanguineous marriage and divorced
Adopted into the family
Adopted out of family
Monozygotic twins
Dizygotic twins
Emotional bonding (bonding is present between mother and daughter)
Extramarital relationship (wife having extramarital relationship)

- **Occupational history**
  - Age of joining the job
  - Relationship with colleagues, subordinates and supervision
  - Frequent change of job, if so, give details with rationale
  - Frequent absenteeism in job
- **Menstrual and puberty history**
  - Age of attaining puberty
  - Menstrual cycles are regular/irregular

- **Sexual history**
    - Source and extent of knowledge about sex
    - Any extramarital relationship (Ask if the information is found to be essential)
- **Marital history**
    - Name, age, education and occupation of spouse
    - Duration of married life
    - Love or arranged marriage
    - Number of marriages
    - Bonding in marital relationship

- **Premorbid personality:** Personality might change after the onset of an illness. Description of the personality before the onset of the illness aims to rule out the change occurred in behavior of individual after illness.
    - **Attitude toward others in social, family and sexual relationship:** Ability to develop trust on others and ability to sustain the relationship with others.
    - **Attitudes toward self:** Selfish, feel proud, over concerned, egocentric, dramatizing, self-conscious, satisfied about self, unhappy or dissatisfied about self.
    - **Moral and religious attitudes and standards:** Identify any specific religious beliefs or having excessive religiosity. Check out the importance given for moral values.
    - **Mood:** Ask regarding the stability of mood, anxious mood, irritable mood, worrying always, mood swings. Ability to express and control anger, depression and anxiety.
    - **Leisure activities and hobbies:** Enquire the patient about the hobbies performed in leisure time.
    - **Fantasy life:** Enquire regarding day dreams and amount of time spent in day dreaming.
    - **Reaction pattern to stress:** Ability to tolerate frustrations or sudden disappointments, and situations causing anger, anxiety or depression. Whether individual might use coping mechanism or defense mechanism to reduce stress.
    - **Habits:** Sleeping, eating and ill-health habits

MENTAL STATUS EXAMINATION

Definition

Assessment performed for the patients/individuals to assess the present mental status which involves mood, thought, speech, perception, cognitive functions and insight.

Purposes

- To assess the mental status of an individual.
- To provide a guideline/pathway to decide the treatment modalities.
- To diagnose the patient's condition.
- To assess the improvement in patient's condition with the treatment regimen.

Format of Mental Status Examination

I. General appearance and behavior

- **Facial expression (Depressed/anxious/smiling/blunted/anger/irritable):** Anger expression denotes the patient might be having chance of getting violent. Smiling is considered normal and also seen in patients with mania. Blunt facial expression is considered neutral and needs further examination. Irritable facial expression denotes the abnormality and sometimes it might be due to the effect of extrapyramidal symptoms in initial stage. Facial expression which denotes extreme sadness, omega sign (furrowed brow due to sustained contraction of corrugator muscle), Otto Veraguth folds (upward inward folds of upper eyelids) and nasolabial folds (lines on the either side of mouth extend from the edge of nose to outer corner of mouth) might suggest depression (Fig. 3.1).
- **Posture (normal/stooped/stiff/guarded):** Stooped posture is seen in patients with Parkinson's disease. Stiff posture may suggest neurological defects and also the extrapyramidal symptoms due to antipsychotics. Guarded posture denotes that the patient is feeling insecure and it may be the sign of phobia or anxiety.
- **Mannerisms (stereotype, negativism/tics/normal):** Negativism is defined as apparently motiveless resistance to all instructions which are seen in catatonic stupor. Repetitive movements which are irregular, purposeless and jerky are considered tics/stereotypical movements.
- **Eye to eye contact (maintained/intermittently maintained/not):** Patients with depression will not

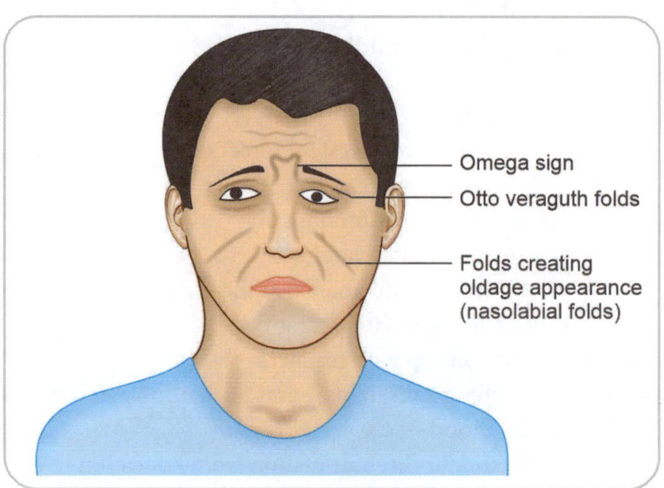

Figure 3.1: Facial expressions

maintain eye contact and native Americans/Alaskan culture might feel that maintaining eye contact is a rude act.

- **Rapport (built easily/not built/built with difficulty):** Difficulty in building up rapport will be there in patients with depression as well the patients who exhibit negative symptoms of schizophrenia and psychosis.
- **Consciousness (conscious/drowsy/unconscious):** Drowsiness might denote the inadequate sleep, sleep disorders or due to the sedative effect of antipsychotics or immediate effect of any substance abuse. Decreased need for sleep is present in patient with mania.
- **Social behavior (overfriendly/disinterested/preoccupied/aggressive/normal):** Patients with mania build rapport and exhibit overfriendliness with everyone. Patients with psychotic disorders/patients with substance use disorder are at high risk of aggression.
- **Dressing and grooming (well-dressed/ appropriate/inappropriate to season and situation/neat/dirty):** Dressing inappropriately especially wearing so colorful dress/ornaments is seen in patients with mania. Depression patients keep themselves dirty and are not well-dressed or groomed well. Wearing dress according to the season can be a triggering factor to identify the seasonal affective disorder.
- **Physical features (look older/younger than age/underweight/overweight/physical deformity):** Overweight denotes obesity might be due to genetic/faulty lifestyle/due to side effects of certain antipsychotics. Underweight condition is seen in patient with anorexia nervosa/bulimia nervosa. Patient with depression might look older than age due to folds seen in the patient's face.
- **Psychomotor activity (normal/increased/decreased/compulsive/echopraxia/stereotyped movements/negativism/automatic obedience):** Increased psychomotor activity is seen in patients with mania. Compulsive acts are due to obsession (repetitive thoughts) seen in obsessive compulsive disorder and also in the patients who exhibit command hallucination. Echopraxia is defined as mimic of activities performed by other individual, seen in schizophrenia. Automatic obedience is performing an action said by others irrespective of thinking about the consequences due to the specified action, this is seen in schizophrenia. *Decreased* psychomotor activity is seen in patients with depression and negative symptoms of schizophrenia.

II. Speech: Write the sample of speech (record as verbatim technique—what patient says exactly)

- **Coherence:** Coherent/incoherent
- **Relevance:** (answer the questions appropriately) Relevant/irrelevant
- **Volume:** Normal/soft/loud/ low
- **Tone:** Normal/high pitch/low pitch/ monotonous
- **Manner:** Excessive formal/relaxed/inappropriately familiar
- **Reaction time** (time taken to answer the question): Normal/increased/decreased.

III. Mood (subjective) and affect (objective)

- Appropriate/inappropriate to the situation
- Congruent/incongruent to the thought.
- **Pleasurable affect:** Euphoria (mild elated mood exhibits hypomania)/Elation (moderate elated mood exhibits psychomotor agitation)/Exaltation (severe elated mood exhibits delusion of grandeur/ecstasy (very severe elated mood or extreme blissfulness; it exhibits delirious or stupor mania).
- **Unpleasurable affect:** Grief (response to loss of beloved ones)/mourning (act of exhibiting great sadness)/depression.
- **Other effects:** Anxiety (apprehension of danger)/fear/panic (anxiety with high level of physiological response such as raised blood pressure, heart rate, etc.)/free floating anxiety (another name of general anxiety disorder)/apathy (lack of emotional expression)/aggression (behavior intended to cause harm due to anger)/mood swing (change of mood from mania to depression or depression to mania)/emotional lability (also known as emotional incontinence or pseudobulbar affect which means uncontrolled expression of emotions such as laughing or crying out suddenly).

IV. Thought

- **Form of thought/formal thought disorder:** Normal/not understandable/circumstantiality/tangentiality/neologism/ambivalence/word salad/perseveration. The concepts of formal thought disorders are explained in the Table 3.3.
- **Stream of thought/flow of thought (pressure of speech/flight of ideas/thought retardation/thought block/mutism/aphonia/clang association):** Pressure of speech is a rapid urge to speak. Speech with pressure is a hallmark symptom of mania. Pressure of speech is also seen in patients with schizophrenia, anxiety disorder and Attention Deficit Hyperactivity Disorder (ADHD).

Table 3.3: Formal thought disorders

Formal thought disorders	Description	Example
Circumstantiality	Speech of the individual reaches the goal or center point toward the question raised only after the unwanted speech	Nurse: Did you have your breakfast? Patient: I like to go home now, I feel sleepy, I would like to see my mother, **I had my breakfast** (At last, patient verbalized the answer that he has had breakfast after an unwanted speech)
Tangentiality	Speech of the individual does not reach the goal or center point	Nurse: Did you have your breakfast? Patient: I like to go home now, I feel sleepy, I would like to see my mother **(Patient talks something but never answered to question whether he had breakfast or not)**
Neologism	Coining of new words	Patient: He says, "Jammba, Kummba, Thangu" (**New words which doesn't have any meaning**)
Ambivalence	Coexistence of two opposing forces or impulses, desires or emotions	Patient says, I want to invite my uncle for function and also feels not to invite his uncle because he will come to function along with his wife.
Word Salad	Mixture of words	Patient verbalizes lion, water, pen, mother...
Perseveration	Persistent repetition of words beyond the point of relevance	Patient verbalizes father, father, father, father....

- Flight of ideas is a rapid shifting of one idea to other ideas seen in mania, schizophrenia and in some patients with ADHD. Thought retardation is a decreased idea identified by decreased content of speech which is seen in patients with depression, dementia, nervousness, memory impairment and schizophrenia. Thought block is a condition of sudden interruption of thoughts exhibited by silence for few seconds to minutes which is commonly seen in patients with schizophrenia. Mutism is complete absence of speech seen in patients with depression, negative symptoms of schizophrenia and in catatonic stupor. Aphonia is defined as the inability to produce voiced sound due to laryngeal nerve damage or secondary thyroidectomy and also due to underlying psychological problems. Clang association is rhyming of words seen in patients with schizophrenia.
- **Content of thought**
  - **Delusion:** Delusion is a strong fixed unshakable belief irrespective of their sociocultural background. However, it is different from overvalued ideas, it means more significance has been given to single ideation. The types are delusion of persecution/delusion of reference/delusion of influence or passivity/hypochondrial delusions/delusions of grandeur/nihilistic delusion/derealization/depersonalization/delusion of infidelity.
  - **Obsession** (repetitive thoughts)
  - **Phobia** (fear of something)
  - **Preoccupation:** Keep on thinking of something.
  - **Fantasy:** Creative/day dreaming.

V. Disorders of perception

- **Illusions**
- **Hallucinations:** Auditory/visual/olfactory/gustatory/tactile or haptic
- **Others:** Hypnogogic/hypnopompic/command or tele-ological/Lilliputian/kinesthetic/macropsia/micropsia

Types of delusion, illusion and hallucination are summarized in the Tables 3.4, 3.5 and 3.6, respectively.

VI. Cognitive functions

- **Consciousness**
  - Conscious/semiconscious/unconscious (or)
  - Alert/confused/somnolent(sleepy)/lethargy/obtunded (difficult to arouse)/stupor (very difficult to arouse)/unresponsive or coma.
- **Attention and concentration**
  - **Digit span test:** For example, repeat the numbers 1, 3, 7, 9
  - **Digit forward test:** For example, say the numbers 1 to 10
  - **Digit backward test:** For example, say the numbers from 10 to 1
    - Method of testing (asking to list the months of the year forward and backward)
    - Serial subtraction test (100 – 7 = 93, Patient is asked to recall the events happened immediately 93 – 7 = 86, 86 – 7 = 79)

Table 3.4: Types of delusion

Types of delusion	Description	Example
Delusion of persecution	Having a strong suspicious belief that others are trying to harm him/her	Patient verbalizes that, "My friend is making a plan to kill me"
Delusion of grandeur	Strong unshakable belief that he/she is an important famous personality or superior knowledge or ideation or power	Patient verbalizes that, 'I am the God'
Delusion of reference	Strong unshakable belief that the other person is referring oneself with a neutral event in the environment	Patient verbalizes that, 'They are talking about me'
Delusion of influence or passivity	Strong unshakable belief that one's thoughts or actions are imposed by someone from outside	Patient verbalizes that, 'My hand is moved by an external source'
Nihilistic delusion	Strong unshakable belief that the world is not existing	Patient verbalizes that, 'World is not existing'
Delusion of infidelity (or) Delusion of jealousy (or) Othello syndrome	Strong unshakable belief that his/her spouse has extramarital relationship with other person	Patient verbalizes that, 'My wife is having a love affair with other guy'
Erotomanic delusion (or) Delusion of love	Strong unshakable belief that some famous personality is having love desire on oneself.	Patient verbalizes that, 'Actor is having love desire toward me'
Somatic delusion	Strong unshakable belief in regard to physical appearance, body functioning and sensation which is unreal but considered real	Patient verbalizes that, 'I feel sound of running water in my stomach'
Delusion of guilt (or) Delusion of sin	Strong unshakable belief that the individual feels more guilt to an extent which is unreal	Patient felt that, he is highly responsible for the disaster happened
Delusion of poverty	Strong unshakable belief that he/she will be deprived of material possessions.	Patient verbalizes that, 'My assets are going to be stolen by my friend'
Delusion of control	Strong unshakable belief that one's own thoughts or actions are controlled from outside	Patient verbalizes that, 'My actions are controlled by ghost'
Delusion of thought broadcasting	Strong unshakable belief that one's own thoughts have been projected/displayed in mass media such as television, newspaper, internet, etc.	Patient verbalizes that, 'My ideas are shown in TV'

Table 3.5: Types of illusion

Types of illusion	Description	Example
Affect Illusion	Misperception with the heightened emotions	Tree moving in a dark place is perceived as a ghost
Completion Illusion	Illusion is mainly due to lack of attention	Misreading the bus route wrongly in the name board of the bus
Pareidolic Illusion	Illusion which is seen over the other illusion	Seeing face like figure in the clouds

Table 3.6: Types of hallucination

Types of hallucination	Description	Example
Auditory	Misperception of hearing. It is of two types: Simple (or) Elementary and Complex. *Simple Auditory Hallucination* means misperception of Sounds and *Complex auditory hallucination* means misperception of words	Patient verbalizes that 'Someone talking to me' is example of complex auditory hallucination. When patient verbalizes that, 'I am hearing the water pouring sound every time' is an example of simple auditory hallucination.
Visual	Misperception of visualization	Patient verbalizes that, 'I am able to see my uncle often who is dead.'
Olfactory	Misperception of smell	Patient verbalizes that, 'I feel always a bad smell'
Gustatory	Misperception of taste	Patient verbalizes that, 'I feel a metallic taste often'
Tactile or Haptic	Misperception of touch	Patient verbalizes that, 'I feel an insect is crawling on my skin'.

Contd...

Types of hallucination	Description	Example
Somatic	Misperception of internal body organs	Patient verbalizes that, 'I am able to feel the blood was circulating in my stomach'.
Functional	Misperception within the same sensory stimuli (For example, hallucination belonging to auditory sensory stimuli)	Patient verbalizes that, 'I am hearing voices when I hear the bird's sound'.
Extracampine	Misperception outside the limits of sensory field	Hearing voices from India when you are in USA
Reflex	Stimulus in one sensory field produces hallucination of another sensory field or modality (For example, one sensory field was touch, i.e., feel of pain and other sensory field was auditory, i.e., hearing sneezing sound)	Patient verbalizes that 'I feel painful when I hear a sneezing sound'.
Command/teleological	Auditory hallucination which is said to be command in nature	Patient verbalizes that, 'Someone is asking me to commit suicide'.
Hypnogogic	Misperception when going into sleep	Patient verbalizes that, 'I feel that a ghost is speaking to me daily while I am getting into sleep'.
Hypnopompic	Misperception while awakening from sleep	Patient verbalizes that 'I feel that a ghost is speaking to me daily when I am awakening from sleep.
Autoscopy (or) Phantom mirror image	Misperception as seeing oneself	Patient verbalizes that 'I am seeing my internal organs often'.
Kinesthetic	Hallucination involves the sense of body movements	Patient verbalizes that 'I feel like my hands are moving often without my control'.
Alice in Wonderland syndrome(or) Todd's Syndrome (or) Lilliputian hallucination (or) Dysmetropsia	• A rare condition that causes temporary episodes of distorted perception and disorientation. • Micropsia (or) Lilliputian: Objects appear smaller than the original size • Macropsia: Objects appear larger than the original size • Pelopsia: People/objects/things appear closer than the original place • Teleopsia: People/objects/things appear far away than the original place	

- **Memory**
  - **Immediate:** Patient is asked to recall the events happened immediately.
  - **Recent memory:** Patient is asked to recall the events happened 24 hours ago.
  - **Remote:** Patient is asked to recall the events happened long back (For example, can you tell your date of birth?).
    - **Amnesia/Paramnesia/Retrograde amnesia/ Anterograde amnesia:** Amnesia means memory loss. Paramnesia means a distorted memory or confusion of facts or fantasy. Retrograde amnesia means loss of memory of the events that happened before the injury or onset of illness. Anterograde amnesia means loss of memory of the events that happened after the injury or onset of illness.
    - **Confabulation:** False filling of memory gaps
    - **Déjà vu:** Familiar of unfamiliar things/**Jamais vu:** Unfamiliar of familiar things.
    - **Hyperamnesia:** Excessive loss of memory
- **Orientation**
  - **Time:** What is the time now? (Ask the patient to answer the approximate time without looking at clock or watch).
  - **Place:** Where he/she is now?
  - **Person:** Who has accompanied him or her?
- **Abstraction:** Patient's ability to answer the exact meaning of the given proverb will identify the presence of abstract thinking (e.g., All that glitters is not gold).
- **Intelligence of general information**
  - **Similarities and differences:** For example, patient will be asked to say the similarities and dissimilarities of apple and orange.
  - **General information:** For example, who is the Prime Minister of India?
- **Judgment**
  - **Personal:** Ask the patient about his/her future plans. For example, what you are planning to do after your discharge from the hospital?
  - **Social:** Observation made by the examiner that how patient is being socialized with others.
  - **Test:** Test the present situation response and ask for his/her responses to different kinds of situations.

- **Rain test:** Ask the client what he/she will do when rain comes.
- **Envelope test:** Ask the client what he/she will do when an envelope is kept on road with stamp and address.
- **Fire test:** Ask the client what he/she will do when there is a fire in his/her home.
- **Child cry test:** Ask the client what he/she will do when a child is crying on a road.

- **Insight:** (Present/Absent/Partially present)
  - **Grading of Insight**
    - **Grade I:** Complete refusal of illness
    - **Grade II:** Slight awareness of being ill
    - **Grade III:** Awareness of being sick attribute toward external or physical factor.
    - **Grade IV:** Awareness of being sick, due to something not known to oneself.
    - **Grade V:** Intellectual insight (aware about one's own mental illness in detail).
    - **Grade VI:** True emotional insight—Awareness of one's own mental illness and how the family members suffer out of it due to patient's illness.

Mental Status Examination of Uncooperative Patients

Psychiatric patients might be uncooperative sometimes and make it difficult to perform the mental status examination by a nurse/doctor. Such challenging situations can be performed using Kirby's method of examination (Table 3.7).

Table 3.7: Kirby's method of performing mental status examination for uncooperative patients

Aspects	Description
General reaction and posture	**Spontaneous action performed** • Any show of activities such as playfulness, assaultiveness or mischievousness occasionally • Whether the patient looks neat or untidy • Whether the patient eats voluntarily or needs assistance • Whether the patient dresses himself or requires assistance • Whether the patient voids or defecates voluntarily or needs assistance • Whether the actions show slowness initially or consistently throughout the day **Behavior toward the examiners** • Resistant, irritable, apathy, complaining others, evasive, etc. **Voluntary postures:** • Comfortable, natural or awkward or constrained. • What does the patient do when placed in an awkward position? **Whether the behavior remains constant or keep on changing with time?**
Facial movement and expression	It is the facial expression of being alert or smiling or mask like face or placid or anxious or perplexed or anger or distressed. Whether the facial expression remains constant or keep changing.
Eyes and pupils	• Eyes are open or closed: Whether it is resistant to open the client's eyes by examiner • Does patient give attention to examiner and move the eyes with that object • Does patient have fixed or evasive gaze • Is there blinking of eyes or flickering of eyelids • Patient responds to examiner if sudden movement of hand has been performed by examiner near to patient's eyes • Presence/absence of corneal reflex
Reaction toward the examiner's questions and tests	• Patient's response to simple commands of the examiner • Presence of negativism—whether active or passive, uncooperativeness exists. • Monitor for automatic obedience, echolalia and echopraxia • Movements of limbs are slow or fast or being interrupted often
Muscular reactions	• Assess for muscle tonicity—waxy flexibility/cog wheel rigidity/Gegenhalten/Mitmachen/Mitgehen. Waxy flexibility is a psychomotor symptom seen in catatonic schizophrenia, bipolar disorder and other psychiatric disorder in which the patient has less response to the stimuli and remains in immobile posture. Cog wheel rigidity is a ratchet-like start-and stop passive movements while performing the physical assessment mainly seen in patients with Parkinson's disease. Gegenhalten is an involuntary resistance to the passive movement seen in cerebral cortical disorders. Mitmachen is a sign in which the patient's body can be put into any posture even though it has been instructed to resist. Mitgehen is a severe form of Mitmachen in which even the slight pressure will move the particular body part. So, it is also called angle-poise effect (or) angle poise lamp sign. • Check out urinary or fecal incontinence • Whether patient speaks spontaneously • Whether patient is mute—Is it consistent or keep changing • Whether patient takes effort to create sounds or whisper

NEUROLOGICAL ASSESSMENT

The various aspects of neurological assessment are as follows:

- Level of consciousness
- Mental status assessment
- Special cerebral function
- Cranial nerve function
- Sensory function
- Motor function
- Cerebellar function
- Reflexes

- **Level of Consciousness**
  - **Alertness:** Awake and respond well to verbal stimuli
  - **Lethargic**: Drowsy, inattentive and frequently sleepy but can be wakened up
  - **Stuporous:** Arise with more difficulty
  - **Semi-comatose:** No response to verbal stimuli, little response to pain and little motor function is seen.
  - **Comatose:** No response to verbal stimuli, pain and no motor function is present
- **Special cerebral function:** Assess for agnosia, apraxia and aphasia
  - **Agnosia:** Inability to recognize the objects with senses
  - **Apraxia:** Inability to perform learned motor activities
  - **Aphasia:** Inability to speak

The Glasgow Coma Scale facilitates nurses to assess the patient's level of consciousness that has been described in Table 3.8.

Neurological effects on cranial nerve have been summarized in Table 3.9.

Table 3.8: Glasgow Coma Scale (GCS)

Glasgow Coma Scale	Categories	Scores	Nurses' responsibility in documentation of GCS
Eye response	• Spontaneous eye opening • To verbal stimuli • To pain stimuli • No response	4 3 2 1	Document 'C'—Swollen eyes due to injury/infection
Verbal response	• Oriented to time, place and person • Confused • Inappropriate speech • Incomprehensive sounds • No response	5 4 3 2 1	V_T—Patient in tracheostomy V_E—Patient is in endotracheal tube
Motor response	• Obeys command • Localizes pain • Flexion withdrawal • Abnormal flexion • Abnormal extension • No response	6 5 4 3 2 1	Record the response in upper extremities (Right/Left) or lower extremities or both
	Total GCS Score	15	
	Minimal GCS Score	3	
	Comatose patient	<7	

Table 3.9: Neurological effects on cranial nerves

Cranial nerves	Sensory/ motor/both	Assessment	Findings
I – Olfactory	Sensory	Ask the patient to identify the odor of some substance from each nostril separately	Anosmia—Absence of smell
II – Optic	Sensory	• Testing visual acuity—Ask the patient to identify numbers/alphabets/signs using Snellen's chart • Assessment of visual fields: Assess the sight of vision on various directions by showing the fingers on various directions and ask the client to see the finger without turning the head • Examine the fundus of eye using ophthalmoscope	• Impaired visual acuity (right eye/left eye/ both) • Impaired visual field (right eye/left eye/both) • Examination of fundus in eye using ophthalmoscope reveals traumatic eyeball, diabetic retinopathy and increased intracranial pressure • Examine the eye for cataract, foreign bodies, infections, inflammation or any other significant abnormalities

Contd...

Cranial nerves	Sensory/ motor/both	Assessment	Findings
III – Occulomotor IV – Trochlear VI – Abducent	Motor	Check for pupillary constriction by showing the torch light from outer canthus of eye to pupil. Assess the accommodation and visual field by checking out whether eyes are focusing the near and far objects or not.	Tumor or trauma in base of the brain Increased Intracranial pressure
V – Trigeminal	Both sensory and motor	Ask the patient to move the mouth against resistance, move the jaw side to side and perform chewing movements. Check the sensation of entire face by: • **Pain:** Using sharp objects • **Touch:** Using wisp of cotton • **Temperature:** Using hot or cold water in a test tube	Asymmetry of temporal muscles and trigeminal neuralgia
VI – Facial	Both sensory and motor	**Motor** • Observe the patient's symmetry of face • Ask the client to smile, frown, raise the eye brows, whistle, puff the cheeks and show teeth	• Bell's palsy • Contusion in parotid region • Temporal bone fracture • Peripheral laceration
VII – Vestibulocochlear (or) Acoustic nerve	Sensory	• It has two divisions—Cochlear for hearing and Vestibular for equilibrium **Cochlear** • Assess ear acuity with whispering voice • Bone conduction and air conduction test should be performed using tuning fork (Weber's test and Rinne's test) • **Weber's test:** Tuning fork is kept in middle of head. Normal individuals will hear the sound equally from both ears. If lateralization is felt on one side it denotes hearing loss (Fig. 3.2) • **Rinne's test:** Keep the tuning fork in mastoid bone and then near to patient's ear after striking it. When air conduction is more than bone conduction, it is normal. If the bone conduction is more than air conduction it denotes conductive hearing loss (Figs 3.3A and B) **Vestibular** • **Romberg test:** This test is performed to assess the balance or equilibrium of body. Ask the patient to stand straight with the eyes closed. Nurse has to be cautious while performing this test, since patient has a risk of fall • **Caloric test** (oculovestibular reflex): This test is performed to assess the coordination of eye and ear muscles. Pouring of cold water in the ear will move the opposite eyeballs and the warm water in ear will move the same side of eyeballs. Mnemonics to remember this is: C—Cold water O—Opposite eye ball movement W—Warm water S—Same side eye ball movement	Meniere's syndrome Acoustic neuroma Hearing loss (sensory-neural, conductive, mixed) Vertigo

Contd...

Cranial nerves	Sensory/ motor/both	Assessment	Findings
IX – Glossopharyngeal and X – Vagus	Both sensory and motor	Ask the patient to: • Open the mouth widely and say 'ah' to observe the movement of uvula and palate. The palate has to raise symmetrical with uvula • Assess gag reflex by touching the side of pharynx with tongue depressor	• Brain tumors • Brain stem trauma • Neck trauma • Stroke
XI – Accessory	Motor	Ask the patient to: • Raise the shoulder with or without resistance • Turn the head to one side • Move the chin away from midline with resistance • Push the head forward with resistance force	• Neck trauma • Torticollis • Drooping of shoulders • Muscle atrophy • Weak shoulders
XII – Hypoglossal	Motor	Ask the patient to move the tongue in, out and side to side	• Deviation of tongue from midline • Neck injury associated with damage to blood vessels

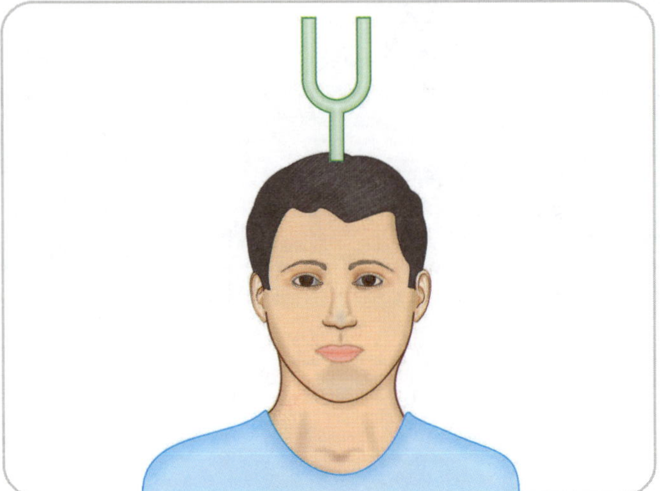

Figure 3.2: Weber's test

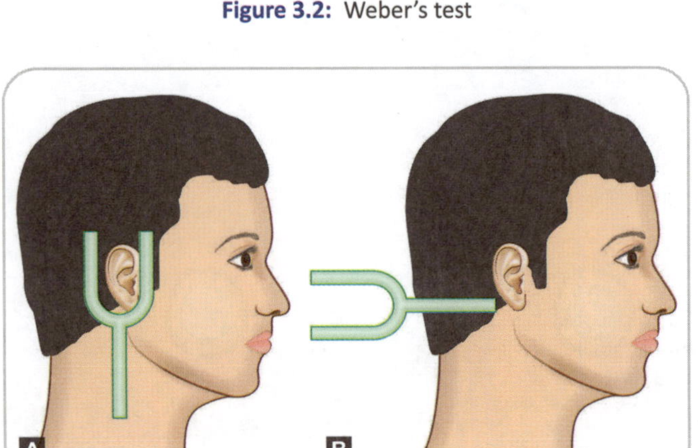

Figures 3.3A and B: Rinne's test: **A.** Air conduction; **B.** Bone conduction

Figures 3.4 and 3.5 show neuroexamination tray arrangement and vital sign examination tray arrangement, respectively.

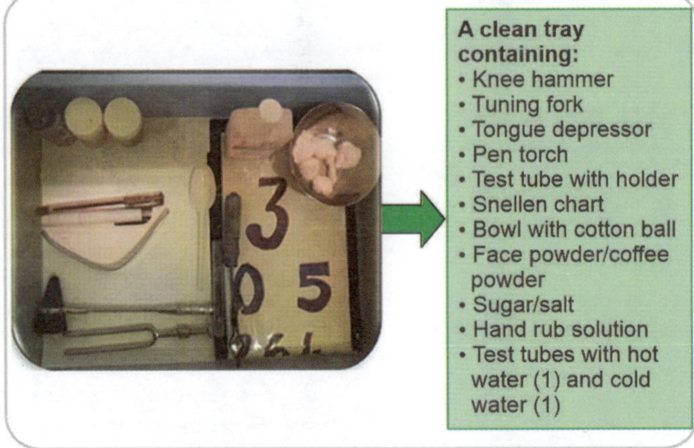

Figure 3.4: Neuroexamination tray arrangement

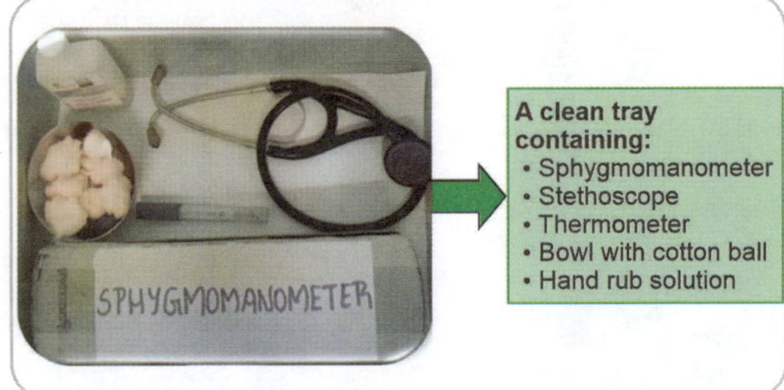

Figure 3.5: Vital signs examination tray arrangement

- **Assessment of motor functions:** It includes assessment of muscle size, muscle tone, muscle strength, muscle coordination, movement and gait. (Table 3.10).

Table 3.10: Muscle strength—Strength's score

Strength's score	Description
5/5	Normal complete strength. Active range of motion against gravity and applied resistance
4/5	Active range of motion is possible against gravity but weak with applied resistance
3/5	Muscle moves active against gravity only
2/5	Muscle moves across surface but unable to overcome gravity
1/5	Muscle contraction is possible; flickering movement is present
0/5	Undetectable muscle contraction or movement

  - **Muscle size:** Check for all muscles in a comparative manner bilaterally either symmetrical or not, assess for atrophy or hypertrophy of muscle.
  - **Muscle tone:** Assess for hypotonicity (muscle tone is decreased), hypertonicity (muscle tone is increased), rigid/spastic muscle.
  - **Muscle coordination:** Deficits in this might be due to cerebellum or posterior column lesion.
  - **Gait:** It means the manner of walking. Ask the patient to stand still, walk slowly and walk in tandem to assess the muscle power and coordination. If the patient is weak, support the patient's arm to prevent fall. Gait abnormalities are commonly seen in depression, sleep disorders, substance abuse, fear of falling, organic brain disorder and use of psychotropics and antidepressants. Common abnormal gaits are mentioned here:
    - **Ataxic gait:** Unsteady, uncoordinated staggering gait happens due to damage of cerebellum (part of brain controls the muscle coordination).
    - **Shuffling gait:** Individual drag his/her feet to walk (seen in disorders associated with dementia, Parkinsonism, etc.).
    - **Propulsive gait (or) Parkinsonian gait:** A stiff and stooped posture with head/neck forward. It is seen in Parkinson's disease, carbon monoxide poisoning and manganese toxicity.
    - **Steppage gait (or) neuropathic gait (or) equine Gait:** Abnormal gait characterized by foot drop due to absence of dorsiflexion of foot.
    - **Sensory gait (or) stomping gait:** It happens when the patient lacks proprioceptive information to the brain when the foot touches the ground. But it lacks in patient with peripheral neuropathy (due to the complications of alcohol, complications of diabetes, and disorders of dorsal columns).
    - **Choreiform gait (or) hyperkinetic gait:** Jerky irregular and involuntary movements in both the extremities. It is seen in Huntington's disease, chorea, athetosis and dystonia.
    - **Hypokinetic gait (or) magnetic gait:** Inability to lift the feet from the floor results in decreased mobility. It is a cardinal sign of normal pressure hydrocephalus.
    - **Cautious gait (or) senile gait:** Excess degree of age-related changes in walking (slow and wide based abducted arm) and having a fear of fall.
    - **Waddling gait (or) myopathic gait:** Individual walks like a duck due to the weakness present in the proximal muscles of pelvic girdle. This gait is seen in congenital hip dysplasia, pregnancy, spinal muscular atrophy and muscular dystrophies.
    - **Scissor gait:** It happens due to the contractures of all spastic muscles (hypertonia of leg muscles), increased adduction of leg. It is seen in spastic cerebral palsy and upper motor neuron lesion.
  - **Muscle movements:** Assess the gross motor movements such as walking, running, jumping, etc. and fine motor movements (using fingers) such as writing, drawing, etc.
- **Assessment of Sensory Function**
  - **Assessment of pain:** It is assessed using the large-headed safety pin with a sharp end and blunt end (Sharp end should not to be sharp enough to puncture the skin). Instruct the patient to close the eyes. Prick the patient's hand with this safety pin and ask the patient where the pain is felt. This helps to rule out hypoalgesia or hyperalgesia or analgesia as shown in Flowchart 3.1.
  - **Assessment of vibration:** Vibration sense is assessed by keeping the tuning fork in the patient's toes or fingers and ask the patient to verbalize when the vibration stops.
  - **Assessment of touch:** Ask the patient to close the eyes. Touch the patient with the wisp of cotton or tissue paper or camel-hair brush. Ask the patient to identify the sense of touch. It may be decreased (hypoesthesia) or increased (hyperesthesia) or absent (anesthesia) as shown in Flowchart 3.1.
  - **Assessment of temperature:** Ask the patient to close the eyes. Keep the hot or cold-water test tube in the patient's arm. Ask the patient to identify whether it is hot water or cold water.

Flowchart 3.1: Sense of touch and pain

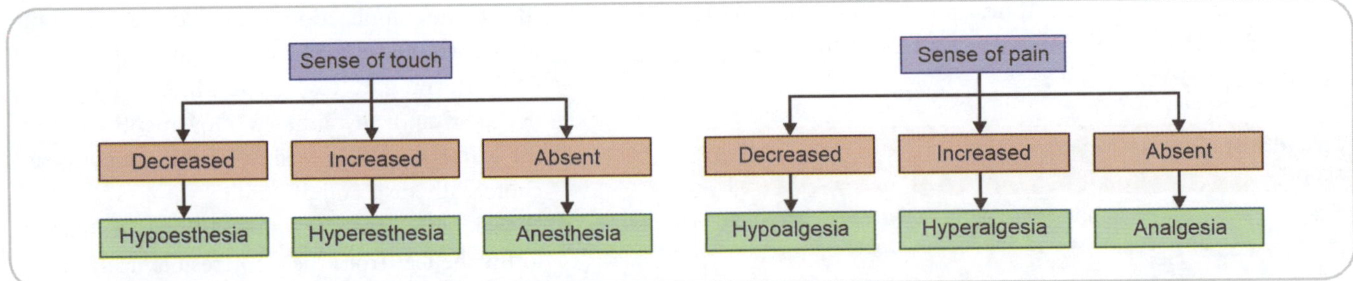

- **Assessment of pressure:** Ask the patient to close the eyes. Apply firm pressure on the patient's skin and ask the patient to identify the place where the pressure is felt.
- **Two-point discrimination:** Ask the patient to close the eyes. Apply firm pressure on the patient's skin at two different points in the same arm simultaneously and ask the patient to explore the distance between two points.
- **Proprioceptive awareness:** Ask the patient to close the eyes. Joint is moved through a range of motion and kept in a static position. Ask the patient to identify the position of the moved arm.

- **Assessment of cerebellar function:**
  - **Finger to finger test:** Patient has to touch nurse's index finger with his/her index finger.
  - **Finger to nose test:** Patient has to touch his/her nose with his/her index finger. This has to be done with opened and closed eyes, respectively. This test will assess the coordination.
  - **Romberg test:** Patient has to stand erect for 10 seconds with the eyes closed. This is done to assess the patient's balance.
  - **Tandem walking test:** Patient is asked to walk over the heel in straight line. This is done to assess for unsteadiness or staggering or imbalance gait.
- **Assessment of reflexes:**
  - The types of reflexes can be superficial or cutaneous and deep tendon or muscle-stretch reflexes as shown in Flowchart 3.2. The responses during assessment of reflexes have been presented in Table 3.11.

Special Tests in Neurological Assessment

- **Stereognosis (or) haptic perception (or) tactile gnosis:** Ability to perceive and recognize the object using tactile sense.
- **Barognosis (or) baresthesia:** It is the ability to evaluate the weight of objects, or to differentiate objects of different weights, by holding or lifting them. It is done to assess loss of the ability to sense weight.

Flowchart 3.2: Classification of reflexes

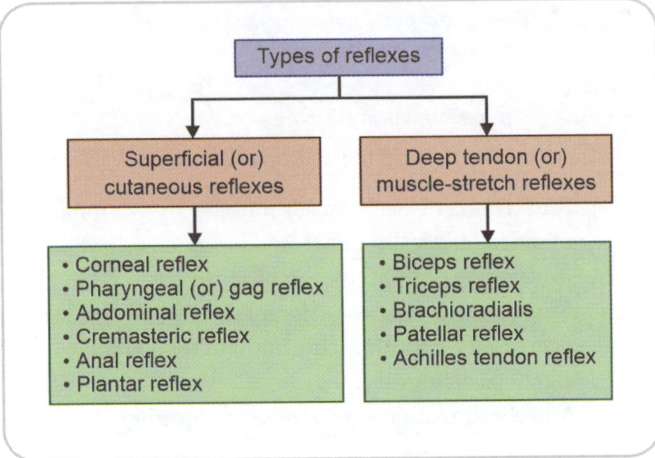

- **Graphesthesia:** Graphesthesia is the ability to recognize writing on the skin purely by the sensation of touch.

MINI MENTAL STATUS EXAMINATION OR FOLSTEIN TEST

Introduction

Mini mental status examination (MMSE) was introduced by Folstein in 1975 to differentiate the organic and functional psychosis.

Definition

Mini mental status examination is a method that uses 30-point questionnaire to assess the cognitive impairment in clinical and research settings (Table 3.12).

Purposes

- To assess the progression and severity of cognitive impairment of an individual.
- To diagnose the patient's condition, administer the treatment.
- To assess the improvement in cognitive status after the treatment regimen.

Table 3.11: Assessment of reflexes and responses

Assessment of reflexes	Description	Response
Corneal reflex	Touching the cornea with wisp of cotton	Blinking of eyes
Pharyngeal (or) gag reflex	Stimulation with tongue blade in back of throat and pharynx	Gagging
Abdominal reflex	Stroking of the skin in the abdominal quadrant	Abdominal muscle contracts and umbilicus move toward the stimulated side
Cremasteric reflex	Stroking the inner thigh of patient	Elevation of Ipsilateral testicle
Anal reflex (or) anal wink (or) perineal reflex (or) anocutaneous reflex	Stroking the skin around the anus	Contraction of rectal sphincter
Plantar reflex	Touching the foot's outer plantar surface from heel toward toes	Contraction of toes
Biceps reflex	Arm gently flexed at elbow, tap the biceps brachii tendon	Flexion of forearm (Fig. 3.6)
Triceps reflex	Tapping of triceps brachii tendon in elbow	Extension of forearm (Fig. 3.7)
Brachioradialis	Tapping of styloid process of radius about 1–2 inches above the wrist	Flexion of elbow/ hand/fingers and supination of forearm (Fig. 3.8)
Patellar reflex	Tapping of quadriceps femoris tendon (present below patella)	Extension of leg
Achilles tendon reflex	Tapping of Achilles tendon	Plantar flexion of foot

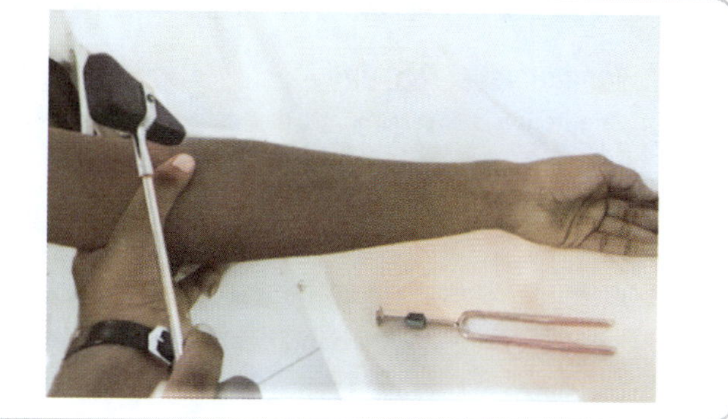

Figure 3.6: Assessment of biceps reflex

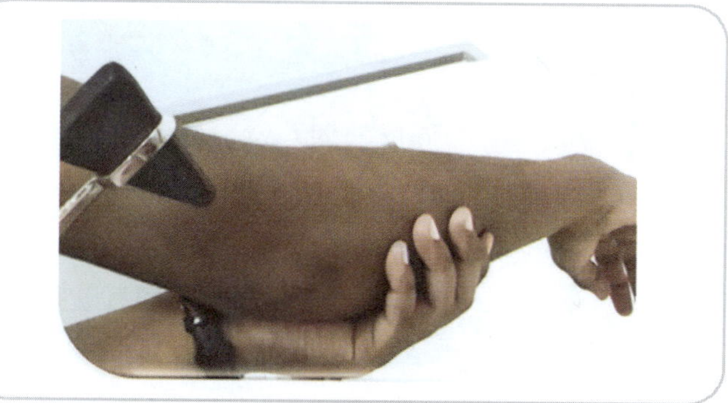

Figure 3.7: Assessment of triceps reflex

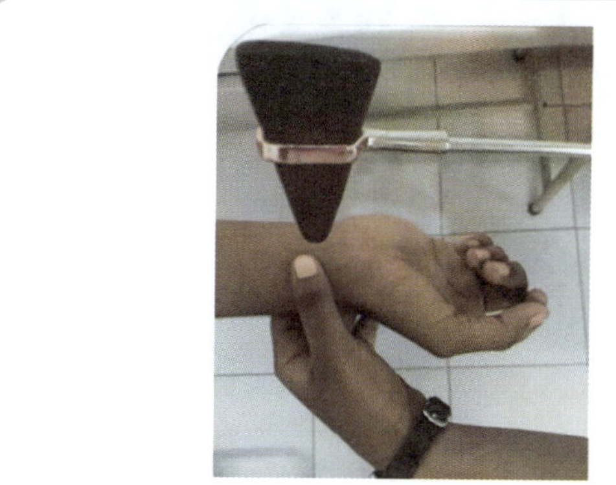

Figure 3.8: Assessment of brachioradialis

Advantages

- No special equipment or instrument is required to administer this test.
- No special training is required to administer this test.
- It has both reliability and validity.
- It is helpful in longitudinal assessment of cognitive status.

Disadvantages

- This test is affected with the demographic factors such as age, education, etc.
- It lacks its sensitivity to assess the patients with mild cognitive impairment; it's difficult to differentiate between patient with mild Alzheimer's disease and a normal person.
- Items in mini mental status examination are highly verbal and little with visuospatial (ability to visualize or imagine the objects) and constructional praxis (ability to build the objects).
- Remembering the physical health problems or other mental disorder or motor deficits that might affect the results of Mini-Mental Status Examination (MMSE).

Table 3.12: **Mini-mental status examination (MMSE) format**

Sl. no.	Components	Description	Max. score	Total score
1.	Orientation	Year, month, day, date, season	5	
		Country, state, town, place, floor	5	
2.	Registration	Examiner names the three objects (example, pen, apple and table). Patient is asked to repeat the objects, one score for each	3	
3.	Attention	Subtract 7 from 100 then repeat from the result for five subtractions	5	
4.	Recall	Ask the name of objects learned earlier	3	
5.	Language	Name a pencil and watch	2	
		Repeat 'No ifs and or buts'	1	
		Give a three-stage command. Score one for each stage. (For example, 'Take this piece of paper in your right hand, fold it in half and place it on the table'	3	
		Ask patient to read and obey a written command on the piece of paper stating: 'Close your eyes'	1	
		Ask patient to write a sentence. Score correct if it has a subject and verb	1	
6.	Copying	Ask the individual to copy the intersecting pentagons. Score if it overlaps and has five sides **Results indicate:** **Total score** – **Cognitive impairment** 24–30 – No cognitive impairment 18–23 – Mild cognitive impairment 0–17 – Severe cognitive impairment	1	
			Grand Total =	_________/30

INVESTIGATIONS IN PSYCHIATRY

Blood Tests

Various blood investigations are carried out on a psychiatry patient which have been presented in Table 3.13.

Table 3.13: **Various blood investigations conducted on psychiatric patients**

Blood investigations	Description
Hemoglobin	Routine screening is helpful to rule out anemia.
Blood glucose level and glycosylated hemoglobin	Increased or decreased blood glucose levels are associated with delirium. Atypical antipsychotics might cause impaired glucose tolerance. Clozapine and olanzapine pose risk of increasing blood glucose. Quetiapine, Risperidone and phenothiazines pose moderate risk of increasing blood glucose. Haloperidol is considered low risk to increase blood glucose. Amisulpride, asenapine, ziprasidone, aripiprazole has only minimal risk to increase the blood glucose.
Total leukocyte count (TLC)	Monitored when the patient is on treatment with following drugs—clozapine, carbamazepine and lithium
Mean corpuscular volume (MCV)	Increased in patients with alcohol dependence syndrome
Renal function test (RFT)	Monitored in treatment with Lithium

Contd...

Blood investigations	Description
Liver function test (LFT)	Monitored in patients with alcohol dependence syndrome. Increased ammonia level may suggest hepatic encephalopathy which includes delirium and lethargic behavior. Treatment with drugs—Benzodiazepines, carbamazepine and sodium valproate.
Total electrolytes panel (TEP)	**Phosphate level** is low in eating disorder due to purging. **Magnesium** is low in agitated, confused, delirious patient and also in patients with alcohol dependence. **Calcium level** might be low in delirium and eating disorder with laxative use, it might be high in psychosis and may be high or low in depression. **Sodium level** is monitored in dehydration and Syndrome of inappropriate secretion of antidiuretic hormone (SIADH) because serotonin plays a vital role in regulation of antidiuretic hormone (ADH) and hence, antidepressants are associated with hyponatremia (usually seen in 30 days of commencement of treatment) Treatment with drugs such as antipsychotics, carbamazepine and lithium is suggestive to monitor electrolyte level.
Thyroid function test (TFT)	• Hyperthyroidism is associated with mania, anxiety and psychosis. • Hypothyroidism is associated with depression and psychosis. Treatment with drugs–Carbamazepine will suppress the thyroid stimulating hormone. • (TSH) and lithium will inhibit the triiodothyronine (T3) and thyroxine (T4).
Triglycerides	Some antipsychotics might cause hyperlipidemia and so, it has to be monitored in patient with psychosis. Beta blockers, corticosteriods and retinoids also increase the level of triglycerides.
Venereal disease research laboratory (VDRL)	It is used to identify syphilis infection because long standing syphilis infection may lead to dementia.
Serum creatine phosphokinase (CPK)	Increased in neuroleptic malignant syndrome.
C-reactive protein (CRP) and troponin	Clozapine might cause Myocarditis so it needs to be monitored on 7th, 14th and 21st days after the commencement of clozapine. If CRP >100 mg/L and troponin (normal range is <0.04 ng/mL) is more than the twice of upper limit, then quit clozapine due to suggestive myocarditis and it is needed to be confirmed with echocardiogram.

Toxicology Screening

Toxicology screening is done in substance abuse disorders such as alcohol, barbiturates, benzodiazepines, cannabis, cocaine, etc. to determine the approximate amount and type of legal or illegal drug in blood of a user (Table 3.14).

Table 3.14: Drug levels in blood

Name of the drug	Blood therapeutic value
Lithium	0.6–1.8 mEq/L
Carbamazepine	6–12 mg/mL
Sodium valproate	50–100 mg/mL
Haloperidol	8–18 ng/mL
Imipramine	200–250 ng/mL
Nortriptyline	50–150 ng/mL

Electrophysiological Tests

A number of electrophysiological tests are performed on psychiatric patients, which have been summarized in Table 3.15.

Table 3.15: Electrophysiological tests

Electrophysiological tests	Description
EEG	Used in patients with dementia and abnormal behavior. It is also used to differentiate seizure with pseudoseizure
Polysomnography/sleep studies	Components include: • Electroencephalogram (EEG) • Electrocardiogram (ECG) • Electrooculogram (EOG) • Electromyogram (EMG), oxygen saturation, airflow measurement, body temperature, galvanic skin response (GSR) and body movements
Holter monitor	Used in panic anxiety disorder

Brain Imaging Tests

Computed tomography (CT scan) is used in patients with psychosis, organic brain disorder and seizure disorder. Magnetic resonance imaging (MRI scan) has high resolution than CT scan. Positron emission tomography (to check brain physiology), Magnetic resonance (MR) angiography and magnetic resonance (MR) spectroscopy may be used for the assessment of disorders in psychiatric patients.

Neuroendocrine Tests

Neuroendocrine tests are given in Table 3.16.

Table 3.16: Neuroendocrine tests

Neuroendocrine tests	Description
Dexamethasone suppression test	If the plasma cortisol level is more than 5mg/100 mL after administering dexamethasone (plasma cortisol level is checked at 8AM, 4PM and 11PM next day). Dexamethasone will suppress the plasma cortisol but it won't suppress the plasma cortisol, if there is a presence of depression. It is a test used to identify the response to antidepressants, ECT and also helpful to differentiate manic depressive disorder with mild dysphoria.
Thyroid releasing hormone (TRH) stimulation test	If the serum Thyroid Stimulating Hormone is more than 35 mIU/mL (following TRH 500 mg administered intravenously), it suggests the test is positive. Test is helpful to monitor lithium-induced hypothyroidism and refractory depression.
Serum prolactin test	Used to differentiate the patients with seizures and pseudoseizures (hysterical fits), Increased prolactin is due to drugs such as antipsychotics, domperidone and methyldopa. Prolactin is also seen to increase in stress, pregnancy, lactation, during exercise, during sleep and coitus. Pathological causes of raised prolactin are primary hypothyroidism, renal failure and prolactinoma
Serum 17-hydroxycorticosteroid	Monitored in organic mood disorder
Serum melatonin	Monitored in seasonal affective disorder
Estrogen	Decreased in menopausal depression and premenstrual syndrome

Further investigations are carried out to identify the sexual disorders in psychiatric patients (Table 3.17).

Table 3.17: Investigations to identify the sexual disorder

Investigations in patients with sexual disorders	Description
Papaverine test	Intracavernosal injection (drug given at the base of penis) of papaverine is used to differentiate organic and nonorganic male erectile dysfunction
Serum testosterone	Decreased in hypoactive sexual desire disorder, impotence and anabolic steroid abuse
Penile Doppler and nocturnal penile tumescence	Done in patients with male erectile dysfunction

Miscellaneous Tests

- **Genetic test:** Tests based on cytogenetics are used in children with mental retardation.
- **Lactate provocation test:** 70% of patients with panic disorders will get panic attack with the infusion of sodium lactate.
- **Amytal interviews:** Administration of drug amytal will help the patient to talk from his/her subconscious mind. It is also helpful in patients with catatonia, dissociative stupor and unexplained mutism.

PSYCHOLOGICAL TESTS

Psychological testing is the administration of psychological tests, which are designed to be "an objective and standardized measure of a sample of behavior." Psychological tests are designed to assess the behavior of psychiatric patients.

Characteristics of Psychological Tests

- **Standardization:** All health team members have to follow the uniform way of administering the test.
- **Objectivity:** Assessment needs to be performed with accurate observation and not with a subjective judgment.
- **Reliability:** Repetition of the test has to be performed to reveal the same results which should be consistent when tested with the same or different evaluator.
- **Validity:** It denotes the accuracy of measurement what it is intended to measure.

Principles of Psychological Tests

- Items for psychological test are prepared by the expertise in a high technical quality.
- It has three basic components: Standardization of the test, content of the test and the protocol or procedure to conduct the test.
- It has norms to compare an individual test with another known group.
- It has to be standardized so that it can be used by all health team members.

Purposes/Uses of Psychological Tests

- It helps to assess the psychopathology, level of functioning, disability and to formulate diagnosis.
- It is a helpful tool to observe the patient's behavior in order to provide the treatment.
- It is helpful to assess the mental status of the individual.
- It is also helpful to identify any academic backwardness and developmental delay in children.

Limitations of Psychological Tests

Need of psychologists or professionals who have knowledge and skills to perform the test. Patient might feel anxiety while performing this test. Few psychological tests lack reliability. Either the patient or the psychologist needs to complete the full test for the best assessment.

Flowchart 3.3: Classification of psychological tests

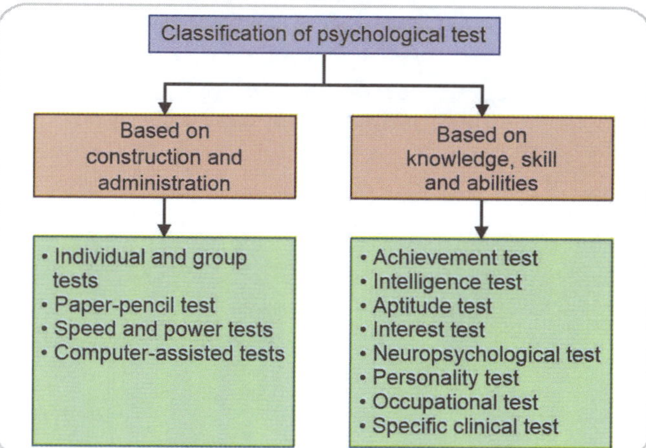

Classification

Classification of psychological tests has been given in Flowchart 3.3 and the summarized description has been explained in Table 3.18.

Table 3.18: Types of psychological tests with their descriptions and examples

Psychological tests	Description	Example
Individual and group test	Test conducted individually is called individual test and as a group is termed group test	Rorschach inkblot test used to assess the personality is an example of individual test and the assessment test to evaluate the academic performance of students as a group is an example of group test
Paper-pencil test	Individual will use paper and pencil to perform this test. Answers will be recorded in the standard sheet	Letter cancellation test in which a single alphabet was told to the participant to cancel the same in a given paragraph within the scheduled time. **Interpretation of the test:** No. of letters correctly identified: No. of letters omitted (or) missed out: No. of letters wrongly identified:
Speed and power test	Speed test is performed within the time limit whereas power test has no time limit to complete it	Sentence completion test administered with time limit is considered speed test and the same test administered without time limit is termed power test
Computer assisted test	Use of computer to assess the group of people in this test	Multiple Choice Questions have been administered to all the participants with the equal level of difficulty in the group, as such it has been programmed in the computer to conduct test.
Achievement test	To assess the level of knowledge in education and in employment sectors	Conducting a university semester examination for a college student
Aptitude test	Helps to assess the attention, accuracy and perceptual speed	General Aptitude Test Battery (GATB) and Differential Aptitude Test (DAT)
Intelligence Test	To assess the intelligence level of individual	**For Children** Wechsler Intelligence Scale for Children (WISC), Stanford-Binet Test Scale
		For Adults Wechsler Adult Intelligence Scale (WAIS), Binet-Kamat test of Intelligence, Bhatia battery test of intelligence

Contd...

Psychological tests	Description	Example
Interest test	To assess the interest and personal preferences	Interest inventory is used to assess the interest of Higher Secondary Board Exam passed students to pursue their higher education
Neuropsychological tests	To assess the cognitive functioning (ability to think, speak and respond)	• Neuropsychological test automated battery (CANTAB) • Wisconsin card sorting test • PGI memory scale • PGI battery of brain dysfunction • Bender gestalt test • Benton Visual Retention Test (BVRT) • Luria-Nebraska Neuropsychological Test Battery • Halstead-Reitan Neuropsychological Test Battery • Wechsler Adult Memory Scale (WAMS) • NIMHANS Neuropsychological Battery of Lobe Dysfunction
Personality test	To assess the personality of the individual	**Rating Scales** • Eysenck's Personality Inventory (EPI) • Minnesota Multiphasic Personality Inventory (MMPI) • Big five personality inventory (neuroticism, extraversion, openness, agreeableness, conscientiousness) • Myer's Briggs Type Indicator (MTBI) Scale (Extroversion-Introversion scale, Sensing-intuition scale, Thinking-feeling scale, Perception-judging scale) • Cattell's 16-personality inventory **Projective Tests** • Rorschach Inkblot test • Thematic Apperception Test (TAT) • Rotter Incomplete Sentence Blank (RISB) • Draw A Person Test (DAP)
Occupational test	To assess the interest of an individual with present employment	McQuaig Occupational Test
Specific clinical test	To assess the specific clinical situation	**Psychosis** • Brief Psychiatric Rating Scale • Psychiatric Symptoms Checklist
		Anxiety • Hamilton Anxiety Rating Scale • Anxiety Self-Rating Scale • Beck's Anxiety Scale • Trait and State Anxiety Scale
		Depression • Hamilton depression scale • Geriatric depression scale • Beck's depression scale
		Schizophrenia • Positive and Negative Symptoms Scale (PANSS) • Extrapyramidal Symptom Rating Scale
		Alcohol Dependence syndrome • CAGE Questionnaire (Cut down, Annoyance, Guilt, Eye opening)
		Mania • Young Mania Rating Scale • Manic State Rating Scale
		OCD • Yale Brown Obsessive Compulsive Scale (YBOCS)
		Suicide • Suicide Intent Scale

Contd...

Psychological tests	Description	Example
		Others • Depression Anxiety Stress Scale (DASS-21) • Global Assessment of Functioning (GAF) Scale • Insight and Treatment Attitude Questionnaire (ITAQ) • Child Behavior Checklist (CBCL) • Nurses' Observation Scale for In-patient Evaluation (NOSIE) • Situational Self-awareness Scale

SUMMARY

- **Psychiatric history collection** includes patient profile, chief complaints, past and present psychiatric history, past and present medical/surgical history, family history, personal history and premorbid personality.
- **Mental status examination** includes assessment of general appearance, behavior, psychomotor activity, perception, speech, thought, mood, affect, judgment, attention/concentration, memory, intelligence, abstract thinking and insight.
- Kirby's method of examination was used to perform **Mental status examination for uncooperative patients.** It includes general reaction, posture, facial movement/expression, eyes/pupils, and reaction to examiner's questions, muscular reactions, emotional responsiveness, writing and vital signs.
- **Neurological assessment** includes level of consciousness, mental status assessment, special cerebral function, cranial nerve function, sensory function, motor function, cerebellar function and reflexes.
- **Mini mental status examination (or) Folstein test** is a 30-point questionnaire test which is used to assess the cognitive status of the patient. The components of test are orientation, registration, attention, recall, language and copying. Score <17 denotes severe cognitive impairment, score 18–23 denotes mild cognitive impairment, and score 24–30 denotes normal.
- **Investigations in psychiatry** include the blood investigations such as hemoglobin, blood glucose level and glycosylated hemoglobin, Total Leukocyte Count, Mean Corpuscular Volume (MCV), Renal Function Test (RFT), Liver Function Test (LFT), Total Electrolytes Panel (TEP), Thyroid Function Test (TFT), Triglycerides, Venereal Disease Research Laboratory (VDRL), serum Creatine Phosphokinase (CPK), C-Reactive Protein (CRP) and troponin. The electrophysiological tests such as EEG, polysomnography/sleep studies and Holter monitor are used for the assessment of psychiatric disorders. The brain imaging tests such as Computed Tomography (CT scan), Magnetic Resonance Imaging (MRI Scan), Positron Emission Tomography, Magnetic Resonance (MR) Angiography and Magnetic Resonance (MR) spectroscopy may be used. Neuroendocrine tests such as dexamethasone suppression test, Thyroid Releasing Hormone (TRH) stimulation test, serum prolactin test, serum 17-hydroxycorticosteroid, serum melatonin and estrogen can be done. Investigations to identify the sexual disorders are papaverine test, serum testosterone, penile Doppler and nocturnal penile tumescence. Other tests such as genetic test, lactate provocation test, amytal interview can be done if required.
- Classification of **psychological tests based on construction and administration** are individual and group tests, paper-pencil test, speed and power tests, computer-assisted tests.
- Classification of **psychological tests based on knowledge, skill and abilities** are achievement test, intelligence test, aptitude test, interest test, neuropsychological test, personality test, occupational test and specific clinical test.

ASSESS YOURSELF

Long Answer Questions

1. Define mental status examination and explain the various components of mental status assessment with appropriate examples.
2. Define neurological examination and explain the various components of neurological examination with appropriate examples.

Short Answer Questions

1. What are the purposes of psychiatric history collection?
2. What are the purposes of mental status examination?

Short Notes

Write short notes on:

1. Mini-mental status examination
2. Psychological tests
3. Psychiatric history collection
4. Investigations in psychiatry
5. Mental status examination for uncooperative patient

Multiple Choice Questions

1. **Description of the personality before the onset of the illness:**

   a. Premorbid personality b. Personality
   c. Personality disorder d. None of these

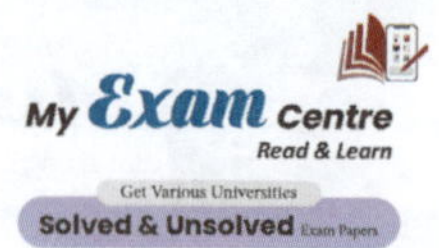

2. **_________ Method of examination was used to perform Mental Status examination for uncooperative patients.**
   a. Kirby's　　b. Folstein
   c. Freud　　d. Hippocrates

3. **Furrowed brow due to sustained contraction of corrugator muscle is _____________.**
   a. Otto Veraguth folds　　b. Omega sign
   c. Nasolabial folds　　d. None of these

4. **Speech of the individual reaches the goal or center point toward the question raised only after the unwanted speech is ______________.**
   a. Circumstantiality　　b. Tangentiality
   c. Neologism　　d. Ambivalence

5. **Strong unshakable beliefs that the world does not exist is ________.**
   a. Delusions of grandeur
   b. Nihilistic delusion
   c. Delusion of guilt
   d. Delusion of control

6. **Misperception with the heightened emotions is known as ________.**
   a. Affect illusion　　b. Completion illusion
   c. Pareidolic illusion　　d. All of these

7. **Misperception of taste is _______ hallucination.**
   a. Auditory　　b. Visual
   c. Functional　　d. Gustatory

8. **Ability to recognize the writing on skin is termed ____.**
   a. Stereognosis　　b. Graphesthesia
   c. Baragnosis　　d. Haptic Perception

9. **Therapeutic drug Lithium level is _________.**
   a. 6–12 mg/mL　　b. 50–100 mg/mL
   c. 8–18 ng/mL　　d. 0.6–1.8 mEq/L

10. **Steppage Gait is also known as __________.**
   a. Neuropathic gait　　b. Propulsive gait
   c. Ataxic gait　　d. Stomping gait

ANSWER KEY

1. a	**2.** a	**3.** b	**4.** a	**5.** b
6. a	**7.** d	**8.** b	**9.** d	**10.** a

Therapeutic Communication and Nurse-Patient Relationship

CHAPTER 4

LEARNING OBJECTIVE

After studying this chapter, the student will be able to gain knowledge regarding the therapeutic communication in order to communicate with the patient effectively using appropriate techniques and to avoid the therapeutic impasses.

CHAPTER OUTLINE

- Communication
- Types of Relationship
- Nurse-patient Relationship or Therapeutic Relationship
- Communication Process and its Barriers
- Therapeutic Impasses
- Therapeutic Communication
- Ethics and Responsibilities
- Dynamics of Therapeutic Nurse-Patient Relationship or Therapeutic use of Self for Gaining Self-awareness
- Johari Window of Interpersonal Relationship
- Process Recording

KEY TERMS

Communication, Ruesch's theory, Transactional analysis, Neurolinguistic programming, Proximity, Posture, Gesture, Restating, Empathy, Focusing, Active listening, False reassurance, Being judgmental, Resistance, Transference, Countertransference, Boundary violations, Johari window of IPR, Nurse-patient relationship, Ethics, Self-awareness, Process recording and verbatim.

COMMUNICATION

Meaning of Communication

The term 'Communication' came from the Latin word 'Communis' which means common understanding.

Definition of Communication

Communication is defined as 'interaction process between the sender and receiver in which the receiver receives the message exactly what the sender intended to say as such, i.e., both the sender and receiver have a common understanding of a message'.

Theories of Communication

- **Ruesch's theory (1961):** Ruesch suggested that communication is a circular process, i.e., sender sends message to receiver and again the message from receiver turn toward the sender as feedback. Ruesch coined the term, "Disturbed communication" as unsuccessful interaction. He also verbalized the unique difference between therapeutic and social relationship, i.e., therapeutic relationship is to bring positive change where as social relationship might not focus in such aspect.
- **Transactional analysis:** The term 'Transactional Analysis' was first used by Dr Eric Berne (1964).

Dr Eric Berne suggests that there are three ego states existing in an individual listed here.

1. **Parent:** Focus on rules/regulations/values
2. **Adult:** Approach based on previous observations
3. **Child:** Focus on emotions and desires

- **Neurolinguistic programming:** Neurolinguistic programming is the item from the concept of Milton H Erickson. Effective communication exists at the state of hypnosis or by alteration of individual person's state of consciousness.

Types of Communication

Types of communication are categorized on the basis of forms, formality, levels, directions and other types. These all are well explained in Flowchart 4.1 and Table 4.1.

Flowchart 4.1: Types of communication

- Types of communication
  - Based on the forms
    - Nonverbal
    - Verbal
      - Oral
      - Written
      - Visual
  - Based on the formality
    - Formal
    - Informal
  - Based on the levels
    - Interpersonal
    - Intrapersonal
    - Transpersonal
  - Based on the directions
    - Horizontal
      - Upward
      - Downward
    - Vertical
    - Chain
  - Miscellaneous types
    - Metacommunication
    - Animal communication
    - Physiological communication
    - Communication through mass media

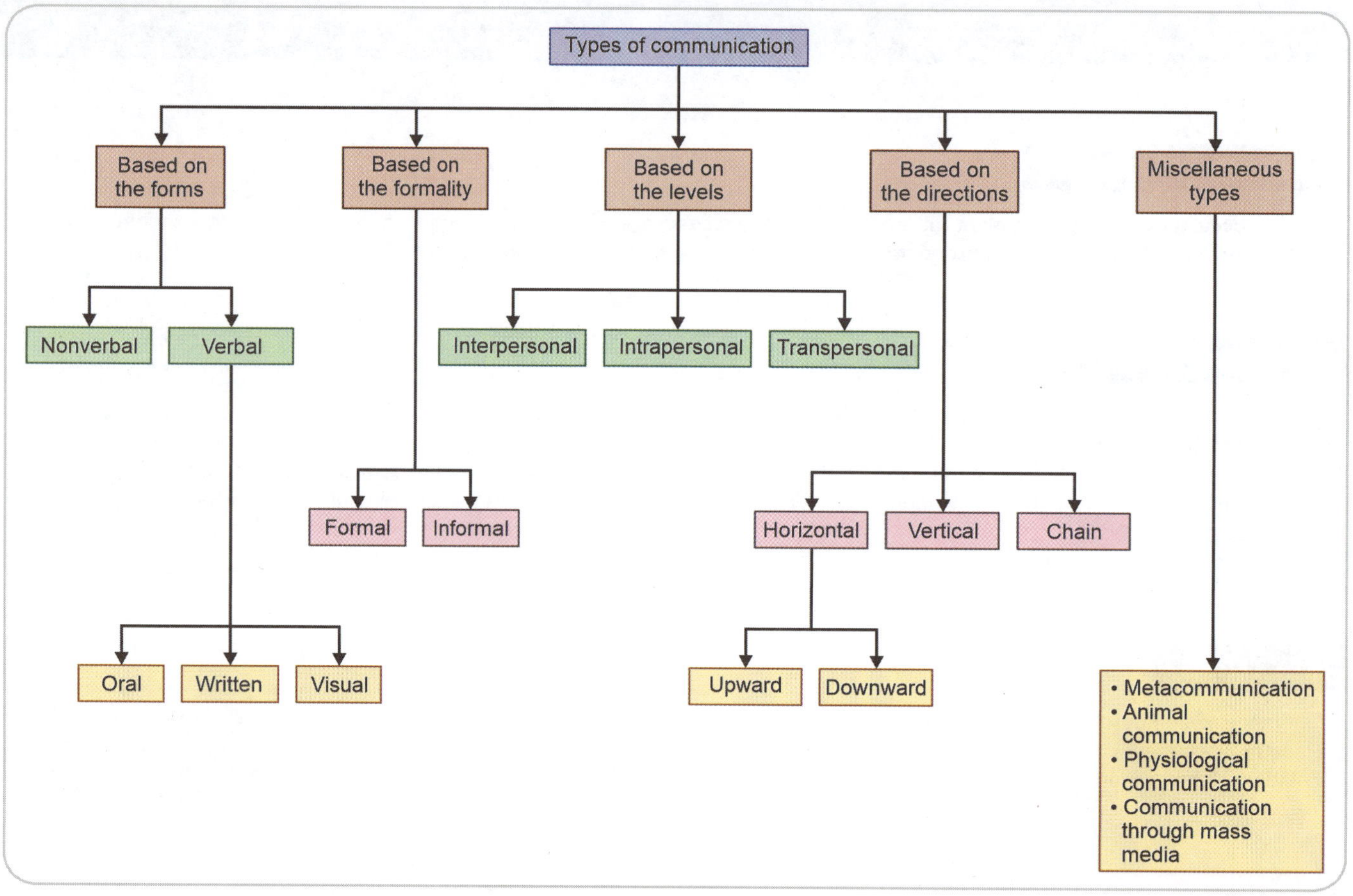

Table 4.1: Types of communication with brief description and example

Types of communication	Description	Example
Verbal communication	**Oral:** Communication by speaking/talking to others	Nurse collects history from the patient
	Written: Communication to others in writing	Nurse documents a post electroconvulsive therapy (ECT) procedure in nurses notes
	Visual: Communication to others with the use of symbols	Nurse kept a 'No Smoking Board' in ward

Contd...

Types of communication	Description	Example
Nonverbal communication	**Facial expression:** Showing sadness/happiness in face	Extreme sad facial expression seen in depression
	Posture: Position that one holds the body while sitting or standing	Stooped posture seen in Parkinson's disease
	Gesture: Movement of body part especially head or hand to convey the ideas	Patient points out the location of abdominal pain with finger
	Gait: Manner of walk	Patient might have irregular involuntary gait if he/she has basal ganglia disorders.
	Eye contact: Receiver giving attention by seeing the sender	Poor eye to eye contact seen in depression
	Body language: Mixture of gesture, posture and expressions	Student might express the unwillingness to participate in a program with body language
	Proximity: Nearness in time, space and relationship	Special care and permission is required if touching the vulnerable zone (face, neck and front of body)
	Personal appearance	Patients with mania wear attractive dress to enhance the personal appearance.
	Touch	Therapeutic touch by nurse heals the patient well
	Silence	Being silence helps the nurse to listen the patient actively
Formal communication	Communication among professionals	Official meetings
Informal communication	Communication among friends	Gossips among friends
Intrapersonal communication	Communication within oneself	Thinking
Interpersonal communication	Communication between two members	Nurse-patient interaction
Transpersonal communication	Communication with God	Prayer
Horizontal communication	**Upward:** Communication from lower hierarchy level to higher level in an institution	Student communicating to the teacher
	Downward: Communication from higher hierarchy level to lower level in an institution	Teacher communicating to the student
Vertical communication	Communication takes place between same hierarchy level in an organization	Students communicating among themselves
Chain communication	Discussion takes place among a group	Group discussion and panel discussion
Metacommunication	Communication within a communication	Raja says to Sita that I am glad to see you with a staring look, denotes Raja is not actually glad to see Sita
Animal communication	Communication takes place between the animals	One dog barks to gather all the dogs
Physiological communication	Communication takes place within the human body	Sneezing happens when a microorganism enters the nose
Communication through mass media	Communication takes place through television, radio, newspaper, social networking (Facebook, WhatsApp, mail, etc.)	Sending a message through WhatsApp

TYPES OF RELATIONSHIP

Relationship means how one is related with other, i.e., the relation is based on purpose. It can be classified as social, intimate and therapeutic as explained in Table 4.2. The zones of space are intimate, personal, social and public zone as explained in Table 4.3. The zones of touch are intimate, vulnerable, consent and social as explained in Table 4.4.

Table 4.2: Types of relationship

Aspects	Social relationship	Intimate relationship	Therapeutic relationship
Meaning	Relationship among friends/ social companionship	Relationship maintained between husband and wife	Relationship maintained between nurse and patient for therapeutic purpose
Zones of space	Social and public zone	Intimate and personal zone	Social and public zone
Zones of touch	Social and consent zone	Intimate and vulnerable zone	Social and consent zone

Table 4.3: Zones of space

Zones	Distance	Example	Relationship maintained
Intimate zone	0–18 inches	Mother-child relationship	Intimate relationship
Personal zone	18 inches–4 feet	Persons who are more familiar	
Social zone	4–12 feet	Business meeting	Social relationship and therapeutic relationship
Public zone	12 feet	Public speaking	

Table 4.4: Zones of touch

Zones	Permission to touch	Body parts can be touched	Relationship maintained
Intimate zone	Yes (great sensitivity needed)	Genitalia and rectum	Intimate relationship
Vulnerable zone	Yes (special care needed)	Face, neck and front side of body	
Consent zone	Yes	Feet, mouth and wrist	Therapeutic and social relationship
Social zone	No	Extremities, shoulders and back	

NURSE-PATIENT RELATIONSHIP OR THERAPEUTIC RELATIONSHIP

Definition

Relationship maintained between nurse and patient in order to gain mutual respect and trust collaboratively is known as nurse-patient relationship (Fig. 4.1).

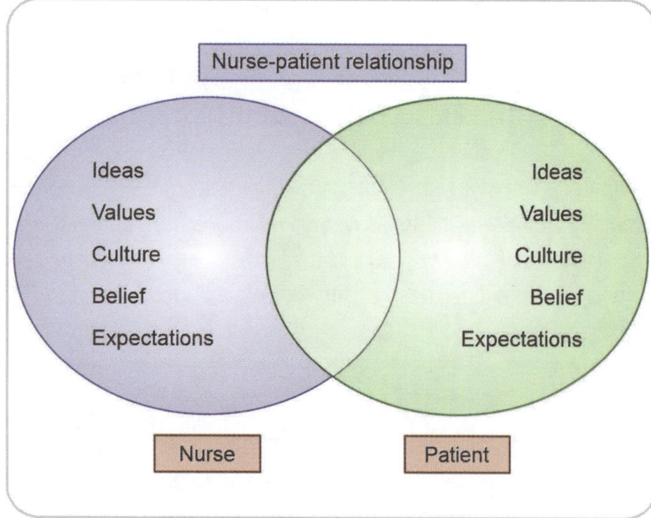

Figure 4.1: Nurse-patient relationship

Purposes

- To bring insight and promote behavioral change in patients.
- To promote self-realization/self-acceptance.
- To develop mutual respect.
- To solve the problems.
- To have genuineness and trustworthiness in relationship.
- To meet the daily routines.
- To develop the coping skills.

Characteristics of Therapeutic Nurse-Patient Relationship

- Able to set and achieve realistic goals.
- It can maintain safe therapeutic environment.
- It maximizes ego strength.
- Relationship is said to be goal oriented.
- Nurse-patient relationship has to follow the phases.
- It has to clarify problems of the patients.
- It has to modify maladaptive behavior into normal behavior.

Principles of Nurse-Patient Relationship

- Nurse has to treat the client as an individual.
- Nurse has to accept the client as he/she is.

- Nurse should be aware of client's complete needs and problems.
- Nurses should have an ability to prioritize the needs.
- Nurse has to maintain limits.
- Nurse has to set goals.
- Nurse has to follow the institutional norms.
- Nurse can establish good rapport.
- Nurse needs to maintain confidentiality.
- Nurse can behave in such a way that it bring confidence in client.

Essential Elements of Therapeutic Relationship

Essential elements of therapeutic relationship are trustworthiness, professionalism, mutual respect, care, empathy, genuineness and unconditional positive regard. These elements have been described in Table 4.5.

Table 4.5: Essential elements of therapeutic relationship

Essential elements of therapeutic relationship	Description
Trustworthy	Nurse can develop the trust with patient. It can be gained with proper interpersonal relationship and step by step explanation of every procedure to the client with high level of clarity
Professionalism	Nurse behaves in a professional way
Mutual respect	Nurse respects the client and client in turn respects the nurse
Caring	Nurse shows caring attitude toward the patient
Empathy	Nurse has to see the situation by thinking from the client's point of view
Genuineness	Nurse has to be truthful in every aspect
Unconditional positive regard	Overall acceptance of the patient irrespective of the nurse's personal opinion. This concept was developed by Carl Rogers (Fig. 4.2), humanistic psychologist.

Figure 4.2 Carl Rogers (1902–1987)

Phases of Nurse-Patient Relationship

Phases of nurse-patient relationship are preorientation phase, orientation, identification, intervention, maintenance and termination phase as shown in Figure 4.3. Each phase has been described in Table 4.6 along with nurses role in each phase of nurse-patient relationship.

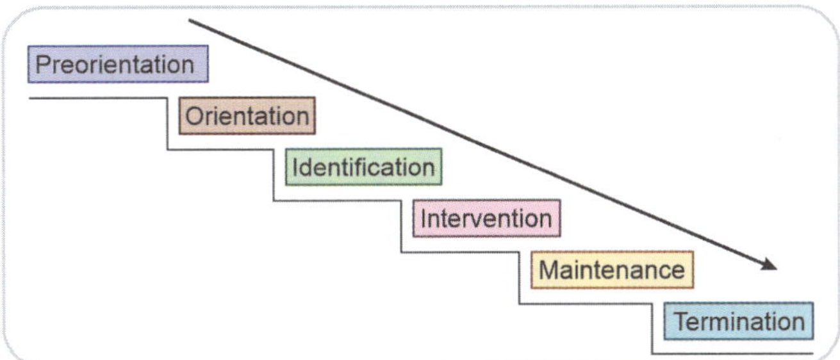

Figure 4.3: Phases of nurse-patient relationship

Table 4.6: Phases of nurse-patient relationship with nurses' role in each phase

Phases of nurse-patient relationship	Description of the tasks	Nurses' role in each phase
Preorientation phase	Nurse has to prepare oneself before interacting with the patient	Nurse is reading the patient's previous file and collecting history from the client's family members
Orientation phase	Nurse orienting the patient in regard with orientation of self, other health team workers and routines of hospital	Nurse explains to the client that visitors are permitted to ward in the evening from 4 pm to 6 pm
Identification phase	Nurse is identifying the client's needs and problems	Nurse identified that the client was unable to consume food due to pain in throat while swallowing food and there is need of Ryle's tube feeding to maintain the nutritional needs of the patient
Intervention phase	Nurse is rendering care/intervention to solve the client's problems	Nurse is rendering therapeutic back massage to prevent bed sore for a bedridden client
Maintenance phase	Nurse has to follow-up the delivered nursing care in this phase	Nurse gives routine nursing care based on client's needs
Termination phase	Examines the level of goal achieved and establishes the plan of continuous assistance	Nurse provides discharge summary, explains regarding the next outpatient department (OPD) visit

Patient's Response in Termination Phase of Nurse-Patient Relationship

The patient might exhibit the three responses in termination phase such as continuation, regression and withdrawal as listed here.

1. **Continuation:** Patient tries to continue the nurse-patient relationship by bringing out the new problem or else seeking help from nurse.
2. **Regression:** Patient returns back to the previous maladaptive behavior.
3. **Withdrawal:** Patient refuses the help from the nurse and tries to quit nurse-patient relationship.

Components of Nurse-Patient Therapeutic Relationship

T – Trust (having faith)
E – Empathy (seeing out things by standing in his/her position)
A – Autonomy (independent)
C – Caring attitude (nurse rendering care to patient)
H – Hopefulness (feeling confident)

Trust

Nurse has to maintain good interpersonal relationship (IPR) with the patient in order to develop trust. Nurse can explain each and every procedure and hospital routines to the client in a way so the patient's anxiety might get reduced and it develops the sense of trust in patient.

Empathy

Nurse has to understand the problems of patient and the nurse has to think if it happens to me, how will I react?—i.e., nurse is visualizing the situations by standing in his/her position.

Autonomy

In the nurse-patient relationship, patient can independently verbalize his/her own point of view at any time.

Caring Attitude

Nurse has to show a caring attitude toward the patient. This will help to maintain a good interpersonal relationship between nurse and patient. This will also help the patient to trust the nurse in all aspects.

Hopefulness

Nurse and patient have to be confident enough in the treatment process so that a good interpersonal relationship can be maintained.

COMMUNICATION PROCESS AND ITS BARRIERS

Barriers of communication process have been explained with each element in a communication process. The barriers in case of a sender are unwillingness or disinterest to communicate, lack of knowledge and problems related to speech or speech deficits. The barriers in case of receiver are unwillingness or disinterest to listen, low level of understanding and hearing problems. Barriers with channeling process as mobile phone is not functioning, no internet connection, etc. Barriers of environment are high noise and extreme hot or cold weather. Concepts of communication barrier related to communication process are shown in Flowchart 4.2.

Flowchart 4.2: Barriers of communication related with communication process

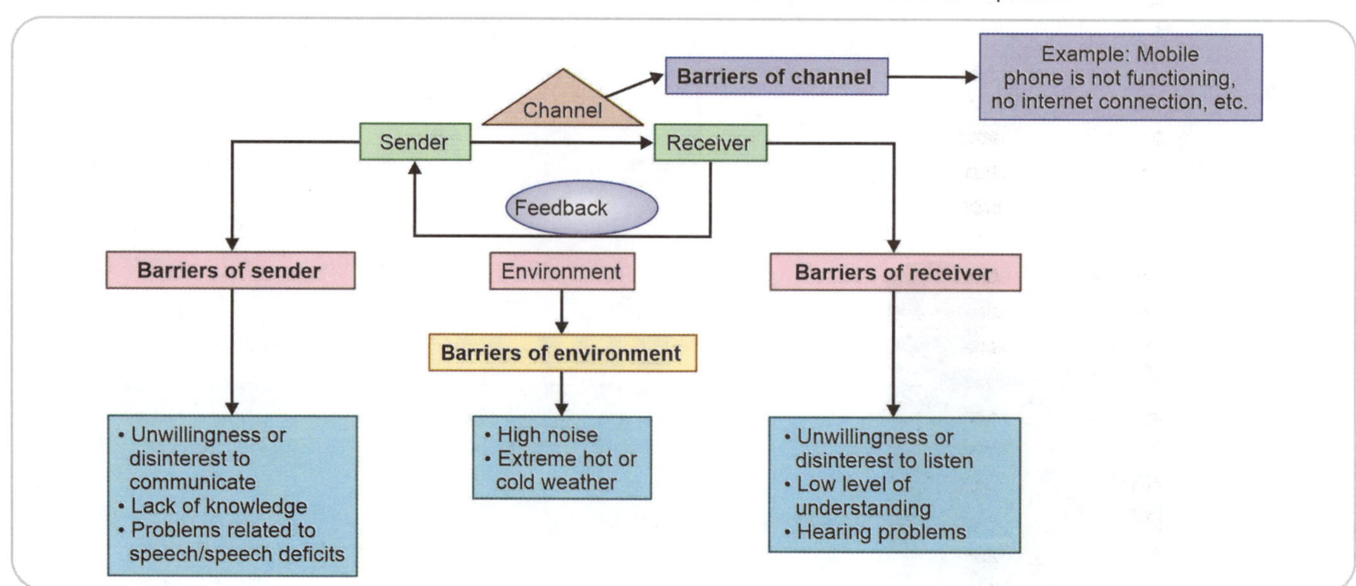

Flowchart 4.3: Barriers of communication

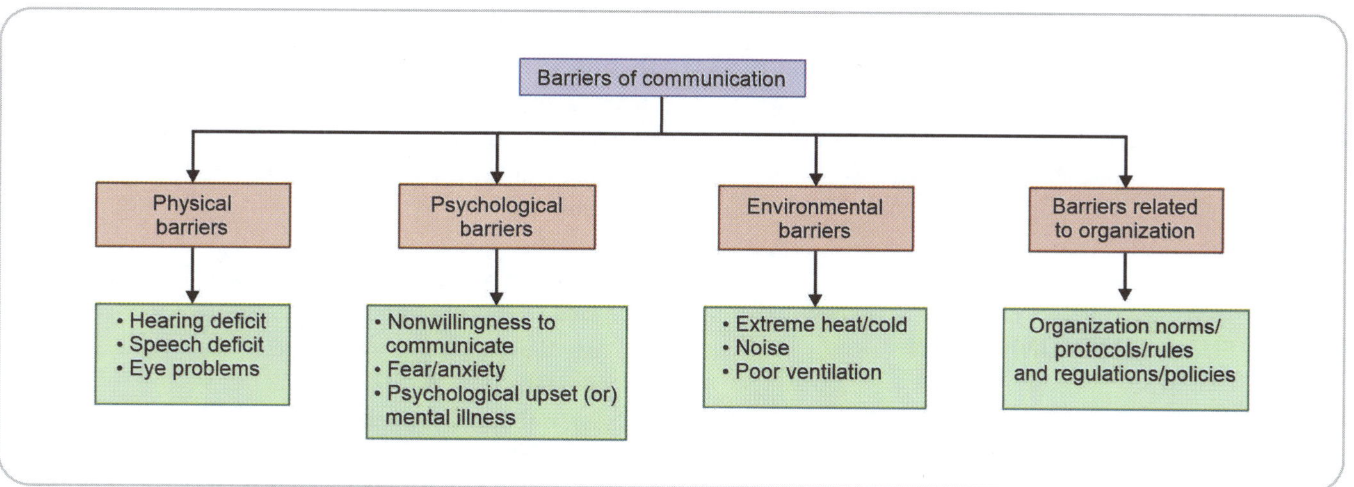

Barriers of communication are further classified into physical, psychological, environmental and barriers related to organization. The examples of physical barriers are hearing deficit, speech deficit and eye problems. The examples of psychological barriers are nonwillingness to communicate, fear/anxiety and psychological upset or mental illness. The examples of environmental barriers are extreme heat/cold, noise and poor ventilation. Barriers related to organization are like organization's norms/protocols/rules and regulations/ policies that have not been communicated within the organization. Barriers of communication have been shown in Flowchart 4.3.

THERAPEUTIC IMPASSES

- **Resistance:** Patient is not willing to communicate the troubling aspect of oneself and patient is not willing to change when the change is expected.
  - Primary (For example, patient takes an inappropriate role model and so the patient is unwilling to change).
  - Secondary (For example, resistance is due to financial problem, unpleasant situation, attention seeking, social pressure, etc.).
- **Transference:** Transfer of client's feeling toward the nurse.
  - Negative or hostile transference (Feel of anger or enmity that the client expresses toward the nurse).
  - Positive or dependent transference (client is emotionally dependent on nurse).
- **Countertransference:** Nurse is emotionally dependent on patient.

  There are three types of countertransferences as mentioned here.

  1. Reactions of intense love or caring.
  2. Reactions of intense disgust or hostility.
  3. Reactions of intense anxiety, especially in response to resistance by the patient.
- **Boundary violations:** The categories of boundary violations are role, time, space, place, money, gifts, clothing, language, self-disclosure, post discharge social boundaries and physical contact boundaries. Categories of boundary violations have been given in Table 4.7.

Table 4.7: Boundary violations

Categories of boundary violations	Description
Role	Nurse or patient performs other than their own specified and accepted role
Time	Patient meets the nurse in inappropriate timings or at night
Space	Nurse and patient have to follow the specified zone of space, if not, it is considered violation of boundaries
Place	Patient meets the nurse in places other than hospital
Money	Nurse accepts money from the patient
Gifts	Nurse accepts gifts from the patient
Clothing	Nurse accepts dress/clothes from the patient
Language	Talking in an unprofessional language
Self-disclosure	Nurse/patient shares their personal information between them
Post discharge social boundaries	Nurse tries to develop social relationship with the patient after discharge or the patient tries to develop social relationship with nurse after discharge
Physical contact boundaries	Patient tries to have a physical contact with the nurse

Management of Therapeutic Impasses

- Maintain limits with the patient.
- Do not use nontherapeutic techniques on the patient while communicating.
- Identify and follow proper zones and spaces.
- Have a proper professional relationship.
- Early identification is important, when the client tends to cross boundaries.
- Accurate documentation is essential.

THERAPEUTIC COMMUNICATION

Definition

Interaction process between nurse and patient with a therapeutic purpose is known as therapeutic communication. This type of communication provides support and information to the patient.

Goals of Therapeutic Communication

The goals of therapeutic communication are listed here.

- Helps to identify the patient needs.
- Assesses the perception of patient's problem.
- Promotes the patient's ventilation of emotions.
- Provides interventions based on patient's needs.
- Establishes a proper therapeutic nurse-patient relationship.

Principles or Characteristics of Therapeutic Communication

The principles or characteristics of therapeutic communication are listed here.

- Patient is a primary focus in the interaction process.
- Maintain the client's confidentiality.
- Avoid unnecessary advice and social relationship with the patient.
- Use self-disclosure only if it is found to be therapeutic.
- Have a nonjudgmental attitude.
- Ask the patient to reinterpret one's own experiences rationally.
- Assess the client's intelligence level to determine the level of understanding.
- Always have a professional attitude.

Therapeutic Communication Techniques

Techniques of therapeutic communication are categorized as techniques helpful in development of description, development of analysis, development of conclusion, development of conclusion to get a meaningful explanation and highlighting the importance of techniques which are helpful in development of solving a problem and making a right. These techniques are helpful in completion of plans. The techniques of therapeutic communication have been presented in Table 4.8.

Table 4.8: Therapeutic communication techniques

Therapeutic communication techniques	Description	Example
Techniques helpful in development of description		
Offering self	Nurse making oneself available to listen the client's problems	Nurse verbalizes to get a meaningful explanation to client as, 'I will stay here to listen you.'
Using silence	Not giving any verbal remarks and allowing the client to talk	Nurse sits silently without any interruption in conversation
Active listening	Paying attention to client's communication **(Mnemonic – SOLER):** S – *Sit facing the client* O – *Open posture* L – *Lean forward toward client* E – *Establish eye contact* R – *Relax*	Nurse while maintaining eye contact with patient conveys the interest through facial expression
Empathy	Talk out by standing or thinking from other's point of view	Nurse verbalizes to client that, 'I am able to understand how much it hurts you, really...'
Offering general leads	Use neutral expressions and encourage the client to talk continuously	Nurse verbalizes to client that, 'I am listening...you can continue...'
Questioning	Asking questions in order to promote discussion	Nurse asks question to the client, 'when? How? What? Why? Where? Who?'
Restating	Repetition of main thoughts expressed by client	Nurse verbalizes to the client, 'You said that you are happy only with your mother nowadays.'
Giving broad openings	Encourage the client to select the topic for discussion	Nurse asking open ended questions such as 'Can you say about your life?'

Contd...

Therapeutic communication techniques	Description	Example
Verbalizing the implied	Rephrasing the client's words to enlighten the underlying message	Patient: I am not interested in studies. Nurse: Are you bored of your subjects?
Techniques helpful in development of analysis		
Seeking clarification and validation or voicing doubt	Asking the client to elaborate or state examples of vague ideas or thoughts	Nurse asking doubts to the client, 'Whether you actually mean this in your conversation?'
Making observations	Verbalizing the observations made	Nurse verbalizes to client, 'You got irritable when I talk about your husband.'
Encouraging description of perceptions	Encourage the patient to verbalize what has been perceived	Nurse verbalizes to client, 'Can you share what is happening to you right now?'
Presenting reality	Clarification of misconceptions, that the client is expressing	Nurse verbalizes to client, 'In reality, what bothers you is wrong thoughts that you have about your family?'
Sharing perceptions	Nurse can share his/her perception to the client during the conversation	Nurse verbalizes to client, 'You are looking dull now.'
Placing the event in time or sequence	Clarifying the relationship of events in time	Nurse verbalizes to client, 'Which event happens first and which one happened next?'
Encouraging comparison	Encourage the patient to compare the similarities and differences in regard with ideas or experiences	Nurse verbalizes to client, 'Which seems to be better when compared with previous one?'
Techniques helpful in development of conclusion		
Summarizing	Highlighting the important points and review back the entire conversation	Nurse verbalizes to client, 'I just summarized the main concepts of our discussions as...'
Theme identification	Encourage the client to identify the recurrent pattern of ideas, behavior and feelings	Nurse verbalizes to client, 'Vital concept of your problems in your life is your anger which makes you deteriorated.'
Techniques helpful in development of conclusion to a meaning and highlight the importance		
Focusing	Focus toward the single idea or word	Nurse verbalizes to client, 'Can you describe that event little more?'
Exploring	Further identification of ideas or experiences	Nurse verbalizes to client, 'Can you elaborate little more?'
Interpreting	Nurse provides the view of meaning or significance of something	Nurse verbalizes to client, 'Actual problem which troubles you is your inferiority complex?'
Techniques helpful in development of solving a problem and making a right decision		
Encourage goal setting	Encourage the client to decide the change needed	Nurse asks to client, 'When did you think the task need to be done?'
Offering help	Nurse offers help to client to solve the problem	Nurse verbalizes to client, 'I am there to help you.'
Encourage decision	Advise the client to make a choice from various options	Nurse asks a client that, 'Can you take decision out of these options?'
Formulating plan of action	Plans are made to perform the next level of action	Nurse asks a client, 'How are you going to do this task?
Techniques helpful in completion of plans		
Giving recognition or Reinforcement	Acknowledging the client for the correct response	Nurse verbalizes to client, 'you have done a good job.'
Limit setting	Discourage the unproductive feelings or behavior	Nurse verbalizes to client that, 'you are becoming angry now. It has to be controlled.'
Supportive confrontation	Convey the difficulties to change and encourage the client to change for a correct action	Nurse verbalizes to client, 'I understand it is difficult to do, but you can perform still.'
Encouraging evaluation	Encouraging the client to provide the view of meaning or significance of something	Nurse verbalizes to client, 'How do you done this in an excellent way?'

Nontherapeutic Communication Techniques

Nontherapeutic techniques of communication are giving false reassurance, rejection, giving advice, unnecessary probing, defending, requesting an explanation, indicating the existence of external source of power, belittling feelings expressed, making stereotyped comments, cliches and trite expressions, using denial, parroting, being judgmental and other techniques which are explained in Table 4.9.

Table 4.9: Nontherapeutic techniques of communication

Nontherapeutic communication techniques	Description	Example
Giving false assurance	Reassurance is different from that of false reassurance.	Nurse verbalizes to HIV patient that taking antiretroviral medications will prolong your life span and enhance the capacity of daily living, is an example of reassurance. If nurse verbalizes to the patient that, HIV will get cured soon, it is an example of false reassurance
Rejection/Rejecting	Refuse the client's ideas/concept/behavior	Nurse verbalizes to client, 'I won't accept your view about your mother.'
Giving advice	Nurse gives advice to the client that whatever is said is the best for him/her	Nurse verbalizes to client, 'You can do better than this instead of that.'
Unnecessary probing	Asking out 'why' often which is not needed actually	Nurse verbalizes to client, 'Why so happened... why so only to you....why you responded as such.....'
Defending	Trying out to defend in such a way that client has no rights to express his/her own thoughts	Nurse verbalizes to client, 'You don't have rights to talk anything about your negative thoughts here.'
Requesting an explanation	Asking 'why' might implies the client to defend one's idea or behavior	Nurse verbalizes to client, 'Why did you do this?'
Indicating the existence of an external source of power	Encourage the client to blame on others for one's own mistake	Nurse verbalizes to client, 'It is not your mistake and it is happened because of your wife.'
Belittling feelings expressed	Make the client feels that the feelings expressed are insignificant.	Nurse verbalizes to client, 'It seems to be very silly.'
Making stereotyped comments, cliches and trite expressions	Meaningless comments with unusual expressions	Nurse verbalizes to client, 'You are powerless when you talk....no life in your speech......inactive talk......powerless speech...'
Using denial	Refusing the discussion with patient	Nurse verbalizes to client, 'I don't like to discuss this.'
Parroting	Continuous repetition of patient's words	Nurse verbalizes to client, 'You said that I feel sad since I am jobless.'
Being judgmental		
Approving or disapproving	Passing judgment as 'good' or 'bad' in regard with client behavior	Nurse verbalizes to client, 'What you have done is so bad.'
Agreeing or disagreeing	Judgment as 'right' or 'wrong' in regard with client ideas	Nurse verbalizes to client, 'What you have done is too wrong?'
Miscellaneous		
Introducing an unrelated topic		
Failure to listen		
Failure to explore the patient's point of view		
Giving inadequate answers		
Vague description		

ETHICS AND RESPONSIBILITIES

Definition

Ethics is a branch of philosophy which deals with the study of values and moral standards related to nursing profession.

Primary Principles in Ethical Decision Making

The American Nurses Association (ANA) has explained the four ethical principles involved in the decision-making process which are discussed as follows:

1. **Autonomy:** Patient taking an independent decision.
2. **Beneficence:** Nurse doing good to patient.
3. **Justice:** Nurse doing which is fair to patient.
4. **Veracity:** Nurse and patient are being truthful.

Responsibilities of the Nurse for Being Ethical in All Aspects

Nurse always has to respect the patient's dignity and cultural belief. Nurse has to provide privacy whenever and wherever necessary. Nurse has to perform the role of an advocate to protect the patient's rights. Nurse has to respect the autonomy or freedom of patient in decision-making process. Nurses working in psychiatric health setup have to take necessary steps to follow the guidelines provided by ANA code of nurses.

DYNAMICS OF THERAPEUTIC NURSE-PATIENT RELATIONSHIP OR THERAPEUTIC USE OF SELF FOR GAINING SELF-AWARENESS

Dynamics is the force which is helpful to produce change in a psychological or social system. It is the vital responsibility of a nurse to understand about these forces which are listed here.

- Therapeutic use of self-awareness
- Improving self-awareness
- Power
- Intimacy
- Trust
- Respect

Therapeutic Use of Self-Awareness

Using the self-awareness in order to provide the nursing interventions. Hildegard Peplau (1952), mother of Psychiatric nursing, concluded that nurses have to understand oneself thereby he/she might improve the patient's health condition.

Improving Self-Awareness

If an individual is aware of oneself, he or she might develop an ability to fight against any issue in his/her day to day life. Self-awareness includes self-concept, values, belief and life experiences. Self-awareness is a vital part for a nurse to aware about oneself. SWOT analysis is an integral part for self-awareness.

S – Strength
W – Weakness
O – Opportunities
T – Threats

Campbell (1980) identified holistic nursing model of self-awareness. It has four aspects which are mentioned here.

1. **Psychological:** Knowledge of motives, emotions, self-concept and personality.
2. **Physiological:** Knowledge of general physiology.
3. **Environmental:** Knowledge of relationship of human with nature or environment.
4. **Philosophical:** Knowledge of sense of life.

Power

Appropriate use of power will help the nurse to work out toward the achievement of goal. Nurse should not consider the power as advantage since the patient is vulnerable.

Intimacy

Kinds of activities that nurses perform to develop the personal and private closeness with patient at various elements such as physical, social, spiritual and psychological aspects.

Trust

Nurse has to develop the sense of trust with the patient. Nurse has to explain the ward routines, and orient the patient. It is always approachable to gain trust.

Respect

Nurse have to respect the patient irrespective of their race, culture, gender, socioeconomic status, occupation, etc. The basic sense of respect given by the nurse will help the nurse to maintain the good nurse-patient therapeutic relationship.

JOHARI WINDOW OF INTERPERSONAL RELATIONSHIP

Joseph Luft and Harry Ingham (1950) described the concept of interpersonal relationship. The prefix of both the names, 'Joseph' and 'Harry', was adjoined together and termed Johari window (Fig. 4.4). Other names are as follows:

- Disclosure or feedback model of self-awareness
- Information processing tool

The Johari window has four quadrants that represent four combinations as follows:

1. **Quadrant 1 (arena or open):** Information was known to the self and also known to others. When Quadrant 1 is

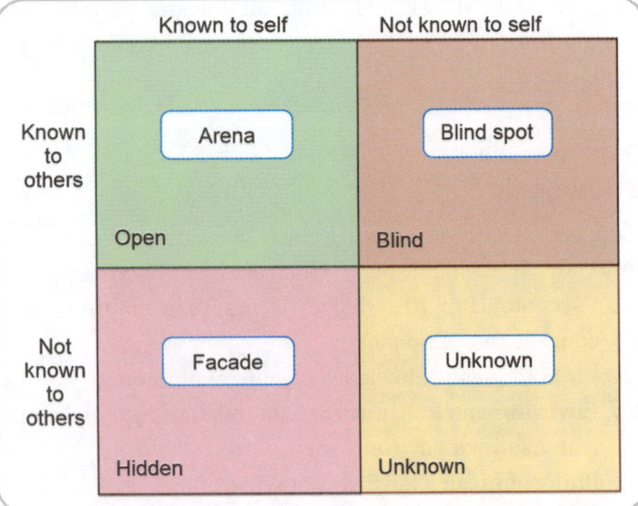

Figure 4.4: Johari Window of interpersonal relationship

large, it denotes nurse is open to others and self. When Quadrant 1 is small, it denotes nurse is partially open to others and self.

2. **Quadrant 2 (blind spot):** Information was not known to the self but known to others. Blind spot denotes the lack of self-awareness. People in the group might learn from the verbal cues, mannerisms or style of speech.
3. **Quadrant 3 (facade or hidden):** Information was known to the self and not known to others. When Quadrant 2 is large, it denotes nurse has higher self-awareness and not opened to others. It is comparable with introvert personality in which the individual does not share anything out due to fear about the group or unwillingness to share to others.
4. **Quadrant 4 (unknown):** Information was not known to self and also to others. When the individual or he/she felt that the information is not known to him/her is the time to remove the ignorance and enlighten the patient with knowledge. When the individual got awareness about oneself, the chances of sharing knowledge will also increase.

PROCESS RECORDING

Definition

It is a method of recording nurse-patient interaction, which has been done by the nurses in psychiatric setup.

Recording Technique

Verbatim recording technique is used for recording the nurse-patient interaction. (The term 'verbatim' denotes record the exact words verbalized by the patient.)

Time of Recording

It should be done either during the nurse-patient interaction or immediately after the nurse as patient interaction.

Purposes

Overall aim of process recording is to improve the quality of interaction process and it also acts as learning experience for the nurse regarding the improvement in interaction process. The specific purposes are as follows:

- Helps to identify the problems and promotes skills to solve those problems.
- Enhances the observational skills during thinking, and categorizing the interaction process into different heading.
- Compares the verbal and nonverbal communication pattern.
- Helps to develop the awareness about the interaction process.
- To plan, structure and evaluate the interaction of nurse and patient.
- Acts as a prerequisite to nursing process.

Thus, process recording is considered teaching or educative tool, diagnostic or assessment tool, therapeutic or intervention tool, evaluative tool and tool for self-awareness.

Prerequisites for Process Recording

- Physical organizational setup
- Good and noise-free environment
- Consent from the patient should be taken if voice recording is needed.
- Willingness of patient should be assessed whether he/she wants to proceed with the interaction process or not.

Format of Process Recording

Patient Profile:

Name:
Age:
Gender:
Education:
Occupation:
Hospital identity number:
Ward/OPD:
Date of admission:
Name of treating doctor:
Chief complaints:

Objectives or Purposes:
Prerequisites or Preparation of Patient and Environment:
Date, time and place of Process recording:

Context of Interaction:

Participants in interaction	Verbal communication	Nonverbal communication	Inference
Nurse: Patient:	Record in verbatim (Document the exact words verbalized by the patient)	Include facial expression, posture, gesture, mannerism, eye contact, tone of voice, pacing and gait of patient during conversation. It is important to include any peculiar behavior such as biting the nail, periods of silence, shouting or exhibiting aggression, etc.	Write the interpretation that what you have interpreted on comparing the verbal and nonverbal communication of nurse and patient interaction

Outline of Process Recording

Introductory Concept

It includes the patient profile, medical/surgical/psychiatric history, date/time/place of interaction, reason for choosing the client and duration of interaction.

Objectives

'SMART' is a Mnemonic to remember the nature of goal setting in process recording.

It has to be:

S – Specific
M – Measurable
A – Achievable
R – Realistic and
T – Timely in nature

Setting the short-term goal is found appropriate in the initial phase of nurse-patient interaction, i.e., on preorientation, orientation and identification phase. Long-term goal has to be set during the intervention, maintenance and termination phase of nurse-patient interaction which includes rehabilitation and follow-up of nursing care as shown in Figure 4.5.

Context of Nurse-Patient Interaction

It includes verbal and nonverbal communication of nurse-patient interaction. It also includes any abnormal behavior elicited during interaction.

Analysis of Interaction

It includes the inference or interpretation of process recording of both the verbal and nonverbal communication of the patient. Identification in terms of thoughts and feelings is more concerned.

Ideal Duration of Interaction

The total time required for process recording is 30 minutes, in which 20 minutes are considered active time and remaining 10 minutes are for conclusion of recording.

Summary of Process Recording

Summarize the entire interaction process and identify the short-term goals whether these have been met or not. If the goals are not met, modify the conversation process and replan/reschedule for the next time.

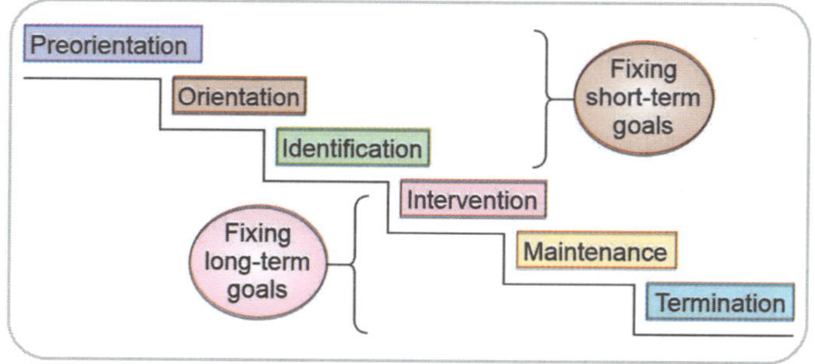

Figure 4.5: Goals of process recording during the phases of nurse-patient relationship

SUMMARY

- Communication is defined as 'interaction process between the sender and receiver in which the receiver receives the message exactly what the sender intended to say as such.
- Theories of communication include Ruesch's theory, transactional analysis and neurolinguistic programming.
- Types of communication are verbal, nonverbal, formal, informal, interpersonal, intrapersonal, transpersonal, horizontal, vertical, animal, physiological, chain, metacommunication and communication through mass media.
- Barriers of communication process have been categorized into barriers related to sender, channel, receiver and environment. Barriers of communication are also categorized as physical, physiological, environment and organization.
- Therapeutic impasses are resistance, transference, countertransference and boundary violations such as role, time, space, place, money, gifts, clothing, language, self-disclosure, post discharge social boundaries and physical contact boundaries.

Contd...

- Therapeutic techniques of communication are offering self, using silence, active listening, offering general leads, empathy, questioning, restating, giving broad openings, verbalizing the implied, seeking clarification and validation or voicing doubt, making observations, encouraging description of perceptions, presenting reality, sharing perceptions, placing the event in time or sequence, encouraging comparison, summarizing, theme identification, focusing, exploring, interpreting, encourage goal setting, offering help, encourage decision, formulating plan of action, giving recognition or reinforcement, limit setting, supportive confrontation, encouraging evaluation.
- Nontherapeutic communications are giving false assurance, rejection/rejecting, giving advice, unnecessary probing, defending, requesting an explanation, indicating the existence of an external source of power, belittling feelings expressed, making stereotyped comments, cliches and trite expressions, using denial, parroting, approving or disapproving, agreeing or disagreeing, introducing an unrelated topic, failure to listen, failure to explore the patient's point of view, giving inadequate answers and vague description.
- Dynamics of nurse-patient relationship includes therapeutic use of self-awareness, improving self-awareness, power, trust, intimacy and respect.
- Joseph Luft and Harry Ingham (1950) described the concept of interpersonal relationship termed Johari window of IPR which has four quadrants as: known to self, known to others, not known to self and not known to others.
- Process recording is a process of recording nurse-patient interaction in psychiatric setup.

ASSESS YOURSELF

Long Answer Questions

1. Define therapeutic communication. Explain the techniques of therapeutic communication with example.
2. Define nurse-patient relationship. Explain the principles, phases and components with appropriate examples.

Short Answer Questions

1. List out the therapeutic techniques of communication?
2. Define Process Recording?

Short Notes

Write short notes on:

1. Types of communication
2. Nurse-patient relationship
3. Barriers of communication
4. Therapeutic impasses and their management
5. Communication process
6. Techniques of therapeutic communication
7. Therapeutic use of self
8. Johari window of IPR

Multiple Choice Questions

1. **Communication takes place among professionals is ________ communication.**
   a. Formal b. Informal
   c. Both a and b d. None of these
2. **Johari window of IPR has _____ quadrants.**
   a. 1 b. 2
   c. 3 d. 4
3. **The below phrase which is best to describe the meaning of communication is _____________.**
   a. Common understanding between the sender and receiver
   b. Interaction between sender and receiver
   c. Two members talking each other
   d. None of the above
4. **Transfer of client's feeling toward the nurse means _____________.**
   a. Transference b. Countertransference
   c. Resistance d. None of these
5. **Johari window of IPR is also known as __________.**
   a. Disclosure or Feedback model of self-awareness
   b. Information processing tool
   c. Both a and b
   d. None of the above
6. **The therapeutic technique of communication is __________.**
   a. Active listening b. Being judgmental
   c. Both a and b d. None of these
7. **The nontherapeutic technique of communication is __________.**
   a. Focusing b. Defending
   c. Both a and b d. None of these
8. **The communication within a communication means ___________ communication.**
   a. Verbal b. Meta
   c. Informal d. Animal
9. **Communication takes place within oneself means ___________ communication.**
   a. Intrapersonal b. Interpersonal
   c. Transpersonal d. Formal
10. **The term 'Blind Spot' in Johari window of IPR denotes ________.**
    a. Not known to self and others
    b. Known to self and not known to others
    c. Not known to self but known to others
    d. None of the above

Answer Key

1. a	**2.** d	**3.** a	**4.** a	**5.** c
6. a	**7.** b	**8.** b	**9.** a	**10.** c

Treatment Modalities and Therapies used in Mental Disorders

CHAPTER 5

LEARNING OBJECTIVE

After studying this chapter, the student will be able to understand the basic concepts of psychological therapies and administer the appropriate psychological therapies to the patient based on the needs and issues.

CHAPTER OUTLINE

KEY TERMS

Antipsychotics or neuroleptics or major tranquilizers or dopamine receptor blockers, Neuroleptic malignant syndrome, Pseudo-Parkinson's disease, Akathisia, Acute dystonia, Rabbit syndrome, Tardive dyskinesia, Antidepressants or thymoleptics or mood elevators, Tricyclic antidepressants, Selective Serotonin Reuptake Inhibitors (SSRI), Serotonin Norepinephrine Reuptake Inhibitors (SNRI), Monoamine Oxidase Inhibitors (MAOIs), Atypical antidepressants, Serotonin syndrome, Hypertensive crisis, Gamma-Amino Butyric Acid (GABA), Antianxiety agents or anxiolytics or minor tranquilizers, Barbiturates, Benzodiazepines, Anti-Parkinson's drugs, Substantia nigra, Mood stabilizers, Stimulants, Amphetamines, Individual psychotherapy, Hypnosis, Abreaction, Reality therapy, Insight psychotherapy, Free association, Psychoanalytical therapy, Cognitive therapy, Behavioral therapy, Classical conditioning, Operant conditioning, Systemic desensitization, Flooding or implosive therapy, Assertiveness training, Aversion therapy, Modeling, covert sensitization, Overt sensitization, Contingency contracting, Token economy, Rational emotive therapy, Meta-cognitive therapy, Dialectical behavior therapy, Mindfulness based cognitive therapy, Acceptance-commitment therapy, Cognitive behavioral therapy, Supportive psychotherapy, Family therapy, Therapeutic community, Milieu therapy, Group therapy, Play therapy, Psycho–drama, Music therapy, Dance therapy, Recreational therapy, Light therapy or phototherapy or heliotherapy, Relaxation therapy, Autogenic training, Jacobson Progressive Muscle Relaxation (JPMR), Guided imagery, Ashtanga yoga, Surya namaskar, Pranayama, Kriyas, Asanas, Acupuncture, Homeopathy, Naturopathy, Ayurveda, Aromatherapy, Herbal therapy, Exercise, Massage therapy, Tai chi technique, Bioelectromagnetic therapy, Reflexology, reiki, Therapeutic touch, Spiritual healing, Art therapy, Sound therapy, Meditation, Biofeedback, Electroconvulsive therapy, Psychosurgery, Deep brain stimulation.

PSYCHOPHARMACOLOGY

ANTIPSYCHOTICS

Antipsychotics are medications used to treat psychotic disorders or psychosis related to other psychiatric and medical disorders.

Synonymous terms
- D_2 receptor blockers
- Major tranquilizers
- Neuroleptic agents
- Ataractics
- Anti-schizophrenic drugs

History of Antipsychotics

Sen and Bose (1931) were the first to introduce Reserpine. Jean Delay and Pierre Deniker (1952) were the first to introduce Chlorpromazine. Janssen (1958) was the first to introduce Haloperidol. Comparison of typical antipsychotics and atypical antipsychotics is explained in Table 5.1.

NOTE

High potency antipsychotics should be avoided in Parkinson and in patients with history of extrapyramidal symptoms. Low potency antipsychotics should be avoided in patients with heart diseases, delirium, benign prostrate hypertrophy in elders and closed angle glaucoma.

Table 5.1: Comparison of conventional (or) traditional (or) typical antipsychotics and atypical antipsychotics (or) second generation antipsychotics

Aspects	Conventional (or) traditional (or) typical antipsychotics	Atypical antipsychotics (or) second generation antipsychotics
Treatment of symptoms	Treat positive symptoms more than negative symptoms	Treat negative symptoms well
Side effects	Cause extrapyramidal side effects	Cause anticholinergic and metabolic side effects
Antagonize the receptors	Antagonize Dopamine (D_2) receptors	Antagonize Dopamine (D_2), serotonin, alpha and histamine receptors
Types/classification/ examples	**High potency medication** (High affinity to dopamine receptors is present and hence low dose is required) • Fluphenazine (Prolixin) • Haloperidol (Haldol) **Moderate potency medication** • Perphenazine (Trilafon) **Low-potency medication** (Low affinity to dopamine receptors, therefore, high dosage is required) • Chlorpromazine (Thorazine) • Thioridazine (Mellaril)	• Risperidone (Risperdal) • Clozapine (Clozaril) • Olanzapine (Zyprexa) • Ziprasidone (Geodon) • Quetiapine (Seroquel) • Aripiprazole (Abilify): Considered Novel (or) Third generation antipsychotics

Types of Antipsychotics

Typical Antipsychotics

- **Phenothiazines**
  - *Aliphatics:* E.g., Chlorpromazine (300–1500 mg/day oral or 50–100 mg/day IM)
  - *Piperidines:* E.g., Thioridazine (300–800 mg/day oral)
  - *Piperazines:* E.g., Fluphenazine (2–20 mg/day oral)
- **Thioxanthenes**
  - *Aliphatics:* E.g., Chlorprothixene (75–600 mg/day oral or 25–75 mg/day IM)
  - *Piperazines:* E.g., Flupenthixol (3–40 mg/day oral)
- **Butyrophenones:** E.g., Haloperidol (5–100 mg/day oral or 5–20 mg/day IM)
- **Diphenylbutylpiperidines:** E.g., Pimozide (4–20 mg oral)
- **Indolic Derivatives (or) Dihydroindolones:** For example, Molindone (50–225 mg/day oral)
- **Dibenzoxazepines:** E.g., Loxapine (25–100 mg/day oral)

Atypical Antipsychotics

- **Dibenzodiazepines:** E.g., Clozapine (50–450 mg/day oral)
- **Benzisoxazole:** E.g., Risperidone (2–10 mg/day oral)
- **Benzisothiazole:** E.g., Ziprasidone (40–160 mg/day oral)
- **Substituted Benzamides:** For example, Amisulpride (400–1200 mg/day oral)
- **Dibenzothiazepine:** E.g., Quetiapine (300–500 mg/day oral)
- **Thienobenzodiazepine:** E.g., Olanzapine (5–20 mg/day oral)

Indications

Organic Mental Disorders

- Delirium
- Dementia with psychotic features/violent behavior
- Organic hallucinosis
- Organic delusional disorder
- Psychosis due to withdrawal of substance/drug

Functional Disorders

- Acute Psychosis
- Schizophrenia
- Schizoaffective disorder
- Delusional disorder

Mood Disorders

- Mania
- Depression with psychotic symptoms

Childhood Disorders

- Autism
- Enuresis
- Attention-deficit hyperactivity disorder (when stimulants are contraindicated)
- Conduct disorder

Neurotic Disorders

- Intractable obsessive compulsive disorder (Thioridazine is drug of choice)
- Intractable anxiety (Olanzapine is drug of choice)

Medical Disorders

- Tics/tourette syndrome
- Tetanus
- Nausea/vomiting
- Eclampsia
- Heat stroke
- Intractable hiccups
- Intractable pruritus
- Huntington's chorea
- Severe pain during malignancies

Contraindications

Contraindications of antipsychotics are illustrated in Flowchart 5.1.

Drug Interactions of Antipsychotics

Drug interactions of antipsychotics are given in Flowchart 5.2.

Classification of Side Effects of Antipsychotics

Antidopaminergic Side Effects

- Extrapyramidal symptoms (Fig. 5.1 and Table 5.2)
- Hyperprolactinemia

Antihistaminic Side Effects

Sedation

Anti-Alpha Adrenergic Side Effects

- Orthostatic hypotension
- Sexual dysfunction
- Cardiac arrhythmias

Flowchart 5.1: Contraindications of antipsychotics

Contraindications of antipsychotics

- Absolute contraindications
  - Central nervous system depression
  - Severe brain damage
  - Hypersensitivity to the drug
- Relative contraindications
  - Glaucoma
  - Intestinal obstruction
  - Severe hyper-tension/hypotension
  - Obesity
  - Diabetes mellitus
  - Seizure
  - Benign prostatic hypertrophy
- Drugs used with caution in
  - Blood dyscrasias
  - Pregnancy and lactation
  - Cirrhosis of liver
  - Heart disease
  - Coma
  - Pheochromocytoma
  - Parkinson's disease

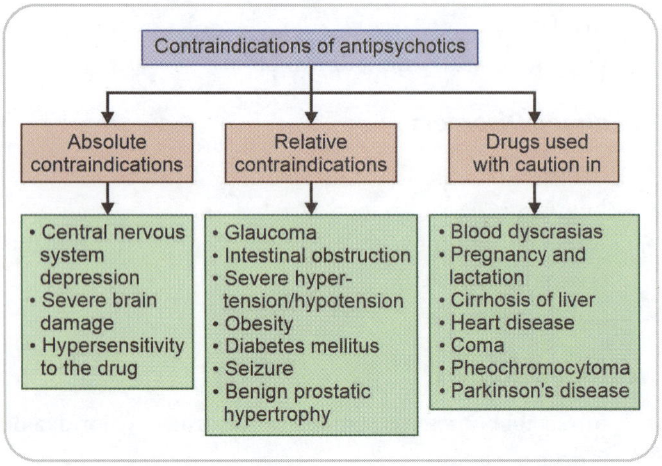

Flowchart 5.2: Drug interactions of antipsychotics

Antipsychotics → WITH

- Antidepressants, Sedatives/hypnotics, Antianxiety drugs, Antihistaminics, Alcohol → CNS depression
- Antidiarrheals, Antacids → Decrease absorption
- Propranolol → Hypotension
- Barbiturates → Increase metabolism

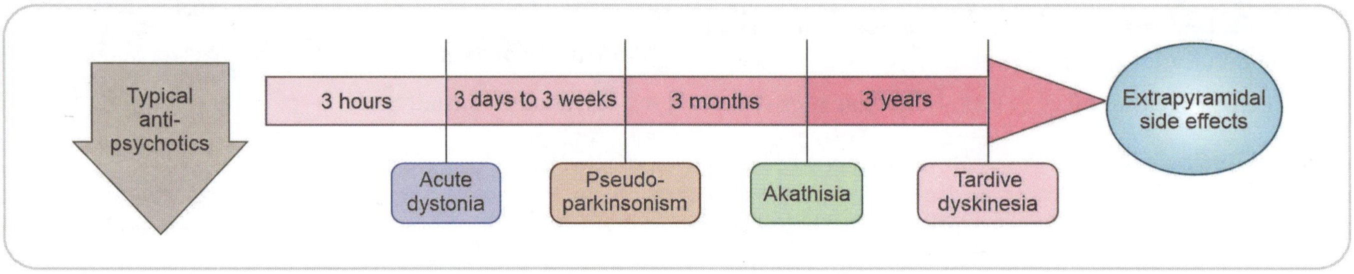

Typical anti-psychotics → 3 hours | 3 days to 3 weeks | 3 months | 3 years → Extrapyramidal side effects

Acute dystonia | Pseudo-parkinsonism | Akathisia | Tardive dyskinesia

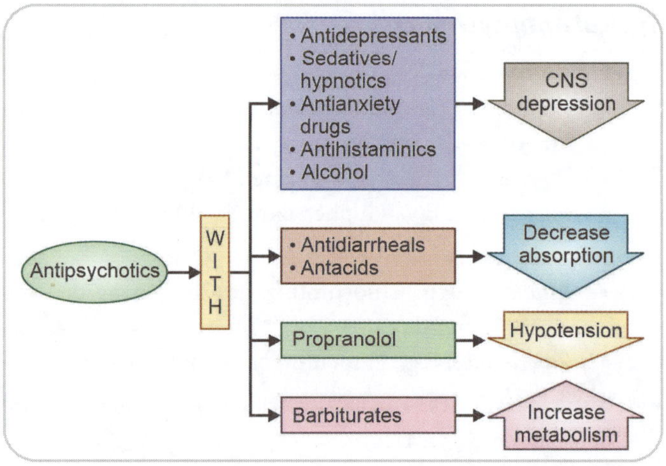

Figure 5.1: Extrapyramidal side effects

Table 5.2: Management of side effects due to antipsychotics

Side effects	Occurring due to	Medical management	Nursing management
Autonomic side effects			
Dry mouth (due to blockage of facial and glossopharyngeal nerve)	Chlorpromazine (thorazine)	• No need of treatment • Pilocarpine 2% (occasionally)	• Maintain oral hygiene • Use sugarless chewing gum
Constipation (due to blockage of vagus nerve)	Chlorpromazine (thorazine)	• No need of treatment • Laxatives (occasionally)	• High fiber diet • More intake of water • Increase physical activity
Orthostatic hypotension (due to blockage of alpha-1 receptor)	• Chlorpromazine (thorazine) • Clozapine (clozaril) • Thioridazine (mellaril)	• Use plasma expanders (when severe) • Raise the leg • Change safer drugs	• Monitor blood pressure regularly • Advise the client to get up from lying or sitting in a slow manner
Central anticholinergic syndrome (delirium)	Chlorpromazine (thorazine)	• Physostigmine • Diazepam (occasionally)	• Prevent falls • Provide safety measures • Orient the patient
Urinary retention	Chlorpromazine (thorazine)	• Assess benign prostrate hypertrophy • If persists, urinary catheterization can be done	• Maintain intake output chart • Assess for bladder distension • Advise the client to report the difficulty in voiding • Pour water on patient's back to stimulate urination
Cycloplegia	Chlorpromazine (thorazine)	• No need of treatment • Pilocarpine 2% (occasionally) • Change the safer antipsychotics	• Report the side effects immediately to the doctor so that safe antipsychotics might be prescribed

Contd...

Side effects	Occurring due to	Medical management	Nursing management
Impotence (due to blockage of α-2 receptor)	Thioridazine (mellaril)		• Document the side effects and measures taken
Mydriasis (due to blockage of Oculomotor nerve)			
Impaired ejaculation (due to blockage of α-2 receptor)			
Extrapyramidal side effects (EPS)			
Neuroleptic malignant syndrome	Traditional (or) typical antipsychotics	• Bromocriptine • Baclofen • Dantrolene • Electroconvulsive therapy (rarely)	• Report the Extrapyramidal side effects immediately to doctor • Quit the next dose of prescribed antipsychotics and inform the same to doctor (stop the drug because it is causing the Extrapyramidal side effects)
Pseudo-Parkinson's disease		• Anti-Parkinson's agents • Benzodiazepines • Anticholinergics	
Akathisia		• Beta blockers	
Acute dystonia		• Anti-Parkinson's agents • Benzodiazepines • Anticholinergics	
Rabbit syndrome			
Tardive dyskinesia	Unknown (equal chance with all antipsychotics)	• Focus on prevention	
Central nervous system side effects			
CNS depression	Unknown	• Antidepressants (occasionally) • Electroconvulsive therapy	
Seizure	Chlorpromazine (thorazine)	• Decrease the dosage • Change to safer antipsychotics	• Safety measures • Put side rails • Prevent falling back of tongue • Don't restrict the movements • Turn head to one side during the seizure to prevent aspiration • Monitor and document the duration and nature of seizure
Sedation	• Olanzapine (zyprexa) • Clozapine (clozaril) • Thioridazine (mellaril)		• Maintain sleep chart • Prevent fall/injury in all activities
Allergic side effects			
Cholestatic jaundice	Chlorpromazine (thorazine)	Change to safer antipsychotics	
Agranulocytosis	Clozapine	Filgrastim	• Weekly checking of White Blood Cells (WBC) count • Isolation • Infection control measures
Metabolic and endocrine side effects			
Weight gain (due to blockage of H1 receptor)	• Chlorpromazine (thorazine) • Clozapine (clozaril) • Thioridazine (mellaril) • Olanzapine (zyprexa)	• Monitor the weight regularly • Diet control • Exercise • Change to other safer medication as prescribed	
Galactorrhea	Haloperidol	Change to other safer medication as prescribed	

Contd...

Side effects	Occurring due to	Medical management	Nursing management
Cardiac side effects			
ECG Changes: Prolonged QTC interval (fatal arrhythmia: Torsades de pointes)	Chlorpromazine (thorazine)	Change to the safer antipsychotics	• Check pulse and blood pressure • Report immediately if chest pain is felt by patient
Ocular side effects			
Granular deposit in cornea and lens	Chlorpromazine (thorazine)	Change to the safer antipsychotics	Ophthalmic examination
Pigmentary retinopathy	Thioridazine (mellaril)		
Dermatological side effects			
Contact dermatitis	Chlorpromazine (thorazine)	• Skin assessment • Symptomatic management	
Photosensitivity reaction		Use of sunscreen and avoid exposure to sunlight	

Antimuscarinic Side Effects

- Blurred vision
- Tachycardia
- Dry mouth
- Urinary retention
- Constipation
- Seizure
- Weight gain
- Increased liver enzymes
- Eye problems
- Skin problems

Extrapyramidal Symptoms

- **Neuroleptic malignant syndrome**
  - Life threatening disorder that occurs in small number of patients receiving antipsychotics.
  - Onset is rapid, within 24–72 hours
  - Mental symptoms
    - Stupor/altered consciousness
  - Autonomic disturbances
    - Tachycardia
    - Increased sweating
    - Urinary incontinence
    - Unstable blood pressure
    - Increased salivation
  - Secondary features
    - Renal failure
    - Cardiovascular collapse
    - Pneumonia
    - Thromboembolism
- **Pseudo-Parkinson's disease**
  - Masked face
  - Cog-wheel rigidity
  - Bradykinesia
  - Stooping posture
  - Drooling of saliva
  - Akinesia
  - Ataxia
  - Pill rolling tremors
- **Akathisia**
  - Agitation
  - Restless (For example, patient tapping the palm on the lap in a fast manner)
- **Acute dystonia**
  - Opisthotonus
  - Oculogyric crisis (upward lateral movement of eye)
- **Rabbit syndrome:** Presence of orofacial tremors
- **Tardive dyskinesia**
  - Abnormal choreoathetoid movements are seen in muscles of head, trunk and limbs
  - Most common in older women
  - Severe form of Extrapyramidal symptoms might lead to disfigurement of face

Pharmacokinetics of Antipsychotics

- **Absorption:** Oral medications are absorbed in GI tract and reach blood stream
- **Distribution:** Lipophilic and bind to proteins
- **Metabolism:** Takes place in liver (hepatic microsomal enzyme)
- **Excretion:** Enterohepatic circulation (liver and kidney)

Pharmacodynamics of Antipsychotics

- **Site of action:** Antipsychotics act on dopamine type 2 (D_2) receptors.

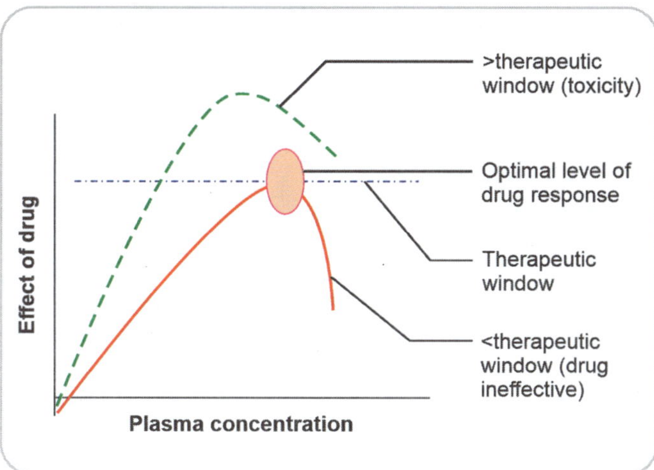

Figure 5.2: Dose-response curve

- **Dose-response curve:** It denotes the drug effect versus plasma concentration (Fig. 5.2).
  Example: Risperidone found more potent than Olanzapine (4 mg of risperidone = 20 mg of olanzapine with same beneficial effects).
- **Therapeutic window:** Blood level of drug below the therapeutic window is not effective and higher than therapeutic window is toxic.

Mechanism of Action

Dopamine (D_2 receptor) blockage on the dopamine pathways will lead to the following effects (Fig. 5.3):

- **Nigrostriatal tract:** Causes extrapyramidal symptoms.
- **Tuberoinfundibular tract:** Modulates pituitary thereby increase prolactin.
- **Mesolimbic tract:** Reduces positive symptoms (hallucinations and delusions).
- **Mesocortical tract:** treats negative and cognitive symptoms.

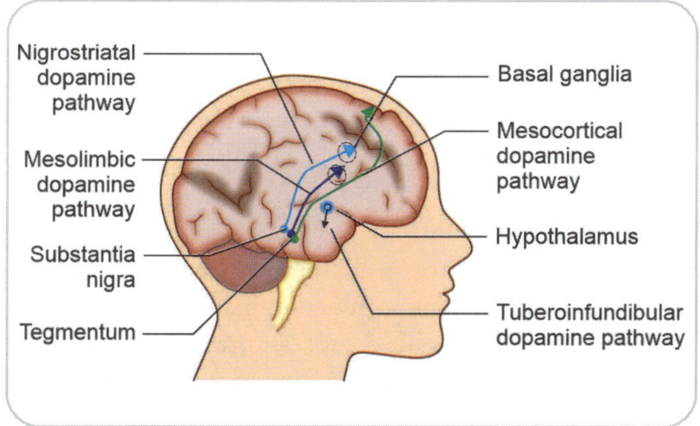

Figure 5.3: Dopaminergic pathways in the brain

NURSING IMPLICATION

Nurses' Responsibility for Patients Receiving Antipsychotics

- Follow the rights of medications.
- Advise the client to take sips of water to prevent xerosis (dryness of mouth).
- Advise the client to take high fiber diet and more intake of water to prevent constipation.
- Advise the client to get up from bed slowly to prevent orthostatic hypotension.
- Observe the client for extrapyramidal symptoms.
- Take seizure precautions.
- Advise the client to take antipsychotic drug at bed time since the drugs might cause sedation.
- Advise the client to use sunscreen, wear full sleeves and use dark glasses for photosensitive reactions.
- Patient receiving clozapine is having risk of developing agranulocytosis. So, WBC count has to be monitored weekly once. If WBC count <3000/mm^3 then stop the drug. Advise the client to report if he/she develops sore throat or fever, since it denotes sign of infection.
- Advise the patient that antipsychotics should not be discontinued suddenly because it leads to antipsychotic withdrawal syndrome characterized by nausea, vomiting, diarrhea, rhinorrhea, and diaphoresis, lack of sleep, agitation and malaise. This withdrawal symptoms occur within 2 weeks when patient quits the drug. So, slow tapering of the drug is advisable.
- Advise the client to have drug compliance in order to prevent the relapse.

ANTIDEPRESSANTS

Synonymous terms
- Thymoleptics
- Mood elevators

History of Antidepressants

- Imipramine was the first discovered antidepressant.
- Iproniazid and antituberculosis medications were found to have antidepressant effects.
- In 1957, tricyclic antidepressants were evolved and so these are referred to as first generation drugs.

Indications for Antidepressants

Neurotic and Stress-Related Disorders

- Endogenous depression
- Panic disorders
- Obsessive compulsive disorder (SSRI)
- Generalized anxiety (SSRI)
- Social phobia
- Panic disorder

- Post-traumatic stress disorder (SSRI)
- Premenstrual dysphoric disorder

Medical Disorders

- Migraine (amitriptyline and nortriptyline)—neuropathic pain
- Chronic pain
- Irritable bowel syndrome
- Premature ejaculation
- Pain related to fibromyalgia (SNRI)
- Pain related to neuropathy (SNRI)

Eating Disorders

- Anorexia nervosa
- Bulimia nervosa
- Obesity

Miscellaneous

- Insomnia (doxepin)
- Schizoaffective disorder
- Nocturnal enuresis in children
- Borderline personality disorder
- Smoking
- Alcoholism

Types of Antidepressants

- First generation antidepressants (or) tricyclic antidepressants (TCA)—drug of choice for severe depression.
- Second generation antidepressants (or) selective serotonin reuptake inhibitors (SSRI)—drug of choice for mild to moderate depression.
- Serotonin norepinephrine reuptake inhibitors (SNRI).
- Monoamine oxidase inhibitors (MAOI).
- Atypical antidepressants.

Tricyclic Antidepressants

- **Tertiary amine tricyclic antidepressants**
  - Amitriptyline 100–200 mg
  - Doxepin 100–200 mg
  - Imipramine 100–200 mg
  - Clomipramine 100–200 mg
- **Secondary amine tricyclic antidepressants**
  - Nortriptyline 75–150 mg
  - Protriptyline 15–40 mg
  - Desipramine 100–200 mg
  - Amoxapine 200–300 mg
  - Maprotiline 100–150 mg

Selective Serotonin Reuptake Inhibitors (SSRI)

- Fluoxetine 20–80 mg
- Sertraline 50–200 mg
- Paroxetine 20–50 mg
- Fluvoxamine 50–300 mg
- Citalopram 20–60 mg
- Escitalopram 10–30 mg

Serotonin Norepinephrine Reuptake Inhibitors (SNRI)

Venlafaxine 75–225 mg

Atypical Antidepressants

- Bupoprion (wellbutrin) 150–450 mg
- Nefazodone (serzone) 200–600 mg

Mechanism of Action for Antidepressants

- **Monoamine hypothesis:** Deficiency of monoamines such as serotonin, norepinephrine and dopamine leads to depression.
- Postsynaptic receptors to upregulate.
- Monoamine hypothesis of gene expression states abnormal functioning of genes that might lead to depression.

Mechanism of Action—Selective Serotonin Reuptake Inhibitors (SSRI)

- SSRI will block serotonin transporter (SERT) and so it will inhibit the reuptake of serotonin in presynapse.
- Serotonin is synthesized in serotonergic neuron by amino acid 'Tryptophan'.
- Tryptophan from vesicles starts to release into synapse and binds with the receptors of postsynapse. At the same time, there will be reuptake process too.
- Serotonin in the synapse is reabsorbed into presynapse by serotonin transporter (SERT).
- When serotonin reuptake takes place, it partially reuptakes into vesicles and partially gets broken down into metabolites by monoamine oxidase (MAO) enzymes.
- Antidepressants will tend to produce maximum benefits by forming the G-protein as cluster in brain cell membrane namely lipid graft. G-Protein lacks access to molecule called Cyclic-AMP which is important to work with the signals of serotonin.
- SSRI will help to release G-protein from lipid raft and reach the membrane to function better. So, in order to carry out all the above processes, antidepressants are taken for 6–8 weeks to get maximum benefits (Fig. 5.4).

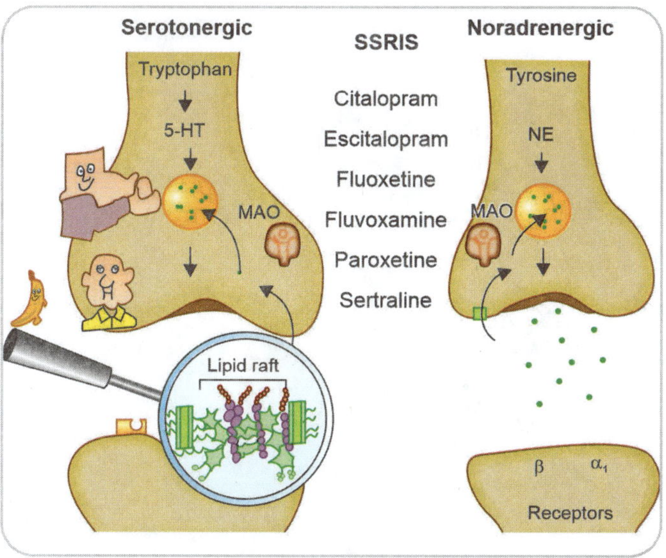

Figure 5.4: Mechanism of action of SSRI

Mechanism of Action—Serotonin Norepinephrine Reuptake Inhibitors (SNRI)

- Serotonin norepinephrine reuptake inhibitors (SNRI) will inhibit the serotonin transporter (SERT) and norepinephrine transporter (NET) and thereby reuptake process will get inhibited.
- Now adequate norepinephrine and serotonin will be present to bind with postsynapse.

Mechanism of Action—Tricyclic Antidepressants (TCA) (Fig 5.5)

- Tricyclic antidepressants (TCA) will block serotonin transporter and norepinephrine transporter primarily.
- Desipramine is more selective in inhibiting norepinephrine transporter than serotonin transporter.
- However, TCA also blocks alpha, histaminic and muscarinic receptors. Thus, serotonin, norepinephrine and dopamine get increased in synapse.

Mechanism of Action—Monoamine Oxidase Inhibitors (MAOI) (Fig. 5.6)

- Monoamine oxidase is present in brain, gut and liver.
- It has MOA-A and MOA-B:
  - **MOA–A:** Preferably metabolizes serotonin but it also metabolizes norepinephrine and dopamine.
  - **MOA–B:** Preferably metabolizes dopamine.
- Monoamine oxidase inhibitors will inhibit the monoamine oxidase enzyme, which then automatically decreases the availability of monoamines such as serotonin, norepinephrine and dopamine.
- Selegiline selectively blocks MAO-B (dopamine metabolism) and so it is helpful in Parkinson's disease.
- MAOI has drug food interactions and is present in the gut/intestines. The inhibited monoamines due to administration of MAOI might metabolize tyramine.

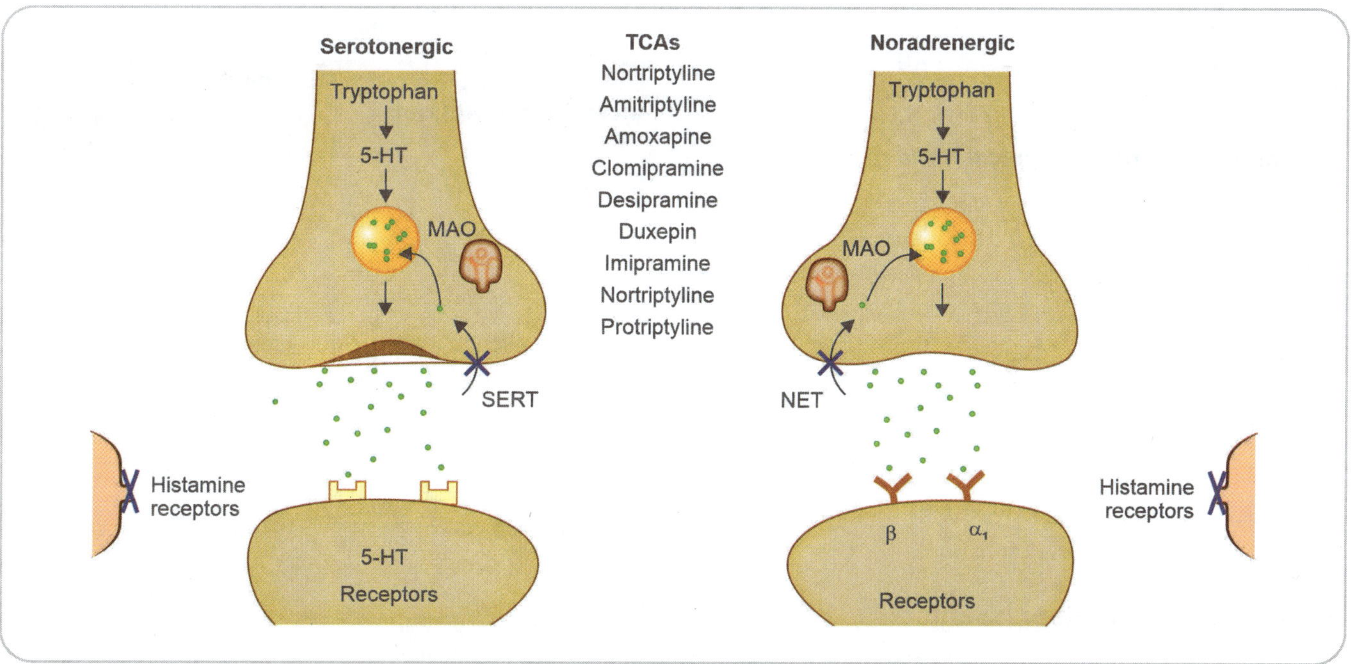

Figure 5.5: Mechanism of action of tricyclic antidepressants

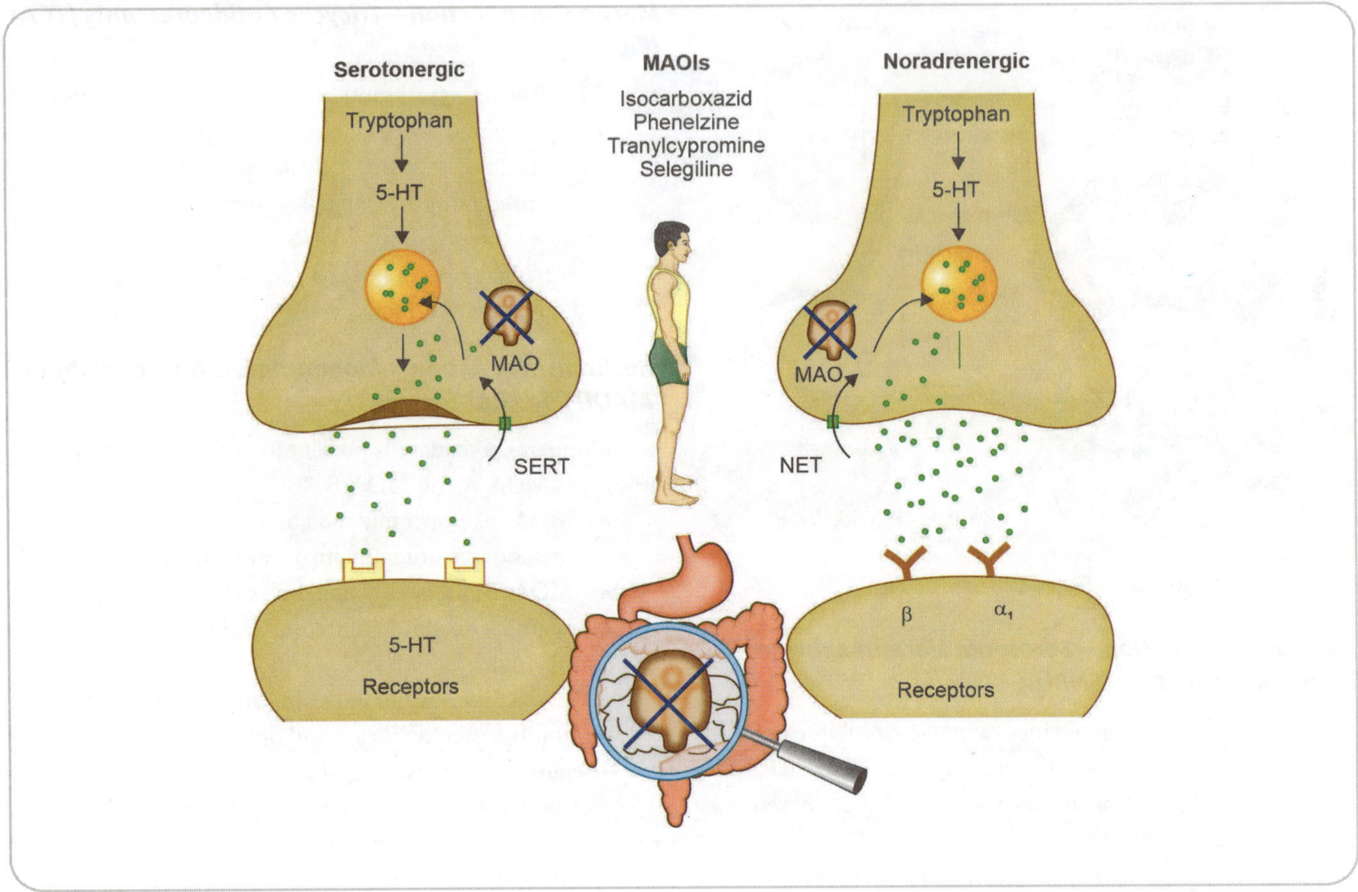

Figure 5.6: Mechanism of action of MAOI

- Increased tyramine acts as catecholamines releasing agent, that leads to hypertensive crisis and further leads to stroke.

Mechanism of Action—Atypical Antidepressants

- Bupropion is a weak norepinephrine and dopamine reuptake inhibitor. It reduces nicotine craving.
- Mirtazapine is an alpha receptor antagonist. It also blocks histamine receptor and serotonin receptor in the postsynapse.
- Trazadone and nefazodone will block serotonin transporter (SERT), 5-HT 2A receptor, histamine and alpha receptor.
- Vilazodone is serotonin (5-HT) partial agonist, i.e., it blocks serotonin transporter (SERT) and also prevents postsynaptic serotonin stimulation.

Side Effects of Antidepressants

The side effects of antidepressants have been given in Table 5.3.

Table 5.3: Side effects of antidepressants

Blockage of receptors by tricyclic antidepressants (TCA)	Side effects
Alpha	• Orthostatic hypotension • Giddiness
Histaminic	• Sedation • Cognitive impairment
Muscarinic	Anticholinergic effects • **Common:** Dry mouth, blurred vision, constipation, sinus tachycardia • **Occasional:** Urinary retention, mental clouding, delirium
Blocks cardiac sodium channels: Cardiac conduction abnormalities (Produce antiarrhythmic effects like clonidine)	
• Allergic rashes are common with drug maprotiline • 5-hydroxytryptamine (5-HT) or serotonin receptors blockage may cause weight gain • 5HT reuptake inhibition might cause nausea, diarrhea and decreased appetite	

Side Effects

Selective Serotonin Reuptake Inhibitors (SSRI):

- Excess stimulation of serotonin in brain will cause insomnia, anxiety and irritability.
- Excess stimulation of serotonin in spinal serotonin receptor will cause sexual side effects (Erectile dysfunction).
- Excess stimulation of serotonin in gastrointestinal system will cause nausea, vomiting and diarrhea.
- Abrupt withdrawal of SSRI will cause headache, nausea, vomiting, agitation and sleep disturbances.

Serotonin Norepinephrine Reuptake Inhibitors (SNRI):

- Hypertension
- Tachycardia

Mnemonics to remember are given in Table 5.4.

Table 5.4: Mnemonics to remember

Mnemonic to remember side effects of SSRI
• **S :** Serotonin syndrome • **S :** Stimulation of CNS • **R :** Reproduction dysfunctions in male • **I :** Insomnia **Serotonin syndrome** • **H :** Hyperthermia • **A :** Autonomic instability (delirium) • **R :** Rigidity • **M :** Myoclonus • Other symptoms are altered sensorium, fluctuating blood pressure, restlessness, tremors and shivering
Mnemonic to remember side effects of Tricyclic Antidepressants (TCA's)
• **T :** Tremors • **C :** Cardiovascular (cardiac arrhythmias, ischemic heart disease, postural hypotension) • **A :** Anticholinergic effects • **S :** Sedation, seizure

Contraindications of antidepressants have been shown in Flowchart 5.3.

Flowchart 5.3: Contraindications of antidepressants

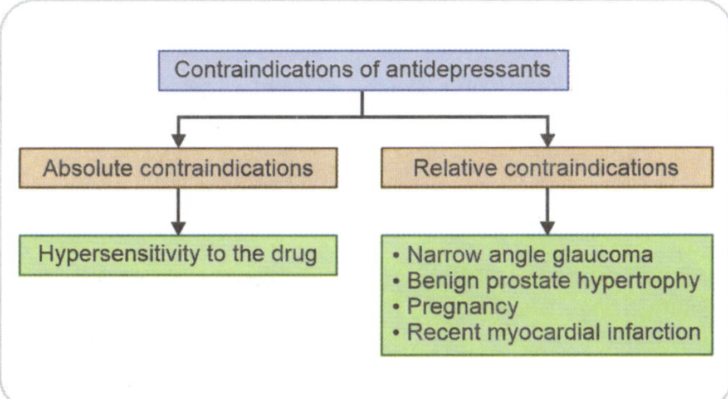

Drug and Food Interactions

Drug and Food Interactions of Monoamine Oxidase Inhibitors

Monoamine oxidase inhibitors (MAOIs) consumed by the patient along with certain medications, tyramine rich food items and other food items (as shown in Figure 5.7) will leads to hypertensive crisis. Monoamine oxidase inhibitors (MAOIs) consumed by the patient along with narcotic analgesics might cause hypertension or hypotension, coma, seizure and death (as shown in Figure 5.7).

Drug Interactions of SSRI

- **Cimetidine:** Raises the concentration of SSRI
- **Diazepam:** Enhances sedation
- **Warfarin:** Increases bleeding time
- When Selective serotonin reuptake inhibitors (SSRI) group of drugs is taken along with Lithium, Dopamine agonist (e.g., bromocriptine) and psychostimulants, they may lead to serotonin syndrome due to increased level of serotonin.

Drug Interactions of TCA

- **Guanethidine and clonidine:** Enhance the effects of guanethidine and clonidine
- **Warfarin:** Increases bleeding time
- **Sympathomimetic:** Hypertension, cardiac arrhythmias
- **Antipsychotics:** Extrapyramidal side effects
- **Levodopa:** Agitation, rigidity and tremors
- **Alcohol and anxiolytics:** Excessive daytime sleepiness
- **Phenytoin, barbiturates and carbamazepine:** Decrease the effect of TCA
- **Guanidine and procainamide:** Prolonged cardiac conduction
- **Anticholinergic agents:** Raised anticholinergic effects
- **MAOI:** Hypertensive crisis, seizure, muscle rigidness, hyperthermia and mania

NURSING IMPLICATION

Nursing Management for Patient with Overdose of Tricyclic Antidepressants

- Check vital signs
- Keep the patient's airway patent
- Gastric lavage/cathartics to prevent further absorption
- Give antidote: Physostigmine (antilirium) is an acetyl cholinesterase inhibitor (prevents the breakdown of acetylcholine)

Role of nurse in managing the side effects of antidepressants are enlisted in Table 5.5.

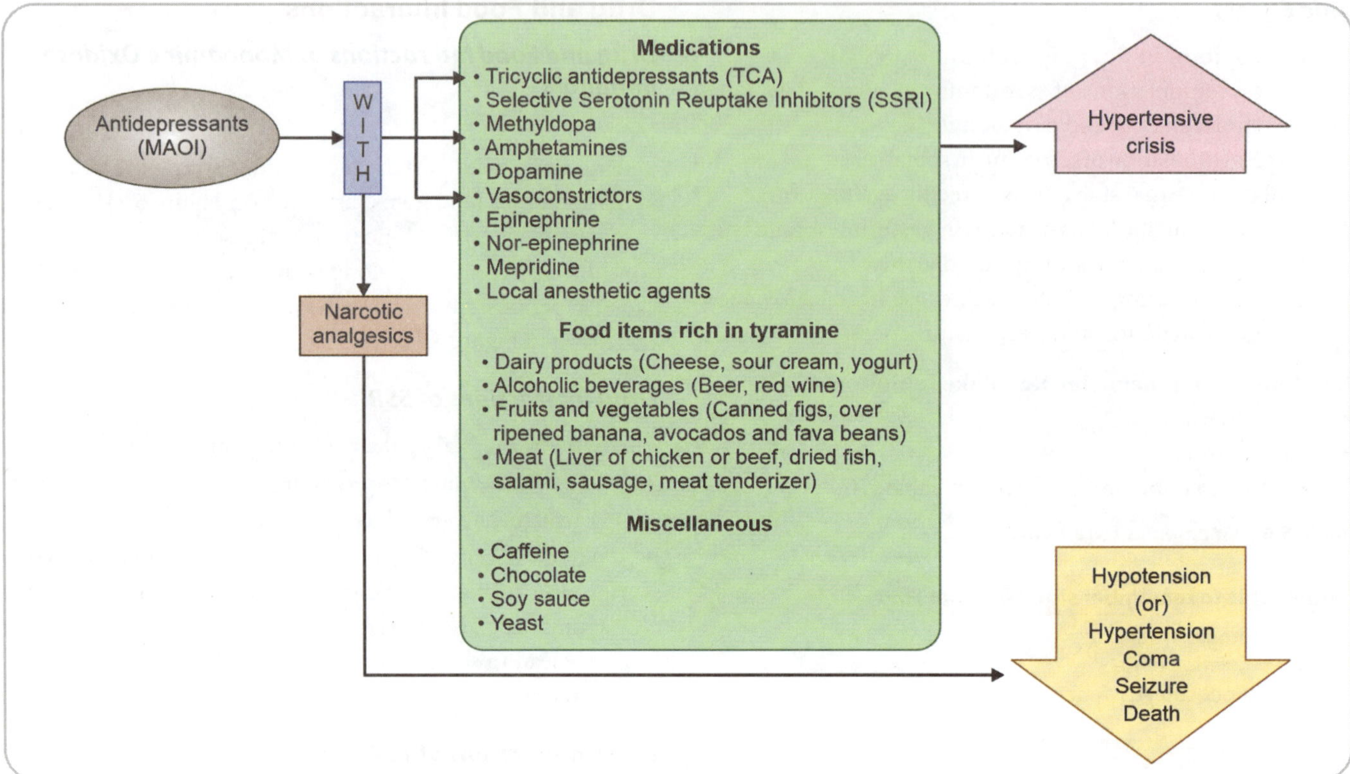

Figure 5.7 Drug and food interactions of MAOI

Table 5.5: Role of nurse in managing the side effects of antidepressants

Common side effects of antidepressants	Nursing management
Dry mouth	Sugarless chewing gum and intake of more fluids
Constipation	More water intake and high fiber diet
Urinary retention	More water intake and pouring water on client's back to stimulate micturition.
Blurred vision	Eye examination, caution while driving, and follow the safety measures. Remove the sharp objects which can cause injury and report any significant visual impairment immediately.
Eye pain	Screen for glaucoma
Reduced lacrimation	Advise to use artificial tears
Mydriasis	Advise to wear sunglasses outside
Weight gain/weight loss	Monitor weight regularly and advise the patient to take balanced diet.
Headache	Advise the patient to drink adequate water and if the headache persists, then report the treating physician.
Insomnia	Maintain sleep chart and provide relaxation therapy
Anhydrosis/decreased sweating	It may increase body temperature. So, adequate fluids and suitable clothing might be helpful
Increased sweating	More water intake to prevent dehydration
Serotonin syndrome	**Prevention** • Aware of drug interactions with serotonin. • Monoamine oxidase inhibitors (MAOI) should not be used with tricyclic antidepressants (TCA) and selective serotonin reuptake inhibitors (SSRI). • If monoamine oxidase inhibitors (MAOI) have been stopped then we need to wait for at least 2 weeks before starting tricyclic antidepressants (TCA)

Contd...

Common side effects of antidepressants	Nursing management
	Management • Discontinue the medication • Monitor vital signs • Inform the doctor immediately • Follow the measures to control fever and seizures
Hyperpyrexia	Check temperature, cold sponging and reassess temperature
Seizure	**Seizure precautions:** Safety measures (put side rails), turn head to side during seizure will prevent the aspiration of oral secretions, avoid falling back of tongue, use bite block to prevent the tongue bite during seizure, don't restrict movements, monitor the nature and duration of seizure, and remove the tight clothing.
Extrapyramidal symptoms	Management has been discussed in the topic of antipsychotics. (Amoxapine is a tricyclic antidepressant which causes extrapyramidal symptoms)
Orthostatic hypotension	Check vital signs, advise the client to take caffeine if he/she prefers, promote supportive stockings, adequate fluid intake, advise the client to get up slowly from lying position.

ANTIANXIETY AGENTS (OR) ANXIOLYTICS

Synonymous terms
- Minor tranquilizers
- Anxiolytics

Benzodiazepines

- **Short acting benzodiazepines**
  - Triazolam
- **Intermediate acting benzodiazepines**
  - Alprazolam
  - Oxazepam
  - Lorazepam
  - Halazepam
  - Temazepam
- **Long acting benzodiazepines**
  - Diazepam
  - Clonazepam
  - Chlordiazepoxide
  - Clorazepate
  - Flurazepam
  - Prazepam
  - Quazepam

Barbiturates

- **Ultra short acting barbiturates (<1 hour—duration of action)**
  - Thiopentone sodium
  - Methohexital
- **Short acting barbiturates (1–5 hours—duration of action)**
  - Secobarbital
- **Intermediate acting barbiturates (5–8 hours—duration of action)**
  - Pentobarbital
  - Amobarbital
- **Long acting barbiturates (>8 hours—duration of action)**
  - Phenobarbital

Nonbarbiturate and Nonbenzodiazepine Anxiolytic Agents

- **Carbamates:** Tybamate, meprobamate and carisoprodol
- **Piperidinediones:** Glutethimide
- **Quinazolines:** Methaqualone
- **Alcohols:** Ethanol, ethchlorvynol and chloral hydrate
- **Cyclic Ethers:** Paraldehyde
- **Beta Blockers:** Propranolol
- **Antipsychotics:** Thioridazine

Miscellaneous Antianxiety Agents

- Buspirone
- Hydroxyzine
- Meprobamate

Antidepressants Causing Antianxiety Effects

- **Selective serotonin reuptake inhibitors (SSRI):** Fluvoxamine, fluoxetine, paroxetine, sertaline, clomipramine.
- **Selective norepinephrine reuptake inhibitors (SNRI):** Venlafaxine.

Indications of Antianxiety Drugs

Anxiety Disorders

- Generalized anxiety disorder
- Post-traumatic stress disorder
- Obsessive compulsive disorder
- Panic disorder

- Social phobia
- Agoraphobia
- School phobia

Mood Disorders

- Bipolar I disorder
- Acute mania
- Depression

Sleep Disorders

- Insomnia
- Nightmares
- Enuresis and somnambulism—Stage 4 [Nonrapid Eye Movement (NREM) sleep disorder].

Psychotic Disorders

- Acute psychoses
- Antipsychotic-induced akathisia
- Violent behavior due to psychosis
- Treatment resistant schizophrenia

Miscellaneous

- Psychosomatic disorders
- Premedication as anesthetic agent
- Endoscopic/obstetric/surgical procedure
- Aggression due to influence of substance abuse
- Adjustment disorder with anxiety
- Status epilepticus/myoclonic seizure
- Alcohol withdrawal syndrome
- Narcoanalysis/abreaction

Mechanism of Action

GABA-A is an ionotropic receptor (or) ligand-gated ion channel. GABA-A is the major inhibitory neurotransmitter present in central nervous system which is linked with chloride channels. GABA-A receptor has two alpha subunits, two beta subunits and two gamma subunits. GABA-B receptor is metabotropic receptor (or) G protein-coupled receptor, which is linked with potassium channels. In anxious situation, there will be rapid excitatory action of neurons in the amygdala (limbic system) of the brain. Administration of the antianxiety drugs stimulates the GABA-A to bind in postsynaptic receptor and thereby releases negatively charged chloride ion in postsynaptic neuron. This chloride ion in postsynaptic neuron will prevent excitatory action of the neurochemicals and so it prevents the action potential. Hence, it calms the central nervous system and reduces anxiety. Benzodiazepine receptors are type I and type II as shown in the Flowchart 5.4.

Flowchart 5.4: Mechanism of action of antianxiety drugs

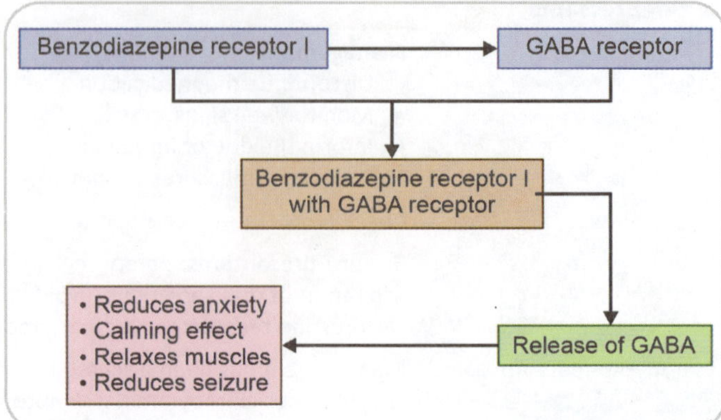

NOTE

- Benzodiazepine receptor I is linked with GABA receptor
- Benzodiazepine receptor II is linked with cognition and motor control.

Drug Interactions

Drug interactions with benzodiazepines are given in Table 5.6.

Table 5.6: Drug interactions of benzodiazepines

Drugs	Effect of drug interactions of benzodiazepines
Tricyclic antidepressants	Confusion, excessive day time sleepiness and altered motor activity
Monoamine oxidase inhibitor	Central nervous system depression
Succinylcholine	Reduced neuromuscular blockage
Phenytoin	Raised anticonvulsant serum value
Disulfiram Cimetidine	Raised benzodiazepines plasma level
Antacids	Alteration in absorption of benzodiazepine
Alcohol	Central nervous system depression and excessive day time sleepiness

Side Effects and their Nursing Management

Side effects of benzodiazepines and their nursing management have been given in Table 5.7.

Signs of Benzodiazepine Toxicity

- Increased sleepiness
- Confusion
- Coma
- Reduced reflexes
- Hypotension

Table 5.7: Side effects of benzodiazepines and their nursing management

Side effects of benzodiazepines	Nursing management
Dry mouth	• Chew the sugarless gum • Drink more water • Rinse the mouth frequently
Giddiness and Drowsy	• Safety measures to be carried out • Be cautious in driving • Take medications preferably at bed time • Help the client in ambulation
Ataxia	Assist the client in walking
Nausea	Medicine has to be taken with food

Benzodiazepine in Pregnancy

- **First Trimester:** Cleft lip and cleft palate
- **Labor:** Floppy infant syndrome (or) benign congenital hypotonic disorder.

Benzodiazepines Among Elders

- Lorazepam and oxazepam are safe drugs.
- Diazepam and chlordiazepoxide are not to be used in elders due to extended half-life and active metabolites.

Contraindications of Antianxiety Drugs

- Hypersensitivity reaction
- Pregnancy and Lactation
- Chronic renal failure
- Liver failure
- Narrow angle glaucoma
- Shock
- Depression/Pre-existing psychosis may worsen

NURSING IMPLICATION

Nurses' Responsibility in Administration of Antianxiety Drugs

- **Oral drug:** Administer with food to prevent nausea/gastric irritation.
- **Intramuscular injection:** Administer deep IM injection for better absorption of drug.
- **Intravenous injection:** Do not mix with other drugs due to harmful effects of drug interaction and slow IV should be given to prevent respiratory arrest/cardiac arrest. Vital signs with oxygen saturation to be monitored. Extravasation of drug might cause phlebitis/thrombosis.
- **Overdose of benzodiazepines:** Administer Flumazenil 0.2 to 1.0 mg IV for 1–2 minutes.
- **Advise the client that abrupt withdrawal of drug might cause irritability, insomnia and seizures.**
- *Remember barbiturates, ethyl alcohol and methaqualone might develop cross-tolerance.*
- Client should not use CNS depressants and other self-medications because they will cause life threatening effects due to drug interactions.

ANTIPARKINSON AGENTS

- Parkinson's disease is a neurodegenerative disorder caused due to degeneration of substantia nigra of midbrain. So, dopamine containing neuron in substantia nigra pathway also gets degenerated and due to the imbalance of dopamine, it leads to Parkinsonism.
- Antiparkinson's agents are the drugs which are used to treat Parkinson's disease and drug-induced extra-pyramidal symptoms.

Common Drugs

- **Anticholinergics**
  - Trihexiphenidyl
  - Procyclidine
  - Benztropine
  - Biperiden
- **Antihistamine**
  - Diphenhydramine
- **Dopaminergic agonists**
  - Bromocriptine
  - Amantadine

Contraindications

- Benign prostrate hypertrophy
- Angle closure glaucoma
- Intestinal obstruction
- Myasthenia gravis

Mechanism of Action

- Imbalance of dopamine will lead to increased cholinergic activity.
- Antiparkinson's agent will help to balance dopamine and acetylcholine in central nervous system.

Side Effects

- Anticholinergic effects
- Orthostatic hypotension
- Sedation
- Giddiness
- Nausea
- Diarrhea
- Worsening of psychosis

NURSING IMPLICATION

- Management of side effects of these drugs has been discussed earlier.
- Maintain intake output chart to watch out the urinary retention.
- Advise the client not to drive because the drug may cause giddiness.
- Advise the client not to take self-medication as it will cause severe drug interaction.

MOOD STABILIZERS

Lithium

This drug has been explained in Chapter 7.

Sodium Valproate

In 1963, Meunier identified the antiepileptic properties of this drug and in 1966, Lambert identified that this drug can be used to treat mania. The various preparations or available forms are:

- Divalproex (enteric coated form or sodium valproate and valproic acid in 1:1 ratio)
- Valproate sodium
- Chrono preparations (enteric coated form or sodium valproate and valproic acid in 3:2 ratio)

Pharmacokinetics

Peak plasma levels will reach at 1–4 hours with a single dose. Half-life period is 8–17 hours. Therapeutic blood level is 50–150 µg/mL.

Dosage

1000–3000 mg/dL oral in divided doses.

Indications

Bipolar Disorder

- Acute mania
- Poor response to lithium
- Mania associated with seizure disorder
- Mixed affective episodes or rapid cycling bipolar disorder or mixed dysphoric mania
- Neurological disorder
- **Seizure disorder:** Absence seizure, myoclonic seizure, complex partial seizure, generalized tonic clonic seizure.
- Migraine
- **Pain syndrome:** Neuropathic pain and trigeminal neuralgia
- Miscellaneous disorders
- Conduct disorder
- Mental retardation
- Attention deficit hyperactive disorder
- Schizoaffective disorder
- Tardive dyskinesia
- Alcohol withdrawal syndrome
- Impulse control disorder
- Borderline personality disorder
- Panic disorder

Mechanism of Action

Sodium valproate dissociates the valproate ion in GI tract and it also increases GABA levels in brain either by reducing reuptake or by reducing the metabolism of GABA. This suppresses the influx of calcium through specified calcium channels.

Drug Interactions

Drugs that increase the serum level of valproate

- Erythromycin
- Aspirin
- Ibuprofen
- Fluoxetine
- Cimetidine
- Phenothiazines
- Fluvoxamine

Drugs that decrease the serum level of valproate

- Phenytoin
- Rifampicin
- Ethosuximide
- Carbamazepine
- Phenobarbital
- Mefloquine

Valproate increases the serum level of below mentioned drugs

- Tolbutamide
- Zidovudine
- Lamotrigine
- Tricyclic antidepressants

Side Effects

- **Common side effects of sodium valproate:** Tremors, nausea, weight gain, sedation, menstrual disturbances in women, alopecia, thrombocytopenia, hyperandrogenism and polycystic ovaries.
- **Uncommon side effects of sodium valproate:** Acute hemorrhagic pancreatitis, hepatic toxicity and Stevens-Johnson syndrome.

Carbamazepine

In 1953, Schindler identified carbamazepine as a tricyclic compound.

Onset of Action

Faster than lithium but slower than sodium valproate.

Dosage

600–1600 mg/day

Therapeutic Blood Level

6–12 µg/mL. Toxic level is >15 µg/mL.

Drug Action

Analgesics, antiepileptic and mood stabilizing agent.

Indications

Mental Disorder

- Bipolar mood disorder (Acute mania or rapid cyclic or lithium intolerant patients)
- Psychosis with mania
- Schizoaffective disorder
- Cocaine withdrawal syndrome
- Borderline personality disorder
- Impulse control disorder

Seizure Disorder

- Complex partial seizure
- Alcohol withdrawal seizure
- Generalized tonic clonic seizure

Paroxysmal Pain Disorders

- Trigeminal neuralgia
- Phantom limb pain
- Neuralgia

Side Effects

- **Major side effects of carbamazepine:** Drowsiness, fatigue, diplopia, nausea, vomiting, skin rashes, ataxia, photosensitivity, Stevens-Johnson syndrome, oliguria, hypertension, cholestatic jaundice, leukopenia, hyponatremia, toxic epidermal necrosis (TEN) and thrombocytopenic purpura.
- **Dangerous side effects of carbamazepine:** Cardiovascular collapse and bone marrow depression.

STIMULANTS (OR) PSYCHOSTIMULANTS

Stimulants are those which enhance the mental and physical function by increasing the alertness, wakefulness, etc. Example for the central nervous system stimulants are caffeine, nicotine, methylenedioxy-methamphetamine (MDMA-Ecstasy), modafinil, ampakines, etc.

Indications

- To reduce the sleep in narcolepsy
- To improve the attention and concentration in attention deficit hyperactive disorder
- To decrease the appetite in obesity
- To reduce lethargy and fatigue
- Sometimes, it is used to treat depression

Contraindications

- Hypersensitivity
- Hypertension
- Hyperthyroidism
- Glaucoma
- Usage of monoamine oxidase inhibitors
- Marked anxiety
- Motor tics or family history of Tourette's disorder
- Acute psychosis
- Heart diseases

Amphetamines

Amphetamines is the group of phenylethylamine stimulants, which increase the level of dopamine and norepinephrine by preventing the reuptake and also the direct release of dopamine and norepinephrine from the storage vesicles in the cells. They elevate the mood and hence, are used to treat major depression.

Modafinil

Modafinil is an approved drug to treat narcolepsy, excessive day time sleepiness associated with the obstructive sleep apnea, attention deficit hyperactive disorder, schizophrenia, depression, Parkinson's disease, cocaine addiction and illness related fatigue. Modafinil increases the release of monoamines and also increases hypothalamic histamine levels and thus promotes the wakefulness.

Ampakines

Ampakines are also called Eugeroics or Good Arousal stimulant. It means, increase in alertness without the peripheral body effects. So, they do not have addiction or abuse potential unlike other stimulants. They do not cause rebound hypersomnolence. These drugs are in the clinical trials and need further research before the usage.

Norepinephrine Reuptake Inhibitor and Norepinephrine-dopamine Reuptake Inhibitor

Norepinephrine Reuptake Inhibitor and Norepinephrine-dopamine Reuptake Inhibitor inhibit the reuptake of dopamine and norepinephrine that leads to increase in the neurotransmission and thereby causes the stimulating effect. Examples for norepinephrine-dopamine reuptake inhibitor (NDRI) are bupropion and methylphenidate. Examples for norepinephrine reuptake inhibitor (NRI) are reboxetine and atomoxetine. These drugs have lower addictive potential as compared to amphetamines.

Effect of Stimulants on the Body

Stimulants constrict the blood vessels and thereby increase the blood pressure. They raise the blood glucose and heart rate. They provide the sense of euphoria. They open the pathways of respiratory system.

Withdrawal Effects of Stimulants

The withdrawal effects of stimulants include sleep disturbances, depression, paranoia, fatigue and feeling of hostility.

Side Effects of Stimulants

Headache, irregular heartbeat, impotence, dizziness, insomnia, dry mouth, constipation or diarrhea, restlessness, confusion, hypertension, anxiety and tremors.

NURSES RESPONSIBILITY

Nurses should monitor the heart rate and blood pressure in order to monitor the side effects of stimulants at early stage. Nurse should observe unexpected symptoms. She should teach the patient and his/her family members in regard with the usage of stimulants and their side effects. She has to teach the patient to avoid the over the counter drugs because the stimulants have high addictive potential.

PSYCHOLOGICAL THERAPIES

PSYCHOTHERAPY

Definition

- Psychotherapy is defined as, 'treating the patient by psychological means, problems of emotional nature, in which the therapist deliberately establishes the professional relationship with patient to modify or remove or reduce the present symptoms, mediate the disturbed patterns of behavior, promote the positive growth and development of the personality.'

  —*Wolberg*
- Psychotherapy is defined as, 'way to help the people with variety of mental illnesses or emotional difficulties. It also helps to control or remove the symptoms which trouble the person, function in a better way, increase the sense of well-being and promote healing.'

  —*American Psychiatric Association*

Common Factors

- **Restoration of morale:** Most clients who are being treated might experience repeated failures and get demoralized. Therefore, continuous motivation by the therapist is necessary for the restoration of morale.
- **Release of emotion:** Therapist encourages the client to ventilate the feelings or emotions, because bottled-up emotions harm a person. The release of negative emotions might reduce the sadness.

Goals of Psychotherapy

Psychotherapy helps the individuals with the Psychiatric disorders by:

- Enhancing the coping skills and problem solving ability
- Promoting the sense of control, self-esteem, positive attitude and psychological well-being.
- Identifying the problems which act as contributing factors to the illness.
- Strengthening the ego
- Creating the deeper insight (or) sense of self-identity
- Developing a therapeutic relationship with patient
- Mediating the disturbed pattern of behavior and modifying the deviated personality
- Understanding the ideas, emotions, and behavior which contribute to mental illness and develop the ability to solve the same.

Contraindications of Psychotherapy

- Acute phase of organic psychosis
- Violent psychotic patient
- Unmotivated and unwilling patients
- Antisocial personality disorders (Patient will not respond back)
- Conversion disorder, hypochondriasis—Group psychotherapy is contraindicated.

Stages of Psychotherapeutic process

First stage is assessment with regard to the necessity of psychotherapy, in which the nurse or the psychotherapist needs to assess the actual need of psychotherapy and its benefits to the patient. The contraindications of the psychotherapy need to be considered before the commencement of therapy. The **second stage** is therapeutic work, in which the psychotherapy is administered actually. **Conclusion** of psychotherapy can be done by the therapist if the desired effect has been achieved or else when the therapist feels the psychotherapy won't work out on the particular patient (Fig. 5.8).

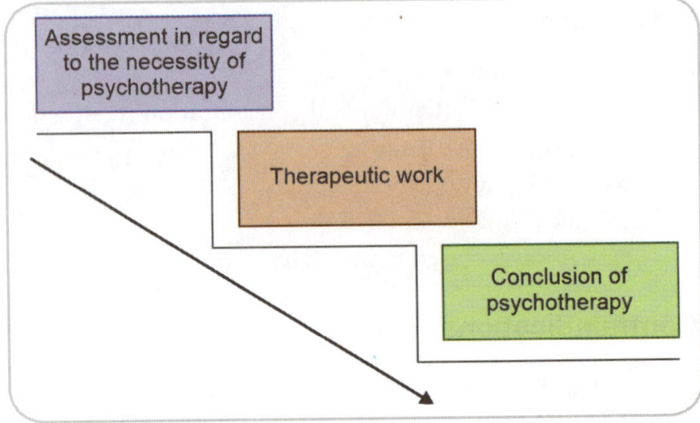

Figure 5.8: Psychotherapeutic process

Classification of Psychotherapy

Classification of psychotherapy is given in Flowchart 5.5.

Flowchart 5.5: Classification of psychotherapy

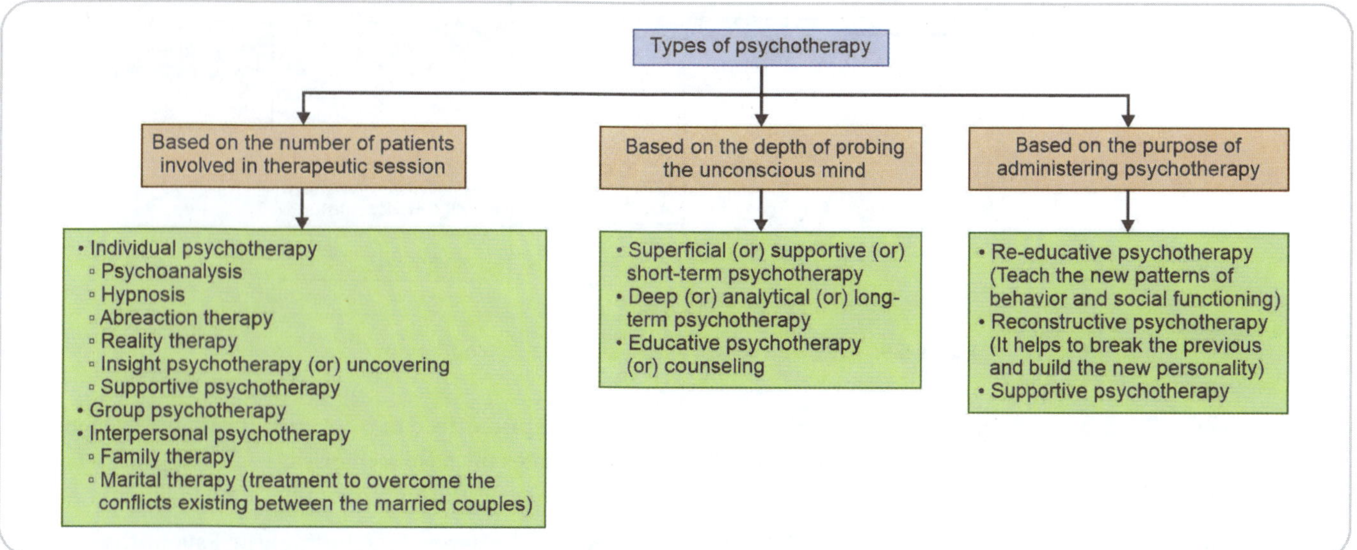

Individual Psychotherapy

Individual psychotherapy is the interaction process (psychotherapy) between the patient and the mental health professional or therapist on one to one basis. The issues addressed in the individual psychotherapy are life adjustment issues, relationship issues, issues related to personal growth or self-esteem or self-confidence, issues related to mental health problems, issues related to stress or coping skills, issues related to sexual problems, issues related to work life balance, issues related to spirituality, issues related to physical disorders, etc.

Psychoanalysis (or) Psychoanalytical Psychotherapy (or) Psychodynamic Psychotherapy

The prefix, 'psycho' denotes mind and the suffix 'analytical' denotes analysis, which means analysis of mind. Hence, it is a psychological therapy which analyses the mind. The suffix, 'dynamic' denotes change. So, change of mind also takes place here.

Definition

Psychoanalytical Psychotherapy is defined as, 'form of insight therapy which aims to overcome the unconscious conflicts and it also aims to identify the relationship between the unconscious motivation and the abnormal behavior.'

Historical Development

Sigmund Freud, a psychoanalyst/Austrian neurologist, framed the therapeutic techniques related to psychoanalytic theory in 1800. Jean-Martin Charcot used a hypnosis for the women suffering with hysteria. Sigmund Freud began to work with Jean-Martin Charcot and continued his work and research activity with Josef Breuer, his colleague. Freud and Josef Breuer published a book namely '*Studies on Hysteria*' and the former developed the concept of talk therapy.

Basic Assumptions of Psychoanalytical Psychotherapy (Fig. 5.9)

- Being aware of one's motivation helps to be more adaptive to acquire the change.
- The causes/reasons behind the maladjustment are unresolved conflicts.

Goal of Psychoanalysis

Psychoanalysis helps to understand the unconscious motives which direct the behavior. Patients are expected to express the healthy impulse during the time of analysis which helps to strengthen the daily activities and develop a positive perception toward the life.

Psychoanalytic Techniques

- **Free association:** Patients are asked to talk freely whatever strikes in their mind in regard with one's own thoughts and feelings. Psychotherapist plays a passive role and performs only observations but at the same time psychotherapist can raise the questions in order to clarify the doubts.
- **Dream analysis:** Analysis of the dreams helps to give insight to the unconscious motivation.

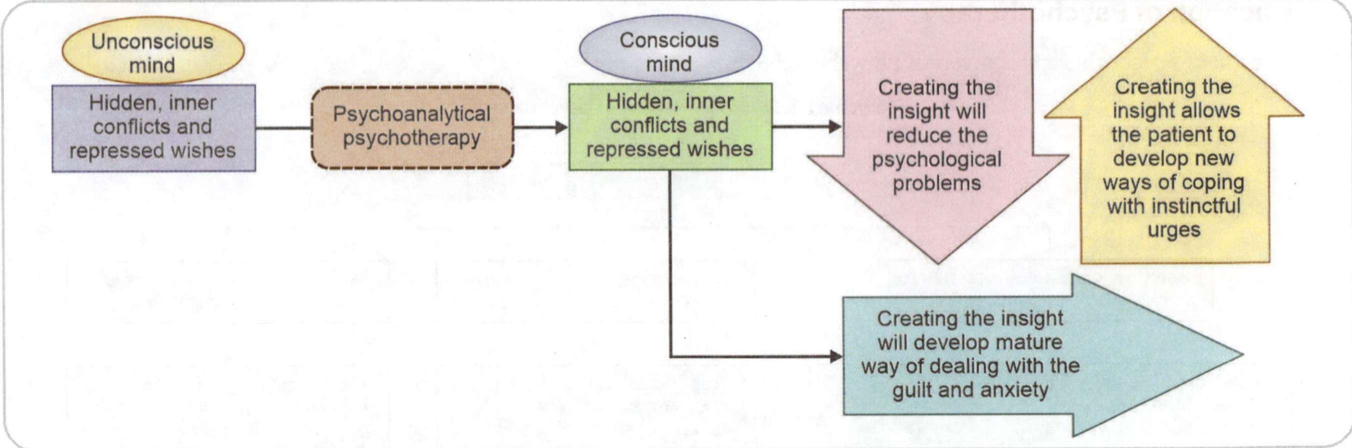

Figure 5.9: Basic concepts of psychoanalytical psychotherapy

- **Treatment alliance:** Therapeutic relationship exists between the therapist and patient which helps in the treatment process.
- **Acting out:** Patient presents the feelings and ideas not in words but in action, i.e., in the form of behavior.
- **Interpretations:** Interpreting the context, cause, idea, feeling, set of behavior and other issues in the session.

Indications

- Neurotic and stress-related disorders such as Panic disorders, obsessive-compulsive disorder, phobias, generalized anxiety disorder and post-traumatic stress disorder
- Persistent feelings of sadness, isolation and loneliness
- Sexual problems
- Borderline personality disorders
- Psychosomatic disorders
- Relationship issues
- Self-destructive behavior
- Emotional trauma
- Depression
- Identity problems

Disadvantages

- Patient needs to be highly motivated and cooperative.
- Patient could afford his/her time and money for this treatment. when compared to other treatment modalities, psychoanalytic psychotherapy takes longer time for treatment.

Myths about Psychoanalytic Psychotherapy

- Psychoanalysis is non-scientific, subjective and not precise.
- Concept of id, ego and superego is not linked with the reality.
- A therapist instead of recovering the repressed memories, inoculates the false memories.
- Psychoanalysis is only about the sex and libido.

Differences between Psychoanalytic Psychotherapy and Cognitive Behavioral Therapy (Table 5.8)

Table 5.8: Major differences between psychoanalytic and cognitive behavioral therapy

Psychoanalytic psychotherapy	Cognitive behavioral therapy (CBT)
Focus on full range of emotions, how they have been expressed	Focus on cognition and behavior
Exploring the reason for avoiding certain topics or thoughts will take place	Reason for avoiding certain topics is not explored
Talk about the past experiences	Focus on the present (here and now concept)
Explore the interpersonal relationship of present and past	Interpersonal relationship of past will not be explored
Focus on the relationship existing between the therapist and patient	Relationship building between the therapist and patient is not a matter of concern
Exploring the fantasy life of patient	CBT is highly structured and goal oriented, therefore, it does not deal with the fantasy life of patient

NURSES RESPONSIBILITY

Nurse should provide and maintain the conflict free and safe environment to render psychoanalytic psychotherapy. She has to ensure whether the psychological needs have been met. She has to take a leadership role and plan the weekly sessions or have a regular follow-up to see the prognosis in the patients. She needs to provide counseling to the patient and his/her family members if required.

Hypnosis

Patient is put into deep trance state with the suggestions of relaxation and is asked to concentrate on a single object. He/she will recall the forgotten memories and it helps to relieve the tension or anxiety. This therapy is used in psychosomatic disorder, dissociative disorder, anxiety disorder, sexual dysfunction, phobias, habit disorder, overeating, pain management and other addictive disorders. The risk of hypnotherapy is that the patient might develop confabulation (false memories). The side effects of hypnosis is headache, dizziness and anxiety.

Abreaction Therapy

The repressed painful experiences are brought back to the conscious mind in abreaction therapy. This can be done with or without the medications. This is extremely helpful in neurotic disorders.

Reality Therapy

Reality therapy is a psychotherapeutic technique focused on the present behavior and the present coping ability of the patient against the stressors. The active relationship between the therapist and patient might focus to promote the realistic behavior at present.

Insight Psychotherapy (or) Uncovering

This therapy or technique is helpful to bring the patient's repressed conflict and traumatic experience into the surface level in order to gain the insight.

Supportive Psychotherapy

This therapy is helpful to provide the basic psychological support to the patient so that, the patient's level of self esteem will improve.

COGNITIVE THERAPY

Historical Background

Cognitive therapy originated in early 1960s when the research on depression was done by Aaron Beck. In his research, he focused on negative cognitive processing in depression patients. Common theme was rejection of passive listening in psychoanalytic methods, behavioral techniques such as modeling and expectancy of reinforcement that have been used within the cognitive domain. The 'Personal appraisal and coping' book written by Lazarus and Folkman (1984) has explored the importance of cognitive approach.

Definition

Cognitive therapy is a form of psychotherapy in which the distorted cognitions are modified into positive cognitions.

Indications

- Depression
- Bipolar disorder
- Panic disorder
- Schizophrenia
- Post-traumatic stress disorder
- Social phobias
- Generalized anxiety disorder
- Obsessive compulsive disorder
- Eating disorder
- Substance abuse
- Personality disorders
- Problems with married couples
- Hypochondriasis
- Somatoform disorder

Goals of Cognitive Therapy

After the successful cognitive therapy sessions, the patient will:
- Observe one's own negative automatic thoughts.
- Identify that a connection exists between cognition, affect and behavior.
- Substitute the realistic interpretation in the biased situations.
- Identify and alter the dysfunctional belief.
- Explore the reason for distorted automatic thoughts.

Principles of Cognitive Therapy

- Cognitive therapy needs a good therapeutic alliance (trusting relationship between therapist and patient)
- It requires active participation and collaboration
- It is problem-focused.
- It is goal-oriented.
- It focuses on the present rather than the past.
- It is completed in limited time (12–16 sessions).
- It has structured sessions.
- It is educative, aimed to teach the patient with a special emphasis on relapse prevention.
- It uses various techniques to modify thinking, behavior and mood.
- It teaches the patient to identify, evaluate and respond to their dysfunctional thoughts.

Basic Concepts

Automatic thoughts (or) Cognitive Errors

Automatic thoughts are rapidly occurring thoughts in response to the situation without any rational analysis. The thoughts are usually negative. The different types of cognitive errors are listed below.

- **Absolutistic thinking (or) over generalization:** Getting into conclusion based on one incident.
- **Arbitrary inference:** Getting into conclusion without any fact to support it or even when there is presence of contradictory evidence.
- **Dichotomous thinking:** Individual views the situations in terms of good or bad, black or white, all or nothing.
- **Selective abstraction (or) Mental Filter:** Getting into conclusion based on selected portion of evidence.
- **Catastrophic thinking:** Always thinking the worst will occur without considering the positive outcome.
- **Magnification:** Exaggeration of the negative significance of an event.
- **Minimization:** Undervaluing the positive aspect of an event.
- **Personalization:** Person takes the complete responsibility of the situation without realizing that the other circumstances also contribute to the outcome.

Schemas (or) Core Beliefs

Concepts might be general or specific, adaptive or maladaptive, become evident when trigger happens by a specific stressful stimulus.

Techniques of Cognitive therapy

The techniques of cognitive therapy have been divided into components such as didactic aspects, cognitive techniques and behavioral interventions (Fig. 5.10).

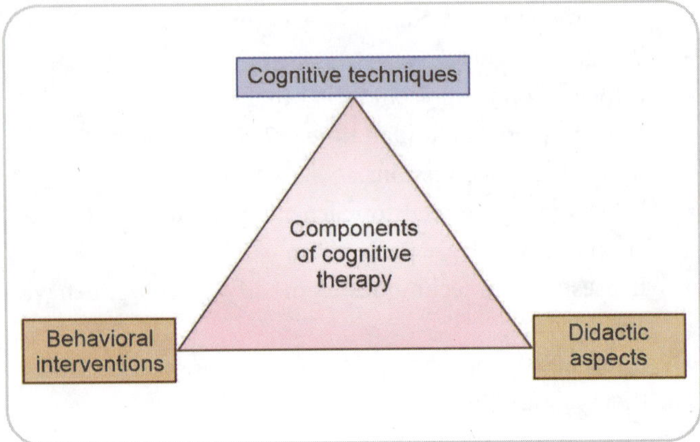

Figure 5.10: Cognitive therapy

Didactic Aspects

Prepare the patient eventually by providing the adequate information about the cognitive therapy either orally or using videos/audio in order to identify the distorted thinking patterns.

Cognitive Techniques

Recognizing the Automatic Thoughts and Schemas

- **Socratic thinking (or) guided discovery:** Therapist raises the question about any particular situation. Client with the socratic thinking is able to explain the feelings associated with the situation.
- **Role play and imagery:** When socratic thinking fails, therapist asks the client to perform imagery exercises or role play to explore the automatic thoughts. With the help of guided imagery, client is asked to relieve the stress by imaging the stress situations and settings in which it has occurred. Client is also asked to participate in role play to recognize the automatic thoughts.
- **Thought recording:** Client is asked to write in a notebook when patient gets the automatic thoughts. This is given as a homework outside the therapy sessions.

Modifying Automatic Thoughts and Schemas

- **Examining the evidences:** Therapist and the client might keep the automatic thoughts as hypothesis and they study the evidence for and against the hypothesis.
- **Generating the alternatives:** Therapist helps the client to generate the alternatives or possibilities toward the automatic thoughts.
- **Decatastrophizing:** Therapist helps the patient to examine the validity of negative automatic thoughts.
- **Reattribution:** This technique helps to reverse the negative attribution into positive one.
- **Daily record of dysfunctional thoughts (DRDT):** Patient is asked to rate the intensity of thoughts and emotions in a 0 to 100 point scale daily.
- **Cognitive rehearsal:** Discussion as a rehearsal or use of mental imagery in order to identify and modify the dysfunctional thoughts.

Behavioral Interventions

- **Activity scheduling:** Client is asked to keep the record of the daily activities and also asked to rate the activity in terms of mastery and pleasure in a 0 to 10 scale.
- **Graded task assignments:** Whole task has been subdivided into small tasks and patient is asked to perform the small task. This completion of small task will enhance the self-esteem of patient and develop the motivation to complete the further tasks.

- **Behavior rehearsal:** This technique is used to perform role-play to rehearse the maladaptive behaviors which contribute to the dysfunctional cognition.
- **Distraction:** Activities are planned to distract and divert the patient from intrusive disturbed thoughts and ruminations.
- **Miscellaneous techniques:** Assertiveness training, relaxation therapy, role modeling and social skills training are also useful. Thought stopping technique (explained in Chapter 8) is used to alter the dysfunctional thinking patterns.

NURSES RESPONSIBILITY

Nurse has to help the patient to identify the distorted thoughts with the use of various techniques as discussed above. She has to plan the cognitive therapy sessions scheduled after coordination with the psychotherapist. She should ensure the patient is attending the sessions as per the scheduled plan (weekly or biweekly). Monitor the improvement in patient when 16 weeks of cognitive therapy session is completed and also ensure that the sessions should not prolong for more than 26 weeks. If the improvement is not satisfactory, then the other therapies have to be considered. She has to follow-up with the patient to ensure the successful completion of therapy sessions.

BEHAVIORAL THERAPY

Definition

Behavioral therapy is defined as 'form of psychotherapy in which the maladaptive behavior is aimed to change as adaptive behavior.'

History

Behavior therapy techniques is based on classical conditioning by Ivan P. Pavlov and operant conditioning by B F Skinner.

Classical Conditioning

Ivan P Pavlov, a russian physiologist, developed the classical conditioning. In his trials, dog began to salivate was an unconditioned response and dog began to eat the food was an unconditioned stimulus. Next time, when the food was shown, the dog started salivating, which was the learned behavior of the dog. Pavlov called this response as conditioned response. When bell alone rings, there is no response from the dog. The combination of unconditioned stimulus (food) and conditioned stimulus (bell) leads to conditioned response (salivation). After this, only with conditioned stimulus (bell), conditioned response (dog salivation) occurs due to learned behavior.

- **Unconditioned stimulus (eating food) → unconditioned response (salivation)**
- **Unconditioned stimulus (seeing food) → conditioned response (salivation)**
- **Conditioned stimulus (bell) → no response**
- **Unconditioned stimulus (food) + conditioned stimulus (bell) → conditioned response (salivation)**
- **Conditioned stimulus (bell) → conditioned response (salivation)**

Operant Conditioning

B F Skinner (1953), American Psychologist, developed the operant conditioning. In classical conditioning, the focus is on behavioral responses but in operant conditioning, the focus is on the consequences of the behavioral responses. A stimulus which gives out a response is called *reinforcing stimulus (or) reinforcer* and the function is termed *reinforcement*. The probability of increasing the desirable behavior with a reinforcing stimulus is called *positive reinforcement* (In Skinner box experiment, giving a food pellet to rat when it presses the lever is the example of positive reinforcement). The probability of increasing the desirable behavior with the help of aversive stimulus is called *negative reinforcement* (In Skinner box experiment, giving a loud noise until the rat presses the lever is the example of negative reinforcement). The behavior which has been reinforced previously is no longer effective when the reinforcing stimulus is stopped, called *Extinction* (In Skinner box experiment, when the rat pushed the lever, it was offered with food pellet. After some time, when food pellet was stopped being offered, it led to the rat not pushing the lever. This is an example of Extinction.)

Indications

- Autism
- Bipolar disorder
- Obsessive compulsive disorder (OCD)
- Post-traumatic stress disorder
- Schizophrenia
- Social anxiety
- Phobia
- Substance abuse
- Personality disorder
- Eating disorder—anorexia nervosa, obesity
- Tics
- Nocturnal enuresis
- Sexual dysfunction
- Tension headache
- Psychosomatic disorders

Contraindications

Mentally ill patients who are acute and symptomatic might not be given behavior therapy because it won't work out and it is ideal waste of time for therapist and sometimes, it might increase the symptoms due to delay in treatment process. Therefore, routine mental status assessment and psychotropic drugs are the first line of treatment to the acute psychiatric patients.

Techniques

Systemic Desensitization

Systemic desensitization is developed by Joseph Wolpe. It has three steps (Fig. 5.11):

1. **Relaxation training:** Relaxation gives the physiological effects which are opposite to the anxiety.
2. **Hierarchy construction:** Arrange the conditions in order of increasing anxiety.
3. **Desensitization of stimulus:** Gradual exposure of the individual from least to most anxiety provoking state.

Systemic desensitization is suitable for anxiety disorders (phobia and obsessive compulsive disorder) and certain sexual disorders.

Examples to explain the systemic desensitization concept for a person who is having fear of dogs.

- Discuss about the dog
- Show the picture of dog
- Show the dog doll
- Play the barking sounds of dog
- Show the dog with a distance of 10 feet
- Take the person near to the dog
- Ask the person to touch the dog
- Ask the person to walk along with the dog

Flooding (or) Implosive Therapy

Flooding is used to desensitize the person to phobic stimuli. It differs from systemic desensitization as instead of working out in hierarchy of anxiety provoking stimuli, the person will be 'flooded' with the continuous presentation of phobic stimulus until the anxiety comes down. Flooding does not exist in practice because this intense anxiety might be dangerous to the individuals and it may lead to heart attack or death. For example, if the individual is having the fear of insects, then the individual is flooded with more phobic stimuli by putting him/her into the room with more number of insects.

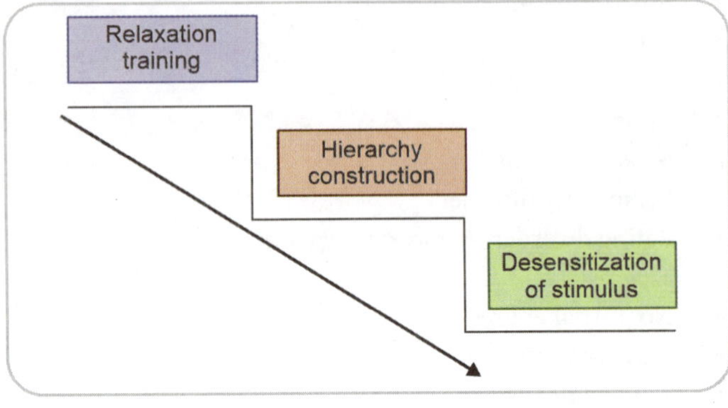

Figure 5.11: Systemic desensitization

Premack Principle

This technique has been named after its originator. The frequently occurring response (R_1) might act as a positive reinforcement for the response (R_2) which is occurring less frequently. For example, Raja is playing with his friends more (frequently occurring response - R_1) and not completing his homework (less frequently occurring response - R_2). Mother asked Raja that, if you complete the homework, you will be allowed to play with your friends; if not; you are not allowed. Hence, Raja is motivated to perform the less frequently occurring response with the help of more frequently occurring response.

Therapeutic Graded Exposure

Therapist helps the patient to construct the fear hierarchy from mild to severe which is ranked according to the difficulties. Therapy begins with mild level and proceeds to the harder ones.

Social Skills Training

Social skills training is a form of behavior therapy which focuses on enhancing the social skills among patients.

The techniques are mentioned below:

- **Instruction:** Modeling of the appropriate social behaviors. For example, teaching the patient how to perform hand shake to others.
- **Behavioral rehearsal (or) role play:** Motivate the patients to practice the new skills in the simulated situations. For example, motivate the patient to start the conversation in front of the mirror by assuming the other person is standing before the patient.
- **Corrective feedback:** Give feedback during practice in order to improve social skills. For example, when the patient is not maintaining eye contact, then the therapist asks to do it as a part of corrective feedback.
- **Positive reinforcement:** Give positive rewards when the patient shows an improvement in social skills. For example, take the patient to an outdoor game as a positive reinforcement when the patient shows an improvement in social skills.

- **Homework assignments:** It helps the patient to practice the new social skills out of the therapy sessions. For example, ask the patient to write 20 open ended questions in a notebook.

Assertiveness Training

Assertiveness training was developed by Andrew Salder in 1961. Training is provided to stand up for one's own rights by expressing one's feelings, thoughts, ideas in an honest and direct manner. By being assertive, one should also respect the feelings, thoughts and ideas of others. The techniques of assertiveness training are as follows:

- **Broken record (or) repeated assertion:** It is the state of continuously repeating the refusal toward the request raised. For example, friends of an alcoholic calling him to consume alcohol, he might respond as, I have taken treatment to quit alcohol, I won't drink, please don't call me.' (Patient says the same answer again and again toward the question raised)
- **Fogging:** Agreeing the truth in the statement even it is limited without being anxious or defensive. For example, I agree, I will take rest for some time during my work due to high stress in my job.
- **Negative assertion:** Agree the negatives or criticism without letting out the demand. For example, I agree I am not willing to listen to the comments of my peer groups.
- **Negative inquiry:** Listen the criticism carefully and clarify the negative feelings so that one can ignore if the information is manipulative. For example, Do you feel that I am not interested in this project?
- **Free information:** Learn to listen the other person's information completely.
- **Self-disclosure:** Assertively disclose about oneself that, how do you feel and think about the information. For example, I feel you can ventilate the hard feelings to your close friends and get solution from them.
- **Workable compromise:** Bargain for the material goals unless the compromise satisfies the personal feel of self-respect. For example, I know you are busy with your work and I too have the same but what about the board meeting scheduled now?

Shaping

Shaping the behavior with the positive reinforcement for the performance of the approximate desired response.

Example

Child with autism was trained for the speech therapy. Positive reinforcement can be given for watching the teacher's lips and imitating the sounds of the teachers (approximate desired response).

Modeling

Modeling is learning out the new behavior by imitating the behavior of the others. We usually take a person as a role model, whom we admire and wish to imitate.

Example

Child with mild mental retardation, learns to button and unbutton his shirt by seeing the therapist how he is performing, this is an example for modeling.

Aversion Therapy

Treatment to arouse the aversion or hatred toward undesirable behavior. For example, aversion therapy for patient with alcohol dependence syndrome can be classified into below types such as:

Electrical Aversion

Ask the client to smell the desired brand of alcohol and low volt electrical stimuli will be administered immediately. Alcohol intake (desired response) will be changed by undesirable electrical stimuli.

Chemical Aversion

Disulfiram therapy (Disulfiram is antabuse drug administered to the alcoholic patients who want to remain in sobriety). The detailed explanation about this drug is discussed in substance abuse chapter.

Aversion Through Emesis

Administer alcohol along with emetics which will induce vomiting after alcohol intake, thereby client develops aversion.

Extinction

A gradual reduction in the frequency or the disappearance of the responses occurs when the positive reinforcement has been withheld.

Example

Temper tantrums are so common among children. When the attention from the parents (positive reinforcement) is withheld then automatically the temper tantrums will get reduced.

Covert Sensitization

Patient will be advised to imagine the unpleasant symptoms whenever required to stop the stimulus of undesirable behavior by self.

Example

Patient with obesity has strong craving to eat more foods, he will be asked to imagine the scene of nausea or vomiting (unpleasant symptoms) when the patient would require to stop the signals of eating more food (undesirable behavior).

Overt Sensitization

Overt sensitization is a kind of aversion therapy in which unpleasant consequences for the undesirable behavior are introduced.

Example

Patient with alcohol dependence syndrome will be taking disulfiram (antabuse therapy) to stop the alcohol. Provide psychoeducation to the patient that if he consumes alcohol while taking disulfiram, it might lead to Disulfiram-Ethanol Reaction (DER) such as dyspnea, palpitations, nausea, vomiting, headache, etc. (unpleasant consequences). Patient consuming alcohol feels undesirable behavior here. So, unpleasant consequences of DER takes place due to the undesirable behavior of consuming alcohol.

Time Out

Time out is an aversive stimulus, in which the patient will be taken out from the particular environment where the unacceptable behavior has been exhibited. Patient will be isolated usually so that the reinforcement from the particular stimulus will be absent.

Example

Patient with obsessive compulsive disorder repeatedly pours hot water on his body for a number of times without having control. Using time out technique, patient will be removed and put in another room where the hot water facility is not available.

Contingency Contracting

Contract has been drawn up between the patient and the health team personnel. The desired behavior change is mentioned in the contract and its reinforcers which will be given after the behavior changes are also mentioned in the contract. Punishment will be provided if the desired behavior change is not met. However, flexibility is vital and renegotiations can be considered if necessary.

Example

Patient with Alcohol Dependence Syndrome signed the contract stating that he won't consume alcohol after the discharge. The treatment cost of ₹ 20,000/- will be paid to the patient after 2 years if he is in abstinence (positive reinforcers). Failing which the patient has to pay ₹ 20,000/- to the hospital as a fine.

Token Economy

Token economy is a kind of contingency contracting in which the contract can be either made orally or signed. Here, tokens will be issued to the patient for performing the desirable behavior. Patient might be allowed to exchange the token for designated privileges.

Example

Patient with negative symptoms of schizophrenia is not taking bath daily. Nurse uses token economy stating that, if the patient takes bath daily, then he will get single token. For three tokens, he is permitted for movie or coffee shop. For six tokens, he is permitted for games or offered with biryani.

NURSES RESPONSIBILITY

Nurse has to identify the behavior which is needed to be modified in the patient and break it out into small manageable segments to proceed. She has to plan the behavior therapy sessions and use the appropriate techniques with the help of the psychotherapist. She needs to observe, record and outline the behavioral changes continuously. Nurse has to plan additional psychotherapies to the patient based on the requirement and need. She has to take measures to enhance the social skills and assertive behavior of the patient. She needs to evaluate the prognosis of patient and re-frame the behavior therapy sessions accordingly.

COGNITIVE BEHAVIORAL THERAPY

Historical Background

- Epictetus, a Greek philosopher, found people were disturbed not because of what was happening around but how an individual perceived the event.
- Aaron beck is pioneer of cognitive behavior therapy. He is Professor in Psychiatry at University of Pennsylvania. He initially developed cognitive therapy and behavior components have been added in it.

Introduction

- Identification of negative cognitions and maladaptive behavior is helpful to improve the client's mood (Flowchart 5.6).
- Cognitive behavior therapy requires active participation of patient.
- ***Cognitive triad*** denotes negative view of self, others and future
- ***Cognitive errors*** denote thinking in the negative schemas

Characteristics of Cognitive Behavioral Therapy

- Thought governs behavior and feelings
- Short term and time limited therapy
- Focus on the current behavior

Flowchart 5.6: Identification of cognition, behavior and mood

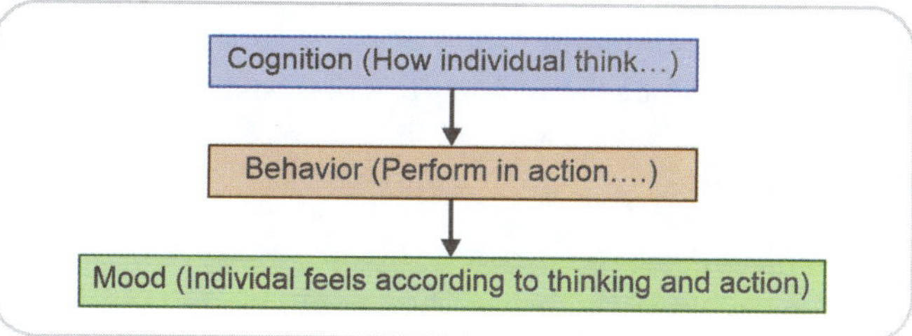

- Plays collaborative role of therapist and patient
- Therapy is based on "Rationale thoughts or facts" and not based on assumptions
- Structured and goal oriented therapy (Table 5.9)

Table 5.9: Sessions in cognitive behavior therapy

Total sessions	12–16
Sequence of session	Once in a week
Duration of each session	1 hour

Indications

- Mild/moderate depression
- Anger management
- Mood swings
- Sleep disorders
- Conduct disorders
- Attention deficit hyperactivity disorder
- Anxiety disorders—obsessive compulsive disorder, post-traumatic stress disorder
- Substance abuse
- Sexual/relationship problems
- Eating disorders
- Childhood and adolescent problems
- Chronic pain
- Facial tics
- Sexual and relationship problems
- Chronic fatigue syndrome

Elements of Cognitive Behavioral Therapy

- **Motivational:** Therapist should motivate the client for behavioral change.
- **Active:** Patient is active key participant in therapy process.
- **Directive:** Therapist develops the treatment plan and directs the client toward therapeutic process.
- **Structured:** Therapy follows the structured treatment plan.
- **Collaborative:** Therapist and patient work collaboratively to achieve the goal.
- **Problem oriented:** Therapy focuses on the discrete problems.
- **Psychoeducation:** Therapist teaches the patient by role play, modeling, instructions, etc.
- **Solution focused:** Therapy focuses on generating the solution and not just gaining the insight.
- **Dynamics:** Schema is a basic template of understanding the individual's world. Dynamic level of this therapy focuses on modifying the schema.

Techniques of Cognitive Behavioral Therapy

- **Cognitive rehearsal:** Client is asked to recall the problematic thoughts of the past. Therapist and client work together to find the solution to the problem.
- **Validity testing:** Therapist tests the validity of the thoughts or beliefs of the patient and the therapist asks the patient to defend his/her thoughts.
- **Writing in a journal:** Ask the patient to maintain a diary of thoughts associated with the situations and the behavior associated with the situations.
- **Guided discovery:** Help the patient to come out of the cognitive distortions. Hence, the change of perception in patient will automatically show a significant change in behavior.
- **Modeling, aversive conditioning and positive reinforcement:** Discussed in the behavior therapy techniques.
- **Self-instructional coping methods:** Therapist aims to teach the coping methods to deal with the stressor.
- **Homework:** Therapist assigns some sort of homework to be performed out of the therapy session in order to overcome the cognitive distortions.
- **Problem solving method:** Therapist suggests the alternative solutions to the problems and picks out the best one to solve the problem.
- **Computer-assisted therapy:** Use of computer-based programs in the cognitive behavior therapy.

Forms of Cognitive Behavioral therapy

- **Cognitive therapy and behavioral therapy:** Discussed in the previous topics.
- **Rational emotive therapy:** Albert Ellis was the proponent for this therapy. It is a short term psychotherapy in which the self-defeating thoughts and feelings are identified, rationalized and replaced with the productive thoughts and ideas.
- **Schema focused therapy:** Jeffrey E Young was the proponent for this therapy. It is an integrative psychotherapy in which the concept of psychoanalytic theory, object relations theory, gestalt therapy, attachment theory and cognitive behavior therapy have been used.

- **Meta-cognitive therapy:** Adrian Wells was the proponent for this therapy. It focuses on modifying the meta-cognitive (higher order thinking) belief which causes worry. It is most commonly used to treat anxiety disorders and depression.
- **Acceptance-commitment therapy:** Steven C Hayes was the proponent for this therapy. It is a concept of clinical behavior analysis which focuses on the acceptance (agreement or positive welcome) and behavioral strategies in order to move toward the valued behavior. Patient is asked to open up unpleasant feelings and move toward the right behavior.
- **Dialectical behavior therapy:** Marsha M Linehan was the proponent for this therapy. It is focused on improving the cognitive and emotional regulation by learning about the triggers that cause stress. This therapy is used to treat borderline personality disorder, mood disorder, depression, substance abuse, post-traumatic stress disorder, binge eating disorder, traumatic brain injury, suicidal ideation and individuals with risk of self-harm.
- **Mindfulness based cognitive therapy:** Jon Kabat-Zinn was the proponent for this therapy. This therapy is rendered with the combination of mindfulness meditation practices along with the cognitive therapy.

THERAPEUTIC COMMUNITY

Introduction

Therapeutic community is done for individuals with substance abuse/addictive behavior for about 40 years. Therapeutic community is a group-based participative approach usually performed by the therapist and patient in a residential unit. It is based on the principles of milieu therapy and group psychotherapy.

History

In 1960, Maxwell Jones and Wilmer developed the concept of therapeutic community retrieved from the therapeutic milieu.

Definitions

Psychiatric nurse structures, gives and maintains the therapeutic environment in collaboration with the patient and other health team workers.

—***American Nursing Association, 2000***

Therapeutic community is a drug free environment in which the individuals with addictive behavior join together in a structured manner in order to promote drug free society. It forms a miniature of society, staff act as facilitators and residents join together to promote the transitional process.

—***Ottenberg, 1993***

Aim

Therapeutic community should be democratic and not authoritative, which focuses on the welfare of the client.

Philosophy

The main philosophy of therapeutic community is that the clients are active participants. The community responsibilities are shared among the health team staff and client.

Objectives

- To utilize the client's social environment for the therapeutic purpose.
- To make the client an active participant and involve in the community-based activities.
- To increase the self-esteem, self-worth, sense of independence and to gain control over the personal activities
- To change the maladaptive behavior into the adaptive one.
- To help the client realize that, one's own negative behavior affects the others.
- To help the client to solve the problems, plan the necessary activities and frame the rules/regulations for the community.

Elements

- Active participation of the client
- Ensure the free communication in the community
- Responsibilities have to be shared among them
- Involvement in the decision-making process
- Understand the roles, responsibilities and limitations of each member.

The components of therapeutic community have been given in Table 5.10.

Length of Treatment

Good outcomes can be expected if the individual completes at least 90 days of stay. Previously the length of treatment was 18–24 months, but presently, duration of the treatment has been reduced to 12 months due to the restrictions of the fund.

Structure

It is a typical set up in the community-based settings with the capacity to accommodate 40 to 80 members. It is designed based on the need, funding and the willingness of the community members. For example, Ground of former camps or sub-urban houses.

Table 5.10: Components of therapeutic community

Components	Description
Daily community meetings	Conduct regular meetings composed of 60 to 90 clients for 1 hour. Frank discussions are encouraged with outburst of emotions. All levels of staff and administrative personnel are involved. Acute patients aren't involved in the meetings.
Patient government (or) ward council	As per the decisions made in the community meetings, a group of 6 patients will be allotted with the specific responsibilities such as meal distribution, physical exercise, housekeeping, personal hygiene, monitoring the patients who have suicidal risk, etc.
Staff meetings (or) reviews	Staff meetings will be conducted following the community meetings in which only the staff is involved and not the patients, in which staff will examine one's own expectations, responsibilities and responses.
Living and learning opportunities	Learning opportunities are given along with social milieu in order to create the realistic learning experience.

Treatment Process

Treatment process involves the components of therapy, education and training. It involves the below written events:

- Treatment of substance abuse
- Education
- Primary medical and dental care
- Vocational skills training
- Job placement
- On-site help to involve in business
- Help in legal activities
- Life skill counseling

Stages of Therapeutic Community

The stages of therapeutic community are shown in Fig. 5.12.

Induction and Treatment

This phase takes place in the first month (30 days) to assimilate the individual into therapeutic community. When the interview or assessment part has been completed, then the individual is allowed to enter into therapeutic community, in which the house constitutes multiple rooms and each room has 6–8 members grouped together. Insisting the individuals with the regular maintenance work, disciplined schedule, and privileges based on the behavior patterns, giving the work which has more physical activity will make the individual feel tired and thereby individual will not have any thoughts to get back to the previous lifestyle.

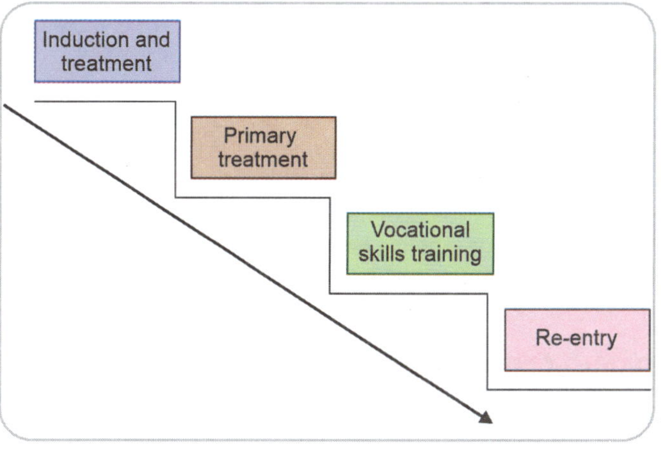

Figure 5.12: Stages of therapeutic community

Primary Treatment

In this, residents are expected to take care of the welfare of others. Vocational training areas are introduced in this stage. Residents will undergo training to develop literacy, computer skills and to obtain general equivalency diploma course, etc. At the end of this phase, residents might complete the diploma program, choose the vocational training area in which they need to specialize, participate in the group activity, deal the daily life and follow the rules or regulations of the facility.

Vocational Skills Training

Vocational training programs are conducted. Money will be saved for the vocational work done by the residents and it will be given when he/she starts his/her new life or when he/she exits the program. Residents are encouraged for the social activities.

Re-entry

Residents need to acquire skills and develop the coping abilities in order to re-enter into the society.

Staffing Pattern

The ratio of staff and resident is 1:15. Staff is the mix up of self-help professionals who have recovered already and other traditional professionals such as staff nurses, doctors, case workers, counselors, etc.

Daily Regimen

An ideal therapeutic community starts at 7 am and concludes at 11 pm. It includes morning and evening house meetings, seminars, job assignments, scheduled personal time, group tasks, individual counseling and recreation. Activities of therapeutic community are organized to enhance the interpersonal and social interactions as the primary purpose, which can be achieved through:

- **Community meetings:** To review goals and functioning of therapeutic community.
- **Clinical groups:** It use various therapeutic approaches to address the problems.
- **Vocational and educational activities:** It will develop the individual through training/education and work.
- **Community and clinical management activities:** To make sure that the life of resident is productive and orderly.

Advantages of Therapeutic Community

- It helps to build self-confidence.
- It helps to develop the harmonious relationship with the community members.
- It builds the leadership ability.
- It improves the problem solving capacity.
- It promotes the ability to live and think collectively along with the members of community.
- It makes the individual as a sociocentric person.

Disadvantages of Therapeutic Community

- Resident may feel the transition to the community is a difficult one.
- Individual concerns/needs have not been met.
- Group responsibility might be no one's responsibility.
- Blurring of role between the staff and resident.

NURSES RESPONSIBILITY

Nurse has to coordinate with the members to select group leader. She has to maintain the environment without conflicts. She has to motivate the patient in decision making process. She has to carry out the supervisory functions. She has to share the responsibilities with the residents.

MILIEU THERAPY

Meaning

The word, 'Milieu' is a French word for 'middle' which denotes the meaning, 'environment or surroundings'.

Definition

Milieu is the scientific structuring of the environment in order to elicit the behavioral changes, enhance the psychological health and functioning of the individual. —*Skinner, 1979*

Historical Background

The historical background has been given in Table 5.11.

Table 5.11: Historical background of milieu therapy

Year	Description
Late 1770s	Pipel in France formulated the term 'moral treatment' to explain the new approach of mental health care on the basis of humanitarianism (For example, by removing the chains/restraints in psychiatric patients).
Early 1800	Tuke in England created York retreat based on the atmosphere of kindness, family environment and treating the patients as guests.
Late 1800	Service pattern in psychiatric organization was domestic service pattern in which the patient care is custodial.
Early 1900	Hospital atmosphere has been declined, results in the development of environment which is custodial.
1930	Sullivan began to experiment with the various milieu by selecting the staff who have good interactions with patient.
1939	Menninger developed the attitude on the basis of psychoanalytical principles which determine the staff patterns.
1940	Medical Intervention pattern was framed, which helped the nurses to provide care.
1946	Thomas main coined term, 'therapeutic community' to describe the resocialization of neurotic patients through social interactions.
1948	Bettelheim coined term 'Milieu therapy' and use of environment for disturbed children.
1953	Maxwell Jones utilized therapeutic community approach in the treatment of antisocial personality disorders.
1990	Milieu therapy has been developed based on the research to explore the milieu structure, which was found effective for the specific treatment groups.

Goals of Milieu Therapy

- Patient is expected to develop the adaptive coping skills, relationship ability and interaction skills to generalize all the aspects of one's life.

- To achieve the patient's level of independence.
- To manipulate the environment in all aspects of patient's hospital experience as therapeutic.

Principles of Milieu Therapy

- It gives opportunities for patient to be a part of unit management.
- It helps to promote socialization, improve the self-esteem and also the fundamental respect to both client as well as staff members.
- This will help to utilize the communication between patient and staff to attain the maximum therapeutic benefit.
- Team approach is helpful but the individual is responsible for one's own actions.
- Peer pressure has been used to reinforce the rules and regulations.
- Clients are motivated to perform the task based on the ability to promote the self-esteem.
- Temporary seclusion is encouraged for acting out behavior.
- Nurse will function consistently to promote the goals of milieu.

Characteristics of Milieu Therapy

Strategies have been formulated to counteract the negative effects of institutionalization and these have been presented below in Table 5.12.

Progressive Levels of Responsibility as per the Self-care Capacity of the Client

Level 1: Exhibiting destructive behavior to self/other/ environment

In level 1, the client exhibits poor personal hygiene without taking care of oneself. Client is disoriented with time, place and person. Client will not get involved in the group therapy.

Level 2: Not Exhibiting Destructive behavior

In level 2, the client attempts to maintain personal hygiene. Client is oriented with time, place and persons. Client will participate in at least one group therapy session.

Level 3: Involve in all the therapeutic activities

In level 3, the client participates in the community meetings and family sessions. Client will develop self-directed behavior to solve the problem. Client will know about the time of medicine that needs to be taken.

Level 4: Take an active role in promoting the changes in other clients

In level 4, the client will develop an active leadership role and act as a good role model to other clients. Client will actively participate in all the scheduled events and group meetings. Client will initiate the discussions with mental health team members regarding the discharge planning.

Progressive levels of responsibility are shown in Figure 5.13.

Table 5.12: Strategies formulated to counteract negative effects of institutionalization

Strategies	Description
Distribution of power	The approach used here is 'flattening,' i.e., all participants might involve in the decision making process. Governing council will take the final decision on the basis of the input from all the small groups. This gives autonomy to every individuals.
Open communication	Open communication is helpful to make the effective treatment decisions. It also helps to create awareness that everyone is working toward the common goal.
Structured interactions	Menninger KA was the first person to introduce the concept of structured interaction approach to all the staff. It helps all the staff members to approach the client in the consistent way toward the treatment goals.
Work related activities	An effective work therapy program is based on three factors: 1. Client has to choose the type of work based on his/her wish. 2. Work activity that improves the skill found necessary in actual job situations. 3. Activities give an opportunity to test out the individual's ability in different areas based on the job interests that are going to be attained in future.
Involvement of community and family members in therapeutic process	Community mental health centers emerge because they help to involve the family members and community people at larger extent. This will help the client to reduce the isolation and enhance the family interaction process.
Adaptation of environment to meet the developmental needs	Adaptation to the environment in order to meet the various needs is a great challenge. This can be done with the inclusion of family members of different age groups in the therapeutic milieu.

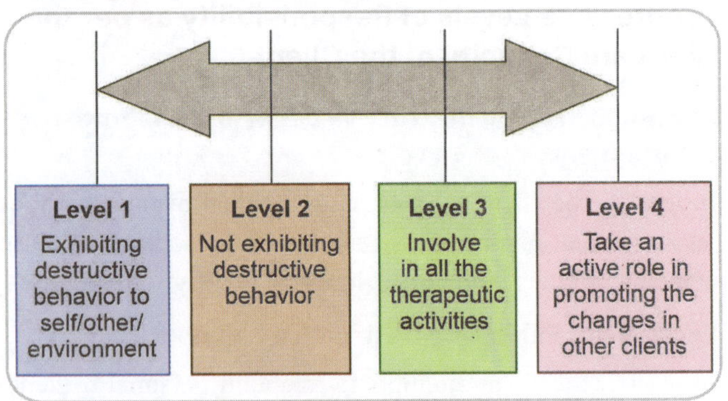

Figure 5.13: Progressive levels of responsibility

Key Concepts of Milieu Therapy

The key concepts include containment, validation, structured interaction and open communication.

- **Containment:** It focuses on safety and security needs of client, attain the basic needs and protect the client against social stigma.
- **Validation:** Interactions between the staff and client should ensure the client's humanity and should protect the human rights. Client has to feel that the communication of the staff is respectful.
- **Structured interaction and open communication:** It is explained in the characteristics of milieu therapy.

Milieu Therapy Team Members

- Psychiatrist
- Psychiatric nurse
- Clinical psychologist
- Psychiatric social worker
- Occupational therapist
- Recreational therapist
- Music therapist
- Art therapist
- Dietician
- Chaplain
- Mental health assistant

Characteristic Features of Milieu Therapist

A good milieu therapist should have:

- Self-respect/self-esteem/self-worth
- Warm and supportive nature
- Empathetic thinking capacity
- Contribute effectively toward the organization goals
- Share problems within the context and work out to solve effectively
- Able to function in various roles and responsibilities
- Visualize the contribution as a whole and not only the tasks
- Accept the responsibilities
- Strong decision making capacity

Programs within the milieu therapy unit have been given below in Table 5.13.

Table 5.13: Programs within the milieu therapy unit

Client government	Work activities
• Conducting the structured meetings at least once in a week • Making decisions for the benefits to the client • Involve the client in planning the activity schedule • Discuss the problems which arise daily	• Create and offer variety of activities • Provide opportunity to the client for selecting the work required to do • Ensure the monetary benefits for the successful completion of the work

NURSES RESPONSIBILITY

Nurses Responsibility in Milieu Therapy

- **Physical dimension:** Nurse has to participate in designing the physical infrastructure or in renovation required to enhance the therapeutic physical environment.
  Example: Bulletin boards are required to display the occupational therapy activities, separate therapy room is required to conduct group therapy and bed side lockers are required to keep the personal items of client, etc.
- **Intellectual dimension:** Nurse has to communicate with the physical design experts regarding the color, lighting and texture of the building, because these factors help to improve the perceptual clarity. Nurse has to coordinate with all the health team members in order to make referrals and promote the participation of client.
- **Social dimension:** Nurse should take the leadership role and promote the interaction process among the clients.
- **Emotional dimension:** Nurse has to create the warm, fruitful, cooperative, relaxed, work with a purpose and rewarding emotional atmosphere to promote the mental health.
- **Spiritual dimension:** Allotment of specific quiet area for worship is vital to promote the spiritual needs.

Advantages of Milieu Therapy

- Client improves the self-confidence and involves in the decision making process.
- Client becomes sociocentric person.
- Client develops the leadership roles.
- Client is able to adopt the behavior which is acceptable to the therapeutic environment.
- A therapeutic milieu is a safe place to develop the strengths and abilities.

- Client develops a fruitful relationship with the other members in community.
- Client learns to live and think collectively for the members in the community.

Disadvantages of Milieu Therapy

- Client finds that transition to the community is a difficult one.
- Individual concerns/needs do not meet.
- Group responsibility might be no one's responsibility.
- Blurring of role between the staff and client.
- Milieu therapy is limited to the hospitalized clients.
- Client and Staff ratio is minimal.
- Open communication is required between the staff and client.

SUPPORTIVE PSYCHOTHERAPY

Definition

Supportive psychotherapy is defined as **psychotherapeutic approach** which integrates various components such as **cognitive-behavioral**, **psychodynamic** and **interpersonal techniques.**

Supportive psychotherapy is defined as a kind of psychotherapy which helps to decrease the psychological conflict and strengthen the patient's defenses with the help of techniques such as suggestion, reassurance, counseling, re-education, etc.

Goals of Supportive Psychotherapy

- To reduce the intensity of the presenting symptoms or distress.
- To decrease the behavioral problems caused by psychic conflicts.
- To reinforce the adaptive patterns of behavior.
- To provide the healthy supportive relationship with the patient.

Do's and don'ts in supportive psychotherapy have been presented below:

Do's	Don'ts
Have an emotional connection	Solve the problems for the patient
Promote catharsis	Interrupt the feelings of the patient
Develop the therapeutic alliance	Interpret the transference
Focus on patient's strength	Assign the homework

Differences between expressive and supportive psychotherapy have been given in Table 5.14.

The supportive psychotherapy includes *advising, comforting, reassuring, encouraging and active listening.*

Table 5.14: Differences between expressive psychotherapy and supportive psychotherapy

Components	Expressive psychotherapy	Supportive psychotherapy
Goal of the therapy	Patient has to gain insight	Patient's symptoms have to be reduced.
Style of the therapist	Not transparent	Therapist converses well with the patient
Regression	Need to be enhanced	Need to be reduced
Transference	Examine it properly	Nurture the positive transference
Level of consciousness	Focus at subconscious and unconscious level	Focus at conscious level
Use of defenses	Interpret the defenses	Reinforce the mature defenses

Techniques of Supportive Psychotherapy

Directive Techniques

- Advice
- Teaching
- Change of environment
- Solving the problems or issues
- Cognitive restructuring
- Modeling (therapist reveals oneself to enhance the patient's identity)

Explanatory Techniques

- Motivation
- Instilling home
- Empathy
- Reassurance
- Promoting self-esteem
- Build therapeutic alliance
- Containment
- Managing transference
- Reality testing

Components of Supportive Psychotherapy

Bloch (1979) explained the key components of supportive psychotherapy as given below:

- Reassurance is vital to clarify the doubts and misconceptions. It has to be realistic and helpful to promote the climate of hope and positive expectation.

- Detailed explanation about the disease has to be focused here and now concept, however, the overall aim is to enhance the coping ability rather than the improvement of self-awareness.
- Individual has to know when to seek help.
- Suggestion by the therapist can result in change of patient's behavior.
- Motivation helps to promote self-esteem and decrease the inferiority complex.
- Environmental change might cause the vital changes in patient.
- Active listening, unconditional acceptance and promoting catharsis is helpful.

FAMILY THERAPY

Historical Development

Family is fundamental unit of the human life. Nathan Ackerman, an American Psychiatrist, coined the term 'family therapy' in 1950. Nathan Ackerman (1958) and Murray Bowen (1978) were the pioneers of family therapy. Sigmund freud explained that, the unconscious process like identification, projection, and introjection are considered individual experiences and might be transmitted across the generations in family. Virginia Satir is an American author/social worker and she is the mother of family therapy (Fig. 5.14).

Definition

Family therapy is defined as, 'a form of psychotherapy in which, the issues or problems or conflicts existing among the family members are addressed and the solution is identified.'

Figure 5.14: Virginia Satir: American author and social worker; mother of family therapy

Goals

- To improve the communication skills among the family members.
- To reduce the existing conflicts within the family.
- To strengthen the ability of the family members to cope with the stressors.
- To integrate the family system along with the social system.
- To decrease the dysfunctional behavior among the family members.
- To raise the awareness about the needs of individuals in the family.
- To establish the empathetic and supportive connection among the family members.

Indications

- Existing family conflicts.
- Interdependence of issues and symptoms (Example: wife is getting depressed because the husband is consuming alcohol; husband is taking alcohol because he/she perceives the wife is having extramarital relationship: Othello syndrome).
- Failure of individual therapy.
- Continuous stressors among family members and lack of coping ability.
- Relationship issues in the family (Existing communication gap or generation gap).

Contraindications

- Unwillingness of the family members to accept the therapy.
- Unavailability of any family member who is involved in the conflicts.
- Family members staying separately.
- Family members who exhibit high level of negative emotions or unwillingness to listen to the conversation.

The functions of family have been presented in Table 5.15.

Types of Family Therapy

- **Individual family therapy:** Each family member in the family will have a separate family therapist and the whole family will meet occasionally with one or two therapist to work out the specific issues.
- **Conjoint family therapy:** It is a psychotherapy in which two or more members in a single nuclear family are involved in the therapy, for example, problems between the parents and children, marriage counseling, etc. are addressed here.

Table 5.15: Functions of a family

Functions of family	Description
Communication function	Communication gap is a major issue for the conflicts existing in the family. So, communication with the family members will give a chance to express the feeling and emotions of the family members.
Boundary function	Boundary will maintain the limits between the individual members in the family. Rigid boundary prevents the innovative ideas and communication within the family and might cause family dysfunction.
Supportive function	It helps to grow and obtain the new roles in the family.
Biological function	Family is the medium for procreation.
Socialization function	Family interaction will improve the social skills and coping skills of the family members.
Psychological function	Love, affection, emotional attachment, belongingness, sympathy, security, intimacy, etc. are the psychological functions existing in the family.
Protective function	Family provides the feeling of safety and security among each other.
Educational function	Parents are the first teachers and care givers. Child's personality will get molded up according to the activities and the teaching from them.
Recreational function	Family creates the atmosphere to recreate, play, entertain and share happiness among them.
Social function	Family provides the identity to maintain the social status.
Religious function	Family gives religious thoughts and ideation toward the God.
Cultural function	Family will mold its members based on their cultural values, belief, tradition and customs.

- **Couple therapy:** This is also called marital therapy in which the problems exist between the married couples, i.e., husband and wife and are discussed here.
- **Multiple family group therapy:** It is a psychotherapy working out with the collection of more families in a group setting.
- **Network therapy:** The network constitutes 40–60 individuals who are experiencing crisis, issues and problems within the family and can attend network therapy. This gathering includes family, neighbors, friends, professional groups and any individual in the community. People who gather will interact regularly regarding their family issues and obtain the solution to the problem.
- **Psychodynamic family therapy:** It is a family therapy which integrates the Sigmund Freud's Psychoanalytical concept (unconscious aspects of individual personality traits integrates with the family context).
- **Structural family therapy:** It is a psychotherapy method developed by Salvador Minuchin. It focuses on the pattern of interactions that create the problems among family members.
- **Strategic family therapy:** Jay Haley is the pioneer of strategic family therapy. In this family therapy, the therapist solves the present problems specific to the interactions between the family members. It is a brief, solution-oriented and process-focused therapy. The key concepts are mentioned in Table 5.16.
- **Cognitive behavioral family therapy:** It is the use of cognitive therapy techniques and behavior therapy techniques within the family context.
- **Family psychoeducational therapies:** It is a health teaching to the family members with the concern of psychological well-being. Nurse should not provide any wrong assurance stating about the cure of mental illness. Instead, the discussion should focus on psychotropic drugs, awareness about the disease, care required, follow-up, rehabilitation, etc.

Family Therapy Assessment

Boyer and Jeffrey (1984) listed six elements which are helpful to assess whether family is functional or dysfunctional.

1. **Family interactions:** Healthy family communication and expressing the family expectations during the interactions will resolve the conflicts.
2. **Family climate:** Positive family climate is based on the trust and openness among the family members.
3. **Communication:** Family members are encouraged to express the honest feelings or opinions, while other members in the family will be active listeners. There are few factors which influence the communication gap within the family such as:
   - **Failing to listen:** Members in the family don't listen the conversation of others or listen very selectively and it would be the reason for wrong interpretation.

Table 5.16: Key concepts of strategic family therapy

Key concepts of strategic family therapy	Description
Avoid paradoxical injunctions	Contradiction between what is said and what is expressed
Avoid paradoxical directives	Direct the patient to continue the behavior
Have a control over one's own behavior	Therapist helps the patient with his/her need and determines the level of control over the behavior
Avoid double bind communication	Conflicting messages are verbalized
Relabeling (positive connotation)	Therapist will change label attached to the person from negative side to positive one, from which the new responses are expected because of the positive perception
Family homeostasis	Families tend to preserve the organization of the family
First order changes	Superficial changes of the behavior in the system is done but the structure of system doesn't change
Second order changes	Changes in the systemic interaction and so the structural and functional changes take place
Avoid faulty family solutions	Ignoring the problem when action is needed and taking action when it is not needed gives faulty solutions
Pretend technique	Therapist motivates the family members to pretend as playful, fantasy, etc.
Neutrality	Therapist has to be neutral with all the family members and avoid coalitions.
Circular questioning	Focus on the connections among family members rather than identifying the differences among them
Reflexive questioning	Help the family members to reflect on the perception, values and beliefs
Hypothesizing	Determining that how the family members have to organize to solve problems

- **Belittling feeling: Members in the family should be encouraged to hold the honest feelings and ignore the hurts or negative feelings caused by others. Example:** Sister developed anger toward the brother because he is scolding continuously. Father asked his daughter to ignore the negative feeling.
- **Indirect communication:** Members in the family should pass the message directly, i.e., sender has to send the message to the receiver directly instead of passing the message to the third person as it might cause improper delivery of messages.

4. **Positive reinforcement is used among the family members:** Family members have to provide the positive reinforcement by using the encouraging words in order to motivate each other for their daily achievements.
5. **Expectations of the family members:** Each family member has different strengths and weaknesses. Every individual might have different expectations from the family and so each member in the family has to be valued independently.
6. **Handling differences:** It is difficult for the two individuals living together to agree with each other all the time. Those differences have to be put into neutral situation for the smooth functioning of the family.

Nurse has to assess the strengths, problems and goals of the family. She has to explore the expectations of the family members. She should pay attention to the needs of the family members. She has to coordinate the treatment process. She has to promote active listening and to have a clear communication among family members. Sessions have to focus toward the resolution of family conflicts. She has to motivate the family members to expand their social support networks and adjust with their expectations. Nurse has to follow-up regularly for the further sessions and render continuous support.

GROUP THERAPY

Human beings are social animals. Social interaction plays the vital role for the human beings. Psychotherapy in the group helps the individual to share the issues or problems to the peer groups and obtain the right solution. It helps the individuals to understand their own deficits in a better way.

Historical Development

In 1905, Joseph Pratt used group therapy for the patient with tuberculosis. Strict hygienic measures have been encouraged

in the nursing homes and so the group health teaching for the patients has been initiated regularly. Cody Marsh, a psychiatrist, was the first person to initiate the dance classes in the group. Later, Sigmund Freud understood the significance of group dynamics. In World War II, many therapists were involved in the group works. Kurt Lewin's work stimulated the interest in group process. The emergence of Gestalt theory, transactional analysis, existential models and bioenergetics developed the group therapy field. Slavson, educationalist of psychoanalytic persuasion developed the group psychodrama/group psychotherapy and he also made efforts to form American Group Psychotherapy Association. In late 1930s, Emmanual Schwartz and Alexander Wolf applied the psychoanalytic concepts in the group therapy.

Definitions

- Group therapy is defined as, 'mentally ill patients are placed into groups, guided by the therapist for the purpose of changing maladaptive behavior.'
- Group therapy is defined as, 'psychosocial treatment where the patients meet regularly to talk, interact and discuss the problems with each other along with the therapist.'
- Group therapy is defined as, 'a type of psychotherapy in which the group sessions are guided by the therapist and the patients will confront their personal problems. Here, the interaction is the integral part of therapy'

Purposes

- To examine and relieve the distortions.
- To treat the psychopathology.
- To improve the coping skills.

Components of Group Therapy

- **Members:** 8–10 members in a group. Not more than 15 members are advised.
- **Duration:** 1–2 hours is the duration of group therapy.
- **Number of sessions:** One group therapy session is held within two weeks.
- **Norms:** Each group may have one's own rules, regulations and standards.
- **Cohesion:** Group members work together to achieve a common goal.
- **Role:** Each patient involved in the group therapy might have separate role to perform.
- **Power:** Individual power may influence over the group.
- **Communication:** Free communication within the group is allowed.

Therapeutic Principles (or) Functions of Group Therapy (or) Factors Contributing the Group Therapy Process

According to Yalom (1985), the therapeutic principles of group psychotherapy are listed below:

- **Instillation of hope:** In the mixed group, a member who solved the problem can be an inspirational person or a motivator to another member who is still struggling with the problem.
- **Imparting the information:** Structured health teaching or psychoeducation is vital to the group members.
- **Universality:** Patient will feel that others in the group have thoughts, problems and feelings similar to his/her own.
- **Corrective recapitulation of the primary family group:** Unconsciously patient perceives the therapist as parents and other members as siblings in the form of transference. The therapist's interpretations can help group members to understand the impact of childhood experiences on their personality, and they may learn to avoid unconsciously repeating unhelpful past interactive patterns in present-day relationships.
- **Altruism:** It is the process of helping each other.
- **Imitative behavior:** Patient attains the growth by the imitation of healthier aspect of behavior from others.
- **Development of socialization:** Role play in the group therapy will enhance the social skills.

Types of Group Therapy

Types of group therapy are given in Table 5.17.

Common Topics Addressed in the Group Therapy

- Addiction
- Behavioral issues
- Anger management
- Communication related issues
- Grief and loss
- Parenting
- Emotional problems like depression, anxiety, etc.
- Relationship issues like trust, intimacy, self-esteem, etc.
- Domestic abuse or violence
- Divorce
- Food and eating related issues

Stages of Group Therapy

In **Initial stage**, the member's involvement is superficial. Structuring the group rules, norms and responsibilities

Table 5.17: Types of group therapy

Types of group therapy	Description
Open group	Members of this group can join at any time.
Closed group	• Members of this group can join only in the initial time of commencement. • Only those participants will attend the meeting for the further sessions.
Small group	Group constitutes 3–4 members.
Large group	Group constitutes more than 4 members.
Primary group	Group where only the family members are involved.
Secondary group	Group where the patients of different families are involved.
Homogenous group	Group where the members with similar problems and issues have been involved, e.g., only the patients with alcohol dependence syndrome were involved.
Heterogeneous group	Group where the members with various problems and issues are involved, e.g., patients with alcohol dependence syndrome, neurotic patients and their family members were involved.
Psychoanalytic group psychotherapy	Application of the psychoanalytical principles in the group therapy. Group communication at conscious, semiconscious and unconscious levels has been focused. Free association, dream interpretation and latent content has been focused in the group therapy. Psychotherapist turns out all these experiences into conscious healthy learning experience to the patient.
Rational emotive therapy	It is aimed to enhance the rational thinking of the group.
Transactional analysis	Three ego states of individuals such as adult, parent and child role is examined in this group.
Interpersonal group therapy	Interactions between the group members help to decrease the anxiety and stress caused due to interpersonal relations.
Psychodrama group	Therapist directs the subject with role play and implement the therapeutic ideas into action.
Encounter group	It is aimed to bring the personal change due to the deep felt experiences.
Community support group	It develops the feeling of togetherness, group cohesion, understanding, social support and thereby it improves the good patterns of behavior.

begin here. Members in the group search out their similarity among them. At **Working Stage,** members in the group work together with co-operation in order to solve the problems. In **Termination stage**, the group members evaluate and summarize their experiences and also explore the positive/negative feelings. The follow-up and next meeting of group session will be planned (Fig. 5.15).

Ethics of Group Therapy

All the group members must protect the identity of fellow members and the information shared in the group should be confidential, until and unless the permission is given, it should not be discussed outside. Therapist needs to inform the authorities if the patient verbalizes 'harm toward self or others'. Therapist should ensure the entire session is non-judgmental and should provide a positive growth to all the members in the group. The sessions have to be free from discrimination, threats, harassment, etc.

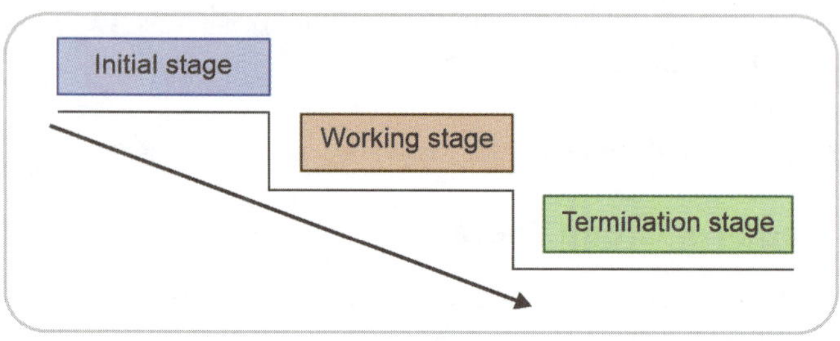

Figure 5.15: Stages of group therapy

Therapeutic Techniques (or) Interventions used in Group Therapy

- **Acceptance:** Accept the participants without implying any approval of particular behavior.
- **Approval:** Encourage the right attitude or action or performance.
- **Clarification:** Restate the statement to clarify the doubts.
- **Identify allies:** Identify tbfhe helpful and co-operative members for the benefit of the group.
- **Information giving:** Saying the facts in regard to the problem.
- **Reinforcement:** Motivate the group members for the positive outlook and to regain the confidence.

- **Encouraging expression of feelings:** Motivate the participants to ventilate the feelings.
- **Support:** Psychological support gives a comfort to the group.
- **Teaching:** Teach the group in regard to the unknown concepts or phenomenon.
- **Listening:** Concentrate the communication of the group without interpretation.
- **Limit setting:** Set the limit when the group members speak out of boundary limits. Therapist has to guide the conversation in group therapy, which has to be related to the context.
- **Use of silence:** Being without speaking.
- **Structuring:** Shaping out the contents to have a group meeting.
- **Themes:** Explore the main concepts in the group discussion.

Group psychotherapy for the special population has been given in Table 5.18.

Advantages of Group Therapy

- It develops the socialization skills.
- It encourages the group members to share their ideas and feelings.
- It is a cost-effective therapy.
- It gives an opportunity for the group members to learn different styles of communication.
- It helps the group members to understand the reason for problems in a better way.
- It helps the group members to learn multiple problem-solving skills from others.

Disadvantages of Group Therapy

- Lack of privacy for the group members.
- Sometimes ethics of the group therapy can be out of control.
- Resistance or showing reluctance to change by the group members may be present.
- Domination by the therapist might take place sometimes, particularly at the time of limit setting.
- Members lack the freedom to join in between the closed group therapy.
- It may consume more time, when the discussion about the different issues in the heterogeneous group take place.

Role of therapist in Group Psychotherapy

According to Lieberman (1973), four basic dimensions of therapist behavior are as follows:

Table 5.18: Group psychotherapy of special population

Disease condition	Description
Alcohol and other substance abuse	**Psychological conflicts, family problems, financial issues, health problems, occupational and legal issues are addressed in the group therapy. Example:** Alcoholic Anonymous (AA) group, Narcotic Anonymous (NA) group, Al-anon, etc.
Schizophrenia and other psychotic patients	Realistic testing, dealing with interpersonal interactions, coping skills, social skills and drug adherence has been discussed. However, group psychotherapy is contraindicated with acute psychotic patients.
Mood disorders	Based on the psychological strengths of the patients, supportive approach or expressive approach of treatment will be provided.
Personality disorders	These patients are usually unaware of maladaptive behavior and at certain extent, patient might irritate or show anger on others. So, this sustained negative behavior pattern is unfolded and confronted with one's own psychopathology. Personality disorder patients perform well in the heterogeneous groups.
Anxiety disorders, eating disorders and somatoform disorders	Patients with high level of anxiety require trusting relationship with the therapist. Patient with post-traumatic stress disorders require homogenous group therapy to address the social phobia. In eating disorders, educational approach, intrapsychic exploration and motivation of interpersonal learning is essential. In somatoform disorders, homogenous group therapy gives adequate psychological support to the patients.
Cancer patients	These patients might face huge psychosocial problems because of cancer. So, the pre-existing coping skills have to be strengthened to handle out the crisis situations and adequate psychological support is essential.
Physically disabled patients	In the rehabilitation centers, issues related to feeling of isolation, loneliness, reduced self-esteem have to be addressed. Group programs have to be conducted to gain the new coping skills.
Mentally retarded-patients	Need of love, sharing, acceptance and closeness is vital for the mentally retarded group. However, therapist has to set limits in patients with hyperactive and impulsive behavior to enhance the realistic socialization.

1. **Emotional stimulation:** Therapist acts as a self-revealing member of the group. Therapist stimulates the group emotionally for the behavior change and not merely by teaching.
2. **Caring:** Therapist shows the cluster of behavior such as love, affection, friendship, support, protection and praise.
3. **Meaning attribution:** The ideas or concepts expressed by the group members might gain the group experience. Therapist might guide the group members to follow the group experience, if found fruitful.
4. **Executive functions:** Therapist directs the group members toward the functioning in the social system.

PLAY THERAPY

Historical development of play therapy is shown in Table 5.19.

Table 5.19: Historical development of play therapy

Year/ Period	Description
429–347 BC	Plato said, 'Person can be discovered within one hour of play, more than one year of conversation.'
18th Century	Rousseau wrote a book, 'Emile' in which it is mentioned that play is a way to understand the children.
1903	In Friedrich Frobel's book, '*The Education of Man*' mentioned the significance of symbolism in play (i.e., Play gives higher development by the way of free expression)
1909	Melanie Klein implemented the play technique to analyze the under 6 children. She strongly believed that children's play is associated with free association used in adults.
1930	David Levy developed the technique or structured approach called 'Release therapy'. He proposed that introducing the play items in stressful situation helped to release the associated emotions.
1946	Anna Freud used play to enhance the positive attachment with therapist and to assess the children's inner life.
1953	Clark Moustakas published first book entitled, '*Children in Play Therapy.*'
1955	Gove Hambidge expanded David Levy's technique, 'Release therapy' (Usage of play items to relieve the stress).
1964–1970	Alexander, Landreth, Muro, Myrick, Holdin, Nelson and Waterland were the counselor-educators who used the play as educative and preventive tool to detect and solve the problems in children.
1973	Moustakas published the novel, '*The child's discovery of himself*,' which focused on the growth experience with play therapy.

Definition of Play Therapy

Play therapy is a form of psychotherapy in which the therapist utilizes the child's fantasy and symbolic meaning as a medium of play to have a communication or understanding about the children. It also gives a chance to the child to express the feelings and experiences.

Theories of Play

- **Natural theory:** Play seems to be natural and instinctive one. Children will play on their basis of age and development. Interests in the particular age is said to be universal. Play can be **correlated** with the chronological age and the physical development.
- **Energy theory:** This theory explains that the concept of play is based on the levels of energy. Children might get involved in active and aggressive play because of high energy level present in them. Children who are inactive exhibit the lack of energy level.
- **Practice theory:** This theory explains the concept of play as a practice or the way of preparing and functioning oneself toward the adult life.
- **Recreation theory:** Play is considered an escape from the fatigue of everyday life. It enhances the physiological needs of relaxation and thereby promotes the recreational value.
- **Catharsis theory:** Play helps to ventilate the bottled up emotions. It decreases the negative emotions such as aggression, anger, hatred, hostile behavior, etc.
- **Discovery theory:** Play gives a chance to the child to discover the environment through the interpersonal relationship with others.
- **Pleasure principle theory:** Sigmund Freud, a psychoanalyst, said that play is a pleasure principle because play gratifies oneself, feel relaxed and happy.

Qualities of Play Therapist

Play therapist should be friendly, appealing and must have good rapport with children. Play therapist has to understand the feelings of the children through the facial expressions. Play therapist should accept their faults. He/she has to make the children comfortable so that they can express their feelings. He/she should have a capacity to reciprocate or reflect the feelings of the child in order to gain insight in the child's behavior. He/she should be free from conflicts to conduct play therapy sessions. He/she must have a zeal that the therapy should help the children to maximum extent. Play therapist should have strong knowledge on child psychology to understand the behavior of the children.

Indications of Play Therapy

- Children with aggression (or) temper tantrums
- Children with sleep disturbances (or) nightmares
- Children with poor bowel and bladder control
- Children who experience physical or sexual abuse
- Children who are neglected
- Children with no care from family members
- Children with excess worries
- Children with low self-esteem
- Children with learning disorder
- Mentally retarded children
- Children with anxiety disorder or having emotional disturbances

Types of Play therapy

- **Controlled (or) situational play:** Therapist creates a variety of toys/dolls and asks the children to speak with the doll assuming the various characters such as parents, teachers, siblings, friends, etc. The various scenes arranged in the play interview will help the child to gain insight into mental mechanisms. Newell said that situational play gives us clues to identify the wishes of parents (when child hides the doll behind), Oedipus wishes regarding masturbatory activities, castration anxiety and other primitive sex theories.
- **Free (or) spontaneous play:** Therapist leaves all the initiation of play toward the child. This type of play will help the child to explore the fear, guilt, anxiety, fantasies regarding birth, death, hostility and sex.
- **Individual play (or) solitary play:** In individual play, child will play with himself/herself.
- **Group play:** Child plays with the group of children.
- **Structured play:** Play is organized based on the situation and the plans.
- **Unstructured play:** Play is not organized on the basis of situation and the plans.
- **Directive play:** Therapist has an active role by directing the children through the play.
- **Non-directive play:** Therapist has a passive role and therapist will not direct the children during the play.

Phases of Play Therapy

Phases of play therapy are shown in Figure 5.16.

- **Introductory phase:** It is the preliminary task of the therapist to establish the trust of the children. It usually takes 5 minutes but might extend depending on the personality of the children.
- **Honeymoon phase:** This phase is helpful to explore the anxiety in the various settings such as school, home setups, entertainment areas, etc.

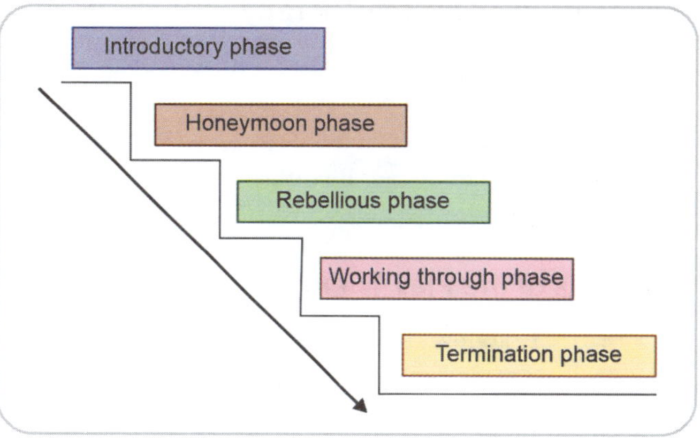

Figure 5.16: Phases of play therapy

- **Rebellious phase:** This phase is helpful for the child to explore the strong anger or repressed feelings or depression which helps to improve the positive mental health.
- **Working through phase:** After the awareness about the feeling of the child, therapist uses the productive methods to develop the healthy behavior in children.
- **Termination phase:** After working out with the child's emotions, when the therapeutic gain occurs, the therapy can be terminated and the next follow-up session can be planned by the therapist.

Duration and Design of Play Therapy

The ideal duration of the play therapy is 30–45 minutes. Play therapy is exclusively designed for the children below 12 years of age.

Principles of Play Therapy

Principles of play therapy are enlisted in Table 5.20.

Table 5.20: Principles of play therapy

Principles	Description
Friendly rapport with the children	This behavior helps to promote the trust between the therapist and the child's relationship.
Accept the child as he/she is	Accepting the child irrespective of his/her intelligence, capacity, socioeconomic background, interests, skills etc. is the ethical norm needed to be followed by the therapist.
Ability toward the problem solving skills	It helps to facilitate the creativity in children
Direct the child toward play	Guidance by the therapist will provoke the child to involve in the play activities at full extent.
Therapist uses the limits sparingly	Build the appropriate required relationship between therapist and children. It also prevents the boundary violations.

Play Items used for the Therapy

- **Preschooler:** Crayons, color pencils, color books, magnetic boards, puppets, story books, recorded videos, safe hospital equipment, etc.
- **Children in school age:** Board games, toys/dolls, crafts, story books, recorded videos, use of computer, etc.

Functions of the Play Therapy

- **Creative function:** It improves the creativity of the child. It gives an opportunity to get rid of one's own conflicts and learn positive qualities as well as emotional growth from other children.
- **Diagnostic function:** It helps to identify the difficulties contributing toward the issues in children. It also helps to understand the child's personality and explore the relationship existing between the siblings. It also helps to explore the intellectual capacity according to the age.

Neuroscience and Play Therapy

Play therapy helps to improve the development of the interconnections between the neurons. Effect of trauma might reside in the nonverbal brain areas such as hippocampus, thalamus, brain stem and amygdala. Play therapy in the form of role playing helps to move out the traumatic experiences from nonverbal brain areas.

Advantages of Play Therapy

Play therapy reduces the level of stress, frustration, fear, tension, aggression, confusion, anxiety, depression and thereby promotes the psychological well-being in children. It helps the therapist to identify and analyze the problems in children. It helps the child to ventilate the negative feelings or thoughts or bottled up emotions. It provokes the thinking and decision making capacity in children. It acts as an add-on therapy to treat the children with mental disorders.

NURSES RESPONSIBILITY

Nurse should select the type of play item and the type of play as per the need and age of the children. She should assess the underlying issue of the children in the honeymoon phase and rebellious phase of play therapy. She has to work out these issues with the help of play therapist. She should remember that children with mental retardation should not be assigned the play task beyond the intellectual level and it should not be conducted in a competitive sense because it can provoke anxiety among them. She should involve the parents in the play therapy which will help in strengthening the mother-child bonding.

PSYCHODRAMA

Historical Development

Jacob L Moreno (1889–1974) was the first person to identify the concepts of psychodrama and sociometry. In 1913, Jacob L Moreno grouped the prostitutes to discuss regarding the social stigma and problems encountered in the form of support group. In 1925, Jacob L Moreno introduced his work done on Psychodrama to the American psychologists. Following this, Wilhelm Reich, Sigmund Freud and Jacob L Moreno developed the concepts of psychodrama. Jacob L Moreno began to work on children and later conducted the psychodrama sessions in a large group in Carnegie Hall.

Definition of Psychodrama

Psychodrama is a form of group psychotherapy, in which the dramatization or dramatic presentation of the group is done to gain self-insight.

Hollander Psychodrama Curve and its Phases

Another pioneer in the psychodrama field is Carl Hollander. He got certification from Jacob L Moreno in psychodrama. He created Hollander Psychodrama Curve, which is used to understand the structure of psychodrama.

Warm-up is the phase of spontaneity and creativity to open the act of psychodrama. Activity is the phase where the enactment of psychodrama takes place. Integration is the phase where discussion and closure of the session are brought together.

The classic psychodrama includes three phases such as (Fig. 5.17):

1. **Warm-up:** Activities done initially to ensure the trust of group members and to promote group cohesion.
2. **Shaping and presentation:** Engaging in the psychodrama scenario. Protagonist and the members of psychodrama actively participate in this phase.

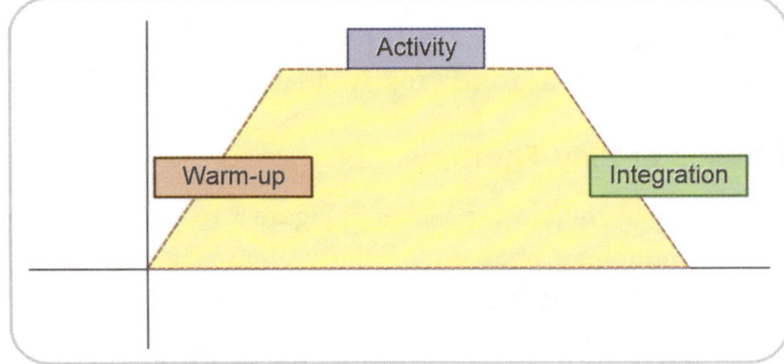

Figure 5.17: Phases of psychodrama

3. **Sharing and discussion:** Group members have to discuss how this enactment is useful to them. Sharing will help to clear the doubts and also analyze the perception of the group regarding the enactment. It will also enhance the social bonding.

Elements of Psychodrama

Elements of psychodrama are given in Table 5.21.

Table 5.21: Elements of psychodrama

Elements	Description
Stage	To enact or play drama.
Protagonist	Person holding the main character in the drama.
Director	Therapist who directs the actors.
Producer	person who narrates the story and uses the appropriate psychodrama techniques such as mirroring, doubling, role playing, soliloquy, role reversal, future projection, magic shop and empty chair.
Auxiliary egos	Participants in the psychodrama who simulate the particular situations for protagonist.
Use of double feedback	Auxiliary Egos express the thoughts/feelings which are difficult to express by the Protagonist

Core Psychodrama Techniques

Core psychodrama techniques have been summarized in Table 5.22.

Psychological applications of Psychodrama

Clinical Arena

- Conditions to decrease psychological trauma
- Neurotic and stress related disorders particularly post-traumatic stress disorders
- Patients with substance abuse/alcohol dependence syndrome
- Autism
- Eating disorders
- Adoption and attachment issues

Nonclinical Arenas

- Education sector
- Business
- Professional training areas

Principles of Psychodrama

- **Action principle:** It helps to understand oneself and is an integrative part in social learning.
- **Social atom principle:** Each individual in the psychodrama is the central person for the social interaction network.
- **Potentiality to grow:** It helps the individual not to get stagnated with the past and to promote the chances of growth potential toward the future.
- **Spontaneity:** It helps to respond the old situation by 'degree of novelty (new thing)' and the new situation by, 'degree of adequacy.'

Table 5.22: Core psychodrama techniques and description

Techniques	Description
Mirroring	Protagonist is asked to act out the experience. Patient will act in the scene and also watch another actor step into his/her role and portray in the scene.
Doubling	It is to bring the thoughts or feelings into conscious mind, which the patient is unable to express due to guilt, shyness, fear, politeness, anger, inhibition, etc. (Doubling denotes, 'one is making attempts to bring the unexpressed or under expressed thoughts or feelings into conscious mind and other is to give a form to unconscious mind).
Role playing	Patient portrays and acts like a person who is problematic to oneself.
Soliloquy	Client speaks his/her thoughts aloud to understand oneself.
Role reversal (or) role training	Patient is asked to portray another person while the second actor portrays patient in a particular scene.
Future projection	Enactment was done by the members to work out regarding the future concerns.
Magic shop	It is a warm-up technique in which the individual imagines to put oneself in the shop which has different personality traits. Participants will express the qualities of different persons.
Empty chair	**It is actually taken from Gestalt therapy technique, in which an individual has to think about a person with whom he would like to converse sitting on an empty chair and starts conversing.** (Example: Mr Raj is the patient who is conversing with his mother imagining that she is sitting on the empty chair. When Raj wants to perform his mother's role, then Raj has to sit on the empty chair and communicates/takes up the role of his mother). It helps to promote mental ventilation or catharsis.

- **Catharsis:** Bursting out of the negative emotions during psychodrama will help toward the positive growth in life pattern.
- **Surplus reality:** Roles enacted in the psychodrama create the surplus chance of reality.
- **Tele principle:** Have a constant interaction to strengthen the existing relationship between people and environment.

Advantages or Benefits of Psychodrama

- It improves the life skills and learning.
- It helps to express the feelings in a safe and supportive environment.
- It identifies the problem clearly; and also identifies the misperceptions, distortions in the realistic perceptions and unrealistic goals.
- It explores the client's adaptive and maladaptive coping response to the problem.
- It helps to promote self-confidence and well-being.
- It promotes healing by overcoming the loss and grief.
- It increases the communication and thereby improves the relationships.
- It promotes the new way of thinking and promotes the acceptable behavior.

NURSES RESPONSIBILITY

Nurse needs to supervise the psychodrama sessions and coordinate with the patients. She has to clarify the doubts of patient and motivate the client to perform the psychodrama using the appropriate techniques. She has to organize or conduct the psychodrama sessions as per the hospital protocol. She has to keep in mind that psychodrama doesn't work out for acute psychotic patients. She should instruct the spectators not to communicate in between the psychodrama, whereas the doubts can be clarified in the discussion phase. She should have clarity about the various roles of the members involved in the psychodrama sessions. Have a regular follow-up with the further sessions to elicit the improvement in patients.

MUSIC THERAPY

Definitions

- Music therapy is defined as, 'utilization of music in treatment, training, education, rehabilitation of children and adults who are suffering from physical or mental disorder'. —*Alvin, 1975*
- Music therapy has been in use to build therapeutic relationship to empower the physical, emotional, cognitive, and social needs of an individual after the assessment done by a professional music therapist. It also promotes the avenues for communication to express the thoughts or feelings into words and thereby it provides the emotional support to the client and families. —***American Music Therapy Association***
- Music therapy is a variety of expressive art therapy which helps to improve physical, psychological and social well-being with the help of listening music, playing musical instrument or by singing songs.

History of Music Therapy

During the time of World War, music groups played music for hospitalized veterans. Doctors began to realize the healing effects of music. Hence, professional musicians have been recruited by the hospitals.

In 1944, Michigan State University included the music therapy in the curriculum. In 1950, first organization for music therapists was formed namely National Association for Music Therapy (NAMT). In 1998, American Music Therapy Association (AMTA) was formed and merging of NAMT and AMTA took place. AMTA focuses on access to music therapy, raising the awareness of services to promote the music therapy in various sectors such as education, training, and research.

Famous Quotes on Music Therapy

- Music expresses, which we can't express in words. —***Victor Hugo***
- Where word fails, music speaks. —***H C Anderson***
- Music washes away from the soul, dust of everyday life. —***Berthold Auerbach***
- Music expresses that which we can't be said and on which it is impossible to be silent. —***Victor Hugo***

Mechanism of Music Therapy

- Stimulation of endorphins, peptides and natural opiates secreted by hypothalamus produce pleasure.
- Synchronization of body rhythms with the musical rhythm takes place in music therapy. This rhythm guides the body to have a slow and deep breathing and thereby it gives calming effect as shown in Figure 5.18.
- Synchronization reduces the activity of sympathetic nervous system.

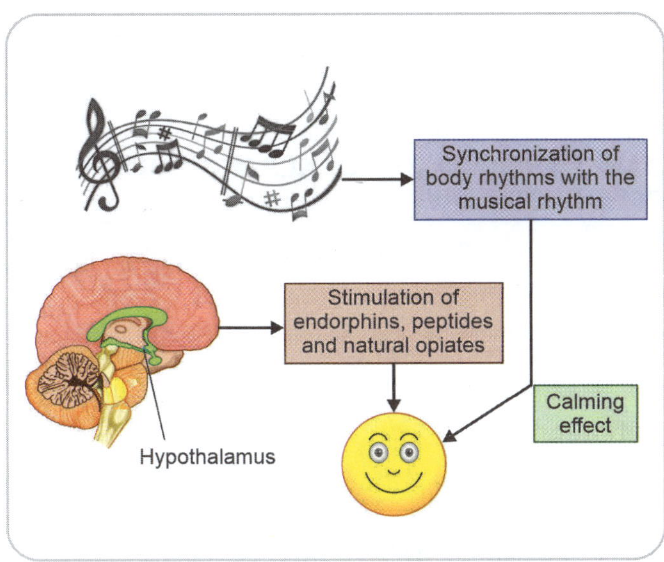

Figure 5.18: Mechanism of music therapy

Types of Music Therapy

Types of music therapy with their benefits have been given in Table 5.23.

Aims of Music Therapy

- It acts as a diversional technique in a stressful situation.
- It helps to relax the mind.
- It encourages patient in promoting the self-expression through music.
- It obtains a specific behavioral change in an individual.
- It reduces pain, stress and isolation.

Indications of Music Therapy

Psychiatric Disorders

- Depression
- Neurotic and stress related disorders (Anxiety)
- Dementia
- Autism
- Developmental disorders
- Insomnia
- Substance dependency
- Personality disorders
- Schizophrenia patients—to decrease aggression, delusions and hallucinations
- Pregnant mothers in labor—to reduce stress level
- Grief and loss

Physical Disorders

- Heart disease
- Stroke
- Aphasia
- Pain management
- Terminally ill patients
- Affective, cognitive and sensory disorders
- Patient with carcinoma
- Hypertension
- Neurological disorders/brain injuries

Effects of Music Therapy

- **Physical effects:** It relieves muscle tension and improves the motor skills.

Table 5.23: Types of music therapy and their benefits

Types	Description	Benefits
Receptive music therapy (or) passive music therapy	**Listening the live or recorded music.** (Example: It decreases stress among patients with post-traumatic stress disorder)	**Decreases/reduces** • Decreases anxiety • Reduces behavioral problems • Decreases the pain • Reduces the stress **Increases/promotes/improves** • Promotes relaxation • Enhances mood • Enhances attention span • Enhances coping skills • Improves motor skills • Increases social skills • Expresses the emotions • Improves communication • Improves memory • Enhances the physical and psychological well-being • Enhances the self-esteem and self-concept • Improves group cohesion
Expressive (or) active music therapy	**Making the music by playing the instrument or by singing songs.** (Example: It increases the speech fluency in the children with attention deficit hyperactive disorder)	

- **Mental effects:** It decreases the level of stress and improves the psychological well-being by keeping the mind in relaxed state.
- **Emotional effects:** Music gives a chance to express the emotions and feelings which cannot be expressed in words.

Guidelines for the Effective Music Therapy

- Choose the slow rhythm of music in general. Fast music is advised for the purpose of stimulation and to enhance the energy level.
- Have a good concentration in music.
- Listen to the sounds in the nature.
- Breathe along with the music.
- Hear the familiar songs.

Aspects of Music Therapy

Merent (1997) explored the healing aspects of music therapy as a restoring agent as follows:

- **Anxiolytic music therapy:** It reduces anxiety.
- **Algolytic music therapy:** It reduces pain.
- **Tensiolytic music therapy:** It decreases tension.
- **Psycholytic music therapy:** It secures the person from evil spirits.
- **Patholytic music therapy:** It aims to relieve grief or loss.

Indian Music Therapy

Indian music is generally very unique due to thousands of raga and tunes. These tunes are the combination of seven notes or *Sapta Swaras* that might derive the base on nine human emotions (or) Navarasas. Stirring of human emotions might increase the human self to experience the joy and bliss.

Areas where the music therapy sessions were conducted:

- Counseling room
- Rehabilitation centers
- De-addiction treatment centers
- Physical therapy units
- Massage therapy rooms
- Labor rooms
- Operation theater
- Patient waiting halls

Limitations of Music Therapy

Music therapy might give positive result by reducing the symptoms and by producing the psychological well-being, but it is not considered only treatment for the serious medical and mental illness. Selection of the music is based on the individual preference and everyone does not find all types of music to be therapeutic. Some forms of music may lead to agitation. So, to get success, music therapist has to ensure the musical preferences and accordingly, the treatment has to be taken into consideration.

DANCE THERAPY (OR) DANCE MOVEMENT PSYCHOTHERAPY

Dance Movement therapy is an expressive art therapy in which psychotherapeutic movements or dance are performed to enhance the emotional, psychological, intellectual and motor functions of the body.

Definitions

- Dance therapy is defined as, 'psychotherapeutic use of movement as a process which promotes physical, emotional and cognitive integration of the individual.
  —***American Dance Therapy Association (ADTA)***
- Dance therapy is defined as, 'therapeutic modality in which, the participants are motivated to express emotions, reduce tensions, improve body image, enhance the body awareness and improve the social interaction with the help of rhythmic exercises and music.' —***Goldenson, 1984***

Historical Development

In 1840–1930, new philosophy of dance has been formulated in USA and Europe, i.e., dance is not merely an expressive art therapy, it also has an effect on movements. In 1916, Jung said that dance or movement is an active imagination. In 1966, Marian Chace formed American Dance Therapy Association to support the emerging professionals in the field of dance therapy. Marian Chace is the Pioneer of Modern Dance Therapy (Fig. 5.19).

Principles of Dance Therapy

- Dance therapy is based on the body-mind interaction.
- The conscious and unconscious movements of a person reflects one's personality.

Figure 5.19: Marian Chace: Pioneer of modern dance therapy

- Dance or movement is a symbolic function of understanding oneself.
- The interaction of body, mind and spirit in the dance therapy gives a sense of wholeness:
  - Body refers to the discharge of energy through the musculoskeletal system as per the stimuli received from the brain.
  - Mind refers to attention, perception, reasoning, decision making, imagery and evaluation.
  - Spirit refers to the feeling or engaging or be empathetic in nature.
- Dance therapy improves the social skills, relationship dynamics and the quality of life.
- Dance therapy creates the deeper sense of awareness about oneself.
- Dance therapy allows the creative expression of thoughts.

Stages of Dance Therapy

Bonnie Meekums, a dance therapist, explained the four stages of dance therapy as follows (Fig. 5.20):

1. **Preparation:** It is a warm-up stage, where the distractions have to be omitted and the client is prepared for movements with the eyes closed.
2. **Incubation:** Therapist asks the participant to get into subconscious mind and to produce the symbolic movements with the relaxed internal atmosphere.
3. **Illumination:** This process focuses on the integration with the conscious awareness. Self-awareness was increased and the *unconscious* motives are resolved.
4. **Evaluation:** Discussion is based on the insight in therapy and process can be ended if the goal is achieved.

Dance Therapy vs Dance

Dance is considered movement or exercise performed according to the music played. In dance therapy, the participant will communicate the conscious and unconscious feelings through dance. Therapist will observe the nonverbal cues, facial expressions, body movements and emotional expressions during the dance in order to frame the interventions.

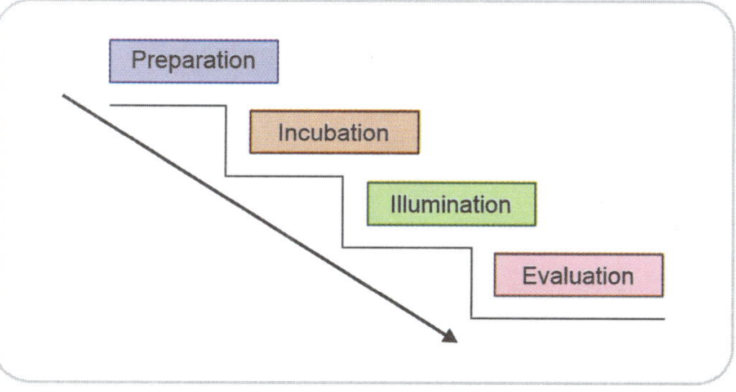

Figure 5.20: Stages of dance therapy

Techniques of Dance Therapy

- **Body movements:** It is the basic technique in which movements are in rhythmic pattern produced by the manipulation of body parts. This technique helps to increase body awareness and flexibility.
- **Props:** Use of some inanimate objects or materials in order to motivate the spectators. This technique is used as an aid to express the emotions of patients.
- **Imagery and movement:** Patient imagines a certain situation and performs the dance accordingly. For example, while dancing, patient imagines oneself as a lion in the forest and performs the dance movements accordingly.
- **Space awareness:** Patient is aware of the space around him/her and uses it appropriately during the dance performance.
- **Memory movements:** Sequence of movements stored in the memory is executed. This will improve cognition/memory/intelligence level.
- **Group coordination:** Two or more participants learn to perform the movements in a synchronized manner. This will improve the social skills and group cooperation.

Settings for Dance Therapy

- Hospitals/nursing homes
- Rehabilitation center
- Psychiatric set ups
- Education sector
- Day care centers

Benefits of Dance Therapy

The benefits of dance therapy in different disease conditions are given in Table 5.24.

Advantages of Dance Therapy

Dance therapy promotes the self-confidence and self-esteem. It helps the patients to express their unconscious motives through the movements. Dance therapy reduces the stress, anxiety and depression. It is helpful for the patients with negative symptoms of schizophrenia to improve the social skills. It is indicated for the patient with Parkinson's disease to improve the gait and balance. It improves the cognition. It helps to maintain the physical fitness. Overall, it promotes the physical, mental, cognitive, emotional and social well-being.

Table 5.24: Benefits of dance therapy in different disease conditions

Disease conditions	Benefits of dance therapy
Visually impaired	Enhances personal awareness, improves body image and motor skills.
Hearing impaired	Decreases the feel of isolation and enhances relationship.
Learning disability	Improves self-confidence and develop learning skills.
Mental retardation	Improves social skills, body image, and motor skills/coordination.
Autism	Enhances cognitive abilities and development of sensory-motor skills.
Physically handicapped	Improves body appearance and motor skills.
Eating disorder	Improves the distorted body image.
Parkinson's disease	Improves motor ability and balance.
Post-traumatic stress disorder	Confronts the painful memories and reduces the level of stress.
Elders with dementia/depression	Decreases the loneliness, isolation and improves social interaction.

RECREATIONAL THERAPY (OR) THERAPEUTIC RECREATION

Definitions

- Recreational therapy is a systematic process which utilizes the recreation and other activity-based interventions based on the needs of individuals with illness or disabling conditions which mean to improve the psychological/ physical health, recovery and well-being.
  —***American Therapeutic Recreation Association (ATRA)***
- Recreational therapy uses education, treatment and recreational services to help the people with disabilities recover or use their leisure in the ways which enhance their health, independence, functional abilities and quality of life.
  —***National Therapeutic Recreation Society (NTRS)***
- Recreational therapy is defined as, 'purposeful or deliberate use of intervention process aimed to help persons with disabilities or illness to improve the health, enhance their capacity to utilize recreation, use of leisure time to improve the ongoing health and quality of life.'
  —***Shank and Coyle, 2002***

History of Recreational Therapy

In 2000 BC, Egyptians used songs, dances and games for recreation for Melancholic patients (patients with depression). Florence Nightingale used the recreation therapy in the hospital for soldiers. At the time of World War I, American Red Cross used recreation therapy in hospitals. From 1920s, recreation therapy was started in the mental hospitals and schools for mentally retarded children. Recreation is a form of amusement, play and relaxation.

Benefits of Recreational Therapy

- Helps to improve physical, mental and social health.
- Reduces the effects of disabilities
- Provides cost-effective treatment
- Enhances the independent functioning of physical, social, cognitive and emotional domains
- Helps to identify and use the community resources which promote the independent functioning
- Improves the quality of life
- Promotes motor development, intellectual development and sensory development
- Aids to promote the psychological expression of thoughts/ ideas
- Reduces the level of stress, anxiety and depression.

Indications

- Psychiatric and medical disorders
- Developmental disabilities
- Rehabilitation
- Childhood disorders
- Substance abuse
- Geriatrics with cognitive deficits

Qualities of Recreational Therapist

- Leadership skills
- Listening skills
- Compassion
- Patience
- Resourcefulness
- Speaking skills

Goals of Recreational Therapy

General Goals

- Administer the structured normal activities of daily living.
- Promote the measures to bridge gap between the hospital and community.
- Assist the patients to use the leisure time suitable to the patient's lifestyle.

Goals Related to Psychological Health

- To help to augment other psychotherapies.
- To improve the memory, attention and concentration.
- To enhance the sense of responsibility by organizing and leading the game well.
- To give a chance to express oneself.
- To improve the self-esteem and self-confidence.
- To develop the psychological well-being.

Goals Related to Physical Health

- It improves muscle power and muscle strength.
- It improves the circulation.
- It stabilizes respiration.
- It increases appetite.
- It develops good posture.
- It improves the overall physical endurance.

Areas of Practice

- Psychiatric hospitals
- Day care centers
- Rehabilitation centers
- Deaddiction centers
- Community mental health centers
- Special schools

Classification of Recreational Therapy

Recreational therapy is classified based on the place of recreational activity performed and based on the benefits of recreational activity (Flowchart 5.7).

- Based on the place of recreational activity performed, it is further classified into indoor activities and outdoor activities.
  - **Examples for indoor activities** are crossword puzzle, reading, debating, carom game, chess, role play, painting, clay modeling, drawing, badminton, board games, ludo, cooking, dancing, stamp collection, etc.
  - **Examples for outdoor activities** are volleyball, hockey, football, badminton, cricket, gardening, basketball, baseball, hide and seek, etc.
- Based on the benefits of recreational activity, it is classified into motor development, sensory development,

Flowchart 5.7: Classification of recreational therapy

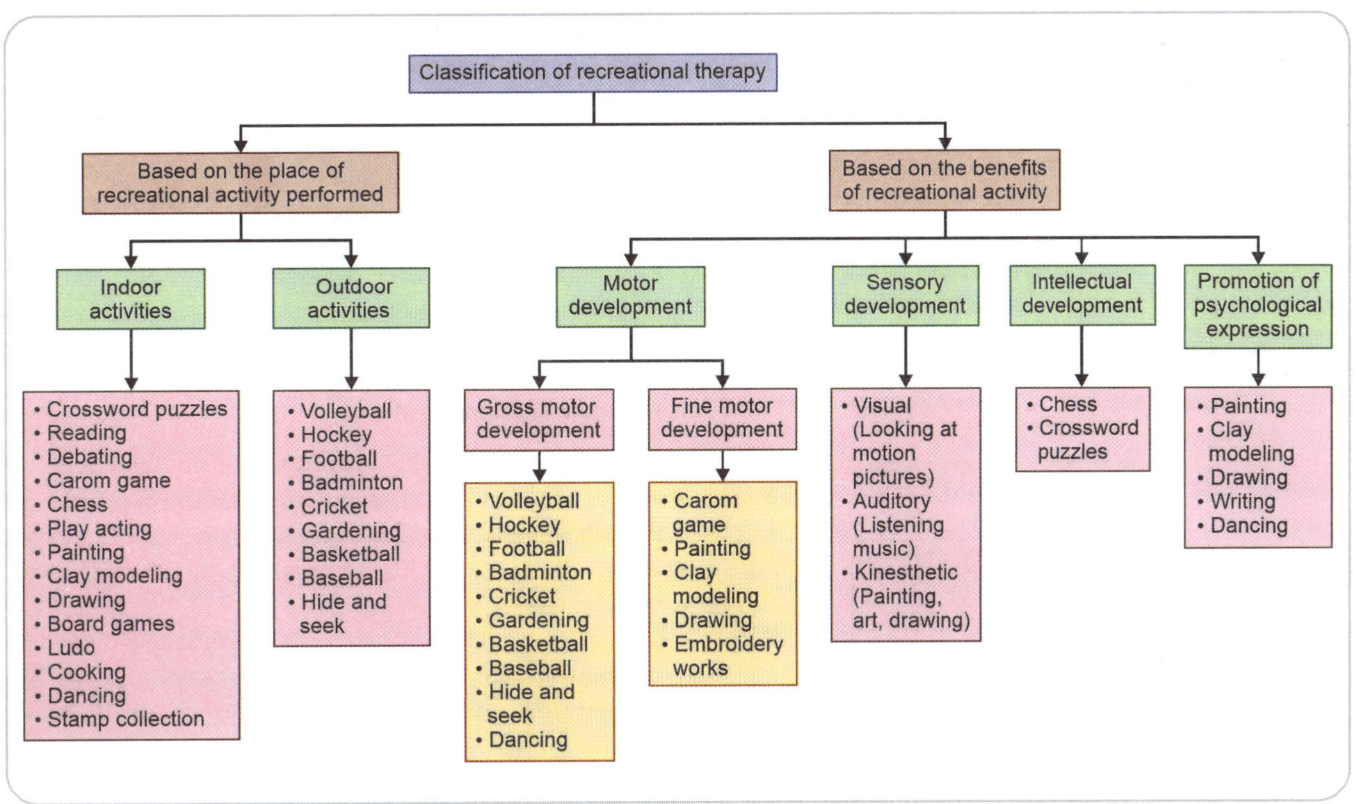

intellectual development and promotion of psychological expression. Promoting gross motor development are volleyball, hockey, football, shuttlecock, cricket, gardening, basketball, baseball, dancing, etc.

- **Activities promoting fine motor development** are carom game, painting, clay modeling, drawing, embroidery works, etc.
- **Activities promoting sensory development** are looking at motion pictures, listening music, painting, art works, drawing, etc.
- **Activities promoting intellectual development** are chess, crossword puzzles, etc.
- **Activities promoting psychological expression** are painting, clay modeling, drawing, writing, dancing, etc.

Recreational therapy is also classified as:

- **Team games:** For example, football
- **Creative play:** For example, role play
- **Curiosity play:** For example, chess
- **Vicarious play:** For example, visualizing the motion pictures
- **Social play:** For example, games in party
- **Aesthetic play:** For example, drawing
- **Acquisition play:** For example, stamp collection
- **Imitative play:** For example, performing a group dance with similar steps
- **Goal games:** For example, hide and seek.

Recreational Therapy Process

Recreational therapy is a systematic process of assessment, planning, implementation and evaluation (Flowchart 5.8). Assess the patient's interests, skills and abilities. Plan the activities according to the domain in which the improvement is required (motor, sensory, intellectual, psychological expression). Implement the recreation activities into practice. Evaluate to what extent the goal of recreational therapy has been achieved (Table 5.25).

Flowchart 5.8: Process of recreational therapy

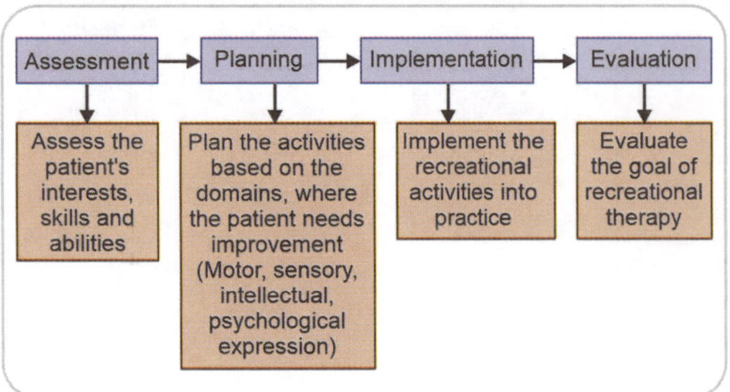

Table 5.25: Recreational activities for various psychiatric disorders

Psychiatric disorders	Recreational activities
Schizophrenia	Social activities that contact with reality. For example, carom, chess, etc.
Depression	Noncompetitive outdoor activities to outlet the anger For example, walking, jogging, etc.
Mania	Individual games on one to one basis are planned to drain out the excess energy, for example, volleyball, football, etc.
Dementia	Concrete activities have familiarization and comfort. For example, craft works, embroidery works, etc.
Anxiety disorders	Activities help to divert the patient from the anxiety provoking situations. For example, listening music, singing songs, etc.
Childhood and adolescent disorders	**Children:** Playing, painting, story telling **Adolescent:** Gross motor activities like volleyball, football, cricket, etc.

NURSES RESPONSIBILITY

Nurse has to motivate the patients to participate in the recreational activities which will help the patient to enhance self-esteem and self-confidence. She should be aware that recreational therapy empowers the patient to develop the existent skills, interests and also to develop the new roles. She has to coordinate with the recreational therapist to assess the patient's expression of interest and plan the activities accordingly. She has to create an opportunity to the patient to enhance their social skills by increasing the social interactions.

LIGHT THERAPY (OR) PHOTOTHERAPY (OR) HELIOTHERAPY

Light therapy is the use of light with the specified intensity for therapeutic purpose.

Historical Development

Ancient Egypt, Ancient Greece and Ancient Rome used the various forms of light therapy. Early Germans, Assyrian and Inca worshiped sun for the healthy living. In 1500 BC, sunlight along with the natural herbs was used to treat nonpigmented skin diseases.

Niels Finsen, a Faroese physician, is the father of modern phototherapy. He is the one to discover the first artificial light therapy. He first used the light with short wavelength to treat lupus vulgaris, 400 nanometers generated reactive oxygen that would kill the bacteria (Fig. 5.21).

Figure 5.21: **Niels Ryberg Finsen:** Father of modern light therapy

Niels Finsen used the red light to treat the small pox lesions. In late 19th century, light therapy was used in medical treatments for varicose ulcers and sick children in the UK.

Indications

- **Skin disorders**
    - Atopic dermatitis
    - Psoriasis
    - Vitiligo
    - Acne vulgaris
    - Skin cancer
    - Cutaneous t-cell lymphoma
    - Eczema
    - Polymorphous light eruption
    - Atopic dermatitis
    - Lichen planus
- **Wound healing**
- **Neonatal jaundice**
- **Bulimia nervosa**
- **Premenstrual syndrome**
- **Migraine headache**
- **Retinal conditions**
    - Diabetic macular edema
    - Diabetic retinopathy
- **Mood- and sleep-related disorders**
    - Seasonal affective disorder
    - Nonseasonal depression
    - Jetlag
    - Chronic circadian rhythm sleep disorders
    - Situational circadian rhythm sleep disorders
    - Sleep disorder in Parkinson's disease
    - Sleep disorder in Alzheimer's disease

> **NOTE**
>
> Light therapy used for skin conditions might emit ultraviolet rays that should not be used for other conditions because it might harm the eyesight.

Contraindications

- Tendency to develop mania (History of hypomania or mania)
- Photosensitive skin conditions
- Marked agitation
- Insomnia
- Eyes vulnerable to get phototoxicity
- Use of photosensitizing herb (E.g., St. John's wort)
- Patients with porphyria
- Patients taking methotrexate or chloroquine (because this drug and light interaction might cause porphyria)

Side Effects

Common Side Effects

- Headache
- Nausea
- Jitteriness
- Eye irritation
- Poor vision
- Skin rashes
- Skin irritation
- Agitation
- Irritability

Rare Side Effects

- Manic episode
- Increased suicidal thoughts

Mechanism of Action of Light Therapy

The mechanism of action of light therapy can be easily understood from Figure 5.22.

The light waves pass through the retina of the eye and activate the hypothalamus in the brain. Hypothalamus sends the signals to pineal gland. This gland suppresses the Melatonin immediately and stimulate the production of serotonin. Serotonin makes the individual to be active and energetic (Fig. 5.22).

Key Elements of Light Therapy

- **Intensity:** Light box intensity is recorded in lux. For seasonal affective disorder, 10,000 lux light box at a

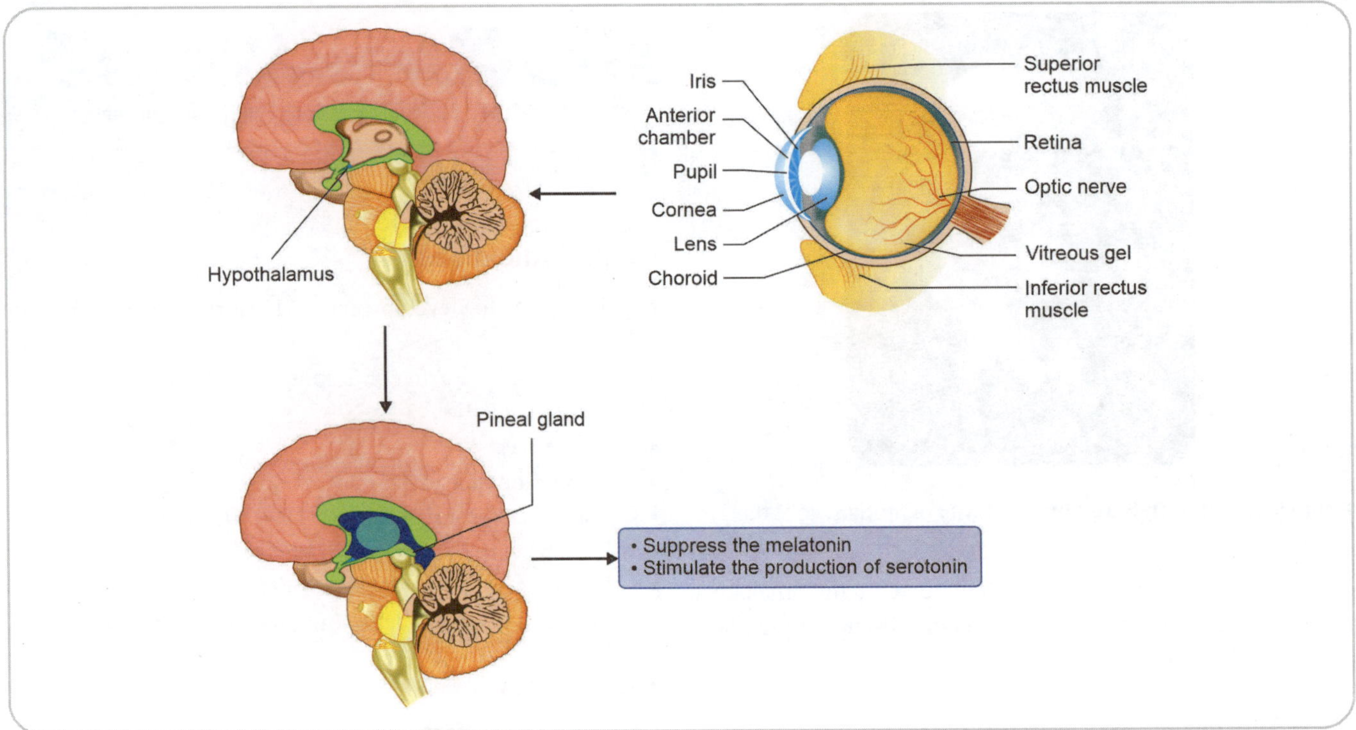

Figure 5.22: Mechanism of action of light therapy

distance of 16–24 inches (or) 41–61 centimeters from the face is recommended.

- **Duration:** Light box with 10,000 lux has to be administered for 20–30 minutes for daily sessions. Administration of lower intensity light box with 2,500 lux requires 2 hours duration in order to obtain treatment efficiency.
- **Timing:** Early in the morning after getting up from bed is the best time to administer light therapy.

Process of Light Therapy

Light box has a set of fluorescent bulbs in a box with diffusion screen. Light box has to be kept on a table at a distance of 16–24 inches. Light should not be seen directly through the eye. Patient is advised to perform regular activities inside the room such as reading, writing, eating, talking over phone, etc. The time and consistency have to be maintained regularly.

Advantages of Light Therapy

Light therapy is a cost-effective, noninvasive procedure with minimal side effects. Routine light therapy might have a quick response in some patients.

Disadvantages of Light Therapy

Patient needs to visit the health care provider regularly and commit to the time for light therapy specifically.

RELAXATION THERAPY

Historical Development

Dr Edmund Jacobson published the book *'Progressive Relaxation'* for doctors/scientists and thereby the concept of relaxation in psychology has been popularized. In 1934, Jacobson published the book called *'You Must Relax'* for general public. In 1908, Jacobson started the research at Harvard University and later proceeded to Cornell and University of Chicago. The research work was aimed to improve the human well-being. In 1932, Wolfgang Luthe and Johannes Schultz developed the method of relaxation called autogenic training. In 1975, Miriam Z Klipper and Herbert Benson published the book called *'The Relaxation Response'*, which explains the concept of integrating the meditation techniques into daily activities.

Definition

Relaxation therapy is a component of body-mind intervention in which the therapist helps the participants at the higher extent of mind relaxation.

Indications

Psychiatric Disorders

- Generalized anxiety disorder

- Post-traumatic stress disorder
- Substance abuse/smoking cessation
- Depression
- Sleep disorder
- Acute stress reaction due to (HIV)/(AIDS).

Medical Disorders

- Hypertension
- Asthma
- Migraine headache
- Chronic pain
- Side effects of chemotherapy
- Fibromyalgia
- Neurocardiogenic syndrome
- Myocardial infarction
- Angina
- Huntington's disease
- Osteoarthritis pain and rheumatoid arthritis
- Facial paralysis
- Menopausal symptoms
- Premenstrual syndrome
- Irritable bowel syndrome

Benefits of Relaxation Therapy

The benefits of relaxation therapy are given in Figure 5.23.

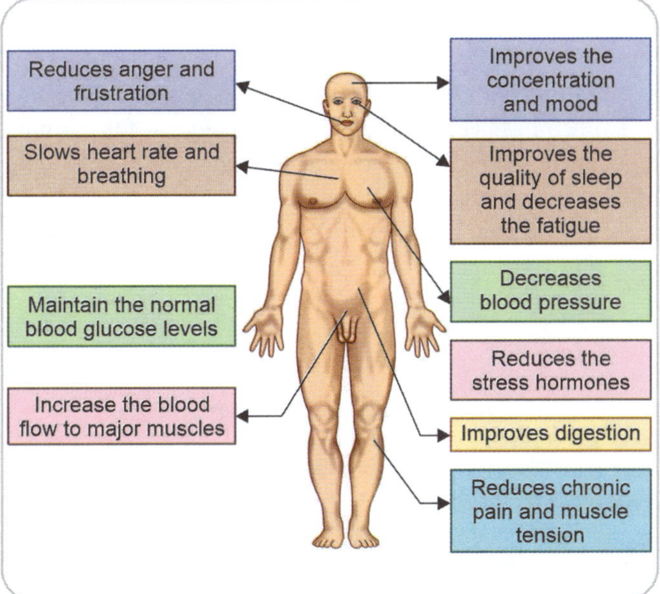

Figure 5.23: Benefits of relaxation therapy

Types of Relaxation Therapy

Autogenic Training

In 1932, Wolfgang Luthe and Johannes Schultz (German Psychiatrist) developed the method of relaxation called autogenic training. This is a relaxation therapy in which the series of self-statements about heaviness and warmth in different parts of the body helps in relaxation.

Preliminary Measures

Patient has to be seated in a calm room. Patient has to remove the watch, belt or anything that could cause constriction. Patient is advised to empty the bowel and bladder before the therapy. Patient is asked to put the cell phone in the silent mode.

Steps

1. Ask the patient to take a few slow and even breaths.
2. Ask the patient to feel that "I am completely calm".
3. Ask the patient to have attention on his/her arms and feel that his/her arms are heavy. Ask the patient to do the same for six times.
4. Ask the patient to have re-attention on his/her arms and feel that his/her arms are warm. Ask the patient to do the same for six times.
5. Ask the patient to have attention on his/her legs and feel that his/her legs are heavy. Ask the patient to do the same for six times.
6. Ask the patient to have re-attention on his/her legs and feel that his/her legs are warm. Ask the patient to do the same for six times.
7. Ask the patient to focus on his/her breathing and feel that his/her breathing is calm and regular. Ask the patient to do the same for six times.
8. Ask the patient to focus on his/her heartbeat and feel that his/her heartbeat is calm and regular. Ask the patient to do the same for six times.
9. Ask the patient to have attention on his/her abdomen and feel that his/her abdomen are calm. Ask the patient to do the same for six times.
10. Ask the patient to have attention on his/her forehead and feel that his/her forehead is cool. Ask the patient to do the same for six times.
11. Ask the patient to enjoy the feel of relaxation, heaviness and warmth. Ask the patient to quietly say to oneself that the arms are firm, breathe deeply and keep the eyes open.

Jacobson Progressive Muscle Relaxation (JPMR)

Definition

This is a relaxation therapy in which the series of guided steps about tension and relaxation of the different body parts helps in relaxation.

Preliminary Measures

Follow all the measures similar to that of autogenic training. Advise the patient not to worry about the thoughts which might arise during the therapy sessions and don't fight over the thoughts because it keeps the individual stressed instead of relaxation.

Steps

1. Clench right and left fist separately and feel the tension in fist and forearm for 5 seconds. Release the fist and feel the relaxation for 10 seconds.
2. Bend right and left arm separately at the elbow and tense the biceps for 5 seconds. Release the arms and feel the relaxation for 10 seconds.
3. Straighten the right and left arm separately and tense the triceps and feel tensing for 5 seconds. Relax and feel the relaxation for 10 seconds.
4. Wrinkle the forehead and try to make the eyebrows touch the hairline which creates tension, feel the tension for 5 seconds. Release the eyebrows and feel relaxation for 10 seconds.
5. Close your eyes and tense the muscles around the eyes for 5 seconds. Release it, relax and feel the relaxation for 10 seconds.
6. Tense the jaw by biting the teeth, feel the tension of jaw muscles for 5 seconds. Release it, relax and feel the relaxation for 10 seconds.
7. Press the tongue against roof of mouth with the lips closed and feel the tension for 5 seconds. Release it, relax and feel the relaxation for 10 seconds.
8. Push the head back as far as possible, feel the tension for 5 seconds. Bring head back to its position, relax and feel relaxation for 10 seconds.
9. Bring the head down and press the chin down on to the chest for 5 seconds. Bring the head to its position, relax and feel the relaxation for 10 seconds.
10. Tense shoulder by shrugging the shoulders up to your ears, feel the tension for 5 seconds. Release it, relax and feel relaxation for 10 seconds.
11. Take a deep breath completely, hold the breath for few seconds and exhale. Relax and feel relaxation for 10 seconds.
12. Pull in the abdomen and tense the abdominal muscle for 5 seconds. Release it, relax and feel relaxation for 10 seconds.
13. Arch the back away and feel the tension for 5 seconds. Relax it and feel relaxation for 10 seconds.
14. Tense both thigh muscles and buttocks by contracting together and feel the tension for 5 seconds. Release it, relax and feel relaxation for 10 seconds.
15. Point the toes toward the head, create the tension in calf muscles, feel tension for 5 seconds. Relax and feel the relaxation for 10 seconds.
16. Point the toes away from the head, feel the tension for 5 seconds. Relax and feel the relaxation for 10 seconds.
17. Relax the complete body for 2 minutes.
18. Keep the eyes closed and remain in the relaxed position.
19. Open the eyes and feel relaxed.

GUIDED IMAGERY OR GUIDED AFFECTIVE IMAGERY (OR) KATATHYM—IMAGINATIVE PSYCHOTHERAPY

Definition

Guided therapy is defined as, 'a form of relaxation therapy in which the therapist helps the participants in relaxation by evoking the mental images which stimulate or recreate the sensory perception of sound, sights, taste, movement, smell and touch.'

Types

Guided therapy is classified based on the ways of generating mental imagery, based on the implementation of guided imagery and based on the numbers of persons involved in the intervention (Flowchart 5.9).

- **Voluntary:** It resembles the previous sensory perception which has been recalled from the memory, for example, patient went to the beach and enjoyed in the past and now has been put into the imagination presently.
- **Involuntary:** Image which is generated from the present sensory stimulation and not from the past memory. For example, therapist shows the object and helps the patient to create the mental image out of it.

Flowchart 5.9: Guided imagery types

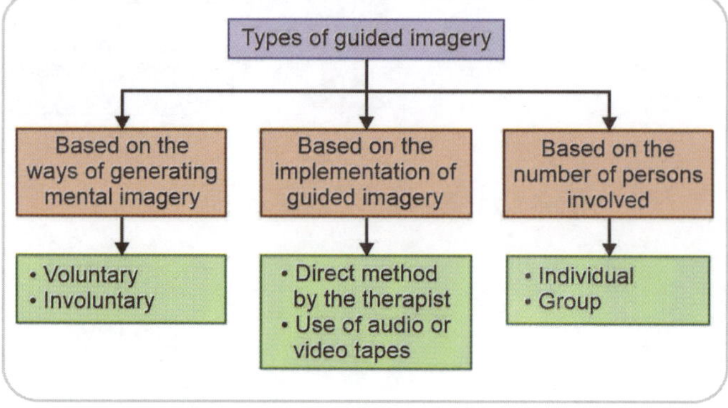

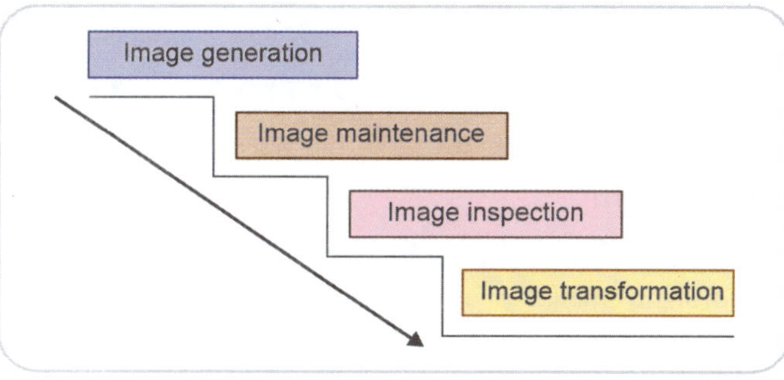

Figure 5.24: Stages of guided imagery

- **Direct method by the therapist:** Steps are guided directly by the therapist.
- **Use of audio or video tapes or recordings:** Steps have been guided with the help of audio or video recordings.
- **Individual:** Only the therapist and single participant are involved in the guided imagery intervention.
- **Group:** Therapist and the group of participants are involved in the guided imagery intervention. This group may be homogenous (with the similar psychiatric disorders) or heterogeneous group (with the different psychiatric conditions).

Stages of Guided Imagery

Stages of guided imagery are shown in Figure 5.24.

- **Image generation:** Generating the mental imagery by sensory stimulation or from past memories or from the fantasy.
- **Image maintenance:** Participant has to maintain the image clearly in mind. Few participants feel difficult to maintain the same and so it is difficult to proceed to the transformation stage. Practice to sustain the attention control that will help to maintain the image.
- **Image inspection:** The maintained image has been inspected on the basis of interpretation and transformation. Here, the participant directs the attention across the image in the perception aspects, i.e., whether the image is generated spontaneously or because of the description given by the therapist during the session.
- **Image transformation:** Finally, with the help of the guided steps from the therapist, the participant transforms the mental image to provoke positive emotion and coping ability.

MISCELLANEOUS

The other therapies which help in the relaxation are Pet therapy (animal assisted therapy), Meditation, Yoga, Bio-feedback, Physical exercises, Aquarium therapy, Occupational therapy, Massage therapy, Tai chi technique, Prayer, etc.

YOGA

'Yoga lets the people discover the sense of oneness with yourself, the world and the nature.' —*Mr Narendra Modi*

Meaning

The word Yoga came from the Sanskrit word 'Yuj' which means union or connect or balance or join, i.e., joining of Jivatma with Paramatma, joining of the individual consciousness with the consciousness of the universe.

Historical Development

Yoga began from the ancient practice of 3000 BC Stone-carved postures of yoga are seen in Indus Valley. Yoga sutras of Patanjali were created in 4th century Common Era. Yoga has become popular in abroad across various cultures and avenues these days. Patanjali Maharishi is the founder of Modern Yoga (Fig. 5.25).

Logo of International Yoga Day

Every year, June 21st is the International Yoga Day celebration. In the logo (Fig. 5.26), the union of hands denotes the joining of the individual consciousness with the consciousness in the universe. Leaves symbolize earth element and nature. Base of the logo symbolizes water element and brightness symbolizes the fire element. On a whole, this symbol denotes the harmony and peace.

Figure 5.25: Patanjali Maharishi—Founder of Modern Yoga

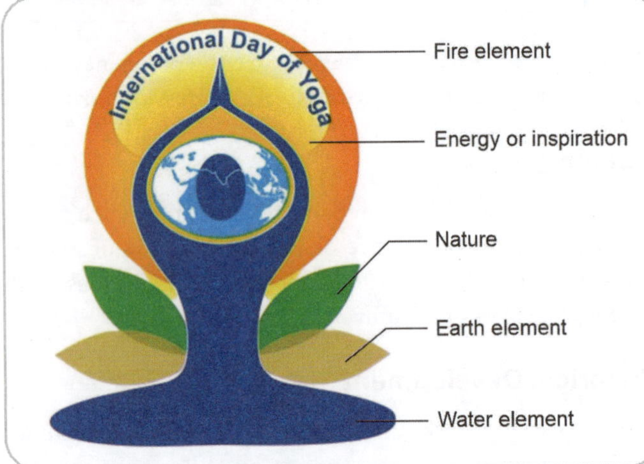

Figure 5.26: Logo of International Yoga Day

Astanga Yoga (or) Eight Limbs or Yoga (or) Eight Folds of Yoga

Patanjali Maharishi has mentioned the 8 limbs of yoga in his yoga sutras which are explained below:

1. Yama
2. Niyama
3. Asanas
4. Pranayama
5. Pratyahara
6. Dharana
7. Dhyana
8. Samadhi

1. Yama

It has five commandments of **Social Discipline**:

1. **Ahimsa:** Nonviolence
2. **Satya:** Truth
3. **Asteya:** Nonstealing
4. **Aparigraha:** Non accumulation of wealth
5. **Brahmacharya:** Celibacy or Continence

2. Niyama

It has five commandments of **Personal Discipline** such as:

1. **Saucha:** Cleanliness
2. **Santhosha:** Contentment
3. **Tapas:** Endurance to face joy or sorrow, regard or disregard
4. **Swadhyaya:** Self-study
5. **Ishwarapranidhana:** Dedication to the god and work without self-motives or not working for the praise.

3. Asanas

Body postures and poses by which **all the impurities** from the body are eliminated that keeps the body in good health.

4. Pranayama

Pranayama is the **control of vital energy** of the body through the breath.

5. Pratyahara

Pratyahara denotes the **willful control of senses** such as sound, sight, smell, touch and taste.

6. Dharana

Dharana is connecting the mind with particular object.

7. Dhyana

Dhyana is the meditation with the constant flow of thoughts or ideas.

8. Samadhi

Samadhi is super-conscious state as the highest stage of yoga in which one will enjoy the external bliss.

Obstacles to Practice Yoga

- **Vyadhi:** Illness
- **Styana:** Unpreparedness
- **Samshaya:** Doubt
- **Pramada:** Indifference
- **Alasya:** Laziness
- **Avirati:** Entanglement of sense object
- **Bhranti Darshana:** Illusion
- **Alabdha Bhumikatva:** Lack of stability
- **Anavasthitatva:** Slackness in practice

Six Branches of Yoga

1. **Hatha yoga:** The word, 'Hatha' came from Sanskrit word, in which the prefix 'Ha' denotes sun and 'Tha' suffix denotes moon. Hatha yoga is the total mastery of the mind and physical bodily functions.
2. **Raja yoga:** It denotes the eight limbs of yoga.
3. **Karma yoga:** It denotes the path of unselfish activities. Karma Yoga says, 'Do your duty and don't expect any benefits out of it.'
4. **Bhakti yoga:** It denotes the path of devotion.
5. **Jnana yoga:** It denotes the path of wisdom.
6. **Tantra yoga:** It came from the Sanskrit word, which means woven together or leading principle. Tantra's rituals encourage their followers to build up the Kundalini energy to the top of the chakras.

Kriyas

Kriya is defined as cleansing techniques used in yoga.

- **Kapalabhati:** Stimulating the brain cells.

- **Neti:** Cleaning the nasal passages.
  - **Jala Neti:** Cleaning the nasal passages by pouring the lukewarm water in one nostril and then the water comes out through opposite nostril.
  - **Sutra Neti:** Cleaning the nasal passages with rubber catheter.
  - **Dugdha Neti:** Milk and ghee is used to clean instead of lukewarm water.
  - **Vyutkrama Kapala Neti:** Similar to Jala Neti, in this the water comes out of mouth instead of opposite nostril.
  - **Sitkarma Kapala Neti:** Take water in the mouth and the water has to come through nostril.
- **Dhouti:** Cleaning the intestinal tract up to the stomach.
- **Nauli:** Control of the abdominal rectus.
- **Trataka:** Fixing the mind by gazing the flame in the candle without blinking of eyes.
- **Shankhaprakshalana kriya:** Complete bowel wash.

Surya Namaskar

Yoga consists of 12 steps which are performed at the time of sunrise by facing the sun with the regulation of breath. At every step of yoga, the forward bending is done with exhaling activity and the backward bending is done with the inhaling activity (Fig. 5.27).

1. Take the hands above the head and bend backward (Inhale).
2. Bend the body toward front and forehead has to touch the knees (Exhale).
3. Take left knee forward and right leg back, keep the left foot and the palm in same line with the heads up (Inhale).
4. Take left leg back and rest only in palm and toes (Exhale).
5. Bend at knee, abdomen at rest on the knee with the arms extended in front (Inhale and Exhale).
6. Come forward. In this position, palms, chest, forehead, knees and feet will be touching the ground and buttocks raised up (Exhale).
7. Raise the head and trunk and make spine in a concave upward position with hands/feet in the ground (Inhale).
8. Push the head down and have a complete arch with heel touching the ground and palms on floor (Exhale).
9. Same as the 5th step (Inhale and Exhale).
10. Same as the 3rd step but here bring the right leg forward instead of left leg (Inhale).
11. Same as the 2nd step (Exhale).
12. Come to stand erect posture.

Figure 5.27: Surya namaskar

Asanas

Asanas are the various forms of postures performed and maintained for few seconds to minutes along with the breathing pattern. Examples of asanas are below:

- **Padmasana:** Lotus posture
- **Dhanurasana:** Bow posture
- **Sarvangasana:** Standing on shoulders
- **Ardhakatichakrasana:** Lateral arc posture
- **Padahastasana:** Forward bend posture
- **Ardha chakrasana:** Half wheel posture
- **Trikonasana:** Triangle posture
- **Parsvakonasana:** Lateral angle posture
- **Vajrasana:** Ankle pose
- **Sasankasana:** Rabbit posture
- **Chakrasana:** Wheel posture
- **Savasana:** Corpse pose

Pranayama

Breathing practices in the yoga are termed pranayama. The types are explained below:

- **Sectional breathing** (only particular section was involved in the inhale and exhale processes)
  - Abdominal or diaphragmatic breathing
  - Thoracic breathing or intercostal breathing
  - Upper lobar breathing or clavicular breathing
- **Anuloma-viloma:** Simple inhalation and exhalation pranayama
- **Chandranuloma-viloma:** Both the inhalation and exhalation through the left nostril (Chandra Nadi)
- **Suryanuloma–viloma:** Both the inhalation and exhalation through the right nostril (Surya Nadi)
- **Surya bhedana:** Inhalation through right nostril by closing the left nostril and exhalation through the left nostril by closing the right nostril.
- **Chandra bhedana:** Inhalation through left nostril by closing the right nostril and exhalation through the right nostril by closing the left nostril.

Bandhas and Mudras

Bandhas and mudras are advanced techniques of hatha yoga. The **Yoga Mudras** are simple rituals used in Hinduism and Buddhist traditions which explain some symbolic gesture. Bandhas are safety locks used in the process of holding the breath. Mula Bandha is contraction of the perineum. Uddiyana bandha is contraction of the abdomen into the rib cage. Jalandhara Bandha means tucking the chin close to the chest. Maha Bandha is the combination all three of the above bandhas.

Yoga in Mental Health

Yoga promotes both the physical and psychological endurance. There is an association between the physical health and mental health, termed psychosomatic concept. Yoga helps in enhancing the attention, concentration, memory and overall psychological well-being. Asana gives physical flexibility so it promotes the mental flexibility. Yoga gives holistic development to an individual. Yoga cures, treats and prevents both the physical and psychological diseases. Thus, the branch of yoga is termed Therapeutic yoga that is evolving nowadays. Yoga can be practiced by any individual from children to old age in order to promote the psychological well-being.

NURSES RESPONSIBILITY

Nurse has to motivate the patient to practice the yoga regularly. She has to coordinate with the yoga therapist to conduct the regular yoga therapy sessions. She has to teach the benefits of yoga to the patient as well as to his/her family members. She has to assess the patient's needs of asana/kriya/pranayama and plan the individual session if required. Nurse has to encourage the patient to practice the yoga in home setup after the discharge.

MEDITATION

The word meditation came from the Latin word "*meditatio*", which indicates the type of physical or intellectual exercise that promotes healing.

Definition

Meditation is defined as 'an experience of relaxing the body, mind and spirit.' Meditation is defined as the process of encouraging and deepening of consciousness or awareness, and also helps in the deeper understanding of self and others.

Benefits of Meditation

- Reduces the level of stress, anxiety and depression.
- Increases the levels of energy, creativity and spontaneity.
- Decreases blood pressure
- Decreases the psychological pain
- Helpful in anger management
- Helps to relax the mind
- Improves the levels of awareness and concentration
- Improves the cognition and thinking ability
- Develops the sense of self and spirituality
- Helps to promote better relationship with others
- Promotes the satisfaction with the life and work done.

Tools Helpful to Practice Meditation

- Quiet place or sound proof room.
- Images or symbols
- Music or audio recordings
- Diary to record about the event of meditation
- Candle with light
- Straight backed chair or mat.

Preliminary Measures before Meditation

The individual has to be seated in the calm room. The constrictive things such as rings, watch, belt, etc. has to be removed. Avoid any distractions such as cellphone sounds, etc. Ask the individual to empty the bowel and bladder. Individual is instructed not to fight with the arising thoughts during the meditation and also instruct to ignore the thoughts.

Types of Meditation

- **Mindfulness meditation (or) breathing meditation:** Meditation is performed by focusing on the breathing (Inhale and Exhale). The breathing has to be slow and deep.
- **Metta meditation (or) loving-kindness meditation:** The concept of Meditation from Theravada Buddhism. Meditation is performed by directing the love and kindness toward the self or other friend or universe.
- **Chakra meditation:** Meditation is performed by focusing on the various chakras in the body. Chakras are the wheels of energy which bundle the nerve roots and organs (Fig. 5.28).
- **Object meditation (or) gazing meditation:** Meditation is done by concentrating on an object or symbol.

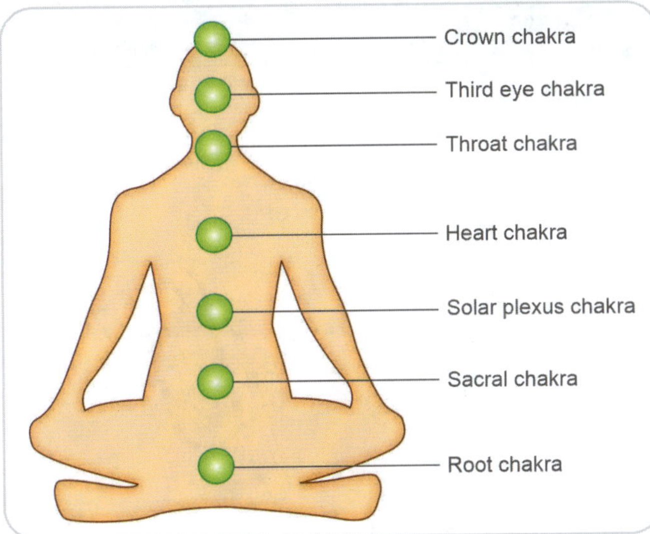

Figure 5.28: Chakra meditation

- **Mantra meditation:** Meditation is performed with the help of mantras such as om, ham, yam, rama, etc.
- **Transcendental meditation:** It is the technique developed by Maharishi Mahesh Yogi. It is a silent mantra meditation performed for 20 minutes.
- **Nada yoga (or) sound meditation:** Meditation is performed with the concentration of sound.
- **Third eye meditation:** Meditation is performed with the concentration of third eye, i.e., forehead, a place between the eyebrows.
- **Taoist emptiness meditation:** Meditation evolved from the Chinese traditional concept in which the negative thoughts, feelings and sensations are to let go out of the body.
- **Meditation with self-inquiry:** Meditation evolved from the Sanskrit concept 'atma viricha,' i.e., investigation is done by exploring the self and answering the questions, 'Who am I?' 'Why am I getting this thought?' 'Why am I feeling like this?'
- **Kundalini meditation:** A concept of meditation in which the energy that has been bundled up in the base of spine will get into the crown by practicing deeper concentration of breathing.

NURSES RESPONSIBILITY

Nurse has to instruct the preliminary measures before the commencement of meditation. She has to select the type of meditation according to the ability and need of the patient. She has to instruct the patient to do the meditation regularly in order to get the fruitful outcome and also instruct that, only regular practice will ensure the psychological well-being. She has to teach the benefits of meditation to the patient as well as to his/her family members. Involve the family members to perform the meditation along with the patient which will be helpful for the entire family to practice in their home after the discharge.

BIOFEEDBACK

Historical Development

Biofeedback is the concept known thousands of years ago. In 1865, scientific evidences for these concepts arose with the research conducted by Claude Bernard, who was the first to introduce the concept of homeostasis. In 1885, J R Tarchanoff demonstrated that voluntary control of heart rate is possible. In 1969, Biofeedback Research Society was formed by Barbara Brown and now it is known today as the Association for Applied Psychophysiology and Biofeedback. Presently, many research activities on Biofeedback is on process.

Definition

Biofeedback is defined as, 'psychophysiological therapy in which the individual is able to monitor the physiological changes in the body which happened due to the psychological stressors.'

Purposes

- To improve the self-regulation and self-monitoring skills to enhance the well-being.
- To be aware about one's own physiological responses due to stress.
- To control the bodily functions or control over the health.
- To improve the benefits of medications and to avoid the medications.

Indications

Psychiatric Disorders

- Generalized anxiety disorder
- Post-traumatic stress disorder
- Substance abuse
- Depression
- Sleep disorder
- Eating disorder
- Attention deficit hyperactive disorder
- Bruxism

Medical Disorders

- Hypertension
- Asthma
- Migraine headache
- Chronic pain
- Side effects of chemotherapy
- Fecal incontinence
- Urinary incontinence
- Fibromyalgia
- Stroke
- Raynaud's disease
- Irritable bowel syndrome
- Constipation
- Temporomandibular joint disorder

Types of Biofeedback Based on the Monitoring of Physiological Functions

Types of biofeedback are given in Flowchart 5.10.

- **Brain waves:** Sensors attached in the scalp with electroencephalogram (EEG) help to monitor the brain waves. This type is used in patients with seizure and attention deficit hyperactive disorder.
- **Breathing:** Bands attached in the chest and abdomen help to monitor the respiratory rate. This type is used in patients with asthma and Chronic Obstructive Pulmonary Disease (COPD).
- **Heart rate:** Sensors attached in the chest with electrocardiogram (ECG) help to monitor the heart rate. This helps to assess irregular heartbeats (Fig. 5.29).
- **Sweat gland activity (or) galvanic skin response:** Sensors attached in the fingers of the palm with the electrodermogram (EDG) help to monitor the sweat gland activity. It is used to assess the level of anxiety and increased sweat due to any physiological changes.
- **Temperature:** Sensors attached in the fingers of the hand help to monitor the blood flow to the skin and thereby surface body temperature can be assessed. This type is used in patients with headache and Raynaud's disease.
- **Muscle contraction:** Sensors attached in the skeletal muscles with the electromyograph (EMG) help to monitor the muscle contraction. This type is used in patients with anxiety disorders, headache, back pain, incontinence and muscle retraining after the injury.

Flowchart 5.10: Types of biofeedback

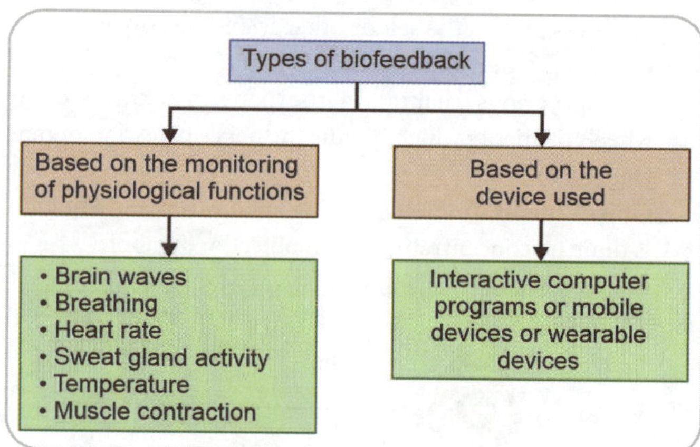

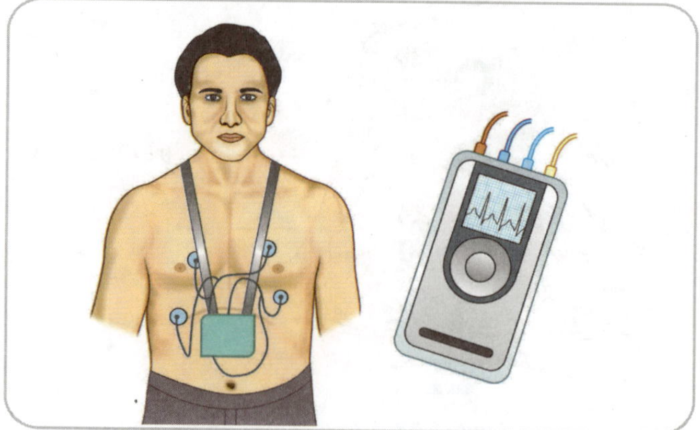

Figure 5.29: Monitoring heart rate

Types of Biofeedback Based on the Devices Used

Interactive computer programs or mobile devices or wearable devices—Band is worn on the wrist, if the individual is tensed, then the application in the mobile phone will send the alert message stating the prolonged tension by tracking out the heart rate, breathing pattern, etc.

Phases of Biofeedback Therapy

Phases of biofeedback therapy is illustrated in Figure 5.30.

- **Initial evaluation:** The patient's psychophysiological profile in response to the moderate stressor is evaluated.
- **Skills training:** Training is provided to learn the readings of biofeedback machine which will ensure the greater control.
- **Therapy:** Biofeedback assisted psychotherapy is the focus in which the emotional change in respect to the sympathetic nervous system is taught. Here, the individual puts oneself into the relaxed state and asks oneself to watch the readings in the biofeedback machine. So, the individual will realize and keep oneself relaxed with the help of biofeedback machine.

Course of Treatment

There are 8–15 sessions and might extend up to 40 or 50 sessions biweekly or monthly or on weekly intervals.

Limitations of the Biofeedback

Using the Biofeedback is difficult for the individuals who have cognitive impairment. Some might feel apprehensive regarding the usage of electrodes and may be unfamiliar with the use of mechanical devices. Poor contact between the sensor/electrodes and skin might show the false readings. Patients who would need to claim insurance for the treatment process might not get coverage of expenses.

NURSES RESPONSIBILITY

Nurse has to assess the need of biofeedback therapy. She has to coordinate with the psychotherapist if the patient requires biofeedback. She has to teach the patient in regard with the usage of biofeedback machine and the way to monitor the readings. She has to follow-up the patient and plan the further therapy sessions that depend on the patient's needs. She has to monitor the level of patient's progress after few sessions. She has to encourage the patient to follow this in the home setup, after the discharge from the hospital.

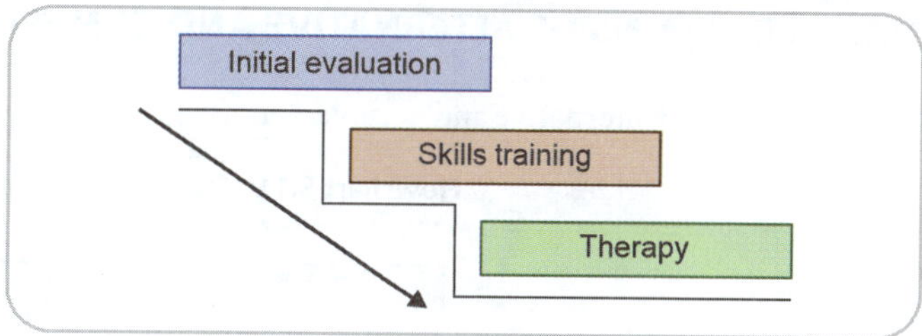

Figure 5.30: Phases of biofeedback therapy

ALTERNATIVE AND COMPLEMENTARY MEDICINE

HISTORY

National Center for Complementary and Alternative Medicine (NCCAM) at National Institute of Health was formed in 1992 to value the alternative and complementary treatment methods.

DEFINITION

Alternative and complementary medicine is defined as, 'a group of diverse medical/health care systems, practices and products that are not presently considered to be a part of conventional medicine.'

—***National Center for Complementary and Alternative Medicine (NCCAM), 2002***

The terms complementary medicine, alternative medicine and integrative medicine are used interchangeably but the exact difference and meaning are as follows:

- **Complementary medicine:** It is a nonmainstream practice used **along with** conventional medicine.
- **Alternative medicine:** It is a nonmainstream practice used **instead of** conventional medicine.
- **Integrative medicine:** Uses both the nonmainstream and conventional medicine appropriately and depends on the patient's need and also focuses on holistic health of an individual.

PRINCIPLES OF ALTERNATIVE AND COMPLEMENTARY MEDICINE

Eliopoulos (1999) explored the five basic principles of alternative and complementary medicine:

1. Body has ability to clean itself.
2. Healing practices are individual centric.
3. Health and healing are related to harmony of body and spirit.
4. Good health practices develop the good healing process.
5. People are responsible for their own healing.

MAJOR DOMAINS OF ALTERNATIVE AND COMPLEMENTARY MEDICINE

Major domains of alternative and complementary medicine have been illustrated in Flowchart 5.11.

Flowchart 5.11: Domains of alternative and complementary medicine

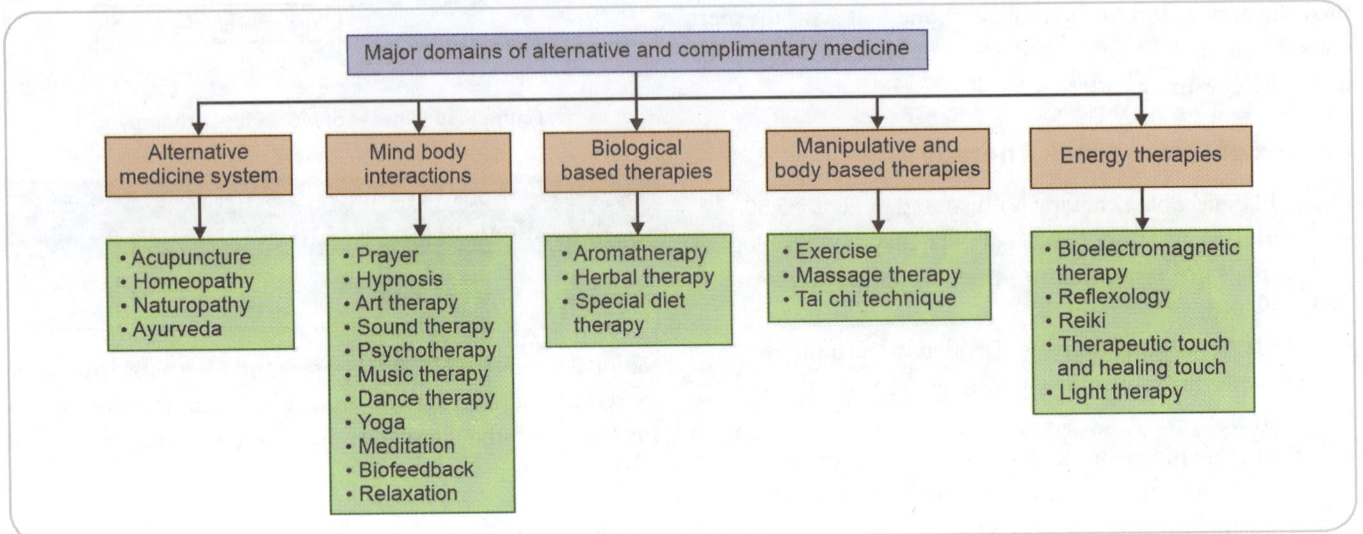

Alternative Medicine System

Acupuncture

Acupuncture is an ancient traditional Chinese medicine that works on the principle of stimulating the points in the body in order to correct the imbalance in energy flow (Qi) through the channels known as meridians. Interaction of five elements such as wood, fire, earth, metal and water have profound effects on internal organs either yin or yang.

Five elements represent five emotions such as:

1. **Fire:** Happiness
2. **Water:** Fear
3. **Wood:** Anger
4. **Earth:** Worry
5. **Metal:** Grief

In the treatment process, acupuncture needles are inserted in acupoints in the skin and left for 20 minutes on average. The benefits of acupuncture include the following:

- It improves the microcirculation
- It relaxes the muscle
- It activates B and T lymphocytes
- It releases encephalin, endorphin, serotonin and adrenocorticotropic hormone
- It improves the complete blood count

Acupuncture helps to reduce the mild level of anxiety by relaxing the muscle. Acupuncture helps to reduce mild level of depression by increasing the serotonin. Modern acupuncture treatment is also useful in treating alcoholism/smoking addiction and eating disorders.

Ayurveda

The word, 'Ayurveda' is a Sanskrit word which means, 'science of life and longevity.' Ayurvedic medicine has a belief that life force is called prana which moves through chakras. Chakras are considered centers of energy in the body. Seven major chakras are present from the head to torso.

Ayurveda recommends the three types of treatment for the mental disorders such as:

1. **Daiva Vyapashraya Chikitsa:** Divine or spiritual therapy (measures like mantras, wearing gems, oblations, vows, prostrations, pilgrimage, etc.)
2. **Yuktivyapashraya Chikitsa: (Logical Therapy):** It denotes usage of ahara (diet) and oushadha (drugs).
   - Ayurvedic diet recommended for psychiatric disorders are milk, ghee, grapes, jack fruit, buffalo meat, cuckoo meat, wood apple, etc.
   - Ayurvedic medicines for psychiatric disorders are brahmi ghrita, panchagavya ghrita, kalyanaka ghrita, ashwagandharishta, brahmyadiyoga, brahmi, tagara, bala, etc.
   - Treatment process includes nasal instillation, enema, purgation, streaming of medicated oil or milk in forehead, application of medicated wet cake in head, etc.
3. **Satvavajaya Chikitsa:** Psychotherapy—this is best achieved by gaining knowledge, memory, courage, analytical thinking and concentration.

Naturopathy

In 1985, the term, 'Naturopathy' was coined by Dr John Scheel and in 20th century, it was formalized by Benedict Lust. Naturopathy is the way of life in which body innately knows to maintain the health and heal oneself. Promotion of health is done by high fiber and low red meat diet pattern. Hope, faith and beliefs are vital in treatment. Hospitalization and usage of drugs are rarely done.

Homeopathy

In 18th century, homeopathy treatment was founded by Dr Samuel Hahnemann. The term homeopathy came from Greek word 'homios' means 'like' and pathos means 'suffering.' Hence, Homeopathy means to 'treat like with like.' It means substance which causes symptoms of disease in healthy individual may, in minute doses, also used to cure the similar symptoms resulting from the disease. It augments the individual's own immune system.

The commonly used homeopathic remedies for anxiety disorder are Aconitum napellus, Cantharis vesicatoria, Gelsemium sempervirens, Ignatia amara, Lycopodium and Spongia tosta.

The commonly used homeopathic remedies for depression are Ignatia amara, China officinalis and Bryonia alba.

Mind-Body Interactions

This domain focuses on the capacity of mind which affects the bodily functions (psychosomatic functions).

Spiritual Healing and Prayer

In 19th century, religion and spirituality have been separated from healing profession. But, later the positive aspects of spirituality in health care were accepted. Patients were asked to use their own songs, poems and inspirational stories with the below segments such as:

- Counting the blessings and saying thanks to the God.
- Requesting the love and protection.
- Requesting to forgive the self and others for the committed mistakes.
- Requesting the needs for self and others.

Hypnosis

Hypnosis is a trance like state in which the patient has been put in a heightened focus and concentration. It is useful to reduce the pain due to cancer, burns, irritable bowel syndrome, childbirth, temporomandibular joint problems, fibromyalgia, dental procedures and headache. It is also useful for the mental disorders such as phobia, anxiety, post-traumatic stress disorder. Hypnosis is also useful to treat some behavioral problems such as bed-wetting, insomnia, over-eating and smoking.

Art Therapy

- Art therapy is defined as 'a form of psychotherapy which uses the art media as a primary mode of expression and communication.' —***British Association of Art Therapists***
- Art therapy promotes the healing process and mental well-being through the expression and psychotherapeutic relationship between the therapist and patient. Art therapy is useful for chronic depression, bipolar disorders, anxiety disorders, dementia, autism, schizophrenia, eating disorders, etc.

Sound Therapy or Vibrational Medicine

Ancient technique in which the sounds of objects such as bell rings, tuning forks, gongs, chants and drum beats have been used to promote vibration in the body and thereby promote the healing process. Vibrations of the human voices are also done.

Psychotherapy, Music therapy, Dance therapy, Yoga, Meditation, Biofeedback and Relaxation: Discussed earlier in this chapter.

Biological Based Therapies

Aromatherapy

In 1937, the term 'Aromatherapy' was first coined by Rene-Maurice Gattefosse (french chemist). It is the use of plant oil for the therapeutic purposes such as antimicrobial, analgesics and psychological effects.

The mode of application of aromatherapy are as follows:

- **Direct inhalation:** Used for respiratory infections, decongestant and for psychological effects.
- **Aerial diffusion:** Fragrance the environment.
- **Topical application:** Used for therapeutic skin care, massage and baths.

Aromatherapy helps to decrease the level of stress and anxiety. It is also helpful for cognitive disorders, insomnia, musculoskeletal disorders and gastrointestinal disorders. In psychotherapy, olfactory stimulation is used to elicit the emotions and memories.

Examples of some aromatherapy oils are rose absolute, sweet almond oil, eucalyptus oil, grapefruit oil, rosewater, chamomile infusion, etc.

- Ylang-ylang, clary sage and chamomile reduces insomnia
- Geranium and helichrysum, lavender and rosemary reduce the depression.
- Bergamot, neroli, jasmine, and orange oil help to reduce anger.

- Bergamot, grapefruit oils and clary sage reduce fear.
- Clary sage, bergamot and patchouli reduce anxiety.
- Peppermint and cypress improve memory and concentration.

Safety Alert

Some essential oils might be affected with the herbicides. Eucalyptus is a commonly used oil which is highly toxic when taken internally. Intake of sage, thuja, cedar oils and hyssop might cause hepatic damage and seizures. Some oils may have interactions with conventional medicine. For example, topical usage of methyl salicylate-heavy oils such as wintergreen and sweet birch might cause hemorrhage in individuals taking the Tab warfarin (anticoagulant).

Herbal Therapy

Treating the diseases with the use of herbs is herbal therapy. The commonly used herbs to treat the psychiatric disorders are St. John's wort, Rosemary, Kava Kava, Ginkgo biloba, Valerian, SAMe (S-adenosylmethionine), Passion flower, Guarana and 5-Hydroxytryptophan (5-HTP).

The herbs used in therapy have been summarized in Table 5.26. The benefits and actions have been discussed along with precautions.

Special Diet Therapy

N-Acetyl Cysteine (NAC), an amino acid, is useful to treat individuals with depression, schizophrenia and bipolar disorders. Diet rich in Omega 3 fatty acids like small fish reduces the level of depression. Foods such as walnuts, bananas, pineapples, nut butters and avocados increase the dopamine and serotonin. So, these foods create happy mood. Foods rich in probiotics such as yogurt, kimchi, pickles, sauerkraut, tempeh, kefler, etc. reduce the social anxiety. Foods rich in vitamin B_{12} such as beef, chicken liver, sardines, salmon, trout, tuna, turkey and lamb increase the neurotransmitter signals.

Eating too much of simple sugars or carbohydrates might reduce the level of serotonin and thereby it causes depression, anxiety and insomnia. Eating the complex carbohydrates such as vegetables, peas, whole grains and beans will increase the level of serotonin and thereby cause mood elevation. Intake of tryptophan (precursor of serotonin) containing foods such as

Table 5.26: Herbal therapy: Benefits, actions and precautions

Herbs	Benefits	Action and precautions
St. John's wort	Treats mild to moderate depression, anxiety, chronic fatigue, immune dysfunction syndrome and anorexia	Hypericin in the leaves and flower is an active ingredient. Don't use the St. John's wort with antiretroviral drugs, psychotropics such as SSRI, MAOIs, tricyclic antidepressants, etc. in order to prevent the herb-drug interactions
Rosemary	Enhances memory and treat dementia. It is an antioxidant, sedative, stabilizes nerve impulse and reduces headache	Acetylcholinesterase Inhibitors
Kava Kava	Decreases the depression, stress and insomnia	It has soothing effect on amygdala of brain. It should not be used with sedatives, tranquilizers and alcohol. Long term usage might lead to dry and scaly skin
Ginkgo biloba	Decreases short term memory loss in elders and increases peripheral circulation	It is an antioxidant. Caution to use with blood thinning agents (aspirin).
Valerian	Decreases anxiety and insomnia	It has sedative and antianxiety effect. It should not be taken with other sedatives, tranquilizers and alcohol due to drug interactions.
SAMe (S-adenosylmethionine)	Treats mild to moderate depression, fibromyalgia and arthritis	Regulates the action of serotonin and dopamine. It should not to be used for bipolar disorder. Folic acid and vitamin B_{12} supplements along with this herb is beneficial
Passion flower	Treats insomnia, nervousness, agitation and restlessness. It causes mild hypnosis.	Central nervous system (CNS) depressant
Guarana	Enhances memory and reduces fatigue	CNS stimulant
5-Hydroxytryptophan (5-HTP) taken from Griffonia simplicifolia seed	It is used to treat depression, insomnia and bipolar disorders.	5-HTP is amino acid considered precursor of serotonin. This can be given along with drug lithium for patients with bipolar disorder.

cottage cheese, tuna, turkey, cashews, salmon (wild), halibut, oatmeal flakes, shrimp, pork, wheat germ, avocado, eggs, spinach, collards, raisins, chicken, yogurt and sweet potato increase the level of serotonin.

Manipulative and Body-Based Methods

Exercise

Physical exercises increase the endorphins and encephalins in the brain. They help to reduce the level of stress, anxiety and depression.

Massage Therapy

Body tissues, superficial and deeper layer of muscle/connective tissue are manipulated to enhance the wellness in massage therapy. It helps to reduce the pain, stress, depression, blood pressure and fatigue. It promotes relaxation, healing process, well-being and immunity.

Tai-chi

The term, 'Tai-chi' denotes 'moving meditation' which consists of series of continuous slow movements along with the mind and breath coordination. Performing this Tai-chi helps the patients to connect the universal (above) energy and the earth (below) energy, thereby it balances the energies inside the body in an equilibrium state. Tai-chi helps to enhance the self-awareness, reduces the stress, improves sleep, enhances socialization, decreases pain and thereby increases the overall quality of life.

Energy Therapies

Bioelectromagnetic Therapy

Bioelectromagnetic therapy is the usage of electromagnetic fields (usage of magnets and electric currents) in the body for a therapeutic purpose. **Example:** Usage of electromagnetic fields to enhance the healing effects of non-uniting bone fracture. Bioelectromagnetic therapy has two methods:

1. **Static method:** Placing of magnets in shoe inserts, belts and mattresses for 2 hours, extending up to 24 hours.
2. **Pulse method:** Machine is used to direct the alternating electromagnetic fields.

Therapeutic Touch and Healing Touch

Therapist will direct the energy flow consciously and intentionally through the hands of the therapist to the patient in order to promote the healing process. This will reduce stress, depression, anxiety, pain, grief. This improves relaxation, wound healing, psychological wellness, etc.

Reiki

Reiki is an ancient, Buddhist healing method rediscovered by Japanese and developed by Tibetans. The term, Reiki is a Japanese word which means, 'Universal life force'. The purpose of Reiki is direct access to universal, transcendental, radiant and light energies at various levels on energy spectrum. Four upper chakras are accessed to get energy for harmony, strength and balance in order to promote healing process. Reiki helps to reduce the stress, recover from illness or injury and decreases the pain.

Reflexology

Dr William Fitzgerald is pioneer of modern reflexology. Reflexology is also called 'Zone therapy.' It consists of massaging the specific areas of hands or feet in order to reduce stress, pain and illness in the corresponding related area in the body. It creates the physiologic changes and thereby promotes the overall wellness.

NURSING RESPONSIBILITY

Nurse should understand the importance of **Complementary** and **Alternative medicines** in the field of psychiatry. She has to assess the needs of the patient and should plan the complementary therapy which is best suited for the particular patient. She has to coordinate with complementary therapy physicians to plan and execute the therapy successfully. She has to follow-up the patient regularly and also motivate the patient to practice these therapies in home settings too after the hospital discharge. She has to teach the patient to report the adverse effects at the earliest stage itself in order to prevent the complications.

OCCUPATIONAL THERAPY

DEFINITIONS

- Occupational therapy is defined as, 'application of goal-oriented and purposeful activity for the assessment and treatment of patients with physical, psychological and developmental disabilities.
- Occupational therapy is defined as, 'therapeutic use of work, play activities, self-care to enhance the development and to prevent disability. It might also include the task adaptation to obtain the maximum level of independence and to improve the quality of life.'

  —*American Occupational Therapy Association*
- Occupational therapy is defined as, 'a goal-directed use of time, interest, energy, attention to get adaptation as well as productivity; to decrease the pathology and to enhance the health status.' —*Kaplan and Sadock*

AIMS OF OCCUPATIONAL THERAPY

The overall aim is to enhance the level of functioning and gain independence. It helps in promoting the recovery of the patients very soon. It reduces the hospital stay. It increases the good habits by involving in the work during leisure time. It helps the client to gain self-confidence and improve the self-esteem. It acts as diversional technique to come out of stress or depression.

PRINCIPLES OF OCCUPATIONAL THERAPY

- Activities have to be selected for the patients based on their interest, intelligence, strength and abilities.
- Positive reinforcement for the achievement of small task is so vital.
- Select the task which gives a new experience to the patient and also it would be useful to perform daily activities.
- Selection of activities for the shorter duration might provoke the sense of accomplishment and promote the self-confidence in patients.
- Utilization of available resources is important to plan and perform the activities.

BASIC ELEMENTS OF PSYCHIATRIC OCCUPATIONAL THERAPY

- **Patient:** Individual who is seeking help.
- **Therapist:** Individual who is rendering or providing help.
- **Purposeful activity:** Occupational therapy activities.
- **Context:** Place where the helping process takes place.

INDICATIONS

- Schizophrenia—paranoid and catatonic
- Substance abuse
- Mood disorders—mania and depression
- Anxiety disorders
- Dementia
- Antisocial personality disorders
- Childhood psychiatric disorders
- Indication for occupational therapy activities are given in Table 5.27.

SETTINGS OF OCCUPATIONAL THERAPY

- Psychiatric hospitals
- Nursing home
- Special schools
- Rehabilitation centers
- Sheltered workshops
- Half-way homes (or) day care centers
- Group homes
- De-addiction centers
- Community mental health centers
- Industrial health centers

OCCUPATIONAL THERAPY ACTIVITIES

Task Activities (or) Activities Enhancing Skills

- Crafts
- Wood works
- Book binding

Table 5.27: Occupational therapy activities for the specific psychiatric disorders

Disease condition	Description of occupational therapy activities	Example
Manic disorders	Activities are planned to get rid of excess energy and promote emotional expression	**Games:** Football/Volleyball
Depressive disorders	Simple tasks which are achievable	Craft works
Paranoid schizophrenia	Tasks which are noncompetitive and meaningful which require concentration	Crossword puzzles
Catatonic schizophrenia	Simple concrete tasks that involve the clients actively	Molding clay
Anti-social personality disorder	Activities which are expressive and creative, one that promotes self-esteem	Painting or art works
Dementia	Group tasks that promote the sense of belongingness	Cover making and packing things as a group task
Childhood psychiatric disorders	Activities can be allotted according to the ability of the children and also as per the interest of the children. The child with Mental retardation are not provided with the competitive nature of tasks because they can provoke anxiety among them.	Drawing, painting, storytelling, playing, etc. **For mental retardation children:** Candle making, cover making, etc.
Anxiety disorders	Simple tasks which have only few steps to perform	Washing clothes

- Chalk making
- Painting
- Mat weaving
- Tailoring
- Operating computer
- Gardening (or) horticulture
- Industrial works
- Candle making
- Leather works
- Sewing
- Ceramic works
- Clay work
- Plastic molding
- Printing
- Baking cakes
- Bamboo making
- Domestic skills
- Basket making
- Carpentry
- Collage

Activities Enhancing Fine Motor Skills

- Drawing
- Embroidery
- Typing

Activities Enhancing the Cognition/Memory

- Poetry
- Newspaper reading
- Discussion
- Puzzles solving

Activities Involving the Communication/Sharing (or) Social Skills

- Drama
- Social skills training
- Assertiveness training
- Activities of daily living
- Recreational activities

CLASSIFICATION OF OCCUPATIONAL THERAPY

- **Diversional:** Activities are planned as diversional techniques aimed to reduce the level of stress and to promote relaxation. For example, recreational activities, drama, poetry, etc.
- **Remedial:** Activities are planned to get a remedy or solution to a problem. For example, embroidery and drawing are activities planned to improve fine motor skills in patients.

SERVICES GIVEN IN OCCUPATIONAL THERAPY

- **Independent living skills (or) self-care:** Patients with the psychiatric disorders might have poor personal hygiene and self-care. Establishing the good habits such as personal hygiene, grooming, etc. has to be done. Psychoeducation is also helpful to develop the independent living skills.
- **Creative or expressive modalities:** Treatment based activities such as craft making, art therapy, drawing, and painting might help the patient to express the unconscious motives and also improve the fine motor skills.
- **Sensorimotor including sensory-integrative and neuromuscular treatment:** Activities such as horticulture, domestic skills, industrial works, leather works, etc. will improve the sensory and motor function together.
- **Miscellaneous:** Therapeutic exercise to improve the functional ability, design and fabrication of orthotic devices, adaptation to the physical environment, planning for discharge and re-entry to community, counseling and education, pre-vocational training, adjustment with employment/home setting, etc.

OCCUPATIONAL THERAPY PROCESS

Occupational therapy process has been illustrated in Figure 5.31.

Selecting a Model

Occupational therapy is a continuous process, in which choosing a right model will help to obtain the good outcome.

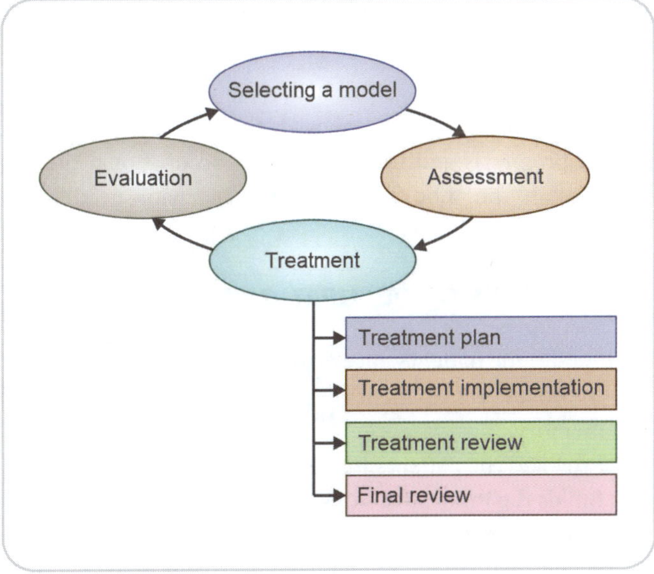

Figure 5.31: Process of occupational therapy

There are many factors which influence the selection of model and we can also use more than a single model in a single setting. The commonly used models are listed below:

- **Adaptive performance model:** Focus on the activation of ego-adaptive skills.
- **Neurobehavioral model:** Focus on sensory motor integration, cognitive orientation, social skills and body integration with the environment.
- **Occupational behavioral model:** Focus on personality development, problem solving, motivation, achievement and social role play.

Assessment

- **Initial assessment:** Identify the major problems in the patient and check out whether the occupational therapy will be helpful for this patient or not.
- **Detailed assessment:** Exploring the strength, needs, interests, short term/intermediate/long term goals, etc.

The basic five methods used in the assessment process are listed below:

1. Specific observation
2. Interview
3. Standardized test
4. Self-rating method
5. Projective tests

Treatment

Occupational therapist needs to plan the activities based on the client's needs and interest. Planned activities need to be executed. Patient's progress needs to be monitored continuously. Treatment reviews should be done, if the required treatment plan has to be modified.

Evaluation

Final treatment review takes place in the evaluation. Patient prognosis and influence of the occupational therapy activities in the modification of the behavior need to be monitored.

ADVANTAGES OF OCCUPATIONAL THERAPY

- Guides the patient's energy toward the work.
- Improves the patient's attention, concentration and memory.
- Provokes the patient's interest.
- Builds the innovative skills.
- Promotes the self-confidence and self-esteem.
- Helps the patient to perform the daily activities after discharge from hospital.
- Develops the positive attitude in patient.
- Improves the decision making ability in the client.
- Reduces the level of stress, anxiety and depression.
- Improves the social skills and learning capacity.

NURSES RESPONSIBILITY

Nurse has to be aware of the specific activities assigned to the patient. She has to coordinate with the occupational therapy department in regard with the treatment process and follow-up. Nurse has to motivate the patient to complete the task successfully. She has to assign the activities as per the interests and needs of the patient by coordinating with occupational therapist. She has to help the client in performing the occupational therapy activities if required. She has to monitor the prognosis of the patient and treatment plan. The Therapeutic process can be modified along with the occupational therapist if required. She has to ensure the patient's safety while the patient is involved in the industrial works or using sharp objects, etc. She has to coordinate with the social worker in order to get employment opportunities for the patient after the discharge.

ELECTROCONVULSIVE THERAPY

HISTORICAL BACKGROUND

- **Initial—20th century**
  - Assumptions that schizophrenia and epilepsy will not occur together.
  - So, artificial induction of convulsion is used for treatment of schizophrenia.
- **Ladislas Meduna (1896–1964)**
  - Pioneer of convulsive treatment.
  - He induced seizure with camphor IM and Metrazol IV.
  - Ugo Cerletti, an Italian Neurologist, discovered the method of electroconvulsive therapy that is used in Psychiatry. Lucino Bini assisted Ugo Cerletti in the discovery of electroconvulsive therapy (ECT).

DEFINITION

Convulsions are induced by passing a brief pulse of electric current through brain *via* electrodes for a therapeutic purpose.

CLASSIFICATION OF ELECTROCONVULSIVE THERAPY

The ECT can be classified depending on the treatment involved and thus has been given in Flowchart 5.12.

- ECT is given in the absence of muscle relaxant and general anesthesia is termed 'Direct ECT' or 'Unmodified ECT'.

Flowchart 5.12: Classification of electroconvulsive therapy

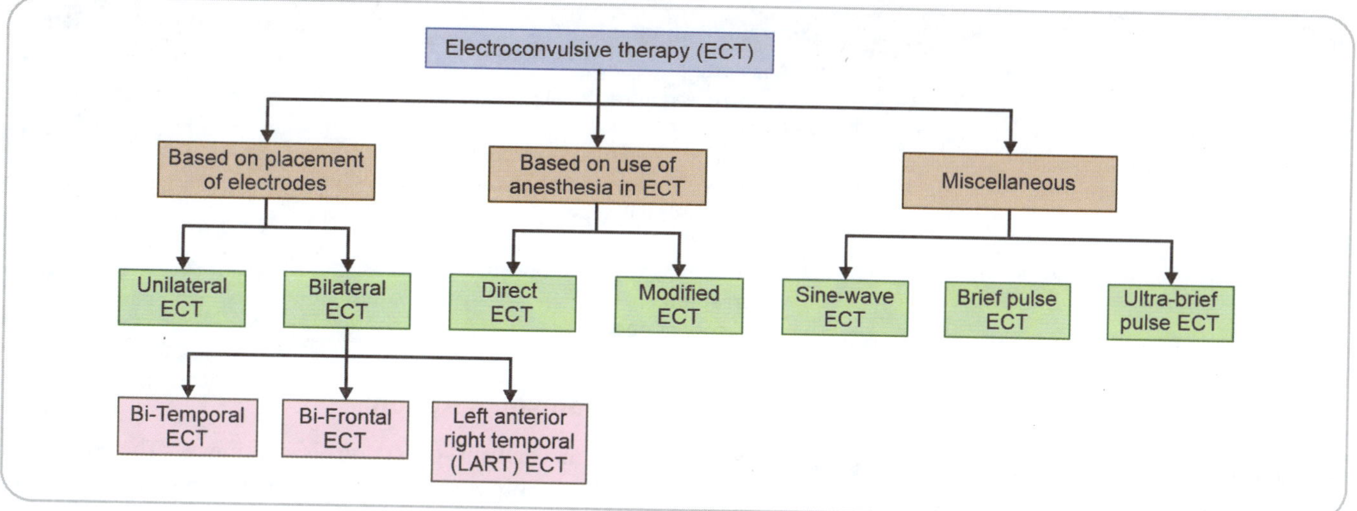

- Based on the placement of electrodes, ECT is classified as Unilateral ECT and Bilateral ECT as shown in Flowchart 5.12. In unilateral ECT, electrode has been placed at one side of the head whereas in bilateral ECT, electrodes are placed at both the sides of head. The electrode placement has been identified as midpoint between the lateral angle of eye and external auditory meatus as shown in Figure 5.34. Right unilateral placement of electrodes (D' Elia placement) is better tolerated than the bilateral ECT and it also has less cognitive impairment. The bilateral ECT such as Bi-temporal ECT, Bi-frontal ECT and Left Anterior Right Temporal (LART) ECT have more cognitive side effects and also have more treatment efficiency when compared with unilateral ECT.

Modified ECT

- ECT is provided along with muscle relaxant and general anesthesia.
- Medications used are as follows:
  - **Anticholinergics:** For example, Glycopyrrolate (0.1–0.4 mg) and Atropine (0.3–0.6 mg).
  - **Anesthetics:** For example, Methohexital Propofol (1 mg/kg).
  - **Muscle relaxant:** For example, Succinylcholine (0.75 mg/kg).

Sine Wave ECT

- Continuous stream of electricity which flows in alternative direction.
- Number of alternatives in direction are considered one positive, and negative current flow is termed frequency of stimulus, measured in Hertz.

Brief Pulse ECT

- Series of instant rising and falling of rectangular pulse of current with adjacent pulse separated by brief period of no electrical activity.

Ultra Brief Pulse ECT

- Use of pulse width of 0.3 ms, comparable with 1.0 ms used in brief pulse ECT.
- Use of smaller dose to induce seizure might reduce cognitive side effects.

Indications and Contraindications

Indications, contraindications and used with precautions of ECT are enlisted in Table 5.28.

Criteria to Use ECT

Criteria to use ECT are given in Table 5.29.

Table 5.28: Indications, contraindications and uses with precautions of ECT

Indications	Contraindications	Uses with precaution
• **Major depression** ▪ High suicidal risk ▪ Psychotic depression ▪ Treatment resistance depression • Catatonic schizophrenia, mania and depression • Postpartum psychosis • Severe neuroleptic malignant syndrome • Augmentation with Anti-psychotics	• **Absolute:** ▪ Increased intracranial pressure (ICP) • **Relative:** ▪ Recent myocardial infarction ▪ Recent stroke/cerebrovascular accident (CVA) • **Major physical illness:** ▪ Cardiac failure ▪ Severe respiratory problems ▪ Brain tumor ▪ History of Aneurysm	• Pregnancy • Patients with cardiac pacemakers

Table 5.29: Criteria to use ECT

Primary criteria	Secondary criteria
• Poor response of psychotropic agents • Need of quick definite response	• Adverse effects with medication is present • Resistance with medications

Biological Effects

Biological effects have been mentioned in Table 5.30.

Table 5.30: Biological effects of electroconvulsive therapy

Increase	Changes
• Plasma catecholamines. • Prolactin release. • Brain derived neuroleptic factor (BDNF). • Permeability of blood brain barrier (BBB)	• 5-hydroxytryptamine or serotonin (5-HT) • Dopamine receptor binding. • Gamma-aminobutyric acid (GABA). • Glutamate neuropeptide Y.

Mechanism of Action

Exact mechanism of action is unknown. The effects of neurotransmitters will get balanced in the monoamine system (serotonin, dopamine and norepinephrine), acetyl choline, GABA, endogenous opioids and adenosine. There is also the effect on neuroendocrine system and hypothalamic pituitary adrenal (HPA) axis.

Frequency of ECT

- ECT can be given on alternative days in a week like, 3 times in a week.
- On an average, 6–10 times ECT can be given.
- Maximum up to 24 ECT is recommended.
- Depends on the diagnosis:
  - **Mania:** >20 times
  - **Depression:** 6–12 times
  - **Catatonia:** 3–5 times

Parameters in ECT is shown in Figure 5.32.

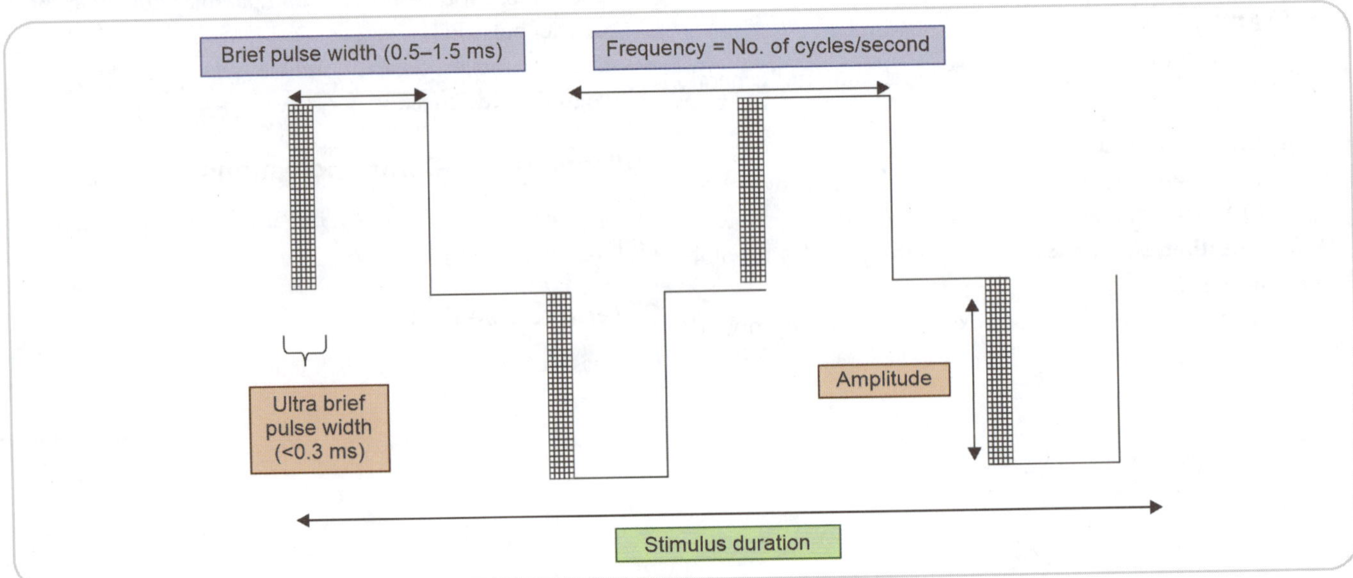

Figure 5.32: Diagram highlighting the parameters in electroconvulsive therapy

Complications

- Memory loss
- Respiratory Arrest
- Fracture
- Dysthymia

Limitations of ECT

- Anesthesia is needed
- Cognitive defects (even though it is temporary it is troublesome)
- Relapse after the ECT course is over (So, maintenance with drugs/psychotherapy is important).

Modern ECT Machine

- Monitor electroencephalograms (EEG), electrocardiogram (ECG) and electromyogram (EMG).
- **Display parameters as shown below:**

Date and time	No of ECT	Date and time of previous ect	Charge (Mc)	Current (A)	Pulse width	Frequency (Hz)	Stimulus duration	Seizure duration

ECT Administration

- Twice a week
- 6–12 sessions (for 3–6 weeks)
- Minimum electrical dose is required to induce generalized seizure.
- Varies from patient to patient.
- Identify seizure threshold in initial session will reduce cognitive effects rather than administering ECT with the standard dose because the seizure threshold differs with every patient.

Rule of Thumb is:

Type of ECT	Electrical dose
Unilateral	1.5 times the seizure threshold (ST)
Bilateral	3 times the seizure threshold (ST)

Seizure threshold varies and is presented in Table 5.31 and Figure 5.33.

Table 5.31: Seizure threshold in electroconvulsive therapy

Increases	Decreases
• Old age • Males • Benzodiazepines (or) barbiturates (avoided or given in lower doses) • Anticonvulsants (if continued then higher ECT stimulus is required)	• Antipsychotics (increased risk of hypotension and post–ECT confusion, clozapine has to be withheld for 24 hours before ECT) • Anti-depressants (tricyclic group of drugs has increased risk of hypotension and post–ECT confusion, moclobemide has to be withheld for 24 hours before ECT) • Lithium (increases the cognitive side-effects and neurotoxic effects)

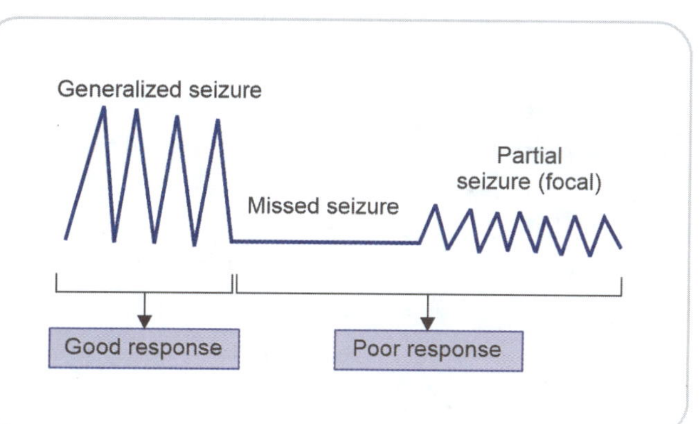

Figure 5.33: Seizure threshold: <100 mc

Process

Process followed for ECT is shown in Flowchart 5.13.

Flowchart 5.13: Process followed for ECT

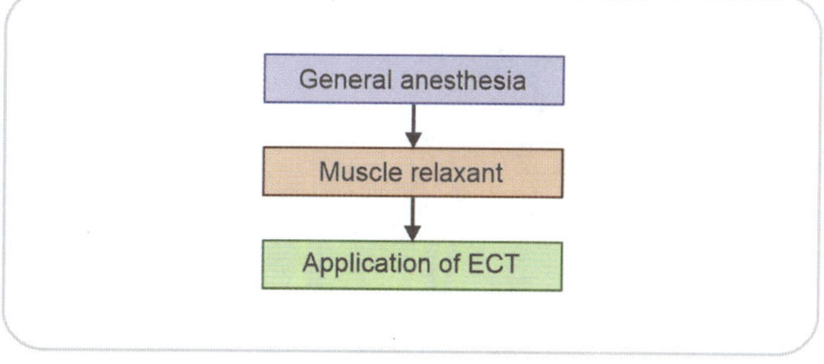

ECT Procedure

Articles required for ECT with rationale are enlisted in Table 5.32.

Table 5.32: Articles required for electroconvulsive therapy with rationale

Articles required for ECT	Rationale
ECG electrodes and monitor	To check the cardiac status during ECT
EEG electrodes and monitor	To check the seizure activity during ECT (Fig. 5.34) EEG monitoring is the gold standard method to assess 'spike and wake activity'.
BP cuff (or) cuff technique	To monitor the ictal motor duration during ECT Cuff is used to isolate the forearm or leg from the muscle relaxant by inflating the cuff. So, that motor seizure will be observed in the particular forearm or leg (seizure has to be at least for 20 seconds that denotes the treatment efficiency)
Pulse oximetry	To monitor oxygen saturation
Peripheral Nerve stimulator	To ensure the adequacy of received muscle blocking agents before ECT which is given especially to the patients with increased musculoskeletal injury.
Stethoscope	To check the heart sounds
Reflex hammer	To check the reflexes in neurological assessment
Venflon	To give intravenous injections
Bite blocks	To prevent tongue bite
Stretchers with side rails	Side rails to prevent the patient from fall.
Suction device	To remove the secretions
Oxygen cylinder	To deliver the required oxygen to patients
Artificial manual breathing unit (AMBU) bag	To provide resuscitation to patient
Oral airways	To maintain the patent airway
Intubation kit	To put endotracheal intubation in case of respiratory arrest
Emergency drugs	To save the life of patient in case of any complication arises due to anesthesia or ECT
Electrode paste	To paste the EEG and ECG electrodes
Gel	For effective conduction of electrodes
Gauze pads	To clean the gel applied after ECT
Distilled water	Helpful to deliver humidified oxygen
Chart paper	To record the ECT procedure

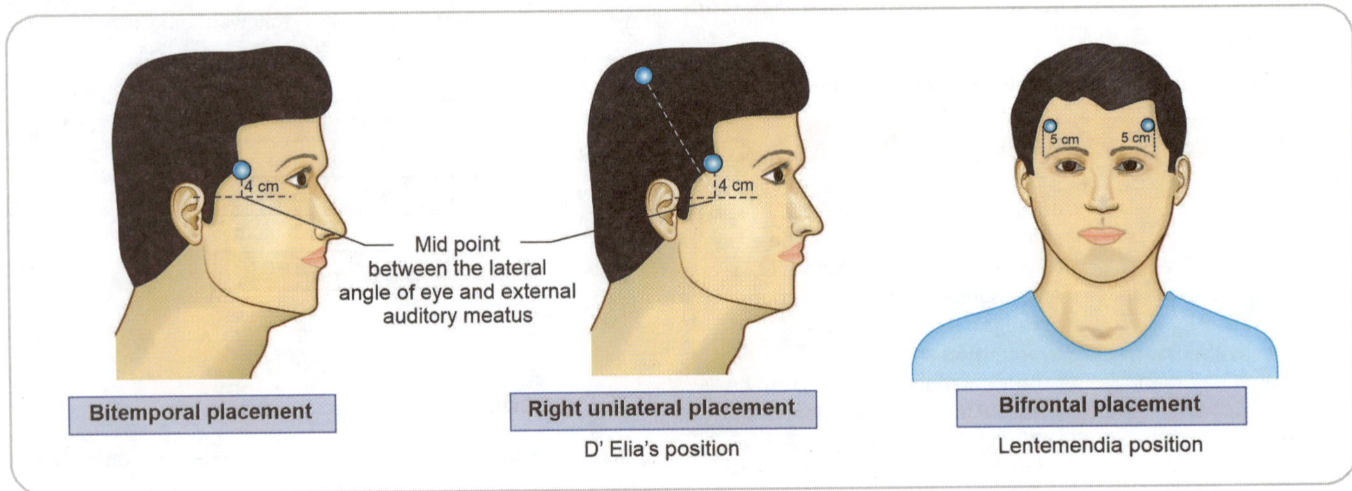

Figure 5.34: Placement of ECT electrodes

The medications given during ECT have been given in Table 5.33.

Table 5.33: Categories of medication

Categories	Medications
Anesthetic drugs	• Thiopental • Propofol • Ketamine • Etomidate
Antihypertensives	• **β-blockers** ▪ Atenolol ▪ Labetalol ▪ Esmolol • **Calcium channel blockers** ▪ Nicardipine ▪ Nifidipine
Narcotics	• Fentanyl • Remifentanyl • Alfentanyl
Anticholinergic agents	• Atropine • Glycopyrrolate
Neuromuscular blocking agents	• Succinylcholine • Atracurium • Mivacurium

Electroconvulsive Therapy Checklist

The ECT checklists are given in Tables 5.34 to 5.36.

Table 5.34: Pre-ECT checklist

Name: **Age:** **Sex:** **Diagnosis:** **IP No.:**
Procedure: **Date:** **Time:** **Ward:**

Checklist	Yes	No	Remarks
Written informed consent (**If psychotic:** Consent from care givers **If Neurotic:** Both from patient and care givers)			
Skin preparation			
Hair wash done			
Hair combed			
Dentures removed			
Nails paired			
Nail polish removed			
Nil per oral (NPO)			
Premedications (If any)			
Preoperative teaching			
Jewels removed			
Investigations • Routine blood test • Chest X-ray • ECG • Echocardiography			

Signature of the Staff Nurse

Table 5.35: Intra-ECT checklist

Name: **Age:** **Sex:** **IP No.:**
Procedure: **Date/Time:** **Diagnosis:** **ECT Room No.:**

Date:
No. of ECT:
Atropine/Glycopyrrolate:
Thiopentone:
Succinylcholine:
Duration:
Frequency:
Pulse width:
Charge (mc):
Seizure duration:
Blood pressure:
Pulse rate:
Remarks:

Signature of the Doctor/Nurse Practitioner

Table 5.36: Post ECT checklist

Name: **Age:** **Sex:** **IP No.:**
Procedure: **Date/Time:** **Diagnosis:** **ECT Room No.:**

Checklist	Yes	No	Remarks
Assessment of memory			
Orientation to patient			
NPO at least 2 hours after ECT			
IV fluids infusion			
Pulse rate checked			
Blood pressure checked			
Any significant complaints elicited (headache, nausea/vomiting, confusion)			
Able to tolerate oral fluids after 2 hours of ECT			
Soft diet after 3 hours of ECT			

Signature of the Nurse

ECT Procedure Steps

Nurses' responsibility before ECT, during ECT and after ECT with steps and rationale are given in Tables 5.37, 5.38 and 5.39 respectively.

Table 5.37: Nurses' responsibility before ECT procedure

Steps	Rationale
Get the informed consent	To check out the willingness before ECT
Check vital signs	It provides the baseline data

Contd...

Steps	Rationale
Get the investigations done as required by anesthetist/doctor	It provides the baseline lab reports
Wear comfortable clothing	Patient will feel comfortable
Maintain NPO from 12 pm	To prevent aspiration
Administer the premedications	To prevent gastric irritation and to have a right seizure threshold during ECT
Remove prosthesis (denture, glasses, contact lens, hearing aids)	To prevent interruptions during ECT
Hair should be clean and dry without oil	Oiled hair leads to poor conduction of electric impulses.
Make patient to void before ECT	To prevent voiding during ECT because the muscle relaxant will relax the bladder sphincter muscle
Provide Pre-ECT teaching to the care givers	To enhance the knowledge about ECT and so it prevents fear regarding procedure
Advise the client to wear sterile dress	To prevent infection
Shift the patient to operating theater or ECT room by wheel chair or stretcher	To start the ECT procedure

Table 5.38: Nurses' responsibility during ECT procedure

Steps	Rationale
Lie the patient in ECT room table	Patient will feel comfortable
Remain with the client throughout the procedure	To reduce the patient's level of anxiety
Place the EEG electrodes	To monitor the brain activity during seizures.
Clip the oxygen saturation probe	To identify the hypoxemia
Give suction in case of oral secretion	To prevent aspiration
Administer medications/anesthesia drugs/muscle relaxants as per doctors order in case of modified ECT	Minimize the side effects of ECT
Monitor Blood pressure throughout the ECT	To identify hypotension or hypertension
Place the bite block in mouth	To prevent tongue bite
Monitor the motor seizure duration	To check out the adequacy of ECT delivered
Document the Intra-ECT checklist	Act as legal evidence and used for further follow-up

Table 5.39: Nurses' responsibility after ECT procedure

Steps	Rationale
Transfer the patient into recovery room	To observe the patient condition
Monitor the oxygen saturation level	To identify the hypoxemia
Check vital signs	It provides the baseline data
Reorient the patient	To reduce cognitive deficits
Allow the patient to sleep	Patient will feel comfortable
Put the side rails of the bed	To prevent the falls
Maintain NPO at least after 2 hours of ECT and introduce the soft diet followed by oral fluids	Step by step introduction of diet will prevent aspiration
Assess the memory impairment	To rule out amnesia as complication of ECT
Document the procedure	It act as a legal evidence.

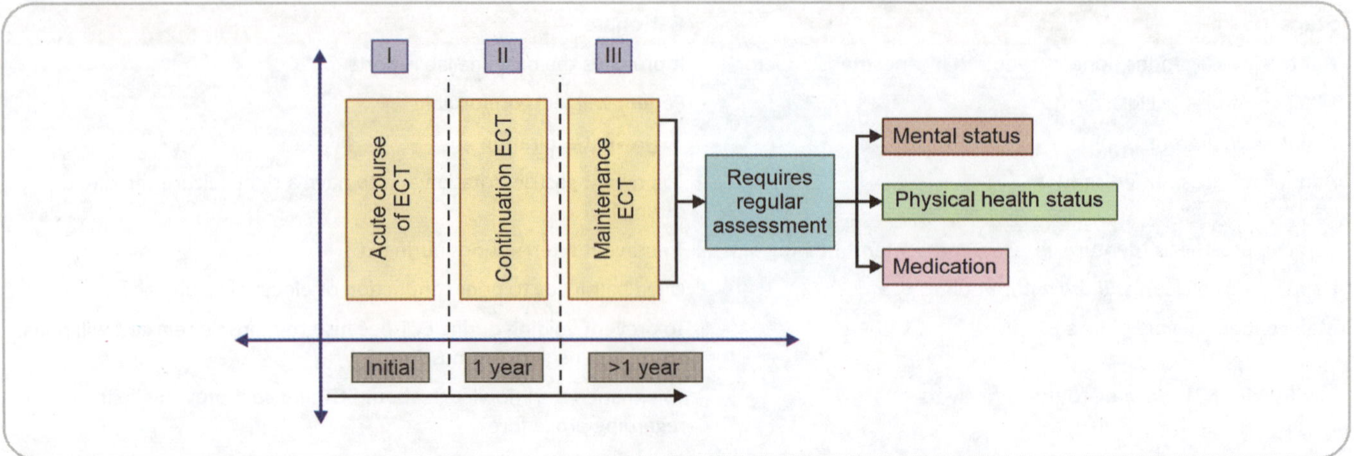

Figure 5.35: Maintenance of electroconvulsive therapy

Maintenance of ECT

Administration of ECT below one year duration is termed, 'Acute course of ECT'. Administration of ECT for one year duration is termed, 'Continuation phase ECT.' Administration of ECT more than one year duration is termed, 'Maintenance phase ECT'. Patient has to undergo the regular physical status and mental health status assessment regularly. Patient also ensure the proper drug adherence and psychotherapy to elicit the good prognosis (Fig. 5.35).

Side Effects

More common side effects are as follows:

- Headache
- Confusion
- Memory disturbances (both anterograde and retrograde amnesia)
- Side effects of general anesthesia and muscle relaxants.

Less common side effects are as follows:

- Muscle weakness/aches
- Nausea
- Anorexia

Side effects are seen prominently immediately after ECT. It is a temporary or short lasting one and so it will be reduced after few hours to days (Fig. 5.36).

The side effects of ECT can be categorized as:

Cardiovascular System

- Palpitations
- Transient changes in cardiovascular system

Cognitive Symptoms

- Confusion
- Memory disturbances
- Poor concentration

Miscellaneous

- Headache
- Nausea and vomiting
- Tongue bite
- Urinary incontinence
- Dry mouth
- Drowsiness

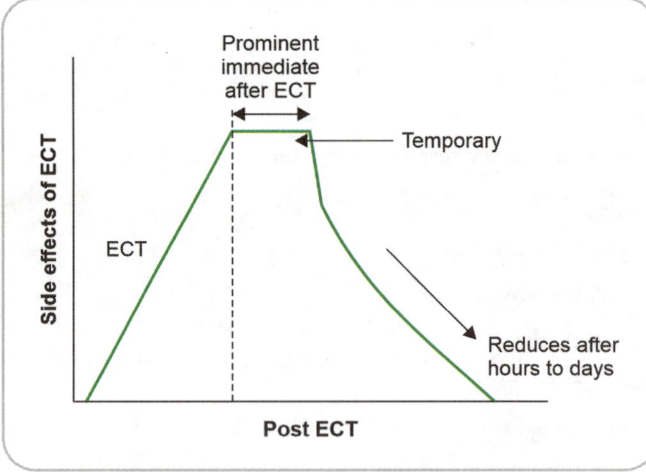

Figure 5.36: Duration of the side effects after electroconvulsive therapy

PSYCHOSURGERY OR FUNCTIONAL NEUROLOGICAL SURGERIES

Psychiatric neurosurgeries are enlisted in Table 5.40.

Table 5.40: Psychiatric neurosurgeries

Name of the psychosurgery	Description	Indicated psychiatric disorders (treatment resistant with psychotropics is present)
Anterior cingulotomy	Anterior cingulate cortex is targeted. Surgery performed to disconnect the thalamic and posterior frontal regions.	• Addictive behavior • Bipolar disorder/depression • Obsessive compulsive disorder (OCD) • Schizophrenia and • Schizoaffective disorder
Anterior capsulotomy	Surgery performed to disconnect the orbitofrontal cortex and thalamic nuclei by producing a lesion in anterior limb of internal capsule	• General anxiety disorder and • Obsessive compulsive disorder (OCD)
Subcaudate tractotomy	Destruction of bifrontal pathways which is present below and in front of the head of caudate nucleus.	• Schizophrenia • Depression and • Obsessive compulsive disorder (OCD)
Hypothalamotomy	Surgical lesions made in the hypothalamus by ultrasonic energy or using knife or by electric impulses or radiation.	• Addictive behavior • Aggression • Sexual disorders
Thalamotomy	The precise destruction is performed in a tiny area of brain called thalamus in order to control the involuntary movements	Tourette syndrome
Amygdalotomy	Destruction of part of the amygdala in the brain	Aggression associated with psychiatric illness.
Limbic leucotomy	It is the combination of anterior cingulotomy and subcaudate tractotomy	

DEEP BRAIN STIMULATION

Definition

Deep brain stimulation is defined as, 'implanting the electrodes in certain parts of brain, the electrodes produce the impulses to regulate the abnormal impulses. The amount of stimulation has been controlled with the pacemaker like device which is kept under the skin of the chest'

Indications

- Parkinson's disease
- Obsessive-compulsive disorder
- Epilepsy
- Dystonia
- Dementia
- Major depression
- Cluster headache
- Huntington's disease
- Traumatic brain injury
- Multiple sclerosis
- Recovery from stroke
- Addiction
- Tourette syndrome
- Chronic pain

Risk of Surgery

Risks include hemorrhage in the brain, misplacement of lead, infection, stroke, breathing difficulty, heart problems, seizure, etc.

Side Effects

- **Side effects related to stimulation:** Speech difficulties, light-headedness, double vision, balance problems, numbness, muscle tightness and mood swings.
- **Side effects after the surgery:** Headache, infection, confusion, difficulty in concentration, stroke, seizure, pain and swelling in implanted site.

Targeted Parts of Deep Brain Stimulation for Psychiatric Disorders

Target parts of deep brain stimulation are enlisted in Table 5.41.

Table 5.41: Target parts of deep brain stimulation

Targeted part of brain in deep brain stimulation	Indicated psychiatric disorders
Lateral habenula	Depression
Nucleus accumbens	Addiction
Subcallosal cingulate	Anorexia nervosa and depression
Ventral capsule or ventral striatum	Addiction Obsessive compulsive disorder Depression
Inferior thalamic peduncle	Obsessive compulsive disorder Depression
Subthalamic nucleus	Obsessive compulsive disorder
Medial forebrain bundle	Depression
Thalamus	Tourette syndrome

PSYCHOLOGICAL THERAPIES

Geriatric Considerations in Psychological Therapies

Nurse has to remember that the psychotherapies will work out slow in elders due to ageing. Nurse should consider that sensory impairment and memory deterioration are the reasons for their slow performance and understanding. The length of the sessions has to be flexible. Nurse needs to fix the small achievable goals in the small group. Physical and mental health of the elders have to be considered before planning out the psychotherapeutic sessions.

Role of Nurse in Psychological Therapies

Nurse has to provide the trusting therapeutic relationship with the patient, to ensure the therapeutic alliance. Nurse has to plan the psychotherapy session in coordination with the therapist based on the needs and problems of the patient. Nurse has to teach the importance of the particular psychotherapy to the patient and his/her family members. Nurse has to work as a liaison officer between patient, therapist and the family members of patient.

Nurse has to observe the improvement or deterioration in patient after the few therapy sessions and report the same to the psychotherapist. Nurse has to explain every step of the psychotherapeutic process to the patient in order to prevent the unnecessary raise in anxiety.

SUMMARY

- Antipsychotics are medications to treat psychotic disorder and psychosis related to other psychiatric and medical disorders.
- The other names of antipsychotics are D_2 receptor blockers, major tranquilizers, neuroleptic agents, ataractics and anti-schizophrenic drugs.
- Types of antipsychotics are conventional (or) traditional (or) typical antipsychotics and atypical antipsychotics (or) Second generation antipsychotics.
- Dopamine (D_2 receptor) pathways in the brain are Nigrostriatal tract, Tuberoinfundibular tract, Mesolimbic tract and Mesocortical tract.
- Extrapyramidal symptoms due to antipsychotics are neuroleptic malignant syndrome, pseudo-parkinson's disease, akathisia, acute dystonia, Rabbit syndrome, Tardive dyskinesia and abnormal choreoathetoid movements.
- The other terms for antidepressants are Thymoleptics and Mood elevators.
- Types of antidepressants are first generation antidepressants or tricyclic antidepressants (TCA), second generation antidepressants or selective serotonin reuptake inhibitors (SSRI), serotonin norepinephrine reuptake inhibitors (SNRI), monoamine oxidase inhibitors (MAOI) and atypical antidepressants.
- The other terms for antianxiety agents are minor tranquilizers and anxiolytics.
- Classification of antianxiety agents are benzodiazepines, barbiturates, nonbarbiturates, non-benzodiazepines anxiolytic agents and antidepressants causing antianxiety effects.
- The common anti-Parkinson's agents are classified into Anticholinergics, Antihistamine and Dopaminergic agonists.
- The common mood stabilizers are Lithium, sodium valproate and carbamazepine.
- Stimulants are those which enhance the mental and physical function by increasing the alertness, wakefulness, etc. Example for the CNS stimulants are Caffeine, Nicotine, Methylenedioxy/methamphetamine (MDMA-Ecstasy), modafinil, Ampakines, etc.
- Psychotherapy is defined as, 'way to help the people with variety of mental illnesses and emotional difficulties and it also helps to control or remove the symptoms which trouble the person, function in a better way, increase the sense of well-being and promote healing.'
- Individual psychotherapy is the interaction process (psychotherapy) between the patient and the mental health professional or therapist on one to one basis.
- Psychoanalytical psychotherapy is defined as insight therapy which aims to overcome the unconscious conflicts and it also aims to identify the relationship between the unconscious motivation and the abnormal behavior.
- Cognitive therapy is a form of psychotherapy in which the distorted cognitions are modified into positive cognitions.
- Behavior therapy is defined as 'form of psychotherapy in which the maladaptive behavior is aimed to change as adaptive behavior.'

Contd...

- Therapeutic community is a drug free environment in which the individuals with addictive behavior join together in a structured manner in order to promote drug free society. It forms a miniature of society, staff act as facilitators, residents join together to promote the transitional process.
- Milieu therapy is the scientific structuring of the environment in order to elicit the behavioral changes and to enhance the psychological health and functioning of the individual.
- Supportive psychotherapy is defined as a kind of psychotherapy which helps to decrease the psychological conflict and strengthen the patient's defenses with the help of techniques such as suggestion, reassurance, counseling and reeducation.
- Play therapy is a form of psychotherapy in which the therapist utilizes the child's fantasy and symbolic meaning as a medium of play to have a communication or understanding about the children. It also gives a chance for the child to express the feelings and experiences.
- Family therapy is defined as, 'a form of psychotherapy in which the issues or problems or conflicts exist among the family members are addressed and the solution has been identified.'
- Psychodrama is a form of psychotherapy (group therapy), in which the dramatization or dramatic presentation of self helps to gain self-insight.
- Music therapy is defined as, 'utilization of music in treatment, training, education and the rehabilitation of children and adults who are suffering from physical and mental disorder.'
- Dance therapy is defined as, 'psychotherapeutic use of movement as process, which promotes physical, emotional and cognitive integration of the individual.'
- Recreational therapy is a systematic process which utilizes the recreation and other activity-based interventions based on the needs of individuals with illness or disabling conditions which means to psychological/physical health, recovery and well-being.
- Relaxation therapy is a component of body-mind intervention in which the therapist helps the participants at the higher extent of mind relaxation.
- Light therapy is the use of light with the specified intensity for therapeutic purpose.
- The word, Yoga came from the Sanskrit word 'Yuj' which means union or connect or balance or join, i.e., joining of Jivatma with Paramatma, joining of the individual consciousness with the consciousness in the universe.
- Biofeedback is defined as, 'psychophysiological therapy in which the individual is able to monitor the physiological changes in the body due to the psychological stressors.'
- Alternative and complementary medicine is defined as, 'group of diverse medical/health care system, practices and products that are not presently considered to be a part of conventional medicine.'
- The major domains of Alternative and complementary medicine are alternative medicine system, mind body interactions, biological based therapies, manipulative or body based therapies and energy therapies.
- Convulsions are induced by passing a brief pulse of electric current through brain *via* electrodes for a therapeutic purpose is defined as ECT.
- Major depression is the most common indication and increased intra-cranial pressure is the absolute contraindication of ECT.
- Poor response of Psychotropic agents is a primary criterion to use ECT.
- Raise in Plasma catecholamines, Prolactin release, BDNF (Brain Derived Neuroleptic Factor), Permeability of blood brain barrier (BBB) are biological effects of ECT.
- Changes in 5-hydroxytryptamine (5 HT) or serotonin, DA receptor binding, Gamma-aminobutyric acid (GABA), glutamate, neuropeptide are also the biological effects of ECT.
- Three times the seizure threshold (ST) in Bilateral ECT and 1.5 times the seizure threshold (ST) in unilateral ECT is rule of thumb.
- Benzodiazepines increase seizure threshold (ST). Lithium, antipsychotics and antidepressants might decrease seizure threshold (ST).
- Memory disturbances are most common cognitive side effects of ECT.
- ECT has been classified as direct ECT, modified ECT, brief pulse ECT, sine wave ECT, ultra brief pulse ECT.
- Based on electrode placement, ECT is classified into unilateral ECT and Bilateral ECT.
- On an average, 6–10 times ECT can be given. Maximum times of ECT administration is 24.
- Informed consent, NPO, Pre-medications, hair wash, removal of prosthesis, check out vital signs is important before ECT.
- Monitor vitals, seizure duration is vital during ECT. Administration of anesthetic drugs is essential in case of modified ECT.
- Reorientation, assessment of memory, soft diet, and adequate rest is vital in post-ECT care.

ASSESS YOURSELF

Long Answer Questions

1. Define antipsychotics. List out the indications, contraindications and their side effects. Classify the antipsychotics and elaborate the nurse's responsibility.
2. Define antidepressants. List out the indications, contraindications and their side effects. Classify the antidepressants and elaborate the role of nurse.
3. Define mood stabilizers. List out the indications, contraindications and their side effects. Classify the mood stabilizers and elaborate the nurse's responsibility.
4. Define anti-anxiety agents. List out the indications, contraindications and their side effects. Classify the antianxiety agents and elaborate the role of nurse.

5. Define psychotherapy. Classify and explain the various psychotherapies along with the nurse's responsibility.
6. Define behavior therapy. Classify and explain the various techniques with appropriate examples.
7. Define cognitive therapy. Classify and explain the various techniques with appropriate examples.
8. Define ECT. List out the indications, contraindications and side effects of ECT. Explain the nurse's responsibility before, during and after ECT.

Short Answer Questions

1. What is the role of nurse in managing the side effects of antipsychotics?
2. Define family therapy.
3. Name the alternative systems of medicine.
4. Write about nurse's role in ECT?

Short Notes

Write short notes on:

1. CNS stimulants
2. Extrapyramidal effects
3. Tricyclic antidepressants
4. Serotonin syndrome
5. Individual psychotherapy
6. Psychoanalytical psychotherapy
7. Supportive psychotherapy
8. Therapeutic community
9. Group therapy
10. Play therapy
11. Psychodrama
12. Music therapy
13. Dance therapy
14. Recreational therapy
15. Light therapy
16. Relaxation therapies
17. Yoga
18. Meditation
19. Biofeedback
20. Classification of ECT

Multiple Choice Questions

1. **Which of the following is not synonymous term of Antipsychotics?**
   a. D_2 receptor blockers
   b. Major tranquilizers
   c. Minor tranquilizers
   d. Neuroleptic agents

2. **_______ used the ECT at first in modern times.**
   a. Egas Moniz b. Kurt Schneider
   c. Ladislas Meduna d. Sigmund Freud

3. **Which of the following is the synonymous term of antianxiety agents?**
   a. Thymolytics b. Major tranquilizers
   c. Minor tranquilizers d. Neuroleptic agents

4. **Which of the following is among the eight limbs of yoga?**
   a. Yama b. Niyama
   c. Asanas d. None of these

5. **The psychoanalytic technique includes:**
   a. Free association b. Dream analysis
   c. Treatment Alliance d. All of these

6. **Most common side effect of ECT is:**
   a. Memory impairment b. Hypertension
   c. Fracture d. Convulsions

7. **Which is not considered atypical antipsychotics?**
   a. Risperidone b. Clozapine
   c. Olanzapine d. Haloperidol

8. **Which type of ECT is highly recommended to prevent memory impairment?**
   a. Direct ECT b. Modified ECT
   c. Both of these d. None of these

9. **The frequently occurring response (R_1) might act as a positive reinforcement for the response (R_2) which is occurring less frequently is ____________ of Behavior therapy.**
   a. Systematic desensitization
   b. Premack principle
   c. Flooding
   d. Assertiveness training

10. **____________ is the psychotherapeutic use of movement as process, which promotes physical, emotional and cognitive integration of the individual.**
    a. Music therapy b. Dance therapy
    c. Yoga therapy d. Biofeedback

11. **____________ group of drug will cause hypertensive crisis if taken with tyramine derivatives.**
    a. Tricyclic antidepressants
    b. Antianxiety drugs
    c. Monoamine oxidase inhibitors
    d. Selective serotonin reuptake inhibitors

12. **____________ group of drug causes extrapyramidal symptoms.**
    a. Antipsychotics b. Anti-anxiety drugs
    c. Stimulants d. Antidepressants

13. **What is the minimum seizure duration required for the efficacy of ECT?**
    a. 30–90 seconds b. 2 minutes
    c. 10–20 seconds d. 20–30 seconds

14. The proponent of Rationale emotive therapy is:

a. Albert Ellis b. Steven C Hayes
c. Marsha M Linehan d. Adrian Wells

15. Most common indication of ECT is:

a. Mania b. Severe depression
c. Schizophrenia d. Anxiety disorder

16. Which of these comes under the category of relaxation therapy?

a. JPMR b. Autogenic training
c. Guided Imagery d. All of these

17. Breathing practices in the yoga is termed:

a. Pranayama b. Asana
c. Kriyas d. Mudras

18. Anticholinergic agent can be given before ECT is:

a. Succinyl Choline b. Atropine
c. Atracurium d. Mivacurium

19. Absolute contraindications of ECT is:

a. Increased intracranial pressure
b. Stroke
c. Recent MI
d. Cardiac failure

20. Drug which decreases seizure threshold is:

a. Lithium
b. Antidepressants
c. Antipsychotics
d. All of the above

Answer Key				
1. c	**2.** c	**3.** c	**4.** c	**5.** d
6. a	**7.** d	**8.** b	**9.** b	**10.** b
11. c	**12.** a	**13.** c	**14.** a	**15.** b
16. d	**17.** a	**18.** b	**19.** a	**20.** d

Notes

Nursing Management of Patients with Schizophrenia and Other Psychotic Disorders

CHAPTER 6

LEARNING OBJECTIVE

After studying this chapter, the student will be able to gain knowledge regarding the schizophrenia and other psychotic disorders in order to render the nursing care of patient with schizophrenia.

CHAPTER OUTLINE

- Introduction and Meaning
- History
- Prevalence and Incidence
- Etiology
- Diagnosis
- Diagnostic Criteria
- Differential Diagnosis of Schizophrenia
- Three Phases of Schizophrenia
- Positive and Negative Symptoms of Schizophrenia
- Other Psychotic Disorders
- Prognosis of Schizophrenia
- Psychosocial Interventions
- Treatment
- Nursing Interventions
- Geriatric Considerations
- Follow-up, Home Care and Rehabilitation of Patients with Schizophrenia

KEY TERMS

Schizophrenia, DiGeorge syndrome, Expressed emotions, Double bind communication, Hallucination, Delusion, Thought broadcasting, Thought withdrawal, Delusion disorder, Catatonia, Anhedonia, Apathy, Acute and transient psychotic disorder, Brief psychotic disorder, Schizoaffective disorders, Schizophreniform disorder, Schizotypal (Personality) disorder.

INTRODUCTION AND MEANING

The word 'schizophrenia' is derived from the Greek word which means 'split mind". Prefix 'Schizo' means 'Split' and Suffix 'Phrenia' means 'mind'. The term 'split mind' does not denote the split personality or multiple personality disorder, it actually means the split in terms of thought, cognition and emotions. Hence, schizophrenia is a psychotic disorder (disorder in which client believes that he/she will not have a base of reality) characterized by abnormalities in emotion, thinking and cognition.

HISTORY

Eugen Bleuler coined the term 'Schizophrenia' in 1908. Emil Kraepelin classified the psychiatric disorders into Dementia praecox and Manic-depressive illness. The term 'Praecox' means onset in young age (early onset) and the term 'Dementia' denotes gradual decrease in cognitive functions. Kurt Schneider was concerned with improving the method of diagnosis in psychiatry. He contributed to diagnostic procedures and the definition of disorders (Fig. 6.1).

Figure 6.1: Pioneers in psychiatry

World schizophrenia day is observed on May 24th every year with an aim to raise public awareness about schizophrenia and to minimize the disgrace associated with the condition.

PREVALENCE AND INCIDENCE

- 1% of total population has life time prevalence rate of schizophrenia and the incidence rate is 0.15–0.25/1,000.
- Usual onset of schizophrenia is adolescence/young adulthood.
- Late-onset schizophrenia is at 45 years of age. Schizophrenia is rarely present before 15 years of age and after 45 years of age.
- Nearly 10% of patients with schizophrenia attempt suicide especially young male adults.
- High rates of schizophrenia are seen in winter season.
- Twin studies of patient with schizophrenia revealed that among twins, monozygotic twins have 47%, dizygotic twins have 12% and nontwin siblings have 8% chance to get schizophrenia as shown in Figure 6.2.

A person is more likely to develop schizophrenia if, someone in his/her family have Schizophrenia. If, the person with Schizophrenia is a parent, brother, or sister, then the chances can go up by 10%. If both the parents are having Schizophrenia, the person can have a 40% chance of getting Schizophrenia. Mostly females around 30 years of age are affected. Mostly males around 20 years of age are affected. Onset of schizophrenia the chances are early in men.

Males and females are equally affected with schizophrenia in general as explained in Table 6.1.

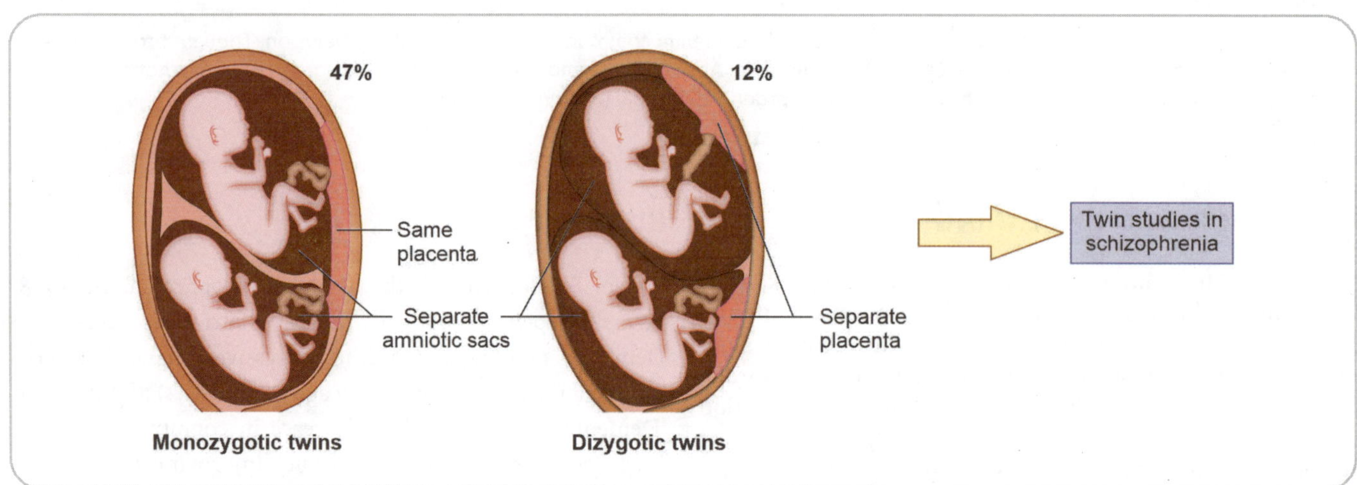

Figure 6.2: Twin studies in schizophrenia

Table 6.1: Gender and schizophrenia

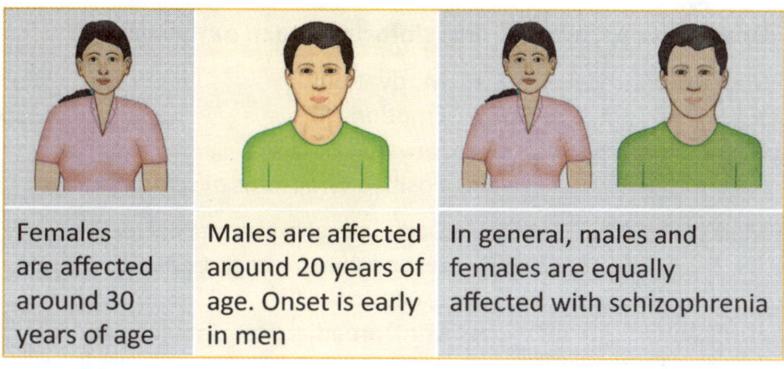

Females are affected around 30 years of age	Males are affected around 20 years of age. Onset is early in men	In general, males and females are equally affected with schizophrenia

ETIOLOGY

Factors

The factors responsible for schizophrenia have been discussed here:

- **Neurochemical factors:** Dopamine hypothesis states presence of excess dopaminergic activity, high serotonin level and imbalance in other neurochemicals such as norepinephrine, GABA, glutamate, acetylcholine and nicotine.
- **Genetic factors:** DiGeorge syndrome or Velocardiofacial syndrome or Shprintzen syndrome or Conotruncal anomaly face syndrome or Takao syndrome or Sedlackova syndrome or Cayler cardiofacial syndrome or 22q11.2 deletion syndrome is defined as deletion of 30 to 40 genes in middle of chromosome 22. The symptoms identified on physical examination are wide spaced eyes (hypertelorism), short broad nose, cardiac malformations, umbilical hernia, intestinal blockage and abnormal pelvis, long forehead, oval shaped low set ears, excess nuchal thickness and edematous feet (Fig. 6.3).

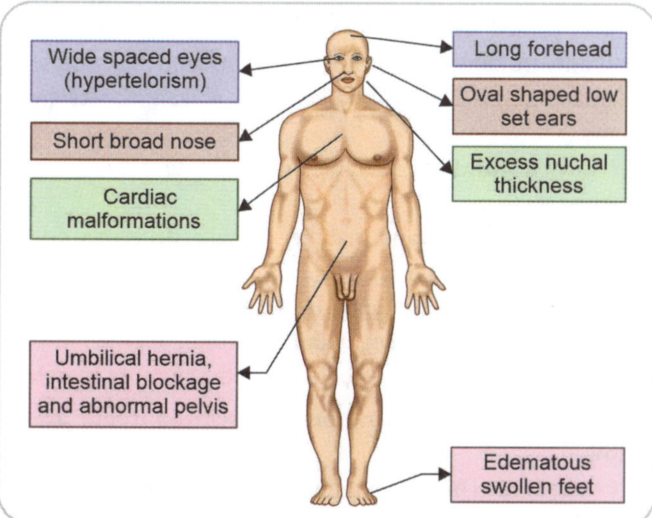

Figure 6.3: Symptoms of DiGeorge syndrome

- **Neuropathological factors:** Enlargement of third and lateral ventricles of cerebrum along with the decreased cerebral volume is seen in patient with schizophrenia. In limbic system, the hippocampus, amygdala and parahippocampal gyrus are in smaller size. In thalamus, loss of neurons in medial dorsal nucleus of thalamus is seen. Anatomical abnormalities in prefrontal cortex, basal ganglia and cerebellum are seen.
- **Neuropeptides:** Imbalance in the neuropeptides such as cholecystokinin, neurotensin, phospholipids, substance P, dynorphin A, neuropeptide Y and peptide YY is risk factor for schizophrenia.
- **Neuroendocrinology:** Imbalance in the hormones such as growth hormone, prolactin, thyroid-releasing hormone and oxytocin.
- **Environmental factors:** Obstetric complications, abnormalities in developmental milestones, prenatal infections, prenatal malnutrition, advanced paternal age, drug abuse, migrated from native place and season of birth in winter or seasonal spring are environmental factors might cause schizophrenia.

Theories and Models

Other theories and models which explain the etiology of schizophrenia have been put forth; some of these are discussed here.

Sociocultural Theory

Downward social drift, i.e., lower social economic background has high chance of developing schizophrenia.

Interpersonal Model

Sullivan explained the interpersonal model, which is highly focused on the mother-child relationship. The internal equilibrium in a body is labeled as self-system. When self-system feels good there will be low level of anxiety, when self-system feels bad it will give rise to high level of anxiety and if self-system feels: it's not me, then it leads to apocalyptic anxiety schizophrenia (Fig. 6.4).

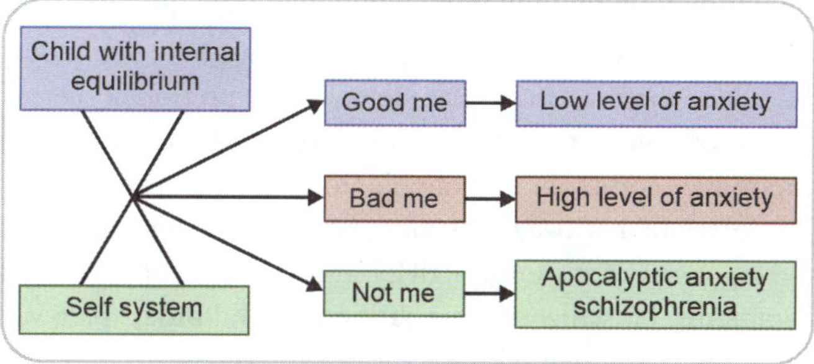

Figure 6.4: Interpersonal model of schizophrenia

Stress-Diathesis Model or Nature-Nurture Model

According to Sandor Rado, genotype (inherited gene) interacts with environment and gives a phenotype namely 'Schizotype'. These are individuals who are unable to cope with the repeated stressors.

Psychoanalytical Theory

In psychoanalytical theory, there is regression to oral stage of psychosexual development, along with use of defense mechanism such as denial, projection, reaction formation and distortion.

Family Theories

- **Double bind communication**: Unable to identify the correct choice (For example, mother says child you can go out to play cricket but your shoes and dress should not get dirty. In this example, mother's nonverbal cues and facial expression denote the child to stay at home).
- **Dysfunctional family:** Hostility between mother and father can lead a child toward schizophrenia.
- **Mother-child relation:** If the mother is overprotective and dominating (try to control the behavior without understanding the feelings—a parenting style).
- **Increased negatively expressed emotion (EE) in family**, i.e., critical comments and emotional over involvement among family members.

Dysfunctional family and Mother-child relation explained above are older theories and are currently not accepted.

Dopamine Pathways

Dopamine pathways are a set of projection neurons in the brain that release dopamine responsible for function, execution, motivation, etc. It has four pathways. Dopamine pathways have been summarized in Table 6.2 and Figure 6.5. Physiology of **mesolimbic pathway** is responsible for motivation, emotion, reward and positive symptoms of schizophrenia. Physiology of **mesocortical pathway** is responsible for negative symptoms of schizophrenia, in which dorsolateral prefrontal cortex is responsible for cognition and execution. Ventromedial prefrontal cortex is responsible for emotions and affect. **Nigrostriatal pathway** constitutes 80% of brain dopamine that is responsible for motor activity and shows extrapyramidal symptoms of schizophrenia. **Tuberoinfundibular** pathway increases prolactin level.

Table 6.2: Dopamine pathways

Dopamine pathways	Physiology of each pathway
Mesolimbic	• Motivation • Emotion • Reward • Positive symptoms of schizophrenia
Mesocortical	• Dorsolateral prefrontal cortex—responsible for cognition and execution • Ventromedial prefrontal cortex—responsible for emotions and affect • Responsible for negative symptoms of schizophrenia
Nigrostriatal	• Constitutes 80% of brain dopamine • Responsible for motor activity • Responsible for extrapyramidal symptoms of schizophrenia
Tuberoinfundibular	Hyperprolactinemia

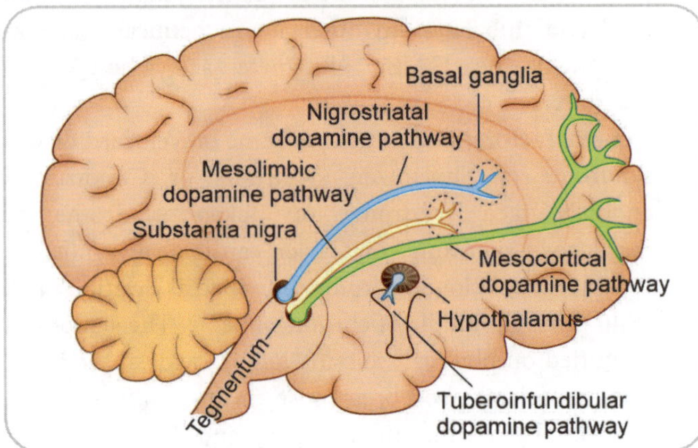

Figure 6.5: Dopamine pathways in brain

A's of Schizophrenia

Bleuler coined the term 'Schizophrenia' in 1908. Four symptoms are considered primary and fundamental symptoms of schizophrenia. Four A's explained by Eugen Bleuler are as follows:

1. **Autistic thinking** and behavior denote excess fantasy thoughts.
2. **Ambivalence** means inability to take decisions due to conflicts existing in mind.
3. **Affect** is inappropriate to the mood.
4. **Associative loosening** (Rapid shifting of one idea to another without any association between those ideas).

Five A's of negative symptoms of schizophrenia are as follows:

1. Anhedonia (Inability to enjoy the pleasure which seems to be pleasurable before).

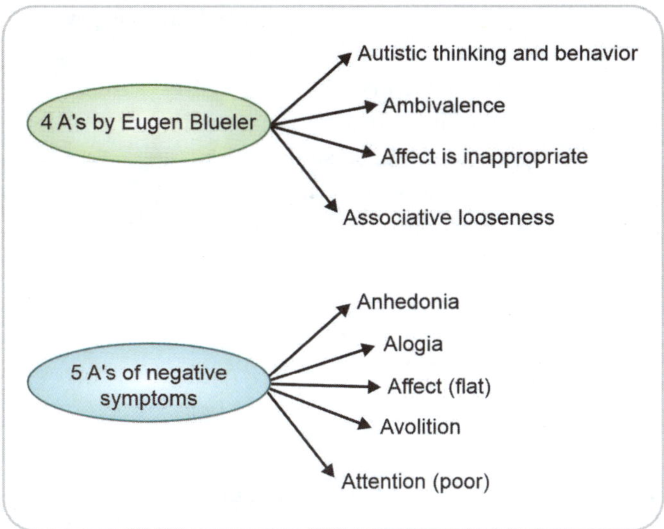

Figure 6.6: A's of schizophrenia

2. Alogia (poverty of speech)
3. Flat affect (lack of emotional expression)
4. Avolition (lack of initiation to perform any action)
5. Poor attention.

Four A's and 5 A's of negative symptoms of schizophrenia have been shown in Figure 6.6.

ICD-11 and DSM-5 Code for Schizophrenia

6A20	ICD-11 code for schizophrenia
295.90	DSM-5 code for schizophrenia

DIAGNOSIS

- **Assessment scales used to identify psychotic symptoms in schizophrenia are as follows:**
  - Brief Psychiatric Rating Scale (BPRS)
  - Scale for Assessment of Negative Symptoms (SANS—Andreasen, 1982)
  - Positive and Negative Syndrome Scale (PANSS—Kay, 1991)
- **Assessment scales used to identify cognitive deficits in schizophrenia are as follows:**
  - Stroop test
  - Trail making test
  - Wisconsin card sorting test
  - Wechsler adult intelligence scale (WAIS)
- **Assessment scales used to identify personality related problems in schizophrenia are as follows:**
  - Rorschach inkblot test
  - Minnesota multiphasic personality inventory (MMPI)
- **CT scan:** Ventricular enlargement and cortical atrophy

> **NOTE**
> Ventricular enlargement is also seen in hydrocephalus, Alzheimer's disease and neurodegenerative disorders.

- **SPECT/PET scan** shows increased D_2 receptor density.
- **Diffusion tensor imaging** reveals the abnormalities in white matter fiber tracts.
- **Functional MRI:** If the patient has positive symptoms, changes can be seen in medial prefrontal cortex and hippocampus. If the patient has negative symptoms, changes can be seen in ventrolateral prefrontal cortex and ventral striatum. If the patient has disorganized symptoms, changes can be seen in dorsolateral prefrontal cortex.

DIAGNOSTIC CRITERIA

DSM-5 Diagnostic Criteria for Schizophrenia

- Two or more of following symptoms present for significant portion of time for 1-month period (or less if successfully treated).
  - Delusions
  - Hallucinations
  - Disorganized speech (e.g., frequent derailment or incoherence)
  - Grossly disorganized or catatonic behavior.
  - Negative symptoms (i.e., diminished emotional expression or avolition)
- Significant impairment in the academic, interpersonal, occupational and social impairment.
- Continuous signs persist for at least 6 months (at least 1 month of symptoms in active phase and then may be only negative symptoms in the prodromal or residual phase).
- There should not be major depressive or manic episodes.
- Sign is not due to consumption of any substance.

Specify if it is:
- First episode or multiple episodes either with full or partial remission
- With or without catatonia
- Severity (use of 5-point scale)

ICD-11 Diagnostic Criteria for Schizophrenia

- Schizophrenia is characterized by disturbances in multiple mental modalities, including:
  - Thinking (e.g., delusions, disorganization in the form of thought)
  - Perception (e.g., hallucinations)

- Self-experience (e.g., the experience that one's feelings, impulses, thoughts, or behavior are under the control of an external force)
- Cognition (e.g., impaired attention, verbal memory, and social cognition), volition (e.g., loss of motivation)
- Affect (e.g., blunted emotional expression) and
- Behavior (e.g., behavior that appears bizarre or purposeless, unpredictable or inappropriate emotional responses that interfere with the organization of behavior)

- Psychomotor disturbances, including catatonia, may be present.
- Persistent delusions, persistent hallucinations, thought disorder, and experiences of influence, passivity, or control are considered core symptoms. Symptoms must have persisted for at least 1 month in order for a diagnosis of schizophrenia to be assigned.
- The symptoms are not a manifestation of another health condition (e.g., a brain tumor) and are not due to the effect of a substance or medication on the central nervous system (e.g., corticosteroids), including withdrawal (e.g., alcohol withdrawal).

DIFFERENTIAL DIAGNOSIS OF SCHIZOPHRENIA

- Schizoaffective disorder
- Delusional disorder
- Post-traumatic disorder
- Hypochondriasis
- Mood disorder with psychotic symptoms
- Sleep-related disorder
- Substance-induced psychotic disorder
- Psychotic disorder due to general medical condition (Metabolic disorders, endocrine disorders, anatomic lesions, infectious diseases, vitamin deficiency)
- Schizophreniform disorder or acute transient psychotic disorder or brief psychotic disorder
- Delirium and dementia
- Body dysmorphic disorder
- Schizotypal personality disorder
- Schizoid personality disorder
- Pervasive developmental disorder
- Obsessive-compulsive disorder
- Anxiety disorder
- Misidentification syndrome
- Induced or shared psychotic disorder
- Factitious disorder
- Bipolar affective disorder

THREE PHASES OF SCHIZOPHRENIA

Three phases of schizophrenia are as follows: (1) Prodromal phase, (2) Psychotic phase, and (3) Residual phase. Prodromal phase is a first phase that occurs before psychotic episode. Social withdrawal and irritability occur in prodromal phase. The second phase is psychotic phase. In psychotic phase, altered thought process, disturbances of perception and delusions are seen. The third phase is residual phase which occurs between psychotic episodes in which patient exhibits flat affect (lack of emotional expression), social withdrawal and odd behavior as shown in Figure 6.7.

POSITIVE AND NEGATIVE SYMPTOMS OF SCHIZOPHRENIA

The positive symptoms of schizophrenia are hallucination, delusion, disorganized thoughts and bizarre behavior which are seen in acute phase and also have good response to treatment. The negative symptoms of schizophrenia are apathy, flat or blunt affect, anhedonia, alogia, avolition, asociality and attention deficit as described in Table 6.3.

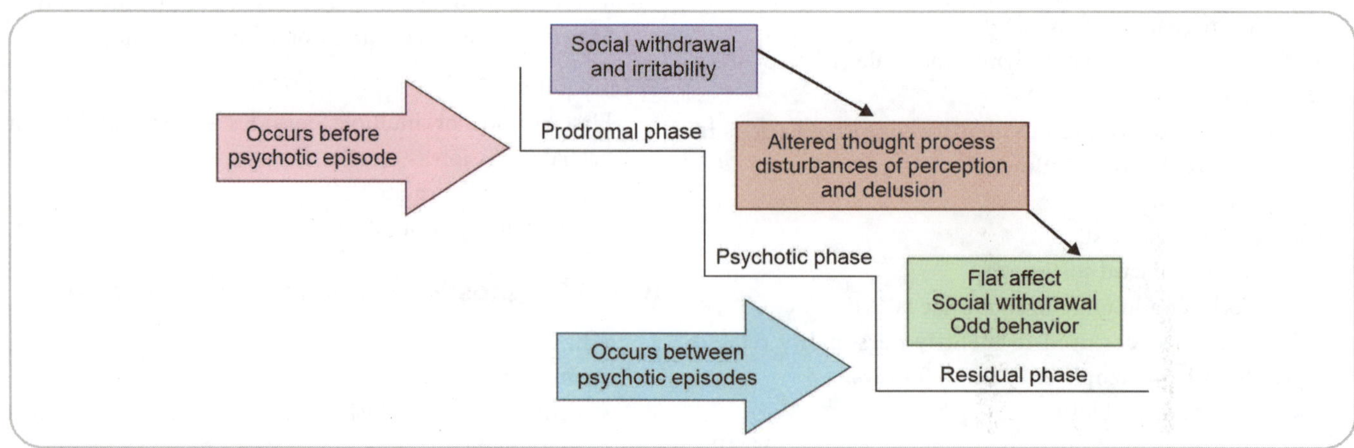

Figure 6.7: Three phases of schizophrenia

Table 6.3: Positive and negative symptoms of schizophrenia

Positive symptoms	Negative symptoms
Hallucination Delusion Disorganized thoughts Bizarre behavior	**Apathy** or **Affective flattening** or **Blunt affect:** Blank facial expression **Anhedonia:** Inability to express pleasure which is pleasurable one previously **Alogia:** Lack of speech output **Avolition:** Lack of initiative to act **Asociality:** Social withdrawal **Attention deficit:** Lack of attention
Seen in acute phase	Seen in chronic phase
Have good response to treatment	Not having good response to treatment when compared with treatment of patient with positive symptoms

Schneider's First-Rank Symptoms: Kurt Schneider, German psychiatrist, enumerated 11 first-rank symptoms of schizophrenia.

- **Three auditory hallucinations:**
  - i. Third person voices giving commentary about patient actions
  - ii. Third person voices arguing or discussing about patient
  - iii. Thought Echo—voices are speaking thoughts a loud
- **Three-thought phenomenon or thought-alienation phenomenon:**
  - i. **Thought broadcasting:** Thoughts escaped into outside world and others are experiencing it.
  - ii. **Thought withdrawal:** Thoughts have been removed by an external source.
  - iii. **Thought insertion:** Thoughts have been inserted by an external source.
- **Three made phenomenon (Client experience emotions, drives and actions influenced by others):**
  - i. **'Made' actions:** Actions performed by outside control.
  - ii. **'Made' feelings:** Feelings are not own, due to external source.
  - iii. **'Made' impulses:** Impulses or drives from an external source.
- **Miscellaneous**
  - **Somatic passivity:** Passive somatic sensation by external source.
  - **Delusional perception:** Illogical meaning attributed toward normal perception.

Symptoms of Schizophrenia

- **Disorders of thought and speech**
  - **Autistic thinking:** Illogical thoughts.
  - **Loosening of association:** Rapid shifting of one idea to other without any association between those ideas.
  - **Thought block:** Interruption in stream of speech before its completion.
  - **Neologism:** Framing new words which do not have any meaning.
  - **Mutism:** Complete absence of speech.
  - **Poverty of ideation:** Speech delivered is adequate but the content of speech is inadequate.
  - **Poverty of speech**: Decreased production of speech.
  - **Echolalia:** Repetition of words by the patient exactly what the examiner says.
  - **Perseveration or verbigeration:** Repetition of words by patient.
  - **Delusions:** False fixed unshakable belief irrespective to their sociocultural values.
- **Disorders of perception**
  - **Auditory hallucinations:** Hearing voices or sounds without external stimuli.
  - **Visual hallucinations:** Visualizing images/shade/ something without external stimuli.
- **Disorders of affect**
  - **Blunt affect:** Reduction in intensity of emotional response.
  - **Inappropriate affect:** Mood and affect are not appropriate.
  - **Apathy:** Lack of facial expression.
  - **Anhedonia:** Inability to experience pleasure which seems to be pleasurable before.
- **Disorders of motor behavior**
  - Decreased psychomotor activity or Increased psychomotor activity.
  - **Stereotype behavior:** Repetitive strange behavior.
  - Catatonic features.
- **Miscellaneous**
  - Reduction in social functioning
  - Decreased self-care
  - Perplexity in regard to own identity

- Multiple somatic complaints
- Suicide if associated with depression
- No disturbances in attention, concentration, memory, cognition and intelligence
- No organic cause
- No prominent mood symptoms (except schizoaffective disorder)

Hallucination

It is defined as misperception without any external stimuli. Common types are auditory, visual, olfactory, tactile and gustatory. Auditory type of hallucination is most common in schizophrenia. Types of auditory hallucination are simple and complex. Simple auditory hallucination is any sound heard whereas complex hallucination is voice heard by the patient. It also referred as second person hallucination and third person hallucination. Hearing voice outside the one's head when the patient is alone clearly identifies auditory hallucination, if not it might be one's own thoughts that refers to pseudo-hallucination.

Dimensions in the Psychopathology of Schizophrenia

The three dimensions in the psychopathology of schizophrenia are: (1) Psychotic dimension, (2) Disorganized dimension, and (3) Negative dimension. Psychotic dimension denotes positive symptoms, disorganized dimension denotes disorganized speech, disorganized behavior and inappropriate affect, and negative dimension denotes negative symptoms as explained in Flowchart 6.1.

Flowchart 6.1: Three dimensions of psychopathology of schizophrenia

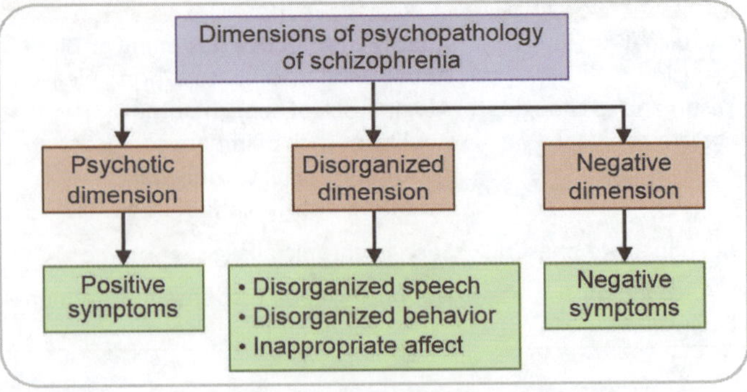

OTHER PSYCHOTIC DISORDERS

As per ICD-11 and DSM-5, the classification of other psychotic disorders is given in Table 6.4.

Acute and Transient Psychotic Disorder

The term 'transient' denotes short lasting. Onset of psychotic symptoms is abrupt and acute with positive symptoms such as delusion, hallucination, disorganized thoughts and perplexity or confusion. This symptom is not a manifestation of another health condition or due to influence or withdrawal of any substances.

Duration of the episode: It does not exceed 3 months, and most commonly lasts from a few days to 1 month.

Table 6.4: ICD-11 and DSM-5 classification of other psychotic disorders

ICD-11	DSM-5	Classification of mental disorders
Schizophrenia spectrum and other psychotic disorders		
6A21	—	Schizoaffective disorder
6A22	301.22	Schizotypal (personality) disorder
6A23	—	Acute and transient psychotic disorder
6A24	297.1	Delusional disorder
—	298.8	Brief psychotic disorder
—	295.40	Schizophreniform disorder
—	295.70	Schizoaffective disorder (bipolar type)
—	295.70	Schizoaffective disorder (depressive type)
—	293.81	Psychotic disorder due to another medical condition (with delusions)
—	293.82	Psychotic disorder due to another medical condition (with hallucinations)
6A40	293.89	Catatonia associated with another mental disorder (catatonia specifier)
—	293.89	Catatonic disorder due to another medical condition
6A41	—	Catatonia induced by psychoactive substances, including medications
6A4Z	293.89	Unspecified catatonia
—	298.8	Other specified schizophrenia spectrum and other psychotic disorder
—	298.9	Unspecified schizophrenia spectrum and other psychotic disorder

Epidemiology: It will appear in early adolescence or early adulthood. Onset may occur anytime throughout the life span. Average age of onset is around 30 years of age.

Recovery and prognosis: Recovery is within 3 months and prognosis is usually better than schizophrenia. It does not fulfill the criteria of schizophrenia so it is categorized as acute transient psychotic disorders.

Rating scale: Rating scale used for the assessment was Clinician-rated dimensions of psychotic symptoms severity. It is 5-point Likert scale with 8 domains such as hallucination, delusion, disorganized speech, negative symptoms, mania, depression, impaired cognition and abnormal psychomotor behavior.

Peculiar Clinical Features

- Types of hallucinations and delusions are seen which are found variable in terms of intensity and nature.
- Marked emotional fluctuations from extreme happiness, sadness, irritability and anxiety.

Specification of Subtypes

- First episode or multiple episodes
- Full remission or partial remission
- Currently symptomatic
- Unspecified

Schizotypal (Personality) Disorder

It is characterized by an enduring pattern (i.e., characteristic of the individual's functioning over several years) of eccentricities in the behavior, appearance and speech, which is accompanied by the unusual beliefs, cognitive distortions, perceptual distortions, often having a reduced capacity for the interpersonal relationships. The symptoms include the paranoid ideas, ideas of reference, or other psychotic symptoms including hallucinations in any modality, may occur (positive schizotypy), and constricted or inappropriate affect, anhedonia (negative schizotypy), but are not of sufficient intensity or duration to meet the diagnostic criteria of schizophrenia, schizoaffective disorder, or delusional disorder. The symptoms might cause the significant personal distress or significant impairment in the personal, family, social, educational, occupational or other vital areas of functioning (Flowchart 6.2).

Flowchart 6.2: Symptoms of schizotypal disorder

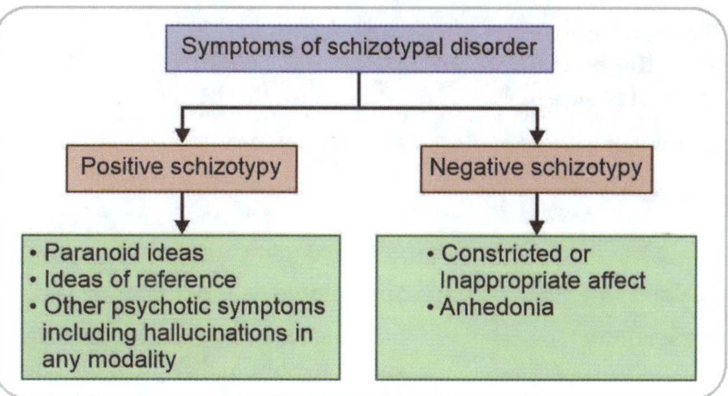

Delusional Disorder

Delusions are well systematized and non-bizarre type stable and chronic in nature. Patient is not able to differentiate between real and imaginary things. Emotional response and patient's behavior is understood well based on delusions. More often social and occupational life is not affected.

The peculiar clinical features are as follows:

- ***Duration:*** Persistent delusions at least for 1 month are longer.
- Not prominent hallucinations may be related to the delusional theme (sensation of being infested with the insects might be associated with delusions of infestation).
- No mood disorders, schizophrenia and organic brain disorders.
- Apart from the impact of the delusion, functioning is not markedly impaired and behavior is not bizarre or odd obviously.
- Disturbances is not due to another mental disorder or medical condition or due to substance abuse/withdrawal.
- If there is a manic or major depressive episode, it is brief relative to the duration of delusional period.

Types of delusional disorder on the basis of central theme of delusions have been given in Table 6.5.

Specify if it is:

- First episode or multiple episodes.
- Currently in acute or chronic episode.
- Currently in partial or full remission.
- Continuous presence of symptoms during the course of illness: Present/absent.
- Severity of symptoms: Very severe/moderate/less severe.
- Mixed type: Lack of any one predominant delusional theme.
- Unspecified: Dominant delusional belief not be clearly determined with any specific type.

Brief Psychotic Disorder

Presence of one or more symptoms such as delusions, hallucinations, disorganized speech, grossly disorganized or catatonic behavior. The duration of an episode of disturbance is at least 1 day but less than 1 month, with the eventual full return

Table 6.5: Delusional disorder on the basis of central theme of delusions

Types of delusional disorder on the basis of central theme	Description	Example
Erotomanic type	Another person is in love with the individual	Patient verbalizes that, 'Actor is having love desire toward me'
Grandiose type	Conviction of having some great or talent or having made some vital discovery	Patient verbalizes that, 'I am the god'
Jealous type	Spouse or lover is not faithful	Patient verbalizes that, 'My wife is having a love with other guy'
Persecutory type	Individual is being cheated, followed, spied on, poisoned or drugged, harassed etc.	Patient verbalizes that, "My friend is having a plan to kill me"
Somatic type	It involves bodily functions or sensations	Patient verbalizes that, 'I feel sound of running water in my stomach'
With bizarre content	Delusions are clearly not understandable and not derived from ordinary life experiences	Individual strongly believes that a stranger has removed one's internal organs and replaced the same with other without any scar in the body

toward the premorbid level of functioning. This disturbance is not well explained by the major depressive or bipolar disorder with psychotic features or other psychotic disorder such as schizophrenia or catatonia, and is not attributable due to the influence of a substance or any other medical condition.

Specify this diagnosis if it is:

- With (brief reactive psychosis) or without stressors
- With postpartum onset (onset is during pregnancy or within 4 weeks' postpartum) or
- With catatonia.

Schizophreniform Disorder

Duration of the episode: This is a mental disorder, diagnosed when symptoms of schizophrenia are at least 1 month but less than 6 months.

Symptoms: At least one of the following symptoms such as delusions, hallucinations, disorganized speech (e.g., frequent derailment or incoherence), grossly disorganized or catatonic behavior, negative symptoms (i.e., diminished emotional expression or avolition). This symptom is not a manifestation of another health condition or due to influence or withdrawal of any substances.

Specify if it is:

- With good prognostic features: Presence of at least two of the features:
    - Onset of prominent psychotic symptoms within 4 weeks of the first noticeable change in usual behavior or functioning.
    - Confusion or perplexity
    - Good premorbid social and occupational functioning and
    - Absence of blunted or flat affect.
- Without good prognostic features: Two or more of the above features are absent.
- With catatonia
- Specify current severity: Clinician-rated dimensions of psychosis symptom severity scale.

Schizoaffective Disorder

Symptoms: It has both symptoms of schizophrenia and mood disorders which are prominently seen in same episode. (Schizo + Affective = Schizophrenic symptoms + Mood symptoms). Mood symptoms may be mania, depression or mixed mania and depression.

Prognosis: good.

Treatment: Injection lorazepam (IV) and electroconvulsive therapy.

Specify if it is:

- Bipolar type: Manic episode is part of the presentation. Major depressive episodes may also occur.
- Depressive type: Major depressive episode is part of the presentation.
- With or without catatonia.
- First episode or multiple episodes.
- Full remission (a period of time after a previous episode during which no disorder-specific symptoms are present) or partial remission (a time period during which an improvement after a previous episode is maintained and in which the defining criteria of the disorder are only partially fulfilled).

Psychotic Disorder due to Another Mental Disorder

There will be presence of prominent hallucinations or delusions with the clear diagnostic evidence states it is due to the direct pathophysiological consequence of another mental disorder. This disturbance causes clinically significant personal distress and impairment in social, occupational or other vital areas of functioning.

Psychotic Disorder due to Another Medical Condition

There will be presence of prominent hallucinations or delusions with the clear diagnostic evidence states it is due to the direct pathophysiological consequence of another medical condition. The disturbance is not better explained by another mental disorder and does not occur during the course of a delirium. This disturbance causes clinically significant personal distress and impairment in social, occupational or other vital areas of functioning.

Specify if it is:

- With hallucinations
- With delusions.

Catatonia

It is a marked disturbance in the voluntary control of movements which is characterized by extreme slowness or absence of motor activity, purposeless motor activity unrelated to external stimuli, mutism, maintenance of rigid or unusual or bizarre postures, resistance to the instructions or attempts to be moved, or automatic compliance with instructions.

Symptoms: Table 6.6 (3 or more following symptoms should be present as per DSM-5 criteria).

It may be diagnosed in the context of certain mental disorders: Schizophrenia, mood disorders and autism spectrum disorder.

Potential risk of catatonia: Malnutrition, Hyperpyrexia, Exhaustion, self-inflicted injury and harming others

Specify if it is:

- Associated with another mental disorder.
- Due to another medical condition.
- Induced by psychoactive substances, including medications.
- Unspecified (full criteria for the catatonia not met or due to insufficient information to have a specific diagnosis—for example, patient admitted in emergency room situations).

Other Specified Schizophrenia Spectrum and Other Psychotic Disorder

Symptoms of a schizophrenia spectrum and other psychotic disorder which cause significant distress or impairment in social, occupational functioning but do not meet full criteria for any of disorders in the schizophrenia spectrum and other psychotic disorders. When there is presence of specific reason for the presentation such as:

- Persistent auditory hallucinations happen in the absence of other features.
- Delusions with predominant overlapping mood episodes.
- Attenuated psychosis syndrome: Psychotic-like symptoms below a threshold for full psychosis (symptoms are less in severity, transient and presence of insight).

Table 6.6: Symptoms of catatonia

Symptoms of catatonia	Description
Stupor	Absence of psychomotor activity or not actively relating to environment
Catalepsy	Passive induction of a posture held against gravity
Waxy flexibility	Slight, even resistance to positioning by examiner
Mutism	Absence or very little verbal response (exclude if there is known aphasia)
Negativism	Opposition or no response to the instructions or external stimuli
Posturing	Spontaneous and active maintenance of a posture against gravity
Mannerism	Odd, circumstantial caricature of normal actions
Stereotypy	Repetitive abnormally frequent non-goal-directed movements
Echolalia	Mimicking another's speech
Echopraxia	Mimicking another's movements
Grimacing	Fixed facial expression
Agitation	A sense of excitement which is not influenced by external stimuli

- Delusional symptoms present in the individual with delusional disorder.

Unspecified Schizophrenia Spectrum and Other Psychotic Disorder

Symptoms of a schizophrenia spectrum and other psychotic disorder which cause significant distress or impairment in social, occupational functioning but do not meet full criteria for any of disorders in the schizophrenia spectrum and other psychotic disorders. When there is presence of insufficient information to make a more specific diagnosis (for example, in emergency room settings).

PROGNOSIS OF SCHIZOPHRENIA

The prognosis of schizophrenia is given in Table 6.7.

Table 6.7: Prognosis of schizophrenia

Aspects	Good prognosis	Poor prognosis
Onset	Acute/abrupt	Insidious
Age of onset	Late	Early
Duration	<6 months	>2 years
Episode	First episode	Previous history of schizophrenia
Gender	Female	Male
Stressor	Absent	Present
Depression	Absent	Present
Symptoms	Positive symptoms	Negative symptoms
Social support	Good	Poor
Types	Acute catatonia (Paranoid has intermediate prognosis)	Disorganized, undifferentiated and simple
Relapse of symptoms	Absent	Present
Drug adherence	Present	Absent
Nature of treatment	Outpatient basis/ community based	Inpatient/ hospitalization
CT scan	Normal	Enlargement of ventricles
Premorbid functioning	Good	Poor

PSYCHOSOCIAL INTERVENTIONS

Psychosocial interventions for schizophrenia have been given in Table 6.8.

Table 6.8: Psychosocial interventions for schizophrenia

Psychosocial interventions for schizophrenia	Description
Psychoeducation	• Regarding the nature and course of schizophrenia • Treatment of schizophrenia
Social skills training	• Patient with negative symptoms of schizophrenia will have lack of social skills • Social skills such as maintaining eye to eye contact, shaking hands with others, making ward rounds, social interaction with others are said to be implied
Cognitive training/Cognitive remediation	Cognitive deficits such as lack in attention/ concentration/memory should be targeted and appropriate training should be provided to improve it
Supportive employment or Vocational rehabilitation	Promotion of vocational guidance and placement in a right job helps the client to cope up with the situation well
Token economy	• Acts as a positive reinforcement in case of desired positive behavior • One token will be issued for one desirable positive behavior • If a number of tokens have been collected by a patient, then a particular gift can be provided to motivate the client
Family interventions	Steps taken to avoid 'Expressed Emotions' in family (i.e., to avoid critical comments, hostile behavior and high emotional involvement)
Psychosocial weight management	• Research data states that tablet Olanzapine might cause increase in weight up to 5 kg within 1 week • Even other antipsychotics might increase the weight • So, balanced high fiber diet has to be maintained
Interventions to enhance drug compliance	• Important cause of relapse of symptoms is drug nonadherence • So, education in regard to drug compliance is needed

Antipsychotics: Discussed in Chapter 5.

TREATMENT

Psychotherapy for Schizophrenia

Individual psychotherapy, group psychotherapy, supportive psychotherapy and cognitive behavior therapy are the first line of treatment which should be started in the patient's suffering from schizophrenia.

Treatment-Resistant Schizophrenia

Clozapine is a drug of choice for the treatment of resistant schizophrenia. If it fails, it can be treated with amisulpride, risperidone, aripiprazole, lamotrigine, topiramate, benzodiazepines, depot preparations and antidepressants (for negative symptoms) (Fig. 6.8).

Repetitive Transcranial Magnetic Stimulation

In this noninvasive technique, changing magnetic field is used to cause electric current to the brain (specific area) through electromagnetic induction. It is a brain stimulation technique and is mainly used to treat depression when applied in prefrontal cortex. However, research evidence suggests auditory hallucination reduces when applied in temporoparietal cortex.

Assertive Community Treatment and Intensive Psychiatric Rehabilitation

Assertive community treatment is defined as group of psychiatric health team workers joins together to render the care to mentally ill patients in a community setup and they do regular follow-ups to promote the holistic mental well-being of patients.

Intensive psychiatric rehabilitation is defined as the structured measures taken for the promotion of mental health of the person (he/she) before the onset of mental illness.

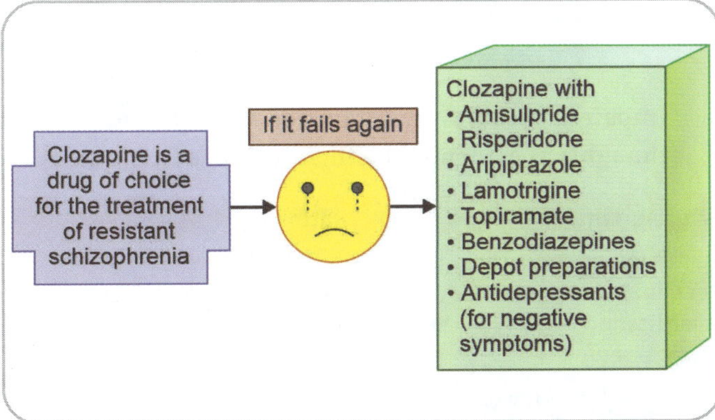

Figure 6.8: Medications for the treatment-resistant schizophrenia

NURSING INTERVENTIONS

- **Disturbed thought process related to neurochemical factors as evidenced by delusion of persecution**

Nursing interventions	Rationale
Assess the intensity, content, frequency and duration of delusion	To obtain baseline data about delusion
Assess the environmental triggering factors	To reduce the environmental triggering factors
Communicate with client calmly and gently	Since the client is having suspiciousness therefore, he/she might have fear of everything
Avoid arguing about delusion	Argument about delusion might put the delusion stronger
Monitor the client carefully	Clients with delusions might harm to self and others
Encourage the client to ventilate the distressing thoughts	To reduce the stress
Encourage the client for group activities	To promote self-esteem
Educate the client and caregivers regarding the importance of psychotropic drugs	To enhance the drug adherence and to prevent the relapse of symptoms
Do's • Assign the same staff for taking care of the patient • Be truthful to the client • Be assertive with patient **Don'ts** • Touch the client unnecessarily • Laughing, murmuring or whispering in front of client	To promote trust

- **Disturbed sensory perception related to genetic or biochemical factors as evidenced by hallucinatory behavior**

Nursing interventions	Rationale
Assess the intensity, content, frequency, duration and type of hallucination	To obtain baseline data about hallucination
Ask the client, 'What the voices saying to you?'	To explore whether the commanding voices will cause any harm to the patient or not
Avoid arguing about hallucination	Argument about hallucination might put the hallucination stronger

Contd...

Nursing interventions	Rationale
Identify the triggering factors	To reduce the severity of hallucination
Interrupt the hallucination by diverting or calling the patient	It helps to divert the patient from hallucination
Encourage the client to say 'stop' or 'go away' or whistle slowly to dismiss the hallucination	It helps to deal the hallucination effectively

- **Social isolation related to negative symptoms of schizophrenia as evidenced by social withdrawal**

Nursing interventions	Rationale
Convey the acceptance attitude to the patient	To promote the feeling of self-worth
Involve the client for group activities	To enhance social skills
Promote positive reinforcement if the client performs voluntary interaction to others	To motivate the client to perform task
Provide social skills trainings such as maintaining eye contact while interacting, shaking hands, talking in polite way, providing a leadership role, etc.	To improve social skills

- **Self-care deficit related to cognitive impairment or lack of trust or anxiety as evidenced by inability to do the tasks such as bathing, grooming, eating, toileting and sleeping**

Nursing interventions	Rationale
Assess the patient ability to perform the self-care activities	To obtain baseline data
Assist the client to perform self-care activities	To promote the comfort and safety
Encourage the patient to perform the task independently	Helps to promote the behavior by motivation
Demonstrate the activities need to be performed in simple steps	Helps to guide the client how to perform the task step by step
Allow enough time to perform the self-care activities	Patient might take more time due to shorter attention span
Withdraw the assistance gradually and supervise the patient's self-care activities	It promotes the sense of independence

- **Ineffective health maintenance related to poor dietary intake or lack of trust or suspiciousness that food is poisonous as evidenced by significant loss of weight**

Nursing interventions	Rationale
Assess the nutritional status of the patient	To obtain the baseline data
Monitor the food intake regularly	It provides a pathway of continuous assessment
If client is suspicious about the food is poisonous, ask the client himself/herself to get the food from shop	It helps to decrease the suspiciousness
Educate the client regarding the nutritious diet	It helps to improve the health status
Provide the menu plan to the patient	Guide the client to eat the food at proper time
Provide food that the client likes	Motivate the client to eat

- **Risk of violence related to command hallucination as evidenced by destruction of nearby objects**

Nursing interventions	Rationale
Observe the client carefully and frequently	To obtain baseline data
Remove the sharp and dangerous objects from the client's room	To ensure the client's safety
Provide scheduled daily activities to patient	To make the client being committed with daily activities
Provide physical restraints to the client. Check the distal pulse rate and color of skin every 15 minutes once	Restraints prevent harm to oneself and also to others. Monitoring pulse and skin color will ensure the proper blood circulation
Encourage the client to ventilate the distressing thoughts	To reduce the aggression
Administer relaxation therapy	To reduce the stress
Redirect the violent behavior into physical outlet. For example, involve the patient in outdoor sports	To redirect the violence into fruitful activity

- **Impaired verbal communication related to unrealistic thoughts as evidenced by flight of ideas**

Nursing interventions	Rationale
Use therapeutic techniques of communication, e.g., clarification—can you clarify it still better	Helps to have clear communication between nurse and patient
Assign the staff nurse consistently with the patient who feels reluctant to talk with other staff nurse	Promote empathy and verbalize the feeling to the nurse after gaining trust

Contd...

Nursing interventions	Rationale
Talk in a simple language	It will help the client to understand properly
Motivate the client to talk to other patients	It will help the patient to improve the communication skills

- **Ineffective family coping related to conflicts among family members, impaired communication among family members and more concern on illness**

Nursing interventions	Rationale
Assess the communication pattern, conflicts and importance of patient among family members	To have a baseline data
Give psychoeducation to the family members regarding the treatment process and prognosis	It will help to reduce the problems among family members
Educate the family members that the conflicts occurring in your family will affect prognosis of the patient	Helps to promote the unity among them
Facilitate the proper communication among family members	Useful to prevent the issues among family members

GERIATRIC CONSIDERATIONS

Late-onset schizophrenia (onset after 45 years of age) characterized by paranoid ideations along with varying degrees of impairment can be observed in older patients. Psychosis in elderly may be comorbid with depression or dementia. Antipsychotics and psychotherapy will be helpful for elders to reduce the psychotic symptoms.

FOLLOW-UP, HOME CARE AND REHABILITATION OF PATIENTS WITH SCHIZOPHRENIA

Follow-up of Patients with Schizophrenia

Regular follow-up by the psychiatric nurse is found vital to prevent the relapse of psychotic symptoms. Follow-up can be done either by home visits or through telephone to provide the necessary guidance and counseling to the patient and family members. Proper documentation of follow-up helps the nurse to promote the quality nursing care.

Home Care of Patients with Schizophrenia

Taking care of patients in home settings will promote the mental health in far better way. Family members have to understand that negatively expressed emotions might provoke the psychotic symptoms so necessary psychoeducation has to be given to the family members. Patient has to be motivated for the right behavior and family members should not express the negative emotions about patient.

Rehabilitation of Patient with Schizophrenia

The term 'Rehabilitation' denotes restoring the health status of mentally ill individuals as early as possible. Nurses can refer to the self-help group or rehabilitative centers in order to promote mental health of patient and to prevent the relapse of psychotic symptoms. The rehabilitative services are as follows:

- Day hospitals
- Half-way homes
- Long-term homes
- Occupational therapy
- Social skills training
- Monetary management skills
- Recreational therapy
- Cognitive training

EXTRA EDGE

ICD-10 Classification of Schizophrenia

- F20.0: Paranoid schizophrenia
- F20.1: Hebephrenic schizophrenia
- F20.2: Catatonic schizophrenia
- F20.3: Undifferentiated schizophrenia
- F20.4: Post-schizophrenic depression
- F20.5: Residual schizophrenia
- F20.6: Simple schizophrenia
- F20.8: Other types of schizophrenia
- F20.9: Schizophrenia, unspecified

EXTRA EDGE

Types of Schizophrenia

Paranoid Schizophrenia

It is most common type of schizophrenia. Onset is late and has good prognosis. Personality is said to be preserved, i.e., client is able to perform activities of daily living (ADLs) and has good social interaction. Hallucination, delusion and thought disorders are peculiarly seen. Examples of hallucinatory themes are commenting, arguing, threatening, body sensations/movements. Examples of thought disorders are irrelevant, incoherent and neologisms in speech. Prognosis is good in case of earlier treatment. Minimal deterioration of personality is seen.

Examples of delusional themes are persecution, grandiose, jealousy and reference.

- Delusion of persecution means patient having strong suspiciousness of being cheated, poisoned, spied on, harassed, etc.

Contd...

- Delusion of reference denotes that the irrelevant or innocent events happen in the surroundings refer to oneself. For example, patient believes that others are talking about him/her.
- Delusion of jealousy means unfaithfulness with individual's sexual partner.
- Delusion of grandiosity means irrational ideas in regard to talent, power or knowledge.

Hebephrenic or Disorganized Schizophrenia

Behavior is aimless and not goal directed in hebephrenic schizophrenia. Hallucinations and delusions are not prominent. Inappropriate and incongruent affects are seen. Speech is incoherent. Early and insidious onset is associated with poor premorbid personality.

Catatonic Schizophrenia

Motor symptoms are present predominantly. Types of catatonic schizophrenia are stuporous, excited and periodic are explained in Flowchart 6.3. Prognosis is good. Treatment includes injection lorazepam (IV) and electroconvulsive therapy.

Simple Schizophrenia

Simple schizophrenia shows prominent negative symptoms of schizophrenia such as amotivation, apathy, social withdrawal, flat or blunt affect and poverty of speech. Positive symptoms are absent. Social functioning gets reduced. Onset is early and insidious. Course is progressive. Prognosis is worst.

Residual Schizophrenia

Progression is from early stage (hallucination and delusions are predominant) to late stage (hallucination and delusions are minimal). Negative symptoms are present.

Undifferentiated Schizophrenia

Schizophrenia not conforming any subtypes will come under the category of undifferentiated schizophrenia.

Postschizophrenic Depression

Depressive episode develops after the resolution of schizophrenic symptoms in post-schizophrenic depression. Patient might be at high suicidal risk.

Schizophreniform Disorder

Features of schizophrenia are present, but when the duration is less than 6 months then it is labeled as schizophreniform disorder.

Pseudoneurotic Schizophrenia

Hoch and Polatin explained this type. Prominent neurotic symptoms are present in initial phase. Classical triad of pseudoneurotic schizophrenia includes pan-anxiety, pan-neurosis and pan-sexuality as explained in Figure 6.9. Pan-anxiety denotes free floating anxiety which will not subside easily. Pan-neurosis includes the predominant neurotic symptoms. Pan-sexuality denotes that patient with pseudoneurotic schizophrenia is preoccupied with sexual desires.

Pfropf Schizophrenia

It occurs with the presence of mental retardation. Behavior disturbance is more prominent than thought disorder. It differs from schizophrenia due to unsystematized delusions and poverty of ideation.

Van Gogh Syndrome

Self-mutilation or self-injurious behavior is seen in this type of schizophrenia. Van Gogh was a famous painter, he cuts his ear in state of acute illness and hence this term is named after him.

Flowchart 6.3: Types of catatonic schizophrenia

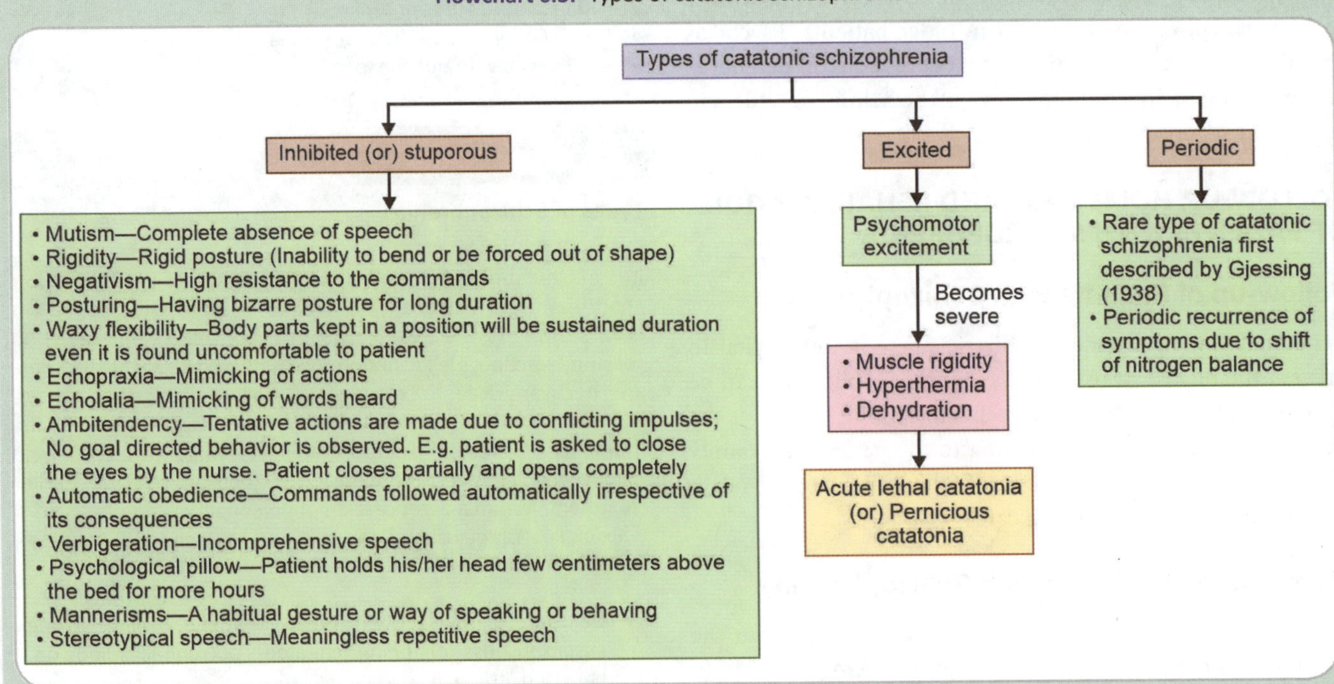

Contd...

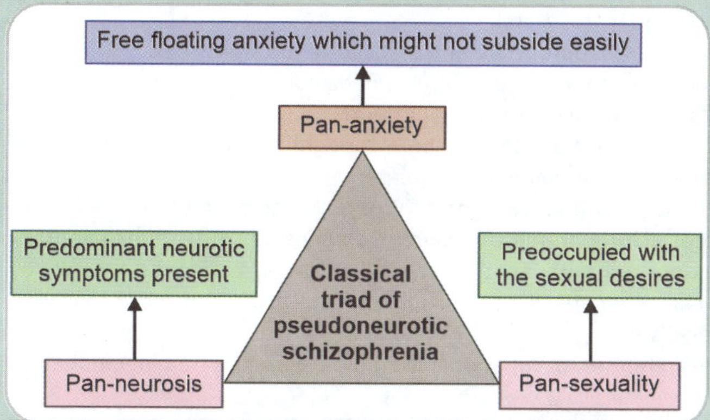

Figure 6.9: Classical triad of pseudoneurotic schizophrenia

Late Paraphrenia

Sir Martin Roth explained this type. Onset is too late. It is common in unmarried or widow women. Delusion of persecution with bizarre/fantasy is present. Visual, auditory, olfactory, gustatory and tactile hallucinations are seen.

Oneiroid Schizophrenia

Mayer-Gross explained this type. Onset is acute and usually the episode is brief. Term 'Oneiroid' means 'dream' so client remains in dream like state. Symptoms are such as clouding of consciousness, perceptual disturbances and disorientation.

Type I and Type II Schizophrenia

TJ Crow is classified schizophrenia as type I and type II. Symptoms, course of illness, cognitive deficit, condition of ventricles, response to medications and prognosis of type I and type II are explained in Table 6.9.

Bouffée Délirante

It is a French term for 'short-lived psychosis'. It is mainly characterized by hallucination, delusion, confused state, amnesia after attack and polymorphous symptoms. Remission takes place within 3 months even without any treatment. It occurs mainly due to consequences of urbanization and westernization.

According to ICD-10, required duration to diagnose schizophrenia is given in Table 6.10.

Table 6.9: Type I and type II schizophrenia

Aspects	Type I schizophrenia	Type II schizophrenia
Symptoms	Positive symptoms	Negative symptoms
Course of illness	Acute	Chronic
Cognitive deficit	Absent	Sometimes present
Ventricles	Normal	Dilated
Response to drugs	Good	Poor
Prognosis	Better	Poor

Table 6.10: Required duration to diagnose schizophrenia as per ICD-10

Types of schizophrenia	Duration
Paranoid schizophrenia	1 month
Hebephrenic or Disorganized schizophrenia	1 month
Catatonic schizophrenia	½ month or 2 weeks
Simple schizophrenia	12 months

Induced Delusional Disorder or Shared Psychotic Disorder

An uncommon delusional disorder in which the delusions have been shared between two individuals due to the emotional bonding is termed folie à deux. If those persons got separated then the dependent individual might be free of the delusions. So, the individual with true delusions has to be treated properly (Fig. 6.10).

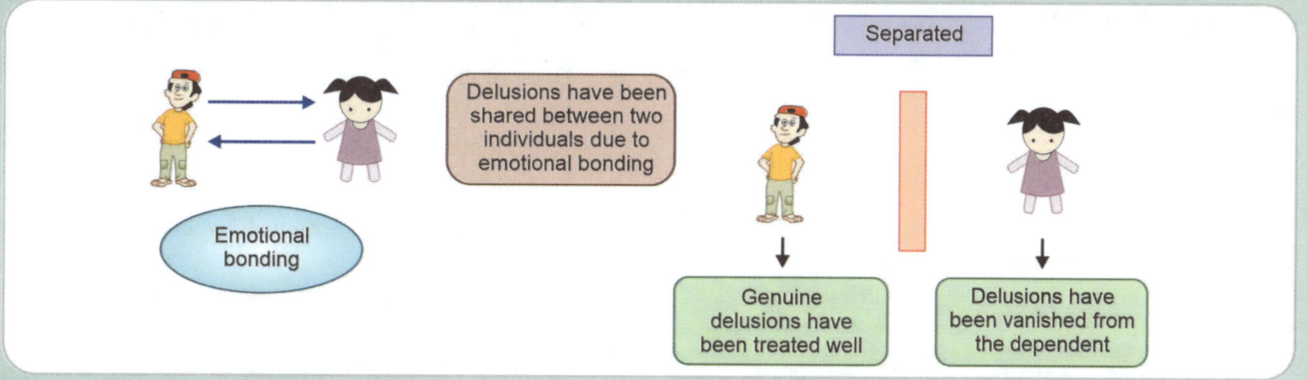

Figure 6.10: Concept map to understand induced delusional disorder

SUMMARY

- Schizophrenia is a psychotic disorder (disorder in which the client believes that he/she not have a basis of reality) characterized by abnormalities in emotion, thinking and cognition.
- 6A20 is ICD-11 code and 295.90 is DSM-5 code for schizophrenia.

Contd...

- Dopamine pathways are mesolimbic, mesocortical, tuberoinfundibular and nigrostriatal.
- 4 A's of schizophrenia by Bleuler are autistic thinking, ambivalence, affect is inappropriate and associative looseness.
- Positive symptoms of schizophrenia are hallucination, delusion, disorganized thoughts and bizarre behavior.
- Negative symptoms of schizophrenia are anhedonia, alogia, affect (flat), avolition and attention (poor).
- Kurt Schneider's first-rank symptoms of schizophrenia are three auditory hallucinations, three thought phenomenon or thought alienation phenomenon, three made phenomenon, somatic passivity and delusional perception.
- Other psychotic disorders are delusional disorder, acute and transient psychotic disorder, schizotypal (personality) disorder, brief psychotic disorder, schizoaffective disorder (bipolar or depressive type), schizophreniform disorder, psychotic disorder due to another medical condition (with delusions or hallucinations), catatonia associated with another mental disorder, catatonia induced by psychoactive substances, including medications, unspecified catatonia, other specified schizophrenia spectrum and other psychotic disorder and unspecified schizophrenia spectrum and other psychotic disorder.
- The rehabilitative services are day hospitals, half-way homes, long-term homes, occupational therapy, social skills training, monetary management skills, recreational therapy and cognitive training.

ASSESS YOURSELF

Long Answer Questions

1. Explain the types, etiology, psychopathology, diagnosis, clinical manifestations and management of patients with schizophrenia.
2. Explain the types, etiology, psychopathology, diagnosis, clinical manifestations and management of patients with catatonia.

Short Answer Questions

1. Define schizophrenia.
2. Define catatonia.

Short Notes

Write short notes on:

1. First-rank symptoms of schizophrenia
2. Delusional disorder
3. Nursing interventions of patient with schizophrenia
4. Etiology of schizophrenia
5. Clinical features of schizophrenia
6. Psychosocial interventions of schizophrenia
7. ICD-11 classification of schizophrenia
8. ICD-11 and DSM-5 diagnostic criteria of schizophrenia

Multiple Choice Questions

1. **Who first coined the term 'schizophrenia'?**
   a. Eugen Bleuler b. Emil Kraepelin
   c. Sigmund Freud d. None of the above
2. **Which dopamine pathway constitutes 80% of brain dopamine?**
   a. Mesolimbic b. Mesocortical
   c. Nigrostriatal d. Tuberoinfundibular
3. **Which dopamine pathway might cause hyperprolactinemia?**
   a. Mesolimbic b. Mesocortical
   c. Nigrostriatal d. Tuberoinfundibular
4. **ICD-11 code for schizophrenia is ________.**
   a. 6A20 b. 5A20
   c. 5A21 d. None of these
5. **Most common type of hallucination in psychiatric disorders is ________.**
   a. Visual b. Auditory
   c. Tactile d. Olfactory
6. **Schizophrenia occurs due to __________ in dopamine level.**
   a. Increased
   b. Decreased
   c. Neither increase nor decrease
   d. Fluctuate
7. **Which of the following are positive symptoms of schizophrenia; except:**
   a. Hallucination b. Delusion
   c. Anhedonia d. Disorganized thoughts
8. **Drug of choice for treatment-resistant schizophrenia is:**
   a. Haloperidol b. Risperidone
   c. Clozapine d. Olanzapine
9. **Thought has been removed by an external source means:**
   a. Thought insertion b. Thought withdrawal
   c. Thought broadcasting d. None of these
10. **Peculiar symptom identified in mental status examination among patients with schizophrenia is:**
    a. Delusion b. Delirium
    c. Sundowning syndrome d. Cogwheel rigidness

Answer Key

1. a	2. c	3. d	4. a	5. b
6. a	7. c	8. c	9. b	10. a

CHAPTER 7

Nursing Management of Patients with Mood Disorders

LEARNING OBJECTIVE

After studying this chapter, the student will be able to gain knowledge regarding mood disorders in order to render the nursing care of patient with mood disorders.

CHAPTER OUTLINE

KEY TERMS

Mood, Affect, Bipolar affective disorder, Depression, Mania, Euphoria, Elation, Exaltation, Ecstasy, Dysthymia, Cyclothymia, Euthymia, Hypomania, Delirious mania, Lithium toxicity, Endogenous depression, Exogenous depression, Involutional melancholia, Seasonal affective disorder, Social skill training, Antidepressants, Mood stabilizers, Electroconvulsive therapy (ECT), Light therapy (or) Phototherapy.

INTRODUCTION

Mood is a persistent and sustained emotional feeling. It is not triggered by a particular experience or event. Mood can be affected by different factors, including fatigue, stress, social interactions, world events, hormones, weather, hunger, and general health.

Mood can leave its impact on different aspects of life, including how people think, feel, and behave. These affective states can affect motivational levels and decision-making. They can also affect relationships and how people interact with others. Before studying mood disorders, it is better to know the differences between mood and its affect, definitions and meaning.

MOOD DISORDERS—MEANING/DEFINITION

It is also known as 'affective disorders'. It is classified as unipolar disorder (Depression) and bipolar disorder. In depression, client may experience one or more episodes of low level of mood known as unipolar disorder. In bipolar disorder, client may experience:

Table 7.1: Concept of mood and affect

Aspects	Mood	Affect
Meaning	It is a sustained and persistent emotional feeling	It is outward expression feelings
Comparable with	Climate (being persistent)	Weather (Keep changing)
Types	Elevated mood Normal mood Depressed mood Elevated mood can range from mild to very severe state as mentioned below. (Refer to Table 7.5) Ecstasy → Very severe Exaltation → Severe Elation → Moderate Euphoria → Mild	• *Flat affect*—No emotional expression • *Constricted or restricted affect*-reduction in the individual's emotional response • *Blunt/shallow affect*—Lack of affect is more severe than constricted or restricted affect but less severe than flat affect • *Labile affect (or) Pseudobulbar affect (PBA) (or) Involuntary Emotional Expression Disorder (IEED)*—Emotional incontinence, i.e., immediate and urge in expression of emotions • *Affect which is appropriate to mood (or) affect which is not appropriate to mood* • *Affect which if congruent (or) noncongruent to thought*

- Both the low mood (depression) and elevated mood (Mania or hypomania).
- Two or more episodes of elevated mood (Mania or hypomania).

Concept of mood and affect is listed in Table 7.1 and continuum of affect (Continuum ranges from no emotion expression to emotional incontinence) is shown in Figure 7.1. It also exhibits explanation of flat affect, constricted affect, blunt affect and labile affect.

History

Hippocrates coined the term 'Mania' and 'Depression'. He identified that mania and depression can occur in the same individual. Emil Kraepelin classified psychiatry as dementia praecox and manic-depressive psychosis. King Saul found that hearing music will help the individual to recover from depression.

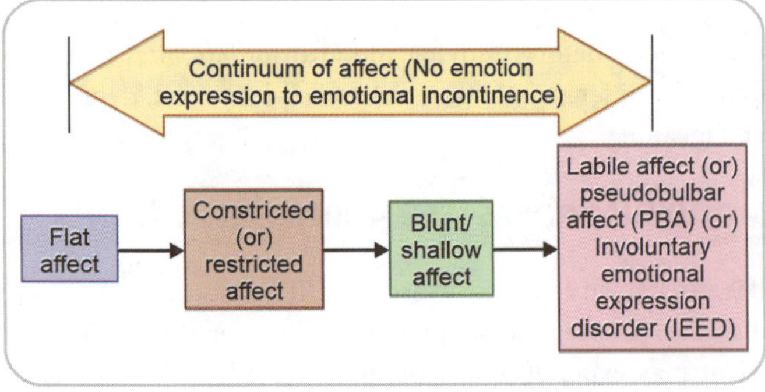

Figure 7.1: Continuum of affect

Incidence and Prevalence

- **Age:** Onset is usually at 25 years of age in bipolar disorder.
- **Gender:** Mania and depression both are more common in females. First episode as depression is common in females and first episode as mania is common in men. As per the **National Mental Health Survey Report**, conducted by National Institute of Mental Health and Neurosciences (NIMHANS), Bengaluru in 2016 explored the life time prevalence rate of Mood disorders: (Male—5.19, Female—6.00); Bipolar Affective disorder (Male—0.58, Female—0.42); and Depressive disorder (Male—4.75, Female—5.72). This report also states that the prevalence rate of mood disorders in urban metro cities is double than the prevalence rate in rural area.
- **Sociocultural:** Incidence is high among unmarried individuals.

Onset, gender and prevalence of bipolar and cyclothymic disorder have been depicted in Table 7.2.

Comorbid illness of mood disorders has been shown in Flowchart 7.1.

Table 7.2: Onset, gender and prevalence of bipolar and cyclothymic disorder

Aspects	Onset (Approx.)	Gender	Prevalence (%)
Bipolar I type	25 years	Males = Females	0.1
Bipolar II type		Females > Males	0.5
Cyclothymic disorder	18–25 years	Males = Females	0.4–1.0

Flowchart 7.1: Comorbid illness with mood disorders

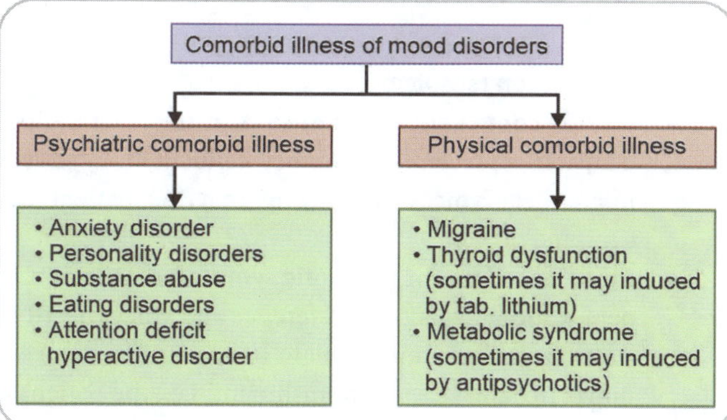

Duration required for the diagnosis of mood disorder has been depicted in Table 7.3.

Table 7.3: Duration of the persisting symptoms required for diagnosis of mood disorder as per DSM-5

Disorder	Duration of the persisting symptoms required for diagnosis of mood disorder as per DSM-5
Hypomanic episode	4 days
Manic episode	1 week
Depressive episode	2 weeks
Cyclothymia	2 years
Dysthymia	2 years

Bipolar Disorder

Either of two poles consists of mania or hypomania in one pole and depression on opposite pole (Flowchart 7.2).

Flowchart 7.2: Types of bipolar disorder

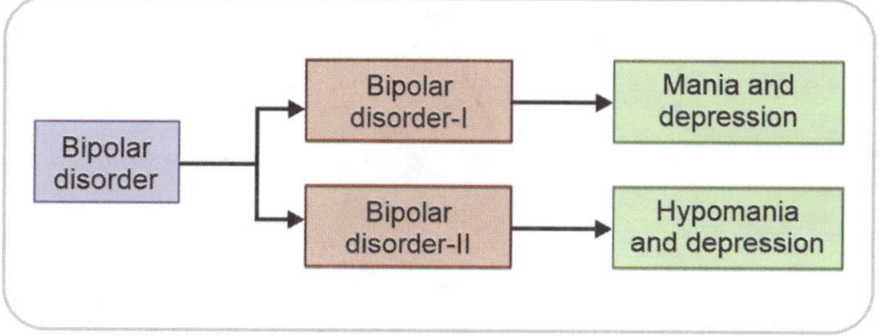

ICD-11 and DSM-5 Classification of bipolar related disorders has been shown in Table 7.4

Stages of Mania

Stage I—Hypomania

Stage II—Acute mania

Stage III—Delirious mania

Hypomania

The mood disorder in which symptoms are not severe to cause significant impairment in social or occupational functioning is known as hypomania. Psychotic features are absent.

Acute Mania

When intensified manic symptoms are present in a patient, the disorder is known as hypomania and if patient requires hospitalization it is known as acute mania. It is characterized by euphoria (or) elation, frequent mood variation, thinking that may have psychotic features, raised sexual interest with poor control of impulse, high energy level and the patient may deny grooming.

Table 7.4: ICD-11 and DSM-5 classification of bipolar related disorders

ICD-11	DSM-5	Bipolar and related disorders
Bipolar I disorder		
—	296.41	Current or most recent episode manic (Mild)
—	296.42	Current or most recent episode manic (Moderate)
—	296.43	Current or most recent episode manic (Severe)
6A60.5	296.44	Current or most recent episode manic (With psychotic features)
6A60.B	296.45	Current or most recent episode manic (In partial remission)
6A60.F	296.46	Current or most recent episode manic (In full remission)
6A60.E	296.40	Current or most recent episode manic (Unspecified)
Bipolar II disorder		
6A61	296.89	Bipolar II disorder
6A62	301.13	Cyclothymic disorder
6A6Y	296.89	Other specified bipolar and related disorder
6A6Z	296.80	Unspecified bipolar and related disorder

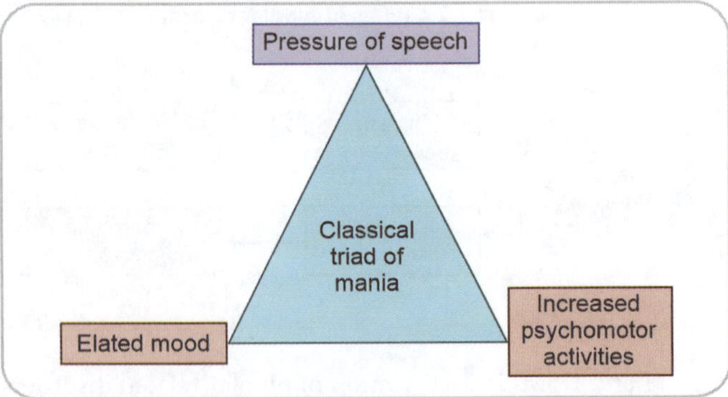

Figure 7.2: Classical triad of mania

Delirious Mania

Severe clouding of consciousness with confusion or disorientation or stupor, extreme labile mood, delusion with grandiosity or religiosity or persecution, auditory or visual hallucinations, increased psychomotor activity which has risk of harming to self or others. If left untreated, death may occur. Classical triad of mania has been given in Figure 7.2.

Types of Bipolar and Related Disorders

- Bipolar I disorder (current or recent manic episode)—mild or moderate or severe; with or without psychotic features; full or partial remission or unspecified.
- Depressive episode.
- Bipolar II disorder—cyclothymic disorder, other specified disorder and Unspecified disorder.

Comparison of hypomania and mania is given in Table 7.5.

Table 7.5: Comparison of hypomania and mania

Aspects	Hypomania	Mania
Duration of symptoms	4 days	>1 week
Psychotic features	Absent	May or may not
Social and occupational dysfunction	Absent	Present
Insight into illness	Present	Absent

Manic Episode (Table 7.5)

- Persistent elated, expansive (non-stop and unselective high-level enthusiasm to interact with others) and irritable mood (easily provoke anger for silly things).
- Increased goal directed activity.
- **Psychomotor activity increased:** Manic patients will be overactive and restless (On the toe—On the Go), excessive planning/doing many activities at the same time, performing high risk activities (Reckless driving in a heavy traffic) and do playful activities (cracking jokes, talking loud, jumping, etc.).
- **Thought**
  - Grandeur (strong unshakable belief that client has acquired a supreme power)
  - Persecution (suspiciousness)
  - **Mood congruent psychotic features:** Grandiose delusion is present. In auditory hallucination, patient might hear voices verbalizing that the patient has supreme power.
  - **Mood incongruent psychotic symptoms:** Delusion of persecution, delusion of reference and voices heard in auditory hallucinations might be telling that, 'you are unworthy and deserve punishment', i.e., the patient is in manic episode, but the psychotic symptoms elicited are not congruent with the patient's mood.
  - Hallucinations (Auditory and visual)
- **Speech:** Mental status examination reveals the flight of ideas that leads to incoherence (rapid shift from one idea to other) and increased pressure of speech (Flight of ideas without pressure is termed prolixity).
- **Perception:** Raised perceptual sensitivity can be seen in patients such as hyperacusis (Little sounds has been heard in higher volume) and seeing vivid colors.
- **Miscellaneous:** Patient will have decreased need for sleep and absence of insight. There is no relation with any organic cause. Patient will have a severe interference in personal functioning and sometimes exhibit irresponsible behavior, e.g., spending too much of money for unnecessary things.

Etiology of Mood Disorders

Neurotransmitter

Levels of norepinephrine, serotonin and dopamine are found to be decreased in depression and increased in mania as shown in Figure 7.3.

Biopsychosocial Factors

Biological causes include imbalance in neurotransmitters and hereditary factors (Primary relatives with mood disorders and monozygotic twins). The psychological causes are hopelessness, helplessness and worthlessness. Social causes are social pressure, stressful life events, loss of loved ones and social isolation as shown in Figure 7.4.

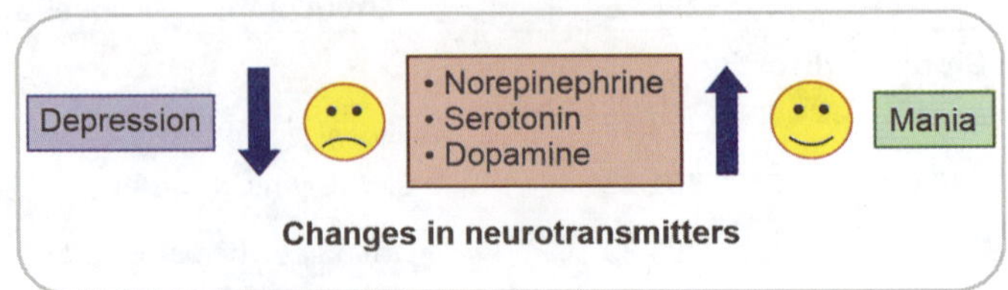

Figure 7.3: Neurotransmitters in mania

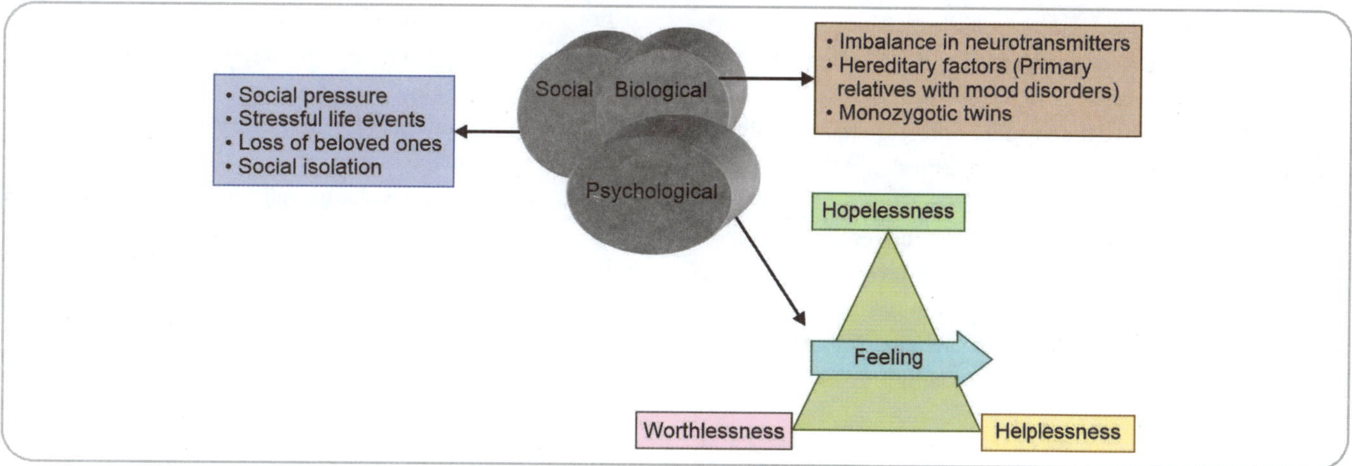

Figure 7.4: Biopsychosocial model

Psychological Factors

- **Psychodynamic theory:** Ambivalence tendency toward the loss of loved object as actual loss or perceived loss leads to emotional conflict which in turn leads to mood disorder.
  - In depression, introjection of ambivalence into the lost object.
  - In mania, inadequacy and worthlessness convert into denial, reaction formation and projection to grandiose feeling.
- **Psychoanalytical theory:** Id, ego, superego (rigid super ego might lead to aggressiveness and the sexual impulses at unconscious state will lead to punishment or suicide).
- **Cognitive triad of depression:** It includes negative view of self, negative view of future and negative view of environment as shown in Figure 7.5.
- **Learned helplessness:** Individual undergoes repeated painful or aversive stimuli, from which the individual is unable to avoid or escape.
- **Stressor:** Factors which cause stress might induce the depression.

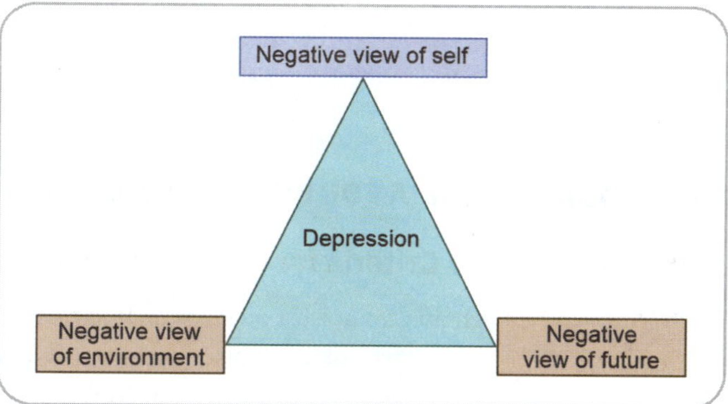

Figure 7.5: Cognitive triad of depression

DIAGNOSTIC CRITERIA FOR BIPOLAR I DISORDER

DSM-5 Diagnostic Criteria for Bipolar I Disorder (Manic Episode)

- Abnormal, persistent, elevated, expansive or irritable mood with the increased goal-directed activity at least one week and present most of the day or every day.
- Three or more of the below symptoms:
  i. Inflated self-esteem (or) grandiosity
  ii. Reduced need for sleep
  iii. More talkative
  iv. Flight of ideas
  v. Distractibility
  vi. Purposeless increase in goal-directed activity or psychomotor agitation
  vii. Involvement in risk taking activities
- Marked impairment in social or occupational functioning or to proceed hospitalization in order to prevent harm to self and others.
- The episode is not due to the physiological effects of a substance.

DSM-5 Diagnostic Criteria for Bipolar I Disorder (Hypomanic Episode)

- A distinct period of abnormally and persistently elevated, expansive, or irritable mood and abnormally and persistently increased activity or energy, lasting at least four consecutive days and present most of the day, nearly every day.
- During the period of mood disturbance and increased energy and activity, three (or more) of the following symptoms (four if the mood is only irritable) have persisted, represent a noticeable change from usual behavior, and have been present to a significant degree:

i. Inflated self-esteem or grandiosity.
ii. Decreased need for sleep (e.g., feels rested after only 3 hours of sleep).
iii. More talkative than usual or pressure to keep talking.
iv. Flight of ideas or subjective experience that thoughts are racing.
v. Distractibility (i.e., attention too easily drawn to unimportant or irrelevant external stimuli), as reported or observed.
vi. Increase in goal-directed activity (either socially, at work or school, or sexually) or psychomotor agitation.
vii. Excessive involvement in activities that have a high potential for painful consequences (e.g., engaging in unrestrained buying sprees, sexual indiscretions, or foolish business investments).

- The episode is associated with an unequivocal change in functioning that is uncharacteristic of the individual when not symptomatic.
- Disturbance in mood and the change in functioning are observable by others.
- Episode is not severe enough to cause marked impairment in social or occupational functioning or to necessitate hospitalization. If there are psychotic features, the episode is, by definition, manic.
- Episode is not due to the physiological effects of a substance (e.g., a drug of abuse, a medication, other treatment).

DSM-5 Diagnostic Criteria for Bipolar I Disorder (Major Depressive Episode)

Five or more of the following symptoms seen during the same two-week period and represent a change from previous functioning; at least one of the symptoms is either (1) Depressed mood or (2) Loss of interest or pleasure.

i. Depressed mood most of the day, nearly every day, as indicated by either subjective report (e.g., feels sad, empty, or hopeless) or observation made by others (e.g., appears tearful). (**Note:** In children and adolescents, can be irritable mood.)
ii. Markedly diminished interest or pleasure in all, or almost all, activities most of the day, nearly every day (as indicated by either subjective account or observation).
iii. Significant weight loss when not dieting or weight gain (e.g., a change of more than 5% of body weight in a month), or decrease or increase in appetite nearly every day. (**Note:** In children, consider failure to make expected weight gain.)
iv. Insomnia or hypersomnia nearly every day.
v. Psychomotor agitation or retardation nearly every day (observable by others; not merely subjective feelings of restlessness or being slowed down).
vi. Fatigue or loss of energy nearly every day.
vii. Feelings of worthlessness or excessive or inappropriate guilt (which may be delusional) nearly every day (not merely self-reproach or guilt about being sick).
viii. Diminished ability to think or concentrate, or indecisiveness, nearly every day (either by subjective account or as observed by others).
ix. Recurrent thoughts of death (not just fear of dying), recurrent suicidal ideation without a specific plan, or a suicide attempt or a specific plan for committing suicide.

The symptoms cause clinically significant distress or impairment in social, occupational, or other important areas of functioning.

Episode is not attributable to the physiological effects of a substance or another medical condition.

ICD-11 Diagnostic Criteria for Bipolar I Disorder

- Bipolar type I disorder is an episodic mood disorder defined by the occurrence of one or more manic or mixed episodes.
- A manic episode is an extreme mood state lasting at least one week unless shortened by a treatment intervention characterized by euphoria, irritability, or expansiveness, and by increased activity or a subjective experience of increased energy, accompanied by other characteristic symptoms such as rapid or pressured speech, flight of ideas, increased self-esteem or grandiosity, decreased need for sleep, distractibility, impulsive or reckless behavior, and rapid changes among different mood states (i.e., mood lability).
- A mixed episode is characterized by either a mixture or very rapid alternation between prominent manic and depressive symptoms on most days during a period of at least two weeks.
- Although the diagnosis can be made based on evidence of a single manic or mixed episode, typically manic or mixed episodes alternate with depressive episodes over the course of the disorder.

DIAGNOSTIC CRITERIA FOR BIPOLAR II DISORDER

DSM-5 Diagnostic Criteria for Bipolar II Disorder

- Criteria have been met for at least one hypomanic episode (criteria A–F under 'Hypomanic Episode' above) and at least one major depressive episode (criteria A–C under 'Major Depressive Episode' above).

- There has never been a manic episode.
- The occurrence of the hypomanic episode(s) and major depressive episode(s) is not better explained by schizoaffective disorder, schizophrenia, schizophreniform disorder, delusional disorder, or other specified or unspecified schizophrenia spectrum and other psychotic disorder.
- The symptoms of depression or the unpredictability caused by frequent alternation between periods of depression and hypomania causes clinically significant distress or impairment in social, occupational, or other important areas of functioning.

Specify current or most recent episode:

- Hypomanic
- Depressed

Specify if:

- With anxious distress
- With mixed features

ICD-11 Diagnostic Criteria for Bipolar II Disorder

- Bipolar type II disorder is an episodic mood disorder defined by the occurrence of one or more hypomanic episodes and at least one depressive episode.
- A hypomanic episode is a persistent mood state characterized by euphoria, irritability, or expansiveness, and excessive psychomotor activation or increased energy, accompanied by other characteristic symptoms such as grandiosity, decreased need for sleep, pressured speech, flight of ideas, distractibility, and impulsive or reckless behavior lasting for at least several days.
- The symptoms represent a change from the individual's typical behavior and are not severe enough to cause marked impairment in functioning. A depressive episode is characterized by a period of almost daily depressed mood or diminished interest in activities lasting at least two weeks accompanied by other symptoms such as changes in appetite or sleep, psychomotor agitation or retardation, fatigue, feelings of worthless or excessive or inappropriate guilt, feelings or hopelessness, difficulty concentrating, and suicidality.
- There is no history of manic or mixed episodes.

DIAGNOSTIC CRITERIA FOR CYCLOTHYMIC DISORDER

DSM-5 Diagnostic Criteria for Cyclothymic Disorder

- For at least 2 years (at least 1 year in children and adolescents) there have been numerous periods with hypomanic symptoms that do not meet criteria for a hypomanic episode and numerous periods with depressive symptoms that do not meet criteria for a major depressive episode.
- During the above 2-year period (1 year in children and adolescents), the hypomanic and depressive periods have been present for at least half the time and the individual has not been without the symptoms for more than 2 months at a time.
- Criteria for a major depressive, manic, or hypomanic episode have never been met.
- The symptoms in criterion A are not better explained by schizoaffective disorder, schizophrenia, schizophreniform disorder, delusional disorder, or other specified or unspecified schizophrenia spectrum and other psychotic disorder.
- The symptoms are not attributable to the physiological effects of a substance or another medical condition.
- The symptoms cause clinically significant distress or impairment in social, occupational, or other important areas of functioning.

Specify if: **With anxious distress**

ICD-11 Diagnostic Criteria for Cyclothymic Disorder

- Cyclothymic disorder is characterized by a persistent instability of mood over a period of at least 2 years, involving numerous periods of hypomanic (e.g., euphoria, irritability, or expansiveness, psychomotor activation) and depressive (e.g., feeling down, diminished interest in activities, fatigue) symptoms that are present during more of the time than not.
- The hypomanic symptomatology may or may not be sufficiently severe or prolonged to meet the full definitional requirements of a hypomanic episode (see Bipolar type II disorder), but there is no history of manic or mixed episodes (see Bipolar type I disorder).
- The depressive symptomatology has never been sufficiently severe or prolonged to meet the diagnostic requirements for a depressive episode (*see* Bipolar type II disorder).
- The symptoms result in significant distress or significant impairment in personal, family, social, educational, occupational or other important areas of functioning.

Treatment

- Lithium (0.6–1.2 mEq/L*)
  - Tab. Lithium carbonate (Eskalith, Lithobid) 40 mg
  - Syrup Lithium citrate 300 mg
- Carbamazepine (6–12 mg/L*)
- Sodium Valproate (50–125 mg/L*)

- Anticonvulsants
  - Gabapentin 300 mg/day at bed time
  - Topiramate (Topamax) 250–500 mg/day
  - Lamotrigine (Lamictal) 100–200 mg/day at bed time
- Calcium channel blockers—Verapamil (Isoptin) 40–360 mg
- Agitated or psychotic patient—Administration of second-generation antipsychotics (olanzapine, risperidone) and benzodiazepines (lorazepam, clonazepam)
- Electroconvulsive Therapy (ECT)

**Therapeutic drug level in blood*

LITHIUM

Discovery of Lithium

Dr John Frederick Joseph Cade AO (1912–1980) an Australian psychiatrist discovered Lithium in 1948. He explored the effects of lithium carbonate as a mood stabilizer and it is also useful in treatment of bipolar disorder.

Basic Information about Lithium (Fig. 7.6)

The half-life of the drug is 24 hours. It is not metabolized in liver and gets excreted by kidneys. Lithium does not bind or minimally bind with protein. The usual dosage is 600–900 mg/day and is given in divided or single dose initially with the maintenance serum level of 0.6–1.2 mmol/L.

Pharmacokinetics

The absorption takes place within 30 minutes and reaches at peak in 3 hours. Antipsychotics/antidepressants might decrease the absorption.

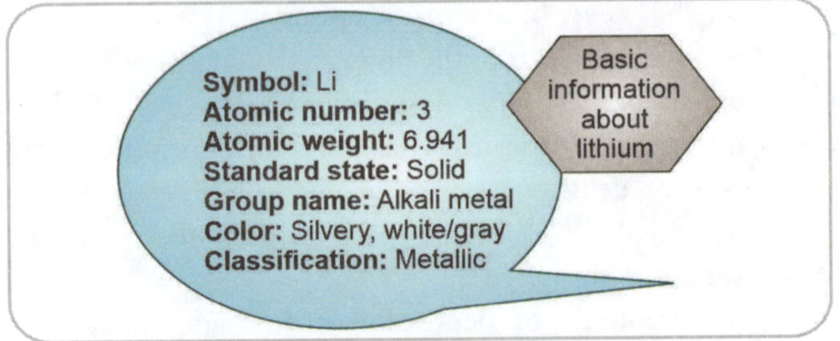

Figure 7.6: Fundamental concepts of lithium

Mechanism of Action

Lithium acts on macroscopic (anatomy of brain) as well as on microscopic level (intracellular) (Fig. 7.7). Lithium is related with neuroprotective effect (or) factors such as:

- Brain-Derived Neurotrophic Factor (BDNF)
- *B-cell lymphoma 2* (BCL2)—*Inhibit the apoptosis in various cells*

Changes in structure of brain during lithium intake are seen in anterior cingulate cortex, ventral prefrontal cortex, hippocampus and amygdala. Lithium modulates the neurotransmitters such as dopamine, glutamate and Gamma aminobutyric acid (GABA). Lithium shows effects at intracellular level by inhibiting proteins such as Phosphoinositol/Protein Kinase C (PKC), Myristoylated Alanine-Rich C Kinase Substrate (MARCKS) and Glycogen Synthase Kinase-3 (GSK-3).

Categories of lithium level in blood has been depicted below in Table 7.6:

Table 7.6: Categories of lithium level in blood

Categories	Lithium level in blood
Therapeutic	0.6–1.2 mEq/L
Prophylactic	0.8–1.2 mEq/L
Toxic	>2 mEq/L

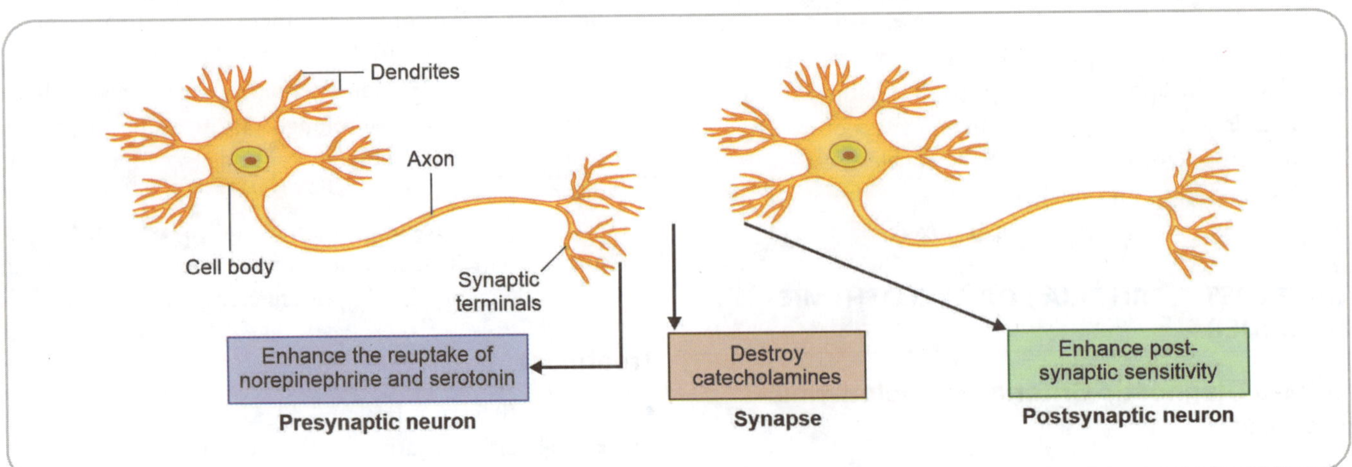

Figure 7.7: Mechanism of action for lithium

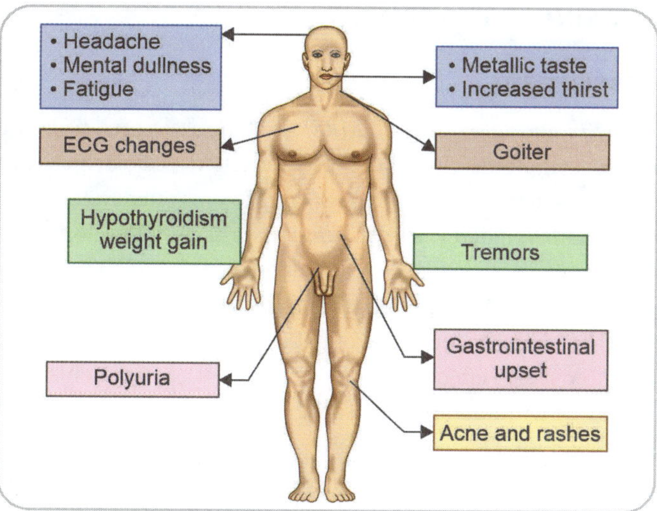

Figure 7.8: Side effects of lithium

Side effects of lithium have been given in Figure 7.8.

Mnemonic

Mnemonic to remember lithium side effects are "LITHUM"

L : Leukocytosis

I : Insipidus (Nephrogenic diabetes insipidus)

T : Tremors (or) thirst (or) taste as metallic (or) teratogenic (Teratogenics–Ebstein anomaly)

H : Hypothyroidism

U : Urinary (Polyuria)

M : Miscellaneous (ECG changes—T wave flattening, QRS widening and sinus node dysfunction, rashes, gastrointestinal (GI) upset, weight gain, fatigue, rashes, ataxia, nystagmus, muscle weakness, delirium, hair loss, psoriasis, peripheral neuropathy, intracranial hypertension, myasthenia gravis like syndrome, lower seizure threshold, neuromuscular irritability, Memory disturbances, dysphoria and slow reaction time)

Factors which increase/decrease serum lithium level have been depicted below in Table 7.7:

Table 7.7: Factors which increase or decrease serum lithium level

Factors increasing serum lithium level	Factors decreasing serum lithium level
Drugs • Thiazide diuretics • Nonsteroidal anti-inflammatory drugs (NSAIDs) • Angiotensin-converting enzyme (ACE) inhibitors • Angiotensin II receptor antagonists • Metronidazole **Miscellaneous** • Low sodium diet • Elderly • Dehydration • Renal disease	**Drugs** • Acetazolamide • Mannitol • Theophylline **Miscellaneous** • Caffeine • Pregnancy

Drug Interactions with Lithium

Drug interactions with lithium are categorized into minor categories, moderate categories and major categories have been summarized in Table 7.8.

Table 7.8: Drug interactions with lithium

Categories	Drugs interact with lithium
Minor interaction with lithium	Carbonic anhydrase inhibitors sympathomimetic medications
Moderate interaction with lithium	• ACE inhibitors • Metrogyl • Methyldopa • Benzodiazepines • NSAID • Caffeine • Carbamazepine • Clozapine • Thiazide diuretics • Loop diuretics • Succinylcholine • Theophylline • Phenothiazines • Fluoxetine • Tricyclic antidepressants
Major interaction with lithium	Haloperidol

Management of Lithium Toxicity

Gastric lavage can be given to remove the contents from gastrointestinal tract. Charcoal helps to bind with lithium. Tab. propranolol decreases the tremors. Sodium and water retention must be avoided. Patients are advised to take more oral fluids/water.

Electrolyte abnormalities have to be corrected. IV fluids can be administered. If the patient has consumed lithium extended-release tablets in last 2–4 hours, in that case, whole bowel irrigation is advisable in order to prevent absorption of lithium. In case of severe lithium toxicity, hemodialysis is the only option. Grades of lithium toxicity with its manifestations and management are given in Table 7.9.

NOTE

Lithium has more chance of toxicity since the drug has narrow therapeutic index (i.e., little variation exists between the therapeutic drug level and toxic drug level).

Table 7.9: Grades of lithium toxicity with its manifestations and management

Level	mEq/L	Clinical manifestations	Management
Grade-1	1.5–2.5	• Nausea • Vomiting • Tremor • Hyperreflexia • Ataxia • Agitation • Muscular weakness	Hydration Kayexalate
Grade-2	2.5–3.5	• Stupor • Rigidity • Hypertonia • Hypotension	Hydration Kayexalate Dialysis (if needed)
Grade-3	>3.5	• Coma • Seizures • Myoclonus • Collapse	Hemodialysis

TREATMENT OF BIPOLAR DISORDER

Anticonvulsants Used to Treat Bipolar Disorder

The action and side effects of mood stabilizers sodium valproate, carbamazepine, lamotrigine and topiramate have been given in Table 7.10.

Antipsychotics Used to Treat Bipolar Disorder

Aripiprazole, risperidone, olanzapine, quetiapine, ziprasidone and clozapine.

NURSING MANAGEMENT

Assessment

Young mania rating scale (YMRS): It is the scale used to assess manic symptoms. It is an observer rated scale which has 11 items. 4 items rated from 0 to 8 and 7 items rated from 0 to 4.

Another mood disorder questionnaire was developed by Hirschfeld, Williams, Spitzer, Calabrese, et al. (2000). It is a screening tool with13-item checklist. It's efficiently lies in the fact that it helps to identify 7 out of 10 patients in case of bipolar disorder. It also effectively screens out 9 out of 10 patients who as may be without bipolar disorder.

Semantic Differential Feelings and Mood Scales (SDFMS) is developed by Maurice Lorr and Richard A Wunderlich. It helps to measure the state of mood. It has 35 differential items which has one-to-five-point scale and they help in assessing and determining the mood. It has five factors as listed below:

1. A = Elated-Depressed
2. B = Relaxed-Anxious
3. C = Confident-Unsure
4. D = Energetic-Fatigue
5. E = Good Natured-Grouchy

Assess the client's mood, level of anxiety and thoughts in regard to harming oneself or others.

NURSING DIAGNOSIS AND INTERVENTIONS

Risk for self-directed violence related to suicidal feelings.

Table 7.10: Mood stabilizers with their actions and side effects

Mood stabilizers	Actions	Side effects
Sodium valproate	• Dissociates the valproate ion in gastrointestinal tract (GI) • Increases GABA levels in brain either by reducing reuptake or by reducing the metabolism of GABA • Suppress the influx of calcium through specified calcium channels	• Alopecia • Pancreatitis • Thrombocytopenia • Hyperammonemia • Inhibition of liver enzymes
Carbamazepine	• Sodium channel blocker (binds with voltage-gated sodium channel and thereby prevents sustained firing of action potential) • It is a serotonin releasing agent and serotonin reuptake inhibitor. • Analgesics • Antiepileptics • Mood stabilizing agent	• Agranulocytosis • Ataxia • Induces liver enzymes • Hyponatremia • Stevens-Johnson syndrome (SJS) • Toxic epidermal necrosis (TEN)
Lamotrigine	• Inhibits • Voltage sensitive sodium ions • Excitatory amino acids (glutamate and asparate)	• Maculopapular skin eruptions • Stevens-Johnson syndrome (SJS) • Toxic epidermal necrosis (TEN)
Topiramate	• Increases GABA • Block voltage gated sodium and calcium channels • Inhibits excitatory neurotransmitters especially glutamate	• Cognitive dulling

Interventions	Rationale
Determine the suicidal risk with the standard tool	It helps to estimate the suicidal risk
Obtain the suicidal contract from the client	It develops in client the feelings of self-realization, not to commit suicide
Decrease the environment stimuli by allotting the single silent room with less lightening effect.	Because the patients are easily distracted even with a slight stimulus
Remove sharp objects	It prevents the self-harm
Provide recreational activities	It helps to divert the patient's mind and decreases the level of stress
When hyperactivity of the patient increases, stay with the client	Staying with the patient might give secure feelings.

Risk for violence directed toward others related to manic excitement, delusion and hallucinations.

Interventions	Rationale
Maintain the low environment stimuli	To reduce anxiety and suspicious ideas
Keep observing the client every 15 minutes	To ensure the patient's safety
Encourage the client to talk	To reduce the bottled-up negative emotions and thereby reduce stress
Divert the client when he/she experiencing hallucination	It acts as diversional technique to reduce hallucination
Involve the client in sports or other activities (e.g., kicking football)	It helps the client to express his violent behavior in a positive way

Impaired nutrition, less than body requirement may be related to refusal of food as evidenced by weight loss.

Interventions	Rationale
Assess the client's likes and dislikes	It provides the client's baseline data
Provide them high calorie diet	Since the client is excited, the level of energy loss will be high in manic patient
Foods has to be colorful and attractive	It motivates the manic patient to eat well
Advice the patient's caregiver to follow small frequent diet as suggested in menu plan	It helps to maintain the nutritional status of the patient
Give more oral fluids and salt adequately to the patient.	To prevent the lithium toxicity
Monitor the weight regularly	To assess the improvement in patient's weight.

DO YOU KNOW

Some Indian celebrities who spoke boldly that they were suffering from mood disorders were Manisha Koirala, Yo Yo Honey Singh, Shahrukh Khan, Deepika Padukone, Anushka Sharma, Varun Dhawan, Randeep Hooda and Ileana D'Cruz.

DEPRESSION

Introduction

The term 'Depression' originated from Latin word '*deprimere*' which means to press down. Hippocrates found the term 'Melancholia' to address the depression initially. Emil Kraepelin said that 'Depressive state is a part of manic-depressive psychosis.' Henry Maudsley used the term, 'Affective disorders'. Kurt Schneider classified the depression as endogenous (melancholic) and reactive (Neurotic) depression.

DSM versions are listed below:

- DSM-I is depressive reaction
- DSM-II is depressive neurosis
- DSM-III, IV and DSM-5 are depressive disorder

Etiology

- **Brain anatomy:** Neuron loss is present in frontal lobe, cerebellum and basal ganglia.
- **Genetics:** First degree relatives of a depression patient have a threefold risk of depression. Abnormality in chromosomes 12 and 15 has been identified in such patients. Polymorphism of serotonin transporter gene in chromosome 17 and chromosomes with short allele of homozygosity or heterozygosity increase the risk of depression.
- **Neurochemical:** Decreased norepinephrine and serotonin are seen in depression. Acetylcholine and Gamma-Aminobutyric Acid (GABA) regulations are impaired.

- **Endocrine theory:** Hypothalamic-pituitary-adrenal (HPA) axis induce stress and thereby cortisol level too increases as shown in Figure 7.9. Nonadrenergic receptors of pineal gland secrete melatonin. Decreased level of melatonin leads to depression. Administration of light therapy will increase the level of melatonin and thereby it decreases the level of depression as shown in Figure 7.10.
- **Circadian rhythm:** Dysregulation of sleep-wake cycle will lead to depression.
- **Psychoanalytical model:** As per Freud (1957) depression is due to loss of 'loved object' and fixed oral sadistic phase of development.
- The hypothalamic pituitary adrenal (HPA) axis is our central stress response system. ACTH binds to receptors on the adrenal cortex and stimulates adrenal release of cortisol. In response to stressors, cortisol will be released for several hours after encountering the stressor.
- Light therapy is a way to treat seasonal affective disorder (SAD) and certain other conditions by exposure to artificial light. SAD is a type of depression that occurs at a certain time each year, usually in the fall or winter. During light therapy, you sit or work near a device called a light therapy box. The light emitted by it reduces depression by decreasing level of melatonin.
- **Psychosocial causes:** Chronic stressors, lack of social support, chronic pain, loneliness, loss of loved ones, poor coping skills, repeated failures, anxious and obsessional personality, family conflicts, use of alcohol or substance abuse and negative view of self or future or environment.
- **Medications:** Psychotropic agent, oral hypoglycemic agents, antihypertensive drugs, anti-Parkinson's medications, antimicrobials, chemotherapeutic drugs, cimetidine, cardiovascular medications, narcotics and non-narcotic analgesics.
- **Organic causes:** Secondary depression is due to various physical disorders listed here:
  - Anemia
  - **Cardiovascular diseases:** Heart failure
  - Cancer (mainly carcinoma in pancreas)
  - **Endocrine disorder:** Diabetes mellitus, Cushing syndrome, hypothyroidism and hyperparathyroidism.
  - **Gastrointestinal disorder:** Irritable bowel syndrome
  - **Genitourinary disorder:** Urine incontinence and chronic renal failure.
  - **Metabolic disturbances:** Hypercalcemia, hypoxia and Wilson's disease.
  - **Viral and bacterial infections:** Influenza, pneumonia, encephalitis, infectious mononucleosis, miliary tuberculosis and brucellosis.
  - **Musculoskeletal disorders:** Arthritis.
  - **Neurological disease:** Alzheimer's disease, Parkinson's disease.
  - **Vascular:** Stroke and coronary artery disease.
  - **Nutritional deficiency:** Iron, folic acid, protein, niacin, vitamin C, thiamine (B_1), pyridoxine (B_6) and cyanocobalamin (B_{12}).

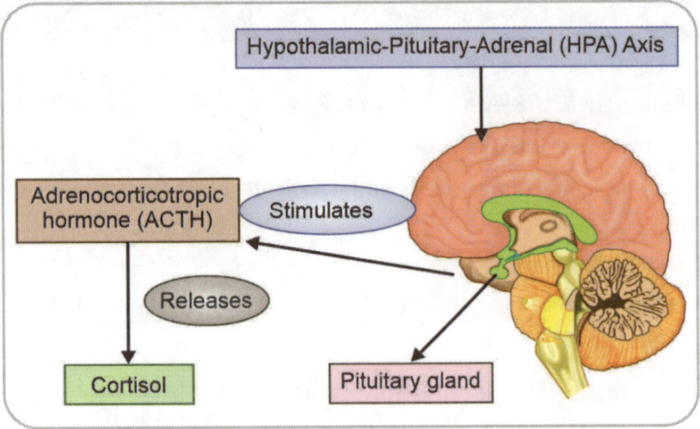

Figure 7.9: Hypothalamic-Pituitary-Adrenal (HPA) Axis and cortisol

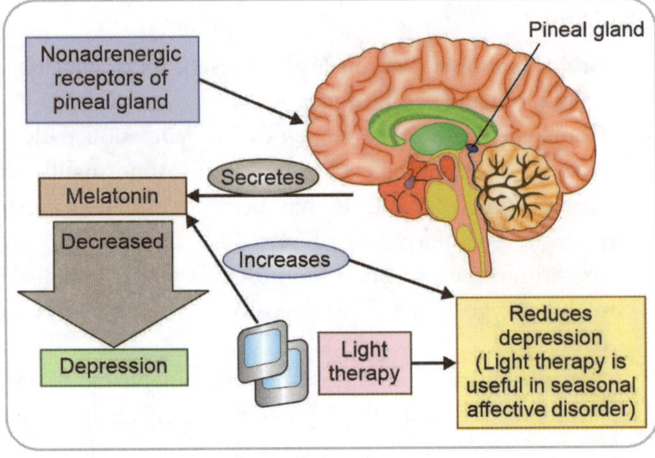

Figure 7.10: Concepts of light therapy

Clinical Features

Physical Symptoms

Blurred vision, dry mouth, giddiness, fatigue, headache, chest pain, breathlessness, numbness, tingling sensation, abdominal discomfort, anorexia, increased urinary frequency, sexual disturbances and constipation (Fig. 7.11).

Psychological and Emotional Symptoms

Depressed mood that is clearly visible abnormal to the individual, anhedonia (Unable to enjoy the events which are considerably joyful before), feel of guilt, anergia, insomnia, psychomotor retardation, decreased concentration, lack of

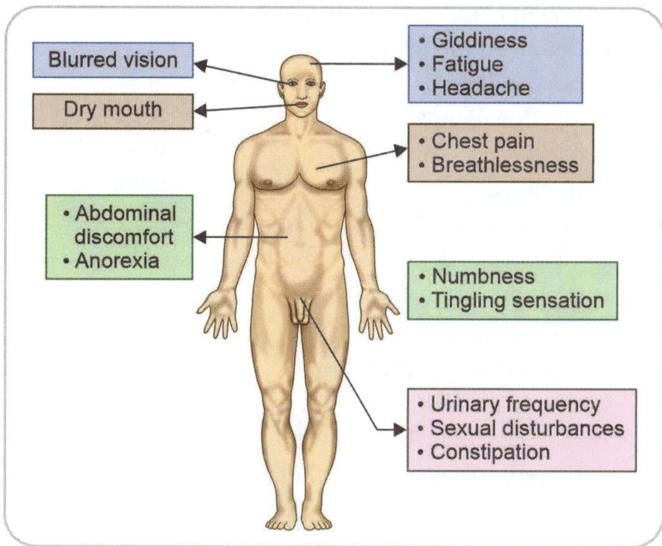

Figure 7.11: Physical symptoms in depression

interest, crying spells, avoiding socialization, diurnal variation (worsening of symptoms in morning), suicidal ideation, feel of hopelessness/helplessness/worthlessness

Mood congruent psychotic symptoms are as follows:

- Delusion of guilt
- Nihilistic delusion
- Delusion of hypochondriasis
- Voices accusing/condemning the client

Mood incongruent psychotic symptoms are as follows:

- Delusion of persecution
- Delusion of reference
- Voices speaks about affectively neutral topic

CLASSIFICATION OF DEPRESSIVE DISORDERS

ICD-11 and DSM-5 classification of depressive disorders is shown in Table 7.11.

Table 7.11: ICD-11 and DSM-5 classification of depressive disorders

ICD-11	DSM-5	Depressive disorders
—	296.99	Disruptive mood dysregulation disorder
6A70.0	296.21	Single episode depression (mild)
—	296.22	Single episode depression (moderate)
6A71.1	—	Single episode depression (moderate without psychotic features)
6A71.2	—	Single episode depression (moderate with psychotic features)
6A71.3	—	Single episode depression (severe without psychotic features)
6A71.4	—	Single episode depression (severe with psychotic features)
—	296.23	Single episode depression (severe)
—	296.24	Single episode depression (with psychotic features)
6A70.6	296.25	Single episode depression (in partial remission)
6A70.7	296.26	Single episode depression (in full remission)
6A70.Z	296.20	Single episode depression (unspecified)
6A71.0	296.31	Recurrent episode depression (mild)
—	296.32	Recurrent episode depression (moderate)
6A71.1	—	Recurrent episode depression (moderate without psychotic features)
6A71.2	—	Recurrent episode depression (moderate with psychotic features)
—	296.33	Recurrent episode depression (severe)
6A71.3	—	Recurrent episode depression (severe without psychotic features)
6A71.4	—	Recurrent episode depression (severe with psychotic features)
—	296.34	Recurrent episode depression (with psychotic features)
6A71.6	296.35	Recurrent episode depression (in partial remission)
6A71.7	296.36	Recurrent episode depression (in full remission)
6A71.Y	296.30	Recurrent episode depression (unspecified)
6A7Z	300.4	Persistent depressive disorder (dysthymia)
—	625.4	Premenstrual dysphoric disorder
—	293.83	Depressive disorder due to another medical condition

DIAGNOSTIC CRITERIA FOR DEPRESSIVE DISORDER

DSM-5 Diagnostic Criteria for Disruptive Mood Dysregulation Disorder

Criteria in Regard to the Recurrent Temper Outbursts

- Severe recurrent temper outbursts manifested either verbally (verbal rages) and/or behaviorally (physical aggression toward other persons or property) that are not proportionate in intensity or the duration to the situation
- Temper outbursts are not consistent with the developmental level.
- Mood between temper outbursts is persistently irritable most of the day or nearly every day.
- Severe recurrent temper outbursts need to be present in at least two of the three settings (i.e., at home, at school, with peers) and need to be severe in at least one of these.

Duration

- On average, temper outbursts happen three or more times in a week.
- All the above criteria's need to present for one year or above.
- Individual should not be present without all of the symptoms for more than three months
- Diagnosis should not be made for first time before 6 years of age or after 18 years.

Miscellaneous

- Symptoms should not reflect any other mental disorders.
- Symptoms are not due to the effects of a substance use or due to another medical condition.

DSM-5 Diagnostic Criteria for Single Episode Depression

- Five or more of the following symptoms present for significant portion of time for 2 weeks period.
  - Depressed mood presents almost most of the day and every day.
  - Lack of interest or pleasure.
  - Significant weight loss (without dieting) or weight gain—5% of body weight loss or gain in a month.
  - Fatigue or energy loss almost every day.
  - Hypersomnia or Insomnia almost every day.
  - Psychomotor retardation or agitation almost every day.
  - Feel or worthlessness or inappropriate guilt.
  - Inability to concentrate almost every day.
  - Frequent thoughts of death.
- Above symptoms cause the significant social and occupational impairment.
- Above symptoms are not due to consumption of any substances.
- There should not be any manic episode.
- Occurrence of depressive episode might not be explained as other psychotic disorders.

Specify if it is:

- With anxious distress
- With atypical features
- With melancholic features
- With mood-congruent psychotic features
- With mood-incongruent psychotic features
- With seasonal pattern

ICD-11 Diagnostic Criteria for Single Episode Depression

- It is characterized by the presence or history of one depressive episode when there is no history of prior depressive episodes.
- Depressive episode is characterized by the period of almost daily depressed mood or lack of interest in activities lasting at least for 2 weeks along with other symptoms such as feelings of worthlessness or excessive or inappropriate guilt, difficulty concentrating, hopelessness, recurrent thoughts of suicide or death, psychomotor agitation or retardation, changes in appetite or sleep and decrease in the energy or fatigue.
- No prior manic, hypomanic, or mixed episodes, which indicate the presence of bipolar disorder.

Specify if it is:

- **Mild:** Less intensity, not considerable difficulty in continuing with work, social, or domestic activities and no delusions or hallucinations.
- **Moderate:** Symptoms of depression for at least 2 weeks and presence difficulty in continuing with work, social, or domestic activities.
- **Severe:** Severe depressive symptoms cause significant distress and have social or occupational impairment.
- With or without psychotic features.
- **Partial remission:** Full definitional requirements for a depressive episode are no longer met but some significant mood symptoms remain.
- **Full remission:** Full definitional requirements for a depressive episode has met.
- Unspecified.

ICD-11 Diagnostic Criteria for Recurrent Episode Depression

- Recurrent depressive disorder is characterized by a history or at least two depressive episodes separated by at least several months without significant mood disturbance.
- A depressive episode is characterized by a period of almost daily depressed mood or diminished interest in activities lasting at least two weeks accompanied by other symptoms such as difficulty in concentrating, feelings of worthlessness or excessive or inappropriate guilt, hopelessness, recurrent thoughts of death or suicide, changes in appetite or sleep, psychomotor agitation or retardation, and reduced energy or fatigue.
- There have never been any prior manic, hypomanic, or mixed episodes, which would indicate the presence of a bipolar disorder.

DSM-5 Diagnostic Criteria for Persistent Depressive Disorder (OR) Dysthymic Disorder

- Depressed mood for most of the day, for more days than not, as indicated by either subjective account or observation by others, for at least 2 years. (In children and adolescents, mood can be irritable and duration must be at least 1 year).
- Presence, while depressed, of two (or more) of the following:
  i. Poor appetite or overeating.
  ii. Insomnia or hypersomnia.
  iii. Low energy or fatigue.
  iv. Low self-esteem.
  v. Poor concentration or difficulty making decisions.
  vi. Feelings of hopelessness.
- During the 2 years period (1 year for children or adolescents) of the disturbance, the individual has never been without the presence of depressive symptoms.
- There has never been a manic episode or a hypomanic episode, and criteria have not met for cyclothymic disorder.
- The disturbance is not better explained by other medical or mental disorder or not due to influence of any substances.
- Symptoms cause clinically significant distress or impairment in social, occupational, or other important areas of functioning.

Specifications on the basis of features: Anxious distress or mixed features or melancholic features or atypical features or mood-congruent psychotic features or mood-incongruent psychotic features or peripartum onset.

Specifications on the basis of remission: Partial or full remission.

Specifications on the basis of onset:

Early onset: If onset is before at age 21 years.

Late onset: If onset is at age 21 years or older.

Specifications on the basis of Severity: Mild or Moderate or Severe.

Other Specifications

- With intermittent major depressive episodes, with or without current episode
- With pure dysthymic syndrome
- With persistent major depressive episode.

ICD-11 Diagnostic Criteria for Persistent Depressive Disorder (OR) Dysthymic Disorder

- Dysthymic disorder is characterized by a persistent depressive mood (i.e., lasting 2 years or more), for most of the day, for more days than not.
- In children and adolescents depressed mood can manifest as pervasive irritability. The depressed mood is accompanied by additional symptoms such as markedly diminished interest or pleasure in activities, reduced concentration and attention or indecisiveness, low self-worth or excessive or inappropriate guilt, hopelessness about the future, disturbed sleep or increased sleep, diminished or increased appetite, or low energy or fatigue. During the first 2 years of the disorder, there has never been a 2 weeks period during which the number and duration of symptoms were sufficient to meet the diagnostic requirements for a depressive episode.
- There is no history of manic, mixed, or hypomanic episodes.

ICD-11 Diagnostic Criteria for Recurrent Depressive Disorder

- Recurrent depressive disorder is characterized by a history or at least two depressive episodes separated by at least several months without significant mood disturbance.
- A depressive episode is characterized by a period of almost daily depressed mood or diminished interest in activities lasting at least two weeks accompanied by other symptoms such as difficulty in concentrating, feelings of worthlessness or excessive or inappropriate guilt, hopelessness, recurrent thoughts of death or suicide, changes in appetite or sleep, psychomotor agitation or retardation, and reduced energy or fatigue.
- There have never been any prior manic, hypomanic, or mixed episodes, which would indicate the presence of a bipolar disorder.

DSM-5 Diagnostic Criteria for Premenstrual Dysphoric Disorder

- Presence of at least five symptoms must be present in the final week before the onset of menses, commence to improve within the few days after the onset of menses, and become less or absent in the week post menses.
- One (or more) of the following peculiar depressive symptoms must be present:
  i. Mood swings
  ii. Marked anger or irritability or interpersonal conflicts.
  iii. Marked depressed mood and feelings of hopelessness.
  iv. Marked anxiety and tension.
- One or more of the following additional symptoms present to reach a total of five symptoms when combined with peculiar depressive symptoms:
  i. Decreased interest in usual activities
  ii. Difficulty in concentration.
  iii. Lethargy or marked lack of energy.
  iv. Marked change in appetite–overeating or craving to eat specific food.
  v. Hypersomnia or insomnia.
  vi. A sense of being out of control.
  vii. Physical symptoms such as tenderness or swelling in breast, joint or muscle pain, a sensation of 'bloating', or weight gain.
- Symptoms are associated with clinically significant distress or interference with usual social activities or relationships with others.
- Symptoms are not attributable to the physiological effects of a substance or other medical condition or other mental disorder.

Diagnosis

Beck Depression Inventory

It is a self-rating scale that consists of 21 items rated on scale of 0–3. Lowest score is 0 and highest score is 63. Score interpretation has been given in Table 7.12.

Table 7.12: Score interpretation of beck depression inventory (BDI)

Score interpretation	Inference
Up to 10	Normal
11–16	Borderline depression
17–20	Mild depression
21–30	Moderate depression
31–40	Severe depression
>40	Extreme depression

Hamilton Rating Scale for Depression

Max Hamilton published the scale in 1960 which was later revised. Original scale had 17 items, later 21 item version of this scale was included. Score inference has been given in Table 7.13.

Table 7.13: Score interpretation of Hamilton rating scale

Score interpretation	Inference
0–7	Normal
20 or higher	Moderate to severe (Require treatment)

Dexamethasone Suppression Test

Cortisol level usually decreases with dexamethasone but it will not reduce in patients with depressive disorder.

Differences between Endogenous and Exogenous Depression

The differences between endogenous and exogenous depression are given in Table 7.14.

Differences between Endogenous and Atypical Depression

The differences between endogenous and atypical depression are given in Table 7.15.

Treatment Modalities

Individual Psychotherapy

When treatment is administered as psychoanalytical oriented manner then the patient develops insight in regard to the factors responsible for depression.

Family Therapy

Interpersonal and intrafamilial conflicts in the life of patient are addressed to reduce the level of depression.

Cognitive Therapy

Cognitive therapy helps to modify the unrealistic or unhelpful thoughts into realistic or helpful thoughts. By driving or walking in the morning hours, the individual will feel hopeful, helpful and worthful as shown in Figure 7.12.

Behavioral Therapy

Social Skills Training

It helps to maintain interpersonal relationship with others. Eye to eye contact has to be maintained while speaking to others. Involving the depression, patients in ward rounds can improve the social skills of the patient.

Table 7.14: Differences between endogenous and exogenous depression

Aspects	Endogenous depression	Exogenous depression
Meaning	Prefix 'Endo' means within (due to hereditary or biochemical imbalance)	Prefix 'Exo' means outside (caused by external factors—unemployment, divorce, sudden death of loved ones)
Other name	• Psychotic depression • Autogenous depression • Biological depression	• Neurotic depression • Reactive depression
Predominant factors	Biological factor	Environmental factor
Stress	Present	Present
Premorbid personality	• Cyclothymic personality • Dysthymic personality	• Anxious personality • Obsessive personality
Insomnia	Early morning awakening	Struggle in getting into sleep
Psychotic feature	• Psychomotor retardation • Suicidal attempt is seen • Delusions is present	• Psychomotor agitation • Suicidal attempts are not common • Psychotic features are absent
Individual feeling	Better when alone	Better in group
Mood	Sad in morning	Sad in evening
Treatment	Antidepressants and ECT	Antidepressants and psychotherapy
Relapse	Common	Not common

Table 7.15: Differences between endogenous and atypical depression

Aspects	Endogenous depression	Atypical depression
Appetite	Decreased	Increased
Weight	Loss of weight	Gain of weight
Worsening of symptoms	Morning	Evening
Insomnia	Insomnia is present in middle or late phase of sleep	Patient may have insomnia at initial phase of sleep and sometimes the patient may have hypersomnia
Interpersonal hypersensitivity (fear of being rejected by others)	Absent	Present

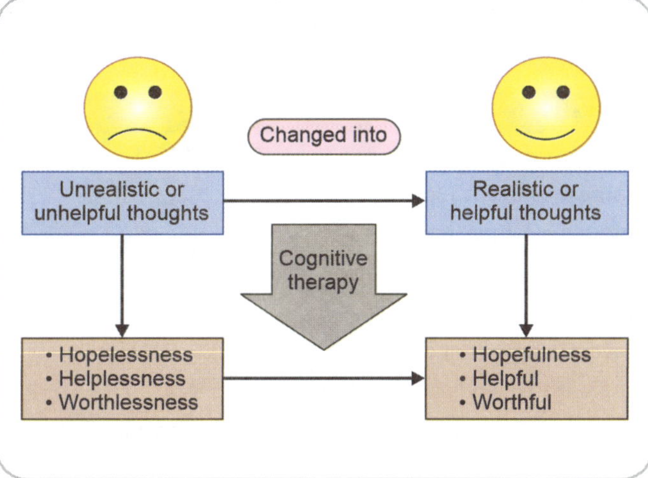

Figure 7.12: Concepts of cognitive therapy

Assertiveness Training

Training is provided to verbalize one's own willingness in polite manner in order to protect one's own rights. Important technique is 'Broken Record'—Speaking the same phrase again and again to another person.

Problem Solving and Decision-Making Skills

Patient is advised to identify the multiple solutions to the problem and to seek help from experts. Patient is thought to check out the benefit–loss ratio for any sort of problem and take decision accordingly.

Activity Schedule

Schedule the activities/daily routines of patient so that the patient occupied. It increases self-esteem of the client.

Psychopharmacology

Antidepressant therapy: Monoamine oxidase inhibitors (MAOIs), tricyclics and selective serotonin reuptake inhibitors (SSRIs). Antidepressants are explained in Chapter 5 (Page No. 111).

Supportive Measures

Reassurance

Nurse has to promote the right psychological support to the patient. Reassurance differs from the false reassurance as it is a wrong assurance (For example, nurse verbalize to the HIV patient that, 'HIV will be cured soon' is an example of false reassurance, instead the nurse is expected to say to the patient that, 'if you take antiretroviral drugs, it will improve your life span' which is reassurance).

Mental Ventilation

If an individual who feels depressed, shares his/her emotional burden with others, then half of the depressed feelings are reduced. Bottled up emotions have to be ventilated.

"Happiness doubles when you share and sorrow reduces to half when you share. Keep sharing to a right person"

Occupational Therapy

Involve the client in activities, so that patient is socialized. It will enhance the cognition, attention, concentration and decision-making skills.

Relaxation Therapy

(Explained in Chapter 5, Page No. 156).

- Jacobson progressive muscle relaxation therapy (JPMR)
- Autogenic training

Miscellaneous

- Electroconvulsive therapy (ECT) *(Explained in Chapter 5, Page No. 172).*
- Light therapy (or) phototherapy *(Explained in Chapter 5, Page No. 154).*
- Deep Brain *(Explained in Chapter 5, Page No. 181).*

Nursing Diagnosis and Interventions for Patient with Mania (Tables 7.16A to E)

Table 7.16A: Risk of injury related to more hyperactivity and impulsive behavior evidenced by performing purposeless and injurious movements

Interventions	Rationale
Have a decreased environmental stimulus	Client is easily distractible and responds even to a slight stimulus
Remove the hazardous objects	Client might harm self
Assist the patient in performing some activities	To relieve from tension
Be with a client when hyperactivity increases	To provide psychological support
Administer psychotropics as per physician's order	For rapid relief of hyperactivity

Table 7.16B: Risk of violence directed to self and others, related to manic excitement

Interventions	Rationale
Maintain the low level of environmental stimuli	To decrease the anxiety
Observe the patient every 15 minutes once	To ensure the patient's safety
Encourage the patient to ventilate the feeling	To relieve the mental tension
Use diversional techniques and engage them in activities	To divert the patients from agitation
Talk to the patient with calm attitude	To prevent anxiety
Apply restraints if the client is harming to self or others	To prevent injury to self or others
Observe the restraints every 15 minutes once	To ensure the patient's safety
Remove the restraints one at a time	To observe the patient's risk of becoming violent and to prevent self-harm
Administer minor tranquilizers as per physician's order	To control the violent behavior

Table 7.16C: Impaired nutritional status less than body requirement, related to inability to sit in a place or to eat as evidenced by significant weight loss

Interventions	Rationale
Calculate the patient's body mass index (BMI)	To get the baseline data
Obtain the information about the patient's likes and dislikes	To encourage the patient to eat the food based on the patient's likes and dislikes
Give high protein and high caloric finger foods which is highly nutritious	To enable the patient eat the foods 'on the run' since the patient will not sit in a place to eat
Maintain intake output chart	To monitor the food intake regularly
Stay with patient when he/she eats	To provide psychological support
Give plenty of fluids/juices/snacks to the patient	To help compensate the caloric requirements which has been lost due to hyperactivity

Table 7.16D: Impaired social interactions related to narcissistic behavior as evidenced by manipulation and inability to sustain the relationship with others

Interventions	Rationale
Identify the manipulative behavior	To obtain the baseline data
Usage of 'Limit setting' as a psychotherapeutic technique (For example, nurse says to the patient that, 'you should not do like this and this is not an acceptable behavior')	To prevent the violation of limits
Provide positive reinforcement of the acceptable behavior	Motivate the patient to do right behavior
Advise the patient about the consequences of manipulative behavior	Help the patient to realize one's mistake
Help the patient to identify the positive aspect of life	To promote self-esteem

Table 7.16E: Impaired family coping skills related to grandiose ideas and manipulative behavior as evidenced by family disputes

Interventions	Rationale
Identify the feelings of the family members such as anger, despair, hostility and powerlessness, etc.	Living along with manic patient might affect the interpersonal relationship among family members
Observe the communication among family members	Helps to identify the undergoing problems among family members
Identify the role of patient in family	If the role was not performed by the patient as per expectation, then family disintegration occurs
Provide family therapy if required	Enhances the family coping skills

Nursing Diagnosis and Interventions for Patient with Depression (Tables 7.16F to J)

Table 7.16F: Risk for suicide related to suicidal ideation as evidenced by suicidal risk determination

Interventions	Rationale
Assess suicidal risk	Provides the baseline data and helps to explore whether the client belongs to mild or moderate or severe risk of suicide
Do not allow the client alone	Monitors the client
Remove the sharp objects from room	Helps to prevent suicidal attempts
Observe the client regularly	Monitoring prevents the suicide
Do not allow the client to put bolt in the door of rest room	For security concern, since the patient is having risk to commit suicide
Ask openly about suicidal ideas	To identify the suicidal thoughts
Allow the client to talk about his/her emotional burden	Expression of negative feeling will reduce the level of depression
Administer antidepressants as ordered	To reduce the level of depression

Table 7.16G: Dysfunctional grieving related to actual or perceived loss as evidenced by inappropriateness in expression of anger and not performing the daily activities

Interventions	Rationale
Identify the stage of grief in which patient is fixed	To obtain the baseline data
Show unconditional positive regard on patients (accept the patient as he/she is)	To develop a therapeutic relationship
Advice the patient to ventilate the feeling of anger	To reduce the emotional burden
Encourage the patient to perform simple activities	An effective way to relieve anger and being involved

Table 7.16H: Self-care deficit related to lack of energy as evidenced by lack of doing activities

Interventions	Rationale
Assess the client's interest and capacity to perform self-care activities	To know about the patient's ability to perform self-care activities
Help the client to do the activities by self	Helping the client will promote interest to do the activities
Assign the daily activities with time schedule	Keep scheduling will make the client to have clear idea about what activity is to be performed at what time
Simple task can be done by the client with supervision	Accomplishment of simple task will motivate the client to perform further activities
Do not rush the client to do activities	It increases the level of anxiety
Reinforce the client to perform activities	Reinforcement will act as a motivation factor to perform the task

Table 7.16I: Hopelessness related to negative view of self as evidenced by mental status assessment

Interventions	Rationale
Nurse has to assess the patient's actual loss and perceived loss	It provides the baseline data about the patient
Reinforce the client supporting system to help the client	Motivate the client to feel that there are supporting systems that will help to get rid of problems
Maintain the therapeutic nurse patient relationship	To maintain basic trust with client
Provide counseling/cognitive behavior therapy	Negative distorted thoughts will be changed into positive way

Table 7.16J: Impaired social interactions related to social isolation as evidenced by poor interpersonal relationship with others

Interventions	Rationale
Nurse has to accept the patient and maintain good interpersonal relationship with client	To promote trust with patient
Provide social skill training	To encourage the socialization
Involve in group activities	To motivate the client to feel the pleasure in talking to others
Help the client to gradually socialize with others	To improve social skills
Avoid competitive tasks	To client may feel discouraged and demotivated

PERSISTENT MOOD DISORDER

ICD-10 Classification includes:
F34.0 Cyclothymia
F34.1 Dysthymia
F34.8 Other persistent mood disorders
F34.9 Persistent mood disorder, not specified

Cyclothymia

It involves the period of depressive symptoms and hypomania. Exact cause is unknown.

- **Onset:** Usually in early adulthood and late childhood.
- **Epidemiology:** Males and females are equally affected. The prevalence is 0.7% at some point of life.

DSM-5 Criteria includes:

- Periods with elevated mood and depressive symptoms have been persisting for half of the time since last two years (for adults) and one year for teenagers.
- Stable mood might last only for two months (mostly).
- Symptoms cause significant distress.
- Symptoms not meeting the criteria of major depression, bipolar disorder or other psychiatric conditions.
- Symptoms not caused by medical conditions or influence of any substance use.

Differential diagnosis includes borderline personality disorder, bipolar disorder and substance use disorder.

Treatment includes psychotherapy and mood stabilizers.

Dysthymia

It is a persistent depressive disorder in which the mild depressive symptoms persist for at least two years (one year in case of children).

Pathophysiology: Brain structural changes in corpus callosum and frontal lobe are seen. Increased activity in amygdala and cingulate gyrus of the brain.

DSM-IV criteria include:

Depressive symptoms persist at least for two years for most of the days. During depression, patient has two or more of the following symptoms:

- Changes in appetite (increased or decreased)
- Sleep disturbances (insomnia or hypersomnia)
- Fatigue
- Reduced self-esteem
- Decreased concentration
- Feel of hopelessness

During the second year, above symptoms are never absent for more than two months. Patient does not have manic/hypomanic/mixed episode. Patient will not the criteria of cyclothymia. Depression does not exist as part of psychosis/schizophrenia/delusion disorder. Symptoms are not caused by medical conditions or influence of any substance use. Depression causes significant personal distress and also social/occupational impairment.

Treatment includes selective serotonin reuptake inhibitors (SSRI) and tricyclic antidepressants (TCA).

GERIATRIC CONSIDERATIONS

Depression is a common psychiatric problem among elders. Geriatric depression scale is used to quantify the severity of depression. Elders residing in old age homes are more prone to depression than elders who stay along with their family members. Empty nest syndrome (loneliness in elderly is common causative factor for depression) is a factor that should be rectified by social skills training. Treatment measure includes psychotherapy and antidepressants which are helpful for elders to recover from depression.

Follow-up, Home Care and Rehabilitation

Psychological therapies rendered to elders with mood disorders have to be followed at regular intervals for higher level of efficiency. Negative expression emotions have to be avoided in home settings to prevent depression. Preventive measures of elderly abuse (physical abuse—beating, emotional abuse—scolding elders, sexual abuse or granny bashing, economical abuse) will also prevent the depression. Rehabilitation helps to restore the elders to live with peace and it helps them to perform the activities of daily living.

EXTRA EDGE

ICD-10 Classification of Mood Disorders

- F30 Manic episode
- F31 Bipolar affective disorder
- F32 Depressive episode
- F33 Recurrent depressive disorder
- F34 Persistent mood (affective) disorders
- F38 Other mood (affective) disorders
- F39 Unspecified mood (affective) disorders

ICD-10 Classification for Bipolar Affective Disorder

- **F30 Manic episode**
  - F30.0 Hypomania
  - F30.1 Mania without psychotic symptoms
  - F30.2 Mania with psychotic symptoms
  - F30.8 Other manic episode
  - F30.9 Manic episode unspecified
- **F31 Bipolar affective disorder**
  - F31.6 Bipolar affective disorder, current episode mixed
- **F32 Depressive episode**
  - F32.0 Mild depressive episode
  - F32.1 Moderate depressive episode
  - F32.2 Severe depressive episode without psychotic symptoms
  - F32.3 Severe depressive episode with psychotic symptoms
  - F32.8 Other depressive episode—atypical depression
  - F32.9 Depressive episode, unspecified
- **F33 Recurrent depressive disorder**

ICD-10 Classification of Depression

- **F32 Depressive episode**
  - F32.0 Mild depressive episode

Contd...

- .00 Without somatic syndrome
- .01 With somatic syndrome
- F32.1 Moderate depressive episode
  - .10 Without somatic syndrome
  - .11 With somatic syndrome
- F32.2 Severe depressive episode without psychotic symptoms
- F32.3 Severe depressive episode with psychotic symptoms
- F32.8 Other depressive episodes
- F32.9 Depressive episode, unspecified

- **F33 Recurrent depressive disorder**
  - F33.0 Recurrent depressive disorder, current episode is mild
    - .00 Without somatic syndrome
    - .01 With somatic syndrome
  - F33.1 Recurrent depressive disorder, current episode is moderate
    - .10 Without somatic syndrome
    - .11 With somatic syndrome
  - F33.2 Recurrent depressive disorder, current episode is severe without psychotic symptoms
  - F33.3 Recurrent depressive disorder, current episode is severe with psychotic symptoms
  - F33.4 Recurrent depressive disorder, currently in remission
  - F33.8 Other recurrent depressive disorders
  - F33.9 Recurrent depressive disorder, unspecified
- **F34 Persistent mood [affective] disorders**
  - F34.0 Cyclothymia
  - F34.1 Dysthymia
  - F34.8 Other persistent mood [affective] disorders
  - F34.9 Persistent mood [affective] disorder, unspecified
  - F38.1 Other recurrent mood [affective] disorders
    - .10 Recurrent brief depressive disorder
  - F38.8 Other specified mood [affective] disorders
- **F39 Unspecified mood [affective] disorder**

EXTRA EDGE

Types of Depression

Endogenous (or) psychotic depression, exogenous (or) neurotic depression (or) reactive depression, mild depression, moderate depression, severe depression. Masked depression, melancholic (or) involutional melancholia, seasonal affective depression, postpartum depression, agitated depression, acute depression, recurrent depression, secondary depression, double depression, atypical depression and mixed anxiety and depressive disorder is shown in Flowchart 7.3.

Flowchart 7.3: Types of depression

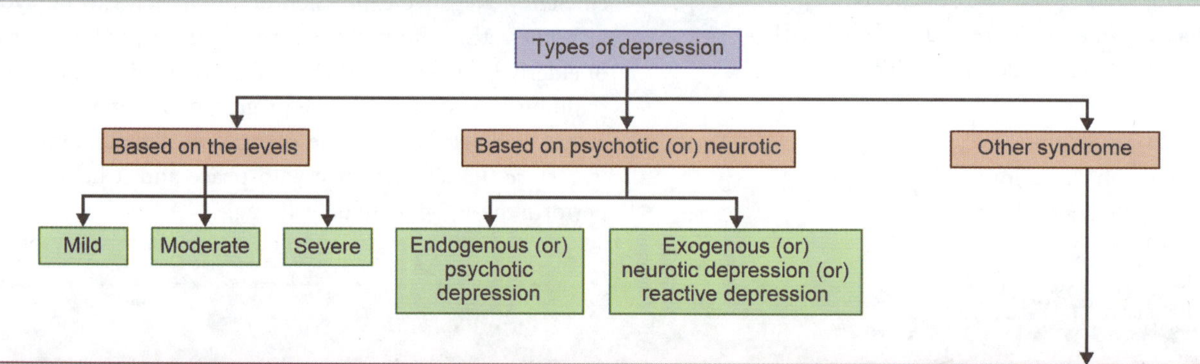

- **Masked depression:** Most clients complain about somatic symptoms such as body ache, lack of energy, pain in the body with less or no psychological symptoms.
- **Melancholic (or) involutional melancholia:** Severe form of major depression occurs above 40 years of age, i.e., at the time of menopause or andropause.
- **Seasonal affective depression:** Depressive symptoms are present in winter season.
- **Postpartum depression:** Major depression is present in post-natal mother within 4 weeks of delivery/postpartum.
- **Agitated depression:** Depression with Psychomotor agitation.
- **Acute depression:** Sudden abrupt onset of depression.
- **Recurrent depression:** Two or more episodes of depression.
- **Secondary depression:** Depression is due to organic causes.
- **Double depression:** Major depressive disorder and persistent depressive disorder occurs at a same time (dysthymia is a chronic low level depression is present for at least of two years and add on to that major depressive symptoms are seen).
- **Atypical depression:** A subtype of major depression or dysthymia characterized by increased appetite, excessive sleepiness, feeling that arms are heavy and interpersonal hypersensitivity (fear of being rejected by others).
- **Mixed anxiety and depressive disorder:** Mixed symptoms of anxiety and depression are present.

SUMMARY

- Mood disorders are also called 'Affective Disorders'.
- Mood disorders are classified as unipolar disorders (depression) and bipolar disorders.
- Mania and depression are bipolar I disorder.
- Hypomania and depression are bipolar II disorder.
- Norepinephrine, serotonin and dopamine—decrease in depression and increase in mania.
- Stages of mania are stage I—Hypomania, Stage II—Acute mania, Stage III—Delirious mania.
- Treatment includes lithium (0.6–1.2 mEq/L), Carbamazepine (6–12 mg/L), sodium valproate (50–125 mg/L), anticonvulsants, calcium channel blockers, antipsychotics and benzodiazepines (lorazepam, clonazepam) and Electroconvulsive Therapy (ECT).
- The term "depression" came from Latin word '*deprimere*' which means to press down.
- Beck depression Inventory (BDI) and Hamilton Rating Scale for depression is the most common rating scales used to assess depression.
- Decreased levels of norepinephrine and serotonin are observed in depression.
- Acetylcholine and Gamma-aminobutyric acid (GABA) regulations are impaired in depression.
- Cortisol level usually decreases with dexamethasone in general but it will not decrease in patients with depressive disorder.
- Behavior therapy includes social skills training, assertiveness training, problem-solving, decision-making skills and activity schedule.
- Antidepressant therapy includes Monoamine Oxidase Inhibitors (MAOIs), tricyclics and Selective Serotonin Reuptake Inhibitors (SSRIs).
- Electroconvulsive therapy (ECT), light therapy (or) phototherapy and repetitive Transcranial Magnetic Stimulation (TMS) and Vagus Nerve Stimulation (VNS) are also helpful to reduce depression.

ASSESS YOURSELF

Long Answer Questions

1. Explain the classification, etiology, psychopathology, diagnosis, clinical manifestations and management of patients with mania.
2. Explain the classification, etiology, psychopathology, diagnosis, clinical manifestations and management of patients with depression.

Short Answer Questions

1. Define Mania.
2. Define depression.

Short Notes

Write short notes on:

1. Lithium
2. Lithium toxicity and its management
3. BPAD
4. Stages of mania
5. Nursing interventions of patient with mania
6. Nursing interventions of patient with depression
7. Etiology of mood disorders
8. Clinical features of mania
9. Symptoms of depression
10. Management of depression
11. Behavioral therapy for depression
12. Differences between endogenous and exogenous depression
13. ICD-11 classification of bipolar related disorders
14. Diagnostic criteria of mania and depression
15. Types of depression

Multiple Choice Questions

1. **Who coined the term mania and depression?**
   a. Hippocrates b. Emil Kraepelin
   c. Aretus d. King Saul
2. **Stage 3 mania is also called _______.**
   a. Hypomania b. Acute mania
   c. Delirious mania d. None of these
3. **Drugs which increase the serum lithium level are ____.**
   a. Acetazolamide b. Mannitol
   c. Theophylline d. Metrogyl
4. **Hypomania and depression is _______.**
   a. Bipolar I disorder b. Bipolar II disorder
   c. Both a and b d. None of these
5. **Decreased Norepinephrine and Serotonin is present in _________.**
   a. Mania
   b. Depression
   c. Both mania and depression
   d. None of the above
6. **Light therapy is indicated for _________.**
   a. Mania
   b. Seasonal affective disorder
   c. Both a and b
   d. None of the above

7. **Stevens-Johnson Syndrome (SJS) is a side effect of __________.**
   a. Sodium valproate b. Carbamazepine
   c. Lamotrigine d. Both b and c
8. **Mania is more common in __________.**
   a. Male b. Female
   c. Both male and female d. None of these
9. **ICD-11 code for current manic episode with psychotic features is __________.**
   a. 6A60.5 b. 6A61
   c. 6A62.5 d. 6A62
10. **Value of Grade-2 lithium toxicity is __________.**
    a. 1.5–2.5 mEq/L b. 2.5–3.5 mEq/L
    c. >3.5 mEq/L d. 0.5 mEq/L

Answer Key				
1. a	**2.** c	**3.** d	**4.** b	**5.** b
6. b	**7.** d	**8.** b	**9.** a	**10.** b

Nursing Management of Patients with Neurotic, Stress-related and Somatoform Disorders

CHAPTER 8

LEARNING OBJECTIVE

After studying this chapter, the student will be able to understand the basic concepts of neurotic disorders. The student will also be able to render the quality nursing care to patients with neurotic, stress-related and somatoform disorders.

CHAPTER OUTLINE

- Neurotic Disorder
- Anxiety Disorders
- Obsessive-Compulsive Disorder and its Related Disorders
- Trauma- and Stressor-Related Disorders
- Dissociative Disorder
- Somotoform or Somatic Symptom and Related Disorders
- Other Neurotic Disorders
- Geriatric Considerations

KEY TERMS

Anxiety disorder, Obsessive-compulsive disorder, Adjustment disorder, Dissociative or conversion disorder, Somatic symptom disorder, Illness anxiety disorder (Hypochondriasis/Health Phobia/Health anxiety disorder), Post-traumatic stress disorder, Somatic autonomic dysfunction, Factitious disorder or Munchausen syndrome by proxy, Malingering, Flashbacks, Trait anxiety, State anxiety, Signal anxiety, Free-floating anxiety, Phobia, Panic attacks, Social phobia, Specific phobia, Agoraphobia, Fear network, Systematic desensitization, Modeling, Exposure/response prevention, Thought-stopping technique, Nightmares, Hyperarousal, Briquet's syndrome or Somatoform disorder, Conversion disorder, Body dysmorphic disorder, Persistent somatoform pain disorder, Dissociative amnesia, Multiple personality disorder, Trance or possession disorder, Ganser syndrome, Dissociative convulsion, Neurasthenia, Depersonalization-derealization syndrome.

NEUROTIC DISORDER

Neurotic disorder is a less severe form of psychiatric disorder, in which the patients exhibit excess or prolong emotional response to the stressors and it is not due to organic brain disease. The major causes of neurotic disorder are overwork, lack of rest, and inability to relax. Neurotic diseases are caused by a disruption in the metabolism of neurotransmitters, hormones, vitamins, and other biologically active chemicals necessary for the regular functioning of the central nervous system.

ANXIETY DISORDERS

Historical Perspectives

In 1871, Jacob Da Costa explained that chronic cardiac syndrome had been included in psychological and somatic symptoms among soldiers. In 1900, Sigmund Freud introduced the concept of anxiety.

Definition

Anxiety is defined as 'feelings of uncertainty, apprehension, uneasiness or tension that an individual shows in a given situation'.

Epidemiology of Anxiety Disorders

- Anxiety disorders are more common in females.
- Lifetime prevalence of anxiety disorders is 25% in females and 15% in males.
- Common anxiety disorder in female is specific phobia followed by social phobia.
- Common anxiety disorder in male is social phobia.
- In general, anxiety disorders are early in onset when compared with psychotic or mood disorders.

Onset of anxiety disorders: These are enlisted in Table 8.1.

Types of Anxiety Disorders

Types of anxiety disorders are summarized in Table 8.2.

When there is a dangerous situation, an individual may fight or flight (escape) or fright (fear) toward the danger. He/she becomes adaptive if there is a presence of coping skills. It may become pathological if it causes significant personal or social distress, interference with normal functioning, disproportionate with the threat and presence of significant avoidance as shown in Flowchart 8.1.

Etiological Factors

Genetic Factors

These factors are enlisted in Table 8.3.

Biological Theory

- **Increased serotonin activity:** Thalamus, raphe nucleus, hypothalamus, basal ganglion and limbic system.
- Increased tidal volume in panic attack.
- Greater activation of amygdala (diamond-shaped structure in limbic system).
- Hyperactivity of insula (portion of cortex buried under lateral sulcus).
- Not activated anterior cingulate cortex (ACC).
- These three structures—amygdala, ACC and insula constitute to form **fear network as shown in Figure 8.1.**
- Abnormalities in cortico-striatal-thalamo-cortical (CSTC) circuit and glutamate transporter gene.
- Deficit in sensory gating, i.e., threat-related stimuli are not filtered out.

Table 8.1: Onset of anxiety disorders

Disorders	Onset of the disorder
Specific phobia	Childhood
Social phobia	Early teenage
Obsessive-compulsive disorder	Mid to late teenage
Agoraphobia	Early 20s age group
Panic disorder	Mid 20s age group
Generalized anxiety disorder	Around 30 years of age
Post-traumatic stress disorder (PTSD)	Depends on the exposure of trauma

Table 8.2: Types of anxiety disorders

Types	Description	Example
Trait anxiety	This type of anxiety is a component of personality and persists for longer duration	Individual with anxious personality disorder
State anxiety	Anxiety which is more specific to the situation	Student becomes anxious during examination
Signal anxiety	Any response to anticipating event	Mother who is relaxed but feels anxious when sending the child to the school for the first time
Free-floating anxiety	Individuals with generalized anxiety disorder often characterize their feelings as 'free-floating anxiety'. Here, the individuals will worry about one thing and when that worry resolves, the individuals might worry about other thing. It is difficult to identify the absolute triggering point.	Ms Sudha having strong worries about her poor academic performance, when it gets solved, now she is worrying about her financial constraints. She is having a racing thought, inability to concentrate or focus on one thing.

Flowchart 8.1: Concept of various responses in anxiety situation

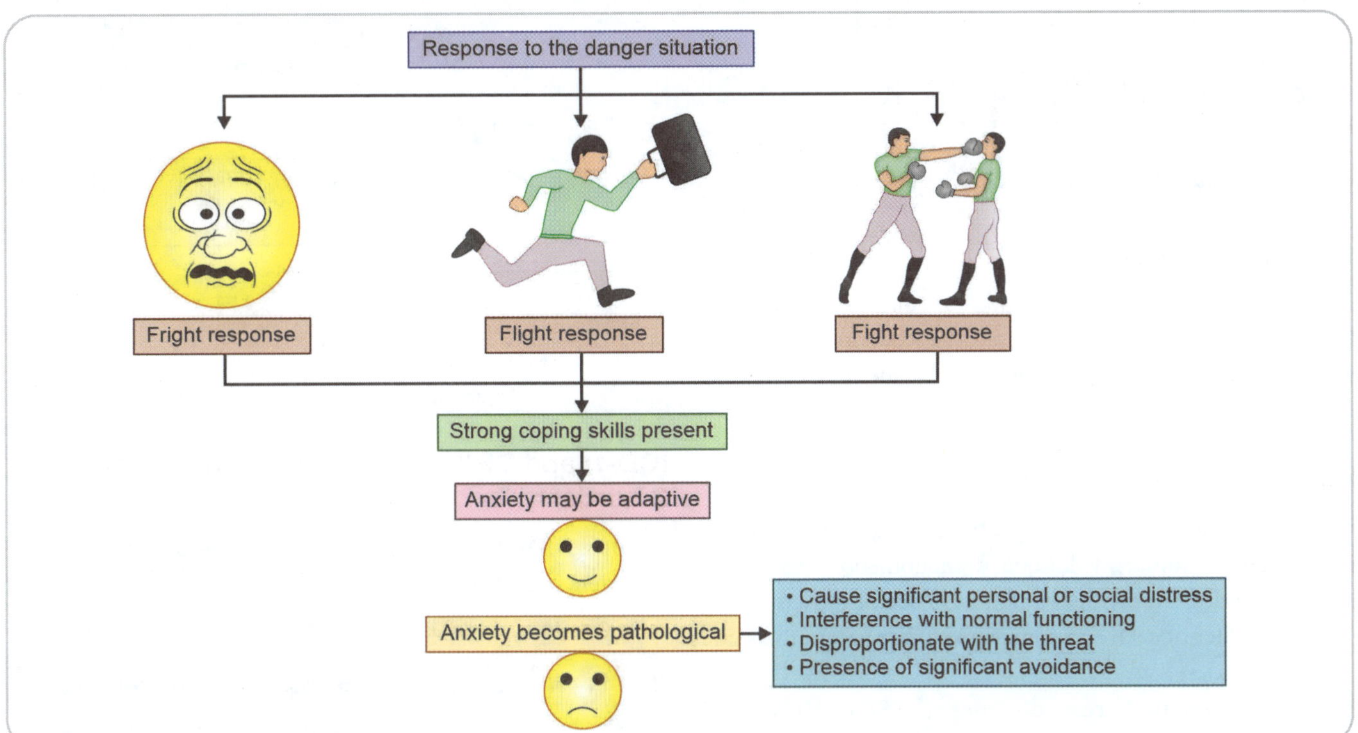

Table 8.3: Genetic factors responsible for anxiety disorder

Chromosome	Linkage of development
1, 9, 11, 13q	Panic disorder
14q	Specific phobia, social phobia, agoraphobia and panic disorder
3q	Agoraphobia
16q	Social and simple phobia

- **Neurotransmitters:** GABA (gamma-aminobutyric acid) underactivity and serotonin dysfunction.
- **Neuroendocrine:** HPA (hypothalamic-pituitary-adrenal) axis overactivity.
- **Neuropeptides:** Creatine phosphokinase (CPK), neuropeptide-Y (NPY), arginine vasopressin (AVP).
- Childhood obsessive-compulsive disorder (OCD) occurs as a part of pediatric autoimmune neuropsychiatric disorders associated with *Streptococcus (PANDAS) syndrome; due to antistreptococcal antibodies acting on basal ganglia.*
- **Positron emission tomography (PET):** Raised metabolic activity and blood flow in frontal lobe, cingulum and basal ganglia are seen in patients with OCD.

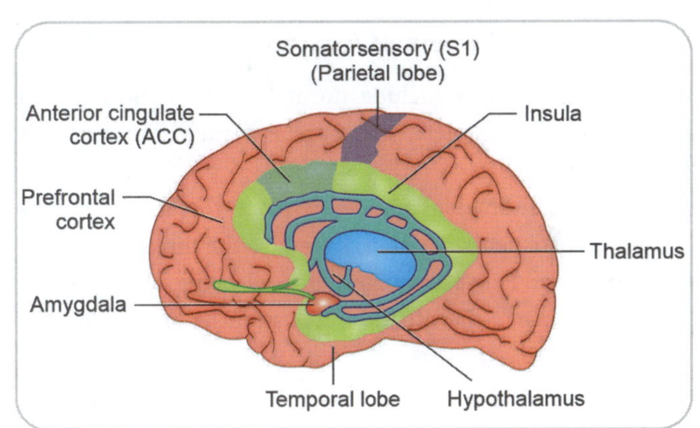

Figure 8.1: Parts involved in fear network

Psychoanalytic Theory

Anxiety is due to unconscious conflicts that exist between impulses of aggressiveness and ego gratification. Example: Child might have unconscious conflict of losing the mother's love.

Cognitive Behavioral Theory

Aaron Beck states that anxiety is a conditioned or learned response toward the stressors. Anxiety is a **learned trait for children from anxious parents.**

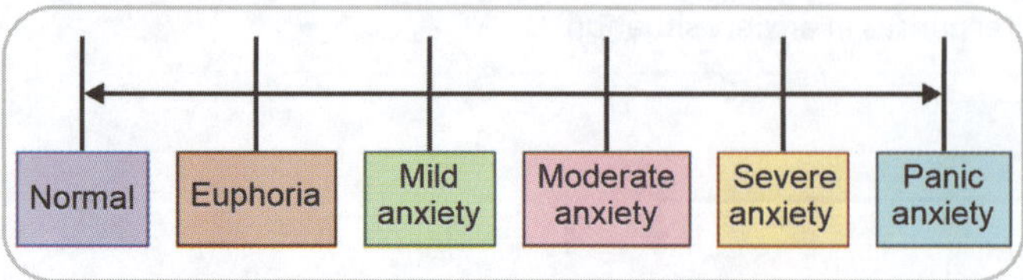

Figure 8.2: Continuum or levels of anxiety

Sociocultural Theory

An individual is unable to meet social or cultural demands due to his low self-concept. For example, if a student is weak in all subjects, he is unable to perform well in academics as good as others.

Etiology Based on the Types

- **Social phobia:** Individual feels humiliated in public places.
- **Specific phobia:** Evolutionary phenomenon **(Example:** Fear of dog—individual might have been exposed to dog bite earlier or seen someone who suffered from the same situation).
- **Post-traumatic stress disorder (PTSD):** History of exposure to traumatic event/events.

Continuum or Levels of Anxiety

The levels of anxiety include normal level, euphoria, mild anxiety, moderate anxiety, severe anxiety and panic anxiety as shown in Figure 8.2.

- **Normal:** Individual may experience threat, but he/she might take necessary steps to reduce the threat.
- **Euphoria:** Exaggerated feel of well-being which is not appropriate to the situation. It is an onset of mild level of anxiety.
- **Mild anxiety:** Increased alertness toward inner feelings. Client might be restless, unable to relax, maintain rigid posture and tremulous motor activity.
- **Moderate anxiety:** Signs like lack of concentration, tremors in voice, physiological changes, pacing and verbalizing about danger are observed.
- **Severe anxiety:** Decreased intelligence, inability to perform the task and inability to communicate clearly, lack of concentration and decreased ability to perceive things.
- **Panic anxiety:** Altered physiological, intellectual and emotional changes take place. Physiological changes peak up and get back to normal within shorter duration followed by a stressor as shown in Figure 8.3.

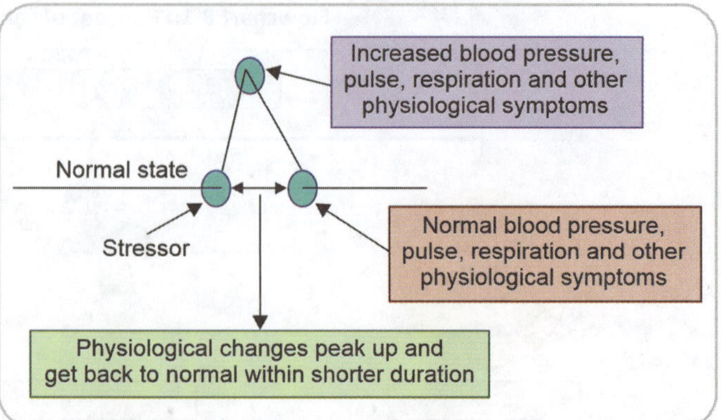

Figure 8.3: Concept of panic anxiety

ICD-11 and DSM-5 Classification of Anxiety Disorders

As per ICD-11 and DSM-5, the classification of anxiety disorders is given in Table 8.4.

Table 8.4: ICD-11 and DSM-5 classification of anxiety disorders

ICD-11	DSM-5	Classification of anxiety disorders
6B00	300.02	Generalized anxiety disorder
6B01	300.01	Panic disorder
6B02	300.22	Agoraphobia
6B03	300.29	Specific phobia
6B04	300.23	Social anxiety disorder (social phobia)
6B05	309.21	Separation anxiety disorder
6B06	312.23	Selective mutism
—	293.84	Anxiety disorder due to another medical condition
6B0Y	300.09	Other specified anxiety disorder
6B0Z	300.00	Unspecified anxiety disorder

Symptoms of Anxiety

They include physiological symptoms, psychological or emotional symptoms, behavioral symptoms and cognitive symptoms. Symptoms of anxiety disorders have been presented in Table 8.5.

Clinical Features of Generalized Anxiety Disorder

- Prominent, persistent and exaggerated worry or tension or apprehension about day-to-day problems or events.
- Restlessness.
- Inability to relax.
- Irritable.

Table 8.5: Symptoms of anxiety disorder

Aspects	Symptoms
Physiological symptoms	• Headache • Tachycardia • Increased blood pressure • Increased respiration • Blurred vision • Diaphoresis • Dilated pupils • Vertigo • Nausea and vomiting • Anorexia • Frequent urination • Increased sweat in palms • Sleep disturbances • Tightness of chest • Dyspnea • Weakness or muscle tension
Psychological or emotional symptoms	• Depression • Irritability • Social isolation • Lack of interest • Anger • Crying spells
Behavioral symptoms	• Hypervigilance • Restless • Pacing
Cognitive symptoms	• Lack of concentration • Inability to perform a task as expected • Memory loss • Unresponsive to external stimuli • Slow in performance • Preoccupied with something

- Difficult to concentrate.
- Initial insomnia (delay in falling into sleep due to continuous worry).

Clinical Features of Panic Disorder

Episodes of panic attacks are characterized by:

- Acute onset of severe anxiety without an obvious trigger.
- Anxiety symptoms and physiological changes might reach at peak within few minutes and get back to normal within few minutes.
- Autonomic symptoms like palpitation, increased heart rate, sweating, tremors, etc.
- Physical symptoms like chest tightness, breathing difficulty, abdominal discomfort, difficult to swallow, hot flushes, cold chills, lump in the throat, numbness or tingling sensation, etc.
- Fear of dying, fear of losing control, fear of fainting, depersonalization and derealization may also be present.

Clinical Features of Agoraphobia

- Marked fear or anxiety about two or more of the following five situations:
  1. Using public transportation (e.g., automobiles, buses, trains, ships, planes)
  2. Being in open spaces (e.g., parking lots, marketplaces, bridges)
  3. Being in enclosed places (e.g., shops, theaters, cinemas)
  4. Standing in line or being in a crowd
  5. Being outside of the home alone
- Agoraphobic situations are actively avoided or almost always provoke fear or anxiety.
- Agoraphobic situations cause significant distress or occupational impairment for at least 6 months or more.

Simple or Specific Phobia

Types of simple phobia are enumerated in Table 8.6.

Table 8.6: Types of simple phobia

Types of simple phobia	Description
Ablutophobia	Fear of washing or bathing
Acarophobia	Fear of itching or of the insects that cause itching
Acerophobia	Fear of sourness
Achluophobia	Fear of darkness
Acousticophobia	Fear of noise
Acrophobia or Altophobia	Fear of heights
Aeronausiphobia	Fear of vomiting secondary to air sickness
Aerophobia	Fear of drafts, air swallowing, or airborne noxious substances
Agraphobia	Fear of sexual abuse
Agrizoophobia	Fear of wild animals
Agyrophobia	Fear of streets or crossing the street
Aichmophobia	Fear of needles or pointed objects
Ailurophobia	Fear of cats
Albuminurophobia	Fear of kidney disease
Alektorophobia	Fear of chickens
Algiophobia or Algophobia	Fear of pain
Alliumphobia	Fear of garlic
Allodoxaphobia	Fear of opinions
Amathophobia	Fear of dust
Amaxophobia	Fear of riding or traveling in a car
Ambulophobia	Fear of walking

Contd...

Types of simple phobia	Description
Amnesiphobia	Fear of amnesia
Amychophobia	Fear of scratches or being scratched
Anablephobia	Fear of looking up
Androphobia	Fear of men
Anemophobia	Fear of air drafts or wind
Anginophobia	Fear of angina, choking or narrowness
Angrophobia	Fear of becoming angry
Ankylophobia	Fear of immobility of a joint
Anthophobia	Fear of flowers
Anthropophobia	Fear of people in the society
Antlophobia	Fear of floods
Anuptaphobia	Fear of staying single
Apeirophobia	Fear of infinity
Aphenphosmphobia or chiraptophobia	Fear of being touched
Apiphobia	Fear of bees
Arachnophobia	Fear of spiders
Asthenophobia	Fear of fainting or weakness
Astrapophobia/ brontophobia	Fear of thunder and lightening
Atelophobia	Fear of imperfection
Automysophobia	Fear of being dirty
Autophobia	Fear of being alone
Bibliophobia	Fear of books
Bromidrosiphobia	Fear of body smells
Cainotophobia	Fear of newness or novelty
Cancerophobia	Fear of cancer
Carnophobia	Fear of meat
Kathisophobia	Fear of sitting down
Catoptrophobia	Fear of mirrors
Chaetophobia	Fear of hair
Cheimatophobia	Fear of cold
Chemophobia	Fear of chemicals
Chorophobia	Fear of dancing
Chromatophobia	Fear of colors
Chrematophobia	Fear of money
Chronophobia	Fear of time
Cibophobia	Fear of food
Claustrophobia	Fear of closed spaces
Climacophobia	Fear of stairs/climbing or falling downstairs
Clinophobia	Fear of going to bed

Contd...

Types of simple phobia	Description
Coitophobia	Fear of coitus
Contreltophobia	Fear of sexual abuse
Coprastasophobia	Fear of constipation
Coprophobia	Fear of aversion of feces
Cyberphobia	Fear of computer or working with use of computer
Cynophobia	Fear of dogs/rabies
Cypridophobia	Fear of venereal disease
Decidophobia	Fear of making decisions
Dermatophobia	Fear of skin lesions
Dentophobia	Fear of dentist
Dextrophobia	Fear of objects/things at right side of the body
Levophobia	Fear of objects/things at left side of the body
Diabetophobia	Fear of diabetes
Diplophobia	Fear of double vision
Didaskaleinophobia	Fear of going to school
Dipsophobia	Fear of drinking
Siderodromophobia	Fear of train travel
Domatophobia	Fear of houses or being in a home
Dromophobia	Fear of crossing streets
Dystychiphobia	Fear of accidents
Ecclesiophobia	Fear of church
Eisoptrophobia	Fear of mirror or seeing oneself in mirror
Emetophobia	Fear of vomiting
Electrophobia	Fear of electricity
Enissophobia/ enosiophobia	Fear of having committed sin
Entomophobia or Insectophobia	Fear of insects
Epistaxiophobia	Fear of nose bleeding
Eosophobia	Fear of daylight
Epistemophobia	Fear of knowledge
Ergophobia	Fear of work
Euphobia	Fear of hearing good news
Gamophobia	Fear of marriage
Geliophobia	Fear of laughter
Genophobia	Fear of sex
Gerascophobia	Fear of growing old
Geumaphobia	Fear of taste
Graphophobia	Fear of writing
Gynephobia	Fear of women

Contd...

Types of simple phobia	Description
Hadephobia	Fear of hell
Harpaxophobia	Fear of being robbed
Hedonophobia	Fear of feeling pleasure
Heliophobia	Fear of sun
Helminthophobia	Fear of worm infestation
Hematophobia	Fear of blood
Heterophobia	Fear of opposite sex
Hippophobia	Fear of horses
Hobophobia	Fear of beggars
Hodophobia	Fear of road travel
Hyelophobia	Fear of glass
Hylephobia	Fear of fits
Hylophobia	Fear of forest
Hypnophobia	Fear of sleep
Hypengyophobia	Fear of responsibility
Latrophobia	Fear of doctors
Ideophobia	Fear of ideas
Iophobia	Fear of poison
Kakorrhaphiophobia	Fear of failure
Kopophobia	Fear of dust
Laliophobia	Fear of speaking
Lachanophobia	Fear of vegetables
Leukophobia	Fear of white color
Melanophobia	Fear of black color
Porphyrophobia	Fear of purple color
Xanthophobia	Fear of yellow color
Ligyrophobia	Fear of loud noises
Logophobia	Fear of words
Lygophobia	Fear of darkness
Maieusiophobia	Fear of childbirth
Mageirocophobia	Fear of cooking
Maniaphobia	Fear of insanity
Meningitophobia	Fear of brain disease
Microbiophobia	Fear of microbes
Methyphobia	Fear of alcohol
Microphobia	Fear of small things
Nephophobia	Fear of clouds
Noctiphobia	Fear of night
Nosocomephobia	Fear of hospitals
Nosophobia	Fear of becoming ill
Numerophobia	Fear of numbers
Obesophobia	Fear of gaining weight
Odynephobia	Fear of pain

Contd...

Types of simple phobia	Description
Olfactophobia	Fear of smells
Oneirophobia	Fear of dreams
Ombrophobia	Fear of rain
Ornithophobia	Fear of birds
Pantophobia	Fear of everything
Papyrophobia	Fear of paper
Ouranophobia	Fear of heaven
Parasitophobia	Fear of parasites
Parthenophobia	Fear of virgins
Pathophobia	Fear of disease
Pharmacophobia	Fear of taking medications
Pedophobia	Fear of children
Pediophobia	Fear of dolls
Peniaphobia	Fear of poverty
Pentheraphobia	Fear of mother-in-law
Phasmophobia	Fear of ghost
Philemaphobia	Fear of kissing
Photophobia	Fear of light
Plutophobia	Fear of wealth
Poinephobia	Fear of punishment
Polyphobia	Fear of many things
Psychophobia	Fear of mind
Pyrexiophobia	Fear of fever
Pyrophobia	Fear of fire
Radiophobia	Fear of radiation
Scabiophobia	Fear of scabies
Soceraphobia	Fear of parents
Sophophobia	Fear of learning
Soteriophobia	Fear of dependent on others
Stasiphobia	Fear of standing or walking
Technophobia	Fear of technology
Telephonophobia	Fear of telephones
Thermophobia	Fear of heat
Thalassophobia	Fear of sea
Thaasophobia or Thassophobia	Fear of sitting or idleness
Tomophobia	Fear of surgery
Trichophobia	Fear of hair
Traumatophobia	Fear of injury
Triskaidekaphobia	Fear of number 13
Trypanophobia	Fear of injection
Urophobia	Fear of urine
Verminophobia	Fear of germs

Contd...

Types of simple phobia	Description
Virginitiphobia	Fear of rape
Vestiphobia	Fear of clothes
Xenophobia	Fear of strangers
Xerophobia	Fear of dryness
Zelophobia	Fear of jealousy
Zeusophobia	Fear of God
Zoophobia	Fear of animals

Clinical Features of Social Anxiety Disorder

- Marked fear or anxiety about one or more social situations.
- Social situations provoke the fear or anxiety always.
- Fear or anxiety is out of proportion to the actual threat posed by the social situation.
- This disturbance is not related to the any other medical or mental disorder.
- Duration of this disturbance—at least 6 months or more
- Muscle tension or tension headache.
- Autonomic symptoms like palpitation, increased heart rate, sweating, tremors, etc.
- Physical symptoms like abdominal discomfort, difficult to swallow, lump in the throat, hot flushes, numbness or tingling sensation, etc.

Clinical Features of Separation Anxiety Disorder

- Recurrent excessive distress when anticipating or experiencing separation from the major attachment figures or from home.
- Persistent and excessive worry of losing the attachment figure.
- Persistent and excessive worry of experiencing the untoward events.
- Repeated nightmare with the themes of separation
- Repeated complaints of physical symptoms when separation from the attachment figures happens.
- Reluctance or refusal to go away from home or sleep away from home.
- Duration involves 4 weeks for children and 6 months for adults.

Clinical Features of Selective Mutism

- Consistent failure to speak in specific social situations (e.g., at school).
- This disturbance interferes with the educational and occupational achievement.
- This disturbance is not better explained in the communication disorder or autism or psychotic disorder
- Duration of this disturbance—at least 1 month.

Differential Diagnosis

- Prodrome or first episode of schizophrenia.
- Behavioral and psychological symptoms of dementia (BPSD).
- Delirium tremens of alcohol withdrawal.
- Anxiety seen in bipolar disorder.
- Hyperthyroidism may mimic anxiety symptoms.

Duration of the Persisting Symptoms Required for Diagnosis

Duration of the persisting symptoms required for the diagnosis of anxiety disorder is given in Table 8.7.

Table 8.7: Duration of the persisting symptoms required for the diagnosis of anxiety disorder

Disorder	DSM-5	ICD-11
Generalized anxiety disorder	At least 6 months	For several months
Phobia	At least 6 months	For several months
Panic disorder	At least 1 month	Not mentioned
Obsessive-compulsive disorder	Not mentioned	
Post-traumatic stress disorder	At least 1 month	At least several weeks

Assessment of Anxiety Disorder

Rating scale in anxiety disorders has been summarized in Table 8.8.

Table 8.8: Rating scale in anxiety disorders

Anxiety disorder	Rating scale
Generalized anxiety disorder	• Hamilton Rating Scale for Anxiety (HAM-A) • State Trait Anxiety Rating Scale
Panic disorder	• Panic Disorder Severity Scale (PDSS) • Panic and Agoraphobia Scale (PAS)
Social phobia	• Social Phobia Inventory (SPIN) • Liebowitz Social Anxiety Scale (LSAS)
Obsessive-compulsive disorder	• Yale-Brown Obsessive-Compulsive Scale (Y-BOCS) • Maudsley Obsessive-Compulsive Inventory (MOCI)
Post-traumatic stress disorder (PTSD)	• Impact of Events Scale (IES) • Clinician-Administered PTSD Scale (CAPS)

- **Routine blood investigations:** Complete blood count, glucose, liver function test, thyroid function test, etc.
- Baseline ECG

- It is important to be aware of the anxiety symptoms may also be present in the major psychiatric illness such as:
  - Unipolar depression
  - Mixed states of bipolar depression
  - Behavioral and psychological symptoms of dementia
  - Delirium tremens of alcohol withdrawal
  - During the prodrome phase in the first episode of schizophrenia.
- Hyperthyroidism may resemble the symptoms of anxiety disorder. So, the features of hyperthyroidism like heat intolerance, tachycardia, etc. need to be checked.

Treatment

Drugs

- **Benzodiazepines:** Useful in simple or specific phobia, e.g., lorazepam and diazepam.
- **Antidepressants:** Selective serotonin reuptake inhibitors (SSRIs) are the first-line treatment for all anxiety disorders (except simple or specific phobia), e.g., fluoxetine and escitalopram.
- **Beta-blockers:** Useful for somatic symptoms of anxiety such as tremors, tachycardia, etc., for example, propranolol.

NOTES

- For OCD, tablet clomipramine can be given. In case of treatment resistant OCD and SSRI augmented with low dose antipsychotics can be given.
- Benzodiazepines might be useful in short-term treatment and SSRI might be used in long-term/maintenance treatment.

Psychotherapy

- **Cognitive behavioral therapy:** Maladaptive cognition/imaginary threat has been identified and maladaptive behavior (escape and avoidance to overcome anxiety) has to be changed.
  - **Cognitive strategies**
    - Help the client to have realistic perception of anxiety.
    - Educate the client that anxiety will not persist forever and it might not kill.
    - Advise the client, avoidance of anxiety may help for short-term reduction of symptoms but for long run it won't help the individual, instead facing the anxiety presently may worsen the symptoms but in long run it might help to overcome the anxiety.
  - **Behavioral strategies**
    - **Panic disorder:** Cognitive behavioral therapy, systematic desensitization, relaxation training, stress management strategies, maintaining the panic diary or journal writing and special training to enhance the coping skills are useful.
    - **Phobia**
      - **Systematic desensitization:** It is developed by Joseph Wolpe. It has three steps:
        1. **Relaxation training:** Relaxation gives the physiological effects which is opposite to the anxiety.
        2. **Hierarchy construction:** Arrange the conditions in order of increasing anxiety.
        3. **Desensitization of stimulus:** Gradual exposure of the individual from least to most anxiety provoking state. In fact, it is a behavior modification technique that is used especially in treating phobias, in which panic or other undesirable emotional response to a given stimulus is reduced or extinguished, especially by repeated exposure to that stimulus. For example, to understand the concept of systemic desensitization in an individual having fear of crossing roads you can discuss the road signals, show the picture of road, show the real road, assist the person to cross the road and at last ask the individual to cross the road alone.
    - **Flooding:** It is also called implosive therapy. It is used to desensitize the persons to phobic stimuli. It differs from systemic desensitization. Instead of working out in hierarchy of anxiety and instead of provoking stimuli, the person is 'flooded' with the continuous presentation of phobic stimuli until the anxiety comes down. Flooding does not exist in practice because this intense anxiety might be dangerous to the individuals and it may lead to heart attack or death. For example, if the individual is having the fear of insect, then the individual is put into the room with a greater number of insects in order to reduce the phobia.
- **Cognitive behavioral therapy for post-traumatic stress disorder**
  - Identify the cognitive distortions
  - Discussion about the trauma
  - Exposure to remind the traumatic incidents (place, activities, person, etc.)
    - By imagination or
    - Direct confrontation
  - Development of skills to deal with future trauma
- Eye movement desensitization and reprocessing for PTSD

- **Self-monitoring technique:** Ask the patient to monitor oneself when he/she becomes anxious
- Relaxation training: Mindfulness meditation, exercise, yoga, progressive muscle relaxation, breathing exercises and autogenic training
- Psychoeducation
- Problem-solving skill training
- Support group
- Bibliotherapy—self-help books

Prognosis of Anxiety Disorder

Prognosis of anxiety disorder is given in Table 8.9.

Table 8.9: Prognosis of anxiety disorder

Aspects	Good prognosis	Poor prognosis
Onset	Late	Early
Severity	Mild/Moderate anxiety	Severe anxiety
Comorbidity	Absent	Present
Drug adherence	Present	Absent
Previous unsuccessful treatment	Absent	Present

OBSESSIVE-COMPULSIVE DISORDER AND ITS RELATED DISORDERS

Definition

- **Obsession:** Repetitive thoughts, images and doubts which make a person absolutely senseless and irrational. Individual tries to resist but finds unable to do so because that restriction might increase the level of anxiety.
- **Obsession versus delusion:** Obsession is ego-alien or ego-dystonic, i.e., opposite to individual's personality whereas delusion is said to be ego-syntonic.
- **Obsession versus thought insertion:** Obsession is one's own idea/thought whereas in thought insertion, someone's idea gets inserted in one's mind.
- **Compulsion:** Repetitive actions are performed followed by obsession in order to avoid the marked distress even though the client knows that behavior is unrealistic, senseless and irrational.

Epidemiology

- Worldwide lifetime prevalence is 2–3%
- Common among unmarried males
- Common with upper socioeconomic individuals
- Onset is late 20s in India.

Classification of Obsessive-Compulsive Disorder and its Related Disorders

As per ICD-11 and DSM-5, the classification of obsessive-compulsive disorder and its related disorders is given in Table 8.10.

Table 8.10: ICD-11 and DSM-5 classification of obsessive-compulsive disorder and its related disorders

ICD-11	DSM-5	Classification of obsessive-compulsive disorder and its related disorders
6B20	300.3	Obsessive-compulsive disorder
—	300.7	Body dysmorphic disorder
6B24	300.3	Hoarding disorder
6B25.0	312.39	Trichotillomania (hair-pulling disorder)
6B25.1	698.4	Excoriation (skin-picking) disorder
—	294.8	Obsessive-compulsive and related disorder due to another medical condition
—	300.3	Other specified obsessive-compulsive and related disorder
6B20.Z	300.3	Unspecified obsessive-compulsive and related disorder

Etiology

Genetic Factors

- **Family studies:** 35% of first-degree relatives of OCD clients might suffer from this disorder.
- **Twin studies:** Monozygotic twins are more prone to it as compared to dizygotic twins.

Psychodynamic Theory

Fixation of anal-sadistic phase in childhood might lead to reaction formation and when it fails it might cause the obsessional personality traits. Anxiety due to oedipal conflicts might lead to regression and when it fails it might cause the aggressive impulses reinforced. Isolation affect (ego removes affect from anxiety occurring thoughts) fails, it might lead to obsessional thoughts. If undoing (prevent the feared consequences of obsession) fails, it might lead to compulsive acts and if displacement fails, it might lead to phobia (Flowchart 8.2).

Flowchart 8.2: Psychodynamic theory of obsessive-compulsive disorder

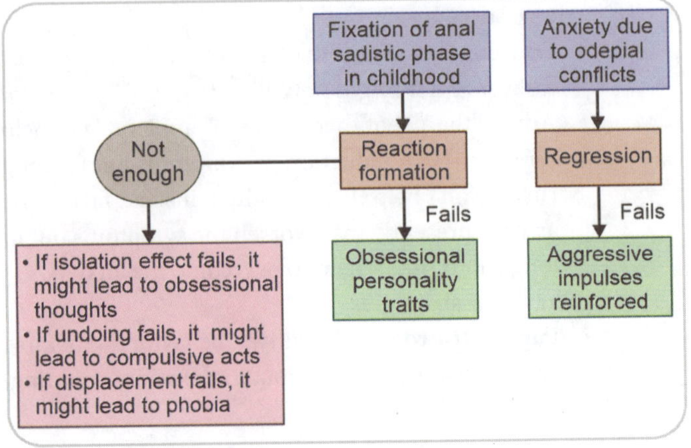

Behavioral Theory

Compulsions are said to be learned behavior to reduce the anxiety related to obsessions.

Biological Theory

- Lesions in hypothalamus, basal ganglia and third ventricles.
- Abnormalities in serotonin (5-HT) system, cortico-striatal-thalamo-cortical circuit and glutamate transporter gene.
- Dysfunction of caudate nucleus (part of striatum).
- OCD secondary to tics and encephalitis.
- Pediatric autoimmune neuropsychiatric disorders associated with *Streptococcus syndrome might cause childhood OCD because of antistreptococcal antibodies which act on basal ganglia of brain.*

Hormonal Factors

Increased incidence during menarche and increased severity of symptoms following the birth of the child.

Psychological Risk Factors

Personality traits such as guilt, excessive doubt, perfectionism, more sense of responsibility, etc.

Types of Obsessive-Compulsive Disorder (Flowchart 8.3)

- **Washers**
  - **Obsession:** Feeling of dirty hands/clothes/rooms.
  - **Compulsive act:** Washing again and again.
- **Checkers**
  - **Obsession:** Feeling of doors is not locked properly.
  - **Compulsive act:** Checking again and again whether door is locked.
- **Pure obsessions**
  - **Obsessive ruminations:** Preoccupied thoughts/images/impulses which ruminate in one's mind.
- **Primary obsessive slowness**
  - Marked slowness in repetitive thoughts will lead to slowness in daily activities.

Clinical Features of Body Dysmorphic Disorder

- Preoccupation with the perceived defects in physical appearance which are not observable by others.
- During the course of the disorder, the person does repetitive behaviors such as mirror checking, skin picking, excessive grooming and seeking reassurance or the mental acts such as comparing his or her appearance with others.
- This preoccupation causes clinically significant distress and impairment in social, occupational, or other vital areas of functioning.
- These symptoms will not meet the diagnostic criteria for an eating disorder.

Clinical Features of Hoarding Disorder

- Persistent difficulty in discarding or parting with possessions, regardless of the actual value.
- Perceived need to save the items and having distress associated with the discarding them.

Flowchart 8.3: Types of obsessive-compulsive disorder

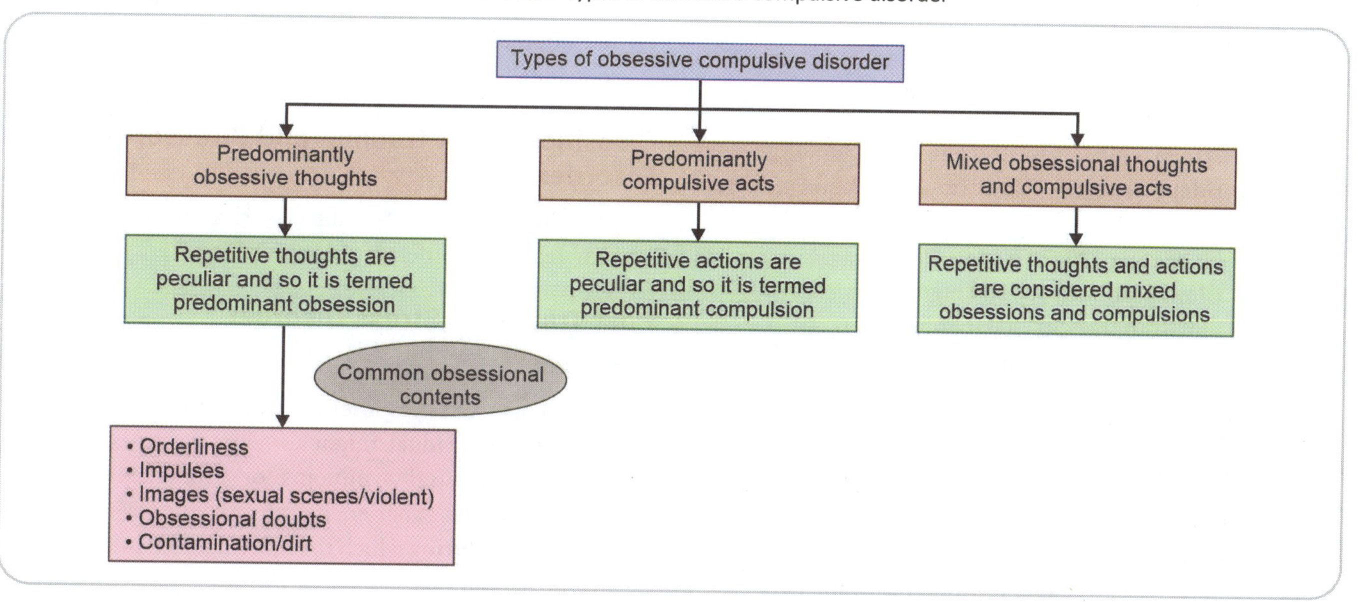

- Hoarding behavior causes the clinically significant distress or impairment in social, occupational or other vital areas of functioning.
- Hoarding behavior is not attributable to another medical condition or other mental disorder.

Clinical Features of Trichotillomania

- Recurrent pulling out of one's hair which results in hair loss.
- Repeated attempt to stop hair pulling.
- Hair pulling behavior causes the clinically significant distress or impairment in social, occupational or other vital areas of functioning.
- Hair pulling behavior is not attributable to another medical condition or other mental disorder.

Clinical Features of Excoriation (Skin-Picking) Disorder

- Recurrent skin picking behavior results in lesions and repeated attempt to stop the same.
- Skin picking behavior causes the clinically significant distress or impairment in social, occupational or other vital areas of functioning.
- Skin picking behavior is not attributable to influence of substance or another medical condition or other mental disorder.

Course and Prognosis

- Good prognosis with social and family support.
- Poor prognosis includes early onset of OCD, more severity of symptoms, bizarre compulsions along with the presence of comorbid illness can be seen.

Treatment

- **Drug therapy**
  - **Benzodiazepines:** Clonazepam, lorazepam, alprazolam
  - **Antidepressants:** Selective serotonin reuptake inhibitors
    - Fluoxetine: 20–80 mg/day
    - Clomipramine: 75–300 mg/day
    - Fluvoxamine: 50–200 mg/day
    - Sertraline: 50–200 mg/day
  - **Antipsychotics:** Haloperidol, olanzapine, risperidone, pimozide
  - **Buspirone**
- **Psychotherapy**
  - Psychoanalytic psychotherapy for patients
  - Supportive psychotherapy for family members
- **Behavior therapy**
  - **Thought-stopping technique**
    - Joseph Wolpe developed this technique.
    - When client gets repetitive thoughts while being alone, then client can shout 'STOP'.
    - When client gets repetitive thoughts in a group, then client can say 'STOP' slowly to oneself.
    - **Rubber band method:** Individual might tie a rubber band in wrist, when he/she gets the repeated thoughts, then strike the rubber band to avoid those distressing thoughts.
  - **Exposure and response prevention**
    - For example, soil the patient's hand visibly dirty (exposure) and ask the client not to perform hand wash (response prevention).
  - **Systematic desensitization:** Step by step graded exposure of fearful stimuli.
  - **Modeling:** Demonstrate the method what has to be done (expected) during obsessions and ask the client to repeat it immediately.
- **Electroconvulsive therapy**

  Indications are as follows:
  - If the client has depression along with OCD
  - Poor response to drug therapy
  - OCD patient with high suicidal risk
- **Psychosurgery**
  - Stereotactic limbic leukotomy
  - Stereotactic subcaudate tractotomy

TRAUMA- AND STRESSOR-RELATED DISORDERS

- The term 'trauma' means injury. Here it denotes the psychological trauma.
- Stressor is something which causes stress. Stressor can be internal (which is present inside) or external (from outside).

Classification of Trauma- and Stressor-Related Disorders

As per ICD-11 and DSM-5, the classification of trauma- and stressor-related disorders is given in Table 8.11.

Post-Traumatic Stress Disorder

Definition

Post-traumatic stress disorder (PTSD) is an anxiety disorder, in which the individual might develop the re-experiencing symptoms or arousal symptoms or avoidance symptoms after witnessing or experiencing an extreme, overwhelming traumatic event during which the individual felt intense fear or helplessness in the past.

Table 8.11: Classification of trauma- and stressor-related disorders

ICD-11	DSM-5	Classification of trauma- and stressor-related disorders
6B40	309.81	Post-traumatic stress disorder
6B41	—	Complex post-traumatic stress disorder
6B42	—	Prolonged grief disorder
6B43	—	Adjustment disorders
6B44	313.89	Reactive attachment disorder
6B45	313.89	Disinhibited social engagement disorder
—	308.3	Acute stress disorder
—	309.0	Adjustment disorders (with depressed mood)
—	309.24	Adjustment disorders (with anxiety)
—	309.28	Adjustment disorders (with mixed anxiety and depressed mood)
—	309.3	Adjustment disorders (with disturbance of conduct)
—	309.4	Adjustment disorders (with mixed disturbance of emotions and conduct)
—	309.9	Adjustment disorders (unspecified)
6B4Y	309.89	Other specified trauma- and stressor-related disorder
6B4Z	309.9	Unspecified trauma- and stressor-related disorder

Etiological Factors

- **Neurochemical factors:** Increased sensitivity of hypothalamic-pituitary-adrenal axis and increased sensitivity to cortisol receptors.
- **Biological factors:** Increased function of sympathetic nervous system, imbalance in dopamine and norepinephrine.
- **Cycle of violence:** Witnessing the child abuse.
- **Miscellaneous**
    - Actual or threatened serious injury or death.
    - Threat to one's physical integrity.
    - Witnessing an event and perceived as life-threatening one, e.g., war, natural disaster, road traffic accident.
    - Learning about unexpected serious harm or violent death or threat of death or injury experienced by a family members or friends.

Symptoms of PTSD

Re-experiencing Symptoms

- Recurrent and distressing recollection of the events (flashback).
- Recurrent dreams of that particular event (nightmares).
- Sudden feeling or acting as if the traumatic event is recurring.
- Intense psychological distress at exposure to things which symbolize or resemble an aspect of the trauma.
- Physiological reactivity when exposed to the internal or external cues of event.

Avoidance Features

- Efforts are made to avoid the thoughts or feelings associated with traumatic event/events.
- Efforts are made to avoid activities, places, situations or people which arouse the recollection of traumatic event.
- Inability to recall the vital aspect of the trauma (psychological amnesia).
- Markedly diminished interest in significant activities.
- Feelings of detachment from others.
- **Restricted range of effect:** Not able to have lovable feelings for others.
- **Sense of foreshortened future:** Not expected to have marriage, children, career, or to lead a normal life span.

Persistent Symptoms of Increased Arousal (Not Present Before Trauma)

- Difficulty in falling asleep or staying asleep
- Irritable (progress to rage) or outburst of anger
- Difficulty in concentrating on any events
- Hypervigilance—resembles like paranoia
- Exaggerated startle response—highly fearful in nature even for small noise.

Diagnostic Criteria for PTSD as per DSM-5

- One or more re-experiencing symptoms
- Two or more increased arousal symptoms
- Three or more avoidance symptoms

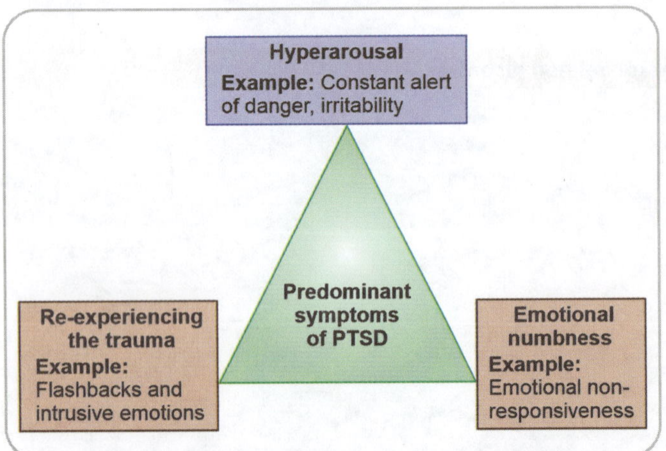

Figure 8.4 Predominant symptoms of PTSD

All the symptoms must be present for more than 1 month duration and clinically cause the significant distress or impairment in social, occupational, or other important areas of functioning.

Predominant symptoms of PTSD have been described in Figure 8.4.

The other common clinical manifestations of PTSD are restlessness, aggressiveness, clinical depression, nightmares, insomnia, memory loss, avoidance, dissociation, hyperarousal, anorexia, anxiety, irritability, hypervigilance, extreme distress and intrusions.

ICD-11 Diagnostic Criteria for PTSD

- Significant evidence of traumatic events
- Onset within 6 months of a traumatic event
- Significant emotional detachment
- Numbness of feelings
- Daytime imagery
- Repetitive, intrusive recollection of the events in memories

Differences between immediate and delayed onset PTSD have been mentioned in Table 8.12. Examples of the post-traumatic events are given in Table 8.13.

Table 8.12: Differences between immediate and delayed onset PTSD

Aspects	Immediate onset PTSD	Delayed onset PTSD
Response to treatment	Better	Poor
Prognosis	Better	Worse
Associated symptoms or complications	Fewer	More
Symptoms are resolved	Within 6 months	More chances to develop into chronic state

Table 8.13: Examples of the post-traumatic events

Witnessed traumatic events	Traumatic events experienced directly	Events experienced by others that are learned about
• Witnessing the serious injury or unnatural death of a person due to road traffic accident, violence, assault, disaster or war • Unexpectedly witnessing a body part or a dead body	• Being kidnapped • Being taken hostage • Terrorist attack • Torture • Violent personal assault • Natural or man-made disasters • Severe accidents • Being diagnosed with a life-threatening illness	• Learned about violent personal assault, serious injury or serious accident, experienced by or a close friend or a family member • Learned about a sudden, unexpected death of a close friend or family member • Learned about one's children have a life-threatening disease

Types of PTSD

Types of PTSD have been displayed in Flowchart 8.4. Traumatic events might occur for individual and group are given in Table 8.14.

Flowchart 8.4: Types of PTSD

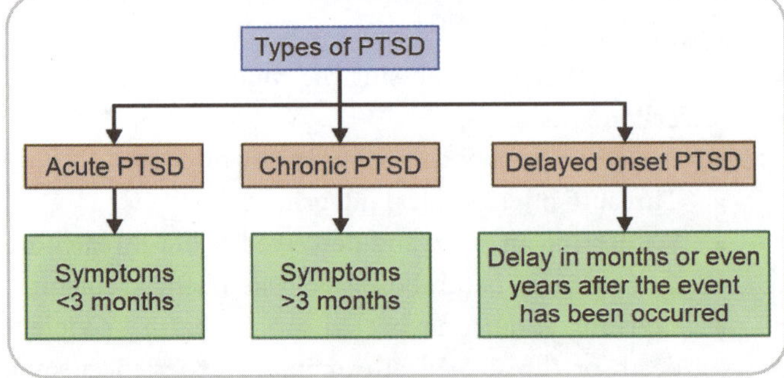

Table 8.14: Traumatic events might occur for individual and group

Traumatic events might occur to an individual	Traumatic events might occur for group or whole population
• Strong threat from stranger • Victim of sexual abuse • Physical abuse • Witness the severe accident • Involved in life-threatening accident • Domestic violence from life partner	• Natural disaster • Earthquake • Tsunami • Hurricane • Drought • Man-made disaster • Bomb threat • War

Assessment of PTSD

- **Interviews**
  - Clinician-Administered PTSD Scale (CAPS)
  - Anxiety Disorder Interview Schedule (ADIS)
  - PTSD Symptom Scale Interview (PSS-I)
  - Structured Interview for PTSD (SI-PTSD)
- **Self-report questionnaires**
  - Impact of Event Scale-Revised (IES-R)
  - The Post-traumatic Diagnostic Scale (PDS)
  - Mississippi Scale for Combat-related PTSD and Mississippi Scale for Civilians
  - Keane PTSD Scale of the MMPI-2
  - PTSD checklist—it has two versions:
    - Version 1: Civilians
    - Version 2: Military personnel and veterans.
- **For children**
  - Child PTSD Symptom Scale (CPSS)
  - Trauma Symptom Checklist for Children (TSCC)
  - Trauma Symptom Checklist for Young Children (TSCYC)
  - Parent Report of Child's Reaction to Stress
  - Child Post-traumatic Stress Reaction Index (CPTS-RI)
  - Children's Impact of Traumatic Events Scale-Revised (CITES-R)
  - Clinician-Administered PTSD Scale for Children and Adolescents (CAPS-CA)

NOTE

In children, the symptoms of PTSD are expressed as nightmares, disturbances in going to sleep, acting out behavior, developmental regression, clinging behavior, withdrawal from friends, poor attention, decline in academic performance, fighting with peers, etc.

Differential Diagnosis

- **Acute stress disorder:** Symptoms might occur within 4 weeks of traumatic event and it might come to an end within that period, when the symptoms persist for more than 4 weeks then it is termed PTSD.
- **Obsessive-compulsive disorder:** Repeated thoughts will be there but not related toward the post-traumatic events in OCD.
- **Adjustment disorder:** Stressor is going to be within the normal human experience in adjustment disorder whereas in PTSD, stressor is a post-traumatic event.
- **Depressive disorders:** Emotional numbness and avoidance features are present in both depression and PTSD whereas hyperarousal or intrusive symptoms are not seen in depression but they are present in PTSD.
- **Others:** Anxiety disorders and substance abuse disorders.

NOTE

Sometimes, the above differential diagnosis might be present as the comorbid conditions of post-traumatic stress disorder.

Treatment

- **Exposure therapy:** Repeated exposure to the post-traumatic events in gradual manner which is aimed to remember the traumatic event without the anxiety.
- **Cognitive therapy:** Separating the intrusive thoughts from the associated anxiety. Therapist will work out to reduce the distress-enhancing cognitions.
- **Stress inoculation training:** Helps the patient to relax while thinking about the traumatic event.
- **Medications**
  - **Selective serotonin reuptake inhibitors:** Sertraline (zoloft), escitalopram (lexapro), paroxetine (paxil fluoxetine (prozac), fluvoxamine (luvox).
  - **Tricyclic antidepressants:** Clomipramine (Anafranil), maprotiline (Ludiomil), nortriptyline (Aventyl), amitriptyline (Elavil), doxepin (Sinequan), desipramine (Norpramin).
  - **Antianxiety agents:** Benzodiazepines, e.g., lorazepam
  - Antihypertensive agents: For example, propranolol, clonidine.
  - **Mood stabilizers:** For example, lithium carbonate, carbamazepine.
- Treatment for children
  - **Critical incident stress management:** Intervention that addresses the traumatic incident to decrease the traumatic effects.
  - **Cognitive behavioral therapy:** Cognitive restructuring and anxiety management can be done.
  - Group therapy
  - Play therapy
  - Involvement of parents in treatment
  - **Medications:** Fluoxetine (prozac) for depression in children and sertraline (zoloft) for OCD in children.

Complex Post-Traumatic Stress Disorder

In addition to the core features of post-traumatic stress disorder, the below features will be present:

- Severe and pervasive problems in affect regulation
- Persistent beliefs about oneself as worthless, accompanied by the pervasive feelings of shame, guilt or failure related to the traumatic event
- Persistent difficulties in sustaining relationships with others.

Prolonged Grief Disorder

(Refer to Grief and Bereavement Topic in Psychiatric Emergency Unit)

Definition of Grief

It is the normal process of reacting to the loss of beloved ones. (Example: At the time of grieving process, any sort of actions or emotions or expressions to loss such as anger, shock, disbelief, depression, resentment, etc. is elicited).

Subtype

Prolonged grief disorder is a subtype of morbid grief or complicated grief.

ICD-11 Diagnostic Criteria

- The disturbance happens following the death of life partner or parent or child or another close person to be bereaved.
- Persistent and pervasive grief response characterized by longing for the deceased.
- Persistent preoccupation with the deceased accompanied by intense emotional pain (e.g., blame, sadness, denial, guilt, anger, feeling one has lost a part of one's self, negative mood, emotional numbness, difficulty in engaging in activities).
- Grief response presents atypically long period of time following the loss (6 months and above at a minimum).
- Grief reactions that have persisted for longer periods that are within a normative period of grieving given the person's cultural and religious context are viewed as normal bereavement responses.
- Disturbance causes significant impairment in personal, family, social, educational, occupational or other important areas of functioning.

Nursing Management

Nurse needs to provide the bereavement counseling to the patient (counseling provided to address the practical issues of living without the loved one who has been dead recently).

Adjustment Disorder

Definition

Presence of significant behavioral or emotional symptoms in response to the psychosocial stressors.

History

Adjustment disorders were previously a part of personality disorder. After 19th century, it is termed 'intrinsic monomania' (fire setting and kleptomania—uncontrolled impulse of stealing things).

Adjustment disorders occur due to the repeated stressors which are experienced by a normal human being such as sudden job loss, marriage, childbirth, divorce, economic problems and not interested in studies which give a maladaptive response to a stressful life event. Emotional and behavioral responses occur within 3 months from the onset of stressors. These emotional and behavioral responses may be present with depression, anxiety, conduct disturbances, mixed depression and anxiety. Adjustment disorders may be acute (with 6 months) or chronic (more than 6 months) (Flowchart. 8.5).

Epidemiology

Adjustment disorders might occur at any age group. Incidence rate is higher in adolescence and women. Approximately 2–3% of people in general population have adjustment disorder. This disorder is more common in individuals with poor coping skills/abilities.

Etiology

- **Genetic factors:** Over reacting to the stressor and high anxiety temperament.
- **Biological factors:** History of serious medical illness or disability.
- **Psychosocial factors:** Poor care from parents and loss of parents in infancy. Decreased frustration tolerance in adult might be due to lack of basic needs in infancy.

Differential Diagnosis

- **Acute post-traumatic stress disorder:** It is outside the range of human experience (e.g., disasters, war or any catastrophic incidents) whereas in adjustment disorder it is within the range of human experience.
- **Brief psychotic disorder:** Brief psychotic disorder delusion, hallucination and disorganized behavior are present whereas these are absent in adjustment disorders.
- **Uncomplicated bereavement:** Symptoms occur after the death of beloved ones in case of uncomplicated bereavement but they occur within the range of human experience in adjustment disorder.
- **Anxiety and mood disorders:** Anxiety and mood disorders do not have direct relation with stressor, whereas adjustment disorder occurs due to the repeated stressors.

Flowchart 8.5: Concept map of adjustment disorder

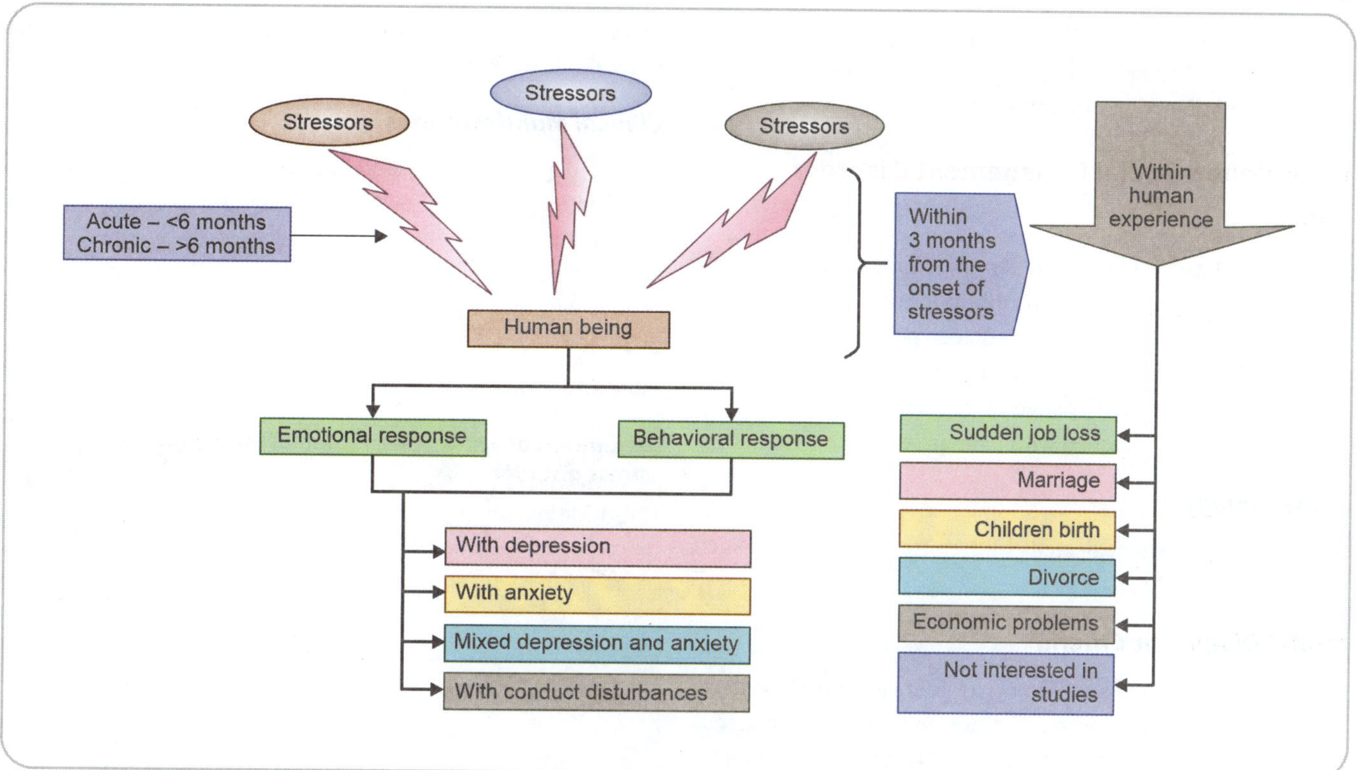

Course and Prognosis

The individual might return to the previous level of functioning within 3-month period. The individual might develop mood disorder or substance abuse disorder in future. Prognosis of adolescence is later than adults.

Treatment

- **Psychological:** Psychotherapy such as biofeedback, relaxation techniques and hypnosis might be helpful. Crisis intervention such as supportive techniques, suggestion, reassurance and environment manipulation might be helpful. Coping skills training and stress management training are essential.
- **Drugs:** Antianxiety and antidepressants.

Reactive Attachment Disorder

Definition

A consistent emotionally withdrawn behavior toward adult caregivers such as rarely seeks or responds to comfort when distressed, persistent emotional or social disturbances such as irritability, sadness, fearfulness, etc. and child experiences the extremes of ineffective care such as social neglect, repeated change of primary caregiver, limited opportunity to get attached with primary caregiver, etc.

Epidemiology

It is seen in severely neglected children (less than 10% of such children).

DSM-5 Diagnostic Criteria

The above-mentioned definition criteria are met but the criteria for autism spectrum disorder are not met. The disturbance is evident before age 5 years and the child has a developmental age of at least 9 months. (Specify as 'Persistent' if the symptoms present more than 12 months).

Functional Consequences

Interpersonal relations with the adult and peers will be greatly impaired.

Nursing Management

Nurse has to teach the parents in regard to the importance of the primary caregiver for the children and functional consequence if the quality of caregiving environment consistently compromised. Ask the caregiver to monitor whether the baby seeks or responds to comfort when distressed and so the progress can be identified.

Prognosis

It depends on the quality of caregiving environment.

Comorbid Disorders

- **Psychological disorders:** Cognitive delay, stereotype behavior, language delay, depressive disorders.
- **Medical disorders:** Malnutrition.

Disinhibited Social Engagement Disorder

Definition

A consistent pattern of behavior in which a child actively approaches and interacts with unfamiliar adults, not limited to impulsivity (as in attention-deficit/hyperactivity disorder). Child experiences the extremes of ineffective care such as social neglect, repeated change of primary caregiver, limited opportunity to get attached with primary caregiver, etc.

Epidemiology

It is seen in severely neglected children (less than 20% of such children).

DSM-5 Diagnostic Criteria

The above-mentioned definition criteria are met but the criteria for autism spectrum disorder are not met. The disturbance is evident before age 5 years and the child has a developmental age of at least 9 months. (Specify as 'Persistent' if the symptoms present more than 12 months).

Functional Consequences

Interpersonal relations with the adult and peers will be greatly impaired.

Nursing Management

Nurse has to teach the child in regard to the negative consequences of having more interaction with the unfamiliar adults. Necessary treatment advice is required to treat the comorbid disorder at the earliest.

Prognosis

It depends on the quality of caregiving environment.

Comorbid Disorders

Cognitive delay, stereotype behavior, language delay and attention-deficit/hyperactivity disorder.

Acute Stress Disorder

Definition

An immediate and clear relation exists between the stressor (e.g., accident, sudden job loss, disaster) and the onset of symptoms such as anger, depression, etc.

Epidemiology

It is common in females, first exposure to traumatic event and individuals with poor coping skills.

Clinical Manifestations

Anger, depression, anxiety, social withdrawal, despair and constricted level of consciousness. Symptoms might resolve within few hours if the individual from stressful environment has been removed. If the stress continues, the symptoms may resolve within 1–3 days. Description of the symptoms is given in Table 8.15.

Table 8.15: Symptoms of acute stress disorder

Symptoms of acute stress disorder	Description of the symptoms
Intrusion symptoms	• Recurrent, involuntary and intrusive distressing memories of traumatic event • Recurrent distressing dreams • Dissociative reactions (e.g., flashbacks) about the traumatic event • Prolonged psychological distress or marked physiological reactions in response to internal or external cues in regard to the traumatic event
Negative mood	Persistent inability to experience positive emotions
Dissociative symptoms	• Altered sense of the reality of one's surroundings or oneself • Inability to remember the vital aspect of the traumatic event (typically due to dissociative amnesia)
Avoidance symptoms	• Efforts to avoid distressing memories, thoughts, or feelings associated with the traumatic event • Efforts to avoid external reminders associated with the traumatic event
Arousal symptoms	• Sleep disturbances • Irritable behavior and angry outbursts • Hypervigilance • Problems with concentration • Exaggerated startle response

Treatment

Antianxiety drugs (benzodiazepines, e.g., diazepam) to reduce the agitation.

DISSOCIATIVE DISORDER

Definition

Dissociative disorder is defined as lack of integration of consciousness, memory and identity.

History

- Mr Pierre Janet (19th century), French Physician and Psychologist, is the first person to identify the concept of dissociation.
- Freud (1962) viewed that the dissociation is an active mechanism of repression.

Epidemiology

Dissociative amnesia (formerly psychogenic amnesia) is the most common type of dissociative disorder. The prevalence of dissociative fugue is 0.2%; however, it is increased during the time of disaster, accidents and war.

Etiology

- **Biological/neurophysiological dysfunction:** Amygdala, hippocampus, frontal cortex, mammillary bodies and thalamus.
- **Psychodynamic factors:** Intrapsychic conflict, sublimation, projection and repression (Flowchart 8.6).
- **Social factors/learning theory:** Nonverbal means of controlling/managing others.
- **Behavioral—reinforcement by:**
  - **Primary gain:** Protect from painful emotional experience.
  - **Secondary gain:** Gratifying response of having a sick role.

Classification of Dissociative Disorders

As per ICD-11 and DSM-5, the classification of dissociative disorders is given in Table 8.16.

Flowchart 8.6: Psychodynamic factors of dissociative disorder

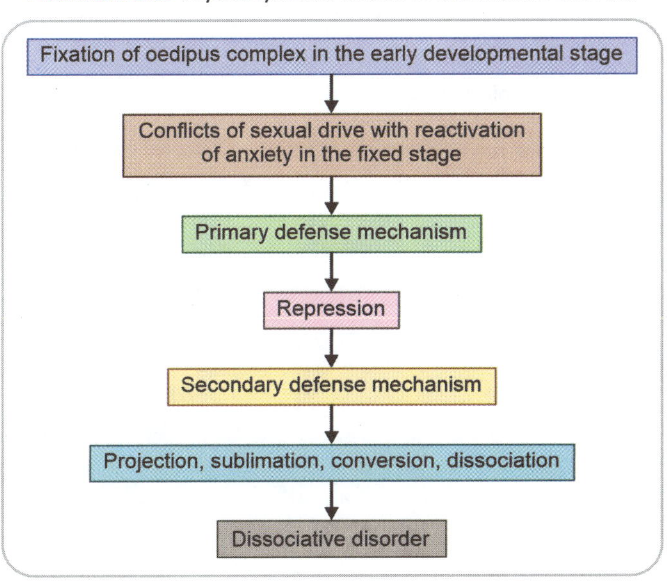

Table 8.16: ICD-11 and DSM-5 classification of dissociative disorders

ICD-11	DSM-5	Classification of dissociative disorders
6B60	—	Dissociative neurological symptom disorder
6B61	300.12	Dissociative amnesia
—	300.13	Dissociative amnesia (with dissociative fugue)
6B62	—	Trance disorder
6B63	—	Possession trance disorder
6B64	300.14	Dissociative identity disorder
6B65		Partial dissociative identity disorder
6B66	300.6	Depersonalization-derealization disorder
6B6Y	300.15	Other specified dissociative disorder
6B6Z	300.15	Unspecified dissociative disorder

Dissociative Neurological Symptom Disorder or Conversion Disorder (Functional Neurological System Disorder as per DSM-5)

(Refer to the Conversion Disorder in the Same Chapter for Full Description)

It is characterized by presentation of motor, sensory or cognitive symptoms which lead to the involuntary discontinuity with the normal integration of motor, sensory or cognitive functions and not consistent with disease of the nervous system, other mental or behavioral disorder or other diseases.

Dissociative Identity Disorder

Individual is dominated with two or more personalities, in which one personality is manifested at a time. One personality is not aware about the other personality (amnesia is present between the personalities). Onset and termination of personalities are sudden in nature.

Partial Dissociative Identity Disorder

One personality state is dominant and normally functions in daily life, but the dominant personality intruded upon by one or more nondominant personality states (dissociative intrusions). This intrusion can be cognitive, affective, motor, perceptual or behavioral. Due to the interfering with the functioning of the dominant personality state may provoke aversiveness. Nondominant personality state will not recurrently take an executive control of individual's consciousness and functioning.

Dissociative Amnesia

It is the most common type of dissociative disorder. It is most commonly seen in young adults and it has been observed that females are more affected as compared to males. Mostly dissociative amnesia has the following stages:

- **Before amnesia:** Stressor or traumatic life event.
- **During amnesia:** Clouding of consciousness.
- **Post amnesia:** Aware of disturbances in memory.

Types of Dissociative Amnesia

- **Localized amnesia:** Unable to recall for specific time period after the event.
- **Selective amnesia:** Unable to recall certain incidents with traumatic event.
- **Continuous amnesia:** Unable to recall from a specific time till date.
- **Generalized amnesia:** Unable to recall entire lifetime incidence including the personal identity.
- **Systematized amnesia:** Unable to recall events with specific category (e.g., any particular person/event/family).

Dissociative Fugue

It is characterized by episodes of wandering away from home. During the wandering, individual assumes new identity along with complete amnesia of previous life. Onset is sudden with presence of stress. Termination is abrupt with remembrance of previous life. Differential diagnosis includes the complex partial seizure and temporal lobe epilepsy (in which assumption of new identity is absent).

Depersonalization-Derealization Disorder

Depersonalization-derealization disorder is persistent or recurrent experiences of depersonalization, derealization, or both.

- Depersonalization is experiencing the self as strange or unreal, or feeling detached from, or as though one were an outside observer of, one's thoughts, feelings, sensations, body, or actions.
- Derealization is characterized by experiencing other persons, objects, or the world as strange or unreal or detached from the surroundings.

Trance Disorder

It is characterized by trance states in which there is a marked alteration in the person's state of consciousness or a loss of the individual's sense of personal identity. Trance state is not replaced by an alternate identity.

Possession Trance Disorder

It is characterized by trance states in which the individual's customary sense of personal identity is replaced by an external 'possessing' identity and in which the individual's movements or behaviors are experienced as being controlled by possessing agent.

Miscellaneous Dissociative Disorder

- **Ganser syndrome or hysterical pseudodementia:** Symptom commonly seen in prison inmates and has a characteristic feature of 'Vorbeireden' called 'saying approximate answer'.
- When client is questioned 6 + 5 = ___. Client might verbalize 10 or 12 but not 11.

Clinical Features of Dissociative Disorder

The clinical features of dissociative disorder have been given in Table 8.17.

ICD-11 Diagnostic Criteria for Dissociative Disorder

- Predominant symptoms should match the description of the specific subtype of dissociative disorder such as dissociative identity disorder or partial dissociative identity disorder or trance or procession trance disorder or dissociative amnesia or dissociative fugue or depersonalization-derealization disorder or dissociative fugue or other specified or unspecified disorder.
- Symptoms are not better explained by another psychiatric, behavioral or the neurodevelopmental disorder.
- Disorder is not due to the influence of any substances or medication on the central nervous system or disease of the nervous system or sleep wake disorder.

Table 8.17: Clinical features of dissociative disorder

Motor symptoms	Sensory deficits	Visceral symptoms
• Involuntary movements • Tics • Blepharospasm • Seizures • Abnormal gait • Torticollis • Opisthotonos • Falling • Weakness • Aphonia • Astasia-abasia • Paralysis	• Anesthesia of extremities • Blindness • Midline anesthesia • Tunnel vision • Deafness	• Psychogenic vomiting • Pseudocyesis • Urinary retention • Diarrhea • Globus hystericus • Swooning or syncope

- Symptoms of this disorder will lead to the significant impairment in personal, family, educational, social, occupational or other vital areas of functioning.

Differential Diagnosis

- Delirium/Dementia
- Epilepsy
- Amnesia with general medical disorder
- Transient global amnesia
- Substance-induced amnesia
- Wernicke-Korsakoff syndrome
- Acute stress
- Somatoform/somatization/conversation disorder
- Malingering

Course and Prognosis

- Usually, acute onset.
- Recovery is complete, few relapses might be there.
- Duration is prolonged if dissociation is due to secondary gain.
- Symptoms might terminate abruptly.
- Prognosis is good when onset is acute and the individual has above average intelligence.

The continuum of dissociation has been presented in Figure 8.5.

Treatment

- **Behavior therapy**
  - Aversion therapy—pressure in tragus of ear
- Psychotherapy with abreaction (Bringing to conscious awareness/thoughts/memories for first time)
  - Hypnosis
  - Free association
  - Intravenous barbiturates (thiopentone/diazepam)
- Supportive psychotherapy
- Insight-oriented supportive or behavior therapy
- Psychodynamic psychotherapy
- Psychoanalysis

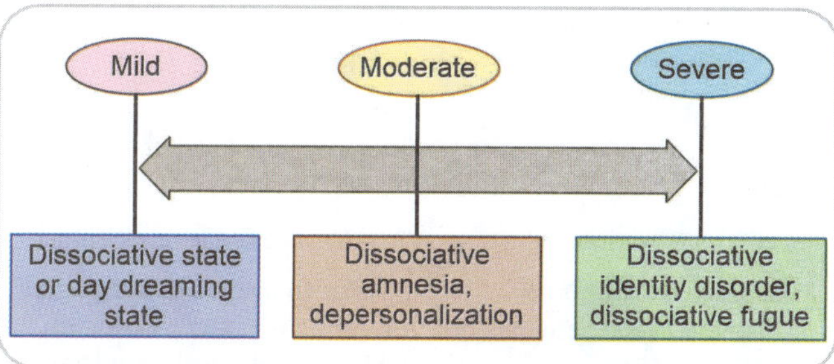

Figure 8.5: Continuum of dissociation

- **Drug therapy:** Short-acting barbiturates (amobarbital) and benzodiazepines.

SOMOTOFORM OR SOMATIC SYMPTOM AND RELATED DISORDERS

Introduction

In the word, 'Somatoform' prefix 'soma' came from Greek word, 'body'. It is a mental illness in which multiple body signs and symptoms are elicited but, the medical evaluation does not reveal any abnormalities. Patients will visit a number of doctors (Doctor shopping), when the doctor says that there is no health problems, then the patient might get face issues like frustration, anxiety and depression.

Classification of Somatic Symptom and Related Disorders

DSM-5 classification of somatic symptom and related disorders is given in Table 8.18.

Somatic Symptom Disorder

Definition

Presence of one or more somatic symptoms which cause significant personal distress in patient.

Epidemiology

It begins in teenage usually before 30 years of age. It is more common in women. Depression and anxiety are the common comorbid illnesses. The common personality traits are paranoid, avoidant, self-defeating and obsessive- compulsive trait.

Etiology

Psychodynamic factors.

Table 8.18: DSM-5 classification of somatic symptom and related disorders

DSM-5 code	Somatic symptom and related disorders
300.82	Somatic symptom disorder
300.7	Illness anxiety disorder
300.11	Conversion disorder (functional neurological symptom disorder)
316	Psychological factors affecting other medical conditions
300.19	Factitious disorder
300.89	Other specified somatic symptom and related disorder
300.82	Unspecified somatic symptom and related disorder

- Learning theory
- Social/cultural factors
- Biological factors
- Genetic factors
- Cytokines

Differential Diagnosis

- True medical illness
- Psychiatric disorders such as depression and anxiety
- Life stressors with associated psychophysiological symptoms.
- Other somatic symptom-related disorders.

Course of Illness

It is usually chronic and relapsing in nature.

DSM-5 Diagnostic Criteria

- One or more somatic symptoms which can be distressing or result in the significant disruption of daily life.
- Excessive feelings or thoughts or behaviors related to somatic symptoms or which are associated with health concerns are manifested by at least one of the following:
    - Disproportionate and persistent thoughts about the seriousness of one's symptoms.
    - Persistently high levels of anxiety about health or symptoms.
    - Excessive time and energy are devoted to these symptoms or health concerns.
- State of being symptomatic persists for more than 6 months.

Individual appears with many physical symptoms which occur over a period of years. It leads to multiple medical consultations and other attempts for seeking treatment. It must cause significant impairment in social, occupational, or other areas of functioning. In spite of appropriate investigations done, the symptoms cannot be fully explained by a known general medical condition. The symptoms are not produced intentionally. There will be four pain symptoms which are related to at least four different sites or functions which are as follows:

- Two gastrointestinal symptoms other than pain
- One sexual or reproductive symptom
- One pseudoneurological symptom

Treatment

Nurse has to help the patient to have a regular monthly visit to the same psychiatrist. Advise the patient to avoid the diagnostic investigations. Raise awareness of these symptoms being responses to psychological pressure. Improve the coping skills/abilities with these symptoms. Provide individual or group psychotherapy. Assist the patient to express the underlying emotions and also help the patient to develop alternative strategies to express feelings of the patient.

Nursing Diagnosis

- Ineffective coping skills related to unresolved psychological conflicts as evidenced by the verbalized somatic symptoms.
- Anxiety related to extreme concern about physical illness/symptoms.
- Low self-esteem related to perceived threat to perform daily functional activities.
- Powerlessness related to perceived lack of ability to improve the physical health as evidenced by high level dependency.
- Social isolation related to lack of ability to participate in social events.
- Interrupted family process related to the assumption of sick role.

Ineffective coping skills related to unresolved psychological conflicts as evidenced by the verbalized somatic symptoms have been given in Table 8.19.

Table 8.19: Ineffective coping skills

Nursing intervention	Rationale
Discuss with the patient to explore the triggering factors	It helps the client to recognize the triggering factor and manage one's own behavior
Show empathy in the patient's distress	To gain the trust from patient
Teach the client to develop coping strategies	It helps to enhance the coping ability
Perform insight-oriented therapy	To promote the insight into behavior patterns

Anxiety related to the extreme concern on physical illness/symptoms has been given in Table 8.20.

Table 8.20: Anxiety related to physical illness

Nursing intervention	Rationale
Assess the level of anxiety and the triggering factor which is provoking anxiety	It gives the baseline data
Provide stress management training	To reduce the level of stress
Teach the relaxation techniques	To decrease the level of anxiety
Encourage the client to participate in the activities of daily living (ADLs)	It helps to involve in activities, thereby the patient's concern on his/her physical symptoms might reduce

Illness Anxiety Disorder (Hypochondriasis/ Health Phobia/Health Anxiety Disorder)

Definition

It is an anxiety disorder which is characterized by being preoccupied with health concerns that might cause significant impairment or personal distress in one's life.

Epidemiology

- Males and females are equally affected.
- Common in all age groups
- In males, symptoms peak around 30 years of age and in females around 40 years of age.

Etiology

- **Psychodynamic factors:** Projection, intrapsychic conflict, pain or suffering as a punishment of guilt and displacement of anger toward self.
- **Social learning model/Learning theory/Social factors:** Symptoms often learned from past experiences or have related medical illness.
- **Biological factors:** Low threshold and low tolerance of physical discomfort.

DSM-5 Diagnostic Criteria

- Preoccupation with having or acquiring a specific illness.
- Usually, somatic symptoms are absent though mild symptoms may be present sometimes.
- Excessive health concern if another medical condition is present or the individual is at high-risk.
- High level of anxiety about health, easily alarmed about personal health status.
- Performs excessive health-related behaviors or exhibits maladaptive avoidance.
- Symptoms last for 6 months or more.
- Preoccupation with health concerns might cause significant impairment or distress in a person's life.

Table 8.21 shows differences between medical and psychiatric disorders.

Table 8.21: Differences between medical and psychiatric disorders

Medical disorders	Psychiatric disorders
• Degenerative diseases of neurons • Myasthenia gravis • Acquired immunodeficiency syndrome (AIDS) • Systemic lupus erythematosus (SLE)	• Depression • Anxiety • Panic disorder • Sexual dysfunction • Malingering • Factitious disorder

Diagnostic Test

All laboratory investigations will reveal the patient's condition is normal. Minnesota Multiphasic Personality Inventory (MMPI) shows the five components on hysteria scale such as poor physical health, shyness, cynicism, headache and neuroticism and it will reveal higher score. More color responses in the Rorschach test might be present and denote the emotional liability.

Nursing Management

Supportive systemic approach with love and care is beneficial. Stress reduction program (deep breathing exercises, relaxation training, healthy lifestyle measures) and enhancement of coping skills are important. Assist the client in performing the daily activities. Do not give any false reassurance to the patient. Support the patient in rehabilitation and refer him/her to the appropriate self-help groups. Inquire the client directly whether he/she is having a suicidal tendency. Group therapy might be helpful to get good social support from others. Regular follow-up of the patients is important. Antidepressants and antianxiety agents are used.

Course and Prognosis

It is usually chronic in nature. The prognosis is good if the individual has a good premorbid personality and prognosis is poor if the individual is superimposed with the physical disorder.

The descriptions of somatoform autonomic dysfunction have been given in Table 8.22. It also shows the symptoms and treatment method of this dysfunction.

The physiology of hyperventilation syndrome has been shown in Flowchart 8.7.

Conversion Disorder

Definition

It is a somatic symptom-related disorder which characterized by the presence of one or more symptoms of altered voluntary motor or sensory function. There is an incompatibility between the symptom and recognized neurological or medical conditions.

Other Names

- This disorder is also called "functional neurological symptom disorder".
- As per ICD-11, this is named as "dissociative neurological symptom disorder".

Epidemiology

- Persistent conversion symptoms are estimated to be 2–5/100,000 per year.
- Two to three times more common in females.

Table 8.22: Descriptions of somatoform autonomic dysfunction

Somatoform autonomic dysfunction	Description	Symptoms	Treatment
Hyperventilation syndrome (HVS) (Flowchart 8.7)	Hyperventilation (loss of too much carbon dioxide) because of fast breathing due to psychosocial stressors	• Mild hyperventilation syndrome • Headache • Fatigue • Chest pain • Sweating • Palpitation • Feel of lightheadedness Moderate to severe hyperventilation syndrome • Paresthesia • Loss of consciousness • Carpopedal spasm (tetany)	• Relaxation therapy • Breathing techniques • Antidepressants • Antianxiety agents • Breathing-in-bag technique (client rebreathes the expired air to increase the pCO_2)
Irritable bowel syndrome (IBS) or irritable colon syndrome or nervous diarrhea or spastic colitis or colon neurosis or mucus colitis	Disturbances in bowel motility are due to psychological factors. It may be hypomotility or hypermotility	• Discomfort, pain or cramps of abdomen • Disturbed bowel habits (diarrhea/ constipation) • Feel of incomplete evacuation	• Antidepressants • Antianxiety • Prokinetic agents (e.g., cisapride) • Supportive psychotherapy
Premenstrual syndrome or premenstrual tension	Presence of physical, behavioral and psychological symptoms occurs in the second half of menstrual cycle (few days after ovulation) due to fault in luteinization increased estrogen and decreased progesterone level	• Psychological Symptoms • Anxiety • Restlessness • Depression • Crying spells • Irritability • Physical Symptoms • Fatigue • Headache • Gastroenterological changes • Pedal edema • Sense of bloating abdomen • Swelling of breast	• Thiazide diuretics (e.g., spironolactone) • Oral/Parental progesterone • Treatment-resistant premenstrual syndrome can be treated with antidepressants, antianxiety drugs, bromocriptine and lithium • Supportive psychotherapy

Flowchart 8.7: Physiology of hyperventilation syndrome

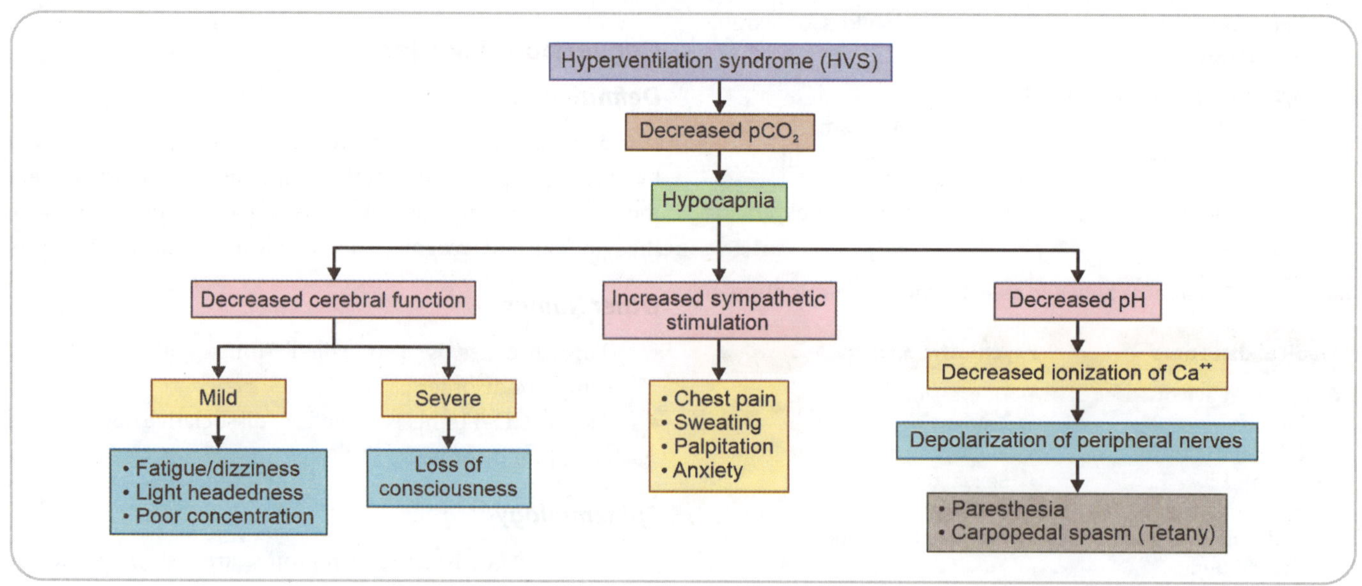

Etiology or Risk Factors

- **Temperamental:** Maladaptive personality traits are commonly associated with this disorder.
- **Environmental:** History of childhood abuse or neglect, stressful life event may be present.
- **Genetic and physiological:** Presence of neurological disease may cause similar symptom (for example, nonepileptic seizure is more common in patients who have epilepsy).

Clinical Features

Motor symptoms:

- Weakness or paralysis.
- Gait abnormalities and abnormal limb posturing.
- Abnormal movements such as tremors or dystonic movements.

Sensory symptoms:

- Altered, reduced or absent skin sensation, vision or hearing
- Episodes of abnormal generalized limb shaking with apparent impaired or loss of consciousness may resemble epileptic seizures (also called psychogenic or nonepileptic seizures)—given in Table 8.23.

Other symptoms:

- Altered articulation (dysarthria).
- Reduced or absent speech volume (dysphonia/aphonia)
- Diplopia (double vision).
- Sensation of a lump in the throat (globus).

Associated features:

- La belle indifference—lack of concern about the nature or implications of the symptom.
- Secondary gain—derive external benefits such as money or release from responsibilities.

NOTE

The associated features are additional but not specific symptom to diagnose the conversion disorder.

Comorbid Disorders

Anxiety disorders (especially panic disorders, depressive disorders and personality disorders are more common comorbid disorders.

Nursing Management

Relaxation program such as deep breathing exercises, relaxation training, healthy lifestyle measures is important. Assist the client in performing the daily activities. Motivate the patients to ventilate the emotions. Support the patient in rehabilitation and refer him/her to the appropriate self-help groups. Teach the coping strategies to patients. Regular follow-up of the patients is important. Antidepressants and antianxiety agents are used.

Table 8.23: Differences between epileptic seizures and psychogenic nonepileptic seizures or hysterical fits

Aspects	Epileptic seizures	Psychogenic nonepileptic seizures or hysterical fits
Clinical pattern	Stereotyped	Purposive body movements
Place of incident	Anywhere	Safe place
Time of day	Anytime. Even happen during sleep	Never happen during sleep
Speech	Absent	May present
Tongue bite	May present	Absent
Injury	May occur	Very rare
Urine and fecal incontinence	May occur	Very rare
Turning duration	Shorter	Prolonged
Turing of head	Unilateral	Side to side turning is present
Eye gaze	Staring gaze if the eyes are open	Avoidant gaze
Neurological signs	Present	Absent
Amnesia	Complete	Partial
Stress	25% of patients have stress	Majority of them have stress
Postictal confusion	Present	Absent
EEG	Abnormal	Normal
Serum prolactin	Raised in postictal period	Normal

Table 8.24: Other specified neurotic disorders (culture-bound syndromes)

Syndromes	Regions commonly affected	Description
Dhat syndrome	India	Belief that there will be presence of semen in urine. There may be sexual dysfunction, depression, anxiety, multiple somatic complaints and asthenia (physical/mental exhaustion)
Amok	Southeast Asia	Sudden onset of rage and killing the persons those who are coming on the way
Koro	Asia	Belief that penis is shrinking and will disappear into abdominal wall
Wihtigo (Windigo)	American-Indians	Belief that the individual is being transferred into cannibal monster mainly during the time of starvation
Piblokto (Arctic hysteria)	Eskimos living in green land arctic circle	Women might tear off clothes and throw oneself into ice. She might cry like bird/animal. It is a type of dissociative disorder and the episode lasts for 1–2 hours followed by amnesia
Latah (Startle reaction)	Japan and Southeast Asia	Presence of echolalia, echopraxia and automatic obedience.

Psychological Factors Affecting Other Medical Conditions

Presence of physical medical condition due to the psychological or behavioral factors may influence the course of the medical condition (exacerbation or delayed recovery), treatment of the medical condition, health risks for the individual, underlying pathophysiology and the precipitating or exacerbating symptoms which seek the medical attention.

Categories

- **Mild category:** Presence of increased medical risk.
- **Moderate category:** Aggravates the underlying medical condition.
- **Severe category:** Results in hospitalization.
- **Extreme category:** Results in life-threatening risk.

Factitious Disorders or Munchausen Syndrome by Proxy

Falsifications of physical or psychological symptoms which project the individual as an ill person. The deception happens even in the absence of obvious external reward. It may happen as a single episode or in a recurrent episode.

In **malingering** (psychiatric disorder), patient plays a similar sick role with the intention of secondary gain (avoiding work, escape from the criminal cases, unwilling to pay the amount, etc.) whereas in factitious disorder playing of sick role is not for the secondary gain.

OTHER NEUROTIC DISORDERS

Neurasthenia: Individual has persistent and distressing complaints of body weakness and he feels exhausted even after a minimal effort. Chronic fatigue syndrome (CFS) is the main differential diagnosis, in which individual has a soft physical sign (present in mild) without the significant medical or psychiatric disorder. Individual with neurasthenia might have any two of these complaints:

- Sleep disturbances
- Muscle aches
- Tension/headache
- Inability to relax
- Dyspepsia
- Fatigue/dizziness
- Irritability

Other specified neurotic disorders (culture-bound syndromes) have been listed in Table 8.24.

GERIATRIC CONSIDERATIONS

The common anxiety disorders seen in elders are general anxiety disorders and phobia. In general, anxiety disorders are comorbid condition of depression, physical illness, dementia and drug toxicity. Drug of choice in geriatrics is selective serotonin reuptake inhibitor group of antidepressants. Drugs have to be initiated in lower dosage in order to check the tolerating capacity among elders.

Follow-Up, Home Care and Rehabilitation

- Teach the stress management techniques and coping skills among patients.
- Encourage the family members to utilize the available community resources.
- Teach the patient to identify the stressors which exacerbate the anxiety and to avoid them.
- Teach the family members about drug compliance.
- Encourage the patient to express the feelings.

- Teach the patient in regard with the lifestyle modifications such as balanced diet, regular exercises, avoidance of smoking and alcoholism.
- Advise the patient and family members to have a regular follow-up in psychiatric OPDs or in community clinics.

EXTRA EDGE

ICD-10 Classification of Neurotic, Stress-related and Somatoform Disorder (F40-F49)

- F40: Phobic anxiety disorder
- F41: Other anxiety disorder
- F42: Obsessive-compulsive disorder
- F43: Reaction to severe stress and adjustment disorder
- F44: Conversion or dissociative disorder
- F48: Other neurotic disorder

EXTRA EDGE

DSM-IV Classification of Somatoform Disorders

- **Somatization disorders or Briquet's syndrome:** Multiple organ system involvement is present.
- **Conversion disorders:** Neurological complaints.
- **Hypochondriasis:** Worried about being sick with a particular illness rather than to focus on physical symptoms (now, hypochondriasis is termed 'illness anxiety disorder' in DSM-5).
- **Body dysmorphic disorder:** Dissatisfaction with any of the body part (now, body dysmorphic disorder has been shifted to obsessive disorders in the DSM-5).
- **Persistent somatoform pain disorder:** Pain is the main complaint (now, persistent somatoform pain disorder is the part of somatic symptom disorder in DSM-5).
- Undifferentiated somatoform disorder.
- Somatoform disorder not otherwise specified.

SUMMARY

- In 1900, Sigmund Freud introduced the concept of anxiety.
- **Anxiety is defined** as 'feelings of uncertainty, apprehension, uneasiness or tension that individual shows in any situation'.
- Anxiety disorders are more common in females.
- Lifetime prevalence of anxiety disorders in females is 25% and in males it is 15%.
- **Types of anxiety disorders**: Trait anxiety, state anxiety, signal anxiety and free-floating anxiety.
- When there is a dangerous situation, individual may fight, flight (escape), fright (fear) toward the danger.
- **Biological factors for anxiety disorders:** Increased serotonin activity in thalamus, raphe nucleus, hypothalamus, basal ganglion and limbic system, greater activation of amygdala (diamond-shaped structure in limbic system), hyperactivity of insula (portion of cortex buried under lateral sulcus), not activated anterior cingulate cortex, three structures (amygdala, anterior cingulate cortex and insula) constitute 'fear network', abnormalities in cortico-striatal-thalamo-cortical circuit and glutamate transporter gene, deficit in 'sensory gating', i.e. threat-related stimuli are not filtered out, neurotransmitters—GABA underactivity and serotonin dysfunction, neuroendocrine—hypothalamic-pituitary-adrenal axis overactivity, neuropeptides—CPK, NPY, AVP.
- Anxiety is due to unconscious conflicts that exist between impulses of aggressiveness or gratification with ego.
- **The levels of anxiety** include normal level, euphoria, mild anxiety, moderate anxiety, severe anxiety and panic anxiety.
- **Symptoms of anxiety** include physiological symptoms, psychological or emotional symptoms, behavioral symptoms and cognitive symptoms.
- **Types of phobias:** Simple or specific phobia, social phobia, agoraphobia, panic disorder with agoraphobia.
- **ICD-11 and DSM-5 classifications of anxiety disorder are** separation anxiety disorder, selective mutism, specific phobia, social anxiety disorder, panic disorder, agoraphobia, generalized anxiety disorder, other specified and unspecified anxiety disorder.
- **Anxiety disorders in DSM-5 are** generalized anxiety disorder, panic disorder, specific phobia/social phobia/agoraphobia, obsessive-compulsive disorder and post-traumatic stress disorder.
- **Differential diagnosis of anxiety disorders is** prodrome or first episode schizophrenia, behavioral or psychological symptoms of dementia, delirium tremens of alcohol withdrawal, anxiety seen in bipolar disorder and hyperthyroidism may mimic anxiety symptoms.
- Hamilton Rating Scale for Anxiety (HAM-A) and State Trait Anxiety Rating Scale are used for assessment of **generalized anxiety disorder.** Panic Disorder Severity Scale (PDSS) are Panic and Agoraphobia Scale (PAS) are used to assess **panic disorder.** Social Phobia Inventory (SPIN) and Liebowitz Social Anxiety Scale (LSAS) are used to assess **social phobia.** Yale-Brown Obsessive-Compulsive Scale (Y-BOCS) and Maudsley Obsessive-Compulsive Inventory (MOCI) are used to assess **obsessive-compulsive disorder.** Impact of Events scale (IES) and Clinician Administered PTSD Scale (CAPS) are used to assess **post-traumatic stress disorder.**
- **Drugs used in anxiety disorders** are benzodiazepines, beta-blockers and antidepressants—selective serotonin reuptake inhibitors are first-line treatment for all anxiety disorders.
- **Psychotherapy for anxiety disorders:** Cognitive behavioral therapy, behavior strategies, systematic desensitization or graded exposure and flooding for phobia, cognitive behavioral therapy for post-traumatic stress disorder (PTSD), eye movement desensitization and reprocessing for PTSD, self-monitoring technique, relaxation training (mindfulness meditation, exercise, yoga, progressive muscle relaxation, breathing exercises and autogenic training), psychoeducation, skill training to solve the problems, support group and bibliotherapy.
- **Obsession** is the repetitive thoughts, images and doubts that one will feel which are absolutely senseless and irrational, individual tries to resist but is unable to do so because that restriction might increase the level of anxiety. Obsession is ego-alien or ego-dystonic. Obsession is one's own idea/thought whereas in thought insertion, someone's idea is inserted in one's mind.

Contd...

- **Compulsion** is repetitive action performed followed by obsession in order to avoid the marked distress even though the client knows that behavior is unrealistic, senseless and irrational.
- Worldwide lifetime prevalence of OCD is 2–3%, common among unmarried males, common with upper socioeconomic individuals and the onset is late 20s in India.
- **Etiology of OCD** includes genetic factors, psychodynamic theory, behavioral theory, biological theory, hormonal factors and psychological risk factors.
- **Types of obsessive-compulsive disorder** include predominantly obsessive thoughts, predominantly compulsive acts and mixed obsessional thoughts and compulsive acts.
- **Good prognosis of OCD** is with social or family support. Poor prognosis of OCD is with early onset, severity of symptoms, bizarre compulsions and presence of comorbid illness.
- **Drug therapy of OCD** includes benzodiazepines (clonazepam, lorazepam, alprazolam), antidepressants—selective serotonin reuptake inhibitors (fluoxetine 20–80 mg/day, clomipramine 75–300 mg/day, fluvoxamine 50–200 mg/day and sertraline 50–200 mg/day), antipsychotics (haloperidol, olanzapine, risperidone, pimozide) and buspirone.
- **Psychotherapy of OCD** includes psychoanalytic psychotherapy for patients and supportive psychotherapy for family members.
- **Behavior therapy of OCD** includes thought-stopping technique, systematic desensitization—step by step graded exposure of fearful stimuli, modeling, exposure and response prevention.
- Electroconvulsive therapy can be administered if the client has depression along with OCD, poor response to drug therapy and OCD patients have high suicidal risk.
- Psychosurgery of OCD includes stereotactic limbic leukotomy and stereotactic subcaudate tractotomy.
- **Acute stress reaction is defined as** 'immediate and clear relation exists between the stressor (e.g., accident, sudden job loss, disaster) and the onset of symptoms'.
- **Post-traumatic stress disorder** is an anxiety disorder in which the individual might develop intense fear or helplessness after witnessing or experiencing an extreme, overwhelming traumatic event.
- **Etiological factors of PTSD** include neurochemical factors (increased sensitivity of hypothalamic-pituitary-adrenal axis and increased sensitivity to cortisol receptors) and biological factors (increased functions of sympathetic nervous system, imbalance in neurotransmitters such as dopamine and norepinephrine).
- **Symptoms of PTSD are classified** as re-experiencing symptoms, avoidance features and persistent symptoms of increased arousal (not present before trauma).
- **ICD-11 Diagnostic Criteria for PTSD** include the significant evidence of traumatic events, onset is within the 6 months of a traumatic event, significant emotional detachment, numbness of feelings, daytime imagery, repetitive or intrusive recollection of the events in memories.
- **Types of PTSD** are acute, chronic and delayed onset type.
- **Assessment of PTSD** includes interviews such as Clinician Administered PTSD Scale (CAPS), Anxiety Disorder Interview Schedule revised (ADIS-R), PTSD Symptom Scale Interview (PSS-I), Structured Interview for PTSD (SI-PTSD). Self-report questionnaires such as Impact of Event Scale-Revised (IES-R), the Post-traumatic Diagnostic Scale (PDS), Mississippi Scale for Combat-related PTSD and Mississippi Scale for Civilians, Keane PTSD Scale of the MMPI-2 and PTSD Checklist Scales used to assess PTSD for Children are Child PTSD Symptom Scale (CPSS), Trauma Symptom Checklist for Children (TSCC), Trauma Symptom Checklist for Young Children (TSCYC), Parent Report of Child's Reaction to Stress, Child Post-traumatic Stress Reaction Index (CPTS-RI), Children's Impact of Traumatic Events Scale-Revised (CITES-R) and Clinician-Administered PTSD Scale for Children and Adolescents (CAPS-CA).
- **Differential diagnosis for PTSD** include acute stress disorder, obsessive-compulsive disorder (OCD), adjustment disorder, depressive disorders, anxiety disorders and substance abuse disorders.
- **Treatment for PTSD** includes exposure therapy, cognitive therapy and stress inoculation training—helps the patient to relax while thinking about the traumatic event.
- **Medications for PTSD** are SSRIs, tricyclic antidepressants, antianxiety agents and antihypertensive agents and mood stabilizers.
- **Treatment for PTSD in children** includes critical incident stress management, cognitive behavioral therapy, group therapy, play therapy, involvement of parents in treatment and medications: fluoxetine (Prozac) for depression in children and sertraline (Zoloft) for OCD in children.
- **Adjustment disorders** are defined as 'presence of significant behavioral or emotional symptoms in response to the psychosocial stressors'.
- **Etiology of adjustment disorders** includes genetic factors, biological factors and psychosocial factors.
- **Differential diagnosis of adjustment disorder** includes acute post-traumatic stress disorder, brief psychotic disorder, uncomplicated bereavement, anxiety and mood disorders.
- **Treatment** of adjustment disorders includes psychotherapy such as biofeedback, relaxation techniques and hypnosis might be helpful. Crisis intervention such as supportive techniques, suggestion, reassurance and environment manipulation might be helpful. Coping skills training and stress management training are essential. Antianxiety and Antidepressants can be administered.
- **Somatoform disorder** is a mental illness in which a multiple body signs and symptoms are elicited but the medical evaluation does not reveal any abnormalities.
- **DSM-5 classification of somatic symptom-related disorders** includes somatic symptom disorder, illness anxiety disorder (hypochondriasis), conversion disorder (functional neurological symptom disorder), psychological factors affecting other medical conditions, factitious disorders, other specified somatic symptoms disorders (pseudocyesis), unspecified somatic symptom and related disorder.

Contd...

- **Dissociative disorder** is defined as lack of integration of consciousness, memory and identity.
- **Types of dissociative disorders** are dissociative amnesia (selective amnesia continuous amnesia, generalized amnesia, systematized amnesia), dissociative fugue, multiple personality (dissociative identity) disorder, trance or possession disorder and other dissociative disorder (Ganser syndrome or hysterical pseudodementia).
- **Treatment** of dissociative disorders includes behavior therapy, abreaction, hypnosis, free association, intravenous barbiturates, supportive psychotherapy, insight-oriented supportive or behavior therapy, psychodynamic psychotherapy and psychoanalysis.
- **DSM-5 Criteria for illness anxiety disorder are** preoccupation with having or acquiring a specific illness, somatic symptoms are absent usually or mildly present sometimes. Excessive health concern if another medical condition is present or the individual at high risk, high level of anxiety about health, easily alarmed about personal health status, performs excessive health-related behaviors or exhibits maladaptive avoidance, symptoms last for 6 months or more and preoccupation with health concerns might cause significant impairment or distress in a person's life.
- **Somatoform autonomic dysfunction** includes hyperventilation syndrome (HVS), irritable bowel syndrome (IBS) or irritable colon syndrome or nervous diarrhea or spastic colitis or colon neurosis or mucus colitis and premenstrual syndrome or premenstrual tension.
- **Factitious disorder** is the falsification of physical or psychological symptoms which project the individual as an ill person. The deception happens even in the absence of obvious external reward.
- **Other neurotic disorders** are neurasthenia, depersonalization disorder or depersonalization-derealization syndrome. Other specified neurotic disorders (culture-bound syndromes) include Dhat syndrome, Amok, Koro, Wihtigo, Piblokto and Latah.

ASSESS YOURSELF

Long Answer Questions

1. Explain its types, etiology, psychopathology, clinical manifestations and management of patient with anxiety disorder.
2. Explain its types, etiology, psychopathology, clinical manifestations and management of patient with obsessive-compulsive disorder.

Short Answer Questions

1. Define anxiety disorder.
2. Define obsessive-compulsive disorder.

Short Notes

Write short notes on:

1. Post-traumatic stress disorder
2. Specific phobia
3. Somatic symptom disorder
4. Dissociative disorder
5. Adjustment disorder
6. Hypochondriasis

Multiple Choice Questions

1. **__________ is the repetitive thoughts, images and doubts that one will feel it's absolutely irrational one.**
   a. Obsession b. Compulsion
   c. Anxiety d. Phobia
2. **Which neurotransmitters underactivity might cause anxiety disorder?**
   a. Dopamine b. GABA
   c. Norepinephrine d. Substance-P
3. **Anxiety which is more specific to the situation is termed __________.**
   a. State anxiety b. Trait anxiety
   c. Signal anxiety d. Free-floating anxiety
4. **Drug of choice for anxiety disorder is __________.**
   a. Chlorpromazine b. Risperidone
   c. Haloperidol d. Lorazepam
5. **Another name for irritable bowel syndrome (IBS) is:**
   a. Nervous diarrhea b. Colon neurosis
   c. Mucus colitis d. All of these
6. **ICD-11 code for dissociative amnesia is:**
   a. 6B61 b. 6B63
   c. 6B62 d. 6B64
7. **Fear of road travel is:**
   a. Acrophobia b. Hydrophobia
   c. Hematophobia d. Zoophobia
8. **Peculiar symptom of PTSD is:**
   a. Nausea b. Fatigue
   c. Flashback d. Crying spells
9. **__________ is characterized by episodes of wandering away from home.**
   a. Dissociative fugue
   b. Dissociative identity disorder
   c. Trance and possession disorder
   d. Dissociative amnesia
10. **________ has characteristic feature of 'Vorbeireden'.**
    a. Ganser syndrome or hysterical pseudodementia
    b. Fatigue
    c. Free-floating anxiety
    d. None of the above

ANSWER KEY

1. a	**2.** b	**3.** a	**4.** d	**5.** d
6. a	**7.** b	**8.** c	**9.** a	**10.** a

Notes

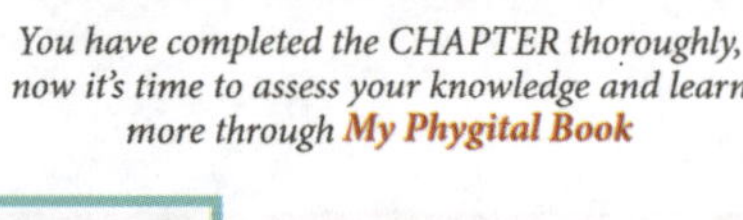

You have completed the CHAPTER thoroughly, now it's time to assess your knowledge and learn more through ***My Phygital Book***

Scan the QR Code to Download the App

Nursing Next Live
The Next Level of Nursing Education
CBS Phygital Books > **Textbook of Psychiatric Nursing PHYGITAL**

Reading is not enough, Now ***Listen, Learn & Practice*** Every Chapter

Golden Points	Solved Exercises	MCQs
Get One Liners of Chapter summary in the PODCAST form	Subjective and objective exercises given in book with their solutions to evaluate and assess the complete chapter knowledge	Chapter-wise extra MCQs in the form of Practice test to give in-depth concept clarity

CHAPTER

9

Nursing Management of Patients with Substance Use Disorders

LEARNING OBJECTIVE

After studying this chapter, the student will be able to gain knowledge regarding the substance abuse in order to render the nursing care of patient with substance use disorders.

CHAPTER OUTLINE

KEY TERMS

Tolerance, Dependence, Abuse, Harmful use, Withdrawal, Intoxication, Detoxification, Codependency, Cross tolerance, Alcohol, Cannabis, Amphetamines, Barbiturates, Cocaine, Hallucinogens, Hypnotics, Sedatives, Opioids, Antianxiety drugs, Addiction reward pathway, Alcoholic anonymous, Stages of change model.

COMMON SUBSTANCE ABUSE IN INDIA

- Alcohol
- Cannabis
- Hypnotics, sedatives and antianxiety drugs
- Amphetamines
- Barbiturates
- Cocaine
- Hallucinogens
- Inhalants
- Nicotine
- Opioids—heroin, morphine and meperidine
- Phencyclidine
- Polysubstance abuse
- Other or unknown substance abuse.

Continued substance use might lead to recurrent interpersonal problems as shown in Flowchart 9.1.

Flowchart 9.1: Concept of dependence and abuse

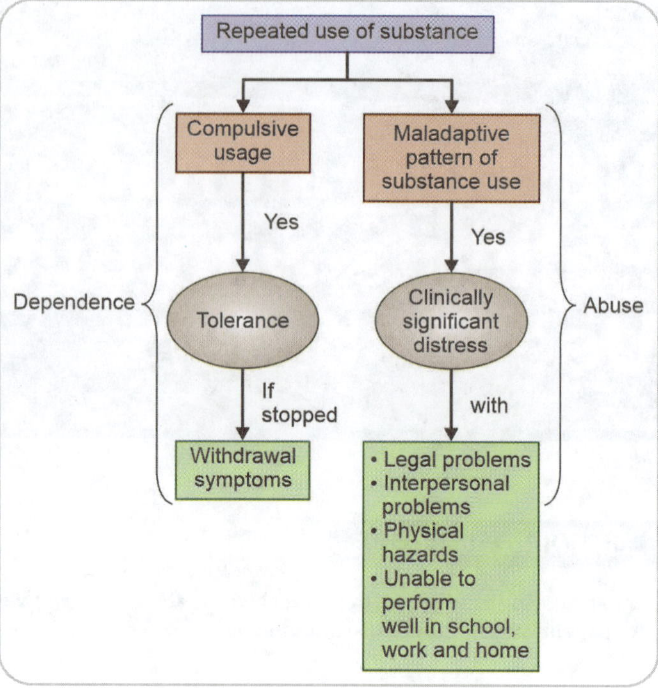

MODIFIED MANN'S INDEX OF ADDICTION

Modified Mann's Index of Addiction denotes the addiction level of various substances which has been arranged from lower to higher, for example, caffeine has low addiction index and heroin is a synthetic opioid derivative with a high addition index as shown in Figure 9.1.

ICD-11 CLASSIFICATION OF SUBSTANCE USE DISORDERS

- 6C40 Disorders due to use of alcohol
- 6C41 Disorders due to use of cannabis
- 6C42 Disorders due to use of synthetic cannabinoids
- 6C43 Disorders due to use of opioids
- 6C44 Disorders due to use of sedatives, hypnotics or anxiolytics
- 6C46 Disorders due to use of stimulants including amphetamines, methamphetamine or methcathinone
- 6C47 Disorders due to use of synthetic cathinones
- 6C48 Disorders due to use of caffeine
- 6C49 Disorders due to use of hallucinogens
- 6C4A Disorders due to use of nicotine
- 6C4B Disorders due to use of volatile inhalants

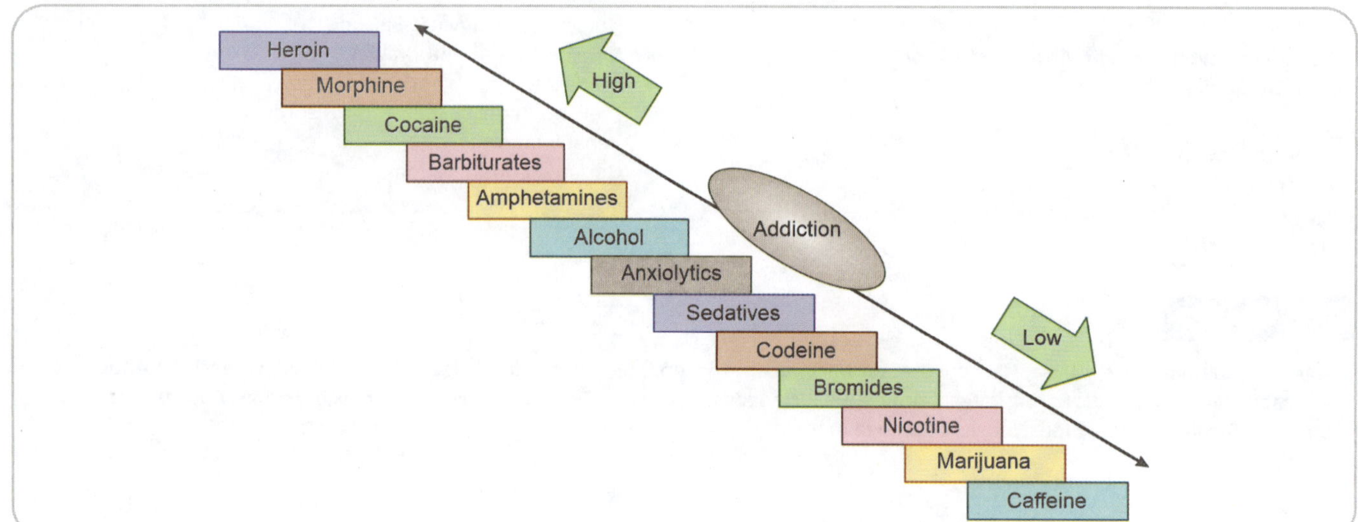

Figure 9.1 Modified Mann's index of addiction

- 6C4C Disorders due to use of MDMA or related drugs, including MDA.
- 6C4D Disorders due to use of dissociative drugs including ketamine and phencyclidine [PCP].
- 6C4E Disorders due to use of other specified psychoactive substances, including medications.
- 6C4F Disorders due to use of multiple specified psychoactive substances, including medications.
- 6C4G Disorders due to use of unknown or unspecified psychoactive substances.
- 6C4H Disorders due to use of nonpsychoactive substances.
- 6C4Y Other specified disorders due to substance use.
- 6C4Z Disorders due to substance use, unspecified.

DSM-5 CLASSIFICATION OF SUBSTANCE USE DISORDERS

Alcohol	
305.00	Alcohol use disorder (mild)
303.90	Alcohol use disorder (moderate or severe)
303.00	Alcohol intoxication
291.81	Alcohol withdrawal
291.9	Unspecified alcohol-related disorder
Caffeine	
305.90	Caffeine intoxication
292.0	Caffeine withdrawal
292.9	Unspecified caffeine-related disorder
Cannabis	
305.20	Cannabis use disorder (mild)
304.30	Cannabis use disorder (moderate or severe)
Inhalants	
292.89	Inhalant intoxication
292.9	Unspecified inhalant-related disorder
Opioids	
305.50	Opioid use disorder (mild)
304.00	Opioid use disorder (moderate or severe)
292.89	Opioid intoxication
292.0	Opioid withdrawal
292.9	Unspecified opioid-related disorder
Sedative, hypnotic or anxiolytic related disorders	
305.40	sedative, hypnotic, or anxiolytic use disorder (mild)
304.10	sedative, hypnotic, or anxiolytic use disorder (moderate or severe)
292.89	sedative, hypnotic, or anxiolytic intoxication
292.0	sedative, hypnotic, or anxiolytic withdrawal
292.9	unspecified sedative-, hypnotic-, or anxiolytic-related disorder
Stimulant-related disorders	
305.70	Stimulant use disorder, mild amphetamine-type substance use (or) use of unspecified substances
305.60	Stimulant use disorder, mild cocaine substance use
304.40	Stimulant use disorder, moderate or severe Amphetamine-type substance use (or) use of unspecified substances
304.20	Stimulant use disorder, moderate cocaine substance use
292.89	Stimulant intoxication
292.0	Stimulant withdrawal
Tobacco	
305.1	Tobacco use disorder, mild
305.1	Tobacco use disorder, moderate
305.1	Tobacco use disorder, severe
292.0	Tobacco withdrawal
292.9	Unspecified tobacco-related disorder
Miscellaneous	
305.90	Other (or unknown) substance use disorder, mild
304.90	Other (or unknown) substance use disorder, moderate
304.90	Other (or unknown) substance use disorder, severe
292.89	Other (or unknown) substance intoxication
292.0	Other (or unknown) substance withdrawal
292.9	Unspecified other (or unknown) substance-related disorder

Contd...

Classification of Substance abuse Based on Psychological Effects

It is classified as CNS depressants and CNS stimulants as shown in Flowchart 9.2.

Patterns of Substance Dependance as per ICD-11

- Current use, continuous—consumption of substance almost daily for at least one month.
- Current use, episodic—intermittent heavy consumption of substance with the period of abstinence during the past one year.
- Early full remission—period of abstinence from substance consumption for 1–12 months after the treatment.
- Sustained Partial remission—significant reduction in substance consumption for more than 12 months.
- Sustained Full remission—abstinent from substance consumption for 12 months or longer.

STAGES OF ADOLESCENT SUBSTANCE ABUSE

Stages of adolescent substance abuse are shown in Flowchart 9.3.

Flowchart 9.2: Substance abuse based on psychological effects

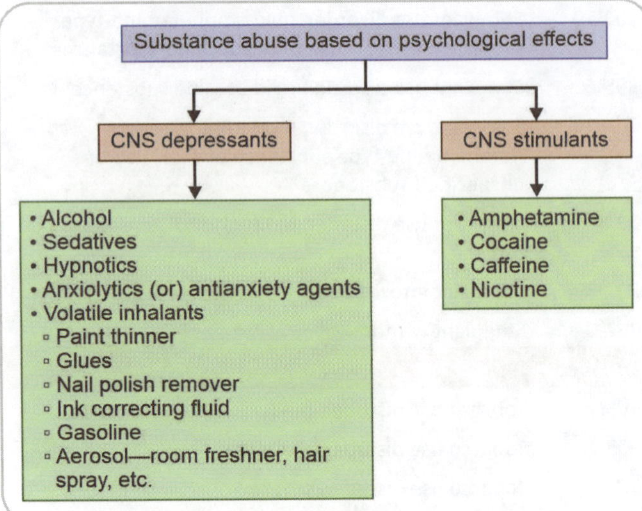

Flowchart 9.3: Stages of adolescent substance abuse

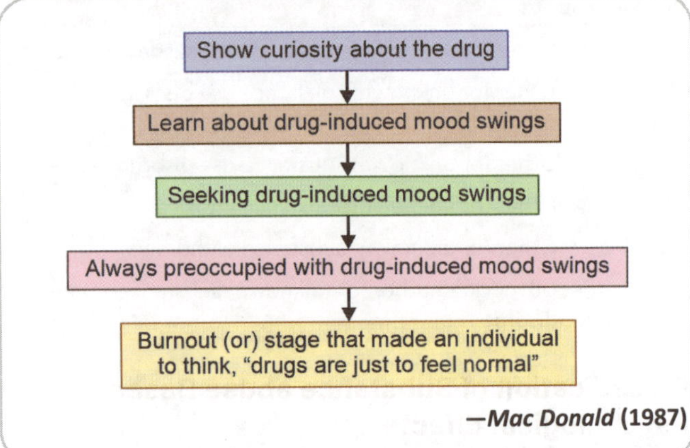

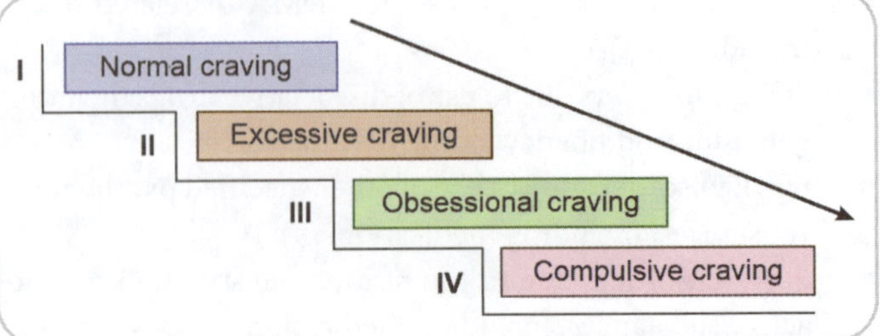

Figure 9.2: Stages of craving

STAGES OF CRAVING

There are four stages of craving. These stages are shown in Figure 9.2. These are as follows:

1. **Normal craving:** It will not cause any distress to individual.
2. **Excessive craving:** It will cause significant distress to individual and not socially acceptable behavior.
3. **Obsessional craving:** Repeated thoughts to consume a particular substance.
4. **Compulsive craving:** With repeated consumption of drug an individual finds difficult to control the behavior of consuming drug.

ETIOLOGY OF SUBSTANCE ABUSE

Etiology of substance abuse is shown in Bio-psychosocial model (Fig. 9.3). Due to repeated consuming of drugs (addictive behavior) an individual becomes stereotyped and it gets difficult for him/her to control an urge to consume the same drug.

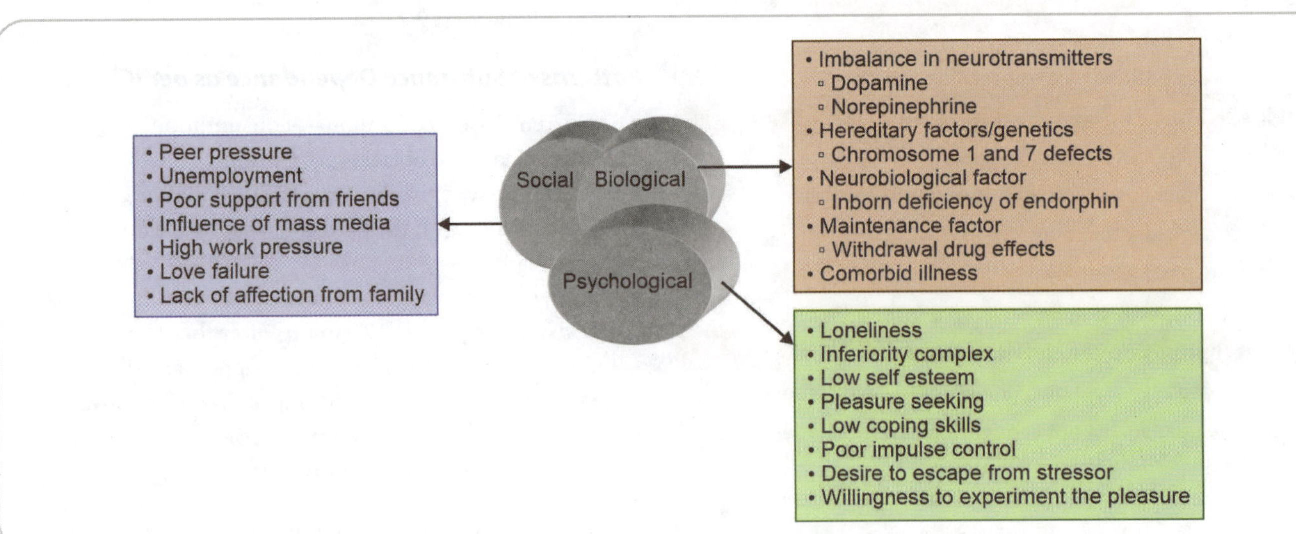

Figure 9.3: Etiology of substance abuse

COMPLICATIONS OF SUBSTANCE ABUSE

Local Effects (In Case of Intravenous Injection)

Thrombophlebitis, vasculitis, skin lesions, abscess and gangrene.

Systemic Effects

- **Neurological complications:** Seizure, Korsakoff's syndrome, Wernicke's encephalopathy, peripheral neuropathy, high blood pressure leads to hemorrhagic stroke, subdural hematoma (common in road traffic accidents, and occur due to influence of alcoholism), intracranial hemorrhage, dementia and delirium tremens.
- **Cardiopulmonary complications:** Hypertension, arrhythmia, cardiomyopathy, subacute bacterial endocarditis, pneumonia, Acute Respiratory Distress syndrome (ARDS), respiratory arrest, respiratory infections, pulmonary emboli and chronic obstructive pulmonary disease (COPD).
- **Musculoskeletal disorders:** Osteoporosis may lead to fracture, osteoarthritis, rheumatoid arthritis, musculoskeletal injury and gout.
- **Gastrointestinal disturbances:** Esophagitis, esophageal varices, peptic ulcer, duodenal ulcer, gastritis, malabsorption syndrome, pancreatitis, hemorrhoids, gastric bleeding leads to hematemesis (or) occult blood (blood in stools), carcinoma of mouth, larynx, throat, esophagus, stomach and intestines.

Reproductive Complications

- **Men:** Sexual dysfunctions such as impotence, decreased libido, oligospermia, decreased sperm motility and infertility.
- **Women:** Miscarriage, stillbirth, premature birth and low birth weight babies.

Psychological Effects

Psychosis, depression, amotivational syndrome (lack of desire to complete task, sense of apathy about future, lack of concentration, reduced interest in social and other activities), suicidal ideation, multiple substance abuse, impaired social and occupational dysfunction.

Miscellaneous

Fetal alcohol syndrome, beriberi, foot ulcer, decrease in blood glucose level, domestic violence, accidents, involving in criminal activities and hypoglycemia.

ALCOHOL

Introduction

Alcohol is a natural product obtained by the reaction of fermented sugar with yeast spores. It is classified as food because it gives calories but there is no nutritive value in it.

Pharmacokinetics of Alcohol

Alcohol absorption is fast and it mostly happens in small intestine. It is highly fat soluble in nature. Its absorption might delay due to food specifically milk. It crosses placenta. It is found in all body fluids such as blood, urine, saliva, cerebrospinal fluid and milk. Ethanol is metabolized by Microsomal Ethanol Oxidizing System (MEOS). Binge drinking of alcohol will affect the absorption of other medications.

Pharmacodynamics of Alcohol

Ethanol is central nervous system depressant. It inhibits cerebral cortex, cerebellum, spinal cord and medulla. It also inhibits antidiuretic hormone of posterior pituitary and thereby causes diuresis. It interferes with the cutaneous vasoconstriction as a response toward cold, so hypothermia develops. The toxic level of alcohol will inhibit regulation of temperature by hypothalamus. Alcohol stimulates the gastric juice along with pepsin and HCl, thereby increasing appetite when consumed in small quantities. However, it is contraindicated with acid peptic disease.

Addiction Reward Pathway

The major parts involved are ventral tegmental area (VTA), nucleus accumbens, and prefrontal cortex shown in Figure 9.4. The VTA is connected with both the nucleus accumbens and prefrontal cortex. Through this pathway, it sends information to neurons. Neurons of VTA contains dopamine (neurotransmitter), which has been released in nucleus accumbens and prefrontal cortex.

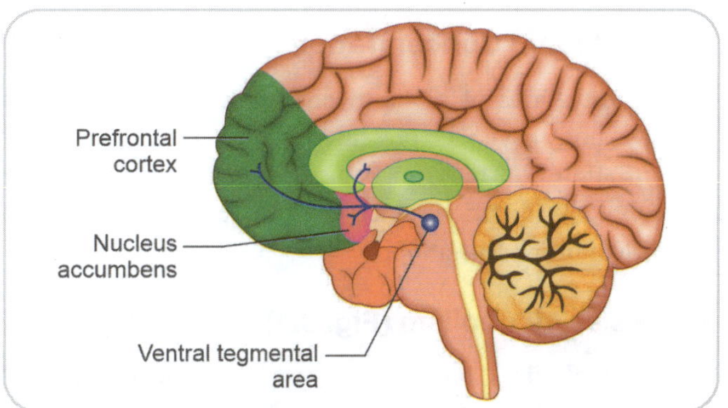

Figure 9.4: Regions of brain related to addiction reward pathway

DSM-IV Classification of Alcoholism

- Alcohol use disorder
- Alcohol dependence syndrome
- Alcohol intoxication
- Alcohol withdrawal syndrome
- Alcohol induced dementia
- Alcohol induced amnesia
- Alcohol induced mood disorder
- Alcohol induced anxiety disorder
- Alcohol induced sexual disorder
- Alcohol induced sleep disorder
- Alcohol induced psychosis:
    - With delusion
    - With hallucination

Common Alcoholic Beverages

Common alcoholic beverages with its source and percentage of alcohol are given in Table 9.1.

Table 9.1: Common alcoholic beverages with its source and percentage of alcohol

Common alcoholic beverages	Source	Percentage of alcohol (approximate)
Beer	Malted barley	3–6%
Wine	Grapes/berry	Fortified: 16–24% Unfortified: 14–16%
Whisky	Malted grains	36–50%
Rum	Molasses	36–50%
Scotch	Malted barley	40–45%
Gin	Distilled spirit with Juniper berries aromatic botanicals	36–50%
Vodka	Grains (Russian vodka from potatoes)	40–95%

Blood Alcohol Concentration

Various categories of blood alcohol concentration with its effects on body have been presented in Table 9.2. Urine alcohol concentration >200 mg% might be used for diagnostic purpose of alcohol consumption which is equivalent to 150 mg% of blood alcohol concentration.

Phases of Alcoholism (Fig. 9.5)

I. **Prealcoholic:** Individual starts to drink alcohol occasionally.

II. **Early alcoholic:** Individual drinks alcohol alone and remains preoccupied with thoughts of alcohol. Individual experiences black out (memory loss of past events after drinking alcohol) and eye opener (strong desire to drink alcohol immediately by after awakening from bed). Individual might use defense mechanism, 'Denial', and he/she may refuse the dependency toward alcoholism.

III. **True alcoholic:** Individual loses control over drinking (physiological dependence). There will be a binge drinking episodes (continuous and routine drinking of alcohol). Individual might be willing to lose anything for alcohol.

IV. **Chronic alcoholic:** Emotional and physical disintegration of the individual might lead to psychosis. Presence of life-threatening complications such as cirrhosis, hepatitis, cardiac myopathy, Wernicke's encephalopathy, Korsakoff's psychosis, ascites, leukopenia, thrombocytopenia, pancreatitis, gastritis, depression, suicidal tendencies might develop.

Table 9.2: Blood alcohol concentration with its effects in body

Blood alcohol concentration (mg/dL)	Effects of alcohol in body
20–30	• Slow motor activity • Slow thinking process
30–80	Decline in cognition
80–200	• Lack of coordination • Decline in cognition • Poor judgment
200–300	• Alcohol black out • Slurring of speech • Nystagmus
300–350	Hypothermia, dysarthria
350–400	Coma, respiratory depression
>400	Death might occur

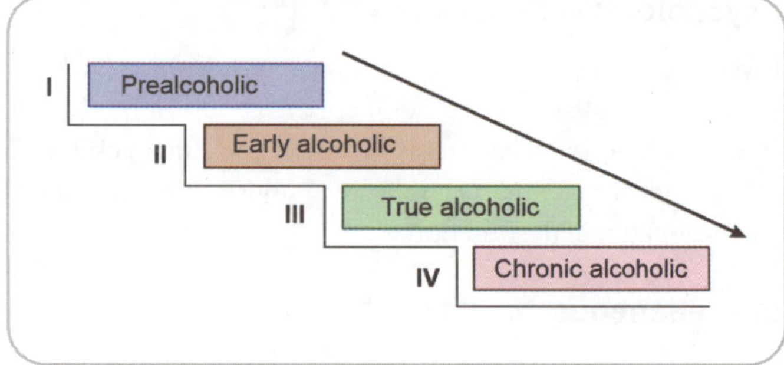

Figure 9.5: Phases of alcoholism

Table 9.3: **Cloninger's classification based on genetics and environmental factors**

Aspects	Type I alcoholism	Type II alcoholism
Causes	Genetic and environmental	Mostly genetic and environmental influence is limited
Gender	Both male and female	Common in male
Usual onset of age	>25 years	<25 years
Family history	May be present	Commonly present
Loss of control	Present	Absent
Premorbid personality traits	Avoidance of harm and reward seeking nature	Novelty seeking behavior
Features	Psychological dependence and guilt present	Aggression followed by drinking alcohol

Table 9.4: **Jellinek's, five species of alcohol dependence based on usage pattern**

Alpha	Beta	Gamma (or) malignant alcoholism	Delta	Epsilon
Increased consumption of alcohol to come out of physical or emotional pain	Increased consumption of alcoholism lead to physical complications but no dependence to alcohol	Physical dependence, psychological dependence tolerance, inability to control and withdrawal symptoms are present	Inability to stop alcohol completely but it can be controlled	Dipsomania (uncontrollable craving of alcohol)

Classification of Alcoholism

Cloninger's classification based on genetics and environmental factors has been given in Table 9.3. Jellinek's, five species of alcohol dependence based on usage pattern are shown in Table 9.4.

ICD-11 Diagnostic criteria for alcohol dependence
- Strong desire to drink alcohol
- Unable to control alcohol intake behavior
- Development of tolerance
- Withdrawal symptoms are present if alcohol consumption is stopped
- Increasing priority given to use alcohol over other activities despite its negative consequences
- Repeated use of alcohol in spite of harmful complications
- Features of dependence present for at least 1 year and the diagnosis is made if features present continuously almost daily for 1 month

Diagnosis of Alcohol Abuse

- **Blood alcohol level:** Accepted legal limit in regard to blood alcohol level (India) is <30 mg/dL (or) 0.03% g/dL.
- **Gamma glutamyl transferase (GGT):** >40 IU/L (seen in 80% of cases and return to normal if alcohol is not consumed (abstinence) >48 hours.
- **Mean corpuscular volume (MCV):** >92 fL/red cell in adult (seen in 60% of cases and it takes few weeks to show as normal value in case of abstinence).
- **Liver function test (LFT):** Increased serum glutamic oxaloacetic transaminase (SGOT), serum glutamic pyruvic transaminase (SGPT), alanine aminotransferase (ALT) and ammonia.
- **Hematologic studies:** Anemia, thrombocytopenia, raised prothrombin and partial prothrombin time (PPT).
- **Serum glucose level:** Decreased in case of severe liver disease.
- **Urine toxicology:** To screen out other diseases.
- **Serum electrolyte analysis:** To analyze the electrolyte imbalance due to alcohol use.
- **ECG:** Cardiac problems due to alcoholism are screened out.

Assessment Tools for Problem Drinkers of Alcoholism

- **CAGE questionnaire:** It is given in Table 9.5

Table 9.5: **CAGE questionnaire**

Mnemonics	Aspects	Questions
C	Cut down	Have you ever felt to stop (cut down) alcohol?
A	Annoyance	Did you feel anger (annoyed) due to other's criticism about your drinking?
G	Guilt	Have you ever felt guilt about drinking?
E	Eye opening	Have you ever felt drinking immediately after awakening from bed (eye opening) in early morning?
Interpretation	Score >2 denotes problem drinkers (possibility of alcoholism dependence and needs further investigations)	

- **Michigan alcoholism screening test (MAST):** Used in courts to screen the individuals who met alcohol related offences.
- **Alcohol use disorders identification test (AUDIT):** Developed by World Health Organization (WHO).
- **Paddington alcohol test (PAT):** Screening tool to assess alcohol-related problems among patients attending emergency department.

Categories of Alcohol Withdrawal

Categories such as mild, moderate and severe is explained in Table 9.6. It is also categorized into complicated alcohol withdrawal and uncomplicated alcohol withdrawal.

Stages of Alcohol Withdrawal

There are three stages of alcohol withdrawal as presented in Figure 9.6.

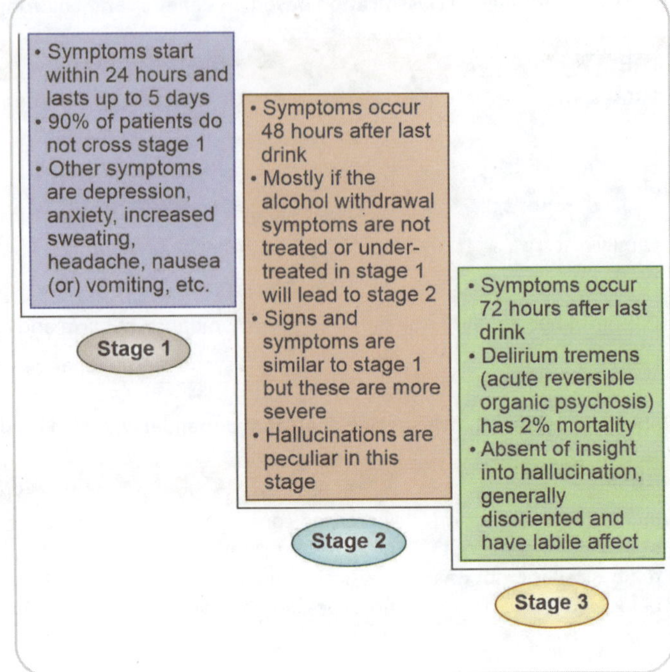

Figure 9.6: Stages of alcohol withdrawal

ICD-11 Diagnostic Criteria for Alcohol Withdrawal

- **Clinically significant cluster of symptoms** present in the varying degree of severity and duration, that happens after the cessation or reduction of use of alcohol in individuals following the alcohol dependence.
- Presenting features are autonomic hyperactivity, tremor, nausea, vomiting, insomnia, psychomotor agitation, anxiety, transient visual or tactile or auditory hallucinations and distractibility.
- Alcohol withdrawal state is complicated by seizures less commonly.
- Alcohol withdrawal state may progress to a very severe form of delirium which is characterized by confusion, disorientation, delusion and prolonged hallucinations (separate diagnosis of alcohol-induced delirium has to be assigned in such cases).
- **Specify it is:**
  - Uncomplicated
  - Complicated with seizures
  - Complicated with perceptual disturbances
  - Complicated with seizures and perceptual disturbances.

Table 9.6: Categories of alcohol withdrawal

Signs/Symptoms	Mild	Moderate	Severe
Appetite	Impaired	Impaired	Complete rejection of all foods
Blood pressure	Normal/slightly raised systolic BP	Increased systolic BP usually	Both systolic and diastolic BP is increased
Confusion and disorientation	Absent	Varies	Present
Dry heaving/retching/ retroperistalsis/nausea and vomiting	Only nausea present	Nausea and vomiting present	Nausea and vomiting present
Hallucinations	Absent Auditory and visual (vague, transient and nocturnal in nature)		Auditory and visual (fearful or threatening in nature); delusional misidentification syndrome present
Motor disturbances	Fine motor disturbances (tremors only seen in hands)	Obvious motor restlessness with hand tremors	Extreme restlessness, agitation and gross motor disturbances
Pulse	Increased	100–120 beats/min	120–140 beats/min
Seizure	Absent	Present	Commonly seen
Sweating	Absent	Sometimes	Increased (hyperhidrosis)

Assessment of Alcohol Withdrawal

- Modified Selective Severity Assessment (MSSA)
- Clinical Institute Withdrawal Assessment for Alcohol Revised (CIWA-AR)

Treatment of Alcohol Withdrawal

Emergency Management

Treatment of trauma, gastrointestinal bleeding and infection.

Symptomatic Management

Give respiratory support in order to maintain airway and administer oxygen. Provide fluid replacement with intravenous normal saline. Intravenous dextrose is administered if hypoglycemia is present. If nutritional deficiency is present, vitamin B supplements (or) Inj. thiamine needs to be administered. If withdrawal symptoms are present, chlordiazepoxide (librium), lorazepam can be given. Antiemetics can be given as required. Psychosis and hyperactivity can be treated with antipsychotics.

Psychological Management

- **Aversion therapy (or) antabuse:** Treatment to arouse the unlikeness or feel likely to be hated of alcoholism. Types include:
  - Electrical aversion
  - Chemical aversion (or) disulfiram therapy
  - Aversion through emesis
  - Covert sensitization (or) covert conditioning
- **Electrical aversion:** Ask the client to smell the desired brand of alcohol. Low volt electrical stimuli will be administered immediately when he smells alcohol. Alcohol intake (desired response) will be changed by undesired electrical stimuli.
- Chemical aversion (or) disulfiram therapy (or) deterrent therapy

  Dosage: Usual dosage of disulfiram is 250 mg/day.

Indications of Disulfiram Usage in Patients with Alcohol Dependence

Abstinence more than 48 hours of alcohol intake, failure or contraindicated with naltrexone, previous good response to disulfiram and client has both cocaine as well as alcohol dependence.

Contraindications

Suspected alcohol intake, rubber/cobalt/nickel allergy, psychotic patients, hypersensitivity, pregnancy/breast feeding, cognitive impairment, uncontrolled hypertension, high suicidal risk, history of stroke/myocardial infarction, severe personality disorder, severe cardiac diseases, severe renal problems and severe hepatic dysfunction.

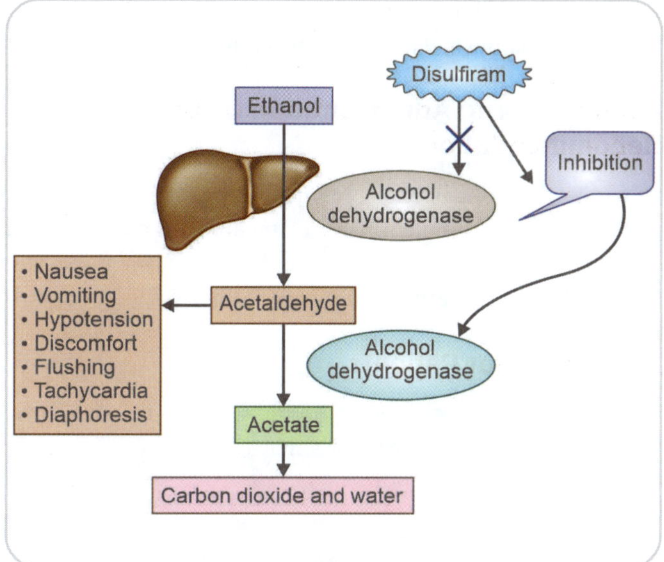

Figure 9.7: Mechanism of action—disulfiram

Mechanism of Action

The drug action of disulfiram is alcohol dehydrogenase Inhibitors. In general, ethanol or alcohol gets converted into acetaldehyde in liver. Acetaldehyde will convert it to acetate. The acetate is converted into carbon dioxide and water. Intake of disulfiram will inhibit the enzyme alcohol dehydrogenase so the conversion of ethanol to acetaldehyde doesn't takes place. This concept has been represented in Figure 9.7.

- **Side effects:** Metallic or garlic taste, headache, drowsiness/fatigue, dermatitis, halitosis, nausea/vomiting and impotence/lack of libido/sexual dysfunction.
- **Adverse reactions:** Polyneuritis, hepatotoxicity, optic neuritis and peripheral neuritis.
- **Drug interactions with disulfiram:** Phenytoin, warfarin, ethanol (cause disulfiram ethanol reaction), metronidazole (flagyl), tricyclic antidepressants (particularly amitriptyline) and benzodiazepines (increase sedative effect).

DISULFIRAM ETHANOL REACTION

Meaning

When client takes disulfiram along with alcohol it might lead to disulfiram ethanol reaction.

Symptoms of Disulfiram Ethanol Reaction (DER)

It includes facial flushing, nausea, vomiting, hypotension, shock, fatigue, general malaise, epigastric pain, sweating, excessive thirst, blurred vision, shortness of breath, liver failure, heart attack, abnormal heart beat and throbbing headache.

Food and Drug Administration (FDA) Recommendations

Client has to avoid alcohol 12 hours before taking disulfiram, during and until completion of treatment for 14 days. Alcohol has to be avoided 48 hours before and after treatment in order to avoid Disulfiram Ethanol Reaction (DER).

Instruction for Patients

Not to use any alcohol content products such as cough syrups, fermented vinegar, sauces, after shave lotions, mouth wash, back rubs, etc.

Treatment

Give reassurance and advice to take adequate oral fluids for mild Disulfiram Ethanol Reaction (DER). In case of severe Disulfiram Ethanol Reaction (DER) intravenous infusions, antihistamines and dopamine infusions are advisable.

Drugs Causing Disulfiram Like Reactions with Ethanol

- **Sulfonylureas (or) antidiabetic agents:** Chlorpropamide, tolazamide, tolbutamide, glipizide, glyburide, gliclazide and glibenclamide.
- **Antimicrobial agents:** Cephalosporin (cefoperazone, moxalactam, cefamandole, cefotetan), isoniazid, sulfonamides, nitrofurantoin, ketaconazole, chloramphenicol, beta-lactams, metrogyl and griseofulvin.
- **Antiviral agents:** Lopinavir (or) ritonavir.
- **Antihypertensive agents:** Beta blockers, vasodilators (Nitrates).
- **Anticoagulants:** Warfarin.

VARIOUS APPROACHES TO QUIT ALCOHOL

Aversion through emesis: Administer alcohol along with emetics which will induce vomiting after alcohol intake, thereby the client develops aversion.

Covert Sensitization (or) Covert Conditioning

Enhance the mental imagination of undesired habits and thereby promote aversion. Success rate of aversion presents with combination of two or more techniques of aversion.

- **Motivational interviewing in alcohol addiction:** It is a form of counseling approach first explained by Prof. William Miller in 1983. It is also called Motivational Enhancement Therapy (or) Brief Intervention. A client-centered approach is followed to improve the readiness to change (quit alcoholism) by resolving ambivalence. It is a technique for motivating the client to quit alcoholism.
- **Cognitive therapy:** Aaron T. Beck introduced this therapy. Unrealistic thoughts in regard to alcoholism might change into realistic thoughts.
- **Behavioral therapy:** Reward for desirable behavior and punishment for undesirable behavior motivates the patient to quit alcohol.
- **Contingency management:** Anker and Crowley described the concepts of contingency management. Use predetermined positive consequences of the abstinence of alcoholism and teach the consequences of continued drinking in order to change the undesired behavior.
- **Group therapy:** Group of alcohol dependents with 5–10 members was involved in the group therapy sessions in order to:
  - Enhance motivation
  - Promote abstinence
  - Establish the stable social and occupational functioning.
  - Prevention of relapse
  - Address any specific psychosocial issue, comment to the group members
  - Psychoeducation

  It helps to observe patient's problems on others in order to work out good ways of coping with problems.
- **Cue exposure therapy:** Nurse might give exposure to the alcoholics with craving, inducing cue and guide the patient, how to prevent the use of alcohol as shown in Figure 9.8.
- **Relapse prevention:** Marlatt and Gordon first explained the concept of relapse prevention. It focuses on cognitive behavior approach to attain a great self-control so that the patients who quit alcohol should never get back into drinking behavior by following guidelines provided with cue exposure therapy.

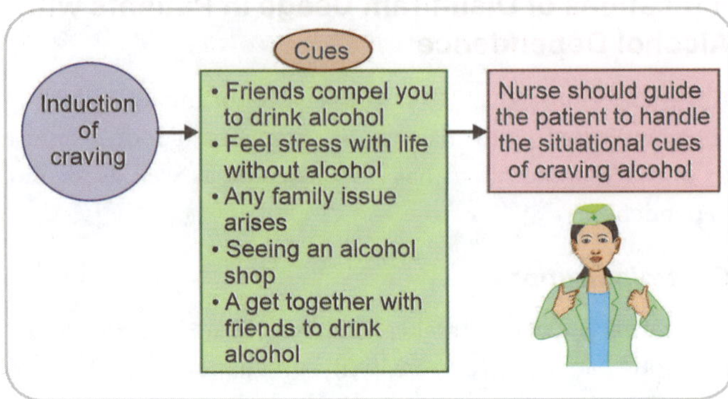

Figure 9.8: Concept of cue exposure therapy

Ethanol Challenge Test
It is performed to create cognitive awareness of disulfiram-ethanol reaction (DER). This test has to be done after informed consent. Patient has to take in 250 mg of disulfiram as initial dose for 5 days. Alcohol has to be administered approximately 40 mL (15 mL for every 15 minutes) as maximum of 90 mL can be given. Monitor the vital signs and keep IV line open so that, if blood pressure drops, vasopressor can be administered.

ALCOHOL WITHDRAWAL SYNDROMES

- **Delirium tremens:** It occurs within 48–72 hours of stopping alcohol. Clinical features are as follows:
  - Clouding of consciousness
  - Disorientation
  - Visual hallucination
  - Illusion
  - Poor attention span
  - Insomnia
  - Autonomic disturbances
  - Dehydration
  - Electrolytes imbalance

  Treatment includes Tab. chlordiazepoxide 100 mg/day in divided doses and Inj. Lorazepam 0.1 mg/kg at 2 mg/min (give lorazepam as slow IV because the intravenous administration of diazepam in a rapid manner might lead to respiratory arrest).
- **Alcohol withdrawal seizures (or) 'Rum Fits':** It occurs within 6–48 hours after the intake of alcohol. It is usually Grand mal type. Around 3–15% of untreated alcohol withdrawal clients might develop seizures and less than 3% of patients will develop status epilepticus.
- **Alcoholic hallucinosis:** Hallucinations are present even in period of abstinence after the regular alcohol intake. It commonly occurs with clear consciousness.
- **Alcoholic pellagra:** The main cause is niacin deficiency due to alcoholism. Initial symptoms include mood changes and neurasthenia. Confusion and lethargy occurs in middle stages of alcoholism. Myoclonus and spastic paresis occur in later stages of alcoholism.

  The mechanism behind this alcoholic pellagra is:
  - **Nutritional:** Vitamin B, protein and zinc deficiency.
  - **Biochemical:** Inhibition of liver tryptophan and niacin precursors.
  - **Physiological:** Disturbances in GABA and Glutamate Neuronal function.
- **Wernicke-Korsakoff syndrome:** Patient with acute phase of Wernicke-Korsakoff syndrome will have Wernicke's encephalopathy and patient with chronic phase of Wernicke-Korsakoff's syndrome will have Korsakoff's

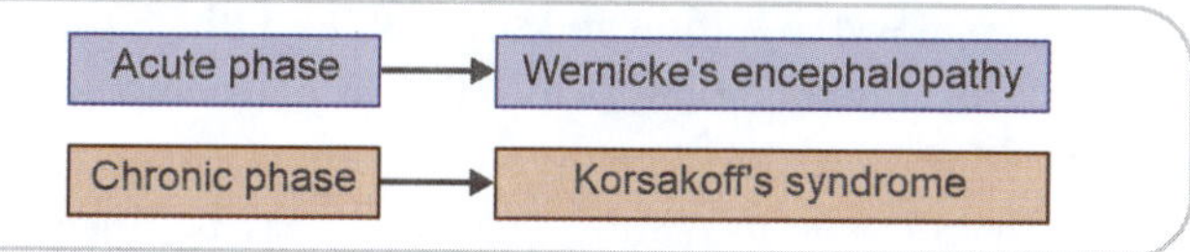

Figure 9.9: Phases of Wernicke-Korsakoff's syndrome

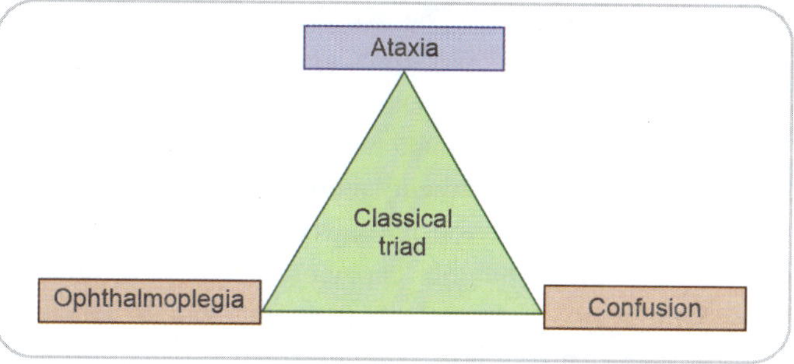

Figure 9.10: Classical triad of Wernicke's encephalopathy

syndrome as shown in Figure 9.9. Damage to neuron occurs secondary to thiamine deficiency so parenteral thiamine for a week of 50–100 mg is helpful.

- **Wernicke's encephalopathy (Fig. 9.10):** Wernicke's Encephalopathy is characterized by cerebellar ataxia, mental confusion, palsy of 6th cranial nerve, hypothermia, cardiac problems, vestibular dysfunction and peripheral neuropathy.
  - **Confusion/encephalopathy:**
    - Disorientation
    - Poor attention span
    - Loss of consciousness in 5% of patients
  - **Occulomotor dysfunction/ophthalmoplegia:**
    - Unequal pupil
    - Nonreactive pupil
    - Nystagmus (involuntary eye ball movements)
    - Lateral rectus palsy
    - Conjugate gaze palsy
    - Light near dissociation (impaired pupillary light reaction but the nearer reaction to light accommodation remains intact)
  - **Gait ataxia:**
    - Stance and gait disturbances are seen as primary symptoms.
    - Wernicke's encephalopathy will not have upper limb ataxia as seen in cerebellar dysfunction.
- In postmortem of Wernicke's encephalopathy, patients might have petechial hemorrhage in mammillary body in brain at third ventricle.
- **Korsakoff's syndrome:** It is characterized by gross memory disturbances (severe retrograde and anterograde amnesia) with a preserved long-term

memory, cognition and social skills. Other symptoms are confabulation (False filling of memory gaps), confusion, disorientation, poor attention span, easily distractible in nature. The client may be unaware of illness.

- **Marchiafava bignami disease:** It is a neurological disease of alcoholism which occurs due to demyelination of corpus callosum, optic tract and cerebellar peduncles. Symptoms include ataxia, disorientation, epilepsy, dysarthria and hallucinations.
- **Morbid jealousy (Othello syndrome):** Morbid jealousy is a delusion that the life partner is not faithful (i.e., suspiciousness that life partner is having extramarital relationship). If it persists, it might lead to domestic violence. Antipsychotics are the drugs of choice with abstinence from alcohol.
- **Alcohol induced disorders**
  - **Amnesia (black out):** Transient short term memory loss may be complete or partial in relation with intoxication state. It doesn't indicate dementia.
  - **Hallucinations:** It is rare with alcohol abuse. The common type is auditory. Voices are derogatory in nature.
  - **Mood disorders:** Alcoholism might lead to persistent depression.
  - **Anxiety disorders:** Panic attacks that occur during acute withdrawal, especially in first 4–6 weeks of abstinence are known as anxiety disorders.
- **Fetal alcohol syndrome:** Alcohol might affect the fetus when consumed by pregnant women. It is a third leading cause of mental retardation and it can be prevented. Risk also depends on the amount and percentage of alcohol consumed by expecting mother. Signs include microcephaly and mental retardation.

ALCOHOLICS ANONYMOUS

Alcoholics anonymous (AA) was founded in 1935 by Bill Wilson and Dr Bob Smith. AA helps people suffering from alcohol addiction disorder. Alcoholics Anonymous Program works under the recovered alcoholics who explain the process of sobriety that they have found in AA, and welcome the newcomers with similar disorder (alcoholics) to join the group.

Types of Alcoholics Anonymous Meetings

- **Closed meeting:** Person only with alcohol problems will participate in this meeting.
- **Open meeting:** Nonalcoholics can also participate in this meeting.
- **Speaker meeting:** Participants can speak their own stories.
- **Discussion meeting:** Narration of brief experiences with detailed discussion.
- **Step meeting:** Any one of 12 steps of alcoholic anonymous is discussed.

Ideology of Alcoholics Anonymous

Theory of alcoholics anonymous focuses on addiction, which means the individual is being powerless over the drug. Abstinence (quitting alcohol) is the primary goal focus on 'emotional sobriety' rather than physical sobriety.

Dynamics of Alcoholics Anonymous

Alcoholics anonymous is nonjudgmental, which means unconditional way of accepting alcoholics. Work out with 12 steps of alcoholic anonymous to stimulate the cognition which was previously unfocused. Elements of group therapy such as group cohesiveness, learning social skills, sharing their experiences and instillation of hope to achieve sobriety are being involved.

Efficacy of Alcoholics Anonymous

Efficacy depends on the following factors such as periodical assessment of achievement, retention of members, active participation of members, active religious life and social adjustment.

Assumptions in Regard with Alcoholics Anonymous

Alcoholics anonymous will help the alcoholics to:

- Get accurate information about the disease
- Obtain guidance and support
- Learn from others to maintain sobriety
- Recognize feelings of everyone
- Provide therapeutic altruism
- Promote group cohesiveness
- Develop social skills
- Involve in activities which could divert them from the use of alcohol.

Twelve Steps of Alcoholics Anonymous

1. Members admit oneself that they were powerless to control alcohol drinking and their lives were not manageable.
2. They believe that a power greater than themselves might restore them to normal mental health.
3. Decisions are taken to change their lives under the care of God and in their understanding of him.
4. They (alcoholics) will keep searching and following moral values by themselves.

5. Admit themselves to God, and to another person in regard to their mistakes.
6. Request the God to remove all defects in their character.
7. Request the God to remove their shortcomings.
8. Prepare the list of all individuals whom they have harmed before and they will try to amend for the harm that happened because of them.
9. Perform direct amendments to people who are psychologically injured.
10. Continue to take self-monitoring and when they found that they were wrong, they will admit it.
11. Do prayer and meditation to enhance their conscious contact with God to have blessings and power to carry out the right behavior.
12. With spiritual awakening as the result of above steps, we will try to carry out the message to alcoholics and to practice these principles in our lives.

Limitations of Alcoholics Anonymous

Alcoholics anonymous does not provide hospitalization, any modalities of treatment, follow-up of the patients, control of drop outs or deal individuals with multiple substance abuse.

Al-anon and Alateen (Table 9.7):

Table 9.7: Al-anon and alateen

Al-anon	Alateen
It is a mutual support group for families and friends of alcoholics.	It is a subgroup of Al-anon. It is a mutual support group for family members and friends of alcoholics especially the teenagers are involved in this group.

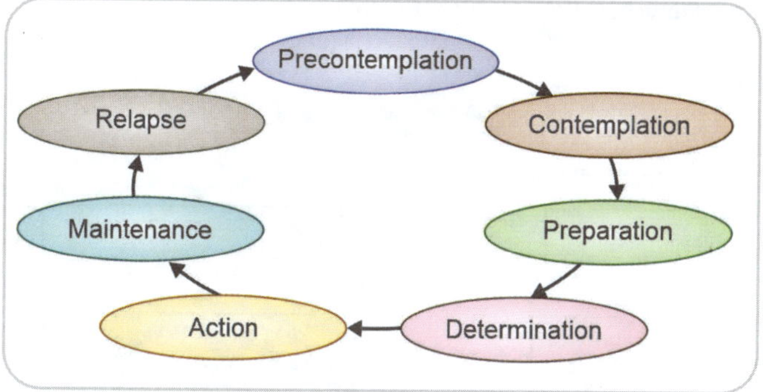

Figure 9.11: Stages of change model

Stages of Change Model

Precontemplation, contemplation, preparation, determination, action, maintenance and relapse are the stages of change model as shown in Figure 9.11. Description of each stage, patient's response and nursing interventions are given in Table 9.8.

SEDATIVES, HYPNOTICS AND ANTIANXIETY AGENTS

INTRODUCTION

Sternbach, discovered chlordiazepoxide (1957): Benzodiazepines was replaced with sedatives-hypnotics. Classification of sedatives, hypnotics and antianxiety agents are shown in Flowchart 9.4. Classification of barbiturates with duration of action and examples explained in Table 9.9 along with street names.

Table 9.8: Stages of change model with description and nursing interventions

Stages of change	Explanation	Patient's response	Nursing interventions
Precontemplation	Patient is unaware of problem	"I don't know what problem I have"	Nurse must create awareness in a patient about one's own problem
Contemplation	Patient had awareness of the problem but not interested to change	"I know that, I am so much addicted to alcohol but I don't want to stop it"	Motivate the patient to quit alcohol.
Preparation	Patient is willing to change and is prepared to change	"I am willing to quit alcohol"	Refer to alcoholic anonymous
Determination	Patient seeks help from others for change process	"I expect the health team members will help me from addiction"	Nurse offers professional help to come out of addiction
Action	Patient is abstaining	"I am not drinking alcohol now a days"	Guide and monitor the efficacy of treatment
Maintenance	Patient takes steps to avoid relapse	"I am avoiding contacts with my friends who drink alcohol"	Promote coping skills and assertive behavior
Relapse	Patient returns to drink alcohol again	"I would like to drink alcohol and so I drank yesterday"	Identify the factors which caused relapse and discuss the steps to prevent it

Flowchart 9.4: Classification of sedatives, hypnotics and antianxiety agents

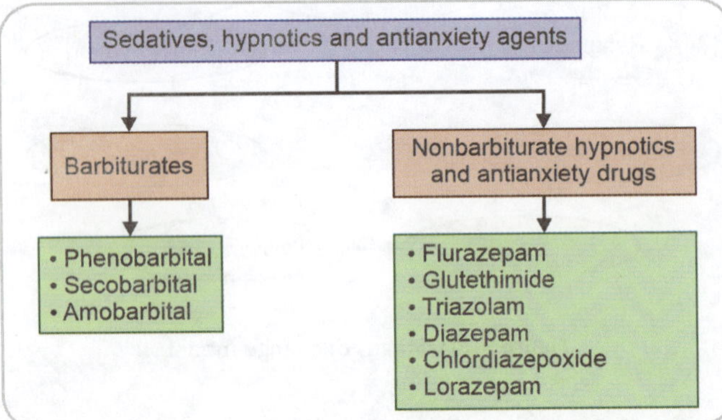

Table 9.9: Classification of barbiturates

Classification of barbiturates	Duration of action	Generic name	Street names
Long acting	>8 hours	Phenobarbital	Purple hearts, goof balls
Intermediate acting	5–8 hours	Amobarbital Pentobarbital	Downers, blue heavers, blue velvet, blue devils Nembies yellow jeckets abbotts mexican yellows
Short acting	1–5 hours	Secobarbital	Reds, red birds, red devils, lily, F-40s, Pinks, pink ladies, seggy
Ultra short acting	<1 hour	Thiopentone sodium	Rainbow, reds and blues, tooies, double trouble gorills pills, F-66s.

Pattern of Usage

- **Pattern I:** Prescribed drug by doctor is used with increased dosage and frequency.
- **Pattern II:** Due to bad company of friends or drugs obtained illegally.

ICD-11 Diagnostic Criteria for Sedatives, Hypnotics and Anxiolytic Dependence

- Disorder of regulation of sedative use arising from repeated or continuous use of these substances.
- The characteristic feature is a strong internal drive to use sedatives, hypnotics, or anxiolytics, which is manifested by impaired ability to control use, increasing priority given to use over other activities and persistence of use despite harm or negative consequences.
- These experiences are often accompanied by a subjective sensation of urge or craving to use these substances.
- Physiological features of dependence may also be present, including tolerance to the effects of sedatives, hypnotics or anxiolytics, withdrawal symptoms following cessation or reduction in use, or repeated use of sedatives or pharmacologically similar substances to prevent or alleviate withdrawal symptoms.
- The features of dependence are usually evident over a period of at least 12 months but the diagnosis may be made if sedative use is continuous (daily or almost daily) for at least 1 month.

Intoxication Effects

These are categorized into psychological effects and physical effects as shown in Flowchart 9.5.

ICD-11 Diagnostic Criteria for Sedatives, Hypnotics and Anxiolytic Intoxication

- A clinically significant transient condition that develops during or shortly after the consumption of sedatives, hypnotics or anxiolytics that is characterized by disturbances in consciousness, cognition, perception, affect, behavior, or coordination.
- These disturbances are caused by the known pharmacological effects of sedatives, hypnotics or anxiolytics and their intensity is closely related to the amount of sedatives, hypnotics or anxiolytics consumed.
- They are time-limited and abate as sedatives, hypnotics or anxiolytics are cleared from the body.

Flowchart 9.5: Intoxication effects of sedatives, hypnotics and antianxiety agents

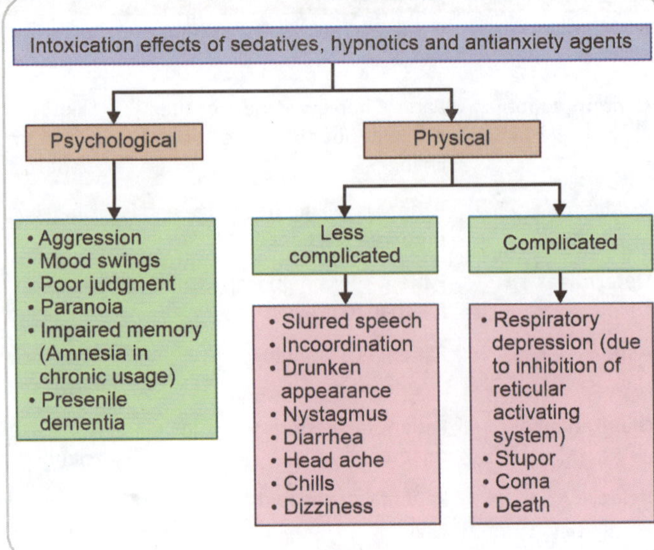

Flowchart 9.6: Withdrawal effects of sedatives, hypnotics and antianxiety agents

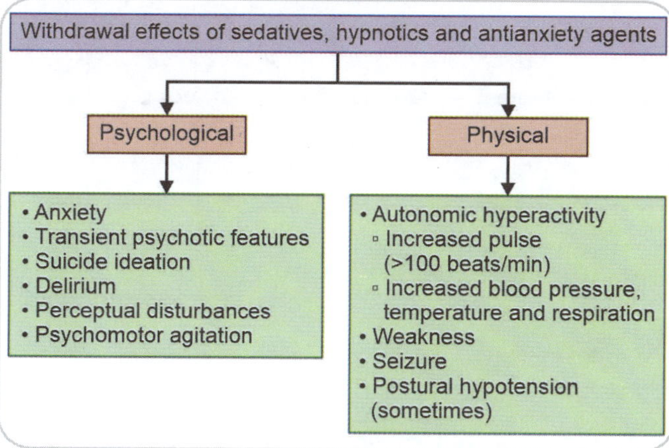

- Presenting features may include somnolence, impaired judgment, slurred speech, impaired motor coordination, unsteady gait, mood changes, as well as impaired memory, attention and concentration. Nystagmus (repetitive, uncontrolled eye movements) is a common physical sign.

Withdrawal Effects

These are categorized into psychological effects and physical effects as shown in Flowchart 9.6.

ICD-11 Diagnostic Criteria for Sedatives, Hypnotics and Anxiolytic Withdrawal

- A clinically significant cluster of symptoms, behavior and/or physiological features, varying in degree of severity and duration, that occurs upon cessation or reduction of use of sedatives, hypnotics or anxiolytics in individuals who have developed dependence or have used sedatives, hypnotics or anxiolytics for a prolonged period or in large amounts.
- Sedative, hypnotic or anxiolytic withdrawal can also occur when prescribed sedatives, hypnotics or anxiolytics have been used in standard therapeutic doses.
- Presenting features of sedative, hypnotic or anxiolytic withdrawal may include anxiety, psychomotor agitation, insomnia, increased hand tremor, nausea or vomiting, and transient visual, tactile or auditory illusions or hallucinations.
- There may be signs of autonomic hyperactivity, or postural hypotension.
- The withdrawal state may be complicated by seizures.
- Less commonly there may be progression to a more severe form of delirium characterized by confusion and disorientation, delusions, and more prolonged visual, tactile or auditory hallucinations.
- In such cases, a separate diagnosis of sedative, hypnotic, or anxiolytic-induced delirium should be assigned.

Treatment

- **Treatment of benzodiazepine overdose**
  - If conscious it could induce vomiting before absorption.
  - Give activated charcoal to decrease absorption.
  - Symptomatic management.
- **Treatment of benzodiazepine dependence**
  - Tapering the drug as 10% per day.
  - **Benzodiazepine substitution:** Long-acting benzodiazepines can be substituted with short acting ones.
  - **Phenobarbital substitution therapy:** Short-acting barbiturates are used.
  - **Antidote of benzodiazepine dependence:** Flumazenil.
- **Treatment of benzodiazepine withdrawal**
  - Carbamazepine to attenuate the withdrawal effects of Benzodiazepines.

CANNABIS

INTRODUCTION

Cannabis is derived from 'hemp plant', *Cannabis sativa* and it produces more than 400 chemicals in which 50 are cannabinoids (active ingredient of 9-tetrahydrocannabinol)

Inhibitory G protein linked with cannabinoid receptors can be substituted in basal ganglion, cerebellum and hippocampus of the brain. Anandamide is endogenous cannabinoid. Tetrahydrocannabinol absorption rate varies depending on the route—Oral (2–3 hours) and smoke (30 minutes), in which effect of single dose lasts for 4–8 hours.

Common Preparations of Cannabis

Common preparation of cannabis with percentage of Tetrahydrocannabinol concentration and street names is given in Table 9.10.

- **Intoxication effects:** Shown in Flowchart 9.7.
- **Complications of cannabis:** Shown in Flowchart 9.8.

Treatment

For detoxification, Inj. lorazepam 1–4 mg/day (or) diazepam 2–10 mg/day can be given. If cannabis induced psychosis is present, Inj. chlorpromazine 50–100 mg IM (or) haloperidol 5–10 mg slow IV is advisable. To prevent extrapyramidal symptoms, trihexyphenidyl (THP) 2–6 mg is administered. Psychotherapy and family therapy are helpful.

Table 9.10: Common preparations of cannabis

Common preparations of cannabis	Percentage of tetrahydrocannabinol concentration	Prepared from	Street names
Marijuana	0.5–1	Leaves, flowers and stem	Mary Jane, joint, weed, locoweed, hay stick, MJ, pot, grass, texas tea
Hashish	2–10	Resin from flowery tops	Ganja, charas, hash, bhang
Hashish oil	15–50	Extract of resin	

Flowchart 9.7: Intoxication effects of cannabis

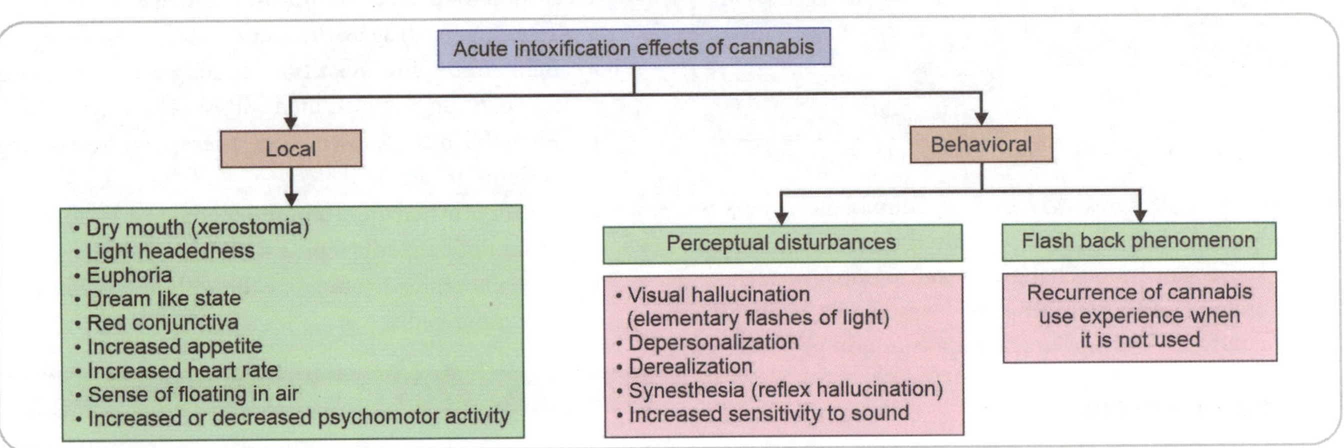

Flowchart 9.8: Complications of cannabis abuse

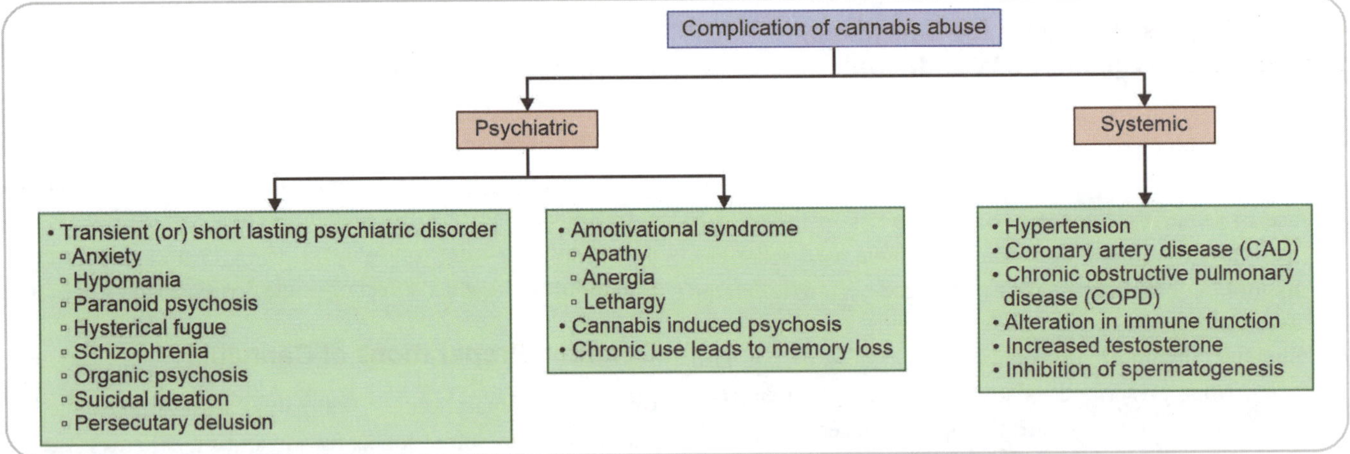

OPIOIDS

It is the exudate from dried seeds of *Papaver somniferum*. The street name is smack and brown sugar.

Synthetic opioid derivatives (Table 9.11) cause more dependence tendency than natural. The withdrawal effects of synthetic opioids are more severe than the natural. Heroin and morphine are commonly high dependence producing agents. Opioid receptors (Table 9.12) have been evenly distributed in central nervous system. However, high density of these receptors is seen in limbic system, neural area and thalamic nucleus.

Table 9.11: Natural and synthetic opioid derivatives

Natural opioid derivatives	Synthetic opioid derivatives
Phenanthrene derivatives • Morphine • Codeine • Thebaine Isoquinoline derivatives • Noscapine • Papaverine	• Heroin • Methadone • Pethidine • Nalorphine • Levallorphan • Hydromorphone • Diphenoxylate • Cyclazocine

Table 9.12: Opioid receptors with its significance

Opioid receptors	Significance
Mu	Most dependent producing opioids bind with Mu receptor
Kappa	E.g., enkephalin
Sigma	E.g., phencyclidine
Epsilon and lambda	—

Acute Intoxication Effects of Opioids

Decreased heart rate, temperature, blood pressure and pulse, pinpoint pupil, apathy, delay in reflexes, coma and mydriasis due to hypoxia are present in a patient in case of severe intoxication.

Withdrawal Effects of Opioids

Withdrawal effects like increase in heart rate/temperature/respiration/pulse, dilated pupil, lacrimation, sweating, rhinorrhea, muscle cramps, body ache, anxiety, nausea/vomiting, piloerection, anorexia and insomnia can be observed.
Complications of opioids dependence: Shown in Flowchart 9.9.

Pharmacodynamics

Opioids depress cerebral cortex, medulla and hypothalamus. They suppresses pain, vomiting center, respiratory center, cough center and chemoreceptor trigger zone (CTZ). Opioid stimulates vagus nerve and causes bradycardia. It stimulates nucleus of oculomotor nerve and causes miosis. Activation of dorsal horn of spinal cord and decrease in release of substance P (pain transmitter) decreases the level of pain. It decreases the secretion of HCl, decreases peristaltic movement and leads to constipation.

Diagnosis

Naloxone challenge test, urine opioid test (radioimmunoassay, thin layer chromatography, pressure liquid chromatography and gas liquid chromatography).

ICD-11 Diagnostic Criteria for Opioids Dependence

- Disorder of regulation of opioid use arising from repeated or continuous use of opioids.
- The characteristic feature is a strong internal drive to use opioids, which is manifested by impaired ability to control use, increasing priority given to use over other activities and persistence of use despite harm or negative consequences.
- These experiences are often accompanied by a subjective sensation of urge or craving to use opioids.
- Physiological features of dependence may also be present, including tolerance to the effects of opioids, withdrawal symptoms following cessation or reduction in use of opioids, or repeated use of opioids or pharmacologically similar substances to prevent or alleviate withdrawal symptoms.
- The features of dependence are usually evident over a period of at least 12 months but the diagnosis may be made if opioid use is continuous (daily or almost daily) for at least 1 month.

Treatment of Opioid Dependence

- **Overdose of opioids:** Narcotic antagonist (intravenous administration of naloxone or naltrexone and it can be repeated after 5–10 minutes).
- **Detoxification**
  - **Use of substitute:** E.g., methadone.

Flowchart 9.9: Complications of opioids dependence

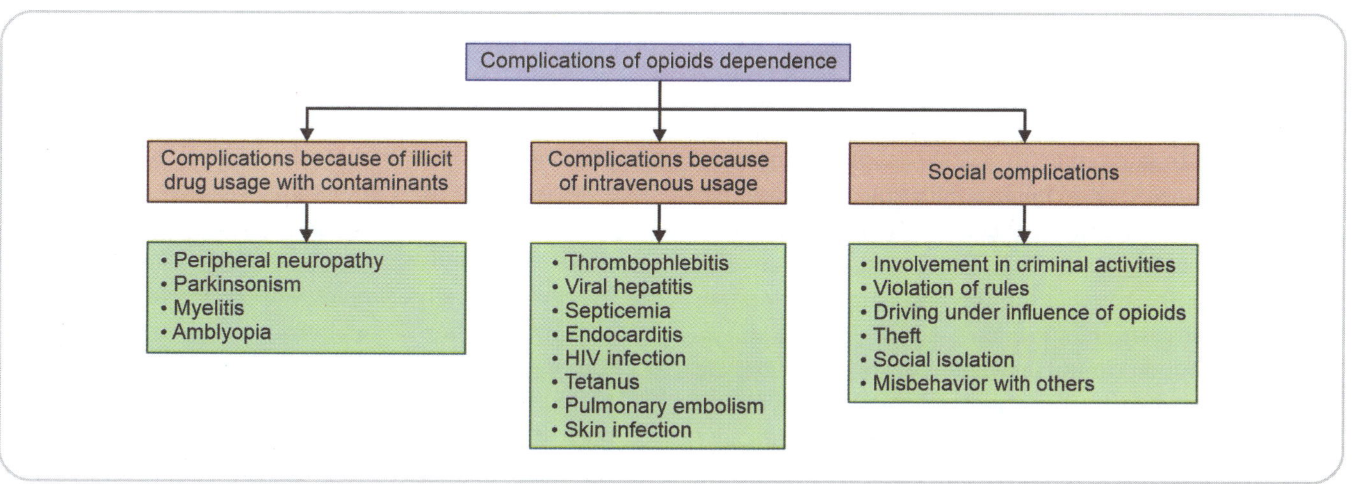

- **Clonidine (0.3–1.2 mg/day):** Inhibit the release of norepinephrine in presynapse. It might lead to excess sleepiness and orthostatic hypotension. So, taper it off within 10–14 days.
- Naltrexone with clonidine
- Levo-Alpha-Acetyl-Methadol (LAAM)
- Propoxyphene
- Buprenorphine
- Diphenoxylate
- Lofexidine

- **Maintenance:** Methadone maintenance (agonist substitution)—20–50 mg/day is helpful to shift out from hard drugs. Opioid antagonist—nalorphine (partial antagonist) 100 mg/day.
- **Miscellaneous:** Individual psychotherapy, behavior therapy, cognitive therapy, interpersonal therapy, motivational interviewing, self-control measures, family therapy, group therapy, narcotic anonymous and psychosocial rehabilitation.

CENTRAL NERVOUS SYSTEM STIMULANTS

Central nervous stimulants are categorized in two types:

1. **Psychomotor stimulants:** Augmentation of norepinephrine, dopamine and serotonin
2. **Cellular stimulants:** Exert the cellular activity (E.g., caffeine and nicotine).

Caffeine inhibits phosphodiesterase enzyme so adenosine 3, 5-cyclin phosphate of cellular metabolism will increase. Nicotine acts at ganglionic synapse so acetylcholine stimulates the nerve impulses toward activation of autonomic nervous system.

Common CNS stimulants are as follows:

- **Amphetamines:** Amphetamine sulfate, dextroamphetamine, methamphetamine.
- **Nonamphetamines:** Benzphetamine, phendimetrazine, pemoline, methylphenidate, sibutramine and phentermine.
- **Miscellaneous:** Cocaine, caffeine and nicotine.

Amphetamine is a stimulant of central nervous system. Its primary action is to release norepinephrine along with dopamine and serotonin. In 1932, amphetamine was introduced in medicine as amphetamine sulfate (benzedrine inhaler) for treating rhinitis, asthma and coryza. Street names of amphetamines are ecstasy, XTC, speed, meth, ice, crank and crystal. As per the metabolism, the oral amphetamines are absorbed well in gastrointestinal tract and excreted by kidneys. At present, common clinical indications of amphetamines are attention deficit hyperactive disorder (ADHD), narcolepsy, obesity (rarely used), mild depression among students and sports personnels and post encephalitic Parkinson's disease.

Acute Intoxication Effects of Amphetamine

- **Neuropsychiatric manifestations:** Panic anxiety, restless, irritability, hostile behavior and bruxism.
- **Cardiovascular manifestations:** Hypertension, cardiac failure, cardiovascular shock, tachycardia and hemorrhage.
- **Psychiatric manifestations:** Prominent visual hallucinations, phobia, euphoria, hypervigilance, hyperactivity, anger, impaired judgment, confused state, talkativeness, absence of thought disorder, paranoid hallucination syndrome and tactile hallucination (present in chronic usage).
- **Miscellaneous:** Ataxia, hyperpyrexia, convulsions, tetany, mydriasis and coma.

Withdrawal Effects of Amphetamine

Depression with suicidal ideation, apathy, fatigue, dysphoria, agitation, increased appetite, unpleasant dreams, psychomotor agitation or retardation, hypersomnia alternative with insomnia and hyperphagia.

Drug Interactions

Decongestants and hay fever medications contain stimulants like sodium bicarbonate (urine alkalinizing agent which decrease amphetamine elimination). Urine acidifying agent increases amphetamine elimination.

ICD-11 Diagnostic Criteria for Amphetamine Dependence

- Disorder of regulation of stimulant use arising from repeated or continuous use of stimulants.
- The characteristic feature is a strong internal drive to use stimulants, which is manifested by impaired ability to control use, increasing priority given to use over other activities and persistence of use despite harm or negative consequences.
- These experiences are often accompanied by a subjective sensation of urge or craving to use stimulants.
- Physiological features of dependence may also be present, including tolerance to the effects of stimulants, withdrawal symptoms following cessation or reduction in use of stimulants, or repeated use of stimulants or pharmacologically similar substances to prevent or alleviate withdrawal symptoms.
- The features of dependence are usually evident over a period of at least 12 months but the diagnosis may be made if stimulant use is continuous (daily or almost daily) for at least 1 month.

Treatment

Management of Amphetamine Intoxication

Induce vomiting as a first aid measure when you suspect amphetamine intoxication. Acidification of urine and diuresis is helpful. If convulsion is there, Inj. diazepam is administered. In case of psychotic symptoms, haloperidol and chlorpromazine can be given. If hypertension is present beta blockers can be given. Administer Tab. paracetamol and give cold sponging if the patient has hyperpyrexia. Nurse should also facilitate the urinary clearance of amphetamines.

Management of Withdrawal Effects of Amphetamine

Symptomatic treatment can be done. Amino acid catecholamine precursors such as phenylalanine and tyrosine is used. Dopamine agonist (For example, bromocriptine) is used to manage withdrawal symptoms of amphetamine. Tricyclic antidepressants and psychotherapy is also helpful.

COCAINE

It is alkaloid derived from coca bush, *Erythroxylum coca*. Karl Koller used this as first effective local anesthetic agent in 1884. Street Name; Coca, Crack, gold dust, coke, cecil, toot, blow, happy dust, snow, dust and flake. It exerts physiological effects on both central and peripheral nervous system which prevents the reuptake of norepinephrine, serotonin and dopamine into presynaptic neurons. Cocaine is commonly used with opioids and amphetamines. Cocaine mixed up with heroin is called speedball. The preparation of cocaine in various forms is given in Table 9.13.

Acute Intoxication Effects of Cocaine

Pupil dilatation, nausea, vomiting, tachycardia, increase or decrease in temperature/blood pressure/pulse/respiration, increased sweating, loss of appetite, weight loss, impaired thinking, seizure, agitation, chest pain, hypomanic state and coma.

Chronic Effects of Cocaine

Psychosis, perforated nasal septum (when snorting is present), disturbances in biological functions, paranoia, crack babies—cause damage to fetus and pseudohallucination.

Withdrawal Effects of Cocaine

Phases of cocaine withdrawal include crash phase, postcrash and extinction phase as explained in Table 9.14.

Complications

- **Psychological:** Anxiety, psychotic symptoms such as tactile hallucination/persecutory delusion, compulsive behavior and out of control behavior.

Table 9.13: Preparation of cocaine in various forms

Final preparation	Mode of administration	Content of cocaine (%)	Content in addition to leaves of Erythroxylum coca
Coca	Chewable	0.5–1.5%	Lime
Coca paste	Smoked Sniffed	40–90% 12–75%	Gasoline or kerosene
Cocaine HCl	Intravenous Smoke with glass pipe	>98%	HCl
Free base or alkaloid	Inhale with glass pipe	Varies	Alkali

Table 9.14: Withdrawal effects of cocaine

Phases of cocaine withdrawal	Duration after discontinuation of cocaine	Substages	Symptoms
Crash	9 hours–4 days	I	Anorexia, agitation, depression and severe craving
		II	Depression, fatigue, sleepiness and moderate craving
		III	Hyperphagia, excessive day time sleepiness with intermediate awareness and mild craving
Postcrash	4 days–1 week	I	Normal sleep, may or may not have craving
		II	Anergia, anxiety, cocaine blues (depression), anhedonia and moderate craving
Extinction	1 week–10 days		Absence of withdrawal symptoms

- **Intranasal:** Nasal septum perforation, mucosal vasoconstriction and anosmia.
- **Systemic:** Gastrointestinal necrosis, respiratory depression, coronary artery disease, arrhythmias, convulsions and fetal anoxia.

ICD-11 Diagnostic Criteria for Cocaine Dependence

- Regulation of cocaine use arising from repeated or continuous use of cocaine.
- Characteristic feature is a strong internal drive to use cocaine, which is manifested by impaired ability to control use, increasing priority given to use over other activities and persistence of use despite harm or negative consequences.
- These experiences are often accompanied by a subjective sensation of urge or craving to use cocaine.
- Physiological features of dependence may also be present, including tolerance to the effects of cocaine, withdrawal symptoms following cessation or reduction in use of cocaine, or repeated use of cocaine or pharmacologically similar substances to prevent or alleviate withdrawal symptoms.
- The features of dependence are usually evident over a period of at least 12 months but the diagnosis may be made if cocaine use is continuous (daily or almost daily) for at least 1 month.

Treatment

- **For overdose of cocaine:**
  - Administration of oxygen
  - Muscle relaxants
  - Antidote is amyl nitrite
  - Diazepam (or) thiopentone IV for seizure (or) severe anxiety
  - Propranolol IV—antagonist of cocaine induced sympathomimetic effect
  - Haloperidol (or) pimozide for treating psychosis
- **For chronic use of cocaine:**
  - Dopaminergic agonist—bromocriptine
  - Antiparkinson agent—amantadine
  - Antidepressants—desipramine, imipramine and trazodone
  - Supportive psychotherapy
  - Behavior therapy
  - Relapse prevention

NICOTINE ABUSE

Nicotine is addictive substance present in tobacco products. Tobacco smoke has around 4,000 chemicals. Available forms are cigarette smoking, pipe smoking, tobacco chewing, snuff and cigar smoking.

Mechanism of Nicotine Dependence

- **Biomolecular:** Nicotine binds with their specified nicotinic receptors in brain and release dopamine or other neurotransmitter which gives pleasure; thereby the dependence to nicotine develops.
- **Psychosocial:** Taking nicotine as a coping mechanism with negative mood or stress.

ICD-11 Diagnostic Criteria for Nicotine Dependence

- Disorder of regulation of nicotine use arising from repeated or continuous use of nicotine.
- The characteristic feature is a strong internal drive to use nicotine, which is manifested by impaired ability to control use, increasing priority given to use over other activities and persistence of use despite harm or negative consequences.
- These experiences are often accompanied by a subjective sensation of urge or craving to use nicotine.
- Physiological features of dependence may also be present, including tolerance to the effects of nicotine, withdrawal symptoms following cessation or reduction in use of nicotine, or repeated use of nicotine or pharmacologically similar substances to prevent or alleviate withdrawal symptoms.
- The features of dependence are usually evident over a period of at least 12 months.

Intoxication effects of nicotine: Lung carcinoma, oropharyngeal carcinoma, emphysema, heart disease, diabetes, macular degeneration of eye, cataract, premature ageing, infertility or impotence, stroke, miscarriage in pregnancy, peptic ulcer, osteoporosis, cancer of kidney, bladder cancer, pancreatic carcinoma, cervical cancer and leukemia.

Withdrawal effects of nicotine: Irritability, headache, insomnia, lack of concentration, memory loss, restlessness, increased appetite, depression, weight gain and decreased heart rate.

Nicotine replacement therapy: Nicotine chewing gum (2 mg dose/gum has to be chewed and kept between the cheek and gums for effective release of nicotine). Nasal spray, inhaler and transdermal patch is also recommended to use. Bupropion hydrochloride (zyban) can be used, but contraindicated with seizure/eating disorders. The second line of treatment is clonidine (antihypertensive) and nortriptyline (antidepressant). Psychosocial interventions include individual and group psychotherapy. Complementary therapies include: acupuncture, yoga, herbs and hypnosis. Tablet varenicline (Trade name: Champix, Chantix)—high affinity partial agonist for nicotinic acetylcholine receptor (nACh) which leads to dopamine release in nucleus accumbens so that nicotine craving is reduced.

Behavior modification (6 D technique): It includes the determination of oneself to quit smoking, deep breathing exercises, drink more water, healthy, diet, daily exercises and diversional techniques as shown in Figure 9.12.

Determine oneself to quit smoking

Drink plenty of water

Deep breathing exercises

Diet should be healthy and balanced

Divert yourself when you get thoughts to smoke

Daily exercises

Figure 9.12: Smoking cessation—6 D technique

Five Major Steps of Intervention (5 A's) (Flowchart 9.10)

Flowchart 9.10: Five major steps to intervention—smoking cessation

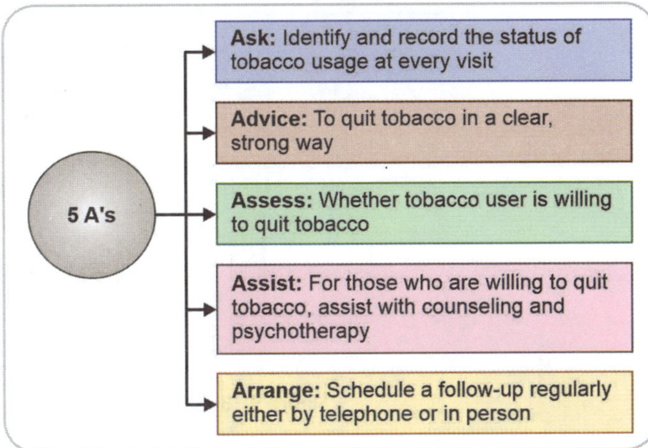

5 R's for Patients Unwilling to Quit Nicotine (Flowchart 9.11)

Flowchart 9.11: Five R's for patients unwilling to quit smoking

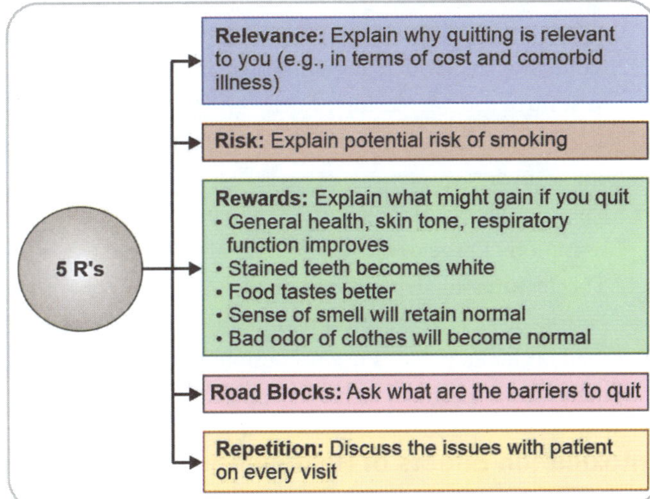

Benefits of smoking cessation: Shown in Figure 9.13

HALLUCINOGENS

Hallucinogens are substances which alter the individual's sensory perception of reality and induce hallucinations. They fall in two categories:

1. **Natural hallucinogens:** Mescaline, Psilocybin, Psilocin and Ololiuqui.
2. **Synthetic hallucinogens:** Lysergic acid diethylamide (LSD), dimethytryptamine (DMT), diethyltryptamine (DET), phencyclidine (PCP), methoxyamphetamine (MDA) and 3, 4-Methylene-dioxyamphetamine (MDMA).

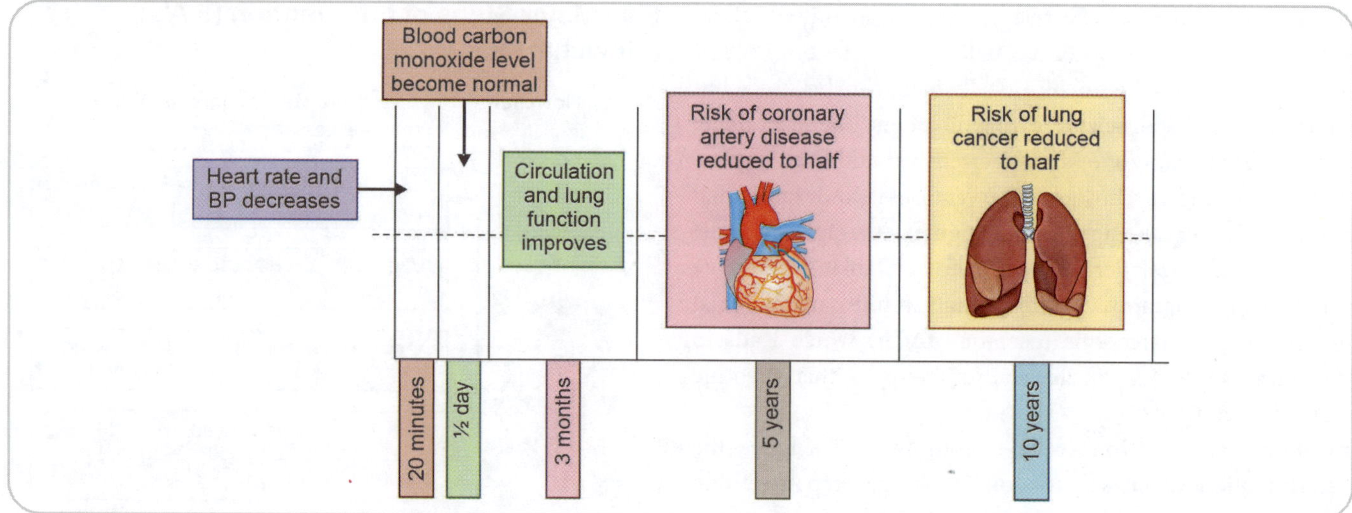

Figure 9.13 Benefits of smoking cessation from 20 minutes to 10 years

ICD-11 Diagnostic Criteria for Hallucinogens Dependence

- Disorder of regulation of hallucinogen use arising from repeated or continuous use of hallucinogens. The characteristic feature is a strong internal drive to use hallucinogens, which is manifested by impaired ability to control use, increasing priority given to use over other activities and persistence of use despite harm or negative consequences.
- These experiences are often accompanied by a subjective sensation of urge or craving to use hallucinogens.
- The features of dependence are usually evident over a period of at least 12 months but the diagnosis may be made if hallucinogens use is continuous (daily or almost daily) for at least 1 month.

Intoxication Effects of Hallucinogens

It includes bad trips [Fear of dying (or) going mad (or) feeling panicky], synesthesia—confusion with sensory modalities (e.g., sound being seen, colors being heard), impaired judgment, paranoid ideas, alertness, full wakefulness, depersonalization, derealization. Physical symptoms such as tachycardia, sweating, palpitation, blurring of vision, pupillary dilatation, tremors, incoordination and raised blood pressure.

Withdrawal Effects of Hallucinogens

No specific withdrawal symptoms. However, flash back phenomenon (repeated occurrence of hallucinogenic state without taking the drug) is seen.

Treatment

Symptomatic management, antidepressants, antianxiety agents–diazepam; antipsychotics-haloperidol and psychotherapy.

CAFFEINE

Caffeine intoxication is a clinically significant transient condition that develops during or shortly after the consumption of caffeine.

- **Intoxication effects:** Disturbances in consciousness, cognition, perception, affect, behavior or coordination.
- **Presenting features:** Restlessness, anxiety, excitement, insomnia, flushed face, diuresis, gastrointestinal disturbances, muscle twitching, psychomotor agitation, perspiration or chills, and nausea or vomiting and panic attacks may occur.
- **Withdrawal effects of caffeine:** Headache, fatigue or drowsiness, anxiety, dysphoric mood, nausea or vomiting, and difficulty in concentrating.
- **Complications on very high doses:** Respiratory distress and seizures
- **Treatment:** Symptomatic management, antidepressants, antianxiety agents and psychotherapy.

SYNTHETIC CATHINONES

- Synthetic cathinones have dependence-inducing properties, resulting in synthetic cathinone dependence and also causes withdrawal symptoms when stopped or reduced.
- **Intoxication effects:**
  - **Presenting features:** Anxiety, anger, hypervigilance, psychomotor agitation, panic, confusion, paranoid

ideation, auditory hallucinations and changes in sociability, perspiration or chills and nausea or vomiting.
  - **Physical signs:** Tachycardia, increased blood pressure, hyperthermia and pupillary dilatation. Seizure may occur rarely.
- **Withdrawal effects:** Dysphoric mood, irritability, fatigue, insomnia or hypersomnia, increased appetite, anxiety and craving for cathinones.
- **Treatment:** Symptomatic management, antidepressants, antianxiety agents and psychotherapy.

DISORDERS DUE TO USE OF METHYLENEDIOXYMETHAMPHETAMINE OR RELATED DRUGS

Methylenedioxymethamphetamine (MDMA) causes a wide range of harms affecting most organs and systems of the body. It also has dependence-inducing properties and withdrawal symptoms when stopped or reduced.

- **Intoxication effects:** Anxiety, Increased or inappropriate sexual interest and activity, restlessness, agitation and sweating. Dystonia and seizure may happen rarely.
- **Withdrawal effects:** Lethargy, fatigue, hypersomnia or insomnia, anxiety, depressed mood, irritability, difficulty in concentrating craving and appetite disturbance.
- **Treatment:** Symptomatic management, antidepressants, antianxiety agents and psychotherapy.

DISORDERS DUE TO USE OF DISSOCIATIVE DRUGS INCLUDING KETAMINE AND PHENCYCLIDINE

The use of dissociative drugs including ketamine and phencyclidine (PCP) will harm the health due to the direct or secondary toxic effects on body organs and systems, behavior related to intoxication, by the harmful route of administration. It also has dependence-inducing properties and withdrawal symptoms when stopped or reduced.

- **Intoxication effects:**
  - **Presenting features:** Aggression, unpredictability, impulsiveness, anxiety, altered judgment, psycho-motor agitation, numbness, slurred speech and dystonia.
  - **Physical signs:** Nystagmus, tachycardia, raised blood pressure, numbness, ataxia, dysarthria, and muscle rigidity.
- **Withdrawal effects:** Dysphoric mood, irritability, fatigue, insomnia or hypersomnia, increased appetite and anxiety.
- **Complications:** Delirium, psychotic features and mood disorder.
- **Treatment:** Symptomatic management, antidepressants, antipsychotics, antianxiety agents and psychotherapy.

INHALANTS (OR) VOLATILE SOLVENTS

The commonly used inhalants (or) volatile solvents are aerosols, varnish remover, thinners, petrol and solvents used in industrial areas.

- **Intoxication effects:** Euphoria, apathy, slurring of speech, belligerence, excitement and impaired judgment.
- **Withdrawal effects:** Anxiety and depression.
- **Complication:** Kidney/liver damage, brain damage, peripheral neuropathy and disturbances in perception.
- **Treatment:** Antianxiety agents, antidepressants and psychotherapy.

NURSING DIAGNOSIS AND INTERVENTIONS FOR PATIENT WITH SUBSTANCE ABUSE

NURSING CARE IN ACUTE EPISODE

- Monitor vital signs.
- Intake output chart is need to be maintained.
- Observe the complications of drug overdose and withdrawal.
- Take precautions to prevent suicide and use restraints if patient is violent/potential for injury to self and others.
- Use limit setting, a psychotherapy technique in order to control the manipulative behavior. Maintain seizure precaution.
- Administer intravenous fluids and medications as per physician order.

NURSING CARE IN WITHDRAWAL

- Observe and monitor the withdrawal symptoms.
- Administer medications as per the doctor's order to reduce the withdrawal symptoms and ensure that the patient has swallowed the medication properly.
- Provide calm environment since noise may agitate the patient.

NURSING DIAGNOSIS AND INTERVENTIONS

- **Imbalanced nutrition less than body's requirements due to the effects of drug dependence.**

Nursing interventions	Rationale
Assess the nutritional requirements of the client and Body mass index	Provide the baseline data about client's nutritional status
Assess the client likes and dislikes	To prepare diet menu accordingly
Plan the adequate and realistic calorie requirement	To improve the health status with adequate calorie
Describe the importance of adequate nutrition to the client	To improve the knowledge regarding nutritious diet thereby weight loss and anemia (physiological effects of drugs) will be corrected
Provide the menu plan to client	To execute the diet plan effectively into practice

- **Ineffective coping identified by the patient verbalization that he consumes drug to relieve stress**

Nursing interventions	Rationale
Assess the situations in which client feels stressful	Provide the baseline data about client's stressful situation
Explore the internal and external stressors	Help to identify the stressor causing stress
Teach the various right coping skills	To cope the stressful situations
Encourage the good relationship with family members	It helps to express the feelings and bottled up emotions to family members instead of consuming drug
Refer the client to alcoholic anonymous, narcotic anonymous, Al-anon, etc.	Self-help group will guide the client to enhance the coping skills
Assist the client to plan the schedule daily	Proper adherence with the schedule will avoid the unnecessary stress

- **Ineffective denial related to underdeveloped ego as evidenced by failure to accept the responsibility and lack of insight**

Nursing interventions	Rationale
Follow the psychiatric nursing Principle 'Accept the patient as he/she is'.	Unconditional acceptance of client will promote self-esteem
Identify the maladaptive behavior and find out how drug act as contributing factor for such behavior	To reduce denial, relation between drug usage and personal problem has to be identified
Don't allow the client to blame others	Helps to promote insight and thereby it reduces denial
Give positive reinforcement when client exhibits insight in his behavior	To promote the desirable behavior

- **Risk of injury related to acute intoxication effects of drug as evidenced by disorientation and confused state**

Nursing interventions	Rationale
Allot the patient's bed near to nurses' station	To have direct observation
Monitor the client's need of restraint	To promote safety measures
Promote seizure precautions (raise the side rails, airway kept ready, padded tongue blade to prevent tongue fall back)	To prevent injury of client
Reorient the client to time, place and person	To orient the patient
Reduce the environment stimuli (switch off the bright lights, restrict the visitors)	To promote the client to take adequate rest

- **Altered health maintenance related to seeking help from others to maintain health as evidenced by feeling exhausted and presence of more physical symptoms due to drug withdrawal.**

Nursing interventions	Rationale
Assess the client health status	Provide the baseline data about client's health status
Provide bland diet	Easily tolerable food for the client with substance abuse
Maintain fluid and electrolyte balance	To rectify the fluids and electrolytes imbalance since, it's common among patients with substance abuse disorder.
Ensure the adequate protein in diet	Hepatic dysfunction is common among patients with substance use disorder so protein metabolism is said to be problematic among these clients
Promote small, frequent and balanced diet	To promote the nutritional status

PREVENTION OF SUBSTANCE USE DISORDER

Primary Prevention

Social changes or governmental measures such as:
- Control the sales of alcohol within the limited hours might decrease the availability.
- Increase in the price of alcohol is helpful to reduce the use of alcohol.

Health education to the public and school/college students:
- Educating in regard with the harmful effects of substance use will be helpful to prevent the usage.
- Consider the cultural belief is important, i.e., tribal group people (Lambani group) might feel 'arrack' manufacture

is said to be normal and certain cultures consider that alcohol consumption in postnatal mother might speedup the retroversion of uterus and some foreigners also consider that drinking little amount of alcohol daily is good for health and to improve the heart function. So, these cultural beliefs have to be addressed properly during the time of health teaching.

Doctors can restrict the over prescription of benzodiazepines: The benzodiazepines have risk of dependence so, it can be either avoided or prescribed in the low doses based on the patient's needs.

Training to enhance the social and personal skills which in turn develops the self-esteem.

Secondary Prevention

Counseling and motivational interviewing (Identify the factors which promote the motivation toward change, i.e., motivation to quit substances).

Detoxification with the benzodiazepines (e.g., Lorazepam, diazepam) will control the withdrawal symptoms and help them to recover from substance abuse.

Tertiary Prevention

Holistic approach of treatment modalities is considered such as assertiveness training, training to promote coping skills, psychotherapy, anger control measures, time management, monetary management, stress management, recreation, sleep hygiene, family counseling, referral to the agencies (alcoholic anonymous, al-anon, al-ateen, narcotic anonymous) and relapse prevention.

REHABILITATION

Measures are taken to improve the new social contacts and avoid the previous contacts who drink alcohol or use substances. Provide them a good social and family support. Engage the patients in work and social activities.

GERIATRIC CONSIDERATIONS

Late onset substance abuse is rare, but if it is present it has to be treated properly because it will increase the grief, stress, depression and social isolation. History of substance use by the same individual with absenteeism might have a chance to use again in old age due to social isolation. Hence, good social and family support are essential.

EXTRA EDGE

ICD-10 Classification of Substance Abuse

F10–F19: Mental and behavioral disorders due to psychoactive substance use and mental and behavioral disorder due to the use of

- F10 — Alcohol
- F11 — Opioids
- F12 — Cannabinoids
- F13 — Hypnotics or sedatives
- F14 — Cocaine
- F16 — Hallucinogens

SUMMARY

- Dependence means compulsive and repeated use of substance, which results in tolerance toward the substance and also leads to withdrawal symptoms, when it is commenced to quit or decrease the dosage of the substance.
- Common substance abuse in India is alcohol, cannabis, hypnotics, sedatives, antianxiety drugs, amphetamines, barbiturates, cocaine, hallucinogens, inhalants, nicotine and opioids.
- Modified Mann's index of addiction denotes the addiction level of various substances which has been arranged from lower level of addiction to higher level of addiction.
- Substance abuse can also be classified based on the psychological effects as depressants and stimulants.
- The major parts involved in addiction reward pathway are ventral tegmental area (VTA), nucleus accumbens and prefrontal cortex.
- DSM-5 classification of alcoholism includes the alcohol use disorder (mild or moderate or severe), intoxication, withdrawal and unspecified alcohol related disorder.
- Cloninger's classified alcoholism as type I and II based on genetic and environmental factors. Jellinek's, five species of alcohol dependence based on usage pattern is alpha, beta, gamma, delta and epsilon.
- CAGE Questionnaire, Michigan Alcoholism Screening Test (MAST), Alcohol Use Disorders Identification Test (AUDIT) and Paddington Alcohol Test (PAT) are the tool used to assess problem of alcoholism.
- Alcohol withdrawal is categorized as mild, moderate and severe. It is also categorized as complicated and uncomplicated.
- Aversion therapy or Antabuse means treatment to arouse unlikeliness.
- Usual dose of disulfiram is 250 mg per day.
- When client takes alcohol along with disulfiram it will cause disulfiram ethanol reaction.
- Ethanol challenge test is done to create the cognitive awareness of disulfiram ethanol reaction.
- Alcoholic anonymous works by the recovered alcoholics to sustain the process of sobriety.
- Precontemplation, contemplation, preparation, determination, action, maintenance and relapse are the stages of change model.

Contd...

- Sedatives, hypnotics and antianxiety agents are classified as barbiturates and nonbarbiturates.
- Flumazenil is antidote of antianxiety agents.
- Cannabis is derived from hemp plant, *Cannabis sativa*.
- Opioids are exudates from dried seeds of *Papaver somniferum*. It is classified as natural and synthetic derivatives. Naltrexone is used to treat the overdose of opioids. Methadone maintenance is the agonist substitution.
- CNS stimulants are two categories—cellular and psychomotor. Common CNS stimulants are classified as amphetamines, nonamphetamines, cocaine, caffeine and nicotine.
- Cocaine is an alkaloid derived from coca bush, *Erythroxylum coca*. Phases of cocaine withdrawal are crash, postcrash and extinction phase. Amyl nitrite is an antidote for cocaine overuse.
- Nicotine is an addictive substance in tobacco product. Mechanism of nicotine dependence is classified as biomolecular and psychosocial. Nicotine replacement therapy is helpful for patients with nicotine dependence.

ASSESS YOURSELF

Long Answer Questions

1. Explain the classification, etiology, psychopathology, diagnosis, clinical manifestations of intoxication and management of patients with alcohol dependence syndrome.
2. Explain the classification, etiology psychopathology, diagnosis, clinical manifestations and management of patients with opioids abuse.

Short Answer Questions

1. Define substance abuse.
2. Write about opioids abuse in brief.

Short Notes

Write short notes on:

1. Cannabis abuse
2. Alcohol withdrawal syndrome
3. Complications of alcoholism
4. Assessment tools used to assess the patient with substance abuse
5. Treatment of alcohol withdrawal
6. Disulfiram
7. Aversion therapy
8. Disulfiram ethanol reaction
9. Alcoholic anonymous
10. Sedatives, hypnotics and antianxiety agents
11. Opioids dependence
12. CNS stimulants
13. Cocaine dependence
14. Nicotine abuse
15. Nursing management of patient with substance abuse

Multiple Choice Questions

1. **_________ is a compulsive and repeated use of substance, which results in tolerance toward the substance and also leads to withdrawal symptoms when it is commenced to quit.**
   a. Dependence b. Abuse
   c. Tolerance d. Codependence
2. **ICD-11 code for mental and behavioral disorders due to psychoactive substance use is ______.**
   a. 6C40 b. 6C41
   c. 6C42 d. 6C43
3. **The major part involved in addiction reward pathway are ______________.**
   a. Ventral tegmental area (VTA)
   b. Nucleus accumbens
   c. Prefrontal cortex.
   d. All of the above
4. **Usual dose of disulfiram is _____ per day.**
   a. 250 mg b. 500 mg
   c. 750 mg d. 1 g
5. **___________ is a first stage in change model.**
   a. Contemplation b. Precontemplation
   c. Preparation d. Determination
6. **_________ works by the recovered alcoholics to sustain the process of sobriety.**
   a. Rehabilitation Center b. Alcoholic anonymous
   c. Psychotropic drugs d. None of these
7. **_________is antidote of antianxiety agents.**
   a. Flumazenil b. Lorazepam
   c. Haloperidol d. Amyl nitrite
8. **_________ is a antidote for cocaine overuse.**
   a. Flumazenil b. Lorazepam
   c. Haloperidol d. Amyl nitrite
9. **________ are exudates from dried seeds of *Papaver somniferum*.**
   a. Cannabis b. Opioids
   c. Nicotine d. Alcohol
10. **_____________is tool used to assess problem drinkers of alcoholism.**
    a. CAGE questionnaire b. AUDIT
    c. MAST d. All of these

ANSWER KEY

1. a	**2.** a	**3.** d	**4.** a	**5.** b
6. b	**7.** a	**8.** d	**9.** b	**10.** d

Nursing Management of Patients with Sexual, Personality and Eating Disorders

CHAPTER 10

LEARNING OBJECTIVE

After studying this chapter, the students will be able to gain knowledge regarding the personality disorders, eating disorders and sexual disorders which will help them in nursing care of patient suffering from personality disorders, eating disorders and sexual disorders.

CHAPTER OUTLINE

Sexual Disorders

- ICD-11 and DSM-5 Classification of Sexual Disorders
- Gender Identity Disorder or Gender Dysphoria or Gender Incongruence
- Disorders Related to Sexual Maturation and Development
- Disorders of Sex Preference/Deviation/Perversions/ Paraphilic Disorders
- Sexual Dysfunction

Personality Disorders

- Introduction
- Definition of Personality Disorder
- Incidence and Prevalence
- Significant Features of Personality Disorders
- Etiology of Personality Disorders
- Classification of Personality Disorders
- Protective and Risk Factors of Personality Disorders
- Antisocial Personality Disorder
- Borderline Personality Disorder
- Geriatric Considerations

Eating Disorders

- Etiology of Eating Disorder
- Comparison of Anorexia Nervosa and Bulimia Nervosa
- Complications of Eating Disorders
- Categories of Eating Disorders
- Assessment of Eating Disorders
- Nursing Diagnosis
- Signs and Symptoms of Eating Disorders Revealed During Physical Assessment
- Treatment of Eating Disorders
- Eating Disorders of Infancy and Childhood
- Obesity

KEY TERMS

Transsexualism, Dual-role transvestism, Gender identity disorders, Fetishism, Fetishistic transvestism, Exhibitionism, Sadomasochism, Multiple disorders of sexual preference, Exhibitionism, Frotteurism, Sadism, Masochism, Pedophilia, Zoophilia (Bestiality), Klismaphilia, Urophilia, Coprophilia, Necrophilia, Telephone or mail scatologia, Voyeurism/Scopophilia, Paranoid personality disorder, Schizoid personality disorder and schizotypal personality disorder, Antisocial personality disorder, Borderline personality disorder, Histrionic personality disorder and Narcissistic personality disorder, Avoidant personality disorder, Dependent personality disorder and Obsessive-compulsive personality disorder, Anorexia nervosa, Bulimia nervosa, Binge eating, Pica, Rumination disorder, Obesity.

SEXUAL DISORDERS

Sexual disorders are classified as gender identity disorders, disorders of sex preference/deviation/perversion, disorders related to sexual maturation or development and sexual dysfunction as shown in Flowchart 10.1.

ICD-11 AND DSM-5 CLASSIFICATION OF SEXUAL DISORDERS

Sexual Dysfunctions		
HA00	302.71	Hypoactive sexual desire disorder
HA01.0	302.72	Female sexual interest/arousal disorder
HA01.1	302.72	Erectile disorder
HA02	302.73	Female orgasmic disorder
HA03.0	302.75	Premature (early) ejaculation
HA03.1	302.74	Delayed ejaculation
—	302.76	Genito-pelvic pain/penetration disorder
HA03.Y	302.79	Other specified sexual dysfunction
Gender Dysphoria (DSM-5) and Gender Incongruence (ICD-11)		
HA60	302.85	Gender dysphoria in adolescents and adults
HA61	302.6	Gender dysphoria in children
HA8Y	302.6	Other specified gender dysphoria
HA6Z	302.6	Unspecified gender dysphoria

Paraphilic Disorders		
6D30	302.4	Exhibitionistic disorder
6D31	302.82	Voyeuristic disorder
6D32	302.2	Pedophilic disorder
6D33	302.84	Sexual sadism disorder
6D34	302.89	Frotteuristic disorder
—	302.83	Sexual masochism disorder
F65.0	302.81	Fetishistic disorder
—	302.3	Transvestic disorder
6D35 and 6D36	302.89	Other specified paraphilic disorder
6D3Z	302.9	Unspecified paraphilic disorder

GENDER IDENTITY DISORDER OR GENDER DYSPHORIA OR GENDER INCONGRUENCE

Transsexualism or Gender Dysphoria

Transsexual people experience gender identity crisis, which is expressed in feeling of discomfort with one's own anatomical sex organs. Individual has preoccupied ideas that he/she will feel better to have opposite sex organs and the person feels marked significant distress. There will be a presence of social and occupational dysfunction. This disorder is being diagnosed after puberty (Table 10.1).

Flowchart 10.1: Classification of sexual disorders

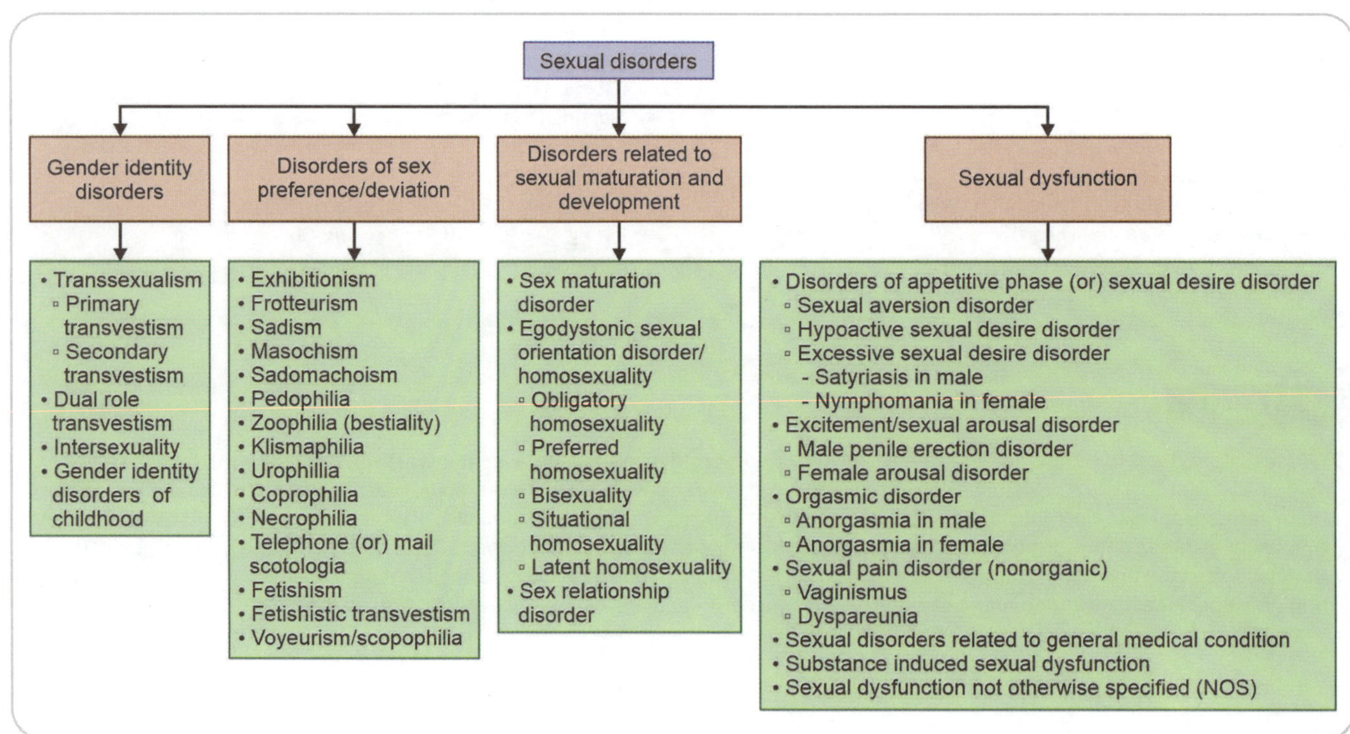

Table 10.1: Primary and secondary transsexualism

Aspects	Primary transsexualism	Secondary transsexualism
Onset	Early childhood	Late
Prognosis	Good	Poor
Category	Homogenous	Heterogenous
Types	• Male to female primary transsexualism • Female to male/ primary transsexualism	Majority are male to female secondary transsexualism
Common feature	Wish to change anatomical sex organ	

Differential Diagnosis

Cross-gender homosexuality or Pseudotranssexualism: Male or female homosexuals sometimes need sex change and even wear the dress of opposite gender.

Transvestism or fetishistic transvestism: Wearing the dress of opposite gender for purpose of sexual excitement is mostly seen in males (transsexuals wear dress of opposite gender because they feel that they are a part of other gender. This is not because of sexual excitement).

Treatment

- **Counseling and psychotherapy:** It is to promote satisfaction with one's own gender (This has been done previously but as per the newer concept, this is no longer advocated if the diagnosis is clear).
  - **Sex reassignment surgery** (if psychotherapy fails).
  - Hormonal therapy.
  - **Mastectomy:** Surgical removal of partial or complete removal of one or two breasts. The main objective of mastectomy is to create an aesthetically pleasing male chest by removing glandular tissue while minimizing chest wall scars.
- **Castration or testiclectomy or oophorectomy:** Action performed to lose the function of the testis or ovaries is known as castration. It can be done either surgically or with the use of chemicals.
- **Phalloplasty:** Surgical reconstruction or artificial modification of penis.
- **Hysterectomy with salpingo-oophorectomy:** Removal of uterus and cervix. Bilateral salpingo-oophorectomy is the removal of both ovaries and fallopian tubes.

Gender Dysphoria of Childhood

Onset of transsexualism can be seen in age group of 2–4 years.

DISORDERS RELATED TO SEXUAL MATURATION AND DEVELOPMENT

Sex Maturation Disorder

Uncertainty with regard to gender identity and sexual orientation (homosexual, heterosexual, bisexual) leads to anxiety or depression. Usual onset of this disorder is in adolescence.

Egodystonic Sexual Orientation Disorder/Homosexuality

Individual wishes to change the sexual orientation because it causes significant distress (egodystonic: Opposite to that of ego, unwillingness to ego). Previously homosexuality was classified as egosyntonic (no distress with regard to homosexual behavior) and egodystonic (distress with regard to homosexual behavior) (Table 10.2).

Table 10.2: Types of homosexuality

Types of homosexuality	Description in regard to the desire to have sex
Obligatory homosexuality	Only homosexuals
Preferred homosexuality	Predominant homosexuals and occasionally heterosexuals
Bisexuality	Both homosexuals and heterosexual
Situational homosexuality	Predominant heterosexual and occasionally homosexual
Latent homosexuality	Only heterosexual and fantasy of homosexuals

Treatment

- **To change sexual orientation:** Psychoanalytic psychotherapy, behavior therapy (systematic desensitization, aversion therapy and covert sensitization), androgen therapy was practiced previously but, it is not practiced nowadays because these methods are considered to provoke the anxiety in patients.
- **To remove psychological distress:** Psychotherapy and psychotropics (antidepressants and benzodiazepines) are used.

DISORDERS OF SEX PREFERENCE/DEVIATION/PERVERSIONS/PARAPHILIC DISORDERS

Disorders of sex preference/deviation/perversions/paraphilic disorders have been described in Table 10.3.

Table 10.3: Disorders of sex preference/deviation or paraphilic disorders

Disorders of sex preference/ deviation/perversion	Description
Exhibitionism	Showing of sex organs to stranger
Frotteurism	Sexual pleasure with rubbing others
Sadism	Sexual pleasure with humiliating others
Masochism	Sexual pleasure with getting or being humiliated
Sadomasochism	Sexual pleasure with humiliating others and getting or being humiliated
Pedophilia	Sexual pleasure with children
Zoophilia (bestiality)	Sexual pleasure with animal
Klismaphilia	Sexual pleasure with enema
Urophilia	Sexual pleasure with urine
Coprophilia	Sexual pleasure with feces
Necrophilia	Sexual pleasure with dead bodies
Telephone or mail Scotologia	Sexual pleasure attained by sending sexual pictures
Fetishism	Sexual pleasure with objects
Fetishistic Transvestism	Sexual pleasure with clothes of opposite sex
Voyeurism/scopophilia	Sexual pleasure with observing the sexual activity of opposite sex/watching naked, etc. (visualizing pornography is not included in this category)

Treatment for Disorders of Sex Preference/Deviation

- **Psychoanalysis:** The aim of psychoanalysis is to release repressed emotions and experiences, that is make the unconscious conscious.
- **Behavior therapy:** Aversion therapy is used to quit undesirable behavior.
- **Drugs:** Antipsychotics are given for aggression with paraphilias and antiandrogens (e.g., cyproterone acetate and medroxyprogesterone acetate) are used for suppressing androgen production.
- **Psychosurgery:** Amygdalotomy involves surgical removal or destruction of amygdala or parts of amygdala. It is mostly last-resort.

SEXUAL DYSFUNCTION

Normal Human Sexual Response Cycle

There are five phases in normal human sexual response cycle such as appetitive phase, excitement phase, plateau phase, orgasmic phase and resolution phase as shown in Figure 10.1 and male/female sexual response in each phase is described in Table 10.4. Sexual dysfunction denotes a significant dysfunction in a human sexual response cycle which is not due to an organic cause.

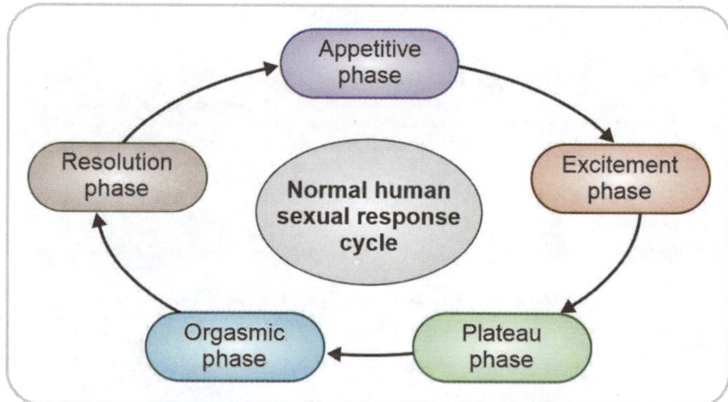

Figure 10.1: Normal human sexual response cycle

Table 10.4: Phases of normal human sexual response cycle

Phases of normal human sexual response	Male	Female
Appetitive phase	Sexual fantasies and desire of sexual activity	
Excitement phase (true phase of sexual response cycle)	• Penile erection • Elevation of testis in scrotum	• Clitoris and nipple erection • Thickening of labia majora • Vagina gets lubricated with transudate
Plateau phase (intermediate state of excitement and orgasm)	• Autonomic hyperactiveness • Erection/ enlargement of penis and testis	• Autonomic hyperactiveness • Lengthening and ballooning of vagina • Breast and labia majora enlarged
Orgasmic phase (peak state of sexual excitement)	• Contraction of penis, urethra, prostate and seminal vesicles • Ejaculation takes place	• Contractions of lower vagina, cervix and uterus • Contractions of external and internal sphincters
Resolution phase	General state of relaxation and vanish of sexual flush	

Disorders Related to Appetitive Phase (Sexual Desire Disorders)

- **Sexual aversion disorder or lack of sexual enjoyment:** Avoidance of sexual activity with life partner or sexual partner.

Thoughts of sexual activities will provoke anxiety and negative feelings.

- **Hypoactive sexual desire disorder:** Decreased sexual desire to initiate sexual activity.
- **Excessive sexual desire disorder:** Excess sexual desire in male is termed 'Satyriasis' and excess sexual desire in female is termed 'Nymphomania'.

Disorders Related to Excitement and Plateau Phase (Sexual Arousal Disorders)

- **Male erectile disorder:** Lack of ability to sustain the penile erection in males. It is classified on the basis of onset, context and etiology factors. Based on onset, it is classified as life-long or acquired (happened few months/years ago). Based on the context, it is classified into generalized (all the time) and situational (only in a particular situation). Based on the etiology, it is classified into biogenic, psychological and combination of both biogenic and psychological as shown in Flowchart 10.2. Previously, it was termed impotence. Tab Sildenafil and Tab Tadalafil might be helpful to treat this disorder.
- **Female sexual arousal disorder:** It is a disorder characterized by a persistent or recurrent inability to attain sexual arousal or to maintain arousal until the completion of a sexual activity. This may be due to biological (postmenopausal) or psychological factors.

Disorders Related to Orgasmic Phase

- **Male orgasmic disorder or male anorgasmia:** Male feels difficult to have orgasm during the coitus. This may be due to biological (drug-induced or after prostate surgery) or psychological factor.
- **Female orgasmic disorder or female anorgasmia:** Female feels difficult to have orgasm during the coitus. This may be due to biological (drug-induced or endocrine disorders like hypothyroidism) or psychological factor.
- **Premature ejaculation:** Ejaculation of sperm occurs before the satisfactory sexual activity. This may be due to biological (not common) or/and psychological factors (performance anxiety).

Sexual Pain Disorders

- **Nonorganic vaginismus:** Spasm of lower vagina will cause interference with the coitus.
- **Nonorganic dyspareunia:** Male or female may have pain in genital area during coitus.

Flowchart 10.2: Classification of male penile erection disorder

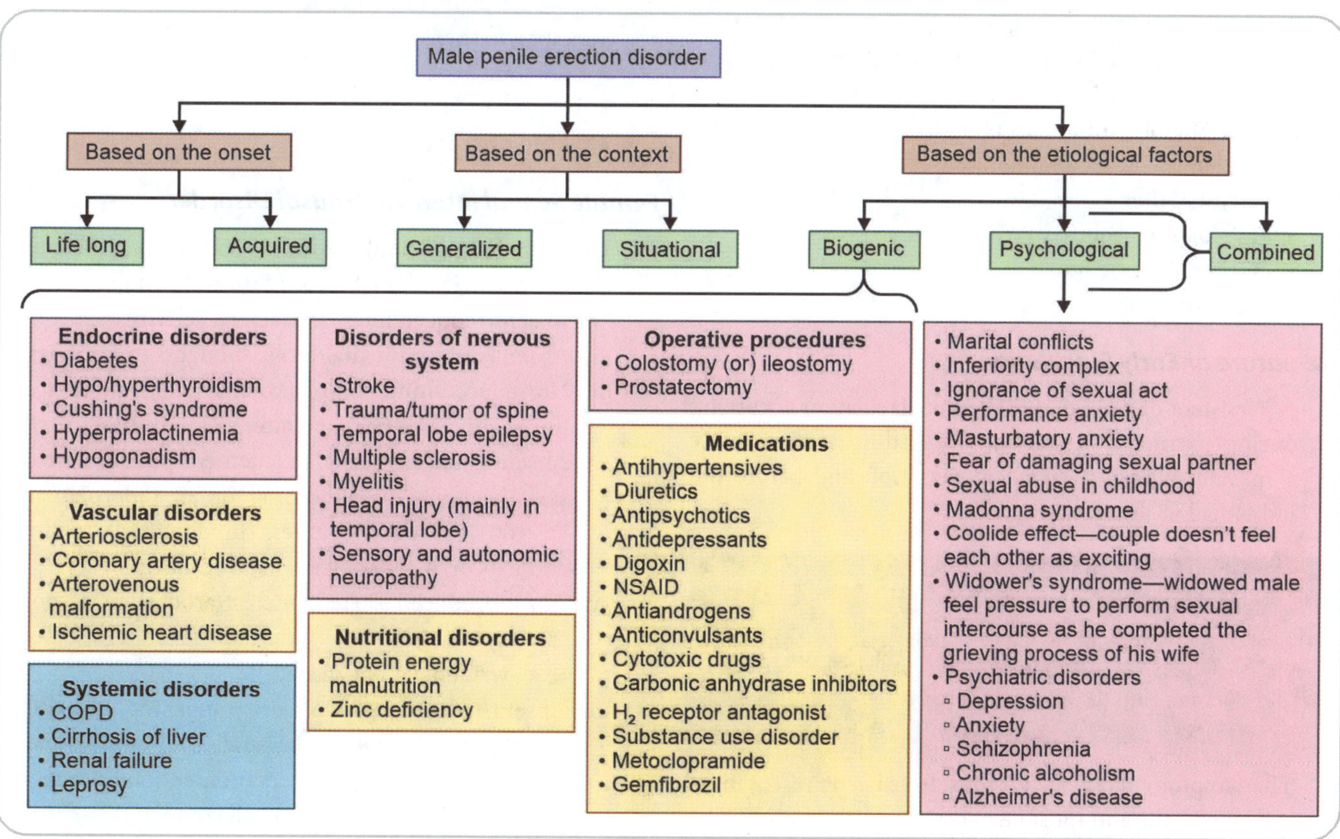

Miscellaneous

- **Sexual disorders related to general medical condition:** Above disorders which occur secondary to general medical conditions come under this category.
- **Substance-induced sexual dysfunction:** Sexual dysfunctions due to substances like nicotine, alcohol dependence or other substances. The drug user loses interest or desire to have sex.
- **Sexual dysfunction not otherwise specified (NOS):** Sexual dysfunctions which have not been discussed above come under this category.

DSM-5 Diagnostic Criteria

Erectile Disorder

- At least one of the following symptoms must be experienced on almost all or all (approximately 75–100%) occasions of sexual activity (in identified situational contexts or, if generalized, in all contexts) such as marked difficulty in obtaining an erection during sexual activity, marked difficulty in maintaining an erection until the completion of sexual activity and marked decrease in erectile rigidity.
- Symptoms are present for minimum duration of 6 months.
- Symptoms cause clinically significant distress in individual.
- Sexual dysfunction is not better explained by a nonsexual mental disorder or as a consequence of severe relationship distress or other significant stressors and is not attributable to the effects of a substance/medication or another medical condition.
- Specify whether
  - Lifelong or acquired
  - Generalized or situational
  - Mild or moderate or severe

Premature or Early Ejaculation

- A persistent or recurrent pattern of ejaculation occurring during partnered sexual activity within approximately 1 minute following vaginal penetration and before the individual wishes it.

NOTE

Although the diagnosis of premature (early) ejaculation may be applied to individuals engaged in nonvaginal sexual activities, specific duration criteria have not been established for these activities.

- The symptom in criterion A must have been present for at least 6 months and must be experienced on almost all or all (approximately 75–100%) occasions of sexual activity (in identified situational contexts or, if generalized, in all contexts).
- The symptom in criterion A causes clinically significant distress in the individual.
- The sexual dysfunction is not better explained by a nonsexual mental disorder or as a consequence of severe relationship distress or other significant stressors and is not attributable to the effects of a substance/medication or another medical conditions.

Delayed Ejaculation

- At least one of the following symptoms must be experienced on almost all or all (approximately 75–100%) occasions of sexual activity (in identified situational contexts or, if generalized, in all contexts) such as marked delay in ejaculation, marked infrequency or absence of ejaculation.
- Symptation of 6 months.
- Symptoms cause clinically significant distress in individual.
- Sexual dysfunction is not better explained by a nonsexual mental disorder or as a consequence of severe relationship distress or other significant stressors and is not attributable to the effects of a substance/medication or another medical condition.
- **Specify whether**
  - Lifelong or acquired
  - Generalized or situational
  - Mild or moderate or severe

Female Sexual Interest /Arousal Disorder

- Lack of, or significantly reduced, sexual interest/arousal, as manifested by at least three of the following:
  - i. Absent/reduced interest in sexual activity.
  - ii. Absent/reduced sexual/erotic thoughts or fantasies.
  - iii. No/reduced initiation of sexual activity, and typically unreceptive to a partner's attempts to initiate.
  - iv. Absent/reduced sexual excitement/pleasure during sexual activity in almost all or all (approximately 75–100%) sexual encounters (in identified situational contexts or, if generalized, in all contexts).
  - v. Absent/reduced sexual interest/arousal in response to any internal or external sexual/erotic cues (e.g., written, verbal, visual).
  - vi. Absent/reduced genital or nongenital sensations during sexual activity in almost all or all (approximately 75–100%) sexual encounters (in identified situational contexts or, if generalized, in all contexts).

- Symptoms present with the minimum duration of 6 months.
- Symptoms cause clinically significant distress in individual.
- Sexual dysfunction is not better explained by a nonsexual mental disorder or as a consequence of severe relationship distress (e.g., partner violence) or other significant stressors and is not attributable to the effects of a substance/medication or another medical condition.

Gender Dysphoria in Adults/Adolescents

- Marked incongruence between one's experienced/expressed gender and assigned gender, of at least 6 months duration, as manifested by at least two of the following:
  - i. A marked incongruence between one's experienced/expressed gender and primary and/or secondary sex characteristics (or in young adolescents, the anticipated secondary sex characteristics).
  - ii. A strong desire to get rid of one's primary and/or secondary sex characteristics because of a marked incongruence with one's experienced/expressed gender (or in young adolescents, a desire to prevent the development of the anticipated secondary sex characteristics).
  - iii. A strong desire for the primary and/or secondary sex characteristics of the other gender.
  - iv. A strong desire to be of the other gender (or some alternative gender different from one's assigned gender).
  - v. A strong desire to be treated as the other gender (or some alternative gender different from one's assigned gender).
  - vi. A strong conviction that one has the typical feelings and reactions of the other gender (or some alternative gender different from one's assigned gender.
- The condition is associated with clinically significant distress or impairment in social, occupational, or other important areas of functioning.

PERSONALITY DISORDERS

INTRODUCTION

Personality is defined as enduring qualities of a person in various circumstances. These qualities develop into personality traits (characters). When these traits become abnormal, inflexible and maladaptive, they cause significant personal distress and cause social/occupational impairment which may lead to personality disorders as shown in Flowchart 10.3.

Flowchart 10.3: Concept of personality disorders

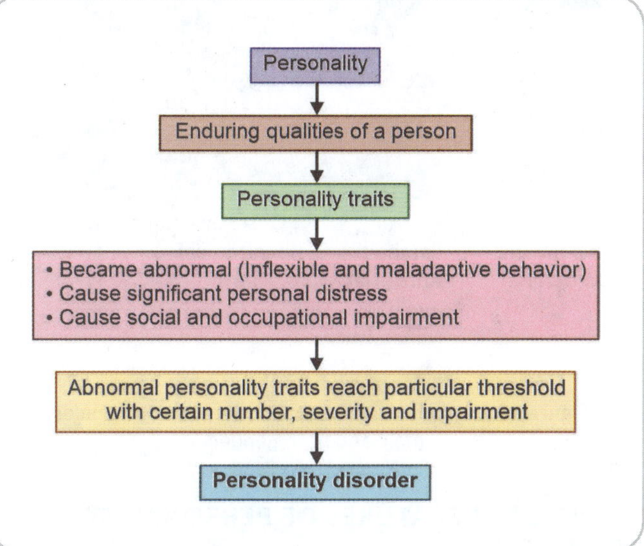

NOTE

Personality is a combination of traits. Abnormal traits do not denote abnormal personality until an abnormal personality trait reaches a particular threshold with certain number, severity and impairment to label it as 'personality disorder.'

DEFINITION OF PERSONALITY DISORDER

- Personality disorder is defined as, "Characteristic and enduring pattern of inner experience or behavior as a whole marked deviation from level of expectation and acceptable range of individual's culture."
  —*International Classification of Diseases (ICD-10)*
- Personality disorder is defined as, "Enduring pattern of inner experience and behavior has marked deviation from expectation individual's culture."
  —*Diagnostic Static Manual (DSM-5)*

INCIDENCE AND PREVALENCE

Around 5–10% of general population suffers from personality disorders. Borderline personality disorder is more common in psychiatric setups. Antisocial personality is common among prison inmates. Mixed personality disorder is more common than single type. Common personality disorders in females and males separately and common in both genders are shown in Figure 10.2.

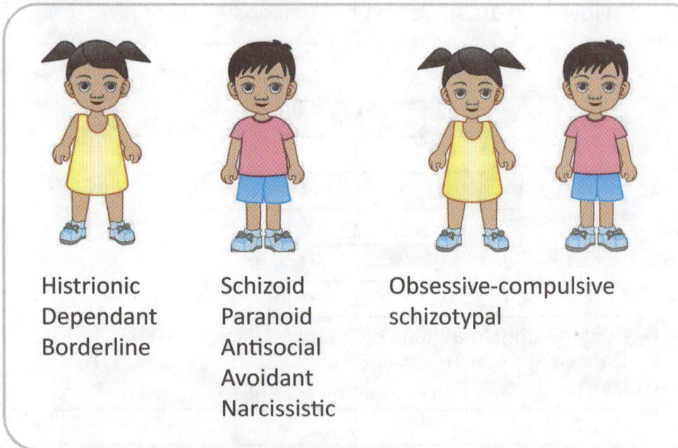

Figure 10.2: Common personality disorders in females, male and both gender

SIGNIFICANT FEATURES OF PERSONALITY DISORDERS

Maladaptive, persistent and inflexible patterns of:
- Thinking (about self and others)
- Feeling (intensity/range of emotions)
- Behavior
- Interpersonal relationship

They cause significant personal distress and impairment in interpersonal or self-functioning. Onset is stable since childhood or adolescence. They do not meet criteria to diagnose other psychiatric disorder or organic disorder.

ETIOLOGY OF PERSONALITY DISORDERS

Increased levels of testosterone, 17-estradiol and estrone and increased level of dopamine and serotonin will cause aggression, impulsivity and change in electrical conductance on EEG seen in antisocial or borderline personality disorder.

CLASSIFICATION OF PERSONALITY DISORDERS

ICD-11 Classification of Personality Disorders

It focuses on core personality dysfunction, while allowing the classification on three levels as mild, moderate and severe personality disorders.

Prominent personality traits or patterns: Trait domain applied to the personality is most prominent which contributes to personality disturbance. Traits are continuous and represent a set of dimensions which correspond to underlying structure of personality. There may be many trait domain qualifiers that are applied to describe personality functioning. Persons with more severe personality disturbance tend to have a greater number of prominent trait domains.

Contd...

DSM-5 Classification of Personality Disorders

In addition to the above 3 clusters, 25 maladaptive traits are divided into five domains:

1. Negative affectivity
2. Detachment
3. Antagonism
4. Disinhibition Vs. Compulsivity
5. Psychoticism

} Reliable to identify the functional impairment in personality disorders

Classification based on maturity is given in Table 10.5.

Comparison of ICD-10 and DSM-IV/5 Classification of Personality disorders has been given in Table 10.6.

ICD-11 and DSM-5 Classification of personality disorders

ICD-11	DSM-5	
6D10	—	Personality disorders
6D10.0	—	Personality disorders, mild
6D10.1	—	Personality disorders, moderate
6D10.2	—	Personality disorders, severe
6D10.Z	—	Personality disorders, unspecified severity
6D11	—	Predominant personality traits
6D11.0	—	Negative affectivity in personality disorder
6D11.1	—	Detachment in personality disorder
6D11.2	—	Dissociality in personality disorder
6D11.3	—	Disinhibition in personality disorder
6D11.4	—	Anankastic personality disorder
6D11.5	—	Borderline pattern personality disorder
Cluster A personality disorders		
—	301.0	Paranoid personality disorder
—	301.20	Schizoid personality disorder
—	301.22	Schizotypal personality disorder
Cluster B personality disorders		
—	301.7	Antisocial personality disorder
—	301.83	Borderline personality disorder
—	301.50	Histrionic personality disorder
—	301.81	Narcissistic personality disorder
Cluster C personality disorders		
—	301.4	Obsessive-compulsive personality disorder
—	301.82	Avoidant personality disorder
—	301.6	Dependent personality disorder
Other personality disorders		
	310.1	Personality changes due to another medical condition
	301.89	Other specified personality disorder

Table 10.5: Classification of personality disorders based on maturity

Immature personality disorder	Mature personality disorder
• Antisocial/Dissocial • Borderline/Emotionally unstable • Histrionic • Dependent • Narcissistic	• Anankastic/Obsessive compulsive • Anxious/Avoidant • Paranoid • Schizoid • Schizotypal

Table 10.6: Comparison of ICD-11 and DSM-5 classification of personality disorders

Types of personality disorders	DSM-5 (Cluster)	ICD-11
Paranoid personality disorder	A	—
Schizoid personality disorder	A	—
Schizotypal personality disorder	A	—
Antisocial personality disorder	B	—
Borderline personality disorder	B	Yes (borderline pattern personality disorder)
Histrionic personality disorder	B	—
Narcissistic personality disorder	B	Yes (dissociality in personality disorder)
Avoidant personality disorder	C	Yes (detachment in personality disorder)
Dependent personality disorder	C	—
Obsessive -compulsive personality disorder.	C	Yes (anankastic personality disorder)

PROTECTIVE AND RISK FACTORS OF PERSONALITY DISORDERS

Protective and risk factors of personality disorders are summarized in Table 10.7.

Table 10.7: Protective and risk factors of personality disorders

Risk factors of personality disorders	Protective factors of personality disorder
• School drop outs • Unemployment • Divorced/separated • Unmarried • History of child abuse • Neglect from parents	• Establishing a strong trusting relationship with parents • Married • Employed • Good interpersonal relationship • Individuals who are extrovert

Types of personality disorders have been given in Table 10.8.

Table 10.8: Types of personality disorders

Types of personality disorders	Psychodynamic factor (defense mechanism)	Signs and symptoms/criteria for diagnosis	Differential diagnosis/comorbid illness
Paranoid personality disorder	Projection	• Suspiciousness/mistrust • Excess sensitive to criticism • Doubts the loyalty of friends • Suspicious of sexual partner fidelity • Interpret remarks as threatening • Hold 'grudges' (Unable to forget/forgive) • Become angry and threaten when he/she perceives as being attacked by someone	• Paranoid schizophrenia • Persistent delusional disorder

Contd...

Types of personality disorders	Psychodynamic factor (defense mechanism)	Signs and symptoms/criteria for diagnosis	Differential diagnosis/comorbid illness
Schizoid personality disorder	Emotional detachment (to relieve from emotional pain)	• Emotional coldness • Blunted or flat affect • Lack of humor sense • Prefer solitary activities • Introspective • Indifference with praise or criticism • Inability to express both positive and negative feelings • Lack of desire to enjoy relationships • Aloof (loneliness) • Prefer to have social distance even with own family members	• Simple schizophrenia • Negative symptoms of schizophrenia • Depression • Autism spectrum disorder
Schizotypal personality disorder	Fantasy (escape from reality)	• Odd, eccentric behavior • Social withdrawal • No close relation with others • Inappropriate and constricted affect • Magical thinking • Paranoid ideation • Ruminations with violence and sexual themes • Vague and circumstantial speech • Depersonalization • Derealization • Illusions	• Schizophrenia • Unspecified psychosis
Antisocial personality disorder	• Denial • Acting out • Externalization	• Violates rules and regulations/social norms • Fails to maintain relationship • Impulsive action • Low frustration tolerance • Absence of guilt • Manipulation in activities to get self-gratification • Unconcern with safety of others • Not able to learn from punishment • Blame others for one's own antisocial activities • Deceitfulness: Frequent lying or cheating others to gain profit as well as pleasure	• Schizophrenia • Unspecified psychosis
Borderline personality disorder or Borderline pattern personality disorder	• Projection • Projective identification • Dissociation • Splitting	• Impulsivity • Chronic feel of emptiness • Unstable affect (intense anxiety/irritable within few hours) • Unstable relationships • Unstable self-image • Self-mutilation (threats of self-harm) • Unable to control anger • Transient dissociative symptoms during stress • Paranoid ideas • Tendency to act out impulsivity without considering the consequences (e.g., driving very fast, binge eating)	• Acute transient Psychosis • Adult attention deficit hyperactive disorder • Mixed state bipolar disorder • Cyclothymia • Rapid cycling bipolar disorder
Histrionic personality disorder	• Regression • Somatization	• Self-dramatization • Attention-seeking behavior • Labile affect • Exaggerated way of expressing emotions • More concern in regard to physical attractiveness • Emotional blackmail/suicide attempts • Crave for excitement • Impulsive behavior • Uncomfortable with situations when other persons are around/being a guest • Easily influenced by others	• Hypomania • Somatization disorder • Narcissistic personality disorder

Contd...

Types of personality disorders	Psychodynamic factor (defense mechanism)	Signs and symptoms/criteria for diagnosis	Differential diagnosis/comorbid illness
Narcissistic personality disorder or Dissociality in Personality disorder	• Reaction formation • Self-importance • Denial • Omnipotence • Fragile self-esteem	• Attention seeking • Arrogance • Strong belief that, he/she is special • Feel to have relation with high status people • Envious of others but, verbalizes that others are envious to self • No empathy • Difficulty to face criticism of others • Preoccupied with fantasy world of success, beauty and power	• Hypomania • Histrionic personality disorder
Avoidant personality disorder or Detachment in personality disorder	• Fixation at oral stage • Parenting style (over-rigid/over-protective) • Childhood attachment problems	• Avoid activities which need to done in interpersonal relationship • Continuous tension and apprehension • Fear of criticism/rejection • Feel inferior than others • Not willing to get along with others • Preoccupied with criticism/rejection by others	• Social phobia • Obsessive compulsive disorder • Somatoform disorder • Schizophrenia • Anxiety • Depression • Schizoid personality disorder
Dependent personality disorder	• Regression • Idealization of others • Devaluation of self	• Depend on others more for psychological support • Inability to take decision • Allow others to take important decisions in life • Subordinating the one's own needs than to the others needs • Difficult to express unwillingness due to fear • Not willing to make reasonable demands to others • Low self esteem • Feel helpless by being alone • Lack of self-confidence	• Dysthymia • Depressive disorder
Obsessive-compulsive personality disorder or Anankastic personality disorder	• Fixation at oral stage • Reaction formation • Undoing	• Preoccupied with perfectionism • Thinking of orderliness always • Excessive doubtfulness • Rigid and stubborn • Preoccupied with rules, list, details, schedules, etc. which interfere with the daily routines • Tendency to hoard/unable to throw the useless object even though he/she doesn't have any sentimental value	Obsessive compulsive disorder

Miscellaneous Personality Disorder as per ICD-11

Comparative diagnostic criteria of mild, moderate and severe personality disorders as per ICD-11 are presented in Table 10.9.

Disinhibition in Personality Disorder or Personality Difficulty

Core feature of this trait domain is the tendency to act rashly based on immediate external or internal stimuli without consideration of the possible negative consequences. Common manifestations include distractibility, impulsivity, recklessness irresponsibility and lack of planning.

Negative Affectivity in Personality Disorder or Personality Difficulty

Core feature of this trait domain is the tendency to experience negative emotions. Common manifestations include experiencing a broad range of negative emotions with a frequency and intensity out of proportion to the situation, negativistic attitude, emotional lability and poor emotion regulation, low self-esteem or self-confidence and mistrustfulness.

Table: 10.9: **Comparative diagnostic criteria of mild, moderate and severe personality disorders as per ICD-11**

Diagnostic criteria as per ICD-11	Mild personality disorder	Moderate personality disorder	Severe personality disorder
Diagnostic requirements of personality disorder are met	Yes	Yes	Yes
Disturbances which affect personality functioning	In some areas	In multiple areas	Severely affected in the functioning of the self
Problems in the Interpersonal relationships	Present	Marked problems in most cases	Seriously affected
Specific manifestations of personality disturbances	Mild degree	Moderate degree	Severe degree
Substantial harm to self or others	Absent	Sometimes	Often
Personal, family, social, educational, occupational or other important areas of functioning	Mild impairment	Marked impairment	Severe impairment

ANTISOCIAL PERSONALITY DISORDER

Patients with antisocial personality disorder mainly violate the social norms and lead to criminal activity. Concept of conduct disorder develops into antisocial personality disorder as shown in Flowchart 10.4. Previously, antisocial personality disorder had four clinical types such as aggressive psychopath, inadequate psychopath, creative psychopath and sexual psychopath.

According to Theodore Millon, five subtypes of antisocial behavior:

1. **Nomadic:** Schizoid and avoidant
2. **Malevolent:** Sadistic and paranoid
3. **Covetous:** Pure form of antisocial behavior
4. **Risk taking:** Histrionic
5. **Reputation defending:** Narcissistic

NOTE

All of the above-mentioned other terms of antisocial personality disorders have been used previously, but are not used these days. The other terms of antisocial personality disorder include psychopathic personality, sociopathic personality, semantic disorder, dangerous and severe personality.

Etiology

- **Psychological factors:** Family having a criminal offender, single parenthood, alcoholism, family disputes, lack of supervision, and history of child abuse.
- **Biological factors:** Presence of monoamine oxidase A (MAO-A) gene, smoking during pregnancy, decreased function of right brain hemisphere and decreased resting heart rate.

Flowchart 10.4: Concept of conduct disorder develops into antisocial personality disorder

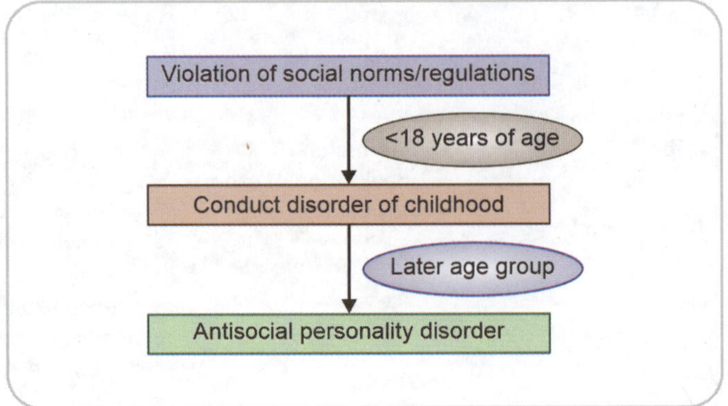

- **Psychodynamic factors:** Use of defense mechanism such as denial, acting out and externalization.

DSM-5 Criteria for Antisocial Personality Disorder

- A pervasive pattern of disregard for violation of the rights of others, occurring since age 15 years, as indicated by three (or more) of the following:
  i. Failure to conform to social norms with respect to lawful behaviors, as indicated by repeatedly performing acts that are grounds for arrest.
  ii. Deceitfulness, as indicated by repeated lying, use of aliases, or conning others for personal profit or pleasure.
  iii. Impulsivity or failure to plan ahead.
  iv. Irritability and aggressiveness, as indicated by repeated physical fights or assaults.
  v. Reckless disregard for safety of self or others.

vi. Consistent irresponsibility, as indicated by repeated failure to sustain consistent work behavior or honor financial obligations.
vii. Lack of remorse, as indicated by being indifferent to or rationalizing having hurt, mistreated, or stolen from another.

- The individual is at least 18-year-old.
- There is evidence of conduct disorder with onset before age 15 years.
- The occurrence of antisocial behavior is not exclusively during the course of schizophrenia or bipolar disorder.

Treatment for Antisocial Personality Disorder

Individual psychotherapy, group psychotherapy, psychoanalysis and use of drugs: Antipsychotics like pericyazine are used for this purpose.

Nursing Interventions for Antisocial Personality Disorder

Nurse has to accept the patient as he/she is. Nurse can maintain calm attitude with patient and convey the message clearly to the patient that he/she is acceptable whereas his abnormal behavior is not acceptable. Nurse has to remove the sharp objects which is present near the patient. Nurse has to set limits with patient when the behavior is found to be out of boundaries. Nurse should provide physical restraint, if patient harms self or others. Nurse can explore the numerous ways of expressing his/her negative emotions in a constructive way and encourage the patient to ventilate hostile feelings. Nurse should show helping attitude to patient and also a positive reinforcement. Nurse can help patient to gain insight into one's behavior and administer sedatives as prescribed, if necessary.

BORDERLINE PERSONALITY DISORDER

Tendency to act out of impulsivity without considering the consequences along with unstable effects. Borderline personality disorder is also called **borderline pattern personality disorder** as per ICD-11 and **emotionally unstable personality disorder** as per ICD-10. Emotionally unstable personality disorder has two subtypes such as:

1. **Impulsive type** is characterized by unstable emotions and unable to control impulses. Anger outburst and violent behavior in response to criticism are common.
2. **Borderline type** is characterized by unstable emotions along with disturbed self-image. Feeling of emptiness and lack of stability in relationship cause emotional crisis and further lead to suicidal threats. Borderline personality was previously known as ambulatory schizophrenia and pseudoneurotic schizophrenia was previously considered subtype of schizophrenia.
   - **Ambulatory schizophrenia** is a mild level of schizophrenia in which the individual can be managed well in community without hospitalization.
   - **Pseudoneurotic schizophrenia** is presence of two or more psychiatric illnesses such as phobia, anxiety, hysteria and obsessive-compulsive neurosis.

Etiology

- **Psychological factors:** History of child abuse, neglect during childhood, family disputes and lack of supervision.
- **Biological factors:** Hypothalamic-pituitary-adrenal axis dysfunction and serotonin dysfunction lead to impulsivity. Other reasons may be the presence of serotonin transporter (5-HTT), tryptophan hydroxylase (TPH) gene, dopamine and noradrenaline dysfunction.
- **Psychodynamic factors:** Defense mechanism such as—projection, projective identification, dissociation, and splitting

ICD-11 Diagnostic Criteria for Borderline Pattern Personality Disorder

Pervasive pattern of instability of interpersonal relationships, self-image, and affects, and marked impulsivity, as indicated by many of the following:

- Frantic efforts to avoid real or imagined abandonment.
- A pattern of unstable and intense interpersonal relationships.
- Identity disturbance, manifested in markedly and persistently unstable self-image or sense of self.
- A tendency to act rashly in states of high negative affect, leading to potentially self-damaging behaviors.
- Recurrent episodes of self-harm; Emotional instability due to marked reactivity of mood; Chronic feelings of emptiness.
- Inappropriate intense anger or difficulty controlling anger
- Transient dissociative symptoms or psychotic-like features in situations of high affective arousal.

DSM-5 Diagnostic Criteria for Borderline Personality Disorder

A pervasive pattern of instability of interpersonal relationships, self-image, and affects, and marked impulsivity, beginning by early adulthood and present in a variety of contexts, as indicated by five (or more) of the following:

1. Frantic efforts to avoid real or imagined abandonment.
2. A pattern of unstable and intense interpersonal relationships characterized by alternating between extremes of idealization and devaluation.
3. Identity disturbance: Markedly and persistently unstable self-image or sense of self.
4. Impulsivity in at least two areas that are potentially self-damaging (e.g., spending, sex, substance abuse, reckless driving, binge eating).
5. Recurrent suicidal behavior, gestures, or threats, or self-mutilating behavior.
6. Affective instability due to a marked reactivity of mood (e.g., intense episodic dysphoria, irritability, or anxiety usually lasting a few hours and only rarely more than a few days).
7. Chronic feelings of emptiness.
8. Inappropriate, intense anger or difficulty controlling anger (e.g., frequent displays of temper, constant anger, recurrent physical fights).
9. Transient, stress-related paranoid ideation or severe dissociative symptom.

Treatment

- Dialectical behavior therapy (DBT)
- Psychodynamic psychotherapy
- Transference-focused psychotherapy (TFP)
- Mentalization-based therapy (MTP)
- Supportive psychotherapy
- Emotion regulation training
- Drugs—Antidepressants, antipsychotics, carbamazepine and lithium.
- Electroconvulsive therapy (ECT)—Occasionally if needed.

Nursing Interventions for Borderline Personality Disorder

Nurse has to observe the patient frequently and not to be suspicious of the patient. Nurse has to establish a no-suicidal contract with the patient to prevent self-mutilation. Nurse can assign one separate staff to observe the patient in case of emergency. Nurse has to encourage the patient to ventilate the stressful feelings and set limits with certain behavior which is unacceptable or out of boundaries. Nurse has to be conscious that patient should not develop dependence on staff nurse and so assigning the different nurse on shift basis is important. Nurse can encourage the patient to explore the situation causing fear and give positive reinforcement to the acceptable behavior.

GERIATRIC CONSIDERATIONS

Personality disorder is not going to be the first diagnosis in old age period. It will be present from young adulthood onwards. Individuals with personality disorders will experience more difficulties in late period of life. Elders with personality disorders are unable to take decisions in regard to their health, finance and their living pattern. They are found dissatisfied with life, difficult to maintain relationships, alienation from friends, relatives and care givers. Constant support and holistic care will be required for taking care of the elders.

Follow-up, Home Care and Rehabilitation

In general, prognosis of these patients is poor so lifelong care is needed. Family members have to be taught that the patient might self-mutilate or attempt suicide or injury to self/others. Limit setting has to be done with the patient in order to control the manipulative behavior. Patient can also verbalize the situation which provokes anger, instead of being aggressive. Nurse should reinforce the realistic perceptions/appraisal every time. Encourage the patient to perform simple decision making. Nurse should identify the stressors and manage them effectively. Drug adherence plays a vital role to control the symptoms.

EATING DISORDERS

Eating disorders are characterized by severe form of disturbances in eating pattern/behavior leading to life threatening conditions.

ETIOLOGY OF EATING DISORDER

- **Neurobiology:** Decreased endogenous opioid, hypothalamus dysregulation (alters gonad or corticoid production leads to amenorrhea), biochemical tests (increased cortisol level), Positron Emission Tomography (PET) shows a decreased metabolism of caudate nucleus, altered function of dopamine, serotonin and norepinephrine.
- **Psychoanalytical:** According to Mahler, restriction of separation-individuation and autonomy (independence) stage in the theory of child development may lead to anorexia nervosa.
- **Social factors:** Influence of mass media or individuals with certain occupation might give importance to their weight, e.g., dancers, beauty contestants.
- **Psychological factors:** Low self-esteem, perfectionism and family disputes.

ICD-11 and DSM-5 Classification of Eating Disorders

ICD-11	DSM-5	Classification of eating disorders
6B80	307.1	Anorexia nervosa
6B80.10	—	Restricting type
6B80.11		Binge eating/Purging type
6B81	307.51	Bulimia nervosa
6B82	307.51	Binge eating disorder
6B83	307.59	Avoidant/Restrictive food intake disorder
6B84	307.52	Pica
6B85	307.53	Rumination disorder
6B8Y	307.59	Other specified feeding or eating disorder
6B8Z	307.50	Unspecified feeding or eating disorder

DSM-5 Diagnostic Criteria for Eating Disorders

Anorexia nervosa

- Restriction of energy intake relative to requirements, leads to the significantly low body weight in context of age, gender, development and physical health.
- Intense fear of gaining weight, even though at a significantly low weight.
- Persistent lack of recognition of the seriousness of the current low body weight.

Bulimia nervosa

- Binge eating within short duration of time
- No control over eating
- Immediate compensatory behavior is present (e.g., inducted vomiting, use of diuretics, etc.)
- Self-evaluation of raised body weight or appearance.
- Disturbances do not occur during the episode of anorexia nervosa.

Binge eating

- Binge eating episodes are associated with three or more of the following features such as:
    i. Eating much more rapidly than normal.
    ii. Eating until feeling uncomfortably full.
    iii. Eating large amounts of food when not feeling physically hungry.
    iv. Eating alone because of feeling embarrassed by how much one is eating.
    v. Feeling disgusted with oneself, depressed, or very guilty afterward.
    vi. Increased food intake within short period of time.
- Unable to control the behavior.
- Marked distress in regard to the Binge eating.
- Binge eating happens at least once a week for 3 months.
- Will not use any compensatory behavior (purging/nonpurging).
- Does not occur exclusively during the course of bulimia nervosa or anorexia nervosa.

Avoidant-restrictive food intake disorder

- Insufficient quantity of food intake to meet the required energy or nutritional requirements.
- Pattern of restricted eating has caused significant weight loss that leads to the dependence on oral nutritional supplements or tube feeding causing the significant functional impairment.
- Pattern of eating behavior does not reflect concerns about body weight or shape.

Restricted food intake is not better accounted for lack of food availability, the effects of medication or substance or another health condition.

Pica

- Regular consumption of non-nutritive non-food objects such as clay, soil, chalk, plaster, plastic, metal and paper or raw food ingredients such as large quantities of salt or cornflour.
- Applicable to the individual who has reached a developmental age approximately 2 years (able to distinguish between edible and non-edible substances).
- Behavior causes damage to health and impairment in functioning.

Contd...

Rumination-regurgitation disorder
- Intentional and repeated bringing up of previously swallowed food back to mouth (i.e., regurgitation), which may be re-chewed and re-swallowed (i.e., rumination), or may be deliberately spat out (but not as in vomiting).
- Regurgitation behavior is frequent and sustained for several weeks.
- Regurgitation behavior is not fully accounted for by another medical conditions which cause regurgitation.
- Applicable to the individual who reached the developmental age of at least 2 years.

Common Comorbid conditions with eating disorder:
- **Affective disorders:** Depression and dysthymia.
- **Personality disorder:** Borderline personality disorder and dependent personality disorder.
- **Substance abuse:** Alcohol, nicotine, cocaine and other substances.
- **Neurosis:** Generalized anxiety disorder, panic disorder and obsessive-compulsive disorder.

COMPARISON OF ANOREXIA NERVOSA AND BULIMIA NERVOSA

Comparison of anorexia nervosa and bulimia nervosa is given in Table 10.10.

Table 10.10: Comparison of anorexia nervosa and bulimia nervosa

Aspects	Anorexia nervosa	Bulimia nervosa
Age of onset	14–16 years	18–24 years
Lifetime prevalence	1–3%	0.5–1%
Gender	Female	
Main symptoms	Fear of being obese	
Weight loss	85% of expected weight	Normal or decreased
Complications	Starvation, Hypotension, Hypothermia and shock	Dental/Enamel erosion, dehydration, hypokalemia, esophageal tear
Post binge anguish	Absent	Present
Awareness of illness	Absent	Present
Types	• Restricted type (Not eating food) • Binge eating/ Purging type	• Purging type ▪ Direct—vomiting ▪ Indirect—use of laxatives or enema • Nonpurging type (starvation and exercise)

COMPLICATIONS OF EATING DISORDERS

The complications of eating disorders have been given in Table 10.11.

Table 10.11: Complications of eating disorders

Aspects	Complications of eating disorders
Cardiovascular	Bradycardia Myocarditis Arrhythmias Heart failure Hypotension } Abuse of Ipecac Syrup
Endocrine	Amenorrhea Imbalance of: • Luteinizing hormone (LH) • Follicle-Stimulating Hormone (FSH) • Cortisol • Estrogen/Testosterone • Thyroxine and Tri-iodothyronine Irregular menses Hypoglycemia
Fluids and electrolytes	Metabolic alkalosis (due to vomiting) Metabolic acidosis (due to diarrhea) Hypokalemia Hypochloremia Hyponatremia Dehydration } Purging/vomiting
Gastrointestinal	Enlargement of parotid gland Severe abdominal pain Esophagitis Raised liver function test } Purging/ vomiting Fungal infection of rectum Irritable bowel syndrome Constipation Rectal prolapse/abscess/ bleeding } Use of enema/ laxatives
Hematology	• Mild anemia • Leukopenia
Dental	Dental and enamel erosion (due to vomiting)
Renal	Renal failure
Musculoskeletal	• Muscle wasting • Osteoporosis
Psychological	• Preoccupied with thoughts of food • Symptoms of depression • Restricted emotional expression • Fear of weight gain
Miscellaneous	• Lethargy • Lanugo • Body image disturbances • Cold intolerance

CATEGORIES OF EATING DISORDERS

- **Anorexia nervosa**
  - **Restricting type:** Weight loss by excess starvation or rigid exercise.
  - **Binge eating/purging type:** Weight loss by binge eating and purging (use of laxatives, diuretics and self-vomiting) in this episode.
- **Bulimia nervosa**
  - **Purging type:** Induce vomiting by self or misuse of enemas, diuretics or laxatives.
  - **Nonpurging type:** Compensatory behaviors such as starvation/fasting or excess exercise but do not induce vomiting by self or misuse of enemas, diuretics or laxatives.

ASSESSMENT OF EATING DISORDERS

- **Questionnaire**
  - Body Image Assessment (BIA)
  - Eating Attitude Test (EAT)
  - Private Body Talk Questionnaire (PBTQ)
  - Eating Habits Questionnaire (EHQ)
  - Body Exposure in Sexual Activity Questionnaire (BESAQ)
  - Body Image Automatic Thoughts Questionnaire (BIATQ)
  - Situational Inventory of Body Image Dysphoria (SIBID)
  - Bulimic Inventory Test, Edinburgh (BITE)
  - Appearance Schemas Inventory (ASI)
- Waist to hip ratio
- Body Mass index or Quetelet's index = Weight (kg)/ Height (m^2)
- Ratio of skin fold
  - Trunk compared with extremities
  - Upper arm compared with upper trunk
- To assess body fat and distribution—USG, MRI, CT scan, body electrical conductivity and dual photon absorptiometry can be used.

NURSING DIAGNOSIS

- Impaired nutrition less than body requirement related to not eating food.
- Impaired nutrition more than body requirement related to improper eating pattern.
- Fluid volume deficit related to compensatory behavior of eating disorder.
- Body image disturbances related to poor ego development.
- Anxiety related to impaired coping skills as evidenced by anxious facial expression.
- Activity intolerance related to poor food intake.
- Low self-esteem related to distorted body image.
- Diarrhea related to laxative use.
- Constipation related to reduced fluid intake.
- Fatigue related to poor intake of food.

SIGNS AND SYMPTOMS OF EATING DISORDERS REVEALED DURING PHYSICAL ASSESSMENT

Enlarged parotid gland, dental and enamel erosion (due to vomiting), muscle wasting, constipation, anemia, severe abdominal pain, lethargy/fatigue and Russell's sign (Callus Knuckles due to self-induced vomiting are seen in eating disorders) (Figure 10.3).

TREATMENT OF EATING DISORDERS

Treatment of Bulimia Nervosa

- **Psychoeducation:** Focus on normal eating patterns:
  - **Self-monitoring technique:** Maintaining food diary which accounts daily food intake/binging and self-vomiting or frequent usage of laxatives.
  - **Nutritional counseling:** Balanced diet, no binge eating, follow regular meal timing, etc.
  - **Cognitive behavior therapy:** Negative cognition about the food needs to be changed into right thoughts and make the patient to perform correct action.
- **Medications:** Antidepressants such as fluoxetine, desipramine, Bupropion, imipramine, trazodone and

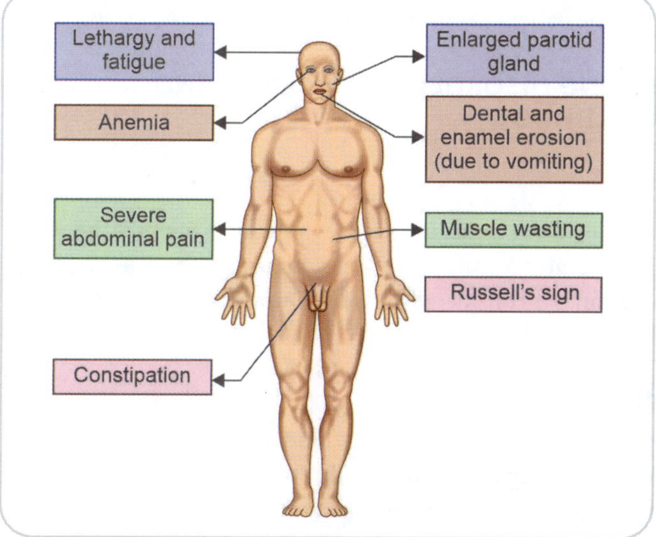

Figure 10.3: Signs and symptoms of eating disorders revealed during physical assessment

Monoamine oxidase inhibitors (MAOIs) are used as medicines. Other medications such as phenytoin (if EEG abnormalities present) and lithium are also useful.
- **Nursing interventions:** Maintain intake output chart. Monitor the weight and ensure the normal weight. Encourage the patient to say about the feelings of fear and anxiety. Supervise the eating pattern, it should be at least 3000 calories per day. Obtain the goal to gain 0.5–1 kg per week. Monitor serum electrolyte level and make the restroom nonaccessible immediately after taking food to prevent vomiting.
- **Miscellaneous:** Relaxation therapy, skills training, stress management and problem solving measures.

Treatment of Anorexia Nervosa

- **Psychological therapies:** Self-monitoring, desensitization, cognitive restructuring and relaxation therapy.
- **Medications:** Antidepressants (tricyclic antidepressants, selective serotonin reuptake inhibitors (fluoxetine), atypical antipsychotics (pimozide, chlorpromazine) and other medications (cyproheptadine, lithium).
- **Nursing interventions:** Advise the patient to self-monitor the food diary to supervise oneself regularly. Nurse can teach the family members to promote trust on the patient. Nurse can keep time limit for each meal. Maintain the eating contract with patient to ensure specific amount of food will be taken on particular timings. Nurse can encourage the patient to ventilate the fear/anxiety about the eating patterns. Nurse can assess the suicidal risk. Ryle's tube feeding can be initiated if the patient is persistently refusing to take food. Nurse has to teach assertiveness and engage the patient in role play and teach the patient about community help groups after discharge.

EATING DISORDERS OF INFANCY AND CHILDHOOD

PICA

Pica is defined as eating the nonedible items. The onset is beyond the milestone development, eating a nonedible substance is considered disorder. Duration of symptoms might last for few months to years.

Types of Pica

- Geophagia—Eating sand, mud and soil
- Xylophagia—Eating wood
- Hyalophagia—Eating glasses
- Tricophagia—Eating hair
- Coprophagia—Eating feces
- Urophagia—Eating urine
- Pagophagia—Eating ice

Epidemiology

- Common in both genders, 15% chances in case of mental retardation.
- Comorbid illnesses: Schizophrenia, anorexia nervosa, bulimia nervosa and autism.

Differential Diagnosis

Zinc and iron deficiency.

Treatment

Positive and negative reinforcement.

Rumination Disorder

Regurgitation of the eaten substances and chewing out without vomiting is called rumination disorder.

Etiology

Link with gastrocolic reflex.

Differential Diagnosis

Pyloric stenosis (will have projectile vomiting).

Treatment

Child guidance clinics, antipsychotics, ranitidine (H_2 receptor antagonist) pantoprazole (proton pump inhibitors) and metoclopramide (to empty the stomach contents).

OBESITY

Excessive accumulation of body fat is termed obesity. In general, obesity is assessed by body mass index or Quetelet's index = Weight (kg)/Height (m^2) (Table 10.12).

Etiology of Obesity

- **Neurotransmitters:** Altered function of dopamine, serotonin and norepinephrine.
- **Hormonal imbalance:** Thyroid stimulating hormone, gonadotropin stimulating hormone and obestatin.
- **Miscellaneous:** Strong stimulation of olfactory bulb by food odors stimulates to eat more.

Factors Contributing to Obesity

Family history of obesity, developmental factors such as increased number of adipocytes with their size, abnormal fat distribution and decreased leptin, decreased physical exercise, ventromedial hypothalamus damage, mood

disorders (atypical depression, seasonal affective disorder), disease such as Cushing disease, myxedema and psychotropic agents (antipsychotics, antidepressants, mood stabilizers and steroids).

Table 10.12: Categories of weight in body mass index

Categories of weight in body mass index	kg/m^2
Normal	18.5–25
Overweight	25–30
Obesity Class I (moderate)	30–35
Obesity Class II (severe)	35–40
Obesity Class III (very severe)	40–45
Obesity Class IV (morbid)	45–50

Differential Diagnosis

- **Night eating syndrome:** Overeating at night time with sleep problems.
- **Pickwickian syndrome or obesity hypoventilation syndrome:** Individual with obesity fails to breathe deeply which results in decreased oxygen supply in blood.
- **Binge eating syndrome:** Recurrent eating of large amount of food.
- **Dysmorphophobia:** Excess dislike of one's own body.

Management of Obesity

- **Lifestyle modification:** Regular exercises, balanced and nutritious diet, yoga, meditation, drink more water, quit alcohol and smoking.
- **Psychological:** Diet counseling.
- **Medical management:** Lorcaserin, phentermine (approved by Food and Drug Administration) and sibutramine (regulate the neurotransmitters thereby regulate the appetite).
- **Surgical management:** Bariatric surgery (liposuction, gastric banding, duodenal-jejunal bypass surgery).

EXTRA EDGE

ICD-10 Classification of Sexual Disorders

- **F64 Gender identity disorders**
  - F64.0 Transsexualism
  - F64.1 Dual-role transvestism
  - F64.2 Gender identity disorder of childhood
  - F64.8 Other gender identity disorders
  - F64.9 Gender identity disorder, unspecified
- **F65 Disorders of sexual preference**
  - F65.0 Fetishism
  - F65.1 Fetishistic transvestism

Contd...

  - F65.2 Exhibitionism
  - F65.3 Voyeurism
  - F65.4 Pedophilia
  - F65.5 Sadomasochism
  - F65.6 Multiple disorders of sexual preference
  - F65.8 Other disorders of sexual preference
  - F65.9 Disorder of sexual preference, unspecified
- **F66 Psychological and behavioral disorders associated with sexual development and orientation**
  - F66.0 Sexual maturation disorder
  - F66.1 Egodystonic sexual orientation
  - F66.2 Sexual relationship disorder
  - F66.8 Other psychosexual development disorders
  - F66.9 Psychosexual development disorder, unspecified

EXTRA EDGE

ICD-10 Classification of Personality Disorders

- **F60-F69 Disorders of adult personality and behavior**
- **F60 Specific personality disorders**
  - F60.0 Paranoid personality disorder
  - F60.1 Schizoid personality disorder
  - F60.2 Dissocial personality disorder
  - F60.3 Emotionally unstable personality disorder
  - F60.4 Histrionic personality disorder
  - F60.5 Anankastic personality disorder
  - F60.6 Anxious personality disorder
  - F60.7 Dependent personality disorder
  - F60.8 Other specific personality disorders
  - F60.9 Personality disorder, unspecified
- **F61 Mixed and other personality disorders**
  - F61.0 Mixed personality disorders
  - F61.1 Troublesome personality changes
- **F62 Enduring personality changes, not attributable to brain damage and disease**
  - F62.0 Enduring personality change after catastrophic experience
  - F62.1 Enduring personality change after psychiatric illness
  - F62.8 Other enduring personality changes
  - F62.9 Enduring personality change, unspecified
- **F68 Other disorders of adult personality and behavior**
- **F69 Unspecified disorder of adult personality and behavior**

DSM-5 Classification of Personality Disorders

- **Cluster A (odd or eccentric disorders):** Paranoid personality disorder, schizoid personality disorder and schizotypal personality disorder
- **Cluster B (dramatic, emotional or erratic disorders):** Antisocial personality disorder, borderline personality disorder, histrionic personality disorder and narcissistic personality disorder
- **Cluster C (anxious or fearful disorders):** Avoidant personality disorder, dependent personality disorder and obsessive-compulsive personality disorder.

SUMMARY

- Gender identity disorders include transsexualism, dual role transvestism, intersexuality and gender identity disorders of childhood.
- Disorders of sexual preference include exhibitionism, frotteurism, sadism, masochism, sadomasochism, pedophilia, zoophilia (bestiality), klismaphilia, urophilia, coprophilia, necrophilia, telephone or mail scotologia, fetishism and fetishistic transvestism.
- Disorders of sexual maturity include sex maturation disorder, egodystonic sexual orientation disorder/homosexuality, obligatory homosexuality, preferred homosexuality, bisexuality, situational homosexuality, latent homosexuality and sex relationship disorder.
- Disorders of sexual dysfunction include sexual aversion disorder, hypoactive sexual desire disorder, excessive sexual desire disorder (satyriasis in male, nymphomania in female), excitement/sexual arousal disorder (male penile erection disorder, female arousal disorder), orgasmic disorder (anorgasmia in male, anorgasmia in female) and sexual pain disorder (non-organic vaginismus, dyspareunia), sexual disorders related to general medical condition, substance-induced sexual dysfunction and sexual dysfunction not otherwise specified (NOS).
- Personality is defined as enduring qualities of a person in different circumstances. These qualities develop into personality traits (character). When these traits become abnormal, inflexible or maladaptive, they can cause significant personal distress and cause social/occupational impairment which leads to personality disorder.
- Cluster A (odd or eccentric disorders) includes paranoid personality disorder, schizoid personality disorder and schizotypal personality disorder.
- Cluster B (dramatic, emotional or erratic disorders) includes antisocial personality disorder, borderline personality disorder, histrionic personality disorder and narcissistic personality disorder.
- Cluster C (anxious or fearful disorders) includes avoidant personality disorder, dependent personality disorder and obsessive-compulsive personality disorder.
- Eating disorders are characterized by severe form of disturbances in eating pattern/behavior leading toward life threatening condition.
- Types of eating disorders include anorexia nervosa, bulimia nervosa, pica, rumination disorder and obesity.

ASSESS YOURSELF

Long Answer Questions

1. Define personality disorders and explain the etiology, diagnostic criteria and management of antisocial personality disorders.
2. Define eating disorders and classify the types and explain the etiology, diagnostic criteria and the management of patient with eating disorders.

Short Answer Questions

1. Differentiate between anorexia nervosa and bulimia nervosa.
2. What are clinical manifestations of eating disorders?
3. Write about nursing management of patient with eating disorders.

Short Notes

Write short notes on:

1. Sexual disorders
2. Etiology of eating disorders
3. Pica
4. Gender identity disorders
5. Clusters of personality disorders
6. Borderline personality disorder
7. Obesity

Multiple Choice Questions

1. **Regurgitation of the eaten substances and chewing out without vomiting is defined as:**
   a. Pica
   b. Rumination disorder
   c. Anorexia nervosa
   d. Bulimia nervosa
2. **Normal Body Mass Index is ________ kg/m^2.**
   a. 18.5–25
   b. 25–30
   c. 30–35
   d. 35–40
3. **Callus Knuckles due to self-induced vomiting seen in eating disorders is ________.**
   a. Omega sign
   b. Russell's sign
   c. Kernig's sign
   d. Cullen's sign
4. **Post binge eating anguish is ________ in bulimia nervosa.**
   a. Present
   b. Absent
   c. Neither present nor absent
   d. None of the above
5. **Psychodynamic factor (defense mechanism) contributing to paranoid personality disorder is ________.**
   a. Regression
   b. Projection
   c. Fantasy
   d. Reaction formation

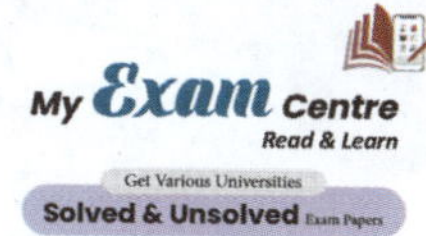

6. **Sexual fantasies and desires of sexual activity occur in:**
   a. Appetitive phase
   b. Excitement phase
   c. Plateau phase
   d. Resolution phase

7. **Eating hair means ________.**
   a. Tricophagia
   b. Urophagia
   c. Coprophagia
   d. Trichotillomania

8. **Wearing the dress of opposite gender for purpose of sexual excitement means _______.**
   a. Transvestism
   b. Transsexualism
   c. Homosexuality
   d. Heterosexuality

9. **Presence of both anatomical and psychological aspect of other sex is called ________.**
   a. Transsexualism
   b. Intersexuality
   c. Sadomasochism
   d. Pedophilia

10. **Common comorbid conditions with eating disorder is __________.**
    a. Substance abuse
    b. Personality disorder
    c. Depression
    d. All of these

ANSWER KEY				
1. b	**2.** a	**3.** b	**4.** a	**5.** b
6. a	**7.** a	**8.** a	**9.** b	**10.** d

Notes

CHAPTER 11

Child Psychiatry

LEARNING OBJECTIVE

After studying this chapter, the student will be able to gain knowledge regarding the child psychiatry in order to render the nursing care to children with psychiatric disorders.

CHAPTER OUTLINE

- Introduction
- Historical Perspectives/Development in Child Psychiatry
- Mental Retardation or Intellectual Disability or Intellectual Developmental Disorder or Mentally Challenged Individuals

Disorders of Psychological Development

- Specific Developmental Disorders of Speech and Language
- Disorders of Language or Specific Language Impairments
- Specific Developmental Disorders of Scholastic Skills
- Autism Spectrum Disorder
- Conduct Disorder
- Juvenile Delinquency
- Separation Anxiety Disorder
- Treatment
- Attention Deficit Hyperactivity Disorder
- Tic Disorder
- Sibling Rivalry
- Enuresis
- Encopresis
- School Refusal or School Phobia
- Sleep Disorders in Children
- Miscellaneous Adult Psychiatric Disorders Present in Children
- Feeding Disorder of Infancy and Childhood
- Pica
- Stereotyped Movement Disorders
- Child Abuse or Child Battered Syndrome
- Follow-up, Home Care and Rehabilitation for Childhood Psychiatric Disorders

KEY TERMS

Mental retardation or Intellectual disability, Specific developmental disorders of speech/language, Scholastic skills, Motor function, Mixed specific developmental disorders, Pervasive developmental disorders, Autism spectrum disorders, Hyperkinetic disorders, Conduct disorders, Juvenile delinquency, Separation anxiety disorder, Phobic anxiety disorder, Social anxiety disorder, Sibling rivalry disorder, Nonorganic enuresis, Nonorganic encopresis, Feeding disorder of infancy and childhood, Pica, Stereotyped movement disorders.

INTRODUCTION

Child psychiatry deals with the assessment and treatment of children's behavioral and emotional problems.

The common child psychiatric disorders are listed here:

- Mental retardation or intellectual disability
- Attention Deficit Hyperactivity Disorder (ADHD)
- Autism spectrum disorder (ASD)
- Tic disorder
- Communication disorder
- Conduct disorder
- Specific learning disorder

HISTORICAL PERSPECTIVES/DEVELOPMENT IN CHILD PSYCHIATRY

Persons with Disability Act, 1995 (PWD) emphasized on education and employment provisions for children with disability. Constitution of India (1950), Article 41 emphasized the 'compulsory education for all children up to 14 years of age and so special schools were established. Milestones of development in child psychiatry are summarized in Table 11.1.

Table 11.1: Historical perspectives/development in child psychiatry

Year	Description
1935	Leo Kanner published a first book about child psychiatry
1954	First graduate program in child psychiatry was introduced
1971	Professional organization for child psychiatric nursing was introduced
1979	American Nurses Association (ANA) certification of child psychiatry commenced
1895	ANA standards of child/adolescent psychiatric nursing practice was established.

Classification of Child Psychiatry (ICD-11 and DSM-5)

Classification of child psychiatry (ICD-11 and DSM-5) are given in Table 11.2.

Table 11.2: Classification of child psychiatry (ICD-11 and DSM-5)

ICD-11	DSM-5	Classification of mental disorders
Neurodevelopmental disorders		
Intellectual disability (intellectual developmental disorder)		
6A00.0	—	Mild intellectual disability
6A00.1	—	Moderate intellectual disability
6A00.2	—	Severe intellectual disability
6A00.3	—	Profound intellectual disability

Contd...

ICD-11	DSM-5	Classification of mental disorders
6A00.4	—	Provisional intellectual disability
—	315	Global developmental delay
6A00.Z	319	Unspecified intellectual disability (intellectual developmental disorder)
Communication disorders		
6A01	315.39	Language disorder
6A01.0	315.39	Speech sound disorder
—	315.35	Childhood-onset fluency disorder (stuttering)
—	307.0	Adult-onset fluency disorder
6A01.22	315.39	Social (pragmatic) communication disorder
6A01.Z	307.9	Unspecified communication disorder
Autism spectrum disorder		
6A02	299.00	Autism spectrum disorder
—	293.89	Autism spectrum disorder with catatonia
Attention-deficit/hyperactivity disorder		
6A05.0	314.00	Predominantly inattentive presentation
6A05.1	314.01	Predominantly hyperactive/impulsive presentation
6A05.2	314.01	Combined presentation
6A05.Y	314.01	Other specified attention-deficit/ hyperactivity disorder
6A05.Z	314.01	Unspecified attention-deficit/ hyperactivity disorder
Specific learning disorder		
6A03.0	315.00	With impairment in reading
6A03.1	315.2	With impairment in written expression
6A03.2	315.1	With impairment in mathematics
Motor disorders		
—	315.4	Developmental coordination disorder
6A06	307.3	Stereotypic movement disorder
Tic disorders		
8A05.00	307.23	Tourette's disorder
—	307.22	Persistent (chronic) motor or vocal tic disorder
—	307.21	Provisional tic disorder
—	307.20	Other specified tic disorder
—	307.19	Unspecified tic disorder
Other neurodevelopmental disorders		
6A0Y	315.8	Other specified neurodevelopmental disorder
6A0Z	315.9	Unspecified neurodevelopmental disorder

MENTAL RETARDATION OR INTELLECTUAL DISABILITY OR INTELLECTUAL DEVELOPMENTAL DISORDER OR MENTALLY CHALLENGED INDIVIDUALS

Introduction

Mental retardation is the most common psychiatric diagnosis among children. The older terms used for mental retardation are as follows:

- **Mental subnormality:** World Health Organization (WHO) used this term which has two categories:
  - i. **Mental retardation:** Subnormal functioning due to pathological cause.
  - ii. **Mental deficiency:** Used for legal purpose when IQ is less than 70.
- **Feeble-mindedness:** It denotes mild mental retardation.
- **Oligophrenia:** This term is used in Western Europe countries.

The term, 'Intellectual disability' is used in DSM-5 and the equivalent term is 'Mental Retardation' as per ICD-10 and intellectual development disorder by ICD-11. Categories of intelligence (ICD-10 concept) are shown in Figure 11.1.

Definition

Mental Retardation is defined as, "sub-average intellectual functioning which results in or is associated with concurrent impairment in adaptive behavior and is manifested during the development."

—*American Association for Mental Retardation, 1983*

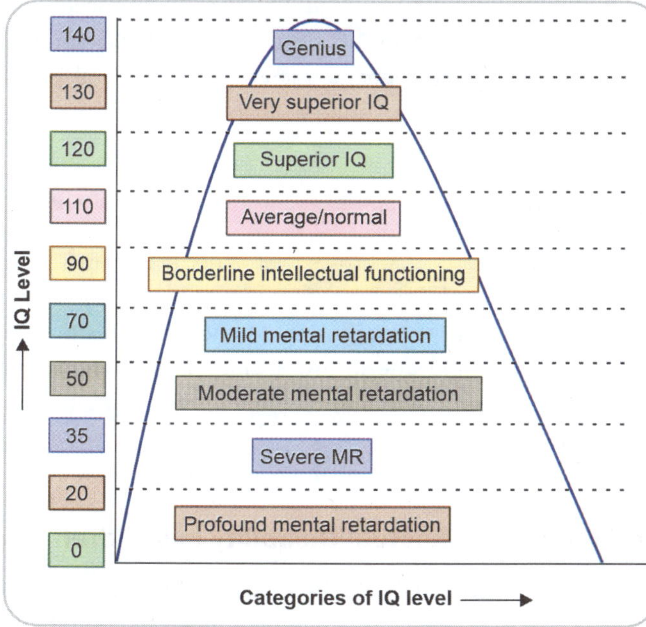

Figure 11.1: Categories of intelligence

Classification

ICD-11	DSM-5	Classification of intellectual disability (intellectual developmental disorder)
6A00.0	—	Mild intellectual disability
6A00.1	—	Moderate intellectual disability
6A00.2	—	Severe intellectual disability
6A00.3	—	Profound intellectual disability
6A00.4	—	Provisional intellectual disability
—	315	Global developmental delay
6A00.Z	319	Unspecified intellectual disability (intellectual developmental disorder)

The classification of intellectual disability has been given in Table 11.3.

Table 11.3: Classification of mental retardation or intellectual disability as per ICD-11 and DSM-5

Classification of intellectual disability	IQ level of intellectual disability	Requirement of support measures
ICD-11		
Mild	Two to three standard deviations below the mean (approximately 0.1–2.3 percentile)	May require appropriate support
Moderate	Three to four standard deviations below the mean (approximately 0.003–0.1 percentile)	Require consistent support
Severe Profound	Four of more standard deviations below the mean (less than approximately the 0.003rd percentile)	Daily support in the supervised environment
Provisional	There is evidence of a disorder of intellectual development but child under the age of four or not possible to conduct a valid assessment of intellectual functioning because of the sensory or physical impairments such as blindness, deafness, locomotor disability, severe behavior problems or co-morbid mental and behavioral disorders.	
DSM-5		
The term, 'Intellectual disability' or 'Intellectual development disorder' is used in DSM-5. It is classified as mild, moderate, severe and profound intellectual disabilities based on the intellectual functions (reasoning, problem-solving, planning, abstract thinking, judgment, academic learning, learning from experience, etc.) and adaptive functioning (communication, social participation, independent living, etc.)		

Contd...

Classification of intellectual disability	IQ level of intellectual disability	Requirement of support measures
Miscellaneous		
Based on the level of intensity of care required for children with intellectual disability, it is categorized as intermittent support (on the need basis), Limited support (with a particular time span), Extensive support (in the required life areas) and pervasive support (constant support across the all-life areas and in all environment).		

Incidence and Prevalence

Mental retardation is seen in 1% of population. It is more common in males. Mild mental retardation is more common in low socioeconomic group. High incidence of mental retardation is seen among school going children in the age group of 10–14 years. Percentage distribution of children with mental retardation is shown in Figure 11.2.

Causes of Intellectual Disability

Biological Factors

- **Prenatal causes:** These include:
  - **Genetic syndromes**
    - **Down's syndrome:** Patients have 47 chromosomes with an additional chromosome number 21.
    - **Fragile X syndrome:** Fragile site in band q27–28 on X chromosome.
    - **Prader-Willi syndrome:** Disorder caused by deletion in the part of chromosome 15.
  - **Errors of inborn metabolism**
    - **Phenylketonuria:** Simple autosomal recessive trait which has deficiency of liver enzyme phenylalanine hydroxylase which leads to lack of ability to metabolize phenylalanine. Screening test to identify phenylketonuria is guthrie test and ferric chloride test.
    - **Lesch-Nyhan syndrome:** It is also called juvenile gout which is caused due to the deficiency of hypoxanthine-guanine phosphoribosyl transferase (HGPRT).
    - **Galactosemia:** Infant is unable to metabolize galactose (It is simple sugar along with glucose it forms lactose), which accumulates in brain and might lead to mental retardation.
    - **Tay-Sachs disease:** A rare fatal inherited disorder that occurs due to the absence of an important enzyme hexosaminidase-A (Hex-A) leads to the *destruction* of nerve cells in brain and spinal cord.
  - **Complications of pregnancy:** Maternal malnutrition, toxemia of pregnancy, placenta previa, vaginal hemorrhage, cord prolapse, premature separation of placenta, iodine deficiency in pregnancy (restricts the growth of brain) and teratogenic effects of drugs, especially in first trimester lead to mental retardation in children.
  - **Maternal infections:** Rubella (German Measles), toxoplasmosis, syphilis, cytomegalic inclusion body disease, HIV infection, maternal hepatitis, influenza, *pneumonia*.
- **Perinatal causes:** Premature birth, intrauterine growth retardation, birth injuries, kernicterus, Rh incompatibility between mother and fetus are responsible for mental retardation.
- **Postnatal causes:** Infections (meningitis, encephalitis), malnutrition, toxins (lead, alcohol), hydrocephalus (abnormal collection of Cerebrospinal Fluid around the brain), macrocephaly, microcephaly, cerebral palsy, Heller's disease, head injury, uncontrolled seizures are some of the causes.

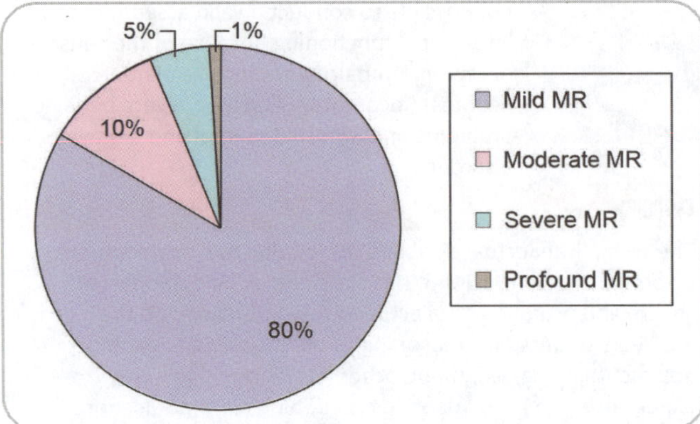

Figure 11.2: Percentage distribution of children with mental retardation

Sociocultural Factors

- **Social adversity:** Lack of social skills may cause mild intellectual disability.
- **Poverty and large family size:** Mother is unable to take care of the child due to low socioeconomic status and increased family size may lead to mental retardation in child.
- Lack of sensory impairment during infancy.

Features of Intellectual Disability in Children

Features of Intellectual disability in children are explained in Table 11.4. 5D's of mental retardation or intellectual disability are given in Flowchart 11.1.

Table 11.4: Features of intellectual disability in children

Aspects	Mild intellectual disability	Moderate intellectual disability	Severe intellectual disability
Standard deviations below mean	2–3	3–4	>4
% of patients	85%	10%	5%
Self-care ability	Independent	Need some help	Limited
Read and write	Acceptable	Basic	Minimum or none
Language	Reasonable	Limited	Minimum or none
Social skills	Normal	Moderate	Little
Ability to work	Semi-skill	Unskilled	Unskilled
Physical problems	Rare	Sometimes	Commonly seen
Causes identified	Sometimes	Often	Usual

Flowchart 11.1: 5D's of mental retardation or intellectual disability

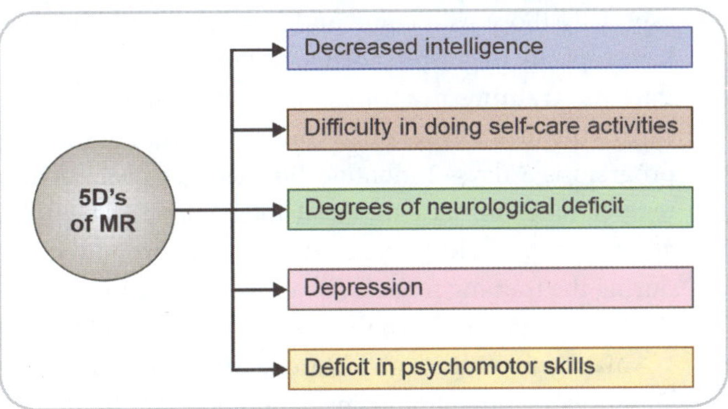

DSM-5 Diagnostic Criteria for Intellectual Disability (Intellectual Developmental Disorder)

Intellectual developmental disorder is a disorder in which the onset happens during the developmental period in both the intellectual and adaptive functioning deficits of conceptual, social and practical domains.

Below given criteria should meet in this case:

- Deficits in intellectual functions (problem-solving, reasoning, abstract thinking, planning, judgment, learning from experience, academic learning, etc.)
- Deficits in adaptive functioning that result in failure to meet developmental or sociocultural standards for personal independence and social responsibility. Without ongoing support, the adaptive deficit limits functioning in one or more activities of daily life [(For example, communication, social participation or independent living) across multiple environments (example—at home, school, work, community)]
- Onset of intellectual and adaptive deficits during the developmental period.

NOTE

Diagnostic term 'Intellectual disability' is the equivalent term for the ICD-11 diagnosis of intellectual developmental disorders. As per United States Law, the term 'Mental Retardation' is replaced with intellectual disability.

Specify if it is:

Mild, moderate, severe or profound on the basis of the adaptive functioning and not on the basis of Intelligence Quotient Level because adaptive functioning is only determining the level of supports required and Intelligence measurement are less valid in the lower end of the Intelligence Quotient range.

ICD-11 Diagnostic Criteria for Intellectual Disability (Intellectual Developmental Disorder)

- Disorders of intellectual development are a group of etiologically diverse conditions originating during the developmental period characterized by significantly below average intellectual functioning and adaptive behavior that are approximately two or more standard deviations below the mean (approximately less than the 2.3rd percentile), based on appropriately normed, individually administered standardized tests.
- Where appropriately normed and standardized tests are not available, diagnosis of disorders of intellectual development requires greater reliance on clinical judgment based on appropriate assessment of comparable behavioral indicators.

Specify if it is:

- **Mild intellectual disability:** Two to three standard deviations below the mean (approximately 0.1–2.3 percentile).
- **Moderate intellectual disability:** Three to four standard deviations below the mean (approximately 0.003–0.1 percentile).
- **Severe and profound intellectual disability:** Four or more standard deviations below the mean (less than approximately the 0.003rd percentile).
- **Provisional intellectual disability:** There is evidence of a disorder of intellectual development but in child under the age of four, it is not possible to conduct a valid assessment of intellectual functioning because of the sensory or physical impairments such as blindness, deafness, locomotor disability, severe behavior problems or comorbid mental and behavioral disorders.

Diagnosis

- **History collection:** Any *consanguineous* marriage in family, faulty parenting style, infant reaction toward the stress, history of head injury/seizures/fever, feeding habits, smiling unnecessarily at others, any cyanosis after birth; also collect history whether baby cried after birth or not.
- **Physical examination:**
  - **Inspection:** General behavior, appearance, facial expression, coordination of movements, skin fold thickness.
  - **Palpation:** Skin texture, muscle tone and pulse rate.
  - **Percussion:** It is done when there is a swelling present in head.
  - **Auscultation:** Cardiovascular sounds.
  - **Measurements:** Height, weight, chest/abdominal circumference and cephalic index (cranial vault).
- **Blood and urine test:** If metabolic disorders are suspected.
- **Karyotyping, amniocentesis and chorionic villus sampling (CVS):** If chromosomal anomaly is suspected.
- **Electroencephalogram (EEG):** To monitor the sleep pattern, assess cognitive status and to detect seizures in mentally retarded children.
- **Assessment of hearing and speech deficits**
- **Psychological test:** To detect brain damage, the tests applied are: Draw a person test, Stanford Binet test, Bender-Gestalt test, Benton visual retention test, Weschler's Adult Intelligence Scale (WAIS), Weschler's Intelligence Scale for Children (WISC), vineland adaptive behavior scale and American Association on Mental Deficiency (AAMD) adaptive behavior scale (Scales used to assess social functioning).

$$\text{Intelligence quotient (IQ)} = \frac{\text{Mental age (MA)}}{\text{Chronological age (CA)}} \times 100$$

American Association on Mental Deficiency (AAMD) explained adaptive behavior skills based on individual's age (Table 11.5).

Table 11.5: American Association of Mental Deficiency (AAMD)–adaptive behavior skills

Categories of age	American Association of Mental Deficiency (AAMD) adaptive behavior skills
Infancy and early childhood	Sensorimotor and social skills
Childhood and early adolescence	Academic, judgment, reasoning and social skills
Late adolescence and adulthood	Performance of task, vocational and social responsibilities

Management of Children with Intellectual Disability or Mental Retardation

- **Adequate support and special needs in schooling:** Special schools are available to improve the academic skill for mild mentally retarded children.
- **Behavior therapy:** Positive and Negative Reinforcement (Flowchart 11.2) might change the maladaptive behavior in children. Aversive stimuli should be avoided. Modeling is a technique used in mild mentally retarded children, i.e., demonstrate the desired behavior to the children. For example, demonstrate the children how-to put-on shirt button and ask the child to repeat the same.
- **Group therapy:** Parents of mentally retarded children share their burdens in group therapy which helps the parents to gain reassurance.
- **Social skills training:** 'Trainable' category of mentally retarded children is capable of acquiring the social skills and require the social skills training.
- **Vocational skills training:** Supportive employment/job placement.
- **Remedial education:** Mentally retarded children especially those who come under category of 'Educable', have capacity to grasp academic skills.
- **Parents' training programs:** Train the parents to take care of the mentally retarded children. Length of training program is 8 days–2 months. Targeted behavior such as temper tantrum, lack of social interaction, inattention, aggressive act, sleep disturbances, etc. are discussed during the training session. It has two main principles:
  1. Parents have to learn the mentally retarded children's management through lectures and demonstration.
  2. Apply the learnt techniques in practice at home and in return have a discussion to verbalize the results and also to sort out the issues.

Flowchart 11.2: Behavior therapy for mentally retarded children

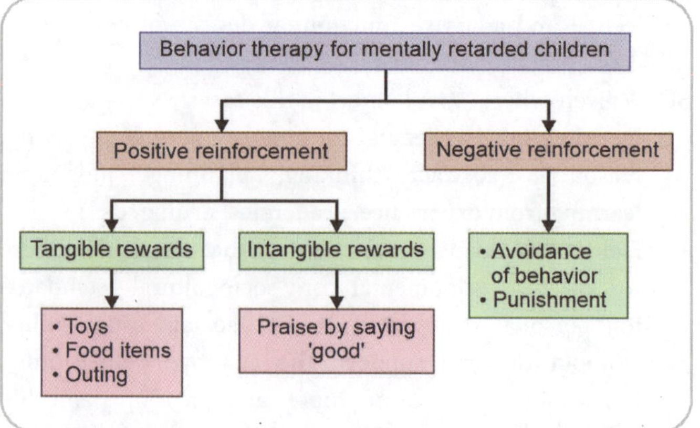

- **Parental counseling:** It helps to promote the positive acceptance of children. It aids the parents to be aware of the importance of social stimulation such as smiling, talking, cuddling, or holding the child while crying. Nurse has to create awareness regarding the special schools, vocational rehabilitation centers and day care centers.
- **Special institution:** Residential care (to take care of profound mentally retarded children) and day care center/ sheltered workshops (to take care of mild and moderate mentally retarded children).
- **If the child is aggressive/agitated:** Mood stabilizers, benzodiazepines and atypical antipsychotics are used. Administer antipsychotics if these are highly essential, in order to avoid the unwanted side effects.
- **Management of psychosocial deprivation:** Nurse has to promote the verbal, emotional and sensory stimulations through play therapy. Play should not be conducted as competition among these children because the failure in the task might demotivate the children. Shared play activities might improve social skills. Firm limits have to be maintained consistently among children with poor impulse control.
- **Management of seizures:** The most common comorbid illness seen in mentally retarded children is seizure. Nurse has to remove the sharp objects away from the children during the seizure. If the seizure occurs in the bed, put the side rails. Remove the tight clothing or chains. Take measures to prevent the tongue fall back. If possible, turn the child's head toward one side during the seizure. It might help to drain the secretions and these secretions will not obstruct the respiratory path. Monitor the timing and type of seizure. Administer benzodiazepines as the physician orders.
- **Medications:**
  - **To control stereotyped motor abnormalities:** Chlorpromazine and haloperidol can be used.
  - **To control aggression:** Antipsychotics, sodium valproate, lithium carbonate, naltrexone and carbamazepine are used.
  - **If child is inattentive:** Stimulants such as amphetamine and methylphenidate can be used.
- **Management of speech deficits:** Lip reading/Speech therapy and assisting with hearing aids are helpful.
- **Management of sexual problems:** Masturbation is common among mentally retarded so the children can be diverted with clay making, finger painting and sand play activities.
- **Miscellaneous:** Supportive counseling to parents and caregivers, physiotherapy and occupational therapy. Identify and treat the comorbid illness.

Differences between mental retardation and mental illness are explained in Table 11.6.

Table 11.6: Differences between intellectual disability and mental illness

Aspects	Intellectual disability	Mental illness
Disease	It is not a disease	It is a disease
Curable	No, it cannot be cured. However, associated vision/hearing/ behavioral problems can be treated	It may or may not be cured.

Myths about Mental Retardation

- It is always hereditary.
- It can be cured.
- It is not common.
- All mentally retarded children are same/alike.
- Mentally retarded children are impossible to train educate.

Prevention of Mental Retardation or Intellectual Disability

Mental retardation or intellectual disability is classified as primary, secondary and tertiary prevention as shown in Flowchart 11.3.

Assessment of Children with Mental Retardation or Intellectual Disability

Common screening tools of mental retardation have been given in Table 11.7. Other screening tools used to assess Mental Retardation are Bharat Raj Developmental Screening Test (DST), Upanayan Early Intervention Programming System (1987) and Functional Assessment Checklist for Programming (FACP-1991).

Table 11.7: Common screening instruments of mental retardation

Common screening instruments	Age group
Denver development scale	0–6 years
Gesell's development scale	4 weeks–6 years
Mental and motor growth of Indian babies (Pramila Pathak, 1976)	1–2 years
Griffith mental development scale	2–8 years
Cattell's infant IQ scale	2 months–2½ years
Stanford binet IQ scale	2½ years–18 years
Bhatia battery of performance test	6–14 years
Raven's Progressive Matrices; Weschler's Intelligence Scale for Children (WISC)	8½ years–16 years
Minnesota Preschool scale	1½ years–6 years
Vineland social maturity scale	0–25 years

Flowchart 11.3: Classification of prevention of mental retardation

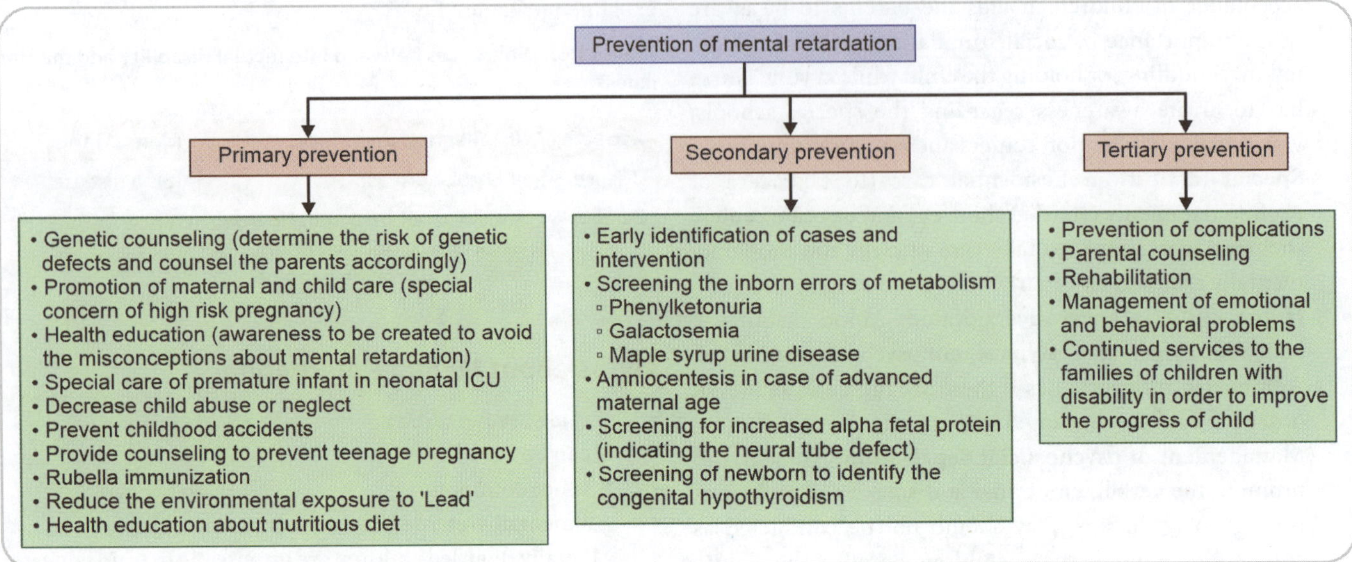

Nursing Management of Patient with Mental Retardation or Intellectual Disability

- **Risk for injury related to aggression as evidenced by signs of impending violence**

Nursing interventions	Rationale
Provide safe environment to client	To promote safety
Store things easily reachable which are used by the client often	To prevent injury
Put side rails if seizure is suspected	To prevent the patient fall
Recognize the signs of impending aggression in early stage	To help the nurse to take precautions/measures
Keep the sharp items out of reach	To prevent injury
Avoid other clients be on their bed	To safeguard other patients
Administer antipsychotics as per the doctor's order	To calm the client

- **Impaired social interaction or verbal communication related to speech deficit as evidenced by inability to communicate**

Nursing interventions	Rationale
Use simple language or words to explain	Helps the client to understand the communication easily.
Use nonverbal gestures/signals appropriately	Helps the client to understand the communication process
Ask the client to participate in group therapy session or with any other interactions.	Helps the patient to listen the interact with other patients.
Provide speech therapy	Promotes speaking ability
Use hearing aids if needed	Helps the client to listen the others' speech
Provide social skills training	Improves social skills
Promote play therapy as a group	Gives a chance to talk with others

- **Self-care deficit related to lack of maturity as evidenced by inability to take care of oneself**

Nursing interventions	Rationale
Identify the aspects of self-care which is deficit	It provides the baseline data
Focus and train the self-care which is found to be deficit	It helps to promote the self-care
Shift to the next self-care activity when one aspect was mastered well	It helps to improve the self-care
Promote positive reinforcement if the client behavior is acceptable	It motivates the desirable behavior

DISORDERS OF PSYCHOLOGICAL DEVELOPMENT

SPECIFIC DEVELOPMENTAL DISORDERS OF SPEECH AND LANGUAGE

Stuttering/Stammering/Childhood Onset Fluency Disorder

Disorders of speech are characterized by disturbances in fluency or rhythm of speech, blocking of speech intermittently, rapid repetition of words, sounds get prolonged and presence of anxiety or distress. Children are usually aware of abnormal speech patterns. The term, 'childhood onset fluency disorder' is given by DSM-5.

DSM-5 Diagnostic Criteria for Childhood Onset Fluency Disorder

- Disturbances in normal fluency and time patterning of speech which is inappropriate for individual's age and language skills, persist over time and are characterized by the frequent and marked occurrences of one (or more) of the following:
  - Sound and syllable repetitions
  - Sound prolongations of consonants as well as vowels.
  - Broken words (e.g., pauses within a word).
  - Audible or silent blocking (filled or unfilled pauses in speech).
  - Circumlocutions (word substitutions to avoid problematic words).
  - Words produced with an excess of physical tension.
  - Monosyllabic whole-word repetitions (e.g., "I-I-I-I see him").
- The disturbance causes anxiety about speaking or limitations in effective communication, social participation, or academic or occupational performance, individually or in any combination.
- The onset of symptoms is in the early developmental period.
- The disturbance is not attributable to a speech-motor or sensory deficit, dysfluency associated with neurological insult (e.g., stroke, tumor, trauma), or another medical condition and is not better explained by another mental disorder.

Management of Stuttering/Stammering/Childhood Onset Fluency Disorder

Simplest measures to control stammering or stuttering is 'Ask the patient to talk more slowly'. Speech and language therapy such as fluency shaping therapy, stuttering modification therapy and use of electronic fluency device are some of the treatment methods. Social skills or communication skill training, assertiveness training, counseling and psychological treatment can also be given.

Cluttering

Erratic and dysrhythmic speech pattern with fast jerky spurting of words. Children are usually not aware of abnormal speech pattern. The comparison of cluttering with stuttering or stammering has been presented in Table 11.8.

Selective Mutism

Complete absence of speech in social situations. It will recover spontaneously, if not recovered then administer cognitive behavior therapy in the form of systematic desensitization (gradual steps taken to ensure the child to talk in front of the strangers). If stammering is the underlying issue, it has to be sorted out by providing speech therapy. Selective serotonin reuptake inhibitors (SSRI) can be given if the symptoms of social phobia are prominent.

Table 11.8: Stuttering/stammering versus cluttering

Aspects	Stuttering/stammering	Cluttering
Features of speech pattern	Disorder of speech is characterized by: • Disturbances in fluency and rhythm of speech • Blocking of speech intermittently • Rapid repetition of syllable or sounds or monosyllabic words (e.g., I...I...I.. want...want...to sleep) • **Circumlocutions:** Substitution of problematic words with the simple words. • Sounds get prolonged • Anxiety or distress present. • Child takes extra effort such as fist clenching, eye blinking, etc. while speaking.	Disorder of speech characterized by: • Erratic • Dysrhythmic speech pattern • Fast jerky spurting of words
Self-awareness of abnormal speech pattern	Present	Absent

DISORDERS OF LANGUAGE OR SPECIFIC LANGUAGE IMPAIRMENTS

Disorders of language such as dysphasia or developmental language disorder, dyslalia or phonological disorder or developmental articulation disorder, receptive language disorder, expressive language disorder and other developmental disorders of language come under these impairments.

- **Causes:** *Hereditary*/Genetics; $FOXP_2$ gene mutation (but it is not common cause); Environmental factors such as Glue ear (*Otitis* media with effusion is present).

Types of Language Disorders

- **Phonologic-Syntactic:** Problem with the articulation or syntax or both (Problem in formation of speech).
- **Pragmatic language impairment (previously termed semantic-pragmatic disorder):** Problem with the use and content of speech and no problem with formation of speech.
- **Landau-Kleffner syndrome or acquired Kleffner syndrome:** Loss of language skills after a normal development. It is a rare disorder which usually starts from 3–9 years of age. 50–70% of children will suffer with seizure attacks. EEG shows paroxysmal discharges in both right and left hemisphere of brain which is more prominently seen during non-rapid eye movement (non-REM) sleep.

Differential Diagnosis

Hearing loss, low intelligence, selective mutism and childhood dementia.

Prognosis

It depends on the type of language disorder and associated cognitive deficits.

SPECIFIC DEVELOPMENTAL DISORDERS OF SCHOLASTIC SKILLS

Specific Learning Disorders (Dyslexia) or Developmental Learning Disorder

Meaning: The term 'Dyslexia' came from Greek word, prefix 'dys' means poor or inadequate and suffix 'lexia' means word or language.

Definitions: A disorder in which the child fails to attain the language skills of reading, writing and spelling commensurate with their intellectual abilities.

—***World Federation of Neurologists, 1968***

A learning disability which hinders the person's ability to read, spell, write and speak.

—***United States National Institute of Health***

It is characterized by slow reading speed, slow acquisition of reading skills, omission of words, distortions, reversal of letters and impaired comprehension. It is clearly differentiated from general backwardness in academics resulting from low intelligence. Flowchart 11.4 shows the sub-categories of dyslexia.

Etiology

Etiology is idiopathic in general.

- **Genetic:** Defects in chromosome 1, 2, 6 and 15 might cause dyslexia.

Flowchart 11.4: Subcategories of dyslexia

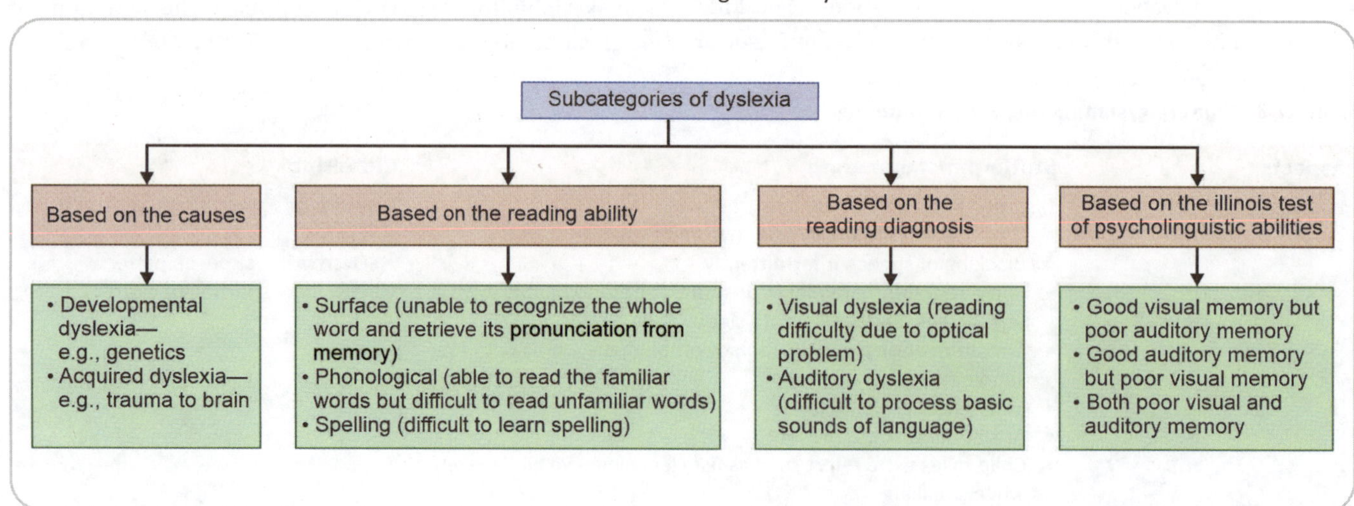

- **Neurological:** Accidents in prenatal/postnatal period or any other birth injuries (particularly injuries of the left hemisphere of brain).

ICD-11 and DSM-5 Classification of Specific Learning Disorder

ICD-11	DSM-5	Developmental learning disorder (ICD-11)/ Specific learning disorder (DSM-5)
6A03.0	315.00	With impairment in reading
6A03.1	315.2	With impairment in written expression
6A03.2	315.1	With impairment in mathematics

Types

- **Trauma dyslexia:** An acquired rare type of mental disorder caused by injury to brain or conductive hearing loss.
- **Deep dyslexia or primary dyslexia:** Usually due to hereditary factors, chromosomal defects affect the left hemisphere and corpus callosum and the child has to compensate this defect using the right brain.
- **Developmental dyslexia or secondary dyslexia:** It occurs in the developmental stages of fetus. The severity decreases as the child grows older.

Diagnosis

It is actually difficult to diagnose. Although it can be diagnosed based on the observations made in the classroom, history collection in regard to the developmental milestones, performance in academics, educational tests to explore the level of functioning related to basic skills and doing special tests to assess the language skills.

DSM-5 Diagnostic Criteria for Specific Learning Disorder

- Difficulties in learning and using academic skills, as indicated by the presence of at least one of the below listed symptoms for at least 6 months, despite the provision of interventions that target those difficulties:
  i. Inaccurate or slow and effortful word reading
  ii. Difficulty understanding the meaning of what is read
  iii. Difficulties with spelling
  iv. Difficulties with written expression
  v. Difficulties mastering number sense, number facts, or calculation
  vi. Difficulties with mathematical reasoning
- Affected academic skills are substantially and quantifiably below those expected for individual's chronological age and cause significant interference with academic or occupational performance, or with activities of daily living, as confirmed by comprehensive clinical assessment.
- The learning difficulties begin during school-age years but may not become fully manifested until the demands for those affected academic skills exceed the individual's limited capacities.
- The learning difficulties are not well accounted by intellectual disabilities, uncorrected visual or auditory acuity, other mental or neurological disorders, psychosocial adversity, lack of proficiency in the language of academic instruction, or inadequate educational instruction.

Specify if

- With impairment in reading
- With impairment in written expression
- With impairment in mathematics
- Level of severity (mild/moderate/severe)

ICD-11 Diagnostic Criteria for Developmental Learning Disorder

- Significant and persistent difficulties in learning academic skills such as reading, writing, or arithmetic.
- Individual's performance in the affected academic skill is markedly below which has been expected for chronological age and general level of intellectual functioning and results in the significant impairment in the individual's academic or occupational functioning.
- Developmental learning disorder first manifests when academic skills are taught during the early school years.
- Developmental learning disorder is not due to a disorder of intellectual development, sensory impairment, neurological or motor disorder, lack of availability of education, lack of proficiency in the language of academic instruction or psychosocial adversity.

Specify if

- With impairment in reading
- With impairment in written expression
- With impairment in mathematics

Treatment

- **Educational techniques:** Teach the children to recognize the smallest sounds that make the words (phonemes) and understand the letters which represent these sounds (phonics). Child has to read aloud which helps in the improvement to develop the reading fluency, accuracy and speed. Child has to be encouraged to comprehend what he/ she is reading.
- **VAKT technique:** Visual, auditory, kinesthetic and tactile techniques. It is a multisensory learning and includes four learning styles such as visual, auditory, kinesthetic and tactile (Table 11.9), in which the child learns through one or other channels of learning.

Table 11.9: Modalities of VAKT technique and its usage to specific modality

Modalities of VAKT technique	Usage of items in order to enhance learning skills among children with dyslexia
Visual	Using images, pictures and spatial understanding
Auditory	Using music and sounds
Kinesthetic or physical	Using body and hand movements
Tactile	Using the sense of touch

Role of Parents and Teachers

- **Do's:** Parents and teachers have to identify the problem at an early stage. Encourage the children to read aloud. Provide adequate additional time for reading. Usage of bullet points, color, flowcharts, more space and white boards are more helpful for easy understanding of auditory, kinesthetic and tactile ways of learning.
- **Don't:** Teachers or parents should not give more instructions to the children and do not use small prints and overcrowded text.
- **Specific spelling disorder:** There is significant speech impairment in saying the spellings of a specific word/ words with absence of a specific reading disorder.
- **Specific arithmetic disorder:** There will be significant impairment in computational skills of addition, subtraction, division and multiplication.

AUTISM SPECTRUM DISORDER

Leo Kanner first described this disorder as **Infantile Autism** and so it is also called Kanner's syndrome. Autism spectrum disorder is characterized by persistent deficits in the ability to initiate and to sustain reciprocal social interaction and social communication, and by a range of restricted, repetitive, and inflexible patterns of behavior and interests.

Causes of Autism

- **Genetics/hereditary factors:** Monozygotic twins have higher concordance than dizygotic twins. Siblings of autistic child shows 2% of prevalence rate. 2–5% might have fragile X syndrome.
- **Neuroanatomical studies:** Enlargement of cerebral ventricles and degeneration of cerebellum is seen.
- **Biochemical factors:** Increased serotonin level is seen in one third of children with autism.
- **Inflammation of central nervous system:** Meningitis and encephalitis.
- **Infection:** Maternal Rubella/cytomegalovirus.
- **Electrophysiological changes:** Autistic children show impairment of sensory modulation in brain stem when observed with brain stem auditory evoked responses (BAERs).
- **Perinatal factors:** Maternal bleeding after first trimester, presence of meconium in amniotic fluid and exposure to sodium valproate or thalidomide may also cause autism.
- **Separation-individuation theory of child development by Margaret Mahler:** Fixation in presymbiotic phase of development according to Mahler might lead to autism.
- **Theory of mind in autism:** This theory denotes that child can understand others' minds what they are thinking, feeling or intending. Children with autism will have 'mind-blind,' i.e., lack of ability to put oneself in others' place and think.
- **Family disputes/conflicts:** Stress among family members, faulty parenting style (a term 'Refrigerator parents' which denotes parents who lack warmth and affection toward the child, is used here), parental rejection, family break up, etc. are examples of it. (Note: Family dispute/conflict has been considered an older concept to cause autism but not widely accepted as a causative factor now).

ICD-11 and DSM-5 Classification of Autism

ICD-11	DSM-5	Classification of autism
6A02	299.00	Autism spectrum disorder
—	293.89	Autism spectrum disorder with catatonia

DSM-5 Diagnostic Criteria for Autism Spectrum Disorder

- Persistent deficits in social communication and social interaction across multiple contexts, as manifested by the following, currently or by history.
  - Deficits in social-emotional reciprocity, ranging to reduced sharing of interests, emotions, or affect; failure to initiate or respond to social interactions.
  - Deficits in nonverbal communicative behaviors used for social interaction, ranging to abnormalities in eye contact and body language or deficits in understanding and use of gestures; to a total lack of facial expressions and nonverbal communication.
  - Deficits in developing, maintaining, and understanding relationships, ranging to difficulties in sharing imaginative play or in making friends; to absence of interest in peers.

  Specify current severity: Severity is based on social communication impairments and restricted, repetitive patterns of behavior.

- Restricted, repetitive patterns of behavior, interests, or activities, as manifested by at least two of the following, currently or by history (examples are illustrative, not exhaustive; see text):
  - Stereotyped or repetitive motor movements, use of objects, or speech.
  - Insistence on sameness, inflexible adherence to routines, or ritualized patterns of verbal or nonverbal behavior.
  - Highly restricted, fixated interests that are abnormal in intensity or focus.
  - Hyper- or hyporeactivity to sensory input or unusual interest in sensory aspects of the environment.

  Specify current severity: Severity is based on social communication impairments and restricted, repetitive patterns of behavior.
- Symptoms must be present in the early developmental period.
- Symptoms cause clinically significant impairment in social, occupational, or other important areas of current functioning.
- These disturbances are not better explained by intellectual developmental disorder or global developmental delay. Intellectual disability and autism spectrum disorder frequently co-occur; to make comorbid diagnoses of autism spectrum disorder and intellectual disability, social communication should be below that expected for general developmental level.

NOTE

Individuals who have marked deficits in social communication, but whose symptoms do not otherwise meet criteria for autism spectrum disorder, should be evaluated for social (pragmatic) communication disorder.

Specify if:
- With or without accompanying intellectual impairment
- With or without accompanying language impairment
- Associated with a known medical or genetic condition or environmental factor
- Associated with another neurodevelopmental, mental, or behavioral disorder
- With catatonia
- Catatonia associated with autism spectrum disorder to indicate the presence of the comorbid catatonia.

ICD-11 Diagnostic Criteria for Autism Spectrum Disorder

- Persistent deficits in the ability to initiate and to sustain reciprocal social interaction and social communication, and by a range of restricted, repetitive, and inflexible patterns of behavior and interests.
- Onset occurs during the developmental period, typically in early childhood, but symptoms may not become fully manifest until later, when social demands exceed limited capacities.
- Deficits are sufficiently severe to cause impairment in personal, family, social, educational, occupational or other important areas of functioning and are usually a pervasive feature of the individual's functioning observable in all settings, although they may vary according to social, educational, or other context. Individuals along the spectrum exhibit a full range of intellectual functioning and language abilities.

NOTE

Above definitional requirements for autism spectrum disorder are met, with or without disorder of intellectual development and with mild or no or significant impairment of functional language (code has to be allotted accordingly).

Main Features of Autism

- **Abnormal social reciprocal relationship:** Poor eye to eye contact, not interested to play with other children, lack of facial expression, lack of ability to establish friendship, live in their own world (lack of attention to parents and sibling), lack of empathy, reciprocal social interaction (prefer to be alone and dislike when cuddled, kissed or picked up) are present. All consider them as easier babies. Due to the lack of parental attention, such children prefer solitary activities and do not participate in social play.
- **Abnormalities in communication:** Children with autism are unable to speak generally, if they speak it might be difficult to understand. There may be an immediate echolalia (immediate repetition of words spoken by others) or delayed echolalia (repetition of words spoken by others will happen but it will be delayed), incoherence of speech, absence of mode of communication such as babbling, gestures and facial expressions. Delay in development and production of speech (rate, rhythm, volume, pitch, etc.) is present. Speech is monotonous, wooden and of mechanical nature. Conversation is like a monologue and not as a dialogue. Pronunciation errors of both syllables and words may be present. Both verbal and nonverbal communication are impaired. Pronominal reversal is seen, e.g., reverse of pronoun, 'I' with 'You,' i.e., instead of saying 'I feel happy' child might say 'You feel happy.'

- **Repetitive and restrictive behavior:** Child with autism insists on 'sameness' (prefers to wear same clothes, eat same food and play with same toy), lack of creativity, stereotyped behavior such as clapping hands, rolling the head, body rocking and making out whirling rounds can be seen. Autistic child may show anger burst out when a toy is moved from its place.

Associated Features

- **Cognitive impairment:** Autistic children might also have mental retardation, in which few may have average and above average intelligence.
- **Abnormal response to sensory stimuli:** Hyperacusis (hypersensitivity to the sound heard), hypersensitivity to touch while the child has no response to stimuli of pain.
- **Self-injurious behavior:** Head banging and self-mutilation are commonly seen. 10–25% of children with autism will have generalized tonic clonic seizure (GTCS) and only few children will have temporal lobe epilepsy (TLE).

Risk Factors of Autism Spectrum Disorder

- **Genetic factors:** Duplication in the section of chromosome 7 (In William's syndrome, same section of chromosome 7 is found deleted which displays the excess sociability behavior).
- Low birth weight
- Increased paternal age
- Exposure to medications during first trimester of pregnancy (e.g., Sodium valproate).
- **Extreme male brain theory:** According to this theory, autism shows an extreme of the typical male profile. Males are usually 'systemizing' than 'empathizing'. Child with autism might have extreme male pattern.

NOTE

Individuals with autism spectrum disorders (ASD) lack in both empathy and theory of mind (ability to assess the mental state of others, that usually starts developing from 3 to 4 years of age. So, autistic individuals are vulnerable for exploitation by others).

Course and Prognosis

Autism has a long course and guarded prognosis (outcome is serious and uncertain). 10–20% of autistic children show improvement by 4–6 years of age in an ordinary school, 10–20% of autistic children will live at home but require special school for training, 60% of autistic children show an improvement but might not lead an independent life.

Management of Autism Spectrum Disorder

Assessment/Diagnosis

- **History collection:** Interview can be conducted with the parents regarding the child's development.
- **Screening Tools:** There is no definite diagnostic tool whereas commonly used rating scales are childhood autism rating scale (CARS), autism diagnostic interview (ADI), autism behavior checklist, Gilliam Asperger's Disorder Scale (GADI) and Child's Social Behavior/ Language Scale. Identify the other comorbid illnesses such as mental retardation, hearing loss, speech defects and neurological disorders.
- **Positive emission tomography (PET):** Impairment in frontal or parietal lobes can be seen.

Psychological Therapies

- **Psychoeducation:** Educate the parents, child and teacher about autism spectrum disorder.
- **Social skills training** *or* **communication skills training** *or* **life skills training.**
- **Counseling and supportive therapy:** Counseling services have to be provided to the family members to cope up with the distress, which happened due to behavior of autistic children.
- **Special schooling:** Refer the autistic children to the special schools for their improvement.
- **Home care:** Teach the caregivers how to manage the behavior of autistic children at home.
- **Behavior therapy:** Unrealistic behavior has to be modified into realistic one.

Psychotropic Medications

Low dose of antipsychotics is used to treat undesirable challenging behavior. Special care must be taken during the time of transition (change of school/home setting/caregivers) because the symptoms might worsen during this transition period.

CONDUCT DISORDER

Definition

A repeated and pervasive pattern of inappropriate behavior in children or adolescence that violates the basic rights of others is known as conduct disorder. Comparison of conduct disorder as per ICD-11 and DSM-5 is given in Table 11.10.

Table 11.10: Comparison of conduct disorder as per ICD-11 and DSM-5

Aspects	Conduct disorder as per ICD-11	Conduct disorder as per DSM-5
Age of onset	**Childhood onset type:** before 10 years of age **Adolescent onset type:** after 10 years of age	Before 13 years
Duration of Symptoms	At least 12 months or more	

Incidence and Prevalence

Prevalence is 5%. It is three times more common in males than females. Severity is more common in males. Early onset in children with conduct disorders are more prone to develop antisocial personality disorder in adulthood.

Etiology

- **Genetic factors:** Child with one particular variant of monoamine oxidase-A (MAO-A) gene are at risk of developing antisocial behavior. Cytogenetics states that, 'Individual with 'XXY Karyotype' are more prone to develop aggression.
- **Biochemical factors:** Increased plasma levels of testosterone might cause aggressive behavior.
- **Organic factors:** Brain damage and seizures may cause conduct disorder.
- **Psychosocial factors:** Low socioeconomic status, large family size, lack of achievement in school, child abuse or neglect, parents involved in criminal activities or substance abuse, parental separation or death of father, inappropriate communication patterns of family and parental conflicts.

ICD-11 and DSM-5 Classification of Conduct Disorder

ICD-11	DSM-5	Classification of conduct disorder
6C91	—	Conduct-dissocial disorder
6C91.0	312.81	Conduct-dissocial disorder, childhood onset
6C91.00	—	Conduct-dissocial disorder, childhood onset with limited prosocial emotions
6C91.01	—	Conduct-dissocial disorder, childhood onset with typical prosocial emotions
6C91.0Z	—	Conduct-dissocial disorder, childhood onset, unspecified
6C91.1	312.82	Conduct-dissocial disorder, adolescent onset
6C91.10	—	Conduct-dissocial disorder, adolescent onset with limited prosocial emotions
6C91.11	—	Conduct-dissocial disorder, adolescent onset with typical prosocial emotions
6C91.1Y	—	Other specified conduct-dissocial disorder, adolescent onset
6C91.Z	312.89	Conduct-dissocial disorder, unspecified

Contd...

DSM-5 Diagnostic Criteria for Conduct Disorder

- A repetitive and persistent pattern of behavior in which the basic rights of others or major age-appropriate societal norms or rules are violated, as manifested by the presence of at least three of the following 15 criteria in the past 12 months from any of the categories below, with at least one criterion present in the past 6 months:

Aggression to people and animals:

1. Often bullies, threatens, or intimidates others.
2. Often initiates physical fights.
3. Has used a weapon that can cause serious physical harm to others.
4. Has been physically cruel to people.
5. Has been physically cruel to animals.
6. Has stolen while confronting a victim.
7. Has forced someone into sexual activity.

Destruction of property:

8. Has deliberately engaged in fire setting with the intention of causing serious damage.
9. Has deliberately destroyed others' property (other than by fire setting).

Deceitfulness or theft:

10. Has broken into someone else's house, building, or car.
11. Often lies to obtain goods or favors or to avoid obligations.
12. Has stolen items of nontrivial value without confronting a victim.

Serious violations of rules:

13. Often stays out at night despite parental prohibitions, beginning before age 13 years.
14. Has run away from home overnight at least twice while living in the parental or parental surrogate home, or once without returning for a lengthy period.
15. Is often truant from school, beginning before age 13 years.

- The disturbance in behavior causes clinically significant impairment in social, academic, or occupational functioning.
- If the individual is age 18 years or older, criteria are not met for antisocial personality disorder.

Specify whether:

- Childhood-onset type: At least one symptom of conduct disorder present prior to age 10 years.
- Adolescent-onset type: No symptom of conduct disorder present prior to age 10 years.
- Unspecified onset: Criteria for a diagnosis of conduct disorder are met, but there is not enough information available to determine whether the onset of the first symptom was before or after age 10 years.
- With limited prosocial emotions.
- Lack of remorse or guilt.
- Callous—lack of empathy.
- Unconcerned about performance.
- Shallow or deficient affect.
- Specify current severity: Mild or moderate or severe.

ICD-11 Diagnostic Criteria for Conduct Disorder

- Repetitive and persistent pattern of behavior in which the basic rights of others or major age-appropriate societal norms, rules, or laws are violated such as aggression toward people or animals; destruction of property; deceitfulness or theft; and serious violations of rules.
- The behavior pattern is of sufficient severity to result in significant impairment in personal, family, social, educational, occupational or other important areas of functioning.
- To be diagnosed, the behavior pattern must be enduring over a significant period of time (e.g., 12 months or more).
- Isolated dissocial or criminal acts are thus not in themselves grounds for the diagnosis.

Specify whether:

- Childhood-onset type: At least one symptom of conduct disorder present prior to age 10 years.
- Adolescent-onset type: No symptom of conduct disorder present prior to age 10 years.
- With limited prosocial emotions.
- With typical prosocial emotions.
- Unspecified.

NOTE

In conduct disorder, aggression is due to low self-esteem and low frustration tolerance in children.

Features

C : Cheating others
O : Obnoxious (very unpleasant or rude) and others are blamed for one's committed mistake
N : No guilt and empathy; nasty behavior/speech
D : Drug and alcohol abuse
U : Unpredictable behavior and usage of dangerous weapons such as gun or knife
C : Cruel to animals and human beings/Criminal activities are performed
T : Truancy
D : Destroy other's property or deliberately set the fire
I : Intimidates (frighten others in order to make them to do)
S : Steal other things
O : Others are forced for sexual act and onset of antisocial personality disorder
R : Repeatedly saying lies and rage
D : Disrespect to others
E : Esteem is low
R : Risk taking behavior or recklessness

Nursing Management of Children with Conduct Disorder

Assessment

4D's in family history of children with conduct disorder or disruptive behavior is shown in Flowchart 11.5. Assess the symptoms using strength and difficulties questionnaire and child behavior checklist. Assess the comorbid disorders such as autism, attention deficit and hyperactivity disorder (ADHD), mental retardation. Perform the risk assessment, if the child has exhibited more antisocial behavior. Assess the cognitive deficits, intellectual functioning and learning disabilities. Neurological examination has to be done if there is history of brain trauma or seizure in present.

Flowchart 11.5: 4D's in family history of children with conduct disorder

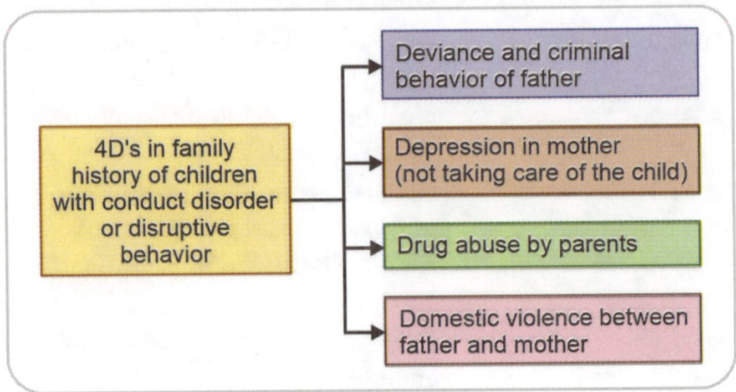

Nursing Interventions

- **Management of violence/aggression:** Nurse should be aware that the child is at risk of being violent any time and so be caution with the children with conduct disorder. Provide physical/mechanical restraints to the children if the aggression is out of control. Chemical restraints or tranquilizers can be administered as per the physician's order.
- **Skill training program for children with conduct disorders:** Skill training program has to be conducted for children with conduct disorder to promote the emotional skill, problem solving skill and social skill as shown in Flowchart 11.6.
- **Control of manipulative behavior:** Reinforce the positive behavior/socially acceptable behavior and gradually reduce the negative behavior. Manipulative behavior has to be controlled using a psychotherapeutic approach namely, 'limit setting'.
- **Self-monitoring technique:** Encourage the children to maintain a diary or log book to enter one's own behavior. A brief statement of anger or any unacceptable behavior has to be noted by oneself with appropriate explanation. It helps the child to identify the patterns of thinking and one's own behavior or action in various situations. Review the diary or log book at the time of discharge and encourage the child to continue this self-monitoring technique even after the discharge.
- **Special considerations:** Aggression can also happen in the school/classroom. Special attention must be given by counselor in the school to sort out cause of aggressive behavior. Truancy has to be considered specifically. Pressurize the child to get back into the school. Resolve the educational and other issues in the school. Nurse has to maintain a good interpersonal relationship with parents and teachers.

Flowchart 11.6: Skill training program for children with conduct disorder

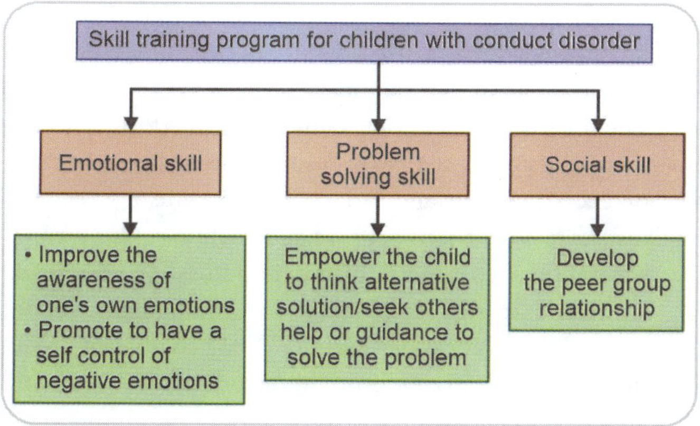

- **Family therapy:** When there is a significant dysfunction in family, which may be expressed by child's behavior has to be treated.
- **Medications:** Atypical antipsychotic (risperidone) is the drug of choice if psychotic symptoms are present. Lithium and carbamazepine for treatment of impulsivity and aggression are given. Anticonvulsants are a diverse group of pharmacological agents that are used in the treatment of epileptic seizures and to central hyperactivity.

JUVENILE DELINQUENCY

Juvenile is an individual who is below the age of 16 (18 years in case of females). Juvenile delinquency implies to the participation by a minor child, usually between the ages of 10–17 years in illegal activities or behavior.

Etiology

- **Psychological factors:** Psychiatric illness, feelings of insecurity, emotional instability and inability to cope up with stressors.
- **Social factors:** Family disputes/conflicts, uncaring attitude of parents, broken family, single parent and bad conduct of parents.
- **Factors related to schooling:** Severe punishment by teachers, ill-treating the child in front of others and following the negative role models.
- **Environmental factors:** Children who live in the area where more criminal activities are present, friends/ parents who have bad conduct may influence the child to perform such activities.
- **Economic factors:** Poverty and low socioeconomic status may lead to get involved in stealing or criminal activities.

Management

Reformatory schools and remand homes can help the child to learn the right moral values. Psychological therapies such as play therapy, art therapy and psychodrama seem to be helpful. Governmental measures such as Children's Act (1977) state that reformatory school and remand homes are made available to develop the child with value education. Vocational training program is helpful to the child to learn the vocational skills for the future employment. Yoga, meditation and relaxation therapy is also needed to reduce the children's level of stress.

Prevention Measures

Educate the parents regarding the proper parenting style. Counsel them in regard with family disputes/conflicts and its importance to avoid them since it promotes the future growth of the children. Empower the teachers to provide positive reinforcement of the child behavior instead of using harsh punishment or hurting words.

SEPARATION ANXIETY DISORDER

Meaning: Children feel excessive anxiety due to separation from home or from the person to whom the child is emotionally attached (mostly the mother, caregiver or siblings).

Definition: An excessive display of fear and distress, when faced with situation of separation from home or any specific emotionally attached figure.

—*American Psychiatric Association*

Epidemiology: It is common in infants and children in the age group of 6 months to 3 years. 75% of children with separation anxiety disorder will have school refusal. Around 50% of anxiety disorders in children suffer from separation anxiety disorder.

Etiology

- **Biological:** High activity of amygdala and defects in ventrolateral and dorsomedial area of prefrontal cortex are linked with separation anxiety disorder.
- **Environmental:** High level of stressors, loss of loved ones, natural disasters, parental separation and change of school or neighborhood.
- **Genetic and physiological:** Researchers have proved that genetic factors are also a cause of separation anxiety disorder in which most of them were girls. Child temperament (timid and shyness in behavior) also leads to separation anxiety disorder.

ICD-11 and DSM-5 Code for Separation Anxiety Disorder

ICD-11 Code	6B05
DSM-5 Code	309.21

ICD-11 Diagnostic Criteria for Separation Anxiety Disorder

- Marked and excessive fear or anxiety about separation from specific attachment figures.
- In children, separation anxiety typically focuses on caregivers, parents or other family members; in adults it is typically a romantic partner or children.
- Thoughts of harm or untoward events befalling the attachment figure, reluctance to go to school or work, recurrent excessive distress upon separation, reluctance or refusal to sleep away from the attachment figure, and recurrent nightmares about separation is present.
- Symptoms persist for at least several months and are sufficiently severe to result in significant distress or significant impairment in personal, family, social, educational, occupational, or other important areas of functioning.

DSM-5 Diagnostic Criteria for Separation Anxiety Disorder

- Developmentally inappropriate and excessive fear or anxiety concerning separation from those to whom the individual is attached, as evidenced by at least three of the following:
    i. Recurrent excessive distress when anticipating or experiencing separation from home or from major attachment figures.
    ii. Persistent and excessive worry about losing major attachment figures or about possible harm to them, such as illness, injury, disasters, or death.
    iii. Persistent and excessive worry about experiencing an untoward event (e.g., getting lost, being kidnapped, having an accident, becoming ill) that causes separation from a major attachment figure.
    iv. Persistent reluctance or refusal to go out, away from home, to school, to work, or elsewhere because of fear of separation.
    v. Persistent and excessive fear of or reluctance about being alone or without major attachment figures at home or in other settings.
    vi. Persistent reluctance or refusal to sleep away from home or to go to sleep without being near a major attachment figure.
    vii. Repeated nightmares involving the theme of separation.
    viii. Repeated complaints of physical symptoms (e.g., headaches, stomachaches, nausea, vomiting) when separation from major attachment figures occur or are anticipated.
- The fear, anxiety, or avoidance is persistent, lasting at least 4 weeks in children and adolescents and typically 6 months or more in adults.
- The disturbance causes clinically significant distress or impairment in social, academic, occupational, or other important areas of functioning.
- The disturbance is not better explained by another mental disorder, such as refusing to leave home because of excessive resistance to change in autism spectrum disorder; delusions or hallucinations concerning separation in psychotic disorders; refusal to go outside without a trusted companion in agoraphobia; worries about ill health or other harm befalling significant others in generalized anxiety disorder; or concerns about having an illness in illness anxiety disorder.

Clinical Features

- Recurrent and excess distress which is anticipated or experienced by separation from the attachment figure.
- Persistent and excess worry about losing the attachment figure.
- Excess worry about experiencing an untoward event (kidnap, accident, become ill) that may happen due to separation from attachment figure.
- Persistent reluctance to go out of home or school due to fear of separation.
- Repeated nightmares.
- Reluctance to be alone without the attachment figure.
- Refusal to sleep alone without the attachment figure.
- Repeated physical complaints such as headache, abdominal pain, leg pain and vomiting occur when separation from the attachment figure takes place.

Nursing Management of Children with Separation Anxiety Disorder

Assessment: Nurse should know about the four different attachment styles.

1. Secure (child relies on caregivers for the emotional support and protection).
2. Anxious-avoidance, insecure (it occurs when infant avoids their parents).
3. Anxious-ambivalent, resistant, insecure (infant feels separation anxiety when separated from caregiver and does not feel reassured when the caregiver returns to the infant).
4. Disorganized (It occurs when there is lack of attachment behavior).

The types of scales used for assessing separation anxiety disorders have been given in Table 11.11.

TREATMENT

- **Cognitive behavior therapy:** It has three phases such as education, application into practice, and relapse prevention. Educate the child that anxiety will affect the physical/mental health. This therapy will enable the child to recognize the anxious reaction and thereby the child will reduce the response. According to Kendall, four components have to be taught to the children undergoing cognitive behavior therapy such as:
  1. Recognize the anxious feeling.
  2. Discuss the situation which provokes anxiety.
  3. Develop the coping plan.
  4. Evaluate the effectiveness of coping plan.

Table 11.11: Types of scale used for assessing separation anxiety disorder

Types of scale used for assessing separation anxiety disorder	Name of the tool used for assessment
Interviews	Diagnostic Interview Schedule for Children, 4th version (DISC-IV), Anxiety Disorders Interview Schedule for the DSM-IV, Child Parent 4th version (ADIS-IV) and Schedule for Affective Disorder (SADS)
Self-report scales	Separation Anxiety Assessment Scale for Children (SAAS-C)
Observation	Dyadic Parent-Child Interaction Coding System II (DPICS II) and Separation Anxiety Daily Diaries (SADD)
Preschool children	Fear survey schedule for infants and preschoolers and Infant–preschool scale for inhibited behaviors

- **Behavior therapy:** It includes contingency management (positive reinforcement with verbal/rewards), systematic desensitization, modelling and guided imagery.
- **Parental counseling:** Give counseling to the parents, so that it is helpful for the child to promote more autonomy and not to be over-protective in nature.
- **Psychotropic medications:** Tricyclic antidepressants, antianxiety drugs and selective serotonin reuptake inhibitors (SSRI).

ATTENTION DEFICIT HYPERACTIVITY DISORDER

Attention deficit hyperactivity disorder (ADHD) is a diagnosis as per DSM-5 and ICD-11 as explained in Table 11.12. The three main features are as follows:

1. Inattention
2. Hyperactivity
3. Impulsivity

Symptoms should persist for at least 6 months. Symptoms have to be present both at home and school. Symptoms have to affect their academic performance and social behavior.

Table 11.12: Attention deficit hyperactivity disorder as per ICD-11 and DSM-5

Aspects	ICD-11	DSM-5
Age of onset	Early to Mid-childhood	12 years
Term	Attention deficit hyperactive disorder	

Epidemiology

Attention deficit hyperactivity disorder is three times more common in males than females. Inattention is more common in females. Impulsivity and hyperactivity are more common in males. ADHD is more common in low socioeconomic group and in children who have been brought up in special homes.

Etiology

Idiopathic: Exact cause is unknown. However, the contributing factors are listed below:

- **Genetic factors:** Family history of ADHD is having greater risk of developing this disease. Monozygotic twins have higher risk. Monozygotic twins are at greater risk than the dizygotic twins. Siblings of hyperactive children are twice at risk of developing ADHD.
- **Biological factors:** Monoamine dysfunction, fronto-striatal dysfunction, delayed cortical maturation and encephalitis.
- **Environmental Factors:** Use of food additives/artificial colors and lead intoxication.
- **Factors related to pregnancy and childbirth:** Prenatal exposure to toxins, smoking in pregnancy, babies with low birth weight, drug exposure during pregnancy, postnatal infections, birth injuries, fetal distress, prolonged labor, birth asphyxia and low APGAR score.

ICD-11 and DSM-5 Classification of ADHD

ICD-11	DSM-5	Classification of ADHD
6A05.0	314.00	Predominantly inattentive presentation
6A05.1	314.01	Predominantly hyperactive/impulsive presentation
6A05.2	314.01	Combined presentation
6A05.Y	314.01	Other specified attention-deficit/ hyperactivity disorder
6A05.Z	314.01	Unspecified attention-deficit/ hyperactivity disorder

Types of ADHD

- **Predominantly hyperactive-impulsive type:** Features of hyperactivity and impulsivity are more prominent.
- **Predominantly inattentive type:** Features of inattention are more prominent.
- **Combined hyperactive impulsive and inattentive type:** Features of hyperactivity, impulsivity and inattention are seen in children with ADHD in combined hyperactive impulsive and inattentive type.

Inattention in ADHD

Inattention in ADHD is characterized by forgetfulness, inability to sustain attention in any task, easily distracted toward an external stimulus, difficulty in organizing the work, doing careless mistakes, often misplacing the objects, unable to follow instructions and avoiding tasks which require more mental effort, e.g., doing homework.

Hyperactivity in ADHD

Hyperactivity in ADHD is characterized by excess motor activity that is inappropriate to a situation, frequent moving from one place to another in a classroom, being restless (commonly seen in older children), noisier and tendency to run inappropriately.

Impulsivity in ADHD

Impulsivity in ADHD is characterized by tendency to act without thinking, excessively talking, interrupting the conversations, answering before the question gets completed and not waiting in a queue.

Diagnostic Criteria

DSM-5 Criteria for ADHD

The persistent pattern of inattention and/or hyperactivity-impulsivity which interferes in the functioning or development, as characterized by points discussed in (1) and/or (2):

1. **Inattention:** Six (or more) of the following symptoms must be present for at least six months with significant impairment in the social and academic/occupational activities:
   i. Doing careless mistakes in school work, or at work, or during other activities.
   ii. He/she may find it difficult to sustain attention in tasks or play activities.
   iii. The child seems like not to listen when spoken directly.
   iv. The child doesn't follow the instructions and fails to finish school work or duties at the workplace.
   v. He/she may often dislike or avoid or feel reluctant to do the tasks which require sustained mental efforts.
   vi. He/she often has a difficulty in organizing the tasks.
   vii. The child will often be forgetful in the daily activities.
   viii. He/she will easily get distracted by external stimuli
   ix. The child often loses necessary things required for the completion of tasks or activities.
2. **Hyperactivity and impulsivity:** Six (or more) of the following symptoms must be present for at least six months to a degree which is inconsistent with the developmental

level and that negatively impacts on social and academic/occupational activities:

i. Fidgeting with or tap hands or feet or squirms in seat.
ii. Often leaving seat in the situations when to remain seated in the place was expected.
iii. Often running around in situations where it was inappropriate.
iv. The child is often unable to play or being involved in leisure activities quietly.
v. He/she is often "on the go", acting as if "driven by a motor".
vi. The child is often talk excessively.
vii. He/she often blurts out an answer before a question has been completed.
viii. The child is often having difficulty in waiting his or her turn.
ix. He/she often interrupts or intrudes on others.

3. Several inattentive or hyperactive-impulsive symptoms should be present prior to 12 years of age.
4. Several inattentive or hyperactive-impulsive symptoms should be present in two or more settings (example–at home, school or work; with friends or relatives; in other activities).
5. There are clear evidences that the symptoms will interfere or decrease the quality of social, academic or occupational functioning.
6. The symptoms may not occur exclusively during the course of schizophrenia or other psychotic disorders but they may not be better explained by another mental disorder (Example–anxiety disorder, mood disorder, personality disorder, dissociative disorder, substance intoxication or withdrawal).

NOTE

Conner's rating scale: Used to assess the severity of ADHD (Parents and Teachers version is available).

ICD-11 Criteria for ADHD

- Inattention refers to significant difficulty in sustaining attention to tasks that do not provide a high level of stimulation or frequent rewards, distractibility and problems with organization.
- Hyperactivity refers to excessive motor activity and difficulties with remaining still, most evident in structured situations that require behavioral self-control. (Predominantly inattentive presentation—inattentive symptoms are predominant).
- Impulsivity is a tendency to act in response to immediate stimuli, without deliberation or consideration of the risks and consequences (predominantly hyperactive/impulsive presentation—impulsivity symptoms are predominant).
- **Combined presentation:** Combination of both hyperactive/impulsive and inattentive symptoms present.
- Persistent pattern (at least 6 months) of inattention and/or hyperactivity-impulsivity, with onset during the developmental period, typically early to mid-childhood.
- Degree of inattention and hyperactivity-impulsivity is outside the limits of normal variation expected for age and level of intellectual functioning and significantly interferes with academic, occupational, or social functioning.
- The relative balance and specific manifestations of inattentive and hyperactive-impulsive characteristics vary across individuals, and may change over the course of development.
- In order to diagnose this disorder, behavior pattern has to be observable in more than one setting.

Nursing Management of Children with ADHD

- Educate the teachers/caregivers/parents that the child is not blamed for his/her behavior.
- Develop a trusting interpersonal relationship with the child. Convey to the child whether the behavior is acceptable or not.
- Keep the sharp items away from the children because the child may get injured during the hyperactive movements.
- Ask the child to repeat the instruction before the commencement of any tasks.
- Ensure that the child is attentive when called by name and also ensure whether the eye contact has been maintained before any instructions.
- Determine the goals daily and provide positive reinforcement step by step for the acceptable completion of tasks.
- Give assistance to the child for the task completion and also reduce the assistance gradually to promote the independent actions.
- Admit the child in special schools with a self-contained classrooms and quiet environment so that the child is not distracted.
- Parents' training program as group sessions need to be arranged and instructional materials have to be provided with step-by-step explanation.
- Balanced diet and regular physical exercises might be helpful.

Flowchart 11.7: Medications for ADHD

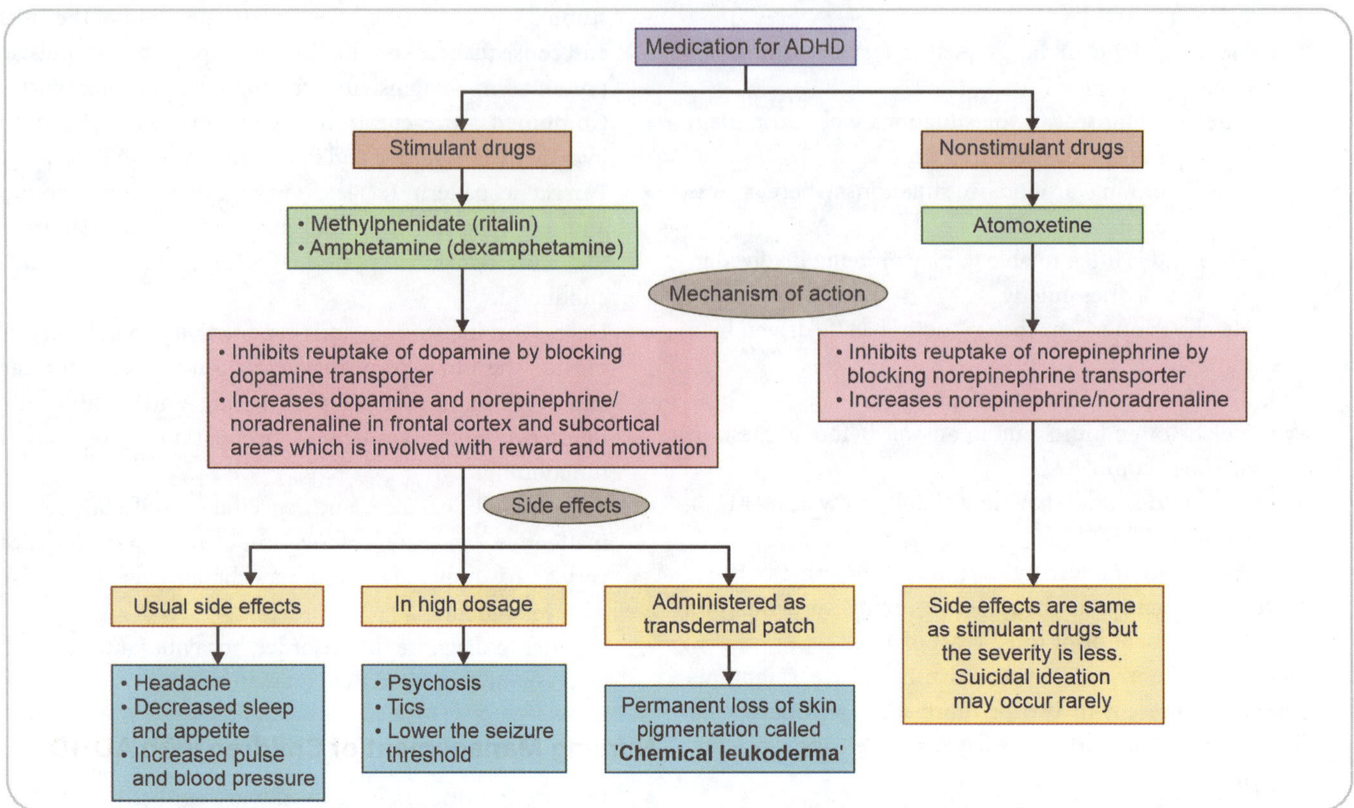

- Behavior therapy is helpful especially if ADHD has comorbid illness of conduct disorder.
- Social skills training (Because children with ADHD lack in social skill with peers due to disruptive behavior).
- Medications for ADHD are shown in Flowchart 11.7.

NOTE

Atomoxetine is a drug of choice if ADHD is comorbid with Tourette syndrome. Atomoxetine and Methylphenidate (Ritalin) might cause priapism in males, i.e., prolonged painful penile erection. Methyphenidate (ritalin) also causes weight loss in children so growth/development has to be monitored regularly.

Course and Prognosis

Severity gets reduced when the child becomes older. ADHD children show good prognosis if the psychosocial interventions and medications are given together. ADHD children have low educational achievements. ADHD comorbid with conduct disorder has high risk of developing antisocial personality disorder and substance abuse disorder.

TIC DISORDER

Tics is defined as sudden, nonrhythmic, involuntary, jerky motor or vocal activity.

Incidence and Prevalence

It is more common in boys than girls. 5% of school children have transient tics. Around 1% of school children have either motor tics or vocal tics. Prevalence of Tourette's syndrome is 4/10,000 population. Among tics, vocal tics are more common than motor tics and are more frequent in boys than girls.

Etiology

- Idiopathic
- May be inherited as autosomal dominant disorder.

ICD-11 and DSM-5 Classification of Tic Disorders

ICD-11	DSM-5	Classification of Tic disorders
8A05.00	307.23	Tourette's disorder
—	307.22	Persistent (Chronic) Motor or Vocal Tic disorder
—	307.21	Provisional Tic disorder
—	307.20	Other Specified Tic disorder
—	307.19	Unspecified Tic disorder

Classification of Tics

Classification of Tics are shown in Flowchart 11.8.

Flowchart 11.8: Classification of Tics

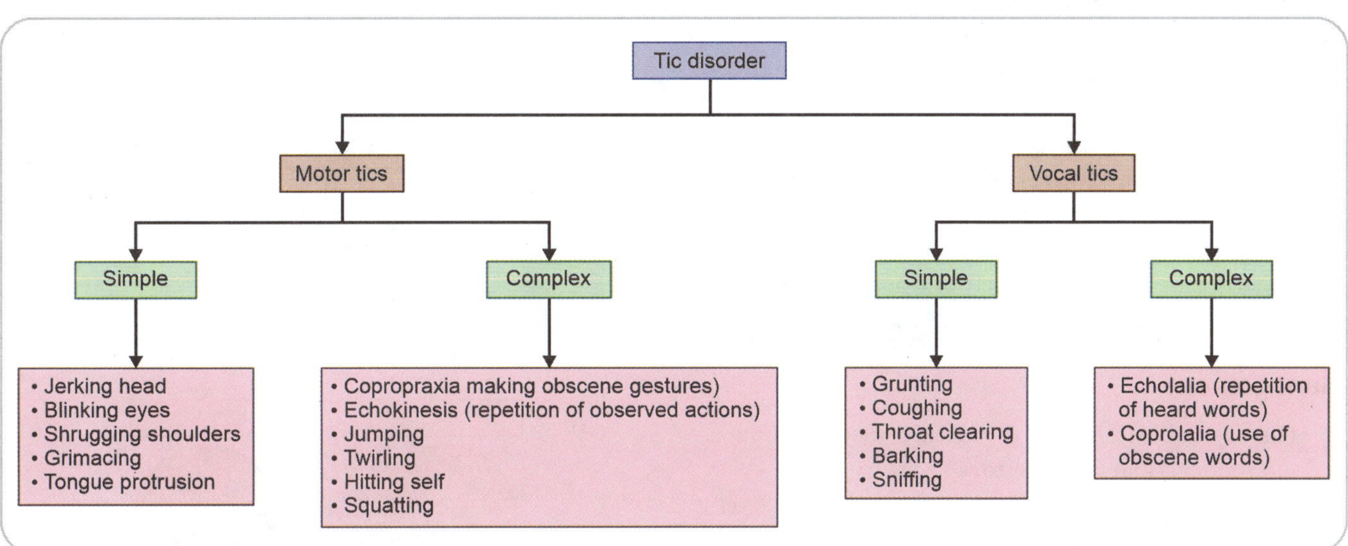

NOTE

Some patients might experience only vocal tics or only motor tics. Many patients might experience Transient tics which will disappear after few months. Few patients may exhibit echolalia and echopraxia.

Features of Tics

Usually occurs in episodes or bouts with an urge or sensation initially before tics and sense of relief after the tics as shown in Figure 11.3.

DSM-5 Diagnostic Criteria of Tic Disorders

Tourette's Disorder

- Both multiple motor and one or more vocal tics have been present at some time during the illness, although not necessarily concurrently.
- Tics may wax and wane in frequency but have persisted for more than 1 year since first tic onset.
- Onset is before age 18 years.
- Disturbance is not attributable to the physiological effects of a substance (e.g., cocaine) or another medical condition (e.g., Huntington's disease, post viral encephalitis).

Classical Tic disorder has been named after Gilles de la Tourette, a French physician, who was first person to describe this disorder. Tourette disorder is chronic, with combined motor and vocal tics. Usually, motor tics precede the vocal tics in Tourette disorder.

Persistent (Chronic) Motor or Vocal Tic Disorder

- Single or multiple motor or vocal tics have been present during the illness, but not both motor and vocal.
- The tics may wax and wane in frequency but have persisted for more than 1 year since first tic onset.
- Onset is before age 18 years.
- Disturbance is not attributable to the physiological effects of a substance (e.g., cocaine) or another medical condition (e.g., Huntington's disease, post viral encephalitis).
- Criteria have never been met for Tourette's disorder.

Specify if

With motor tics only with vocal tics only.

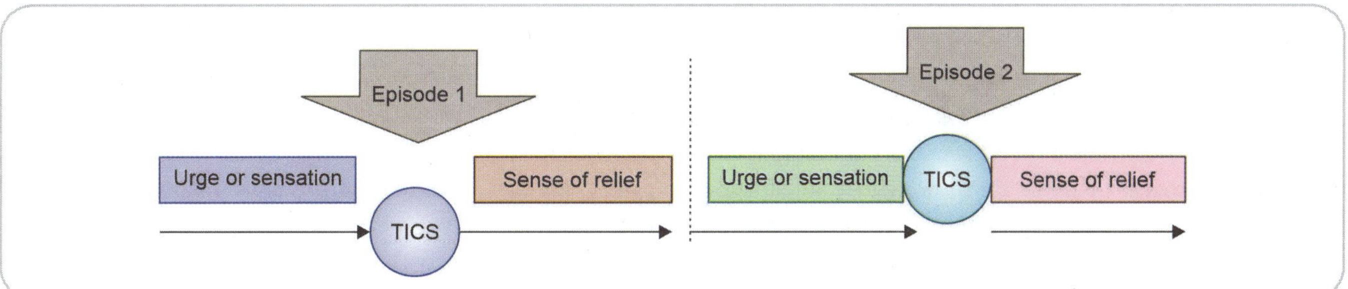

Figure 11.3: Episodes of Tic disorder

Provisional Tic Disorder

- Single or multiple motor and/or vocal tics.
- Tics have been present for less than 1 year since first tic onset.
- Onset is before age 18 years.
- Disturbance is not attributable to the physiological effects of a substance (e.g., cocaine) or another medical condition (e.g., Huntington's disease, post viral encephalitis).
- Criteria have never been met for Tourette's disorder or persistent (chronic) motor or vocal tic disorder.

Management

- **History collection:** Age of onset, course (continuous/intermittent) and family history.
- **Assessment:** Rating scale used is Yale Global Tic Severity Scale (YGTS). Assess for comorbid illnesses such as Attention Deficit and Hyperactivity Disorder (ADHD), Obsessive Compulsive Disorder (OCD), Autism spectrum disorder and depression. If children have atypical features, rule out dystonia or myoclonus or other neurological symptoms.
- **Reassurance:** Transient tics can be managed with reassurance and routine monitoring.
- **Behavior therapy**
    - **Habit reversal training:** *It is the multi-component behavior treatment which is administered to treat the repetitive behavior of tics.* It includes awareness training, competing response training (action performed to replace the tic or impulsive behavior. For example, purse the lips for one who sticks out the tongue repeatedly), contingency management, relaxation training and generalization of new skills (Encouraging to practice new skills might control the impulsive behavior).
- **Medications:** Antipsychotics—haloperidol, risperidone, pimozide, aripiprazole and other drugs such as clonidine, guanfacine and tetrabenazine can be used.
- **Deep brain stimulation:** In case of treatment resistant tics, deep brain stimulation can be administered.

SIBLING RIVALRY

Sibling rivalry refers to significant competition or animosity among the siblings for the love and affection from parents and is associated with unusual negative feelings. For example, elder son will think that my parents are showing love and affection to the younger ones only.

- **Onset:** It occurs following the birth of younger sibling.

Flowchart 11.9: Concept of sibling rivalry versus happy family

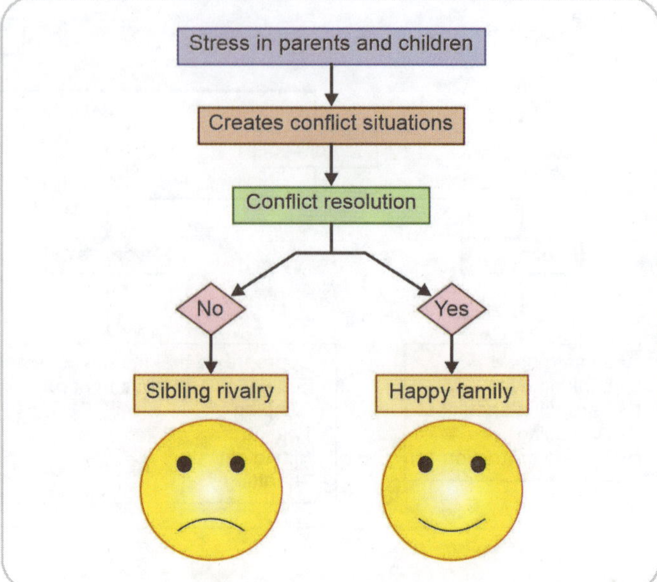

- **Intensity:** Rivalry increases when the age of both siblings is closer and when they are of same gender. When the severity increases, the expression of hostility (feel of enmity) will be present toward the siblings.
- **Behavior of children with high intensity:** This in turn enhances the oppositional behavior toward the parents, dysphoria and temper tantrums in the form of anxiety or social withdrawal.
- **Causes:** Child might feel that parents have love and affection toward the other child but not to self. Unresolved conflicts might also lead to sibling rivalry as shown in Flowchart 11.9.
- **Preventive strategies of sibling rivalry:** Parents are advised to perform fun activities with feel of togetherness. Parents are advised to spend time specifically with each child. Teach the children how to gain the positive attention from parents in a positive way instead of expressing aggressively. Additional teaching is required to improve the problem-solving skills and emotional intelligence. Encourage the children to focus on win-win solutions as a teamwork.

ENURESIS

Introduction

Enuresis means urinary incontinence (involuntary passing of urine). Bladder incontinence usually remains till the age of four years. If continence has not developed beyond four years, it is called enuresis.

NOTE

Purely diurnal enuresis is very rare condition and the secondary enuresis might be due to some underlying emotional disorder.

Incidence and Prevalence

Around 10% of children have enuresis at 5 years of age, 5% of children have enuresis at 10 years of age, 1% of children have enuresis at 15 years of age. In regard to gender, diurnal enuresis is common in females, nocturnal enuresis is common in males and secondary enuresis is common in older children as shown in Figure 11.4.

Etiology of Enuresis

- **Genetic factors:** Family history of enuresis might be the risk factor for the child to suffer with enuresis.
- **Biological factors:**
  - **Neurological**—delay in the brain development, Epilepsy and other neurological problems.
  - **Endocrine**—reduced antidiuretic hormone and diabetes.
  - **Renal/urological anomalies**—unstable bladder and overactive bladder.

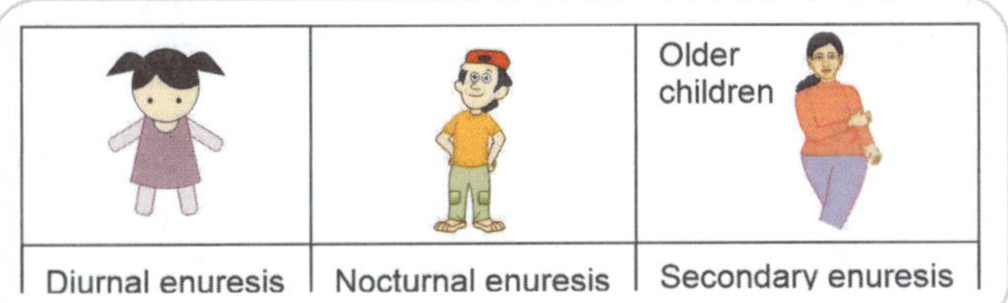

Figure 11.4: Common types of enuresis in females, male and older children

  - **Side-effects of medications:** Diuretics and antipsychotics.
  - **Urinary tract infection**
- **Psychological factors:** Death of parents, child of a divorced parent, family disputes/conflicts and sexual abuse.
- **Social factors:** Low socioeconomic status, improper toilet training, etc.

Types of enuresis: Shown in Flowchart 11.10.

ICD-11 and DSM-5 Classification of Enuresis

ICD-11	DSM-5	Classification of Enuresis
6C00	307.6	Enuresis
6C00.0	—	Nocturnal enuresis
6C00.1	—	Diurnal enuresis
6C00.2	—	Nocturnal and diurnal enuresis
6C00.Z	—	Enuresis, unspecified

DSM-5 Diagnostic Criteria of Enuresis

- Repeated voiding of urine into bed or clothes, whether involuntary or intentional.
- The behavior is clinically significant as manifested by either a frequency of at least twice a week for at least three consecutive months or the presence of clinically significant distress or impairment in social, academic (occupational), or other important areas of functioning.
- Chronological age is at least 5 years (or equivalent developmental level).
- The behavior is not attributable to the physiological effects of a substance (e.g., a diuretic, an antipsychotic medication) or another medical condition (e.g., diabetes, spina bifida, a seizure disorder).

Flowchart 11.10: Types of enuresis

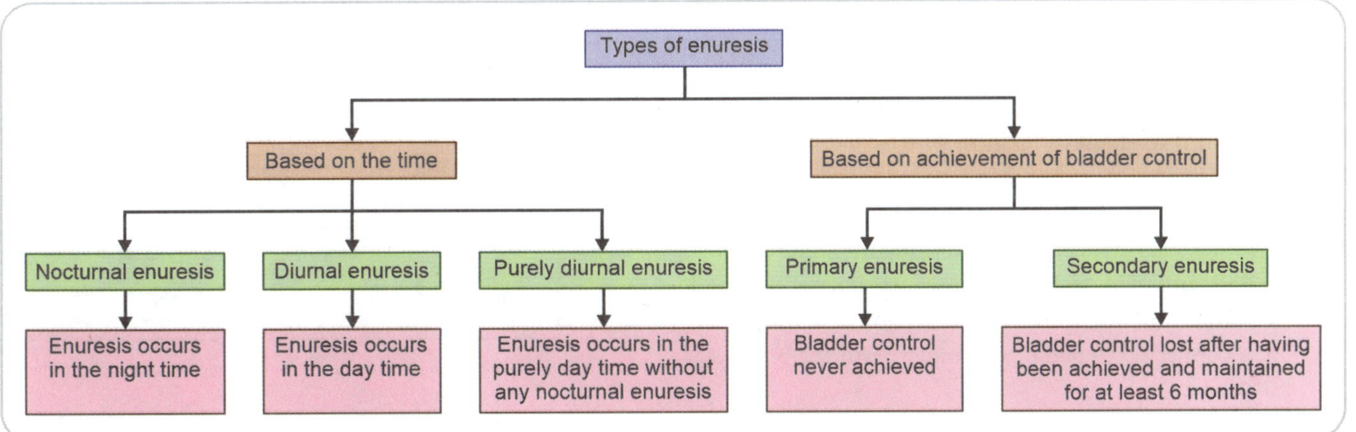

Specify whether:

- **Nocturnal only:** Passage of urine only during nighttime sleep.
- **Diurnal only:** Passage of urine during waking hours.
- **Nocturnal and diurnal:** A combination of the two subtypes above.

ICD-11 Diagnostic Criteria of Enuresis

- Repeated voiding of urine into clothes or bed, which may occur during the day or at night, in an individual who has reached a developmental age when urinary continence is ordinarily expected (5 years).
- Urinary incontinence may have been present from birth (i.e., an atypical extension of normal infantile incontinence), or may have arisen following a period of acquired bladder control.
- Behavior is involuntary but in some cases it appears intentional.
- Enuresis should not be diagnosed if unintentional voiding of urine is due to a health condition that interferes with continence (e.g., diseases of the nervous system or musculoskeletal disorders) or by congenital or acquired abnormalities of the urinary tract.

Specify whether:

- **Nocturnal only:** Passage of urine only during nighttime sleep.
- **Diurnal only:** Passage of urine during waking hours.
- **Nocturnal and diurnal:** A combination of the two subtypes above.

Management of Enuresis

- **History collection:** It helps to explore the family history of enuresis.
- **Physical examination:** It helps to rule out the underlying organic cause for enuresis. It also helps to assess the type of enuresis as primary, secondary, nocturnal, diurnal and purely diurnal.
- **Reassurance:** Reassure the parents and children that enuresis is a common condition.
- **Behavioral strategies**
  - **Positive reinforcement:** Motivate the children with appreciation and reward for the absence of bed wetting rather than criticizing or punishing the children.
  - **Bell and pad technique/enuresis alarm:** Bell and pad technique involves the activation of alarm which is connected to pad placed underneath the bedsheet. The alarm rings when urine makes contact with a sensor placed in the alarm.
  - **Star chart:** Child will get a star in calendar for each non-enuresis night.
- **Medications:** Tricyclic antidepressants (For example, imipramine) and intranasal desmopressin (synthetic antidiuretic hormone).

ENCOPRESIS

Introduction

Encopresis is defined as repeated passage of feces at inappropriate places or times after the bowel control is physiologically possible. There is no organic cause for this. It is also called fecal incontinence. Toilet training is achieved in 2–3 years of age whereas encopresis is termed when toilet training has not been achieved even after 4 years of age.

Epidemiology

Encopresis is more common in males. 1–1.5% of children develop encopresis by the age of 5 years. 25% of patients with encopresis might also have enuresis.

Etiology

- **Nonorganic cause:** Mental retardation, autism, childhood schizophrenia, attention deficit and hyperactive disorder (ADHD), sibling rivalry, inadequate/inconsistent toilet training.
- **Organic cause:** Overflow diarrhea with constipation, inflammatory bowel disease, Hirschsprung's disease, hypothyroidism and neurological lesions

Types of Encopresis are shown in Flowchart 11.11.

Flowchart 11.11: Types of encopresis

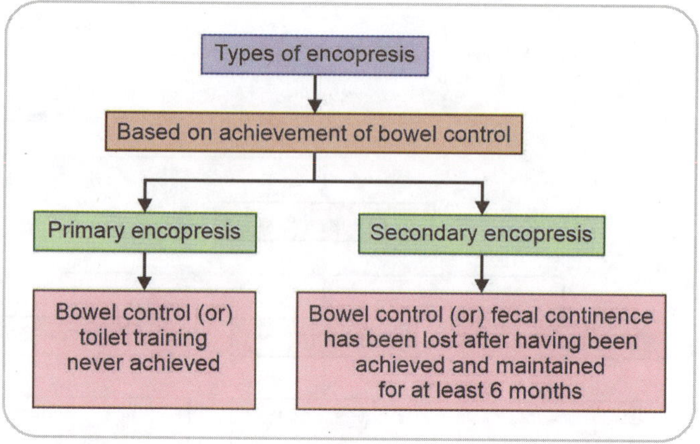

ICD-11 and DSM-5 Classification of Encopresis

ICD-11	DSM-5	Classification of encopresis
6C01	307.7	Encopresis
6C01.0	—	Encopresis with constipation or overflow incontinence
6C01.1	—	Encopresis without constipation or overflow incontinence
6C01.Z	—	Encopresis, unspecified

DSM-5 Diagnostic Criteria of Encopresis

- Repeated passage of feces into inappropriate places (e.g., clothing, floor), whether involuntary or intentional.
- At least one such event occurs each month for at least 3 months.
- Chronological age is at least 4 years (or equivalent developmental level).
- The behavior is not attributable to the physiological effects of a substance (e.g., laxatives) or another medical condition except through a mechanism involving constipation.

Specify whether:

- With constipation and overflow incontinence.
- Without constipation and overflow incontinence.

ICD-11 Diagnostic Criteria of Encopresis

- Repeated passage of feces in inappropriate places.
- Encopresis should be diagnosed if inappropriate passage of feces occurs repeatedly (e.g., at least once per month over a period of several months) in an individual who has reached the developmental age when fecal continence is ordinarily expected (4 years).
- The fecal incontinence may have been present from birth (i.e., an atypical extension of normal infantile incontinence), or may have arisen following a period of acquired bowel control.
- Encopresis should not be diagnosed if fecal soiling is fully attributable to another health condition (e.g., aganglionic megacolon, spina bifida, dementia), congenital or acquired abnormalities of the bowel, gastrointestinal infection, or excessive use of laxatives.

Specify whether:

- **With constipation and overflow incontinence:** There is evidence of constipation on physical examination or by history.
- **Without constipation and overflow incontinence:** There is no evidence of constipation on physical examination or by history.

Treatment

Provide a consistent and adequate toilet training to the children. Family support has to be given with proper understanding and family members might have a direct communication. Emotional disturbances of child have to be identified early and treated on priority.

- **Behavior therapy:** Provide positive and negative reinforcement to correct the maladaptive behavior.
- **Antidepressants:** Imipramine is the drug of choice.
- **Miscellaneous:** Psychotherapy and biofeedback.

SCHOOL REFUSAL OR SCHOOL PHOBIA

Introduction

Children with school phobia refuse to go to school because of fear. If parents attempt to convince the child, then the child may start pleading, crying, etc. and prefer to stay at home. Child may also verbalize the multiple somatic complaints such as headache, backache, abdominal pain, etc. and tries to give excuses so that the child is allowed to stay at home. These somatic symptoms only occur when the child is leaving the home and starting to go to the school (Table 11.13).

Table 11.13: School refusal versus truancy

School refusal	Truancy
Children refuse to go to school because of fear.	Children leave the school and go somewhere else without the knowledge of parents

Epidemiology

Prevalence is about 1% among school going children. Prevalence is equal in boys and girls.

Management

Behavior therapy is helpful to a large extent. Involve the parents and teachers in health teaching so that teacher might offer extra time for special coaching to the child in order to compensate for the missed hours of classes. If school refusal is found chronic, 'Systematic Desensitization' has to be done by gradual increase in the duration of time spent at school. Changing the school is generally not advisable until the teachers are unable to tackle this problem. Administer antidepressants if the depressive symptoms are identified.

SLEEP DISORDERS IN CHILDREN

Nightmares

Children may wake up after the frightening dreams. The themes of dreams are threat to survival or self-esteem. Dreams are recalled but they are vivid in nature and also cause marked distress. It occurs in second half of night time sleep (REM Sleep). It is more common in females and usually starts at the age of 3–6 years.

Management: Identify the root cause because in some individuals, nightmares may be due to sudden stoppage of psychotropics (REM rebound) or as a symptom of Post-Traumatic Stress Disorder (PTSD).

Night Terrors or Sleep Terrors

Child gets up from the sleep with panic, screaming and high level of anxiety. It occurs in third stage of night time sleep (NREM Sleep). An episode of amnesia after awakening from the bed with a short duration of confusion is present.

Somnambulism

Somnambulism refers to walking during the sleep. Child rises from the bed and walks during night time. Blank staring face and unresponsiveness are present during Somnambulism. Child can be woken up during walking in sleep with a considerable effort. It occurs in first third stage of night time sleep (NREM Sleep).

Management of Night Terrors and Somnambulism

'Scheduled Awakenings'—Awake the child prior to the expected time of episode and allow the child to get back to the sleep again.

Drugs: Benzodiazepine is advisable.

Other sleep disorders such as Obstructive Sleep apnea, Insomnia, Narcolepsy, REM sleep disorder, etc. are also commonly seen in adults.

MISCELLANEOUS ADULT PSYCHIATRIC DISORDERS PRESENT IN CHILDREN

- Childhood onset schizophrenia
- Anxiety disorders
- Mood disorders
- Eating disorders
- Dissociative disorders

FEEDING DISORDER OF INFANCY AND CHILDHOOD

Refusal of food and more food fads (highly adhere to one food item) in the presence of variety of available foods. There is no organic disease. This may or may not be associated along with rumination disorder (regurgitation and chewing of food items without nausea or gastric problems).

PICA

Pica is characterized by eating the nonedible substances. It has already been explained in detail in Chapter 10 (eating disorder).

STEREOTYPED MOVEMENT DISORDERS

These are characterized by repetitive, voluntary, rhythmic and nonfunctional movements which are not considered peculiar psychiatric or neurological issues.

Signs of stereotyped movement disorders are movements such as body rocking, finger flicking, hair plucking, hand twisting, head banging and hand flapping.

Treatment focuses on steps taken to modify this unacceptable behavior using scheduled behavior strategies and individual/family psychotherapy.

CHILD ABUSE OR CHILD BATTERED SYNDROME

Child abuse is defined as physical, psychological or sexual maltreatment of child or neglecting the child by caregivers.

Classification as per World Health Organization

- **Physical abuse:** For example, beating, biting, burning, poisoning and suffocating the child.
- **Sexual abuse:** For example, stimulating a child for sex, action toward physical gratification, etc.
- **Emotional or psychological abuse:** For example, scolding, exploiting and isolating the child.
- **Child neglect:** For example, mother not taking care the child. It involves two acts:
    i. **Act of omission or neglect:** Not taking care of child (For example, not giving feed or clothing or education, etc.).

    Sub-Categories of Neglectful Act are as follows:
    - **Supervisory neglect:** Absence of parent's supervision leads to harm/abuse or any involvement in criminal activities.

- **Physical neglect:** Fails to provide basic physical things such as safe home, clothing, etc.
- **Medical neglect:** Fails to provide the medical care
- **Emotional neglect:** Lack of encouragement and psychological support from caregivers.
- **Educational neglect:** Fails to provide education.
- **Abandonment:** Caregivers leave the child alone for long period of time.

ii. **Act of commission or performing abuse:** When a parent/caregiver severely/violently abuses the child either physically or sexually, it leads to subdural hemorrhage, cerebral edema and cerebral hemorrhage. This problem is termed **shaken baby syndrome.**

Nursing Management

Nurse has to involve the child in activities like playing and drawing in order to ventilate the feelings related to abuse. Communicate the children honestly as per age. Do not blame the children for the abuse happened to them. Provide psychological support and ensure safe environment. Identify limits and boundaries. Explain the appropriate behavior to children. Give counseling. Blood test has to be done to identify the toxicity. Drugs have to be administered to combat Hepatitis B and HIV/AIDS. Antidepressants, antianxiety and antibacterial drugs have to be administered based on the needs.

Legal Support to Prevent Child Abuse

Protection of Children Against Sexual Offences Act (POCSO –2012) and Immoral Traffic Prevention Act, 1956 are aimed to fight for child rights to prevent the child abuse

Parents and Nurse's Role to Prevent Sexual Abuse in Children

Teach the children, differences between Good Touch and Bad Touch when strangers or any family members are allowed to touch the body parts such as hands, legs and forehead. For example, Strangers are not allowed to touch the private parts. If so happened, the child has to say 'STOP' and also say 'You are not allowed to touch me here' as such.

FOLLOW-UP, HOME CARE AND REHABILITATION FOR CHILDHOOD PSYCHIATRIC DISORDERS

- Teach the parents regarding the milestone development, disorders of childhood with their symptoms, behavior, treatment strategies and age-appropriate development tasks.
- Educate the family members regarding the importance of reinforcing the acceptable behavior to the child in order to promote the positive qualities in children.
- Teach the family members to identify the possible stressors that affect the children to behave in aggressive or disruptive way.
- Adequate information needs to be given to the parents in regard to the special schools and local self-help groups which are available for mentally challenged children and also create awareness about government policies which are available to uplift those children in the society.

EXTRA EDGE

Classification of Child Psychiatry (ICD-10)

- **F70-F79 Mental retardation**
  - F70 Mild mental retardation
  - F71 Moderate mental retardation
  - F72 Severe mental retardation
  - F73 Profound mental retardation
- **F80-F89 Disorders of psychological development**
  - F80 Specific developmental disorders of speech and language
  - F81 Specific developmental disorders of scholastic skills
  - F82 Specific developmental disorders of motor function
  - F83 Mixed specific developmental disorders
  - F84 Pervasive developmental disorders
- **F90-F98 Behavioral and emotional disorders with onset usually occurring in childhood and adolescence**
  - F90 Hyperkinetic disorders
  - F91 Conduct disorders
  - F93 Emotional disorders with onset in childhood
  - F94 Disorders of social functioning specific to adolescence and childhood
  - F95 Tic disorders
  - F98 Other behavioral and emotional disorders with onset in childhood and adolescence

SUMMARY

- Child psychiatry deals with the assessment and treatment of children's behavioral and emotional problems.
- Mental retardation is defined as, 'sub-average intellectual functioning that results in or is associated with concurrent impairment in adaptive behavior and manifested during the development.'
- Stuttering/stammering/childhood onset fluency disorder is a disorder of speech characterized by disturbances in fluency or rhythm of speech, blocking of speech intermittently, rapid repetition of words, sounds get prolonged and anxiety or distress is present.
- Disorders of language include dysphasia or developmental language disorder, dyslalia or phonological disorder or developmental articulation disorder, receptive language disorder, expressive language disorder and other developmental disorders of language.
- Pervasive developmental disorder is characterized by abnormalities in social interaction and communication skills. It includes autism, Asperger's syndrome, Rett's syndrome and childhood disintegrative disorder.
- ADHD is a persistent pattern of inattention and/or hyperactivity seen in children.
- Conduct disorder is defined as a repeated and pervasive pattern of age-inappropriate behavior that violates the basic rights.
- Juvenile delinquency refers to an act committed by an individual who is below the age of 16 (18 years in case of females) but is involved in antisocial activities.
- Separation anxiety disorder occurs in children when separation takes place from the attachment figure.
- Tics is an abnormal involuntary movement which is sudden, repetitive, rapid and purposeless. It is classified into verbal and motor tics. When tics are chronic, it is termed Tourette's syndrome.
- Involuntary voiding of urine is enuresis and involuntary defecation is encopresis.
- School refusal means the children refuse to go to school because of fear. Truancy means the child will leave the school and go elsewhere.
- Pica is characterized by eating the nonedible substances.
- Stereotyped movement disorder is characterized by repetitive, voluntary, rhythmic and nonfunctional movements which is not considered a peculiar psychiatric or neurological issue.
- Sleep disorders in children include Night terrors or Sleep Terrors, Somnambulism and Nightmares.

ASSESS YOURSELF

Long Answer Questions

1. Define intellectual disability. Write the etiology, classification, manifestations, prevention and management of children with mild intellectual disability.
2. Define pervasive developmental disorders. Describe the etiology, classification, manifestations, prevention and management of children with autism.
3. Define ADHD. Write the etiology, classification, manifestations, prevention and management of children with ADHD.

Short Answer Questions

1. Write about nursing management of patient with mental retardation.
2. Define school phobia and school refusal.
3. What is separation anxiety disorder?

Short Notes

Write short notes on:

1. Tics disorder
2. Enuresis and encopresis
3. Sibling rivalry disorder
4. Conduct disorder
5. Juvenile delinquency
6. Child abuse
7. Dyslexia

Multiple Choice Questions

1. **Drug of choice for children with ADHD is ____________.**
   a. Methylphenidate b. Haloperidol
   c. Lorazepam d. Chlorpromazine
2. **Craving and eating of nonedible items are:**
   a. Polyphagia b. Pica
   c. Enuresis d. Anorexia nervosa
3. **IQ level with two to three standard deviations below the mean (approximately 0.1 – 2.3 percentile) denotes ____________.**
   a. Mild MR b. Moderate MR
   c. Severe MR d. Profound MR
4. **____________ is defined as a repeated and pervasive pattern of age-inappropriate behavior that violates the basic rights.**
   a. Conduct disorder b. Mental retardation
   c. Autism d. ADHD
5. **An abnormal involuntary movement which is sudden, repetitive, rapid and purposeless is termed ____________.**
   a. Tics
   b. Conduct disorder
   c. Juvenile delinquency
   d. Neurological disorder

6. **Drug of choice to treat enuresis is ____________.**
   a. Antianxiety drugs b. Antidepressants
   c. Sedatives d. Antipsychotics

7. **Pervasive developmental disorder includes ________.**
   a. Autism
   b. Asperger's syndrome
   c. Rett's syndrome
   d. All of the above

8. **A child is educated about the good touch and bad touch in order to prevent ____________.**
   a. Child abuse b. Suicide
   c. Sibling rivalry d. Conduct disorder

9. **Bell pad technique is a behavioral strategy used to prevent ____________.**
   a. Nail biting b. Enuresis
   c. Insomnia d. nightmares

10. **Prioritized nursing management for children who involve in head banging ____________.**
   a. Safety measures b. Psychotropic drugs
   c. Counseling d. Psychotherapy

ANSWER KEY				
1. a	**2.** b	**3.** a	**4.** a	**5.** a
6. b	**7.** d	**8.** a	**9.** b	**10.** a

Notes

Nursing Management of Patients with Organic Brain Disorders or Neurocognitive Disorders

CHAPTER 12

LEARNING OBJECTIVE

After studying this chapter, the student will be able to understand the concepts of organic brain disorders and render the quality nursing care to patients with organic brain disorders.

CHAPTER OUTLINE

- Organic Brain Disorders or Neurocognitive Disorders
- Delirium
- Proper Communication Strategies for Patients with Organic Brain Disorders
- Nursing Management
- Amnesia
- Dementia (ICD-11) or Mild and Major Neurocognitive Disorders (DSM-5)
- Nursing Management of Patients with Organic Brain Disorders
- Geriatric Considerations

KEY TERMS

Delirium, Dementia, Amnesia, Alzheimer's disease, Lewy body dementia, Vascular dementia, Pick's disease, Huntington's chorea, Parkinson's disease, Tryptophan regulation Concept, Hypoactive delirium, Hyperactive delirium, Mixed delirium, Sundown syndrome, Dyssomnia, Dysarthria, Prosopagnosia, Bradyphrenia, Klüver-Bucy syndrome, Catastrophic reaction, Bradyphrenia, Binswanger's disease.

ORGANIC BRAIN DISORDERS OR NEUROCOGNITIVE DISORDERS

Definition

Organic brain disorders are disorders of mental function in which the causative factor might be physiological rather than purely related to mind. The psychological dysfunction happens due to the damage which had occurred in brain. Two main causes of organic brain disorders are brain injury and diseases that affect brain.

Organic brain disorders are neuropsychiatric disorders that have a strong biological basis or a significant brain dysfunction.

Classification of Organic Brain Disorders

Organic brain disorders are classified into delirium, dementia, amnesia and others as shown in Flowchart 12.1.

- **Based on the etiology,** it is classified into primary (intracranial causes) and secondary causes such as systemic infections, metabolic causes, endocrine causes, nutritional factors and medications.

Flowchart 12.1: Classification of organic brain disorder

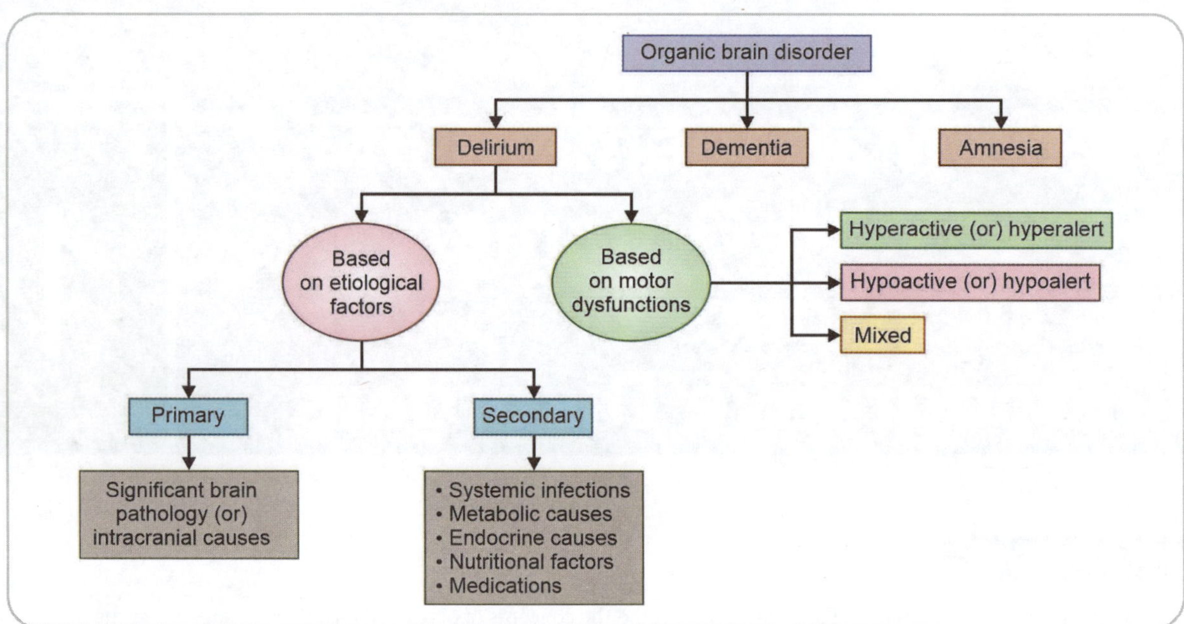

- **Based on motor dysfunctions,** it is classified into hyperactive, hypoactive and mixed.
- Classification of amnesia and dementia have been displayed through figures later in this chapter. Other types of organic brain disorders are classified into organic hallucinosis, organic delusional disorder, organic mood disorder, organic personality disorder, organic dissociative disorder, organic emotionally labile disorder.

ICD-11 Classification of Neurocognitive Disorders or Organic Brain Disorders (Block L1-6D7)

- 6D70 Delirium
- 6D71 Mild neurocognitive disorder
- 6D72 Amnestic disorder
- 6D80 Dementia

DSM-5 Classification of Neurocognitive Disorders or Organic Brain Disorders

- Delirium
- Major and mild neurocognitive disorder

Features of Organic Brain Disorders

The classical features of organic brain disorders are listed below:

- First episode
- Acute onset
- Older age of onset
- History of alcohol or substance abuse
- Neurological signs and symptoms
- Memory impairment
- Prominent visual or nonauditory hallucination

Predisposing Factors

- **Demographic status:** Presence of age extremes (very old or young) and being a male person.
- **Functional status:** Immobility, history of falls, functional dependent and low performance in activity.
- **Cognitive status:** History of delirium, dementia and memory impairment.
- **Sensory problems:** Visual disturbances and hard of hearing.
- **Surgery:** Orthopedic surgery and cardiac surgery (cardiopulmonary bypass).
- **Environmental factors:** Admission in intensive care unit, stress, use of physical restraints, patients on urinary catheterization and having disturbances in sleep pattern.
- **Neurological, endocrine and metabolic disorders**
- **Miscellaneous:** Fever, hypothermia, infections, hypoxia, shock, anemia, dehydration, poor nutritional status and decreased serum albumin level.

Synonymous terms for delirium and dementia have been given in Table 12.1.

Table 12.1: Synonymous terms for delirium and dementia

Delirium	Dementia
• Acute confusion state • Organic brain syndrome • Acute organic reaction • Toxic psychosis • Metabolic encephalitis	• Chronic brain syndrome • Chronic brain failure

Etiology of Organic Brain Disorders

The causes of organic brain disorders have been described in Flowchart 12.2. In general, the causes are classified into primary (intracranial) and secondary (other than brain related causes). The secondary causes are metabolic causes, endocrine causes, nutritional deficiency, systemic infections, medications, etc.

DELIRIUM

Definition

- An acute confusional state with disturbances in level of consciousness and reduced ability to focus, sustain, or shift attention.
- A change in the level of cognition, perceptual disturbances which are not due to preexisting dementia.

Etiology

Mnemonic

I WATCH DEATH

I : Infections (Urinary tract infections, pneumonia, septicemia, endocarditis)

W : Withdrawal (Opioids, alcohol)

A : Acute metabolic (Acidosis/alkalosis, renal failure)

T : Trauma

C : CNS pathology (Epilepsy, cerebral hemorrhage, head injury, encephalitis, Subarachnoid hemorrhage, migraine, stroke, focal lesions)

H : Hypoxia

D : Deficiencies (Cyanocobalamin, thiamine, folic acid, niacin, pyridoxine)

E : Endocrine (Thyroid, parathyroid, pituitary, adrenal)

A : Acute vascular (Stroke, myocardial infarction, pulmonary embolism, heart failure)

T : Toxins/drugs (Tramadol, digoxin toxicity, antianxiety agents, sedatives, hypnotics, anticholinergics, corticosteroids, antihypertensives, anticonvulsants, barbiturates, furosemide, theophylline, cimetidine, prednisolone, captopril, tricyclic antidepressants)

H : Heavy metals

Flowchart 12.2: Etiology of organic brain disorder

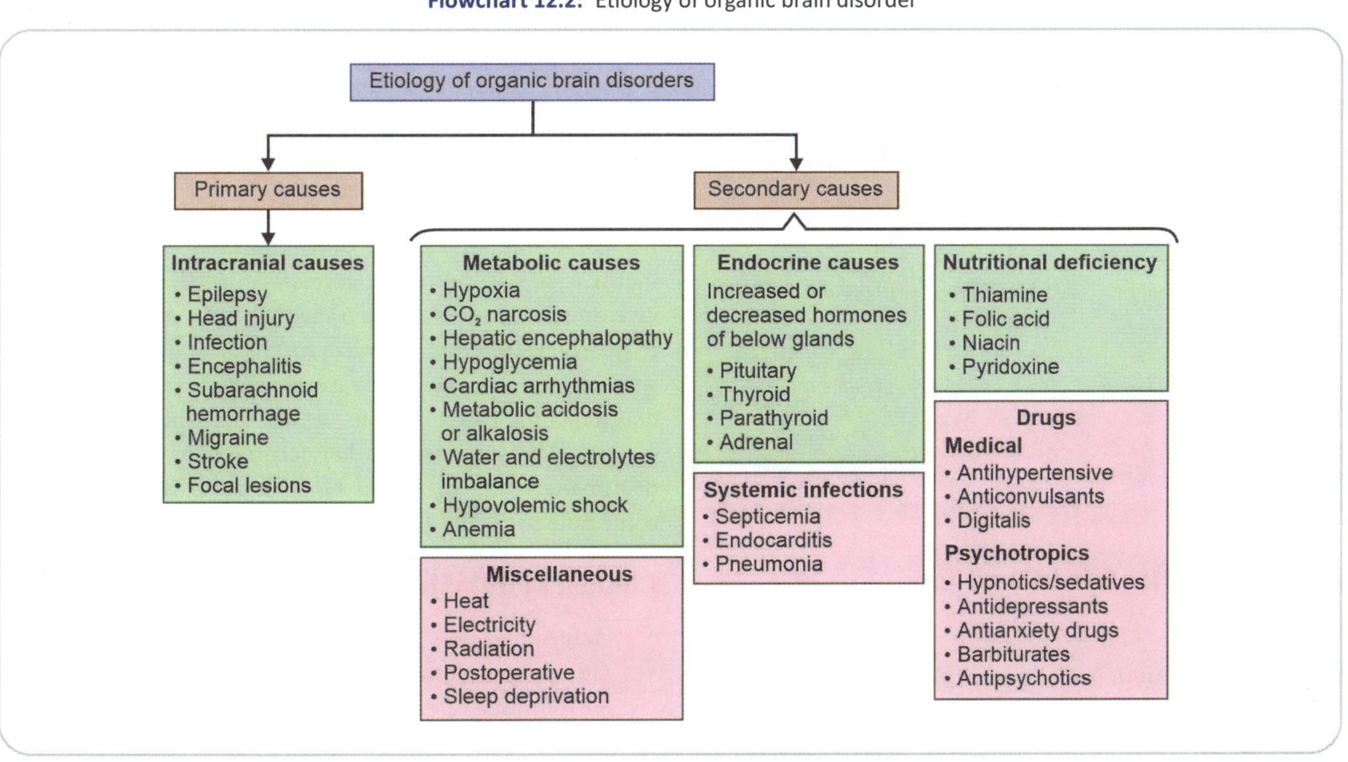

Mnemonic

DELIRIUM

D : Drugs
E : Eyes/ears
L : Low oxygen
I : Infection
R : Retention of urine/stool
I : Ictal
U : Under-hydration and Under-nourishment
M : Metabolic

CLINICAL IMPLICATION

Tryptophan Regulation Concept

Stimulation of serotonin will increase melatonin. The melatonin will enhance sleep (hypersomnia) and further it will lead to hypoactive delirium. Increased N-dimethyltryptamine might lead to agitation which is seen in hyperactive delirium. A combination of both hypoactive delirium and hyperactive delirium is termed mixed delirium. Symptoms of hypoactive and hyperactive delirium have been described in Flowchart 12.3.

Flowchart 12.3: Tryptophan regulation concept

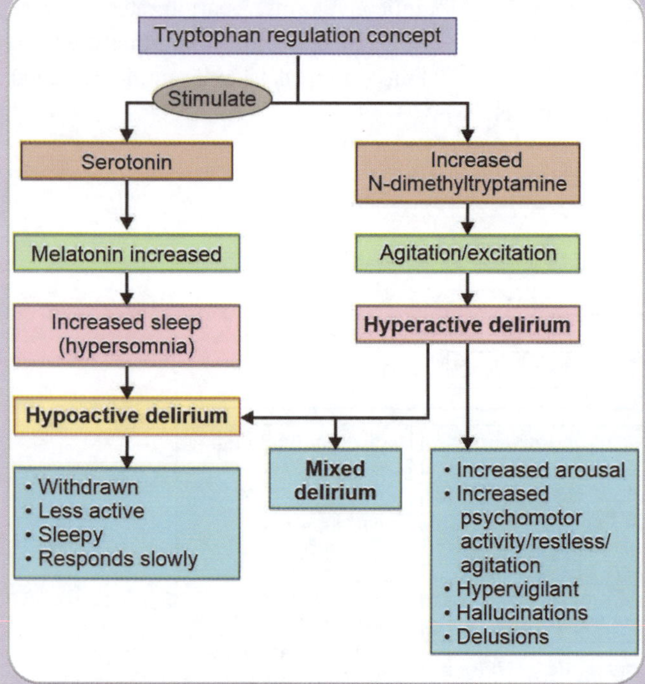

ICD-11 Classification of Delirium

6D70 Delirium

- 6D70.0 Delirium due to disease classified elsewhere.
- 6D70.1 Delirium due to psychoactive substances including medications.
- 6D70.2 Delirium due to multiple etiological factors.
- 6D70.3 Delirium due to unknown or unspecified etiological factors.

DSM-5 Classification of Delirium

Table 12.2 shows the classification of neurocognitive disorders.

Table 12.2: Neurocognitive disorders

Neurocognitive disorders	
292.81	Medication-induced delirium
293.0	Delirium due to another medical condition or delirium due to multiple etiologies
780.09	Other specified delirium or unspecified delirium

Types of Delirium According to DSM-5 on the Basis of Activity Level

Hypoactive Delirium

Patient will have intermittent sleep on and off for entire day. Patient will also have inattention while awake and fall into sleep very soon. Patient might miss medications/appointments/meals.

Hyperactive Delirium

Patient will be highly active due to response of increased internal stimuli.

Mixed Delirium

It is a combination of both hypoactive and hyperactive forms. Majority of elders with delirium (80%) belong to mixed and hypoactive type (Fig. 12.1).

Pathophysiology

In general, pathophysiology of delirium is idiopathic. The neurotransmitters such as dopamine and serotonin might increase in delirium. Inflammatory mechanism such as cytokines, e.g., release of interleukin-1 from cells might occur in delirium. Cerebral oxidative metabolism decreases. Elders with impaired cholinergic transmission are prone to develop delirium. Increased action of the hypothalamic-pituitary adrenal (HPA) axis and other factors such as stress, sleep disturbances and disturbed blood-brain barrier (BBB) also contribute to the development of delirium.

Clinical Manifestations of Delirium

- Acute onset (less than 6 months).
- Clouding of consciousness (decreased awareness to the surrounding or external stimuli).
- Disorientation to time and place is common; and disorientation to person is rare.

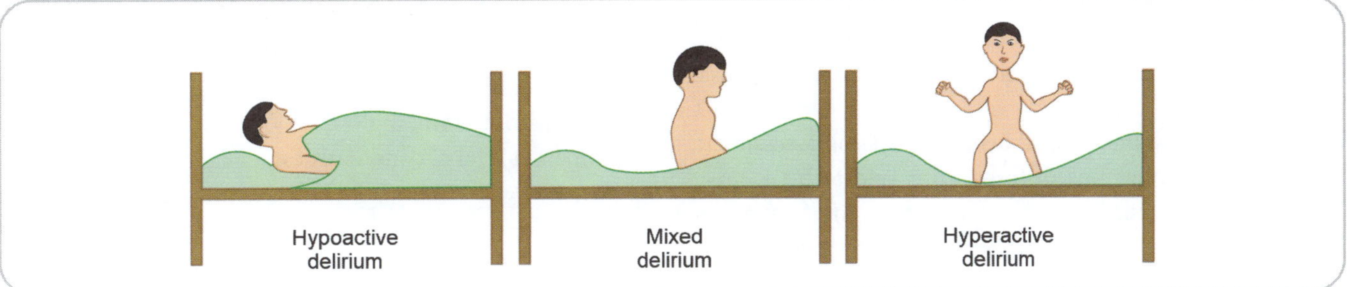

Figure 12.1: Types of delirium

- **Perceptional disturbances:** Illusion and visual hallucination.
- **Sleep wake cycle disturbances:** Insomnia during night time and drowsiness in day time.
- **Sundown syndrome or sundowning:** Worsening of symptoms in evening (diurnal variation). Symptoms of sundown syndrome such as wandering, mood swings, disorientation, insomnia, resistance, confusion and hallucination are present as shown in Figure 12.2.
- **Memory disturbances:** Impairment in registration and retention.
- **Speech disturbances:** Slurring of speech, Incoherence in speech, dysarthria (motor speech disorder/difficult in articulation of speech) and fleeting delusion (short lasting delusion).
- **Motor disturbances:** Asterixis, multifocal myoclonus and flocculation/carphologia.
- Labile affect

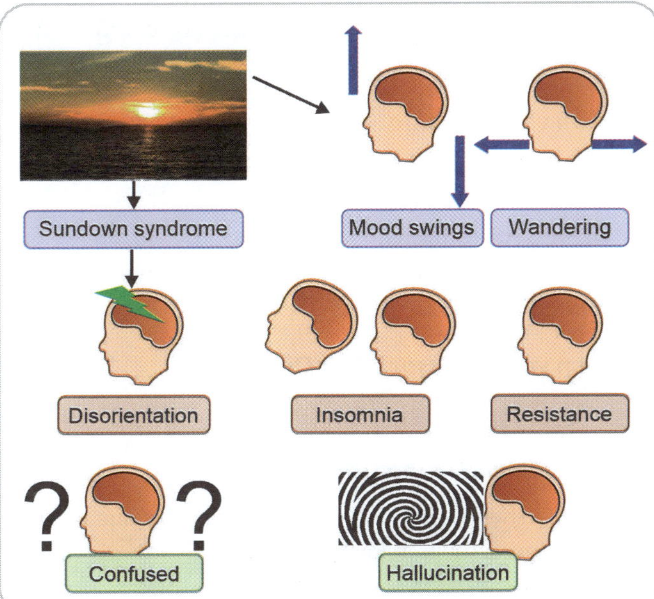

Figure 12.2: Symptoms of sundown syndrome

- **Occupational delirium:** It refers to the repetitive behavior seen in patients who act as if they are continuing their usual occupation.
- Motor/verbal perseveration
- **Dyssomnia:** Primary sleep disorder, difficulty in initiation or maintenance of sleep.
- **Agraphia:** Inability to write (language disorder due to brain damage).
- Impairment in comprehension
- Mood alteration (dysphoria/euphoria)

DSM-IV and 5 criteria of delirium have been given in Table 12.3.

Table 12.3: **DSM-IV and 5 criteria of delirium**

DSM-IV criteria of delirium	DSM-5 criteria of delirium
• Disturbances in consciousness with decreased ability to focus, sustain or shift attention • Change in cognition or development of perceptual disturbance that is not accounted well for a pre-existing, existing or evolving dementia • Rapid onset and fluctuation in the course of illness	• Disturbance in attention or cognition • Acute abrupt onset • Changes from the baseline • Fluctuating in nature • Unable to explain completely by chronic psychiatric disorder • Impairment levels do not • occur in context of coma

DSM-5 Diagnostic Criteria for Delirium

- A disturbance in attention (decreased ability to focus, direct, sustain, and shift attention) and awareness (decreased orientation to environment).
- Disturbances present over a short duration of time (hours to a few days), represent a change from the baseline attention and awareness, may tend to fluctuate in severity during the course of a day.
- Presence of additional disturbance in cognition such as memory deficit, language, disorientation, visuospatial ability and perception.

- The disturbances in attention and cognition are not better explained by another neurocognitive disorder and will not occur in context of severely decreased level of arousal such as coma.
- Evidence obtained from history, physical assessment, lab findings that this disturbance is said to be a direct physiological consequence of substance intoxication or withdrawal, another medical condition or due to multiple etiologies.

Specify if:

- Delirium due to substance intoxication
- Delirium due to substance withdrawal
- Delirium due to another medical condition
- Medication-induced delirium
- Delirium due to multiple etiologies
- Acute (lasting for a few hours or days) or persistent (lasting for weeks or months)
- Hypoactive or hyperactive or mixed level of activity.

ICD-11 Diagnostic Criteria for Delirium

- Delirium is characterized by disturbed attention (decreased ability to focus, direct, sustain and shift attention) and awareness (reduced orientation to environment) which develops over a short period of time and tends to fluctuate during the course of a day.
- Disturbed attention and awareness are accompanied by other cognitive impairment such as disorientation, memory deficit, language impairment, visuospatial ability or perception.
- Disturbance in the sleep-wake cycle (decreased arousal of the acute onset or the total sleep loss with the reversal of sleep-wake cycle) may be present.
- Symptoms attributable to disease are not classified under the mental and behavioral disorders or due to substance intoxication or withdrawal or due to a medication.

Diagnosis

History Collection

Collateral history from family members or friends with regard to baseline functions, pre-morbid personality and psychiatry history must be collected from the patient.

Interview

Structured interview focuses on concentration, somnolence deficit, mood lability, ability of execution, short-term memory deficits and mobility.

Confusion Assessment Method (CAM)

1. Acute onset and fluctuating course
2. Inattention
3. Disorganized thinking
4. Impaired level of consciousness

Along with 1 and 2 criteria, 3 or 4 has to be present to diagnose delirium.

Mini mental status examination (MMSE) is used to assess cognition.

CT Scan/MRI

Dysfunction in prefrontal cortex, frontal/temporoparietal cortex, fusiform cortex, subcortical region, basal ganglion, thalamus and lingual gyri (particular with nondominant part of brain).

Miscellaneous

Complete blood count (CBC), urine analysis, electrocardiogram (ECG) and electroencephalogram (EEG) show slowing of brain activity and sometimes focal areas of hyperactivity.

Differential Diagnosis

Delirium versus Schizophrenia

Onset of schizophrenia is rare after 50 years of age. Auditory hallucinations are common in schizophrenia, whereas visual hallucinations are common in delirium. Memory is found to be grossly intact in schizophrenia. Disorientation occurs rarely in schizophrenia. Dysarthria (difficult in articulation of speech) is not present in schizophrenia. No significant fluctuations are seen over the course of the day in schizophrenia.

Delirium versus Mania

- In mania, client may be very agitated; however, cognition usually does not decline.
- Flight of ideas in mania usually has little coherence and is not as distractible in nature. Disorientation is not common in mania.

Delirium versus Dissociative Disorder

Spotty amnesia due to cognitive impairment.

Delirium versus Depression

Table 12.4 shows the differences between dementia and pseudodementia (depression).

Table 12.4: Differences between dementia and pseudodementia (depression)

Aspects	Dementia	Pseudodementia (Depression)
Complaints of cognitive impairment	Rarely	Mostly
Emphasis achievements	• Patient emphasizes achievements • Patient is unconcerned about symptoms	• Patient emphasizes disability • Patient communicates distress
Mood	Labile affect	Depressed
Mental status exam	• Makes mistakes • Impairment of recent memory • Confabulation • Poor performance test	Patient says, 'Don't know' as answer to most of the questions
History	No such history of dementia	History of depression
Age group (More common)	Elders	Nonspecific
Organic symptoms	Yes	No
CT and EEG	Abnormal	Normal
Cooperation of the patient	Cooperative	Uncooperative
Cognitive impairment	Present	Absent
Benzodiazepines and barbiturates	Worsen the disease	May improve sleep only

Delirium versus Dementia

Table 12.5 shows the differences between delirium and dementia.

Table 12.5: Delirium versus dementia

Aspects	Delirium	Dementia
Onset	Acute	Gradual/insidious
Nature	Reversible	Irreversible
Duration	Days to weeks	Months to year
Course	Fluctuating	Progressive
Attention	Impaired	Normal until severe
Consciousness	Fluctuating/altered	Rarely alters/clear
Decreased awareness of self	Present	Present
Perception	Illusions and hallucinations are common	Hallucinations not common
Speech	Slow and incoherent	Repetitive difficulty in finding words
Disorientation	Disorientation to time is common	Disorientation to time, person and place occurs
Illness, medicine toxicity	Often	Rarely
Outcome	Excellent, if corrected early	Poor
Diurnal disruptions	Present	Present
Psychomotor changes	Increased/decreased	Often normal

PROPER COMMUNICATION STRATEGIES FOR PATIENTS WITH ORGANIC BRAIN DISORDERS

- **Getting patient's attention:** Stand in front of patient, maintain eye to eye contact and turn off noise in environment.
- **Use closed-ended questions:** For example, are you having pain? are you feeling hungry?
- **Tone of voice:** Do not shout and speak slowly.
- **Use of language:** Use short phrases and simple language.
- **Repeat, rephrase and repair**
  - **Repeat:** Help to fill speech. For example, I would like to eat ____. If nurse repeats this, elders might add rice, dosa, etc.
  - **Rephrase:** Help the elders to get correct response. E.g., if elder says juice, nurse might point out the juice and say that, do you like to have a glass of juice?

  - **Repair:** Use tactics to fill the missing information. For example, if elders point out canteen, nurse can ask the elder, are you feeling hungry?
- **Orient and reorient frequently:** Use of visual and hearing aids, orientation is needed toward place, person and time using calendar/clock.
- **Use therapeutic touch**
- **Be a good listener**
- **Do not argue with elders**

NURSING MANAGEMENT

Identify the underlying cause and treat it. Complete lab investigation is required to identify the comorbid illness. Medications are not first line treatment because psychotropics may increase delirium. Nursing care of agitated/violent/noncooperative patients is included.

Reorient training with the use of:

- **Calendar:** Orientation of date/day
- **Clock:** Orientation of time
- **Family photos:** Orientation of person
- **Windows/clouds:** Orientation of place/season (Fig. 12.3)

Antipsychotics

- Haloperidol 0.5–1 mg (must be avoided in patients with hypotension, tachycardia and arrhythmias).
- Risperidone (risperdal 0.5–2 mg) used in elders with dementia and it increases risk of stroke by three times.
  i. Quetiapine 12.5–50 mg
  ii. Olanzapine 2.5–10 mg
  iii. Benzodiazepines—For example, lorazepam 0.5–1 mg orally. Physostigmine (antidote for anticholinergics) will help to reverse the delirium that occurs due to anticholinergics.

Music therapy, light therapy, use of hearing or visual aids and involvement of family members in rendering nursing care are found helpful. Steps have to be taken to normalize sleep-wake cycle.

AMNESIA

Definition

Amnesia refers to complete or partial loss of memory. Cognitive functions of brain have been given in Table 12.6.

Table 12.6: Cognitive functions of brain

Parts of brain	Cognitive functions
Frontal	Understanding behavior of others, problem solving, plan ahead
Parietal	Control hearing, speech, language
Amygdala	Emotional responses are directed
Corpus callosum	Passing information from one part to other

Functions and malfunctions of memory systems along with parts of brain involved have been given in Table 12.7.

Table 12.7: Memory systems—its functions, parts involved and its malfunctions

Memory systems	Functions	Parts of brain involved	Malfunctions
Working memory	Execution	Prefrontal cortex	Anterograde and retrograde amnesia
Episodic memory	Recall	Diencephalon, medial and temporal lobe	
Semantic memory	Funds of knowledge	Temporoparietal	Impairment in intelligence
Procedural memory	Learning the skills	Basal ganglion	Impairment in skill learning

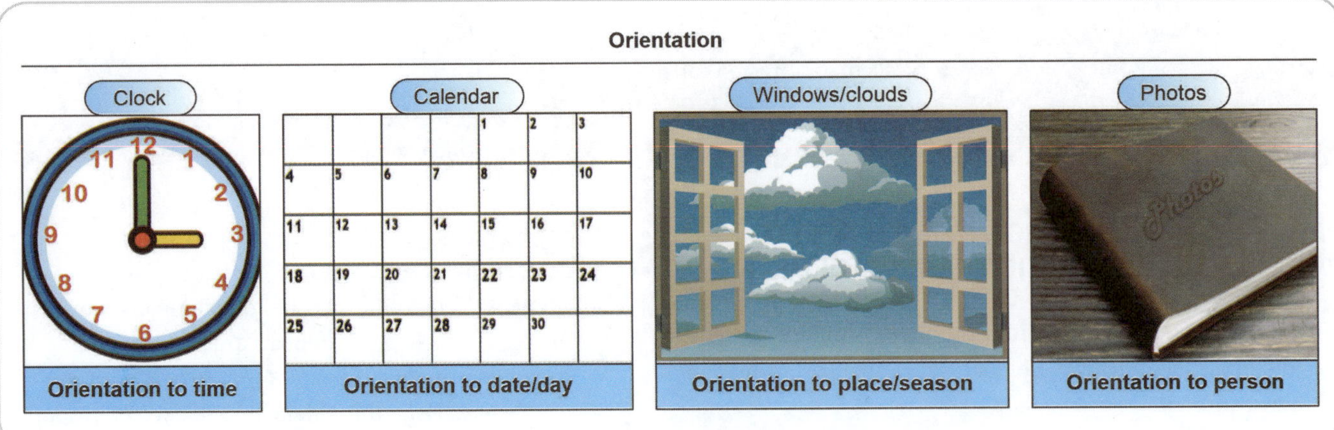

Figure 12.3: Reorientation training for patients with organic brain disorders

Types of Amnesia

Amnesia is classified into acute and chronic based on the duration. On the basis of causative factors, amnesia could be classified into amnesia due to general medical condition, due to effect of chemicals, thiamine deficiency and others. In general, amnesia is classified into transient global amnesia, transient epileptic amnesia, anterograde amnesia, retrograde amnesia, lacunar amnesia and dissociative amnesia as described in Flowchart 12.4.

- **Transient global amnesia:** Sudden temporary episode of memory loss.
- **Transient epileptic amnesia:** Memory loss due to epilepsy either in ictal or postictal period.
- **Anterograde amnesia:** Inability to create new memories due to brain damage.
- **Retrograde amnesia:** Inability to recall before the onset of amnesia.
- **Lacunar amnesia:** Partial loss of memory or memory loss of specific events.
- **Dissociative amnesia:** Amnesia is purely psychogenic due to intrapsychic conflicts.
- **Prosopagnosia or face blindness or facial agnosia:** A neurological disorder characterized by the inability to recognize faces.

ICD-11 Classification of Amnestic disorder

6D72 Amnestic disorder

- 6D72.0 Amnestic disorder due to diseases classified elsewhere.
- 6D72.1 Amnestic disorder due to psychoactive substances including medications.
- 6D72.10 Amnestic disorder due to use of alcohol.
- 6D72.11 Amnestic disorder due to use of sedatives, hypnotics or anxiolytics.
- 6D72.12 Amnestic disorder due to other specified psychoactive substances including medications.
- 6D72.13 Amnestic disorder due to use of volatile inhalants.
- 6D72.2 Amnestic disorder due to unknown or unspecified etiological factors.
- 6D72.Y Other specified amnestic disorder.
- 6D72.Z Amnestic disorder, unspecified.

ICD-11 Diagnostic Criteria

- Amnestic disorder is characterized by severe memory impairment relative to individual's age and general level of intellectual functioning which is disproportionate to the impairment in other cognitive domain.
- It is manifested by severe deficit in memories or learning new concepts or inability to recall the previously learned one, without disturbance of consciousness or cognitive impairment.
- Recent memory is more disturbed than the remote memory; and immediate recall is usually preserved.
- Memory impairment may be due to underlying neurological condition, injury, infection, tumor or other disease which affect the specific areas of brain or due to chronic use of specific substances or medications.

Flowchart 12.4: Types of amnesia

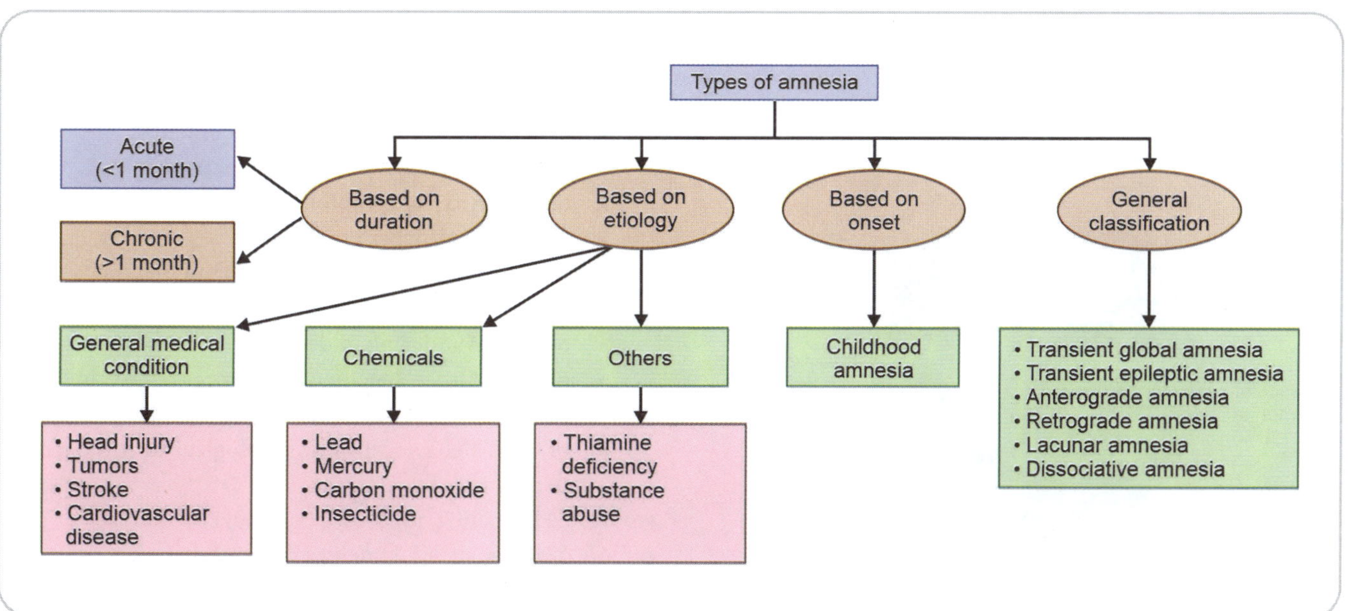

Treatment

- Cognitive training is helpful to certain extent to improve memory. **If transient global amnesia** is present, the patient recovers after a short period.
- **For alcohol-induced amnesia,** administer Inj. thiamine.

DEMENTIA (ICD-11) OR MILD AND MAJOR NEUROCOGNITIVE DISORDERS (DSM-5)

Definition

Dementia is a group of heterogeneous and neurodegenerative disorders with presence of significant decline in memory, cognitive abilities (planning, organizing, executing, thinking, judgment, etc.), emotional control (lability, apathy, irritability) and social behavior. It is a chronic memory impairment with clear consciousness. It is progressive deterioration of intelligence, behavior and personality due to consequences of impairment in the brain hemispheres, particularly cerebral cortex and hippocampus to a large extent.

Incidence of Dementia

Alzheimer's disease is the most common type of dementia (60%). Vascular dementia is the second most common type of dementia (20%). Lewy body dementia is the third most common type of dementia (15%) Figure 12.4 shows the incidence of dementia.

ICD-11 Classification of Dementia

6D80 Dementia

- 6D80 Dementia due to Alzheimer's disease.
  - 6D80.0 Dementia due to Alzheimer's disease with early onset.
  - 6D80.1 Dementia due to Alzheimer's disease with late onset.

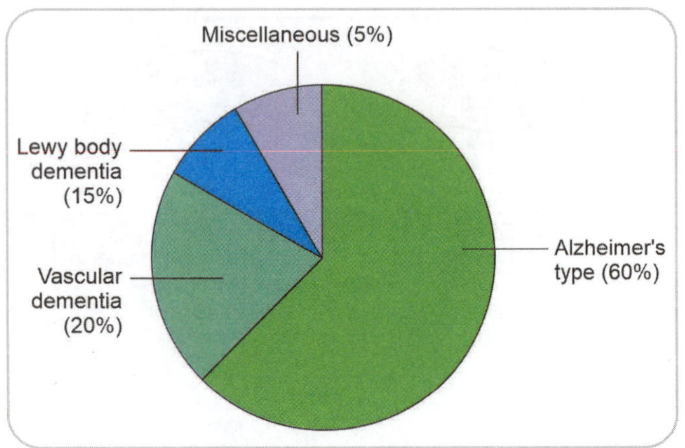

Figure 12.4: Incidence of dementia

  - 6D80.2 Alzheimer's disease dementia, mixed type, with cerebrovascular disease.
  - 6D80.3 Alzheimer's disease dementia, mixed type, with other nonvascular etiologies.
  - 6D80.Z Dementia due to Alzheimer's disease, onset unknown or unspecified.
- 6D81 Vascular dementia
- 6D82 Dementia due to Lewy body disease.
- 6D83 Frontotemporal dementia.
- 6D84 Dementia due to psychoactive substances including medications.
  - 6D84.0 Dementia due to use of alcohol.
  - 6D84.1 Dementia due to use of sedatives, hypnotics or anxiolytics.
  - 6D84.2 Dementia due to use of volatile inhalants.
  - 6D84.Y Dementia due to other specified psychoactive substance.
- 6D85 Dementia due to diseases classified elsewhere.
  - 6D85.0 Dementia due to Parkinson's disease.
  - 6D85.1 Dementia due to Huntington's disease.
  - 6D85.2 Dementia due to exposure to heavy metals and other toxins.
  - 6D85.3 Dementia due to human immunodeficiency virus.
  - 6D85.4 Dementia due to multiple sclerosis.
  - 6D85.5 Dementia due to prion disease.
  - 6D85.6 Dementia due to normal pressure hydrocephalus.
  - 6D85.7 Dementia due to injury to the head.
  - 6D85.8 Dementia due to pellagra.
  - 6D85.9 Dementia due to Down syndrome.
  - 6D85.Y Dementia due to other specified diseases classified elsewhere.
- 6D86 Behavioral or psychological disturbances in dementia.
  - 6D86.0 Psychotic symptoms in dementia.
  - 6D86.1 Mood symptoms in dementia.
  - 6D86.2 Anxiety symptoms in dementia.
  - 6D86.3 Apathy in dementia.
  - 6D86.4 Agitation or aggression in dementia.
  - 6D86.5 Disinhibition in dementia.
  - 6D86.6 Wandering in dementia.
  - 6D86.Y Other specified behavioral or psychological disturbances in dementia.
  - 6D86.Z Behavioral or psychological disturbances in dementia, unspecified.
- 6D8Z Dementia, unknown or unspecified cause.
- 6E0Y Other specified neurocognitive disorders.
- 6E0Z Neurocognitive disorders, unspecified.

DSM-5 Classification of Major and Mild Neurocognitive Disorders (Dementia)

Table 12.8 shows the classification of major and mild neurocognitive disorders.

Table 12.8: Classification of major and mild neurocognitive disorders

Major and mild neurocognitive disorders	
294.11	Probable major neurocognitive disorder due to Alzheimer's disease with behavioral disturbance
294.10	Probable major neurocognitive disorder due to Alzheimer's disease without behavioral disturbance
331.9	Possible major neurocognitive disorder due to Alzheimer's disease
331.83	Mild neurocognitive disorder due to Alzheimer's disease
294.11	Major or mild frontotemporal neurocognitive disorder with behavioral disturbance
294.10	Major or mild frontotemporal neurocognitive disorder without behavioral disturbance
331.9	Possible major neurocognitive disorder due to frontotemporal lobar degeneration
331.83	Mild neurocognitive disorder due to frontotemporal lobar degeneration
294.11	Major or mild neurocognitive disorder with Lewy Bodies with behavioral disturbance
294.10	Major or mild neurocognitive disorder with Lewy Bodies without behavioral disturbance
331.9	Possible major neurocognitive disorder with Lewy Bodies
331.83	Mild neurocognitive disorder with Lewy Bodies
290.40	Probable major vascular neurocognitive disorder with behavioral disturbance
290.40	Probable major vascular neurocognitive disorder without behavioral disturbance
331.9	Possible major vascular neurocognitive disorder
331.83	Mild vascular neurocognitive disorder
294.11	Major neurocognitive disorder due to traumatic brain injury with behavioral disturbance
294.10	Major neurocognitive disorder due to traumatic brain injury without behavioral disturbance
331.83	Mild neurocognitive disorder due to traumatic brain injury
294.11	Major neurocognitive disorder due to HIV infection with behavioral disturbance
294.10	Major neurocognitive disorder due to HIV infection without behavioral disturbance
331.83	Mild neurocognitive disorder due to HIV infection
294.11	Major neurocognitive disorder due to prion disease with behavioral disturbance
294.10	Major neurocognitive disorder due to prion disease without behavioral disturbance
331.83	Major neurocognitive disorder due to prion disease
294.11	Major neurocognitive disorder probably due to Parkinson's disease with behavioral disturbance
294.10	Major neurocognitive disorder probably due to Parkinson's disease without behavioral disturbance
331.9	Major neurocognitive disorder probably due to Parkinson's disease
331.83	Mild neurocognitive disorder probably due to Parkinson's disease
294.11	Major neurocognitive disorder due to Huntington's disease with behavioral disturbance
294.10	Major neurocognitive disorder due to Huntington's disease without behavioral disturbance
331.83	Mild neurocognitive disorder due to Huntington's disease
294.11	Major neurocognitive disorder due to another medical condition with behavioral disturbance
294.10	Major neurocognitive disorder due to another medical condition without behavioral disturbance
331.83	Mild neurocognitive disorder due to another medical condition
294.11	Major neurocognitive disorder due to multiple etiologies with behavioral disturbance
294.10	Major neurocognitive disorder due to multiple etiologies without behavioral disturbance
331.83	Mild neurocognitive disorder due to multiple etiologies

Flowchart 12.5: Basic forms of dementia

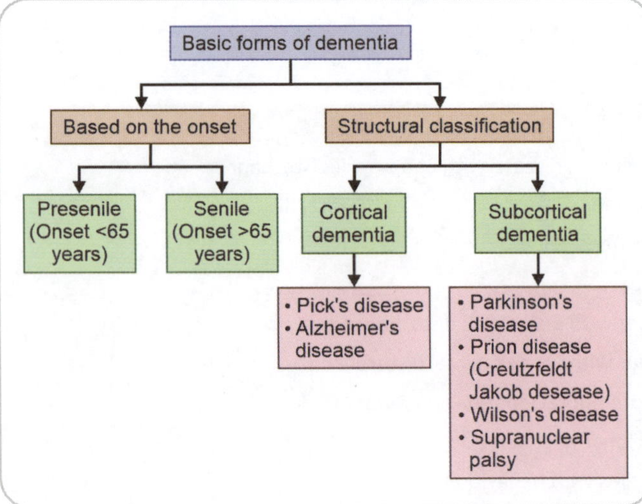

Basic Forms of Dementia

Based on onset, dementia is classified into presenile and senile type. The onset of presenile dementia is below 65 years of age; and the onset of senile dementia is above 65 years of age. The structural classification of dementia is cortical and subcortical type. Pick's disease and Alzheimer's disease are subtypes of cortical dementia. Parkinson's disease, prion disease (Creutzfeldt-Jakob disease), Wilson's disease, supranuclear palsy are subtypes of subcortical dementia (Flowchart 12.5).

Diagnosis of Dementia

Diagnosis of dementia is only done when there is presence of consistent symptoms for at least 6 months; and it should not be done when patient is delirious or in confused state. Collateral history collection has to be done from care givers/relatives/friends. Decline from previous level of functioning has to be established.

Assessment of Cognition

Categories of Mini Mental Status Examination (MMSE) have been explained in Table 12.9. Montreal Cognitive Assessment (MoCA) and Clinical Dementia Rating Scale (CDRS) can also be used.

Table 12.9: Categories of mini mental status examination

Categories	Score
Normal	26–30
Mild dementia	21–25
Moderate dementia	15–20
Severe dementia	11–15
Profound dementia	£10

Blood Tests

Complete blood count, thyroid hormones, urea, creatinine, electrolytes, liver function test, lipid profile, glucose, vitamin B_{12}/thiamine/folate levels and HIV confirmation tests are performed.

Neuroimaging

Magnetic Resonance Imaging (MRI) shows bilateral temporal lobe atrophy in Alzheimer's disease and checks out sub-cortical vascular changes. **Single-Photon Emission Computerized Tomography (SPECT)** shows temporoparietal hypoperfusion in Alzheimer's disease. **DAT scan** is a dopamine transporter scan to assess function of dopamine transportation and Nigrostriatal pathway. It is an accurate way to diagnose Parkinson's disease. **Positron Emission Tomography (PET) scan and Pittsburgh compound B** (PiB) are used to identify the amyloid deposition in Alzheimer's disease. **Computerized Tomography (CT) scan** shows cortical atrophy and ventricular enlargement. It also helps to check out treatable causes such as tumors, subdural hematoma and normal pressure hydrocephalus.

Electroencephalogram

Electroencephalogram (EEG) shows slow activity waves in Alzheimer's disease and multi-infarct dementia. EEG waves are normal in pseudodementia; and periodic complexes are seen in Creutzfeldt-Jakob disease).

Genetic Testing

Apolipoprotein E4 mutation in Alzheimer's disease; the mutation seen in Huntington's chorea. Mutant gene defects result in malformed huntingtin protein which is prone to clumping in the brain and cause nearby cell death.

Miscellaneous

Midstream urine (MSU) for culture and sensitivity, syphilis serology, HIV test, brain biopsy and CSF analysis (β amyloid and tau protein) can be done, if required.

Decline of Memory and Cognition in Dementia

Learning capacity to group new information declines in initial stage of dementia. The patient is unable to recall the events in middle stage of dementia. Unable to recognize close relatives or even self is the advanced stages of dementia (Fig. 12.5). The patient is unable to do complicated tasks which he/she could do earlier in initial stage of dementia. He/she seeks assistance for simple tasks in middle stage of dementia. He/she is unable to do any activity which requires cognitive function even with help, in advanced stages of dementia as shown in Figure 12.6.

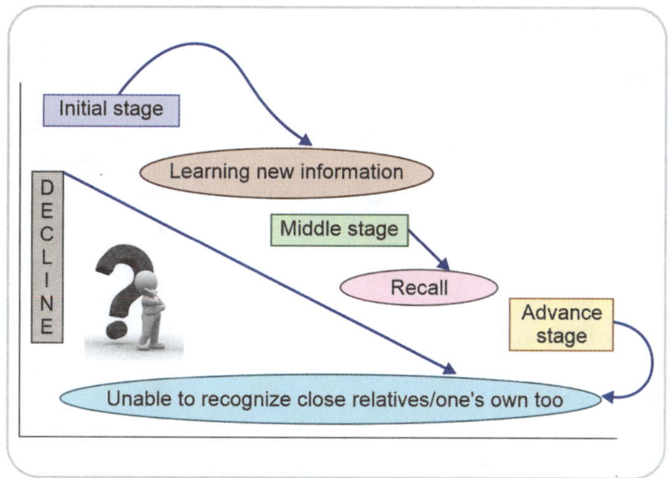

Figure 12.5: Decline of memory in dementia

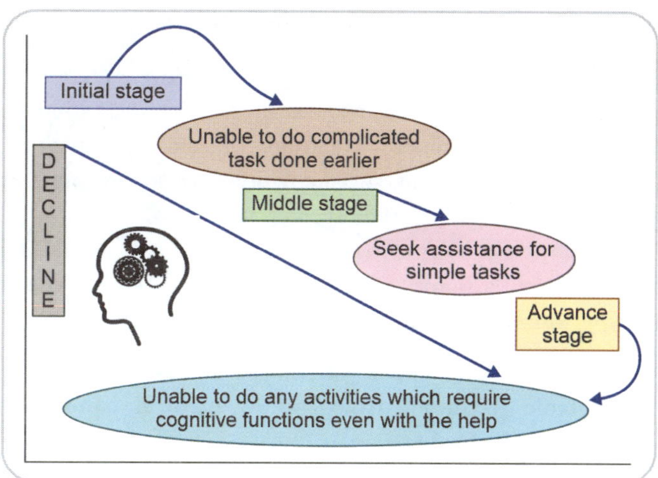

Figure 12.6: Decline of cognition in dementia

Differences between cortical and subcortical dementia have been given in Table 12.10.

Table 12.10: Differences between cortical and subcortical dementia

Aspects	Cortical dementia	Subcortical dementia
Presence of lesion in	• Frontal • Parietal • Temporal • Occipital • Hippocampus	• Thalamus • Basal ganglion • Brain stem
Severity	Severe	Mild to moderate
Motor activities	Normal	• Tremors • Dystonia • Dysarthria • Flexed or extended Posture • Chorea • Ataxia • Rigidity
Decline in short-term memory/ cognition/ recall	Bradyphrenia (Decreased cognitive speed) and recall by cues can be done to very little extent	Recall by cues done in partial way
Depressive symptoms	Not common	Common
Delusions	Simple	Complex
Miscellaneous (5 As)	• Aphasia • Amnesia • Agnosia • Apraxia • Acalculia	Nil

DSM-5 Diagnostic Criteria for Major Neurocognitive Disorder (Dementia)

- Significant cognitive decline from a previous level in one or more cognitive domains, such as complex attention, learning, memory, executive function, perceptual-motor or social cognition, language) based on:
  - Concern of the individual or treating doctor or reliable informant that there is a significant decline in cognitive function.
  - A clear impairment in cognitive performance, documented by standardized neuropsychological testing.
- Cognitive deficits interfere with everyday activities.
- Cognitive deficits do not occur exclusively in the context of a delirium.
- Cognitive deficits are not better explained by another mental disorder (e.g., major depressive disorder, schizophrenia).
- Specify whether due to:
  - Alzheimer's disease
  - Frontotemporal lobar degeneration
  - Lewy body disease
  - Vascular disease
  - Traumatic brain injury
  - Substance/medication use
  - HIV infection
  - Prion disease
  - Parkinson's disease
  - Huntington's disease
  - Another medical condition
  - Multiple etiologies
  - Unspecified

ICD-11 Diagnostic Criteria for Dementia

- Decline from a previous level of cognitive functioning with impairment in two or more cognitive domains such as memory, attention, executive functions, language, judgment, social cognition, visuoperceptual or visuospatial ability and psychomotor speed.
- Cognitive impairment is not entirely attributable to normal aging and it significantly interferes with independence in person's performance with activities of daily living.

Cognitive impairment is attributed or assumed to be attributable to the neurological or medical conditions which affect the brain.

Differential Diagnosis of Dementia

Hypothyroidism, normal pressure hydrocephalus, vitamin B_{12} deficiency and folic acid deficiency, depression and chronic subdural hematoma.

Behavioral and Psychological Symptoms of Dementia

About 90% of behavioral psychological symptoms in dementia (BPSD) occur in one or other stages of dementia. They cause significant distress to patients. In Lewy body dementia, visual hallucination is most common. In vascular dementia, emotional instability is most common. Kurt Goldstein coined the term **"catastrophic reaction"** to explain this overreaction to minor stressors which happens in a cognitive impaired individual. These outbursts are precipitated by misinterpretation of a request, misinterpretation of sensory stimuli, inability to perform a task, overstimulation and fatigue.

- **Common behavior symptoms are as follows:**
  - Aggression
  - Agitation
  - Restlessness
  - Wandering
  - Hostile behavior
  - Cursing
  - Hoarding
  - Screaming
- **Common psychological symptoms are as follows:**
  - Mood changes
  - Apathy
  - Anxious
  - Hallucination
  - Delusion
  - Sleep disturbances
  - Problems with appetite

Management of Dementia

General Considerations

Provide the patient a safe and comfortable environment. Regular social interactions with family members have to be made. Promote adequate sleep. Advise the patient to eat healthy foods with high nutrients and antioxidants. Mental exercises, such as puzzles, aptitude, finding solutions to problems, are found to be helpful. It is important for the patient to relax well either by hearing music or by involving in other recreational activities. Patient can be advised to perform yoga and physical exercises.

Psychological Treatment Modalities

Cognitive Stimulation

Cognitive stimulation is found useful in mild to moderate dementia. The objective of this therapy is to stimulate cognitive function. It can be administered twice a week as group activity. For example, group discussion, games by identification of words, letter cancellation test, etc.

Reality Orientation

Orient the patients with time, place and person. Discuss current events with patients. For example, use of calendars, clock, newspaper reading, watching TV, consistent daily schedules, labeling the rooms, etc.

Validation Therapy

Naomi Feil, a social worker from Germany, explored validation therapy, which is a method of therapeutic communication used in patients with moderate to late-stage dementia. It emphasizes emotional aspects of conversation rather than the factual content. Therefore, it imparts respect to the patient's feelings and beliefs. Techniques of validation therapy include listening to the patients in an empathetic manner, reminisce with elders, use therapeutic touch, maintain eye contact, use clear or low or loving tone of speech and avoid arguing with them. Feeling validated, respected and understood will prevent argumentative or agitative behavior in patients with dementia.

Alzheimer's Dementia

Neuropathological changes in Alzheimer's dementia were explained by Alois Alzheimer (Fig. 12.7). Alzheimer's dementia is the most common type of dementia. Females are more commonly affected with Alzheimer's disease than males. Risk is high if family history of dementia is present. Incidence of Alzheimer's disease increases as the age increases.

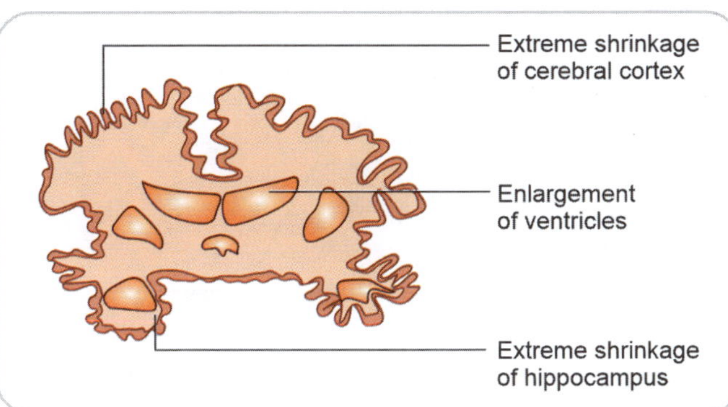

Figure 12.7: Peculiar changes in brain seen in Alzheimer's dementia

Types of Alzheimer's Dementia

Early Onset

Onset is usually <65 years of age (mostly in late 40s and early 50s). Nearly 5% of patients have early onset of Alzheimer's disease. It is very severe with rapid progression in nature. Three genes commonly implicated in early onset of dementia are Presenilin 1 Gene, Presenilin 2 Gene and Amyloid Precursor Protein (APP) gene.

Late Onset

Onset is usually >65 years of age. It is gradually progressive in nature. Commonly, 95% of patients suffer with late onset of Alzheimer's disease. Apo E4 (Apolipoprotein E4) gene has been implicated in this type.

Types of Alzheimer's dementia can also be classified based on: with behavioral symptoms and without behavioral symptoms. Behavioral symptoms include anger, aggression, emotional distress, verbal or physical outburst, restlessness, hallucinations, delusions, sleep problems, irritability and anxiety.

Risk Factors and Etiology

- Pathological stress
- Cardiovascular diseases
- Hypertension
- Obesity
- Depression
- Traumatic brain injury
- Presence of family history
- Smoking
- Monozygotic twins
- Down syndrome
- Amyloid (Precursor of chromosome 21)
- Hypoactive neurotransmitters such as acetylcholine and norepinephrine
- Cholinergic hypothesis
- Decreased corticotrophin and somatostatin
- Aluminum toxicity
- Cell membrane phospholipids metabolism
- Abnormal glutamate metabolism
- Apo E4 (Apolipoprotein E4) allele
  - Single Apo E4 (Apolipoprotein E4) allele, heterogeneous with double risk of Alzheimer's disease
  - Two Apo E4 (Apolipoprotein E4) allele, homogeneous increase in the risk of Alzheimer's disease (five folds).

Protective Factors against Alzheimer's Dementia

- Physical exercises
- **Intellectual stimulation:** Puzzles, mind games, aptitude testing, etc.
- Foods rich in antioxidants and polyunsaturated fatty acid (PUFA)
  - Fruits
  - Vegetables
  - Sea foods (fish)
  - Curcumin (ingredient of turmeric)

Diagnosis

- **Macroscopic view:** Cerebral ventricles are enlarged, cerebral cortex shrinks; and shrinkage of hippocampus and widening of cerebral sulci are seen.
- **Microscopic view:** Senile plaques, granulovacuolar degeneration, neurofibrillary tangles and cell loss in cortical nerves are seen.
- Neurochemical changes include a decrease in choline acetyltransferase or acetylcholinesterase (Ach).
- CT/MRI
  - Enlargement in ventricles.

Neuropathological changes in Alzheimer's Dementia

Deposits of β-amyloid lead to plaque formation outside the neuron. Hyperphosphorylation of tau protein causes neurofibrillary tangles (NFT) inside the neuron. There may be nonspecific changes such as oxidative stress and inflammation that happen in Alzheimer's disease (Fig. 12.8).

Treatment

Acetylcholinesterase Inhibitors

Drugs inhibit acetylcholinesterase, which will break acetylcholine (Ach). Acetylcholine decreases in Alzheimer's disease. Acetylcholine is important for learning and memory.

- Rivastigmine (Exelon) 5–6 mg
- Donepezil (Aricept) 5–10 mg/day
- Galantamine (Reminyl) 8 mg
- Tacrine

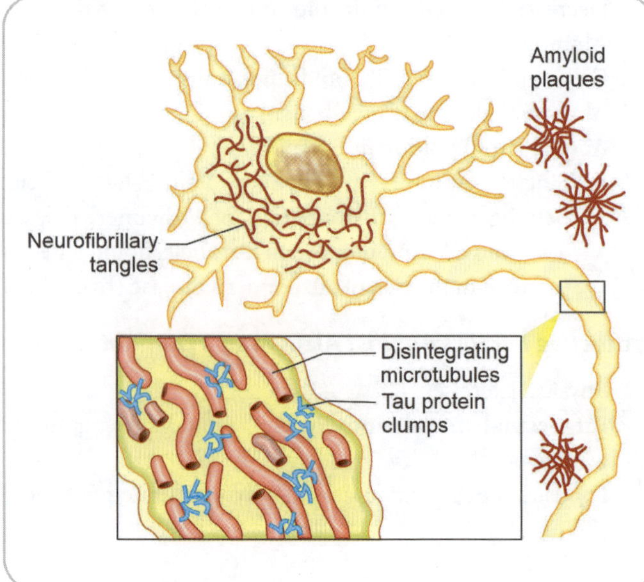

Figure 12.8: Neurons in Alzheimer's disease

N-methyl-D-aspartate receptor (NMDA) Receptor Antagonist

Glutamate is the excitatory neurotransmitter released by nerve cells in the brain. **NMDA** (N-methyl-D-aspartate) receptor allows the glutamate to connect with the nerve cell and therefore, calcium enters the cell which carries the electrical or chemical signals. In Alzheimer's disease, nerve cells make increased quantities of glutamate. So, increased amount of calcium that enters the nerve cells damages the neurons. Hence, NMDA receptor antagonists block the connection of the glutamate with the nerve cell and they maintain healthy neurons. Memantine (Ebixa, Axura, Namenda) is the drug of choice for patients with Alzheimer's disease.

Miscellaneous

- Antidepressants
- Antipsychotics (used with caution because of higher risk of stroke when they are used in dementia patients)
- Benzodiazepines
- Mood stabilizers
- Avoid anticholinergics or drugs with similar effects of anticholinergics, such as tricyclic antidepressants, because they can worsen the cognitive impairment leading to confusion.

Prognosis

Prognosis is progressive and irreversible. Deterioration rate varies among individuals. Early onset Alzheimer's disease will progress faster. Death usually occurs within 20 years of onset; and the cause of death is usually bronchopneumonia.

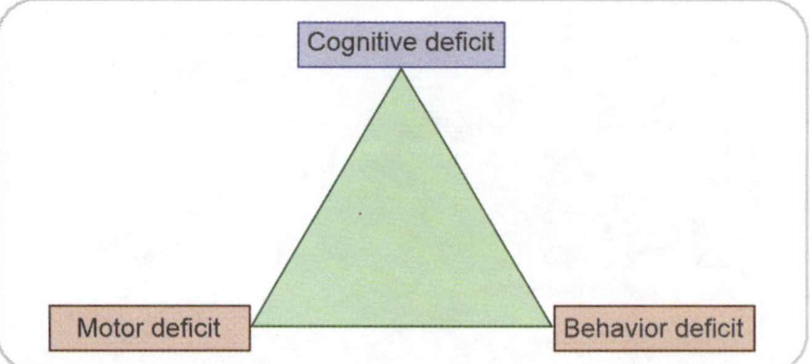

Figure 12.9: Main diagnostic criteria for AIDS dementia complex

AIDS Dementia Complex

Acquired immunodeficiency syndrome (AIDS) is caused by human immunodeficiency virus (HIV) which is a retrovirus that crosses the blood-brain barrier (BBB). HIV infected macrophages and lymphocytes lead to decreased cognition, motor, behavioral and neurological functions. Approximately two-third of patients with AIDS will develop dementia. Main diagnostic criteria for AIDS dementia complex are deficits of behavior, motor and cognition as shown in Figure 12.9. HIV proteins or virotoxins have direct toxic effects toward nerve cells by initiating astrocytes, macrophages and microglia to release chemokines, cytokines and neurotoxic substances. Prognosis is generally variable. Poor prognosis is seen in low or decreased CD4 count, platelet count, hemoglobin level and body mass index (BMI). CT scan reveals cortical atrophy in the initial period of onset (1–4 months). Treatment includes zidovudine, which partially helps to reduce neuropsychological deficit.

Lewy Body Dementia

In Lewy body dementia, decline in cognition comes with three more features:

1. Fluctuations in alertness.
2. Recurrent and vivid visual hallucinations in early stages of disease.
3. **Features of Parkinson's disease:** Muscle rigidity, loss of spontaneous movement, mask-like face, bradykinesia, etc.

Other features include syncope, autonomic symptoms, rapid eye movement (REM) sleep behavior disorder and severe neuroleptic sensitivity.

Medial temporal atrophy is not a vital feature in this type of dementia since memory impairment is not a prominent one. Family history is also not an essential part in this type of dementia. Lewy bodies are also seen in Parkinson's disease. Single-photon emission computed tomography (SPECT) scan shows occipital hypoperfusion or hypometabolism.

Pathophysiology

Accumulated components of alpha-synuclein protein within nucleus of neurons in the brain control various aspects of memory and motor control, so that the particular functions of brain get affected.

Treatment

Acetylcholinesterase inhibitors (rivastigmine, donepezil, galantamine) and N-methyl-D-aspartate (NMDA) receptor antagonist (memantine) are used. Avoid antipsychotics because of neuroleptic sensitivity. Levodopa will not help in improving the motor symptoms in this type of dementia, though it works well in Parkinson's disease.

Vascular Dementia or Multi-infarct Dementia (MID)

Vascular dementia is considered the second most common type of dementia. It is more common in men. It can be prevented by managing the risk factors well. Primary risk factors are stroke and transient ischemic attack. Secondary risk factors are diabetes, hypertension, smoking, coronary artery diseases and dyslipidemia (Fig. 12.10).

Mechanism

There is presence of occlusive plaque or thromboembolism or hemorrhage in blood vessels. Multiple small cortical infarcts are present in vascular dementia. Small vessel vascular dementia due to damage of white matter is termed **Binswanger's disease (Subcortical leukoencephalopathy)**. **Lacunar state/Lacunar syndrome/status lacunaris** is defined as more minute infarcts called lacunae which are seen in vascular dementia and in severe hypertension.

Characteristic Features

- Abrupt onset and usual age of onset is between 60 and 75 years.
- Acute exacerbations (because of repeated infarctions)
- Deterioration is step wise (Pattern as step-ladder)
- Course is fluctuating
- History of stroke or transient ischemia
- Focal neurological signs
- Presence of insight
- Emotionally labile

Diagnosis

Carotid bruit, fundoscopic abnormalities, EEG shows focal slowing and CT scan shows multiple infarcts in brain and enlarged cerebral ventricles.

Treatment

Treatment modalities include prevention of primary and secondary risk factors, control of high blood pressure. Medications, such as antiplatelet (aspirin), antipsychotics, antidepressants, psychostimulants and benzodiazepines, can be used.

Pick's Disease or Frontotemporal Dementia

Frontal lobe is prominently involved (frontal signs are inhibited). Atrophy, neuronal loss, gliosis and intraneural bodies (pick bodies) can be seen in frontal temporal lobe.

Klüver-Bucy syndrome is represented by lesions in medial temporal lobe and it is common in Pick's disease in which insertion of inappropriate things in mouth (hyperorality), high sexual desire (hypersexuality) and poor response to emotional stimuli (placidity) can be seen (Fig. 12.11).

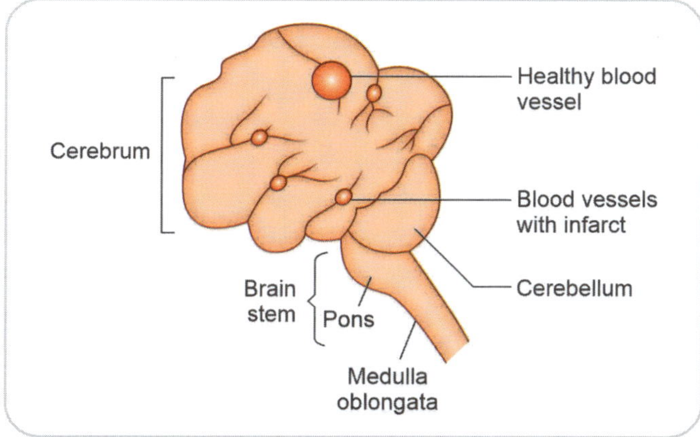

Figure 12.10: Healthy blood vessel and blood vessel with multiple infarction in vascular dementia

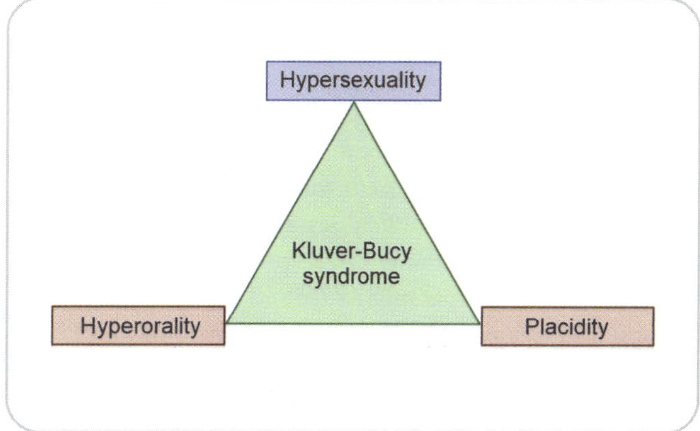

Figure 12.11: Kluver-Bucy syndrome

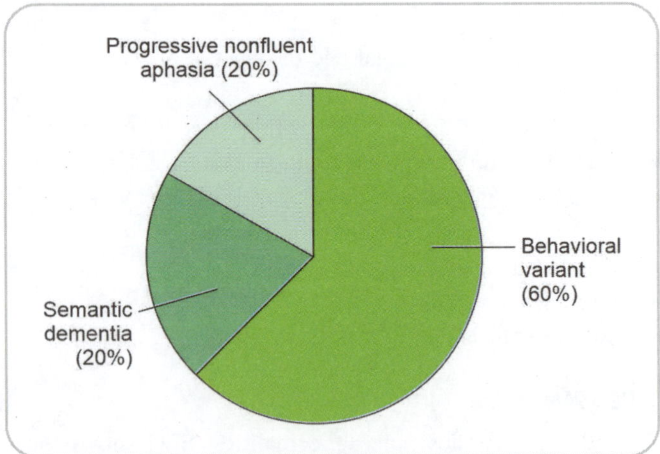

Figure 12.12: Subdivision of Pick's disease based on presentation

Subdivision of Pick's disease on presentation basis shows that 60% are behavioral variants, 20% have semantic dementia and 20% show progressive nonfluent aphasia (Fig. 12.12).

- **Behavioral variant:** Frontal lobe is mainly involved; so, executive function, personality and emotional control are affected.
- **Semantic dementia:** Temporal lobe is mainly involved. Language comprehension is said to be poor but the expression is fluent.

Progressive Nonfluent Aphasia

Progressive nonfluent aphasia (PNFA) is a clinical syndrome associated with frontotemporal lobar degeneration. It is insidious in onset. The specific degeneration of frontal and temporal lobe might create peculiar language deficit. This disorder commonly has a primary effect on the left hemisphere, which causes the symptomatic display of expressive language deficit and sometimes may disrupt the receptive abilities while comprehending complex language. The main clinical features are progressive difficulties with speech production. There may be problems with different parts of speech production. Hence, the patients may present with articulation breakdown, phonemic breakdown (difficulties with sounds) and other features such as hesitant or effortful speech, stuttering, apraxia of speech, phonemic paraphasia (sound errors in speech, for example 'cat' was pronounced as 'gat'), apraxia of speech and agrammatism (usage of wrong grammar or tense).

Differences between Alzheimer's disease and pick's disease have been depicted in Table 12.11.

Table 12.11: Differences between Alzheimer's disease and Pick's disease

Aspects	Alzheimer's disease	Pick's disease or frontotemporal dementia
Age of onset	Commonly above 65 years	50–60
Speech problems	Most common	Less
Memory impairment	Early	Late
Behavior changes	Late	Early

Prion Disease

Replicative protein mutates and causes a variety of spongiform diseases. It can transmit through use of contaminated dura mater, corneal graft and ingesting meat from cattle (Bovine spongiform encephalopathy).

Huntington's Chorea or Huntington's disease

A genetically dominant disease due to chromosome four defect. Onset is around 30–40 years of age.

Epidemiology

Male and female are equally affected. 6 members in 1 lakh population are affected with Huntington's chorea.

Signs

Choreoathetoid movements are an early sign of Huntington's chorea and dementia is a late sign.

Pathophysiology

- Brain atrophy is seen in basal ganglia and caudate nucleus.
- Associated psychiatric symptoms are mood disorders (50%), personality disorders (25%) and schizophrenia (25%).

Differential Diagnosis

Psychosis, depression.

Course and Prognosis

Progressive.

Treatment

Antipsychotics, antidepressants, benzodiazepines and genetic counseling.

Parkinson's Disease

Parkinson's disease is a neurodegenerative disease caused by degeneration of neurons in brain particularly in nigrostriatal pathway of the basal ganglia. The cells in substantia nigra will release dopamine.

Basal ganglia pathway is responsible for regulation of movement. Cells of substantia nigra degenerate; and movement disturbances are present in Parkinson's disease.

Motor symptoms are as follows:

- Tremors
- Bradykinesia
- Muscle rigidity
- Lack of facial expression
- Unstable posture
- Stooped and shuffling gait

Other symptoms include:

- Decreased sense of smell
- Low voice tone
- Foot cramps
- Sleep disturbances
- Depression
- Constipation
- Drooling of saliva

Differences between lewy body dementia and Parkinson's disease have been given in Table 12.12.

Table 12.12: Differences between Lewy body dementia and Parkinson's disease

Aspects	Lewy body dementia	Parkinson's disease
Onset of dementia	Mostly precedes motor symptoms or at the onset of motor symptoms	Mostly follow motor symptoms
Type of dementia	Cortical	Sub-cortical
Motor symptoms at diagnosis	50%	100%
Cognitive fluctuation	Present	Absent
Visual hallucination	Present	Absent
Resting tremors	Not prominent	Prominent

Medical treatment includes:

- Levodopa
- Carbidopa
- Monoamine oxidase inhibitors, e.g., selegiline
- Catechol-O-Methyl Transferase (COMT) inhibitors, e.g., entacapone, tolcapone.
- Anticholinergics

Surgical treatment includes

- Deep brain stimulation—implanting a pacemaker-like unit, transmit the impulses to electrodes placed in subthalamic nucleus.

Points to Remember

- Do not use benzodiazepine for delirium unless the delirium is due to alcohol or benzodiazepine withdrawal.
- **Black box warning:** Atypical and typical antipsychotics are not considered approved drugs for dementia-related psychosis because they have higher risk of death. Avoid using haloperidol *via* IV since it increases the risk of cardiac arrest.

Stages of Dementia

- **Early stage of dementia** occurs usually at 2–4 years after the onset of dementia. The common symptoms are forgetfulness, poor performance in work, decreased interest in environment and reluctance to initiate action.
- **Middle stage of dementia** occurs usually at 2–12 years after the onset of dementia. The common symptoms are anxiousness, irritability, progressive memory loss, wandering, difficulty in following simple instructions, social isolation and neglect of personal hygiene.
- **Late stage of dementia** occurs usually more than 12 years after the onset of dementia. The common symptoms are significant weight loss, unable to recognize the family members, inability to communicate, inability to stand or walk. Death may occur due to aspiration pneumonia. Stages of dementia have been presented in Flowchat 12.6.

Flowchart 12.6: Stages of dementia

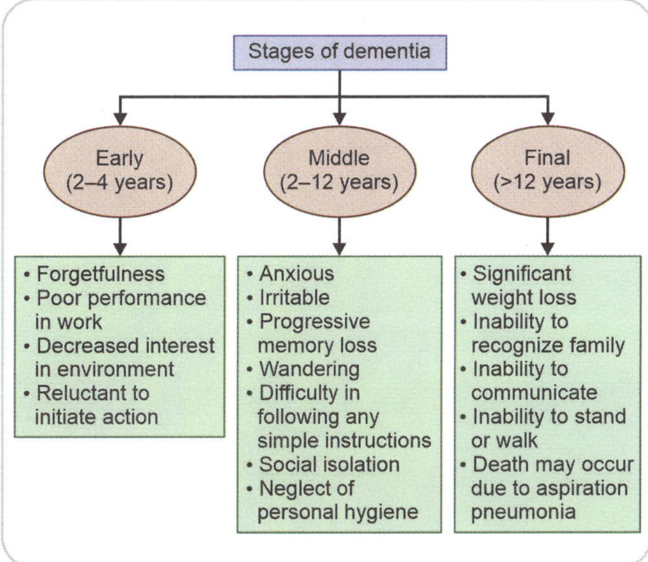

Mild Cognitive Impairment

Mild cognitive impairment (MCI) is an intermediate state between normal aging and dementia. Mild cognitive impairment will develop into dementia usually within three years. Types of mild cognitive impairment have been listed below:

1. **Amnestic mild cognitive impairment:** Affects memory function. It is a risk factor for Alzheimer's disease.
2. **Nonamnestic mild cognitive impairment:** Does not affect memory function. It is a risk factor for frontal temporal dementia and Lewy body dementia.
3. **Mixed mild cognitive impairment:** It is a combination of both amnestic and nonamnestic type. It is a risk factor for vascular dementia.

Continuum from Normal Aging to Dementia

Normal aging process takes place among all elders, whereas patients with dementia will undergo the intermediate state which includes mild cognitive impairment and it slowly develops into dementia within three years as shown in Figure 12.13.

NURSING MANAGEMENT OF PATIENTS WITH ORGANIC BRAIN DISORDERS

Nursing Assessment

Nurse has to assess the cognitive functions, safety needs of patients, social interaction with others, activities of daily living, nutritional needs, hygienic needs and need for sleep and rest.

Nursing Diagnosis

Biological Perspective

- Self-care deficit
- Impaired physical mobility
- Sleep pattern disturbances

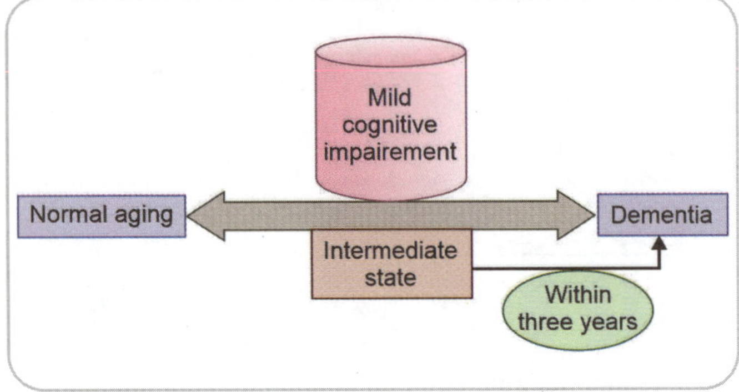

Figure 12.13: Continuum from normal aging to dementia

- Risk of infection
- Risk of aspiration
- Risk of injury

Psychological Perspective

- Disturbed thought process
- Memory impairment
- Anxiety
- Disturbed identity of self
- Powerlessness

Social Perspective

- Poor social interaction
- Interrupted family process
- Impaired verbal communication

NURSING INTERVENTIONS

Memory impairment related to declined cognitive functions as evidenced by impairment of recent memory revealed by mental status examination.

Nursing interventions	Rationale
Orient the patients to time, place and person	To help the patient become aware of time, place and person
Use calendars to remind the daily routines	Help to know the daily routines
Use reminders in phone to remember the work schedules on time	It helps the patient to be reminded of the work schedules
Do Mini-Mental State Examination (MMSE) or Folstein test periodically	To review the client's cognitive functions
Check lab reports to rule out contributing factors	It helps to identify the factors which affect cognition

- **High risk of injuries to elderly patients who lack coordination and balance evidenced by Romberg test in neurological assessment.**

Nursing interventions	Rationale
Stick the safety stickers on case files	To make all the health team workers aware of high-risk patients who need safety measures
Provide non-slippery shoes	To prevent the patient from falling
Ensure the holders are attached in bathrooms/toilet	It gives the grip to hold while the patient is walking in the bathroom. Therefore, it will prevent the patient's fall

Contd...

Nursing interventions	Rationale
Provide 'low bed' to the patient	It will help the patient claim the bed easily
Store the things near patients which are repeatedly used by them	It provides easy access to patient
Provide call bell near the patient in order to seek help from nurse, if needed	Bell helps to call the nurse immediately in case of emergency
Put on side rails when client is sleeping	To prevent the patient's fall from the bed

- **Self-care deficit related to lack of ability for brushing, bathing, grooming, putting dress as evidenced by patient verbalization.**

Nursing interventions	Rationale
Identify the areas of dysfunction in self-care	To get the baseline data
Motivate the patient to perform daily activities	To improve the skills and abilities of the patient
Assist the patient in all activities, if necessary	It will help the patient perform the activities
Be consistent in assignment of daily care givers	Remaining consistent in assignment will avoid confusion in patients
Involve family members in patient care	It promotes a feeling of well-being among family members
Provide structural schedule of activities	Guide the patient in a structured way without any confusion

- **Poor social interactions related to lack of socialization with others as evidenced by poor social judgment in mental status examination.**

Nursing interventions	Rationale
Observe the patient and perform mental status examination	To get the baseline data
Provide social skills therapy	To improve social skills
Involve the patient and family members to participate in psychodrama	It gives an opportunity to the patient to talk with others
Promote group therapy	It enhances the social skills
Organize games involving all patients	It gives an opportunity to the patient to mingle with others

Administer IV fluids to the patient in order to promote hydration, apply physical restraints, if the patient is uncontrollable or exhibiting violent behavior. Administer oxygen to the patient, if required.

GERIATRIC CONSIDERATIONS

Assess the cognitive status of elders in order to identify the cognitive dysfunction in early stage itself. Identify the suicidal thoughts verbalized to friends or relatives. Assess the capacity to perform the task independently. Feelings of loneliness, worthlessness, hopelessness and helplessness need to be identified at an early stage because these are symptoms of depression that may lead to suicide. Disorders of language or aphasia are due to organic lesions in brain. Consider sensory deprivation such as loss of vision, hearing, touch, smell and taste in elders. Elderly abuse (granny bashing) needs to be assessed and prevented (psychological abuse, sexual abuse and physical abuse must be assessed). Special care is needed for elders residing in nursing homes. Teach true coping mechanism to the elders so that they can handle the stressors.

Follow-up, Home Care and Rehabilitation

- Reminiscence therapy helps the elders to hold up good memories.
- Social skills training is helpful to enhance social skills.
- Psychological support from caregivers and family members is essential.
- Recreational and relaxation therapies help the elders enhance coping skills and deal with stressors.
- Promotion of self-esteem is a vital part and can be improved by promoting the activities of daily living.
- Memory training is helpful to improve the cognition.
- Orientation to time, place and person is essential.
- Take steps to promote individuality and make them to feel that elders are a part of society. Promotion of physical, psychological and social wellness will promote them in holistic way.
- Treat depression at early stages to prevent suicidal thoughts.
- Psychotropic drugs have to be followed if prescribed by a physician; and drug adherence has to be monitored.
- Positively expressed emotions of care givers will promote psychological well-being of elders.

EXTRA EDGE

ICD-10 Classification of Organic Brain Disorders

F00-F09 Organic, including symptomatic, mental disorders

- **F00 Dementia in Alzheimer's disease**
  - F00.0 Dementia in Alzheimer's disease with early onset
  - F00.1 Dementia in Alzheimer's disease with late onset
  - F00.2 Dementia in Alzheimer's disease, atypical or mixed type
  - F00.9 Dementia in Alzheimer's disease, unspecified
- **F01 Vascular dementia**
  - F01.0 Vascular dementia of acute onset
  - F01.1 Multi-infarct dementia
  - F01.2 Subcortical vascular dementia
  - F01.3 Mixed cortical and subcortical vascular dementia
  - F01.8 Other vascular dementia
  - F01.9 Vascular dementia, unspecified
- **F02 Dementia in other diseases classified elsewhere**
  - F02.0 Dementia in Pick's disease
  - F02.1 Dementia in Creutzfeldt-Jakob disease
  - F02.2 Dementia in Huntington's disease
  - F02.3 Dementia in Parkinson's disease
  - F02.4 Dementia in Human Immunodeficiency Virus [HIV] disease
  - F02.8 Dementia in other specified diseases classified elsewhere
- **F03 Unspecified dementia-A fifth character may be added to specify dementia in F00-F03, as follows:**
  - x0 Without additional symptoms
  - x1 Other symptoms, predominantly delusional
  - x2 Other symptoms, predominantly hallucinatory
  - x3 Other symptoms, predominantly depressive
  - x4 Other mixed symptoms
- **F04 Organic amnestic syndrome, not induced by alcohol and other substances**
- **F05 Delirium, not induced by alcohol and other psychoactive substances**
  - F05.0 Delirium, not superimposed on dementia
  - F05.1 Delirium, superimposed on dementia
  - F05.8 Other types of delirium
  - F05.9 Delirium, unspecified
- **F06 Other mental disorders due to brain damage or dysfunction and due to physical disease**
  - F06.0 Organic hallucinosis
  - F06.1 Organic catatonic disorder
  - F06.2 Organic delusional [schizophrenia-like] disorder
  - F06.3 Organic mood [affective] disorders
    - .30 Organic manic disorders
    - .31 Organic bipolar affective disorders
    - .32 Organic depressive disorders
    - .33 Organic mixed affective disorder
  - F06.4 Organic anxiety disorder
  - F06.5 Organic dissociative disorder
  - F06.6 Organic emotionally labile [asthenic] disorder
  - F06.7 Mild cognitive disorder
  - F06.8 Other specified mental disorders due to brain damage or dysfunction and due to physical disease
  - F06.9 Unspecified mental disorder due to brain damage and dysfunction and due to physical disease

SUMMARY

- Organic brain disorders are neurological and psychiatric disorders with strong biological basis.
- Organic brain disorders are classified into delirium, dementia, amnesia and others (organic hallucinosis, organic delusional disorder, organic mood disorder, organic personality disorder, organic dissociative disorder, organic emotionally labile disorder).
- Delirium is an acute confusion state, whereas dementia is chronic.
- Predisposing factors of delirium are extreme ends of age (very old or young), male gender, immobility, history of falls, functional dependent, low performance in activity, history of delirium or dementia, memory impairment, visual disturbances, hard of hearing, orthopedic surgery, cardiac surgery or cardiopulmonary bypass, intensive care unit (ICU) admission, stress, use of physical restraints, patient's urinary catheterization, sleep disturbances, neurological or endocrine or metabolic disorders, fever, hypothermia, infections, hypoxia, shock, anemia, dehydration, poor nutrition and decreased serum albumin level.
- Delirium can be classified into hyperactive, hypoactive and mixed.
- Melatonin is increased in hypoactive delirium; and N-Dimethyltryptamine is increased in hyperactive delirium.
- Increased dopamine and serotonin, release of interleukin-1 from cells, decreased cerebral oxidative metabolism, elders with impaired cholinergic transmission, stress, sleep disturbances, increased action of the hypothalamic-pituitary adrenal (HPA) axis might lead to delirium.
- Acute onset, clouding of consciousness, perceptional disturbances, sleep wake cycle disturbances, sundown syndrome, memory disturbances, speech disturbances, motor disturbances, labile affect, occupation delirium, motor/verbal perseveration, dyssomnia, agraphia, impairment in comprehension, mood alteration and disorientation (disorientation to time and place is common, whereas disorientation to person is rare) are clinical manifestations of delirium.
- Confusion assessment method, mini mental status examination, CT scan, MRI, CBC, urine analysis, EKG, EEG are helpful to diagnose delirium.
- Dementia, schizophrenia, depression, mania, dissociative disorders are differential diagnosis of delirium.

Contd...

- Repeat, rephrase, repair, speaking slowly, using therapeutic touch, be a good listener, do not argue with elders, using closed-ended questions, using small sentences are the proper communication strategies used in patients with organic brain disorder.
- **Management of patients with delirium includes:** Identify the underlying cause, complete lab investigation, nursing care of agitated/violent/noncooperative patients, reorientation training with the use of drugs such as benzodiazepine, antipsychotics, physostigmine etc., music therapy, light therapy, normalize sleep-wake cycle, use of hearing and visual aids, involvement of family in nursing care.
- Complications of delirium are falls, aspiration pneumonia, pressure ulcer, malnourishment, fatigue and decreased ability or functioning.
- Complete or partial loss of memory is called amnesia.
- Types of amnesia include transient global amnesia, transient epileptic amnesia, anterograde amnesia, retrograde amnesia, lacunar amnesia dissociative amnesia and prosopagnosia or face blindness or facial agnosia.
- If alcohol-induced delirium occurs, then administer Inj. thiamine.
- Alzheimer's disease is the most common type of dementia.
- **Neuropathological changes in Alzheimer's disease:** Deposits of β amyloid lead to plaque formation outside the neuron; and hyperphosphorylation of tau protein causes neurofibrillary tangles (NFT) inside the neuron.
- Acetylcholinesterase inhibitors are used to treat Alzheimer's disease.
- Cognitive deficit, behavior deficit and motor deficit are the main diagnostic criteria for AIDS dementia complex.
- Decline in cognition with fluctuations in alertness, recurrent and vivid visual hallucinations in early stages of disease and features of Parkinson's disease are seen in Lewy body dementia.
- Nursing management of organic mental disorders includes enhancement of cognitive functions, prevent the patient's fall, promote self-esteem, orientation training, improve the patient's self-care, social skills, etc.

ASSESS YOURSELF

Long Answer Questions

1. Define delirium. Explain the classification, etiology, psychopathology, diagnosis, clinical manifestations and management of patients with delirium.
2. Define dementia. Explain the classification, etiology, psychopathology, diagnosis, clinical manifestations and management of patients with dementia.

Short Answer Questions

1. What are the different types/forms of dementia based on onset and structural classification?
2. What are the features of organic brain disorders?
3. What are the different types of delirium according to DSM-5 on the basis of activity level?
4. What are the proper communication strategies for patients with organic brain disorders?
5. What are the different types of neuroimaging for diagnosing dementia?
6. What are the behavioral and psychological symptoms of dementia?
7. What are the characteristic features of vascular dementia or multi-infarct dementia (MID)?

Short Notes

Write short notes on:

1. Alzheimer's disease
2. Differences between delirium and dementia
3. Differences between dementia and pseudodementia
4. Types of amnesia
5. Types of dementia
6. Etiology of delirium
7. Nursing management of patients with dementia
8. Complications of delirium
9. ICD-11 classification of organic mental disorders
10. Clinical manifestations of delirium
11. Assessment of cognitive functions
12. Psychopathology of organic mental disorders
13. Differences between cortical and subcortical dementia
14. Pick's disease
15. Lewy body dementia

Multiple Choice Questions

1. **__________ is an acute confusional state in organic brain disorder.**
   a. Delirium b. Dementia
   c. Amnesia d. None of these
2. **Which type of hallucination is predominant in organic brain disorders?**
   a. Visual b. Auditory
   c. Gustatory d. Tactile
3. **Increased N-dimethyltryptamine will lead to _______ delirium.**
   a. Hypoactive b. Hyperactive
   c. Mixed d. None of these
4. **Toxic psychosis is also called:**
   a. Delirium b. Dementia
   c. Amnesia d. None of these

5. **Which is the proper communication technique used in patients with organic brain disorders?**
   a. Use of open-ended questions
   b. Use of closed-ended question
   c. Use of small sentences
   d. Both b and c
   e. Option a, b and c

6. **Sundown syndrome means:**
   a. Worsening of symptoms in evening
   b. Improvement of symptoms in evening
   c. Worsening of symptoms in morning
   d. Improvement of symptoms in morning
   e. Both a and d

7. **_________ is an antidote for anticholinergic that will help to reverse the delirium due to anticholinergics.**
   a. Neostigmine b. Physostigmine
   c. Atropine d. Pilocarpine

8. **__________________ is the most common type of dementia.**
   a. Alzheimer's disease b. Vascular dementia
   c. Lewy body dementia d. Pick's disease

9. **Hyperphosphorylation of tau protein in intracellular areas is seen in _______**
   a. Alzheimer's disease b. Vascular dementia
   c. Lewy body dementia d. Pick's disease

10. **Which of the following is NOT TRUE about Lewy body dementia?**
   a. Fluctuation of cognition is present
   b. Visual hallucination is prominent
   c. It is mostly a subcortical type
   d. Motor symptoms are seen

11. **_________ used in elders with dementia will increase risk of stroke by three times.**
   a. Antidepressants b. Antipsychotics
   c. Anxiolytics d. Mood stabilizers

12. **Usual age of onset in Pick's disease is _________**
   a. >60 years b. 50–60 years
   c. 40–50 years d. 30–40 years

13. **Kluver-Bucy Syndrome is common in __________**
   a. Alzheimer's disease b. Vascular dementia
   c. Lewy body dementia d. Pick's disease

14. **_________ lobe in brain is predominantly involved in Pick's disease.**
   a. Frontal b. Temporal
   c. Parietal d. Occiput

15. **Amnesia which is purely psychogenic due to intrapsychic conflicts is called _________**
   a. Anterograde amnesia b. Retrograde amnesia
   c. Lacunar amnesia d. Dissociative amnesia

16. **Wandering behavior is seen in _________ stage of dementia.**
   a. Early b. Middle
   c. Final d. None of these

17. **Which is the second most common type of dementia?**
   a. Alzheimer's disease b. Vascular dementia
   c. Lewy body dementia d. Pick's disease

18. **Replicative protein that mutates and causes a variety of spongiform diseases is seen in ________**
   a. Prion disease b. Huntington's chorea
   c. Vascular dementia d. Lewy body dementia

19. **Which of the following is cortical dementia?**
   a. Parkinson's disease
   b. Creutzfeldt-Jakob disease
   c. Wilson's disease
   d. Pick's disease

20. **The course of disease is ______________ in delirium.**
   a. Fluctuating
   b. Progressive
   c. Intermittently fluctuating and progressive
   d. None of the above

ANSWER KEY

1. a	2. a	3. b	4. a	5. d
6. a	7. b	8. a	9. a	10. c
11. b	12. b	13. d	14. a	15. d
16. b	17. b	18. a	19. d	20. a

Psychiatric Emergencies and Crisis Intervention

CHAPTER 13

LEARNING OBJECTIVE

After studying this chapter, the student will be able to gain knowledge regarding the psychiatric emergencies in order to render the nursing care to the patients with psychiatric emergencies.

CHAPTER OUTLINE

- Introduction
- Common Psychiatric Emergencies
- Aggression/Violence
- Transient Situational Disturbances
- Victims of Disaster
- Catatonic Stupor
- Victim of Rape

Medical Emergency in Psychiatry

- Neuroleptic Malignant Syndrome
- Overdose of Psychotropic Agents
- Substance Intoxication and Withdrawal
- Serotonin Syndrome
- Delirium
- Epileptic Furor

Maladaptive Behaviors of Individuals and Groups: Crisis, Stress and Disasters

- Adaptive Behavior
- Maladaptive Behavior
- Crisis
- Grief and Bereavement
- Counseling
- Stress
- Coping Mechanism
- Geriatric Considerations

KEY TERMS

Suicide, Aggression/Violence, Catatonic stupor, Hysterical attacks, Delirium tremens, Transient situational disturbances, Epileptic furor, Neuroleptic malignant syndrome, Drug toxicity, Victims of disaster, Rape victim, Stress adaptation model, Crisis and grief.

INTRODUCTION

- **Emergency:** It is a serious, unexpected and often dangerous situation, which requires an immediate action.
- **Psychiatric emergency:** A psychiatric emergency is an acute disturbance of behavior, thought or mood of a patient that negatively impacts a patient's ability to function in his/her environment. It must be treated properly otherwise individual may harm himself or herself or to the others.
- **Crisis:** An emerging situation which causes significant distress either to the individual group or society

that leads to sudden disability and needs immediate management is called crisis. When this crisis situation causes psychological distress to an individual, it is called psychiatric emergency.

Characteristics of Psychiatric Emergencies

- Psychiatric emergency is a situation that causes significant psychological distress.
- Presence of disharmony within an individual and toward environment (danger toward the self or others or society or property).
- Condition of the individual that needs immediate crisis intervention.
- Abrupt or sudden disorganization within the individual might lead to lack of coping skills in day-to-day situations.

Objectives to Treat Psychiatric Emergencies

The following are the objectives to treat psychiatric emergencies:

- To develop the emotional security of an individual and others
- To reduce the anxiety of family members
- To safeguard the life of individual
- To enhance the coping ability

Types of Psychiatric Emergencies

Types of psychiatric emergencies have been given in Figure 13.1.

Classification of Psychiatric Emergency

The classification of psychiatric emergency has been given in Flowchart 13.1.

Figure 13.1: Types of psychiatric emergencies

Flowchart 13.1: Classification of psychiatric emergency

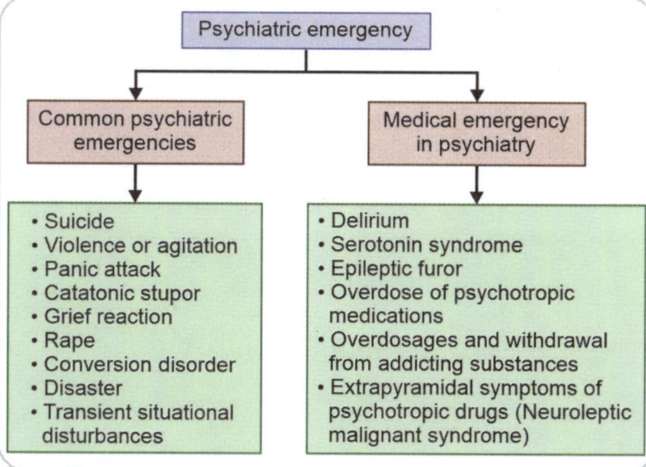

COMMON PSYCHIATRIC EMERGENCIES

Suicide

The term 'suicide' has been derived from the Latin word '*Suicidium*', which means killing of oneself.

- Prefix 'Sui' denotes oneself.
- Suffix 'Cidium' denotes killing.

Definition

Suicide is defined as "intention to kill oneself" or "self-inflicted cessation of life" which ends in a fatal outcome.

Attempted Suicide

Attempt for suicide is widely seen among patients suffering from different types of psychiatric issues. Suicide is the act of causing one's own death intentionally, whereas the attempted suicide is the deliberate infliction of injury on oneself or an attempt to commit suicide but the individual survives.

Epidemiology

In India, suicide is one of the top ten leading causes of death. Incidence of suicide is 10.8/1,00,000 population. Suicide is more common in males than in females. It is common in the age group of 18–30 years.

Etiology (Fig. 13.2)

Psychiatric Disorders

- Major depression
- Schizophrenia
- Bipolar mood disorder
- Substance or alcohol abuse
- Delirium
- Dementia
- Personality disorders

Physical Disorders

- Patients with chronic diseases like acquired immunodeficiency syndrome (AIDS), cancer, etc.
- Unbearable pain, epilepsy, multiple sclerosis, etc.

Biological Factors

Imbalance in release of neurotransmitter, namely serotonin might provoke suicidal ideation.

Psychosocial Factors

- Long-term difficulties in relationships toward friend and family.

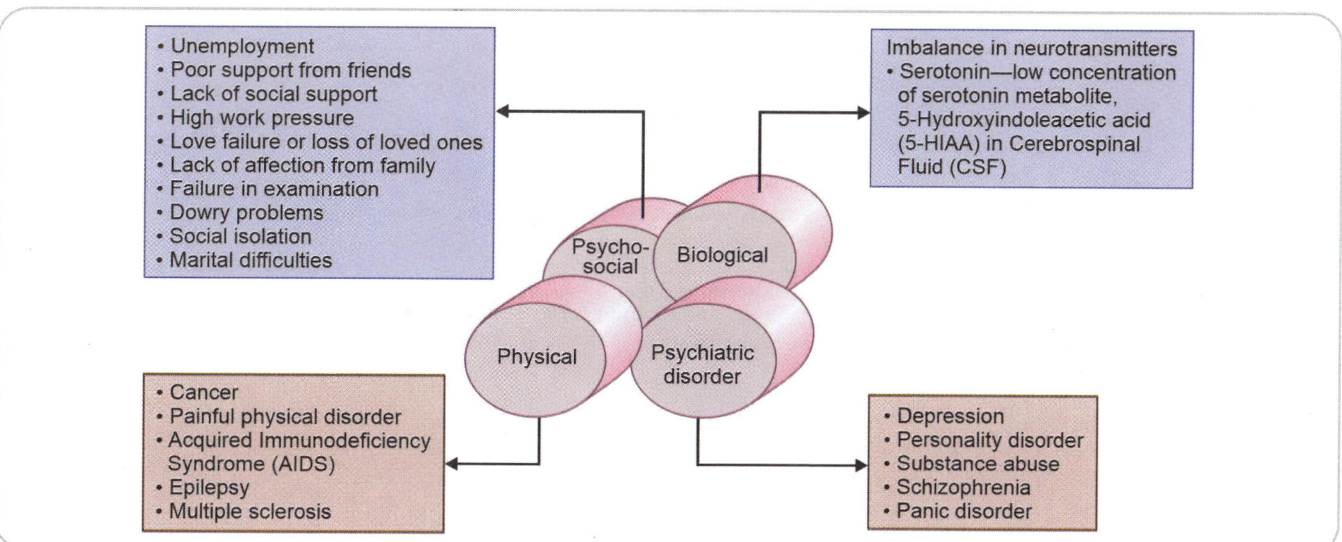

Figure 13.2: Etiology of suicide

- Losing hope or the will to live.
- Significant losses in a person's life, such as death of loved ones.
- Loss of important relationship, loss of employment, etc.
- Failure in exams.
- Financial losses.
- Poor anger management (unable to control anger).
- Frustrations.
- Aiming to threaten others.

Methods of Committing Suicide

Methods of committing suicide have been given in Flowchart 13.2.

Types of suicide have been tabulated in Table 13.1.

Suicide Intention Model

World Health Organization (WHO) and Institute of Health Metrics and Evaluation (IHME) used the model given by Center for Suicide Prevention, Canadian Mental Health Association to get a clarity in regard to the interchange of terms

Flowchart 13.2: Methods of committing suicide

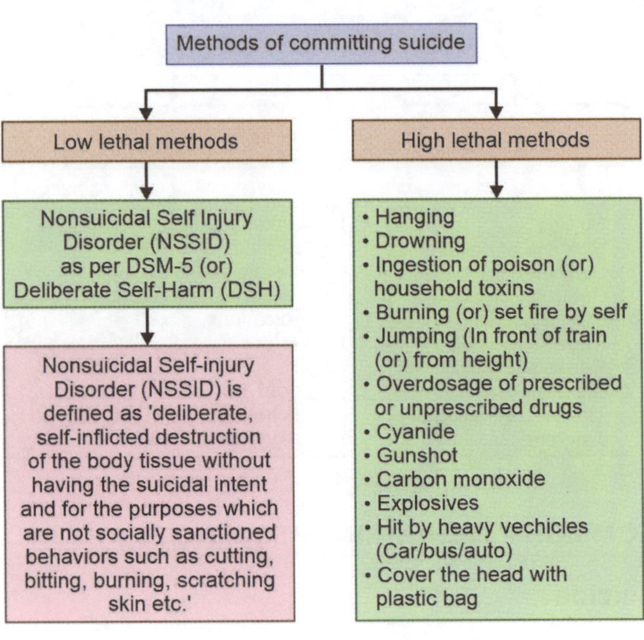

Table 13.1: Types of suicide

Types of suicide	Description	Examples
Based on social categories as per Emile Durkheim (1951)		
Egoistic suicide	Suicide due to lack of social integration.	Divorce
Altruistic suicide	Sacrifice of one's life for the benefit of others or to preserve the traditions and honor of society.	Mr Raj is recently diagnosed with end stage cancer, committed suicide because he never wanted to become an economic burden for his family.
Anomic suicide	Suicide due to occurrence of sudden changes in individual's life	Loss of job
Samsonic suicide or suicide of revenge	Suicide due to sudden unfriendly experiences	Wife is not faithful to husband and husband attempted suicide to take revenge.
Miscellaneous types		
Parasuicide	Injure himself/herself due to self-motivation but does not wish to die	Ms Raji attempted suicide to threaten her parents in order to accept her love affair; does not wish to die.
Cyber-suicide	Suicide happens due to internet-related issues	Blue whale game
Copycat suicide	Suicide attempt was made by copying a peer group or friend or family member who attempted suicide previously.	Ms Sumathi attempted suicide by adopting the same method as her mother had attempted.
Anniversary suicide	Suicide has taken place on the same anniversary date of family member or friend who was dead.	Ms Sushma attempted suicide on the anniversary date of her husband's death.

Flowchart 13.3: Suicide intention model by Canadian Mental Health Association, Center for Suicide Prevention (2016)

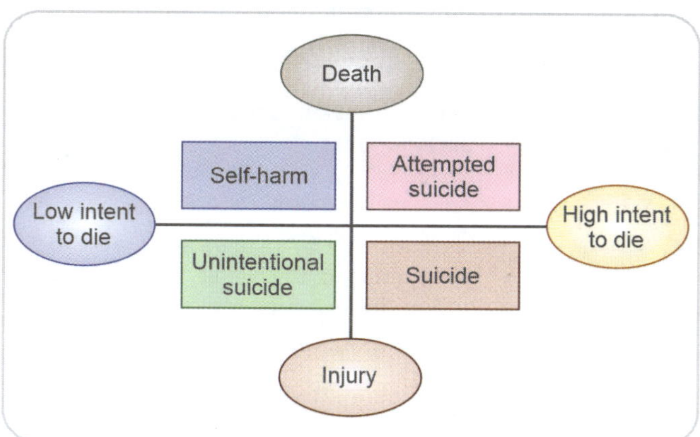

'self-harm and suicide'. Self-harm is not done with high intent to die, whereas suicidal attempts are done with high intent to die. The term 'unintentional suicide' denotes the lifestyle changes or ill-health habits, such as smoking, alcoholism, lack of exercises, eating junk foods, riding a bike without helmet, that might cause injury or death (Flowchart 13.3).

The differences between self-harm and suicide have been given in Table 13.2.

Table 13.2: Differences between self-harm and suicide

Aspects	Self-harm	Suicide
Purpose	Performed to avoid suicide impulses	Performed with the intention to die
Methods commonly used	Cutting, self-hitting, burning	Poisoning by self
Frequency of incident	More frequent	Less frequent
Severity	Less	High

Suicidal Barometer Model

Suicidal barometer model describes various suicidal levels such as nonsuicidal, low suicidal, moderate suicidal and high suicidal (Fig. 13.3).

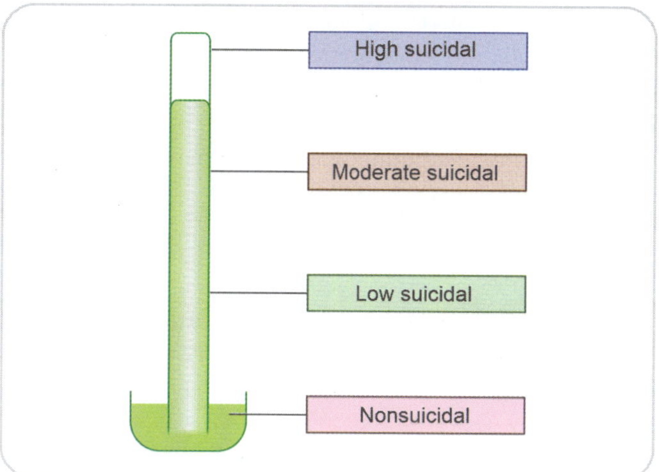

Figure 13.3: Suicidal barometer model

The features of suicidal levels as per suicidal barometer model have been given in Table 13.3.

Risk Factors and Warning Signs of Suicide

Risk factors denote the probability to increase the risk of suicidal crisis.

The following are signs of clinical depression:

- Withdrawal or isolation from friends and family
- Sadness and hopelessness
- Feeling trapped with unbearable pain
- Talking in such a way as being burden to others
- Lack of interest in previous activities or in what is going on around them
- Physical changes such as lack of energy, different sleep patterns, change in weight or appetite
- Loss of self-esteem
- Increased use of alcohol or drugs
- Presence of mood swings
- Being anxious, agitated or reckless
- Exhibiting rage or talking about revenge
- Negative comment about self-worth
- Speaking or writing about death or suicide
- Giving their valuable possessions to somebody
- More interest in personal wills or life insurances

Table 13.3: Features of suicidal levels

Features	High suicidal	Moderate suicidal	Low suicidal	Nonsuicidal
Wish to live	Very low	Low	Moderately high	Very high
Wish to die	Very high	Moderately high	Low	Very low
Prediction of future suicidal attempts	High	High	Low	Absent
Attempts with intent to die	High	Present	low	Absent
Life/death debate	Frequent	Frequent	Infrequent	Absent

American Foundation for Suicide Prevention emphasizes that the suicide determination is to be done with the help of three factors such as health factors, environmental factors and history-related factors.

Factors that determine suicidal risk have been given in Table 13.4.

Table 13.4: Factors that determine the suicidal risk as per American Foundation for Suicide Prevention

Health-related factors	Environmental factors	History-related factors
• Mental illness • Substance abuse • Chronic pain • Sleep pattern difficulties • Serious health problems	• Financial loss • Exposure to suicidal attempts among family members or media • Stressful life events such as loss of loved ones, loss of job, divorce, etc. • Access to lethal means such as drugs etc. • Prolonged stressors such as harassment, relationship problems, etc.	• Previous suicide attempts • Family history of suicide • Cultural beliefs that support suicide • History of deliberate self-harm • Recent hospitalization

Aspects of suicidal risk have been given in Table 13.5.

Table 13.5: Aspects of suicidal risk

Aspects	Description
Demographic profile	• Gender: Male • Marital Status: Single, widow, divorced, *Separated* • Age: Adolescence and old age
Psychological dimension	• Hopelessness, helplessness and worthlessness (depressed) • Agitation • Psychic pain or turmoil • Low self-esteem • Fragile narcissism and perfectionism
Psychosocial dimension	• Socioeconomic status: High • Job: Unemployment • Social support: Absent
Behavioral dimension	• Aggression • Panic attacks • Severe anxiety • Intoxication • Impulsivity • Prior suicidal attempts
Cognitive dimension	• Thought constriction • Polarized thinking
Psychiatric dimension	• Borderline personality disorder • Psychotic illness • Reactive depression
Physical Illness	• Functional impairment • Pain syndromes • HIV/AIDS • Malignant neoplasm • Any terminal illness
Genetic and Familial	• Family history of suicide • Previous suicidal attempts • Family history of psychiatric illness or abuse

Suicidal Risks in Ward

- Attempted suicides are the most common among psychiatric patients, who suffer from major depressions due to their delusions, feeling of worthlessness and hopelessness.
- Schizophrenic patients are highly prone especially when they develop postschizophrenic depression; they may also attempt suicide due to delusions and hallucinations.
- Manic patients may also attempt/commit suicide due to their grandiose delusions, i.e., to prove their supernatural powers.
- **Drugs or alcohol:** Alcoholic adult patients commit suicide due to development of depression during withdrawal phase. Few other drugs or substances may provoke suicidal ideation among addicts.

Warning Clues of Suicide

There are certain warning clues of suicide that are helpful in predicting the suicidal attempts (Table 13.6).

Table 13.6: Aspects of warning clues of suicide

Warning clues of suicide	Description
Behavioral clues	• Writing suicidal notes • Abrupt changes of mood • Making the will • Giving out the valuable possessions • Buying some lethal drugs
Verbal clues	Passing negative comment directly or indirectly • Use of overt statement (Passing direct comments) • For example: I wish, I want to die. This is the last time you are seeing me. • Use of covert statement (Passing indirect comments) For example: Everything will be fine very soon. I won't be a problem to anyone.

Contd...

Warning clues of suicide	Description
Situational clues	Certain life experiences associated with major stress denote the situational clues, e.g., diagnosis of fatal diseases, loss of job, sudden death of beloved ones, heavy financial losses, etc.
Syndromic clues	Psychological disturbances associated with suicide, psychotic illness, acute delirium, depression, etc.
Nonverbal clues	• Sleeping excessively or sleeping too less • Depressive mood • Lack of attention and concentration • Addictive behavior • Lack of interest in all activities • Poor performance in school or job • Boredom • Restlessness
Emotional and behavioral changes associated with suicide	• Hopelessness, helplessness and worthlessness • Feeling of shame and guilt • Self-neglect • Withdrawal from friends and family members • Being preoccupied with dying

SAD PERSONS rating scale can be used to determine the suicidal risk (Table 13.7).

Table 13.7: SAD PERSONS rating scale

Letter	Characteristics	Score
S	Sex (male)	1
A	Age (25–44 years or 65 years)	1
D	Depression	1
P	Previous suicidal attempts	1
E	Ethanol usage	1
R	Rationale thinking loss	1
S	Lacking social support	1
O	Organized plan	1
N	No spouse	1
S	Sickness is present	1

Based on the SAD PERSONS rating score, the guidelines for clinical action have been given in Table 13.8.

Protective Factors for Suicidal Attempts

Protective factors are responsible for decreasing the risk of suicidal crisis. The following are the factors which help to prevent an individual from attempting suicide.

Table 13.8: Guidelines for clinical action based on the score obtained in SAD PERSONS rating scale

Score	Guidelines for clinical action
0–2	Can send to home with follow-up
3–4	Follow-up closely and consider hospitalization
5–6	Strongly consider hospitalization
7–10	Hospitalize immediately

- Strong family and social support
- Easy access to clinical interventions
- Skills in problem solving and conflict resolution
- Restricted access to lethal means of suicide
- Strong support from the health care professional
- Cultural and religious beliefs that discourage suicide.

Three levels of prevention of suicide are shown in Flowchart 13.4.

Suicide prevention and stress helpline numbers of different regions are given in Table 13.9.

Flowchart 13.4: The levels of prevention of suicide

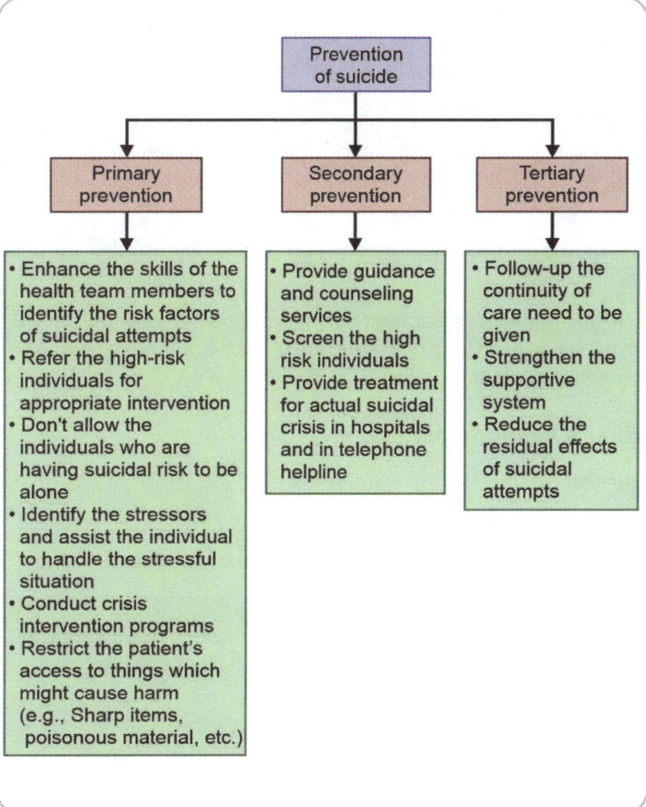

Table 13.9: Suicide prevention and stress helpline numbers (Updated till September 2019)

Region*	Name of the suicide prevention phone center*	Helpline numbers
Delhi	Sumaitri	011-23389090
	Sanjivini Society for Mental Health	011-24311918, 243118883
	Fortis National Helpline	91-8376804102
Gangtok	Sikkim Helpline Number	1800-3453225, 03592-202111
Kolkata	Serve	9830785060
	Clippings	98300 27976
	Defeat depression	9830027975
	AASRA	91-22-27546669
	Singing Soulz	9892003868
Mumbai	Samaritans	8422984528/ 8422984529/ 8422984530
Chennai	Sneha Suicide Prevention Helpline	044 2464 0050
	Jeevan Suicide Prevention Hotline	044 2656 4444
Bangalore	Sahai	080-25497777
Hyderabad	One Life	78930 78930
Kochi	Maithri	91-484-2540530
Nagpur	Nagpur Suicide Prevention Helpline	8888817666
All-India	Vandrevala Foundation	1860-266-2345/ 1800-233-3330/ 0261-2662700

*(*Suicide prevention helplines [online] available from http:// www.healthcollective.in/suicide-prevention-helplines) [Access Sep. 2019]*

Nurse's Responsibilities

The responsibilities of a nurse in prevention of suicide have been given in Table 13.10.

Table 13.10: Responsibilities of a nurse in prevention of suicide

Do's	Don'ts
Closely monitor the patient	Do not leave the patient alone
Accompany the patient wherever he/she goes	Do not allow patient to lock inside the bathroom
Avoid keeping dangerous objects near the patient	Don't keep ties, belt, sharp instruments, shoe laces, long towels near the patient, etc.
Sedate the patient, if uncontrollable	Do not scold patient in front of others for his/her behavior
Teach the family members or care givers that patient needs to be monitored continuously due to the increased suicidal risk	Do not allow the patient to take medicine by self
Encourage the patient to verbalize his/her thoughts related to suicide	Never keep syringes and needles in patient's room
Apply restraints, if necessary	Do not keep drug cupboards within the reach of patients

Medicolegal issues related to Suicide

Section 309 of Indian Penal Code (IPC) states that whoever attempts to commit suicide and does any act toward the commission of such offence shall be punished with simple imprisonment for a term which may extend to 1 year or fine or both.

Nursing Management

Management of Attempted Suicide

Attempted suicide is not only psychiatric emergency, but also a medical emergency. Firstly, do not panic and also do not make other panicky. Inform the psychiatrist immediately. Monitor the vital signs. Nurse should act fast depending on the method of suicidal attempt done by the patient. Nurse should change the rooms of other patients, if necessary. Treat the underlying psychiatric conditions, e.g., depression or schizophrenia. If necessary, give antidepressants, antipsychotics and electroconvulsive therapy (ECT) as per the order of psychiatrist.

Nurse plays an important role in management of attempted suicide. Nurse should maintain good rapport with the patient. Ward should have sufficient number of staff to monitor a patient with suicidal risk. Nurse should encourage the patient to express his/her plans of suicide and also encourage the patient to develop socialization. Nurse needs to record the behaviors or the behavior changes seen in patient. Nurse can involve the patient in group games in order to relax and divert from the suicidal ideation. Nurse can also encourage the patient to get involved in spirituality, relaxation exercises, watching TV, etc. Nurse needs to give appropriate counseling to the patient. If the patient has attempted suicide, inform the psychiatrist immediately and then start life-saving procedures to preserve patient's life. If the patient is dead, inform the police and proceed with further legal or clinical actions.

Nursing Diagnosis

- High-risk of suicide or self-directed violence related to feelings of desperation.
- Hopelessness or lack of self-esteem related to lack of social support system.
- Ineffective coping skills related to lack of coping ability with stressors as evidenced by suicidal attempts.
- Masked depression related to guilt.

Nursing interventions with rationales are given in Table 13.11.

Table 13.11: Nursing interventions with rationales

Nursing interventions	Rationales
Encourage the patient to stay with friends and family members	To reduce isolation and to divert him/her from the suicidal thoughts
Advise the patient not to take any decision in crisis situation	In case of crisis situation, individual is unable to think and take decision correctly.
Encourage the patient to talk and verbalize the feelings	Mental ventilation helps to ventilate the inbuilt suicidal ideas and therefore, minimizes the occurrence of suicide. It further helps to minimize the suicidal tendencies.
Maintain accurate and timely records	It acts as evidence for the rendered nursing care or treatment.

AGGRESSION/VIOLENCE

Anger: "Anger is a normal human emotion that may be handled or expressed assertively to solve the problem and show a productive change." —*Horton-Deutsch, 2003*

Aggression: Aggression is an expression of anger by physical or psychological or verbal means in a socially inappropriate manner, which may or may not cause significant harm to self or others.

Risk Factors for Violence

- **Demographic factors:** Male gender, young age, unemployment and illiteracy.
- **Family history:** Involvement in criminal activity, antisocial behavior, cruelty to other human beings/ animals and violence among family members.
- **Biological factors:** Central nervous system dysfunction/ infections, abnormalities in neurotransmitters, frontal or temporal lobe dysfunction, limbic system dysfunction and traumatic brain injury.
- **Biochemical factors:** Decreased serotonin level.
- **Socioenvironmental factors:** Friends/relatives who have association with antisocial elements, access to lethal weapons and living in a community where violence is predominant.
- **Sociocultural factors:** Unemployment, poverty, disruption in marital life and single parent in a family.
- **Cognitive factors:** Negative perception/attitude that induces aggression/hostile behavior.
- **Psychological factors:** Low self-esteem, severe emotional deprivation, overt rejection in childhood and low frustration tolerance.
- **Behavioral factors:** Agitation, poor impulse control, shouting at others and damaging the nearby things.

Etiology of Violence

Organic Psychiatric Disorders

- Acute organic brain syndrome or delirium, e.g., delirium tremens.
- Chronic organic brain syndrome or dementia, e.g., catastrophic reaction.
- Wernicke-Korsakoff's psychosis.

Nonorganic Psychiatric Disorders

- Psychotic disorder (schizophreniform disorder, schizophrenia-paranoid and catatonic type).
- Mania
- Depression
- Substance abuse (intoxication and withdrawal syndrome)
- Epilepsy (epileptic furor, complex partial seizure and postictal confusion).
- Neurotic disorder (panic disorder, posttraumatic stress disorder).
- Impulsive violent behavior (Borderline personality disorder and intermittent explosive disorder).
- Reactive psychosis.

Medical Disorders Associated with Violent Behavior

- **Neurologic illnesses**
  - Head injury with intracerebral, subarachnoid or subdural hematoma.
  - Cerebral infarction.
  - Brain infections such as encephalitis, meningo-encephalitis.
  - Seizure disorders (interictal, postictal or temporal lobe epilepsy).
  - Huntington's disease.
  - Hepatic encephalopathy.

- Wilson's disease
- Parkinson's disease due to levodopa toxicity.
- **Endocrine disorders:** Hypothyroidism, thyrotoxicosis, hyperparathyroidism and Cushing's syndrome.
- **Metabolic disorders:** Hypoglycemia, electrolyte imbalance, hypoxia and hypocholesterolemia.
- **Vitamin deficiencies:** Folic acid, niacin, pyridoxine and vitamin B_{12}.
- **Infections**: Acquired Immunodeficiency Syndrome (HIV/AIDS), syphilis and tuberculosis.
- **Temperature disturbances:** Hyperthermia and hypothermia.

Sources and Expressions of Anger

The signs of anger are categorized into subjective and objective (Table 13.12).

Behavior Associated with Aggression

- **Verbal behavior signs:** Pressure of speech, verbal threat to real or imagined object, demand of attention and thought content with a paranoid ideation.
- **Motor agitation:** Clenching fists, inability to sit still for a long time, increased respiratory rate, pacing and sudden cessation of motor activity.

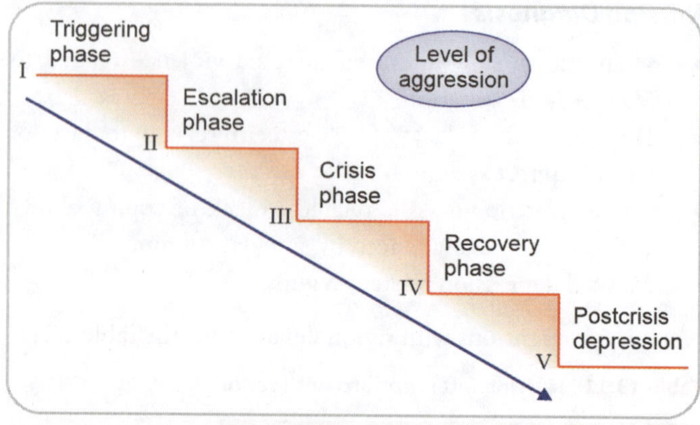

Figure 13.4: Assault cycle

- **Level of consciousness:** Confusion, disorientation, memory impairment and changes in mental status.
- **Affect:** Hostile behavior, anger, irritability, extreme anxiety, labile affect and inappropriate or excessive euphoria.

Assault Cycle

Smith's stress model (1981) explained the assault cycle which has five stages of aggressive response to physical or emotional stress (Figure 13.4).

Different phases of assault cycle are given in Table 13.13.

Table 13.12: Category-wise signs of anger

Anger turned outward		Anger turned inward	
Subjective signs	**Objective signs**	**Subjective signs**	**Objective signs**
• Impatience • Annoyance • Negative attitude • Feeling Jealous • Feeling of harming others • Want to scold others • Domination	• Irritation • Hostile behavior • Tensed facial expression • Verbal abuse • Verbalization of anger • Temper tantrums • Rage • Screaming • Assault • Damage to property • Beating others • Argumentativeness • Use of weapons as threat	• Guilt • Tensed • Disappointment • Feeling inferior • Lack of self-confidence • Low self-esteem • Depression • Powerlessness • Helplessness • Somatic symptoms • Feeling hurt	• Substance abuse • Crying often • Suicidal attempts • Self-mutilation • Apathy

Table 13.13: Phases of assault cycle

Phases of assault cycle	Description	Level of anxiety	Behavioral response	Nursing interventions
Triggering phase	Stressors trigger the individual	Mild	Irritable, perspiration, suspiciousness, change in voice/breathing pattern, restlessness	• Encourage the client to ventilate the feelings • Give support empathically • Use small, clear and simple sentences • Encourage the client to maintain control

Contd...

Phases of assault cycle	Description	Level of anxiety	Behavioral response	Nursing interventions
Escalation phase	Escalating behaviors such as movement toward the loss of control	Moderate	Agitation, screaming, demanding, clenched fists, flushed face	• Direct the client toward a quiet room • Administer the oral medications as ordered • Ask the staff nurse to stand at a distance and motivate the client to have a control over his/her behavior
Crisis phase	Physical and emotional crisis causes the complete loss of control	Severe	Fighting or kicking others, throwing things, rage	Physical or chemical restraints
Recovery phase	Cooling down period in which the individual moves toward calming effect	Moderate or Mild	Lowering voice, reduced body tension, feeling relaxed	Evaluate the client's progress toward the loss of control
Post-crisis depression phase	Individual attempts reconciliation with others	Mild	Crying, asking sorry, realizing the mistakes committed	• Decrease the degree of seclusion and restraints • Discuss alternative solutions to problems

Management of Violence

- **Assessment:** Assess the signs of impending violence such as shouting at others, throwing things, running or chasing others, etc. in early stage itself so that the nurse can be alert to manage the violent behavior effectively.
- **Reassurance:** Approach the patient in firm and kind way. Always talk to the patient in a soft manner. Nurse should ask direct and concise questions in patient's language, which helps the patient to understand easily. Ask open-ended questions to the patient. Try to reassure the patient in calm and soft manner.
- **Medications**
  - Inj. haloperidol 4–10 mg IM/IV
  - Tab. chlorpromazine 50–100 mg/oral
  - Inj. diazepam 5–10 mg/Slow IV
- **Psychological well-being:** Advise the client to 'talk out' the feelings which cause aggression rather than acting them out. Stay with the patient which decreases the level of anxiety.

NURSES RESPONSIBILITY

Collect the history and perform the physical examination. Administer IV fluids to assess the level of dehydration. Keep the decreased environmental stimuli and keep less furniture in the patient's room. Remove all sharp instruments from the room.

The do's and don'ts in violence management have been given in Table 13.14.

Table 13.14: Do's and don'ts in violence management

Do's in management of violence
• Assess the signs of impending violence at the earliest. • Protect yourself first • Secure the nearby patients (Instructing them not to stand near the violent patient) • Keep the nearby doors open • Show the concern and establish adequate rapport • Apply restraints, if necessary • Call for help, if required
Don'ts in management of violence
• Don't keep any sharp objects near the patient • Don't sit when the patient is at your back (Keep the patient always in front of you) • Don't stand/sit very near to the patient • Don't wear any neck chain/tie/jewelry • Don't keep any family members who provoke violence in patient's room • Don't tie the physical restraints in bed side rails (instead tie securely in bed cradle)

Restraints

Restraints are used during certain medical procedures to restrain the patients with minimum discomfort and pain. There are two types of restraints: physical and chemical (Flowchart 13.5).

Flowchart 13.5: Types of restraints

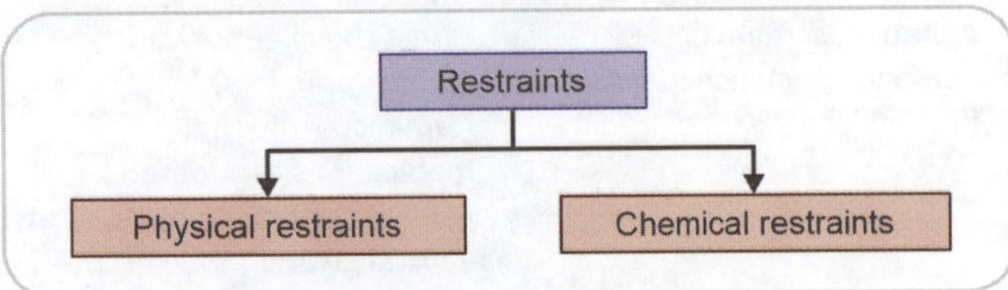

Physical Restraints

- **Guidelines to apply physical restraints:** Obtain the written order from the treating physician to apply physical restraint. Get the written consent from the patient's care givers to perform the same. Apply the physical restraints one by one tying the joints of upper and lower extremities with the bed cradle (don't tie the restraints in side rails). Restraints should not be too tight or too loose. Restraints that are too tight might obstruct the blood flow leading to necrosis. Restraints that are too loose might have chance of removal.
- **Guidelines to monitor physical restraints:** Check the peripheral pulse and the color/warmth of all the extremities every 5 minutes once for first half an hour, 10 minutes once for second half an hour and 15 minutes once for the next one hour (Table 13.15).
- **Guidelines to remove physical restraints:** Remove physical restraints one by one from all the extremities after making adequate observations. For example, in case of four-point restraint, first remove the restraint in right foot, secondly the left foot, then right wrist and lastly the left wrist after making adequate intermittent observations.

Table 13.15: Time frame to monitor physical restraints

Time frame to monitor the physical restraints	Observations made
5 minutes once for 1st half hour	• Check the peripheral pulse • Assess the color/ temperature of all extremities
10 minutes once for 2nd half hour	
15 minutes once from one hour onward	

Chemical restraints: Chemical restraints are defined as the medications/drugs which are helpful to control the violent behavior of patient. For example, injection Haloperidol 4–10 mg IM/IV, injection Chlorpromazine 50–100 mg/IM and injection Diazepam 5–10 mg/slow IV can be administered.

Strategies to Manage and Prevent Violence

Communication strategies used to prevent aggressive behavior are as follows:

- Listen to the patient
- Show respect to the patient
- Speak softly to the patient
- Be calm
- Have an adequate space between yourself and patient.
- Have an intermittent eye-to-eye contact with patient.
- Encourage the patient to talk.
- Don't make any unnecessary promises, which are unable to be kept.
- Talk in a nonjudgmental and nonprovocative manner.

Strategies to manage violence/aggression have been tabulated in Table 13.16.

Table 13.16: Strategies to manage violence

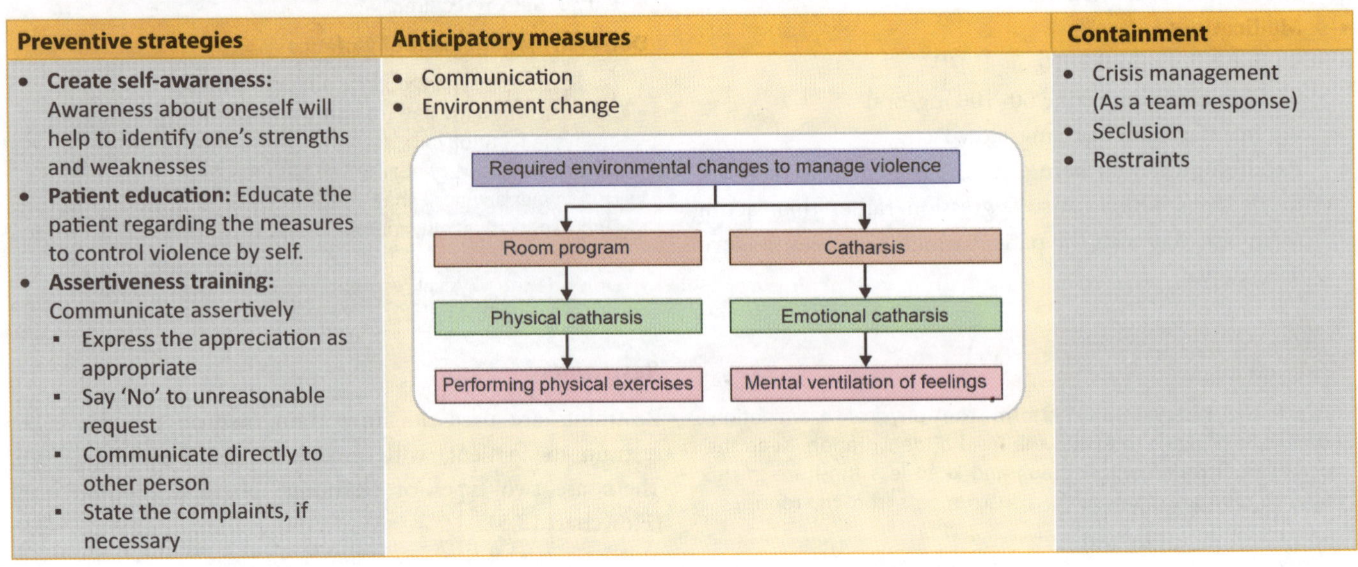

Preventive strategies	Anticipatory measures	Containment
• **Create self-awareness:** Awareness about oneself will help to identify one's strengths and weaknesses • **Patient education:** Educate the patient regarding the measures to control violence by self. • **Assertiveness training:** Communicate assertively ▪ Express the appreciation as appropriate ▪ Say 'No' to unreasonable request ▪ Communicate directly to other person ▪ State the complaints, if necessary	• Communication • Environment change Required environmental changes to manage violence Room program → Physical catharsis → Performing physical exercises Catharsis → Emotional catharsis → Mental ventilation of feelings	• Crisis management (As a team response) • Seclusion • Restraints

Strategies to prevent assault have been given in Table 13.17.

Table 13.17: Strategies to prevent assault

Strategies to prevent verbal assault	Strategies to prevent physical assault
• Answer in a soft, simple and honest way to all the questions asked by the patient • Be calm and empathic in nature • Use nonthreatening body language • Use reflective statements rather than the judgmental ones	• Call for help, if required • Nurse has to keep his/her hands visible • Always keep the door open • Stay at least an arm's length away from the patient • Escape from the place, if required • Face the person in the sideways • If patient is choked, use head tilt and chin lift maneuver to the chest and maintain the airway

TRANSIENT SITUATIONAL DISTURBANCES

Transient situational disturbances are characterized by disturbed behavior and feelings due to repeated external stimuli. The term 'transient' denotes short term.

Management

- Reassure and allow the patient to ventilate his/her feelings.
- Provide counseling.
- Administer mild sedation, if required.

Panic Attacks

Panic attacks refer to episodes of acute anxiety as a part of psychotic or neurotic disorders.

Symptoms

- Palpitations
- Tremors
- Sweating
- Feel of choking, abdominal distress, fear of dying
- Nausea, paresthesia and hot or chill flushes.

Management

Reassure the patient and administer Inj. diazepam 10 mg or lorazepam 2 mg.

VICTIMS OF DISASTER

Victims of disaster are the persons who survived disasters such as earthquakes, riots, flood, drought, cyclone, terrorism, etc. They usually undergo a severe form of sudden and unexpected stress.

Clinical Manifestations

Guilt, anger or aggression, irritable, frustration, confusion and numbness.

First Aid Management

- First treat the life-threatening physical problem and then refer to the mental health service.
- Provide counseling.
- Teach coping patterns to prevent crisis. (Teach the strategies to the survivors on how to get help, request information, access resources and get required support).

Medications

Administer benzodiazepines to reduce anxiety.

Critical Incident Debriefing

Critical incident debriefing is a special technique used to decrease the discomfort of disaster victims. It has the following five phases:

1. **Fact phase:** Participants are asked to share their perception about the incident. When they share, new information is noted and integrated for a common understanding.
2. **Thought phase:** Participants are asked to reflect on the incident and tell how they felt personally at different stages of crisis.
3. **Reaction phase:** Participants are asked to identify the emotional aspect of incident. (For example, asking the participant which is worst part of incident). When participants come to know that 'others are also experiencing the same', it might make them realize that these kinds of feelings are normal behavioral responses to abnormal situations/circumstances.
4. **Teaching phase:** Emotional, cognitive and spiritual strategies are used to decrease stress.
5. **Re-entry phase:** Facilitator summarizes the process and clarifies the doubts of participants. Referral for further counseling sessions can be done, if required.

CATATONIC STUPOR

Catatonic stupor is a clinical syndrome with a combination of akinesis (absence of movements) and mutism (absence of speech).

Signs and Symptoms

- **Mutism:** Absence of speech completely.
- **Rigidity:** Rigid posture maintained against the force tried for movement.

- **Negativism:** High resistance to commands
- **Posturing:** Having bizarre posture for a long duration
- **Waxy flexibility:** Body parts placed in a position will be kept for a longer duration even if they are found uncomfortable to patient.
- **Echopraxia:** Mimicking of actions
- **Echolalia:** Mimicking of words heard
- **Ambitendency:** Tentative actions are made due to conflicting impulses. No goal-directed behavior is observed, for example, a patient is asked to close eyes by the nurse; the patient closes partially and opens completely.
- **Automatic obedience:** Commands followed automatically irrespective of their consequences.
- **Verbigeration:** Incomprehensive speech.
- **Psychological pillow:** Patient holds his/her head a few centimeters above the bed for many hours.
- **Mannerisms**
- **Stereotypical speech:** Meaningless repetitive speech.

Nursing Management

- Collect the history from the patient's family members.
- Perform physical examination and send the blood samples to identify the patient's health problems.
- Nurse has to ensure the patent airway in order to prevent the tongue from falling back as it might cause respiratory arrest.
- Administer intravenous fluids in order to meet the fluid balance.
- Other nursing care is similar as that for an unconscious patient.

VICTIM OF RAPE

Rape is a traumatic experience for victim in which the perpetrator coerces or physically forces a female for sexual intercourse against her consent.

Types of Rape

- **Date rape:** Rape done by a person whom the victim knows already.
- **Marital rape or spousal rape:** Rape done by husband toward his wife.
- **Gang rape:** Rape done by a group of individuals.
- **Statutory rape:** Rape done to an individual who is unable to give consent as per the law (minors below the age of 18). Here, there will not be any physical force by perpetrator.
- **Payback rape or punishment rape or revenge rape:** Rape done by the rapist with intent to give punishment.
- **Custodial rape:** Rape done to an individual who is in custody (e.g., in police station, hospital, etc.)

Nicholas Groth classified rape based on the goal of the rapist (types of perpetrators) as follows:

- **Anger rapist:** Rape is done in order to show the anger toward victim.
- **Power rapist:** Rape is done in order to show the power toward victim.
- **Sadistic rapist:** Rape is done in order to enjoy or to get pleasure by harming the victim.

Signs and Symptoms

Low self-esteem, self-blame, fear of being killed, social isolation, feeling of depersonalization or derealization, fear of degradation, recurrent intrusive thoughts, sleep disturbances, loss of appetite, depression and anxiety. It might lead to post-traumatic stress disorder (PTSD) if persists for long term.

Nursing Management

- Provide reassurance and give adequate psychological support.
- Perform physical assessment to identify any injury.
- Send blood samples to rule out any sexually transmitted diseases (STDs), especially HIV infection and initiate the appropriate medications as per the order, if the infection is present.
- Give contraceptive pills to prevent pregnancy.
- Encourage the patient to ventilate the feelings related to the rape trauma.
- Provide counseling services to enhance the psychological well-being of victim.

MEDICAL EMERGENCY IN PSYCHIATRY

NEUROLEPTIC MALIGNANT SYNDROME

Neuroleptic malignant syndrome is an extrapyramidal syndrome/hypermetabolic reaction to the dopamine antagonists, especially antipsychotics. It usually occurs in the early phase of treatment and rarely occurs in the maintenance phase. It occurs in around 3% of patients who are under treatment with antipsychotics. Risk of developing neuroleptic malignant syndrome increases in agitated patients who get increased dosage of drugs.

Signs and Symptoms

Hyperpyrexia, hypertension, muscle rigidity, tachycardia, tachypnea, autonomic dysfunction and changes in the mental status.

Diagnosis

Laboratory findings include respiratory and metabolic acidosis, increased *creatine kinase* (CK), myoglobinuria and leukocytosis.

Treatment

Stop the antipsychotic drugs. Treat the myoglobinuria/fever/acidosis, by providing supportive care. The dopamine agonist—Tab. bromocriptine 2.5–2.0 mg tds or Inj. dantrolene up to 10 mg/kg IV/4th hourly is used as a muscle relaxant. Patient needs to be treated in intensive care unit.

Miscellaneous

Reintroduction of antipsychotics after recovery may retrigger the syndrome in one-third of patients. Mortality rates are around 10–20%.

OVERDOSE OF PSYCHOTROPIC AGENTS

History

Collect history from the patient regarding the intention of taking over-dosage of drug whether it is suicidal or accidental. Identify the amount of the drug consumed.

First Aid Management

If a patient has taken toxic dosage of psychotropics and is awake, then induce vomiting followed by administering the activated charcoal.

Monitoring and Treatment

Overdose with carbamazepine or tricyclic antidepressants needs a regular cardiac monitoring. Overdose with benzodiazepines or barbiturates and alcohol may cause respiratory arrest. Therapeutic as well as toxic dosage of antipsychotics may cause acute extrapyramidal symptoms such as akinesia, oculogyric crisis, dystonia and torticollis. Akathisia is the most adverse effect of high-potency antipsychotic and it might be accompanied by extreme anxiety or terror, if it gets severe. Acute onset of orofacial dystonia or oculogyric crisis might suggest purposeful or inadvertent ingestion of antipsychotics. Immediate relief from orofacial dystonia or oculogyric crisis can be provided with administration of parenteral antihistaminic agents (e.g., promethazine 25 mg IM). Administer oxygen in case of breathing difficulty. Start the intravenous line, administer anticonvulsants and proceed with hemodialysis, if required.

SUBSTANCE INTOXICATION AND WITHDRAWAL

Substance intoxication may happen as a primary presenting complaint or it may happen along with any psychiatric disorder. Withdrawal from barbiturates, sedatives, hypnotics, benzodiazepines and alcohol is clinically similar.

Alcohol Withdrawal Effects

Withdrawal of alcohol may be life-threatening, if the patient has seizures. Delirium tremens is a withdrawal symptom that starts within 7 days of alcohol withdrawal (usually within 24–72 hours). It is a medical emergency and needs to be treated in critical care unit. Management of alcohol withdrawal is usually with high dose of benzodiazepines, maintenance of fluid/electrolyte balance and administration of parenteral thiamine.

Management of Violent Behavior During Substance Withdrawal

Alcohol, phencyclidine and cocaine are the substances that commonly lead to aggression or violent behavior. Patients should be kept under observation in a separate room, away from stimulation. Physical restraints or chemical restraints (sedation) may be needed for patients who are aggressive. Inj. Lorazepam 2–4 mg or diazepam 10–20 mg is recommended to be administered at once to treat agitation.

Treatment Modalities

Treatment in a hospital is safe and mandatory if the patient is febrile (>101°F), not taking oral fluids and is having a severe underlying physical disorder.

SEROTONIN SYNDROME

Definition

Serotonin syndrome is defined as over activation of serotonergic receptors which leads to increased secretion of serotonin.

Etiology

Serotonin syndrome happens due to use of two or more serotonergic medications.

Drugs that induce serotonin syndrome have been given in Table 13.18.

Table 13.18: **Drugs inducing serotonin syndrome**

Class	Drugs that induce Serotonin syndrome
Antidepressants	• Monoamine oxidase inhibitors (MAOIs) • Tricyclic antidepressants (*TCAs*) • Selective serotonin reuptake inhibitors (*SSRIs*) • Serotonin and norepinephrine reuptake inhibitors (SNRIs) • Atypical antidepressant—nefazodone • Miscellaneous—trazodone and mirtazapine
CNS Stimulants	• Methylenedioxy methamphetamine (MDMA) • Amphetamine • Methylphenidate • Phentermine • Methamphetamine • Lisdexamfetamine • Cocaine
Opioids	• Tramadol • Pethidine • Fentanyl • Dextropropoxyphene • Pentazocine • Oxycodone • Hydrocodone • Buprenorphine
Serotonin agonists	Triptans (tryptamine based drug used to treat migraine and cluster headache)
Psychedelics	• Lysergic acid diethylamide (LSD) • 5-Methoxy-diisopropyltryptamine
Antihistamine	Chlorpheniramine
Antipsychotics	Risperidone and olanzapine
Mood stabilizers	Sodium valproate and lithium
Antiretroviral drugs	Ritonavir
Muscle relaxants	Metaxalone
Antiemetics	Granisetron and ondansetron
Miscellaneous	Tryptophan, 5-hydroxytryptophan, Buspirone and linezolid
Herbs	• St John's Wort • Nutmeg • Panax ginseng • Yohimbe • Syrian rue

Clinical Manifestations

A sudden increase in serotonin might lead to a life-threatening condition, which manifests as hyperthermia, excitement or increased motor activity, tachycardia, altered mental state (delirium), mood changes, myoclonus, dilated pupils, abdominal pain, diarrhea, diaphoresis, hyperreflexia, tremors and hypertension.

Flowchart 13.6: Clinical triad of abnormalities in serotonin syndrome

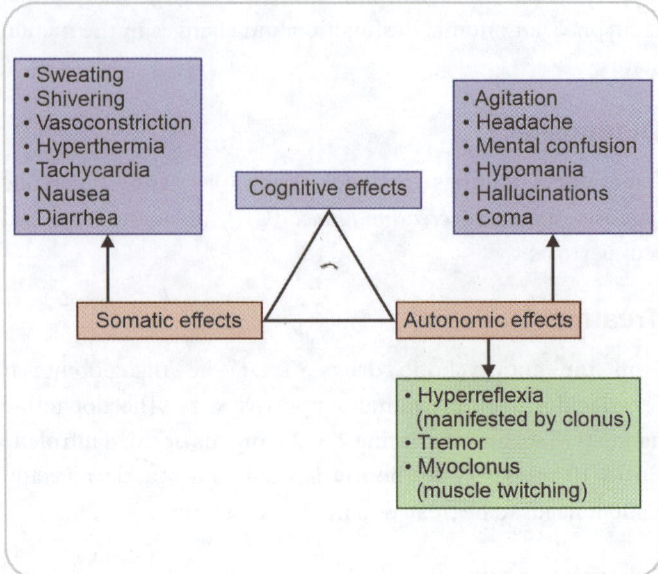

The clinical triad of abnormalities in serotonin syndrome is shown in Flowchart 13.6.

Complications

Serotonin syndrome may lead to cardiovascular collapse, *disseminated intravascular coagulation (DIC)* and rhabdomyolysis (damaged muscles will release myoglobin into bloodstream which causes damage to kidney).

Prevention

Use the drugs with caution that might induce serotonin syndrome. Give adequate washout period while changing one group of antidepressants to another group. For example, if the drug from tricyclic antidepressants (*TCAs*) group to monoamine oxidase inhibitors (MAOIs) group needs to be changed in order to enhance the prognosis of patient, then give washout period (waiting period) for 2 weeks in order to prevent serotonin syndrome. Similarly, change of medicine from MAOIs to SSRI requires 14 days of washout period and change of medicine from SSRI to MAOIs requires 5 weeks of washout period.

Treatment

Medications such as dantrolene (a potent muscle relaxant) and periactin (serotonin antagonist) can be administered.

DELIRIUM

Nursing Management

Environmental manipulation, frequent orientation (time, person and place) and medications might be helpful to reduce severity of delirium.

Medications

Low dose of haloperidol (0.5–2 mg) is the drug of choice. When delirium is due to substance withdrawal, Tab. lorazepam (0.5–2 mg) is the drug of choice to control agitation.

Used with Caution

Anticholinergic drugs (e.g., benztropine) must be used with caution in patients with delirium, especially among elders, because the drug may cause anticholinergic toxicity (atropine psychosis).

EPILEPTIC FUROR

Patient has sudden unprovoked attacks of anger and gets violent or agitated with psychomotor epilepsy. Treatment includes administration of sedatives (Inj. diazepam 10 mg IV), oral anticonvulsants to treat epilepsy and Inj. haloperidol 10 mg IV to control psychotic symptoms.

MALADAPTIVE BEHAVIORS OF INDIVIDUALS AND GROUPS: CRISIS, STRESS AND DISASTERS

Behavioral problems or maladaptive behaviors can occur from childhood to adulthood. If not treated or managed, they can be harmful not only to the society and people but also to the person manifesting maladaptive behaviors. It is important for the person to be given help and support by professionals, society and family members.

ADAPTIVE BEHAVIOR

Adaptive behavior is a collection of skills that the people learn and employ to function in everyday life. They allow us to adapt to the demands of life and fulfil our needs.

MALADAPTIVE BEHAVIOR

Maladaptive behavior refers to the type of behavior that inhibits a person's ability to adjust with certain situations. We must adapt our behavior to face challenges and conflicts in daily life. However, people can develop a tendency to escape from these challenges rather than dealing with them.

There are several types of maladaptive behaviors, ranging from relatively minor impairments (such as nail-biting and separation difficulties) to more severe impairments (such as self-harm) in response to crisis. The following are the common maladaptive behaviors in general.

- **Avoidance coping:** It is a type of behavior in which someone avoids stressful thoughts or feelings in order to protect himself/herself from psychological damage. It involves seeking situations which have less stressors, and avoiding situations which have more stressors. A common disease condition of avoidance coping is panic disorder, which can itself lead to agoraphobia, a condition in which sufferers become anxious in unfamiliar environments.
- **Self-harm (SH):** Self-harm is the deliberate, direct, self-inflicted destruction of body tissue without suicidal intent and for the purposes which are not socially sanctioned (Gratz, 2001). It used to be known as 'deliberate self- harm' or DSH. The most common forms of self-harm are skin-cutting, burning oneself, causing physical trauma to oneself, scratching oneself, pulling one's own hair, interfering with healing wounds, and so on. It can be spontaneous or planned, and it can be a regular occurrence or a one-off event.
- **Disordered eating:** Disordered eating refers to a range of abnormal eating behaviors, including binge-eating, excessive dieting, bulimia, and attachment of well-being to body image. The most common form of disordered eating is dieting, i.e., severely restricting the amount of food you eat. Disordered eating can have profound destructive consequences on someone's life; and research has shown a relationship between disordered eating and the ability to deal with stress or conflict. There is also a relationship between suicidal thoughts or behaviors and disordered eating in adolescents.
- **Substance misuse:** Substance misuse can be the use of illicit drugs, or the use of prescribed medications in ways other than the intended purpose, or problematic use of alcohol. Generally, it is defined as, 'taking of any substance (including alcohol) in such a way that it leads to harm'. Substance misuse has been found in some cases to correlate with anti-social behavior, criminal behavior and changes in one's personality. Addiction, death, injury, violence, accidents, homicide and suicide are linked (to varying degrees) to the misuse of substances. For example, the rate of suicide frequently increases with alcoholism.

Maladaptive Behaviors in Response to Stress

Stress is a nonspecific response of the body to any demand made upon it, either caused by the results of pleasant or unpleasant situations. Initially, people attempt to cope with stressful situations by using a number of adaptive coping strategies. However, when the impact of stress exceeds their coping ability, they resort to maladaptive behavior. At first, these strategies might seem useful, but in the end, the situation gets worse. Here are some maladaptive behaviors exhibited by individuals in response to stress.

Maladaptive behaviors in response to stress	• Substance abuse • Attention-seeking behavior • Sex addiction • Anger conversion • Addiction to exercise • Workaholism • Internet addiction

Substance Abuse

People use drugs or medications excessively often to reduce pain, to decrease the level of anxiety and get temporary relief from problems or bad experiences. However, this can lead to changes in the brain functions and increase the chances of dependency.

Attention-Seeking Behavior

Attention-seeking behavior is a type of maladaptive behavior in which an individual seeks attention or wants to be the center of attention by making excessive actions that can draw attention of others toward him/her. Manipulation, admitting to crimes or doing the wrong things he/she is not intended to commit but to seek the attention of others toward oneself are considered maladaptive behaviors.

Sex Addiction

Some people have an excessive desire to have sexual relations, which is also an example of maladaptive behavior. Such people rely on sex to escape, relieve pain and even manage stress. These actions may lead to harming other people and oneself to the point of losing jobs, missing school and engaging in unprotected sex with numerous individuals.

Anger Conversion

When a person converts his/her anger to violence such as hurting someone else, committing crimes and inflicting physical harm to oneself or other people, this becomes an inappropriate and maladaptive behavior.

Addiction to Exercise

Excessive exercise can be considered a compulsive maladaptive behavior, especially if a person manifests certain signs like being restless or anxious if the person quits exercise. Engaging in strenuous physical activities that can be detrimental to health and can cause pain and injury is a maladaptive behavior.

Workaholism

Spending too much time at work can be a maladaptive behavior when it becomes an addiction. At first, it can be an unconscious way to cope with psychological issues, but it progresses and eventually impairs the functions of the individual when he/she comes to non-working environment. Over a period of time, a workaholic individual will be in conflict with family members, burned-out at work and will have impaired health.

Internet Addiction

Compulsive use of the internet is a maladaptive behavior. These individuals manifest reactions such as depression when not using the internet, anger, forgetting to eat, denying excessive spending of time on internet and preferring to be online instead of being with family and friends.

Patterns of Maladaptive Coping Among Children

- It has been recognized that maladaptive coping apparently stems from adverse childhood experiences and predicts the psychopathology across lifespan. However, same research has addressed how maladaptive styles of coping develop (Fig. 13.5).
- Zimmer-Gembeck and Skinner's integrative review showed that older children and adolescents may continue to use **less mature or primitive forms of coping** (e.g., escaping from the situation and seeking contact with a caregiver) when they face extremely stressful events.
- Children develop **problematic coping** to protect themselves from overwhelming stress or maltreatment.
- Children develop **negative coping** and thinking patterns from invalidating interactions with caregivers.
- Thus, repeated use of developmentally primitive coping, lack of exposure to healthy alternatives, or

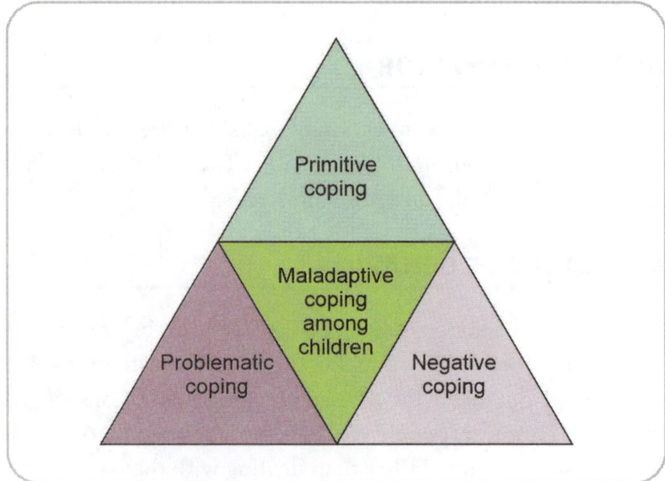

Figure 13.5: Maladaptive coping among children

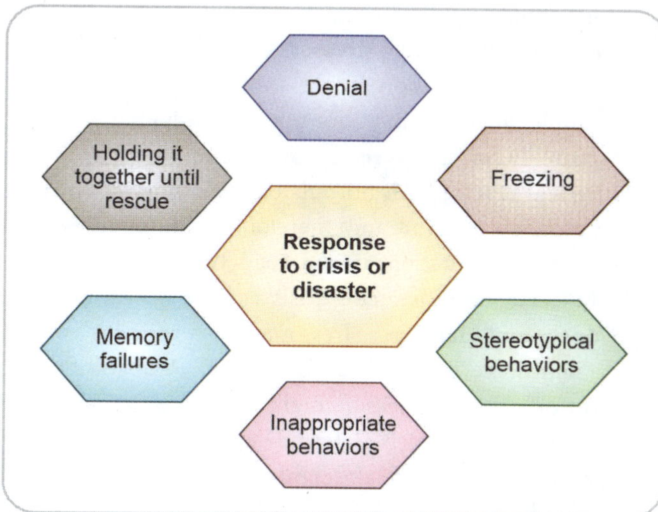

Figure 13.6: Maladaptive behaviors in response to crisis or disasters

repeated exposure to overwhelming stress may solidify a maladaptive style of coping—one that relies too much on primitive strategies such as avoidance and denial.

Maladaptive Behaviors in Response to Crisis or Disasters

People can behave in an appropriate manner during an emergency. They become indecisive and act in a stunned and bewildered manner. Some victims will display serious maladaptive behavior, including confusion, crying, paralyzing anxiety and hysteria. People may be passively standing by or running aimlessly here and there (Fig. 13.6).

Denial

Denial is one of the main maladaptive behaviors for the people who fail to respond toward the danger because they enter a state of denial. Denial can result if people do not trust the source of the disaster warning signal. Generally, people do not respond to disaster signs because they don't want to deviate from what others are doing.

For example, during Chennai flood, many persons were reluctant to vacate to safer places because people from their own locality were not vacating. One more reason people do not respond to threat is because it becomes very difficult to create new behaviors under threat.

Freezing

During disasters, freezing (also known as cognitive paralysis) is commonly seen as a struggling behavior of people to generate new appropriate behaviors. Stunned behavior has been reported in many disaster situations from fires to flood.

Stereotypical Behaviors

Sometimes people can avoid freezing by engaging in a pre-existing schema during the disaster. For example, while evacuating a building during a disaster, people may pass by the emergency exits as they use their normal preplanned exit route.

For example, during the September 11, 2001 attacks on the World Trade Center, people took time to shut down their computers before exiting. Since the victims did not have a preplanned schema for leaving under emergency conditions, they implemented their normal 'leaving' behavioral schema, which included the switching off of their computers.

Inappropriate Behaviors

People in threat situations can also make poor decisions which leads to inappropriate action. Due to time pressure, victims can be faced with a large amount of ambiguous, incomplete and novel information. Under these types of conditions, people are more likely to make errors in judgment. Obviously, poor decision making in a life-threatening situation can increase the risk of injury or death.

For example, during the Japanese earthquake in March 2011, people in a supermarket were running to save bottles of alcohol from smashing rather than carrying out the correct earthquake drill.

Memory Failures

Disaster victims often report failures in memory under threat. One theory states that the victims of disasters have memory problems since the body releases high levels of the stress hormone cortisol that might affect the parts of the brain which are responsible for memory processing. Another theory is that the worry and anxiety caused by the disaster occupies the area of the brain which is responsible for processing memories.

For example, failing to remember where you left your front door keys during a fire will have more serious implications. Whatever the reason, it is clear that memory failures during disasters can cause people to forget how to use emergency equipment or how to follow emergency procedures.

Holding it Together Until Rescue

One interesting observation of disaster victims is that some are able to take prompt and effective actions under threat but at the point of rescue, they become dazed. For example, Chilean mine survivors who acted in a rational manner while trapped underground but became stunned and dazed upon rescue.

CRISIS

Crisis Intervention

Meaning of Crisis

The term, 'crisis' came from the Chinese word, 'weiji', which means 'danger at a point of juncture'. Crisis came from the Greek word, 'Krisis', which means 'decision' or 'judgment' or 'dispute'.

Definitions of Crisis

- Crisis is an immediate compulsive act, which alters the homeostasis of an individual and it remains unresolved act at a moment due to loss of control.
- Crisis is a sudden event in one's life which disturbs homeostasis during which the usual coping mechanism can't resolve the problem. —*Lagerquist, 2001*

Characteristics of Crisis

- Crisis is personal in nature.
- It is precipitated by a specific event.
- It contains the potential factor for growth and deterioration.
- Crisis is a disturbance caused by a stressful event or a perceived thought.
- Crisis also depends on the perception of event and the perceived event can be identified.
- Crisis can be equated with psychopathology.
- Crisis can be a challenge or a positive outcome.

Factors Influencing Crisis

- **Psychological factor:** Psychological causes might induce stress, thereby leading to crisis, if not resolved at a time. For example, severely depressed individual has to be treated with antidepressants, so that the psychological problem can be resolved; if not done, it might lead to crisis situation.
- **Chronic and repeated stressor:** Continuous and repeated stressor in all action might influence the crisis. For example, unemployment for a longer period after trying repeatedly can cause crisis.
- **Physical factor:** Health-related issues might cause continuous stressor and therefore, lead to crisis. For example, amputation after a road traffic accident is a physical factor influencing crisis.
- **Concurrent factors:** Stressors are the ones which influence the stress on an individual. Along with one stressor, another stressor might influence the stress on the individual which is termed concurrent factor. For example, an individual might meet with an accident suddenly (stressor), additionally, the individual's wife dies suddenly (additional stressor). This puts the individual in crisis (Flowchart 13.7).

Types of Crises

Different types of crises along with their description and examples have been given in Table 13.19.

Phases of Crisis

Caplen Phases of Crisis

Caplen (1964) classified crisis into four phases as described below (Figure 13.7):

1. **Phase I** takes place when an event is perceived as a threat, then the normal coping mechanism gets activated. If the coping mechanism works well, then there will not be any crisis. If it fails, then entry to the second phase of crisis takes place.
2. In **Phase II,** an individual experiences a sense of vulnerability because the failure of coping mechanism

Flowchart 13.7: Factors influencing crisis

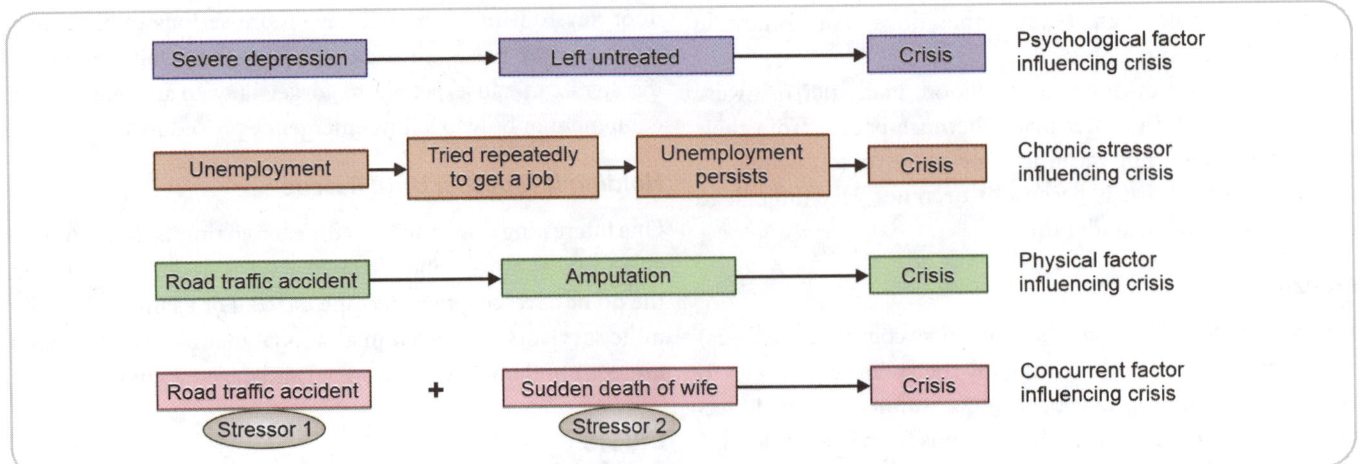

Table 13.19: Types of crises along with their description and examples

Types of crises	Description	Examples
Maturational crisis or developmental crisis	Transitional point, when an individual needs to adjust and adapt to the new life responsibilities but fails to do so resulting in maturational crisis. Common transitional periods having high chances of crisis potential are new job, early adolescence, marriage, parenthood and retirement. Changes in relationship, emotional growth and adjustment are required to prevent this type of crisis.	Mr X got newly married, unable to adopt the pattern of lifestyle, adjust with wife, sudden unexpected expenses, etc. leading to maturational crisis
Situational crisis	It is precipitated by a stressful event which is unanticipated or suddenly creates a disequilibrium, which acts as a threat to biological, physical, psychosocial integrity	• Sudden economical loss • Abrupt role changes • Death of loved ones • Premature death of baby • Psychological or physical illness • Poor academic performance • Loss of ability to work • Transfer to another work environment
Social crisis	An accidental and unanticipated loss causes drastic negative changes in the environment	**Natural disasters such as:** • Earthquake • Flooding • Tsunami • Drought • Cyclone **Man-made disasters such as:** • Nuclear accidents or bomb blast • Violence/war • Mass attack/Terrorism • Contamination using toxic waste in huge areas
Crisis reflecting psychopathology	Psychological illness of family members might affect other individuals in the family	Mother might have high risk of depression who is taking care of her son with mental illness
Post-traumatic crisis	Crisis that happens after a physical or psychological trauma	Individual is suffering with depression after a road traffic accident
Anticipated crisis	Crisis which is expected or emerging, requires a timely action	Pregnant women need to undergo the anticipated crisis
Transcultural crisis	An individual experiencing sudden transition from his/her culture to a different culture might undergo cultural shock or transcultural crisis	A girl married to a person of other religion may experience transcultural crisis if there is lack of adjustment between them.

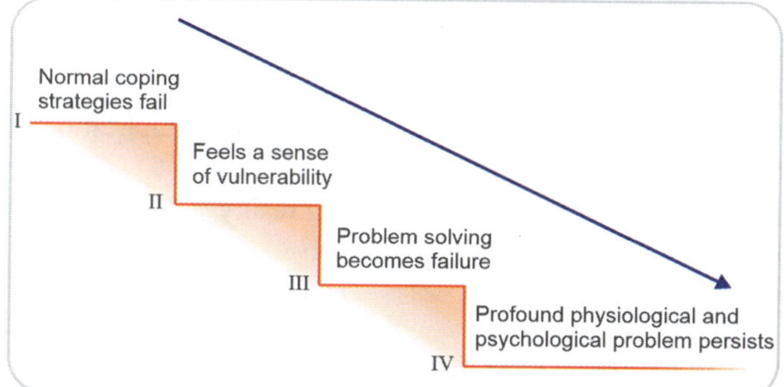

Figure 13.7: Caplen's phases of crisis

still persists. So, anxiety might continue.

3. In **Phase III,** an individual tries to use problem-solving skills but he/she tends to fail in this phase. So, further disorganization takes place.
4. In **Phase IV,** there will be profound physiological and psychological problems. Therefore, an individual might have severe to panic level of anxiety. Referral to the appropriate treatment measures is essential.

Donna's Model or Phases of Crisis

Donna's model includes the following four phases:

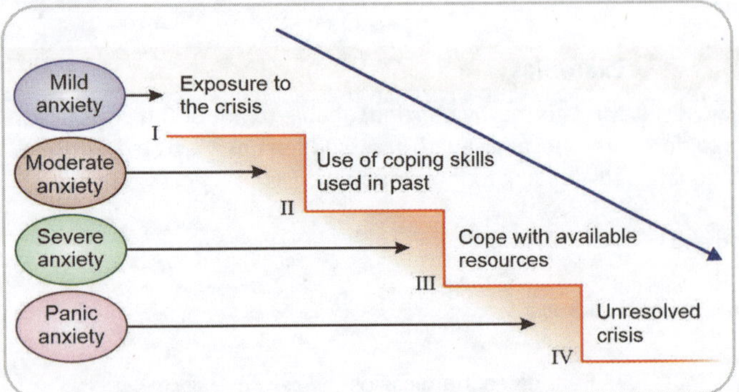

Figure 13.8: Donna's phases of crisis

1. **Phase I** takes place when an individual is exposed to the crisis, he/she might get mild anxiety.
2. In **Phase II,** individual tries to use the coping mechanism, which has been used in the past in order to prevent the crisis; he/she might have a chance to have moderate anxiety.
3. In **Phase III,** individual tries to cope with the available internal or external resources; he/she might experience severe anxiety.
4. In **Phase IV,** individual's crisis might be unresolved; so, he/she might experience panic anxiety (Figure 13.8).

Theories Related to Crisis Intervention

Emil Kraepelin Theory of Crisis Intervention

Emil Kraepelin emphasized that therapeutic intervention or adherence to proper therapeutic regimen has been considered a vital phenomenon during crisis.

Aguilera model of crisis response has been shown in Flowchart 13.8.

Flowchart 13.8: Aguilera (1998) model of crisis response

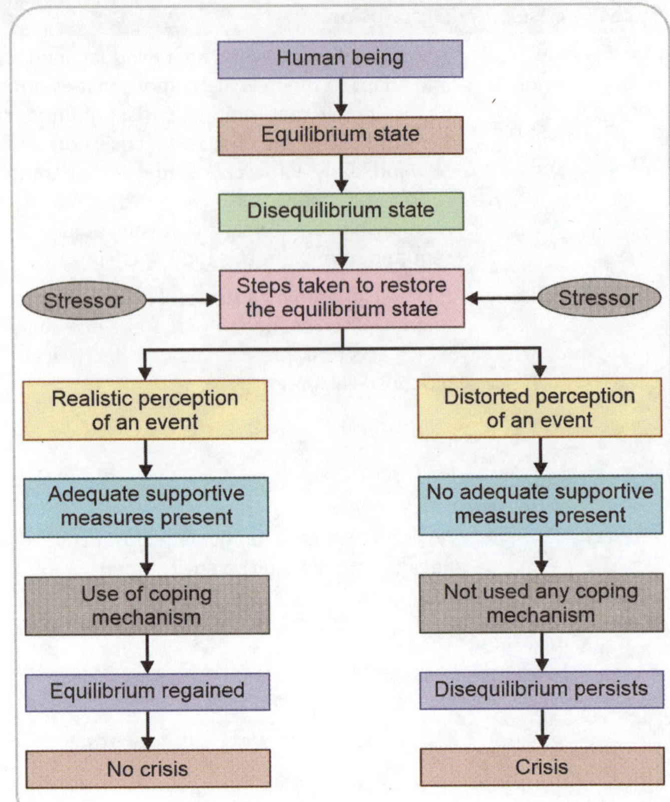

Gerald Kaplan's Theory of Crisis Sequence

- Gerald Kaplan described that individuals undergo the crisis sequence, which are pre-crisis, impact of crisis, crisis stage and post-crisis.
- Precrisis is the duration that exists before the crisis phase.
- Crisis is an emerging situation which requires immediate action.
- Impact of crisis denotes the psychological and physical trauma that an individual undergoes due to crisis.
- Postcrisis is the phase after the crisis, where an individual might have a chance of growth or deterioration (Figure 13.9). Growth occurs when he/she utilizes the supportive measures and coping mechanism in a better way; and deterioration occurs when supportive measures and coping mechanism are not utilized properly.

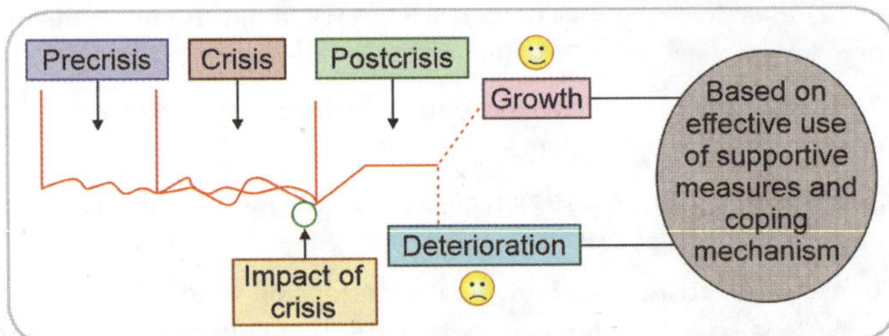

Figure 13.9: Kaplan's theory of crisis sequence

Principles of Crisis Intervention

- Motivate the patient to express feelings
- Listen to facts and feelings
- Guide the patient in confronting reality
- Motivate the patient to focus on particular implication at a time
- Clarify distortions by focusing on reality
- Allow the patient to clarity doubts
- Use specific and concise statements during conversation.

Steps of Effective Crisis Intervention

- **Listen:** Maintain a proper interpersonal relationship with the patient and listen to his/her problems, which cause the crisis situation.
- **Assess:** Assess the precipitating factors such as low self-

esteem, substance abuse, decreased cognition, low ability to handle situations, etc. Assess the perception of the event such as unresolved problem, anxious, depressed, stress, etc.

- **Develop the action plan:** It can be developed using various coping patterns, family/social resources and supportive measures used in past. Action plan consists of individual approach, generic approach, general supportive measures and environment manipulation. The characteristics of action plan are simple, manageable, short term (24 hours to 3 days), achievable, focused and should have a provision of follow-up.

Steps of effective crisis management are shown in Figure 13.10.

1. **Individual approach:** An individual might provide social support to promote coping skills, correct the misconceptions, provide adequate information and help restore psychological health.
2. **Generic approach:** Identification of homogeneity in the problems and handle them with critical incident debriefing using the following steps:
    i. **Fact:** Find out or identify the reason for crisis situation
    ii. **Thought:** Allow the individual to think why, what and when it happens
    iii. **Reacting:** Promote mental ventilation or catharsis
    iv. **Teaching:** Teach by providing adequate suggestions but don't force the individual to decide the suggestion provided as a final one.
    v. **Re-entry:** Enter into first phase of generic approach, if the crisis remains unresolved.
3. **General support:** It includes the following aspects of supportive measures:
    - **Group work:** A group of people affected with common traits of stressors is addressed here. Group members are given chances to express the common experiences and concerns to foster hope and develop mutual support. Health promotion activities need to be provided by family members, friends and individuals who have had previous exposure to the crisis situation.
    - **Disaster response:** Nurse has to extend his/her hands in helping out during the time of floods, earthquake, drought, nuclear accidents, fire and airplane crashes. Nurse plays a vital role in helping people to deal with psychosocial stress.
    - **Mobile crisis program:** It includes on-site assessment, management of crisis, referral services to the appropriate centers and educational services to an individual, families and community.
    - **Telephone contact:** Counseling services through telephone help an individual to enhance the coping skills and self-confidence. They also act as timely help to prevent crisis (For example, Sneha Suicide Prevention Center at Chennai promotes counseling service via telephone to prevent suicidal attempt).
        - **Victim outreach program:** Nurse has to identify the needs of victims and connect them with appropriate referrals as required. Nurse helps the victims to undergo proper assessment, have right psychological support and regular follow-up.
        - **Health education:** Educating the public helps them to be aware of available services in order to deal with problems happened due to the crisis.
    - **Environmental manipulation:** Change of environment from crisis exposed place to the other place helps them to vanish from the remembrance. 'Out of sight, out of mind' is a proverb stating the importance of environmental manipulation.
4. **Close:** This is the final step of crisis intervention required to plan the follow-up care. Summarize and review the action plan which is completed. Do anticipatory planning for building new resources.

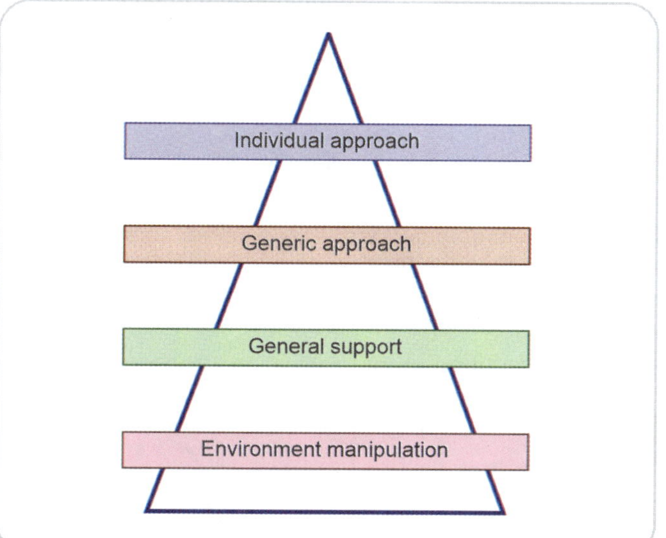

Figure 13.10: Steps of effective crisis management

Nurse's Responsibilities

- Determine the severity of crisis, which has happened
- Nurse should be empathetic while talking to an individual who is affected due to crisis
- Explore the problem as much as possible
- Advise the individual to express emotions
- Nurse has to teach the importance and benefits of coping skills that will help the individual recover from crisis.
- Offer the alternative possible solution to build the coping skills.

Techniques of Crisis Intervention

Techniques of crisis intervention along with description and examples have been given in Table 13.20.

Table 13.20: Techniques of crisis intervention along with description and examples

Techniques of crisis intervention	Description	Examples
Catharsis	Emotional ventilation helps an individual get rid of stress. When you ventilate, your troubles become half and the happiness becomes double. So, keep sharing opinions and troubles with others who are genuine to you	Nurse: Can you please share with me what made you feel distressed? Patient: Cried out and said, 'I miss my wife so much after this accident'
Clarification	Motivating the client to express doubts	Nurse: Do you have any doubts regarding this
Suggestion	Nurse can give suggestion to the client to recover from crisis situation but it should not be forced as a decision to be opted by the client	Nurse: I would suggest you that...
Reinforcement of positive behavior	Reinforcement is a part of motivation; it helps the client promote positive behavior. It can be either verbal (saying good) or material based (giving token/food)	Nurse: Excellent, you have done a good job (verbal reinforcement)
Exploring the solution	Motivate the client to identify the possible solution, which is available for a particular problem	Nurse: Can you verbalize the possible solution to this problem?
Use of adaptive coping mechanism	Use of appropriate stress management strategies helps the client recover from crisis	Nurse: you can perform yoga and meditation to relax yourself
Raising self-esteem	Promotion of self-concept and self-esteem will help the client to be confident and move forward to the next step of life	Nurse: I am damn sure you are capable of performing this task.

Crisis Resolution

Crisis resolution refers to the steps or measures taken to solve a crisis situation (Flowchart 13.9).

Flowchart 13.9: Seven steps intervention model to resolve the crisis

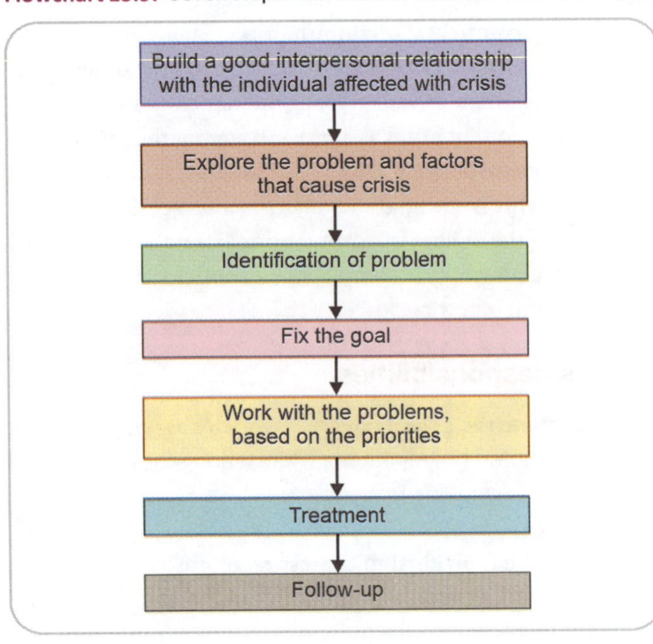

Characteristics

- Crisis resolution is a rapid response.
- It requires supportive measures and education.
- Crisis resolution services should be available round the clock (24 hours).
- Crisis resolution measures act like a gatekeeper between outpatient and in-patient services.
- Services should end up with level of goal achieved and the follow-up measures.

Key Principles

- Crisis needs to be worked out to resolve it as early as possible.
- Holistic biopsychosocial approach needs to be adopted to resolve crisis.
- Success of crisis resolution is highly dependent on adherence to treatment.
- Education is highly required in order to enhance mental health.
- Early identification of problem that causes a crisis will help to resolve the crisis in earlier stage.

Factors Affecting the Effectiveness of Crisis Resolution Services

- **Length of involvement:** Duration of working togetherness between the nurse and patient in order to resolve the crisis plays a vital role in solving crisis.
- **Previous exposure to psychological services:** Client with previous exposure to psychological services might have knowledge to understand the services in a better way.
- **Hours of service rendered:** Crisis resolution services performed round the clock (24 hours) must be ready and available to resolve crisis in a better way.
- **Referral services:** Services referred to certain department should have attitude of acceptance in order to perform effective crisis resolution service.
- **Crisis resolution team:** *Genuineness* in the work of team members such as psychiatrist, psychiatric nurse, psychologist, social worker, occupational therapist plays a vital role in resolving the crisis.
- **Miscellaneous:** Realistic appraisal of the event, availability of support systems and coping skills.

Crisis resolution may be successful or unsuccessful depending on the use of coping skills and problem-solving ability. If an individual uses pathological adaptation of crisis by ruminating about the loss without accepting it, this might lead to prolonged grief reaction and depression. Sometimes, individual uses repression (defense mechanism) and tries to push out the stressors (incident and intense emotions) out of consciousness, which leads to pseudo-resolution (Flowchart 13.10).

Flowchart 13.10: Crisis resolution

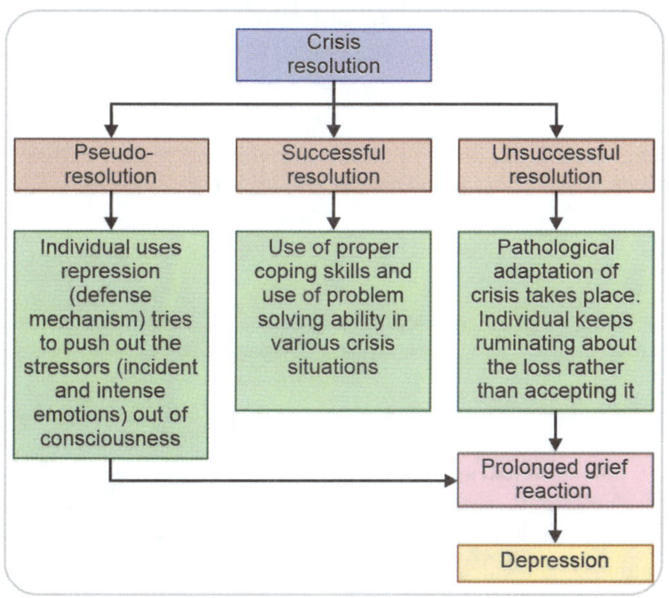

NURSES RESPONSIBILITY

Nurse should maintain a good interpersonal relationship and follow the principles of crisis resolution. Nurse has to work along with the crisis resolution team members in order to resolve the crisis effectively. Nurse should act as an educator to teach the supportive services which are readily available to solve the crisis. Nurse should make an action plan based on criteria and follow the steps correctly. Check out the level of goal achieved intermittently and proceed with the services till the goal has been achieved. Nurse has to take steps in order to enhance the coping skills of the patient. Nurse should follow-up the client in order to guide and provide the supportive services.

GRIEF AND BEREAVEMENT

Meaning

The term 'grief' came from the Latin word '*gravare*' which means burden or something that causes distress. Differences among grief, bereavement and mourning have been listed in Table 13.21.

Table 13.21: Differences among grief, bereavement and mourning

Grief	Bereavement	Mourning
It is a normal process of reacting to the loss of loved ones.	It is the period after a loss during which grief is experienced and mourning occurs	It is the outward expression of loss and grief.
Example: At the time of grieving process, any sort of actions or emotions or expressions to loss such as anger, shock, disbelief, depression, resentment etc. is elicited.	**Example:** Grief has been experienced for a period of two months	**Example:** Crying out due to pain of loss

Definition

Grief is defined as physical, somatic, spiritual, emotional and intellectual responses to the nature of loss. —***Worden, 2005***

Types of Grief

Grief is considered a normal reaction due to loss unless it is not morbid (pathological and complicated). Presence of one or more symptoms and duration of grief for >6 months are considered the characteristics of **morbid grief**, which is classified into pathological grief, complicated grief and grief at death anniversary (Flowchart 13.11).

Flowchart 13.11: Types of grief

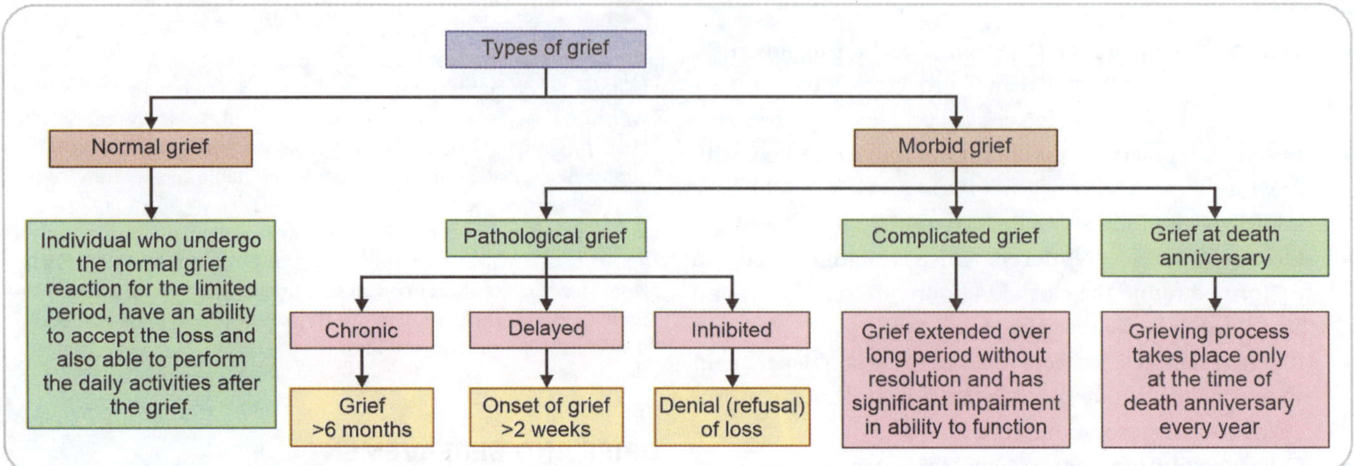

- **Pathological grief** is further classified into chronic grief, delayed grief and inhibited grief.
  - **Chronic grief** is the term used when grief reaction persists for more than 6 months.
  - **Delayed grief** is onset after 2 weeks of actual loss.
  - **Inhibited grief** means the denial/refusal of loss.
- Grief extended over a long period without resolution is considered **complicated grief.**
- Grief at death anniversary means the grieving process takes place only at the time of death anniversary every year.

Miscellaneous griefs along with their description and examples have been given in Table 13.22.

Table 13.22: Miscellaneous griefs

Miscellaneous types of grief	Description	Example
Anticipatory grief	Grieving process takes place before the loss itself since the loss has been expected by the individual	Ms Sudha's mother health has been deteriorating and doctor informed Ms Sudha that her mother will die within 2 weeks. Grieving process starts when she gets this information from the doctor.
Disenfranchised or ambiguous grief	Grief felt by an individual but not acknowledged by others	Mr Raj is undergoing grieving process due to the death of his pet animal but the grieving process is not acknowledged by his family members.
Time-limited grief	Grieving process takes place within a limited time period	Ms Sudha exhibited grief response only for 4 hours after the death of her father.
Private or forbidden or absent grief	Individual who does not exhibit any signs of grief. Grieving process takes place but neither not shown outside nor identified by others	Mr Raj does not show any grief sign after the death of his close friend but the grieving process takes place within him.
Collective grief	Grief which is felt by the group or community	Natural disaster, death of any famous personality in that area, terrorist attack, etc.
Masked grief	Grieving process is exhibited in terms of symptoms or negative behavior, which is not said to be the actual character of the person. Connection between those physical symptoms or negative behavior and grief is difficult to identify	Mr Raj becomes more silent most of time and sleeps a lot during the grieving process but this behavior is out of his character.
Exaggerated or distorted grief	Grief present with extreme feeling of anger, guilt, self-destructive behavior and hostility toward a particular individual	Mr Raj develops a feeling of enmity toward a person because he feels that the person is responsible for the loss.
Cumulative grief	Grief takes place when multiple losses happen within a short duration of time	Ms Sudha experiences pathological grief due to sudden death of four members in her family.

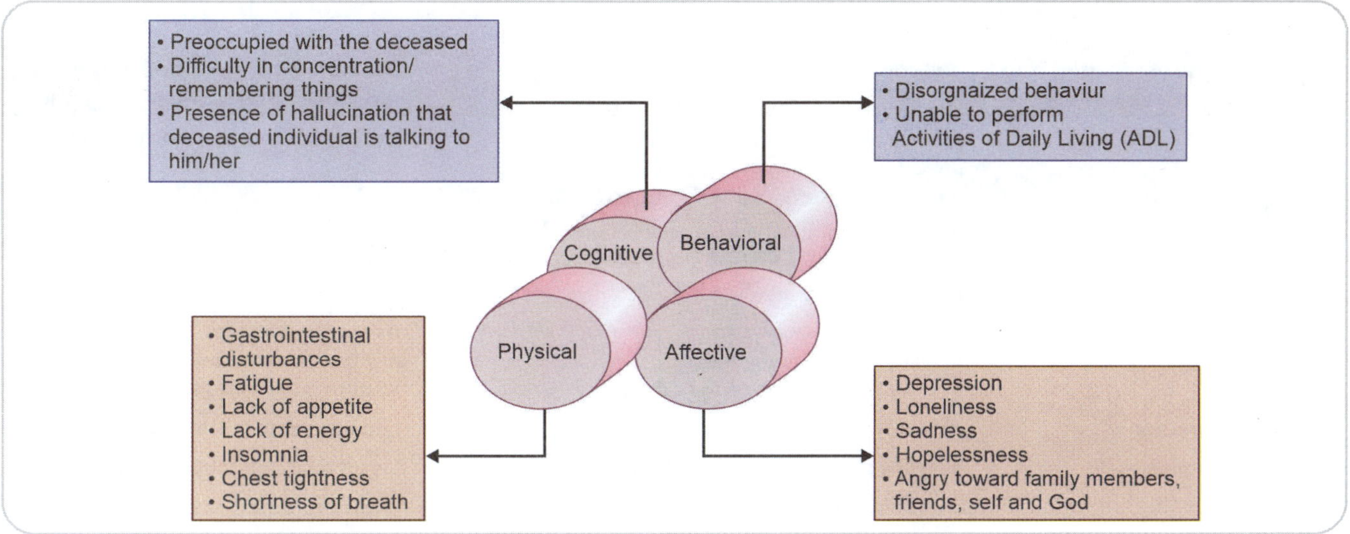

Figure 13.11: Responses to grief and loss

Responses to grief and loss have been given in Figure 13.11.

Grief Experiences

- **Hurting:** Individual feels hurt due to the painful experiences during grief.
- **Missing:** Individual feels that he/she is missing the loved ones.
- **Holding:** Individual feels like holding the memories of deceased.
- **Being stopped:** Individual feels like that he/she is unable to perform all the activities.
- **Seeking:** Individual seeks help from others during grief.

Theories of Grief

Kubler-Ross Theory of Grief

Kubler Ross (1969) identified five stages of behavior and feelings that an individual experiences in response to the actual or perceived or anticipated loss, which are as follows (Fig. 13.12):

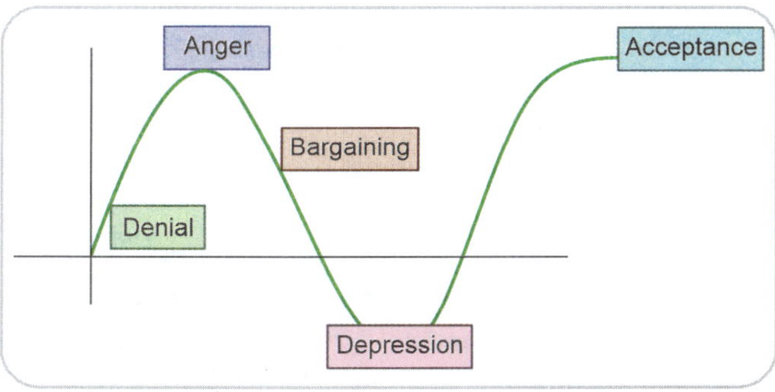

Figure 13.12: Responses to grief-Kubler-Ross theory

- Denial
- Anger
- Bargaining
- Depression
- Acceptance

Different stages of grief along with their description and examples have been described in Table 13.23.

Dr Rando's 6 Rs of Mourning

Table 13.24 shows different phases of grief along with their description.

John Bowlby's Four Stages of Grief

John Bowlby used the Freud perspectives to describe grief. It is a biological instinct for attachment.

1. Urge to recover the lost person
2. Disequilibrium
3. Disorganization
4. Reorganization

Worden's Four Tasks of Mourning

Worden views the bereavement as active or self-determining rather than a passive process. Worden explained that with the use of social support and dealing with the problems, coping process takes place.

1. Accepting the reality of loss
2. Working through the pain of grief
3. Adjusting to an environment which has changed due to loss
4. Move on with present life

Table 13.23: Stages of grief along with their description and examples

Stages	Name of the grief stage as per Kubler Ross	Description	Example (Phrase verbalized by the individual who is undergoing grief)
I	Denial	Refusing that it has not happened to me. It is a projective defense mechanism that allows adequate time frame to develop the coping skills/ability	No, it is not true and it will not happen to me....
II	Anger	A negative emotion directed toward self or displaced to others (family members, caregivers, loved ones, friends, God)	Shout and say....Why did it happen to me?
III	Bargaining	A state of bargain with God or supreme power in order to reverse or postpone the loss	Asking the God that, 'I have never done any bad things to any one, why you want to punish me like this?'
IV	Depression	A state where the full impact of loss has been realized	I don't want to talk to anyone else......
V	Acceptance	A feeling of peace and complete realization in regard with the loss happened	I want to accept this...what to do...

Table 13.24: Phases of grief along with their description as per Dr Rando

Phases of grief as per Dr Rando	6'R's of Mourning	Description
Avoidance	Recognize the loss	Understanding what has happened and really accepting that loved one has been lost
Confrontation	React to the separation	Acknowledging the secondary losses. E.g., death of spouse also tends to loss of financial security, loss of future ideas and lack of romantic intimacy.
	Recollect and re-experience	Remembering the memories of loved one
	Relinquish old attachments	Slowly begin to process the impact of loved one's absence
Accommodation	Readjust to the new world without forgetting the old world	Readjusting to new roles and responsibilities and also understand how the loss of loved one has changed your life pattern
	Reinvest emotional energy	Act of enjoying life with new friends or roles but it does not mean that this is a replacement for loved ones.

Parke's Four Phase Model of Grief

1. Shock and numbness—similar to somatic distress
2. Yearning and searching (strong negative emotions might express the anger toward the deceased)
3. Anguish, disorganized and identification
4. Reorganization

COUNSELING

Definition

Counseling is an interactive process between the counselor and counselee. Counselor is a person who provides help and counselee is a person who seeks help.

Types of Counseling

Based on the ***number of members involved in counseling***, it is classified into:

- **Individual counseling:** Nurse counsels a single patient.
- **Group counseling:** Nurse counsels a group of patients.

Based on the ***purposes of counseling***, it is classified into:

- **Bereavement counseling:** Counseling is provided to address the practical issues of living without the loved one who has died recently.
- **Family counseling:** Counseling is provided to solve the family issues.
- **Premarital counseling:** Counseling provided before marriage is termed premarital counseling. This helps to prevent marital disputes.
- **Problem solving counseling:** Counseling is provided to solve a problem.
- **Crisis intervention:** Counseling is provided to resolve the crisis situation.

Counseling to relieve personal distress:

- **Special counseling:** It is done to discuss the risks and benefits.

Based on the ***approaches of counseling,*** it is classified into:

- **Directive or counselor-centered counseling:** Counselor directs the counselee (patient) to solve the problem and take decision (counselor plays a predominant role in this type).
- **Nondirective or patient-centered counseling:** Counselee (patient) himself or herself solves the problem and takes decision (patient plays a predominant role in this type).
- **Eclectic counseling:** Counselor will guide to take decision; at the same time counselee is also actively involved in the decision-making process.

Principles of Counseling

- **Principle of acceptance:** Accept the patient with his/her physical, psychological, economical, social and cultural conditions.
- **Principle of communication:** Communication should be relevant, appropriate to the problem raised by the patient.
- **Principle of empathy:** Nurse has to think from the patient's point of view by standing in patient's position and then give reflections accordingly.
- **Principle of nonjudgment:** Nurse should not criticize or comment in a negative way with regard to the patient's complaints.
- **Principle of confidentiality:** Nurse has to keep all the information about the patient secretly and assure the patient about the same.
- **Principle of individuality:** Nurse has to treat each and every patient as unique and respect everyone.
- **Principles of nonemotional involvement:** Nurse should not get involved with the patient emotionally and not get carried away by their feelings.

Table 13.25 shows different techniques of counseling along with their description.

Table 13.25: Techniques of counseling along with their description

Techniques of counseling	Description
Active listening	Therapist actively listens and shows attentive interest during counseling. **Mnemonics** **SOLER:** **S**: Sit facing the client **O**: Open Posture **L**: Lean forward toward client **E**: Establish eye contact **R**: Relax
Capping	It is the universal skill of the therapist to change the direction of conversation from emotional to cognitive in order to cut off the patient's emotion.
Clarification	Asking the patient to elaborate or state examples of vague ideas or thoughts. For example, nurse asking doubt to the patient, whether did actually mean this?
Confrontation	Counselor gently brings into the patient's awareness that something is overlooked or avoided
Empathy	Recognizing the patient's feeling by standing up in patient's situation. For example, nurse is saying to the patient that, 'I can feel how painful it is?'
Exploring	Delving further into the idea or subject. For example, nurse is asking the patient, 'can you explain it fully'?
Encouraging the description of perceptions	Asking the patient's view about the present situation. For example, nurse is asking the patient, 'what do you think about the present situation'?
Focusing	Focus toward a single idea or word. For example, nurse verbalizes to client that 'Can you describe the event a little more'?
Immediacy	Therapist talks immediately and openly with the patient in regard with any happenings that occur in the therapy session. For example, nurse verbalizes to the patient that you look tensed when we talk about your father.
Linking the patient to the social support	Involving the family members of the patient in counseling process will enhance the patient's social support to solve problem.
Open-ended questions	This will help the patient to put into detailed discussion. For example, nurse can ask 'How do you feel today'? (Open-ended question) instead of asking 'Are you happy today'? (closed-ended question)
Paraphrasing	Nurse attempts to give feedback about what the patient has just said in order to convey to the patient that nurse or therapist is listening.

Contd...

Techniques of counseling	Description
Proxemics	Counselor analyzes the spatial movements of patient; by understanding the body orientation, counselor can determine feelings, mood and reactions of the patient.
Reinforcement	Providing feedback about the positive behaviors. For example, nurse is saying to the patient that 'Good, you have done a wonderful job'
Self-disclosure	Counselor discloses personal information to the client during the counseling process if the patient gets benefit out of this.
Trustworthiness	Therapist has to be empathetic, warm and deliver unconditional positive regard in order to develop trustworthiness with the patient so that rapport is developed.
Working alliance	Counselor and patient work together in order to achieve a common goal in treatment process.

STRESS

Stress Adaptation Model

Schafer (2000) defined stress as 'arousal of body and mind in response to the demand made upon them'.

- Stress can be classified into **Eustress** and **Distress**.
- **Eustress** is a normal level of stress that everyone undergoes in day-to-day life. **Distress** is a negative perception of event/situation that might lead an individual to have a significant distress.

Stressor

Stressor is defined as an event or situation or person which causes stress. Stressor can be classified into internal stressor and external stressor.

- **Internal stressor** arises from inside. (Example: Hunger).
- **External stressor** arises from outside (Example: Teacher forcing the student to study well). Stressors can also be classified based on the etiological factors such as environmental factors, physiological factors, social factors and thoughts.

Extrinsic Factors

- **Environmental factors:** Air/water/noise pollution, crowd, heavy traffic, bad weather (extremely hot or cold climate).
- **Social factors:** Loss of loved ones, unemployment, financial problems, participation in social events due to compulsion of others, forced to work in a job which is not willing to him/her.

Intrinsic Factors

- **Thoughts:** Negative thoughts/ideation, high perfectionism, lack of self-motivation.
- **Physiological factors:** Lack of sleep or nutrition, more hunger, sickness, physical injuries and hormonal imbalance.

Models of Stress

Models of stress help the nurses to identify the productive and unproductive responses to the stressors. Knowledge of these models helps the nurses to promote the patient's coping skills in order to adjust the unhealthy and unproductive responses (Table 13.26).

Table 13.26: Models of stress

Models of stress	Author	Year
Stimulus-based model	Holmes and Rahe	1960
Response-based model	Hans Selye	1945
Transaction-based model	Lazarus	1966

Stimulus-Based Model

As per stimulus-based model, stress is due to stimuli or life events or circumstances which enhance the physiologic and psychological reactions that might enhance the chance of individual's vulnerability to get rid of stress.

Social Readjustment Rating Scale (SRRS) consists of 43 life changes which are positive and negative in nature considered to be stressful. This scale helps an individual in regard with the stressor that he/she experiences within the life period. Low score in this scale does not mean that the individual is free from stress; and high score in this scale does not mean that the individual might experience serious problems. Mediating factors such as the individual's perception about the event and coping skills with the stressor play a vital role in determining the impact of stress.

Response-Based Model

As per response-based model, stress might affect a set of bodily changes described as general adaptation syndrome. This syndrome has the following three stages:

1. Alarm Reaction Stage

Stimulation of hypothalamus, sympathetic nervous system and adrenal medulla might release catecholamine (epinephrine and norepinephrine), which leads to alarm reaction.

In the alarm reaction, there are two responses to the stress, namely **flight response** and **fight response**. When an individual feels stressed, either he/she should develop the ability to fight against the stress or else the individual should use the flight response by running away from the stressor. For example, Mr Raj fails in all exams, it has been informed by the class teacher that if it persists, he will not be permitted to next year of course. Mr Raj has a chance to discontinue the course (flight response) or else put his efforts by understanding the subject and study well (fight response) (Fig. 13.13).

Stress responses in alarm reaction have been given in Table 13.27.

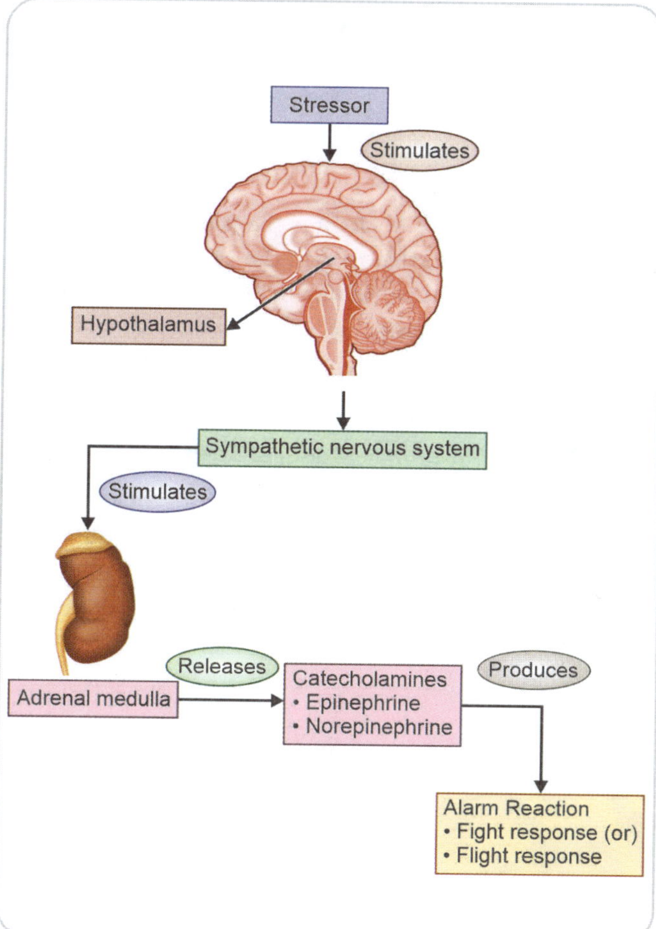

Figure 13.13: Alarm reaction

Table 13.27: Stress responses in alarm reaction

Organs	Physiological responses in alarm reaction
Heart	• Heart rate increases • Strength of cardiac muscle contraction increases and so, blood circulation quickly takes place
Lungs	• Respiratory rate increases • Respiratory passages widen to get more oxygen
Gastrointestinal system	• Digestive enzymes decrease • Production of saliva occurs • Liver converts the glycogen into glucose and releases it into • bloodstream (so that it provides energy to fight with the stressor)
Blood vessel	• Blood supply to skin and viscera • gets constricted • Blood supply to heart, lungs, skeletal muscles and brain gets dilated. • RBC production increases

2. Resistance Reaction Stage

Resistance reaction is the **second stage of stress response**. The regulating hormones secreted by hypothalamus in resistance reaction are growth hormone releasing hormone (GHRH), corticotropin releasing hormone (CRH) and thyrotropin releasing hormone (TRH). The regulating hormones stimulate the anterior pituitary to release adrenocorticotropic hormone (ACTH), human growth hormone and thyroid stimulating hormone (TSH). ACTH stimulates the adrenal cortex to release the adrenal hormones such as glucocorticoids and mineralocorticoids. Human growth hormone stimulates the liver and therefore, it supplies energy through glyconeogenesis and lipolysis. Thyroid stimulating hormone stimulates the thyroid gland and it supplies energy through increased breakdown of carbohydrates.

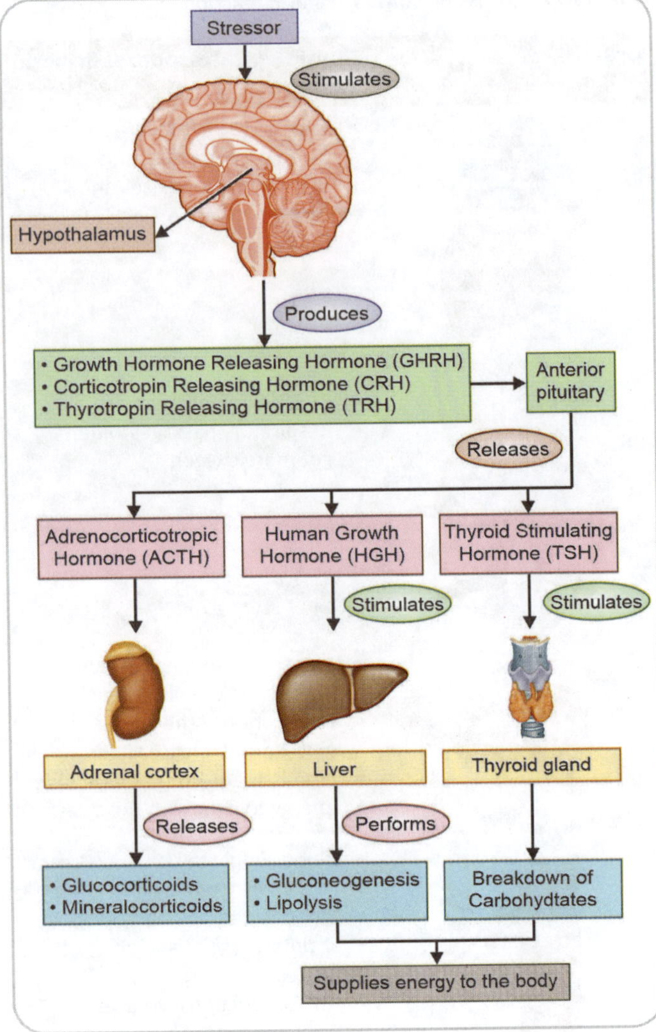

Figure 13.14: Resistance reaction

Resistance reaction allows the body to fight with stressors for a long time and so, it is helpful to cope with a stressful situation. If this fighting mechanism with the stressors fails, then it will get into the next stage, namely exhaustion (Fig. 13.14).

3. Exhaustion Reaction Stage

In this stage, tissues start dying and organs become weak due to the long-term resistance which puts higher demand on lungs, heart, blood vessels, glands and gastrointestinal system. These organs might have higher chance to fail because of the extreme strain given to that organ.

Transaction-Based Model

Transaction-based model has been shown in Flowchart 13.12.

Flowchart 13.12: Transaction-based model

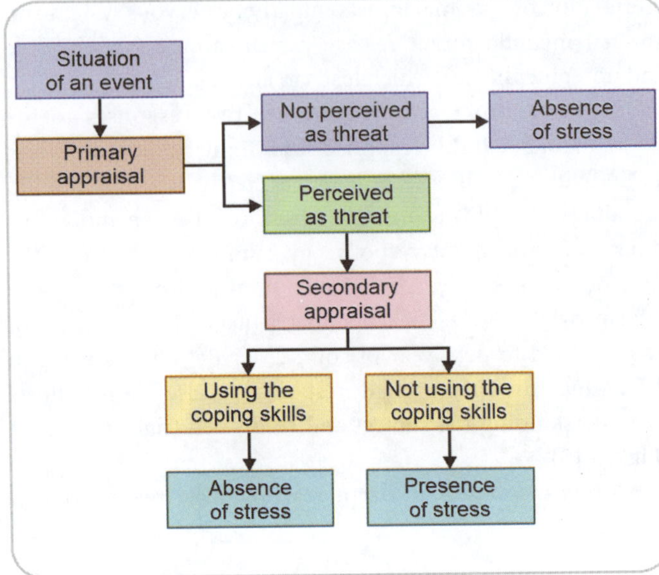

ABC Model of Stress (Prof. Cooper)

(A+B = C)

A : Activating event
B : Belief
C : Consequences

An activating event for Mr Ram is "he failed in two subjects". The belief is "he is unable to pass the examination" and the consequence is "continuous failure in exams" which lead to physiological responses such as his heart rate and blood pressure increase and psychological response such as always being depressed.

Effort Reward Imbalance Model of Stress

An organization getting more work from the employees but not paying wages properly, when there is no professional growth and not promoting them to next level it might lead an individual to have stress (Fig. 13.15).

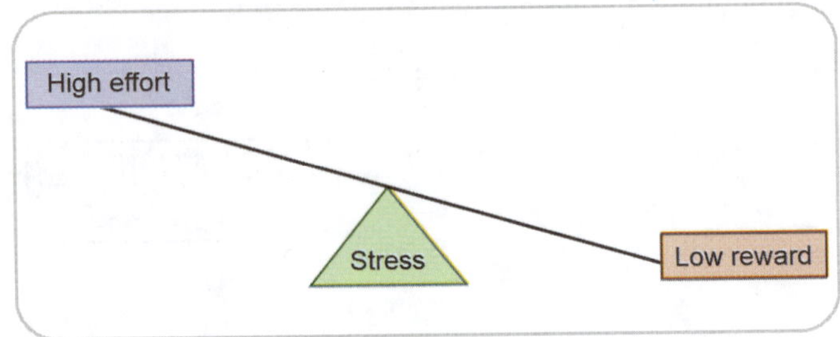

Figure 13.15: Effort reward imbalance model of stress

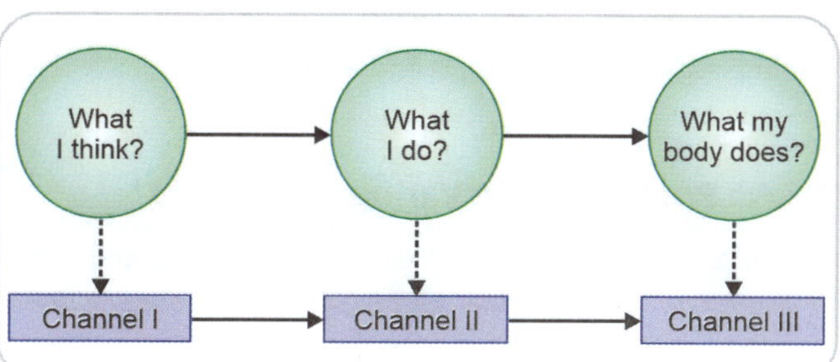

Figure 13.16: Three channel model of stress reaction

Three Channel Model of Stress Reaction

Stress always depends on the perception of an event. 'What the individual thinks about it?' is said to be first channel to cause stress reaction. In Channel II, based on his/her thoughts, he/she may perform flight or fight response, i.e., fight against the stressor or else flight (escape) out of stressor. Channel III denotes 'What body does due to the stressor?' i.e., physiological response, e.g., heart rate and blood pressure increase and the psychological response, e.g., being depressed may occur (Fig. 13.16).

Psychosomatic Model of Stress

Udupa (1977) explained the concept of psychosomatic model of stress, which has four phases, namely psychic phase, psychosomatic phase, somatic phase and organic phase (Table 13.28).

Table 13.28: Psychosomatic model of stress

Phases	Description	Example
Psychic phase	Psychological symptoms are predominant	Crave to smoke cigarettes
Psychosomatic phase	Psychological condition alters the bodily function	Smoking causes lung damage
Somatic phase	Impairment of the bodily function damages the organ	Lung damage persists
Organic phase	Damage to an organ leads to disease	Chronic obstructive pulmonary disease (COPD)

Socioenvironmental Model of Stress

Pestonjee (1930) described that there are three factors which cause the stress, namely job and organization, intrapsychic factor and social factor (Flowchart 13.13). An individual with strong stress tolerance limit can cope with stressors but repeated stressors might break the stress tolerance limit (STL) further leading to extreme level of stress.

Flowchart 13.13: Socioenvironmental model of stress

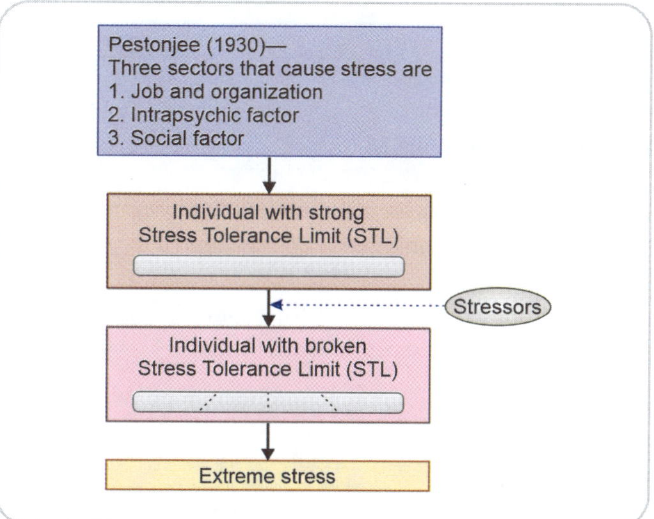

Flowchart 13.14: Bounce model of stress

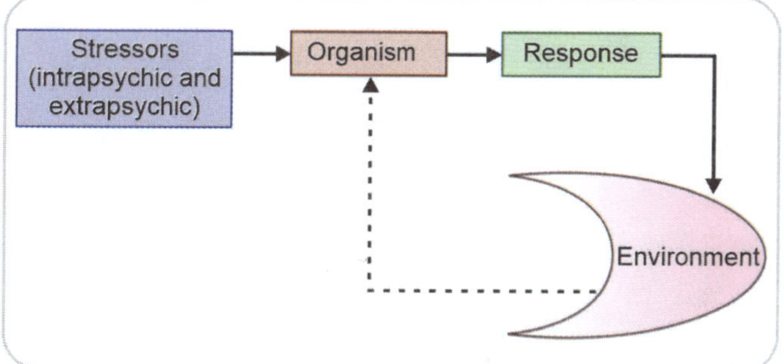

Bounce Model of Stress

An individual might take stress as adaptive response or a maladaptive response depending on the individual's perception. If an individual perceives a maladaptive response (negative sense) toward environment, then it also reflects back the maladaptive response toward him/her (Flowchart 13.14).

S-O-R Model of Stress

S stands for stimuli, O stands for organism and R stands for response (Flowchart 13.15). A stimulus is a provoking factor which motivates the organism to perform a desired response. For example, parents act as stimuli who motivate the children (organism) to secure good marks in exam (response). Organism might perceive this in a positive sense (eustress) or in a negative sense (distress). If the child perceives as adaptive response, then child will perceive the parents' motivation in a right way and secure good marks in exam. If the child perceives as maladaptive response, then child will perceive the parents' motivation in a wrong way by taking it as distress and will not secure good marks in exam.

Flowchart 13.15: S-O-R model of stress

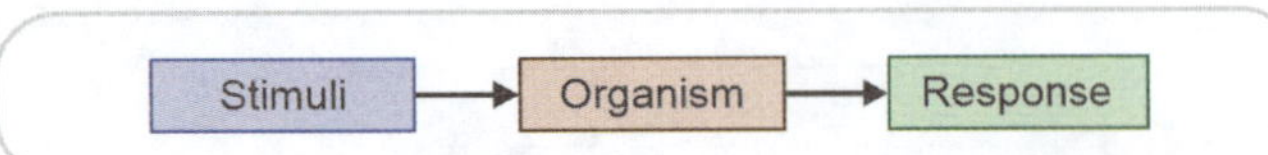

COPING MECHANISM

- According to Suzanne Lego (1996), coping mechanism is defined as a conscious method adopted by a person to solve a problem.
- According to Lazarus (1999), coping is an individual's effort to overcome psychological stress.

Lazarus and Folkman (1984) defined three types of coping as:

1. **Problem focused coping:** Use of coping skills to deal with an existing problem.
2. **Emotion focused coping:** Use of coping skills by dealing with emotions that arise out of problem.
3. **Cognitive focused coping:** Use of coping skills by dealing with stress with the help of existing knowledge.

Flowchart 13.16 shows the coping mechanism.

Flowchart 13.16: Coping mechanism

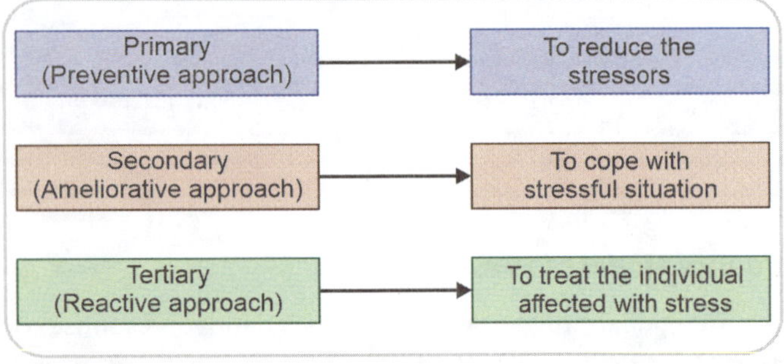

Examples for three types of coping are given in Table 13.29. Coping styles as per Nash and Roger (1995) have been presented in Table 13.30.

Stress Busters Using Various Therapies

Psychological therapies are found helpful to an individual to come out of stress such as relaxation training (Jacobson progressive muscle relaxation and autogenic training), breathing, meditation or mindfulness training, animal assisted therapy or pet therapy, yoga, music therapy, guided imagery, physical exercises, laughter therapy, diversional therapy, occupational therapy, talk therapy, hypnotherapy, light therapy, dance therapy, etc.

Role of Nurse in Teaching the Coping Mechanism to Patient

Advise the patient to adhere to the following instructions in order to use the coping mechanism and it might be helpful in managing the stress.

- Engage in some personal growth-oriented activities
- Adopt healthy lifestyle practices such as maintaining the quality of sleep, eating healthy diet, doing yoga or exercises, etc.
- Perform relaxation training such as Jacobson Progressive muscle relaxation and autogenic training.
- Hear music to relax oneself.
- Use cognitive restructuring to avoid the negative view of oneself and the problems in life.
- Avoid using substances such as alcohol, cigarettes, etc.
- Spend time with family members.
- Develop aesthetic sense within oneself

Table 13.29: Examples for three types of coping

Problem focused coping	Emotion focused coping	Cognitive focused coping
Individual leaves the job and plans to proceed to do business, since there is no proper salary or no job satisfaction present, even though the organization promised to give the required salary.	Father had a fear that child did not come home from the school and later he remembered that he gave permission to participate in sports today and then father felt better.	Mr Ram felt stressed due to his sudden loss of property, instead he put his hard work and used appropriate tactics in order to regain his property

Table 13.30: Coping styles as per Nash and Roger

Adaptive coping style (adjustment with environment)		Maladaptive coping style (nonadjustment with environment)	
Detached	**Rationale**	**Emotional**	**Avoidance**
• Not perceive the problems as a threat • Use sense of humor • Steps taken to solve the issues • Have a take it easy policy	• Treat problem as challenge • Have a logical approach to a problem • Use a past experience to solve the problem	• Seeks attention and Sympathy from others • Feel depressed, anxious, fearful, frustrated and being worried.	• Think everything as impossible • Have more trust on fate • Lack of self-confidence • Not verbalizing the problems to others.

- Enjoy the day-to-day life
- Always remember there is no problem without a solution
- Have a take it easy policy in life
- Perceive the threat as challenging one
- Have a healthy relationship with friends and relatives
- Keep sharing the problems with a genuine friend.

GERIATRIC CONSIDERATIONS

Elders might attempt suicide due to various issues in family or else secondary to depression. Elderly abuse or assault (Granny Bashing) is also increasing day by day. Social isolation is an important key factor for depression. Elderly persons who experience more loss and are not able to complete the grief reaction have overload of bereavement which in turn leads to depressive disorders. Stress management techniques will be helpful to treat mild level of depression. Periodical screening and assessment are essential to identify the elderly mental health issues at an early stage so that they do not lead to the stage of psychiatric emergency.

SUMMARY

- A **psychiatric emergency** is an acute disturbance of behavior, thought or mood of a patient that negatively impacts a patient's ability to function in his/her environment.
- **Suicide** is defined as 'intentional way of killing oneself' or 'self-inflicted cessation of life which ends in a fatal outcome'.
- Imbalance in release of neurotransmitter, namely serotonin might provoke suicidal ideation
- **Types of suicide based on social categories as per Emile Durkheim (1951)** are egoistic suicide, altruistic suicide, anomic suicide and Samsonic suicide or suicide of revenge. **Miscellaneous types are** parasuicide, cyber-suicide, copycat suicide and anniversary suicide.
- **Risk factors and warning signs of suicide** are signs of clinical depression, withdrawal or isolation from friends and family, sadness and hopelessness, feeling trapped with unbearable pain, talking as being burden to others, lack of interest in previous activities or in what is going on around them, physical changes such as lack of energy, different sleep patterns, change in weight or appetite, lack of self-esteem, increased use of alcohol or drugs, presence of mood swings, being anxious, agitated or reckless, exhibiting rage or talks about taking revenge, negative comment about self-worth, speaking or writing about death or suicide, giving their valuable possessions to somebody and having more interest in personal wills or life insurances.
- **Protective factors** against suicide attempts are strong family or social support, easy access to clinical interventions, skills in problem solving and conflict resolution, restricted access to the lethal means of suicide, strong support from the health care professional, cultural and religious belief that discourage the suicide.
- **Section 309 of IPC** states that suicide attempt will be punishable with simple imprisonment which may extend to one year or fine or both.
- **SAD PERSONS rating scale** is used to determine the suicidal risk.
- **Nurse's role to prevent suicide:** Monitor the patient closely, accompany the patient wherever he/she goes, avoid keeping dangerous objects near patient, sedate the patient if uncontrollable, encourage the patient to verbalize his/her thoughts related to suicide, if necessary apply restraints to control the patient.
- **Anger** is a normal human emotion that may be handled and expressed assertively to solve the problem and it shows a productive change. Aggression is an expression of anger in a socially inappropriate manner, may or may not cause significant harm to self or others either physically, psychologically or verbal means of expressing anger.
- **Biological risk factors of violence** are central nervous system dysfunction/infections, imbalance in neurotransmission, frontal or temporal lobe dysfunction, limbic system dysfunction and traumatic brain injury.
- **Etiology of violence** includes organic psychiatric disorders, nonorganic psychiatric disorders, medical disorders associated with violent behavior such as neurologic illness, endocrine disorders, metabolic disorders, vitamin deficiencies, infections and temperature disturbances.
- Smith's stress model (1981) explained the assault cycle which has five stages of aggressive response to physical or emotional stress. Stages are triggering phase, escalation phase, crisis phase, recovery phase and post-crisis depression phase.
- **Management of violence** includes reassurance, medications (Inj. haloperidol, Inj. chlorpromazine, Inj. diazepam), promotion of psychological well-being and restraints (physical and chemical).
- **Other psychiatric emergencies** are panic attack, catatonic stupor, grief reaction, rape, conversion disorder, disaster victim and transient situational disturbance.
- **Medical emergencies related to psychiatry** are delirium, serotonin syndrome, epileptic furor, overdose of psychotropic medications, overdoses and withdrawal from addicting substances and extrapyramidal symptoms of psychotropic drugs (neuroleptic malignant syndrome).
- **Crisis** is a sudden event in one's life which disturbs homeostasis during which the usual coping mechanism can't resolve a problem.
- **Types of crises** are maturational crisis or developmental crisis, situational crisis and social crisis, crisis reflecting psychopathology, post-traumatic crisis, anticipated crisis and transcultural crisis.
- **Steps of crisis intervention** include individual approach, generic approach (handle with critical incident debriefing with the steps: fact, thought, reacting, teaching and re-entry), general supportive measures such as group work, disaster response, mobile crisis program, telephone contact (suicide prevention center), victim outreach program, health education and environmental manipulation.

Contd...

- **Techniques of crisis intervention are** catharsis, clarification, suggestion, reinforcement of positive behavior, exploring the solution, use of adaptive coping mechanism and raising self-esteem.
- **Grief** is defined as physical, somatic, spiritual, emotional and intellectual responses to the nature of loss.
- **Types of grief** are normal grief and morbid grief. Morbid grief classifies into pathological grief, complicated grief and grief at death anniversary. Other types of grief are anticipatory grief, disenfranchised or ambiguous grief, time-limited grief, private or forbidden or absent grief, collective grief, masked grief, exaggerated or distorted grief and cumulative grief.
- Kubler Ross (1969) identified the five stages of grief: denial, anger, bargaining, depression and acceptance. Other theories are Dr Rando's 6 Rs of mourning, John Bowlby's four stages of grief, Worden's four tasks of mourning and Parke's four phase model of grief.
- Schafer (2000) defined stress as 'arousal of body and mind in response to the demand made upon them'.
- **Models of stress** are stimulus-based model, response-based model and transaction-based model. In response-based model, stress might affect a set of bodily changes described as general adaptation syndrome. This syndrome has three stages, namely alarm, resistance and exhaustion.

ASSESS YOURSELF

Long Answer Questions

1. Define psychiatric emergencies. Explain the common psychiatric emergencies in India.
2. Define crisis. Explain the techniques of crisis intervention and nurses' responsibility during the crisis.

Short Answer Questions

1. What are the characteristics of psychiatric emergencies?
2. What are the psychosocial factors in the etiology of suicide?
3. What is SAD PERSONS rating scale?
4. What are the symptoms of panic attacks?

Short Notes

Write short notes on:

1. Stress adaptation model
2. Theories of grief
3. Warning signs of suicide
4. Management of violent behavior
5. Types of suicide

Multiple Choice Questions

1. **Imbalance in ___________ neurotransmitters might provoke suicide.**
   a. Serotonin b. Dopamine
   c. Acetylcholine d. Norepinephrine
2. **Types of suicide based on social categories as per Emile Durkheim are the following; EXCEPT ___________.**
   a. Egoistic suicide b. Altruistic suicide
   c. Anomic suicide d. Parasuicide
3. **Suicide attempt will be punishable with simple imprisonment as per _________ of IPC.**
   a. Section 309 b. Section 308
   c. Section 307 d. Section 306
4. **___________ is defined as physical, somatic, spiritual, emotional and intellectual responses to the nature of loss.**
   a. Grief b. Stress
   c. Stressor d. Distress
5. **___________ is the first phase in Smith's Stress Model (1981) of assault cycle.**
   a. Escalation phase b. Crisis phase
   c. Triggering phase d. Recovery phase
6. **When the serotonergic agents are used along with Monoamine Oxidase Inhibitors (MAOI), it leads to:**
   a. Neuroleptic malignant syndrome
   b. Serotonin syndrome
   c. Rabbit syndrome
   d. Sundowning syndrome
7. **___________must be used with caution in patients with delirium, mainly the elderly, because it may cause anticholinergic toxicity (atropine psychosis).**
   a. Benztropine b. Neurobion forte
   c. Haloperidol d. Lorazepam
8. **Overdose with carbamazepine or tricyclic antidepressants needs _________ monitoring.**
   a. Cardiac b. Respiratory
   c. Temperature d. None of these
9. **An accidental and unanticipated loss that causes drastic negative changes in the environment is called:**
   a. Situational crisis b. Maturational crisis
   c. Social crisis d. Post-traumatic crisis
10. **Stages of General Adaptation Syndrome are:**
   a. Alarm b. Resistance
   c. Exhaustion d. All of these

Answer Key

1. a	2. d	3. a	4. a	5. c
6. b	7. a	8. a	9. c	10. d

CHAPTER 14

Legal Issues in Mental Health Nursing

LEARNING OBJECTIVE

At the end of this chapter, student will be able to explain the legal aspects of psychiatric nursing and will be able to apply them in clinical practice.

CHAPTER OUTLINE

- Indian Lunacy Act (1912)
- Mental Health Act (1987)
- Protection of Child from Sexual Offences (POCSO) Act (2012)
- Offences Covered as per the Act
- Punishment for Offences Covered Under the Act
- Mental Health Care Act (2017)
- Rights of Mentally Ill Patients
- Forensic Psychiatry
- Narcotic Drugs and Psychotropic Substance Act (1985)
- Role of Mental Health Nurse as per the Mental Health Care Act (2017)
- Nurse's Responsibility in Admission Procedure
- Nurse's Responsibility in Discharge Procedure
- Nurse's Responsibility in Regard to Legal Aspects

KEY TERMS

Mental Health Act (1987), Mental Health Care Act (2017), Indian Lunacy Act (1912) POSCO Act (2012), Rights of Mentally Ill Clients, Forensic psychiatry, M'Naghten's rule, Irresistible Impulse Act, Durham's rule/Product rule, American Law Institute (ALI) test, Narcotic and Psychotropic Substances Act (1985), Protection of Children from Sexual Offence (POSCO) Act (2012).

INDIAN LUNACY ACT (1912)

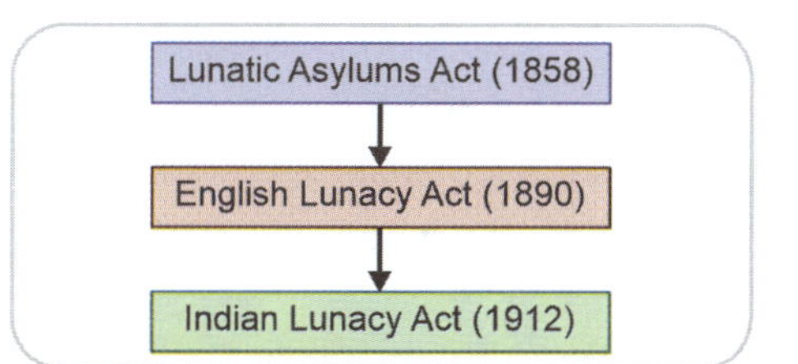

It consists of four Parts, eight chapters and hundred sections. Objectives of Indian Lunacy Act (1912) are improvement of asylums and care of lunatics in asylums.

The eight chapters Indian Lunacy Act (1912) are as follows:

1. **Chapter I:** Preliminary Information and Definition
2. **Chapter II:** Admission Procedure of Mentally Ill (Refer to Table 14.5)
3. **Chapter III:** Procedure for Treatment and Discharge of Mentally Ill
4. **Chapter IV:** Proceedings of Lunatics in Presidency Town
5. **Chapter V:** Proceedings of Lunatics Outside Presidency Town
6. **Chapter VI:** Establishment of Asylums
7. **Chapter VII:** Expenses of Lunatics

8. **Chapter VIII:** Rules of State Government regarding the Care of Lunatics.

Acts for Mentally Ill

- **Mental Health Act (1987) Chapter VIII** focuses on protection of rights for mentally ill.
- **In Universal Declaration of Human Rights (UDHR)**
  - **Article 5:** Mentally ill should not be tortured or treated in cruel way.
  - **Article 24(1):** Everyone has a right for standard living for oneself as well as family including food, shelter, clothing, medical and social services.
- **In Persons with Disability Act (1995)**
  - **Section 2:** Mental illness is considered disability.
  - **Article 66(1):** Government and local authorities might take care of expenses for rehabilitation to take care of person with disabilities.

Rights of Mentally Ill

Rights of Self

- Right to spend reasonable money for one's own expenses
- Right to see visitors
- Right to have reasonable use of communication media
- Right to use personal storage space
- Right to wear own clothes
- Right to marriage.

Rights in Regard to In-patient Treatment

- Right to have voluntary admission and voluntary discharge from hospital, if he/she is major.
- Right to treat the patients with dignity, kindness and compassion.
- Right to refuse electroconvulsive therapy.
- Right to refuse restraints/seclusion unless the emergency situation arises.
- Right to recreation.
- Right to eat nutritious food.
- Right to have environmental sanitation (clean toilets).
- Right to access books, periodicals, newspaper in their own language.

Rights Related with Legal Aspects

- Right to manage/dispose property/execute the wills.
- Right to get informed consent.
- Right to witness.
- Right to access the one's own records upon request.
- Right to maintain confidentiality of records.

Nursing Implications

A nurse has to protect the patient's rights in all circumstances. Nurse has to ensure that nursing procedures in ward should not violate the patient rights. Nurse can discuss the rights with mental health team.

MENTAL HEALTH ACT (1987)

Introduction

Indian Mental Health Act was initiated by Parliament in 1987 and came into effect in all states of India in 1993. Enactment of this Act has been revised as Indian Lunacy Act (1912). It has 10 chapters with 98 sections.

Objectives

- To protect mentally ill persons.
- To guide the admission and discharge procedure in psychiatric hospital/nursing homes.
- To give legal aid to psychiatric patients
- To build the strong state and central mental health authorities.
- To have a proper maintenance charges of psychiatric hospital/nursing homes.
- To prevent unnecessary hold of any individual labeled as mentally ill without proper proof.

Chapter I (Preliminary Information and Definition)

- **Mentally ill person:** Individual seeking treatment for a mental disorder.
- **Mentally ill prisoner:** Mentally ill prisoner is placed in a safe custody.
- **Cost of maintenance:** Cost required to maintain the mental hospital/mentally ill person.
- **Inspecting officer:** Person appointed by State Government to inspect psychiatric hospital.
- **License:** Document issued by the government when a hospital meets the required standards.
- **Licensee:** Holder of license.
- **Licensed psychiatric hospital:** Psychiatric hospital licensed to perform as per act.
- **Licensing authority:** Authority specified by the state government to provide licensure.
- **Medical officer:** Registered medical practitioner.
- **Medical officer in-charge:** In-charge of psychiatric hospital/nursing home.
- **Medical practitioner:** Person who has recognized medical qualification and is registered under Medical Council of India.

- **Minor:** Individual below 18 years of age.
- **Psychiatric hospital/Nursing home:** Hospital established by the government for the treatment of mentally ill.
- **Psychiatrist:** Medical practitioner with postgraduation (or) Diploma in Psychiatry and registered under Medical Council of India.
- **Reception order:** Order is made under this act for admission and detention of mentally ill in psychiatric hospital.

Chapter II (Mental Health Authority)

Central and State Authority appointed by government to coordinate the services related to mental health as mentioned below:

- To provide advice to government in regard to mental health.
- To supervise the psychiatric hospitals/nursing homes.
- To issue/renew/cancel the license to psychiatric hospitals/nursing homes.

Chapter III

Regulations to establish and maintain the psychiatric hospitals/nursing homes.

Chapter IV (Regulations of Admission under Various Circumstances)

- **Admission on voluntary basis**
  - **Major:** When an individual feels himself/herself in need of being admitted for the treatment in psychiatric hospital, then he/she can approach to medical officer. Medical officer will enquire within 24 hours and if the individual requires treatment, then he/she will be admitted.
  - **Minor:** If volunteer is minor then guardian can apply to medical officer for the treatment in psychiatric hospital.
- **Admission under special circumstances (Involuntary admission)** When an individual is not willing for admission to get treatment in psychiatric hospital, then his/her guardian or relative can apply to medical officer. Medical officer will enquire within 24 hours and if the individual requires treatment, then he/she will be admitted.
- **Admission under authority or order:** A mentally ill person is admitted in psychiatric hospital as per the order passed by court/authority.

  It has four main categories:
  1. **Reception order on application:** Relative or friend can apply to magistrate along with two medical certificates. Magistrate will obtain the consent from medical officer in-charge of psychiatric hospital/nursing home and admission under reception order is made.
  2. **Reception order on producing the mental illness before magistrate:** Individual behaving violently will be detained by the police and was produced in court within 24 hours. Application has to be supported with the medical certificates and magistrate will issue the reception order.
  3. **Reception order after inquest:** District court directs the individual for admission.
  4. **Admission and detention of mentally ill prisoner:** Mentally ill prisoner will be admitted in psychiatric hospital as per the order of court.
- **Admission in emergencies:** Summary of the admission procedure is shown in Table 14.6.

Chapter V (Regulations of Discharge under Various Circumstances)

- **Discharge of patient admitted on voluntary basis:** On the recommendation of two medical practitioners (one of these has to be a psychiatrist), medical officer in-charge can provide the directions to discharge the patient.
- **Discharge of patient admitted under special circumstances:** Relatives/friends of mentally ill can request discharge to the medical officer with a bond assuring that mentally ill will not cause any harm to self or others.
- **Discharge of patient admitted on reception order:** Patient who recovered from mental illness can apply for discharge to magistrate along with a certificate from medical officer in-charge of psychiatric hospital/nursing home. If magistrate feels that patient is fit, the discharge can be issued.
- **Discharge of patient admitted by police:** For patients detained by police, patient might be discharged if the family members of patient has given in writing that they will take care of patient after discharge and also medical officer in-charge of psychiatric hospital/nursing home found that the patient is fit, discharge will be granted.
- **Discharge of mentally ill prisoner:** Hospital in-charge has to report about the condition of patient every 6 months to the authority. When patient is fit for discharge, the same has to be reported to authority so as to hand over the patient to prison officer for further proceedings.
- **Leave of absence:** As per section 45, mentally ill person in hospital can be given limited time period (maximum of 6 months) to visit the family members provided the relatives of patient have signed the bond, stating that

patient will not cause any harm to self or others and take good care in leave period. It helps the patient to gain the required skills in community-based treatment.

Chapter VI (Appointment of Guardian)

As per Section 54, Guardian needs to be appointed for the mentally ill patient who is unable to look after self and property. As per Section 97, if the mentally ill is not represented by legal practitioner before court, then the district court or magistrate can assign a legal practitioner for the same.

Chapter VII (Cost of Treatment)

As per Section 78, Government of the particular state will bear the cost of treatment for mentally ill patient who is detained in the hospital, if the mentally ill doesn't have any property or money.

Chapter VIII (Protection of Human Rights)

Section 81 states that mentally ill should not be treated in undignified or cruel manner and mentally ill should not be used for research purpose until the research is found beneficial to them after getting a consent from patient (in case of voluntary admission) and consent from relatives (in case of involuntary admission).

Chapter IX (Establishment and Maintenance of Psychiatric Hospital/Nursing Home)

Article 6 (1) states that the psychiatric hospital/nursing home needs license to run successfully. Article 11(1b) states that license of psychiatric hospital/nursing home can be cancelled, if maintenance doesn't meet the standards.

Chapter X (Procedure Followed by Medical Officer In-charge)

It deals with the clarification in regard to the procedure/ procedures followed by the medical-officer in-charge of Psychiatric hospital/Nursing home.

Nursing Implications

Knowledge on legal aspects in Psychiatry will guide the nurse in:

- Ethical decision making
- Protecting the rights of mentally ill
- Admission and discharge procedures of mentally ill
- Role of mental health authority
- Quality treatment of mentally ill

PROTECTION OF CHILD FROM SEXUAL OFFENCES (POCSO) ACT (2012)

Ministry of Women and Child Development introduced the Protection of Children from Sexual Offences (POCSO) Act, 2012. The act was passed in Indian Parliament on 14.11.2012. It also gives the details of special courts in regard to the protection against the sexual offenses. The basic concepts of this Act are explained in the Table 14.1.

Table: 14.1 Basic concepts of POCSO Act, 2012

Act no.	32
Year of Act	2012
Date of enactment	19/06/2012
Date of enforcement	14/11/2012
Ministry	Ministry of Women and Child Development
Short title	The Protection of Children from Sexual Offences Act, 2012
Long title	An Act to protect children from offences of sexual assault, sexual harassment and pornography and provide for establishment of Special Courts for trial of such offences and for matters connected therewith or incidental thereto.
Total no. of chapters	9
Total no. of sections	46

Primary Features of POCSO ACT, 2012

- The Act is a statute comprises 9 chapters and 46 sections (Table 14.2).
- The Act defines the child as any person below age of eighteen years old.
- The whole Act focuses on ensuring a healthy physical, mental and social development of child.
- The Act has set of laws which helps to protect the child from sexual abuse, harassment and pornography.
- The Act provides a child-friendly reporting and investigating procedure. In every step of the psychological condition of abused child has been given the much-required devotion.

Table: 14.2 Chapters and Sections of POCSO Act, 2012

Chapters	Title of Chapter	Sections
I	**Preliminary**	1. Short title, extent and commencement 2. Definitions
II	**Sexual Offences Against Children**	**A. Penetrative Sexual Assault and Punishment Therefor** 3. Penetrative Sexual Assault. 4. Punishment for Penetrative Sexual Assault. **B. Aggravated Penetrative Sexual Assault and Punishment Therefor** 5. Aggravated Penetrative Sexual Assault. 6. Punishment for Aggravated Penetrative Sexual Assault. **C. Sexual Assault and Punishment Therefor** 7. Sexual Assault. 8. Punishment for Sexual Assault. **D. Aggravated Sexual Assault and Punishment Therefor** 9. Aggravated Sexual Assault. 10. Punishment for Aggravated Sexual Assault. **E. Sexual Harassment and Punishment Therefor** 11. Sexual harassment. 12. Punishment for sexual harassment
III	**Using Child for Pornographic Purposes and Punishment Therefor**	13. Use of child for pornographic purposes. 14. Punishment for using child for pornographic purposes 15. Punishment for storage of pornographic material involving child.
IV	**Abetment of and Attempt to Commit an Offence**	16. Abetment of an offence. 17. Punishment for abetment. 18. Punishment for attempt to commit an offence.
V	**Procedure for Reporting of Cases**	19. Reporting of offences. 20. Obligation of media, studio and photographic facilities to report cases. 21. Punishment for failure to report or record a case. 22. Punishment for false complaint or false information. 23. Procedure for media.
VI	**Procedures for Recording Statement of the Child**	24. Recording of statement of a child. 25. Recording of statement of a child by Magistrate. 26. Additional provisions regarding statement to be recorded. 27. Medical examination of a child.
VII	**Special Courts**	28. Designation of Special Courts. 29. Presumption as to certain offences. 30. Presumption of culpable mental state. 31. Application of Code of Criminal Procedure, 1973 to proceedings before a Special Court. 32. Special Public Prosecutors.
VIII	**Procedure and Powers of Special Courts and Recording of Evidence**	33. Procedure and powers of Special Court. 34. Procedure in case of commission of offence by child and determination of age by Special Court. 35. Period for recording of evidence of child and disposal of case. 36. Child not to see accused at the time of testifying. 37. Trials to be conducted in camera. 38. Assistance of an interpreter or expert while recording evidence of child.
IX	**Miscellaneous**	39. Guidelines for child to take assistance of experts, etc. 40. Right of child to take assistance of legal practitioner. 41. Provisions of sections 3–13 not to apply in certain cases. 42. Alternative punishment. 42A. Act not in derogation of any other law. 43. Public awareness about Act. 44. Monitoring of implementation of Act. 45. Power to make rules. 46. Power to remove difficulties.

OFFENCES COVERED AS PER THE ACT

Penetrative Sexual Assault

If a man penetrates his penis or any body part into the vagina, mouth, urethra or anus of a child or makes the child to do so with him or any other person; or he applies his mouth to the penis, vagina, anus, urethra of the child or makes the child to do so to such person or any other person.

Aggravated Penetrative Sexual Assault

One who commits the penetrative sexual assault in the following conditions:

- If he is a police officer or armed or security force.
- Staff of jail or remand home or protection home or observation home.
- Staff in the hospital, educational or religious organization. It may be Government or private.
- Individual uses deadly weapon or fire or heated substance or a corrosive substance to hurt the sexual organ of the child.
- When the sexual assault causes the child mentally ill.
- Individual makes the female child pregnant as the consequence of penetrative sexual assault.
- Individual who causes the child with human immunodeficiency virus or any other life-threatening infection or disease or which might cause a death of the child or attempt to murder the child.
- Individual who commits the assault by taking the advantage of a child's mental or physical disability.
- Relative of child through blood adoption or guardian or in foster care or a person has a domestic relationship with a parent of child or living in the same house commits penetrative sexual assault on child.
- Individual who commits during the communal (or) sectarian violence (or) at any natural calamity.
- Person who makes the assaulted child to strip or parade naked in public.

Sexual Assault

Individual with the sexual intent touches child's vagina, anus, penis or breast (or) does any other act with sexual intent which involves physical contact without penetration.

Aggravated Sexual Assault

The provisions of aggravated penetrative sexual assault are when an individual induces or coerces a child to get administered of any drug or chemical substance, to a child with an intention of the child attains an early sexual maturity.

Sexual Harassment

Individual commits sexual harassment, under this Act with the sexual intent of:

- Using any word or making a gesture or exhibiting any object or a body part with intention to be heard or seen by the child.
- Making a child to exhibit his or her body parts.
- Showing any object to a child which provokes or give gratification for pornographic purposes.
- Constantly and repeatedly watching the child either directly (or) through digital means.

PUNISHMENT FOR OFFENCES COVERED UNDER THE ACT

- Aggravated penetrative sexual assault: Not less than 20 years and fine.
- Penetrative sexual assault: Not less than 10 years (in case of child below 16 years, not less than 20 years).
- Sexual assault: Not less than three years which may extend up to 5 years.
- Aggravated sexual assault: Not less than 5 years which may extend to seven years.
- Sexual harassment of the child—Imprisonment of 3 years and fine.
- Involving the child for propagating pornographic material - imprisonment of either up to 3 years of imprisonment, or with fine, or both.

MENTAL HEALTH CARE ACT (2017)

The Mental Health Care Act (2017) superseded the previous Mental Health Act (1987). In India, Mental Health Care Act commenced in 7.4.17 and came into force on 7.7.18. It has 16 chapters as described in Table 14.3.

The revisions made in this act are listed here:

- Individuals who tried to commit suicide need to be given an opportunity for rehabilitation from government side, instead of giving punishment for suicidal attempt.
- Agency of people with mental illness is given a chance to take decision with regard to health matters.
- Aims to protect the rights of mentally ill and assess the treatment for mental illness without any discrimination.
- In addition, insurance company has a provision for mental illness as they are providing for physical ailment.
- Electroconvulsive therapy (ECT) can be given only in case of emergency along with anesthesia and muscle relaxant.
- ECT should not be given for minors. Other agencies and police have to respect the people with mental illness. Various measures are suggested to tackle the stigma of mental illness.

Table 14.3: **Chapters and description of Mental Health Care Act (2017)**

Chapter	Description of Mental Health Care Act (2017)
I	It has basic definitions and it includes postgraduate AYUSH doctors in mental health team
II	Capacity to decide mental health treatment without any discrimination
III	**Advance directives** • Patient has a right to appoint a representative in order to take treatment decisions • In case of minor, parents or care givers might act as representative • It is not applicable in case of emergency • If the psychiatrist or caregivers are not satisfied, they might approach the concerned board
IV	Guidelines of choosing nominated representative
V	**Rights of mentally ill** • Right to access mental health care • Right to community living • Right to protect from cruel, inhuman and degrading treatment • Right to equality and nondiscrimination • Right to information • Right to confidentiality • Restriction on release of information in respect of mental illness • Right to access medical records • Right to have personal contacts and communication • Right to legal aid • Right to make complaints in regard to the deficiencies in provision of services
VI	Gives direction to the government to implement the program
VII	Gives provision of forming central mental health authority
VIII	Gives provision of forming state mental health authority
IX	Finance, accounts and audit
X	**Mental health establishments** • All mental health institutions have to be registered • Provisions to commence the new mental health institutions
XI	**Constitution of mental health review boards. Board constitutes of:** • District judge as chair person • Two members (one was psychiatrist and other was registered medical practitioner) • Two members who are care givers of mentally ill represent the organizations of individual with mental illness
XII	**Admission, treatment and discharge** (Table 14.7)
XIII	**Duties of police officer in respect to mentally ill:** Police has to give protection to the wandering individuals with mental illness at nearest police station
XIV	It restricts unauthorized duty and medication
XV	It deals with penalty and punishment • Institutions which are unauthorized can be punished from ₹5000 – ₹50,000 as penalty for first time and up to ₹2 lakhs for second time • Individuals of who violate this Act are liable to penalty of ₹10,000 or jail or both.
XVI	**Miscellaneous:** Power of central government to issue directions

RIGHTS OF MENTALLY ILL PATIENTS

As per the Indian Lunacy Act (1912), the rights of mentally ill patients are as follows:

Rights of Self

- Right to spend reasonable money for one's own expenses
- Right to see visitors
- Right to have reasonable use of communication media
- Right to use personal storage space
- Right to wear own clothes
- Right to marriage

Rights in Regard with In-Patient Treatment

- Right to have voluntary admission and voluntary discharge from hospital, if he/she is major.

- Right to treat the patients with dignity, kindness and compassion.
- Right to refuse electroconvulsive therapy
- Right to refuse restraints/seclusion unless the emergency situation arises
- Right to recreation
- Right to eat nutritious food
- Right to have environmental sanitation (clean toilets)
- Right to access books, periodicals, newspaper in their own language.

Rights Related with Legal Aspects

- Right to manage/dispose property/execute the wills
- Right to get informed consent
- Right to witness
- Right to access the one's own records upon request
- Right to maintain confidentiality of records.

As per the Mental Health Act (1987), the rights of mentally ill patients are as follows:

Chapter VIII address about the rights of mentally ill patients. Section 81 states that mentally ill should not be treated in undignified or cruel manner and mentally ill should not be used for research purpose until the research is found beneficial to them after getting a consent from patient (in case of voluntary admission) and consent from relatives (in case of involuntary admission).

As per the Mental Health Care Act (2017), the rights of mentally ill patients are as follows:

- **Right to access mental health care:** Mentally ill patients have rights to access high quality, cost effective, affordable mental health care which is accessible geographically without any discrimination on basis of gender, religion, culture, social class, sexual orientation, caste, political beliefs, disability provided in a good manner which is acceptable by the mentally ill patients.
- **Right to community living:** Mentally ill patients have a right to live in, to be part of society and not be segregated from society. Patients should not continue to remain in the mental health facilities merely not because of that he or she does not have family support or homeless or due to the absence of community-based facilities. Government shall provide legal aid and to facilitate exercising his right to the family home and living in the family home.
- **Right to protect from cruel, inhuman and degrading treatment:** Mentally ill patients have the rights:
  - To live in safe and hygienic environment
  - To have adequate sanitary conditions
  - To have reasonable facilities for recreation, education and religious practices.
  - To privacy
  - For proper clothing to maintain his dignity
  - To not be forced to undertake work in a mental health establishment and to receive appropriate remuneration for work when undertaken.
  - To have adequate provision for living in the community
  - To have adequate provision for wholesome food, space and access to articles to maintain the personal hygiene, in particular, women's personal hygiene be adequately addressed by providing access to items that may be required during menstruation.
  - To say no to tonsuring (shaving of head hair)
  - To wear own personal clothes if so wished and to not be forced to wear uniforms provided by the hospital.
  - To be protected from all the forms of physical, verbal, emotional and sexual abuses.

Right to Equality and Nondiscrimination

Every individual with the mental illness should be treated equally as that of the individuals with physical illness. Patients has to be treated without any discrimination on basis of gender, religion, culture, social class, sexual orientation, caste and disability.

- **Right to information:** Mentally ill individual can appoint a representative to review the reason for admission in the concern board and also can obtain the information about the treatment progress if the language explained by the doctors are not understandable. It is the duty of the treating doctor or psychiatrist to provide the complete information to the patient about the treatment.
- **Right to confidentiality:** It is the right of the mentally ill patient to maintain confidentiality. The information is only transferred to others for the public security or safety, treatment purpose, when there is harm to others, when there is threat to life and only to the nominated representative.
- **Restriction on release of information in respect of mental illness:** Photograph or any other information about the mentally ill should not to be released in the media without the consent of the person with mental illness. The information of mentally ill either in the digital or virtual platform should be protected, i.e., confidentiality need to be maintained.

- **Right to access medical records:** Mentally ill patients have right to access their own medical records. The nurse in-charge has to withhold the records from access in case the patient causes harm to self or others.
- **Right to personal contacts and communication:** Mentally ill patients have right to make telephone calls, send or receive e-mails, allow or restrict the visitors after the hospital admission.
- **Right to legal aid:** An individual with mental illness shall be entitled to receive free legal services to exercise any of his rights given under this act.
- **Right to make complaints about deficiencies in provision of services:** Any person with mental illness or his/her nominated representative, has the right to complain in regard to the deficiencies in provision of care, treatment and service.

FORENSIC PSYCHIATRY

It is a branch of medicine that deals with mental disorders and related legal aspects. The core aspects are as follows:
- Criminal responsibility
- Crime due to psychiatric disorder
- Civil responsibility
- Laws related to psychiatric disorder
- Admission and discharge procedure in psychiatric hospital (Tables 14.5, 14.6 and 14.7)

Criminal Responsibility

Indian Penal Code (1860), Section 84 states that, "Nothing is offence which is done by individual with unsound mind".

M'Naghten Rule

On 20th January 1843-Daniel M'Naghten, 29-year-old Scotsman planned to murder Sir Robert Peel, Prime Minister. But, he mistakenly gunshot Edward Drummond, Secretary of Sir Robert Peel. Lord Chancellor put panel of 14 judges, five hypothetical questions were asked and "M'Naghten Rules" were framed based on these. Judge found two rules to identify the criminal responsibility of person by keeping M'Naghten Rules in mind.
- **Rule 1:** Person does not know/aware of nature and quality of action performed during the crime.
- **Rule 2:** When a person does not know what he has done at the time of crime, then he might not be aware of what was wrong.

It is also called 'Legal Test'. Psychiatrist found that Daniel performed the act due to delusion of persecution and not with healthy mind. M'Naghten's Rule—"not felt guilty on grounds of insanity" So, he was not punishable under the law.

Irresistible Impulse Act

As per the rule, person might know that, the action is illegal but is unable to control the action due to mental illness.

Durham's Rule/Product Rule

In 1954, Durham test was framed on the basis of decision in District of Columbia. Accused is not liable as criminal for action due to effect of mental disease.

American Law Institute (ALI) Test

Person is not responsible for criminal activity if he/she has done the act as a result of 'mental disease/defect'. The term 'mental disease/defect' referred, does not include the criminal activity or antisocial conduct.

Crime Due to Psychiatric Disorder

Individuals might be involved in criminal activity due to:
- Psychosis (due to delusions and hallucinations).
- Drug dependence and drug related violence.
- Antisocial personality disorder.
- Mood disorder.
- Confused/Excited mental state.

Civil Responsibility

Contract

As per Indian Contract Act (1872), contract is an agreement enforced by law. Section 11 states, "every individual can perform contract provided one who is major and having sound mind." Section 12 states that "person with unsound mind and occasionally with sound mind (lucid interval) can make contract. However, person who is sound mind usually and occasional unsound mind, should not make contract when he/she is in unsound mind state."

Management of Property

If the relative of mentally ill filed a case that property of mentally ill individual was not managed due to incapacity of individual being mentally ill, then the court can appoint a manager to look after the property to sell/dispose in order to settle the debt or expenses.

Marriage

Hindu Marriage Act (1955) states, "if one of them among the couple was of unsound mind at the time of marriage is considered null as per law. Party can file for divorce if his/her mental illness is continuous for the period of two years. If divorce has been filed for more than three years, then divorce can be granted with the condition that, other party needs to pay maintenance charges for mentally ill person."

Adoption

Hindu Adoptions and Maintenance Act (1956) states, Section 7—"Hindu male, who is major and sound minded can adopt a child with consent of wife unless the wife is of unsound mind." Section 8—"Hindu female, who is major and sound minded can adopt a child with consent of husband unless the husband is of unsound mind." Person giving in adoption also has to be with sound mind.

Witness

As per Indian Evidence Act (1872), mentally ill is not competent to give evidence, provided the evidence can be considered if given in lucid interval.

Testamentary Capacity

Indian Succession Act states that testamentary capacity of mentally ill is considered valid, provided psychiatrist has to assess concentration, memory and orientation of testator was normal before making will. Even the mentally ill with delusions can make will if the delusions are not related with disposal of property.

Right to Vote and Right to be a Member in Parliament

Under Act 326 by constitution of India, person with mental illness does not have privilege of voting. Under Act 102 by Constitution of India, "Individual is not qualified for being a member of parliament when he/she is unsound mind."

Laws Related to Psychiatry

Laws related to psychiatry are mentioned in Table 14.4.

Table 14.4: Laws related to psychiatry

Year	Laws related to psychiatry
1869	Indian Divorce Act
1912	Indian Lunacy Act
1925	Indian Evidence Act Indian Succession Act
1939	Dissolution of Muslim Marriage Act
1954	Special Marriage Act
1955	Hindu Marriage Act
1984	Family Court Act
1985	Narcotic Drugs and Psychotropic Substance Act
1986	Consumer Protection Act Juvenile Justice Act
1987	Indian Mental Health Act
1992	Rehabilitation Council of India Act
1996	Person with Disabilities Act

NARCOTIC DRUGS AND PSYCHOTROPIC SUBSTANCE ACT (1985)

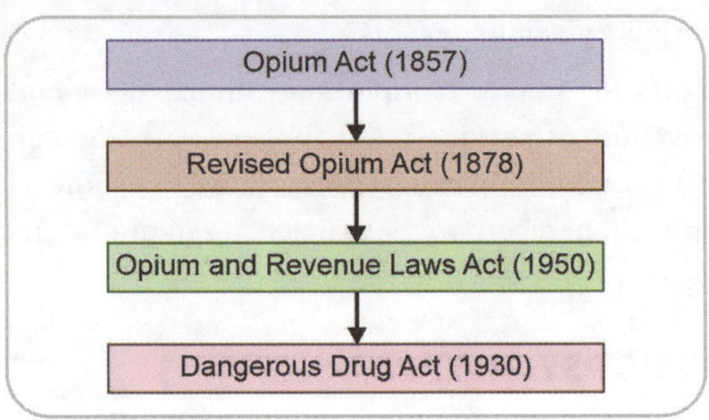

It has 6 chapters with 83 sections.

Chapter I (Preliminary Information and Definition of Terms)

- **Addict:** Individual addicted to narcotic drug/psychotropic substance.
- **Narcotic drug:** Cannabis, cocaine, opium and all manufactured drugs.
- **Manufactured drug:** Opium derivatives, medicinal cannabis, poppy straw and other narcotic substance.
- **Psychotropic substance:** Seventy-six substances are mentioned in schedule which are natural or synthetic that change brain function and results in alterations in perception, mood, consciousness, cognition, or behavior.

Chapter II (Authorities and Officers)

Narcotics Control Bureau is the authority and its headquarter is located at New Delhi. It is headed by Director General. It has five zonal offices at Chennai, Varanasi, Mumbai, Kolkata and New Delhi. Committee appointed by Central Government is Narcotic Drugs and Psychotropic Substance Consultative Committee which consists of Chairman (Head of Committee) and Committee Members (not more than 20 members).

Chapter III (Prohibition, Control and Regulation)

As per Section 8, no one can cultivate cannabis, coca and opium or possess or consume any psychotropic substances or narcotic drugs except for the specified scientific or medicinal reason.

Chapter IV (Offences and Penalties)

If an individual uses narcotic drug or substance he/she is punishable with:

- Imprisonment not less than 10 years and it can be extended up to 20 years.
- In case of repeated offence, imprisonment for not less than 15 years which can be extended up to 30 years.
- Fine not less than one lakh which can be extended up to two lakh rupees.
- In case of repeated offence, fine not less than 1.5 lakh which can be extended up to three lakh rupees.
- Possessing small quantities of heroin, opium or cocaine is liable to simple imprisonment that can be extended to one year or fine or both.

Chapter V (Details the Procedure)

This chapter deals with power to issue warrant or authorization, duty of land holder or certain officers to give information about illegal cultivation of substances, disposal of seized narcotic drugs and psychotropic substances, etc.

Chapter VI (Miscellaneous Issues)

Government has to establish the de-addiction centers to identify and treat the addicts.

Admission and discharge procedure summary as per Indian Lunacy Act (1912) is depicted in Table 14.5.

- **Voluntary patients—** Patient has insight and seeking admission.
- **In volitional patients—** Patient not having insight and refuse admission, e.g., psychosis.

Non volitional patients—Patient not giving/refusing consent for admission, e.g., mental retardation (severe).

Admission and discharge procedure summary as per Mental Health Act (1987) is given in Table 14.6.

- Admission of person with mental illness as independent patient in mental health establishment.
- Independent admission and treatment.
- Discharge of independent patients.
- Admission and treatment of persons with mental illness, with high support needs, in mental health establishment, up to thirty days (supported admission).
- Admission and treatment of persons with mental illness, with high support needs, in mental health establishment, beyond thirty days (supported admission beyond thirty days).
- Leave of absence.

Table 14.5: Summary of admission and discharge procedure as per Indian Lunacy Act (1912)

Type of admission	Type of patient	Admission application by	Admitting authority	Discharge application by	Discharge authority
Voluntary	Voluntary	Mentally ill	Asylum in-charge with two visitors	Volunteer	Asylum in-charge
Under special circumstances	In volitional and nonvolitional	Guardian/relative/friend of mentally ill	Medical officer in-charge	Guardian/relative/ friend of mentally ill	Magistrate
Reception order on application/ petition	In volitional and nonvolitional	Husband/wife or close relative		No application	Three or more visitors
				Petitioner	Asylum in-charge
				Inquisition	Magistrate
Reception order without application/ petition	Dangerous/ neglected/ wandering mentally ill	Police	Magistrate	No application	Three or more visitors
				Guardian/relative/ friend of mentally ill	Asylum in-charge
				Inquisition	Magistrate
Inquisition	Any mentally ill	Guardian/relative/friend of mentally ill (or) advocate general (or) district collector (or) public curator		Inquisition	Magistrate
Criminal lunatics	Criminal lunatic	Any order under Prisoners Act/Army Act	Order	Visitor might recommend discharge	Under the appropriate Section

Table 14.6: Summary of admission and discharge procedure as per Mental Health Act (1987)

Type of admission	Type of patient	Admission application by	Admitting authority	Discharge application by	Discharge authority
Voluntary	Voluntary		Medical officer in-charge	Volunteer	Medical officer in-charge
Under special circumstances		Guardian/relative/friend of mentally ill		Guardian/Relative/ Friend of mentally ill	Magistrate
Reception order on application/ petition	In volitional and nonvolitional	Guardian/relative/friend of mentally ill (or) medical officer in-charge		No application	Medical officer in-charge and two medical practitioners (one is Psychiatrist)
				Guardian/Relative/ Friend of mentally ill	Medical officer in-charge
				Petitioner	Medical officer in-charge
			Magistrate	Inquisition	Magistrate
				Mentally ill with certificate from medical officer in-charge	Magistrate
Reception order without application/ petition	Dangerous/ Neglected/ wandering mentally ill	Police		No application	Medical officer in-charge and two Medical Practitioners (one is Psychiatrist)
				Guardian/Relative/ Friend of mentally ill	Medical officer in-charge
				Petitioner	Medical officer in-charge
				Inquisition	Magistrate
				Mentally ill with certificate from medical officer in-charge	Magistrate
Inquisition	Any mentally ill	Guardian/relative/ friend of mentally ill (or) advocate general (or) district collector (or) public curator		Inquisition	Magistrate
Criminal lunatics	Criminal lunatic	Any order under Prisoners Act/Air Force Act/Army Act/ Navy Act	Order	Visitor might recommend discharge	Under the appropriate section (as per Act)

- Absence without leave or discharge.
- Transfer of persons with mental illness from one mental health establishment to another mental health establishment.
- Discharge planning
- Emergency treatment.

ROLE OF MENTAL HEALTH NURSE AS PER THE MENTAL HEALTH CARE ACT (2017)

Member of Mental Health Authority

Mental Health Nurse with 15 years of experience is nominated as member of Central Mental Health Authority and State Mental Health Authority.

Teaching to Patient (or) Caregivers (or) Public

- Providing health teaching to the patient and family members.
- Promotion of mental health and preventive programs can be organized in order to create awareness to the public.
- Educate the caregivers in regard to the importance of making advance directives and nominate the representative to protect the patient rights. Provide information about the Insurance coverage (similar to physical illness, coverage is applicable to patient suffering with mental illness).
- Inform the patient and caregivers that there will not be any discrimination or torturing in any means and there is no compulsion to wear hospital patient uniforms.

Treatment

- Rendering quality nursing care to the patient.
- Electroconvulsive therapy should not be administered without anesthesia (i.e., Direct ECT should not to be administered).
- Electroconvulsive therapy can be administered to minors in exceptional cases after the prior intimation to the board and after obtaining the informed consent from the guardian.
- Psychosurgery can be done if required after obtaining the informed consent and approval from the board.
- No physical restraints to patient and if indicated, it has to be in least restrictive manner with the very close monitoring for the patient to prevent any injuries.
- Mental health nurse will ensure that the women with mental illness will not be separated from her child if the age of the child is below 3 years.

Miscellaneous

- Assisting in the admission and discharge procedures (Table 14.7).
- Protecting out the rights of mentally ill patients.
- If mental health nurse found the patient is incapable of take care oneself or found wandering then, nurse can approach the in-charge of police to protect the patient.
- Proper documentation should be done to protect the nurse and to avoid the legal consequences.

NURSE'S RESPONSIBILITY IN ADMISSION PROCEDURE

Nurse has to welcome the patient to the ward. Nurse has to maintain interpersonal relationship with the patient to gain trust. Ensure the legal issues before admission. Nurse needs to tie the identity band on the patient's wrist. Nurse can collect the

Table 14.7: Summary of admission and discharge procedure as per Mental Health Care Act (2017)

Type of admission	Type of patient	Admission application by	Admitting authority	Discharge application by	Discharge Planning /Procedure
Independent admission (major)	Voluntary	Patient	Medical officer in-charge	Patient	Medical officer in-charge (or) psychiatrist of the Hospital. Patient can discharge into the community or to a different mental health establishment or where a new psychiatrist is to take responsibility of the person's care and treatment **Leave of absence** Medical officer or mental health professional in-charge may grant leave to any person with mental illness can absent from the establishment subject to such conditions, if any, and for such duration **Absence without leave or discharge** If any person absents oneself without leave or without discharge from hospital, he or she shall be taken into protection by any Police Officer at the request of the medical officer and shall be sent back to the mental health hospital immediately **Transfer of persons with mental illness from one mental health hospital to another hospital** It may subject to any general or special order of Board, that the patient can be removed from such mental health hospital and admitted to another hospital with consent of Central Authority and also consent from the nominated representative of the patient.
Independent admission (minor)	Voluntary	Guardian/ parents/ relatives	Medical officer in-charge	Guardian/ parents/ relatives	
Supported admission up to 30 days	Person who are incapable to make mental health care and treatment decisions	Guardian/ relative/friend of mentally ill (or) medical officer in-charge	Medical officer in-charge	Guardian/ relative/ friend of mentally ill	
Supported admission beyond 30 days		Application by the nominated representative of a person with mental illness	Medical officer or mental health professional in charge of a mental health establishment (two psychiatrists have independently examined the person with mental illness)		

communication address/permanent address/contact details of patient. Nurse collects history from the patient, relatives, friends, guardian, police, etc. Nurse has to perform head to toe assessment (physical examination) including vital signs and mental status examination. Orient the ward routines/rules, e.g., activities in ward, meal timings, daily schedule, etc. Assign the bed to the patient depending on the patient's condition, e.g., patient with high suicidal risk/psychiatric emergencies has to be assigned infront of nurse's station for continuous observation/monitoring. Nurse has to document the admission notes and enter the admission in nominal register.

NURSE'S RESPONSIBILITY IN DISCHARGE PROCEDURE

Nurse has to provide discharge teaching to the patient and his family members in regard to the treatment regimen and next follow up in outpatient department (OPD) visit. Nurse has to ensure the that patient leaves the ward with all his personal belongings. Nurse has to give discharge summary to the family members along with the investigation reports carried out in the ward, provided the proper signature is obtained in nursing documents.

Nurse might explain the nearby rehabilitation centers for routine care and also offer help to arrange wheel chair, if needed. Nurse can promote a right psychological support to the client. In case of parole or leave of absence, patient has to be given permission to attend family functions or any specific purpose. During parole, relatives have to be explained about the medications to be followed and regular monitoring of patient is also required (sleep pattern, communication, side effects/extrapyramidal symptoms, allergy to medication). Advice the caregivers to intimate any other specific issues found during the parole.

NURSE'S RESPONSIBILITY IN REGARD TO LEGAL ASPECTS

A nurse has to protect **patient rights** and she should also be aware of the **criminal and civil responsibility** of psychiatric patients. Nurse has to protect the legal records properly and keep the patient information confidential (nondisclosure of information).

A nurse has to **take informed consent or substitute consent** (patient with unsound mind is unable to give consent so substitute consent from relatives/guardian can be considered) as follows:

- Admission and discharge of psychiatric patient
- Before electroconvulsive therapy
- Prior to psychosurgery
- Before any invasive investigations
- Narco-analysis
- Special drug therapy—disulfiram, clozapine
- Involving the client in drug trial for research purpose.

If the Patient Escaped from Mental Hospital

Give immediate information to the nursing supervisor/medical superintendent/security officer of hospital. Family members/relatives/guardian has to be informed that patient escaped from hospital. Incident report has to be sent to supervisor in writing regarding the same. Hospital in-charge has to be informed about the same to the local police.

If Patient with Mental Illness Dead

Nurse has to hand over the dead body to the family members/relatives/guardian. Postmortem is only needed if death is due to accident/poisoning/assault/unknown bites, etc. If family members/relatives/guardian are not nearby, information can be given telephonically and dead body can be kept for three days in mortuary. If family members/relatives/guardians do not arrive to hospitals within three days, then the dead body can be handed over to municipal authority.

If Mentally Ill Patient is Pregnant

Detailed gynecological examination has to be performed during the admission process. If pregnancy occurs due to rape and the pregnant women is with unsound mind, then abortion can be done on considering humanitarian aspect. If baby has developed and abortion is considerable risk to mother, then necessary arrangements have to be made to hand over the baby to social welfare organization.

In Case of Criminal Lunatics

Care has to be taken in same way as that of other patients. Strict security has to be provided considering safety of self and others.

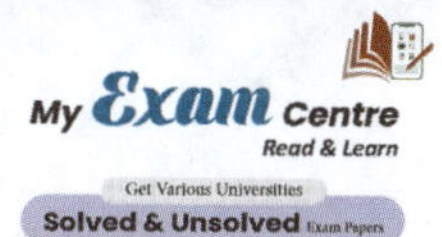

SUMMARY

- Indian Mental Health Act initiated by Parliament in 1987. It has 10 chapters with 98 sections.
- The Mental Health Care Act (2017) superseded the previous Mental Health Act (1987). It has 16 chapters.
- Indian Lunacy Act (1912) consists of four Parts, eight Chapters and 100 Sections. Objective of this Act focus on the improvement of asylums and care of lunatics in asylums.
- Mental Health Act (1987) Chapter VIII focuses on protection of rights for mentally ill.
- Protection of Children from Sexual Offence (POSCO) Act enacted in 2012. It consists of 9 chapters and 46 sections.
- Rights of mentally ill is categorized into rights of self, patient rights related to in-patients, rights related with legal aspects.
- Forensic psychiatry is a branch of medicine that deals with mental disorders with its related legal aspects. Forensic Psychiatry is categorized into criminal responsibility and civil responsibility. Criminal responsibility are M'Naghten's rule, Irresistible Impulse Act, Durham's rule/Product rule and American Law Institute (ALI) Test. Civil responsibility includes contract, management of property, marriage, adoption, witness, testamentary Capacity, right to vote and right to be a member in parliament.
- Narcotic Drugs and Psychotropics Substance Act (1985) has 6 chapters and 83 sections.
- Various categories of admission procedure in Indian Lunacy Act/Mental Health Act are admission on voluntary basis, admission under special circumstances, reception order with petition as well as without petition, inquisition and admission of criminal lunatics.

ASSESS YOURSELF

Long Answer Questions

1. Describe the admission and discharge procedures as per Mental Health Act.
2. Explain the concepts of forensic psychiatry.

Short Answer Questions

1. List out the chapters and sections of POCSO Act?
2. List out the name of the chapters in Narcotics Drugs and Psychotropics Substance Act?

Short Notes

Write short notes on:

1. Rights of mentally ill
2. Mental Health Act
3. Indian Lunacy Act
4. M'Naghten's Rule
5. Nurses' responsibility in admission and discharge procedure
6. Narcotic Drugs and Psychotropics Substance Act
7. Nurses' responsibility in legal aspects

Multiple Choice Questions

1. Indian Mental Health Act initiated by parliament in ________.

a. 1912 b. 1987
c. 1988 d. 1908

2. Indian Lunacy Act enacted in __________.

a. 1912 b. 1987
c. 1988 d. 1908

3. Number of chapters in Indian Mental Health Act is ___.

a. 8 b. 10
c. 12 d. 14

4. Number of chapters in Indian Lunacy Act is ______.

a. 8 b. 10
c. 12 d. 14

5. Narcotic Drugs and Psychotropics Substance Act is enacted in ______.

a. 1985 b. 1988
c. 1987 d. 1912

6. Rehabilitation Council of India Act enacted in __________.

a. 1912 b. 1992
c. 1914 d. 1985

7. Regulations of admission under various circumstances is explained in chapter ________ in Mental Health Act.

a. I b. II
c. V d. IV

8. Protection of Human Rights is explained in chapter ______ in Mental Health Act.

a. V b. VI
c. VIII d. VII

9. Protection of Children from Sexual Offence (POCSO) Act enacted in ________.

a. 2012 b. 1912
c. 2000 d. 1987

10. Protection of Children from Sexual Offence (POCSO) Act has ______ chapters and ______ sections.

a. 10, 46 b. 9, 46
c. 9, 48 d. 10, 48

ANSWER KEY

1. b	**2.** a	**3.** b	**4.** a	**5.** a
6. b	**7.** d	**8.** c	**9.** a	**10.** b

Notes

It's time to do self-assessment. Are you ready for the competition!

Mini Test (Topic-wise) 6 Tests based on important topics of the respective subjects	Semester-wise Test (All semester subject) 2 Tests based on all the subjects of particular semester	Mega Grand Test (All subject) 2 Tests based on all the UG subjects (1 Test from Target High book)

CBS Phygital Books >
Textbook of Psychiatric Nursing PHYGITAL

CHAPTER 15

Community Mental Health Nursing

LEARNING OBJECTIVE

After studying this chapter, student will be able to understand and practice the concepts of community mental health nursing.

CHAPTER OUTLINE

- Introduction
- Definition of Community Mental Health Nursing
- Principles of Community Mental Health Nursing
- Issues in Community Mental Health Nursing
- Development of Community Mental Health Services
- National Mental Health Policy
- National Health Policy, 2002
- National Mental Health Program, 1982
- District Mental Health Program, 1996
- Institutionalization versus Deinstitutionalization
- Preventive Psychiatry
- Psychiatric Rehabilitation
- Mental Health Services by Various Agencies
- Agencies/Organization Supporting to Promote Mental Health—Abroad
- Issues in Mental Health Nursing for Special Populations
- Victims of Violence
- Psychiatric Aspects of HIV/AIDS

KEY TERMS

Psychiatric rehabilitation, Preventive psychiatry, National Mental Health Program, District Mental Health Program, Partial hospitalization, Quarter way homes, Group homes, Foster homes, Sheltered workshop, Self-help group, Suicide prevention centers, Premenstrual syndrome, Postpartum depression, Postpartum psychosis, Cycle of violence, HIV/AIDS.

INTRODUCTION

Community Mental Health Centers Act (1963) was initiated by 35th United States' President, John F Kennedy (Fig.15.1), who brought the change in shifting the mental health care from hospitals to the community.

Figure 15.1: John F Kennedy

DEFINITION OF COMMUNITY MENTAL HEALTH NURSING

Community Mental Health Nursing is defined as, 'decentralized pattern of rendering mental health services/care to the needy person in the community, further it focuses on prevention of mental illness, promotion of mental health and rehabilitation of patients with mental disorder in the community'.

PRINCIPLES OF COMMUNITY MENTAL HEALTH NURSING

- Community mental health nursing uses holistic approach with the people residing in community by the integration of mind, body and spirit.
- Community mental health nursing must consider the social setting where the client and family members live together. The care should be based on their capabilities for the promotion of mental health.
- Community mental health nursing focuses on providing the psychosocial support, removal of stigma/ discrimination, prevention of mental illness and treatment of mentally ill-using accessible health care services.
- Community mental health nursing focuses to strengthen the available resources with the required training and education.

ISSUES IN COMMUNITY MENTAL HEALTH NURSING

- Lack of trained manpower and uneven distribution of manpower.
- Lack of budget to promote mental health in community area.
- Lack of knowledge and skills in general medical practitioner about taking care of mentally ill patients in community.
- Lack of awareness about the psychiatric illness in community.
- Poor access to primary health centers to get treatment for mental illness.
- Persistence of stigma and discrimination about mental illness.

DEVELOPMENT OF COMMUNITY MENTAL HEALTH SERVICES (TABLE 15.1)

Table 15.1: Development of community mental health services

Phase	Period	Year	Milestones of development
I	Colonial period (before independence)	1745	First mental asylum was started in Bombay
		1781	First mental asylum was started in Calcutta
		1794	First mental asylum was started in Madras
		18th century onwards	More lunatic asylums were built
		1841	Dorothea Dix was appointed as inspector of mental asylums to promote humanity-based treatment measures. It resulted in establishment of 32 psychiatric hospitals in USA.
		1908	'A Mind that Found Itself'—Book was written by Clifford W Beers. He was a mentally ill patient who exposed awful conditions of psychiatric hospitals. So, 'National Mental Health Association in USA' was formulated and 'Mental Hygiene Movement' began.
		1900	Adolf Myer emphasized on the community mental health approach.
		1955–1980	Era of deinstitutionalization in USA and other Western countries.
		1940	Boston psychopathic hospital was launched in USA (This hospital is pioneer to develop Milieu Therapy).
		1946	• Col M Taylor, Superintendent of European Mental Hospital (Ranchi) surveyed 17 hospitals and found that poor care was rendered in them. Based on this survey report, Bhore Committee recommended to promote mental health care in the hospitals. • President Harry S Truman (33rd president of USA) passed the Mental Health Act. President Harry S Truman

Contd...

Phase	Period	Year	Milestones of development
II	After Independence	1950	All India Institute of Mental Health (Now it is NIMHANS) was institutionalized at Bangalore.
		1955	Joint Commission on Mental Illness and health was formed.
		1957	First mental hospital was started in Hyderabad. Dr Vidyasagar, Medical Superintendent of Amritsar Mental Hospital involved the family members in mental health care of a mental patient as it leads to faster recovery. Hence, family wards were initiated in CMC Vellore and Mental hospital at Bangalore.
		1958	First mental hospital was started in Srinagar.
		1960	First mental hospital was started in Jamnagar.
III	1961–1969	1961	Joint Commission on Mental Illness and Health (1955) published a book 'Action for Mental Health'.
		1962	Mudaliar Committee recommends to establish Psychiatric Units in all districts of India.
		1963	Community Mental Health Centers Act was passed. Rural Mental Health Program was started at Sakalwara, Bengaluru.
		1966	First mental hospital was started in Shahdara, New Delhi.
		1961–1969	Development of General Hospital Psychiatric Unit (GHPU).
IV	1970–1982	1970	Expert Committee of World Health Organization (WHO) and Indian Psychiatric Society focuses on the development of General Hospital Psychiatric Unit (GHPU) into Primary Health Centers (PHC) and Community Health Centers (CHC). Community care approach was followed first in the below mentioned centers. • Sakalwara village at Bengaluru • Raipur Rani Block in Ambala District at Haryana.
		1975	Community Mental Health Construction Act was passed to extend seven more services 1. Services for children and adolescent 2. Services for elders 3. Services for patients with alcohol abuse 4. Services for patients with drug abuse 5. Screening the community people 6. Transitional services (Services framed to assist the person who had transition from hospital to community) 7. Follow-up
		1980	Community Mental Health Systems Act was passed. District Mental Health Program at Bellary district in Karnataka was started.
		1982	National Mental Health Program was launched.
V	1987–2012	1987	Indian Lunacy Act (1912) was replaced by Mental Health Act (1987).
		1990's	• Increased in funding to promote mental health services in hospitals. • Nongovernmental Organizations (NGO's) took an active lead to improve mental health. • Growth of private sector in mental health services.
		2008	WHO's Mental Health Action Gap Program was launched
		2011	WHO's World Health Atlas demonstrated that mental health services were poor because of inequitable distribution and insufficient resources.

Contd...

Phase	Period	Year	Milestones of development
VI	2013–2020		Dr Margaret Chan, Director-General of **World Health Organization (WHO)** formulated the comprehensive **Mental Health Action Plan with five main objectives** 1. Empower the leadership and governance for mental health. 2. Provide the comprehensive, integrated and responsive mental health services. 3. Health/Social care services in community-based settings. 4. Implement the strategies for promotion of mental health and prevention of mental illness. 5. Empower the information systems, evidence and research for mental health. **Mental Health Action Plan have six core principles** listed below: 1. **Universal health coverage**: Equal treatment is rendered to all irrespective of their religion, gender, race, age, social status and sexual orientation, etc. 2. **Evidence-based practice**: Treatment, preventive measures and promotion of mental health services based on the current evidence. 3. **Human rights**: Protection of the rights of mentally ill. 4. **Life course approach**: Policies and protocols needs to be considered at all stages of life course such as infancy, childhood, adolescence, adulthood and old age. 5. **Multisectoral approach**: Coordination with the private sector and public sector (health, employment, education, judicial, housing, etc.) 6. **Empowerment of patients with mental disorders and psychosocial disabilities.**

National Institute of Mental Health and Neurosciences (NIMHANS)

National Institute of Mental Health and Neurosciences (NIMHANS) at Bengaluru has developed alternative measures instead of hospital-based care, which are as follows:

- **Domiciliary Care Program:** Mental health professionals and nurses render the mental health care at patient's home in order to develop the social functioning and overall improvement in health.
- **Extensive use of outdoor services:** Family members are encouraged to treat the mentally ill patients in home set-up. The patient's mental health can be improved by exposure to nature and by doing outdoor activities. There should be periodical visiting in Out Patient Departments (OPD's) and the patient should spend short-stay in hospital, if needed.
- **Organizing short-term course to private general practitioners:** Mental health professionals train the private general practitioners by organizing the short-term courses in order to enhance the knowledge and skills.
- **Extension program by satellite clinics:** Mental health professionals conduct monthly or weekly clinics at district headquarters or taluks. Local NGO's help to conduct such camps regularly.
- **Promotion of mental health by training the school teachers in regard to mental health care:** Teachers are trained to identify the mental health or behavioral problems in children and to manage the psychosocial problems of students by providing counseling to them.
- **Training of village leaders, student volunteers and lay volunteers:** Training the village leaders might guide them to act as a changing agent in society. College students who are involved in National Social Service (NSS) activities can extend their social service to render mental health services.
- **Student Development Program:** Poor academic performance is a common problem among students, so special training program for school students in regard to study habits, tips for learning, writing pattern in examination and the role of emotional factors in the learning are considered.
- **Involvement of Integrated Child Developmental Services (ICDS) personnel in children mental health care:** Anganwadi workers are trained in regard to the mental health care. It helps them to identify the children with behavior problems or mental disorders and refer them to appropriate psychiatric hospital.
- **Nongovernmental voluntary organization:**
  - Schizophrenia Research Foundation (SCARF), Chennai.
  - Medico-Pastoral Association
  - Richmond Fellowship of India, Bengaluru
  - Suicide Prevention Centers (e.g., Sneha at Chennai, Maithreyi at Puducherry).

NATIONAL MENTAL HEALTH POLICY

The policy has the plan of action that is required for promoting mental health.

- **Reformulating the National Mental Health Policy, 1982:**
  - District Mental Health Program (DMHP) was field tested in 1985 in Bellary District of Karnataka under the guidance of National Institute of Mental Health and Neurosciences (NIMHANS).
  - After pilot project, District Mental Health Program (DMHP) was implemented during 9th Five-Year Plan (1997–2002).
  - National Mental Health Program (NMHP) failed due to its one-dimensional nature.
  - After in-depth situation analysis and extensive consultations with stakeholders, the NMHP (1982) underwent radical restructuring.
  - It aimed at striking a judicious balance between various components of the mental health care delivery system, with the specified budgetary allocations.
- **Revised NMHP, 2003:** It is comprised of five closely networked or interdependent strategic components, with a total outlay of ₹19 billion during the 10th Five-Year Plan. The components of Revised National Mental Health Program are as follows:
  - Redesigning the DMHP around a modal institution (Zonal Medical College)
  - Strengthening the medical colleges with a view to develop:
    - The manpower in psychiatric department.
    - Psychiatric treatment facilities at secondary level.
    - General Hospital Psychiatric Unit (GHPU).
  - Streamlining and modernization of mental hospitals to transform from custodial care to:
    - Tertiary centers of excellence
    - Provide psychodynamic orientation
    - Enhance the research and development in the field of community mental health.
  - Strengthening of central and state mental health authorities:
    - To fulfill their role in monitoring the ongoing Mental Health Program.
    - Determine intersectoral collaboration and linkages with other national programs.
  - Research and training aim at:
    - Building an extensive database of epidemiology
    - Therapeutic needs of community.
    - Development of better and most cost-effective intervention models.
    - Promote intersectoral research.
    - Provide the necessary inputs/conceptual framework for health and policy planning.
    - Focused Information Education Communication (IEC) activities in collaboration with Indian Institute of Mass communication.
    - Enhancing public awareness.
    - Eradicating the stigma/discrimination related mental illness.
- **Organizing services**
  - Providing mental health care in primary care setting.
  - Make psychotropic drugs available at all levels of health care.
- **Community mental health care facilities**
  - Community care is more effective and cost-effective.
  - It leads to early intervention.
  - Removes stigma.
  - Different services such as day care centers, half way homes and long stay homes, sheltered workshops, de-addiction center and suicide prevention center were provided.
- **Support to families**
  - Providing financial support to families.
  - Offering public places to the community for the meeting and organization of day care activities.
  - Nurses has to visit the patient's home in order to support patient's family members.
  - Involving them in the planning of the Mental Health Program.
- **Human resource development:** It involves short-term training of:
  - Medical students
  - General psychologists'
  - General social workers
  - General nurses
  - Rehabilitation professionals
- **Public mental health education:** The goal of providing mental health education to the public is:
  - To reduce the barriers to treatment
  - To reduce the stigma and discrimination
  - To recover human rights
- **Private sector mental health care:** Role of private sector is identified as the following:
  - Systematic recording
  - Clarifying treatment utilization
  - Working in medical colleges as consultants
  - Training Primary Health Center (PHC) personnel
  - Supporting Nongovernmental Organizations (NGOs)
  - Encouraging public health education

- **Support to voluntary organization**
  - Developing suicide prevention and crisis support cells
  - Formation of self-help groups
  - Organizing community-based housing facilities
  - Setting up day care centers
  - Sheltered employment facilities
  - Public mental health education
- **Promotion and preventive interventions**
  - Life skill education programs for school children
  - Psychosocial care for the survivors of the disasters
- **Administrative support:** At all levels in directorate of health services:
  - One administrative officer (psychiatrist)
  - Additional staff—statistician

  At district level
  - Two mental health teams
    - One is District Medical Officer (DMO)
    - One in district hospital

NATIONAL HEALTH POLICY, 2002

The National Health Policy (NHP) was formulated in 1983 since the marked changes were required in the determinant factors relating to the health sector. Some of the policy initiatives outlined in the NHP, 1983 have yielded results while in several other areas the outcome has not been as expected. The NHP was revised in 2002.

Objective of NHP, 2002

To achieve an acceptable standard of good health among the general population of the country.

Approaches of NHP, 2002

- To increase access to the decentralized public health system by establishing new infrastructure in deficient areas and by upgrading the infrastructure in the existing institutions.
- To ensure a more equitable access to health services across the social and geographical expansion of the country.
- To increase the aggregate public health investment through a substantial increase in contribution by the Central Government.
- To strengthen the capacity of the public health administration at the state level to render effective service delivery.
- To enhance the contribution of the private sector in providing health services to the society.
- Primacy will be given to the preventive and first line curative initiatives at the primary health level through increased sectoral share of allocation.

The revised NHP, 2002 draft discusses the following:

- **Extending public health services:** India has a vast reservoir of practitioners in the Indian systems of medicine and homeopathy, who have undergone formal training in their own disciplines. The possibility of using such practitioners in the implementation of state/central government public health programs in order to increase the reach of basic health care in the country was addressed in the NHP, 2002.
- **Norms for health care personnel:** It is observed that the deployment of doctors and nurses in both public and private institutions is ad-hoc and significantly short of the requirement for minimal standards of patient care. NHP, 2002 makes a specific recommendation in regard to this deficiency.
- **Nursing personnel:** The ratio of nursing personnel in the country *vis-a-vis* doctors/bed is very low according to professionally accepted norms. There is also an acute shortage of nurses, trained in super-specialty disciplines for deployment in tertiary care facilities. NHP, 2002 addresses these problems.
- **Mental health:** Serious mental disorders require hospitalization and treatment under trained supervision. Mental health institutions are woefully deficient in physical infrastructure and trained manpower. NHP-2002 addresses itself to these deficiencies in the public health sector.
- **Alternative systems of medicine:** The policy focuses on building up the credibility to the alternative systems, by encouraging evidence-based research to determine their efficacy and safety. It also encourages certification and quality-marking of products to enable a wider popular acceptance of these systems of medicine.

Specific recommendations with regard to:

- **Nursing personnel**
  - Improving the skills of nurses.
  - Increasing the ratio of degree holding nurses *vis-a-vis* diploma holding nurses.
  - Need for Central Government subsidy for setting up, the running of and training facilities for nurses.
- **Mental health**
  - Decentralizing mental health services.
  - Upgrading the physical infrastructure of mental health institutions.
  - Primary health care with emphasis on preventive, promotive and rehabilitative aspects.
  - Restructuring of health services.

NATIONAL MENTAL HEALTH PROGRAM, 1982

The National Mental Health Program (NMHP) was an initiative of development in various fields, e.g., The Alma-Ata declaration on Primary Health Care, the commitment of the country to provide health services to all, the awareness regarding the magnitude of psychiatric disorders in the community and the availability of a large infrastructure for general health services.

Aims of NMHP

During planning of mental health services for India, the following three aims were taken into account:

1. Prevention and treatment of mental and neurological disorders with their associated disabilities.
2. Use of mental health technology to improve general health services.
3. Application of mental health principles in total national development to improve quality of life.

Objectives of NMHP

- To ensure availability and accessibility of minimum mental health care for all in the foreseeable future particularly to the most vulnerable and under privileged sections of the population.
- To encourage application of mental health knowledge in general health care and in social development.
- To promote community participation in the mental health service development.

Targets of NMHP

- Representatives from all the states of India, in the field of psychiatry unites to form a national coordinating body.
- Include the mental health as a component for the health workers in their curriculum.
- Doctors in Primary Health Centers (PHCs) will have two weeks training program regarding the mental health care.
- Psychiatrist will be appointed at district level to organize and supervise the mental health training program.
- Inclusion of community mental health components in teaching institution.
- Psychotropic medications should be included in the list of essential medications in India.

Approaches to Achieve the Objectives

In order to achieve the objectives formulated above, the program will adapt the following approaches:

- **Diffusion of mental health skills to the periphery of the health care service system:**
  - Instead of exclusively centralizing and concentrating mental health skills in specialized facilities, mental health care will be spread over the existing network of services.
  - The aim is to incorporate mental health awareness and skills at the levels of health care.
  - Mental health care must start at the grass-root level.
- **Appropriate appointment of tasks in mental health care:** The tasks have to be performed at each level:
  - Community health volunteer (1/1000 population)—to act as liaison between mental health care and the community.
  - Multipurpose worker (1/5000 population)—Multipurpose worker is a first level full time health personnel to provide health care service and act as the first person to link with health service system by providing first aid care and follow-up service.
  - Senior and more experienced primary health personnel (Health Supervisor, health inspectors, Lady health visitors, etc.)—Entrusted with the tasks of early recognition and management of psychiatric conditions on priority basis.
  - Medical Officer—has the responsibility of organizing and supervising the primary level mental health care for the entire population under Primary Health Center (PHC).
  - The referral system will operate to help the individuals with mental health problems.
- **Equitable and balanced territorial distribution of resources:**
  - Coverage of unserved or underserved population with highest priority.
  - Strengthen the mental health care in the regions with deficient or deprived mental health.
- **Integration of mental health care into general health services:** This will facilitate the application of mental health skills when dealing with patients without gross psychiatric disturbances. It will also enable the health worker to identify psychosocial problems under the disguise of physical complaints and manage them more adequately.
- **Linkage to community development:** An important approach would be the involvement of State, District and Block leadership in the implementation of the mental health program to ensure community involvement in preventive efforts directed toward psychosocial problems like alcohol or drug abuse, behavior problems of childhood and adolescence including delinquency, etc.
- **Mental health care:** The service component will include three subprograms:

1. **Treatment subprogram:** Multiple levels of this subprogram are given below:
   i. **Village and subcenter level:** Multipurpose workers and health supervisors under the supervision of Medical Officer (MO) to be trained for:
      - Management of psychiatric emergencies.
      - Administration and supervision of maintenance treatment for chronic psychiatric disorders.
      - Diagnosis and management of grand mal epilepsy, especially in children.
      - Liaison with local school teachers and parents regarding mental retardation and behavioral problems in children.
      - Counseling problems related to alcohol and drug abuse.

   ii. **Medical Officer of Primary Health Center (PHC) aided by health supervisor to be trained for:**
      - Supervision of multipurpose worker's performance.
      - To diagnose the patient's condition.
      - Treatment of functional psychosis.
      - Treatment of uncomplicated cases of psychiatric disorders associated with physical diseases.
      - Management of uncomplicated psychosocial problems.
      - Epidemiological surveillance of mental morbidity.

   iii. **District hospital:** It was recognized that there should be at least one psychiatrist attached to every district hospital as an integral part of the district health services. The district hospital should have 30–50 beds. The psychiatrist in a district hospital was envisaged to devote only a part of his time in clinical care and greater part in training or supervision of nonspecialist health workers.

   iv. **Mental hospitals and teaching psychiatric units:** The major activities of these higher centers of psychiatric care include:
      - Help in care of 'difficult' cases
      - Teaching
      - Specialized facilities like occupational therapy units, psychotherapy, counseling and behavior therapy.
2. **Rehabilitation subprogram:** The components of this subprogram include the maintenance treatment of epileptics and psychotics at the community level. Rehabilitation centers at the district level and also the higher referral centers were developed.
3. **Prevention subprogram:** The prevention component is to be community-based, with the initial focus on prevention and control of alcohol-related problems. Later, problems like addictions, juvenile delinquency and acute adjustment problems like suicidal attempts are to be addressed.

- **Mental health training:** Mental health specialists like psychiatrists would not be enough in the near future in our country to deliver mental health care to all those who immediately require it. As an immediate solution, we have to train a large number of health personnel of all categories as much as possible in the minimum essentials of mental health tasks at their own level of performance.
- **Mental retardation and drug dependence:** Mental retardation is not mental illness but often associated with it as well as physical illness.

Often the mentally retarded first come to the notice of the medical services. Therefore, health workers are able to counsel the parents, provide public education in this subject, teaching them how to approach social welfare agencies for rehabilitation. Simultaneously, Integrated Child Development Services (ICDS) personnel should know to refer the mentally retarded recognized by them to medical agencies when indicated.

DISTRICT MENTAL HEALTH PROGRAM, 1996

Government of India funded to launch the District Mental Health Program (DMHP) as per the guidelines of National Mental Health Program. In 1996, DMHP was launched in four districts under 9th Five-Year Plan and it extended to 123 districts in 12th Five-Year Plan. In 1997, DMHP was launched in Trichy, extended to Ramanathapuram and Madurai in 2003. District Mental Health Program (DMHP) is further extended into 13 districts.

Aims to Launch District Mental Health Program by Government of India

- To develop the awareness about mental health in public.
- To Promote the community participation in the mental health services by self-help group.
- To integrate the mental health care with general health services.
- To provide the accessible mental health services to the vulnerable and under-privileged people.

Objectives

- To early detection of cases and to provide the prompt treatment within the community.
- To decrease the stigma and discrimination.
- To reduce the work pressure of mental hospitals.

- To give treatment and to provide rehabilitation services to the patient after the discharge from psychiatric unit.

Components

District Mental Health Program was developed based on the 'Bellary Model'. It emphasized on the following components such as:

- Early detection of cases and providing necessary treatment.
- Conduct short-term training program for general physicians regarding the treatment process of mental illness. Health workers also need to be trained.
- **Information Education Communication (IEC):** Creating awareness among public.
- Monitoring and having a complete documentation.

Administrative Plan of District Mental Health Program

DMHP has Central Mental Health Authority at National level, State Mental Health Authority at state level, District Mental Health Team (DMHT) at district level and Community Health Centers (CHCs)/Primary Health Centers (PHCs)/Trained staff members at sub-district or state level. DMHT includes program officer/psychiatrist, psychiatric nurse/trained general nurse, clinical psychologist, psychiatric social worker, community nurse/case manager, case registry assistant and record keeper as shown in the Flowchart 15.1.

Milestones and Achievements in District Mental Health program

- Psychiatrist has been appointed in all districts. Appointments of psychologist/psychiatric social worker is in progress.
- Basic psychotropic agents/drugs are made available in Primary Health Centers (PHC).
- Suicide prevention centers have been established in 16 districts.
- Survey has been conducted all over India to ensure the quality of services rendered through DMHP. Madurai in Tamil Nadu is leading with high satisfactory score.
- Regular supervision is done by the district collector.
- Ten bedded psychiatric wards equipped with Boyle's machine, BP apparatus and ophthalmoscope have been established.
- 60% of districts are able to render mental health care at district level and 20% of them are able to render mental health care at primary health level.
- At present DMHP has been achieved in 123 districts which is extendable to all districts (on progress).

Initiatives Taken and the Presence of Treatment Gap

Treatment gap is present among the general health physicians due to lack of knowledge so NIMHANS organizes three months training program to the doctors. It was observed that primary care doctors were reluctant of telepsychiatric services.

Mental Health Care Act (2017) states that, only the emergency treatment can be provided by the general physician (72 hours) and the further treatment has to be referred to the higher-level center. There is no provision for the nonmental health professionals to treat the psychiatric patient in their follow-up. Hence, the resource building, workforce development with adequate proper legal framework is essential for the successful progress of DMHP.

INSTITUTIONALIZATION VERSUS DEINSTITUTIONALIZATION

Institutionalization means treating the patients in psychiatric ward after the admission procedure. Patients remains in the custodial care in this situation.

Deinstitutionalization means treating the patients in the community area whereas the patients visit the OPD's or

Flowchart 15.1: Administrative plan of district mental health program

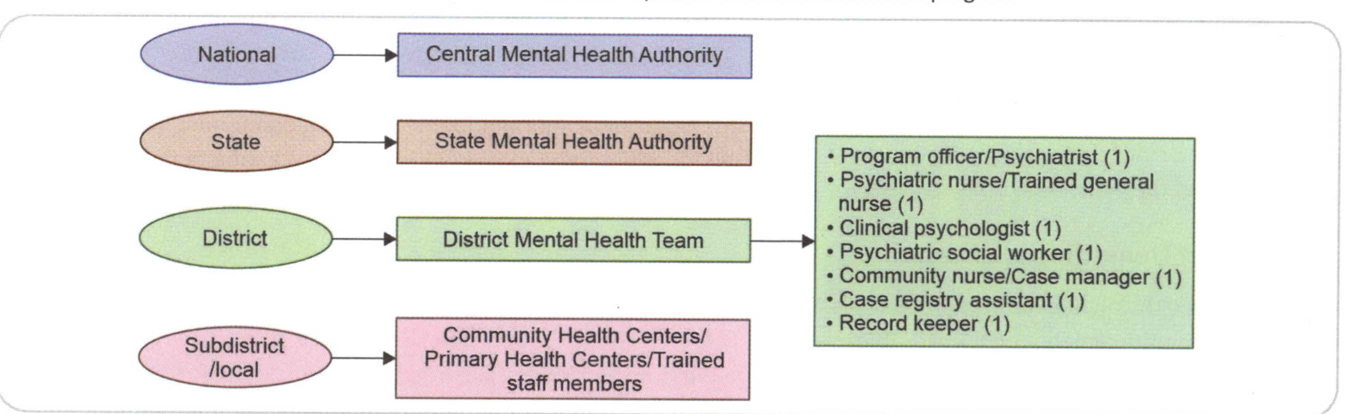

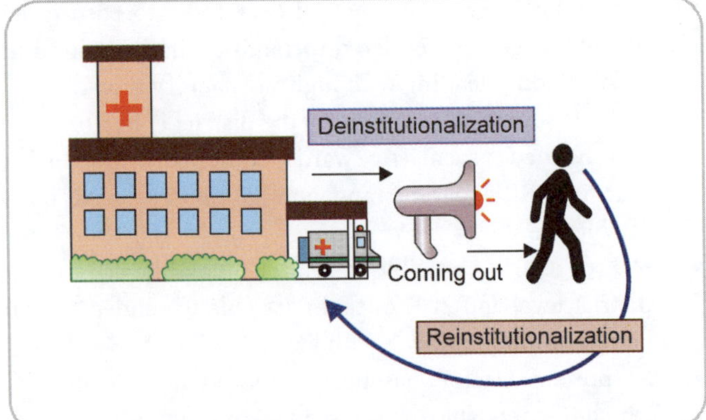

Figure 15.2: Concepts of deinstitutionalization and reinstitutionalization

Primary Health Centers (PHC) or day care centers or short stay units for the continuity of treatment process. President John F Kennedy brought a change of shifting the mental health care from hospitals to the community by the initiation of Community Mental Health Centers Act (1963) (Fig. 15.2).

World Health Organization (WHO): Conducted a survey in 2014 with 78 mental health experts representing 42 regions from the World. World Health Organization (WHO) identified the five principles of deinstitutionalization:

1. Need to implement community-based services.
2. Health workforce should be committed to change.
3. Political support is required at the highest and broadest level.
4. Timing is a key factor.
5. Additional financial resources are required.

Causes of Deinstitutionalization

There are three causes which made the changes in the society in regard with deinstitutionalization:

1. Development of psychotropic drugs.
2. Society has accepted that mentally ill should not be in custodial care, instead proper treatment has to be given.
3. Initiation of funding to the community health centers.

Benefits of Deinstitutionalization

It helps the patient to integrate with the society and it also helps to protect the patient's rights.

Demerits of Deinstitutionalization

It is difficult for the mental health professionals to coordinate with the community centers with the available resources. There may be chances that the client misses out the regular treatment to maintain drug adherence. Patients have to be taken care by their family members/relatives. It is unable to take care all the acute mentally ill patients in the community area.

PREVENTIVE PSYCHIATRY

Introduction

Mental illness is a leading cause of disability. So, it is found vital to have a disease prevention and health promotion program. This will help to prevent the mental illness and promote the good mental health.

Definitions

- Preventive psychiatry is defined as, 'services rendered in the community in order to prevent the mental illness and promote the mental health'.
- Preventive psychiatry is defined as, 'prevention of mental illness by having an aim to reduce the incidence, prevalence, relapse, symptoms and risk factors of mental illness and is also aimed to decrease the impact of illness on the affected person's family and community'.

—Mrazek and Haggerty, 1994

Main Features of Preventive Psychiatry

- Focus on prevention as well as treatment.
- Rendering continuity of care.
- Multidisciplinary team approach.
- Promotion of comprehensive services.
- Rendering care by coordinating with the accessible nearby community health centers

Model of Preventive Psychiatry

Gerald Caplan (1960) described the levels of prevention specific to psychiatry. Levels of prevention are classified into primordial, primary, secondary and tertiary as shown in Flowchart 15.2.

Primordial Prevention

The primordial prevention denotes the prevention of modifiable and nonmodifiable risk factors. The modifiable risk factors are smoking, alcoholism, continuous stressors, lack of exercise/yoga/meditation, obesity, eating junk foods, etc. The nonmodifiable risk factors have genetic history/family history of mental illness.

Primary Prevention

Primary prevention denotes the promotion of health status and specific protection by immunization. **Primary prevention interventions** are shown in Table 15.2.

Flowchart 15.2: Model of preventive psychiatry

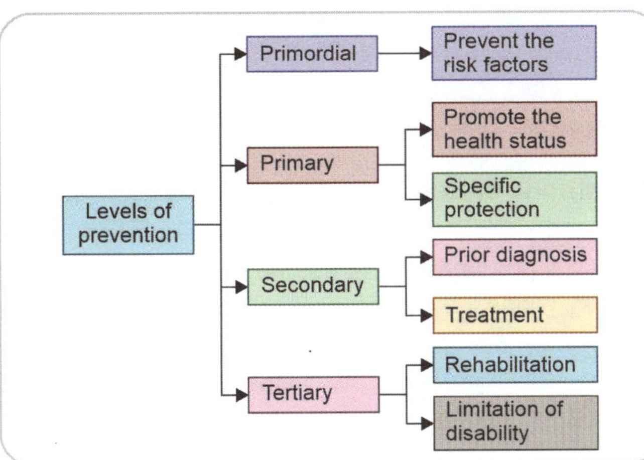

Table 15.2: Primary prevention interventions

Interventions	Description
Individual centered Interventions	**At home** • Provide antenatal care to mother. • Dietary rectification to the infants who suffer with metabolic disorders. • Liberalize the laws of medical termination of pregnancy, if required. • Training to the physically and mentally challenged children. • Provide counseling to the parents if the child is physically or mentally challenged.
	At school • Teaching the growth/development chart to the parents and teachers. • Identify the problems of children in school and provide timely intervention.
Family centered interventions	• Teach the significance of having harmonious relationship among family members • Help them to have an open healthy communication among the family members • Develop the parents-teachers association • Encourage the child guidance clinic to improve the child rearing practices • Develop the educational services in mental health • Administer the marital therapy in case of any marital problems • Administer family therapy to develop the healthy relationship among family members • Give crisis intervention to mentally challenged children ▪ First aid centers ▪ Walk in clinics ▪ Mental health check-up • Empower the social support for elders • Encourage the mental health education programs with the use of audio-visual aids.

Contd...

Interventions	Description
Society centered interventions	• Development of the community • Steps taken to fulfill of basic needs to society ▪ Food ▪ Water ▪ Shelter ▪ Clothing ▪ Education ▪ Health • Promote the epidemiological investigation ▪ Data collection ▪ Analysis of data ▪ Interpretation/findings from data.

Secondary Prevention

Secondary prevention denotes the early diagnosis and treatment. The health team members need adequate training, so that they could conduct the general health checkup regularly, examine the high-risk population periodically and monitor the patients regularly. The health team members can get help from community leaders, balwadis, mahila mandals, industries/work areas and schools to perform a regular health check-up/do referral services. Conducting this screening programs will help to do further consultation with the specialist doctor and can also perform the crisis intervention programs as shown in Flowchart 15.3.

Flowchart 15.3: Concept of secondary prevention in model of preventive psychiatry

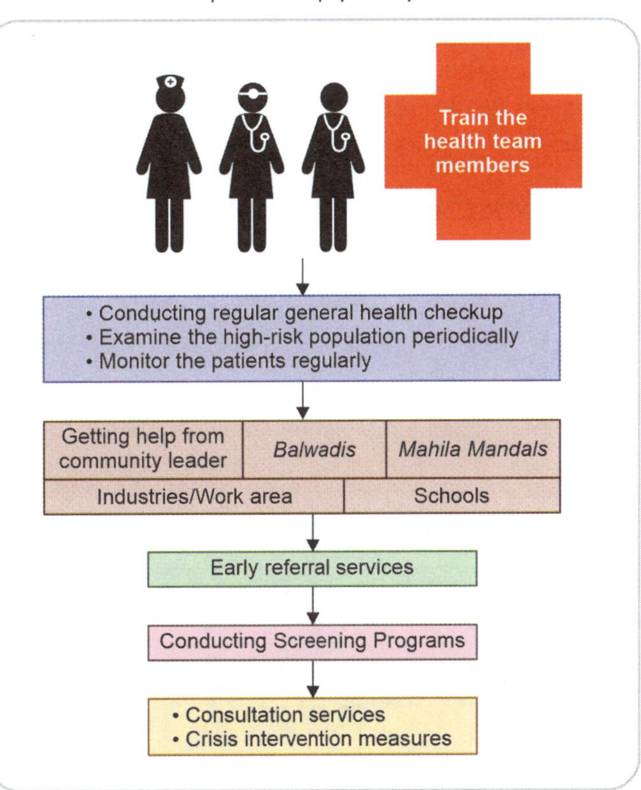

Tertiary Prevention

Tertiary prevention focuses on the rehabilitation and limitation of disability. Training in community living (TCL) concept was provided by "Stein and Test".

Description of this Model

After the identification of high-risk patients, the nurse needs to go to the community area to be with the client and approach the hospital along with the patient.

Purposes of this Model

It will help the nurse and patient to have a mutual agreement to set the realistic goals. The key concepts of this model are as follows:

- Involvement of family members in the treatment program.
- Organize the recreational activities in hospital.
- Implementing the community-based programs
  - Day hospitals
  - Night hospitals
  - After care clinics
  - Half-way homes
  - Ex-patient hostels
  - Foster care homes
- Liaison between the community health nurse and mental hospital.
- Collaboration with the nearby agencies available in community.
- Health education to demolish the stigma about mental illness.
- Monitor the attitude of community people toward mental illness.

Nurses should create awareness in the community people in order to develop healthy attitude toward mentally ill.

PSYCHIATRIC REHABILITATION

Rehabilitation will help the individual to return to his/her previous highest level of functioning. It is a vital part of the community mental health program at tertiary level of prevention. The combined as well as coordinated utilization of medical, physical, psychological, educational, social and vocational measures will help to ensure the functional ability of the individual. Rehabilitation helps to retain greatest amount of function and independence as far as possible.

Definitions of Rehabilitation

- Rehabilitation is defined as the restoration of the person's health to his/her former capacity.
- Rehabilitation is defined as, 'attempt to render best possible role in community area in order to achieve the maximum range of activity, compatible with one's personality and interest'. —*Maxwell Jones, 1952*

Rehabilitative Nursing

It focuses on preventive activities, maintenance activities and restoration activities as explained in the Flowchart 15.4.

Goals of Psychiatric Rehabilitation

- To help the patient to achieve the highest level of independence and maintain a satisfying, productive life.
- To reduce the disability
- To build the coping skills
- To improve the social functioning
- To provide good psychological support.

Principles of Psychiatric Rehabilitation

- Psychiatric rehabilitation is a vital part of tertiary prevention, which focuses on disability limitation related to the course/episode of the disease.
- Psychiatric rehabilitation should start with assessment of skills in regard to the patient's abilities.
- Psychiatric rehabilitation focuses on rebuilding the strength of patient's ego and build the psychological well-being in order to perform the assigned job/occupation.

Flowchart 15.4: Concept of rehabilitative nursing

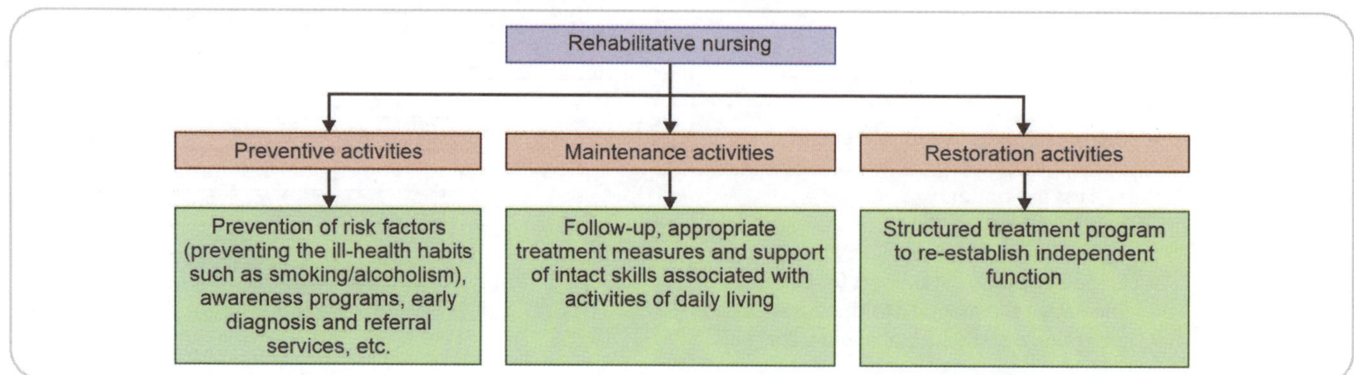

Community Rehabilitation Facilities (Table 15.3)

Table 15.3: Community rehabilitation facilities

Community rehabilitation facilities	Description
Partial hospitalization (or) day care hospital/centers (or) day treatment program	It is an outpatient facility where clients undergo the assessment, treatment and rehabilitation during day time. Patient can return to his/her home after the treatment. This partial hospitalization is advised when the symptoms of mentally ill patients are in control and show a good prognosis in treatment.
Halfway homes (or) sober house (or) recovery house	It is an institution in which the patients with physical, emotional and mental disabilities or individuals with criminal backgrounds learn or relearn the required skills to reintegrate in society. In general, halfway homes are in two models: • **In first model:** At the time of admission, patients are categorized based on the types of disability, abilities to reintegrate with society, and the expected time-frame for performing this. • **In second model:** At the time of admission, patients are allotted separate individual rooms to provide one-to-one services.
Quarter way homes	It provides lower level of supervision than the half way homes. Here, mostly patient has to take care of himself. In India, NIMHANS have an inbuilt quarter way home.
Group homes	It is a small residential care facility present in the community, which has been allotted to take care of the children and adults with chronic disabilities. These homes usually have six or fewer occupants. Trained caregivers are present full time over there.
Foster homes	When the parents are unable to take care of their children due to variety of reasons, foster home is the place where the children are taken care of. Foster care may be the informal one or arranged by the courts or by a social service agency.
Sheltered workshop	It is an environment or organization which employs the persons with disabilities separately from the other individuals.
Self-help group	It is a voluntary association of persons who have common desire to overcome the mental illness and promote the mental health. For example, Alcoholic anonymous group, Al-anon and narcotic anonymous group. (Groups consist of recovered patients from substance abuse who joined together to help the patients to recover from addiction.
Suicide prevention centers	• Sneha Suicide Prevention Center and Jeevan Suicide Prevention—Chennai • One Life—Hyderabad • Maithri—Kochi • Medico-Pastoral Association and Sahai—Bengaluru • AASRA, Sahara, Singing Soulz, Samaritans and Karma Holistic Café—Mumbai • Serve, Lifeline Foundation and Defeat Depression—Kolkata • Sanjivini Society for Mental Health, Sumaitri and Fortis—New Delhi • The Mind Research Foundation—Chandigarh

- Psychiatric rehabilitation should enhance the competencies and capacities of the individual with the mental disorders.
- Psychiatric rehabilitation should influence the positive expectations to the individual and family.
- Psychiatric rehabilitation focuses on the improvement of abilities more than that of improving good insight.
- Psychiatric rehabilitation focuses on the components such as development of resources in patient's environment, improvement of skills and interventions to improve the functional ability.

Areas of Rehabilitation

The health care delivery system at various levels to promote mental health has been shown in Figure 15.3.

In general, area of rehabilitation is categorized into domestic, occupational and social aspects as shown in Flowchart 15.5. It is also classified into eight areas as mentioned below:

1. **Psychiatric:** Management of symptoms and providing psychological treatment measures.
2. **Health and medical:** Maintaining consistency in rendering health care.

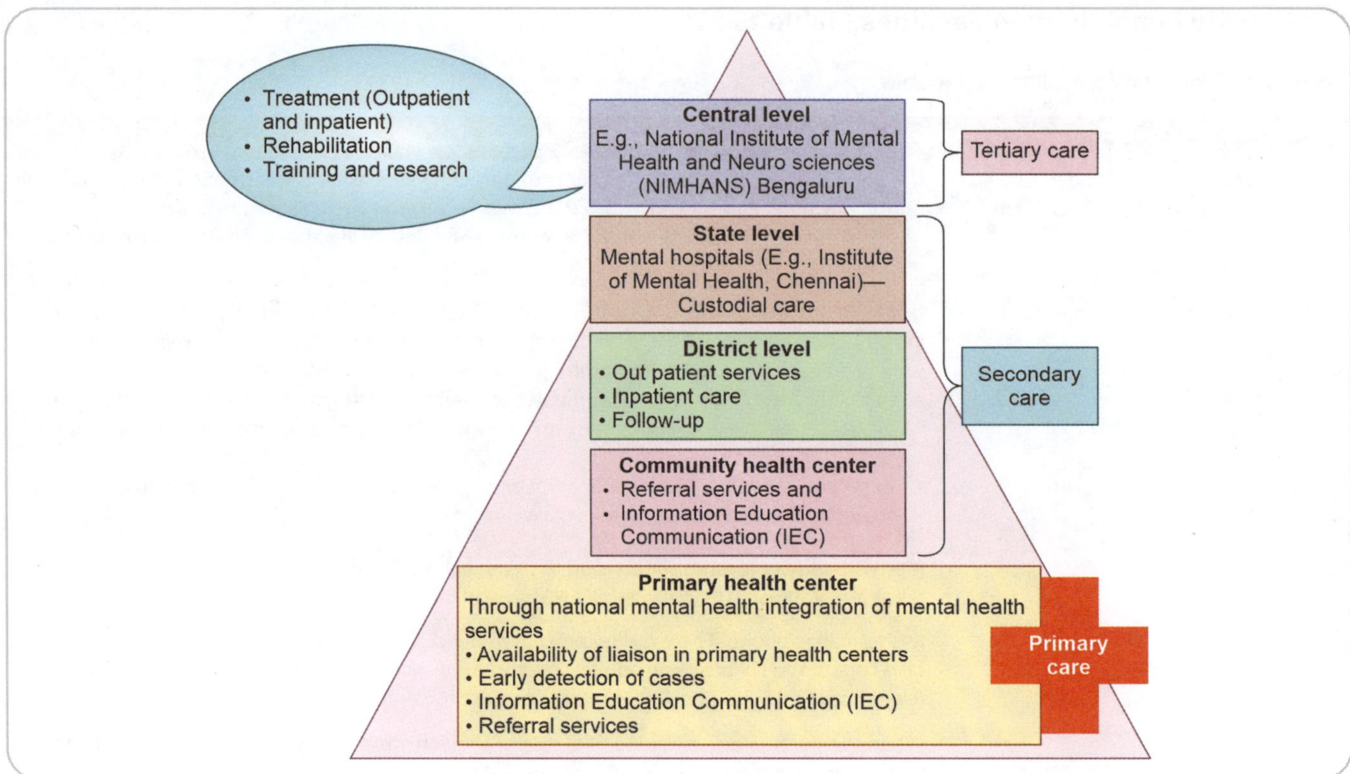

Figure 15.3: Health care delivery system at various levels to promote mental health

Flowchart 15.5: Areas of rehabilitation

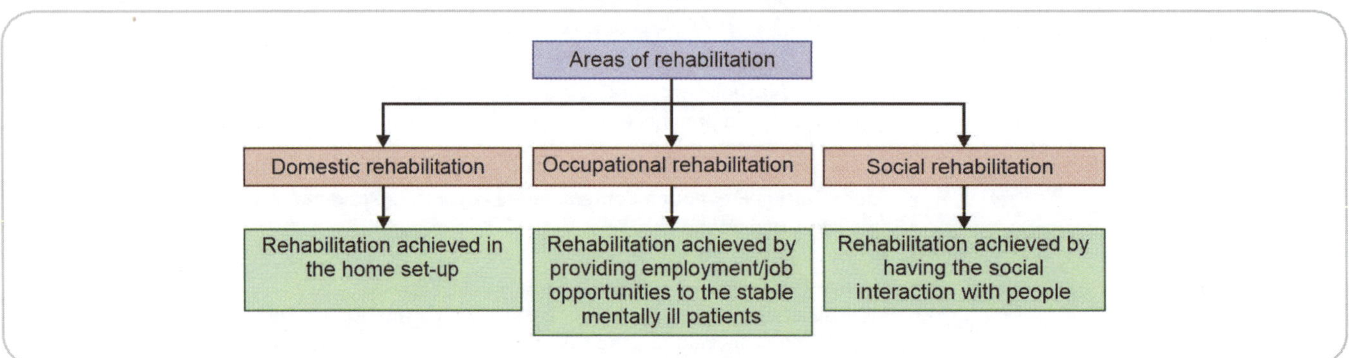

3. **Basic living skills:** Maintaining personal hygiene, development of skills to cook food, safety measures during travel, etc.
4. **Social skills:** Relationship with the family members, friends, etc.
5. **Vocational skills:** Assistance in the preparation for employment.
6. **Educational skills:** Participating in the educational activities and teaching programs.
7. **Financial skills:** Planning own personal budget.
8. **Community and legal:** Usage of community resources and helping out in legal activities.

Rehabilitation Team

Health care professionals consists of:

- Psychiatric/mental health nurse
- Psychiatrist
- Clinical psychologist/counselor
- Psychiatric social worker
- Occupational therapist
- Recreational therapist and
- Other health professionals involved in mental health rehabilitation.

Domains of Psychiatric Rehabilitation

Psychiatric Rehabilitation Association (PRA) at Virginia states that, there are seven domains focused for the successful rehabilitation process as shown in Table 15.4.

Role of Nurse in Rehabilitation

Assessment

Nurse has to collect history from the individual and family members in order to obtain the baseline data. Nurse has to assess their values, health beliefs, cultural background, etc. Nurse also needs to assess the nearby available community resources for mentally ill. Nurse has to assess the severity of illness, onset, duration, factors contributing the mental illness, its impact on social/occupational impairment, its impact on activities of daily living, expectations of the patient and family members in regard with treatment, etc.

Interventions

- Create awareness among patients and their family members regarding the available resources in the community to promote mental health and to treat the mental illness.
- Teach the patient and family members about stress management/coping skills and problem-solving techniques.
- Take measures to reduce the stigma and discrimination about the mental illness in community.
- Develop the structured daily activity schedule for the patient in order to promote the activities of daily living.
- Encourage the patient to participate in the group activities to promote the social skills and also motivate the patient to be part of self-help group.
- Provide assistance to the patient for employment opportunities meant for the mentally ill with the help of social worker.
- Advice the patient and family members in regard with the importance of drug adherence.
- Monitor the patient and have a regular follow-up.

MENTAL HEALTH SERVICES BY VARIOUS AGENCIES

Components of Support Systems/Available Services in Community

- Identification of mentally ill patients
- Protection and advocacy to protect patient's rights
- Mental health treatment
- Support to the family members
- Rehabilitation services
- Income support and entitlement
- Health and dental services
- Housing
- Peer support
- Crisis response services

Governmental Organizations

- **Central or state mental health authority** protects the mentally ill from discrimination and stigma.
- **National Human Rights Commission** monitor the structure and functions of mental hospitals in all the states of India.
- **National Mental Health Program** (1982) helps in the modernization of government psychiatric hospitals, promotes the manpower development scheme in 11th Five-Year Plan. Child and adolescent mental health care was rendered through National Rural Health

Table 15.4: Domains of psychiatric rehabilitation

Domains	Focus	Description
I	Interpersonal competencies	Skills to communicate, collaborate to have healthy relationships
II	Professional role	Practitioners need to provide the evidence-based best practices
III	Community integration	Community integration is designed to promote the personal, vocational and social competency of the people in order to live successful life in the community. Practitioners need to develop skills in order to promote community integration
IV	Assessment, planning and outcomes	Assess the strength and weakness of the individuals in order to promote his/her skills and achieve the goal.
V	Strategies for promoting resilience and recovery	Helping the individuals to achieve their goals. It focuses on relapse prevention and outreach programs
VI	Systems competencies	Helping the practitioners to improve the working knowledge on systems in order to remove stigma, discrimination and to integrate the individual with the society
VII	Supporting health and wellness	Develop the healthy connections between body, mind and spirit to have a sustained wellness life style

Mission (NRHM) in order to promote the school health, Reproductive child health (RCH) and adolescence friendly clinic under 12th Five-Year Plan.

- **District Mental Health Program** is incorporated to enhance the promotive and preventive action plan in order to achieve positive mental health. It focuses on the:
  - School mental health services such as life skill education and counseling.
  - Suicide prevention services such as help lines, Information Education Communication (IEC), promotion of counseling centers and conducting the sensitization workshops.
  - Promoting the college counseling services.
  - Focus the stress management strategies in work place.

Nongovernmental Organization

- Disability special schools and disability rehabilitation services for example, Sathya Special School in Puducherry and School for Special Children in Chennai.
- **Community facilities** such as partial hospitalization, halfway homes, quarter way homes, group homes, foster homes, sheltered workshop, self-help groups and suicide prevention centers as shown in Table 15.3.
- National trust for welfare of persons with mental retardation, autism, cerebral palsy and multiple sclerosis.
- NGOs promoting mental health in India are enlisted in Table 15.5.

Table 15.5: NGO's in India promoting mental health

Sl. no.	Place	Name of the NGO	Focus
1.	New Delhi	Sumaitri Voluntary Organization	NGOs with the primary focus on mental health and social service
		Sanjivani Society for Mental Health	
		Manas	
		Snehi	
		Aanchal Charitable Trust	
		Aasha Kiran	
		Indo Global Social Service Society (IGSSS)	
		The Earth Saviours Foundation	
		National Alliance for Access to Justice for Persons with Mental Illness	
		Nav Jyoti Center	
		Association for Advancement and Rehabilitation of Handicapped	
		Ashray Adhikar Abiyan	NGO's working for homeless children
		Sudhinalaya	
		Mother NGO (MNGO)	
		Servants of the People Society, Model School for Mentally Deficient Children, YMCA Institute for Special Education and Eclat Society for the Welfare of Mentally Retarded	School for mental retardation
		Parents Association for the Welfare of Mentally Handicapped	Vocational training for mental retardation
		Hindustan Scouts and Guides Association, Association for Social Health in India, Association of National Brotherhood for Social Welfare, Youth and Masses	Treatment and counseling center for drug deaddiction
		Jeevan Jyoti Missionaries of Charity	Care of mental illness and orthopedically handicapped individuals
		Forum for Autism and Action for Autism	Training and development of children with autism/developmental disorders
		Society of Social Services	Day care center for elders

Contd...

Sl. no.	Place	Name of the NGO	Focus
2.	Chennai	Banyan	Mental health
		Schizophrenia Research Foundation (SCARF)	Schizophrenia
		Ashaa Family	Psychiatric Rehabilitation
		Atma Nirbhar	Mental illness and employment projects
3.	Madurai	Akshaya trust	Helping out the homeless, sick, elders and mentally ill
4.	Coimbatore	HCA Mental Health Care Center	Care of mental health
5.	Kerala	Alzheimer's and related disorders society India	Dementia
6.	Bengaluru	White Swan Foundation	Knowledge services for mental health and well-being
		Amba for life	Economic empowerment of the intellectually challenged
		Athma Sakthi Vidhyalaya Society	Therapeutic community
		Banjara Academy	Counseling and mental health training
7.	Kolkata	Turning Point Mental Rehabilitation Center	Psychiatric rehabilitation
		Paripurnata, halfway home, center for psychosocial rehabilitation	
		Antara	
		Anjali	Mental health and human rights organization
8.	Goa	Sangath, improving health across the life-span	Mental health
9.	Bangladesh	Bangladesh Association for Child and Adolescent Mental Health (BACAMH)	Mental health of children and adolescence
10.	West Bengal	Manas	Society for mentally disturbed persons, their family and friends

AGENCIES/ORGANIZATION SUPPORTING TO PROMOTE MENTAL HEALTH—ABROAD

Agencies in Africa

- Farm Radio Integrated Mental Health Project
- Treatment Not Chains, Campaign to Raise Funds
- Mental Health Innovation Network Africa
- Neuro and Mental Health Organization
- African Mental Health Research Initiative (AMARI)
- Nairobi Parenting Clinic
- New life rehabilitation for those addicted to drugs or alcohol
- Community Association for Psychosocial Services (CAPS)
- Mentally Aware Initiative
- The Mandate Health Empowerment Initiative
- Sociotherapy Rwanda
- Mabel Mental Care Foundation, health care for the mentally challenged patients.
- Gede Foundation, bringing stigmatized health burdens out of the shadows, Mercy for Life Foundation.
- Friendship Bench Project, CBT for Depression
- Support for Addiction and Prevention
- Center for Child and Adolescent Mental Health University of Ibadan
- Clowns Without Borders South Africa
- Kamili Mental Health Organization
- Befrienders Uganda, Crisis Intervention and Suicide Prevention
- Habeeb Mental Health Foundation
- Thandanani Center for Persons with Severe Psychiatric Disability
- Healing Through Art, Stories from Swaziland
- Kenya Psychological Association
- Hugs for better Mental Health
- Reconnect-Health Development Initiative
- South African Federation for Mental Health
- Basic needs
- NASM Afrique—New Approach Mental Health Africa
- Talisman Foundation, temporary home and rehabilitation support for those with a mental illness
- Bring joy to needy

- My Mind My Funk, Mental Health Information and Support Hub—Mental Health in Primary Care Project
- Somalia Mental Health Foundation
- Alan J Flisher Center for Public Mental Health (CPMH)
- Community Mental Health Initiatives (CoMHI)
- Street Angels Foundation Uganda, to better the lives of slum and street children
- Hope and Health Vision, creating a better world for vulnerable children
- Trauma Center for Survivors of Violence and Torture
- Uvira Psycho-Social Rehabilitation Center
- Liberian Behavioral Health Services
- Open Society Initiative for Eastern Africa: Encouraging open and informed dialogue about issues of public importance
- Enabling Access to Mental Health, Mental Health Coalition Sierra Leone
- Mental Health Awareness Nigeria, fighting stigma
- Zimbabwe National Association for Mental Health
- Babungo Integrated Mental Health Care (BIMEHC)
- HOPE organization for Chronic Disease and Mental Health Development
- For All Africa Foundation, advocacy and support for people with a mental illness
- Normal Difference Mental Health Project, a group of mental health activists
- Kintampo Project, improving community mental health services
- Carter Center building Mental Health Care in Liberia
- Mental Health Society Ghana (MEHSOG)
- General Assistance and Volunteer Organization (GAVO)
- Bhaso, support groups for people living with HIV
- Horizon, Social Assistance Development Organization
- GSH-HIV Mental Health Group
- One Mind Kenya, Mental Health Awareness Campaign
- Lagos State Mental Health Team
- Mental Health Foundation Nigeria
- African Palliative Care Association
- Cape Mental Health Society
- Comcare, affordable, stable accommodation for adults with chronic psychiatric disabilities
- International Network Toward Alternatives and Recovery (INTAR)
- Central Gauteng Mental Health Society
- National Organization of Users and Survivors of Psychiatry Rwanda
- Kenya Society for the Mentally Handicapped (KSMH)
- Youth on the Move, Empower Talents with Epilepsy
- Tiyatin Health
- Regional Psychosocial Support Initiative for Children
- Aanhouwen, Work and Care Center
- South African Depression and Anxiety Group
- Africa Mental Health Foundation
- Community Mental Health and Psychiatry

Agencies in USA

- The American Psychiatric Association
- Orchid Mental Health Policy Global
- Substance Abuse and Mental Health Services Administration
- A Billion Minds and Lives
- The National Association of Psychiatric Health Systems
- Me too Orchestra, music organization created for individuals with mental illnesses
- The National Alliance on Mental Illness
- American Psychological Association
- Psychological artificial intelligence for mental health care
- The Joint Commission
- Crazywise documentary film on new ways of recovery
- Parity Implementation Coalition
- Gaza Mental Health Foundation
- International Bipolar Organization
- Heart Mind International, psychosocial services and mental health at South Asia
- Agency for Health care Research and Quality
- Project Semicolon, faith-based NGO in love and hope
- American Association of Suicidology
- Western Mass, Recovery Learning Community
- American Psychiatric Nurses Association
- Haitian Mental Health (HMH) Network
- Anxiety Disorders Association of America
- Yale University Global Mental Health Program
- Bazelon Center for Mental Health Law
- Centers for Disease Control and Prevention
- Postpartum Support International (PSI)
- Centers for Medicare and Medicaid Services
- Global Mental Health News website
- Depressive and Bipolar Support Alliance
- ASHA International, Promoting Mental Health Awareness, Hope and Holistic Wellness
- Institute of Medicine
- The NGO Committee on Mental Health in consultative relationship with United Nations
- Mental Health America (previously National Mental Health Association)
- International Mental Health Research Organization (IMHRO)
- Mental Health Liaison Group
- The Marcé Society for Perinatal Mental Health
- National Association for Rural Mental Health

- Trust Circle—International Peer-Centered Mental Health Network
- National Association of Anorexia Nervosa and Associated Disorders
- Psychologists for Social Responsibility
- National Association of Country Behavioral Health and Developmental Disability Directors
- Center for Victims of Torture, care for those who have been tortured and advocacy
- National Association of State Mental Health Program Directors
- National Center for Health Statistics
- The Citizens Commission on Human Rights (CCHR)
- National Council for Community Behavioral Health care
- Peers Envisioning and Engaging in Recovery Services (PEERS)
- National Guidelines Clearinghouse
- The Chester M Pierce, MD Division of Global Psychiatry
- National Institute of Mental Health
- International Association for Women's Mental Health
- The National Institute of Alcoholism and Alcohol Abuse
- The Minds Foundation, Mental Health Care in Rural India
- National Institute on Drug Abuse
- Peter Alderman Foundation
- The World Mental Health Organization
- The Siwe Project—Promoting mental health education and awareness among the global black community
- Salus World, Psychosocial Care after Emergencies
- International Medical Corps, Mental Health Program

Agencies in Australia

- Mandala Foundation
- Mental Health First Aid Australia
- Asia Australia Mental Health
- Prahran Mission
- International Association for Youth in Mental Health
- Center for International Mental Health
- Trauma Recovery Blog of Eva Alisic

Agencies in Europe

- Lisbon Institute of Global Mental Health
- International Psychosocial Organization
- World on the Ground—Mental Health Platform
- Fracarita International for Mental Health Projects World Wide
- Samaritans—24 hours Emotional Support Helpline
- Global Alliance of Mental Illness Advocacy Networks
- Center for Crisis Psychology
- International Society for Psychological and Social Approaches to Psychosis
- Psycho-Rehabilitation Center for Victims of Violence, Torture and Stress Impact
- Gulbenkian Global Mental Health Platform
- Global Mental Health-Map
- Epapsy
- Mental Disability Advocacy Center
- Cares, Brothers of Charity and Mental Health Care
- St Camille de Lellis Foundation—Psychiatric Rehabilitation
- Association for the Improvement of Mental Health Programs
- Antares Foundation
- Reference Centers for Psychosocial Support
- Mental Disability Rights Initiatives Serbia

Agencies in UK

- Promise Global (Alliance of humane care in mental health)
- International Mental Health Collaborative Network
- Clowns without Borders (joy with the children in crisis)
- Men Tell Health (concern on men and mental health)
- Social felt, touch and care
- Richmond Psychosocial Foundation
- International Center for Recovery Action in Education, Research and Practice
- McPin Foundation—Mental Health Research
- Amadou UK Mental Health Matters
- Careif—International Mental Health Charity
- Black Dog Tribe—social place to share mental health issues.

ISSUES IN MENTAL HEALTH NURSING FOR SPECIAL POPULATIONS

Mental Health Problems in Women

World Health Organization (WHO) states the mental health facts about women as listed below:

- Unipolar depression might be 2nd leading cause of worldwide disability by 2020, which is twice commonly seen in women.
- One in five men and one in 12 women develop dependence to alcohol during their lives in the developed countries.
- Lifetime prevalence of violence against women is 16–50%. In the lifetime of women, at least one in five suffers from rape or attempted rape.
- Increased prevalence rate of sexual violence in women might increase the chances of Post-traumatic Stress Disorder (PTSD) in women.

- 41.9% of depressive disorders are due to neuropsychiatric disorders, especially among women when compared to men (29.3%).
- Leading mental health problems of elders (majority are women) are depression, dementia and organic brain syndrome.

Premenstrual Syndrome

Definition

It is the combination of physical, emotional, mood and behavioral disturbances present in women before few days of menstrual flow due to the interaction of neurochemicals in brain and the sex hormones.

Epidemiology

Around 80% of women experience premenstrual syndrome, in which 2–5% will experience severe symptoms.

Clinical Features

Psychological symptoms such as irritability, anger, high level of stress/fear/anxiety, restlessness, depression, being more sensitive, episodes of crying and presence of mood swings. Physical symptoms such as weight gain, fatigue, breast tenderness, ache, bloating, sleep disturbances and changes in appetite (over craving of food or loss of appetite).

Treatment

Mostly natural methods such as exercise, emotional support, relaxation, decreased intake of salt, quit smoking/alcohol is sufficient. Medications are required only if the symptoms are complicated. Antianxiety drugs, drugs to suppress ovulation/oral contraceptives, analgesics and diuretics (decrease the water retention) might be helpful.

Premenstrual Dysphoric Disorder

Definition

A severe form and disabling extension of premenstrual syndrome.

Epidemiology

Prevalence of Premenstrual Dysphoric Disorder (PMDD) is estimated to affect 5–8% of menstruating women.

Clinical Features

In addition to the clinical features of premenstrual syndrome, extreme mood shifts which interrupts the work and the relationship issues, may be present.

Treatment

- **Antidepressants:** Selective Serotonin Reuptake Inhibitors (SSRI) such as fluoxetine and sertraline will decrease the emotional symptoms, food cravings, fatigue and sleep pattern disturbances.
- **Nutritional supplements:** Taking 1200 mg of dietary calcium will reduce the symptoms of premenstrual dysphoric disorder. Intake of magnesium, vitamin B6 and L-tryptophan is also helpful to decrease the symptoms of premenstrual dysphoric disorder.
- **Birth control pills:** Consuming the birth control pills with no pill-free interval or else with a shortened pill-free interval will decrease the symptoms of Premenstrual syndrome and Premenstrual dysphoric disorder in some women.
- **Life style modification:** Quit smoking, caffeine and alcohol. Avoid stressful triggers. Practice regular exercises, yoga and meditation.

Puerperal Blues (or) Postpartum Blues (or) Baby Blues

Definition

It is a less severe form of postpartum depression. Onset of depressive episode happens within few days after the delivery of baby and the depressive symptoms reduce within one or two weeks.

Epidemiology

Around 70% of women who delivered baby suffer with postpartum blues.

Clinical Features

Crying spells, irritability, fatigue, anxiety, restlessness, insomnia, mood changes, poor concentration, sadness, etc.

Treatment

Eating a balanced diet, relaxation techniques and to ensure psychological support.

Postpartum Depression

Definition

Episodes of depression occurs after the delivery. If the depression episode is present during pregnancy and within one year after the delivery, it is termed as perinatal depression.

Epidemiology

About 13% of women who delivered baby suffers with postpartum depression.

Risk factors

low self-esteem, poor social support, stressful life events, depression or anxiety during pregnancy, low socioeconomic status, poor relationship with husband, negative cognitive attributions, history of depression, etc.

Etiology

Hormonal changes (decreased estrogen), unbearable stressors, sleep deprivation, fragile baby, difficulty in breast feeding and lack of family support, etc.

Clinical Features

It includes all the classic features of depression. Edinburgh Postnatal Depression Scale can be used as a screening tool.

Treatment

- **Antidepressants:** Tricyclic antidepressants such as nortriptyline and desipramine, Selective Serotonin Reuptake Inhibitors (SSRIs) group of antidepressants such as fluoxetine and sertraline, Serotonin and Norepinephrine Reuptake Inhibitors (SNRIs) group of antidepressants such as venlafaxine and duloxetine are useful to treat postpartum depression.
- **Psychological treatment:** Interpersonal psychotherapy, cognitive behavioral psychotherapy, couples therapy and family therapy are helpful.
- **Nutritional supplements and herbal supplement:** Adequate intake of vitamin B_2 (Riboflavin) will prevent the risk of developing postpartum depression. Diet rich in omega 3 fatty acids will reduce the symptoms of postpartum depression. Herbal supplements such as St. John wort is useful to treat postpartum depression.

Comparison of postpartum blues and postpartum depression is given in Table 15.6.

Table 15.6 Comparison of postpartum blues and postpartum depression

Characteristics	Puerperal blues (or) postpartum blues (or) baby blues	Postpartum depression
Onset	Within a week	Weeks to months
Duration	Days to weeks	Weeks to year if not treated
History of mood disorder	Absent	Mostly present
Family history of mood disorder	Absent	Mostly present
Anhedonia	No	Often
Sleep disturbances	Sometimes present	Mostly present
Guilt feeling	Absent/mild	Excessive and often seen
Thoughts to harm baby	Rare	Often
Mood liability	Yes	Often (sometimes with unipolar depression)
Tearful eyes	Yes	Yes

Postpartum Psychosis (or) Puerperal Psychosis

Definition

It is a serious mental illness in which the episodes of depression occur after the delivery. Here, depressive symptoms accompany psychotic illness.

Epidemiology

About 13% of women who have delivered baby suffer with postpartum depression.

Risk factors

Family history of mental illness, history of depression or bipolar disorder or schizophrenia, trauma during pregnancy, prenatal depression, autoimmune thyroid dysfunction, abnormal mutation of chromosome 16, and complications related to delivery, etc.

Clinical Features

Hallucinations, delusions, manic mood, low mood, suspiciousness, restlessness, confusion, phobia, etc.

Treatment

Antidepressants, antipsychotics and mood stabilizers (lithium) can be administered. Psychotherapy such as cognitive behavior therapy is useful. Electroconvulsive therapy (ECT) is indicated if there is a presence of strong suicidal risk.

Prognosis

Symptoms may be seen from 2 to 12 weeks. It takes 6 months to year for complete recovery. It is considered complicated mental illness when compared with postpartum depression.

Mental Health Problems in Elders

World Health Organization (WHO) in 2017, stated that approximately 15% of elders suffer with mental illness. WHO also added that, there is 6.6% disability (Disability Adjusted Life Years—DALY) among elders. Unipolar depression occurs in 7% of general population and it accounts for 5.7% individuals living with disability. Around 50 million people worldwide are living with dementia and it is expected to increase to 82 million in 2030 and 152 million by 2050.

Chicago Methodist Senior Services, USA states that there are four warning signs that need to be observed earlier to identify the mental health problems as listed below:

1. Memory problems
2. Social withdrawal
3. Changes in personal care
4. Changes in mood

Delirium, dementia, depression and paranoid disorders are common mental disorders seen in elders. Delirium and dementia have been described in Chapter 12 (organic brain disorders). Depression is described in Chapter 7 (Mood disorders). Paranoid disorders have been described in chapter 6 (Schizophrenia). Anxiety and stress might be comorbid disorders among elders who are suffering with depression. Late-onset schizophrenia may also occur among elders. The causes of depression in elders is loneliness, widowed/separated spouse/death of spouse, retirement, loss of income, health deterioration, presence of physical illness, sensory deficits, low social status, etc. Antidepressants and psychosocial therapies are helpful.

Mental Health Problems in Children and Adolescent

The common psychiatric illness in children and adolescent age group are mental retardation, autism spectrum disorder (ASD), Attention Deficit Hyperactive Disorders (ADHD), anxiety disorders, eating disorders, mood disorders, schizophrenia, Oppositional Defiant Disorder (ODD), Tourette syndrome and conduct disorder. The warning signs of poor mental health in children are mood changes, behavioral changes, lack of concentration, unexplained weight loss, self-harm, verbalizing more physical symptoms and influence of substance abuse. Counseling, psychotherapy and psychotropic agents based on the diagnosis are helpful. The above said childhood disorders have been described in Chapter 11 (Child Psychiatry). Child Abuse has been explained in Chapter 11 (Child Psychiatry).

VICTIMS OF VIOLENCE

Violence is the expression of physical force or verbal force toward self or other with intention to hurt or to cause pain. Domestic violence (or) domestic abuse (or) spouse abuse (or) intimate partner abuse is the violence that takes place against the women by men/husband.

World Health Organization states that, one in three women (or) girls experience the physical (or) sexual violence in their lifetime, mostly by her husband/intimate partner. Only 52% of married women can take their own decisions in regard with sexual relations, use contraceptive devices and take health care. Percentage of women who experience the physical or sexual violence by the intimate partner or husband in their life period ranges from 15% to 17%

United Nations General Assembly has designated 25th November as the International Day for the Elimination of Violence Against Women as depicted in Figure 15.4.

The various forms of violence against women are as follows:

- Honor killings

Figure 15.4: International day to eliminate violence against women

- Female genital mutilation
- Trafficking
- Force and early marriage
- Intimate partner violence includes physical, sexual and emotional abuse.
- Sexual violence due to conflicts between husband and wife.

The health consequences of violence are as follows:

- Physical injuries
- Death
- Sexually transmitted diseases
- Unintended pregnancies
- Depression
- Post-traumatic stress disorder
- Harmful use of substances

Violence against women is preventable and the risk factors at multiple levels have been explained in Table 15.7.

Cycle of Violence

Dr Lenore Walker in 1979 developed the cycle of violence. It has three phases (Figure 15.5) as mentioned below:

Table 15.7: Risk factors and interventions for violence against women at various levels

Level	Risk factor	Interventions
Individual	History of violence in childhood	Parenting program to prevent the maltreatment of child
Relationship	Men have more control over women	Create the gender equality attitudes to men
Family	Inequality in gender norms that create violence against women	Steps taken to promote equality in gender norms
Community/ Society	Lack of education and employment opportunities for women	Policies and law is made to promote the education and employment chances to women

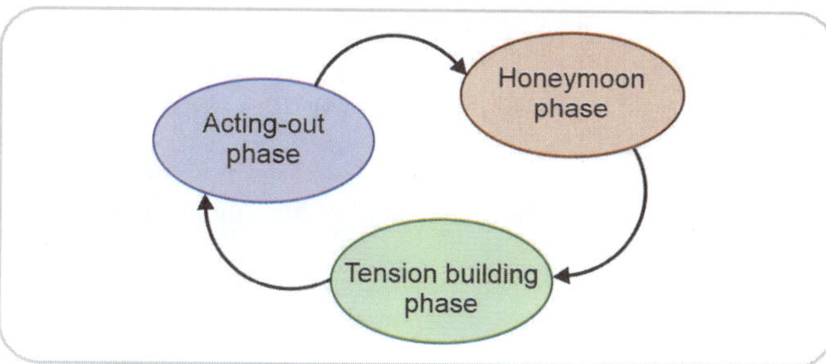

Figure 15.5: Cycle of violence

Phase 1: Tension building phase

- **Build-up:** Tension between the individuals in the relationship will rise and abusing each other begins.
- **Stand-over:** A threat or frightening takes place for the individual who experiences the abuse. Behavior of the abuser increases and the victim feels that the release of tension is impossible one.

Phase 2: Acute explosion (or) Acting out phase

The violence will reach peak level in this phase. Perpetrator might experience a release of tension and this behavior might become habitual.

Phase 3: Honeymoon Stage

- **Remorse:** Here, perpetrator may feel ashamed, withdrawn in oneself and try to justify the actions to self and others.
- **Pursuit:** Perpetrator may promise to never be violent again and perpetrator also tries to say that the violence happened due to alcohol, job stress or some other cause, etc. Perpetrator try to compensate the violence by providing gift or helping out the victim well. At this point, the victim who experiences violence, feels confused.
- **Denial phase:** Both the individuals in the relationship might refuse about the abuse and violence. Intimacy might increase and they live happy during this phase.

Over the period of time, this phase may pass and the cycle may begin again.

Role of nurse to prevent the violence against women is to give the comprehensive health care to the survivors. Nurse has to gather data, prevalence in regard with violence against women. Nurse has to foster and inform the preventable programs and help out in framing the policies to prevent the violence against women. Nurse has to play the role of an advocate to voice out the violence against women as a public health problem.

PSYCHIATRIC ASPECTS OF HIV/AIDS

Acquired Immunodeficiency Syndrome (AIDS) is caused by Human Immunodeficiency Virus (HIV). The virus is called retrovirus because the molecular structure always keeps on changing so no medication has been found to cure AIDS, however, the life span of AIDS patient can be increased by taking the antiretroviral (ART) drugs such as didanosine, lamivudine, stavudine, zidovudine, doravirine, nevirapine, etc. **World Health Organization** insists to start the ART drugs irrespective of their CD4 count. WHO also recommends to start the pre-exposure prophylaxis to the individuals at substantial risk of HIV.

National AIDS Control Society (NACO) initiated the Integrated Testing and Counseling Center (ITCC) in 1977 in the government hospitals. Their main functions are conducting diagnostic tests, creating awareness in regard with the modes of HIV transmission and promoting the behavioral changes to decrease the vulnerability and to promote the treatment services.

Around 60–70% of patients with HIV infection suffer with AIDS related dementia. They suffer with forgetfulness, lack of concentration, mental slowness, disorientation and problem with short-term memory. Around 10% of HIV patients present with neurological complaints. The comorbid psychiatric disorders among AIDS patients are depression, mood disorders, adjustment disorders, anxiety disorders and presence of psychotic symptoms.

Role of Psychiatric Nurse

Nurse has to provide counseling to the patient before and after testing the HIV. Nurse needs to assess the patient's risk of getting HIV infection and educate the patient to reduce the transmission of HIV infection. Psychiatric nurse should watch the HIV patients for signs indicating the mental status, emotional and negative behavioral changes. Early treatment is the best way to reduce the impact of the behavioral/psychological changes in HIV patients in order to promote their sense of well-being. The multimodal approach such as antiretroviral medications, symptomatic management, treatment of comorbid neurological/psychiatric disorders, counseling services, etc. are helpful to take care of the patient with HIV infection.

SUMMARY

- **Community Mental Health Centers Act (1963)** initiated by 35th United States President John F. Kennedy brought a change of shifting the mental health care from hospitals to the community.
- **Community mental health nursing** is defined as, 'decentralized pattern of rendering mental health services/care to the needy in the community, further it focus on prevention of mental illness, promotion of mental health and rehabilitation of patients with mental disorder in the community'.
- Lack of trained manpower, budget constraints, lack of knowledge and skills of general physicians, poor access to PHC's, Persistence of stigma and discrimination about mental illness are the **issues prevailing in community mental health nursing**.
- **Development of community mental health services categorized as** Colonial Period (Before Independence), after Independence, 1961–1969, 1970–1982, 1987–2012 and 2013–2020.
- **Mental Health Action Plan by WHO have six core principles** such as universal health coverage, evidence-based practice, human rights, life course approach, multisectoral approach and empowerment of patients with mental disorders and psychosocial disabilities.
- **NIMHANS, Bengaluru developed the alternative measures instead of hospital-based care such as** Domiciliary Care Program, Extensive use of outdoor services, organizing short-term course to private general practitioners, extension program by satellite clinics, promotion of mental health by training the school teachers with regard to mental health care, training of village leaders, student volunteers, tertiary. Student development program, Involvement of Integrated Child Developmental Service (ICDS) personnel in children mental health care and Nongovernmental voluntary organization.
- **Institutionalization** means treating the patients in psychiatric ward after the admission procedure. Patients will be in the custodial care.
- **Deinstitutionalization** means treating the patients in the community area whereas the patient will visit the OPD's or Primary health centers or day care centers or short stay units for the continuity of treatment process.
- **National Mental Health Program** was launched in 1982, Revised National Mental Health Program was launched in 2003, and District Mental Health Program (DMHP) was launched in 1996.
- Preventive Psychiatry is defined as, 'services rendered in the community in order to prevent the mental illness and promote the mental health'.
- **Gerald Caplan** (1960) described the levels of prevention such as primordial, primary, secondary and tertiary.
- Rehabilitation is defined as the restoration of the person's health to his/her former capacity.
- **Rehabilitative nursing** focuses on preventive activities, maintenance activities and restoration activities.
- **Psychiatric rehabilitation** helps to gain independence, reduce the disability, to build the coping skills/social functioning and to get good psychological support.
- **Areas of rehabilitation** is categorized into domestic, occupational and social aspects. The other eight areas are psychiatric, health or medical, basic living skills, social skills, vocational skills, educational skills, financial skills, community and legal aspects.
- **Rehabilitation team** consists of psychiatric/mental health nurse, psychiatrist, clinical psychologist/counselor, psychiatric social worker, occupational therapist, recreational therapist and other health professionals involved in mental health rehabilitation.
- **Psychiatric Rehabilitation Association (PRA)** at Virginia states that, there are seven domains for the successful rehabilitation process such as interpersonal competencies, professional role, community integration, assessment, planning and outcomes, strategies for promoting resilience and recovery, systems competencies, supporting health and wellness.
- The **governmental organizations** helping to promote the mental health are Central or State Mental Health Authority, National Human Rights Commission, National Mental Health Program and District Mental Health Program.
- **Mental health problems in women** are premenstrual syndrome, puerperal blues (or) postpartum blues (or) baby blues, postpartum psychosis (or) Puerperal Psychosis.
- Delirium, Dementia, Depression and paranoid disorders are common **mental disorders seen in elders.**
- The common **psychiatric illness in children** and adolescent age group was mental retardation, Autism Spectrum Disorder (ASD), Attention-deficit/hyperactivity disorder (ADHD), anxiety disorders, eating disorders, mood disorders, schizophrenia, oppositional defiant disorder (ODD), Tourette syndrome and conduct disorder.
- International day to eliminate violence against women is celebrated on 25th November, every year.
- Dr Lenore Walker in 1979 developed the **cycle of violence—tension-building phase, acting out phase and honeymoon phase.**
- **National AIDS Control Society (NACO)** initiated the Integrated Testing and Counseling Center (ITCC) in 1977 at government hospitals to diagnose the HIV infection, counsel and treat the patients living with HIV.

ASSESS YOURSELF

Long Answer Questions

1. Write the principles and issues in community mental health nursing. Explain the development of community mental health services in India.
2. Discuss the levels of prevention in psychiatry.
3. Explain the goals, principles, domains and role of nurse in psychiatric rehabilitation.

Shotrt Answer Questions

1. Define Community Mental Health Nursing.
2. Define psychiatric rehabilitation.

Short Notes

1. Revised National Mental Health Program
2. Institutionalization versus Deinstitutionalization
3. Role of nurse in rehabilitation
4. Mental health services by various agencies
5. Mental health problems in women
6. Mental health issues among elders
7. Mental health issues among children
8. District Mental Health Program (DMHP)
9. Psychiatric aspects of HIV/AIDS
10. Community facilities in psychiatry

Multiple Choice Questions

1. **Revised National Mental Health Program was launched in ______.**
   a. 1996 b. 1982
   c. 2003 d. 2005
2. **________ level of prevention focuses on the prevention of risk factors.**
   a. Primordial b. Primary
   c. Secondary d. Tertiary
3. **The other names of postpartum blues ___________.**
   a. Puerperal blues b. Baby Blues
   c. Both a and b d. Premenstrual syndrome
4. **District Mental Health Program (DMHP) was launched in _______________.**
   a. 1996 b. 1982
   c. 2003 d. 2005
5. **Perpetrator may promise to never be violent again in ________ phase of violence cycle.**
   a. Tension-building phase b. Acting out
   c. Honeymoon stage d. None of these
6. **National AIDS Control Society (NACO) initiated the Integrated Testing and Counseling Center (ITCC) on __________.**
   a. 1977 b. 1966
   c. 1955 d. 1982
7. **Anhedonia is present in________.**
   a. Puerperal blues b. Puerperal depression
   c. Both a and b d. None of these
8. **First mental asylum was started in Madras in_____.**
   a. 1792 b. 1794
   c. 1894 d. 1795
9. **________level of prevention focuses on psychiatric rehabilitation.**
   a. Primordial b. Primary
   c. Secondary d. Tertiary
10. **Community Mental Health Centers Act was started in**
    a. 1992 b. 1994
    c. 1999 d. 1963

ANSWER KEY				
1. c	2. a	3. c	4. a	5. c
6. a	7. b	8. b	9. d	10. d

Notes

Do you Know?

- Anaclitic depression means the infant will develop the symptoms of crying, lack of sleep, weight loss, developmental delay, apathy and will become susceptible to get infection followed by the death of mother.
- Lesions in the left frontal lobe of the brain are seen in post-stroke depression, whereas lesions in the right frontal lobe are seen in post-stroke mania.
- Individuals have higher risk of depression during cocaine withdrawal.
- Thought stopping techniques will be helpful for the long-lasting auditory hallucination.
- Age of onset for childhood schizophrenia is around 6 years and age of onset for late onset schizophrenia is more than 45 years of age.
- Drug amoxapine has both antipsychotic and antidepressant effects.
- Use of tricyclic antidepressants has to be avoided in patients with human immunodeficiency virus infection due to the increased risk of oral candidiasis.
- Sexual dysfunction related to the alcohol and psychotropics is listed in the following table:

Alcohol and psychotropic agents	Sexual dysfunction
Alcohol	Prolong the penile erection with no ejaculation
Antipsychotics (thioridazine)	Retrograde ejaculation
Tricyclic antidepressants	Delay the ejaculation
Selective serotonin reuptake inhibitors (SSRI)	Delay the orgasm

- SSRI and Clomipramine are effective in the treatment of obsessive compulsive disorder (OCD).
- Alprazolam is the benzodiazepine which has antidepressant effect.
- Fluoxetine (SSRI) has the longest half-life (4–6 days).
- Imipramine is the drug of choice for nocturnal enuresis.
- Imipramine and fluoxetine in smaller doses are helpful in treating panic attack.
- Monoamine Oxidase Inhibitors (MAOIs) should not be given with amphetamine or any Central Nervous System acting drug because they lead to hypertension.
- Tricyclic antidepressants (TCAs) are contraindicated in Narrow Angle Closure Glaucoma.
- Electroconvulsive therapy (ECT) is highly effective in patients suffering from psychotic depression with suicidal risk and patients with catatonic schizophrenia.
- Headache is the most common complaint by the patients after ECT.
- Drug Lithium has to be avoided before ECT because it will reduce the seizure threshold and also cause postictal delirium.
- Ugo Cerletti and Lucio Bini were the first psychiatrists who used ECT for patients with schizophrenia. Jarvie was the first psychiatrist who used ECT for treating depressive patients. Friedman and Wilcox were the first psychiatrists to use unilateral ECT.
- Drug Donepezil can be used to decrease the cognitive side effects after ECT.
- Thiamine improves the post-ECT recovery.
- D' Elia Position is the best site to place the electrodes in unilateral ECT.
- Clozapine and Olanzapine are the only antipsychotics which are helpful to treat both positive and negative symptoms in the same patient.

- Dopamine receptor blockage due to antipsychotics leads to suppression of testosterone in males, hyperprolactinemia (breast enlargement) and galactorrhea (discharge of milk from breast) in females.
- Use of Carbamazepine and Sodium Valproate in the first trimester of pregnancy will increase the risk of neural tube defects in fetus.
- Use of lithium in pregnancy has risk of Ebstein anomaly in fetus.
- Lithium is the drug of choice for treatment of resistant depression or refractory depression.
- Long term use of Lithium might cause renal side effects and hypothyroidism.
- Use of Methylphenidine in children with attention deficit hyperactive disorder (ADHD) may cause Tourette syndrome and growth suppression.
- Amphetamine is used for the treatment of ADHD, endogenous obesity and narcolepsy.
- Amphetamine will decrease the effect of hypoglycemic agents.
- Nurse has to administer the long acting psychotropics (Flupenthixol decanoate, Fluphenazine decanoate, Haloperidol decanoate, Risperidone decanoate, Pipothiazine decanoate, etc.) in a Z track method of Intramuscular injection (deep IM injection) in order to prevent the skin irritation.

Syndromes in Psychiatry

Punch-drunk syndrome or boxer's syndrome or dementia pugilistica, also called Chronic Traumatic Encephalopathy (CTE), is commonly seen in alcoholics and boxers due to the repeated cerebral concussions which result in weakness of limb, unsteady gait and mental dullness.

Ekbom syndrome or delusional parasitosis is a mental disorder characterized by patient's conviction that he or she is infested with parasites.

Amotivational syndrome is similar to the signs of depression in which individual lacks interest to complete the task, poor concentration and sense of apathy is seen. This syndrome is commonly seen among patients with Marijuana abuse.

De clerambault syndrome or erotomania is a delusional idea in which an individual thinks that a higher professional and social standard person is in love with him/her.

Cotard syndrome or corpse syndrome or cotard delusion is a rare psychiatric disorder in which the person strongly believes that he is dead or does not exist or has lost the internal organs or blood.

Clumsy child syndrome is a term not in use nowadays, instead the term has been changed to Developmental Coordination Disorder (DCD) or Dyspraxia which means perceptomotor dysfunction characterized by difficulty in jumping, delay in sitting and walking.

Savant syndrome or idiot savant or autistic savant is defined as individuals with significant mental disabilities able to demonstrate certain abilities excess than the average. For example, artistic ability, doing fast calculation, good music ability, etc.

Empty nest syndrome denotes the symptoms of depression elicited due to the loneliness or isolation.

Ganser syndrome or nonsense syndrome or balderdash syndrome, syndrome of approximate answers or hysterical pseudodementia or prison psychosis is defined as rare dissociative disorder characterized by saying the approximate answers to the question raised along with other dissociative symptoms such as amnesia, fugue and visual pseudohallucination.

Diogenes syndrome or **senile squalor syndrome refers to** presence of self-neglect, withdrawal from others and tendency to hold the rubbish things due to the dysfunction of frontal lobe.

Other syndromes which have been discussed in the chapters and Glossary are as follows:

- **DiGeorge syndrome** or Velocardiofacial syndrome or Shprintzen syndrome or Conotruncal anomaly face syndrome or Takao syndrome or Sedlackova syndrome or Cayler cardiofacial syndrome or 22q 11.2 deletion syndrome
- **Othello syndrome** or delusion of infidelity or Delusion of jealousy or Morbid Jealousy
- **Alice in Wonderland syndrome** or Todd's syndrome or Lilliputian hallucination or Dysmetropsia
- Asperger's syndrome
- Capgra syndrome
- Child battered syndrome or child abuse
- Down syndrome
- Munchausen syndrome by proxy or factitious disorders
- Depersonalization—derealization syndrome
- Fetal alcohol syndrome
- Fragile X syndrome
- Kluver-Bucy syndrome

- Korsakoff syndrome
- Lacunar syndrome or status lacunaris or Lacunar state
- Lesch-Nyhan syndrome
- Neuroleptic malignant Syndrome
- Night eating syndrome
- Pickwickian syndrome or obesity hypoventilation syndrome
- Prader willi syndrome
- Premenstrual syndrome
- Rett's syndrome
- Serotonin syndrome
- Sun downing syndrome
- Tourette syndrome
- Van gogh syndrome
- Widower's syndrome

Psychotropic Drugs

Name of the drugs	Dosage and route	Action	Indications	Contraindications	Side effects	Nurse's responsibility
Chlorpromazine ***Trade name:*** Largactil ***Classification:*** Dopamine receptor antagonist ***Functional Classification:*** Antipsychotics ***Chemical Classification:*** Phenothiazines	***Oral*** 300–1500 mg/day ***IM*** 25–100 mg/day **Frequency** bd or tds	Depresses the cerebral cortex, hypothalamus and limbic system which controls the activity, aggression and blocks neurotransmission produced by dopamine at synapse and also exhibits a strong alpha adrenergic anti-cholinergic action.	Schizophrenia, Schizoaffective disorder, Mania, depression, Delusional disorder, Delirium, dementia, Tourette syndrome, Huntington's disease, Borderline personality disorder, Substance and induced psychotic disorder	Comatose state, myelosuppression, severe cardiovascular disease, central nervous system depression, subcortical brain damage, liver damage, closed angle glaucoma, hypertension or hypotension	***Central nervous system:*** EPS-akathisia, dystonia, tardive dyskinesia, Parkinson's disease. ***Cardiovascular system:*** Orthostatic hypotension, ECG changes, tachycardia ***Eye:*** Blurred vision, glaucoma ***Gastrointestinal system:*** Nausea, vomiting, Diarrhea ***Genitourinary system:*** Urinary retention, enuresis, amenorrhea, impotence ***Hematology:*** Anemia, leucopenia, leukocytosis, agranulocytosis ***Integumentary system:*** Rash, dermatitis ***Respiratory system:*** Dyspnea, respiratory depression	***Assess or Monitor*** • Patient's behavior and emotional status. • Extrapyramidal symptoms (EPS) • Blood pressure for hypotension • Complete Blood Count (CBC) to explore blood dyscrasias • Patient producing fine tongue movement to evaluate the signs of tardive dyskinesia. • Serum drug level. (Therapeutic serum level is 50–300 mcg/mL. Toxic serum level is >750 mcg/mL). ***Patient Teaching*** • Advise to take high fiber diet and more intake of water. • Avoid excessive exposure to sunlight while on drug and use protective sunscreens. • Advise the patient to get up from the bed slowly. ***Miscellaneous*** • Don't give this drug subcutaneously because it causes severe tissue necrosis • Avoid skin contact with oral concentrate and syrup to prevent contact dermatitis. • Dilute the injection with Normal saline to prevent irritation at the injection site.

Name of the drugs	Dosage	Action	Indications	Contraindications	Side effects	Nurse's responsibility

Haloperidol
 	
Trade name:
Serenace
 	
Classification:
Dopamine receptor antagonist
 	
Functional Classification:
Typical antipsychotics
 	
Chemical Classification:
Butyrophenone
	Oral
	5 mg
	
	Parental
	5–100 mg
		Antipsychotic, Antiemetic and Antidyskinetic agent which blocks postsynaptic dopamine receptors, interrupts nerve impulse movement and raises the turnover of dopamine in the brain.	Schizophrenia, Schizoaffective disorder, Mania, depression, Delusional disorder, Borderline personality disorder, Substance induced psychotic disorder, Delirium, Dementia, Tourette's syndrome, Huntington's disease.	Angle-closure Glaucoma, Central nervous System depression, Myelosuppression, Parkinson's disease, Severe cardiac problems, hepatic disease	***Central nervous system:***
					EPS-akathisia, dystonia, tardive dyskinesia, pseudo-Parkinsonism, drowsiness, headache.
					Seizures, neuroleptic malignant syndrome.
					
					Cardiovascular system:
					Orthostatic hypotension, Hypertension, ECG changes, Tachycardia.
					
					Eye: Blurred vision, glaucoma, dry eyes
					
					Gastrointestinal system: Dry mouth, nausea, vomiting, anorexia, constipation, diarrhea, jaundice, weight gain, hepatitis.
					
					Genitourinary system:
					Urinary retention, dysuria, enuresis, impotence, amenorrhea
					
					Integumentary system:
					Rash, dermatitis.
					
					Respiratory system:
					Laryngospasm, dyspnea, respiratory depression
						Assess or monitor
						• Patient's behavior and emotional status.
						• Extrapyramidal symptoms (EPS)
						• Blood pressure in standing and lying posture
						• Monitor the patient for fine tongue movements, mask like facial expression, rigidity, and tremors.
						• Serum drug level.
						  ▪ Drug therapeutic serum level is 0.2–1 mcg/mL
						  ▪ Toxic serum level >1 mcg/mL.
						
						Patient teaching
						• Avoid alcohol during therapy.
						• Avoid exposure to sunlight and any condition may cause dehydration.
						• Take sips of water to prevent dry mouth.
						• Avoid hot water bath to prevent the hypotension.

Name of the drugs	Dosage	Action	Indications	Contraindications	Side effects	Nurse's responsibility
Quetiapine ***Trade name:*** Seroquel ***Classification:*** Atypical Antipsychotic agent ***Chemical Classification:*** Dibenzothiazepine	***Adults*** 300–400 mg /day ***Children and adolescents*** 100–350 mg/day Route Oral	Combination of dopamine type 2 (D2) and serotonin type 2 (5-HT2) antagonisms.	• Schizophrenia • Schizoaffective disorders • Autism • Bipolar disorders • Mania and Psychosis.	***Be cautious*** in Parkinson's disease, hemodynamic instability, previous myocardial infarction, Increased cholesterol level in blood, thyroid problems, seizures, renal impairment, respiratory disease. ***Not to be used in patients with*** hypersensitivity to blood dyscrasias, bone marrow suppression, severe hepatic dysfunction or coma.	• Excess sleep • Weight gain • Headache • Increased pulse rate • Palpitations • Dizziness • Rashes • Blurred vision • Abdominal pain • Postural hypotension • Constipation • Anorexia • Vertigo • Weakness • Diabetes mellitus • Yellowish discoloration of eyes • Dysuria • Hyperlipidemia and Hypothyroidism	***Assess or monitor*** Side effects ***Patient teaching*** • Advise to take medication with food in order to avoid the stomach upset • Don't stop the medicine suddenly • Drug may cause fainting so avoid driving • Avoid drinking alcohol • Take plenty of water
Ziprasidone ***Trade name:*** Zeldox, Ziprasidone Hydrochloride, Ziprasidone Mesylate ***Classification:*** Atypical antipsychotic.	***Adults – Oral*** 20–100 mg bd ***Intramus-cular*** 10 mg in Q2H or 20 mg Q4H	• Combination of its antagonistic function at D_2 receptors in mesolimbic pathways at $5HT_2$ receptors in frontal cortex. • Reduction of positive symptoms is due to antagonism at D_2 receptors and reduction in negative symptoms because of $5HT_2A$ antagonism.	• Schizophrenia • Bipolar affective disorder • Acute mania • Depression • Anxiety • Aggressive behavior • Dementia • Attention deficit hyperactivity disorder (ADHD) • Obsessive compulsive disorder (OCD) • Autism • Post-Traumatic Stress disorder.	• Hypersensitivity • Recent Myocardial Infarction • Previous Arrhythmias and use of antiarrhythmics • Cardiac failure. ***Use with caution*** • Seizures • Dementia • Diabetes • Obesity	• Dry mouth • Dizziness • Somnolence • Drowsiness • Headache • Vomiting • Nausea • Hypertension • Postural hypotension • Cough • Running nose • Mood changes • Extrapyramidal symptoms • Rashes • Dysmenorrhea • Constipation • Abdominal pain	**Assess or *monitor*** • Serum potassium and magnesium • Check out extrapyramidal symptoms (neuroleptic malignant syndrome), fever, confusion, stiffness ***Miscellaneous*** • Take medication with food to prevent gastric upset. • Don't give this drug to the patients with heart attack or congestive heart failure history.

Name of the drugs	Dosage	Action	Indications	Contraindications	Side effects	Nurse's responsibility
Imipramine ***Trade name:*** Antidep, tofranil ***Classification:*** Tertiary tricyclic antidepressant drugs	***Oral*** 75–300 mg/day	Blocks the reuptake of norepinephrine (NE) and serotonin (5-HT) in nerve terminals, thereby it increases level of NE and 5-HT at receptor site.	• Depression with psychotic symptoms • Depressive episode • Dysthymia • Secondary depression due to hypothyroidism • Reactive depression • Cushing's Syndrome • Pathological grief • Separation anxiety disorder • Enuresis • Somnambulism • Night terrors • Panic attacks • Social phobia • Agoraphobia • Chronic pain • Obsessive Compulsive disorder • Depersonalization • Post-traumatic stress disorder • Migraine headache • Gastric ulcer.	• Heart disorders • Recovery period after myocardial infarction • Not to be given to younger children less than 6 years of age • Usage within 2 weeks of MAOIs.	• Sedation • Dry mouth • Tremors • Constipation • Tachycardia • Urinary retention • Arrhythmias • Mydriasis • Agranulocytosis • Orthostatic hypotension • Cholestatic jaundice • Sedation • Tremors • Withdrawal • Syndrome • Acute organic syndrome • Seizures • Weight gain • Tiredness • Drowsiness and insomnia.	***Assess or monitor*** • Complete Blood Count • Blood Glucose level • Liver and Renal Function test • Baseline ECG (If risk of Arrhythmias is present) • Suicidal risk in patients • Sleep pattern, mood and behavior • Bowel and bladder function • Blood pressure • Pulse rate ***Patient teaching*** • Take medicines with food or milk to prevent gastric upset. • Don't crush the film-coated tablets • Take sips of water and use chewing gums to prevent dry mouth • Ask patient to change the position slowly to prevent fainting

Name of the drugs	Dosage	Action	Indications	Contraindications	Side effects	Nurse's responsibility
Clomipramine ***Trade name:*** Anafranil ***Classification:*** Tertiary tricyclic antidepressant	150–250 mg/day ***oral***	Blocks the reuptake of neurotransmitters (norepinephrine and serotonin) at Central Nervous System presynaptic membranes by increasing their availability at postsynaptic receptor sites.	• Obsessive compulsive disorder • Depression • Panic disorder • Phobias • Pain disorders.	• Heart disorders • Recovery period after myocardial infarction • Pregnancy • Hepatic and renal disease • Usage of clomipramine within the 2 weeks of MAOI medication intake.	• Somnolence • Dizziness • Xerostomia • Blurry vision • Constipation • Sexual dysfunction • Impotence • Hyperpyrexia • Increased weight • Delay in urination and Urinary retention • Orthostatic hypotension • Palpitation • Seizures • Tachycardia • Profuse sweating • Altered concentration • Increased appetite • Arrhythmias	***Assess or monitor*** • Complete blood count • Blood glucose level • Liver and renal function test • Baseline ECG (If risk of arrhythmias is present) • Suicidal risk in patients • Sleep pattern, mood and behavior • Bowel and bladder function • Blood pressure • Pulse rate ***Patient teaching*** • Take medicines with food or milk to prevent gastric upset. • Don't crush the film-coated tablets • Take sips of water and use chewing gums to prevent dry mouth • Ask patient to change the position slowly to prevent fainting
Lamotrigine ***Trade name***: Apo-lamotrigine, Lamictal, Lamictal XR ***Classification***: Anticonvulsant	50 mg/ Day ***Oral***	Inhibits the glutamate (excitatory neurotransmitter) release, at voltage sensitive sodium channels, thus decreasing seizures.	• Generalized tonic-clonic seizures • Bipolar disorder.	• Hypersensitivity • Pregnancy • Lactation ***Use with caution*** • Altered cardiac function • Hepatic and renal impairment • Patients below 16 years of age	***Central nervous system*** Dizziness, Ataxia, headache and tremors ***Eye***: Nystagmus, diplopia and blurred vision **Hematology:** Anemia, disseminated intravascular Coagulation, leukopenia and thrombocytopenia. ***Gastrointestinal system***: Nausea, vomiting, and Hepatotoxicity. ***Miscellaneous***: Stevens-Johnson syndrome, Toxic epidermal necrosis, Multiple organ failure and Suicidal ideation.	***Assess or monitor*** • Duration, type and intensity of Seizure. • Sign of skin rashes • Renal and hepatic function test ***Patient teaching*** • Advise the patient to do periodic ophthalmic examination • Taper the drug for 2 weeks before discontinuing and do not discontinue the drug abruptly • Advise the client to report, if yellowish skin discoloration, change in the urine color, fever, rashes, unusual bleeding and abdominal pain occur

Name of the drugs	Dosage	Action	Indications	Contraindications	Side effects	Nurse's responsibility
Sertraline ***Trade name:*** Zoloft ***Classification:*** Selective Serotonin Reuptake Inhibitors -Antidepressant	25–50 mg ***Oral***	Inhibits reuptake of serotonin in Central Nervous System by increasing the serotonergic function	Major depressive disorder, Obsessive compulsive disorder, Panic disorder, Bulimia Nervosa, Post-traumatic stress disorder, Social anxiety disorder, Premenstrual dysphoric disorder	Hypersensitivity, Pruritus with Cholestatic Liver Disease, Premature Ejaculation, Breast Cancer Patients Taking Tamoxifen, Hot Flashes During Menopause, Men with Prostate Cancer secondary to Androgen Deprivation Therapy.	***Central nervous system:*** Insomnia, Agitation, Tremor, Seizure, Neuroleptic Malignant Syndrome. ***Cardiovascular system:*** Palpitations, chest pain. **Eye:** Vision abnormalities, yawning. ***Endocrine system:*** Syndrome of Inappropriate Antidiuretic Hormone Secretion (SIADH) ***Gastrointestinal system:*** Diarrhea, nausea and constipation. ***Genitourinary system:*** Micturition disorder. **Skin:** Increased sweating, rash, hot flashes.	***Assess or monitor*** • Complete blood count • Renal function test • Bowel activity • Stool consistency • Suicidal risk • Mental Status Examination (Mood and Affect) • Pulse rate • Blood pressure • Weight ***Patient teaching*** • Take this medicine with food to prevent gastric distress • Avoid taking the drug at night time to prevent insomnia • Care givers of patient have to monitor the patient due to increased suicidal risk because as the energy level comes up in the depressive client, there is an increased risk of suicide • Teach the patient and his family members that drug will take 2–4 weeks to get the complete therapeutic effect • Avoid taking alcohol • Take sips of water to prevent dry mouth • Report Headache, fatigue, tremors and sexual dysfunction immediately

Name of the drugs	Dosage	Action	Indications	Contraindications	Side effects	Nurse's responsibility
Olanzapine ***Trade name:*** Zyprexa ***Classification:*** Atypical antipsychotic-Serotonin dopamine antagonists	***Oral*** 5–10 mg/day	Antagonizes dopamine histamine muscarinic, alpha-adrenergic and serotonin receptors.	Positive and negative symptoms of schizophrenia, schizoaffective disorders, depression (when combine with other drugs), bipolar mania.	Narrow angle glaucoma, urinary out flow obstruction and paralytic ileus. ***Use with caution*** Low WBC count, Smoking, alcohol consumption, high cholesterol level, sleep apnea, family history of diabetes and cardiac disorder ***Drug interactions*** Antianxiety agents, Muscle relaxants, Opioids, cough relievers and Antihistamine drugs	***Central nervous system:*** Agitation, headache, sleep deficit, nervousness, hostile behavior. ***Cardiovascular system:*** Tachycardia and Orthostatic hypotension. ***Other adverse effects:*** Weight gain, constipation, Seizures and neuroleptic malignant syndrome.	***Assess or monitor*** • Liver function test before starting olanzapine • Patient's behavior and mental status. • Blood pressure. ***Patient teaching*** • Don't stop drug abruptly • Avoid tasks which require mental alertness because the drug causes drowsiness • Instruct the patient to notify if become pregnant. • Avoid dehydration mainly during exercise or exposure to extreme heat. • Take sips of water and use chewing sugarless gum to prevent dry mouth. • Diet and exercises are important to prevent weight gain. • Take olanzapine early in the day to reduce insomnia.
Alprazolam ***Trade name***: Alprax, Apo-Alpraz, Novo-Alprazolam ***Classification***: Antianxiety drug (Benzodiaz-epines), Sedatives and hypnotics	***Oral*** 0.25–0.5mg	Enhance the inhibiting effect of gamma aminobutyric acid (GABA)—inhibitory neurotransmitter	Anxiety disorder, insomnia, premenstrual, syndrome and irritable bowel syndrome.	• Hypersensitivity • Acute angle closure glaucoma. • Severe chronic obstructive pulmonary disease (COPD) • Myasthenia gravis • Pregnancy and lactation • Acute alcohol intoxication with reduced vital signs.	• Ataxia • Transient mild somnolence • Light-headedness or Headache • Slurred speech • Dry mouth • Confusion • Depression • Blurred vision • Restlessness • Constipation • Abdominal cramps • Diarrhea • Nausea • Vomiting • Tremors • Irritability • Seizure • Diaphoresis • Insomnia	***Assess or monitor*** • Patient motor response (agitation). ***Patient teaching*** • Use of alprazolam in pregnancy might lead to Central Nervous System depression • Don't stop drug abruptly • Take sips of water and use chewing sugarless gum to prevent dry mouth. • Drowsiness usually disappears with the continued therapy. • Patient has to change the position slowly • Stop smoking and consuming alcohol

Name of the drugs	Dosage	Action	Indications	Contraindications	Side effects	Nurse's responsibility
Acamprosate ***Trade name:*** Acamprol	Tablet available form is 333 mg.	Anti- craving medication (Enhances the GABA neurotransmitter system. It interferes with glutamate action. It also act on calcium channel and decreases CNS excitability that might lead to decrease in the craving effect)	To reduce craving effect in patients with alcohol dependence syndrome	• Hypersensitivity • Cirrhosis with severe hepatic dysfunction • Pregnancy and lactation • Renal disease	***Central nervous system:*** Headache and dizziness ***Cardiovascular system:*** Chest pain and vasodilation ***Gastrointestinal system:*** Nausea, vomiting, diarrhea and dry mouth. ***Respiratory system:*** Dyspnea **Skin:** Pruritus **Miscellaneous:** Weight loss, dehydration	***Assess or monitor*** • Mood changes • Depressive symptoms • Suicidal risk ***Patient teaching*** • Drug adherence is vital • Avoid tasks which require mental alertness because the drug causes drowsiness • Report the doctor if the patient has side effects.
Clozapine ***Trade name:*** Sizopin ***Classification:*** Atypical Antipsychotics	***Oral*** 25 mg may gradually increase to 300 mg per day in divided doses.	Antagonizes Alpha-Adrenergic, Histamine, Dopamine, Muscarinic and Serotonin Receptors.	• Positive and negative symptoms of schizophrenia • Schizoaffective disorders • Schizophrenia is not effective with typical antipsychotic drugs • Side effects of typical antipsychotics	• Hypersensitivity • Bone marrow suppression • Central nervous system depression • Coma • Lactation • Patients below 16 years of age	• Agranulocytosis • Decreased WBC • Fatigue • Polymorphonuclear leukocytes • Hypotension • Seizure • Sialorrhea • Sedation • Constipation • Tachycardia • Weight gain • Anticholinergic effects ***Use with Caution*** • Glaucoma • Heart disease • History of seizures • Myocarditis • Liver failure • Urine retention • Renal dysfunction • Benign prostrate Hyperplasia • Altered respiratory function	***Assess or monitor*** • Liver function test and Renal function test and complete blood count before starting Clozapine. • Weekly monitor the WBC count for the first six months and then biweekly monitoring can be done if the WBCs are in the acceptable range. If level of WBCs is less than 1500/mm^3, discontinue the drug. ***Patient teaching*** • Avoid tasks which require mental alertness and motor skills because the drug causes drowsiness and the drowsiness will subside with the continued therapy • Don't discontinue the drug abruptly • Take seizure precautions • Ask the client to report the symptoms such as sore throat, weakness, fever and lethargy

Name of the drugs	Dosage	Action	Indications	Contraindications	Side effects	Nurse's responsibility
Donepezil ***Trade name:*** Aricept	5–10 mg/day	Acetylcholinesterase inhibitor (Increase acetylcholine concentration by inhibiting hydrolysis of cholinesterase enzyme)	Mild to moderate Dementia (Alzheimer's type)	Hypersensitivity	***Central nervous system*** Headache, insomnia, seizures and dizziness. ***Cardiovascular system:*** Chest pain and vasodilation ***Gastrointestinal system:*** Nausea, vomiting, anorexia and diarrhea. ***Genitourinary system:*** Urinary frequency. ***Respiratory system:*** Dyspnea and bronchitis ***Miscellaneous*** Weight loss and dehydration	***Assess or monitor*** • Cognitive ability of the client. • Heart rate because bradycardia may occur. • Side effects of this drug ***Patient teaching*** • Importance of taking the medication regularly. • This drug may cause dizziness; so, take medication before going to bed. • Avoid alcohol and other drugs such as sedatives and tranquilizers. • Take small and frequent meals, frequent mouth care, use chewing gum, which may reduce nausea. • Advise the client to intimate suicidal thoughts and nervousness.
Phenergan ***Generic name:*** Promethazine	50 mg for sedation and 10–25 mg every 4 hours for antiemetic action	Sedative/hypnotics, Anti-emetics, H_1 receptors blockers, antihistamines effect. It also blocks the cholinergic receptors in vomiting center which prevents nausea and vomiting	To sedate the patient, prevent vomiting, used to reduce pain and for the purpose of anesthesia	Hypersensitivity, prostate hypertrophy, comatose patient, bladder neck obstruction and narrow angle glaucoma	• Sedation • Disorientation • Confusion • Fatigue • Dizziness • Nervousness • Bradycardia or Tachycardia • Hypertension or hypotension • Dry mouth • Hepatitis • Constipation • Blood dyscrasias • Extrapyramidal symptoms • Blurred vision • Rashes • Tinnitus • Diplopia • Photosensitivity	***Assess or monitor*** • Vital signs • Level of sedation • Nausea and vomiting ***Miscellaneous*** • Give deep intramuscular injection because administration into subcutaneous tissue will cause necrosis • Arteriospasm and gangrene of artery may happen when this drug is administered through intra-arterial route.

Name of the drugs	Dosage	Action	Indications	Contraindications	Side effects	Nurse's responsibility
Risperidone ***Trade name:*** Sizodon ***Classification:*** Atypical antipsychotics	***Oral*** 0.5–6 mg per day	Antiadrenergic, antiserotonergic, antidopaminergic and antihistaminergic action.	Schizophrenia, Schizoaffective disorder, bipolar disorder, irritable behavior associated with autism and other psychotic disorders.	Hypersensitivity, cardiac diseases, seizure disorder, Parkinson's disease, hyperprolactinemia, kidney and liver dysfunction. ***Use with Caution*** Low WBC count, dementia, sleep apnea, high cholesterol level, QT prolongation (heart rhythm) glaucoma and cataract ***Drug Interactions*** Antihistamine agents, Opioids, cough relievers, antianxiety agents and muscle relaxants.	***Central nervous system:*** Headache, Hypersomnia and epilepsy ***Cardiovascular system:*** Dizziness, tachycardia, orthostatic hypotension and syncope. ***Gastrointestinal system:*** Constipation, abdominal pain and vomiting ***Miscellaneous:*** Erectile dysfunction, weight gain, mood changes, sleep apnea, tremors, hyperglycemia, Skin rashes, tardive dyskinesia and neuroleptic malignant syndrome.	***Assess or monitor*** • Blood urea nitrogen levels • Renal and liver function test • Serum alkaline phosphate • Mental status examination • Blood pressure • Heart rate • Weight ***Patient teaching*** • Avoid tasks which require mental alertness and motor skills because the drug causes drowsiness • Drink more water to reduce constipation. • Notify the doctor if there are gait disturbances, palpitations, breathing difficulty, severe dizziness, pain or swelling in breasts, unusual movements, trembling fingers, rashes and visual disturbances • Avoid drinking alcohol • Change the position slowly as this drug causes orthostatic hypotension.
Fluoxetine hydrochloride ***Trade name:*** Auscap, fluohexal, Levan, Novo-fluoxetine, Prozac ***Classification:*** Antidepressants Serotonin-Specific reuptake inhibitors	20 mg/day and maximum 80 mg/day	Inhibits the serotonin uptake in the central nervous system by increasing serotonergic activity.	Depressive disorder, Bulimia nervosa, anxiety disorder especially obsessive-compulsive disorder (OCD) and Panic attacks ***Use with caution*** Cardiac problems, seizure disorder, Diabetes Mellitus, Pregnancy and Patient with high suicidal risk	Hypersensitivity, pregnancy, lactation, history of seizure, severe liver dysfunction and renal impairment.	***Central nervous system:*** Nervousness, headache, drowsiness and fatigue ***Cardiovascular system:*** Palpitations. **ENT:** Nasal congestion, pharyngitis and sinusitis. ***Gastrointestinal system:*** Dry mouth, nausea, anorexia and diarrhea or constipation. ***Genitourinary system:*** Sexual dysfunction.	***Assess or monitor*** • Complete Blood Count (CBC) • Renal Function test • Liver Function test • Bowel and Bladder function • Patient's Behavior, mood and sleep pattern • Suicidal risk determination ***Patient teaching*** • Take medication with milk and food to prevent gastric distress. • Take the last dose of medication before 4 pm to prevent insomnia at night. • Quit alcohol

Name of the drugs	Dosage	Action	Indications	Contraindications	Side effects	Nurse's responsibility
					Musculoskeletal system: muscle pain. ***Respiratory system***: Upper Respiratory tract infection, respiratory distress and cough **Skin:** Rashes and Pruritus	• Ask the patient to report headache, fatigue, sexual dysfunction and tremors. • Take adequate water to prevent dry mouth.
Disulfiram	***Oral*** 250 mg/day once a day.	Alcohol dehydrogenase inhibitors (alcohol dehydrogenase is the enzyme which prevents the conversion of ethanol into acetaldehyde)	Abstinence for more than 48 hours of alcohol intake, failure or contraindicated with naltrexone, previous good response to disulfiram and client has both cocaine and alcohol dependence	Suspected alcohol intake, rubber/cobalt/nickel allergy, psychotic patients, hypersensitivity, pregnancy/breastfeeding, cognitive impairment, uncontrolled hypertension, high suicidal risk, history of stroke/myocardial infarction, severe personality disorder, severe cardiac, renal and hepatic dysfunction. ***Drug interactions*** Phenytoin, Warfarin, ethanol (cause disulfiram ethanol reaction), metronidazole (flagyl), tricyclic antidepressants (particularly amitriptyline) and benzodiazepines (increase sedative effect)	Metallic or garlic taste, headache, drowsiness/fatigue, dermatitis, halitosis, nausea/vomiting and impotence/lack of libido/sexual dysfunction ***Adverse reactions*** Polyneuritis, hepatotoxicity, optic neuritis and peripheral neuritis	***Assess or monitor*** • Complete Blood Count (CBC) • Liver function test • Mental status examination ***Patient teaching*** • Disulfiram is not to be taken if patient has consumed alcohol within 12 hours because it leads to Disulfiram-Ethanol Reaction (DER). • Disulfiram-Ethanol Reaction (DER) includes trouble in breathing, nausea, vomiting, throbbing pain in head and neck, sweating, increased thirst, dizziness, palpitations, blurred vision, confusion and weakness. Severe Disulfiram-Ethanol Reaction includes unconsciousness, cardiac failure, respiratory failure, seizures and death • Don't use hand sanitizer, perfume, alcoholic beverages and food (vinegars, marinades, sauces, extracts, etc.), perfumes, after shave lotions, cough syrup, etc. which have alcohol content.

Name of the drugs	Dosage	Action	Indications	Contraindications	Side effects	Nurse's responsibility
Lithium (Lithium Carbonate, Lithium Citrate)	600–900 mg/day given as divided or single dose initially	Lithium enhances the reuptake of Norepinephrine and Serotonin in presynapse, destroy the *catecholamines* in synapse and enhance post synaptic sensitivity	Bipolar disorder, Schizophrenia, Eating disorder, Neutropenia, Headache, Epilepsy, Asthma, Overactive thyroid, Tourette's syndrome, Tardive Dyskinesia, Aggression, Attention Deficit Hyperactive Disorder (ADHD)	Cardiovascular disease, renal disease, severe dehydration or sodium depletion, Patients on diuretics, patients with the high risk of lithium toxicity	Headache, Mental dullness, Fatigue, ECG Changes (T wave flattening, QRS widening and sinus node dysfunction), Hypothyroidism, Weight gain, Polyuria, Metallic taste, Increased Thirst, Goiter, Tremors, Gastrointestinal Upset, acne, rashes, Ataxia, Nystagmus, Muscle weakness, Delirium, hair loss, psoriasis, Peripheral Neuropathy, Intracranial hypertension, Myasthenia gravis like syndrome, lower seizure threshold, neuromuscular irritability, Memory disturbances, dysphoria and slow reaction time	***Assess or monitor*** • Therapeutic lithium level has to be 0.6–1.2 mEq/L; and >2 mEq/L is said to be toxic level. • WBC count • Renal function test • Thyroid function test • Glucose level ***Patient teaching*** • Retention of sodium and water has to be avoided. • More intake of oral fluids/water. • Follow up and regular check-up is vital to prevent lithium toxicity
Amphetamine ***Trade name(s):*** • Adzenys ER (Extended Release) • Adzenys OET (Oral Disintegrating Tablet) • Evekeo • Dyanavel XR	Adult Narcolepsy - 5–60 mg; Obesity – 5–10 mg maximum up to 30 mg; Attention Deficit Hyperactive disorder Adzenys ER – 12.5 mg/day	It is a noncatecholamine sympathomimetic amine which enhances the release of catecholamines (mainly dopamine and norepinephrine) from the storage site at presynaptic terminals. Anorexigenic effect is mainly secondary to the central nervous system-stimulating effect and the site of action is hypothalamic center.	Attention deficit Hyperactive disorder (ADHD), Narcolepsy, Depression and Obsessive-Compulsive disorder (OCD)	Hypersensitivity, Heart disease, Arteriosclerosis, Hypertension, Agitation, history of depression, tics, or Tourette's syndrome, Bipolar disorder, Suicidal ideation, glaucoma, hyperthyroidism and use of Monoamine Oxidase Inhibitors (MAOIs) within the past 14 days	***Physical effects*** • Hypertension or Hypotension • Raynaud's phenomenon • Erectile dysfunction • Tachycardia • Abdominal pain • Anorexia • Weight loss • Nausea • Rashes • Acne • Xerostomia • Nose bleeding • Profuse sweating • Seizures • Tics • Dysuria	***Patient teaching*** • Don't take amphetamines along with the fruit juices rich in vitamin C because it decreases absorption • Inform the doctor immediately if there are signs of heart problems such as chest pain, breathing difficulty, etc. signs of psychosis such as hallucination, aggression, hostile behavior, paranoia, etc., signs of circulatory problems such as bluish or pale colour skin, numbness, feel cold, etc. • Take the missed dose as early as possible but don't take double dose. • Don't share amphetamine with others because it has addiction potential.

Name of the drugs	Dosage	Action	Indications	Contraindications	Side effects	Nurse's responsibility
					Psychological effects • Increased alertness • Mood swings • Change in libido • Insomnia • Obsessive behavior • Grandiose • Anxiety • Irritability	
Diazepam ***Trade name:*** Valium, Valpam ***Classification:*** Antianxiety drug, Sedatives/ Hypnotics -Benzodiazepines	Oral 2–10 mg	Gamma–Aminobutyric acid (GABA) and other inhibitory neurotransmitters will bind with the specific benzodiazepine receptors in limbic and cortical areas of the Central Nervous System, GABA inhibits the excitatory stimulation and therefore, it controls emotional behavior. This drug also suppresses the spread of seizure activity which is caused by seizure producing foci in the thalamus, cortex and limbic system	Anxiety disorder, preanesthetic medication, skeletal muscle relaxants, alcohol withdrawal syndrome, tremors, status epilepticus, panic attack, tension and headache.	Pre-existing CNS depression, Angle Closure glaucoma, Coma, respiratory depression and severe uncontrolled pain.	***Central nervous system:*** Dizziness, confusion, drowsiness, headache, anxiety, tremors, fatigue, depression, insomnia, hallucinations, ataxia, fatigue. ***Cardiovascular system:*** Orthostatic hypotension and tachycardia ***Eye:*** Blurred vision, mydriasis and nystagmus ***Gastrointestinal system:*** Dry mouth, nausea, vomiting, anorexia and diarrhea or constipation. ***Hematology:*** Neutropenia ***Skin***: Rashes, dermatitis and Itching ***Respiratory System:*** Respiratory depression.	***Assess or monitor*** • Patient's Blood Pressure, Pulse rate, respiratory rate, rhythm before giving diazepam • Motor responses such as trembling, agitation, autonomic responses such as cold, clammy extremities and diaphoresis. ***Patient teaching*** • Ask the client to lie in recumbent position for up to 3 hours after the parenteral administration of diazepam to decrease the hypotensive effect. • Teach the patient that drowsiness disappears with continued therapy. • Ask the patient to change position slowly to prevent dizziness. • Ask patient to take the diazepam with food to reduce gastric distress. • Abrupt withdrawal of diazepam may cause irritability, insomnia and sometimes seizures. • Avoid tasks which require mental alertness and motor skills because the drug causes drowsiness • Avoid alcohol or other CNS depressants along with diazepam

Name of the drugs	Dosage	Action	Indications	Contraindications	Side effects	Nurse's responsibility
						During the time of administration • Intramuscular administration has to be given as deep IM. • Do not mix IV diazepam with any other drug. • Give slow IV injection because respiratory or cardiac arrest can occur • Monitor vital signs during IV administration. • Prevent extravasation because it can cause phlebitis and venous thrombosis.

Know the Differences

1. **Defense mechanism and coping mechanism**

Defense mechanism	Coping mechanism
It is a false coping mechanism that gives a temporary relief from the psychological stressors.	It helps to deal with the stressors and cope with situations.
Example: Rationalization, sublimation, regression, repression, etc.	Example: Yoga, meditation, relaxation therapy, play therapy, etc.

2. **Psychosis and neurosis**

Categories	Aspects	Psychosis	Neurosis
Etiology	Stressful events	More significant	Less significant
	Genetic factors	More significant	Less significant
Clinical manifestations	Personality	Affected	Not as a whole (only part of the personality is involved)
	Disorganized speech	Present	Absent
	Disorganized behavior	Present	Absent
	Delusions and hallucinations	Present	Absent
	Cognitive disturbances	Common	Rare
	Disturbances in perception and thinking	Common	Rare
	Insight	Absent	Present
	Reality testing and Judgment	Absent	Present
	Risk of self–harm	High	Low
Treatment	Medications	Major Tranquilizers	Minor tranquilizers
	ECT	Useful	Not useful
	Psychotherapy	Not much useful	Very useful
	Prognosis	Poor	Good
Example		Schizophrenia, Schizoaffective disorder and bipolar disorder	Anxiety disorder, Phobia and obsessive-compulsive disorder

3. **Hallucination and illusion**

Hallucination	Illusion
Misperception without an external stimulus. Types—Auditory, visual, olfactory, gustatory, tactile or haptic, hypnagogic, hypnopombic, command or telological, liliputian, kinesthetic, functional, reflex, extracampine and autoscopy.	Misperception with an external stimulus. Types—Pareidolic, completion and affect.

4. **Echopraxia, echolalia, perseveration and coprolalia**

Echopraxia	Echolalia	Perseveration	Coprolalia
Mimic the activities done by others	Mimic the words spoken by others	Persistent repetition of words beyond the point of relevance	Repeated use of obscene words

5. **Ambivalence and conflict**

Ambivalence	Conflict
Coexistence of two opposing forces or impulses, desires, ideas or emotions in one individual.	Coexistence of two opposing forces or impulses, desire, ideas or emotions between two individuals.

6. **Flight of ideas and loosening of association**

Aspects	Flight of ideas	Loosening of association
Definition	Rapid shifting of one idea to other idea with the presence of common context.	Rapid shifting of one idea to other idea without having any common context.
Example	Nurse asking patient, did you have breakfast? Answer: I like to eat idly. I feel biryani is good always. Sweets are available in the canteen.	Nurse asking patient, did you have breakfast? Answer: I like to travel more. I hate the rich persons. I feel sleepy now. I don't know where my mother went now.
Explanation of the Example	The common context in the above example is 'food'. Patient is shifting from one idea to other but all are about food whereas association is not good. There is no common context.	There is no common context in the above said example.

7. **Circumstantiality and tangentiality**

Circumstantiality	Tangentiality
Speech of the individual reaches the goal or center point of the question raised only after the unwanted speech.	Speech of the individual does not reach the goal or center point.
Nurse: Did you have your breakfast? Patient: I like to go home now, I feel sleepy, I would like to see my mother, I had my breakfast (At last, patient verbalized the answer that he had breakfast after unwanted speech).	Nurse: Did you have your breakfast? Patient: I like to go home now, I feel sleepy, I would like to see my mother (Patient talks something but never answers to question whether he had breakfast or not).

8. **Delusion and overvalued idea**

Delusion	Overvalued ideas
Delusion is a strong fixed unshakable belief irrespective of their socio-cultural background.	Overvalued ideas give more importance to one's own idea.
E.g., when patient says, 'I strongly believe that I am a God' denotes the Delusion of grandeur.	E.g., when patient says, 'It is mandatory to pray to God before every meal' denotes overvalued idea.

9. Functional and reflex hallucination

Functional hallucination	Reflex hallucination
Misperception within the same sensory stimuli (For example, each hallucination belongs to auditory sensory stimuli).	Stimulus in one sensory field produces hallucination in another (For example, one sensory field was touch, i.e., feel of pain and other sensory field was auditory, i.e., hearing sneezing sound).
Patient verbalizes that, 'I am hearing voices when I hear the birds sound.'	Patient verbalizes that 'I feel painful when I hear a sneezing sound'.

10. Hypnogogic and hypnopompic hallucination

Hypnogogic hallucination	Hypnopompic hallucination
Misperception when going to sleep.	Misperception while awakening from sleep.
Patient verbalizes that, 'I feel that a ghost is speaking to me daily when I am getting into sleep'.	Patient verbalizes that 'I feel that a ghost is speaking to me daily when I am awakening from sleep'.

11. Micropsia and macropsia

Micropsia	Macropsia
Objects appear smaller than the original size.	Objects appear larger than the original size.

12. Pelopsia and teleopsia

Pelopsia	Teleopsia
People/objects/things appear closer than the original place.	People/objects/things appear far away than the original place.

13. Retrograde amnesia and anterograde amnesia

Retrograde amnesia	Anterograde amnesia
It means loss of memory to the events happened before the injury or onset of illness.	It means loss of memory to the events happened after the injury or onset of illness.

14. Delirium and dementia

Aspects	Delirium	Dementia
Other Names	Acute confusion state, Organic brain syndrome, Acute organic reaction, Toxic psychosis and Metabolic encephalitis	Chronic brain syndrome and chronic brain failure.
Onset	Acute	Gradual/insidious
Nature	Reversible	Irreversible
Duration	Days to weeks	Months to years
Course	Fluctuating	Progressive
Attention	Impaired	Normal until severe
Consciousness	Fluctuating/altered	Rarely alters/clear
Decreased awareness of self	Present	Present
Perception	Illusions, hallucinations common	Hallucinations not common
Speech	Slow, incoherent	Repetitive difficulty finding words
Disorientation	To time is common	To time, person and place occurs
Illness, med. toxicity	Often	Rarely
Outcome	Excellent if corrected early	Poor
Diurnal disruptions	Present	Present
Psychomotor changes	Increased/decreased	Often normal

15. **Dementia and pseudodementia (depression)**

Aspects	Dementia	Pseudodementia (Depression)
Complaints of cognitive impairment	Rarely	Mostly
Emphasis achievements	Patient emphasis achievements Patient be unconcerned on symptoms	Patient emphasis disability Patient communicates distress
Mood	Labile affect	Depressed
Mental status exam	• Makes mistakes • Impairment recent memory • Confabulation • Poor performance test	• Say don't know • Not such
History	No such history	History of depression
Age	Elders	Non-specific
Organic symptoms	Yes	No
CT and EEG	Abnormal	Normal
Cooperation	Cooperative	Uncooperative
Behavior	With cognitive impairment	Not such
Benzodiazepam Barbiturates	Worsen the disease	May improve sleep only

16. **Cortical and subcortical dementia**

Aspects	Cortical dementia	Subcortical dementia
Presence of lesion in	• Frontal • Parietal • Temporal • Occipital • Hippocampus	• Thalamus • Basal ganglion • Brain stem
Severity	Severe	Mild to moderate
Motor activities	Normal	• Tremors • Dystonia • Dysarthria • Flexed or extended posture • Chorea • Ataxia • Rigidity
Decline in short term memory/ cognition/recall	Bradyphrenia (Decreased cognitive speed) and recall by cues done in very little way	Recall by cues done in partial way
Depressive symptoms	Not common	Common
Delusions	Simple	Complex
Miscellaneous (5A's)	• Aphasia • Amnesia • Agnosia • Apraxia • Acalculia	Nil

17. **Lewy body dementia and Parkinson's disease dementia**

Aspects	Lewy body dementia	Parkinson's disease dementia
Onset of dementia	Mostly precedes motor symptoms or within onset of motor symptoms	Mostly follows motor symptoms
Type of dementia	Cortical	Sub-cortical

Contd...

Aspects	Lewy body dementia	Parkinson's disease dementia
Motor symptoms at diagnosis	50%	100%
Cognitive fluctuation	Present	Absent
Visual hallucination	Present	Absent
Resting tremors	Not prominent	Prominent

18. Mood and affect

Mood	Affect
It is a sustained and persistent emotional feeling.	It is outward expression of thoughts as feelings.

19. Hypomania and mania

Aspects	Hypomania	Mania
Duration of symptoms	4 days	>1 week
Psychotic features	Absent	May or may not
Social and occupational dysfunction	Absent	Present
Insight into illness	Present	Absent

20. Endogenous and exogenous depression

Aspects	Endogenous depression	Exogenous depression
Meaning	Prefix 'Endo' means within (due to hereditary or biochemical imbalance)	Prefix 'Exo' means outside (caused by external factors—unemployment, divorce, sudden death of loved ones)
Other names	• Psychotic depression • Autogenous depression • Biological depression	• Neurotic depression • Reactive depression
Predominant factors	Biological factor	Environmental factor
Stress	Present	Present
Premorbid personality	• Cyclothymic personality • Dysthymic personality	• Anxious personality • Obsessive personality
Insomnia	Early morning awakening	Struggle in getting into sleep
Psychotic feature	• Psychomotor retardation • Suicidal attempts • Delusions	• Psychomotor agitation • Suicidal attempts are not common • Other features are absent
Individual feeling	Better when alone	Better in group
Mood	Sad in morning	Sad in evening
Treatment	Antidepressants and ECT	Antidepressants and psychotherapy
Relapse	Common	Not common

21. Endogenous and atypical depression

Aspects	Endogenous depression	Atypical depression
Appetite	Decreased	Increased
Weight	Loss of weight	Gain of weight
Worsening of symptoms	Morning	Evening
Insomnia	Middle or in late phase of sleep	Initial phase of sleep and sometimes hypersomnia
Interpersonal hypersensitivity (fear of being rejected by others)	Absent	Present

22. **Primary and secondary transsexualism**

Aspects	Primary transsexualism	Secondary transsexualism
Onset	Early childhood	Late
Prognosis	Good	Poor
Category	Homogenous	Heterogenous
Types	• Male to female primary transsexualism • Female to male primary transsexualism	Majority are male to female secondary transsexualism
Common feature	Wish to change anatomical sex organ	

23. **Anorexia nervosa and bulimia nervosa**

Aspects	Anorexia nervosa	Bulimia nervosa
Age of onset	14–16 years	18–24 years
Lifetime prevalence	1–3%	0.5–1%
Gender	Female	
Main symptoms	Fear of being obese	
Weight loss	85% of expected weight	Normal or decreased
Menses	Amenorrhea (3 consequent cycles)	Irregular menses (sometime amenorrhea)
Sexual desire	Absent or decreased libido	Normal or increased libido
Complications	Starvation, decreased blood pressure and temperature and shock	Dental/enamel erosion, dehydration, hypokalemia, esophageal tear
Post binge anguish	Absent	Present
Awareness of illness	Absent	Present
Types	Restricted type (not eating food) Binge eating/Purging type	Purging type Direct—Vomiting Indirect—Laxatives usage, Enema Non-purging type (starvation, Exercise)

24. **Type I and Type II schizophrenia**

Aspects	Type I schizophrenia	Type II schizophrenia
Symptoms	Positive symptoms	Negative symptoms
Course of illness	Acute	Chronic
Cognitive deficit	Absent	Sometimes present
Ventricles	Normal	Dilated
Response to drugs	Good	Poor
Prognosis	Better	Poor

25. **Transference and Counter transference**

Aspect	Transference	Counter transference
Meaning	Transfer of client's feeling toward the nurse.	Nurse is emotionally dependent on patient.
Types	• Negative or hostile transference (feeling of anger or enmity that the client has expressed toward the nurse). • Positive or Dependent transference (client is emotionally dependent on nurse).	• Reactions of intense love or caring. • Reactions of intense disgust or hostility. • Reactions of intense anxiety, especially in response to resistance by the patient.

26. Reassurance and false assurance

Reassurance	False assurance
It is a therapeutic technique of communication or counseling.	It is a non-therapeutic technique of communication.
Giving psychological support by providing assurance with the original fact.	Assurance given to the patient with manipulation of fact.
Nurse verbalizing to HIV patient that taking antiretroviral medications will prolong your lifespan and enhance the capacity of daily living is an example of reassurance.	If nurse verbalizes to the patient that HIV will get cured soon, it is an example of false reassurance.

27. Phobia and anxiety

Phobia	Anxiety
Phobia is irrational fear of something.	Anxiety is defined as, 'feeling of uncertainty, apprehension, uneasiness or tensed feeling of an individual to any situation'.

28. Obsession and thought insertion

Obsession	Thought insertion
It is one's own intrusive thoughts that put an individual into compulsive acts.	Thoughts of others are inserted into patient's mind.

29. Adjustment disorder and post-traumatic stress disorder

Adjustment disorder	Post-traumatic stress disorder
Presence of significant behavioral or emotional symptoms in response to the psychosocial stressors.	It is an anxiety disorder, in which the individual might experience stress after an extreme overwhelming traumatic event.
Here, the stressors are within the human experience such as job loss, marriage, childbirth, divorce, economic problems, etc.	Here, the stressors are outside the human experience such as sudden disaster (e.g., earthquake, flood, drought, etc.), or terrorist attack, severe accidents, etc.

30. Depersonalization and derealization

Depersonalization	Derealization
Detachment from one's own identity or oneself.	Individual feels that people or things around him/her are unreal.

31. Abstract thinking and concrete thinking

Abstract thinking	Concrete thinking
It refers to the hidden meaning of the concept or phrase which is not directly seen.	It gives the literal meaning of the words or sentences and do not go beyond the level to explain it.

32. Autistic thinking and realistic rhinking

Autistic thinking	Realistic thinking
Thinking which is not real or logical, composed of fantasies and day dreaming.	Thinking which is logical and based on the reality.

33. Déjà vu, Jamais vu, Deja pense, Deja entendu and Jamais entendu

Déjà vu	Jamais Vu	Deja pense	Jamais pense	Deja entendu	Jamais entendu
Familiar of unfamiliar situations	Unfamiliar of the familiar situations	Familiar of unfamiliar thoughts	Unfamiliar of the familiar thoughts	Familiar of unfamiliar auditory perception	Unfamiliar of the familiar auditory perception

34. Tics and Tourette syndrome

Tics	Tourette syndrome
It is a sudden, repetitive and nonrhythmic motor movement or vocalization which involves discrete muscle groups.	Georges Gilles de la Tourette was the first to identify this neurodevelopmental disorder. Tic disorder for at least one year duration with the presence of one vocal tics and two motor tics denotes Tourette syndrome.

35. Eustress and distress

Eustress	Distress
Perceives the stress in positive way which improves the overall performance with the effective use of coping mechanism.	Feels unpleasant due to the stress which decreases the overall performance which might lead to physical or mental fatigue.

36. Mental ventilation and catharsis

Mental ventilation	Catharsis
Sharing of thoughts or ideas which may or may not be felt as psychological burden to an individual.	Technique to release the emotional tension by ventilating the psychological burden along with emotions.

37. Attention and concentration

Attention	Concentration
Focus on the particular thing or concept.	Sustained attention is termed concentration.

38. Normal, abnormal and maladaptive behavior

Normal behavior	Abnormal behavior	Maladaptive behavior
Behavior which adheres to the socially acceptable norms.	Behavior which has strong deviation from the socially acceptable norms.	Abnormal behavior persists for the longer duration.

39. Suicide and homicide

Suicide	Homicide
Killing oneself	Killing others

40. Conversion disorder and somatization disorder

Conversion disorder	Somatization disorder
Internal psychological conflicts are exhibited as physical symptoms.	Complaints of recurring and multiple somatic symptoms which are no longer considered diagnosis.

41. Conduct disorder and antisocial personality disorder

Conduct disorder	Antisocial personality disorder
Disorder in which the patterns of disruptive and violent or antisocial behavior are present. Individual will have problems in following rules. It is usually termed when the antisocial behavior is elicited below 18 years of age.	It is a type of personality disorder in which the patterns of disruptive and violent or antisocial behavior are present. It is usually termed when the antisocial behavior is elicited above 18 years of age.

42. ICD-11 and DSM-5

ICD-11	DSM-5
International Classification of Diseases – 11th revision Codes given by World Health Organization	Diagnostic Static Manual 5th edition Codes given by American Psychiatric Association

43. Decorticate and decerebrate posture

Aspects	Decorticate posture	Decerebrate posture
Arms	Adducted, flexed	Adducted and extended
Wrist	Flexed on the chest	Pronated
Feet	Plantar flexion of the feet	Plantar flexion of the feet
Problems in the brain	Cerebral hemisphere and cervical spinal tract	Pons and midbrain

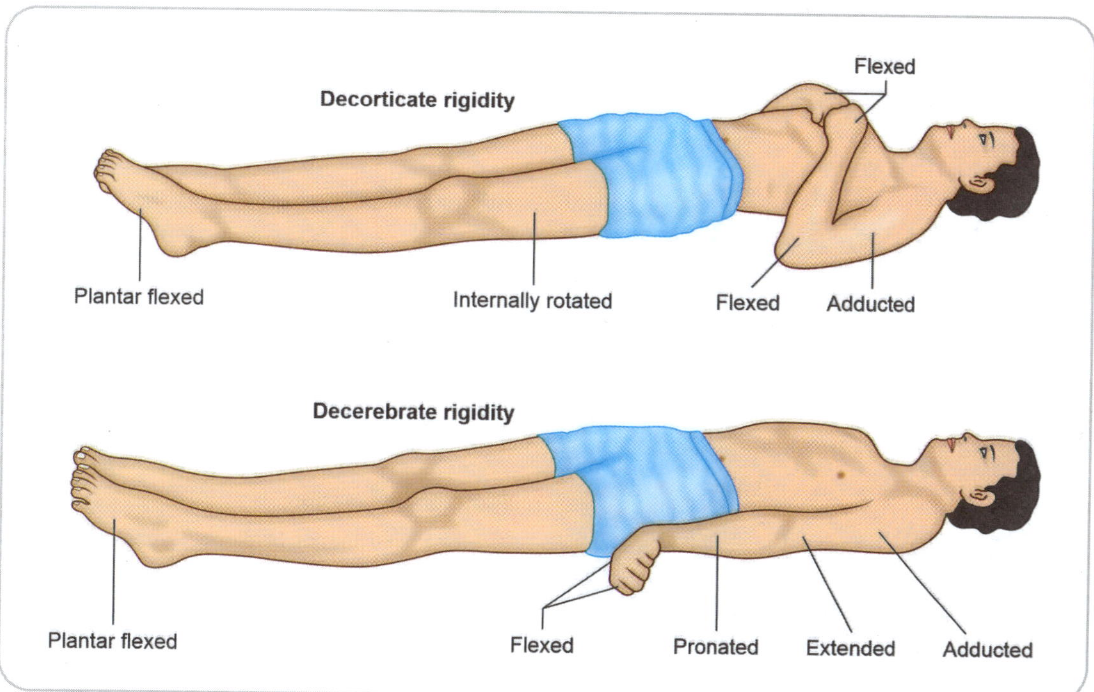

44. Typical and atypical antipsychotics

Aspects	Typical antipsychotics	Atypical antipsychotics
Other names	First generation Antipsychotics or older Antipsychotics	Second generation antipsychotics or newer antipsychotics
Extrapyramidal symptoms	High risk to get	Low risk to get
Side effects	More likely to cause neurological side effects	More likely to cause metabolic side effects
Withdrawal symptoms	High	Less
Example	Haloperidol, Chlorpromazine, Thioridazine, fluphenazine, etc.	Clozapine, olanzapine, risperidone, quetiapine, etc.

45. Stereognosis and barognosis

Aspects	Stereognosis	Barognosis
Other names	Haptic perception or tactile gnosis	Baresthesia
Definition	Ability to perceive the object with tactile perception in the absence of auditory and visual perception.	Ability to evaluate the weight of the objects

46. Grief and depression

Grief	Depression
Intense emotional pain due to the loss of loved ones.	
Loss of interest or pleasure due to loss of loved ones.	Pervasive loss of interest or pleasure.
Withdrawal from the activities or meeting the person or situations due to death.	Withdrawal from the activities in general.
Intrusive images about the deceased.	Intrusive images are uncommon.
Preoccupied with the deceased. Sense of guilt, shame and low self-esteem related to the deceased.	Preoccupied with the sense of guilt, shame and low self esteem.
Pervasive dysphoric mood is present.	Emotions might be triggered by the reminders of loss.

47. Sedatives and hypnotics

Sedatives.	Hypnotics
Drugs produce the calming and relaxing effect.	Drugs that induce sleep.
It reduces anxiety.	It initiates and maintains the sleep.
Sedatives in larger dose produce hypnotic effect.	Hypnotics in larger doses produce the effect of general anesthesia.
Site of action of this drug is Limbic system.	Site of action of this drug is reticular activating system.

48. Hallucination and pseudohallucination

Hallucination	Pseudohallucination
Misperception without any external stimuli which occurs in objective space.	It is false hallucination involuntary sensory experience which occurs in subjective space.
Example: Voices heard from outside is termed complex auditory hallucination.	Example: One's own thought being heard is termed pseudohallucination.

49. Yoga and exercise

Aspects	Yoga	Exercises
Meaning	Integration of body, mind and spirit	Physical activity which promotes the health
Oxygen consumption	Reduced	Increased
Calorie consumption	Moderate to high	Low
Movements	Rapid	Slow and dynamic
Toning of muscle tone	Enhances muscle strength but it is not a primary concern	Primary concern
Special equipment	Not required	Required
Risk of injury	Low	High
Age restrictions	No	Elders need to avoid the strenuous activities

50. Euthymia, euphoria, elation, exaltation and ecstasy

Euthymia	Euphoria	Elation	Exaltation	Ecstasy
Normal Mood	Mild elevation of mood (Seen in hypomania)	Moderate elevation of mood with psychomotor agitation	Severe elevation of mood with grandiose delusion	Very severe elevation of mood with extreme blissfulness

51. Weber's test and Rinne's test

Weber's test	Rinne's test
Test is performed to assess cochlear nerve function. Tuning fork is kept in middle of head. Normal individuals will hear the sound equally by both ears. If lateralization toward one side is felt it denotes hearing loss.	Test is performed to assess cochlear nerve function. Keep the tuning fork in mastoid bone and then near to patient's ear after striking it. When air conduction is more than bone conduction, it is normal. If the bone conduction is more than air conduction it denotes conductive hearing loss.

52. Indian Lunacy Act and Mental Health Act

Aspects	Indian Lunacy Act	Mental Health Act
Year of commencement	1912	1987
Chapters	8	10
Act number	4	14
Terms involved	Lunatics, Lunatic asylum and Criminal Lunatics	Mentally ill, Psychiatric Hospital, and Nursing homes
Authority	No such provision	Central and State Mental Health authority established
License system		License has to be obtained to commence and maintain the psychiatric hospital or nursing homes.
Out patient facility		Established for those who doesn't need admission.
Psychiatrist and social workers involved as visitors board member		Included
Voluntary admission	Medical officer can admit the voluntary patient with the permission obtained from at least two boards of visitors.	Medical officer has power to admit the voluntary patient.
Involuntary admission	No such provision	Medical officer can admit the involuntary patient with two medical certificates.
Human rights protection	No such provision	Guidelines established
Inspecting officer		Appointed to monitor the hospital facilities, medical records, patient care and report the same to licensing authorities.
Leave of absence	Guidelines made are less flexible	Permitted to all patients except the patients in prison.

53. Epileptic seizures and dissociative convulsions or hysterical fits

Aspects	Epileptic seizures	Dissociative convulsions or hysterical fits
Clinical pattern	Stereotyped	Purposive body movements
Place of incident	Anywhere	Safe place
Time of day	Anytime, even happen during sleep	Never happen during sleep
Speech	Absent	May present
Tongue bite	May present	Absent
Injury	May occur	Very rare
Urine and fecal incontinence	May occur	Very rare
Duration	Shorter	Prolonged
Turning of head	Unilateral	Side to side turning is present
Eye gaze	Staring gaze if the eyes are open	Avoidant gaze

Aspects	Epileptic seizures	Dissociative convulsions or hysterical fits
Neurological signs	Present	Absent
Amnesia	Complete	Partial
Stress	25% of patients have stress	Majority of them have stress
Post-ictal confusion	Present	Absent
Eeg	Abnormal	Normal
Serum prolactin	Raised in postictal period	Normal

54. Oral movements in rabbit syndrome and tardive dyskinesia

Oral movements in rabbit syndrome	Oral movements in tardive dyskinesia
Chewing movements are regular and rapid	Orofacial choreoathetoid movements are present with decreased rapidness. Tongue and other parts of the mouth are not involved

Objective Structured Clinical Evaluation (OSCE)

INTRODUCTION

Curriculum requires students to integrate basic and clinical sciences. No single method of assessment can effectively test the three individual aspects of learning, namely knowledge, attitudes and skill. A vast variety of evaluation procedures are available for measuring the results of teaching and learning. Evaluation procedure can be classified into qualitative and quantitative techniques.

The teaching learning process and evaluation in nursing education are designed on the basis of three domains-cognitive, affective and psychomotor in varying degrees. Providing fair and reasonable clinical evaluation is one of the most important and most challenging faculty roles. Objective structured clinical evaluation was designed to test the clinical competence while simultaneously improving objectivity and reliability.

MEANING

OSCE is a method of clinical/practical examination where predetermined decisions are made based on the competencies to be tested with the use of checklists incorporating important skills. The candidates rotate through a number of stations at which they are asked to carry out a specific task.

- 'O' stands for **Objective.**
  Every student gets the same patient (same chance).
- 'S' stands for **Structured.**
  - Several skills are tested at one time.
  - Each skill is tested at a separate station.
  - The examiner has a checklist for doing the marking.

PURPOSES OF OSCE

- To test each component of clinical competence uniformly and objectively for all students.
- To assess the extent of achievement of each student in every practical skill.
- To improve the objectivity and reliability of clinical evaluation.
- To evaluate a set of predetermined clinical competencies.
- To reduce patient and examiner variability.

IMPORTANCE OF OSCE

- OSCE allows the student to appreciate more on its purpose.
- Learners can benefit more from its pedagogical values.
- OSCE allows to institute different modalities including the traditional method of studying anatomy on cadavers, by dissection, manipulation.
- Exploration of surface anatomy, medical imaging methods and therapeutic procedures such as open surgery, laparoscopy and arthroscopy.
- In OSCE, multiple stations are designed and each station has a specific objective.
- OSCE is more objective, reliable and a valid tool to assess practical aspects of integrated problem-based curriculum.
- Organization of OSCE requires team work, logistics but at the same time a large number of students can be tested with standard setting in a short period of time.
- OSCE appropriately tests students' grasping power.
- OSCE is motivating, inspiring and interesting.

- OSCE is based on the curriculum which demands higher cognitive skills.
- There is a need to develop objective tools to assess higher cognitive skills like clinical application.
- Objectives tested in an OSCE assess higher cognitive and psychomotor skills, i.e., ability to relate clinical information with structural material (plastic models, cadaveric specimen, photomicrographs, etc.).

SKILLS TESTED BY OSCE

- OSCE helps to assess the capacity for observation, analysis and interpretation.
- OSCE can be structured to achieve the desired mix of different elements being assessed, each element receiving the desired weightage.

STATIONS

- The students during the examination move around a number of stations spending a specific amount of time at each station.
- On a signal, he/she moves on to the next station.
- The time allowed is the same for all the stations.
- The stations must be designed accordingly. 4–10 minutes are given at each station.

OSCE PROCESS

- The questions for each station are written in accordance with the blueprint of the block.
- Organization of OSCE for the "end of block" examination.
- The answer key is prepared before examination. The OSCE questions (stations) are reviewed by a multidisciplinary committee before they are administered.
- A clinical scenario is given at each station and students are informed about integrated questions.
- These would incorporate knowledge components including structural, functional, clinical, radiological and microscopic aspects.
- For example, for a given clinical scenario, students are asked to:
    - Identify the labeled or tagged structures involved
    - Interpret physiological/pathological laboratory data.
    - Identify the labeled structure on a radiograph.

BLUEPRINT FOR OSCE

- Organize a meeting with the appropriate resource persons, HODs and faculty.
- Identify the important learning needs.
- The blueprint of OSCE is developed as a part of the master blueprint.
- Formulates a blueprint.
- Prepare table of specification.
- Represent every aspect of the course.
- Faculty member is assigned for a particular unit/block.
- Prepare objectives (Unit/block committee).
- Write questions in accordance with specific objectives.
- The members through a concerted effort correct the questions as needed.
- Ensure clarity, sound factual content and appropriate emphasis on the clinical application.
- Ensure that the questions are not ambiguous and the students are able to answer each question within time limit.
- Test skills of identification, interpretation of results in clinical context.
- Finally, the questions are sent to the Phase Director who appoints three to six judges to evaluate the questions and set up minimum pass level, the questions are then handed over to assessment office for execution.
- (A) related to identification of a structure
- (B) a secondary question involving application of knowledge.

MERITS OF OSCE

- It is objective, reliable, valid and discriminatory.
- All students are exposed to same standardized questions.
- It covers a wide spectrum of learning domains.
- It tests a wide range of skills in a short period of time.
- Learning objectives can be achieved.
- The content and complexity of the exam can be controlled by the examiners.
- It gives a reasonable idea of the achievement of the student in every objective of practical exercises.
- It helps to test the analytical abilities of students.
- Organization is easy.
- Questions bank can be made.
- A large number of students can be examined in a short time.

DEMERITS OF OSCE

- Substantial faculty hours are required to construct, review and develop integrated multidisciplinary questions.
- The availability of quality cadaveric dissections, images, laboratory and physiological data sets.

- It takes a lot of time, effort and team work on the part of examiners.
- All stations must invariably demand equal time, and they require careful organization.

INSTRUCTIONS TO STUDENTS

Before the start of OSCE, the following instructions are given to students:

- Bring your own pen/pencils and wear white lab coats.
- Electronic devices like mobile phones, tabs, etc. are not allowed in the examination hall.
- Cheating in any respect is strictly prohibited and the regulation of the university will be applied.
- Write your name and ID on each sheet of answer books.
- Upon entering the OSCE examination hall, stand on each station with face opposite to station.
- Encircle the station number in your answer books. This will be your first station and then follow the sequence.
- A bell will ring at the beginning of OSCE marking the start of examination.
- Rotate clockwise around 28 stations including 4 rest stations spending 90 seconds (1.5 minutes) at each station.
- Clear instructions are given at each station as to what you should do.
- Do not touch or move the models, specimens or plastinated specimen.
- Do not move the microscopic slides, only fine adjustments knobs can be used.
- A bell will ring at the end of examination and remain at your station from where the answer books will be collected.

EXAMPLE FOR OSCE IN MENTAL HEALTH NURSING

SET: 1 (OSCE Stations)

OBJECTIVE STRUCTURED CLINICAL EVALUATION (OSCE)
TEST MAP (BASED ON BLUEPRINT)

Blueprint cell		Item title (Condition)	Competence tested	Proposed test item
A	1	Anxious personality disorder	Examination	Mental status examination
B	2	Couplet (A) assessment on suicidal ideas	Diagnostic measures	Simulated patient with suicidal ideas
C	3	Couplet (B) psychotherapeutic counseling	Therapeutic procedure	Simulated patient with suicidal ideas
D	4	Violent behavior	Identification	Simulated patient with violent behavior by VideoShow (video editing software)
E	5	Paranoid personality disorder	History collection	Simulated patient with paranoid personality disorder
F	6	Obsessive compulsive disorder (OCD) personality order	Therapeutic procedure	Simulated patient with OCD personality disorder
G	7	Histrionic personality disorder	Data interpretation	Case scenario
H	8	Narcissistic personality disorder	Identification of abnormal finding	Case scenario
I	9	Dependent personality disorder	Data interpretation	Case scenario

Sl. no.	Program component	Domains of clinical experience										
		No. of stations	Communication		Examination		Procedure			Cognitive skills		
			HT	OC	MSE	VSI	TP	DP	IATF	DI	DM	PS
			A	B	C	D	E	F	G	H	I	J
1.	Anxious personality disorder	1			1							
2.	Couplet (A) assessment on suicidal ideas	2							1			
3.	Couplet (B) psychotherapeutic counseling	3		1							1	1
4.	Violent behavior	4								1	1	1
5.	Paranoid personality disorder	5	1									
6.	OCD personality disorder	6		1		1					1	1
7.	Histrionic personality disorder	7									1	
8.	Narcissistic personality disorder	8								1	1	
9.	Dependent personality disorder	9						1				
	Total											

Key Words:

- **HT** : History taking
- **DI** : Data interpretation
- **OC** : Other communication
- **IATF** : Identification of abnormal test finding
- **PE** : Physical examination
- **DP** : Diagnostic procedure
- **VSI** : Virtual sign identification
- **DM** : Decision making
- **TP** : Therapeutic procedure
- **PS** : Problem solving

Artifacts for every station:

Simulation	Examiner	Examinee
Scenario printout	Examiner instruction Sheet printout Evaluation scoring sheet printout Table Chair Writing pad Pen Eraser Pencil Gong bell	Simulation client Student response sheet Response sheet collection box

STATION 1–ANXIOUS PERSONALITY DISORDER

Instructions to the Examinee

Ms X aged 28 years came with complaint of avoiding social gathering and family functions. Her mind is preoccupied with being criticized or rejected and she also shows extreme anxiety, nervousness and low self-esteem. She wants to be alone always and feels embarrassed, blushes and cries. Perform mental status examination.

Participant number: ________ **Date:** ___________

Instructions to the Examiner

- Observe the examinee, check whether the examinee makes appropriate assessment of the client.
- Consult the examinee about the assessment performed.

Skill Station

Mental status examination

Objectives

At the end of simulation, the examinee:
- Observes and assesses the client
- Documents the disorder

CRITERIA FOR IDENTIFICATION OF TYPES OF PERSONALITY DISORDER

Steps	Tasks	Scores	Yes	No
1.	Greet the client/establish the rapport	1		
2.	The examinee asks questions and explores verbal comments/ information 1. Social withdrawal 2. Fear of criticism 3. Excessive preoccupation with being rejected. 4. Extreme anxiety and aloofness	 2 2 2 2		
3.	Interprets signs and symptoms and infers the diagnosis.	1		
	Total	**10**		

Pass score = 8/10 (80%)
Student score = ____
Pass – Yes/No

Signature of the examiner **Signature of the OSCE coordinator**

Instructions for the Simulated Anxious/Avoidant Personality Disorder

You are playing the role of a 28-year-old female having complaint of avoiding social gathering and family functions. Your mind is preoccupied with being criticized or rejected and you also show extreme anxiety, nervousness and low self-esteem. You want to be alone always and feel embarrassed, blush and cry and show signs of anxiety in front of others.

OSCE—Response Sheet

Station 1: Mental Status Examination—Anxious personality disorder
Registration No: Documentation—Assessment of mood disturbances for anxious personality disorder

STATION 2–SUICIDAL IDEATION

Instruction to the Examinee

Mr X aged 30 years is a divorcee with complaints of suicidal ideas, sudden changes in mood, passing negative comments on her parents about future, feeling of extreme sadness, hopelessness and lack of interest in personal appearance, friends and social activities. He says repeatedly that I want to die and end my life. Assess the warning signs or clues of suicidal ideas.

STATION 2 –COUPLET-(A) SUICIDAL IDEAS (ASSESSMENT)

Register number: ________ **Date:** ______

Instruction to the Examiner

- Kindly check whether the examinee interprets correctly.
- If the student assesses and identifies the warning signs of suicidal ideas, give 1 mark. If no warning signs are seen, 0 mark has to be given.

Objectives

At the end of simulation, the examinee:
Assesses and observes the response of the client carefully.

Sl. no.	Tasks	Scores	Yes	No
1.	Greet and welcome the client with warmth	2		
2.	Identify the warning signs of suicidal ideas			
	Behavioral clues: Sudden changes in mood, sadness	2		
	Verbal clues: I want to die and end my life	2		
	Situational clues: Client got divorce recently **Nonverbal clues:** Lack of interest in personal appearance, family and social activities	2		
3.	The examinee documents the inference regarding the client's signs and symptoms	2		
	Total	**10**		

Pass score = 8/10 (80%)
Student score =____
Pass – Yes/No

Signature of the examiner **Signature of the OSCE coordinator**

STATION 2–COUPLET-(A) ASSESSMENT ON WARNING SIGNS OF SUICIDAL IDEAS

Instruction to the Simulated Suicidal Ideas Patient

You are playing the role of a 30-year-old divorcee with complaints of suicidal ideas, sudden changes in mood, passing negative comments on your parents about future, feeling of extreme sadness, hopelessness and lack of interest in personal appearance, friends and social activities. You say repeatedly that I want to die and end my life.

OSCE–RESPONSE SHEET

Station 2 –Couplet-(A) Assessment
Registration no:
Documentation: Assessment

STATION 3-PSYCHOANALYTICAL COUNSELING

Instruction to the Examinee

Mr X aged 30 years is a divorcee with complaints of suicidal ideas, sudden changes in mood, passing negative comments on her parents about future, feeling of extreme sadness, hopelessness and lack of interest in personal appearance, friends and social activities. He says repeatedly that I want to die and end my life. There is a need of counseling for behavior modification.

STATION 3–(PSYCHOANALYTICAL COUNSELING)

Register number: ________ **Date:** _______

Instruction to the Examiner

Observe the examinee while counseling the client and assess whether counselor adheres to the steps involved in the checklist during counseling.

Skill Station

Therapeutic

Objectives

At the end of simulation, the examinee:
Observes, assesses and counsels the client for behavior modification.

CHECKLIST: COUNSELING

Sl. no.	Tasks	Scores	Yes	No
1.	Greet and welcome the client with warmth	1		
2.	The examinee tends to promote insight and awareness	2		
3.	The examinee explores whether the client has reduced resistance in behavior	2		
4.	The examinee examines and helps the client for open communication	2		
5.	The examinee promotes the client to change behavior through counseling	2		
6.	The examinee interprets the change of behavior	1		
	TOTAL	10		

Pass score = 8/10 (80%)
Student score = ____
Pass – Yes/No

Signature of the examiner **Signature of the OSCE coordinator**

Instruction to the Simulated Patient with Suicidal Ideation

You are playing the role of a 30-year-old divorcee with complaints of suicidal ideas, sudden changes in mood, passing negative comments on your parents about future, feeling of extreme sadness, hopelessness and lack of interest in personal appearance, friends and social activities. You say repeatedly that I want to die and end my life.

STATION 4–VIOLENT BEHAVIOR AND SELECTION OF APPROPRIATE MEDICINE

Instruction to the Examinee

Mrs X aged 25 years has a history of domestic violence toward others and violence to self, and her behavior is cruel toward others and animals. She frequently engages in assault behavior. She is uncooperative, irrational and feels humiliated. Identify the condition and write appropriate drug.

Register number: ___________ **Date:** ___________

Instructions to the Examiner

Observe the examinee and consult whether the selection of drug displayed is appropriate.

Skill Station

Virtual identification of diagnosis and analyze the appropriate medication.

Objectives

At the end of simulation, the examinee:
Observes the video and selects the medication displayed.

CRITERIA FOR IDENTIFICATION OF THE DIAGNOSIS AND SELECTION OF APPROPRIATE MEDICATION

Sl. no.	Tasks	Scores	Yes	No
1.	Assess the client status	2		
2.	The examinee observes and identifies the symptoms of violent behavior: • Domestic violent act • Cruel behavior toward others • Assault behavior • Uncooperativeness • Irrational • Feels humiliated	6		
3.	Identify the client diagnosis and analyze the appropriate medication.	2		
	Total	**10**		

Pass score = 8/10 (80%)
Student score = ____
Pass – Yes/No

Signature of the examiner **Signature of the OSCE coordinator**

Artifacts

- Video tap
- Laptop
- Headset

STATION 5–PREMORBID PERSONALITY ASSESSMENT (HISTORY TAKING)

Instruction to the Examinee

Mrs X aged 38 years has mistrust about all realms of life, has difficulty in maintaining job, feels insecure, assumes her partner to be unfaithful, and she is stubborn about her suspiciousness. She finds it difficult to maintain intimate relationship with others. She likes to be alone and self-thinking. She has lack of proper sleep and diet. Assess the premorbid personality of the client.

Register number:_________ **Date:**________

Instruction to the Examiner

- Observe the examinee while assessing and identifying the personality of the client.
- If the student assesses and identifies the component of personality, give 1 mark. Else, 0 mark has to be given.

Skill Station

Assessment—History collection

Objectives

At the end of assessment, the examinee:
- Identifies the personality of the client
- Documents the inference of the client

Sl. no.	Tasks	Scores	Yes	No
1.	Establish rapport with the client	1		
2.	The examinee asks lead questions and explores verbal comments/information:	1		
	• On attitude to self (hopes and attitude)	1		
	• Social relationships (relationship with family, friends and others)	1		
	• Moral and religious standards	1		
	• Responsibility at work place (relationship with coworkers, job satisfaction)	1		
	• Mood (love, anger, frustration)	1		
	• Habits (sleeping, eating, elimination)	1		
	• Fantasy life (daydreaming)	1		
3.	The examinee documents the inference regarding the client's premorbid personality.	1		
	TOTAL	**10**		

Pass score = 8/10 (80%)
Student score = ____
Pass – Yes/No

Signature of the examiner **Signature of the OSCE coordinator**

Instruction to the Simulated Patient

You are playing the role of a 38-year-old female who has mistrust about all realms of life, difficulty in maintaining job, feels insecure and assumes her partner to be unfaithful. You are stubborn about your suspiciousness. You find it difficult to maintain intimate relationship with others. You like to be alone and self-thinking. You have lack of proper sleep and diet.

Instruction to the Informant of Simulated Patient

You are playing the role of a parent of a 38-year-old female who has mistrust about all realms of life, difficulty in maintaining job, feels insecure and assumes her partner to be unfaithful. She is stubborn about her suspiciousness. She faces difficulty in maintaining intimate relationship with others. She likes to be alone and self-thinking and has lack of proper sleep and diet.

STATION 6–COUNSELING FOR BEHAVIOR MODIFICATION (PATIENT WITH OCD PERSONALITY DISORDER)

Instruction to the Examinee

Ms X aged 25 years washes hands at regular intervals throughout the day due to fear of contamination and arranges household things perfectly. She performs tasks to seek relief from anxiety. She has some stereotyped behavior such as repeated clearing of throat and counting steps.

Participant number:________ **Date:___________**

Instructions to the Examiner

Observe the examinee while counseling the client and assess whether counselor adheres to the steps provided in the checklist during counseling.

Skill Station

Therapeutic

Objectives

At the end of simulation, the examinee:

- Observes and assesses the client
- Counsels the client for behavior modification

CHECKLIST: COUNSELING

Sl. no.	Tasks	Scores	Yes	No
1.	Greet and welcome the client with warmth	1		
2.	Assess the client's symptoms and confirm the condition	1		
3.	The examinee explains the situation and encourages to utilize coping strategies to overcome problems	2		
4.	The examinee encourages the client to constantly observe his/her behavior and teaches to utilize "self-control technique" to overcome ritualistic behavior.	2		
5.	The examinee explores some diversional activities to divert the client's mind	2		
6.	The examinee examines and helps the client for open communication	1		
7.	The examine interprets the change of OCD behavior	1		
	Total	**10**		

Pass score = 4/5 (80%)
Student score = ____
Pass – Yes/No

Signature of the examiner **Signature of the OSCE coordinator**

Instructions to the Simulated Client

You are playing the role of a 25-year-old female who washes hands at regular intervals throughout the day due to fear of contamination and arranges household things perfectly. You perform tasks to seek relief from anxiety. You have some stereotyped behavior such as repeated clearing of throat and counting steps.

STATION 7–DIAGNOSIS AND MANAGEMENT OF HISTRIONIC PERSONALITY DISORDER

Instruction to the Examinee

Ms X aged 25 years is admitted in female ward with complaints of excessive emotionality and attention-seeking behavior, excessive concern about her physical appearance, and self-centeredness. She shows very poor tolerance of frustration and delayed gratification, and exhibits suicidal attempts frequently.

Answer the following questions:

1. Identify the condition.
2. List out any two symptoms.
3. Write any three nursing management steps.

Participant number: ________ **Date:** ____________

Instructions to the Examiner

Identify the correct answer and give scores.

Skill Station

Unmanned

Objective

At the end of assessment, analyze the examinee's critical thinking and decision making.

CRITERIA FOR IDENTIFICATION OF DIAGNOSIS AND APPROPRIATE MANAGEMENT

Sl. no.	Tasks	Scores	Yes	No
1.	Histrionic personality disorder	2		
2.	• Traumatic emotionality • Constance seeking of reassurance Others: self-centered, poor tolerance	2		
3.	Nursing management. • Establish and maintain therapeutic nurse-client relationship	2		
	• Provide immediate positive feedback	2		
	• Provide safe and calm environment Others: Promo te effective communication strategies	2		
	Total	10		

Pass score = 8/10 (80%)
Student score = ____
Pass – Yes/No

Signature of the examiner **Signature of the OSCE coordinator**

STATION 8–IDENTIFY THE TYPES OF NARCISSISTIC PERSONALITY

Instruction to the Examinee

Read the scenario carefully and identify the type of narcissistic personality and document it.

- **Scenario 1:** People who are more self-centered.
- **Scenario 2:** Intense contempt for themselves, but projects outward into others: drives other people away from them by hypercritical and jealous comments and behavior
- **Scenario 3:** Enjoys with superiority feelings by manipulating the situations.
- **Scenario 4:** People who tend to be aggressive, athletic, exhibitionistic, enjoy by showing off body, clothes and overall manliness.

STATION 8

Participant number: ________ **Date:** ___________

Instructions to the Examiner

Identify the correct answer and give scores.

Skill Station

Unmanned

Objective

At the end of assessment, analyze the examinee's critical thinking and decision making.

CRITERIA FOR IDENTIFICATION OF SUBTYPES OF NARCISSISTIC PERSONALITY DISORDER

Sl. no.	Tasks	Scores	Yes	No
1.	Craving narcissists	2		
2.	Paranoid narcissists	2		
3.	Manipulative narcissists	2		
4.	Phallic narcissists	2		
5.	Inference and documentation	2		
	Total	10		

Pass score = 8/10 (80%)
Student score = ____
Pass – Yes/No

Signature of the examiner **Signature of the OSCE coordinator**

STATION 9–DEPENDENT PERSONALITY DISORDER

Instruction to the Examinee

Mrs X aged 35 years came with complaints of fear of separation, strong need for constant reassurance and support. She expects subordination for her own needs, faces difficulties in decision making and exhibits low self-esteem and self-confidence.

Answer the following:

1. Identify the type of personality disorder.
2. Mention any two drug therapy.
3. Mention any two therapeutic management needed.
4. Write one possible nursing diagnosis based on symptoms.

STATION 9

Participant number: ________ **Date:**___________

Instructions to the Examiner

Identify the correct answer and give scores.

Skill Station

Unmanned

Objective

At the end of assessment, analyze the examinee's critical thinking and decision making.

CHECKLIST FOR SCORING

Sl. no.	Tasks	Scores	Yes	No
1.	Dependent personality disorder	2		
2.	Antidepressants Sedative and tranquilizers	4		
3.	Psychotherapy Cognitive behavior therapy	2		
4.	Fear and anxiety related to separation as evidenced by facial expression	2		
	Total	**10**		

Pass score = 8/10 (80%)
Student score = ____
Pass – Yes/No

Signature of the examiner **Signature of the OSCE coordinator**

TEST MAP (BASED ON BLUEPRINT)

Blueprint cell		Item title (condition)	Competence tested	Proposed test item
A	1	Positive reinforcement	Examination	Simulated child with habit of thumb sucking
B	2	Amnesia	Assessment	Visual image
C	3.	Psychometric Assessment	Assessment	Visual image
D	4	Admission procedure	Examination	Simulated patient
E	5	Paraphilias	Assessment	
F	6	Dysgraphia	Assessment	Simulated video
G	7	Dyscalculia	Assessment	Simulated video
H	8	Discharge procedure	Assessment	

Sl. no.	Program component	Domains of clinical experience									
		Communication		Examination		Procedure			Cognitive skills		
		HT	OC	MSE	VSI	TP	DP	IATF	DI	DM	PS
		A	B	C	D	E	F	G	H	I	J
1.	Positive reinforcement					1					
2.	Amnesia					1		1			
3.	Psychometric assessment	1				1					
4.	Admission procedure			1						1	
5.	paraphilia							1			
6.	Dysgraphia					1		1			
7.	Dyscalculia					1					
8.	Discharge procedure								1		
	Total										

Key words:

- **VSI** : Virtual sign identification
- **HT** : History taking
- **DI** : Data interpretation
- **DM** : Decision making
- **OC** : Other communication
- **IATF** : Identification of abnormal test finding
- **TP** : Therapeutic procedure
- **PE** : Physical examination
- **DP** : Diagnostic procedure
- **PS** : Problem solving

STATION 10–BEHAVIOR THERAPY- POSITIVE REINFORCEMENT

Instruction to the Examinee

Mr X aged 8 years is brought to the child guidance clinic by his parents, with the habit of thumb sucking. He is not able to concentrate on his studies, has poor academic performance, does not interact with others, and shows frustration and sleeplessness.

- Identify the problems of the child.
- Use the appropriate behavior technique to resolve his problem.
- Implement appropriate behavior technique.
- Mention any two suggestions for family counseling.

Participant number: ________ **Date:** ___________

Instructions to the Examiner

- Observe the examinee, check whether the examinee makes appropriate assessment of the client.
- If the student assesses and identifies the behavior technique give 1 mark. If the student does not identify the behavior technique, 0 mark has to be given.

Skill Station

Manned station–behavior therapy – Positive reinforcement

Objective

At the end of simulation, the examinee assesses and observes the response of the client carefully.

Criteria for Using Behavior Therapy—Positive Reinforcement

Steps	Tasks	Scores	Yes	No
1.	Greet the child and parents/establish rapport	2		
2.	Assess the problems of the child by observing and obtaining information from parents Thumb sucking	2		
3.	Identify the appropriate behavior technique to resolve his thumb sucking Behavior therapy-positive reinforcement Give some token for his inappropriate behavior (not sucking the thumb)	2		
4.	Give any two appropriate suggestions to the family • Always start by talking to your child about why thumb sucking is a bad habit. Positive motivation to quit is half the battle. • Thumb and finger sucking spreads germs and makes people sick. • Sucking pushes teeth forward and can make you look funny, and you might need brace. • Other kids will think you are still a baby or might tease. • As long as you suck your thumb, it is hard to learn how to speak the right way. You might sound funny. **Sticker chart or positive reward system:** Make a sticker chart and provide lots of praise and positive rewards for success. At first, your child might need a sticker for every hour he or she goes without sucking. **Praise, all day:** Find a way to remind yourself or your child's caregiver to praise your child for not sucking at least once an hour. Consider setting an alarm or reminder on your phone.	4		
	Total	**10**		

Pass score = 4/ 5(80%)
Student score = ____
Pass – Yes/No

Signature of the examiner **Signature of the OSCE coordinator**

Instructions to the Simulated Child with Habits of Thumb Sucking

You are playing the role of a 8-year-old child who has the habit of thumb sucking, is not able to concentrate on his studies, has poor academic performance, does not interact with others, and shows frustration and sleeplessness.

Station 10: Behavior therapy

Registration no:

Documentation: Asses the problems of the child and provide family counseling.

STATION 11–AMNESIA

Instruction to the Examinee

Mr Surya aged 40 years who met with an accident was admitted in male acute ward with complaints of head injury, inability to recall, and confusion about time and place.

- Identify the symptoms and mention the condition
- Formulate a nursing diagnosis
- Write three nursing interventions.

STATION 11

Register number: _______ **Date:** ______

Instruction to the Examiner

- Kindly check whether the examinee interprets correctly.
- If the student assesses and identifies the symptoms, give 1 mark. If the student does not assess and identify the symptoms, 0 mark has to be given.

Skill Station

Unmanned Station–Amnesia

Objectives

At the end of simulation, the examinee:

- Identifies the symptoms
- Formulates a nursing diagnosis
- Writes nursing interventions

Sl. no.	Tasks	Scores	Yes	No
1.	Identify the picture and mention the symptoms Amnesia	2		
2.	Impaired memory as evidenced by memory loss/ behavioral changes Chronic confusion related to memory impairment	2		
3.	**Nursing interventions:** • Using memory aid • Use object cues: A timer set to remind the persons to turn off the stove • Use telephone reminders for a person who remains unsupervised at home • Identify family members or support systems • Use reminiscence therapy	6		
	Total	**10**		

Pass score = 4/5 (80%)

Student score = ____

Pass – Yes/No

Signature of the examiner **Signature of the OSCE coordinator**

STATION 12–PSYCHOMETRIC ASSESSMENT

Instruction to the Examinee

Identify the types of psychological tests in psychometric assessment and abbreviate the questionnaire.

Picture completion test

Ink blot test

Arrangement of equipment

Fire accident—what is your immediate action?

MMPI stands for?

STATION 12

Register number: ________ **Date:** ________

Instruction to the Examiner

Identify the appropriate type of psychological test and abbreviate the questionnaire.

Skill Station

Unmanned Station — Identify the name of the test by visualization

Objectives

At the end of simulation, the examinee:

- Identifies the appropriate psychological test
- Abbreviates the questionnaire.

Sl. no.	Tasks	Scores	Yes/No
1.	**Identify the appropriate psychological test**		
	Picture completion test—Intelligence test	2	
	Ink blot test—Personality test	2	
	Arrangement of equipment—Aptitude test	2	
	Fire accident—what is your immediate action?—Attitude test	2	
	MMPI—Minnesota Multiphasic Personality Inventory	2	
	TOTAL	10	

Pass score= 4/5 (80%)
Student score=____
Pass – Yes/No

Signature of the examiner **Signature of the OSCE coordinator**

STATION 13–ADMISSION PROCEDURE

Instructions to the Examinee

A woman aged 45 years is looking untidy, wandering on the street, and does not know about her identity.

- What is your immediate action?
- Mention any three types of admission.
- Which type of admission you will prefer?

Register number: _______ **Date:** ______

Instruction to the Examiner

- Observe the examinee, check whether the examinee makes appropriate assessment of the client.
- If the student assesses and identifies the types of admission, each type give 1 mark, else 0 mark has to be given.

Skill Station

Manned Station—Admission Procedure

Objectives

At the end of assessment, the examinee:

- Is able to take immediate response
- Enlists the types of admission
- Documents the admission type.

Sl. no.	Tasks	Scores	Yes	No
1.	Immediate response of the examinee Calling the police	2		
2.	Any three types of admission • Admission on voluntarily basis • Admission under special circumstances • Admission under reception order • Admission through police	 2 2 2		
3.	Which type of admission will suit this scenario? Admitted by police	2		
	TOTAL	**10**		

Pass score = 4/5 (80%)
Student score = ____
Pass – Yes/No

Signature of the examiner **Signature of the OSCE coordinator**

STATION 14–SEXUAL DISORDER

Instructions to the Examinee

Mr X aged 45 years comes with complaints that he is very fond of nonliving objects associated with human body, frequently wears the clothes of opposite sex and has intimate relationship with pet animals.

- Identify the classification of disorder.
- Mention three signs and symptoms.
- What type of therapy can be given?

STATION 14

Participant number: ________ **Date:** ___________

Instructions to the Examiner

- Observe the examinee, check whether the examinee makes appropriate assessment of the client.
- If the student assesses and identifies the sexual disorder, its signs or symptoms and therapy, each type give 2 mark, else 0 mark has to be given.

Skill Station

Unmanned Station—Analyze the appropriate types of disorder.

Objective

At the end of simulation, the examinee identifies the disorder and symptoms.

Criteria for Examinee Regarding Identification of Symptoms and Therapy

Sl. no.	Tasks	Scores	Yes	No
1.	Classifications of disorder Sexual disorder	2		
2.	Three sign and symptoms • Fetishism • Transvestism • Zoophilia	 2 2 2		
3.	Therapy Aversion therapy	2		
	TOTAL	10		

Pass score = 4/5 (80%)
Student score =____
Pass – Yes/No

Signature of the examiner **Signature of the OSCE coordinator**

STATION 15–PERVASIVE DEVELOPMENTAL DISORDER-DYSGRAPHIA

Instructions to the Examinee

- Observe the video and identify the disorder
- Make a nursing diagnosis
- Write three possible nursing interventions

Participant number: ________ **Date:** ___________

Instructions to the Examiner

- Observe the examinee, check whether the examinee makes appropriate assessment of the client.
- If the student assesses and identifies the name of disorder, its skill deficit and any three nursing interventions; each type give 2 mark, else 0 mark has to be given.

Skill Station

Unmanned Station—Virtual identification and analysis of the disorder

Objectives

At the end of simulation, the examinee:
- Identifies the type of disorder
- Identifies the skill which is deficient in the child
- Writes three nursing interventions for improving skill

Sl. no.	Tasks	Scores	Yes	No
1.	Classifications of disorder Pervasive developmental disorder—dysgraphia	2		
2.	Skill deficit Difficulty in writing	2		
3.	Any three nursing interventions:	6		
	• Helps the child to hold pen			
	• Additional time to copy			
	• Don't penalize spelling error			
	• Breakdown the assignments			
	Total	**10**		

Pass score = 4/5 (80%)
Student score =____
Pass – Yes/No

Signature of the examiner **Signature of the OSCE coordinator**

STATION 16–DYSCALCULIA

Instruction to the Examinee

- Observe the video and identify the disorder.
- Which skill is deficient for the child?
- Write three possible nursing interventions for improving the skill.

STATION 16

Participant number: ________ **Date:** ___________

Instructions to the Examiner

- Observe the examinee, check whether the examinee makes appropriate assessment of the client.
- If the student assesses and identifies the name of disorder, its skill deficit and any three nursing interventions; each type give 2 mark, else 0 mark has to be given.

Skill Station

Unmanned station and virtual identification

Objectives

At the end of simulation, the examinee:
- Identifies types of disorder
- Makes a nursing diagnosis
- Writes three nursing interventions

Sl. no.	Tasks	Scores	Yes	No
1.	Classifications of disorder Pervasive developmental disorder- dyscalculia	2		
2.	Skill deficit: Difficulty in working with numbers or maths	2		
3.	Any three nursing interventions:			
	• Allow extra time	2		
	• Use games, colors, images to identify the number	2		
	• Use fingers to count the numbers	2		
	TOTAL	10		

Pass score = 4/5 (80%)
Student score = ____
Pass – Yes/No

Signature of the examiner **Signature of the OSCE coordinator**

STATION 17– DISCHARGE PROCEDURE

Instruction to the Examinee

Mr X is 45 years old man was admitted in psychiatric hospital. After the treatment he is about to discharge. mention the different types of discharge has been possible to Mr X
Mention different aspects of discharge procedure.

STATION 17

Participant number: ________ **Date:** __________

Instruction to the Examiner

If the student assesses and identifies the types of admission, each type give 1 mark. Else 0 mark has to be given.

Skill Station

Assessment—Discharge

Objectives

At the end of assessment, the examinee enlists the types of discharge procedure

Sl. no.	Tasks	Scores	Yes	No
1.	Types of procedure • Discharge on voluntary basis	2		
	• Discharge under special circumstances	2		
	• Discharge under reception order	2		
	• Discharge admitted by police	2		
	• Leave absence	2		
	TOTAL	10		

Pass score = 4/5 (80%)
Student score =____
Pass – Yes/No

Signature of the examiner **Signature of the OSCE coordinator**

STATION 18–PREMORBID PERSONALITY ASSESSMENT (HISTORY TAKING)

Instruction to the Examinee

Mrs X aged 45 years shows loss of interest, helplessness, hopelessness, lack of activity, inappropriate guilt, and feels tired and worthless. Assess the premorbid personality of the client.

Instructions to the Examiner

- Observe the examinee while assessing and identifying the personality of the client.
- If the student assesses and identifies the component of personality, give 1 mark. Else 0 mark has to be given.

Skill Station

Manned station: Assessment—History collection

Objectives

At the end of assessment, the examinee:
- Identifies the personality of the client.
- Documents the inference of the client.

Sl. no.	Tasks	Max. marks	Registration no. and marks obtained										
1.	Establishes rapport with the client	1											
2.	The examinee asks lead questions and explores verbal comments/information	1											
3.	• On attitude to self (hopes and attitude)	1											
	• Social relationships (relationship with family, friends and others)	1											
	• Moral and religious standards	1											
	• Responsibility at work place (relationship with coworkers, job satisfaction)	1											
	• Mood (love, anger, frustration)	1											
	• Habits (sleeping, eating, elimination)	1											
	• Fantasy life (daydreaming)	1											
4.	The examinee documents the inference regarding the client's premorbid condition.	1											
	TOTAL	**10**											

Pass score = 8/10 (80)

Signature of the internal examiner **Signature of the external examiner**

STATION 19–CAGE QUESTIONNAIRE AND PSYCHOLOGICAL TEST

Instruction to the Examinee

Mr X aged 35 years has complaints of hand tremors and visual hallucination, and has been diagnosed with chronic alcoholism, Identify the appropriate psychological test and abbreviate the questionnaire.

Instruction to the Examiner

Observe the examinee while identifying the appropriate psychological test and abbreviating the questionnaire.

Skill Station

Therapeutic

Objectives

At the end of simulation, the examinee:

- Identifies the appropriate psychological test.
- Abbreviates the questionnaire.

Sl. no.	Tasks	Max. marks	Registration no. and marks obtained																	
1.	Identify the appropriate psychological test	2																		
2.	**Abbreviation** C – Have you ever had to cut down alcohol intake? A – Have you ever been annoyed by people criticizing alcohol? G – Have you ever felt guilty about drinking? E – Have you ever needed an eye opener drink?	2 2 2 2																		
	TOTAL	10																		

Pass score = 8/ 10 (80)

Signature of the internal examiner

Signature of the external examiner

STATION 20–OBSESSIVE COMPULSIVE DISORDER, CHECKERS

Instruction to the Examinee

Mrs X aged 45 years has repeated multiple doubts of the door not being locked and gas knob being left open, and she continues to check to remove her doubt.

- Identify the clinical type.
- Mention three psychopharmacological treatment.
- Write the appropriate therapy for the particular condition.

Instruction to the Examiner

Kindly check whether the examinee identifies the symptoms correctly and infers the diagnosis and its pharmacological treatment, therapies.

Skill Station

Therapeutic

Objectives

At the end of assessment, the examinee:

- Identifies the clinical type.
- Specifies the psychopharmacological treatment and its therapy.

Sl. no.	Tasks	Max. marks	Registration no. and marks obtained
1.	Obsessive Compulsive Disorder—Checkers	2	
2.	Psychopharmacological Treatment		
	• Antidepressants—Clomipramine 75–300 mg/day, Fluoxetine 20–80 mg/day	2	
	• Benzodiazepines—Alprazolam, Clonazepam.	2	
	• Antipsychotics—Haloperidol, risperidone, Olanzapine.	2	
3.	Therapy Thought stoppage technique	2	
	TOTAL	**10**	

Pass score = 8/10 (80)

Signature of the internal examiner

Signature of the external examiner

STATION 21–SOMATOFORM DISORDER–THERAPEUTIC PROCEDURE

Instruction to the Examinee

Ms Y, a 19-year-old student of college, always takes 4–5 days leave prior to menstruation and complains of headache, irritability, depression, crying spells, anxiety and restlessness. From college, it was reported that she has been unable to write examination due to lack of attendance. Identify the possible diagnosis and write three possible etiological factors.

Instruction to the Examiner

Observe the examinee for identification of provisional diagnosis and plan for nursing interventions.

Skill Station

Simulated patient for identification of diagnosis and three etiological factors.

Objectives

At the end of simulation, the examinee enhances the Client's ability to cope with her menstruation process.

Sl. no.	Tasks	Max. marks	Registration no. and marks obtained
1.	Greet the patient and establish rapport with the patient.	2	
2.	Identification of provisional diagnosis—Somatoform autonomic dysfunction—Premenstrual syndrome	2	
3.	**Etiology:** • Biological factors—Faulty luteinization, Excess of estrogen and progesterone deficiency. • Psychological factors—education, expectations and attitudes toward menstruation and femineity. • Social factors—environmental factors	6	
	Total	10	

Pass score = 8/10 (80)

Signature of the internal examiner **Signature of the external examiner**

STATION 22–OBSESSIVE COMPULSIVE DISORDER

Instruction to the Examinee

Ms Y aged 25 years washes hands at regular intervals throughout the day due to fear of contamination and arranges household things perfectly. She performs tasks to seek relief from anxiety. She has some stereotyped behavior such as repeated clearing of throat and counting steps. Counsel the client with appropriate measures.

Instructions to the Examiner

Observe the examinee while counseling the client and assess whether counselor adheres to the steps given in the checklist during counseling.

Skill Station

Manned Station: Therapeutic

Objective

At the end of simulation, the examinee observes, assesses and counsels the client for behavior modification.

CHECKLIST: COUNSELING

Sl. no.	Tasks	Max. marks	Registration no. and marks obtained																	
1.	Greet and welcome the client with warmth	1																		
2.	Assess the client's symptoms and confirm the condition	1																		
3.	The examinee explains the situation and encourages to utilize coping strategies to overcome problems	1																		
4.	The examinee encourages the client to constantly observe his/her behavior and teaches to utilize "self-control technique" to overcome ritualistic behavior.	2																		
5.	The examinee explores some diversional activities to divert the client's mind	2																		
6.	The examinee examines and helps the client for open communication	2																		
7.	The examinee interprets the change of OCD behavior	1																		
	TOTAL	**10**																		

Pass score = 4/5 (80%)

Signature of the internal examiner **Signature of the external examiner**

STATION 23–HISTRIONIC PERSONALITY DISORDER

Instruction to the Examinee

Ms X aged 25 years is admitted in female ward with complaints of excessive emotionality and attention-seeking behavior, excessive concern about her physical appearance, and self-centeredness. She shows very poor tolerance of frustration and delayed gratification, and exhibits suicidal attempts frequently.

Answer the following questions:
- Identify the condition.
- List out any two symptoms.
- Write any three nursing management steps.

Instruction to the Examiner

Identify the correct answer and give scores.

Skill Station

Unmanned

Objective

At the end of assessment, analyze the examinee's critical thinking and decision making.

CRITERIA FOR IDENTIFICATION OF DIAGNOSIS AND APPROPRIATE MANAGEMENT

Sl. no.	Tasks	Max. marks	Registration no. and marks obtained															
1.	Histrionic personality disorder	2																
2.	• Traumatic emotionality • Constance seeking of reassurance Others: self-centered, poor tolerance	2																
3.	Nursing management: • Establish and maintain therapeutic nurse-client relationship	2																
	• Provide immediate positive feedback	2																
	• Provide safe and calm environment Others: Promote effective communication strategies	2																
	TOTAL	10																

Pass score = 8/10 (80)

Signature of the internal examiner **Signature of the external examiner**

STATION 24–PICA

Instruction to the Examinee

Mr X aged 7 years is admitted to the child psychiatry ward with complaints of abdominal pain and distension. Examination shows long pink and round worms in stool. Blood count shows eosinophilia. Her mother told he has a habit of eating non-food items such as mud and paper.

Answer the following:

- What is the diagnosis related to these problems?
- Mention any two etiologies.
- Draw three possible nursing diagnosis based on the complaints.

Instructions to the Examiner

- Kindly check whether the examinee interprets correctly.
- If the student answers correctly, give 1 mark. Else 0 mark has to be given.

Objectives

At the end of simulation, the examinee:

- Is able to identify the symptoms
- Formulates a nursing diagnosis

Sl. no.	Tasks	Max. marks	Registration no. and marks obtained
1.	PICA	2	
2.	Nutritional deficiency Psychological factors	2	
3.	**Nursing Diagnosis** • Acute pain (abdomen) related to disease condition as evidenced by facial expression	2	
	• Imbalanced nutrition pattern less than body requirement related to unhealthy eating habit as evidenced by weight loss	2	
	• Disturbed bowel elimination related to worm infestation as evidenced by the presence of round worm in stool	2	
	TOTAL	**10**	

Pass score= 8/10 (80)

Signature of the internal examiner **Signature of the external examiner**

STATION 25–IDENTIFICATION OF TYPES OF DELUSIONS

Instruction to the Examinee

Observe the images and identify the types of delusions.

(1)

(2)

(3)

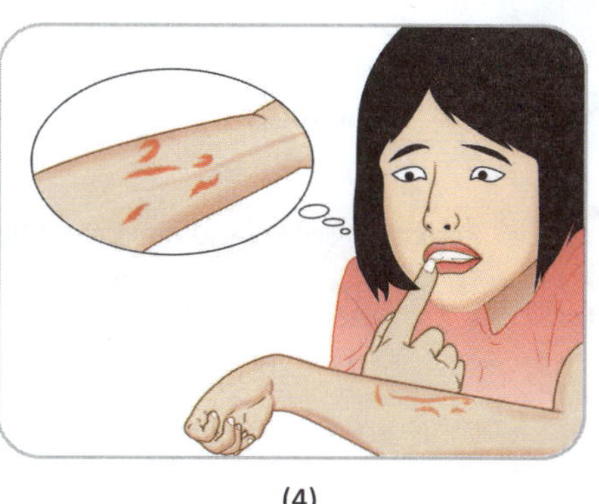

(4)

(5)

Instruction to the Examiner

- Kindly check whether the examinee interprets correctly.
- If the student answers correctly, give 1 mark. Else 0 mark has to be given.

Objectives

At the end of simulation, the examinee:

- Is able to identify the types of delusions
- Is able to document the types of delusions

Sl. no.	Tasks	Max. marks	Registration no. and marks obtained																	
1.	Delusion of grandeur	2																		
2.	Delusion of persecution	2																		
3.	Delusion of infidelity	2																		
4.	Hypochondriacal delusions	2																		
5.	Delusion reference	2																		
	TOTAL	10																		

Pass score = 8/10 (80)

Signature of the internal examiner **Signature of the external examiner**

STATION 26–IDENTIFICATION OF THERAPY (THERAPEUTIC PROCEDURE)

Instruction to the Examinee

Identify the name of the therapy which involves the patient in his/her own environment to provide therapeutic experience.

Answer the following:
- Name of the therapy.
- Write any one objective of the therapy.
- List out two elements of the therapy.
- List out two advantages of the therapy.
- Enlist two disadvantages of the therapy.

Instructions to the Examiner

- Kindly check whether the examinee interprets correctly.
- If the student answers correctly, give 1 mark. Else 0 mark has to be given.

Objective

At the end, the examinee identifies the name of the therapy which involves the patient in his/her own environment to provide therapeutic experience.

Sl. no.	Tasks	Max. marks	Registration no. and marks obtained																	
1.	Milieu therapy	2																		
2.	**Objective:** To use patient's social environment to provide a therapeutic experience.	2																		
3.	**Two elements:** 1. Free communication 2. Shared responsibilities	2																		
4.	**Two advantages:** 1. Gains self-confidence 2. Develops leadership skills	2																		
5.	**Two disadvantages:** 1. Role blurring between staff and patients. 2. Group responsibilities can easily become nobody's responsibility.	2																		
	TOTAL	**10**																		

Pass score = 8/10 (80)

Signature of the internal examiner

Signature of the external examiner

STATION 27–DRUG IDENTIFICATION (THERAPEUTIC PROCEDURE)

Instruction to the Examinee

Mr X aged 45 years shows loss of interest, helplessness, hopelessness, lack of activity, inappropriate guilt, and feels tired and worthless. Identify the diagnosis and the type of drug prescribed for Mr X.

Read the questions carefully and document the answers.

- Identify the diagnosis.
- Identify the type of drug.
- Enlist two indications of the drug.
- Enumerate two contraindications of the drug.
- Enlist two side effects of the drug.

Instructions to the Examiner

- Kindly check whether the examinee interprets correctly.
- If the student answers correctly, give 1 mark. Else 0 mark has to be given.

Objectives

Examinee will be able to identify the anti-depressants has been appropriate to treat depression. Moreover examinee will list out the indications, contra-indications and side effects of the same.

Skill Station

Assessment (Drug identification)

The examinee has to identify the disorder and prescribe the type of drug, and observe indications, contraindications, actions and side effects.

Sl. no.	Tasks	Max. marks	Registration no. and marks obtained																	
1.	Depression	2																		
2.	Antidepressants	2																		
3.	Two indications: 1. Depressed mood 2. Agitation	2																		
4.	Two contraindications: 1. Type 1 and Type 2 diabetes mellitus 2. Epilepsy	2																		
5.	Two side effects of the drug: 1. Blurred vision 2. Drowsiness	2																		
	TOTAL	10																		

Pass score = 8/10 (80)

Signature of the internal examiner **Signature of the external examiner**

STATION 28–GENERALIZED ANXIETY DISORDER

Instruction to the Examinee

Ms X aged 15 years is studying in 10th standard and waiting for public examination. She is admitted in inpatient ward with complaints of tremors, sweating, poor concentration in studies and unpleasant and vague sense of apprehension.

- Identify the possible diagnosis.
- Formulate one nursing diagnosis.
- Write three possible nursing interventions.

Instructions to the Examiner

Observe the examinee for identification of provisional diagnosis and plan nursing intervention.

Skill Station

Identification of diagnosis and planning nursing interventions.

Objective

At the end, the examinee prepares the client to cope with her studies.

Sl. no.	Tasks	Max. marks	Registration no. and marks obtained																	
1.	Identification of provisional diagnosis – Generalized anxiety disorder.	2																		
2.	Nursing diagnosis: 1.	2																		
3.	Nursing interventions: Specify the client's identification of threat. Discuss the reality of situation wopith the client Include the client in making decisions related to selection of alternative coping strategies.	6																		
	TOTAL	10																		

Pass score = 8/10 (80)

Signature of the internal examiner **Signature of the external examiner**

STATION 29–DEPRESSIVE DISORDER

Instructions to the Examinee

You have video in the laptop, switch on and watch it.

- Observe the symptoms and infer the provisional diagnosis.
- Formulate appropriate nursing diagnosis for this video.
- Write three nursing interventions for this diagnosis.

Instructions to the Examiner

Kindly check whether the examinee observes the video, identifies the symptoms correctly and infers the diagnosis and its nursing interventions promptly.

Skill Station

(Virtual Sign Identification)

Objectives

At the end of the VideoShow, the examinee observes and documents the response about the VideoShow carefully.

Sl. no.	Tasks	Max. marks	Registration no. and marks obtained
1.	Infers the diagnosis—Depression	2	
2.	Nursing diagnosis—Disturbed mood (Depressed) related to disease condition as evidenced by facial expression	2	
3.	Nursing interventions: • Assess the client's coping abilities • Help the client meet psychological needs • Help the client cope with current situation	6	
	TOTAL	10	

Pass score = 8/10 (80)

Signature of the internal examiner **Signature of the external examiner**

STATION 30–MANIA

Instruction to the Examinee

Ms Y aged 36 years came with complaints of having severe elevation of mood, restless with on – the - toe –on – the - go activity, having increased thoughts and talks about politics, cine field, normal public, economics and so on for the past one month. Collect the history from the informant, write the presenting chief complaints and document the provisional diagnosis.

Participant number: ________ **Date:** ________

Instructions to the Examiner

- Observe the examinee, check whether the examinee collects appropriate history from the informant.
- Consult the examinee about the provisional diagnosis of the patient.

Skill Station

History Taking

Objectives

At the end of the session, the examinee communicates, collects history from the informant and identifies the provisional diagnosis.

Criteria for Identification of Mania

Steps	Tasks	Scores	Yes	No
1.	Greet the client and informant/establish rapport with them.	2		
2.	The examinee asks questions and specifies verbal comments/information • Exaltation • Increased psychomotor activity • Thought racing	6		
3.	Document the provisional diagnosis.	2		
	Total	**10**		

Pass score = 8/10 (80%)
Student score = ____
Pass – Yes/No

Signature of the examiner **Signature of the OSCE coordinator**

Instructions to the Simulated Patient—Mania

You are playing the role of Ms Y aged 36 years who came with complaints of having severe elevation of mood, restless with on – the – toe – on – the – go activity, having increased thoughts and talks about politics, cine field, normal public , economics and so on for the past one month.

Instruction to the Informant

You are the mother of Ms Y, who has chief complaints of having severe elevation of mood, restless with on – the – toe – on – the – go activity, having increased thoughts and talks about politics, cine field, normal public, economics and so on for the past one month. Narrate the chief complaints about the patient when examinee collects history.

STATION 31–BIPOLAR MOOD DISORDER-VIRTUAL SIGN IDENTIFICATION

Instructions to the Examinee

You have video in the laptop, switch on and watch it.

- Write the clinical picture of bipolar affective disorder.
- Observe and identify the symptoms.
- Infer the provisional diagnosis.

Participant number: ________ **Date:** ________

Instruction to the Examiner

Kindly check whether the examinee writes the clinical picture, identifies the symptoms correctly and infers the diagnosis promptly.

Objectives

At the end of the VideoShow, the examinee observes and documents the response about the VideoShow carefully.

Sl. no.	Tasks	Scores	Yes	No
1.	The examinee writes the clinical picture about bipolar affective disorder Mania Hypomania Mixed episode Normal mood Subsyndromal depression Depression	2		
2.	The examinee identifies the signs and symptoms: • Mood swings • Speech disturbances • Hyperactivity	 2 2 2		
3.	Infers the diagnosis—Bipolar affective disorder	2		
	Total	**10**		

Pass score = 4/5 (80%)
Student score =____
Pass – Yes/No

Signature of the examiner **Signature of the OSCE coordinator**

STATION 32–PHOBIA-DIAGNOSTIC PROCEDURE

Instruction to the Examinee

Ms X aged 19 years is unable to perform activities in the college in front of faculty including classmates and does not participate in group activities and avoids these activities by being continuously absent from the college. She is diagnosed to have social phobia.

- Define social phobia.
- Specify the ICD-10 Classification.
- Mention the specific psychosocial therapy which can be used to alleviate the symptoms.

Register number: _________ **Date:** _________

Instruction to the Examiner

Observe the examinee whether she is able to define and specify the ICD-10 Classification and mention the specific psychosocial therapy which can be used to alleviate the social phobia.

Skill Station

Diagnostic procedure

Objectives

At the end of simulation, the examinee is able to define and specify the ICD-10 Classification and mention the specific psychosocial therapy which can be used to alleviate the social phobia.

Sl. no.	Tasks	Scores	Yes	No
1.	Greet the patient and maintain rapport with the patient	2		
2.	**Definition:** Social phobia is characterized by irrational fear of performing activities in the presence of others or interacting with others often leading to persistent avoidance of the feared activity.	2		
	ICD – 10 Classification: F40.1 – Social Phobia	2		
	Psychosocial treatment: Behavior therapy	2		
3.	Documentation	2		
	TOTAL	10		

Pass score = 4/5 (80%)
Student score =____
Pass – Yes/No

Signature of the examiner **Signature of the OSCE coordinator**

Instruction to the Simulated Phobic Patient

You are playing the role of a 19-year-old woman who is unable to perform activities in the college in front of faculty including classmates and does not participate in group activities and avoids these activities by being continuously absent from the college. You are diagnosed to have social phobia.

STATION 33–POST-TRAUMATIC STRESS DISORDER-IDENTIFICATION OF SYMPTOMS

Instruction to the Examinee

Mr Z aged 32 years is working in the Indian Army. Six months ago, he was caught by Pakistan Army and was made to undergo physical and mental torture, where he was forced to tell secrets of the Indian Army's plan. Presently, he is experiencing recurrent, intrusive recollection of that particular torture event. He feels detached from reality and is unable to experience pleasure. Identify the possible diagnosis and also identify three abnormal symptoms he is experiencing.

Participant number: ________ **Date:** ___________

Instructions to the Examiner

Observe the examinee for identification of provisional diagnosis and also abnormal symptoms.

Skill Station

Simulated patient for identification of diagnosis and also abnormal symptoms.

Objective

At the end of simulation, the examinee will be able to identify the abnormal symptoms.

Sl. no.	Tasks	Scores	Yes	No
1.	Greet the patient and establish rapport with the patient.	2		
2.	Identification of provisional diagnosis—Post-Traumatic Stress Disorder.	2		
3.	**Abnormal Symptoms:** • Flashbacks • Numbness • Anhedonia	 2 2 2		
	TOTAL	**10**		

Pass score = 4/5 (80%)
Student score =____
Pass – Yes/No

Signature of the examiner **Signature of the OSCE coordinator**

Instructions to the Simulated Client

You are playing the role of Mr Z, who is aged 32 years and working in the Indian Army. Six months ago, you were caught by Pakistan Army and were made to undergo physical and mental torture, where you were forced to tell the secrets of the Indian Army's Plan. Presently, you are experiencing recurrent, intrusive recollection of that particular torture event. You feel detached from reality and are unable to experience pleasure.

STATION 34–SCHIZOID PERSONALITY DISORDER-VIRTUAL SIGN IDENTIFICATION

Instruction to the Examinee

Ms Y aged 26 years is working in an IT company, has ingrained characteristics of being alone, humorless and is unable to experience pleasure in the working area along with her coworkers. Identify the personality type and also specify three common signs and symptoms based on the characteristics.

Participant number: ________ **Date:** ___________

Instructions to the Examiner

Observe the examinee for identification of personality type and specify three common signs and symptoms.

Skill Station

Laptop with video for virtual sign identification.

Objectives

At the end of the VideoShow, the examinee:
- Is able to identify the personality type.
- Specifies three common signs and symptoms.

Sl. no.	Tasks	Scores	Yes	No
1.	Greet the patient and establish rapport with the patient.	2		
2.	Identification of provisional diagnosis—Schizoid Personality Disorder.	2		
3.	**Signs and symptoms:** • Aloof • Apathy • Anhedonia	 2 2 2		
	TOTAL	**10**		

Pass score = 4/5 (80%)
Student score =____
Pass – Yes/No

Signature of the examiner **Signature of the OSCE coordinator**

Instructions to the Simulated Client

You are playing the role of Ms Y, who is 26-year-old and works in an IT company. You have ingrained characteristics of being alone, humorless and are unable to experience pleasure in the working area along with your coworkers.

BASICS OF MENTAL HEALTH NURSING

1. **Define mental health.**
   "An adjustment of human beings to the world and to each other with a maximum of effectiveness and happiness."
   — ***Karl Menninger, 1983***

2. **Define mental illness.**
   Mental illness is a maladjustment in living which produces disharmony in life.

3. **List out the members of mental health team.**
   Psychiatrist, mental health nurse, psychologist, counselor, psychiatric social worker, occupational therapist, pharmacist, speech therapist, etc.

4. **List out the roles of mental health nurse.**
   Psychiatric home care nurse, forensic psychiatric nurse, geropsychiatric nurse, psychiatric nurse educator, community mental health nurse.

5. **What are the main features of mental illness?**
   - Disturbances in body (decreased sleep, appetite, libido)
   - Disturbances in mental functions (abnormal thoughts/perception/attention/concentration)
   - Changes in activities (neglected physical care, poor social sense and strange behavior)
   - Somatic complaints (aches or pain)

6. **What is the continuum of mental health?**
   - From low mental health to high mental health.
   - From high mental disorder to low mental disorder.

7. **What are the models used to explain the concept of normal and abnormal behavior?**
   Medical, statistical, sociocultural and behavior models.

8. **What is the scope of psychiatric nursing?**
   - **Basic roles**
     - Patient care
     - Education
     - Supervision
     - Ward management
     - Interpersonal relationship
     - Communication
     - Role in other therapies
   - **Expanded roles**
     - Registered psychiatric nurse
     - Nurse practitioner
     - Clinical nurse specialist
     - Nurse clinician
     - Nurse researcher
     - Nurse counselor
     - Case manager
   - **Extended roles**
     - Community mental health nurse
     - Psychiatric home care nurse
     - Forensic psychiatric nurse
     - Psychiatric consultation—liaison nurse
     - Geropsychiatric nurse
     - Parish nurse

9. **What are the characteristics of a mentally healthy person?**
   - Has the ability to make adjustments
   - Has a sense of personal worth
   - Solves his own problems
   - Can make own decisions
   - Has a sense of responsibility
   - Can give and accept love
   - Lives in the world of reality

- Has emotional maturity
- Has a variety of interests in life
- Has developed a philosophy of life

10. What are the standards of psychiatric nursing?

- **Standards of Care**
    - Standard I: Assessment
    - Standard II: Diagnosis
    - Standard III: Outcome identification
    - Standard IV: Planning
    - Standard V: Implementation
        - Standard Va: Counseling standard
        - Standard Vb: Milieu-therapy standard
        - Standard Vc: Self-care activities standard
        - Standard Vd: Psychobiological interventions
        - Standard Ve: Health teaching
        - Standard Vf: Case management
        - Standard Vg: Health promotion and health maintenance
        - Standard Vh: Psychotherapy
        - Standard Vi: Prescription of pharmacological agents
        - Standard Vj: Consultation
    - Standard VI: Evaluation
- **Standards of Professional Performance**
    - Standard I: Quality of care
    - Standard II: Performance appraisal
    - Standard III: Education
    - Standard IV: Collegiality
    - Standard V: Ethics
    - Standard VI: Collaboration
    - Standard VII: Research
    - Standard VIII: Resource utilization
- **Indian Nursing Council Standards (2019)**
    - **Standards of Practice**
        - Standard 1: Assessment
        - Standard 2: Nursing diagnosis
        - Standard 3: Expected outcomes of care
        - Standard 4: Planning
        - Standard 5: Implementation
            - Standard 5a: Nursing care delivery to health care consumers
            - Standard 5b: Assistance in the delivery of biological therapies
            - Standard 5c: Psychotherapeutic interventions
            - Standard 5d: Safe and therapeutic environment
            - Standard 5e: Health education
            - Standard 5f: Community mental health nursing services, including reintegration of health care consumers into the community
        - Standard 6: Evaluation
    - **Standards of Education**
        - Standard 7: Academic excellence
            - Standard 7a: Personal academic development
            - Standard 7b: Capacity building
    - **Standards of Administration**
        - Standard 8: Administrative efficiency
            - Standard 8a: Personalvision,commitment, technical expertise
            - Standard 8b: Team building
            - Standard 8c: Quality assurance
            - Standard 8d: Continuing nursing education
            - Standard 8e: Leadership
            - Standard 8f: Performance appraisal
            - Standard 8g: Organizational and professional advancement
    - **Standards of Evidence-Based Practice and Research**
        - Standard 9: Responsible and ethical conduct of research and integration into practice
            - Standard 9a: Research ethics
            - Standard 9b: Integration of research into practice
            - Standard 9c: Teaching scientific rigor to young nurse investigators
    - **Other Standards of Professional Performance**
        - Standard 10: Self-care and self-awareness
        - Standard 11: Ethics
        - Standard 12: Communication
        - Standard 13: Culturally sensitive care
        - Standard 14: Legally safe practice

11. What are the conceptual models in psychiatric nursing?

Existential model, psychoanalytical model, behavioral model and interpersonal model.

12. What are the principles of psychiatric nursing?

- Accept the client exactly as he/she is
- Use self-understanding as a therapeutic tool
- Use of consistent behavior might contribute to the client's security

- Give reassurance in an acceptable and subtle manner
- Change the client's behavior by emotional experience rather than rational interpretation
- Avoid unnecessary increase in client's anxiety
- Use objective observation to understand client's behavior
- Maintain a realistic nurse-client relationship
- Avoid physical and verbal forces as much as possible
- Provide nursing care to the patient as a person not on the control of symptoms
- Give all explanations of procedures and routines according to the client's level of understanding
- Many procedures are modified but basic principles remain unchanged

CLASSIFICATION OF PSYCHIATRIC DISORDERS

1. **What is meant by ICD Classification?**
   ICD stands for International Classification of Diseases. This classification list is provided by World Health Organization (WHO).

2. **What are the components of ICD-11 and DSM-5 Classification?**
   - Schizophrenia spectrum and other psychotic disorders
   - Bipolar and related disorders
   - Depressive disorders
   - Anxiety disorders
   - Obsessive-Compulsive and related disorders
   - Trauma- and Stressor-related disorders
   - Dissociative disorders
   - Somatic symptom and related disorders
   - Feeding and eating disorders
   - Elimination disorders
   - Sleep-wake disorders
   - Sexual dysfunctions
   - Gender dysphoria
   - Disruptive, impulsive and conduct disorders
   - Substance-related and addictive disorders
   - Neurocognitive disorders
   - Personality disorders
   - Paraphilic disorders
   - Other mental disorders

3. **What is meant by DSM Classification?**
   DSM stands for Diagnostic and Statistical Manual of Mental Disorders. It was published by American Psychiatric Association (APA).

4. **What is the Indian Classification of Mental disorders?**
   - **Psychosis:** Functional (Schizophrenia), Affective (Mania and Depression), Organic (Delirium, Dementia and Amnesia)
   - **Neurosis:** Anxiety disorders, Phobia, Obsessive Compulsive Disorders (OCD), somatoform disorders, post-traumatic stress disorder (PTSD) and conversion disorders.
   - **Others:** Child psychiatric disorders, substance abuse, personality disorders and Psychophysiological disorders.

5. **What is the ICD-11 code for schizophrenia?**
   6A20

6. **What is the ICD-11 code for acute and transient psychotic disorder?**
   6A23

7. **What is the ICD-11 code for personality disorder?**
   6D10

8. **What is the ICD-11 code for generalized anxiety disorder?**
   6B00

9. **What is the ICD-11 code for bipolar II disorder?**
   6A61

10. **What is the ICD-11 code for cyclothymic disorder?**
    6A62

11. **What is the ICD-11 code for bipolar affective disorder?**
    F31

12. **What is the ICD-11 code for panic disorder?**
    6B01

13. **What is the ICD-11 code for anorexia nervosa?**
    6B80

14. **What is the ICD-11 code for bulimia nervosa?**
    6B81

15. **What is the ICD-11 code for binge eating disorder?**
    6B82

16. **What is the ICD-11 code for hypoactive sexual desire disorder?**
    HA00

17. **What is the ICD-11 code for OCD?**
    6B20

18. **What is the ICD-11 code for amnestic disorder?**
    6D72

19. **What is the DSM-5 code for schizophrenia?**
    295.90

20. **What is the DSM-5 code for bipolar II disorder?**
    296.89
21. **What is the DSM-5 code for OCD?**
    300.3
22. **What is the DSM-5 code for bulimia nervosa?**
    307.51
23. **What is the DSM-5 code for generalized anxiety disorder?**
    300.02

HISTORICAL DEVELOPMENT OF PSYCHIATRIC NURSING

1. **Who is known as mother of psychiatric nursing?**
   Hildegard Peplau
2. **Who is referred to as the father of modern psychiatry?**
   Philippe Pinel
3. **Who is considered the father of American psychiatry?**
   Benjamin Rush
4. **Who is the father of psychobiology?**
   Adolf Meyer
5. **When is the World Mental Health Day celebrated?**
   October 10
6. **When is the World Schizophrenia Day celebrated?**
   May 24
7. **When is the World No Tobacco Day celebrated?**
   May 31
8. **When is the World Suicide Prevention Day celebrated?**
   September 10
9. **When is the World Alzheimer's Day celebrated?**
   September 21
10. **Who is the father of therapeutic community?**
    Maxwell Jones
11. **Who is the founder of interpersonal theory?**
    Harry Sullivan
12. **Who were the proponents of Alcoholics Anonymous?**
    Dr. Bob and Bill Wilson
13. **Name the proponent of cognitive therapy.**
    Aaron Beck
14. **Name the proponent of group therapy.**
    Joseph Pratt
15. **When did the Indian Nursing Council (INC) incorporate the Psychiatric Nursing subject in BSc Nursing curriculum?**
    1965
16. **List out the phases in the evolution of mental health nursing.**
    - Phase 1: Emergence of Mental Health Nursing
    - Phase 2: Development of Work Role of Psychiatric Nurses
    - Phase 3: Development of Undergraduate Psychiatric Nursing Education
    - Phase 4: Development of Graduate Psychiatric Nursing Education
    - Phase 5: Development of Research in Psychiatric Nursing

PERSONALITY THEORIES

1. **What are different personality theories?**
   Psychoanalytic theory, Jung's theory, Erikson's theory, Roger's theory, Bandura's theory.
2. **Which is the pleasure principle for psychoanalytical theory?**
   Id
3. **How many stages of personality development are there as per Erickson?**
   8 stages:
   1. Trust vs Mistrust
   2. Autonomy vs shame
   3. Initiative vs Guilt
   4. Industry vs Inferiority
   5. Identity vs Role confusion
   6. Intimacy vs Isolation
   7. Generativity vs Stagnation
   8. Ego integrity vs Despair
4. **What are the structures of mind?**
   Id, Ego and Superego

STRUCTURE OF BRAIN

1. **What are the different parts of brain?**
   Cerebrum, cerebellum, brain stem, limbic system.
2. **Which is the structural and functional part of the brain?**
   Neuron
3. **What are the parts of a neuron?**
   Axon, Dendrites, Myelin sheath, Schwann cells, Nucleus, cell body

4. Which part of brain is considered emotional brain?
Limbic system

5. What are the components of limbic system?
'BATCH' – Mnemonic to remember
- B : Basal ganglia
- A : Amygdala
- T : Thalamus and hypothalamus
- C : Cingulate gyrus
- H : Hypothalamus

6. How many lobes are there in brain?
Brain has four lobes, namely frontal lobe, temporal lobe, parietal lobe and occipital lobe.

7. What constitutes brain stem?
Brain stem includes midbrain, pons, medulla oblongata and cranial nerves.

8. What is pineal body?
Pineal body is located in the thalamus and contains secretory cells that emit melatonin hormone.

9. What is neurotransmission?
Neurotransmission is the fundamental process that transfers information between neurons.

10. What are the steps that occur in neurotransmitters?
Neurotransmitter
1. Synthesis
2. Package
3. Release
4. Binding
5. Stopping of chemical signal

11. Name some neurotransmitters.
Some examples of neurotransmitters are dopamine, norepinephrine, epinephrine, serotonin, GABA, acetylcholine.

PSYCHIATRIC HISTORY COLLECTION

1. What is psychiatric history collection?
His + story= History means inquiry or the knowledge acquired by investigations. History is collected from friends, police and strangers who might know the patient. It is vital to have strong knowledge about patient.

2. What are the purposes of history collection?
- To know about the patient
- Pathway for health assessment
- Provides baseline data about the patient
- To understand the past treatment and outcomes
- To compare the patient symptoms before the onset of illness

3. What are the various aspects in history collection format?
- Demographic data
- Presenting chief complaints
- Present psychiatric history
- Medical, surgical history, obstetrical history [for females]
- Family history
- Personal history

4. What is the genogram symbol for pregnancy?

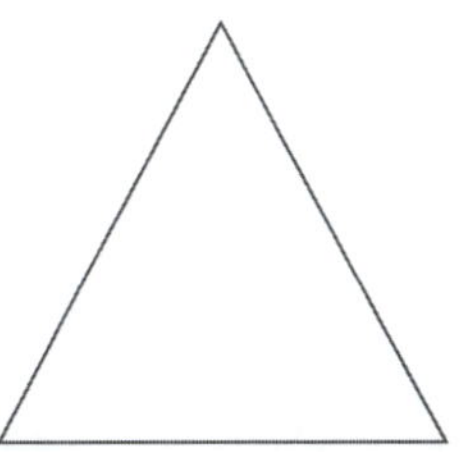

5. What are the genogram symbols for monozygotic and dizygotic twins?

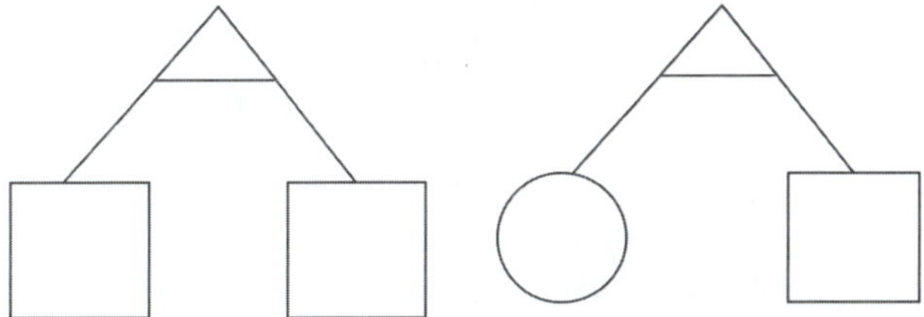

MENTAL STATUS EXAMINATION

1. What is mental status examination (MSE)?
Assessment of the patient to assess the present mental status and to diagnose patient condition.

2. What are the purposes of mental status examination?
- Provide a guideline to decide the treatment modalities
- To assess the patient condition with the treatment regimen.

3. What is the format of mental status examination?
- General appearance and behavior
- Speech
- Mood
- Thought
- Disorders of perception
- Cognitive functions

4. What is the method of performing MSE for uncooperative patients?
Kirby's method

5. **What is omega sign?**
Omega sign is a peculiar sign of depression in which the patient has furrowed brow due to sustained contraction of corrugator muscle.

6. **Define echopraxia.**
Echopraxia is defined as desire to mimic activities performed by other individual; it is seen in schizophrenia.

7. **Define automatic obedience.**
Automatic obedience is performing an action instructed by other irrespective of thinking about the consequences due to the specified action which is seen in schizophrenia.

8. **Define circumstantiality.**
Circumstantiality is the result of a nonlinear thought pattern and it is a pattern of speech which has a mix of relevant and irrelevant information. It happens when the focus of a conversation drifts, but often comes back to the point.

9. **Define tangentiality.**
Tangentiality is a phenomenon in which a person deviates from one topic/idea to another without ever reaching a conclusion.

10. **Define neologism.**
Neologism refers to coining of new words.

11. **Define ambivalence.**
Ambivalence refers to the coexistence of two opposing forces or impulses, desires or emotions.

12. **Define "word salad".**
Word salad refers to mixture of words that are incoherent.

13. **Define perseveration.**
Perseveration refers to persistent repetition of words beyond the point of relevance.

14. **What is pressure of speech?**
Pressure of speech is a rapid speech delivered with urgency that is apparently inappropriate to the situation. It is a hallmark symptom of mania. Pressure of speech is also seen in patients with schizophrenia, anxiety disorder and attention deficit hyperactivity disorder.

15. **What is thought retardation?**
Thought retardation is defined as the reduction of thoughts in one's mind leads to reduced content of speech, which is seen in patients with depression, dementia, nervousness, memory impairment and schizophrenia.

16. **Define thought block.**
Thought block is a condition of sudden interruption of thoughts exhibited by silence from a few seconds to minutes which is commonly seen in patients with schizophrenia.

17. **What is mutism?**
Mutism is complete absence of speech seen in patients with depression, negative symptoms of schizophrenia and in catatonic stupor.

18. **Define aphonia.**
Aphonia is defined as the inability to produce voiced sound due to laryngeal nerve damage or secondary thyroidectomy and also due to underlying psychological problems.

19. **What is clang association?**
Clang association is grouping of rhyming words irrespective of their meaning; it is seen in patients with schizophrenia.

20. **What is delusion?**
Delusion is a strong fixed unshakable belief irrespective of sociocultural background.

21. **What is the delusion of persecution?**
Delusion of persecution refers to having a strong suspicious belief that others are trying to harm him/her.

22. **What is the delusion of grandeur?**
Strong unshakable belief that he/she is an important famous personality or has superior knowledge or ideation or power.

23. **What is delusion of infidelity or delusion of jealousy or Othello Syndrome?**
Strong unshakable belief that his/her spouse has extramarital relationship with another person.

24. **What is delusion of thought broadcasting?**
Strong unshakable belief that one's own thoughts have been projected/displayed in mass media such as television, newspaper, internet, etc.

25. **What is delusion of control?**
Strong unshakable belief that one's own thoughts or action has been controlled from outside.

26. **Define nihilistic delusion?**
Strong unshakable belief that the world does not exist.

27. **What is delusion of reference?**
Strong unshakable belief that the other person is referring oneself with a neutral event in the environment.

28. **What is amnesia?**
Memory loss

29. **What is retrograde amnesia?**
Retrograde amnesia means loss of memory of the events that happened before the injury or onset of illness.

30. **What is anterograde amnesia?**
Anterograde amnesia means loss of memory of the events that happened after the injury or onset of illness.

31. **What is Déjà vu?**
Familiarity with unfamiliar things.

32. **What is Jamais Vu?**
Unfamiliarity with familiar things.

33. **What is confabulation?**
False filling of memory gaps.

34. **What is illusion?**
Misperception of an external stimulus.

35. **What are the types of illusion?**
Affect illusion, completion illusion, pareidolic illusion.

36. **What is hallucination?**
Misperception without an external stimulus.

37. **List out the types of hallucination.**
Auditory, visual, olfactory, gustatory, tactile or haptic, functional, reflex, extracampine, hypnogogic, hypnopompic, command or teleological, Lilliputian, kinesthetic, macropsia and micropsia.

38. **How do you assess personal judgment?**
Asking the patient about his/her future plans.

39. **How do you assess social judgment?**
Observation made by the examiner that how patient is being socialized with others.

40. **What are the various test judgments?**
Rain test, fire test, envelope test and child cry test.

41. **Define insight.**
Patient's awareness of his/her own mental illness.

42. **How do you grade the insight?**
- Grade I: Complete refusal of illness
- Grade II: Slight awareness of being ill
- Grade III: Awareness of being sick attribute toward external or physical factor
- Grade IV: Awareness of being sick, due to something not known to oneself
- Grade V: Intellectual insight (awareness about one's own mental illness in detail)
- Grade VI: True emotional insight—Aware of one's own mental illness and how the family

NEUROLOGICAL EXAMINATION

1. **What are the various aspects of neurological assessment?**
- Level of consciousness
- Mental status assessment
- Cerebral function
- Cranial nerve function
- Sensory function
- Motor function
- Cerebellar function
- Reflexes

2. **List down the cranial nerves.**
- Olfactory
- Optic
- Oculomotor
- Trochlear
- Abducent
- Trigeminal
- Facial
- Vestibulocochlear
- Glossopharyngeal
- Vagus
- Accessory
- Hypoglossal

3. **What is Weber's test?**
Tuning fork is kept in the middle ear. If lateralization is felt on one side, it denotes hearing loss. Normal individuals will hear sound in both ears equally.

4. **Define Rinne's test.**
Keep the tuning fork in mastoid bone and then to patient's ear. After striking, air conduction is more than bone conduction, which is normal. If bone conduction is more than air conduction, it denotes conductive hearing loss.

5. **What is Romberg test?**
To assess the balance or equilibrium of the patient's body. Ask the patient to stand straight when the eyes are closed. Aware of patient has a risk of fall.

6. **How do you advise the patient to perform tandem walk test?**
Patient is asked to walk over the heel in straight line. This is done to assess unsteadiness or staggering or imbalance gait.

7. **What is stereognosis or haptic perception or tactile gnosis?**
   Ability to perceive and recognize the object using tactile sense.

8. **Define baragnosis or baresthesia.**
   It is the ability to evaluate the weight of objects, or to differentiate objects of different weights, by holding or lifting them. It is done to assess the loss of ability to sense weight.

9. **How do you perform Caloric test (test to assess oculovestibular reflex)?**
   Caloric test is performed to assess the coordination of eye and ear muscles. Pouring of cold water in the ear will move the opposite eyeballs, and the pouring of warm water in the ear will move the same side of eyeballs.

10. **How do you assess biceps reflex?**
    Arm gently flexed at elbow, tap the biceps brachii tendon. It leads to flexion of forearm.

11. **How do you assess triceps reflex?**
    Tapping of triceps brachii tendon in elbow. It leads to extension of forearm.

12. **How do you assess patellar reflex?**
    Tapping of quadriceps femoris tendon (present below patella). It leads to extension of leg.

13. **How do you assess the gag reflex?**
    Stimulation with tongue blade at the back of throat and pharynx.

14. **What is agnosia?**
    Inability to recognize the objects with senses.

15. **What is apraxia?**
    Inability to perform learned motor activities.

16. **What is Glasgow Coma Scale (GCS)?**
    GCS is the scale to assess the level of consciousness. It consists of eye response, verbal response and motor response. Total score is 15.

17. **What is the minimal Score of GCS?**
    3

18. **What is the score of GCS determining comatose patient?**
    <7

THERAPEUTIC COMMUNICATION

1. **Define communication.**
   Communication is an interaction process between the sender and receiver. The receiver receives the message exactly what the sender intended to say. Both receiver and sender have a common understanding of a message.

2. **What are the types of communication?**
   - Verbal
   - Nonverbal
   - Formal
   - Nonformal
   - Intrapersonal
   - Interpersonal
   - Horizontal
   - Vertical
   - Chain
   - Meta

3. **What is therapeutic relationship?**
   Relationship maintained between the nurse and patient to gain mutual respect and trust.

4. **What are the phases of nurse-patient relationship?**
   - Pre-orientation phase
   - Orientation phase
   - Identification phase
   - Intervention phase
   - Maintenance phase
   - Termination phase

5. **List out the types of psychological tests.**
   - Paper pencil test
   - Individual and group test
   - Speed and power test
   - Computer assisted test
   - Aptitude test
   - Intelligence test
   - Interest test
   - Personality test

6. **What are the components of nurse-patient relationship?**
   TEACH
   - T : Trust
   - E : Empathy
   - A : Autonomy
   - C : Caring attitude
   - H : Hopefulness

7. **What are the barriers of communication?**
   Physical, psychological and environmental barriers.

8. **What are the therapeutic impasses?**
   - Resistance
   - Transference
   - Countertransference

9. **Mention some therapeutic communication techniques.**
   - Offering self
   - Silence
   - Listening
   - Empathy
   - Questioning
   - Restating
   - Broad openings
   - Verbalizing
   - Seeking clarification
   - Sharing perceptions
   - Summarizing

10. **What are the nontherapeutic communication techniques?**
    - Defending
    - Requesting
    - Indicating the external source
    - Belittling feelings
    - Stereotyped comments
    - Denial
    - Parroting

11. **Define ethics.**
    Ethics is a branch of philosophy that deals with the study of values and moral standards related to nursing profession.

12. **What is SWOT Analysis?**
    - S : Strength
    - W : Weakness
    - O : Opportunities
    - T : Threats

13. **What is Johari window? How many quadrants are there in Johari window?**
    - Joseph Luft and Harry Ingham (1950) described the model of interpersonal relationship.
    - Other names are Disclosure or Feedback Model of Self-Awareness and Information Processing Tool.
    - It has four quadrants. Quadrant 1- Arena, Quadrant 2- Blind spot, Quadrant 3- Hidden and Quadrant 4- Unknown

14. **Define process recording.**
    Process recording is a method of recording nurse-patient interaction, done by nurses in psychiatric setup.

15. **What is the format of process recording?**
    - Patient profile
    - Objectives
    - Preparation of patient and environment
    - Date, time and place of recording
    - Context of interaction

16. **Name few theories of communication.**
    Ruesch's theory, transactional analysis, neuro-linguistic programming

DEFENSE MECHANISM

1. **Define defense mechanism.**
   Defense mechanism is an unconscious psychological mechanism that reduces anxiety from harmful stimuli.

2. **Name some defense mechanisms.**
   Displacement, repression, denial, rationalization, reaction formation, undoing, acting out, etc.

3. **Define displacement.**
   Unconscious manner of letting the feelings toward a less threatening object.

4. **Define rationalization.**
   Try to make excuses to convince self that he/she is not wrong.

5. **Define reaction formation.**
   Converting the unconscious wishes or ideas or impulses which are perceived as dangerous or unacceptable by their opposites.

6. **Define regression.**
   Temporary state of the ego put into the earlier stage of development instead of handling the unacceptable impulses as an adult.

7. **Define repression.**
   Unconscious way of suppressing the negative feelings which pose threat.

8. **Define suppression.**
   A conscious way of pushing out the negative thoughts or feelings.

9. **Define altruism.**
   Constructive social service to others which gives personal satisfaction.

10. **Define sublimation.**
    Sublimation refers to transformation of socially unacceptable impulses or thoughts into socially acceptable actions or behavior, resulting in a long-term conversion of the initial impulse.
11. **Define identification.**
    Unconscious modeling of one's self toward another person's character and behavior.

LEGISLATIONS IN MENTAL HEALTH NURSING

1. **When was the Indian Mental Health Act enacted?**
   1987
2. **When was the Indian Lunacy Act enacted?**
   1912
3. **When was the Mental Health Care Act enacted?**
   2017
4. **When was the Rehabilitation Council of India Act enacted?**
   1992
5. **When was the Persons with Disability Act enacted?**
   1996
6. **When was the Narcotics and Substance Abuse Act enacted?**
   1985
7. **When was the POCSO Act enacted?**
   2012
8. **How many chapters and sections are there in the Indian Mental Health Act?**
   10 chapters and 98 sections
9. **How many chapters, parts and sections are there in the Indian Lunacy Act?**
   8 chapters, 4 parts and 100 sections
10. **How many chapters are there in the Mental Health Care Act?**
    16 chapters
11. **How many chapters and sections are there in the Narcotics and Substance Abuse Act?**
    6 chapters and 83 sections
12. **When was the National Mental Health Policy formulated?**
    2002
13. **When was the National Society for Mental Hygiene founded?**
    2002
14. **What is M'Naghten Rule?**
    Daniel M'Naghten murdered Edward Drummond, secretary of Sir Robert Peel, Prime Minister in his insane mind. But he was not punished under law because the gun shot happened due to the delusion of persecution.
15. **What are the various types of admission procedure as per the Mental Health Act?**
    - Admission on voluntary basis
    - Admission under special circumstances (Involuntary admission)
    - Admission in emergencies
    - Admission under authority or order
      - Reception order on application
      - Reception order on producing the mental illness before magistrate.
      - Reception order after inquest: District court directs the individual for admission.
      - Admission and detention of mentally ill prisoner: Mentally ill prisoner will be admitted in psychiatric hospital as per the order of court.
16. **What are the various types of discharge procedure as per the Mental Health Act?**
    - Discharge of patient admitted on voluntary basis
    - Discharge of patient admitted under special circumstances
    - Discharge of patient admitted on reception order
    - Discharge of patient admitted by police
    - Discharge of mentally ill prisoner
    - Leave of absence
17. **What is the nurse's role in regard to the legal aspects in psychiatry?**
    - Ethical decision making
    - Protecting the rights of mentally ill
    - Admission and discharge procedures of mentally ill
    - Role of mental health authority
    - Quality treatment of mentally ill

ADJUSTMENT DISORDER, SOMATOFORM DISORDER AND PHOBIA

1. **Define adjustment disorder.**
   Adjustment disorder is defined as the presence of significant behavioral or emotional symptoms in response to the psychosocial stressors.

2. **Define somatoform disorder.**
   Somatoform disorder is a mental illness in which multiple bodily signs and symptoms are elicited but the medical evaluation does not reveal any abnormalities.

3. **Classify somatoform disorders.**
   - Somatization disorder
   - Conversion disorder
   - Hypochondriasis
   - Body dysmorphic disorder
   - Persistent somatoform pain disorder

4. **Define somatic symptom disorder.**
   Presence of one or more somatic symptoms which cause significant personal distress in patient.

5. **Define dissociative disorder.**
   Dissociative disorder is defined as lack of integration of consciousness, emotions and identity.

6. **Who identified the concept of dissociation?**
   Mr Pierre Janet

7. **Which is the most common type of dissociative disorder?**
   Dissociative amnesia

8. **Which is an active mechanism of repression?**
   Dissociation

9. **What are the clinical features of dissociative disorder?**
   - **Motor symptoms:** Tics, abnormal gait, aphonia, paralysis
   - **Sensory symptoms:** Blindness, deafness
   - **Visceral symptoms:** Urinary retention, diarrhea, vomiting

10. **Define dissociative amnesia.**
    Dissociative amnesia is most commonly seen in young adults. Before amnesia caused by stressors, during amnesia caused by clouding of consciousness and post amnesia due to aware of disturbances in memory.

11. **What are the different types of dissociative amnesia?**
    - Localized amnesia
    - Selective amnesia
    - Continuous amnesia
    - Generalized amnesia
    - Systematized amnesia

12. **Define dissociative fugue.**
    Dissociative fugue is characterized by episodes of wandering away from home. During wandering, individual assumes new identity along with complete amnesia of previous life.

13. **Define multiple personality disorder.**
    Individual is dominated with one or two personalities in which one personality is manifested at a time.

14. **Define trance and possession disorder.**
    Control of one's personality by spirit. One personality is aware. It is different from other personality disorders.

15. **What is Ganser's syndrome?**
    Commonly seen in prison inmates having characteristic feature of 'Vorbeireden'.

16. **What is the meaning of Vorbeireden?**
    Saying approximate answer

17. **What are the different treatment therapies for dissociative disorder?**
    - Behavior therapy
    - Psychotherapy
    - Insight oriented therapy
    - Psychodynamic psychotherapy
    - Psychoanalysis
    - Drug therapy

18. **Define hypochondriasis.**
    Hypochondriasis is an anxiety disorder which is characterized by being preoccupied with health concerns that might cause impairments or personal distress in one's life.

19. **Name some somatoform autonomic dysfunction.**
    - Hyperventilation syndrome
    - Irritable bowel syndrome
    - Premenstrual syndrome

20. **Define neurasthenia.**
    In neurasthenia, individual has persistent and distressing complaints of body weakness and he feels exhausted even after a minimal effort.

21. **Define depersonalization disorder.**
    Depersonalization disorder occurs when you repeatedly feel that you are observing yourself from outside your body and the individual feel that he/she is not real one.

22. **What is the drug of choice for anxiety disorders.**
    Lorazepam
23. **What is claustrophobia?**
    Fear of closed places
24. **What is the name given for extreme fear of travel?**
    Hodophobia
25. **What is the peculiar symptom of post traumatic stress disorder (PTSD)?**
    Flashbacks
26. **What are the two characteristic features of Vorbeireden?**
    Ganser's syndrome and hysterical pseudodementia

ANXIETY DISORDERS

1. **Which is called central stress response system?**
   The Hypothalamic Pituitary Adrenal [HPA] axis
2. **What is circadian rhythm?**
   Sleep-wake cycle
3. **What is neurotic disorder?**
   Neurotic disorder is a less severe form of psychotic disorder in which the patient exhibits excess of prolonged emotional response to the stressors.
4. **Who introduced the concept of anxiety?**
   Sigmund Freud
5. **Define anxiety.**
   Anxiety is defined as feelings of uncertainty, apprehension, uneasiness or tension that an individual shows in a given situation.
6. **What are the different types of anxiety disorders?**
   - Trait anxiety
   - State anxiety
   - Signal anxiety
   - Free floating anxiety
7. **What is the concept of anxiety response?**
   Responding to a dangerous situation leads to Fright response, Flight response and Flight response
8. **What are the etiologic factors for anxiety?**
   - Genetic factors
   - Biological factors
   - Psychoanalytical factors
   - Sociocultural factors
   - Cognitive factors
9. **What is the continuum or levels of anxiety?**
   - Normal
   - Euphoria
   - Mild anxiety
   - Moderate anxiety
   - Severe anxiety
   - Panic anxiety
10. **What are the symptoms of anxiety disorders?**
    - **Physiological symptoms:** Headache, vertigo, nausea and vomiting, tachycardia
    - **Psychological symptoms:** Depression, irritability, social isolation, anger
    - **Behavioral symptoms:** Hypervigilance, restless, pacing
    - **Cognitive symptoms:** Lack of concentration, memory loss, inability to perform a task, preoccupied with something.
11. **What are the clinical features of anxiety disorders?**
    - Exaggerated worry and tension
    - Restlessness
    - Irritable
    - Difficulty in concentrating
    - Insomnia
    - Tension headache
    - Palpitation
    - Sweating, tremors
12. **What are the clinical features of panic disorder?**
    - Acute onset of severe anxiety
    - Palpitation, increased heart rate, tremors
    - Chest tightness, breathing difficulty
    - Hot flushes, cold chills, fear of dying, fear of fainting
13. **What are the clinical features of post-traumatic stress disorders?**
    - Flashbacks while awake
    - Nightmares during sleep
    - Hypervigilance
    - Startled easily
    - Emotional numbness, irritability
    - Lack of concentration
14. **What are the clinical features of phobic anxiety?**
    - Acute anxiety
    - Tension
    - Irritability
    - Individual tries to escape from triggers
15. **What are different types of phobias?**
    - Simple phobia

- Social phobia
- Agoraphobia

16. Name some simple phobias.
- Acrophobia
- Algophobia
- Claustrophobia
- Hematophobia
- Leukophobia
- Zoophobia
- Nosophobia

17. What is the duration of persisting symptoms required for diagnosis of anxiety disorders?
- **Generalized anxiety disorder:** at least 6 months
- **Phobia:** at least 6 months
- **Panic disorder:** at least 1 month
- **Obsessive compulsive disorder:** at least 2 weeks
- **PTSD:** at least 1 month

18. Mention some rating scales in anxiety disorders.
- Hamilton Rating Scale
- State trait anxiety rating scale—Generalized anxiety disorders
- Panic disorder severity scale—panic disorder
- Social phobia inventory—social phobia
- Yale-Brown Obsessive Compulsive Scale [Y-BOCS]-OCD
- Impact of Event Scale- PTSD

19. What is the pharmacotherapy for anxiety disorders?
- Benzodiazepines
- Antidepressants
- Beta blockers

20. What are the treatment modalities for anxiety disorders?
- Cognitive behavior therapy
- Behavior strategies
- Relaxation training
- Psychoeducation
- Skill training
- Bibliotherapy

21. Define obsessive obsession and compulsion.
- **Obsession:** Repetitive thoughts, images, doubts make a person senseless and irrational.
- **Compulsion:** Repetitive actions are performed followed by obsessions.

22. What are the etiological factors for OCD?
- Genetic factors
- Psychodynamic factors
- Behavioral factors
- Hormonal factors
- Psychosocial factors

23. What are the different types of obsessive-compulsive disorders?

Washers, Checkers, Pure obsessions, Primary obsessive slowness.

24. What is the pharmacotherapy for OCD?
- Benzodiazepines
- Antidepressants
- Antipsychotics

25. What are the different therapies used for treating OCD?
- Psychotherapy
- Behavior therapy
- Thought stopping technique
- Rubber band method
- Electroconvulsive therapy
- Psychosurgery

26. Define acute stress reaction.

An immediate and clear relation exists between the stressor and the onset of symptoms such as anger, depression.

27. Define post-traumatic stress disorder (PTSD)?

PTSD is an anxiety disorder in which an individual might develop the re-experiencing symptoms or avoidance symptoms after witnessing extreme, overwhelming traumatic event when the individual felt intense fear.

28. What are the predominant symptoms of PTSD?
- Hyperarousal
- Re-experiencing the trauma
- Emotional numbness

29. What are the types of PTSD?
- Acute PTSD
- Chronic PTSD
- Delayed onset PTSD

30. Name a few etiological factors of PTSD.
- Serious injury
- Unnatural death
- Kidnapped
- Terrorist attack
- Natural or man-made disaster
- Life-threatening illness

31. **How is PTSD assessed?**
    - **Interviews:** PTSD symptom scale interview
    - **Self-report Questionnaire:** Post-Traumatic Diagnostic Scale
    - **For children:** Child PTSD Symptom Scale
32. **What are the treatment modalities for PTSD?**
    - Exposure therapy
    - Cognitive therapy
    - Stress inoculation training
    - Behavior therapy
    - Pharmacotherapy: SSRIs, antianxiety drugs, mood stabilizers, tricyclic antidepressants

COMMUNITY MENTAL HEALTH NURSING

1. **When was the National Mental Health Program (NMHP) launched?**
   1982
2. **What are the roles of community psychiatry nurse?**
   Counselor, crisis worker, educator, researcher, community consultant
3. **What are the components of the Mental Health Program?**
   Treatment, rehabilitation, prevention
4. **What are the objectives of NMHP?**
   - To ensure availability and accessibility of mental health care for vulnerable and underprivileged population.
   - To encourage mental health knowledge in general health care
   - To promote community participation.

MOOD DISORDERS

1. **Define mood.**
   Mood is a persistent and sustained emotional feeling.
2. **Define affect.**
   Affect is an outward expression of feeling.
3. **What are different types of mood?**
   - Elevated mood
   - Normal mood
   - Depressed mood
4. **What is the continuum of affect?**
   - Flat affect
   - Restricted affect
   - Blunt affect
   - Labile affect
5. **Define mood disorder.**
   Mood disorder is a mental health condition in which an individual experiences long periods of extreme happiness, extreme sadness or both.
6. **Who coined the terms "mania" and "depression"?**
   Hippocrates
7. **What is the duration required to diagnose mood disorders?**
   - **Hypomania:** 4 days
   - **Mania:** 1 week
   - **Depression:** 2 weeks
   - **Cyclothymia and dysthymia:** 2 years
8. **What are the stages of mania?**
   - **Stage I:** Hypomania
   - **Stage II:** Acute mania
   - **Stage III:** Delirious mania
9. **Define hypomania.**
   Hypomania is a mood disorder in which the symptoms are not severe, and it does not cause noticeable impairment in social and occupational functioning.
10. **Define acute mania.**
    In acute mania, intensified symptoms such as euphoria, elation are present in a patient and the patient requires hospitalization. The patient has psychotic features and poor impulse control.
11. **What are different types of mood disorders?**
    - Manic episode
    - Depressive episode
    - Bipolar mood disorder
    - Recurrent mood disorder
    - Mixed mood disorder
12. **What are the levels of manic episodes?**
    - Euphoria
    - Elation
    - Exaltation
    - Ecstasy
13. **What are the signs and symptoms of mania?**
    - Irritable mood
    - Increased psychomotor activity
    - Grandeur thought
    - Pressure of speech
    - Raised perceptual activity
    - Decreased sleep
    - Absence of insight

14. What are the etiologies of mood disorder?
- **Neurotransmitters:** Serotonin and dopamine decrease in depression and increase in mania
- **Biopsychosocial factors:** Social pressure, social isolation, feeling of helplessness, worthlessness, hopelessness.
- **Psychological factors:** Loss of loved ones, aggressiveness, negative view, stressors

15. What is the pharmacotherapy for mood disorders?
- Lithium
- Carbamazepine
- Sodium valproate
- Anticonvulsant
- Calcium channel blockers

16. Who discovered lithium?
Johan August Arfwedson

17. What is the mechanism of action of lithium?
Lithium causes changes in the structure of brain, anterior cingulate, hippocampus, amygdala. It modulates the neurotransmitters such as dopamine, GABA and shows effects at intracellular level by inhibiting proteins.

18. What are the side effects of lithium?
- L- Leukocytosis
- I-Insipidus
- T-Tremors
- H-Hypothyroidism
- U-Urinary [Primary]
- M-Miscellaneous [weight gain, ECG changes, fatigue, nystagmus, muscle weakness]

19. What are the grades of lithium toxicity?
- **Grade I:** 1.5- 2.5
- **Grade II:** 2.5-3.5
- **Grade III:** > 3.5

20. What are the scales used to assess mania?
- Young mania rating scales
- Mood disorder questionnaire
- Semantic differential feelings and mood scales

21. Frame some nursing diagnosis for mania.
- Risk of self-directed violence
- Risk for violence towards others
- Impaired nutrition less than body requirements

22. Define depression.
Depression is a part of manic-depressive psychosis.

23. What is the etiology of depression?
- Brain anatomy
- Genetics
- Neurochemical factors
- Endocrine theory
- Psychosocial factors
- Organic causes
- Circadian rhythm imbalances

24. What are the clinical symptoms of depression?
- *Physical symptoms*
  - Blurred vision
  - Dry mouth
  - Headache
  - Chest pain
  - Abdominal discomfort
- *Psychological and emotional symptoms*
  - Anhedonia
  - Feeling of guilt
  - Insomnia
  - Psychomotor retardation
  - Lack of interest
  - Crying spells

25. What are the types of depression?
- Mild depression
- Moderate depression
- Severe depression
- Endogenous depression
- Exogenous depression

26. Mention the scales used to assess depression.
- Beck Depression Inventory
- Hamilton Rating Scale for depression

27. Define endogenous depression.
The prefix 'Endo' in the term 'Endogenous' means 'within'. Endogenous depression can be hereditary or due to biochemical imbalance. Other name is psychotic depression. The individual feels sad in morning, experiences psychomotor retardation and delusion. Relapse is common.

28. Define exogenous depression.
The prefix 'Exo' in the term 'Exogenous' means 'outside'. Exogenous depression is caused by external factors. Other name is neurotic depression. The individual feels sad in evening. Psychotic features are absent. Stress is present. Relapse is not common.

29. What are the treatment modalities for depression?
- Individual psychotherapy
- Family therapy
- Cognitive therapy
- Behavior therapy
- Occupational therapy
- Relaxation therapy

30. **Frame some nursing diagnosis for patients with depressive disorder.**
    - Risk of injury
    - Risk of violence
    - Impaired nutrition less than body requirements
    - Impaired social interaction
    - Impaired family coping skills
    - Risk of suicide
    - Self-care deficit
    - Hopelessness related to negative view
31. **What is cyclothymia?**
    Cyclothymia is characterized by a period of depressive symptoms and hypomania.
32. **Define dysthymia.**
    Dysthymia is a persistent depressive disorder in which mild depressive symptoms persist for at least two years.
33. **What is empty nest syndrome?**
    Empty nest syndrome refers to the feelings of sadness and anxiety that some parents feel when their children move out of the family home. Such a situation makes parents prone to depression and anxiety.
34. **What is the other name for stage 3 mania?**
    Delirious mania
35. **What is bipolar II disorder?**
    Bipolar II disorder involves periods of hypomania and periods of depression.
36. **Carbamazepine is a major side effect of which syndrome?**
    Stevens-Johnson syndrome
37. **What is the other name for mood disorder?**
    Affective disorders
38. **Classify mood disorders.**
    - Unipolar disorders
    - Bipolar disorders
39. **What is bipolar I disorder?**
    Bipolar I disorder involves mania and depression.

PSYCHOPHARMACOLOGY

1. **Define psychopharmacology.**
   Psychopharmacology is the study of drugs used to treat psychiatric disorders with psychoactive medications.
2. **How are psychotropic drugs classified?**
   - Antipsychotics
   - Antidepressants
   - Mood stabilizers
   - Anxiolytics
   - Antiepileptics
   - Antiparkinsonian
3. **Define antipsychotics.**
   Antipsychotics are the medications used to treat psychotic disorders.
4. **How are antipsychotics classified?**
   - Typical antipsychotics
   - Atypical antipsychotics
5. **What are other names used for antipsychotics?**
   - D_2 receptor blockers
   - Neuroleptics
   - Antischizophrenic drugs
   - Major tranquilizers
6. **What is the mechanism of action of antipsychotics?**
   Antipsychotics block the D_2 receptors in the mesolimbic and mesofrontal systems.
7. **Name any two drugs of typical antipsychotics.**
   Chlorpromazine and haloperidol.
8. **Name any two drugs of atypical antipsychotics.**
   Clozapine and ziprasidone.
9. **Define extrapyramidal symptoms.**
   Extrapyramidal symptoms are the serious neurologic symptoms and major side effects of antipsychotics.
   - Acute dystonia
   - Pseudoparkinsonism
   - Akathisia
   - Tardive dyskinesia
10. **What are the indications for antipsychotics?**
    - Organic mental disorders
    - Functional disorders
    - Mood disorders
    - Childhood disorders
    - Neurotic disorders
11. **What is rabbit syndrome?**
    Rabbit syndrome is presence of orofacial tremors.
12. **Define antidepressants.**
    Antidepressants are the drugs which are used for the treatment of depressive illness.
13. **What are the indications of antidepressants?**
    - Neurotic and stress related disorders
    - Medical disorders
    - Eating disorders
    - Childhood psychiatric disorders

14. How are antidepressants classified?

- Tricyclic antidepressants
- Selective serotonin reuptake inhibitors
- Serotonin norepinephrine reuptake inhibitors
- Monoamine oxidase inhibitors
- Atypical antidepressants

15. What is the mechanism of action of antidepressants?

Antidepressants increase catecholamine levels in the brain, block the reuptake of norepinephrine at the nerve terminals, thus increase the norepinephrine levels at the receptor site.

16. What is the mnemonic of serotonin syndrome?

HARM

- H : Hyperthermia
- A : Autonomic instability
- R : Rigidity
- M : Myoclonus

17. What are anxiolytics?

Anxiolytics are otherwise called antianxiety drugs. Most of them belong to benzodiazepine group of drugs.

18. What are indications for antianxiety?

Anxiety disorders, mood disorders, sleep disorders and psychotic disorders.

19. What is the mechanism of action for antianxiety drugs?

Antianxiety drugs stimulate the GABA to bind in postsynaptic receptor and release negativity ion in postsynaptic neuron.

20. How are antianxiety drugs classified?

- Benzodiazepines
- Barbiturates
- Nonbarbiturates
- Nonbenzodiazepines

21. Define Parkinson's disease.

Parkinson's disease is a neurogenerative disorder caused due to degeneration of substantia nigra of midbrain and caused imbalance of dopamine.

22. What is the mechanism of action for antiparkinsonian drugs?

Antiparkinsonian drugs help to balance dopamine and acetylcholine in central nervous system.

23. What are mood stabilizers?

Mood stabilizers are used for the treatment of bipolar affective disorder.

24. Which is the drug of choice for mood stabilizer?

Lithium

25. Mention blood lithium levels.

Therapeutic levels = 0.8–1.2 mEq/L
Prophylactic level= 0.6–1.2 mEq/L

26. What is the Lithium toxic level?

> 2.0 mEq/L

27. Define psychostimulants.

Stimulants are those which enhance the mental and physical function by increasing the alertness and wakefulness. For example, Caffeine and Nicotine.

28. What are antabuse drugs?

Antabuse drugs are used in the treatment of substance abuse, e.g., Disulfiram is the Antabuse drug used for patient with Alcohol dependence syndrome.

PSYCHOTHERAPY

1. Define psychotherapy.

Psychotherapy is defined as the way to help the people with mental illness or emotional difficulties. It helps to control or remove the symptoms and increase the sense of well-being.

2. What are the stages of psychotherapy?

- First stage is the assessment
- Second stage is therapeutic work
- Third stage is conclusion

3. What are the psychoanalytic techniques?

- Free association
- Dream analysis
- Treatment alliance
- Acting out interpretation

4. What are the indications for psychotherapy?

- Stress related disorder
- Personality disorder
- Psychosomatic disorder
- Neurotic disorders
- Depression
- Identity problems

5. Define catharsis.

Freud and Breuer defined catharsis as "the process of reducing or eliminating a complex by recalling it to conscious awareness and allowing it to be expressed."

6. What are the types of psychotherapy?

- Individual psychotherapy

- Group psychotherapy
- Interpersonal psychotherapy
- Superficial psychotherapy
- Deep psychotherapy
- Educational psychotherapy
- Re-educative psychotherapy
- Reconstructive psychotherapy
- Supportive psychotherapy

7. What are the goals of psychotherapy?
- Enhance the coping skills
- Problem solving ability
- Promote the sense of control
- Strengthen the ego
- Create the deeper insight
- Provide a therapeutic relationship with patients
- Promote the positive attitude

8. Define cognitive therapy.

Cognitive therapy is a form of psychotherapy in which the distorted cognitions are modified into positive cognitions.

9. What are the indications of cognitive therapy?
- Depression
- Bipolar disorder
- Panic disorder
- Post-traumatic stress disorder
- Generalized anxiety disorder
- Eating disorder

10. What are the components of cognitive therapy?
- Cognitive techniques
- Behavioral interventions
- Didactic aspects

11. Name some cognitive techniques.
- Guided discovery
- Role play
- Imagery
- Thought recording
- Daily records of thoughts
- Cognitive rehearsal
- Activity scheduling
- Assertiveness techniques
- Relaxation therapy

12. Define behavior therapy.

Behavior therapy is a form of psychotherapy in which various techniques are used to change maladaptive behaviors.

13. What are the types of behavior therapy?
- Classical conditioning
- Operant conditioning

14. What are the techniques of behavior therapy?
- Systemic desensitization
- Flooding
- Social skill training
- Shaping
- Aversion therapy
- Token economy
- Time out

15. What are the indications for behavior therapy?
- Bipolar disorder
- Obsessive compulsive disorder
- Social anxiety
- Phobia
- Substance abuse
- Tics
- Nocturnal enuresis
- Sexual dysfunction

16. Who is the pioneer of cognitive behavior therapy?

Aaron beck

17. What are the techniques of cognitive behavior therapy?
- Cognitive rehearsal
- Validity testing
- Writing in a journal
- Guided discovery
- Self-instructional coping methods
- Homework
- Problem solving methods
- Computer assisted therapy

18. Define therapeutic community.

Therapeutic community is a drug free treatment in which the individuals with addictive behavior join together in a structured manner to promote drug free society.

19. What are the components of therapeutic community?
- Daily community meetings
- Patient government
- Staff meetings
- Living and learning opportunities

20. What are the stages of therapeutic community?
- Induction and treatment
- Primary treatment
- Vocational skill training
- Re-entry

21. Define Milieu therapy.

Milieu means environment or surroundings. It is the scientific structuring of the environment to elicit the behavioral changes and enhance the psychological health and functioning of the individual.

22. What are the characteristics of Milieu therapy?

- Distribution of power
- Open communication
- Structured interactions
- Work related activities

23. What are the concepts of Milieu therapy?

- Containment
- Validation
- Structured interaction
- Open communication

24. Who are all the Milieu team members?

- Psychiatrist
- Psychiatric nurse
- Clinical psychologist
- Occupational therapist
- Recreational therapist
- Music therapist
- Art therapist
- Chaplin

25. Define supportive psychotherapy.

Supportive psychotherapy is defined as psychotherapeutic approach which integrates various components as, cognitive behavioral, psychodynamic and interpersonal techniques which help to decrease psychological conflict and strengthen the patient's defenses.

26. What are the techniques of supportive therapy?

Directive techniques	Explanatory techniques
Advice	Motivation
Teaching	Empathy
Change of environment	Reassurance
Cognitive restructuring	Containment
Modeling	Reality testing

27. What is the fundamental unit of human life?

Family

28. Who is the mother of family therapy?

Virginia satir

29. Define family therapy.

Family therapy is a form of psychotherapy in which the issues, problems or conflicts existing among the family members are addressed and the solution is identified.

30. Who are the indicators for family therapy?

- Family conflicts
- Issues of families
- Stressors among family members
- Relationship issues
- Generation gap

31. What are the functions of family?

- Communication function
- Boundary function
- Supportive function
- Biological function
- Socialization function
- Psychological function
- Protective function
- Educational function
- Recreational function

32. What are types of family therapy?

- Individual family therapy
- Conjoint family therapy
- Couples family therapy
- Multiple family therapy
- Network therapy
- Psychodynamic family therapy
- Structural family therapy
- Strategic family therapy

33. Define group therapy.

Group therapy is a type of psychotherapy in which the mentally ill patients are placed in groups, guided by therapist, to talk, interact and discuss the problems with the therapist for the purpose of changing maladaptive behavior.

34. List out the components of group therapy.

- Members
- Duration
- No. of sessions
- Norms
- Cohesion
- Role
- Power
- Communication

35. List out the types of group therapy.

- Open group therapy
- Closed group therapy
- Small group therapy
- Primary group therapy
- Large group therapy
- Secondary group therapy
- Homogenous group therapy

- Heterogenous group therapy
- Psychodrama
- Interpersonal group therapy
- Encounter group therapy
- Community group therapy

36. What are the stages of group therapy?
- Initial stage
- Working stage
- Termination stage

37. What are the therapeutic techniques of group therapy?
- Acceptance
- Approval
- Clarification
- Information giving
- Reinforcement
- Support
- Teaching
- Listening
- Limit setting
- Silence
- Structuring
- Themes

38. Define play therapy.

Play therapy is a form of psychotherapy in which the therapist utilizes the child's fantasy and symbolic medium of play to have communication with him and understand him.

39. What are the theories of play?
- Natural theory
- Energy theory
- Practice theory
- Recreation theory
- Catharsis theory
- Discovery theory
- Pleasure principle theory

40. Enlist the indications for play therapy.
- Children with:
  - Aggression
  - Temper tantrums
  - Poor bladder and bowel control
  - Who are neglected
  - Excess worries
  - Low self esteem
  - Learning disorder
  - Differently abled children

41. Mention the types of play therapy.
- Controlled play
- Free play
- Individual play
- Group play
- Structured play
- Unstructured play
- Directive play
- Nondirective play

42. What are the phases of play therapy?
- Introductory phase
- Honeymoon phase
- Rebellious phase
- Working through phase
- Termination phase

43. Define psychodrama.

Psychodrama is a form of psychotherapy in which the dramatization or dramatic presentation of the group is done to gain self-insight.

44. What are the phases of psychodrama?
- Warm-up
- Shaping
- Discussion

45. Mention the psychodrama techniques.
- Mirroring
- Doubling
- Role play
- Role training
- Future projection
- Magic shop
- Empty chair

46. List out the principles of psychodrama.
- Action principle
- Social atom principle
- Potentiality
- Spontaneity
- Catharsis
- Surplus reality
- Tele principle

47. Define music therapy.

Music therapy is defined as utilization of music in treatment, training, education and rehabilitation of children and adults who are suffering from physical or mental disorder.

48. What is the mechanism of action of music therapy?

Stimulation of endorphins, peptides and natural opiates leads to the synchronization of body rhythms with musical rhythms, thereby it gives calming effect.

49. What are the types of music therapy?
- Active music therapy
- Passive music therapy

50. Enlist the various aspects of music therapy.
- Anxiolytic music therapy
- Algolytic music therapy
- Tensolytic music therapy
- Psychotic music therapy
- Patholytic music therapy

51. Name the areas where music therapy sessions are conducted.
- Counseling rooms
- Rehabilitation centers
- Physical therapy units
- Massage therapy rooms
- Labor rooms
- Operation rooms
- Patient waiting halls

52. Define dance therapy.

Dance therapy is defined as psychotherapeutic use of movement as process which promotes physical, emotional, cognitive integration of the individual.

53. Who is the pioneer of modern music therapy?

Marian chace.

54. What are the Stages of dance therapy?
- Preparation
- Incubation
- Illumination
- Evaluation

55. What are the techniques of dance therapy?
- Body movements
- Props
- Imagery movement
- Space awareness
- Memory movements
- Group coordination

56. What are the settings of dance therapy?
- Hospitals
- Rehabilitation center
- Psychiatric setups
- Education sector
- Day care centers

57. Define recreational therapy.

Recreational therapy is a systematic process which utilizes the recreation and other activity-based interventions based on the needs of individuals with illness to improve the psychological, physical health, recovery and well-being.

58. What are the indications for recreational therapy?
- Psychiatric disorders
- Developmental disability
- Childhood disorders
- Substance abuse
- Geriatrics with cognitive deficits

59. How do you classify recreational therapy?
- Based on the place of recreational activity:
  - Indoor activity
  - Outdoor activity
- Based on the benefits of recreational activity:
  - Motor development
  - Sensory development
  - Intellectual development

60. What are the recreational activities for psychiatric disorders?
- Schizophrenia—Carrom, chess
- Depression—Walking, jogging
- Mania—Volley ball, football
- Dementia—Craft works
- Anxiety disorders—Music listening
- Childhood and adolescent disorders—Gross motor activities

61. Who is the father of modern phototherapy?

Niels Finsen

62. What are the indications for Light therapy?
- Skin disorders
- Retinal conditions
- Mood and sleep related disorders

63. What is the mechanism of action of Light therapy?

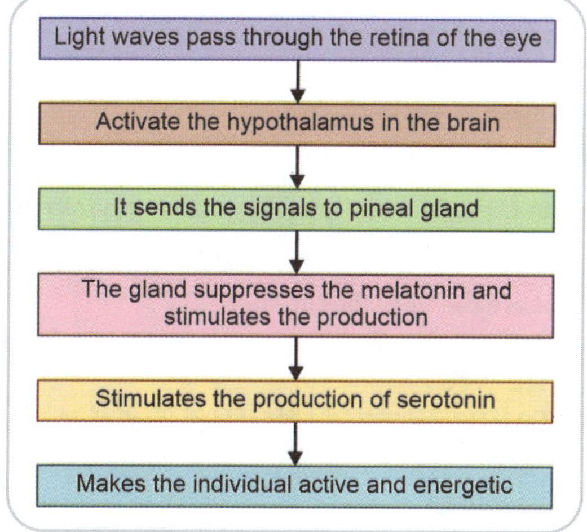

64. Define relaxation therapy.

Relaxation therapy is a component of body mind intervention which the therapist provides to the participants for mind relaxation.

65. Define autogenic training.

Autogenic training is defined as relaxation therapy that involves the daily practice of sessions of around 15 minutes usually thrice a day. The technique helps alleviate symptoms of stress. During each session, a series of self-statements or visualisations is repeated that induces a state of relaxation.

66. What is assertiveness training?

Assertiveness training is a training to verbalize one's own willingness in polite manner in order to protect one's own rights. Important technique is 'Broken record.'

67. What is Jacobson Progressive Muscle Relaxation?

Jacobson Progressive Muscle Relaxation is a relaxation therapy in which a series of guided steps focus on tightening and relaxing specific muscle groups that help in dealing with anxiety.

68. Define Guided imagery.

Guided imagery is a form of relaxation therapy in which the therapist helps the participants relax by evoking the mental images or recreating the sensory perception of sound, taste, movement and smell.

69. What are the types of guided imagery?

- Voluntary
- Involuntary
- Direct method
- Use audio or video tapes
- Individual
- Group

70. What are the stages of guided imagery?

- Image generation
- Image maintenance
- Image inspections
- Image transformations

71. When is the International Yoga Day celebrated?

June 21

72. What are the branches of Yoga?

- Hatha yoga
- Raja yoga
- Karma yoga
- Bhakthi yoga
- Jnana yoga
- Tantra yoga

73. Name some asanas.

- Padmasana
- Dhanurasana
- Sarvangasana
- Savasana
- Vajrasana
- Sasankasana
- Chakrasana

74. What is pranayama?

Breathing practices in the Yoga.

75. Define meditation.

Meditation is defined as an experience of relaxing the body, mind and spirit.

76. List out the types of meditation.

- Breathing meditation
- Metta meditation
- Chakra meditation
- Gazing meditation
- Object meditation
- Mantra meditation
- Sound meditation
- Third eye meditation

77. Define biofeedback.

Biofeedback is defined as the psychophysiological therapy in which the individual is also able to monitor the physiological changes in the body due to psychological stressors.

78. What are the phases of biofeedback?

- Initial evaluation
- Skills training
- Therapy

79. List out the types of biofeedback.

On the basis of physiological function - brain waves breathing, heart rate, galvanic skin response, temperature and muscle contraction.

On the basis of devices used – mobile device, wearable device.

80. Define Alternative and Complementary Medicine.

Alternative and Complementary Medicine is defined as group of diverse health care systems, practices and products that are not presently considered to be a part of conventional medicine.

81. What are the major domains of alternative and complementary medicines?

- Alternative medicine system
- Mind body interactions
- Biologically based therapies

- Body based therapies
- Energy therapies

82. Define Acupuncture.

Acupuncture is stimulating the points in the body to correct the imbalance in energy flow through the channels known as Meridians.

83. What is Naturopathy?

Naturopathy is the way of life in which the body innately maintains the health and heals oneself.

84. What is homeopathy?

Homeopathy means 'treat like with like.'

85. What is hypnosis?

Hypnosis is a trance like state in which the patient has been put in a heightened focus and concentration.

86. What are the modes of application of aromatherapy?

- Direct inhalation
- Topical application
- Aerial diffusion

87. Define Tai-chi.

Tai-chi means 'moving meditation.' A series of continuous slow movements with the mind and breath coordination.

88. Define bioelectromagnetic therapy.

Bioelectromagnetic is the usage of electromagnetic fields in the body for a therapeutic purpose by Static and Pulse method.

89. What is Reiki?

Reiki means Universal life force. The purpose is direct access to universal, transcendental, radiant and light energies at various levels of energy.

90. Define reflexology.

Reflexology is called 'Zone therapy.' Massaging the specific areas of hands or feet in order to reduce stress, pain and illness in the body.

91. Define occupational therapy.

Occupational therapy is defined as application of goal-oriented and purposeful activity for the assessment and treatment of patients with physical, psychological and developmental disabilities.

92. What are the basic elements of occupational therapy?

- Patient
- Therapist
- Purposeful activity
- Context

93. What are the indications of occupational therapy?

- Substance abuse
- Mood disorders
- Anxiety disorders
- Childhood psychiatric disorders
- Antisocial personality disorders

94. Mention the various settings of occupational therapy.

- Psychiatric hospitals
- Nursing homes
- Special schools
- Rehabilitation centers
- Group homes
- Halfway homes

95. What are all the occupational therapy activities?

- Task activities, e.g., crafts, wood works
- Activities enhancing fine motor skills, e.g., drawing, typing
- Activities enhancing the cognition, e.g., poetry, discussion
- Activities involving communication, e.g., drama, social skill training

96. What are all the occupational therapy activities for psychiatric disorders?

- Manic, e.g., games
- Depression, e.g., craft works
- Anti-social personality disorder, e.g., painting
- Dementia, e.g., cover making
- Childhood psychiatric disorder, e.g., drawing, painting
- Anxiety disorders, e.g., washing clothes

97. Enlist the process of occupational therapy.

- Selecting a model
- Assessment
- Treatment
- Evaluation

98. Define Electroconvulsive therapy.

Electroconvulsive therapy is defined as therapy in which convulsions are induced by passing a brief pulse of electric current through brain via electrodes for a therapeutic purpose.

99. List out the types of Electroconvulsive therapy (or) How can you classify ECT?

- Sine wave ECT
- Brief pulse ECT
- Ultra-brief pulse ECT
- Direct ECT
- Modified ECT

- Unilateral ECT
- Bilateral

100. What are the indications of ECT?
- Depression
- Schizophrenia
- Postpartum psychosis

101. What are the contraindications of ECT?
- Absolute contraindications—Increased intracranial pressure
- Relative contraindications—Myocardial infarction, cerebrovascular accident
- Major physical illness, Cardiac and Respiratory problems

102. What is the mechanism of action of ECT?
Exact mechanism is unknown. The effects of neurotransmitters get balanced in the monoamine system and affect the neuroendocrine and HPA axis.

103. What is the frequency of ECT?
3 times a week, 6–10 times ECT can be given and the maximum of 24 ECT.

104. What is the protocols for ECT administration?
Twice a week, 6–12 sessions, minimum electrical dose is required to induce generalized seizures.

105. What are the complications of ECT?
- Memory loss
- Respiratory arrest
- Fracture
- Dysrhythmia

106. What are the articles required for ECT administration?
- ECG electrodes and monitor
- Pulse oximetry
- Stethoscope
- Reflex hammer
- Venflon
- Suction device
- Oxygen cylinder
- AMBU bag
- Airways
- Intubation kit

107. What are the medications used for ECT?
- Anticholinergics, e.g., Atropine
- Anesthetics, e.g., Methohexital propofol
- Muscle relaxant, e.g., Succinylcholine

108. What is the placement of ECT electrodes?
- Bitemporal placement
- Right unilateral
- Bifrontal

109. Mention some psychiatric neurosurgeries.
- Anterior cingulotomy
- Anterior capsulotomy
- Thalamotomy
- Hypothalamotomy
- Amygdalotomy
- Limbic leucotomy

110. Define deep brain stimulation.
Deep brain stimulation is defined as implanting the electrodes in central parts of the brain, the electrodes produce the impulses to regulate the abnormal impulses. The stimulation is controlled by the pacemaker like device that implanted under the skin of the chest.

111. What are the indications of deep brain stimulation?
- Parkinson's disease
- Epilepsy
- Dementia
- Cluster headache
- Major depression

112. Who used ECT at first in modern times?
Ladislas Meduna

113. What is the minimum seizure duration required for the efficacy of ECT?
10–20 seconds

SCHIZOPHRENIA

1. Who coined the word 'schizophrenia'?
Eugen Bleuler

2. What is the meaning of schizophrenia?
The prefix in the term 'Schizophrenia'—'Schizo' means 'split' and, the suffix 'phrenia' means 'mind'. So, Schizophrenia means split mind.

3. Define schizophrenia.
Schizophrenia is a psychotic disorder characterized by abnormalities in emotion, thinking and cognition.

4. What are the etiological factors for schizophrenia?
- Neurochemical factors
- Genetic factors
- Neuropathological factors

- Neuroendocrinology factors
- Environmental factors

5. **What are the 4 As of schizophrenia?**
   1. Autistic thinking
   2. Ambivalence
   3. Affect
   4. Associative loosening

6. **What is the diagnostic evaluation of schizophrenia?**
   - Assessment scales for psychotic symptoms—Brief Psychiatric Rating scale
   - Assessment scales for cognitive deficits—Wechsler Adult intelligence scale
   - Assessment scales for personality problem—Rorschach inkblot test
   - Single photon emission computed tomography (SPECT) and positron emission tomography (PET)
   - Magnetic resonance imaging (MRI)
   - Diffusion tensor imaging

7. **What are the three phases of schizophrenia?**
   1. Prodromal phase
   2. Psychotic phase
   3. Residual phase

8. **What are the positive and negative symptoms of schizophrenia?**

Positive Symptoms	Negative Symptoms
Hallucination	Apathy
Delusion	Blunt affect
Bizarre behavior	Anhedonia
Disorganized thoughts	Alogia

9. **What are the types of schizophrenia?**
   - Paranoid schizophrenia
   - Hebephrenic schizophrenia
   - Catatonic schizophrenia
   - Simple schizophrenia
   - Residual schizophrenia
   - Undifferentiated schizophrenia

10. **What are the treatment modalities for schizophrenia?**
    - Pharmacotherapy
    - Psychotherapy
    - Transcranial magnetic stimulation
    - Community-based treatment
    - Psychiatric rehabilitation

11. **Frame nursing diagnosis for schizophrenia.**
    - Disturbed thought process
    - Disturbed sensory perception
    - Social isolation
    - Self-care deficit
    - Ineffective health maintenance
    - Impaired verbal communication
    - Ineffective family coping

12. **Which is the most common type of schizophrenia?**
    Paranoid schizophrenia

13. **Which rate of Dopamine level caused schizophrenia?**
    Increased level of dopamine

14. **Which is the most common type of hallucination in psychiatric disorders?**
    Auditory

15. **Define rehabilitation.**
    Rehabilitation means restoring the health status of mentally ill patients as early as possible.

16. **What is bouffee delirante?**
    Bouffee delirante means short lived psychosis. It is characterized by hallucination, delusion, confused state and amnesia after attack and polymorphous symptoms.

17. **What is the classical trial of psychoneurotic schizophrenia?**
    - Pan anxiety
    - Pan neurosis
    - Pan sexuality

18. **Mention some psychosocial intervention for schizophrenia.**
    - Psychoeducation
    - Social skill training
    - Cognitive training
    - Token economy
    - Family intervention
    - Psychosocial weight management

19. **What is the required duration to diagnose paranoid schizophrenia?**
    1 month

20. **What is Capgras syndrome?**
    Capgras syndrome is defined as the delusion of doubles or delusional misidentification syndrome.

21. **What is another name for Capgras syndrome?**
    Imposter syndrome

22. **Who classified the schizophrenia as Type I and Type II?**
    T J Crow

23. **Define Pfropf schizophrenia.**
    Schizophrenia occurs with mental retardation.

SEXUAL DISORDERS

1. **How can you classify the sexual disorder?**
   - Gender identity disorder
   - Disorders of sex deviation
   - Disorders related to sexual maturation
   - Sexual dysfunction
2. **What is transsexualism?**
   People having the feeling of discomfort with one's own anatomical sex organs.
3. **What is transvestism?**
   Wearing the dress of opposite gender for the purpose of sexual excitement.
4. **What are the treatment options for transvestism?**
   - Counseling and psychotherapy
   - Sex reassignment surgery
   - Mastectomy
   - Castration
   - Phalloplasty
5. **What is dual-role transvestism?**
   Dual-role transvestism is wearing opposite gender's dress to enjoy the experience of opposite sex on temporary basis.
6. **Name the types of homosexuality.**
   - Obligatory homosexuality
   - Preferred homosexuality
   - Bisexuality
   - Situational homosexuality
   - Latent homosexuality
7. **What is the normal human sexual response cycle?**
   - Appetitive phase
   - Excitement phase
   - Plateau phase
   - Orgasmic phase
   - Resolution phase
8. **Define exhibitionism.**
   Exhibitionism is showing of sex organs to stranger.
9. **Define frotteurism.**
   Frotteurism is sexual pleasure with rubbing others.
10. **Define sadism.**
    Sadism is sexual pleasure with humiliating others.
11. **Define masochism.**
    Masochism is sexual pleasure with getting humiliated.
12. **Define pedophilia.**
    Pedophilia is sexual pleasure with children.
13. **Define zoophilia.**
    Zoophilia is sexual pleasure with animals.
14. **Define necrophilia.**
    Necrophilia is sexual pleasure with dead bodies.
15. **Define fetishism.**
    Fetishism is sexual pleasure with objects.
16. **Define fetishistic transvestism.**
    Fetishistic Transvestism is sexual pleasure with clothes of opposite sex.
17. **Define voyeurism.**
    Voyeurism is sexual pleasure by observing the sexual activity of opposite sex.
18. **What is sexual dysfunction?**
    Sexual dysfunction is a significant dysfunction in human response cycle which is not due to an organic cause.
19. **What are the disorders related to appetitive phase?**
    - Sexual aversion disorder
    - Hypoactive sexual desire disorder
    - Excessive sexual desire disorder
20. **What are the disorders related to excitement phase?**
    - Male erectile disorder
    - Female sexual arousal disorder
21. **What are the disorders related to orgasmic phase?**
    - Male orgasmic disorder
    - Female orgasmic disorder
    - Premature ejaculation
22. **What is nonorganic vaginismus?**
    Spasm of lower vagina causes interference with the coitus.
23. **What is nonorganic dyspareunia?**
    Male or female has pain in genital area during coitus.
24. **Which is the peak state of sexual excitement?**
    Orgasmic phase
25. **What are gender identity disorder?**
    - Transsexualism
    - Dual-role transvestism
    - Intersexuality
    - Gender identity disorders of childhood

26. Define personality.

Personality is an enduring quality of a person and these qualities develop into personality traits.

27. Define personality disorders.

Personality disorders are types of mental disorders in which an individual has rigid and unhealthy pattern of thinking, functioning and behaving.

28. Which personality disorder is more common in psychiatric setups?

Borderline personality disorders

29. Which personality disorder is more common than single type?

Mixed personality disorders

30. Which personality disorder is more common among prison inmates?

Antisocial personality disorders

31. What is the etiology of personality disorders?

- Increased levels of testosterone
- Increased levels of dopamine and serotonin
- Impulsivity
- Change in electrical conductance

32. What is the DSM-5 classification of personality disorders?

- Cluster A [odd and eccentric]
- Cluster B [dramatic, emotional]
- Cluster C [anxious or fearful]

33. What is DSM-5 classification of personality disorders?

- Negative affectivity
- Detachment
- Antagonism
- Disinhibition
- Psychoticism

34. What are the risk factors of personality disorders?

- School dropouts
- Unemployment
- Unmarried
- Divorced
- History of child abuse
- Neglect from parents

35. What are the protective factors of personality disorders?

- A string trusting relationship
- Married
- Employed
- Good IPR
- Extrovert

36. What are types of personality disorders?

- Paranoid personality disorder
- Schizoid paranoid personality disorder
- Schizotypal paranoid personality disorder
- Antisocial paranoid personality disorder
- Borderline paranoid personality disorder
- Histrionic paranoid personality disorder
- Narcissistic paranoid personality disorder
- Avoidant paranoid personality disorder
- Dependent paranoid personality disorder
- Obsessive compulsive paranoid personality disorder

37. Define antisocial personality disorders.

Antisocial personality disorders violate the social norms and lead to criminal activities.

38. What are the criteria of antisocial personality disorders?

- No concern for others
- Decreased frustration
- No guilty
- Blame others with rationalization
- Violation of social norms

39. What are borderline personality disorders?

Borderline personality disorders consist of tendency to act out of impulsivity without considering the consequences along with unstable effects.

40. What is the other name for borderline personality disorders?

Emotionally unstable personality disorder.

41. What are the types of Borderline personality disorders?

- Impulsive type—unstable emotions
- Borderline type—unstable emotions along with self-image

42. What is the treatment for borderline personality disorders?

- Dialectical Behavior therapy
- Psychotherapy
- Mentalization based therapy
- Emotional regulation training
- ECT
- Pharmacotherapy

43. Define eating disorders.

Eating disorders are characterized by severe form of disturbances in eating pattern leading to life-threatening conditions.

44. What are the types of eating disorders?

- Anorexia nervosa

- Bulimia nervosa
- Binge eating

45. What are the complications of eating disorders?
- Cardiovascular
- Endocrine
- Fluids and electrolytes
- Gastrointestinal
- Dental
- Renal
- Musculoskeletal
- Psychological

46. What are the types of anorexia nervosa?
- Restricted type
- Binge eating/ Purging type
- What are the types of bulimia nervosa?
- Purging type
- Non purging type

47. What is the assessment of eating disorders?
- Questionnaires: Eating attitude test, body image assessment
- Waist to hip ratio
- Body mass index
- Ratio to skin fold
- Assess the body fat

48. What are the signs and symptoms of eating disorders?
- Lethargy and fatigue
- Anemia
- Severe abdominal pain
- Constipation
- Enlarged parotid glands
- Dental and enamel erosion
- Muscle wasting

49. Define Russel's sign.

Russel's sign are callus knuckles due to self-induced vomiting.

SUBSTANCE ABUSE

1. Define substance abuse.

Substance abuse is the maladaptive pattern of substance use leading to clinically significant distress or impairment in recurrent substance use.

2. Define tolerance.

Tolerance is the increase in the level of substance use in order to get the same desired effect.

3. Define dependence.

Dependence is the compulsive and repeated use of substance, which results in tolerance toward the substance and leads to withdrawal symptoms.

4. Define withdrawal.

Withdrawal symptoms occur when blood level of abused drug gets decreased and the symptoms ceased when that substance has been taken by the individual.

5. Define intoxication.

Intoxication occurs when substance-related symptoms occur due to the strong exposure to the substances.

6. Define detoxification.

Detoxification is the process of eliminating or neutralizing the toxins from the human body.

7. What is the common substance abuse in India?
- Alcohol
- Cannabis
- Hypnotics
- Cocaine
- Barbiturates
- Nicotine
- Opioids

8. What is modified Mann's Index of addiction?

Modified Mann's Index of addiction denotes the addiction level of various substances which has been arranged from lower to higher; Caffeine has low addiction index and heroin has high addiction index.

9. What are the stages of craving?
- Normal craving
- Excessive craving
- Obsessional craving
- Compulsive craving

10. What are the etiological factors for substance abuse?
- **Social causes:** Peer pressure, unemployment, high work pressure, love failure, lack of affection
- **Biological causes:** Imbalance in neurotransmitters, hereditary factors, co-morbid illness
- **Psychological factors:** Loneliness, low self-esteem, low coping skills, poor impulse control

11. What are the complications of substance abuse?

Neurological, Cardiopulmonary, Musculoskeletal, Gastrointestinal and Reproductive.

12. Define alcohol.

Alcohol is a natural product obtained by the reaction of fermented sugar with yeast spores.

13. What is the DSM-5 Classification of Alcoholism?
- 305.00 Alcohol use disorder (mild)

- 303.90 Alcohol use disorder (moderate or severe)
- 303.00 Alcohol intoxication
- 291.81 Alcohol withdrawal
- 291.9 Unspecified alcohol-related disorder

14. What are the common alcoholic beverages?
- Beer
- Wine
- Whisky
- Rum
- Scotch
- Gin
- Vodka

15. What are the blood alcohol concentration levels?
- 20–100—Slow motor activity
- 100–200—Lack of coordination
- 200–300—Alcohol blackout
- 300–350—Hypothermia
- 350–400—Coma
- >400—Death might occur

16. What are the phases of alcoholism?
- Pre alcoholic
- Early alcoholic
- True alcoholic
- Chronic alcoholic

17. Name five species of Jellinek's alcohol dependence.
Alpha, Beta, Gamma, Delta and Epsilon.

18. What is the diagnostic evaluation for alcohol abuse?
- Blood alcohol levels
- Liver function test
- Hematologic studies
- Urine toxicology
- Serum electrolytes
- Electrocardiogram (ECG)

19. Define CAGE questionnaire.
- C : Cutdown
- A : Annoyance
- G : Guilt
- E : Eye opening

20. What are the assessment tools for problem drinkers of alcoholism?
- Michigan Alcoholism Screening Test [MAST]
- CAGE questionnaire
- Alcohol Use Disorders Identification Test [AUDIT]
- Paddington Alcohol Test [PAT]

21. What are the assessment tools for alcohol withdrawal?
- Modified Selective Severity Assessment [MSSA]
- Clinical Institute Withdrawal Assessment for Alcohol Revised [CIWA-Ar]

22. Define aversion therapy.
Aversion therapy is the treatment to arouse the unlikeness or feel likely to be hated of alcoholism.

23. What is electrical aversion?
Ask the client to smell the alcohol. Low volt electrical stimuli administered immediately when he smells alcohol. Desired response will be changed by undesired electrical stimuli.

24. What are the approaches to quit alcohol?
- Aversion therapy
- Motivational interview
- Cognitive therapy
- Behavior therapy
- Contingency management
- Cue's exposure therapy
- Relapse prevention

25. What are the alcohol withdrawal syndromes?
- Delirium tremens
- Alcohol withdrawal seizures
- Alcohol hallucination
- Alcohol pellagra

26. What is Wernicke's Korsakoff syndrome?
Wernicke's Korsakoff syndrome is a neurological disorder caused by the lack of thiamine (vitamin B1) in which damage to neuron occurs.

27. What is Wernicke's encephalopathy?
Wernicke's encephalopathy is characterized by cerebellar ataxia, mental confusion, palsy of 6th cranial nerve, hypothermia and peripheral neuropathy.

28. What are the classical triad of Wernicke's encephalopathy?
- Ataxia
- Confusion
- Ophthalmoplegia

29. Define Korsakoff's syndrome.
Korsakoff's syndrome is characterized by gross memory disturbance, confabulation, confusion, disorientation, poor attention span.

30. What is Marchiafava bignami disease?
Marchiafava bignami disease is a neurological disease of alcoholism which occurs due to demyelination of corpus callosum, optic tract and cerebellar peduncles.

31. Define Othello syndrome.
Othello syndrome is called morbid jealousy. It is a delusion that a life partner is not faithful.

32. **What is blackout?**
    Blackout is transient short term memory loss that may be partial or complete in relation with intoxication state.
33. **What is fetal alcohol syndrome?**
    Alcohol affects the fetus when consumed by pregnant women. It leads to mental retardation.
34. **Define alcoholic anonymous [AA].**
    Alcoholic Anonymous helps the people suffering from alcohol addiction disorder.
35. **Who founded alcoholic anonymous [AA]?**
    Bill Wilson and Dr Bob Smith
36. **What are the types of Alcoholic Anonymous [AA] Meetings?**
    - Closed meetings
    - Open meetings
    - Speaker meetings
    - Discussion meetings
    - Step meetings
37. **What is Al-Anon?**
    Al-Anon is a mutual support group for families and friends of alcoholics.
38. **What is Alateen?**
    Alateen is a subgroup of Al-Anon. It is a mutual support group for families and friends of alcoholics especially teenagers.
39. **What is the usual dose of Disulfiram per day?**
    250 mg.
40. **What is the action of Disulfiram?**
    Aldehyde Dehydrogenase Inhibitors
41. **What is Cannabis?**
    Cannabis is derived from 'hemp plant'. It has more than 400 chemicals and the cannabinoid receptors can be substituted in basal ganglia, cerebellum and hippocampus of the brain.
42. **What is the common preparation of cannabis?**
    - Marijuana
    - Hashish
    - Hashish oil
43. **What are the complications of cannabis use?**
    - **Psychiatric complications:** Anxiety, Hypomania, Paranoid psychosis, Organic psychosis, Schizophrenia.
    - **Systemic complications:** Hypertension, CAD, COPD, Alteration in immune response.
44. **Which are the Central Nervous Stimulants?**
    - **Psychomotor stimulants:** Dopamine, Serotonin
    - **Cellular stimulants:** Caffeine, Nicotine
45. **What are the common CNS stimulants?**
    - Amphetamines
    - Nonamphetamines
    - Miscellaneous—Caffeine, Cocaine and Nicotine
46. **What is cocaine?**
    Cocaine is an alkaloid and it has physiological effects on central and peripheral nervous system. It is commonly used with opioids and amphetamines.
47. **What are the phases of cocaine withdrawal?**
    - Crash
    - Post-crash
    - Extinction
48. **Define Nicotine abuse.**
    Nicotine is an addictive substance present in tobacco products. It has 4000 chemicals. Cigarette smoking, pipe smoking, tobacco chewing are the ways of nicotine abuse.
49. **What are the intoxication effects of Nicotine?**
    Lung carcinoma, Emphysema, Heart disease, Oropharyngeal carcinoma.
50. **What are the 6 D techniques in smoking cessation?**
    - Decide to quit smoking
    - Drink plenty of water
    - Deep breathing exercise
    - Diet in balanced proportion
    - Diversional activities
    - Daily activities
51. **What is meant by Hallucinogen?**
    Hallucinogens are substances which alter the individual's sensory perception of reality and induce hallucinations.
52. **What are types of Hallucinogens?**
    - Natural hallucinogens
    - Synthetic hallucinogens
53. **What are the common inhalants?**
    Aerosols, varnish remover, thinners, petrol and solvents.
54. **Which is an antidote for Cocaine overdose?**
    Amyl nitrite.

Multiple Choice Questions

1. **What is the antidote of narcotics or heroin poisoning?**
(AIIMS Jodhpur Nursing Officer Exam – 2020)
a. Naloxone b. Atropine sulphate
c. Digibind d. Flumazenil

2. **Which of the following is a delusional disorder?**
(NIMHANS – 2019)
a. Trance b. Capuras syndrome
c. Dissociative fugue d. Ganser's syndrome

3. **What is the purpose of using Succinylcholine in ECT?**
(AIIMS Jodhpur Nursing Officer Exam – 2020)
a. Muscle relaxant b. Muscle contraction
c. Both a and c d. Reduces oral secretion

4. **According to psychosocial theory of Erikson, which behavior is seen in toddler age group?**
(AIIMS Jodhpur Nursing Officer Exam – 2020)
a. Autonomy Vs Shame
b. Trust Vs Mistrust
c. Generativity Vs Stagnation
d. Ego integrity Vs despair

5. **Normal value of Serum Lithium test is:**
(AIIMS Jodhpur Nursing Officer Exam – 2020)
a. 0.6–1.2 mEq/L
b. 0.10–0.32 mEq/L
c. 1–1.8 mEq/L
d. 1.2–2.2 mEq/L

6. **Drug of choice for alcohol withdrawal symptoms are:**
(AIIMS Jodhpur Nursing Officer Exam – 2020)
a. Labetalol b. Metoclopramide
c. Digoxin d. Chlordiazepoxide

7. **Which antipsychotics is most common to cause amenorrhea?** *(AIIMS Jodhpur Nursing Officer Exam – 2020)*
a. Risperidone b. Sertraline
c. Paroxetine d. Citalopram

8. **Parkinson's disease is characterized by deficiency of ______________ neurotransmitter.**
(AIIMS Jodhpur Nursing Officer Exam – 2020)
a. Dopamine b. GABA
c. Serotonin d. Acetylcholine

9. **__________causes Extra Pyramidal Symptoms.**
(AIIMS Jodhpur Nursing Officer Exam – 2020)
a. SSRI b. Antipsychotics
c. Mood Stabilizers d. Antianxiety agents

10. **Which of the following causes delirium?**
(AIIMS Jodhpur Nursing Officer Exam – 2020)
a. Alcohol consumption b. Brain tumor
c. Head trauma d. All of these

11. **Paranoid thoughts are described as:**
(AIIMS Jodhpur Nursing Officer Exam – 2020)
a. Hallucinations b. Anxiety disorders
c. Illusions d. Delusions

12. **Which of the following conditions is example for acute organic mental disorder?** *(JIPMER – 2020)*
a. Schizophrenia b. OCD
c. Manic Psychosis d. Delirium

13. **A patient is brought to emergency unit after RTA. Patient's motor response is 3 on GCS. This means the patient's response is:** *(JIPMER – 2020)*
a. Decorticate posture b. Decerebrate posture
c. Withdraws from touch d. Withdraws to pain

14. **Disulfiram is used for the treatment of:**
(JIPMER – 2012)
a. Hallucination b. Mania
c. Catatonia d. Alcoholism

15. **Another term for superego is:** *(JIPMER – 2012)*
a. Self b. Ideal self
c. Conscience d. Subconscious

Ans.
1. a
2. b
3. c
4. a
5. a
6. d
7. a
8. a
9. b
10. d
11. d
12. d
13. a
14. d
15. c

16. Making up stories to fill the memory gaps is: *(JIPMER – 2012)*
a. Reaction formation b. Sublimation
c. Confabulation d. Lying

17. Persistent fear of severe medical illness: *(JIPMER – 2012)*
a. Conversion b. Regression
c. Sublimation d. Hypochondriasis

18. Use of Carbamazepine in psychiatry is: *(JIPMER – 2012)*
a. Mood stabilizer b. Antidote
c. Anticonvulsant d. Neuroleptics

19. An irreversible side effect of antipsychotics is: *(JIPMER – 2012)*
a. Akathisia
b. Tardive dyskinesia
c. Tremor
d. Sleeplessness

20. Type of speech in which one repeats, what the others just said is: *(JIPMER – 2012)*
a. Neologism b. Echopraxia
c. Echolalia d. Association

21. Antipsychotics decrease the psychotic symptoms by: *(RRB – 2019 Shift I)*
a. Blocking the action of dopamine in brain
b. Blocking the reuptake of NE and 5-HT
c. Inhibiting MOA
d. Depressing the CNS

22. Normal IQ for the human being is: *(RRB – 2019 Shift I)*
a. 80–100 b. 90–110
c. 110–120 d. 120 and above

23. Standards of mental health practices are published by: *(RRB – 2019 Shift I)*
a. State Nursing Council
b. TNAI
c. INC
d. American Nurses Association

24. What are the immediate side effects of ECT? *(RRB – 2019 Shift I)*
a. Fractured and dislocated bones
b. Permanent memory loss and brain damage
c. Myocardial infarction and cardiac arrest
d. Temporary memory loss and confusion

25. Which disease is the fatal brain disorder caused by Prion Protein? *(RRB – 2019 Shift I)*
a. Pick's disease
b. Lewy body
c. Creutzfeldt-Jakob disease
d. Mad Cow disease

26. A client with paranoid schizophrenia has a delusion of persecution. He tells the nurse, "The CIA is out to get me. They are spying on me.' The nurse's best initial response is: *(AIIMS Bathinda 2019)*
a. I didn't want to hurt you
b. How would they spy on you here?
c. Tell me how they are trying to get you
d. I know the CIA wound not want to hurt you

27. False sensory perception in the absence of real external stimuli is: *(AIIMS Bathinda 2019)*
a. Illusion b. Hallucination
c. Depersonalization d. Déjà vu

28. For most nurses, the difficult part of nurse client relationship is: *(AIIMS Bathinda 2019)*
a. Developing an awareness to self and professional role in relationship
b. Remaining therapeutic and professional at all times
c. Accepting responsibility in identifying and evaluating the real needs of the client
d. Being able to understand and accept the client behavior

29. Vital aspect of crisis resolution is: *(AIIMS Bathinda 2019)*
a. Meet all dependency needs
b. Encourage socialization
c. Involve the person in therapy sessions
d. Support ego strengths

30. Vital component in nursing care plan of patient with organic brain deterioration is: *(AIIMS Bathinda 2019)*
a. Extensive Re-education Program
b. Introduction of new leisure activities
c. Details of protective and supportive care
d. Plans to involve the new client in group therapy

31. Defense mechanism in which the emotional conflicts are expressed through sensory, motor or somatic disability is: *(AIIMS Bathinda 2019)*
a. Dissociation b. Compensation
c. Psychosomatic d. Conversion

32. In approaching the client with the period of over activity is: *(AIIMS Bathinda 2019)*
a. Use of firm, warm and consistent approach
b. Physically control the hyperactivity
c. Allow the patient to participate in any activity
d. Let the client know the staff will not tolerate the destructive behavior

33. A 19-year-old female was admitted in ICU after being found unconscious. Her BP is 82/50 mm Hg. She is 5'4" tall and weighs 35.8 kg. She appears malnourished and dehydrated. After regaining consciousness, she reported difficulty in eating and she can't remember

Ans.
16. c
17. d
18. a
19. b
20. c
21. a
22. a
23. d
24. d
25. c
26. c
27. b
28. b
29. d
30. c
31. d
32. a
33. a

what she ate for the last 24 hours. She has irregular menstrual period for past 1 year. She refused food since she feels that she was obese. The nurse suspects the case of: *(AIIMS Bathinda – 2019)*

a. Anorexia nervosa b. Bulimia nervosa
c. Reactive depression d. Schizophrenia

34. Nurse demonstrates the active listening by: *(AIIMS Bathinda – 2019)*

a. Repeating everything what the client says
b. Agreeing with the client
c. Assuming relaxed posture and leaning toward the client
d. Smiling and nodding continuously through the interview

35. Meaningless and incoherent mixture of words and phrases is: *(AIIMS Raipur Shift I – 2019)*

a. Word salad b. Verbigeration
c. Paralalia d. Neologism

36. Normal therapeutic value of Serum Lithium test is: *(AIIMS Raipur Shift I – 2019)*

a. 0.8 – 1.2 mEq/L b. 0.1 – 1.0 mEq/L
c. 2 – 4 mEq/L d. 1 – 3 mEq/L

37. What is the normal intracranial pressure? *(AIIMS Raipur Shift I – 2019)*

a. 0–10 mm Hg b. 5–10 mm Hg
c. 5–15 mm Hg d. 30–40 mm Hg

38. What is the 'Problem defining phase' of interpersonal relationship as per 'Peplau's theory'? *(AIIMS Raipur Shift I – 2019)*

a. Orientation phase b. Identification phase
c. Resolution phase d. Exploitation phase

39. The period of acceptance of loss during which the person learns to deal with loss is known as: *(AIIMS Raipur Shift I – 2019)*

a. Idealization b. Bereavement
c. Mourning d. None of these

40. Flow of information between the persons at the same hierarchical level helps in improving ________ communication. *(AIIMS Raipur Shift III – 2019)*

a. Oral b. Horizontal
c. Upward d. Downward

41. Nerve that maintains the hearing and balance is: *(AIIMS Raipur Shift II – 2019)*

a. Vestibulocochlear b. Vagus
c. Facial d. Trochlear

42. Nerve that conveys the special sensory information to the smell is: *(AIIMS Raipur Shift II – 2019)*

a. Optic b. Olfactory
c. Oculomotor d. Trochlear

43. As adult, throwing a temper tantrum when he does not get his own way is an example of: *(AIIMS Raipur Shift II – 2019)*

a. Regression b. Repression
c. Sublimation d. Undoing

44. Which mental disorder is characterized by fantasy, extreme withdrawal, hallucination, delusion and inability to communicate especially in children? *(AIIMS Raipur Shift II – 2019)*

a. Juvenile delinquency
b. Autism
c. Social anxiety disorder
d. Mutism

45. Which of the following is not a physical assessment finding in Parkinson's disease? *(AIIMS Bhubaneswar Shift II – 2019)*

a. Absence of cognitive impairment
b. Mask like expression
c. Pill rolling tremors
d. Dysarthria

46. Which of the following is not true about brief cognitive therapy? *(AIIMS Bhubaneswar Shift II – 2019)*

a. It uses here and now approach
b. It uses goal directed approach
c. It uses time limited approach
d. It puts great emphasis on cause of problem

47. Which one of the following theories states that integrated social or cultural factors cause anxiety? *(AIIMS Bhubaneswar Shift II – 2019)*

a. Psychoanalytic theory
b. Biological theory
c. Integrated theory
d. Cognitive behavioral theory

48. The type of loss in which the client is aware that a loss will occur is known as: *(AIIMS Bhubaneswar Shift II – 2019)*

a. Anticipatory loss b. Observable loss
c. Actual loss d. Perceived loss

49. In Schizophrenia, gradual subtle behavior changes occur in: *(AIIMS Bhubaneswar Shift II – 2019)*

a. Premorbid phase b. Prodromal phase
c. Onset phase d. Progressive phase

50. Antidepressant used in children for depression is: *(NIMHANS – 2019)*

a. Amitriptyline b. Fluoxetine
c. Benzodiazepines d. Naloxone

51. Antidote of opioids is: *(NIMHANS – 2019)*

a. Naloxone b. Fluphenazine
c. Benzodiazepines d. Flumazenil

Ans.

34. c
35. a
36. a
37. c
38. a
39. c
40. b
41. a
42. b
43. a
44. b
45. a
46. d
47. c
48. a
49. b
50. b
51. a

52. Immediate management of Wernicke's encephalopathy is to: *(NIMHANS – 2019)*
a. Administer Thiamine
b. Administer steroids
c. Order EEG
d. Prescribe Tab. Disulfiram

53. Delusion of grandiosity is present in: *(NIMHANS – 2019)*
a. Depression b. Mania
c. Dissociative disorder d. Schizophrenia

54. False fixed ideas or belief is known as: *(NIMHANS – 2019)*
a. Hallucination b. Delusion
c. Illusion d. Confabulation

55. Which of the following is not an antipsychotic medication?
a. Haloperidol b. Risperidone
c. Imipramine d. Olanzapine

56. Parents of autistic child should be taught to: *(NIMHANS – 2019)*
a. Be consistent
b. Set limit
c. Change the routine frequently
d. All of the above

57. Disulfiram Ethanol reaction is characterized by: *(NIMHANS – 2019)*
a. Bradycardia, sweating and hypertension
b. Bradycardia, blurred vision and hypertension
c. Tachypnea, vomiting and hypertension
d. Headache, hypotension and chest pain

58. Global loss of memory, cognition and personality is known as: *(NIMHANS – 2019)*
a. Delirium
b. Alzheimer type of dementia
c. Dissociative disorder
d. Conversion disorder

59. A recurrent recollection of flashbacks/images/thoughts in dream is: *(NIMHANS – 2019)*
a. Acute stress disorder
b. Post-traumatic stress disorder
c. Sleep disorder
d. Psychosomatic disorder

60. Preoccupation with details/rules, lists, order is seen in which type of personality? *(NIMHANS – 2019)*
a. Narcissistic b. Histrionic
c. Obsessive-Compulsive d. Borderline

61. Cluster A personality disorder includes: *(NIMHANS – 2019)*
a. Antisocial, borderline and narcissistic
b. Paranoid, schizoid and schizotypal
c. Avoidant, obsessive and dependent
d. Avoidant, schizoid and antisocial

62. Major cause of mortality associated with anorexia nervosa: *(NIMHANS – 2019)*
a. Obesity b. Malnutrition
c. Electrolyte imbalance d. Nausea and vomiting

63. Drug of choice for catatonia is: *(NIMHANS – 2019)*
a. Benzodiazepines b. Carbamazepine
c. Haloperidol d. Sodium valproate

64. Directive counseling is also known as: *(NIMHANS – 2019)*
a. Personal counseling
b. Group counseling
c. Client centered counseling
d. Counselor centered or prescriptive counseling

65. Neurotransmitter between neuron and muscle cell is: *(Kerala PSC – 2018)*
a. Serotonin b. Acetylcholine
c. Dopamine d. Endorphin

66. A strategy of effective communication where the interviewer validates the information from the client without changing out the meaning of the statement is: *(Kerala PSC – 2018)*
a. Clarifying b. Focusing
c. Summarizing d. Paraphrasing

67. A process of redirecting the energy produced by unacceptable desires or activities so that they become acceptable is: *(Kerala PSC – 2018)*
a. Reaction formation b. Sublimation
c. Projection d. Identification

68. Suitable method to handle the overactive aggressive patient is: *(Kerala PSC – 2018)*
a. Accept the criticism and verbal attack without punishment
b. Avoid the person and neglect him for a while
c. Fire the person and apply restraints
d. Try to cheer up, give praise

69. Extrapyramidal side effects of antipsychotics are managed with the following drugs except: *(Kerala PSC – 2018)*
a. Anticholinergic drugs b. Antihistamines
c. Dopamine drugs d. Barbiturates

70. A 47-year-old female client with the diagnosis of depression has been hospitalized for three days. During this time, she has not maintained her personal hygiene and shows no interest in wearing a clean dress and combing her hair. In working with a depressed client, the nurse should understand that depression is most directly related to person's: *(NIMHANS – 2019)*

Ans.
52. a
53. b
54. b
55. c
56. a
57. d
58. b
59. b
60. c
61. b
62. c
63. a
64. d
65. b
66. d
67. b
68. a
69. d
70. c

a. Experiencing poor IPR with others
b. Remembering his/her traumatic childhood
c. Having experienced a sense of loss
d. Stage in life

71. A client has been on long term phenothiazine (Thorazine) 400 mg/day. Patient had jerky choreiform movements, lip smacking, neck and back tonic contractions. This indicates that the patient has developed: *(NIMHANS – 2019)*
a. Tardive Dyskinesia b. Dystonia
c. Parkinsonism d. Akathisia

72. A patient diagnosed as BPAD is being discharged from hospital with lithium medication. Most important information to impart to the client and his family in the discharge teaching is the patient should: *(NIMHANS – 2019)*
a. Have adequate sodium intake
b. Restrict sodium intake
c. Restrict his fluid intake
d. Avoid tyramine rich foods

73. Publication of a false statement about an individual made either verbally or in some other form to the third person: *(Kerala PSC – 2018)*
a. Battery b. Displacement
c. Depersonalization d. Defamation

74. Anxiety is caused by:
a. Subjectively perceived threat
b. An objective threat
c. Masked depression
d. Hostility turned to oneself

75. Which of the following is used in drug dependence to prevent relapse? *(Kerala PSC – 2018)*
a. Naloxone b. Naltrexone
c. Neuroleptic d. Nomifensine

76. Informal communication is also known as __________ communication. *(Kerala PSC – 2018)*
a. Diagonal b. Grape wine
c. Cross wine d. Horizontal

77. A chronic alcoholic patient blames his family environment for his alcoholism. Which of the following defense mechanism was used by the patient? *(AIIMS Delhi – 2018)*
a. Denial b. Projection
c. Rationalization d. Sublimation

78. Which drug is used for prophylaxis of manic-depressive disorder? *(AIIMS Delhi – 2018)*
a. Lithium b. Valproate
c. Haloperidol d. Phenytoin

79. Which electrolyte has to be maintained in lithium therapy? *(AIIMS Delhi – 2018)*
a. Sodium b. Potassium
c. Calcium d. Magnesium

80. Delirium tremens are withdrawal symptoms of: *(AIIMS Delhi – 2018)*
a. Alcoholism b. Cocaine
c. Opioid d. Cannabis

81. Drug of choice for Bipolar Affective Disorder is: *(AIIMS Delhi – 2018)*
a. Lithium carbonate
b. Chlorpromazine
c. Bupropion
d. Benzodiazepines

82. Which of the following is the negative symptom of Schizophrenia? *(AIIMS Delhi – 2018)*
a. Delusion b. Anhedonia
c. Hallucination d. Clang association

83. Which of the following is the positive symptom of Schizophrenia? *(AIIMS Delhi – 2018)*
a. Stupor b. Apathy
c. Delusion d. Alogia

84. Major depressive episodes are characterized by low mood for at least: *(AIIMS Delhi – 2018)*
a. 1 week b. 2 weeks
c. 4 weeks d. 8 weeks

85. All of the following are assessed in mental status examination, except: *(AIIMS Delhi – 2018)*
a. General appearance b. Judgment
c. Prejudice d. Intelligence

86. Which of the following food should be avoided when the patient is on Mono-amine Oxidase Inhibitors (MAOIs)? *(AIIMS Delhi – 2018)*
a. Calcium rich food
b. Gluten rich food
c. Tyramine containing food
d. Alanine containing food

87. Parrot like repetition of word spoken by another person is known as: *(AIIMS Jodhpur SNO – 2018)*
a. Echolalia
b. Neologism
c. Echopraxia
d. Dyscalculia

88. Which part of mind is associated with practical reality principle? *(AIIMS Jodhpur SNO – 2018)*
a. Hyper-ego b. Super-ego
c. Ego d. Id

Ans.
71. a
72. a
73. d
74. a
75. b
76. b
77. b
78. a
79. a
80. a
81. a
82. b
83. c
84. b
85. c
86. c
87. a
88. c

89. The part of mind copes with quarreling among young children by placing them in separate rooms is using: *(AIIMS Jodhpur SNO – 2018)*
a. Time out b. Reinforcement
c. Shaping d. Punishment

90. A nurse who enters the patient's room with cognitive impairment asks what is the date, month, year and where the patient is. The nurse is attempting to assess: *(AIIMS Jodhpur SNO 2018)*
a. Perseveration b. Confabulation
c. Orientation d. Delirium

91. False sensory perception with no basis in reality are known as: *(AIIMS Jodhpur SNO – 2018)*
a. Delusions b. Illusions
c. Hallucination d. Loose association

92. Deficiency of which neurotransmitters in brain will cause Alzheimer's disease? *(AIIMS Jodhpur SNO – 2018)*
a. Acetylcholine b. GABA
c. Serotonin d. Dopamine

93. Drug of choice for nocturnal enuresis is: *(AIIMS Jodhpur SNO – 2018)*
a. Imipramine b. Trazodone
c. Chlorpromazine d. Sertraline

94. Unshakable and persistent ideas are: *(AIIMS Jodhpur SNO – 2018)*
a. Compulsions b. Delusions
c. Hallucinations d. Illusions

95. The part of mind that distinguishes right from wrong and acts as a censor of behavior is known as: *(AIIMS Jodhpur SNO – 2018)*
a. Libido b. Id
c. Super-ego d. Ego

96. Omega sign is seen in: *(AIIMS Bhopal – 2018)*
a. Anxious to specific b. Depressed patient
c. Deluded patient d. Negativistic patient

97. Disorder of recurrent pulling out one's hair is called: *(AIIMS Bhopal – 2018)*
a. Pyromania b. Kleptomania
c. Trichotillomania d. Rhinotillexomania

98. Diagnostic interview with sodium amytal or hypnosis is a special feature of: *(AIIMS: Bhopal – 2018)*
a. Post-traumatic neurosis
b. Mania
c. Hyperventilation syndrome
d. Phobia

99. Which of the following is a long-term effect of 'Medical complication of Alcoholism'? *(AIIMS Bhopal – 2018)*
a. Korsakoff psychosis b. Depression
c. Delirium tremens d. Paranoia

100. Which of the following features is present only in dementia when compared to delirium? *(AIIMS Bhopal – 2018)*
a. Misperception
b. Hallucination
c. Vivid illusions
d. Systematized delusions occur early

101. Movement of eyeballs is the function of which cranial nerve? *(AIIMS Bhopal – 2018)*
a. Olfactory b. Oculomotor
c. Optic d. Accessory

102. "No, not me" reaction of patient is seen in which stage of terminal illness or death? *(AIIMS Bhopal – 2018)*
a. Bargaining b. Denial
c. Anger d. Acceptance

103. In Alzheimer disease, plagues are more common in:
a. Thalamus b. Hypothalamus
c. Hippocampus d. Brain stem

104. Which of the following is not a medico-psychiatric condition? *(AIIMS Bhopal – 2018)*
a. Hyperthyroidism b. Agitated depression
c. Angina d. Insulinoma

105. What is the difference between Direct ECT and Modified ECT?
a. Low volt shock is given
b. Anesthesia or Muscle relaxant will be given
c. Pain killer will be given
d. No such differences

106. Example of Sublimation is: *(AIIMS Bhopal – 2019)*
a. Blaming the teacher for failing in exam
b. Women has no memory of being sexually assaulted as child
c. Child starts bedwetting after the birth of sibling
d. A young man who is dealing with aggression by playing football

107. Correct order of response to stress is: *(AIIMS Bhopal – 2019)*
a. Alarm-Resistance-Exhaustion
b. Resistance-Exhaustion-Alarm
c. Exhaustion-Resistance-Alarm
d. Resistance-Alarm-Exhaustion

Ans.
89. a
90. c
91. c
92. a
93. a
94. b
95. c
96. b
97. c
98. a
99. a
100. d
101. b
102. b
103. c
104. b
105. b
106. d
107. a

108. From the age group of 1–3, stages of development are: *(AIIMS Bhopal – 2019)*

a. Oral stage b. Anal stage
c. Genital stage d. Phallic stage

109. Behavior of diabetic patient who eats sweets regularly indicates: *(AIIMS Bhopal – 2019)*

a. Displacement b. Fixation
c. Denial d. Dislocation

110. Separation of thought or memory from its associated feeling or emotion is known as: *(AIIMS Bhopal – 2019)*

a. Idealization b. Projection
c. Intellectualization d. Isolation

111. An organic mental disorder among the following is: *(AIIMS Bhopal – 2019)*

a. Bipolar disorder b. Conversion disorder
c. Schizophrenia d. Vascular dementia

112. As per Erickson's psychosocial theory, development task of toddler is: *(AIIMS Bhopal SNO – 2018)*

a. Trust/Mistrust
b. Autonomy/Shame and doubt
c. Industry/Inferiority
d. Initiative/Guilt

113. Which is not a part of 4 A's of Bleuler? *(AIIMS Bhopal SNO – 2018)*

a. Ambivalence b. Associative learning
c. Avolition d. Autistic thinking

114. When MAOIs are administered, patient has to be caution against: *(AIIMS Bhopal SNO – 2018)*

a. Involving in active physical exercises
b. Use of medicine with elixir base
c. Prolonged sun exposure
d. Ingesting wine and aged cheese

115. As per the Kubler-Ross theory of grief, which behavior is being observed in stage II? *(AIIMS Bhopal SNO – 2018)*

a. Depression b. Anger
c. Bargaining d. Denial

116. Crisis which is precipitated by unanticipated stressful event which creates the disequilibrium by threatening one's sense of biological, social or psychological integrity is: *(AIIMS Bhopal SNO – 2018)*

a. Situation crisis b. Adventitious crisis
c. Social crisis d. Maturational crisis

117. A person changing the subject or cracking joke in an attempt to compensate for defects by using strategies to avoid demonstrating failures in intellectual performance is called: *(AIIMS Bhopal SNO – 2018)*

a. Catastrophic reaction
b. Sundowner syndrome
c. Affective impairment
d. Thought insertion

118. Neurotransmitter released by motor neuron at the neuromuscular junction is: *(AIIMS Bhopal SNO – 2018)*

a. Dopamine b. Adrenaline
c. Noradrenaline d. Acetylcholine

119. Presenting the patient with 'hypothetical situation' helps in the assessment of: *(AIIMS Bhopal SNO – 2018)*

a. Insight b. Abstract thinking
c. Judgment d. Comprehension

120. Concept of health which emphasizes the health as 'sound mind in a sound body in a sound family in sound environment' is: *(AIIMS Bhopal SNO – 2018)*

a. Ecological concept
b. Physical concept
c. Psychological concept
d. Holistic concept

121. Perception without stimulus is: *(AIIMS Bhubaneswar – 2018)*

a. Delirium b. Illusion
c. Delusion d. Hallucination

122. Formed visual hallucination are seen in the lesion of: *(AIIMS Bhubaneswar – 2018)*

a. Occiput b. Parietal
c. Temporal d. Frontal

123. Biochemical etiology of Alzheimer's disease is:

a. Epinephrine b. Acetylcholine
c. Serotonin d. Dopamine

124. Stranger anxiety develops by the age of:

a. Birth b. 6 months after birth
c. 8 months after birth d. 3 months after birth

125. Best test to diagnose the organic mental disorder is:

a. Bender gestalt test
b. Sentence completion test
c. Rorschach test
d. Thematic appreciation test

Ans.

108. b
109. c
110. d
111. d
112. b
113. c
114. d
115. b
116. a
117. c
118. d
119. c
120. a
121. d
122. c
123. b
124. c
125. a

Notes

Appendices

APPENDIX 1

HISTORY COLLECTION FORMAT

I. **Demographic data**
- Name
- Age
- Gender
- Education
- Occupation
- Monthly income
- Universal Hospital Identity Number (UHID No.)/In Patient Number (IP No.)/Out Patient Number (OP No.)
- Ward/OPD
- Unit
- Marital status
- Nationality
- Religion
- Date of admission and time
- Diagnosis
- Doctor's in-charge
- Address
- Informant (Name/Relationship)
- **Reliability of informant:** Criteria's to collect history from reliable informant are as follows:
  - Informant must be living with patient for at least last two years
  - Informant should not have any communication deficit (hearing/vision problems)
  - Informant should be sound minded person (i.e., not suffering from mental illness)
- Information (reliable or not, adequate or not)

II. **Chief complaints/presenting complaints (list with duration)**
- Use verbatim technique (write the patient's complaint exactly what the patient verbalized or note down what the informant verbalized, exactly in his/her words)
- According to patient:
- According to informant:

  e.g., Unable to sleep properly for past 10 days;
  Hearing voices for past eight days;
  Loss of appetite for past three days.

Organize and write the chief complaints in such a way that, 'complaint with longer duration are written first and of shorter duration at last'.

III. **Present psychiatric history/nature of the current episode**
- Onset
  - Abrupt (symptoms occur within 48 hours)
  - Acute (symptoms occur within two weeks)
  - Insidious (symptoms occur from several weeks to months)
- Intensity—Same/increasing/decreasing
- Duration—Days, weeks or months
- Course—Continuous/episodic
- Precipitating factors—Yes/no (if yes, describe the factors such as stressful events of life, non-adherence to medications)
- History of current episode (write in detail about the presenting complaints)
- Associated disturbances—It includes the present medical problems (e.g., Disturbances in sleep pattern, problems with appetite, interpersonal relations with others, social functioning with others, problems faced in occupation, etc.)

IV. Past psychiatric history

- Number of episodes with onset, duration of each episode, intensity and course
- Complete or incomplete remission of symptoms
- Treatment details and its side effects of extrapyramidal effects, if any
- Prognosis of the previous treatment/hospitalization
- Previous suicidal attempts
- Description of any precipitating factors if present.

V. Medical history, surgical history, obstetrical history (If the patient is female)

- **Medical history:** Significant medical problems or previous hospitalization
- **Surgical history:** Any previous surgeries
- Obstetrical history (if the patient is female)
  - Last menstrual period (LMP)
  - Number of children
  - Problems associated with pregnancy, delivery and puerperium
  - Abortion (if any):

VI. Family history

- **Family genogram:** Draw three generation chart include grandparents. Include the particular generation which has specific psychiatric family history.
- **Types of family:** Joint/nuclear/extended
- **Consanguinity:** Present/absent

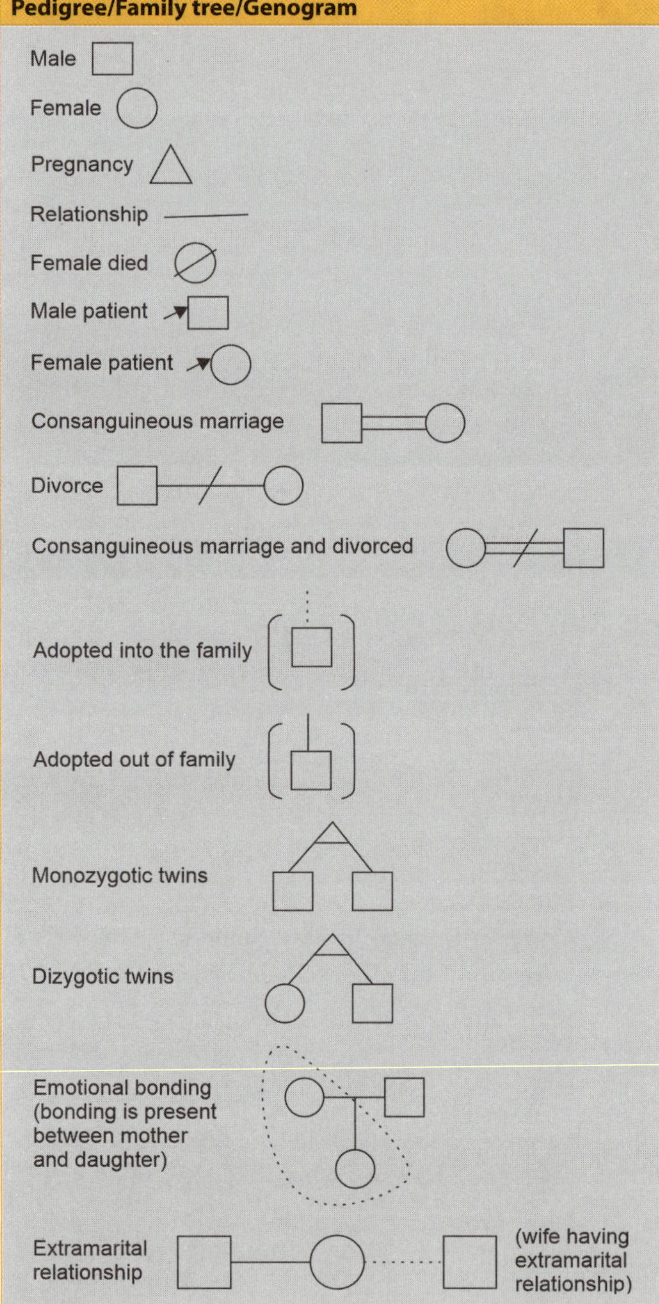

VII. Personal history

Birth history:

- **Prenatal history:** Fetus having exposure to radiation, maternal infections and other maternal complications
- **Natal history:** Type of delivery (Normal/caesarean/vacuum/forceps), newborn cried at birth, neonatal infections and other complications
- **Birth defects:** If yes, specify
- **Postnatal complications:** Convulsions/cyanosis/neonatal infections/jaundice/any other
- **Milestones:** Normal or delayed

Childhood history

- Primary care giver:
- Feeding pattern: Breast feed/Artificial feed
- Age at weaning

Behavior during childhood

- Excessive temper tantrum: Yes/No
- Feeding habits or pica: Yes/No
- Habit disorders: Yes/No (if yes specify)

Illness during childhood

- Seizures
- Neurotic disorders
- Central nervous system infections
- Malnutrition

Schooling/educational history

- Age of joining in school
- Academic performance in the school
- Relationship with peer group
- Relationship exist with teachers
- Learning disability and attention deficit in childhood
- Reason for discontinuation from school

Play history
- Games interested to play
- Relationship with playmates

Emotional problems during adolescence

Smoking/alcoholism/drug abuse/delinquency/running away from home/any others

Occupational history
- Age of joining the job
- Relationship with colleagues, subordinates and supervisors
- Frequent change of job—if so, give details with rationale
- Frequent absenteeism in job.

Menstrual history
- Age of attaining puberty
- Menstrual cycles are regular/irregular
- Abnormalities if any (dysmenorrhea, menorrhagia, etc.)

Sexual history
- Source and extent of knowledge about sex
- Any extramarital relationship (ask if the information is found to be essential)

Marital history
- Name, age, education and occupation of spouse
- Duration of marriage life
- Love or arranged marriage
- Number of marriage
- Bonding in marital relationship

Premorbid personality
- **Attitude to others in social, family and sexual relationship**
- **Attitudes to Self:** Selfish/feel proud/over concerned/egocentric/dramatizing/self-conscious/satisfied about self/unhappy or dissatisfied about self.
- **Moral and religious attitudes and standards**
- **Mood**
  - **Stability of the mood:** Stable/anxious/irritable/worrying/mood swings.
  - Ability to express and control anger, depression and anxiety—Yes/No
- **Leisure activities and hobbies**
- **Fantasy life**
  - Amount of time spent in day dreaming
  - Content of the day dreams
- **Reaction pattern to stress**
  - Tolerate frustrations or sudden disappointments, and situations causing anger, anxiety or depression: Yes/No
  - Use coping mechanism or defense mechanism: Yes/No
- Habits
  - **Sleeping pattern:** Regular/insomnia/early morning awakening/sleep disorders (specify)
  - **Eating pattern:** Regular/binge eating/crave to eat more/frequent starvation/eating disorders (specify)
  - **Elimination pattern:** Regular/dysuria/oliguria/anuria/constipation/fecal incontinence/any diagnosed diseases.
  - **Ill health habits:** Use of drug, smoking, alcohol, tobacco

APPENDIX 2

HISTORY COLLECTION FORMAT FOR PATIENT WITH ALCOHOL DEPENDENCE SYNDROME

I. Demographic data:
- Name
- Age
- Gender
- Education
- Occupation
- Monthly income
- Universal Hospital Identity Number (UHID No.)/In Patient Number (IP No.)/Out Patient Number (OP No.)
- Ward/OPD
- Unit
- Marital status
- Nationality
- Religion
- Date of admission and time:
- Diagnosis
- Doctor's In-charge
- Address
- Informant (name/relationship)
- Reliability of informant

II. Chief complaints/presenting complaints (list with duration)

III. Present psychiatric history
- Reason for starting the first drink
- First experience with alcohol
- Amount of alcohol commenced initially
- Brand of alcohol started
- History of tolerance
- History of craving
- History in regard with loss of control
- Presence of withdrawal symptoms
- Social and occupational impairment due to alcohol

- Reason for increasing the amount of alcohol
- Brand of alcohol preferred
- History of black out
- History of abstinence
- Money spent daily for alcohol
- Usual time of drinking alcohol
- Preferred drinking pattern (Individual/group)
- Level of motivation to quit alcohol
- Feel of guilt in regard with drinking alcohol
- Medical problems due to alcohol
- Psychiatric problems due to alcohol
- Previous admission and treatment undergone in de-addiction center.

IV. Past psychiatric history

V. Medical and surgical history

VI. Family history

- Family history of alcoholism
- Interpersonal relationship with family members
- Family genogram
- Family history of mental illness

VII. Marital History

- Bonding in marital relationship
- Extramarital relationship
- Sexual dysfunction

VIII. Premorbid personality

APPENDIX 3

HISTORY COLLECTION FORMAT—CHILDREN AND ADOLESCENT WITH PSYCHIATRIC DISORDERS

I. Demographic data

- Name
- Age
- Gender
- Education
- Universal Hospital Identity Number (UHID No.)
- Ward/OPD
- Unit
- Nationality
- Religion
- Date of admission and time
- Diagnosis
- Doctor's In-charge
- Address
- Informant (name/relationship)

II. Chief complaints/presenting complaints (list with duration).

III. Present and past psychiatric history

IV. Co-morbid illness

V. Family history

- Type of family
- Type of marriage (consanguineous/non-consanguineous)
- Interpersonal relationship with family members
- Family genogram
- Family history of mental illness

VI. Personal history

- Antenatal history
- Postnatal history
- Milestones development
- Behavior at home
- Behavior at school
- Habits
- Special interests
- Hobbies
- Intelligence level

- Performance in school or academics
- Performing the self-care (toileting, eating, bathing, dressing).

APPENDIX 4

HISTORY COLLECTION FORMAT—GERIATRIC PSYCHIATRY

I. Demographic data

- Name
- Age
- Gender
- Education
- Previous occupation
- Pension
- Nationality
- Religion
- Address
- Informant (name/relationship)

II. Chief complaints/presenting complaints (list with duration)

III. Present and past psychiatric history

- Cognitive function
- Current psychiatric problems

IV. Medical and surgical history (Medications are taken for the chronic illness)

V. Family history

- Type of family
- Number of members in the family
- Monthly income of the family (socioeconomic status)
- Interpersonal relationship with family members
- Family genogram
- Family history of mental illness

VI. Personal history
- Educational history
- Occupational history before retirement
- Source of income
- Residence: Living alone/with spouse/old age home
- Performing the self care (toileting, eating, bathing, dressing).

VII. Premorbid personality (social, occupational and biological functioning)

VIII. Psychological support by the family members or relatives or friends

IX. Attitude towards aging and death

APPENDIX 5

MENTAL STATUS EXAMINATION (MSE) FORMAT

I. General appearance and behavior
- Facial expression (e.g. anxiety, pleasure, confidence, blunted, pleasant)
- Posture (stooped, stiff, guarded, normal)
- Mannerisms (stereotype, negativism tics, normal)
- Eye to eye contact (maintained or not)
- Rapport (built easily or not built or built with difficulty)
- Consciousness (conscious or drowsy or unconscious)
- Behavior (includes social behavior, e.g., over friendly, disinherited, preoccupied, aggressive, normal)
- Dressing and grooming—Well-dressed/appropriate/inappropriate (to season and situation)/neat and tidy/dirty.
- **Physical features:** Look older/younger than his or her age/underweight/overweight/physical deformity.

Psychomotor activity: (Increased/decreased/compulsive/echopraxia/stereotyped/negativism/automatic obedience)

II. Speech: Write the sample of speech (verbatim in 2 or 3 sentences)
- Coherence—Coherent/incoherent
- Relevance (answer the questions appropriately)—Relevant/irrelevant
- Volume (soft, loud or normal)
- Tone (high pitch, low pitch, or normal/monotonous)
- Manner—Excessive formal/relaxed/inappropriately familiar
- Reaction time (time taken to answer the question) —increased, decreased or normal.

III. Mood (subjective) and affect (objective)
- Appropriate/inappropriate (relevance to situation and thought congruent.
- Pleasurable affect—Euphoria/Elation/Exaltation/ecstasy.
- **Unpleasable affect:** Grief/mourning/depression
- **Other affects:** Anxiety/fear/panic/free floating anxiety/apathy/aggression/moods swing/emotionally labile.

IV. Thought
- Form of thought/formal thought disorder—not understandable/Normal/Circumstantiality/tangentiality/neologism/Word Salad/Perseveration/ambivalence).
- Stream of thought/flow of thought—Pressure of speech/flight of ideas/thought retardation/mutism/aphonia/thought block/clang association.)
- Content of thought
  - Delusions—Specify type and give example – Persecutory/delusion of reference/delusion of influence or passivity/hypochondriacal delusions/delusions of grandeur/nihilistic delusion/derealization/depersonalization/delusion of infidelity.
  - Obsession
  - Phobia
  - Preoccupation
  - Fantasy—Creative/day dreaming.

V. Disorders of perception
- Illusion
- Hallucinations—(specify type and give example)—auditory/visual/olfactory/gustatory/tactile
- Others—hypnogogic/hypnopompic/lilliputian/kinesthetic/macropsia/micropsia

VI. Cognitive functions
- **Attention and Concentration:**
  - **Digit span test:** e.g., Repeat the numbers 1, 3, 7, 9
  - **Digit forward test:** e.g., Say the numbers 1 to 10
  - **Digit backward test:** e.g., Say the numbers 10 to 1
  - **Serial subtraction test:** e.g., (100 – 7 = 93, then 93 – 7 = 86, 86 – 7 = 79)
- **Memory**
  - **Immediate:** Recall the events happened immediately
  - **Recent memory:** Recall the events happened 24 hours before.
  - **Remote:** Asking for date of birth or events which are occurred long back
    - Amnesia (memory loss)/Paramnesia (distorted memory or confusion of facts or fantasy)/Retrograde amnesia (loss of memory to the events happened before the injury or onset of illness)/Anterograde amnesia (loss of memory to the events happened after the injury or onset of illness).

- Confabulation (false filling of memory gaps)
- Déjà vu (familiar of unfamiliar things)/Jamais Vu (unfamiliar of familiar things)
- Hyperamnesia (excessive loss of memory)

- **Orientation**
  - Ask the time approximately without looking at the watch, what time is it?
  - Place—Where he/she is now?
  - Person—Who has accompanied him or her?
- **Abstract thinking:** Patient's ability to answer the exact meaning of the given proverb will identify the presence of abstract thinking (e.g., all the glitters are not gold)
- **Intelligence of general information**
  - **Similarities and differences:** E.g., Say the similarities and dissimilarities between pen and pencil?
  - **General information:** E.g., Who is the Prime Minister of India?
- **Judgment**
  - Personal judgment (ask about the patients future plans)
  - Social judgment (lobservation made by the examiner that how patient is being socialized with others)
  - Test judgment (test the present situation and ask his/her response to the situation)
    - **Rain test:** Ask the client what he/she will do when rain comes?
    - **Envelope test:** Ask the client what he/she will do when envelope remains in road with stamp?
    - **Fire test:** Ask the client what he/she will do when there is a fire in his/her home?
    - **Child cry test:** Ask the client what he/she will do when a child remains crying in a road?
- **Insight:** (Aware of one's own mental illness)

  Grade I : Complete refusal of illness

  Grade II : Slight aware of being ill

  Grade III : Awareness of being sick attribute toward external or physical factor

  Grade IV : Awareness of being sick, due to something not known to oneself

  Grade V : Intellectual insight (aware about the one's own mental illness in detail)

  Grade VI : True emotional insight—Aware of ones own mental illness and how the family members suffer out of it due to patient's illness.

APPENDIX 6

MENTAL STATUS EXAMINATION OF UNCOOPERATIVE PATIENTS (KIRBY'S METHOD)

Aspects	Description
General reaction and posture	**Spontaneous action performed** • Any show of activities occasionally—playfulness/assaultiveness/mischievousness • Appearance of patient—neat/untidy • Patient eats—voluntarily/needs assistance • Patient dress himself/herself—voluntarily/needs assistance • Patient voids or defecates—voluntarily/needs assistance • Actions show slowness—initially/consistently throughout the day **Behavior toward the examiners:** Resistant/irritable/apathy/complaining others/evasive, etc. **Voluntary postures:** Comfortable/natural/awkward/constrained (What does the patient do when placed in an awkward position?) **Whether the behavior remains constant or keeps on changing with time?**
Facial movement and expression	**Facial expression:** Being alert/smiling/mask like face/placid/anxious/perplexed/anger/distressed Whether the facial expression remains constant or keeps changing?
Eyes and pupils	• Eyes—Open/closed/resistance to open the client eyes by examiner • Patient give attention to examiner and move the eyes with that of object—yes/no • Gaze—Fixed/evasive • Blinking or flickering of eye lids—yes/no • Patient responds to examiner if sudden movement of hand has been performed by examiner near to patient's eyes—yes/no • Corneal reflex—present/absent

Contd...

Aspects	Description
Reaction to examiners questions and tests	• Patient response to simple commands of the examiner • Presence of negativism—whether active or passive uncooperativeness exists • Monitor for automatic obedience, echolalia and echopraxia • Movements of limbs are slow or fast or being interrupted often
Muscular reactions	• Assess for muscle tonicity—waxy flexibility/cogwheel rigidity, gegenhalten, mitmachen and mitgehen. • Check out urinary or fecal incontinence
Speech	• Whether patient speaks spontaneously? • Whether patient is mute—Is it consistent or keep changing? • Whether patient takes effort to create sounds or whisper?
Emotional responsiveness	• Emotional response of patient when family members speak? ◆ Response of patient toward the unexpected stimuli by examiner such as clapping hands or switching on the light.
Writing	Ask the patient to write one's wishes on a plain paper
Vital signs	Temperature, pulse, respiration and blood pressure

Inference:

APPENDIX 7

HINDI MENTAL STATUS EXAMINATION (HMSE)

For illiterate demention patients

Sl. no.	Components	Score	
		Correct	Wrong
1.	Is it morning (or) afternoon (or) evening?	1	0
2.	What day of the week is today?	1	0
3.	What date is it today?	1	0
4.	Which month is today?	1	0
5.	What season of the year is this?	1	0
6.	Under which post office does your village come?	1	0
7.	Which district does your village fall under?	1	0
8.	Which village are you from?	1	0
9.	Which block (If village has only blocks) or which numbered area is this?	1	0
10.	Which place is this?	1	0

Sl. no.	Components	Score
11.	(I went to Delhi and brought three things such as chair, coin and mango) Can you say the three things what I got from Delhi?	1 2 3
12.	A. Can you say the name of the days starting from Sunday? B. Now can you tell me names of the days backwards?	1 2 3 4 5
13–15	Can you name the three things what I got from Delhi?	1 2 3

Contd...

Sl. no.	Components	Score	
16.	(Show the patient the wrist watch and pen) Can you tell me these objects? (If yes, items 17 and 18 apply) (If No, Item 17(a) apply)		
17. 17.(a).	Show him the wrist watch and say what is this? (or) If necessary, identify the watch by touching what is this?	1	0
18. 18.(a).	Show him the pen and say what is this? (or) If necessary, identify the pen by touching what is this?	1	0
19.	Now I am going to say a phrase, listen carefully and repeat it exactly as I say after I finish Phrase: 'NEITHER THIS NOR THAT'	1	0
20.	Now look at my face and do exactly what I do. Close your eyes?	1	0
21.	First you take the paper in your right hand, then with your both hands, fold it into half once and then give the paper back to me.	1 2 3	
22.	Now say a line about your house?		
23.	Copy the drawing exactly as shown in the space below. [drawing: square with a diamond inscribed] **Score:** Must draw four sided figure = 1 One figure should be mostly inside the other = 2 Orientation of the figures should be obviously appropriate = 3	1 2 3	
	Total Score =	/31	

APPENDIX 8

MINI MENTAL STATUS EXAMINATION (OR) FOLSTEIN TEST FORMAT

Sl. no.	Components	Description	Max. Score	Total Score
1.	Orientation	Year, month, day, date, season	5	
		Country, state, town, place, floor	5	
2.	Registration	Examiner names the three objects (example: pen, apple and table). Patient is asked to repeat the objects, one score for each	3	
3.	Attention	Subtract 7 from 100 then repeat from the result for five subtractions	5	
4.	Recall	Ask the name of objects learned earlier	3	
5.	Language	Name a pencil and watch	2	
		Repeat 'No its and or buts'	1	
		Give a three stage command. Score one for each stage. (For example, 'Take this piece of paper in your right hand, fold it in half and place it on the table')	3	
		Ask patient to read and obey a written command on the piece of paper stating: 'Close your eyes'	1	
		Ask patient to write a sentence. Score correct if it has a subject and verb.	1	
6.	Copying	Ask the individual to copy the intersecting pentagons. Score if it overlaps and has five sides	1	
			Grand Total =	________/30

Total Score	Cognitive impairment
24–30	No cognitive impairment
18–23	Mild cognitive impairment
0–17	Severe cognitive impairment

APPENDIX 9

NEUROLOGICAL ASSESSMENT

Level of consciousness: Alertness/lethargic/stuporous/semicomatose/comatose

Glasgow Coma Scale	Categories	Scores	Nurse's responsibility in Documentation of GCS
Eye response	• Spontaneous eye opening • To verbal stimuli • To pain stimuli • No response	4 3 2 1	Document 'C'—Swollen eyes due to injury/infection
Verbal response	• Oriented to time, place and person • Confused • Inappropriate speech • Incomprehensive sounds • No response	5 4 3 2 1	V_T – Patient in tracheostomy V_E – Patient is in endotracheal tube

Contd...

Glasgow Coma Scale	Categories	Scores	Nurse's responsibility in Documentation of GCS
Motor response	• Obeys command • Localizes pain • Flexion withdrawal • Abnormal flexion • Abnormal extension • No response	6 5 4 3 2 1	Record the response in upper extremities (right/left) or lower extremities or both
Total GCS score		15	
Minimal GCS score		3	
Comatose patient		<7	

- **Special cerebral function:** Assess for agnosia, apraxia and aphasia
- Cranial nerve assessment
    - Olfactory – Sense of smell: Present/absent
    - Optic
        - Visual acuity test (Snellen's chart)
        - Assessment of visual fields (right and left eye)
        - Examine the fundus of eye with ophthalmoscope

- Oculomotor, trochlear and abducens
  - Pupillary size—Equal/unequal
  - Pupillary reaction to light—Reacting/not reacting
  - Accommodation and visual field—Normal/abnormal
  - Diplopia—Present/absent
  - Nystagmus—Present/absent
- Trigeminal
  - Corneal reflex—Present/absent
  - Mandibular strength—Normal/Hypotonia
  - Facial sensory response (pain, temperature and touch)—Present/absent.
- Facial—Assess symmetry of face; ask the client to smile, frown, raise the eye brows, whistle, puff the cheeks and show teeth
- Vestibulocochlear (or) acoustic nerve
  - Cochlear
    - Hearing acuity test
    - Bone conduction and air conduction test—Weber's test and Rinne's test
  - Vestibular
    - Romberg test
    - Caloric reflex test (oculovestibular reflex)
- Glossopharyngeal and vagus
  - Gag reflex—Present/absent
  - Movement of uvula and palate—Symmetrical/Deviation
  - Sensation of taste—present/absent
- Spinal accessory
  - Strength of Sternocleidomastoid muscle—Normal/Hypotonia
  - Shoulder elevation—Adequate/Weak
- Hypoglossal

- Tongue movement—Normal/Abnormal
- **Motor function assessment**
  - **Muscle size:** Symmetrical/Nonsymmetrical/Atrophy/Hypertrophy
  - **Muscle tone:** Hypotonicity/Hypertonicity/Rigid/spastic muscle.
  - **Muscle strength:** 0/5 to 5/5
  - **Muscle Coordination:** Present/Absent
  - **Gait:** Normal/Abnormal
  - Muscle movements (gross and fine motor movements)
- **Assessment of Sensory Function**
- Sense of Touch—Hypoesthesia/Hyperesthesia/Anesthesia
- Sense of Pain—Hypoalgesia/Hyperalgesia/Analgesia
- Temperature sensation—Present/Absent
- Vibration sensation—Present/Absent
- **Assessment of cerebellar function**
- Finger to finger test
- Finger to nose test
- Romberg test
- Tandom walking test
- **Assessment of reflexes**
- Superficial (or) Cutaneous Reflexes—Corneal reflex /Pharyngeal (or) Gag reflex/Abdominal reflex/Cremasteric reflex/Anal reflex/Plantar reflex
- Deep Tendon (or) Muscle-Stretch Reflexes—Biceps reflex/Triceps reflex/Brachioradialis/Patellar reflex/Achilles tendon reflex
- Abnormal reflexes—Present/Absent
- **Special Tests**
- Stereognosis (or) Haptic perception (or) Tactile gnosis
- Baragnosis
- Graphesthesia

Summary

APPENDIX 10

PROCESS RECORDING FORMAT

Demographic Data

- Name
- Age
- Gender
- Education
- Occupation
- Monthly income
- Universal Hospital Identity Number (UHID No.)/In Patient Number (I.P.No.)/Out Patient Number (O.P.No.)
- Ward/OPD
- Unit
- Marital Status
- Nationality
- Religion
- Date of admission and Time:
- Diagnosis:
- Doctor's In-charge
- Address
- Languages known
- Summary of patient problem

Objectives (or) Purposes

Prerequisites (or) preparation of patient and environment:

Date, time and place of process recording:

Place of Interaction:

Reason for selecting the patient:

Context of interaction:

Participants in interaction	Verbal communication	Non-verbal communication	Inference
Nurse: Patient:	Use verbatim technique	Include facial expression, posture, gesture, mannerism, eye contact, tone of voice, pacing and gait of patient during conversation. It is important to include any such peculiar behaviour such as biting the nail, periods of silence, shouting or exhibiting aggression, etc.	Write the interpretation of process recording (nurse-patient interaction)

Summary:

APPENDIX 11

NURSING CARE PLAN FORMAT

History Collection

I. **Demographic data**
- Name
- Age
- Gender
- Education
- Occupation
- Monthly income
- Universal Hospital Identity Number (UHID No.)/ In Patient Number (I.P.No.)/Out Patient Number (O.P.No.)
- Ward/OPD
- Unit
- Marital Status
- Nationality
- Religion
- Date of admission and time:
- Diagnosis:
- Doctor's in-charge
- Address
- Informant (name/relationship)
- Reliability of informant

II. **Chief complaints/presenting complaints (list with duration)**
- According to patient:
- According to informant:

III. **Present psychiatric history**

IV. **Past psychiatric history**

V. **Medical history**
Surgical history
Obstetrical history

Vi. **Family history**

Vii. **Personal history**
- Birth History
- Childhood history
- Schooling/Educational history
- Play history
- Emotional problems during adolescence
- Occupational history
- Menstrual history
- Sexual history
- Marital history

VIII. **Premorbid personality**
- Attitude to others in social, family and sexual relationship
- Attitudes to Self
- Mood
- Leisure activities and hobbies
- Fantasy life
- Reaction pattern to stress
- Habits

Physical Examination

Head to toe assessment and focus assessment

Mental Status Examination

- General appearance and behavior
- Psychomotor activity:
- Speech:
- Mood (subjective) and affect (objective):
- Thought:
- Disorder of perception:
- Cognitive functions:
- Attention and concentration:
- Memory:
- Orientation:
- Abstract thinking:
- Intelligence:
- Judgment:
- Insight:

NOTE

If the patient is uncooperative, write Kirby's method of mental status examination.

Neurological Examination

- Level of consciousness
- Special cerebral function
- Cranial nerve assessment
- Motor function assessment
- Assessment of sensory function
- Assessment of cerebellar function
- Assessment of reflexes
- Special tests

Investigation

Sl. no.	Diagnostic tests	Patient value	Normal value

Treatment

Sl. no.	Name of the medication	Dosage	Route	Frequency	Drug action

- Psychotherapy
- ECT

Nursing Process

Assessment	Nursing diagnosis	Goal	Planning	Implementation	Rationale	Evaluation
Subjective data Objective data						

Process Recording

Objectives (or) purposes:
Prerequisites (or) preparation of patient and environment:
Date, time and place of process recording:
Place of interaction:
Reason for selecting the patient:
Context of interaction:

Participants in interaction	Verbal communication	Non-verbal communication	Inference
Nurse: Patient:			.

Summary:
Psychoeducation
Conclusion
Bibliography

APPENDIX 12

NURSING CARE STUDY/CLINICAL PRESENTATION FORMAT

History collection
Physical examination
Mental status examination (If the patient is uncooperative, write Kirby's method of mental status examination)
Neurological examination (If required)

Compare the disease condition with book picture

- Introduction
- Definition
- Epidemiology
- Etiology

Book picture	Patient picture

- Psychopathology
- Clinical manifestation

Book picture	Patient picture

- Investigations (or) Diagnostic studies

Book picture	Patient picture

- Treatment

Book picture	Patient picture

Nursing process
Process recording
Psychoeducation
Conclusion
Bibliography

APPENDIX 13

HEALTH EDUCATION FORMAT

Health teaching topic:
Group:
Date:
Time:
Place:
Duration of health teaching:
Student name:
Name of the clinical instructor:
Method of teaching:
Av aids prepared:
General objective:
Specific objective:

Sl. no.	Specific objective	Content	A.V. aids	Evaluation

Conclusion
Bibliography

APPENDIX 14

ASSESSMENT AND CHECKLIST USED FOR THE PATIENT UNDERGOING ELECTROCONVULSIVE THERAPY (ECT)

History collection
Physical examination
Mental status examination
Assessment of patient and family member's knowledge of therapeutic effects

Table: Pre-ECT checklist

Name: **Age:** **Sex:** **Diagnosis:** **IP No.:**
Procedure: **Date:** **Time:** **Ward:**

Checklist	Yes	No	Remarks
Written informed consent (If psychotic – Consent from care givers If neurotic – Both from patient and care givers)			
Skin preparation			
Hair wash done			
Hair combed			
Dentures removed			
Nails paired			
Nail Polish removed			
Nil per oral (NPO)			
Premedications (If any)			
Preoperative teaching			
Jewels removed			
Investigations • Routine blood test • Chest X-ray • ECG • Echocardiography			

Contd...

Signature of the staff nurse

Table: Intra-ECT checklist

Name: **Age:** **Sex:** **IP No.:**
Procedure: **Date/Time:** **Diagnosis:** **ECT Room No.:**

No. of ECT:
Atropine/ Glycopyrrolate:
Thiopentone:
Succinylcholine:
Duration:
Frequency:
Pulse width:
Charge (mc):
Seizure duration:
Blood pressure:
Pulse rate:
Remarks:

Signature of the Doctor/Nurse practitioner

Table: Post-ECT checklist

Name: **Age:** **Sex:** **IP No.:**
Procedure: **Date/Time:** **Diagnosis:** **ECT Room No.:**

Checklist	Yes	No	Remarks
Assessment of memory			
Orientation to patient			
NPO at least 2 hours after ECT			
IV fluids infusion			
Pulse rate checked`			
Blood Pressure checked			
Any significant complaints elicited (Headache, Nausea/Vomiting, Confusion)			
Able to tolerate oral fluids after 2 hours of ECT			
Soft diet after 3 hours of ECT			

Signature of the nurse

Informed Consent to Electroconvulsive Therapy (ECT)

I. (Patient name with hospital identification number) with the diagnosis of ________________ and ICD-10 code ____________ hereby understand the following aspects

- Nurse has explained my diagnosis for which ECT is proposed
- Nurse has explained how ECT will benefit me
- I understands that ECT is given under general anesthesia with muscle relaxant
- Nurse has explained risks or side effects of ECT, general anaesthesia and muscle relaxant
- I have cleared my queries from the doctor regarding the ECT
- I understand all the information given by the nurse in regard with ECT
- I understand that results of ECT are not guaranteed
- Any changes in my ECT treatment will be intimated to me and the informed consent will be obtained in regard to the changes
- I had enough time to take decision in regard to my ECT treatment
- I know that, I can withdraw my ECT at any time, even the course of ECT has started.

I hereby agree to have specified Electroconvulsive Therapy (ECT), general anaesthesia and muscle relaxant.

Signature of the person giving informed consent:

Name of the person giving informed consent:

Date and time:

Witness signature:

Witness name:

APPENDIX 15

INDIVIDUAL PSYCHOTHERAPY FORMAT

History collection
Findings of the mental status examination
Indications for psychotherapy
Problems identified from the patient
Description of the psychotherapy

- Session no.
- Venue
- Date and time
- Type of psychotherapy
- Techniques used by the psychotherapist
- Outcome of the session
- Homework given to the patient
- Plan for next session

Summary

APPENDIX 16

GROUP PSYCHOTHERAPY FORMAT

History collection
Findings of mental status examination
Size of the group
Duration of the session
Norms of the group therapy
Type of group therapy
Purposes of group therapy
Topic addressed in the group therapy
Indications for group psychotherapy
Problems encountered from the group
Techniques used in group therapy
Plan for the next session
Summary

APPENDIX 17

FAMILY THERAPY FORMAT

History collection
Findings of the mental status examination
Goals of the family therapy
Indications for family therapy
Type of the family therapy
Problems identified among the family members
Description about the family therapy

- Session no.
- Venue
- Date and time:
- Name and relationship of the family members participated in the session:
- Communication pattern of the family members
- Techniques used by the family therapist
- Outcome of the session
- Homework given to the patient
- Plan for next session

Summary

APPENDIX 18

CLOZAPINE SIDE EFFECT CHART

Patient name:

Age:

Gender:

UHID No. (or) I.P. No. (or) O.P. No.

Diagnosis:

Date						
Dosage						
Weight						
Body mass index (BMI)						
Chest pain						
Breathlessness						
Blood pressure						
Pulse						
Fever						
Sore throat						
Palpitation						
Sedation						
Hypersalivation (or) sialorrhea (or) ptyalism						
Constipation						
Incontinence						
Skin rashes						
Jerks						
Chest pain						
Total count (white blood cells)						
Absolute neutrophil count (ANC)						

APPENDIX 19

PSYCHIATRIC NURSING CARE DAILY CHECKLIST

Name:
Age:
Gender:
IP No.
Diagnosis:
Chief complaints:

Sl. no.	Components	Yes	No	Not applicable
1.	Oral care			
2.	Shave off the beard			
3.	Hair care			
4.	Nail care			
5.	Voided urine			
6.	Stool passed			
7.	Taken Bath			

Contd...

Sl. no.	Components	Yes	No	Not applicable
8.	Blood samples obtained (specify)			
9.	Plan for any investigations (e.g., CT scan, MRI – Specify)			
10.	Vital signs monitored			
11.	Had Breakfast (specify the diet)			
12.	Taken the prescribed medications (morning, afternoon and night)			
13.	Performed Exercises			
14.	Participated in Yoga or Meditation sessions			
15.	Performed in occupational therapy sessions			
16.	Had lunch (specify the diet)			
17.	Had short nap in afternoon (mention the number of hours)			
18.	Involved in recreational activities			
19.	Attended psychotherapy			
20.	Taken adequate oral fluids			
21.	Presence of suicidal risk			
22.	Presence of aggressive behavior			
23.	Use of restraints			
24.	Any psychotropic drugs given as oral orders			
25.	Health teaching provided to the care givers			
26.	Had dinner (specify the diet)			
27.	Sleep window (duration of time patient lies in the bed with the intent to sleep and the number of hours patients slept)			
28.	Any peculiar behaviour observed (specify)			
29.	Plan for ECT			
30.	Presence of Extrapyramidal symptoms (specify)			
31.	Any other nursing care given (specify)			
32.	Any other sentinel events (specify)			
33.	Any other (specify)			

APPENDIX 20

DISULFIRAM CONSENT FORM

Disulfiram is an antabuse medication which is used to prevent the relapse to alcohol. The body is unable to process the alcohol while taking disulfiram. This includes even a small dose that may be absorbed from hand sanitizer, perfume, alcoholic beverages or food (vinegars, marinades, sauces, extracts, etc.). It is vital to check the labels of items that will be either consumed or used on the surface of the body. Disulfiram should **NOT** be taken if you drank alcohol within 12 hours, because it leads to Disulfiram-Ethanol Reaction (DER). Disulfiram-alcohol reaction may last up to 2 weeks after stopping the Disulfiram.

Disulfiram-Ethanol Reaction (DER) includes trouble in breathing, nausea, vomiting, throbbing pain in head and neck, sweating, increased thirst, dizziness, palpitations, blurred vision, confusion and weakness. Severe DER includes the unconsciousness, cardiac failure, respiratory failure, seizures and death. Allergic reactions due to disulfiram includes chest pain, skin rashes, trouble in breathing or wheezing, fainting, dizziness, swelling of eyes, tongue, mouth or face. The most common side effect of disulfiram is drowsiness. The adverse reactions may occur in some patients having health problems like, psychosis, liver failure, neuropathy, skin rash, acne, impotence and optic neuritis.

Disulfiram can affect your liver so blood test should be done before and after the treatment to ensure that liver is healthy. Approach the doctor or seek emergency treatment if you develop any of these symptoms such as yellow discoloration of the skin or eyes, dark urine, diarrhea, white stool, unusual tiredness, abdominal pain and loss of appetite.

Some medications which should not be taken with disulfiram are metronidazole, phenytoin, dronabinol, some cough syrups, etc. Don't change your medications without consulting with the doctor. Store the disulfiram at room temperature and in a light-resistant container. All your family members and friends should be aware that you are on disulfiram and the risk associated with it can be relapse. I hereby agree to have Disulfiram Therapy.

Signature of the person giving informed consent:

____

Name of the person giving informed consent:

____

Date and Time:

________________.

Witness Signature: ....

Witness Name: ....

APPENDIX 21

OCCUPATIONAL THERAPY FORMAT

History collection

Findings of mental status examination

Goal (or) objectives of occupational therapy

Problems identified from the patient

Assessment of patient's interest

Description of the occupational therapy

- Session no.
- Venue
- Date and time
- Description of the activities with its therapeutic value
- Difficulties faced by the patient during the occupational therapy
- Area or part where the assistance is required for the patient during the therapy
- Outcome of the session
- Plan for next session

Summary

APPENDIX 22

RECREATIONAL (OR) PLAY THERAPY FORMAT

History collection

Findings of mental status examination

Goal (or) objectives of recreational therapy

Problems identified from the patient

Assessment of patient's interest

Description of the recreational therapy

- Session no.
- Venue
- Date and time
- Indications of recreational therapy
- Description of the activities with its therapeutic value
- Advantages of the recreational therapy
- Outcome of the session
- Plan for next session

Summary

APPENDIX 23

CHECKLIST FOR ADMISSION PROCEDURE

Name:

Age:

Gender:
IP No.
Diagnosis:
Address:
Education:
Occupation:
Income:
Chief complaints:
Date of Admission:
Type of Admission:

Sl. no.	Components	Yes	No	Remarks
1.	Preparation of patient unit			
2.	Introduce the health team members			
3.	Tie the identification band in patient's hand			
4.	Orient the hospital routines or policies or regulations of the ward such as visiting hours, diet timings, etc.			
5.	Prepare the patient record			
6.	Obtain the admission consent from the patient or relative			
7.	Collect history from informant			
8.	Perform physical assessment and mental status assessment			
9.	Monitor vital signs			
10.	Obtain the necessary investigations done			
11.	Administer the medications as per the order			
12.	Write the admission notes in the patient record			

Name and Signature of Nursing Officer

APPENDIX 24

CHECKLIST FOR DISCHARGE PROCEDURE

Name:
Age:
Gender:
IP No.
Diagnosis:
Address:
Education:
Occupation:
Income:
Chief complaints:
Date of admission:
Date and Type of Discharge:

Sl. no.	Components	Yes	No	Remarks
1.	Check the discharge order of the treating doctor			
2.	Hand over the patient's valuables which has been taken at the time of admission			
3.	Give discharge summary			
4.	Give the prescription of medications			
5.	Provide information about the follow-up visits			
6.	Explain the importance of drug adherence			
7.	Arrange transportation for the patient and family members to reach home			
8.	Payment of the hospital bill is done			
9.	Discharge teaching is done			
10.	Remove the patient's Identification band			
11.	Allow the patient and family members to clarify the doubts			
12.	Document the discharge procedure in Nurses Notes.			
13.	Monitored the vital signs at the time of discharge			

Name and Signature of Nursing Officer

APPENDIX 25

FORMAT FOR WRITING OBSERVATIONAL VISIT REPORT

Name of the organization:
Date of visit:
Location of the organization (or) institution (or) center:
Philosophy of the organization:
Objectives:
Various departments exist in the organization:
Various services rendered in the organization:
Organizational pattern (or) organogram:
Staffing pattern:
Physical layout:
Admission and discharge procedure:
Daily schedules (or) routines:
Learning experiences gained from the observational visit:

APPENDIX 26

PSYCHOMETRIC ASSESSMENT REPORT

Patient Identification Data

Name:

Age:

Gender:

IP No.

Diagnosis:

Address:

Education:

Occupation:

Income:

Chief complaints:

Psychometric Assessment

Name of the psychological test:

Date and venue of the psychometric test done:

Indications and purposes of the psychometric assessment:

Preparation of the patient and equipment (rating scales/cards):

Description about the psychometric test:

Score interpretation:

APPENDIX 27

IMPORTANT DAYS RELATED TO MENTAL HEALTH

Month	Date	Event/Day
March	11th	No Smoking Day
	20th	International Day for Happiness
	30th	World Bipolar Day
April	7th	World Health Day
	11th	World Parkinson's Day
May	1st	World Maternal Mental Health Day
	12th	International Nurses Day
	24th	World Schizophrenia Day
	31st	Anti-tobacco Day (or) World No Tobacco Day
June	26th	International Day against Drug abuse and Illegal Trafficking
September	10th	World Suicide Prevention Day
	21st	World Alzheimer's Day
October	1st	World Elderly Day (or) International Day for Elderly (or) International Day for Older Persons
	2nd	National Anti-drug Addiction Day and International Day of Non-violence
	10th	World Mental Health Day and World Homeless Day
	11th	World Obesity Day
November	25th	International Day for Elimination of Violence Against Women
December	3rd	World Disability Day (or) International Day for Disabled Persons

Contd...

APPENDIX 28

PROPONENTS IN PSYCHIATRY

Therapies in psychiatry	Proponent
Alcoholic anonymous	Dr Bob and Bill Wilson
Aversion therapy	L V Kantorovich
Cognitive therapy	Aaron Beck
Client centered psychotherapy	Carl Rogers
Family therapy	Nathan Ackerman
Group therapy	Joseph Pratt
Gestalt therapy	Frederick Peris
Hypnosis	James Braid
Interpersonal psychotherapy	Klerman
Psychodrama	Jacob Moreno
Psychotherapy	Walter Cooper Danny
Psychosurgery	A Egas Moniz (Won Nobel Prize)
Rational emotive therapy	Albert Ellis
Sexual counseling	William H masters and Virginia E Johnson
Therapeutic community	Maxwell Jones
Transactional analysis	Eric Berne
Token economy	Ayllon and Azrin

Medications in psychiatry	Proponent
Chlorpromazine	Jean Delay and Pierre Deniker
Clozapine	Bern
Fluoxetine	Lilly
Haloperidol	Paul Janssen
Imipramine	Ronald Kuhn
Lithium	John Cade
Olanzapine	Elli Lilly
Sertraline	Roerig
Tranquilizers	Yonkman

Mental illness/psychiatric symptoms	Proponent
Agoraphobia	Westphal
Akathisia	Haskovec
Alcoholic delirium	Thomas Salton
Bulimia nervosa	Gerald Russell
Catatonia, cyclothymia and verbigeration	KL Kahlbaum
Dementia precox	Emil Kraepelin
Hysteria	Jean Martin Charcot
Neurosis	William Cullen
Pica	Ambroise Pare
Postpartum psychosis	Robert Gooch
Psychosis for LSD	Hoffman
Sadism, masochism and sexual bondage	Richard Von Krafft-Ebing
Schizophrenia	Eugen Bleuler
Stress	Hans Selye
Trichotillomania	Francois Hallopeau
Kleptomania	Charles Henri Marc and Jean Etienne

Assessment in psychiatry	Proponent
Intellectual development	Jean Piaget
Mental status assessment for uncooperative patients	Kirby
Minnesota multiphasic personality inventory (MMPI)	S.R. Hathaway and J.C. McKinley
Mini-mental status examination	Folstein
Inkblot test	Hermann Rorschach
IQ development	Jean Piaget
Thematic apperception test	Henry A Murray

Theories or Miscellaneous concepts related to Psychiatry	Proponent
Behaviorism	J. Watson
Biopsychosocial model	George Engel and Iohn Romano
Interpersonal theory	Harrystack Sullivan
Classical conditioning	Pavlov
Operant conditioning	B.F. Skinner
Term psychiatry coined	Johann Reil
Founder of modern psychiatry	J.E.D. Esquirol
Father of psychobiology	Adolf Meyer
Father of suicidology	Edward Shneidman
Theory of humor to describe emotions and mood	Galen
Seat of mind is present in brain	Hippocrates
Object relations theory	Melanie Klein

APPENDIX 29

THERAPEUTIC SERUM LEVELS OF PSYCHOTROPIC MEDICATIONS

Name of the drugs	Reference value
Amitriptyline plus Nortriptyline	95–250 ng/mL
Clozapine	200–700 ng/mL
Carbamazepine	4–12 mg/mL
Chlorpromazine	50–300 mcg/ml
Lithium	0.6 to 1–8 mEq/L
Lamotrigine	2.5–15 μg/mL
Desipramine	150–300 ng/mL
Imipramine	200–250 ng/mL
Desipramine plus imipramine	150–300 ng/mL
Nortriptyline	50–150 ng/mL
Haloperidol	8–18 ng/mL
Valproic acid (or) sodium valproate	50–125 mg/ml

APPENDIX 30

IMBALANCE OF NEUROTRASMITTERS IN VARIOUS PSYCHIATRIC DISORDERS

Psychiatric disorders	Neurotransmitters	
	Increased	Decreased
Schizophrenia	Dopamine, Epinephrine and norepinephrine	Gamma-Amino Butyric Acid (GABA)
Mania	Dopamine, Epinephrine and Norepinephrine	—
Depression	Acetylcholine	Epinephrine, Norepinephrine and Histamine
Parkinson's disease	—	Dopamine
Anxiety disorder	Serotonin	Gamma-Amino Butyric Acid (GABA), Epinephrine and Norepinephrine
Aggression, Suicide and Impulsivity	—	Serotonin
Huntington's disease	Somatostatin	—
Alzheimer's disease	—	Somatostatin
Eating disorder and Sleep disorder	Gamma-Amino Butyric Acid (GABA)	—

APPENDIX 31

ICD-11 AND DSM-5 CLASSIFICATION OF MENTAL DISORDERS

ICD-11	DSM-5	Classification of mental disorders
Neurodevelopmental disorders		
Intellectual disability (intellectual developmental disorder)		
6A00.0	—	Mild intellectual disability
6A00.1	—	Moderate intellectual disability
6A00.2	—	Severe intellectual disability
6A00.3	—	Profound intellectual disability
6A00.4		Provisional intellectual disability
—	315	Global developmental delay
6A00.Z	319	Unspecified intellectual disability (intellectual developmental disorder)
Communication disorders		
6A01	315.39	Language disorder
6A01.0	315.39	Speech sound disorder
—	315.35	Childhood-onset fluency disorder (stuttering)
—	307.0	Adult-onset fluency disorder
6A01.22	315.39	Social (pragmatic) communication disorder
6A01.Z	307.9	Unspecified communication disorder
Autism spectrum disorder		
6A02	299.00	Autism spectrum disorder
—	293.89	Autism spectrum disorder with catatonia
Attention-deficit/hyperactivity disorder		
6A05.0	314.00	Predominantly inattentive presentation
6A05.1	314.01	Predominantly hyperactive/impulsive presentation
6A05.2	314.01	Combined presentation
6A05.Y	314.01	Other specified attention-deficit/ hyperactivity disorder
6A05.Z	314.01	Unspecified attention-deficit/ hyperactivity disorder
Specific learning disorder		
6A03.0	315.00	With impairment in reading
6A03.1	315.2	With impairment in written expression
6A03.2	315.1	With impairment in mathematics
Motor disorders		
—	315.4	Developmental coordination disorder
6A06	307.3	Stereotypic movement disorder

Contd...

ICD-11	DSM-5	Classification of mental disorders
Tic disorders		
8A05.00	307.23	Tourette's disorder
—	307.22	Persistent (chronic) motor or vocal tic disorder
—	307.21	Provisional tic disorder
—	307.20	Other specified tic disorder
—	307.19	Unspecified tic disorder
Other neurodevelopmental disorders		
6A0Y	315.8	Other specified neurodevelopmental disorder
6A0Z	315.9	Unspecified neurodevelopmental disorder
Schizophrenia spectrum and other psychotic disorders		
6A20	295.90	Schizophrenia
6A21	—	Schizoaffective disorder
6A22	301.22	Schizotypal (personality) disorder
6A23	—	Acute and transient psychotic disorder
6A24	297.1	Delusional disorder
—	298.8	Brief psychotic disorder
—	295.40	Schizophreniform disorder
—	295.70	Schizoaffective disorder (bipolar type)
—	295.70	Schizoaffective disorder (depressive type)
—	293.81	Psychotic disorder due to another medical condition (with delusions)
—	293.82	Psychotic disorder due to another medical condition (with hallucinations)
6A40	293.89	Catatonia associated with another mental disorder (catatonia specifier)
—	293.89	Catatonic disorder due to another medical condition
6A41	—	Catatonia induced by psychoactive substances, including medications
6A4Z	293.89	Unspecified catatonia
—	298.8	Other specified schizophrenia spectrum and other psychotic disorder
—	298.9	Unspecified schizophrenia spectrum and other psychotic disorder
Bipolar and related disorders		
Bipolar I disorder		
—	296.41	Current or most recent episode manic (mild)
—	296.42	Current or most recent episode manic (moderate)
—	296.43	Current or most recent episode manic (severe)

Contd...

ICD-11	DSM-5	Classification of mental disorders
6A60.5	296.44	Current or most recent episode manic (with psychotic features)
6A60.B	296.45	Current or most recent episode manic (in partial remission)
6A60.F	296.46	Current or most recent episode manic (in full remission)
6A60.E	296.40	Current or most recent episode manic (unspecified)
Bipolar II disorder		
6A61	296.89	Bipolar II disorder
6A62	301.13	Cyclothymic disorder
6A6Y	296.89	Other specified bipolar and related disorder
6A6Z	296.80	Unspecified bipolar and related disorder
Depressive disorders		
—	296.99	Disruptive mood dysregulation disorder
6A70.0	296.21	Single episode depression (mild)
—	296.22	Single episode depression (moderate)
6A71.1	—	Single episode depression (moderate without psychotic features)
6A71.2	—	Single episode depression (moderate with psychotic features)
6A71.3	—	Single episode depression (severe without psychotic features)
6A71.4	—	Single episode depression (severe with psychotic features)
—	296.23	Single episode depression (severe)
—	296.24	Single episode depression (with psychotic features)
6A70.6	296.25	Single episode depression (in partial remission)
6A70.7	296.26	Single episode depression (in full remission)
6A70.Z	296.20	Single episode depression (unspecified)
6A71.0	296.31	Recurrent episode depression (mild)
—	296.32	Recurrent episode depression (moderate)
6A71.1	—	Recurrent episode depression (moderate without psychotic features)
6A71.2	—	Recurrent episode depression (moderate with psychotic features)
—	296.33	Recurrent episode depression (severe)
6A71.3	—	Recurrent episode depression (severe without psychotic features)

Contd...

ICD-11	DSM-5	Classification of mental disorders
6A71.4	—	Recurrent episode depression (severe with psychotic features)
—	296.34	Recurrent episode depression (with psychotic features)
6A71.6	296.35	Recurrent episode depression (in partial remission)
6A71.7	296.36	Recurrent episode depression (in full remission)
6A71.Y	296.30	Recurrent episode depression (unspecified)
6A7Z	300.4	Persistent depressive disorder (dysthymia)
—	625.4	Premenstrual dysphoric disorder
—	293.83	Depressive disorder due to another medical condition
Anxiety disorders		
6B00	300.02	Generalized anxiety disorder
6B01	300.01	Panic disorder
6B02	300.22	Agoraphobia
6B03	300.29	Specific phobia
6B04	300.23	Social anxiety disorder (social phobia)
6B05	309.21	Separation anxiety disorder
6B06	312.23	Selective mutism
—	293.84	Anxiety disorder due to another medical condition
6B0Y	300.09	Other specified anxiety disorder
6B0Z	300.00	Unspecified anxiety disorder
Obsessive-compulsive and its related disorder		
6B20	300.3	Obsessive-compulsive disorder
—	300.7	Body dysmorphic disorder
6B24	300.3	Hoarding disorder
6B25.0	312.39	Trichotillomania (hair-pulling disorder)
6B25.1	698.4	Excoriation (skin-picking) disorder
—	294.8	Obsessive-compulsive and related disorder due to another medical condition
—	300.3	Other specified obsessive-compulsive and related disorder
6B20.Z	300.3	Unspecified obsessive-compulsive and related disorder
Trauma- and stressor-related disorders		
6B44	313.89	Reactive attachment disorder
6B45	313.89	Disinhibited social engagement disorder
6B40	309.81	Post-traumatic stress disorder
—	308.3	Acute stress disorder

Contd...

ICD-11	DSM-5	Classification of mental disorders
6B43	—	Adjustment disorders
—	309.0	Adjustment disorders (with depressed mood)
—	309.24	Adjustment disorders (with anxiety)
—	309.28	Adjustment disorders (with mixed anxiety and depressed mood)
—	309.3	Adjustment disorders (with disturbance of conduct)
—	309.4	Adjustment disorders (with mixed disturbance of emotions and conduct)
—	309.9	Adjustment disorders (unspecified)
6B4Y	309.89	Other specified trauma- and stressor-related disorder
6B4Z	309.9	Unspecified trauma- and stressor-related disorder
Dissociative disorders		
6B60	—	Dissociative neurological symptom disorder
6B61	300.12	Dissociative amnesia
—	300.13	Dissociative amnesia (with dissociative fugue)
6B62	—	Trance disorder
6B63	—	Possession trance disorder
6B64	300.14	Dissociative identity disorder
6B65	—	Partial dissociative identity disorder
6B66	300.6	Depersonalization-derealization disorder
6B6Y	300.15	Other specified dissociative disorder
6B6Z	300.15	Unspecified dissociative disorder
Somatic symptom and related disorders		
—	300.82	Somatic symptom disorder
—	300.7	Illness anxiety disorder
—	300.11	Conversion disorder (functional neurological symptom disorder)
—	316	Psychological factors affecting other medical conditions
—	300.19	Factitious disorder
—	300.89	Other specified somatic symptom and related disorder
—	300.82	Unspecified somatic symptom and related disorder
Feeding and eating disorders		
6B80	307.1	Anorexia nervosa
6B80.10	—	Restricting type
6B80.11	—	Binge eating/purging type
6B81	307.51	Bulimia nervosa

Contd...

ICD-11	DSM-5	Classification of mental disorders
6B82	307.51	Binge eating disorder
6B83	307.59	Avoidant/Restrictive food intake disorder
6B84	307.52	Pica
6B85	307.53	Rumination disorder
6B8Y	307.59	Other specified feeding or eating disorder
6B8Z	307.50	Unspecified feeding or eating disorder
Elimination disorders		
6C00	307.6	Enuresis
6C01	307.7	Encopresis
—	788.39	Other specified elimination disorder (with urinary symptoms)
—	787.60	Other specified elimination disorder (with fecal symptoms)
6C00.Z	788.30	Unspecified elimination disorder (with urinary symptoms)
6C01.Z	787.60	Unspecified elimination disorder (with fecal symptoms)
Sexual dysfunctions		
HA00	302.71	Hypoactive sexual desire disorder
HA01.0	302.72	Female sexual interest/arousal disorder
HA01.1	302.72	Erectile disorder
HA02	302.73	Female orgasmic disorder
HA03.0	302.75	Premature (early) ejaculation
HA03.1	302.74	Delayed ejaculation
—	302.76	Genito-pelvic pain/penetration disorder
HA03.Y	302.79	Other specified sexual dysfunction
Gender dysphoria		
—	302.6	Gender dysphoria in children
—	302.85	Gender dysphoria in adolescents and adults
—	302.6	Other specified gender dysphoria
—	302.6	Unspecified gender dysphoria
Disruptive, impulse-control and conduct disorders		
6C90	313.81	Oppositional defiant disorder
6C73	312.34	Intermittent explosive disorder
6C91.0	312.81	Conduct disorder (childhood-onset type)
6C91.1	312.82	Conduct disorder (adolescent-onset type)
6C91.Z	312.83	Conduct disorder (unspecified onset)
—	301.7	Antisocial personality disorder

Contd...

ICD-11	DSM-5	Classification of mental disorders
6C70	312.33	Pyromania
6C71	312.32	Kleptomania
6C7Y	312.89	Other specified disruptive, impulse-control, and conduct disorder
6C7Z	312.9	Unspecified disruptive, impulse-control, and conduct disorder
Personality disorders		
6D10	—	Personality disorders
6D10.0	—	Personality disorders, mild
6D10.1	—	Personality disorders, moderate
6D10.2	—	Personality disorders, severe
6D10.Z	—	Personality disorders, unspecified severity
6D11	—	Predominant personality traits
6D11.0	—	Negative affectivity in personality disorder
6D11.1	—	Detachment in personality disorder
6D11.2	—	Dissociality in personality disorder
6D11.3	—	Disinhibition in personality disorder
6D11.4	—	Anankastic personality disorder
6D11.5	—	Borderline pattern personality disorder
Cluster A personality disorders		
—	301.0	Paranoid personality disorder
—	301.20	Schizoid personality disorder
—	301.22	Schizotypal personality disorder
Cluster B personality disorders		
—	301.7	Antisocial personality disorder
—	301.83	Borderline personality disorder
—	301.50	Histrionic personality disorder
—	301.81	Narcissistic personality disorder
Cluster C personality disorders		
—	301.4	Obsessive-compulsive personality disorder
—	301.82	Avoidant personality disorder
—	301.6	Dependent personality disorder

ICD-11	DSM-5	Classification of mental disorders
Other personality disorders		
	310.1	Personality change due to another medical condition
	301.89	Other specified personality disorder
Medication-induced movement disorders and other adverse effects of medication		
—	332.1	Neuroleptic-induced parkinsonism
—	333.92	Neuroleptic malignant syndrome
—	333.72	Medication-induced acute dystonia
—	333.99	Medication-induced acute akathisia
—	333.85	Tardive dyskinesia
—	333.72	Tardive dystonia
—	333.99	Tardive akathisia
—	333.1	Medication-induced postural tremor
—	333.99	Other medication-induced movement disorder
Gender dysphoria (DSM-5) and gender incongruence (ICD-11)		
HA60	302.85	Gender dysphoria in adolescents and adults
HA61	302.6	Gender dysphoria in children
HA8Y	302.6	Other specified gender dysphoria
HA6Z	302.6	Unspecified gender dysphoria
Paraphilic disorders		
6D30	302.4	Exhibitionistic disorder
6D31	302.82	Voyeuristic disorder
6D32	302.2	Pedophilic disorder
6D33	302.84	Sexual sadism disorder
6D34	302.89	Frotteuristic disorder
—	302.83	Sexual masochism disorder
F65.0	302.81	Fetishistic disorder
—	302.3	Transvestic disorder
6D35 and 6D36	302.89	Other specified paraphilic disorder
6D3Z	302.9	Unspecified paraphilic disorder

Contd...

Clinical Case Scenarios

CASE 1 PATIENT WITH MANIA

Mr M, 52-year-old male, married, completed Secondary School Leaving Certificate (SSLC) and is currently unemployed. Mr M talks too much, often sings songs, over grooming, uses abusive language, has reduced need for sleep, has sudden shift of one idea to other, being authoritative, cleaning often and raised psychomotor activities. Mr M has no significant history of depressive ideation, repeated intrusive thoughts, images, impulses or acts, substance abuse, head injury, infections and convulsions. Mr M has nonconsanguineous marriage and belongs to low socioeconomic background. He has similar episodes of mania in the past and discontinued the medication twice. He is married but he is separated from his wife. He is a shy personality even before the onset of illness. His vital signs are stable. In regard to blood values, total count, Erythrocyte Sedimentation Rate (ESR) and platelets are increased. The current medications are trihexyphenidyl, lithium, risperidone, chlorpromazine and paracetamol.

History Collection

Demographic Profile

Mr M, 52-year-old male, married, completed SSLC and currently unemployed. He is diagnosed with mania with psychotic symptoms. The information gathered from patient and mother was adequate, reliable and relevant.

Chief Complaints for Seeking Admission

- Over talkativeness
- Shifting of one idea to other
- Increased activities
- Collecting things
- Over religiosity
- Singing songs
- Cleaning
- Over grooming
- Authoritative and demanding
- Abusive and assaultive
- Decreased need for sleep

} for three months

History of Present Illness

His illness is of insidious onset and episodic course of illness. He was apparently normal three months before he developed symptoms like elated mood with excessive speech and flight of ideas. He also picked things outside the house and did excessive activities, and was over involved in religious rituals, said that he had the power of God and he can help the poor people. He was involved in cleaning and over grooming, sang songs often religious songs, sometimes he demands money from mother and if it is not given, he is abusive and assaultive. He also had decreased need for sleep and poor appetite. He is not on regular treatment. No history of physical illnesses.

Negative History

No history of depressive ideation, repeated intrusive thoughts, images, impulses or acts, substance abuse, organic causes like head injury, infections and convulsions.

Current Treatment History

- Tab. Trihexyphenidyl (THP), 4 mg, BD

- Tab. Risperidone (RSPN), 6 mg, HS
- Tab. Lithium, 300 mg, 1-0-3
- Tab. Chlorpromazine (CPZ), 100 mg, HS
- Tab. Paracetamol, 500 mg, BD

Past History

Similar episodes in the past.

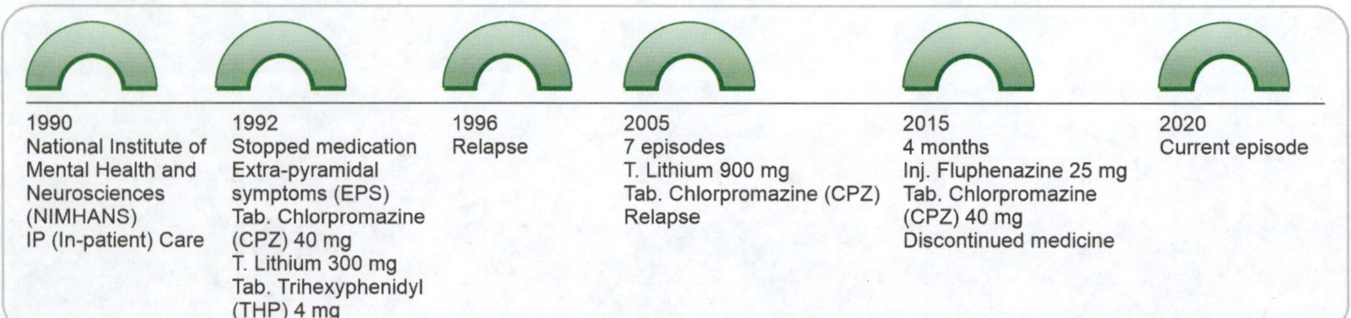

Family History

Nonconsanguineous marriage, he is from low socioeconomic status. Family history of mental illnesses in maternal uncle and Alcohol Dependence Syndrome (ADS) among 1st and 2nd degree relatives.

Genogram

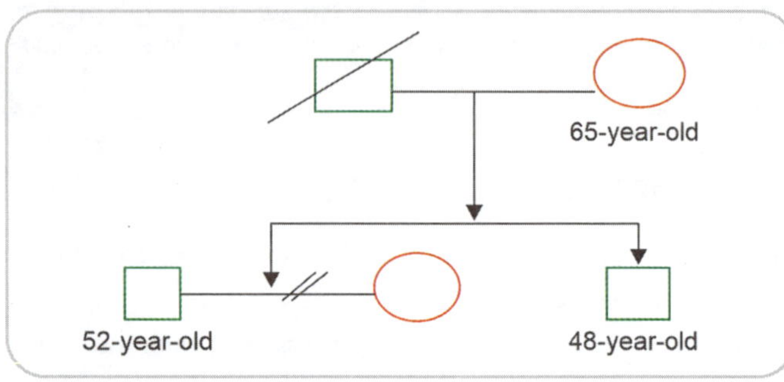

Personal History

- **Birth and early development:** He was reported to be born full term with normal vaginal delivery which was conducted at hospital. No complications were reported during the periods of antenatal, intranatal and neonatal periods. Birth weight was reported to be normal. Baby cried soon after delivery and breastfeeding was initiated soon after delivery. Milestone development was reported to be normal.
- **Behavior during childhood:** He was temperamentally an easy child; he possessed only few friends in his childhood. He was shy type and did not involve in any play activities. He was closely attached with family members. He was emotionally controlled and calm and quiet.
- **Physical illnesses:** No physical illness during childhood was reported.
- **Schooling:** He started schooling at the age of four, concentrated on his studies, few friends. Not good in scholastic performances. He studied up to SSLC. Occupation: No specific jobs held.
- **Sexual and marital history:** Married but her wife separated, reason not known.
- **Substance use:** No significant history.

Premorbid Personality: Well Adjusted

- **Social relationships:** Fewer friends in school, closely attached with his mother.
- **Intellectual activities:** Reading books. Not good in academic activities.
- **Mood:** Bright, calm and relaxed.
- **Character:** Attitude to work and responsibility, worried when responsibility comes, meticulous and methodical.
- **Interpersonal relationships:** Shy, few friends, no play in schools; perform household activities, concentrates on studies, emotionally controlled and quiet.
- **Energy and imitativeness:** Sluggish in doing household activities: would always insist on studying.
- **Fantasy life:** Not present
- **Habits:** Normal sleep and rest pattern. Regular bowel and bladder habits.

Mental Status Examination

- **General appearance and behavior:** He looks irritable, well kempt, groomed and restless, establishes eye to eye contact, he is cooperative, and establishes rapport.
- **Psychomotor activity:** Psychomotor activities observed as increased.
- **Speech:** Speech is spontaneous. Reaction time is decreased. Tone, tempo, and volume are normal. Speech is relevant and coherent. Prosody was maintained throughout.
- **Thought:** Flight of ideas is present, possession normal; no repeated thoughts reported. Delusion of grandiosity present "God has given power and to help the poor."
- **Mood**
  - Subjectively: "I am very happy."
  - Objectively: Elated. Range and reactivity increased, congruent and appropriate, occasionally lability present.
- **Perception:** Hearing voice of God and his brother. He may have auditory hallucination.
- **Cognitive function:**
  - **Orientation:** He is grossly oriented to time, place and person.
  - **Attention and concentration:** Attention is aroused and concentration is not sustained.
    Digit span test:
    Digit forward test: 4 digits
    Digit backward test: 4 digits
    Serial subtraction till 31
  - **Memory:** Immediate, recent and remote intact.
  - **Intelligence** General information, Comprehension, Arithmetic ability, Abstraction intact.
  - **Judgment:** Personal, social and test judgment are impaired.
- **Insight:** It is absent; as he completely denies that he is ill and requires treatment.

Psychometric Assessment

The Young Mania Rating Scale (YMRS)

1. **Elevated mood** [3]
   0 Absent
   1 Mildly or possibly increased on questioning
   2 Definite subjective elevation; optimistic, self-confident; cheerful; appropriate to content
   3 Elevated; inappropriate to content; humorous
   4 Euphoric; inappropriate laughter; singing
2. **Increased motor activity-energy** [4]
   0 Absent
   1 Subjectively increased
   2 Animated; gestures increased
   3 Excessive energies; hyperactive at times; restless (can be calmed)
   4 Motor excitement; continuous hyperactivity (cannot be calmed)
3. **Sexual interest** [3]
   0 Normal; not increased
   1 Mildly or possibly increased
   2 Definite subjective increases on questioning
   3 Spontaneous sexual content; elaborates on sexual matters; hypersexual by self-report
   4 Overt sexual acts (toward patients, staff, or interviewer)
4. **Sleep** [4]
   0 Reports no decrease in sleep
   1 Sleeping less than normal amount by up to one hour
   2 Sleeping less than normal by more than one hour
   3 Reports decreased need for sleep
   4 Denies need for sleep
5. **Irritability** [6]
   0 Absent
   2 Subjectively increased
   4 Irritable at times during interview; recent episodes of anger or annoyance on ward
   6 Frequently irritable during interview; short, curt throughout
   8 Hostile, uncooperative; interview impossible
6. **Speech (rate and amount)** [8]
   0 No increase
   2 Feels talkative
   4 Increased rate or amount at times, verbose at times
   6 Push; consistently increased rate and amount; difficult to interrupt
   8 Pressured; uninterruptible, continuous speech
7. **Language-thought disorder** [3]
   0 Absent
   1 Circumstantial; mild distractibility; quick thoughts
   2 Distractible, loses goal of thought; changes topics frequently; racing thoughts
   3 Flight of ideas; tangentiality; difficult to follow; rhyming, echolalia
   4 Incoherent; communication impossible
8. **Content** [8]
   0 Normal
   2 Questionable plans, new interests
   4 Special project(s); hyper-religious
   6 Grandiose or paranoid ideas; ideas of reference
   8 Delusions; hallucinations
9. **Disruptive-aggressive behavior** [8]
   0 Absent, cooperative
   2 Sarcastic; loud at times, guarded
   4 Demanding; threats on ward

6 Threatens interviewer; shouting; interview difficult
8 Assaultive; destructive; interview impossible

10. Appearance 1

0 Appropriate dress and grooming
1 Minimally unkempt
2 Poorly groomed; moderately dishevelled; overdressed
3 Dishevelled; partly clothed; garish make-up
4 Completely unkempt; decorated; bizarre garb

11. Insight 4

0 Present; admits illness; agrees with need for treatment
1 Possibly ill
2 Admits behavior change, but denies illness
3 Admits possible change in behavior, but denies illness
4 Denies any behavior change

Patient's Score = 50 (Severe mania) N <20

General Physical Examination

- **General appearance:** He is thin-built, conscious, good hygiene.
  - Height: 166 cm
  - Weight: 49 kg
  - Body mass index (BMI): 17
- **Vital signs:** Stable
  - Temperature : 98.6°F
  - Pulse : 86 beats/min
  - Respiration : 20 breaths/min
  - Blood pressure : 120/80 mm Hg
- **Head and scalp:** Size and shape of the head is normal. Hair distribution is even, no palpable mass or tenderness; small wound on lower lip on mucosal surface is noted.
- **Eyes:** No pallor present, Symmetrical in size and shape. Pupils equal in round and reacting to light. No infections or color changes observed.
- **Nose:** Nostrils patent; though labored breathing persists. Nasal flaring is present, frontal and maxillary sinuses non tender.
- **Ears:** Both ears are equally placed. Pinna is soft and flexible. Auditory canal patent, no discharges observed.
- **Mouth and throat:** Lips are dry and patchy. Buccal mucosa pink and moist; teeth normally aligned; no missing teeth. Gum is pink and moist; uvular elevation normal and midline. Gag reflux present. Tongue midline and movements normal. Throat congestion is present. He is having hoarseness of voice.
- **Neck:** Trachea is in midline, nontender. Range of motion (ROM) is of full range, strong. No palpable tender lymph nodes or masses. Thyroid is palpable; smooth and not enlarged. Carotid pulses present.
- **Thorax**
  - **Anterior thorax:** Breathing movements bilaterally equal. No visible pulsations. Apical impulses are palpable. No tender lymph nodes to palpate. Heart sounds S1 and S2 heard; rate 86 beats/min; regular rate and rhythm. No murmurs, rubs or clicks.
  - **Posterior thorax:** Anterioposterior diameter is less than Transverse diameter; muscular development normal. No spinal abnormalities noticed; no increase in tactile fremitus. Lungs are resonant and clear throughout.
- **Abdomen:** No visible gastric pulsations. Rounded; bowel sounds present no tenderness or palpable mass, liver and spleen; non palpable, nontender. Femoral pulses feeble. Inguinal- femoral nodes tender as reported.
- **Upper and lower extremities:** Well developed; no muscle wasting. No edema, injuries noted, ROM; full strength and possible in all directions. Pedal and radial pulses palpable equal bilaterally.
- **Genitals and rectum:** Normal as reported; no examination done.

Investigations

Sl. no.	Date	Investigation	Patient's value	Normal value	Remarks
1.		• Hemoglobin • Total count (TC) • Platelet • Erythrocyte sedimentation rate (ESR)	• 13.9% • 12,800 cells/mm^3 • 4.92 lakhs/ mm^3 • 33 mm/hr	• 12–16 g/dL • 4–9000 cells/mm^3 • 2.5–4.5 lakhs/ mm^3 • 5–15 mm/hr	• Normal • Elevated • Elevated • Elevated
2.		Sr. Lithium	0.8 mg/dL	0.5–1.5 mg/dL	Normal

Medication

Name of the drug	Dose/ frequency	Action	Side effects	Nurses' responsibility
Tab. Trihexy-phenidyl	4 mg 1-1-0	Trihexyphenidyl blocks efferent impulses in parasympathetically innervated structures like smooth muscles (spasmolytic activity), salivary glands and eyes (mydriasis).	• **Cardiovascular:** Tachycardia • **Central nervous system:** Confusion, agitation, euphoria, drowsiness, headache, dizziness, nervousness, delusions, hallucinations, paranoia. • **Dermatologic:** Dry skin, increased sensitivity to light, rash. • **Gastrointestinal:** Constipation, xerostomia, dry throat, ileus, nausea, vomiting, parotitis. • **Genitourinary:** urinary retention **Neuromuscular and skeletal weakness** • **Ocular:** Blurred vision, mydriasis, increase in intraocular pressure, glaucoma, blindness (long-term use in narrow-angle glaucoma). • **Respiratory:** Dry nose • **Miscellaneous:** Diaphoresis (decreased)	• Give Intra-muscular injections deep into muscle. • Do not administer subcutaneously; as tissue necrosis may occur. • Do not administer intra-arterially; arteriospasm and gangrene of the limb may result. • Reduce dosage of barbiturates given concurrently with promethazine by at least half; arrange for dosage reduction of opioid analgesics given concomitantly by one-fourth to one-half.
Tab. Risperi-done	4 mg 0-0-$1_{1/2}$	It blocks postsynaptic mesolimbic dopaminergic D_1 and D_2 receptors in the brain; depresses the release of hypothalamic and hypophyseal hormones; believed to depress the reticular activating system, thus affecting basal metabolism, body temperature, wakefulness, vasomotor tone, and emesis.	• Altered cardiac conduction, arrhythmias. • **Anticholinergic effects:** (constipation, xerostomia, blurred vision, urinary retention); use with caution in patients with decreased gastrointestinal motility, paralytic ileus, urinary retention, Benign prostatic Hypertrophy (BPH), xerostomia, or visual problems. • **Blood dyscrasias:** Extrapyramidal symptoms including pseudo parkinsonism, acute dystonic reactions, akathisia, and tardive dyskinesia. • **Hepatic effects:** Hepatitis, hyperprolactinemia • **Hypotension:** Neuroleptic malignant syndrome • **Orthostatic hypotension:** Sedation	• Monitor addiction-prone patients carefully because of their predisposition to habituation and drug dependence. • Monitor liver function and blood counts periodically in patients on long-term therapy.

Contd...

Name of the drug	Dose/ frequency	Action	Side effects	Nurses' responsibility
Tab. Lithium	300 mg 1-0-3	Alters sodium transport in nerve and muscle cells; inhibits release of nor epinephrine and dopamine from stimulated neurons; slightly increases intra neuronal stores of catecholamines; decreases intra neuronal content of second messengers and may thereby selectively modulate the responsiveness of hyperactive neurons that might contribute to the manic state.	• **CNS:** Lethargy, slurred speech, muscle weakness, fine hand tremor. • **GI:** Nausea, vomiting, diarrhea, thirst. • **GU:** Polyuria • **1.5–2 mEq/L (mild to moderate toxic reactions)** • **CNS:** Coarse hand tremor, mental confusion, hyperirritability of muscles, drowsiness, incoordination. • **CV:** ECG changes • **GI:** Persistent GI upset, gastritis, salivary gland swelling, abdominal pain, excessive salivation, flatulence, indigestion. • **2–2.5 mEq/L (moderate to severe toxic reactions)** • **CNS:** Ataxia, giddiness, fasciculation, tinnitus, blurred vision, clonic movements, seizures, stupor, coma. • **CV:** Serious ECG changes, severe hypotension with cardiac arrhythmias. • **GU:** Large output of dilute urine. • **Respiratory:** Fatalities secondary to pulmonary complications. • **2.5 mEq/L (life-threatening toxicity)** • **General:** Complex involvement of multiple organ systems, including seizures, arrhythmias, CV collapse, stupor, coma. • **Reactions unrelated to serum levels** • **CNS:** Headache, worsening of organic brain syndromes, fever, reversible short-term memory impairment, dyspraxia. • **CV:** ECG changes; hyperkalemia associated with ECG changes; syncope; tachycardia-bradycardia syndrome; rarely, arrhythmias, CHF, diffuse myocarditis, death. • **Dermatologic:** Pruritus with or without rash; maculopapular, acneiform, and follicular eruptions; cutaneous ulcers; edema of ankles or wrists. • **Endocrine:** Diffuse nontoxic goiter; hypothyroidism; hypercalcemia associated with	• Regular monitoring of serum lithium levels to patients with renal or cardiovascular disease, debilitation, or dehydration or life-threatening psychiatric disorders. • Give drug with food or milk or after meals. • Monitor for therapeutic serum levels of 0.6–1.2 mEq/L. • Advise patient that this drug may cause serious fetal harm and cannot be used during pregnancy; urge use of barrier contraceptives. • Decrease dosage after the acute manic episode is controlled • Ensure that patient maintains adequate intake of salt and adequate intake of fluid (2,500–3,000 mL/day).

Contd...

Name of the drug	Dose/ frequency	Action	Side effects	Nurses' responsibility
			hyperparathyroidism; transient hyperglycemia; irreversible nephrogenic diabetes insipidus, which improves with diuretic therapy; impotence or sexual dysfunction. • **GI:** Dysgeusia (taste distortion), salty taste; swollen lips; dental caries. • **Other:** Weight gain (5–10 kg); chest tightness; swollen or painful joints, eye irritation, worsening of cataracts, disturbance of visual accommodation, leukocytosis.	
Tab. Chlor-promazine	100 mg 0-0-1	Interference with central dopaminergic pathways in the mesolimbic and medullary chemoreceptor trigger zone areas of the brain, respectively. It is a dopamine blocker.	• Tardive dyskinesia, extrapyramidal symptoms, anxiety, drowsiness, depression, hallucinations, anorexia. • Transient tachycardia, its effects on the ECG include prolongation of the PR and QT intervals, blunting of the T wave and depression of the S-T segment, postural hypotension. • Agranulocytosis, leukopenia, granulocytopenia, eosinophilia, thrombocytopenia, anemia, aplastic anemia, pancytopenia. • Lowered seizure threshold. • Increased prolactin secretion; gynecomastia, galactorrhea, mastalgia, altered libido, menstrual irregularities, weight gain, alterations in glucose tolerance and false positive pregnancy tests have occurred.	• Do not administer intra-arterially; arteriospasm or gangrene may result. • Give IM injections of undiluted drug deep into muscle mass, monitor injection sites. • Do not use solutions that are discolored or contain a precipitate. • Protect drug from light, and refrigerate oral solution.
Tab. Paraceta-mol	500 mg 1-0-1	**Antipyretic:** Reduces fever by acting directly on the hypothalamic heat-regulating center to cause vasodilatation and sweating, which helps dissipate heat.	• **CNS:** Headache • **CV:** Chest pain, dyspnea, myocardial damage when doses of 5–8 g/day are ingested daily for several weeks or when doses of 4 g/day are ingested for 1 year. • **GI:** Hepatic toxicity and failure, jaundice. • **GU:** Acute kidney failure, renal tubular necrosis. • **Hematologic:** Methemoglobinemia—cyanosis; hemolytic anemia—hematuria, anuria; neutropenia, leukopenia, pancytopenia, thrombocytopenia, hypoglycemia. • **Hypersensitivity:** Rash, fever	• Do not exceed the recommended dosage. • Avoid using multiple preparations containing acetaminophen. • Carefully check all over the counter (OTC) products. • Give drug with food if GI upset occurs. • Discontinue drug if hypersensitivity reactions occur. • Treatment of overdose: Monitor serum levels regularly, *N*-acetylcysteine should be available as a specific antidote; basic life support measures may be necessary.

Nursing Management

Client Assessment

Elated mood with excessive speech, flight of ideas, picks things outside the house and excessive involvement in religious rituals. He says that he had the power of God and he can help the poor people, involved in cleaning and over grooming, sings songs often religious songs, sometimes he demands money from mother and if it is not given, he becomes abusive and assaultive, he also has decreased need for sleep and poor appetite, unemployed, separated from his wife.

Diagnostic Studies

Complete blood count reveals elevated white blood cell count and erythrocyte sedimentation rate (ESR) and normal Sr. Lithium.

Nursing Priorities

- Protect client/others from the consequences of hyperactive behavior.
- Provide for client's basic needs.
- Support client/family participation in follow-up care/community treatment.

Nursing Diagnosis

- Disturbed thought process related to inability to think and process information and evaluate reality as evidenced by delusion of grandiosity and exaggerated responses.
- Risk for violence, self-directed or toward others related to lack of impulse control, self-destructive strategies as evidenced by grandiose ideas and increased psychomotor activities.
- Imbalanced Nutrition: Less than body requirements related to decreased intake of nutrients sufficient to meet metabolic needs.
- Ineffective therapeutic regimen management pattern of regulating and integrating into daily living: A program for treatment of illness and the sequelae of illness that is unsatisfactory for meeting specific health goals.
- Knowledge deficit related to the management of the symptoms and about the hallucinations.
- Interrupted family processes, situational crises (illness, economic, change in roles).
- Disturbed sleep pattern related to biochemical changes in the brain and hyperactivity and increased environmental stimuli as evidenced by decreased sleep.

Nursing Care Plan

Assessment	Nursing diagnosis	Objectives	Nursing intervention	Implementation	Evaluation
Subjective Data: Patient says, "I have the power of God, I can help the poor." **Objective data:** • Nonreality-based thinking • Labile affect • Impaired judgment • Distractibility	Altered thought process related to inability to think and process information and evaluate reality as evidenced by delusion of grandiosity and exaggerated responses.	The client will be able to free from delusions or demonstrate the ability to function without responding to persistent delusional thoughts.	• Do not make promises that you cannot keep. • Encourage the client to talk with you, but do not try only for information. • Explain procedures, and try to be sure the client understands the procedures before doing it. • Recognize the client's delusions as the client's perception of the environment. • Do not argue with the client or try to convince the client that the delusions are false or unreal. • Interact with the client on the basis of real things; do not dwell on the delusional material.	• Not made any promises to the patient • Encouraged the client to talk with his thoughts. • Explained the procedures (medication administration) to the patient. • Did not make any argument to the patient • Interaction made with the client on the basis of real things. • Engaged the client in one-to-one activities (cleaning). • Showed empathy regarding the client's feelings; reassured the client.	Client demonstrated normal thought process as evidenced by the participation in activities for reduction in delusions.

Contd...

Assessment	Nursing diagnosis	Objectives	Nursing intervention	Implementation	Evaluation
			• Engage the client in one-to-one activities at first, then activities in small groups, and gradually activities in larger groups • Show empathy regarding the client's feelings; reassure the client of your presence and acceptance.		
Objective data: • Lack of impulse control • Wounds in lips • Abusive and assaultive • Feelings of anger or hostility	Risk for violence, self-directed or toward others related to lack of impulse control, self-destructive strategies as evidenced by grandiose ideas and increased psychomotor activities.	The client will not harm himself or others and identify alternative ways of dealing with stress and emotional problems.	• The client has one-to-one contact with a staff member at all times • Assess the client's suicidal potential, and evaluate the level of suicide precautions at least daily. • Do not argue with the client. • Ask the client if he or she has a plan for suicide. • The client's room should be near the nurse station and within view of the staff. • Be especially alert to sharp objects and other potentially dangerous items. • Involve the client as much as possible in planning his or her own treatment. • Be alert to the client's behaviors, especially excessive communication, flight of ideas, etc. • Observe, record, and report any changes in the client's mood.	• The client had one-to-one contact with a staff member at all times. • He is not having suicidal ideas and the environment is safe. • Not involved in any argument with patients by the staff and family members. • He was kept near the nurse station and free from other patients. • The room and the surroundings were free of dangerous objects. • Involved the client in planning his or her own treatment. • Paid more attention to his conversations. • His mood changes and behavior were recorded periodically.	Client was prevented from self and other's harm as evidenced by reduction in abusive behavior and help the ward people.
Objective data: • Inappropriate behavior related to self-care • Inadequate retention of information presented • Inadequate under-standing of information presented	Knowledge deficit related to the management of the symptoms and about the hallucinations.	The client will be able to understand about the illness, its chronic nature, treatment, and safe use of medications.	• Teach the client and family or significant others about manic behavior, bipolar disorder, and other problems as indicated • Teach the client and family or significant others about signs of relapse, such as insomnia, decreased nutrition, and poor personal hygiene.	• Taught the client and family or significant others about manic behavior. • Taught the client about signs of relapse, such as insomnia, decreased nutrition, and poor personal hygiene.	Client got adequate knowledge about the disease process and the side effects of medications.

Contd...

Assessment	Nursing diagnosis	Objectives	Nursing intervention	Implementation	Evaluation
			• Inform the client and family or significant others about psychotropic drugs, dosage, need to take the medication only as prescribed, the toxic symptoms, the need to monitor blood levels, and other considerations. • Reinforce teaching with written material as indicated.	• Informed the client about medications: dosage, need to take the medication only as prescribed, the toxic symptoms, the need to monitor sr. lithium levels, and other considerations. • Stressed to the client that medications must be taken regularly and continually to be effective; medications should not be discontinued just because the client's mood is has shown an improvement.	
Objective data: • Lack of appetite • Weight loss-49 kg. • Refusal to eat • Delusions and other psychotic symptoms	**Imbalanced Nutrition:** Less than body requirements related to decreased intake of nutrients sufficient to meet metabolic needs.	The client will be able to establish adequate nutrition.	• Give positive support and attention when the client eats; withdraw your attention when he or she refuses to eat. • Encourage the client to eat at appropriate meal and snack times; allow food only at those times. • Make culturally or ethnically appropriate foods available to the client • Try to accommodate the client's normal or previous eating habits as much as possible • Gradually decrease the frequency of suggestions, and allow the client to take responsibility for eating. • It may be necessary for you to feed the client, accompany the client to get food, or sit with the client through meal time. Nasogastric tube feedings or intravenous therapy also may be necessary. • Administer intravenous (IV) fluids as per order.	• Positive support and attention was given to him, when he ate the food; withdrew the attention when he refuses to eat. • Encouraged the client to eat at appropriate meal and snack times; allow food only at those times. • Provided finger foods and plenty of oral fluids according to his likes • Instructed the family members to feed the client, by accompanying him, or sit with the client through meal time.	The client maintained normal nutritional status as evidenced by weight gain.

Psychoeducation

Name of the Patient: Mr M
Topic: Compliance to treatment
Name of student teachers:
Language: English

Venue: Male Psy. Ward
Date: ______________
Time: ______________

Objectives

- **General objective:** At the end of the health education, the participants will be able to understand compliance to treatment.
- **Specific objectives**: At the end of the health education, the participants will be able to:
  - Define compliance.
  - List the outcomes of noncompliance.
  - Measures to promote compliance.

Specific objectives	Time	Contents	Teaching and learning activities	Audio visual aids	Evaluation
At the end of the health education, the participants will be able to:	2 minutes	**Introduction** Not taking medicine properly can be dangerous!!! Noncompliance to medicine is the number one cause of increasing disability in chronic mental illnesses.	Discussion	Charts	Can you outline the basics of compliance?
Define compliance	2 minutes	**Definiton** Compliance is defined as, "The extent to which a person's behavior—taking medication, following a diet, and/or executing lifestyle changes, corresponds with agreed recommendations from a health care provider."	Lecture	Roller board	What is compliance?
List the outcomes of noncompliance	10 minutes	**Outcomes of Noncompliance** • 5–20% mental illness patients relapse every year • 20–30% patients do not have adequate recovery on treatment. • Maximum loss of ability to work • Not able to take care of oneself • If not treated earlier with appropriate doses for sufficient time, the illness becomes chronic • Frequent and longer admissions to hospital are needed • Illness can become more resistant to treatment • Increased risk of self-harm and homelessness • Loss of self-esteem • Social relations wither and vocational progress is lost • Increased burden on families, caregivers.	Discussion	Handouts	List the outcomes of noncompliance

Contd...

Specific objectives	Time	Contents	Teaching and learning activities	Audio visual aids	Evaluation
Describe the measures to promote compliance	10 minutes	**Measures To Promote Compliance** • Understand mental illness is chronic • Patient has to continue medication for longer duration • If patient develops side effects, notify to the doctor • Never stop medication abruptly • Medication is given under supervision • If patient refuses oral medication, injectables or implants are available • Provide counseling to the patient regarding its benefits • Effectively manage oneself in case of crisis • Encourage regular follow-up **Conclusion** I hope that you understand the importance of compliance to medication, this will help you to prevent relapse.	Lecture cum discussion	Flannel board	What are the ways to promote compliance?

Recording and Reporting

Date	Time	Nursing care/activities	Name with signature
	8:00 am	Assessment of the patient	Ms X
	8:50 am	Patient has taken breakfast (2 pieces of bread) and 1 cup tea	Ms X
	9:00 am	• Administration of Oral Medication ▪ Tab. Trihexyphenidyl 4 mg ▪ Tab. Lithium, 300 mg. ▪ Tab. Paracetamol, 500 mg. • He has taken the medications and tolerated well.	Ms X
	9:15 am	He participated in exercise program	Ms X
	10:00 am	He participated in garden activities	Ms X
	10:35 am	Health education given to family members on "Compliance to treatment"	Ms X

CASE 2 PATIENT WITH DEPRESSIVE DISORDER

Mr K, 63-year-old male, unmarried, he is a carpenter, completed Higher Secondary Certificate (HSC). Mr K has a pervasive low mood, poor appetite, decreased sleep, fearfulness, lack of interest in activities, decreased self-care and social withdrawal. He attempted suicide twice, he was involved in alcohol consumption, not going to work and has fearfulness toward others. He occasionally expresses the death wishes. Beck's depression inventory reveals severe depression. Vital signs are stable. His complete blood count (CBC) is normal, sodium value is decreased and liver enzymes are increased. He has similar episodes of depression in the past. He is on tricyclic antidepressants.

History Collection

Demographic Profile

Mr K, 63-year-old male, unmarried, he is a carpenter, completed HSC. He was diagnosed with chronic depression with super imposed dysthymia. Information was given by patient and his mother, the information given was adequate, reliable and relevant.

Chief Complaints For Seeking Admission:

- Pervasive low mood
- Poor appetite
- Decreased sleep
- Fearfulness
- Lack of interest in activities
- Decreased self-care
- Social withdrawal

} for two months

History of Present Illness

His illness is of insidious onset and continuous course of illness. He was apparently normal 44 years back, with repeated episodes of depression, super imposed of being depressed always from 1974 onwards. From 1982 to 1992, he was reported of two suicidal attempts of high intentionality and lethality. From 1976, he was treated with adequate dosage of three antidepressants (TCA) and two selective serotonin re-uptake inhibitors (SSRIs). He reported of no improvement in depressive ideations. He has developed severe depressive mood for two months, no interest in activities, decreased sleep, not interested in taking food, always sits alone and passes the days, involved in alcohol consumption, not going to work, fearfulness toward others, no interaction with others. Occasionally expresses death wishes. No history of physical illnesses. He is on regular follow-up.

Negative History

No history of elevated mood, grandiosity, repeated intrusive thoughts, images, impulses or acts, suicidal attempts, organic causes like head injury, infections convulsions.

Current Treatment History

Tab. Chlorpromazine 200 mg, HS (one tablet before bed time at night)
Tab. Amitriptyline 150 mg, HS (one tablet before bed time at night)

Past History

Similar episodes in the past.

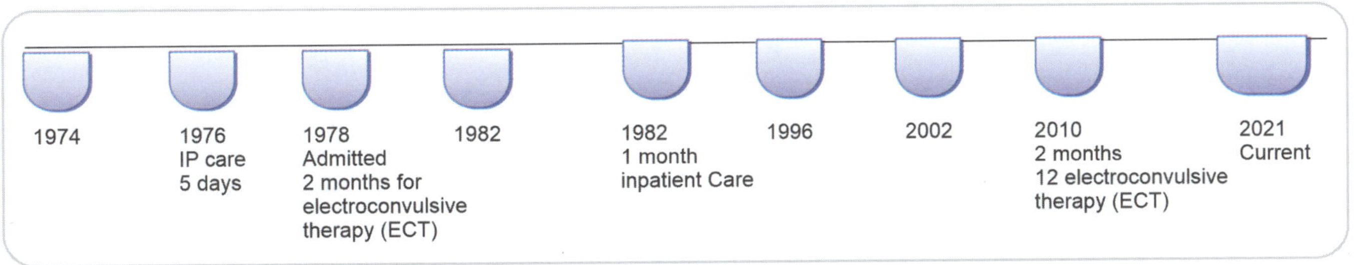

Family History

Nonconsanguineous marriage, he is from low socioeconomic status. Positive family history of mental illnesses and elder sister died by suicide, father died at early age, mother got second marriage, stepfather is cruel to him, bitter early childhood experiences, alcohol dependence syndrome (ADS) among 1st and 2nd degree relatives.

Genogram

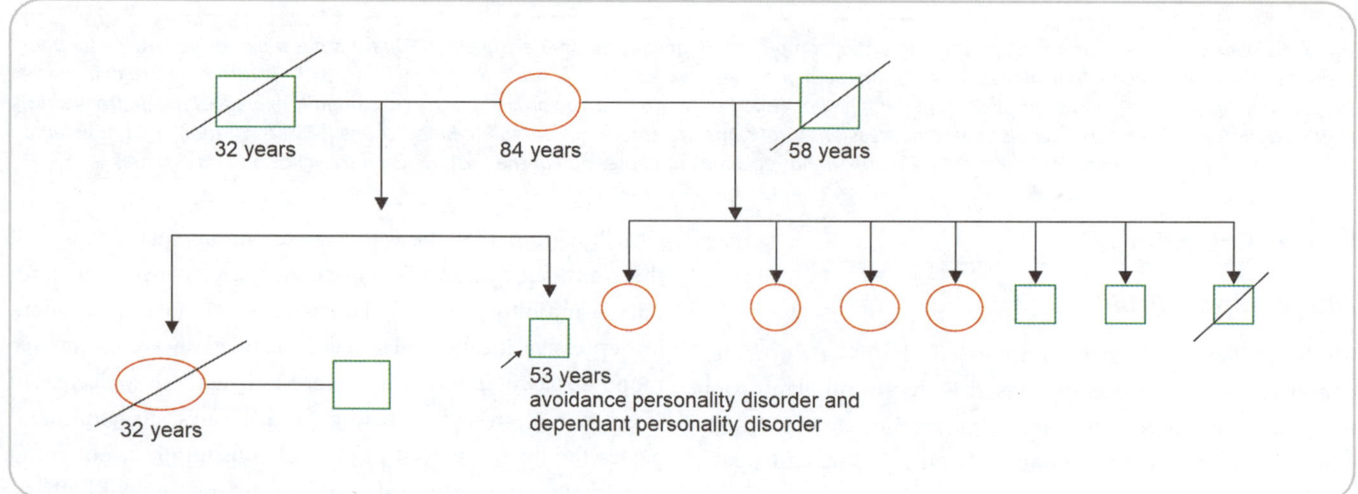

Personal History

- **Birth and early development:** He was reported to be born full term with normal vaginal delivery which was conducted at hospital. No complications were reported during the periods of antenatal, intranatal and neonatal periods. Birth weight was reported to be normal. Baby cried soon after delivery and breastfeeding was initiated soon after delivery. Milestone development was reported to be normal.
- **Behavior during childhood:** He was temperamentally an easy child; he possessed only a few friends in his childhood. He was shy type and did not involve in any play activities. He was closely attached with family members. He was emotionally intolerant, fearful, calm and quiet.

Significant Stressors

- **Physical illnesses:** No physical illness during childhood was reported.
- **Schooling:** He started schooling at the age of five, concentrated on his studies and had few friends. Not good in scholastic performances. He studied up to HSC.
- **Occupation:** Carpenter.
- **Sexual and marital history:** He is unmarried
- **Substance use:** Nicotine and alcohol dependence syndrome substance abuse.

Premorbid Personality

Anxious avoidant personality traits and dependent person

- **Social relationships:** Fewer friends in schools, closely attached with his mother.
- **Intellectual activities:** Reading books. Not good in academic activities.
- **Mood:** Dull, anxious and worried.
- **Character:** Attitude to work and responsibility; worried by responsibility, meticulous and methodical.
- **Interpersonal relationships:** Shy, few friends, no play in schools; perform household activities, concentrates on studies, emotionally controlled and quiet.
- **Energy and imitativeness:** Sluggish in doing household activities: would always insist on studying.
- **Fantasy life:** Not present
- **Habits:** Normal sleep and rest pattern. He has regular bowel and bladder habits.

Mental Status Examination

- **General appearance and behavior:** He looks ill-kempt, groomed, fearful, and appears to be restless, establishes eye to eye contact, he is cooperative and establishes rapport.
- **Psychomotor activity:** Psychomotor activities observed as retarded.
- **Speech:** Speech is on prompting. Reaction time is increased. Tone, tempo, and volume are decreased. Speech is relevant and coherent. Prosody was maintained throughout.
- **Thought:** No formal thought ideas, no flight of ideas is present, possession of thought is normal and no repeated thoughts. No delusion present. He is having depressive cognition, sense of worthlessness, hopelessness and uselessness. No death wishes.
- **Mood:**
  - **Subjectively:** "I am sad"
  - **Objectively:** Depressed mood. Range and reactivity decreased, congruent and appropriate.

- **Perception:** No illusion or hallucination present
- **Cognitive Function**
  - **Orientation:** Grossly oriented to time, place and person.
  - **Attention and concentration:** Attention can be aroused but concentration is not sustained.

  Digit span test:

  Digit forward test: 5 digits

  Digit backward test: 4 digits

  Serial subtraction till 42
- **Memory:** Immediate, recent and remote intact.
- **Intelligence:** General information, comprehension, arithmetic ability, abstraction intact and proverb test was done well by the patient.
- **Judgment:** Personal and social are impaired and test judgment is normal.
- **Insight:** Insight is present

Psychometric Assessment

Beck's Depression Inventory

This depression inventory can be self-scored. The scoring scale is at the end of the questionnaire.

Sl. no.	Score	Items	Patient score
1.	0	I do not feel sad	
	1	I feel sad	
	2	I am sad all the time and I cannot snap out of it	√
	3	I am so sad and unhappy that I cannot stand it	
2.	0	I am not particularly discouraged about the future	
	1	I feel discouraged about the future	√
	2	I feel I have nothing to look forward to	
	3	I feel the future is hopeless and that things cannot improve	
3.	0	I do not feel like a failure	
	1	I feel I have failed more than the average person	
	2	As I look back on my life, all I can see is a lot of failures	√
	3	I feel I am a complete failure as a person	
4.	0	I get as much satisfaction out of things as I used to	
	1	I do not enjoy things the way I used to	
	2	I do not get real satisfaction out of anything anymore	√
	3	I am dissatisfied or bored with everything	
5.	0	I do not feel particularly guilty	
	1	I feel guilty a good part of the time	
	2	I feel quite guilty most of the time	√
	3	I feel guilty all of the time	
6.	0	I do not feel I am being punished	
	1	I feel I may be punished	
	2	I expect to be punished	√
	3	I feel I am being punished	
7.	0	I do not feel disappointed in myself	
	1	I am disappointed in myself	√
	2	I am disgusted with myself	
	3	I hate myself	
8.	0	I do not feel I am any worse than anybody else	
	1	I am critical of myself for my weaknesses or mistakes	
	2	I blame myself all the time for my faults	
	3	I blame myself for everything bad that happens	√
9.	0	I do not have any thoughts of killing myself	
	1	I have thoughts of killing myself, but I would not carry them out	
	2	I would like to kill myself	√
	3	I would kill myself if I had the chance	
10.	0	I do not cry any more than usual	
	1	I cry more now than I used to	
	2	I cry all the time now	√
	3	I used to be able to cry, but now I cannot cry even though I want to	
11.	0	I am no more irritated by things than I ever was	
	1	I am slightly more irritated now than usual	
	2	I am quite annoyed or irritated a good deal of the time	√
	3	I feel irritated all the time	
12.	0	I have not lost interest in other people	
	1	I am less interested in other people than I used to be	√
	2	I have lost most of my interest in other people	

Contd...

Sl. no.	Score	Items	Patient score
	3	I have lost all of my interest in other people	
13.	0	I make decisions about as well as I ever could	
	1	I put off making decisions more than I used to	√
	2	I have greater difficulty in making decisions more than I used to	
	3	I cannot make decisions at all anymore	
14.	0	I do not feel that I look any worse than I used to	
	1	I am worried that I am looking old or unattractive	
	2	I feel there are permanent changes in my appearance that make me look unattractive	√
	3	I believe that I look ugly	
15.	0	I can work about as well as before	
	1	It takes an extra effort to get started at doing something	
	2	I have to push myself very hard to do anything	√
	3	I cannot do any work at all	
16.	0	I can sleep as well as usual	
	1	I do not sleep as well as I used to	
	2	I wake up 1–2 hours earlier than usual and find it hard to get back to sleep	√
	3	I wake up several hours earlier than I used to and cannot get back to sleep.	
17.	0	I do not get more tired than usual	
	1	I get tired more easily than I used to	
	2	I get tired from doing almost anything	√
	3	I am too tired to do anything	
18.	0	My appetite is no worse than usual	
	1	My appetite is not as good as it used to be	√
	2	My appetite is much worse now	
	3	I have no appetite at all anymore	
19.	0	I have not lost much weight, if any, lately	
	1	I have lost more than five pounds	√
	2	I have lost more than ten pounds	
	3	I have lost more than fifteen pounds	
20.	0	I am no more worried about my health than usual	
	1	I am worried about physical problems like aches, pains, upset stomach, or constipation	√
	2	I am very worried about physical problems and it is hard to think of much else	
	3	I am so worried about my physical problems that I cannot think of anything else	
21.	0	I have not noticed any recent change in my interest in sex	
	1	I am less interested in sex than I used to be	√
	2	I have almost no interest in sex	
	3	I have lost interest in sex completely	

Contd...

Interpreting the Beck Depression Inventory

- 1–10 These ups and downs are considered normal
- 11–16 Mild mood disturbance
- 17–20 Borderline clinical depression
- 21–30 Moderate depression
- 31–40 Severe depression
- Over 40 Extreme depression
- Total score is **35**
- Mr K is having Severe Depression.

General Physical Examination

- **General appearance:** He is moderately built, conscious, poor hygiene.
  - Height: 156 cm
  - Weight: 60 kg
  - Body mass index (BMI): 21
- **Vital signs:** Stable
  - Temperature : 98.6°F
  - Pulse : 80 beats/min
  - Respiration : 22 breaths/min
  - Blood pressure : 120/70 mm Hg
- **Head and scalp:** Size and shape of the head is normal. Baldness present, hair distribution is even, no palpable mass or tenderness; no scar or injuries present.
- **Eyes:** No pallor present, symmetrical in size and shape. Pupils equal, round and react to light. No infections or color changes observed.
- **Nose:** Nostrils patent; though labored breathing persists. Nasal flaring is present, frontal and maxillary sinuses nontender.

- **Ears:** Bilaterally equally placed. Pinna is soft and flexible. Auditory canal patent, no discharges observed.
- **Mouth and throat:** Lips are dry and patchy. Buccal mucosa pink and moist; teeth normally aligned; no missing teeth. Gum is pink and moist; uvular elevation normal and midline. Gag reflux present. Tongue midline and movements normal. Throat congestion is present. He is having hoarseness of voice.
- **Neck:** Trachea is in midline, nontender. ROM is of full range, strong. No palpable tender lymph nodes or masses. Thyroid is palpable; smooth and not enlarged. Carotid pulses present.
- **Anterior thorax:** Breathing movements bilaterally equal. No visible pulsations. Apical impulses are palpable. No tender lymph nodes to palpate. 80 heart sounds S1 and S2 heard; rate 70 beats/min; regular rate and rhythm. No murmurs, rubs or clicks.
- **Posterior thorax:** AP is less than transverse diameter; muscular development normal. No spinal abnormalities noticed; no increase in tactile fremitus. Lungs are resonant and clear throughout.
- **Abdomen:** No visible gastric pulsations. Rounded; bowel sounds present no tenderness or palpable mass, liver and spleen; nonpalpable, nontender. Femoral pulses feeble. Inguinal; femoral nodes tender as reported.
- **Upper and lower extremities:** Well developed; no muscle wasting. No edema injuries noted, ROM; full strength and possible in all directions. Pedal and radial pulses palpable equal bilaterally. Clubbing present.

Investigations

Sl. no.	Date	Investigation	Patient's value	Normal value	Remarks
1.		• Hemoglobin (Hb) • Total count (TC) • Platelet • Neutrophils • Lymphocyte • Basophil • Monocyte • Eosinophil	• 14% • 9000 cells/mm³ • 3 lakhs/mm³ • 48% • 35% • 02% • 05% • 10%	• 12–16 g/dL • 4–9000 cells/mm³ • 2.5–4.5 lakhs/ mm³ • 45–75% • 20–40% • 0.5–1% • 2–8% • 0–6%	• Normal • Normal • Normal • Normal • Normal • Normal • Normal • Normal
2.		• Glucose • Urea • Creatinine • Total bilirubin • Alkaline phosphatase • Serum glutamic-oxaloacetic transaminase (SGOT) • Serum glutamic pyruvic transaminase (SGPT) • Sodium • Potassium • Chloride	• 65 mg/dL • 19 mg/dL • 1.2 mg/dL • 0.2 mg/dL • 45 IU/mL • 27 IU/mL • 17 IU/mL • 134 mEq/L • 4.1 mEq/L • 104 mEq/L	• 60–100 mg/dL • 17–43 mg/dL • 0.6–1.4 mg/dL • 0.3–1.2 mg/dL • 40–129 IU/mL • 8–40 IU/mL • 6–40 IU/mL • 135–145 mEq/L • 3.5–5.4 mEq/L • 95–106 mEq/L	• Normal • Normal • Normal • Normal • Normal • Elevated • Normal • Decreased • Normal • Normal

Medications

Name of the drug	Dose/ frequency	Action	Side effects	Nurses' responsibility
Tab. Amitrip-tyline	150 mg/HS	Tricyclic antidepressants (TCAs) inhibit the reuptake of the neurotransmitters norepinephrine and serotonin, leading to an increase in their effects; anticholinergics at central nervous system (CNS) and peripheral receptors; sedative.	• **CNS:** Disturbed concentration, sedation and anticholinergic, confusion, hallucinations, disorientation tinnitus, altered electroencephalogram (EEG) • **CV:** Orthostatic hypotension, hypertension, syncope, tachycardia, chronic heart failure (CHF), cereberovascular accident (CVA) • **Endocrine:** Elevated or depressed blood sugar, elevated prolactin levels	• Restrict drug access for depressed and potentially suicidal patients. • Give intramuscular injection only when oral therapy is impossible. • Do not administer intravenous injection.

Contd...

Name of the drug	Dose/ frequency	Action	Side effects	Nurses' responsibility
			• **GI:** Dry mouth, constipation, paralytic ileus. • **GU:** Urinary retention, gynecomastia, testicular swelling; breast enlargement, menstrual irregularity and galactorrhea; increased or decreased libido; impotence. • **Hematologic:** Bone marrow depression, including agranulocytosis; eosinophilia, purpura, thrombocytopenia, leukopenia. **Hypersensitivity** • **Withdrawal:** Symptoms • **Other:** Nasal congestion, excessive appetite.	• Administer major portion of dose at bedtime if drowsiness, severe anticholinergics effects occur. • Reduce dosage if minor side effects develop; discontinue if serious side effects occur. • Arrange for CBC if patient develops fever, sore throat, or other sign of infection.
Tab. Chlor-promazine	200 mg/HS	Phenothiazines are thought to elicit their antipsychotic and antiemetic effects via interference with central dopaminergic pathways in the mesolimbic and medullary chemoreceptor trigger zone areas of the brain, respectively. Although often termed dopamine blockers, the exact mechanism of dopaminergic interference responsible for the drugs antipsychotic activity has not been determined.	• Tardive dyskinesia, extrapyramidal symptoms, anxiety, drowsiness, depression, hallucinations, anorexia. • Transient tachycardia, its effects on the ECG include prolongation of the PR and QT intervals, blunting of the T wave and depression of the S-T segment and postural hypotension. • Agranulocytosis, leukopenia, granulocytopenia, eosinophilia, thrombocytopenia, anemia, aplastic anemia, pancytopenia. • Lowered seizure threshold. • Increased prolactin secretion; gynecomastia, galactorrhea, mastalgia, altered libido, menstrual irregularities, weight gain, alterations in glucose tolerance and false positive pregnancy tests have occurred.	• Do not administer intra-arterially; arteriospasm or gangrene may result. • Give IM injections of undiluted drug deep into muscle mass, monitor injection sites. • Do not use solutions that are discolored or contain a precipitate. Protect drug from light, and refrigerate oral solution.

Nursing Management

Client Assessment

Pervasive low mood, poor appetite, decreased sleep, fearfulness, lack of interest in activities, decreased self-care and socially withdrawn, he is involved in alcohol consumption, not going to work, occasionally expresses death wishes for 2 months.

Diagnostic Studies

CBC is normal, elevated liver enzymes and decreased Sr. Sodium.

Nursing Priorities

- Promote physical safety with special focus on suicide prevention.
- Provide for client's basic needs, promoting highest possible level of independent functioning.
- Provide experience/interactions that enhance self-esteem, sense of personal power.
- Support client/family participation in follow-up care/community treatment.
- Provide information about condition, prognosis, and treatment needs.

Nursing Diagnosis

- Risk for violence, self-directed, related to depressed mood, feelings of worthlessness and hopelessness.
- Anxiety moderately related to disturbed thought processes, related to unconscious conflict about essential values/goals of life, and threat to self-concept.
- Social isolation related to preoccupation with thoughts as evidenced by withdrawn and less interaction with others.
- Knowledge deficit related to the electroconvulsive therapy (ECT).
- Deficient self-care related to disinterest or unconcern; lack of energy/inertia; psychomotor retardation.
- Disturbed sleep pattern related to biochemical alterations (decreased serotonin), unresolved fears and anxieties.

Nursing Care Plan

Assessment	Nursing diagnosis	Objectives	Nursing intervention	Implementation	Evaluation
Subjective data: • Patient says "I am not interested in anything." • Previous history of self-harm severe in intentionality and lethality.	Risk for violence, self-directed related to depressed mood, feelings of worthlessness and hopelessness.	Client verbalizes a decrease/ absence of suicidal ideas. State two reasons for not harming self.	• Identify degree of risk/ potential for suicide through direct questions • Re-evaluate potential for suicide periodically at key times. • Implement suicide precautions • Create a time-specific contract with client on what client and nurse will do to provide for client's safety • Provide close observation (1:1 or random checks every 10–15 minutes for most acute risk). • Check all items brought in to or by the client as indicated. • Maintain special care in administration of medications. • Administer medications as indicated, e.g., Selective serotonin reuptake inhibitors. • Prepare for/assist with ECT as indicated.	• Helped in expressing feeling of hopelessness and worthlessness • Maintained one to one observation and kept him near the nurses' station • Communicated suicide precautions and provided sense of protection. • Written contract is made that he won't hurt himself. • His mother and father stayed with him alternatively and nurses visited him one in every half an hour. • Harmful objects have been removed from the patient's room • Oral medications are administered and confirmed the intake of medicines by the patient. • Tab. AMN, 150 mg, HS administered • Patient had taken 1 ECT	He verbalized absence of self-harm, showed interest in activities as evidenced by the calm and relaxed look.
Subjective data: Patient says, "I am having fear and anxiety, I don't know how it occurs to me I fear for everybody." **Objective data:** He looks fearful, not interacting with others.	Anxiety moderate related to disturbed thought processes, related to unconscious conflict about essential values/goals of life, and threat to self-concept.	Verbalize awareness of feelings of anxiety, changes in thinking/ behavior. Identify ways to deal effectively with decision-making.	• Evaluate/re-evaluate level of anxiety. • Recognize and deal with own feelings in response to client's anxiety. • Listen nonjudgmentally to client's expressions; convey empathy; acknowledge or label feelings for client. • Use short, concrete communication. Assume calm, "in-control-of-things" manner. • Decrease environmental stimulation; remove to quiet area away from other clients. Suggest activity that may be relaxing. • Maintain a calm attitude and use physical touch, if acceptable to client. • Assist client to learn relaxation/imagery exercises. • Encourage participation in regular exercise program.	• He is having moderate level of anxiety. • Maintained the emotion diary. • Spent time while interacting with him, listening to his problems and concerns. • Provided appropriate explanations directly as required. • Stayed in a separate room and visitors were restricted. • Maintained a calm and gentle approach. • Provided large motor exercises for discharging pent-up tensions. • He is actively participating in group therapy and indoor games.	He understood his feelings and thinking and involved in relaxation activities.

Contd...

Assessment	Nursing diagnosis	Objectives	Nursing intervention	Implementation	Evaluation
			• Involve in group settings, encouraging and reinforcing appropriate participation. Redirect into activities. • Deal with physical complaints in matter-of-fact style.	Attention given to his physical problems.	
Objective data: • Not willing for ECT • Repeatedly asks doubts regarding ECT	Knowledge deficit related to ECT.	The client will be able to understand about ECT.	• Teach the client and family or significant others about symptoms of depression. • Teach the client and family about treatment of depression. • Inform the client and family about ECT, types and indications of ECT. • Teach client and family about preparation to be done before ECT. • Inform them about the procedure involved in ECT. • Teach the client and family members about the post ECT care and its complications. • Teach the client and family about medications must be taken regularly along with ECT. • Reinforce teaching with written material as indicated.	• Taught the client and family or significant others about symptoms of depression. • Taught them about the treatment for depression. • Informed the client and family about ECT, Types and Indication of ECT. • Taught the client and family about preparation to be done before ECT. • Informed them about the procedure involved in ECT. • Taught the client and family members about the post ECT care and its complications.	Client got adequate knowledge about the ECT.

Psychoeducation

Name of the patient: Mr K **Venue:** Male Psy. Ward

Topic: Care of patient undergoing ECT **Date:** ______________

Name of student teachers: **Time:** ______________

Language: English

Objectives

- **General objective:** At the end of the health education, the participants will be able to understand ECT.
- **Specific objectives:** At the end of the health education, the participants will be able to:
  - Define ECT
  - Mention the types of ECT
  - Explain the duration of ECT
  - List the side effects of ECT
  - Discuss the pre ECT care
  - Explain the care during ECT
  - Describe the post ECT care

Specific objectives	Time	Contents	Teaching and learning activities	Audio visual aids	Evaluation
At the end of the health education, the participants will be able to	1 minute	**Introduction:** Electroconvulsive therapy (ECT), or electroshock, is the most effective modern treatment for those with severe and persistent emotional disorders.	Discussion	Charts	What is ECT?
Define ECT	1 minute	**Definition:** Electroconvulsive therapy (ECT), also known as electroshock, is a well-established, psychiatric treatment in which seizures are electrically induced in anesthetized patients for therapeutic effect.	Lecture	Power-point presentation	
Mention the types of ECT	2 minutes	**Types of ECT** • Direct ECT • Modified ECT	Lecture	Power-point presentation	List the side effects of ECT
Explain the duration of ECT	1 minute	**Duration:** Treatments are usually given three times a week for 2–7 weeks. For a sustained recovery, weekly or biweekly continuation treatments are administered for several months. The duration of the treatment is similar to that of the psychotropic medications frequently used for the same conditions.	Lecture	Power-point presentation	
List the side effects of ECT	1 minute	**Risks/Side effects:** Transient confusion, headache, nausea, myalgia, retrograde and anterograde amnesia.	Lecture	Power-point presentation	
Discuss the pre ECT care	2 minutes	**Pre ECT care** • Educate the patient concerning the procedure and explain the patient about the necessary tasks associated with ECT. • Patient will not eat or drink anything after midnight the night before scheduled ECT. • Do not smoke in the morning of ECT. • Carefully follow doctor's instructions about which medications you should take, or not take, before treatments.	Lecture	Charts	
Explain the care during ECT	3 minutes	**During ECT** • Nurse will place a needle into a vein in your arm (IV). • Place sensors called electrodes on head • Wrap a blood pressure cuff around your arm, so that they can monitor your blood pressure during the procedure. • Give you oxygen through a mask or a tube • Doctor or nurse will inject you with a medication (such as methohexital or propofol) that will make you go to sleep for 5–10 minutes. When you are asleep, you will get another injection, of a muscle relaxant (succinylcholine). • Doctor will administer the ECT treatment.	Demonstration	Model	

Contd...

Specific objectives	Time	Contents	Teaching and learning activities	Audio visual aids	Evaluation
Describe the post ECT Care	2 minutes	**After ECT care** • Patient will be transferred to recovery unit • Doctor and nurses will check vital signs, oxygen saturation and ECG • They will check and maintain the airway. • Administer fluids per order • Position patient to maintain airway patency and comfort; groom as needed. • Maintain quiet environment, privacy, and side rails up. • Orient patient to person and place. • Administer supplemental oxygen per order and patient's oxygen saturation (SPO_2) levels. Document oxygen flow rate and SPO_2 levels. • Observe for and report cyanosis, perfuse dieresis, nausea/vomiting, delirium, psychomotor agitation, seizure activity, or other unexpected activity. **Conclusion** I hope, you have understood about the ECT and its care and will use these techniques effectively while caring your beloved ones.	Discussion cum demonstration	Model	Mention the post ECT care

Recording and Reporting

Date	Time	Nursing care/activities	Name with signature
	8:00 am	Assessment of the patient	Ms X
	8:50 am	Patient has taken breakfast (2 rotis with vegetable curry) and 1 cup tea	Ms X
	9:00 am	Administration of Oral Medication Tab. Chlorpromazine 200 mg, HS (one tablet before bed time at night) Tab. Amitriptyline 150 mg, HS (one tablet before bed time at night)	Ms X
		He has taken the medications and tolerated well.	
	9:15 am	He participated in exercise	Ms X
	10:00 am	He participated in group therapy, and interacted with the group members	Ms X
	10:35 am	Health education given to family members on "Care of patient undergoing ECT"	Ms X

CASE 3 PATIENT WITH BIPOLAR AFFECTIVE DISORDER *(Depression with Psychotic Symptoms)*

Mrs S, 24-year-old female, married, housewife, she completed higher secondary education, she is from middle socioeconomic status, got admitted in psychiatric emergency ward with the complaints of irrelevant talk, smiling to self, with crying spells, talking to self and hearing voices for two months. She also attempted to commit suicide by hanging herself. It is of high intentionality and lethality. She has significant neglect of self-care and decreased appetite and sleep. The symptoms are insidious onset and continuous course of illness. She was a known case of bipolar affective disorder (BPAD) past 7 years. Significant family history of mental illnesses in paternal uncle committed suicide and BPAD in second degree relatives. Normal birth and early development, she was temperamentally an easy child; she possessed only a few friends in his childhood. She was shy type and did not involve in any play activities. She started schooling at the age of four, not good in scholastic performances. No specific jobs held. Attained menarche at the age of 13 years, irregular and no reactions reported, arranged marriage with cordial relationship. Her premorbid personality shows that she was shy, anxious, would seek reassurance, sensitive to criticism, responsible, anxious avoidant personality, and fewer friends in school, closely attached with her mother. Mental Status Examination revealed that attention could be aroused, but difficult to sustain, tone, tempo of speech was decreased, depressed mood and range restricted. She hears voices which were derogating and criticized, she hears multiple voices, both genders, known people from objective space, all the times, second person auditory hallucination. Grossly oriented to time, place and person, judgment is impaired and insight is absent. On physical examination, inguino-femoral nodes tenderness reported and mild edema over the right wrist. Investigation shows elevated Triglycerides (511 mg/dL), Sr. Cholesterol (222 mg/dL) and very low density lipoprotein (102 mg/dL), Alk. Phosphatase (680 U/L), serum glutamic-oxaloacetic transaminase (41U/L), serum glutamic pyruvic transaminase (42U/L) chloride (109 mEq/L) and Thyroid test normal and normal blood sugar levels. She is on Tab. Flumod, OD, Tab. Nexipride 50 mg, BD, Tab. Topinol 100 mg, HS, Tab. Clopam, HS and Tab. Sebelium 5 mg, OD.

History Collection

Demographic Profile

Mrs S, 24-year-old female, married, she is housewife and completed Pre-University Course (PUC). She got admitted in Female psychiatric ward. She was diagnosed with bipolar affective disorder-depression with psychotic symptoms. The information was collected from patient's brother and husband given was adequate, reliable and relevant.

Chief Complaints for Seeking Admission

Smiling to self	2 months
Crying 2 months	
Talking to self	
Hearing voices	

History of Present Illness

Her illness was insidious onset and has continuous course of illness. She was apparently normal 7 years back then she had an episode characterized by smiling to self, irrelevant talking, crying, decreased self-care, decreased need for sleep, excessive grooming, disorganized behavior like putting nails on head. She also attempted to commit suicide by hanging herself. This is of high in intentionality and lethality. Her treatment was started 3 months back, later she gradually improved in 3–4 months. According to brother, there was 90% improvement. In 2015, after 2–3 months of childbirth, she tried to harm the baby and herself by cutting her throat; high intentionality and lethality, since then she has behavior of smiling to self, talking to self, irritability, periods of increased speech, increased level of energy, excessive grooming, decreased sleep and increased appetite, irritable mood, lasting for 7–10 days and periods of crying spells, talking, smiling to self, decreased speech, decreased self-care, decreased sleep and appetite, lasting for about 15–20 days. Mood is irritable, Deliberate self-harm (DSH) attempt about 3–4 months back. Her self-care is not adequate, has to be prompted. Sleep is decreased and appetite is increased. She also tends to wash her hands repeatedly, several times after touching anything, increases when periods of sad mood. She also hears abusive voices and threatening discussions about her among themselves. No history of physical illnesses.

Negative History

No thought alienation phenomenon, no history of grandiose ideas, substance abuse, organic causes like head injury, infections, convulsions.

Current Treatment History

- Tab. feno fibrate, 100 mg, OD
- Tab. quetiapine, 100 mg, HS
- Tab. lamotrigine, 50 mg, BD
- Tab. levosulpride, 50 mg, BD
- Tab. clonazepam, 1 mg, HS

Past History

Similar episode in the past. Seven years before information not available.

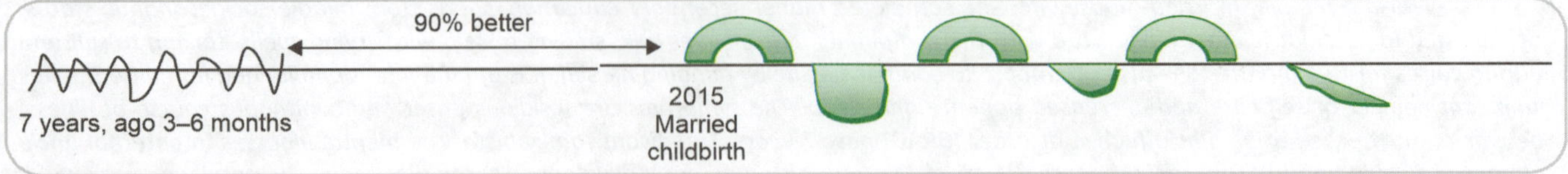

Family History

She is the first-born child, nonconsanguineous marriage, from middle socioeconomic status. Family history of mental illnesses in paternal uncle who died by committing suicide and presence of bipolar affective disorder (BPAD) in second degree relatives.

Genogram

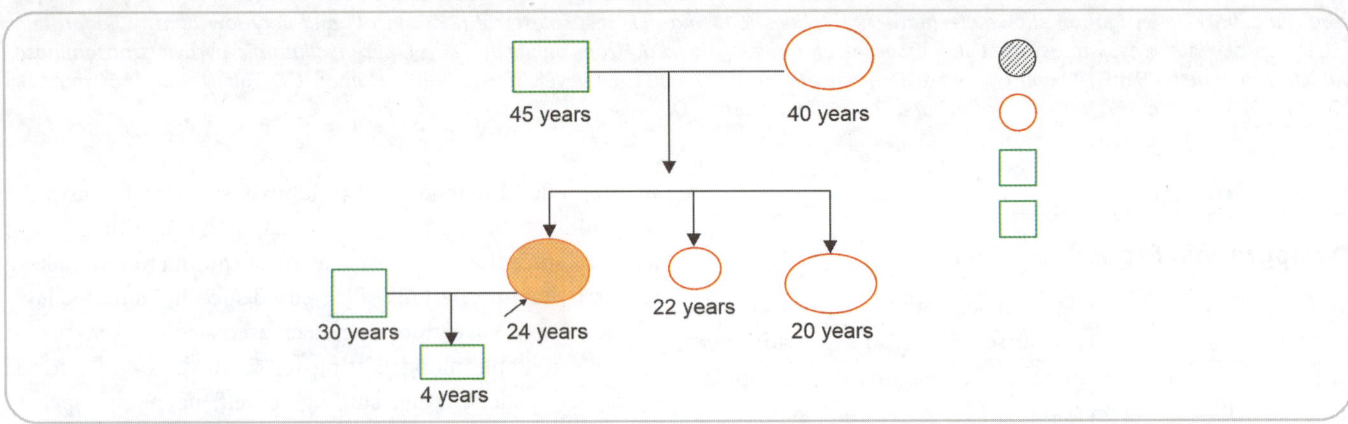

Personal History

- **Birth and early development:** She was reported to be born full term normal vaginal delivery which was conducted at hospital. No complications were reported during the periods of antenatal, intranatal and neonatal periods. Birth weight was reported to be normal. Baby cried soon after delivery and breastfeeding was initiated soon after delivery. Milestone development was reported to be normal.
- **Behavior during childhood:** She was temperamentally an easy child; she possessed only a few friends in her childhood. She was shy type and did not involve in any play activities. She was closely attached with family members. She was emotionally controlled and calm and quiet.
- **Physical illnesses:** No physical illness during childhood was reported.
- **Schooling:** She started schooling at the age of four, concentrated on her studies, few friends. Not good in scholastic performances. She studied up to Pre-University Course.
- **Occupation:** No specific jobs held.
- **Sexual and marital history:** Age at menarche was 13 years, irregular and no reactions reported. Married in 2004, arrange marriage with cordial relationship.
- **Substance use:** No substance abuse.

Premorbid Personality: Well Adjusted

- **Social relationships:** Shy type, anxious, would seek reassurance, sensitive to criticism, responsible, anxious, avoidant personality, and fewer friends in college, closely attached with her mother.
- **Intellectual activities:** Reading books. Not good in academic activities.
- **Mood:** Bright, calm and relaxed.
- **Character:** Attitude to work and responsibility; worried by responsibility, meticulous and methodical.
- **Interpersonal relationships:** Shy, few friends, no play in schools; performs household activities, concentrates on studies, emotionally controlled and quiet.
- **Energy and imitativeness:** Sluggish in doing household activities: would always insist on studying.
- **Fantasy life:** Not significant.
- **Habits:** Normal sleep and rest pattern and having regular bowel and bladder habits.

Mental Status Examination

- **General appearance and behavior:** She is ill kempt and not clean, establishes eye to eye contact, attention can be aroused, but difficult to sustain, establishes rapport, no tics and mannerism noted, no catatonic symptoms.
- **Psychomotor activity:** Psychomotor activities are observed as normal.
- **Speech:** She was replying to the questions alone. Reaction time is normal. Tone, tempo decreased, volume and reaction time are normal. Speech is relevant and coherent. Prosody was maintained throughout.
- **Thought:** No formal thought disorders elicited. She is having normal stream of thoughts. No flight of ideas, retardation in thinking, circumstantialities, or thought block. No thought interpolation.
- **Mood:** Subjectively: Patient says, "Sometimes good and sometimes bad." Objectively: Looks depressed, congruent to thought process, reaction present, range restricted.
- **Perception:** Hears voices which were derogating and criticized. Patient also at times commands her. Multiple voices, both gender, known people from objective space, all the times; second person auditory hallucination.

Cognitive Function

- **Orientation:** Grossly oriented to time, place and person.
- **Attention and concentration:** Attention can be aroused but concentration is not sustained.

  Digit span test:

  Digit forward test: 5 digits

  Digit backward test: 3 digits

  Serial subtraction till 43
- **Memory:** Immediate, recent and remote intact.
- **Intelligence:** Average, General information, Comprehension, Arithmetic ability, proverb and similarities concrete.
- **Judgment:** Impaired
- **Insight:** Insight is absent

General Physical Examination

- **General appearance:** She is moderately built, conscious, poor hygiene.
  - Height: 153 cm
  - Weight: 44 kg
  - Body mass index (BMI): 23
- **Vital signs:** Stable
  - Temperature : 98.2°F
  - Pulse : 90 beats/min
  - Respiration : 18 breaths/min
  - Blood pressure : 110/70 mm Hg
- **Head and scalp:** Size and shape of the head is normal. Hair distribution is even, no palpable mass or tenderness, no surgical scars or injuries noted.
- **Eyes:** Severe pallor present, symmetrical in size and shape. Pupils are equal, round and react to light. No infections or color changes observed.
- **Nose:** Nostrils patent; though labored breathing persists. Nasal flaring present, frontal and maxillary sinuses nontender.
- **Ears:** Ears bilaterally equally placed. Pinna soft and flexible. Auditory canal patent, no discharges observed.
- **Mouth:** Lips are dry and patchy. Buccal mucosa pink and moist; teeth normally aligned; no missing teeth. Gum; pink and moist; uvular elevation normal and midline. Gag reflux present. Tongue midline and movements normal.
- **Neck:** Trachea; midline, nontender. Range of Motion (ROM) full range, strong. No palpable tender lymph nodes or masses. Thyroid palpable; smooth and not enlarged. Carotid pulses present.
- **Thorax:**
  - **Anterior thorax:** Breathing movements bilaterally equal. No visible pulsations. Apical impulses are palpable. No tender lymph nodes to palpate. Heart sounds S_1 and S_2 heard; rate 82 beats/min; regular rate and rhythm. No murmurs, rubs or clicks.
  - **Posterior thorax:** Anteroposterior <transverse diameter; muscular development normal. No spinal abnormalities noticed; no increase in tactile fremitus. Lungs resonant and clear throughout.
- **Abdomen:** No visible gastric pulsations. Rounded; bowel sounds (+) no tenderness or palpable mass, liver and spleen; nonpalpable, nontender. Femoral pulses feeble. Inguino-femoral nodes tender as reported.
- **Upper and lower extremities:** Well developed; no muscle wasting. Contusions over the left upper arm near the elbow joint. Mild edema over the right wrist, range of motion: full strength and possible in all directions. Pedal and radial pulses palpable equal bilaterally.
- **Genitals and rectum:** Normal as reported; no examination done.

Investigations

Sl. no.	Date	Investigation	Patient's value	Normal value	Remarks
1.		• Fasting blood glucose • Post prandial blood glucose	• 77 mg/dL • 105 mg/dL	• 60–100 mg/dL • 100–160 mg/dL	• Normal • Normal
2.		• Triiodothyronine (T_3) • Thyroxine (T_4) • Thyroid Stimulating Hormone (TSH)	• 130 ng/dL • 6.54 µg/dL • 0.86 µ IU/mL	• 60–200 ng/dL • 4.5–12 µg/dL • 0.30–5.5	• Normal • Normal • Normal
3.		• Glucose • Urea • Creatinine • Triglycerides • Cholesterol • High-density lipoprotein (HDL) • Low-density lipoprotein (LDL) • Very low density lipoprotein (VLDL) • Total bilirubin • Alk. phosphatase • Serum glutamic-oxaloacetic transaminase (SGOT) • Serum glutamic pyruvic transaminase (SGPT) • Sodium • Potassium • Chloride	• 81 g/dL • 22 mg/dL • 0.7 mg/dL • 511 mg/dL • 222 mg/dL • 42 mg/dL • 79 mg/dL • 102 mg/dL • 0.2 mg/dL • 680 U/L • 41 U/L • 42 U/L • 138 mEq/L • 4.5 mEq/L • 109 mEq/L	• 60–100 g/dL • 14–40 mg/dL • 0.6–1.4 mg/dL • 50–150 mg/dL • 110–220 mg/dL • 40–60 mg/dL • 60–130 mg/dL • 10–40 mg/dL • 0.3–1.2 mg/dL • 40–129 U/L • 31 U/L • 39 U/L • 135–145 mEq/L • 3.5–5.2 mEq/L • 95–106 mEq/L	• Normal • Normal • Normal • Elevated • Elevated • Normal • Normal • Elevated • Normal • Elevated • Elevated • Elevated • Normal • Normal • Elevated

Medications

Name of the drug	Dose/ frequency	Action	Side effects	Nurses' responsibility
Tab. fenofibrate	100 mg 1-0-0	Inhibits triglyceride synthesis in the liver resulting in a reduction in very-low-density lipoprotein (VLDL) released into circulation; may also stimulate the breakdown of triglyceride-rich lipoproteins.	• **CV:** Angina, arrhythmias, swelling, phlebitis, thrombophlebitis. • **Dermatologic:** Rash, alopecia, dry skin, dry and brittle hair, pruritus, urticaria. • **GI:** Nausea, vomiting, diarrhea, dyspepsia, flatulence, bloating, stomatitis, gastritis, pancreatitis, peptic ulcer, GI hemorrhage. • **GU:** Impotence, decreased libido, dysuria, hematuria, proteinuria, decreased urine output. • **Hematologic:** Leukopenia, anemia, eosinophilia, increased alanine transaminase (ALT) and aspartate transaminase (AST), increased creatine phosphokinase (CPK). • **Other:** Myalgia, flulike syndromes, arthralgia, weight gain, polyphagia, increased perspiration, systemic lupus erythematosus, blurred vision, gynecomastia.	• Administer drug with meals. • Monitor patient carefully. • Ensure that patient continues strict dietary restrictions and exercise program. • Arrange for regular follow-up including blood tests for lipids, liver function, and CBC during long-term therapy. • Give frequent skin care to deal with rashes and dryness. • Monitor patient for muscle weakness, aches, especially if patient takes Tricor in combination with other cholesterol lowering drugs.

Contd...

Name of the drug	Dose/ frequency	Action	Side effects	Nurses' responsibility
Tab. quetiapine.	100 mg 0-0-3	Blocks dopamine and serotonin receptors in the brain; also acts as a receptor antagonist at histamine and adrenergic receptor sites.	• **Autonomic:** Dry mouth, salivation, nasal congestion, nausea, vomiting, anorexia, fever, pallor, flushed faces, sweating, constipation. • **CNS:** Drowsiness, insomnia, vertigo, headache, weakness, tremor, tardive dyskinesia, Neuroleptic malignant syndrome. • **CV:** Hypotension, orthostatic hypotension, syncope. • **Hematologic:** Increased alanine transaminase (ALT), total cholesterol and triglycerides. • **Other:** Risk of development of diabetes mellitus.	• Administer small quantity to any patient with suicidal ideation. • Monitor elderly patients for dehydration and institute remedial measures promptly; sedation and decreased sensation of thirst related to central nervous system (CNS) effects of drug can lead to severe dehydration. • Monitor patient closely in any setting that would promote overheating. • Regularly monitor patient for signs and symptoms of diabetes mellitus. • Consult physician about dosage reduction and use of Anticholinergic antiparkinsonians (controversial) if extrapyramidal effects occur.
Tab. lamotrigine	25 mg 2-0-4	It acts on sodium channels, inhibits voltage-sensitive sodium channels, thereby stabilizing neuronal membranes and consequently modulating presynaptic transmitter release of excitatory amino acids (for glutamate and aspartate).	Skin reactions, including Stevens-Johnson Syndrome and Toxic Epidermal Necrolysis. Headaches, dizziness and insomnia, acne and skin irritation, vivid dreams or nightmares, night sweats, body aches and cramps, muscle aches, dry mouth, mouth ulcers, damage to tooth enamel, fatigue, memory and cognitive problems, irritability, weight changes, hair loss, changes in libido, frequent urination, nausea, appetite changes.	• Assess for the side effects • Watch for skin rashes • Re-orient the patient • Provide oral care • Encourage to take nutritious diet. • Monitor weight regularly
Tab. levosulpride	50 mg 1-0-1	Antidopaminergic (Selective dopamine D_2 receptors) activity on both central and peripheral levels. It is an atypical Neuroleptic and a prokinetic agent.	• Amenorrhea, gynecomastia, galactorrhea, changes in libido. • Neuroleptic malignant syndrome.	• Regularly monitor patient for signs and symptoms of Neuroleptic symptoms. • Consult physician about dosage reduction and use of Anticholinergic antiparkinsonians (controversial) if extra pyramidal effects occur. • Reassurance about changes in the breast. • Monitor for side effects.
Tab. clonazepam benzodiazepine	1 mg 0-0-1	Benzodiazepines potentiate the effects of Gamma-aminobutyric acid (GABA), an inhibitory neurotransmitter.	• **CNS:** Sedation, depression, lethargy, apathy, fatigue, light-headedness, disorientation, anger, hostility, episodes of mania and hypomania, restlessness, delirium, headache, slurred speech, dysarthria, stupor, rigidity, tremor, dystonia, vertigo, euphoria, nervousness, difficulty in concentration, vivid dreams, psychomotor retardation, extrapyramidal symptoms; mild paradoxical excitatory reactions during first 2 weeks of treatment.	• Monitor addiction-prone patients carefully because of their predisposition to habituation and drug dependence.

Contd...

Name of the drug	Dose/ frequency	Action	Side effects	Nurses' responsibility
			• **CV:** Bradycardia, tachycardia, CV collapse, hypertension and hypotension, palpitations, edema. • **EENT:** Visual and auditory disturbances, diplopia, nystagmus. • **GI:** Constipation, diarrhea, dry mouth, salivation, hepatic dysfunction. • **GU:** Incontinence, urinary retention, changes in libido, menstrual irregularities. • **Hematologic:** Elevations of blood enzymes—lactate dehydrogenase (LDH), alkaline phosphatase, aspartate transaminase (AST); blood dyscrasias: agranulocytosis, Leukopenia. • **Other:** Hiccups, fever.	• Monitor liver function and blood counts periodically in patients on long-term therapy. • Taper dosage gradually after long-term therapy, especially in patients with epilepsy; substitute another antiepileptic. • Monitor patient for therapeutic drug levels: 20–80 ng/mL. • If the patient has epilepsy, arrange for patient to wear medical alert identification indicating the patient has epilepsy and is receiving drug therapy.

Nursing Management

Client Assessment

Mrs S, 24-year-old female, married, a housewife and completed Pre-University Course. Her illness was insidious onset and has continuous course of illness. She had an episode characterized by smiling to self, irrelevant talk, crying, decreased self-care, decreased need for sleep, excessive grooming, disorganized behavior like putting nails on head. She also attempted to commit suicide by hanging herself. It is of high in intentionality and lethality. She also hears voices abusive and threatening discussing about her among them. She was a known case of bipolar affective disorder for 7 years.

Diagnostic Studies

Elevated blood cholesterol levels and elevated liver enzymes.

Nursing Priorities

- Promote physical safety with special focus on suicide prevention.
- Provide for client's basic needs, promoting highest possible level of independent functioning.
- Support client/family participation in follow-up care/community treatment.

Nursign Diagnosis

- Altered thought process related to inability to think and process information.
- Risk for violence, self-directed related to lack of impulse control, self-destructive strategies as evidenced by severe depression and loss of interest to live.
- Social isolation related to preoccupation with thoughts as evidenced by withdrawn and less interaction with others.
- Ineffective therapeutic regimen management pattern of regulating and integrating into a daily living program for treatment of illness and the sequelae of illness that is unsatisfactory for meeting specific health goals.

Nursing Care Plan

Assessment	Nursing diagnosis	Objectives	Nursing intervention	Implementation	Evaluation
Objective data: • Nonreality-based thinking • Laughing to self • Talking to self • Hearing voices • Poor self-care	Altered thought process related to inability to think and process information	The client will be able to maintain normal thought process	• Do not make promises that you cannot keep. • Encourage the client to talk with you, but do not try only for information. • Explain procedures, and try to be sure the client understands the procedures before doing it. • Recognize the client's delusions as the client's perception of the environment. • Do not argue with the client or try to encourage nonverbal communication. • Interact with the client on the basis of real things; do not dwell on the delusional material. • Engage the client in one-to-one activities at first, then activities in small groups, and gradually activities in larger groups. • Show empathy regarding the client's feelings; reassure the client of your presence and acceptance.	• Did not make any promises to the patient. • Encouraged the client to talk with her thoughts. • Explained the procedures to the patient before doing it. • Recognized the client's delusions as the client's perception of the environment. • Did not make any argument to the patient. • Interaction made with the client on the basis of real things. • Engaged the client in one-to-one activities at first, then activities in groups slowly. • Showed empathy regarding the client's feelings; reassured the client.	She maintained normal thought process as evidenced by decreased hearing voices improved self-care.
Subjective data: patient says "I don't want to live." **Objective data:** • Self-destructive tendencies • Feelings of anger or hostility	Risk for violence, self-directed related to lack of impulse control, self-destructive strategies as evidenced by severe depression and loss of interest to live.	The client will not harm herself or others and identify alternative ways of dealing with stress and emotional problems.	• The client has one-to-one contact with a staff member at all times • Assess the client's suicidal potential, and evaluate the level of suicide precautions at least daily. • Do not argue with the client. • Ask the client if he or she has a plan for suicide. • The client's room should be near the nurse station and within view of the staff.	• Client was observed frequently every 15–20 minutes. • Client is not verbalizing about suicidal thoughts. • Accepted her and not involved in any arguments by staff and family members. • She is staying near to the nurse station. • Sharp objects, drugs and long clothes removed. • She was provided care based on her preference.	She was prevented from deliberate self-harm (DSH) and violence.

Contd...

Assessment	Nursing diagnosis	Objectives	Nursing intervention	Implementation	Evaluation
			• Be especially alert to sharp objects and other potentially dangerous items. • Involve the client as much as possible in planning his or her own treatment. • Be alert to the client's behaviors, especially decreased communication, conversations about death or the futility of life. • Observe, record, and report any changes in the client's mood.	• She communicated with her parents and staff. • Daily and shift wise record maintained regarding her mood.	
Subjective Data: patient says "My mother doesn't want me and I am alone." **Objective data:** • Inappropriate or inadequate emotional responses • Poor interpersonal relationships • Feeling threatened in social situations • Difficulty with verbal communication • No responses to stimuli	Social isolation related to preoccupation with thoughts as evidenced by; withdrawn and less interaction with others.	The client will be able to demonstrate appropriate emotional responses	• Provide attention in a sincere, interested manner. • Support any successes or responsibilities fulfilled, projects, interactions with staff members and other clients, and so forth. • Avoid trying to convince the client verbally of his own worth. • Teach the client social skills and demonstrate specific skills, such as eye contact, attentive listening, and so forth. • Help the client improve his grooming; assist, when necessary, in bathing, doing laundry, and so forth. • Help the client accept as much responsibility for personal grooming as she can (do not do something for the client that she can do alone).	• Provided attention to the client and spent more time with the patient. • Positive reinforcement given if she talks to others and performs activities of daily living • Taught the client social skills and demonstrated specific skills, such as eye contact, attentive listening, and so forth. • Helped the client in grooming, she takes bath on prompting. Kept her bed clean and tidy • She accepts responsibilities in taking food, medication and self-care.	Client is able to mingle with the other patients and to me by increased speaking and active participation in games.
Subjective data: patient says "I don't think I need to take the medications."	• Ineffective Therapeutic Regimen Management	The client will be able to take medications as given and establish an adequate balance of rest, sleep, and activity.	• Tell the client that the medications are a part of the treatment plan and you expect him or her to take them as prescribed. Check the client's mouth if necessary, after giving oral medications	• Encouraged the patient and family members to continue treatment. Medications were given on observation	Patient understood the importance of taking the medications and agreed to take it regularly.

Contd...

Assessment	Nursing diagnosis	Objectives	Nursing intervention	Implementation	Evaluation
Objective data: • Reluctance or refusal to take medications • Inability to carry out responsibilities at work, home, and so forth • Inadequate attention to need for nutrition, rest, or sleep • Inability to carry out activities of daily living	• Pattern of regulating and integrating into a daily living program for treatment of illness and the sequelae of illness that is unsatisfactory for meeting specific health goals.		• Be straightforward with the client when giving information about the medications, including the name desired effects • Observe the client's eating, drinking, and elimination patterns, and assist the client as necessary • Monitor the client's sleep patterns, and prepare him or her for bedtime by decreasing stimuli and administering comfort measures or medications • Assess and record the client's caffeine intake and limit it if necessary	• Information were given about the medications, including the name and desired effects • She takes regular meals but in smaller quantity, frequently drinks fluids and have regular elimination. • She sleeps 6 hours at night and 1 hour in the daytime.	

Psychoeducation

Name of the Patient: Mrs S

Topic: Suicide prevention

Name of student teachers: Ms X

Language: English

Venue: Female Psy. Ward

Date: ______________

Time: ______________

Objectives

- **General objective:** At the end of the health education, the participants will be able to understand suicide prevention and help to protect the patients from committing suicide.
- **Specific objectives:** At the end of the health education, the participants will be able to:
  - Define suicide.
  - List the causes of suicide.
  - Describe the preventions of suicide.

Specific objectives	Time	Contents	Teaching and learning activities	Audio visual aids	Evaluation
At the end of the health education, the participants will be able to.	2 minutes	**Introduction:** Suicide is a major public health concern. Suicide is a leading cause of death in India. Among 15–24-year-old 12.0 per 100,000 for females and 14.2 per 100,000 for males commit suicide. Suicide is complicated and tragic, but it is often preventable. Knowing the warning signs for suicide and how to get help can help save lives.	Discussion	Charts	Can you outline the basics of suicide?
Define suicide.	1 minute	**Definiton:** Suicide can be defined as the intentional taking of one's own life in a culturally nonendorsed manner	Lecture	Roller board	Explain the meaning of suicide?

Contd...

Specific objectives	Time	Contents	Teaching and learning activities	Audio visual aids	Evaluation
List the causes of suicide.	5 minutes	**Cause:** Genetic factors (18% in monozygotic twins); Biochemical factors (low levels of 5-HIAA); Physical factors (Patients with incurable or painful physical disorders, like cancer and AIDS); Social factors (a divorced male, who has no children and who lives alone); Psychological factors (failures in examination, failure in love, dowry difficulties, marital difficulties, illegitimate pregnancy, family dispute, loss of a loved object by death or others means, occupational and financial difficulties and social isolation).	Lecture	Handouts	What are the causes of suicide?
Describe the preventions of suicide.	10 minutes	**Prevention** **Risk identification** (Talking about wanting to die, feeling empty, hopeless, or having no reason to live, withdrawing from family and friends, making a plan or looking for a way to kill themselves, such as searching online, stockpiling pills, or buying a gun). **Five step action:** 1. **Ask:** "Are you thinking about killing yourself?" 2. **Keep them safe:** Reducing a suicidal person's access to highly lethal items or places is an important part of suicide prevention. 3. **Be there:** Listen carefully and learn what the individual is thinking and feeling. Findings suggest acknowledging and talking about suicide 4. **Help them connect:** Save the National Suicide Prevention Lifeline's number in your phone so it's there when you need it: 1-800-8255 (TALK). 5. **Stay Connected:** Staying in touch after a crisis or after being discharged from care can make a difference. **Conclusion:** People who want to kill themselves are only suicidal for a limited time, most suicides occur within about 3 months after the beginning of "improvement," hence, it is important to prevent suicide.	Discussion	Power-point presentation	How to prevent suicide?

Recording and Reporting

Date	Time	Nursing care/activities	Name with signature
	8:00 am	Assessment of the patient	Ms X
	8:50 am	Patient has taken breakfast (2 dosas with sambar) and 1 cup tea	Ms X
	9:00 am	• Administration of Oral Medication ▪ Tab. Fenofibrate, 100 mg ▪ Tab. Lamotrigine, 50 mg ▪ Tab. Levosulpride, 50 mg • She has taken the medications and tolerated well.	Ms X
	9:15 am	She went to occupation training unit	Ms X
	10:00 am	She participated in group therapy, she responded very minimally	Ms X
	10:35 am	Health education given to family members on "Prevention of Suicide"	Ms X

CASE 4 PATIENT WITH MULTIPLE SUBSTANCE USE DISORDER

Mr C, 19-year-old male, unmarried, residing in Bengaluru, working as a construction worker, studied up to 7th standard. Mr C is dependent to alcohol, nicotine and cannabis. He has symptoms of fearfulness, suspiciousness, fearfulness, reduced socialization, decreased sleep and appetite, attempted suicide, hearing voices of people saying that he will be killed when he goes out of the jail, for past 3.5 months. He has two similar episodes in the past. He is on Tab. Risperidone, Tab. Trihexyphenidyl (THP) and Cap. Fluoxetine.

History Collection

Demographic profile: Mr C, 19-year-old male, unmarried, residing in Bengaluru, working as a construction worker, studied up to 7th standard, admitted in male psychiatric ward with the diagnosis of multiple substance abuse disorders (Alcohol, cannabis and nicotine dependence syndrome). Source of information from patient, the information given was inadequate, not reliable.

Chief Complaints for Seeking Admission:

For 3.5 months:

- Fearfulness
- Suspiciousness
- Decreased socialization
- Decreased sleep and appetite
- Attempted suicide
- Sadness
- Hearing voices

History of Present Illness

His illness is of insidious onset and episodic course of illness. He was apparently normal 4 months back before he was brought to the prison, then he developed pervasive sadness, lack of interest in all activities, lack of energy, hearing voices for 3 months, sleeplessness, decreased appetite, voices of people telling that he will be killed when he goes out of the jail, when he see the prisoners talking he thinks they are talking about him, he made a suicidal attempt two days back, had two episodes in the past, one in 2015 in the prison (sadness, death wishes and decreased sleep) another episode one year back with increased talkativeness, irritable and thinking high about him. He had socio-occupational dysfunctioning and substance abuse disorders. He had legal issues for attempt to theft.

Negative History

No history of repeated intrusive thoughts, images, impulses or acts, organic causes like head injury, infections convulsions.

Current Treatment History

- Tab. Risperidone 8 mg HS
- Tab. Trihexyphenidyl 2 mg BD
- Cap. Fluoxetine 40 mg HS

Past History

Similar episodes in the past. Nicotine dependence syndrome for 6–7 years and cannabis dependence syndrome 3–4 years.

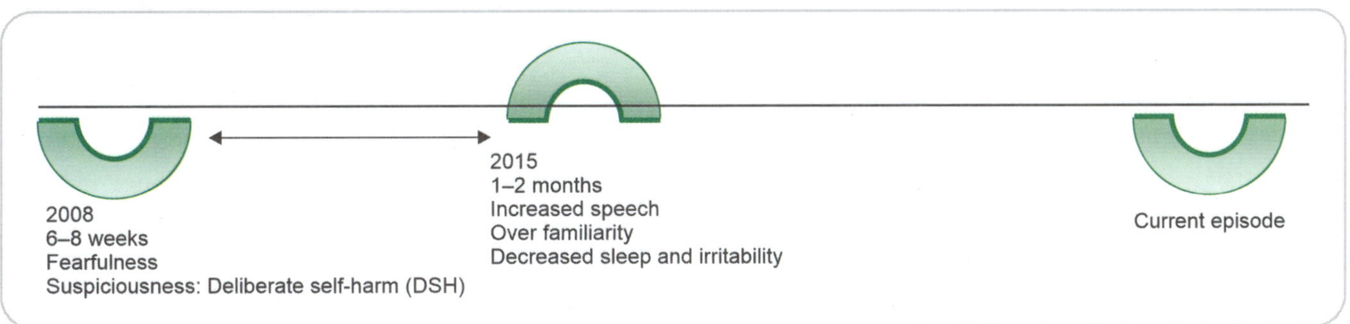

Family History

Nonconsanguineous marriage, he is from low socioeconomic status and family history of alcohol dependence syndrome (ADS) among 1st-degree relatives.

Genogram

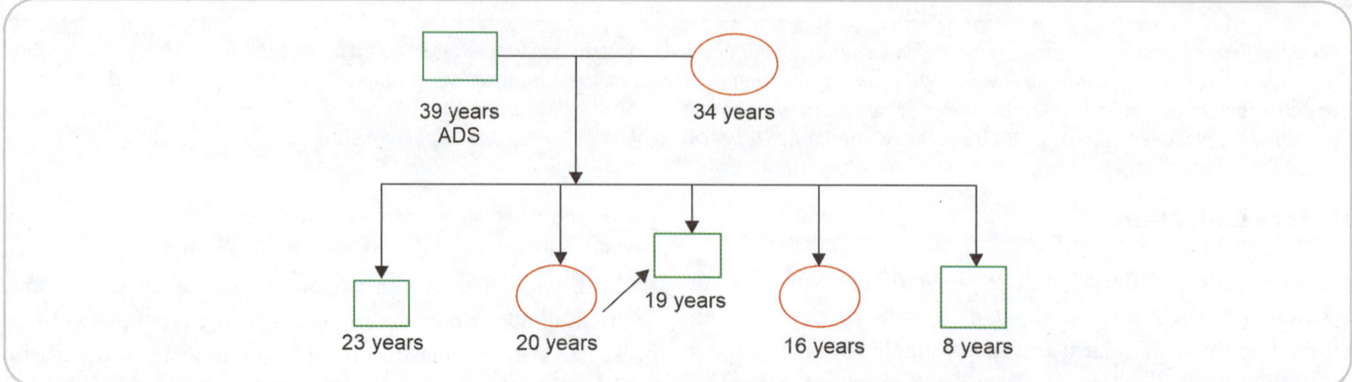

Personal History

- **Birth and early development:** He was reported to be born full term normal vaginal delivery which was conducted at hospital. No complications were reported during the periods of antenatal, intranatal and neonatal periods. Birth weight was reported to be normal. Baby cried soon after delivery and breastfeeding was initiated soon after delivery. Mile stone development was reported to be normal.
- **Behavior during childhood:** He was temperamentally an easy child; he possessed only a few friends in his childhood. He was shy type and did not involve in any play activities. He was closely attached with family members. He was emotionally controlled and calm and quiet.
- **Physical illnesses:** No physical illness during childhood was reported.
- **Schooling:** He started schooling at the age of five, concentrated on his studies, few friends. Not good in scholastic performances. He studied up to 7th standard. No specific jobs held.
- **Sexual and marital history:** Married but her wife separated reason not known.
- **Substance use:** He is a chronic alcoholic and smoker and occasionally uses cannabis.

Premorbid Personality—Dissocial

- **Social relationships:** Fewer friends in school, quarrelled with friends, not attached with parents.
- **Intellectual activities:** Reading books. Not good in academic activities.
- **Mood:** Dull, irritable and troubling.
- **Character:** Attitude to work and responsibility—worried by responsibility, meticulous and methodical.
- **Interpersonal relationships:** Shy, few friends, no play in schools; perform household activities, not concentrates on studies, emotionally uncontrolled and dissocial.
- **Energy and imitativeness:** Sluggish in doing household activities.
- **Fantasy life:** Not present.
- **Habits:** Normal sleep and rest pattern. He is having regular bowel and bladder elimination habits.

Mental Status Examination

- **General appearance and behavior:** He appears to be irritable, poorly kempt and poor hygiene. Not able to establish eye to eye contact, rapport not established.
- **Psychomotor activity:** Psychomotor activities observed as retarded.
- **Speech:** Speech is not spontaneous. Reaction time is increased. Tone, tempo, and volume are decreased. Speech is relevant and coherent. Prosody was maintained throughout.
- **Thought:** Possession of thought is normal; no repeated thoughts reported. Delusion of persecution presents—single, nonelaborative, nonsystematized—"people are planning to kill me once I am released from jail". Delusion of references—"people are talking about me". He is having depressive ideation, such as feeling of worthlessness, hopelessness and suicidal ideation present.
- **Mood:**
  - **Subjectively:** "I am sad".
  - **Objectively:** He looks depressed. Range restricted and reactivity absent, not congruent.
  - **Perception:** He hears voices of people discussing about him and they are threatening. Auditory hallucination presents.
- **Cognitive functions:**
  - **Orientation:** He is not oriented to time, place and person.
  - **Attention and concentration:** Poor attention and concentration.

    Digit span test:

    Digit forward test: 3 digits

    Digit backward test: 2 digits

    Serial subtraction for 50–3, completed till 31.

- **Memory:** Immediate, recent and remote intact.
- **Intelligence:** General information, comprehension, arithmetic ability and abstraction were intact.
- **Judgment:** Personal, social and test judgment are impaired.
- **Insight:** Awareness of being sick, insight is absent.

Psychometric Assessment

The Alcohol Use Disorders Identification Test (AUDIT)

1. **How often do you have a drink containing alcohol?**
   (0) Never
   (1) Monthly or less
   (2) 2–4 times a month
   (3) 2–3 times a week √
   (4) 4 or more times a week
2. **How many drinks containing alcohol do you have on a typical day when you are drinking?**
   (0) 1 or 2
   (1) 3 or 4 √
   (2) 5 or 6
   (3) 7, 8, or 9
   (4) 10 or more
3. **How often do you have six or more drinks on one occasion?**
   (0) Never
   (1) Less than monthly
   (2) Monthly √
   (3) Weekly
   (4) Daily or almost daily
4. **How often during the last year have you found that you were not able to stop drinking once you had started?**
   (0) Never
   (1) Less than monthly
   (2) Monthly √
   (3) Weekly
   (4) Daily or almost daily
5. **How often during the last year have you failed to do what was normally expected from you because of drinking?**
   (0) Never
   (1) Less than monthly
   (2) Monthly √
   (3) Weekly
   (4) Daily or almost daily
6. **How often during the last year have you been unable to remember what happened the night before because you had been drinking?**
   (0) Never
   (1) Less than monthly
   (2) Monthly
   (3) Weekly √
   (4) Daily or almost daily
7. **How often during the last year have you needed an alcoholic drink first thing in the morning to get yourself going after a night of heavy drinking?**
   (0) Never
   (1) Less than monthly
   (2) Monthly
   (3) Weekly √
   (4) Daily or almost daily
8. **How often during the last year have you had a feeling of guilt or remorse after drinking?**
   (0) Never
   (1) Less than monthly
   (2) Monthly
   (3) Weekly √
   (4) Daily or almost daily
9. **Have you or someone else been injured as a result of your drinking?**
   (0) No √
   (2) Yes, but not in the last year
   (4) Yes, during the last year
10. **Has a relative, friend, doctor, or another health professional expressed concern about your drinking or suggested you cut down?**
    (0) No
    (2) Yes, but not in the last year
    (4) Yes, during the last year √

Scoring

- A total score of less than 8: No harmful drinking behavior or alcohol dependence.
- A total score of 8 or more: Harmful drinking behavior.
- A score of 13 or more in women: Alcohol dependence.
- A score of 15 or more in men: Alcohol dependence.

Mr C scored: 23 (Alcohol dependence)

General Physical Examination

- **General appearance:** He is thin built, conscious, poor nutritional status, poor hygiene.
  - Height: 168 cm
  - Weight: 52 kg
  - Body mass index (BMI): 18
- **Vital signs:** His BP is low.
  - Temperature : 98.2°F
  - Pulse : 70 beats/min
  - Respiration : 20 breaths/min
  - Blood pressure : 90/70 mm Hg

- **Head and scalp:** Size and shape of the head is normal. Hair distribution is even, no palpable mass or tenderness; numerous wound scars seen.
- **Eyes:** No pallor present, symmetrical in size and shape. Pupils equal in round and reacting to light. No infections or color changes observed. Conjunctivitis is present.
- **Nose:** Nostrils patent; though labored breathing persists. Nasal flaring is present, frontal and maxillary sinuses—nontender.
- **Ears:** Ears are bilaterally equally placed. Pinna is soft and flexible. Auditory canal patent, no discharges observed.
- **Mouth and throat:** Lips are dry and patchy. Buccal mucosa pink and moist; teeth normally aligned; no missing teeth. Gum is pink and moist; uvular elevation normal and midline. Gag reflux is present. Tongue midline and movements normal. Throat congestion is present. He is having hoarseness of voice.
- **Neck:** Trachea is in midline, nontender. Range of motion is of full range, strong. No palpable tender lymph nodes or masses. Thyroid is palpable; smooth and not enlarged. Carotid pulses present.
- **Thorax:**
  - **Anterior thorax:** Breathing movements bilaterally equal. No visible pulsations. Apical impulses are palpable. No tender lymph nodes to palpate. Heart sounds S_1 and S_2 heard; rate 64 beats/min; regular rate and rhythm. No murmurs, rubs or clicks.
  - **Posterior thorax:** Anteroposterior diameter is less than transverse diameter; muscular development normal. No spinal abnormalities noticed; no increase in tactile fremitus. Lungs are resonant and clear throughout.
- **Abdomen:** No visible gastric pulsations, bowel sounds present, no tenderness or palpable mass, liver and spleen are nonpalpable, nontender. Femoral pulses are normal. No tenderness of inguinal and femoral nodes is reported.
- **Upper and lower extremities:** No muscle wasting, numerous wound scars present in the anterior aspect of forearms, no edema, injuries noted, range of motion; full strength and possible in all directions. Pedal and radial pulses are bilaterally palpable.
- **Genitals and rectum:** Normal as reported; no examination done.

Investigations

Sl. no.	Date	Investigation	Patient's value	Normal value	Remarks
1.		Hemoglobin	15.4%	12–16 g/dL	Normal
		Red blood cells (RBC)	4.38 cells/mm^3	1.5–4.5 lakh cells/mm^3	Normal
		Total count (TC)	7,700 cells/mm^3	4–9,000 cells/mm^3	Normal
		Platelet	2.33 lakhs/mm^3	2.5–4.5 lakhs/mm^3	Normal
		Neutrophils	70%	45–70%	Normal
		Lymphocytes	20%	20–40%	Normal
		Basophils	02%	0.5–1%	Normal
		Monocytes	05%	1–10%	Normal
		Eosinophils	10%	0–6%	Elevated
		Erythrocyte sedimentation rate (ESR)	10 mm/hr	0–20 mm/hr	Normal
		Postprandial blood glucose	110 mg/dL	80–140 mg/dL	Normal
		Glucose (random)	81 mg/dL	60–100 mg/dL	Normal
2.		Urea	13 mg/dL	17–43 mg/dL	Normal
		Creatinine	0.9 mg/dL	0.6–1.4 mg/dL	Normal
		Total bilirubin	1.1 mg/dL	0.3–1.2 mg/dL	Normal
		Alkaline phosphatase	84 IU/mL	40–129 IU/mL	Normal
		Serum glutamic-oxaloacetic transaminase (SGOT)	23 IU/mL	8–40 IU/mL	Elevated
		Serum glutamic pyruvic transaminase (SGPT)	78 IU/mL	6–40 IU/mL	Normal
		Sodium	130 mEq/L	135–145 mEq/L	Decreased
		Potassium	4.4 mEq/L	3.5–5.4 mEq/L	Normal
		Chloride	984 mEq/L	95–106 mEq/L	Normal

Medication

Name of the drug	Dose	Action	Side effects	Nurses' responsibility
Tab. Trihexyphenidyl	4 mg 0-0-2	Trihexyphenidyl blocks efferent impulses in parasympathetically innervated structures like smooth muscles (spasmolytics activity), salivary glands and eyes (mydriasis).	Tachycardia, confusion, agitation, euphoria, drowsiness, headache, dizziness, delusions, hallucinations, paranoia, dry skin, increased sensitivity to light, rash, constipation, xerostomia, dry throat, ileus, nausea, vomiting, urinary retention, blurred vision, increase in intraocular pressure.	• Give intramuscular injections deep into muscle • Do not administer subcutaneously; tissue necrosis may occur • Do not administer intra-arterially; arteriospasm and gangrene of the limb may result • If patient develops side effects, it should be reported • Take plenty of oral fluids
Tab. Risperidone	4 mg 0-0-2	It blocks postsynaptic mesolimbic dopaminergic D_1 and D_2 receptors in the brain; depresses the release of hypothalamic and hypophyseal hormones; believed to depress the reticular activating system, thus affecting basal metabolism, body temperature, wakefulness, vasomotor tone, and emesis.	• Cardiac: arrhythmias • Anticholinergic effects: (constipation, xerostomia, blurred vision, urinary retention); use with caution in patients with decreased gastrointestinal motility, paralytic ileus, urinary retention, BPH, xerostomia, or visual problems. • Blood dyscrasias • Extrapyramidal symptoms: pseudoparkinsonism, acute dystonic reactions, akathisia, and tardive dyskinesia. • Hepatic effects: hepatitis • Hyperprolactinemia • Hypotension • Neuroleptic malignant syndrome • Orthostatic hypotension • Sedation	• Monitor addiction, habituation and dependence • Monitor liver function • Monitor blood counts periodically in patients on long-term therapy • If serious effects, the drugs should be discontinued • Monitor temperature • Regular follow-up
Cap. Fluoxetine	20 mg 0-0-2	Selective serotonin reuptake inhibitors (SSRIs). Preventing the reuptake of one neurotransmitter, serotonin, by nerve cells after it has been released.	Changes in sex drive or ability; coma (loss of consciousness for a period of time); confusion; difficulty breathing or swallowing; dizziness; drowsiness; dry mouth; excessive sweating; fainting; fever; hives; joint pain; loss of appetite; nausea; nervousness; rapid, irregular, or pounding heartbeat; rash; seeing things or hearing voices that do not exist (hallucinating); seizures; sore throat; weakness; weight loss.	• Restrict drug access for depressed and potentially suicidal patients • Give intramuscular only when oral therapy is impossible • Do not administer intravenous injection • Administer major portion of dose at bedtime if drowsiness, severe anticholinergic effects occur. • Reduce dosage if minor side effects develop; discontinue if serious side effects occur. • Arrange for complete blood count (CBC) if patient develops fever, sore throat, or other sign of infection.

Nursing Management

Client Assessment

He is having pervasive sadness, lack of interest in all activities, lack of energy, hearing voices for 3 months, sleeplessness, decreased appetite, history of suicidal attempt two days back. He is separated from his wife. He has socio-occupational dysfunctioning and substance abuse disorders. He has legal issues for attempt theft.

Diagnostic Studies

Complete blood count and differential count are normal, renal function test found to be normal and elevated liver enzymes and decreased Sr. sodium are seen.

Nursing Priorities

- Provide support for decision to stop substance use/harm reduction.
- Strengthen individual coping skills.
- Facilitate learning of new ways to reduce anxiety.
- Promote family involvement in rehabilitation program.
- Facilitate family growth/development.
- Provide information about condition, prognosis, and treatment needs.

Nursing Diagnosis

- Ineffective denial related to weak, underdeveloped ego evidenced by "I don't have a problem with (substance). I can quit any time I want to."
- Ineffective coping related to inadequate coping skills and weak ego evidenced by use of substances as a coping mechanism.
- Altered thought process related to inability to think and process information and evaluate reality as evidenced by delusion of grandiosity and exaggerated responses.
- Deficient knowledge (effects of substance abuse on the body) related to denial of problems with substances evidenced by abuse of substances.
- Anxiety moderate related to unconscious conflict about essential values/goals of life, unmet needs and threat to self-concept.
- Disturbed sensory perception—auditory related to change in the amount or patterning of incoming stimuli accompanied by an exaggerated, distorted, or impaired response to such stimuli.
- Risk for violence, self-directed related to lack of impulse control, self-destructive strategies as evidenced by severe depression and loss of interest to live.

Nursing Care Plan

Assessment	Nursing diagnosis	Nursing objectives	Nursing interventions	Implementation	Evaluation
Subjective data: Patient says, "I can stop taking substance as my will, it is not a problem for me." **Objective data:** Dependence to substance is clear He is having physical problems of substance use Impaired judgment and insight were absent.	Ineffective denial related to weak, underdeveloped ego evidenced by "I don't have a problem with (substance). I can quit any time I want to".	The client will be able to accept that substance taking behavior is a maladaptive and decided to quit.	• Develop trust. • Convey an attitude of acceptance. • Ensure that client understands it is not the person but the behavior that is unacceptable. • Correct any misconceptions, such as "I don't have a drinking problem. I can quit any time I want to". • Be matter-of-fact, nonjudgmental manner. • Identify recent maladaptive behaviors or situations that have occurred in the client's life, and discuss how use of substances may be a contributing factor. • Do not allow client to rationalize or blame others for behaviors associated with substance use.	• Developed trusting relationship with the patient. • Accepted the patient as he is. • Made him aware that everyone like him but not his substance taking behavior. • Explained about facts about substance abuse. • Given care in a nonjudgmental manner. • Discussed the laboratory report with him and related that the abnormal finding is due to substance use. • Discouraged rationalizing behavior such as blaming others for his maladaptive behaviors associated with substance use.	Client demonstrated acceptance of substance use as maladaptive behavior as evidenced by he voluntarily participates in activities to quit substance use.

Contd...

Assessment	Nursing diagnosis	Nursing objectives	Nursing interventions	Implementation	Evaluation
Objective data: Believe that substance use is a normal behavior Inadequate retention and understanding of information presented.	Knowledge deficit related to the management of the substance use disorder (SUD) and impact of substance use.	The client will be able to understand about the illness, its chronic nature, impact of substance uses on health treatment, and safe use of medications.	• Teach the client and family about substance use disorder (SUD). • Teach the client and family about signs of relapse, such as substance taking behavior, insomnia, decreased nutrition, and poor personal hygiene. • Inform the client and family about psychopharmacology. • Inform about the impact of substance abuse on health. • Reinforce teaching with written material as indicated.	• Taught the client and family about meaning, causes, psychopathology and clinical presentation of SUD. • Taught the client about signs of relapse, such as insomnia, decreased nutrition, and poor personal hygiene. • Informed the client and family about psychopharmacology; dosage, need to take the medication only as prescribed, the toxic symptoms, the need to monitor blood levels, and regular intake. • Explanation given on the impact of SUD on physical health, psychological health, vocational and legal issues.	Client gained adequate knowledge about the disease process, medications and impact of SUD.
Subjective data: Patient says "I have lots of family problems and not getting any job". **Objective data:** He quarrels with parents and abusive and assaultive.	Ineffective coping related to inadequate coping skills and weak ego evidenced by use of substances as a coping mechanism.	Client will be able to develop effective coping skills an able to use to solve the daily stressors in life.	• Set limits on manipulative behavior. • Administer consequences when limits are violated. • Obtain routine drug screening for identifying substances. • Explore options available to assist with stress rather than resorting to substance use. • Teach problem solving techniques. • Give positive reinforcement for ability to delay gratification and respond to stress with adaptive coping strategies. • Teach about relaxation techniques.	• Identified manipulative behavior and advised his parent not to listen such behaviors. • Outing and watching TV was restricted for not crossing the limits. • Explored options available to assist with stress. • Taught about the steps in problem solving. • Positive reinforcement schedule was followed. • Involved him in Yoga, listening to music and participated in badminton.	Client developed effective coping skills and kept him away from substance use.

Psychoeducation

Name of the patient: Mr C
Topic: Ill effects of Alcoholism
Name of student teachers:
Language: English

Venue: Male psychiatric ward
Date: ____________________
Time: ____________________

Objectives

- **General objective:** At the end of the health education, the participants will be able to understand the ill effects of alcoholism.
- **Specific objectives:** At the end of the health education, the participants will be able to:
  - Define alcoholism.
  - List the causes of alcoholism.
  - Describe the various effects of alcoholism.
  - Explain the treatment for alcoholism.

Specific objectives	Time	Contents	Teaching and learning activities	Audiovisual aids	Evaluation
At the end of the health education, the participants will be able to:		**Introduction:** Alcohol exerts a depressant effect on the central nervous system, resulting in behavioral and mood changes. An individual is legally intoxicated with a blood alcohol level of 0.08–0.10%. Long-term and uncontrollable harmful consumption can cause alcohol-related disorders. It is estimated that about 62.5 million alcohol users.	Discussion	Charts	Can you give an outline about alcoholism?
Define alcoholism.	2 minutes	**Definition:** Alcoholism is defined as alcohol seeking and consumption behavior that is harmful.	Lecture	Roller chart	What is alcoholism?
List the causes of alcoholism.	10 minutes	**Causes:** Behavioral related to the internal feedback: Shame or hangover; external feedback: Reprimands, criticism, or encouragement. Other external factors: peer pressure, acceptance in a peer group. Specific moods (easygoing, relaxed, calm, sociable) that are related to the formation of intimate relationships. • **Environmental factors:** Severe childhood trauma, lack of peer and family support. • **Biological factors:** Repeated use of alcohol can impair the brain levels of a "pleasure" neurotransmitter called dopamine. Norepinephrine modulates reward dependence or the resistance to extinction of previously rewarded behavior. A high testosterone concentration during pregnancy may be a risk factor for the alcohol dependence syndrome in future. • **Genetic factors:** Alcoholism recognized to be run in the family. Sevenfold risk of alcoholism in first-degree relatives of alcohol-dependent individuals predominantly among males.	Lecture cum discussion	Handout	Mention the list of causes of alcoholism.

Contd...

Specific objectives	Time	Contents	Teaching and learning activities	Audiovisual aids	Evaluation
Describe the various effects of alcoholism.	10 minutes	**Effects of Alcohol:** • Peripheral neuropathy • Alcoholic myopathy • Wernicke's encephalopathy • Korsakoff's psychosis • Alcoholic cardiomyopathy • Esophagitis • Gastritis • Pancreatitis • Alcoholic hepatitis • Cirrhosis of the liver • Leukopenia • Thrombocytopenia • Sexual dysfunction • Alcohol intoxication • Socio-occupational dysfunction • Legal issues	Discussion cum brainstorming sessions	Flannel board	Describe the effects of alcoholism.
Explain the treatment for alcoholism.	8 minutes	**Treatment of Alcoholism:** Medication: Alcohol-sensitizing drugs (Disulfiram 125–500 mg) Cognitive and behavior therapies: • Relapse prevention • Social skills and assertiveness training • Contingency management • Deep muscle relaxation • Self-control training • Cognitive restructuring • Motivational Enhancement Therapy (MET) Teach more adaptive coping strategies alter to the conditions that precipitate and reinforce drinking • Self-help groups **Conclusion** I hope that you all understood alcoholism as a disorder, its causes and its effects, this discussion helps you to quit alcohol.	Lecture	PowerPoint Presentation	What is the treatment for alcoholism?

Recording and Reporting

Date	Time	Nursing care/activities	Name with signature
	8:00 am	Assessment of the patient	Mr X
	8:50 am	Patient has taken breakfast (2 *pooris* with *sambar*) and 1 cup tea	Mr X
	9:00 am	Administration of oral medication, Tab. Trihexyphenidyl 2 mg BD, he has taken the medications and tolerated well	Mr X
	9:15 am	He involved in playing badminton	Mr X
	10:00 am	He participated in group therapy, and actively participated	Mr X
	10:35 am	Health education given to patient and family members on "Impact of Alcoholism"	Mr X

CASE 5 PATIENT WITH UNDIFFERENTIATED SCHIZOPHRENIA

Ms K, 37-year-old female, unmarried, completed 9th standard, got admitted in female psychiatric ward with the complaints of muttering to self, laughing to self, irritability, crying spells with fearfulness, abusive toward neighbors and family members and tear newspaper, throw articles, says that bad smell from her body, complaints of obstruction in the throat, she is irritable at that time. She says that some people are trying to harm her. She hears voices abusive and threatening discussing about her among them. Her illness was insidious in onset and continuous course of illness. She was a known case of schizophrenia past 14 years. She is from low socioeconomic status and no significant family history of mental illnesses, normal birth and early development; she possessed only a few friends in her childhood. She did not involve in any play and group activities, not well in scholastic performances. Premorbid well adjusted. MSE reveals that she is irritable, moderately kempt not groomed, she is having blunted affect; range restricted, decreased reactivity, inappropriate and noncongruent mood, denies of any delusion, she has auditory and visual hallucination. Personal and social judgment was impaired and lacks insight. On physical examination, it was found that she had severe pallor and no other significant findings. Investigations done are Hemoglobin (8 g/dL), white blood cells (7,400 cells/mm^3) and platelet (2.88 lakh cells/mm^3). She is on medications such as Tab. Chlorpromazine 100 mg HS, Tab. Clozapine 25 mg OD, Tab. Trihexyphenidyl 2 mg OD and Inj. Fluphenazine 25 mg IM fortnightly.

History Collection

Demographic profile: Ms K, 37-year-old female, unmarried, unemployed, completed 9th standard, diagnosed as undifferentiated schizophrenia. The information given by patient and mother, it was adequate, reliable and relevant.

Chief Complaints for Seeking Admission

- Muttering to self
- Laughing to self
- Irritability
- Crying spells
- Abusive
- Fearfulness
- Delusion of persecution
- Third person hallucination
- Visual hallucination

} For 2 months

History of Present Illness

Her illness is of insidious onset and continuous course of illness. She was apparently normal 14 years back, then she developed muttering to self and laughing to self, she was irritable and abusive toward neighbors and family members, she occasionally expresses fearfulness without any cause, she is withdrawn, sit alone not interacting to the people previously she was over talkative, not performing the household activities, 1 week before she went away from home but brought back. Not sleep at night, again she tried to escape from home stopped food intake 3 days back, wake up at 2 am, puts all lights and take bath in the night. Tear newspaper, throw articles, says that bad smell from her body, complaints of obstruction in the throat, she is irritable at that time. She says that some people are trying to harm her. Hears voices abusive and threatening discussing about her among them. Currently she is having disorganized behavior. No history of physical illnesses.

Negative History

No history of grandiose ideas, over spending, elevated mood, increased activity, over religiosity, depression, repeated intrusive thoughts, images, impulses or acts, substance abuse, organic causes like head injury, infections, convulsions.

Current Treatment History

- Tab. Clozapine 125 mg 0-0-1
- Tab. Trihexyphenidyl 2 mg 1-0-0
- Inj. Fluphenazine 25 mg IM fortnightly

Past History

Similar episodes in the past.

Year	Signs and symptoms	Diagnosis	Treatment	Side effects/compliance
2005	Muttering to self, laughing to self, irritability, crying spells, abusive, fearfulness, delusion of persecution, third person hallucination, visual hallucination.	Psychosis NOS ↓ Paranoid schizophrenia	T. CPZ (Chlorpromazine) 400 mg + Inj. FFZ (Fluphenazine) 25 mg ↓ Tab. Risperidone 2 mg ↓ Tab. Olanzapine 10 mg ↓ Tab. Chlorpromazine 100 mg + Inj. Fluphenazine 25 mg ↓ Inj. Fluphenazine increased to 50 mg + Tab. Chlorpromazine 300 mg for disorganized behavior Tab. Chlorpromazine 600 mg	60% improvement Gastritis/poor. Developed increased weight gain and increased appetite/poor Similar complaints of symptoms masked face, constipation, tremor, slowness/poor.
2015	Similar complaints 6 months later developed amotivation, apathy, anhedonia, affect flattening.	Schizophrenia with negative symptoms	Tab. Clozapine 200 mg + Inj. FFZ 25 mg ↓ Stopped T. Clozapine T. Trihexyphenidyl 4 mg + Inj. Fluphenazine (Fluphenazine) 25 mg	Hypersalivation, drowsiness withdrawn/poor Dysphagia.

Family History

She is the second born child, nonconsanguineous marriage, from low socioeconomic status. No family history of mental illnesses.

Genogram

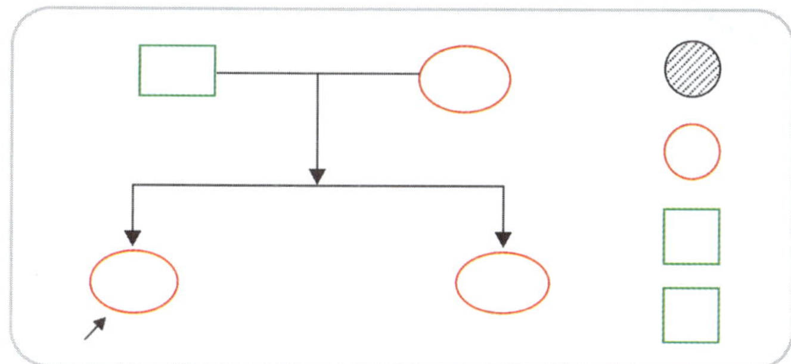

Personal History

- **Birth and early development:** She was reported to be born full term normal vaginal delivery which was conducted at hospital. No complications were reported during the periods of antenatal, intranatal and neonatal periods. Birth weight was reported to be normal. Baby cried soon after delivery and breastfeeding was initiated soon after delivery. Milestone development was reported to be normal.
- **Behavior during childhood:** She was temperamentally an easy child; she possessed only a few friends in her childhood. She was shy type and did not involve in any play activities. She was closely attached with family members. She was emotionally controlled, calm and quiet.
- **Physical illnesses:** No physical illness during childhood was reported.
- **Schooling:** She started schooling at the age of four, concentrated on her studies, few friends. Not good in scholastic performances. She studied up to 9th standard. Occupation: No specific jobs held.
- **Sexual and marital history:** Age at menarche was 13 years, regular and no reactions reported. She is unmarried.
- **Substance use:** No substance abuse.

Premorbid Personality—Well Adjusted

- **Social relationships:** She had fewer friends in college, closely with her mother.
- **Intellectual activities:** She spent times in reading books. Not good in academic activities.
- **Mood:** She was bright, calm and relaxed.
- **Character:** She is worried of responsibility, meticulous and methodical.
- **Interpersonal relationships:** She is shy, has few friends, she is emotionally controlled and quiet.

- **Energy and imitativeness:** Sluggish in doing household activities.
- **Fantasy life:** Wants to become IAS officer.
- **Habits:** She is having normal sleep and rest pattern. She is having regular bowel and bladder habits.

Mental Status Examination

- **General appearance and behavior:** She looks irritable, moderately kempt, not groomed. Not able to establish eye to eye contact, she is cooperative, rapport established.
- **Psychomotor activity:** Psychomotor activities observed as normal.
- **Speech:** She only responds to the questions. Reaction time is normal. Tone, tempo, and volume are normal. Speech is relevant and coherent. Prosody was maintained throughout.
- **Thought:** No formal thought disorders elicited. No flight of ideas, retardation in thinking, circumstantiality, or thought block. Possession normal; no repeated thoughts reported. Denies delusion predominantly occupied by thoughts of obstruction in throat. No thought interpolation and no obsession.
- **Mood:** Subjectively: "I am OK". Objectively: Blunted affect; range restricted, decreased reactivity, inappropriate and congruent.
- **Perception:** Patient denies hallucination? Olfactory hallucination.
- **Cognitive functions:**
    - **Orientation:** Grossly oriented to time, place and person.
    - **Attention and concentration:** Attention can be aroused, but concentration is not sustained.
    - Digit span test:
    - Digit forward test: 4 digits
    - Digit backward test: 4 digits
    - Serial subtraction till 31.
    - **Memory:** Immediate, recent and remote intact.
    - **Intelligence:** General information, comprehension, arithmetic ability, and abstraction were intact.
    - **Judgment:** Personal, social and test judgment are normal.
    - **Insight:** Insight is absent.

Psychometric Assessment

Indian Disability Evaluation and Assessment Scale (IDEAS)

Items:

- **Self-care:** Includes taking care of body hygiene, grooming, health including bathing, toileting, and dressing, eating, and taking care of one's health.
- **Interpersonal activities (social relationships):** Include initiating and maintaining interactions with others in contextual and socially appropriate manner.
- **Communication and understanding:** Include communication and conversation with others by producing and comprehending spoken/written/nonverbal messages.
- **Work:** Three areas are Employment/Housework/ Education. Measures on any aspect.
    1. **Performing in work/job:** Performing in work/ employment (paid) employment/self-employment/ family concern or otherwise. Measures ability to perform tasks at employment completely and efficiently and in proper time includes seeking employment.
    2. **Performing in housework:** Maintaining household including cooking, caring for other people at home, taking care of belongings, etc. Measures ability to take responsibility for and perform household tasks completely and efficiently and in proper time.
    3. **Performing in school/college:** Measures performance education-related tasks.

Scores for Each Item

Items	0 No disability	1 Mild disability	2 Moderate disability	3 Severe disability	4 Profound disability
Self-care			√		
Inter-personal activities				√	
Communi-cation and under-standing				√	
Work					√

- 0: No disability (none, absent, negligible **Scores for Each Item**
- 1: Mild disability (slight, low)
- 2: Moderate disability (medium, fair)
- 3: Severe disability (high, extreme)
- 4: Profound disability (total, cannot do)

Total score: 12

Add scores of the four items and obtain a total score.

Weightage for duration of illness (DOI): **15 years of illness**

- <2 years : score to be added is 1
- 2–5 years : add 2
- 6–10 years : add 3
- >10 years : add 4

Global disability: Total disability score + Duration of illness (DOI): score = Global disability score percentages: **12 + 4 = 16**

- 0 : No disability = 0%
- 1–6 : Mild disability = <40%
- 7–13 : Moderate disability = 40–70%
- 14–19 : Severe disability = 71–99%
- 20 : Profound disability = 100%

Inference: Ms K is having severe disability

General Physical Examination

- **General appearance:** She is moderately built, conscious, poor hygiene.
  - Height : 146 cm
  - Weight : 50 kg
  - Body mass index (BMI): 23
- **Vital signs:** It is stable
  - Temperature : 99°F
  - Pulse : 86 beats/min
  - Respiration : 20 breaths/min
  - Blood pressure : 120/80 mm Hg
- **Head and scalp:** Size and shape of the head is normal. Hair distribution is even, no palpable mass or tenderness, no surgical scars or injuries noted.
- **Eyes:** Symmetrical in size and shape. Pupils equal in round and reacting to light. No infections, no pallor, or color changes observed.
- **Nose:** Nostrils patent; though labored breathing persists. Nasal flaring is present, frontal and maxillary sinuses—nontender.
- **Ears:** Ears bilaterally equally placed. Pinna is soft and flexible. Auditory canal patent, no discharges observed.
- **Mouth:** Lips are dry and patchy. Buccal mucosa pink and moist; teeth normally aligned; no missing teeth. Gum appears to be pink and moist; uvular elevation normal and midline. Gag reflux is present. Tongue midline and movements normal.
- **Neck:** Trachea is in midline, nontender. Range of motion is in full range, no palpable tender lymph nodes or masses. Thyroid gland is not palpable, carotid pulse is felt.
- **Thorax:**
  - **Anterior thorax:** Breathing movements bilaterally equal. No visible pulsations. Apical impulses are palpable. No tender lymph nodes to palpate. Heart sounds S_1 and S_2 heard; rate 86 beats/min; regular rate and rhythm. No murmurs, rubs or clicks.
  - **Posterior thorax:** Anteroposterior < transverse diameter; muscular development normal. No spinal abnormalities noticed; no increase in tactile fremitus. Lungs are resonant and clear throughout.
- **Abdomen:** No visible gastric pulsations, bowel sounds heard, no tenderness or palpable mass, liver and spleen are not palpable and nontender.
- **Upper and lower extremities:** Well, developed; no muscle wasting. Mild swelling was present over the right wrist, Range of motion is on full strength and possible in all directions. Pedal and radial pulses on both sides were palpable.
- **Genitals and rectum:** Normal as reported; no examination done.

Investigation

Sl. no.	Date	Investigation	Patient's value	Normal value	Remarks
1.		Hemoglobin Total count Platelet	14% 7,400 cells/mm³ 2.88 lakhs/mm³	12–16 g/dL 4–9,000 cells/mm³ 2.5–4.5 lakhs/mm³	Normal Normal Normal

Medication

Name of the drug	Dose	Action	Side effects	Nurses' responsibility
Tab. clozapine	125 mg 0-0-1	It blocks receptors in the brain for several neurotransmitters, including dopamine type 4 receptors, serotonin type 2 receptors, norepinephrine receptors, acetylcholine receptors, and histamine receptors.	Agranulocytosis, infections, seizures, dizziness, orthostatic hypotension, drowsiness. Increased heart rate, increased salivation, headache, tremor, low blood pressure, and fever. Blurred vision and difficulty urinating, constipation, paralytic ileus	• Assess for any allergy, CNS depression and CV disease • Monitor Electrocardiogram, Blood pressure, renal function and liver function. • Regularly check WBCs count and temperature • Report lethargy, fever, sore throat, oral ulcer, etc.

Contd...

Name of the drug	Dose	Action	Side effects	Nurses' responsibility
Inj. fluphenazine	50 mg 1-0-0	It blocks postsynaptic mesolimbic dopaminergic D_1 and D_2 receptors in the brain; depresses the release of hypothalamic and hypophyseal hormones; believed to depress the reticular activating system, thus affecting basal metabolism, body temperature, wakefulness, vasomotor tone, and emesis.	• Altered cardiac conduction, arrhythmias; • Anticholinergic effects: (constipation, xerostomia, blurred vision, urinary retention); use with caution in patients with decreased gastrointestinal motility, paralytic ileus, urinary retention, BPH, xerostomia, or visual problems. • Blood dyscrasias • Esophageal dysmotility/aspiration use with caution in patients at risk of pneumonia (i.e., Alzheimer's disease).	• Monitor and report neuroleptic malignant syndrome • Monitor signs of agranulocytosis • Assess motor function and check for extra-pyramidal symptoms • Monitor allergic reactions • Check blood pressure for hypotension • Assess heart rate and electrocardiogram • Frequently check for weight gain • Protect against fall and trauma.
			• **Extrapyramidal symptoms:** Including pseudoparkinsonism, acute dystonic reactions, akathisia, and tardive dyskinesia. • **Hepatic effects:** Hepatitis • Hyperprolactinemia • **Neuroleptic malignant syndrome (NMS):** Mental status changes, fever, muscle rigidity, and/or autonomic instability. • **Ocular effects:** May cause pigmentary retinopathy, and lenticular and corneal deposits. • Orthostatic hypotension • **Sedation:** Impaired core body temperature regulation.	
Tab. trihexyphenidyl	2 mg 1-0-0	The exact mechanism of action in parkinsonian syndromes is not precisely understood, but it is known that trihexyphenidyl blocks efferent impulses in parasympathetically innervated structures like smooth muscles (spasmolytic activity), salivary glands and eyes (mydriasis).	• Frequency not defined. • **Cardiovascular:** Tachycardia; central nervous system: confusion, agitation, euphoria, drowsiness, headache, dizziness, nervousness, delusions, hallucinations, paranoia. • **Dermatologic:** Dry skin, increased sensitivity to light, rash. • **Gastrointestinal:** Constipation, xerostomia, dry throat, ileus, nausea, vomiting, parotitis. • **Genitourinary:** Urinary retention • **Neuromuscular and skeletal:** Weakness • **Ocular:** Blurred vision, mydriasis, increase in intraocular pressure, glaucoma, blindness (long-term use in narrow-angle glaucoma). • **Respiratory:** Dry nose • **Miscellaneous:** Diaphoresis (decreased).	• Assess for contraindication • Perform thorough physical examination. • Monitor Electrocardiogram and renal functions • Administer drug along with meals. • Provide safety measures to prevent injuries.

Nursing Management

Client Assessment

She is having muttering to self and laughing to self, she was irritable and abusive toward neighbors and family members; she is withdrawn, and having wandering behavior. Lack of sleep at night, hears voices abusive and threatening discussing about her among them. She is having disorganized behavior.

Diagnostic Studies

Blood test values are within normal range.

Nursing Priorities

- Provide for client's basic needs, promoting highest possible level of independent functioning.
- Support client/family participation in follow-up care/community treatment.
- Provide information about condition, prognosis, and treatment needs.

Nursing Diagnosis

- Disturbed thought processes related to disruption in cognitive operations and activities.
- Disturbed sensory perception—auditory related to change in the amount or patterning of incoming stimuli accompanied by an exaggerated, distorted, or impaired response to such stimuli.
- Impaired social interaction related to aloneness experienced by the individual and perceived as imposed by others and as a negative or threatening state.
- Deficient knowledge related to deficiency of cognitive information related to a specific topic.

Nursing Care Plan

Assessment	Nursing diagnosis	Nursing objectives	Nursing interventions	Implementation	Evaluation
Subjective data: Client says "Some people near to her tries to kill her". **Objective data:** She is abusive toward her neighbors, looks fearful and having crying spells.	Disturbed thought process related to disruption in cognitive operations and activities.	Client will be able to maintain normal thought process.	• Be sincere and honest when communicating with the client. Avoid vague or evasive remarks. • Be consistent in setting expectations, enforcing rules, and so forth. • Do not make promises that you cannot keep. • Encourage the client to talk with you, but do not pry for information. • Explain procedures, and try to be sure the client understands the procedures before carrying them out. • Give positive feedback for the client's successes. • Recognize the client's delusions as the client's perception of the environment. • Initially, do not argue with the client or try to convince the client that the delusions are false or unreal. • Interact with the client on the basis of real things; do not dwell on the delusional material.	• Maintained honest communication with her and talked with purpose. • Consistency was maintained in ward routine, rules and regulation. • Not given false assurance. • Collection information about her abnormal thoughts only once and never discussed about it later. • Explanation was given during medication administration. • Positive reinforcement given as she was involved in self-care. • Informed that delusions were her own, not really it exists. • Not involved in arguments regarding her delusional thinking. • Involved in interactions with her other that about her delusions.	She maintained normal thought process as evidenced by reduction in fear and crying spells.

Contd...

Assessment	Nursing diagnosis	Nursing objectives	Nursing interventions	Implementation	Evaluation
			• Engage the client in one-to-one activities at first, then activities in small groups, and gradually activities in larger groups. • Show empathy regarding the client's feelings; reassure the client of your presence and acceptance. • Never convey to the client that you accept the delusions as reality • Administer antipsychotics as prescribed.	• She was involved in indoor games and group therapy. • Conveyed acceptance of the clients. • She is on Tab. clozapine 125 mg HS and Inj. fluphenazine 25 mg IM fortnightly.	
Subjective data: Client says "She hears voices that are abusive and threatening her". **Objective data:** Hallucinatory behavior like talking to self and gesturing Listening intently to no apparent stimuli Feelings of insecurity and confusion.	Disturbed sensory perception—auditory related to neurochemical imbalances in brain accompanied by an exaggerated, distorted, or impaired response to such stimuli.	Client will be able to demonstrate decreased hallucinations Interact with others in the external environment.	• Be aware of all surrounding stimuli, including sounds from other rooms (such as television or stereo in adjacent areas). • Try to decrease stimuli or move the client to another area. • Avoid conveying to the client the belief that hallucinations are real. Do not converse with the "voices" or otherwise reinforce the client's belief in the hallucinations as reality. • Explore the content of the client's hallucinations during the initial assessment to determine what kind of stimuli the client is receiving, but do not reinforce the hallucinations as real. You might say, "I don't hear any voices-what are you hearing?" • Use concrete, specific verbal communication with the client. • Avoid gestures, abstract ideas, avoid asking the client to make choices. Don't ask "Would you like to talk or be alone?" Rather, suggest that the client talk with you. • Respond verbally and reinforce the client's conversation when he or she refers to reality.	• Made her aware about her environment. • She is placed in separate room and visitors are limited. • Client was informed that only she hears the voices and others were not hearing such voices. • Details about the hallucination were collected only during the initial assessment. • Interacted with the client on purpose. • Spoken to her in simple and in local language. • Positive reinforcement given when she speaks about herself and family. • Involved her in watching TV. • She was involved in painting.	She demonstrated normal perceptual functioning and she interact well with others.

Contd...

Assessment	Nursing diagnosis	Nursing objectives	Nursing interventions	Implementation	Evaluation
			• If the client appears to be hallucinating, attempt to engage the client's in conversation or a concrete activity. • Provide simple activities that the client can realistically accomplish (such as uncomplicated craft projects).		
Objective data: Poor interpersonal relationships, sits alone, and has difficulty with verbal communication.	Impaired social interaction related to aloneness experienced by the individual and perceived as imposed by others and as a negative or threatening state.	Client will be able to report increased feelings of self-worth, identify strengths and assets Engage in social interaction.	• Provide attention in a sincere, interested manner. • Support any successes or responsibilities fulfilled, projects, interactions with staff members and other clients, and so forth. • Avoid trying to convince the client verbally of her own worth. • Teach the client about communication skills. • Teach the client social skills. Describe and demonstrate specific skills, such as eye contact, attentive listening, and so forth. Discuss the types of topics that are appropriate for casual social conversation, such as the weather, local events, and so forth. • Help the client improve his or her grooming; assist when necessary, in bathing, doing laundry, and so forth.	• Actively listen to her problems and helped her in fulfilling her daily needs. • Appreciated her for a small conversation with family member, staffs and other patients. • Demonstrated her about the communication skills. • Client was actively participating in social skills training program. • Client was encouraged to have a one to interaction. • Client was instructed to do daily bathing, grooming and wear clean clothes.	She developed sense of self-concept and interacts with others.

Psychoeducation

Name of the patient: Ms K

Topic: Prevention of side effects of antipsychotics

Name of student teachers:

Language: English

Venue: Female psychiatric ward

Date: ____________________

Time: ____________________

Objectives

- **General objective:** At the end of the health education, the participants will be able to understand the prevention of side effects of antipsychotics.
- **Specific objectives:** At the end of the health education, the participants will be able to:
  - Define antipsychotics.

- List the common antipsychotics.
- Describe the side effects and its prevention.

<table>
<tr><th>Specific objectives</th><th>Time</th><th>Contents</th><th>Teaching and learning activities</th><th>Audiovisual aids</th><th>Evaluation</th></tr>
<tr><td>At the end of the health education, the participants will be able to:</td><td>2 minutes</td><td>Introduction: An antipsychotic (or neuroleptic) is a psychiatric medication primarily used to manage psychosis (e.g., delusions or hallucinations), particularly in schizophrenia and bipolar disorder.</td><td>Discussion</td><td>Charts</td><td>Can you outline the basics of anti-psychotics?</td></tr>
<tr><td>Define antipsychotics.</td><td>2 minutes</td><td>Definition: All antipsychotic drugs tend to block D_2 receptors in the dopamine pathways of the brain. It is the blockade of dopamine receptors in this pathway that is thought to control psychotic experiences.</td><td>Lecture</td><td>Roller board</td><td>What is antipsychotics?</td></tr>
<tr><td>List the common antipsychotics.</td><td>6 minutes</td><td>List of common antipsychotics:
• Chlorpromazine (Largactil, Thorazine)
• Trifluoperazine (Stelazine)
• Haloperidol (Haldol, Serenace)
• Fluphenazine (Prolixin)
• Clozapine (Clozaril)
• Olanzapine (Zyprexa)
• Quetiapine (Seroquel)</td><td>Discussion</td><td>Handout</td><td>List two antipsychotics.</td></tr>
<tr><td>Describe the side effects and its prevention.</td><td>20 minutes</td><td>Prevention of side effects:
<table>
<tr><th>Side effects</th><th>Preventive measures</th></tr>
<tr><td>Dystonic reactions</td><td>Administer medications as ordered for effectiveness, reassure client if frightened.</td></tr>
<tr><td>Tardive dyskinesia</td><td>Notify physician</td></tr>
<tr><td>Neuroleptic malignant syndrome (NMS)</td><td>Stop medication and notify physician.</td></tr>
<tr><td>Akathisia</td><td>Administer medication as ordered, assess for effectiveness.</td></tr>
<tr><td>Extrapyramidal syndrome</td><td>Administer medication as ordered, assess for effectiveness.</td></tr>
<tr><td>Seizures</td><td>Stop medication, notify physician, protect client form injury during seizure, provide reassurance and privacy.</td></tr>
<tr><td>Sedation</td><td>Caution about activities requiring client to be fully alert such as driving a car.</td></tr>
<tr><td>Photosensitivity</td><td>Caution client to avoid sun exposure, advise client when in the sun, to wear protective clothing and sun-blocking lotion.</td></tr>
<tr><td>Weight gain</td><td>Encourage balanced diet, regular exercise.</td></tr>
</table></td><td>Lecture</td><td>Flannel board</td><td>How to prevent dystonic reactions?</td></tr>
</table>

Contd...

<table>
<tr><th>Specific objectives</th><th>Time</th><th>Contents</th><th>Teaching and learning activities</th><th>Audiovisual aids</th><th>Evaluation</th></tr>
<tr><td></td><td></td><td>
<table>
<tr><th>Side effects</th><th>Preventive measures</th></tr>
<tr><td>Dry mouth</td><td>Use ice chips or hard candy for relief.</td></tr>
<tr><td>Blurred vision</td><td>Assess side effect, which should improve with time, report to physician if no improvement.</td></tr>
<tr><td>Constipation</td><td>Increase fluid and dietary fiber intake, client may need a stool softener if unrelieved.</td></tr>
<tr><td>Urinary retention</td><td>Report any frequency or burning with urination, report to physician.</td></tr>
<tr><td>Orthostatic hypotension</td><td>Instruct client to rise slowly from sitting or lying position, wait to ambulate until no longer dizzy or lightheaded.</td></tr>
</table>
</td><td>Brainstorming session</td><td>Charts</td><td>What immediate measures to be taken if patient develop NMS?</td></tr>
<tr><td></td><td></td><td>Conclusion: I hope that all of you have understood the prevention of side effects of antipsychotics; it will help you to identify at the earliest and prevent it. This will help for mediation compliance and thereby prevent the relapse of the illness.</td><td>Lecture</td><td>PowerPoint Presentation</td><td>How to prevent weight gain?</td></tr>
</table>

Recording and Reporting

Date	Time	Nursing care/activities	Name with signature
	8:00 am	Assessment of the patient	Ms X
	8:50 am	Patient has taken breakfast (2 *rotis* with vegetable *curry*) and 1 cup tea	Ms X
	9:00 am	Oral medication given, Tab. THP 2 mg, she has taken the medications and tolerated well	Ms X
	9:15 am	She participated in vocational training activities	Ms X
	10:00 am	She participated in painting activities, and interacted well during the session	Ms X
	10:35 am	Health education given to patient and family members on "Prevention of Side Effects of Antipsychotics".	Ms X

CASE 6 BIPOLAR AFFECTIVE DISORDER—MANIA WITH PSYCHOTIC SYMPTOMS

Mr X, a 19-year-old single male, admitted in male psychiatric ward. He is undergoing his graduation and domiciled in Chennai from middle socioeconomic status. His mother complains that he was normal 1 month before then he developed wandering out behavior, suspiciousness toward his mother that he has immoral affair with the neighbor, over talkative and over familiarity and decreased interest to sleep and personal care neglect. Past history of bipolar affective disorder for about 3 years with three previous episodes of manic features; 3 years ago, met with a road traffic accident. Maternal uncle committed suicide at the age of 25. No significant personal history. Mental Status Examination finding reveals that he is well hygienic and wears colorful dresses. Not able to establish eye contact, increased psychomotor activities, pressured speech, patient says "I love staying here rather going home that I hate my mother who is not good," paranoid delusion present. He says, "I am very happy and feel great energy today," appears to be euphoric. Poor attention and concentration, he says that he is admitted to treat his eye problem. Laboratory investigation shows Hb—11.8 g/dL, WBCs—7,000 cells/mm^3, Sr. lithium is 1.2 mEq/L, and he is on Tab. Lithium 1050 mg TDS and Tab. chlorpromazine 200 mg BD.

CASE 7 MULTIPLE SUBSTANCE ABUSE DISORDER—ADS, CDS, NDS

Mr C, 28-year-old male, married, and from low socioeconomic background got admitted in psychiatric emergency ward with the complaints of attempt suicide, pervasive sadness and fearfulness, suspiciousness, hearing voices, decreased socialization, lack of interest in all activities, lack of energy and decreased sleep and appetite for 3.5 months. His illness is of insidious onset and episodic course of illness. On MSE, he looks sad, irritable and poorly kempt not involving in any activities, psychomotor activities observed as retarded, Speech is not spontaneous, reaction time is increased. Tone, tempo, and volume are decreased. He had delusion of persecution nonelaborative, nonsystematized—"people are planning to kill me once I am released from jail", delusion of references— "people are talking about me". He had depressive ideation such as feeling of worthlessness, hopelessness and suicidal ideation present, personal, social and test judgment are impaired. Insight is absent. He had two episodes of mood disorders in the past. He had a history of multiple substance abuse such as alcohol, cannabis and tobacco. He was imprisoned for attempted theft. His father is a chronic alcoholic. Normal birth and development, he was temperamentally easy child; he possessed only a few friends in his childhood. He was shy type and did not involve in any play activities. He was closely attached with family members. Not good in scholastic performances. No specific jobs held. His wife was separated; the reason is not known. Physical examination revealed that he is thin body built, and malnourished (BMI–17). He underwent investigations Hb (15.4%), blood urea (52 mg/dL), SGOT (231 IU/mL), Sr. sodium (137 mEq/L). He is on Tab. risperidone 4 mg HS, Tab. trihexyphenidyl, 2 mg BD, and Cap. fluoxetine 20 mg HS.

CASE 8 MAJOR DEPRESSIVE DISORDER

Mr K, 53-year-old male, unmarried, completed SSLC, got admitted in male psychiatric ward with the complaints of pervasive low mood, fearfulness, socially withdrawn, lack of interest in any activities, poor self-care associated with poor appetite, and decreased sleep for 2 months. His illness is of insidious onset and episodic course of illness. He is known case of depressive disorder past 4 years with past history of suicidal attempt with high intentionality and severely lethal. He is from low socioeconomic status. His elder sister died by committing suicide, father died at early age, mother got second marriage, step father is cruel to him, bitter early childhood experiences, ADS among 1st- and 2nd-degree relatives. Normal birth and early development, he was temperamentally an easy child; he possessed only few friends, he was introvert and did not involve in any play activities. He was closely attached with family members; he had emotional intolerance and fearful. He had significant stressors during his childhood. He is a chronic smoker and chronic alcoholic. He has anxious avoidant personality traits and dependent person. MSE revealed that he was ill kempt, fearful, restless, psychomotor activities were observed as retarded. He speaks on prompting. Reaction time is increased. Tone, tempo, and volume are decreased. He has depressed mood, range and reactivity decreased. He is grossly oriented to time, place and person. He has good insight about his illness. On physical examination, he has clubbing. He underwent following investigation: Hb (13%), WBCs (8,900 cells/mm^3), platelet (2.16 lakh cells/mm^3), SGOT (52 IU/L), Sr. sodium (130 mEq/L) and blood urea and creatinine are normal. He was on Tab. Chlorpromazine 100 mg and Tab. Amitriptyline 75 mg OD and underwent six episodes of ECT and psychotherapy.

CASE 9 MENTAL RETARDATION

Mr J, 21-year-old male, educated up to 6th standard, belongs to joint family. He got admitted in male psychiatric ward with the complaints of wandering behavior, self-injury, he cuts his upper limb with no intention to die, he tried to burn himself and he harms people around him, associated with lack of sleep. History of delayed milestones, not cried soon after his birth, he started sitting and walked with support at the age of 1.5-year-old. At the age of 4 years, he played with toys but could not play with children around him. He started his schooling at the age of 7-year-old in Government school and continued till Class 5th. In primary school, he did not find interest in studies and left school after 6th standard, had low grades in subjects. He left school and worked in a shop; he left the job after some time. Then he got unemployed and used to stay at home. He is a chronic smoker. No significant family history. On physical examination, he was found malnourished (BMI–17), burn scars present over his both arms and cut injury present inner aspect of left inner arm. MSE reveals that he is ill kempt, irritable, not interested and responsive and highly distractive in nature. The eye contact was not maintained and sustained. His emotional expression is labile. He responds to questions, speech is loud, tempo is decreased, and flow of speech is decreased and not clear. Patient is not fully oriented to time, place and person. Attention was not sustained. Immediate memory is impaired, intelligence is below average, abstraction is poor, personal, social and test judgment are poor. Insight is partially absent. Investigation reported are WBCs (7,000 cells/mm^3), neutrophils (32%), eosinophils (15%), monocytes (1%), normal blood sugar, blood urea (22 mg/dL) and creatinine (1 mg/dL), and urinalysis reported normal findings.

He is taking medications such as Tab. Risperidone 2 mg HS, Tab Amisulpride 100 mg OD, Tab. Trihexyphenidyl 2 mg OD, Tab. Quetiapine 40 mg BD and Tab. Haldol 15 mg OD.

CASE 10 OBSESSIVE-COMPULSIVE DISORDER

Mrs K, 47-year-old female, married, belongs to a middle-class family. The patient got admitted to the female psychiatry ward with the complaints of repetitive thoughts of temple-related objects such as murti, bell entering through her urinary tract which were repeated, intrusive and distressing causing anxiety and restlessness, her symptoms worsened and started affecting her activities of daily living, decreased appetite and sleep in the past 2 months. The onset is insidious and progressive. No significant family history of mental illnesses, she is well adjustable, actively involved in household activities, maintains good relationship with family members, her mood is cheerful and optimistic. MSE reveals that she is well kempt, dresses properly, but she looks restless and worried, depressed mood, anxious and is congruent. She responds to the questions, volume is normal, rhythm and expressive intonation are clear and flow of speech is normal. Speech is understandable and clear. There is no evidence though disturbances such as of flight of ideas, word salad, clang association, neologism and circumstantiality. No suicidal thoughts, intent, or plan. No evidence of auditory and visual hallucination, and also there is no illusion, depersonalization and derealization present in the patient. She is conscious, alert and responsive, she is oriented to time, place and person. The attention can be aroused but sometimes cannot be sustained. Concentration was good. The immediate, recent memory is intact and remote partially intact. Intelligence is good and average, abstraction is intact, personal, social and test judgment are intact, fully aware about her illness, and participates in her treatment. No significant finding on physical examination. She underwent following investigations such as Hb (10 g/dL), WBCs (4,000 cells/mm^3), RBCs (3.38 lakh cells/mm^3), normal differential count and platelet (1.3 lakh cells/mm^3). She is on Tab. Sertraline 50 mg BD, Tab. Lorazepam 2 mg HS and Tab. B-complex OD; she is participating in cognitive behavioral therapy.

Notes

Glossary

A

Abasia: It is inability to walk due to lack of motor coordination.

Abdominal reflex: In this reflex, abdominal muscle contracts and umbilicus move toward the stimulated side while stroking of the skin in the abdominal quadrant

Abnormal Behavior: It's a kind of behavior which is not socially acceptable.

Abreaction: It is the release and expression of emotional tension associated with the repressed ideas by bringing those ideas into conscious mind.

Abstract thinking: It is the ability to think about things which are not actually present. Individuals who think in an abstract way look at the broader significance of ideas and information rather than the concrete details.

Abulia (or) aboulia (or) blocq's disease: It's an absence of initiative or act to take decisions independently which is seen in Disorder of Diminished Motivation (DDM). Abulia might be seen in Depression, Progressive supranuclear palsy, Parkinson's disease, Huntington's disease, Normal pressure hydrocephalus, Schizophrenia, Frontotemporal dementia, Pick's disease, Traumatic brain injury and Stroke.

Acetylcholine: It is biological amine (cholinergics) category of neurotransmitter which mediates cognitive functioning directly or by modulating another neurotransmitter indirectly; contributes to sleep-wake cycles. It is increased in depression and decreased in Alzheimer's disease.

Achilles Tendon Reflex: It's plantar flexion of foot while tapping of Achilles tendon.

Acupuncture: It is an ancient traditional Chinese medicine that works on the principle of stimulating the points in body in order to correct the imbalances in energy flow (Qi) through the channels known as meridians.

Acute and transient psychotic disorders (or) brief psychotic disorder: Short-lasting psychotic symptoms which are abrupt and acute with positive symptoms such as delusion, hallucination, disorganized thoughts and abnormal psychomotor movements. It may or may not be due to acute stressors.

Acute depression: It's a sudden abrupt onset of depression.

Acute Mania: It's an intensified manic symptom which requires hospitalization. It is characterized by euphoria (or) elation, frequent mood variation, thinking may have psychotic features, raised sexual interest with poor control of impulse, high energy level and may deny grooming.

Acute Stress Reaction: It's an immediate and clear relation exists between the stressor (e.g., Accident, sudden job loss, disaster) and the onset of symptoms such as anger, depression, etc.

Adjustment disorder: Presence of significant behavioral or emotional symptoms in response to the psychosocial stressors is called adjustment disorder.

Affect: It's an outward expression of emotions in a given time.

Affect illusion: A type of illusion in which the misperception remains present with heighten emotions or with the changes of mood, e.g., in night time, the shadow has been perceived as ghost.

Aggression: It is an expression of anger by physical or psychological or verbal means, in a socially inappropriate manner which may or may not cause significant harm to self or others.

Agitated depression: It's a kind of depression with Psychomotor agitation.

Agitation: Presence of severe motor restlessness arises out of individual's anxiety or frustration is called agitation.

Agnosia: It's the inability to recognize the sounds or objects or shapes or persons or smells where there is no defect in specific sense or no memory loss. It is associated with the neurological problems or brain injury.

AIDS Dementia Complex: HIV stands for Human Immunodeficiency Virus. It is a retrovirus which crosses Blood Brain Barrier (BBB) as HIV infected macrophages and lymphocytes will lead to decreased cognition, motor, behavioral and neurological functions.

Al-anon: It's a mutual support group for families and friends who has been affected by someone else drinking

Alateen: It's a subgroup of Al-anon. It's a mutual support group for individuals, especially teenagers who have been affected by someone else drinking.

Alcohol: Natural substance formed with the reaction of fermented sugar and yeast spores. It's classified as food because it gives calories but no nutritive value in it.

Alcoholic hallucinosis: Hallucinations present even in abstinence after the regular alcohol intake. It commonly occurs with clear consciousness.

Alcoholic Pellagra: The main cause is Niacin deficiency due to alcoholism.

Alcoholics anonymous: Recovered alcoholics help the new alcoholics to join the group in order to achieve sobriety.

Alcohol withdrawal seizures (or) rum fits: It occurs within 6-48 hours of last intake of alcohol. It is usually Grand mal seizures type. Around 3-15% of untreated alcohol withdrawal clients might develop seizure. Less than 3% of patients will get status epilepticus.

Alexithymia: It's an inability to describe the one's feelings verbally.

Alice in Wonderland syndrome (or) Todd's Syndrome (or) Lilliputian hallucination (or) Dysmetropsia: Disorienting neurological dysfunction which affects the perception (Subcategories are Micropsia (or) Lilliputian, Macropsia, Pelopsia and Teleopsia).

Alogia: It is an inability to speak or reduction in the amount of speech due to mental defect, mental confusion or aphasia. It is seen in patients with dementia and negative symptoms of schizophrenia. This is also called Poverty of Speech.

Alternative medicine: It is a non-main stream practices used instead of conventional medicine.

Alzheimer's dementia: Neuropathological changes was explained by Alois Alzheimer. Deposits of β amyloid will lead to Plaque formation outside the neuron. Hyperphosphorylation of tau protein will cause Neurofibrillary Tangles (NFT) inside the neuron.

Ambivalence: It's a coexistence of two opposing impulses to a single person at the same time put the person inability to take decision.

American Law Institute (ALI) Test: Person is not responsible for criminal activity if he/she has done it as the result of 'mental disease/defect'. The term 'mental disease/defect' does not include the criminal activity or antisocial conduct.

Amnesia: Loss of memory.

Amphetamine: It is a stimulant of central nervous system. Its primary action is to release Norepinephrine along with dopamine and serotonin.

Anergia: It's a complete lack of energy seen in depression.

Anger: It is a normal human emotion which is mishandled and expressed assertively may solve the problem and show a productive change.

Anhedonia: It's a kind of depression in which the patient becomes unable to enjoy the pleasurable things which seem to be enjoyed before the onset of depression.

Anorexia nervosa: It is an eating disorder with the symptoms of having less than 85% of expected weight, fear of increase in body weight, complete denial about the morphology of body when said by others and amenorrhea (3 cycles of menses after menarche). It has 2 types: Restricted and Binge eating/purging.

Anterograde amnesia: It's an inability to create new memories due to brain damage.

Antianxiety agents: These are drugs to treat anxiety disorders.

Antidepressants: These are drugs to treat depression.

Antimanic drugs: These are drugs to treat mania.

Antipsychotics: These are drugs to treat psychosis (Schizophrenia). Antipsychotics are also called Major tranquilizers.

Antisocial personality disorder: It's a type of personality disorder with the diagnostic criteria. The patient violates rules/regulations/social norms, fails to maintain relationship, impulsive action, low frustration tolerance, absence of guilt, manipulation in activities to get self-gratification, unconcerned with safety of others, not able to learn from punishment, blame others for one's own antisocial activities and deceitfulness (Frequent lying or cheating others to gain profit as well as pleasure).

Anxiety: It is defined as 'feelings of uncertainty, apprehension, uneasiness or tensed that individual's response to any situation.'

Apathy: Absence of emotional expression. It exhibits the lack of interest or concern or enthusiasm. This is a sign of seen in depression.

Aphasia: Absence in the production of speech.

Aphonia: Absence of sound that produces speech due to laryngeal nerve damage or secondary to thyroidectomy and also due to underlying psychological problems.

Apraxia: Inability to perform learned motor activities.

Aromatherapy: It is the use of plant oil for the therapeutic purposes such as antimicrobial, analgesics and psychological effects.

Art therapy: It is defined as 'a form of psychotherapy which uses the art media as a primary mode of expression and communication'.

Asociality: Social withdrawal seen in negative symptoms of Schizophrenia

Asperger's syndrome: It is also called 'High functioning Autism' (i.e., capable to perform functioning in daily life). It is usually diagnosed from 3–9 years of age. Children who are diagnosed might have normal to advanced intelligence, normal to advanced verbalization skills or language development but severely impaired social skills.

Assertiveness training: It is provided to stand up for one's own rights by expressing the one's feelings, thoughts, ideas in an honest and direct manner.

Associative loosening: Rapid shift of ideas without having any central theme or concept is termed associative loosening.

Astasia-Abasia: The term 'Astasia' refers to inability to stand normally and 'Abasia' refers to inability to walk due to lack of motor coordination.

Ataxic gait: Unsteady, uncoordinated staggering gait happened due to damage of cerebellum (part of brain controls the muscle coordination)

Attention Deficit Hyperactivity Disorder (ADHD): It is child psychiatric disorder with three main features such as inattention, hyperactivity and impulsivity.

Atypical depression: A subtype of major depression or dysthymia characterized by increased appetite, excessive sleepiness, feeling that arms are heavy and interpersonal rejection, sensitiveness.

Auditory hallucination: Commonest type of hallucination in psychiatric disorders, in which the voice or sounds are heard by the patient without any external stimuli. Sounds heard are termed simple or elementary auditory hallucination. Voice heard is termed complex auditory hallucination. Voice speaking to him/her addressing 'you' is termed second person hallucination. Voice speaking to him/her addressing 'he' or 'she' is termed third person hallucination. Individual hearing one's own thoughts speaking aloud is termed thought echo.

Autism spectrum disorder: It consists of Autism and Asperger's syndrome or Asperger's disorder (Language or intellectual impairment is not prominent). ICD-10 denotes this disorder as pervasive developmental disorder.

Autistic thinking: Thinking which is preoccupied with the inner experience. It differs from dereistic thinking by having disconnection with the reality.

Automatic obedience: Exaggerated co-operation of the examiner's request in obeying the commands which is seen in patients with Schizophrenia.

Autoscopy (or) phantom mirror image: Misperception as seeing oneself.

Aversion therapy (or) antabuse: Treatment to arouse the unlikeness or feel likely to be hated of substance usage or any behavior.

Avoidant personality disorder: Type of personality disorder with the diagnostic criteria such as avoidance of activities which needs to be done with interpersonal relationship, continuous tension and apprehension, fear of criticism/ rejection, feel inferior than others, not willing to involve with others and preoccupied with criticism/rejection by others.

Avolition: Inability to take initiative in performing the goal directed activity which is seen in negative symptoms of Schizophrenia.

Ayurveda: The word, 'Ayurveda' is a Sanskrit word which means, 'science of life and longevity'. Ayurvedic medicine has a belief that life force called 'prana' moves through chakras. Chakras are considered a center of energy in the body.

B

Baragnosis: It denotes the loss of ability to estimate the differences in weight or pressure.

Behavior therapy: It is defined as 'form of psychotherapy in which the maladaptive behavior is aimed to change as adaptive behavior'.

Biceps reflex: Flexion of forearm occurs when arm is gently flexed at elbow, tap the biceps brachii tendon.

Binge eating: It is an eating disorder with the symptoms of increased food intake within short period with increased rate, feel of guilt within short duration, unable to control the behavior, food intake still the feel of discomfort increases, feel disgust or guilt and doesn't use any compensatory behavior (purging/non-purging)

Binswanger's disease (or) Subcortical leukoencephalopathy: Small vessel vascular dementia occurs due to damage of white matter.

Bioelectromagnetic therapy: It is the usage of electromagnetic fields (usage of magnets and electric currents) in the body for a therapeutic purpose.

Biofeedback: It is defined as, 'psychophysiological therapy in which the individual is able to monitor the physiological changes in the body due to the psychological stressors'.

Bipolar disorder: Either of two poles consists of mania or hypomania in one pole and depression in opposite pole.

Black out (or) alcohol-induced amnesia: Transient short-term memory loss may be complete or partial in relation with intoxication state and does not indicate dementia.

Blunt/shallow affect: Lack of affect is more severe than constricted or restricted affect and less severe than flat affect.

Body Language: Type of nonverbal communication which means the mixture of gesture, posture and expressions.

Borderline personality disorder: A type of personality disorder with the diagnostic criteria such as impulsivity, chronic feel of emptiness, unstable affect (intense anxiety/irritable within few hours), unstable relationships, unstable self-image, self-mutilation (threats of self-harm), unable to control anger, transient dissociative symptoms during stress, paranoid ideas and tendency to act of out impulsivity without considering the consequences (e.g., Driving very fast, binge eating).

Bouffee delirante: It is a French term for short-lived psychosis. It is mainly characterized by hallucination, delusion, confused state and amnesia after attack and paranoia, aggression and psychomotor excitement. It is a culture bound syndrome of west Africa. Remission takes place within 3 months even without any treatment. It occurs mainly due to consequence of urbanization and westernization.

Boundary violations: A kind of therapeutic impasses in which a nurse or patient crosses over the limits in the therapeutic relationship. The categories of boundary violations are role, time, space, place, money, gifts, clothing, language, self-disclosure, post discharge social boundaries and physical contact boundaries.

Brachioradialis reflex: Flexion of elbow/hand/fingers and supination of forearm occurs when tapping of styloid process of radius about 1–2 inches above the wrist.

Bulimia nervosa: It is an eating disorder with the symptoms of binge eating within short duration of time, having no control over eating, immediate compensatory behavior is present. There is self-evaluation of raised body weight or appearance. It has two types: Purging and nonpurging.

C

Caloric Reflex Test (Oculovestibular reflex): This test is performed to assess the coordination of eye and ear muscles. Pouring of cold water in the ear will move the opposite eye balls and the warm water in ear will move the same side of eye balls.

Cannabis: It is derived from 'hemp plant', *Cannabis Sativa*. It produces more than 400 chemicals in which 50 are cannabinoids (active ingredient of 9-tetrahydrocannabinol).

Capgra syndrome: It is defined as delusion of doubles or delusional misidentification syndrome in which patient strongly believes that the other person is not real and he/she is doubles of self.

Catalepsy: Individual maintains the body posture in the position which has been placed. The end result of waxy flexibility leads to catalepsy.

Cataplexy: It's an abrupt loss of muscle tone without the loss of consciousness which is seen in Narcolepsy.

Catatonic excitement: It is type of Catatonic Schizophrenia, in which the patient has increased psychomotor activity.

Catatonic schizophrenia: Type of Schizophrenia in which the motor symptoms are predominantly present. Types include: stuporous, excited and periodic.

Catatonic stupor: It is a clinical syndrome or type of Catatonic Schizophrenia, with the combination of akinesis (absence of movements) and mutism (absence of speech).

Catharsis: Emotional ventilation will help the individual to come out of stress.

Cautious gait (or) senile gait: Excess degree of age-related changes in walking (slow and wide based abducted arm) and having a fear of fall.

Child abuse (or) child battered syndrome: It is defined as physical, psychological or sexual maltreatment of child or neglecting the child by care givers.

Choreiform gait (or) hyperkinetic gait: Jerky irregular and involuntary movements in both the extremities. It is seen in Huntington's Disease, Chorea, Athetosis and dystonia.

Circumstantiality: Speech of the individual reaches the goal or center point toward the question raised only after the unwanted speech.

Clang association: It is rhyming of words seen in patients with schizophrenia.

Cluttering: Disorder of speech characterized by erratic, dysrhythmic speech pattern and fast jerky spurts of words (e.g.: 'Machine-gun' speech with irregular rate).

Cocaine: It is alkaloid derived from coca bush, *erythroxylum coca*.

Cognitive therapy: It is a form of psychotherapy in which the distorted cognitions are modified into positive cognitions.

Cog wheel rigidity: It is a ratchet-like start-and stop passive movements while performing the physical assessment mainly seen in patients with Parkinson's disease.

Communication: It is defined as 'interaction process between the sender and receiver in which the receiver receives the message exactly what the sender intended to say as such, i.e., both the sender and receiver have a common understanding of a message'.

Community Mental Health Centers Act (1963): It is initiated by 35th United States President, John F. Kennedy which brought a change of shifting the mental healthcare from hospitals to the community.

Community mental health nursing: It is defined as, 'decentralized pattern of rendering mental health services/ care to the needy in the community, further it focuses on prevention of mental illness, promotion of mental health and rehabilitation of patients with mental disorder in the community'.

Complementary medicine: It is a nonmainstream practice used along with conventional medicine.

Completion illusion: Illusion is mainly due to lack of attention.

Compulsion: Repetitive actions performed are followed by obsession in order to avoid the marked distress even though the client knows that behavior is unrealistic, senseless and irrational.

Conduct disorder: A repeated and pervasive pattern of age-inappropriate behavior that violates the basic rights of others.

Confabulation: False filling of memory gaps.

Constricted or restricted affect: Reduction in the individual's emotional response.

Coolidge effect: Married couples do not feel each other as excited during the sexual intercourse.

Coprophilia: Sexual pleasure with feces.

Corneal reflex: Blinking of eyes while touching the cornea with wisp of cotton.

Counseling: It is an interaction process between the counselor and counselee. Counselor is the person who provides help and counselee is the person who seeks help.

Counter transference: Nurse is emotionally dependent on patient. There are three types of counter transference reactions of intense love or caring, reactions of intense disgust or hostility and reactions of intense anxiety, especially in response to resistance by the patient.

Covert sensitization: Patient will be advised to imagine the unpleasant symptoms whenever required to stop the stimulus of undesirable behavior by self.

Cremasteric reflex: Elevation of ipsilateral testicle while stroking the inner thigh of patient.

Crisis: It is a sudden event in one's life which disturbs homeostasis during which the usual coping mechanism can't resolve the problem.

Crisis resolution: These are the steps or measures taken to solve the crisis situation.

Cross-gender homosexuality (or) Pseudo-transsexualism: Male or Female homosexuals sometimes need a sex change and wear the dress of opposite gender.

Cue exposure therapy: Expose the alcoholics with craving inducing cue and guide the patient how to prevent the use of alcohol.

Cyclothymia: Mood swing is present between the short periods of mild depression and hypomania or an elevated mood.

D

Dance therapy: It is defined as, 'psychotherapeutic use of movement as process which promotes physical, emotional and cognitive integration of the individual'.

Deep brain stimulation: It is defined as, 'implanting the electrodes in certain parts of brain, the electrodes produce the impulses to regulate the abnormal impulses. The amount of stimulation has been controlled with the pacemaker like device which is kept under the skin of the chest'.

Defence mechanism: It is an unconscious psychological mechanism that reduces anxiety which arises from unacceptable or potential harmful stimuli.

Deinstitutionalization: Bringing the mental health patients out of the hospital and shifting the care to community.

Déjà entendu: It's a false feel or sense of familiarity with the unfamiliar words heard newly.

Déjà vu: It's a false feeling or sense of familiarity with the unfamiliar scenes or circumstances.

Deliberate self harm (or) Nonsuicidal self injury disorder: It is defined as 'deliberate, self-inflicted destruction of the body tissue without having the suicidal intent and for purposes not socially sanctioned, includes the behaviors such as cutting, biting, burning and scratching skin'.

Delirious mania: Severe clouding of consciousness with confusion, disorientation and may be stupor, extreme liable mood, delusion with grandiosity, religiosity and/or persecution, auditory and/or visual hallucinations, increased psychomotor activity has risk for harming to self and to others, even death may occur if left untreated.

Delirium: An acute confusional state with disturbances in level of consciousness and reduced ability to focus, sustain, or shift attention is called delirium.

Delirium Tremens: It is the alcohol-withdrawal syndrome that occurs within 48–72 hours of stopping alcohol. Clinical features are clouding of consciousness, disorientation, visual hallucination, illusion, poor attention span, insomnia, autonomic disturbances, dehydration and electrolytes imbalance.

Delusion: False fixed unshakable belief irrespective of their socio-cultural background is called delusion.

- **Nihilistic delusion:** Strong unshakable belief that the world is not existing is referred to nihilistic delusion.

Delusion of control: It's a strong unshakable belief that one's own thoughts or action are controlled from outside.

Delusion of guilt (or) delusion of sin: It's a strong unshakable belief that the individual feels more guilt to an extent which is unreal.

Delusion of infidelity (or) delusion of jealousy (or) othello syndrome: Strong unshakable belief that his/her spouse has extra-marital relationship with other is called delusion of infidelity (or) delusion of jealousy (or) Othello syndrome.

Delusion of influence or passivity: Strong unshakable belief that active movements are considered passive which is imposed by someone from outside.

Delusion of love (or) erotomanic delusion: It's a strong unshakable belief that some famous personality is having love desire on oneself.

Delusion of persecution: Having a strong suspicious belief that other individual will cause harm is delusion of persecution.

Delusion of poverty: It's a strong unshakable belief that he/she will be deprived of material possessions.

Delusion of reference: Strong unshakable belief that the other person is referring oneself with a neutral event in the environment is called delusion of reference.

Delusion of thought broadcasting: It's a strong unshakable belief that one's own thoughts have been projected/displayed in mass media such as television, newspaper, internet, etc.

Delusions of grandeur: Strong unshakable belief that he/she is an important famous personality or superior knowledge or ideation or power is termed delusions of grandeur.

Dementia: It is a group of heterogeneous and neurodegenerative disorder with presence of significant decline in Memory, Cognitive abilities (Planning, organizing, executing, thinking, judgment, etc.), emotional control (lability, apathy, irritability) and social behavior. It is a chronic memory impairment with clear consciousness. The progressive deterioration of intelligence, behavior and personality is due to consequences of impairment in the brain hemispheres. The cerebral cortex and hippocampus are affected to higher extent.

Dependent personality disorder: It's a type of Personality Disorder with the diagnostic criteria such as to depend on others more for psychological support, inability to take decision, allow others to take important decisions in life, difficult to express unwillingness due to fear, not willing to make reasonable demands on others, low self-esteem, feel helpless by being alone and lack of self-confidence.

Depersonalization: Alteration in the perception of self as unreal one.

Depersonalization disorder (or) Depersonalization-Derealization syndrome: Alteration in the perception or experience of self and alteration in the perception or experience of others seems to be unreal.

Depression: It is a mood disorder characterized by anhedonia, feel of guilt, anergia, insomnia, psychomotor retardation, decreased concentration, lack of interest, crying spells, avoid socialization, diurnal variation (worsening of symptoms in morning), suicidal ideation and feel of hopelessness/helplessness/worthlessness.

Derealization: Alteration in the perception of external environment as unreal one.

Dexamethasone suppression test: Cortisol level usually decreases with dexamethasone but it will not reduce in patients with depressive disorder.

Dhat syndrome: Belief that there will be a presence of semen in urine. There may be sexual dysfunction, depression, anxiety, multiple somatic complaints and Asthenia (Physical/Mental Exhaustion).

DiGeorge syndrome (or) Velocardiofacial syndrome (or) Shprintzen syndrome (or) Conotruncal anomaly face syndrome (or) Takao syndrome (or) Sedlackova syndrome (or) Cayler cardiofacial syndrome (or) 22q 11.2 deletion syndrome: It is defined as deletion of 30–40 genes in middle of chromosome 22.

Disorientation: Lack of orientation to time, place and person.

Dissociative amnesia: Amnesia is purely psychogenic due to intrapsychic conflicts.

Dissociative disorder: It is defined as lack of integration of consciousness, memory and identity.

District Mental Health Program, 1996: Government of India funded to launch this District Mental Health program as per the guidelines of National Mental Health Program. In 1996, DMHP was launched in 4 districts under 9th five-year plan and it extended to 123 districts in 12th five-year plan. In 1997, District Mental Health program (DMHP) was launched in Trichy and it has been extended to Ramanathapuram, Madurai in 2003 and it has been further extended into 13 districts.

Disulfiram ethanol reaction (DER): When client takes disulfiram along with alcohol it might lead to disulfiram ethanol reaction.

Disulfiram therapy (or) deterrent therapy (or) chemical aversion: Administration of Disulfiram will inhibit the Alcohol Dehydrogenase enzyme thereby it promotes the aversion to alcoholism.

Double depression: Major depressive disorder and Persistent depressive disorder occurs at the same time (Dysthymia is a chronic low-level depression at least of 2 years and add on to that major depressive symptoms)

Down syndrome: Patients have 47 chromosomes with an additional chromosome 21.

Dual role transvestism: Wearing opposite gender dress to enjoy the experience of opposite sex on temporary basis and not having a desire to change the anatomical sex organs as like transsexualism and also sexual excitement is absent with cross dressing which is present in fetishistic transvestism.

Durham's rule/Product rule: In 1954, Durham test was framed on the basis of decision in District of Columbia. Accused is not liable as criminal for his/her action due to product of mental disease.

Dyslexia (or) specific reading disorder: A disorder of children who fails to attain the language skills of reading, writing and spelling commensurate with their intellectual abilities.

Dysmorphophobia: Excess dislike of one's own body.

Dysthymia: It is a persistent depressive disorder in which the mild depressive symptoms persist for at least 2 years (1 year in case of children).

E

Eating disorders: It is characterized by severe form of disturbances in eating pattern/behavior which leads the life-threatening condition.

Echolalia: Repetition of words spoken by others as mimicking the words or phrases.

Echopraxia: Repetition or mimicking of actions performed by others, seen in patients with schizophrenia.

Ecstasy: Very severe elevation of mood seen in stuporous or delirious mania.

Elation: Moderate elevation of mood in which the individual feels confident with increased psychomotor activity.

Elective mutism: Complete absence of speech in social situations.

Electroconvulsive therapy: Convulsions are induced by passing a brief pulse of electric current through brain via electrodes for a therapeutic purpose.

Emotional lability (or) emotional incontinence (or) pseudobulbar affect: Uncontrolled expression of emotions such as laughing or crying out suddenly.

Encopresis: It is defined as repeated passage of feces in inappropriate place or time after the bowel control is possible physiologically and not due to organic cause. It is also called fecal incontinence.

Endogenous depression: Depression is due to hereditary or biochemical imbalance.

Enuresis: It means urinary incontinence (involuntary passing of urine).

Epileptic furor: Attacks of anger seen in patients with epilepsy in certain occasions without disturbances of consciousness.

Ethanol challenge test: It is performed to create cognitive awareness of Disulfiram Ethanol Reaction (DER). Patient has to be on 250 mg of disulfiram as initial dose for 5 days. Alcohol has to be administered approximately 40 mL (15 mL for every 15 minutes) or maximum of 90 mL can be given.

Euphoria: Mild elevation of mood seen in hypomania. Happiness is present but not related to ongoing events.

Euthymia: Normal mood

Exaltation: Severe elevation of mood is seen in severe mania. Intense elation along with the delusion of grandeur is present.

Excessive sexual desire disorder: Excess sexual desire in male is termed 'Satyriasis' and excess sexual desire in female is termed 'Nymphomania'.

Exhibitionism: Showing of sex organs to stranger.

Exogenous depression: Depression caused by external factors such as unemployment, divorce, sudden death of loved ones, etc.

Extinction: A technique of behavior therapy, in which the gradual reduction in the frequency or the disappearance of the responses occurs when the positive reinforcement has been withheld.

Extracampine hallucination: Misperception outside the limits of sensory field (e.g., I hear voices from USA when I am in India).

F

Factitious disorders (or) munchausen syndrome by proxy: Falsification of physical or psychological symptoms which project the individual as an ill person. The deception is evident even in the absence of obvious external reward. It may happen as a single episode or in a recurrent episode.

Family therapy: It is defined as, 'a form of psychotherapy in which the issues or problems or conflicts exist among the family members are addressed and the solution is identified.

Female orgasmic disorder or female anorgasmia: Females feel difficult to have orgasm during the coitus. This may be due to biological (drug induced or endocrine disorders like hypothyroidism) and psychological factor.

Female sexual arousal disorder: Vaginal dryness due to absence of lubrication. This may be due to biological or (postmenopausal) psychological.

Fetal alcohol syndrome: Pregnant women who drink alcohol might affect the fetus and cause microcephaly or mental retardation in children.

Fetishism: Sexual pleasure with objects.

Fetishistic transvestism: Sexual pleasure with clothes of opposite sex.

Flat affect: No emotional expression.

Flight of ideas: Rapid shift of one idea to other idea with the presence of central theme as seen in mania, schizophrenia and in some patients with ADHD.

Flooding (or) implosive therapy: It is used to desensitize the persons to phobic stimuli. It differs from systemic desensitization that instead of working out in hierarchy of anxiety provoking stimuli, the person will be 'flooded' with the continuous presentation of phobic stimuli until the anxiety comes down.

Folie a deux: Delusions are shared between two closely related or connected individuals. (When it happens among three individuals, it is termed folie a trio. When it happens among four individuals, it is termed folie a quatre).

Forensic psychiatry: It is a branch of medicine which deals with mental disorders with its related legal aspects. The core aspects are criminal responsibility, crime due to psychiatric disorder, civil responsibility, laws related to psychiatric disorder, admission and discharge procedure in psychiatric hospital.

Formication: Type of tactile hallucination in which the individual feels that the insects are crawling underneath the skin which may be associated with the prolonged use of cocaine.

Foster homes: It is the place where the children are taken care, when the parents are unable to take care of their children due to a variety of reasons. Foster care may be the informal one or arranged by the courts or by a social service agency.

Fragile X syndrome: Fragile site in band q27–28 on X chromosome

Frotteurism: Sexual pleasure with rubbing others

Fugue: It is a loss of awareness in regard with one's identity, often coupled with flight from one's usual environment, which is seen in dissociation disorder and epilepsy.

Functional hallucination: Misperception within the same sensory field, e.g., Patient verbalizes that, 'I am hearing voices when I hear the birds sound'. (Sensory field is auditory).

G

Gag reflex (or) pharyngeal reflex: It is a reflex contraction of the back of the throat, evoked by touching the root of the month, the back of the tongue, area around tonsils or back of the throat.

Gait: Manner of walk, it is a rare genetic disorder that affects on individual's ability to metabolize galactose properly.

Galactosemia: Infant unable to metabolize Galactose (It is simple sugar along with glucose it forms lactose), which might accumulate in brain and lead to mental retardation.

Gegenhalten: It is an involuntary resistance to the passive movement, which is seen in cerebral cortical disorders.

Gesture: Movement of body part, especially head or hand to convey the ideas.

Glasgow coma scale: It is the scale used to measure the level of consciousness.

Graphesthesia: Ability to recognize the writing in skin.

Grief: It is defined as physical, somatic, spiritual, emotional and intellectual responses to the nature of loss.

Group homes: These are small, residential facilities present in the community, which are allotted to take care of the children and adults with chronic disabilities.

Group therapy: It is defined as, 'psychosocial treatment where the patients meet regularly to talk, interact and discuss the problems with each other along with the therapist'.

Guided imagery (or) guided affective imagery (or) Katathym: Imaginative psychotherapy—It is defined as, 'a form of relaxation therapy in which the therapist helps the participants in relaxation by evoking the mental images which stimulate or recreate the sensory perception of sound, sights, taste, movement, smell and touch.

Gustatory hallucination: Perception of taste without an external stimulus.

H

Half way homes (or) sober house (or) recovery house: It is an institution in which the patients with physical emotional and mental disabilities or individuals with criminal backgrounds learn or relearn the required skills to re-integrate into society for the needed support and care.

Hallucinogens: Substances which alter the individual's sensory perception of reality and induce hallucinations.

Hebephrenic (or) disorganized schizophrenia: Behavior is aimless and not goal-directed one, in hebephrenic schizophrenia. Hallucinations and delusions are not prominent. Inappropriate and incongruent affects are seen. Speech is incoherent. Early and insidious onset is associated with poor premorbid personality.

Herbal therapy: Treating the diseases with the use of herbs is herbal therapy. The commonly used herbs to treat the psychiatric disorders are St. John's wort, Rosemary, Kava Kava, Ginkgo biloba, Valerian, SAMe (S-adenosylmethionine), Passion flower, Guarana and 5-Hydroxytryptophan (5-HTP).

Hindu Adoptions and Maintenance Act (1956): It states that, Section 7 – Hindu male, who is major and sound minded can adopt a child with consent of wife unless the wife is of unsound mind. Section 8 - Hindu female, who is major and sound minded can adopt a child with consent of husband unless the husband is of unsound mind. Person giving in adoption also has to be with sound mind.

Hindu having an Marriage Act (1955): Among the couples, any other who is unsound mind is considered null as per law. Party can file for divorce if spouses' mental illness continues for the period of 2 years. If divorce has been filed for more than 3 years, then divorce can be granted with the condition that, party need to pay maintenance charges.

Histrionic personality disorder: Type of Personality Disorder with the diagnostic criteria's such as self-dramatization, attention-seeking behavior, labile effect, exaggerated way of expressing emotions, more concern in regard to physical attractiveness, emotional blackmail/suicide attempts, crave for excitement, impulsive behavior and discomfort with situations where the other person is being a guest and he/she is easily influenced by others.

Homeopathy: It means to 'treat like with like' i.e., substance which causes symptoms of disease in healthy individual may in smaller doses is also used to cure the similar symptoms resulting from the disease. It helps to augment the individual's own immune system.

Homosexuality (or) egodystonic sexual orientation disorder: Individual wishes to change the sexual orientation because it is causing significant distress (ego-dystonic: Opposite to that of ego).

Huntington's Chorea: A genetically dominant disease due to 4 defects in chromosome.

Hyperesthesia: Individual perceives highest intensity of sensations seen in hypochondriasis, anxiety personality disorder and in intense emotions. (e.g., Sounds are heard louder, colors are seen brighter, pain is perceived with high intensity, etc.)

Hypermnesia: Excessive loss of memory.

Hypnogogic hallucination: Misperception happens when the individual is getting into sleep.

Hypnopompic hallucination: Misperception happens when the individual is awakening from sleep.

Hypnosis: Individual is directed into state of subconsciousness, assisted through suggestions in order to recall the events which he/she was unable to recall at conscious time.

Hypoactive sexual desire disorder: Decreased sexual desire in sexual activity.

Hypokinetic gait (or) magnetic gait: Inability to lift the feet from the floor results in decreased mobility. It is a cardinal sign of Normal Pressure Hydrocephalus.

Hypomania: Manic symptoms which are not severe to cause significant impairment in social or occupational functioning. Psychotic features are absent.

I

Illness anxiety disorder (hypochondriasis/health phobia/ health anxiety disorder): Excessive health concern and preoccupation with having or acquiring a specific illness. Somatic symptoms are absent usually, mild symptoms may be seen sometimes.

Illusion: False perception with an external stimulus.

Imperative hallucination: Voices give instructions to the patient who may or may not feel obliged to carry out.

Indian Contract Act (1872): Contract is an agreement enforced by law. Section 11 states, every individual can perform contract, provided he/she is major and having sound mind. Section 12 states that person with unsound mind and occasionally with sound mind (lucid interval) can make contract. However, person who is in sound mind usually and occasional in unsound mind, should not make contact when he/she is in unsound mind state.

Indian Evidence Act (1872): As per this Act, mentally ill is not competent to give evidence, provided the evidence can be considered if given in lucid interval.

Indian Lunacy Act (1912): It consists of 4 Parts, 8 Chapters and 100 Sections. Objectives of this act are improvement of asylums and care of lunatics in asylums.

Indian Mental Health Act (1987): It is initiated by Parliament in 1987 and came into effect in all states of India in 1993. Enactment of this act revised the Indian Lunacy Act (1912). It has 10 chapters with 98 sections.

Insight: Aware of one's own mental illness.

Insight psychotherapy (or) uncovering: This therapy or technique is helpful to bring the patient's repressed conflict and traumatic experience on the surface level in order to gain the insight.

International Classification of Diseases (ICD-10): It is the 10th revision and a medical classification is done by the World Health Organization (WHO). It contains codes for diseases, signs and symptoms, abnormal findings, complaints, social circumstances, and external causes of injury or diseases.

Intersexuality: Presence of both anatomical and psychological aspect of other sex. They are seen in Pseudo-Hermaphroditism, Ovatestes, True Hermaphrodite, Congenital Adrenal Hypoplasia, Testicular Feminization Syndrome, Temporal Lobe Disorder, Turner's Syndrome and Klinefelter's Syndrome.

Irresistible Impulse Act: As per the rule, person might know that the action is illegal still is unable to control the action due to presence of mental illness.

J

Jacobson progressive muscle relaxation (JPMR): It is defined as relaxation therapy in which the series of guided steps about tension and relaxation of the different parts of body helps in relaxation.

Johari window of IPR: Joseph Luft and Hary Ingham (1950) described the model of interpersonal relationship. Other names are Disclosure or Feedback Model of Self Awareness and Information Processing Tool. Components are known to self, known to others, not known to self and not known to others.

Judgment: The ability to make logical decisions.

Juvenile delinquency: An individual below 18 years of age involved in antisocial activities is called Juvenile Delinquent.

K

Kinesthetic hallucination: Hallucination involves the sense of body movements.

Klismaphilia: Sexual pleasure obtained by the use of enema.

Kluver-bucy syndrome: This syndrome includes insertion of inappropriate things in mouth (hyperorality), high sexual desire (hypersexuality) and poor response to emotional stimuli (placidity). It is due to the lesions present in medial temporal lobe. It is commonly seen in Pick's disease.

Korsakoff syndrome: It is the complication of alcoholism characterized by gross memory disturbances (Severe retrograde and anterograde amnesia) with preserved long-term memory, cognition and social skills. Other symptoms are confabulation (False filling of memory gaps), confusion, disorientation, poor attention span, easily distractible in nature and client may be unaware of illness.

L

Labile affect (or) pseudobulbar affect-PBA (or) involuntary emotional expression disorder (IEED): Emotional Incontinence, i.e., immediate urge in expression of emotions.

Lacunar amnesia: Partial loss of memory (or) memory loss of specific events.

Lacunar state/lacunar syndrome/status lacunaris: It is defined as more minute infarcts called lacunae that are seen in vascular dementia and in severe hypertension.

Late paraphrenia: Type of Schizophrenia with the late onset, delusion of persecution with bizarre/fantasy are present. Visual, auditory, olfactory, gustatory and tactile hallucination are seen.

Lesch-nyhan syndrome: It is also called juvenile gout caused due to deficiency of hypoxanthine-guanine phosphoribosyltransferase (HGPRT).

Lewy body dementia: A type of dementia having decline in cognition with three more features such as fluctuations in alertness, recurrent vivid visual hallucinations at early stages of disease and features of Parkinson's disease such as muscle rigidity, loss of spontaneous movement, Mask-like face, Bradykinesia, etc. Other features include syncope, autonomic symptoms, REM Sleep behavior disorder and Severe neuroleptic sensitivity.

Light therapy: Use of light with the specified intensity for therapeutic purpose.

Lithium: It is a mood stabilizer.

Lunatics: Individuals with unsound mind (or) mentally ill individuals.

M

M'Naghten Rule: Daniel M'Naghten murdered Edward Drummond, secretary of Sir Robert Peel, Prime Minister in his insane mind. But he was not punished under law because the gun shot happened due to the delusion of persecution.

Macropsia: Objects appear larger than the original size

Maladaptive behavior: Abnormal behavior persists for the longer duration.

Male erectile disorder: Lack of ability to sustain the penile erection in males.

Male orgasmic disorder or male anorgasmia: Males feel difficult to have orgasm during the coitus. This may be due to biological (drug induced or after prostate surgery) or psychological, cause/causes.

Malingering: It is a psychiatric disorder in which the patient plays a similar sick role to get secondary gain (avoiding work, escape from the criminal cases, unwilling to pay the amount, etc.).

Mania: It is a mood disorder, a state of abnormally elevated arousal, energy level and affect.

Marchiafava-bignami disease: It is a neurological disease of alcoholism which occurs due to demyelination of corpus callosum, optic tract and cerebellar peduncles. Symptoms include ataxia, disorientation, epilepsy, dysarthria and hallucinations.

Masked depression: Most clients complaint of somatic symptoms such as body ache, lack of energy, pain in the body with less or no psychological symptoms.

Masochism: Sexual pleasure by humiliating others or being humiliated

Massage therapy: Body tissues, superficial and deeper layer of muscle/connective tissues are manipulated to enhance the wellness in massage therapy.

Meditation: It is defined as 'an experience of relaxing the body, mind and spirit'.

Melancholic (or) involutional melancholia: Severe form of major depression occurs above 40 years of age, i.e. at the time of menopause or andropause.

Mental health: State of well-being in which every person realizes one's own potential, able to cope with the normal stresses of life, able to work productively or fruitfully, and is able to make a valuable contribution to the community.

Mental Health Care Act (2017): It superseded the previous Mental Health Act (1987). In India, Mental Health Care Act commenced in 7.4.17 and came into force on 7.7.18. It has 16 chapters.

Mental health nurse (or) psychiatric nurse: An expert in performing mental status assessment, crisis intervention, administering psychotropics, therapies and providing the patient assistance. Psychiatric nurses work with patients to help them in order to manage their psychiatric illness and live a productive fulfilling life.

Mental health nursing: Mental health nursing is defined as 'branch of nursing which deals with the study of measures in order to prevent the mental illness, promote mental health and restore of the patient with mental illnesses'.

Mental health team: Members include Psychiatrist, Psychiatric Nurse, Clinical Psychologist, Psychiatric Social Worker, Occupational Therapist, Counsellor, Pharmacist and Psychiatric Paraprofessionals or Technical Staff such as Psychiatric Nursing Aid, ECT technician, Dietician, Clergy Men/Chaplain and Speech Therapist.

Mental illness: A clinically significant behavioral or psychological syndrome or pattern that occurs in an individual which is associated with present distress or disability.

Mental retardation (or) intellectual disability (or) mentally challenged individuals: It is defined as, 'sub-average intellectual functioning that results in or is associated with concurrent impairment in adaptive behavior and is manifested during the development"

Micropsia (or) lilliputian: Objects appear smaller than the original size

Mild cognitive impairment (MCI): It is an intermediate state between normal ageing and dementia.

Milieu therapy: The scientific structuring of the environment in order to elicit the behavioral changes and to enhance the psychological health and functioning of the individual.

Mini mental status examination (or) folstein test: It was introduced by Folstein in 1975. It is 30-point questionnaire used to assess the cognitive impairment apparently.

Mitgehen (or) Angle-Poise Effect (or) Angle Poise Lamp Sign: Severe form of Mitmachen in which even the slight pressure will move the particular body part. So, it is also called angle-poise effect (or) angle poise lamp sign.

Mitmachen: It is a sign in which the patient's body can be put in any posture even though it has been instructed to resist.

Modeling: It is a technique of behavior therapy in which, learning out new behavior takes place by imitating the behavior of the others.

Mood: It is a sustained and persistent emotional feeling.

Motivational enhancement therapy (or) brief intervention: A client-centered approach to improve the readiness to change by helping the client in solving ambivalence.

Mourning: Act of exhibiting great sadness.

Music therapy: It is defined as, 'utilization of music in treatment, training, education and the rehabilitation of patient with mental disorder'.

Mutism: Complete absence of speech seen in patients with depression, negative symptoms of schizophrenia and catatonic stupor.

N

Narcissistic personality disorder: Type of Personality Disorder with the diagnostic criteria such as attention seeking, arrogance, strong belief that, he/she is special, feel to have relation with high status people, envious of others but verbalizes that others are envious to self, no empathy, difficulty to face criticism of others, preoccupied with fantasy world of success/beauty and power.

Narcolepsy: It is a sleep disorder characterized by excessive daytime sleepiness, sleep paralysis, hallucinations and cataplexy.

Nasolabial folds: Lines on the either side of mouth extend from the edge of nose to outer corner of mouth might suggest depression.

National Mental Health Policy: Policy formulated in 1982, consists of the plan of action that is required for promoting mental health.

National Mental Health Program: It was initiated in 1982. Aims taken into account were prevention/treatment of mental and neurological disorders, use of mental health technology to improve general health services and application of mental health principles in total national development to improve quality of life.

Naturopathy: It is the way of life in which body innately knows to maintain the health and heal oneself.

Necrophilia: Sexual pleasure with dead bodies.

Negativism: It is defined as apparently motiveless resistance to all instructions which is seen in catatonic stupor.

Neologism: Coining of new words.

Neurasthenia: Individual will have a persistent and distressing complaints of body weakness and feel exhausted even after a minimal effort.

Neuroleptic malignant syndrome: It is an extrapyramidal symptom/hypermetabolic reaction to the dopamine antagonists especially with typical antipsychotics.

Neurolinguistic programming: It is item from the concept of Milton Hyland Erickson. Effective communication exists at the state of hypnosis or by alteration in the individual's state of consciousness.

Neurotransmission: It is the fundamental process that transfers information between neurons.

Neurotransmitters: They are the endogenous chemicals which enable the neurotransmission.

Nicotine: It is addictive substance seen in tobacco products.

Night eating syndrome: Overeating in night time with sleep problems.

Nightmares: Children may wake up after the frightening or unpleasant dreams. The themes of dreams are threat to survival or self-esteem. Dreams are recalled but they are vivid in nature and also cause marked distress. It occurs in second half of night time sleep (REM Sleep).

Night terrors (or) sleep terrors: Child gets up from the sleep with panic screaming and high-level anxiety. It occurs in the deepest stage of Nonrapid Eye Movement (NREM) sleep.

Non-organic dyspareunia: Male or Female might have pain in genital area during coitus.

Non-organic vaginismus: Spasm of lower part of vagina interferes the coitus.

Normal behavior: Behavior performed as per the socially acceptable norms.

Nursing ethics: It is a branch of philosophy which deals with the study of values and moral standards related to nursing profession.

O

Obesity: Excessive accumulation of body fat is termed obesity. In general, Obesity was assessed by Body Mass Index (or) Queenlet's Index = Weight (Kg)/Height (m^2)

Obsession: To control one's thoughts by a continuous, powerful idea or feeling or the ides of feeling itself. These are repetitive thoughts, images and doubts (that one feels it's absolutely senseless and irrational, individual tries to resist but unable to do so because that restriction might increase the level of anxiety.)

Obsessive-compulsive personality disorder: Type of Personality Disorder with the diagnostic criteria such as preoccupied with perfectionism, thinking of orderliness always, excessive doubtfulness, rigid and stubborn, preoccupied with rules, list, details, schedules, etc. which interfere the daily routines and tendency to hoard/unable to throw the useless object even it may not have any sentimental value.

Occupational therapy: It is defined as, 'therapeutic use of work, play activities and self-care to enhance the development and to prevent disability. It might also include the task adaptation to obtain the maximum level of independence and to improve the quality of life'.

Olfactory hallucination: Type of Hallucination in which the individual smells the odors without any external stimuli. Commonly felt unpleasant odors are vomit, rotten flesh, smoke, feces, urine, etc.

Omega sign: Furrowed brow due to sustained contraction of corrugator muscle, which is seen in depression.

Oneiroid schizophrenia: Type of Schizophrenia with acute onset, brief episodic dream-like state. Symptoms include clouding of consciousness, perceptual disturbances and disorientation.

Opioids: It is the exudate from dried seeds of *Papaver somniferum*. The street name is smack and brown sugar.

Oral communication: Communication by speaking/talking to others.

Organic brain disorder: A neuropsychiatric disorder which has a strong biological basis or a significant brain dysfunction. This is classified as delirium, dementia, amnesia and other disorders such as organic hallucinosis, organic delusional disorder, organic mood disorder, organic personality disorder, organic dissociative disorder and organic emotionally labile disorder.

Othello syndrome (or) morbid jealousy: Delusion that life partner is not faithful (i.e. suspiciousness that life partner is having extramarital relationship). If it persists, it might lead to domestic violence.

Otto veraguth's folds: Upward inward folds of upper eyelids, which are seen in depression

Overt sensitization: It is a kind of aversion therapy in which introduction of unpleasant consequences for the undesirable behavior can be observed.

P

Panic anxiety (or) panic attacks: Anxiety with high level of physiological response such as raised blood pressure, heart rate, etc.

Paranoid personality disorder: Type of Personality Disorder with the diagnostic criteria such as suspiciousness/mistrust, excess sensitive to criticism, doubts the loyalty of friends, suspicious of sexual partner fidelity, interpret remarks as threatening and holding "grudges" (Unable to forget/forgive).

Paranoid Schizophrenia: It is commonest type of Schizophrenia in which patient has hallucination, delusion and thought disorder. Examples of hallucinatory themes are commenting, arguing, threatening, body sensations/movements. Examples of thought disorders are irrelevant, incoherent and neologisms in speech. Examples of delusional themes are persecution, grandiose, jealousy and reference.

Pareidolic illusion: Illusion which is seen over the other illusion.

Parkinson's disease: It is a neurodegenerative disease caused by degeneration of neurons in brain, particularly in nigrastriatal pathway of the basal ganglia.

Partial Hospitalization (or) Day care Hospital/Centers (or) Day Treatment Program: It is an outpatient facility where clients undergo the assessment, treatment and rehabilitation during day time and then patient can return to home at later times.

Patellar reflex: Extension of leg while tapping of quadriceps femoris tendon (present below patella).

Pedophilia: Sexual pleasure with children.

Pelopsia: People/objects/things appear closer than the original place.

Perseveration: Persistent repetition of words beyond the point of relevance.

Persistent delusional disorders: Delusions are well-systematized and nonbizarre type which is stable and chronic in nature.

Personality: Personality is defined as the characteristic set of behaviors, cognitions, and emotional patterns that evolve from biological and environmental factors.

Personality disorder: It is defined as, "enduring pattern of inner experience and behavior which has marked deviation from the expectation of individual's culture"

Pervasive developmental disorder: It denotes the group of disorders characterized by abnormalities in social interaction and communication skills.

Pfropf schizophrenia: Schizophrenia occurs with the presence of mental retardation. Behavior disturbance is more prominent than thought disorder. It differs from schizophrenia due to unsystematized delusions and poverty of ideation.

Phenylketonuria: Simple autosomal recessive traits which have deficiency of liver enzyme, 'phenylalanine hydroxylase' leads to lack of ability to metabolize phenylalanine.

Pica: It is defined as eating the non-edible items.

Pickwickian syndrome (or) obesity hypoventilation syndrome: Individual with obesity will fail to breathe deeply which results in decreased oxygen supply to blood.

Pick's disease (or) frontotemporal dementia: Frontal lobe is prominently involved (Frontal signs are inhibited). Atrophy, Neuronal loss, Gliosis and Intraneural bodies (Pick bodies) seen in Frontal or temporal lobe.

Plantar reflex: Contraction of toes while touching the foot's outer plantar surface, from heel toward toes.

Play therapy: It is a form of psychotherapy in which the therapist utilizes the child's fantasies and uses the symbolic meaning as a medium of play to have a communication or understanding about the children. It also gives a chance to the child to express feelings and experiences.

Postschizophrenic depression: Depressive episode develops after the resolution of schizophrenic symptoms. Patient might be in high suicidal risk.

Post-Traumatic Stress Disorder (PTSD): It is an anxiety disorder, in which the individual might develop after witnessing or experiencing an extreme, overwhelming traumatic event during which the individual has intense fear or helplessness.

Postpartum depression: Episode of depression occurs after the delivery. If the depression episode is present during pregnancy and within one year after the delivery it is termed perinatal depression.

Postpartum depression: Major depression appearing within 4 weeks of delivery/postpartum

Postpartum psychosis (or) puerperal psychosis: It is a serious mental illness in which the episode of depression occurs after the delivery. Here, there will be presence of depressive symptoms and psychotic features.

Poverty of ideation: Speech delivered is adequate but the content of speech is inadequate.

Poverty of speech: Decreased production of speech.

Prader-Willi syndrome: This disorder is caused by a deletion in the paternal chromosome 15. It is a complex genetic condition in children, characterized by poor muscle tone (hypotonia), feeding difficulties, poor growth, and delayed development.

Premack principle: This technique has been named after its originator. The frequently occurring response (R1) might act as a positive reinforcement for the response (R2) which is occurring less frequently.

Premature ejaculation: Ejaculation of sperm occurs before the satisfactory sexual activity. This may be due to biological (not common) or psychological (Performance anxiety) pressure.

Premenstrual syndrome: It is combination of physical, emotional, mood and behavioral disturbances present in women before few days of menstrual flow due to the interaction between the neurochemicals in brain and the sex hormones.

Pressure of speech: Rapid speech with an urgent quality. It is often noted in patients with mania.

Preventive psychiatry: It is defined as, 'services rendered in the community in order to prevent the mental illness and promote the mental health'.

Prion disease: Replicative protein mutates and causes a variety of spongiform diseases. It can transmit through use of contaminated duramater, Corneal graft and ingesting meat from infected cattle (Bovine Spongiform Encephalopathy).

Process recording: It is a method of recording the nurse-patient interaction, which has been done by the nurses in psychiatric setup.

Propulsive gait (or) Parkinsonian's gait: A stiff and stooped posture with head/neck forward. It is seen in Parkinson's disease, carbon monoxide poisoning and manganese toxicity.

Prosopagnosia (or) face blindness (or) facial agnosia: A neurological disorder characterized by the inability to recognize faces.

Proximity: Nearness in time, space and relationship.

Pseudohallucination: It is an involuntary sensory experience vivid enough to be regarded as hallucination, but recognized by the patient not as a result of external stimuli.

Pseudoneurotic schizophrenia: A type of Schizophrenia which has classical triad features such as pan-anxiety, pan-neurosis and pan-sexuality. Pan-anxiety denotes free floating anxiety which will not subside easily. Pan-neurosis includes the predominant neurotic symptoms. Pan-sexuality is preoccupied with sexual desires.

Psychiatric nursing: It is the branch of nursing which deals with the study of nursing care required for the mentally ill patients.

Psychiatry: It is a branch of medicine with deals with the study of prevention, diagnosis and treatment of patient with mental illness.

Psychoanalytical psychotherapy: It is defined as form of insight therapy which aims to overcome the unconscious conflict and it also aims to identify the relationship between the unconscious motivation and the abnormal behavior.

Psychodrama: It is a form of psychotherapy (group therapy), in which the dramatization or dramatic presentation of self helps to gain self–insight.

Psychological pillow: A characteristic feature of Catatonic Schizophrenia in which the patient hold his/her head few centimeters above the bed for long hours.

Psychosurgery (or) psychiatric neurosurgery: It is functional neurological surgery for treatment of mental disorders. It is done when there is presence of strong treatment resistance with psychotropic agents and ECT.

Psychotherapy: It is defined as, 'way to help the people with variety of mental illnesses and emotional difficulties and it also helps to control or remove the symptoms which troubles the person, function in a better way, increase the sense of well-being and promote healing'.

Puerperal blues (or) postpartum blues (or) baby blues: It is a less severe form of postpartum depression, in which the onset of depressive episode is present within few days and ends up within one or two weeks.

Q

Quarterway homes: It provides lower-level supervision than the half way homes. Here, mostly patients have to take care of themselves.

R

Reality therapy: It is a psychotherapeutic technique focused on the present behavior and the present coping ability of the patient against the stressors. The active relationship between the therapist and patient might promote the realistic behavior which is focused on the present.

Recreational therapy: It is a systematic process which utilizes the recreation and other activity-based interventions based on the needs of individual with illness or disabling conditions which means psychological/physical health recovery and well-being.

Recurrent depression: Two or more episodes of depression.

Reflex hallucination: Stimulus in one sensory field produces hallucination in another in other sensory field. (For example, patient says that, 'I feel pain when I am hearing the sneeze sound'. One sensory field is tactile i.e., feel of pain and other sensory fields are auditory i.e., hearing sneezing sound, in the given example).

Rehabilitation: It is defined as the restoration of the person's health to his/her former capacity.

Reiki technique: The term, Reiki is a Japanese word which means, 'Universal life force'. The purpose of Reiki is to direct access to universal, transcendental, radiant and light energies at various levels on energy spectrum.

Relaxation therapy: It is a component of body-mind intervention in which the therapist helps the participants at the higher extent of mind relaxation.

Residual schizophrenia: Progression from early stage (Hallucination and delusions are predominant) to late stage (Hallucination and delusions are minimal). Negative symptoms are present.

Resistance: It is a kind of therapeutic impasses. Patient is not willing to communicate the troubling aspect of oneself and is not willing to change when the change is expected. Primary resistance (e.g., Inappropriate role model). Secondary resistance (e.g., financial problem, unpleasant situation, attention seeking and Social pressure).

Restraints: Restricting the violent behavior of patient either by physical or chemical (use of drugs) modality.

Retrograde amnesia: Inability to recall before the onset of amnesia.

Rett's syndrome: Syndrome due to autosomal dominant mutation. Girls are more affected. The main symptoms are hypotonia, muscle spasm, loss of speech in 1–2 years, abnormal gait, mixed receptive and expressive language development in 1–4 years of age, severe psychomotor retardation, apraxia, hand flapping, presence of microcephaly, Toe walking, lack of eye contact, scoliosis and peripheral motor disturbances.

Rinne's test: Keep the tuning fork in mastoid bone and also near to patient's ear after striking it. When air conduction is more than bone conduction, it is normal. If the bone conduction is more than air conduction it denotes conductive hearing loss.

Romberg test: It is performed to assess the balance or equilibrium of body. Ask the patient to stand straight with the eyes closed. Nurse has to be cautions while performing this test, since patient has a risk of fall.

Russel sign: Callus knuckles due to self-induced vomiting, seen in eating disorders.

S

Sadism: Sexual pleasure by humiliating others.

Sadomasochism: Sexual pleasure by humiliating others and getting or being humiliated.

Schizoaffective disorders: It has both symptoms of schizophrenia and mood disorders which are prominently seen in same episode.

Schizoid personality disorder: Type of Personality Disorder with the diagnostic criteria such as having emotional coldness, blunted or flat affect, humorless, preferably solitary activities, introspective, indifference with praise or criticism, inability to express both positive and negative feelings, lack of desire to enjoy relationships and being aloof (loneliness).

Schizophrenia: It is a psychotic disorder (disorder in which client believes that he/she will not have a base of reality, characterized by abnormalities in emotions, thinking and cognition.

Schizophreniform disorder: Presence of symptoms of schizophrenia for up to 6 months.

Schizotypal personality disorder: Type of Personality Disorder with the diagnostic criteria such as odd/eccentric behavior, social withdrawal, no close relation with others, inappropriate/constricted affect, magical thinking, paranoid ideation, ruminations with violence and sexual themes, vague/circumstantial speech, depersonalization and prefer to have social distance even to his/her own family members.

School refusal (or) school phobia: Children refuse to go to school because of fear.

Scissor gait: It happens due to the contractures of all spastic muscles (hypertonia of leg muscles), increased adduction of leg. It is seen in spastic cerebral palsy and upper motor neuron lesion.

Seasonal affective depression: Depressive symptoms in winter season.

Secondary depression: Depression is due to organic causes.

Sedatives: Drugs that promote sleep.

Sensory gait (or) stomping gait: It happens when the patient lacks proprioceptive information to the brain when the foot touches the ground. But it lacks in patient with peripheral

neuropathy (due to the complications of alcohol, complications of diabetes and disorders of dorsal columns).

Separation anxiety disorder: An excessive display of fear and distress when faced with situation of separation from home or any specific attachment figure.

Serotonin syndrome: It is defined as, 'over activation of serotonergic receptors which leads to increased serotonin.

Sexual aversion disorder (or) lack of sexual enjoyment: Avoidance of sexual activity with life partner or sexual partner. Thoughts of sexual activities provoke anxiety and negative feelings.

Sheltered workshop: It is an environment or organization which employs the persons with disabilities separately from the other individuals.

Shuffling gait: Individual drags his/her feet to walk (Seen in disorders associated with dementia, Parkinsonism, etc.)

Sibling rivalry disorder: It refers to significant competition or animosity among the siblings for the love and affection from parents associated with unusual negative feelings (e.g., elder son will think that, only my parents are showing love and affection to the younger ones only).

Simple schizophrenia: Prominent negative symptoms of Schizophrenia such as amotivation, apathy, social withdrawal, flat or blunt affect and poverty of speech. Positive symptoms are absent. Social functioning is reduced. Onset is early and insidious. Course is progressive. Prognosis is worst.

Social skills training: A form of behavior therapy which focuses to enhance the social skills among patients.

Somatic delusion: Strong unshakable belief in regard to the one's bodily function or appearance is grossly abnormal.

Somatic hallucination: False sensation of movement occurs inside the body usually which is visceral in origin.

Somatic symptom disorder: Presence of one or more somatic symptoms which cause significant personal distress in patient.

Somatoform disorder: It is a mental illness in which multiple bodily signs and symptoms are elicited but the medical evaluation does not reveal abnormalities.

Somnambulism: It refers to walking during the sleep.

Steppage gait (or) neuropathic gait (or) equine gait: Abnormal gait characterized by foot drop due to absence or dorsiflexion of foot.

Stereognosis (or) haptic perception (or) tactile gnosis: Ability to perceive and recognize the object using tactile sense.

Stereotype behavior: Repetitive strange behavior

Stereotypical movements: Repetitive movements which are irregular, purposeless and jerky.

Stereotypical speech: Meaningless repetitive speech

Stuttering/stammering/childhood onset fluency disorder: Normal flow of speech interrupted by the pause or by repeating the fragments of the word.

Substance abuse: Maladaptive pattern of substance use leading to clinically significant distress or impairment with recurrent substance use results in failure to perform well in home, school or at work, recurrent substance use in situation which is physically hazardous (e.g., While driving), recurrent substance related legal problems and continued substance use might lead to recurrent or continuous social/interpersonal problems.

Substance codependency: Behavior of one family member affects the other because of the substance abuse.

Substance cross tolerance: Effect of one drug produces tolerance of another drug; usually it happens between the two drugs with same functions.

Substance dependence: Compulsive and repeated use of substance which results in tolerance toward the substance and also leads to withdrawal symptoms when commenced to quit or decrease the dosage of the substance.

Substance detoxification: It is the process of eliminating or neutralizing the toxins from the human body.

Substance harmful use: A pattern of psychoactive substance use which harms the physical health (liver cirrhosis due to alcohol use) or psychological health (depression due to alcohol use)

Substance intoxication: Substance-related syndrome occurs due to the strong exposure to the substance.

Substance withdrawal: Symptoms occur when blood level of abused drug gets decreased and symptoms cease when that substance has been taken by the individual.

Suicide: It is defined as, 'intentional way of killing oneself' (or) 'Self-inflicted cessation of life ends with a fatal outcome'.

Sundowning syndrome: Worsening of symptoms in evening (Diurnal variation). Symptoms of sun downing syndrome such as wandering, mood swings, disorientation, insomnia, resistance, confusion and hallucination are present.

Supportive psychotherapy: It is defined as psychotherapeutic approach which integrates the various components such as cognitive-behavioral, psychodynamic and interpersonal techniques of psychotherapy.

Systemic desensitization: It is the technique of behavior therapy developed by Joseph Wolpe. It has three steps such as Relaxation training (Relaxation gives the physiological effects which is opposite to the anxiety), Hierarchy Construction (Arrange the conditions in the order of increasing the anxiety) and Desensitization of stimulus (Gradual exposure of the individual from least to most anxiety provoking state).

T

Tactile hallucination: Type of Hallucination in which the individual feels that someone is touching without any external stimuli. It may be superficial (touching the skin), kinesthetic (movement of the body parts) or visceral (pain felt due to the separation or twisting of internal organs).

Tai-chi' technique: The term, 'Tai-chi' denotes 'moving meditation' which consists of a series of continuous slow movements performed along with the mental and breath co-ordination.

Tandem walking test: Patient is asked to walk over the heel in straight line. Assess for unsteadiness or staggering or imbalance gait.

Tangentiality: Speech of the individual does not reach the goal or center point.

Tay-Sachs disease: A rare fatal inherited disorder occurs due to absence of an important enzyme hexosaminidase-A (Hex-A) leads to the destruction of nerve cells in brain and spinal cord.

Teleopsia: People/objects/things appear far away from the original place.

Telephone (or) mail scotologia: Sexual pleasure attained by sending sexual pictures.

Testamentary capacity: It is a legal term used to explain the person's legal and mental ability to make (or) alter a valid will.

Therapeutic communication: Communication maintained between nurse and patient for therapeutic purpose.

Therapeutic community: Psychiatric nurse structures, give and maintain the therapeutic environment. It is done in collaboration with the patient and other health team workers.

Therapeutic impasses: Barriers in therapeutic communication or relationship.

Therapeutic relationship: Relationship maintained between nurse and patient for therapeutic purpose.

Thought alienation phenomenon: Thought insertion, thought broadcasting and thought withdrawal.

Thought block: It is a sudden interruption of thoughts exhibited by silence for few seconds to minutes which is commonly seen in patients with schizophrenia.

Thought broadcasting: It is a symptom of schizophrenia. The patient believes that his/her thoughts have been shared with other people without the patient's willingness, through an unknown or known medium (Here, the known medium is mass media such as television, newspaper, radio, etc.)

Thought echo: Voices are speaking thoughts aloud

Thought insertion: Thoughts have been inserted by an external source

Thought retardation: It is decreased idea identified by decreased content of speech which is seen in patients with depression, dementia, nervousness, memory impairment and schizophrenia.

Thought withdrawal: Thoughts have been removed by an external source.

Tics: It is defined as sudden, nonrhythmic, involuntary, jerky motor (or) vocal activity.

Token economy: It is a kind of contingency contracting in which the contract can be either made orally or signed. Here, tokens will be issued to the patient for performing the desirable behavior.

Tolerance: Increase in the amount of substance use in order to get the same desired effect.

Tourette syndrome: Classical Tic disorder named after Gilles de la Tourette, a French Physician was first person to describe this disorder. Tourette Syndrome is chronic, combined motor and vocal tics. Usually, motor tics precede the vocal tics in Tourette syndrome.

Transactional analysis: The term 'Transactional Analysis' was first used by Dr Eric Berne (1964). Dr Eric Berne suggests that there are three ego states that exist in individual. Parent—Focus on rules/regulations/values. Adult—Approach based on previous observations. Child—Focus on emotions and desires.

Transference: Transfer of client's feeling toward the nurse. Negative or hostile transference denotes feel of anger or enmity that the client has expressed toward the nurse. Positive or dependent transference denotes the client is emotionally dependent on nurse.

Transient epileptic amnesia: Memory loss due to epilepsy either during the ictal or post-ictal period.

Transient global amnesia: Sudden temporary episode of memory loss.

Transsexualism: Anatomical sex is normal. Feeling of discomfort with one's own anatomical sex organs. Individual will have preoccupied ideas that to feel better to have opposite sex organs and have marked significant distress. There will be a presence of social and occupational dysfunction.

Transvestism (or) fetishistic transvestism: Wearing the dress of opposite gender for purpose of sexual excitement; mostly seen in males (Transsexuals wear dress of opposite gender because they feel they are a part of that gender and not because of sexual excitement).

Triceps reflex: Extension of forearm while tapping of triceps brachii tendon in elbow.

Truancy: Children leave the school and go somewhere else without the knowledge of parents.

U

Undifferentiated schizophrenia: Schizophrenia not conforming any subtypes comes under the category of undifferentiated schizophrenia.

Unipolar depression: Presence of depressive episode; patient will not experience mania or hypomania.

Urophilia: Sexual pleasure with urine.

V

Van Gogh syndrome: Self-mutilation (or) Self-injurious behavior in this type of Schizophrenia. Van Gogh was a famous painter. He cut his ear in acute illness state and hence this term is named after this incident after his name.

Vascular dementia (or) Multi-infarct dementia (MID): Presence of occlusive plaque or thromboembolism or hemorrhage in blood vessels. Multiple small cortical infarcts are present in vascular dementia.

Verbal communication: It's a type of communication through oral, written and visual means.

Verbigeration: It's a senseless repetition of words or phrases.

Vibrational medicine (or) sound therapy: It's an ancient technique in which the sounds of objects such as bell rings, tuning forks, gongs, chants, drum beats are used to promote vibrations in the body which further promote the healing process. Vibrations of the human voices are also used.

Visual communication: It refers to communication to others by symbols.

Visual hallucination: A type of hallucination in which the individual visualizes or sees the things without any external stimuli. It may be elementary (flashes of light), partially organized pattern (blurred images) or fully organized pattern (people, animal or objects).

Voyeurism/scopophilia: A kind of sexual pleasure by observing the sexual activity of opposite sex/watching naked, etc. (Visualizing Pornography is not included in this category).

W

Waddling gait (or) myopathic gait: Individual walks like a duck due to the weakness present in the proximal muscles of pelvic girdle. This gait is seen in congenital hip dysplasia, pregnancy, spinal muscular atrophy and muscular dystrophies.

Waxy flexibility: Body parts placed in the fixed position are maintained for a long duration even if the position is uncomfortable.

Weber's test: It is a test a lateralization. Tap the tuning fork strongly on your palm and then press the butt of the instrument on the top of the patient's head in the midline, and ask the patient where he/she hears the sound normally, the sound is heard in the center of the head or equally in both ears. If there is a conductive hearing loss present, vibrations will be louder on one side (lateralization).

Wernicke's encephalopathy: It is the complication of Alcoholism characterized by cerebellar ataxia, mental confusion, palsy of 6th cranial nerve, hypothermia, cardiac problems, vestibular dysfunction and peripheral neuropathy.

Widower's syndrome: Widowed male feels pressure to perform sexual intercourse when he has completed the grieving process of his wife.

Word salad: It refers to mixture of words.

Y

Yoga: It means union, i.e., joining of the individual consciousness with the consciousness in the universe.

Z

Zone therapy: It is also called Reflexology. It consists of massaging the specific areas of hands or feet in order to reduce stress, pain and illness in the corresponding related areas in the body.

Zoophilia (Bestiality): It relates to sexual pleasure with animal.

Index

Refer 'f' for figure, 'fc' for flowchart and 't' for table, respectively.

B

D

E

H

I

J

K

L

M

N

O

P

Q

R